10,000
Dreams
EXPLAINED

10,000

Dreams

EXPLAINED

HOW TO USE YOUR DREAMS TO ENHANCE
YOUR LIFE AND RELATIONSHIPS

PAMELA J. BALL

ARCTURUS

I would like to thank all those who have made this book possible. Firstly, Fiona who has balanced the dual roles of daughter and editor with admirable aplomb and who has realized that the frustration is not directed at her; secondly, Jacob who epitomizes the generations to come and hopefully will find the book useful in future years; thirdly, my publishers, who gave me the confidence to set out on this labyrinthine road in the first place and, finally of course, you the readers, who continue to be the source of much of the material in the book itself.

ARCTURUS

This edition published in 2008 by Arcturus Publishing Limited
26/27 Bickels Yard, 151–153 Bermondsey Street,
London SE1 3HA

ISBN: 978-1-84837-087-6

Printed in Great Britain

CONTENTS

KEY TO ENTRIES

🏵 spiritual meaning
♥ psychological, emotional perspective
🖼 everyday material aspects
🎴 gender-specific meanings

INTRODUCTION

'The man who will not listen to the sublime whisper of his Overself during his waking hours will respond more easily during his dreaming ones, when the veil is thinner, partly because his egoistic will is more relaxed and partly because he is actually nearer the source of consciousness.'

PAUL BRUNTON

Paul Brunton was one of the finest mystics of the 20th century, bridging the gap between the spiritual and physical realms in his own inimitable way. For him, dreams began within the spiritual and manifested in the physical. We are more able to listen to, and understand, the inner self in sleep in ways we are not able to do in waking life.

He went on to say, 'It is dreams of this superior and spiritual character which bear good fruit after the man awakes.' He, then, was aware that interpretation of dreams was an integral part of understanding the spiritual dimensions and the spiritual self.

Dreams are perhaps one aspect of the human mind which are an integral part of all aspects of knowledge, but which still hold their mystery no matter which way we look at them. Regarded from a spiritual perspective they help us to understand the Divine; from the psychological point of view they enhance our understanding of ourselves and from a mundane viewpoint they make sense of the world in which we live.

Following Brunton's lead, we lay out each interpretation as follows:

First, there is the spiritual meaning indicated by the symbol 🜚, then the psychological/emotional perspective with the image ♥, followed by the more everyday material aspects with the 🔲 emblem. Some entries also have a fourth interpretation which gives gender-specific meanings ⚥. There can never be a 'one-fits-all' theory – we must all be honest enough to admit that we do not know and then be prepared to take from each theory what seems right for us.

We can use this book then as a dictionary, first listing those components that we need to understand and then, if necessary, reconstructing the dream so we understand the whole story. To enhance your understanding and your dream vocabulary there is extensive cross-referencing throughout the A to Z section: sometimes to similar images, sometimes to other entries which have similar meanings. Often, the entries refer back to this introduction to the

Archetypes (a proven source of images) and to Symbology and Spiritual Imagery. Gradually you will build up your own categories of meaning and hopefully will find as you do so that the content of your dreams becomes more meaningful and part of your everyday life.

MODERN DREAM INTERPRETATION AND ANALYSIS

The word 'interpret' is, we discover, of unknown origin but probably comes from a Sanskrit word meaning 'to spread among'. Therefore dream interpretation would mean 'to spread our dreams among others'. The common factor that is shared by all dream interpreters is that the original material from which dreams are fashioned is hidden.

The renowned and extremely influential psychoanalyst Sigmund Freud's work was based on the belief that dreams were disguised expressions of what went on below the surface of the mind. Carl Jung, who was originally a pupil of Freud's, had a more spiritual perspective and said, 'Dreams may give expression to ineluctable truths, to philosophical pronouncements, illusions, wild fantasies... anticipations, irrational experiences, even telepathic visions and heaven knows what besides.' Herbert Silberer, a contemporary of the two, took a much more mystical approach and studied the state between waking and sleeping. He formed the theory of Intraversion, which necessitates the descent of the individual into the soul/psyche from which a great deal of information and knowledge can be drawn.

Calvin Hall in the mid-20th century developed a cognitive (relating to intellectual activity) theory of dreams which states that dreams express 'conceptions' of self, family members, friends and social environment. With Robert van de Castle he developed the quantitative analysis of dream content, perhaps the first time that truly scientific methods had been applied to dream analysis. He also saw dream content as metaphor – one thing conceived as representing another: a symbol.

Then, in the late 1960s, Fritz Perls developed his own philosophy of Gestalt which means 'wholeness'; he believed that it was possible to reclaim those parts of our personalities which had become lost or hidden. He called dreams 'the royal road to integration'. If each image in the dream is an alienated part of ourselves, then it is wise to look at the necessity of giving each part of the dream its own voice and the opportunity to express itself, and therefore to become whole. Those wholenesses can then be integrated to become a greater whole. This approach ties in with Jung's theory of Archetypes about which we shall learn more later.

Calvin Hall's method of dream analysis gave rise to much research, and arguments still rage today as to whose theories of dreaming are right. For the layman, it would seem that the arguments can be divided into two camps, broadly how we dream and why. Much still remains hidden because those who believe that dreaming is purely neurological in origin cannot give a reasonable answer as to how the images are put together to form a dream. They appear to believe that the process is essentially chaotic and possibly meaningless. Those who believe that dreaming is a function of the cognitive brain – that which knows – have difficulty in explaining the randomness of the images.

G William Domhoff of the University of California, who has used Hall's methods to good effect, has come to probably the most easily understood conclusion that:

'Dreaming is best understood as a developmental cognitive achievement that depends upon the maturation and maintenance of a specific network of forebrain structures. The output of this neural network for dreaming is guided by a "continuity principle" linked to current personal concerns on the one hand and a "repetition principle" rooted in past emotional preoccupations on the other.' [Domhoff, G. W. (2001). A new neuro-cognitive theory of dreams. *Dreaming, 11,* 13–33.]

It has been discovered that, in the front part of the brain (forebrain), the necessary nerve connections for what might be called coherent dreaming are not really sufficiently mature until around the age of nine years old. This suggests that the night terrors that very young children have are a function of the immature brain.

The personal concerns of the dreamer – that which is happening to him in the here and now – is linked by the dreaming mind with what has happened in the past and had an effect on him emotionally. Setting aside for the moment the argument that the brain itself must mature before it can process information, one supposes that a child would not have enough waking life experience to be able to make such links.

When the dreaming mind makes connections and brings together images from similar experiences (Freud called it condensation), this is metaphor. Metaphor in dreams is basically a noting and expressing of similarities. Dreams then, according to Ernest Hartmann, one of the chief proponents of this idea, are explanatory metaphor. Through the highlighting of the similarity we gain understanding. Mostly, dreams will work with what is occurring at the time in our lives, but they will also pick up past images, ideas and concepts in an effort to have us understand and deal with what disturbs us. This then allows us to uncover the hidden meaning more objectively.

Dream metaphor takes a somewhat abstract idea such as fear and turns it into a recognizable picture (a monster). The best interpreter of these pictures obviously is the dreamer himself, but it can be of help to know the common meanings of such pictures. The language of dreams is universal.

SPIRITUAL DREAMING

Dreams can be a useful tool, giving us a much wider perspective and fuller appreciation of what is happening both in our world and the wider world in general. The knowledge and information that we acquire in dreams opens up a whole library of creativity which is ours to use if only we have the courage. Unfortunately, it is all too easy to forget the content of a dream on waking. We need to learn to record our dreams and an easy-to-follow method is shown below.

Dreams also give us access to another dimension of being – spirituality and the intrinsic use of power. Many Eastern cultures see sleep as a preparation for death and therefore a learning experience. One definition of spirituality is 'the awareness of other dimensions of existence beyond that of the purely physical, tangible realms'.

Dreams are an expression of the spiritual realm and also a bridge between that and the tangible. Interestingly, many authors, artists, poets, scientists and engineers are able to use their dreams creatively. Such people tend to be more lateral in their thought processes and are more likely to remember their dreams, which allows them to make something of a quantum leap in understanding. Scientists and engineers do tend to be more logical and linear in their thought processes and will not necessarily accept their dreams without being able to prove the reality in waking life.

However, it has happened. An excellent example of this process is scientist Friedrich Kekule's dream of the structure of the benzene molecule. Trying to solve the mystery of this structure, Kekule dreamt that the most important aspect was that the molecules formed a complete ring which he saw as a snake eating its own tail. Remembering that this dream occurred in the latter part of the 19th century when less was known about chemistry, this dream certainly constituted a breakthrough in knowledge.

This benzene ring provided the basis for the whole science of molecular chemistry. This particular dream symbol echoes the ouroborus (the symbol of the cycle of existence), which is often used in magical workings as a protective device.

INSPIRED DREAMING

Today, many people will admit to having creative flashes of inspiration following dreams. It is as though a missing piece of jigsaw suddenly fits into place, allowing them to see the whole picture and therefore to make sense of a creative problem. Often a fragment of music, poetry or apparent doggerel will linger in the mind, which on consideration is not as beautiful or pertinent as it once seemed in the dream, but it may contain the key for moving an idea or a project forward.

The mind can open up to possibilities and potentials far beyond the waking consciousness. Meditation can often aid in this process of creative dreaming, whether we use it before sleep to open up to the creative self or use it after dreaming to gain a greater understanding.

Part of the process of using inspiration as a dream tool is to be able to remove the restrictions placed on us by the society in which we live. We need to know and understand ourselves what makes us the unique individuals that we are, as well as what we need to do to bring out our best qualities. The way a child grows in understanding as it matures is a good matrix for spiritual and creative growth.

As adults, with the realization that we are very much part of a greater whole, we can begin to take responsibility for the creation of a better, fuller existence for ourselves and finally accept that, by doing so, we can build a better and more stable future. Whatever stage of understanding we may have reached, dreams can help and encourage us or indicate that we are going down a particular route which may not be worthwhile.

Dreams can be taken as events in their own right and be interpreted as such. Whether they make sense, or whether we choose to act on the information given, is decided by us and us alone. We can also accept dreams as an expression of the unconscious creative self, which can contain a message given either in an easy-to-understand form or in the language of symbolism, where initially the meanings are not easily discernible.

It is when we begin to recognize the creativity behind the process of dreaming that we open ourselves up to different ways of approaching our own talents and abilities in a novel way.

THE HYPNAGOGIC AND HYPNOPOMPIC STATES

With practice, the states between waking and sleeping (or indeed sleeping and waking) can also be a time when wishes and desires can be given substance and brought into reality in a particularly magical way.

Briefly, the hypnagogic state is one which occurs between waking and sleeping, whilst the hypnopompic occurs between sleeping and waking. The best explanation of these two states comes from the realms of Spiritualism. The Astral Planes are those levels of awareness where the various thought-forms which have occurred are stored, and in the hypnagogic and hypnopompic states the mind has some access to those realms, without actually seeing spirit form.

Herbert Silberer sought to fuse contemporary ideas with mystical thought processes using the 'in-between states'. This is part of the process of the spiritual 'transmutation of the soul' found in most of the mystical traditions of the world. His book, *Problems Of Mysticism And Its Symbolism,* becomes a work of mysticism in its own right and is no longer a purely scientific work or psychological study.

While dream interpretation itself does not necessarily require an understanding of the 'hypno' states or vice versa, we can often use dream images and the hypno states to enhance our spiritual workings. The half-and-half awareness of consciousness and the semi-dream state that we have within the hypnagogic state gives us an opportunity to follow a line of thought which can clear away problems in an almost magical way. Learning to use incantations, blessings or prayers as well as colour and symbolism in this state can be highly productive. One such mantra might be:

May the good I have done remain,
May the wrongs I have done be washed away.

During the hypnogogic state, the mind is in idling mode when a review of the day can lead to insights about our behaviour or beliefs in surprising ways. By using this pre-sleep state to 'download' each day's material, the mind can then bring forward deeper and more meaningful images in dreams, the understanding of which eventually allow us to take more control of our lives. We learn to dream spiritually and creatively rather than simply using dreaming as a dumping ground. We then start the next day with a clean slate and can use the hypnopompic state to bring order to the coming day.

This can be an exciting time, and can open up all sorts of possibilities, such as the exploration of telepathy, ESP (Extra Sensory Perception), healing and so on. It is our choice which route of exploration we wish to undertake.

By their very nature, flashes of ESP are symbolic and indistinct and take on a hallucinatory quality. When they occur spontaneously in the 'hypno' states, they are more readily accepted as valid and open to interpretation in the same way as dream images. By becoming more practised at working in that state, we become more able to use the magically spiritual and psychic senses if we so wish. We are able to make use of a far more creative input than our 'normal' awareness.

Hallucinations

When dreaming, there is an hallucinatory quality about everything that we see anyway. We usually accept what we experience as real and, in the actual dream state, do not question it. It is only when we consider the dream afterwards that we realise how odd this may be. During dreams, things can take on qualities of other objects and of other feelings.

Dreams can create a reality of their own, they do the unexpected – which in normal waking life would be totally illogical and surreal; it seems simply that we observe what is going on. Even our own actions can take on an oddness about them and we can be liberated enough to create a totally different concept of our own abilities, our thought patterns and even our own past. We can often dream that we have done things in the past which we have never done, or more importantly we can prepare ourselves to do things in the future which again we would never expect to do.

The hallucination that we experience in dreams can also be the result of direct messages from the unconscious – psychologically freeing the mind so it can 'roam' at its own speed, allowing hidden memories, images and thoughts to surface in such a way that we can handle the input when perhaps in real life we might not have been able to do so. We create a reality which suits an action, rather than creating an action which suits the reality.

SLEEP DISORDERS

There are a number of sleep disorders that are worthy of note, particularly since any such disorder affects the quality and quantity of our dreaming.

Insomnia

This is probably the best-known sleep disorder and one from which many people suffer. The causes range from depression through stress to physical problems. To understand our own insomnia it would be necessary to recognize the underlying causes and to do what we can about them. In the case of physical problems, ensuring habits such as regular bedtimes can be helpful, as can all the well-known ways of handling the problem which include hot baths and massage.

It is worth noting that Chinese medicine holds the theory that some energy lines within the body are soothed or stimulated at certain times of the day and night, and that certain imbalances when identified and treated, will aid the management of insomnia. The organs of the body each govern certain psychological and physiological processes and understanding this, working with the principle and using alternative methods of management such as acupuncture, creative visualization or meditation can help. It has been said that ten minutes of meditation is worth four hours' sleep at night, so being able to make adjustments to our lifestyle could be of great help. Insomnia is a very difficult thing to deal with, not least because it can affect not only the individual's life, but also the lives of others round about.

Sleep Apnoea

Another sleep disorder is sleep apnoea. This occurs when the sleeper stops breathing for anything up to a minute. This then brings arousal from sleep, and the individual seldom has restful sleep. This condition does need qualified medical attention.

Narcolepsy

The study of narcolepsy, which is a condition where people can fall asleep in the middle of conscious activity, has yielded information on muscular movement in sleep. Under normal circumstances there is an area in the brain which suppresses muscular movement. This is called the *pons*. If this part is damaged or suppressed, then full muscular movements in connection with the dream occur. Such movements do not seem to be survival techniques or socially motivated, but are a form of release mechanism to enable the dreamer to deal with emotions and trauma. As part of that process, spontaneous movement and speech can occur. This is akin to automatism which can occur in changes of consciousness connected with many religious practices.

Nightmares

Nightmares and anxiety dreams have an intensity of emotion about them which we seldom feel at any other time. The commonest characteristic is the need for flight, i.e. to run away from the situation. The physiological reaction to fear of fright, fight, flight (then in the waking state, submission) seems to be involved here, except that we usually wake up before submission. It is almost as though it would be too painful to get into that submission state. Almost inevitably, on waking there is huge relief that one has escaped. Nightmares do appear to arise from six main causes. These are:

a Childhood memories of intense emotions. These are often centred around loss, and it has been suggested that such dreams are to do with the birth process and the severance from mother.

b Childhood fears, perhaps also centred around the same situation, though the fears at this stage also include the fear of being attacked, and also anxiety about our internal drives. This may be to do with the child's need for survival and to satisfy the basic needs for food, warmth and shelter. (It has been noted that, if those needs are not satisfied, the child withdraws into a world of its own. If, therefore, the rage it experiences is suppressed, this could surface later in nightmares.)

c In Post-Traumatic Stress Syndrome, where again the basic need for survival is threatened, it has been found that the anxiety experienced can still surface a long time afterwards. Some people are still experiencing such nightmares many years after the event. It would appear that the brain has not been able to discharge the trauma sufficiently for the sufferer to be at peace.

d The ordinary everyday drive to survive can surface in adults as fear of the future, or fear of change and growth. Essentially, it is fear of the unknown.

e Some nightmares are centred around an apparent sense of foreboding. Whether these come under the title of precognitive dreams is not decided. What does seem true is that the human being is capable of picking up information on a subliminal level, without being able to understand that information.

f Serious illness with all its fear surrounding death can obviously cause nightmares. Some help could be gained from therapy and counselling.

Recurring Dreams

Recurring dreams can have an element of anxiety about them. Indeed, it may be that they are triggered off by anxiety. The setting of the dream may always be the same. The characters in the dream may not vary, or the theme may always be the same. It is often not until we begin to explore our dreams that the anxieties and attitudes begin to change, and there is no longer a habitual response.

Sleep Talking and Walking

Sleep talking and sleep walking both seem to occur as part of a response to stimuli. Sleep talking seems to play a part in clearing the mind of worries and concerns.

Sleep walking also apparently has a purpose, in that if left alone the sleepwalker will attempt to complete whatever action was started.

TYPES OF DREAM

It is generally recognized that dreams tend to be of two types, those that Jung called 'big' and 'little' dreams. With practice we can record these in different ways; for example if we choose to write down our dreams by using two different books. Important dreams are usually easily remembered and we recognize the relevance fairly quickly, whereas the significance of lesser dreams may not become apparent until all the themes and dimensions have been explored. Frequently, it is worthwhile comparing important and less important dreams. The themes which are first presented in 'big' dreams are often enhanced and better understood by subsequent 'little' dreams. The more proficient we become at recording our dreams, the more easily they are remembered.

A further way of categorizing dreams is by dividing them into 'good' or 'bad' dreams. With a greater degree of knowledge, the dreamer can often change the outcome of a bad dream into a good one. This is called RISC technique and was developed in America as a therapeutic tool. The four steps are:

1) Recognize a bad dream while it is occurring.
2) Identify the bad feeling.
3) Stop the dream.
4) Change negative into positive. Initially, it may be necessary to wake up in order to undertake any of these steps. Gradually, with a greater proficiency, we are able to do this while remaining asleep.

Because change takes approximately six weeks to occur on a psychological level, we need to be patient with ourselves while learning these new techniques. Often, we notice changes in attitude fairly quickly, but they do not become habit until about six weeks later, since it takes time for them to become fixed in our minds. Given that we are prepared to change, it is often we ourselves who are most surprised by the shift in awareness. We may become better able to deal with issues which have previously proved difficult, or find that inner conflict is more easily and efficiently handled. By beginning to work with opposites – however they may present themselves – those opposites become more easily appreciated and handled in waking life.

Sometimes in dreams there is an intensity of emotion which can be extremely frightening. We may be incapable of feeling such an emotion in everyday life, but for some reason we can allow ourselves, for instance, to be terrified in nightmares. It is almost as though we know we can escape from the situation simply by waking up.

Anxiety Dreams

One of the most frequent dream themes is that of some form of anxiety. Anxiety dreams – while less intense than nightmares – often allow us to replay, and thus capture, those aspects of our lives which cause us difficulty. Disturbing elements in our dreams arise from our memories, stray thoughts or impressions and our own emotions which we deliberately suppress during waking hours.

Subliminal worries and problems can be allowed to surface with safety in anxiety dreams. While the images may appear to be the important part of such a dream, it is actually the emotion experienced which needs to be faced and recognized. By doing this, we are able to handle ordinary, everyday anxieties. Dreams associated with grief, particularly surrounding the death of a partner, are a particularly poignant form of anxiety dream and are a necessary part of recovery.

Dreaming can allow us deliberately to access and explore our anxieties. If we cannot meet our feelings of fear or emotional pain we allow ourselves to be controlled by them. Often by deliberately facing our hidden anxieties, dreams will give us information on what action needs to be taken to enable us to avoid making mistakes. Expectations of the future may be revealed through hidden anxieties.

Precognitive Dreams

Precognitive dreams are an interesting phenomenon. Opinions vary as to whether there really are such things. Suffice to say that when anxieties are dealt with and further insights gained, the dream function will often access the best course of action available and give the information through images. That course of action is then usually chosen by the dreamer, though it may be that the conscious mind does not readily accept the situation.

Magical and Spiritual Dreams

Magical dreams and spiritual dreams are also part of the framework of awareness, though there are those who will deny their existence. Dreams have often been proved to give information in more esoteric ways. Number and colour, and all of the symbolism contained therein, are a valid part of dream interpretation and, with a little knowledge, can create a structure which allows access to what would otherwise be hidden information.

Tradition which is based on wisdom, and rituals and ceremonies built around a knowledge of symbolism, are thus accessed. Personal management of the creative side of oneself becomes possible both through dreams and the directed use of power in the waking state, and dreams can act as a monitor for correct behaviour.

KEEPING A DREAM JOURNAL

Keeping a dream journal – that is, recording each and every one of the dreams we can recall – can be a fascinating but somewhat difficult task. Over a period of time, while it can give us information from all sorts of angles, it is an extremely efficient tool in dream interpretation.

We may find that we go through a period when most or all of our dreams seem to be around a particular theme, for instance that of the gods and goddesses. When we feel that we have understood that series of dreams, we can explore the same theme in waking life and enhance our knowledge.

It can be interesting to discover months or perhaps years later that the same pattern and theme recurs, with additional information and clarity. By keeping a dream journal at the same time as recording the methods and results of our contemplations, we are able to follow and chart our own progress in becoming a spiritual adept.

The dreaming self is highly efficient in that it will keep presenting information in different ways until we have finally got the message. Equally, that same dreaming self can be very inefficient in that the information can be shrouded in extraneous material and symbolism which will need teasing out of the rubbish. It is up to you to decide which explanation is more relevant, so if you are using your dreams as a spiritual or psychic tool you will interpret them in that light.

There are now a number of software programmes to help in the quantifying of dream content. Some people are prolific dreamers, others less so, and many more have 'big' dreams very rarely. In fact, we all dream at some point every night, often without remembering, though it does appear that the more we learn to remember our dreams, the more proficient we become at dreaming. It is as though the more we use the 'muscle', the better it responds.

A dream journal allows us to assess not just the content of our dreams, but also the pattern of our dreaming. Below are several steps necessary for you to keep a dream journal efficiently:

Any paper and writing implements can be used – whatever you prefer, although it will probably make things easier for you if you just use one journal at a time. You might also like to keep your writing implements separate from any others.

Always keep your recording implements at hand. You can also if you wish use a tape recorder to record your dream. 'Speaking' the dream fixes it in your mind in a particular way, enabling you to be in touch with the feelings and emotions of the dream. It is sometimes easier to explain the dream in the present tense. For instance, 'I am standing on a hill' rather than 'I was standing on a hill'.

Write the account of the dream as soon as possible after waking. Keeping an account – particularly of the more inexplicable or 'way-out' kind – is helpful.

Use as much detail as you can remember. A hastily scribbled dream is much less easy to decipher than one which goes into more detail.

Be consistent in the way that you record your dreams. One simple scheme is given below.

RECORDING YOUR DREAM

This is an easy way for you to record your dreams, which echoes that used by Calvin Hall. Obviously, the first three parts only need to be recorded if you intend to share your dream with others who do not know you.

If you intend to keep your dream journal private, this method gives you the opportunity to look carefully at each of your dreams and return to them at a later date if necessary, perhaps to compare content, scenarios or other aspects. It can also allow you to assess your progress in the art of self-development.

Name

Age

Gender

Date of dream

Where were you when you recalled the dream?

What was the content of your dream?

Write down anything that strikes you as odd about the dream (e.g. size, bizarre situations etc.).

What were your feelings in/about the dream?

DREAM MANAGEMENT

If you are just beginning to record your dreams, the important thing is not to try too hard. Being relaxed about the whole thing will give you far more potential for success than getting worked up because you cannot remember your dream or because you do not appear to have dreamed at all. The more you practise, the easier it becomes.

If you do decide to keep a journal, it is worthwhile incorporating it in the preparation for your night's sleep. Making these preparations into something of a ritual can help to concentrate your mind on the activity of dreaming, and thinking over a situation before you go to sleep, or meditating on it, can help to open the doors of the unconscious to some of the answers you are seeking. So, carefully laying out your tools, re-reading some of your old dreams, using deep relaxation methods, assisted by relaxing oils or herb teas, and even asking the superconscious for useable material can all assist in the creative dreaming process.

Try to wake up naturally, without the shrill call of an alarm clock or booming music. There are various devices on the market such as daylight simulators which come on gradually, dimmer switches, and clocks which have a soft alarm, graduating in intensity, which can help with this. Even a radio, tape recorder or mobile phone programmed to play soft relaxing music can be used. Using such waking aids can help us eventually to hold on to the hypnopompic state and use it creatively. Some dreamers report that the spoken word seems to chase away a dream, so gentle music is probably best.

On waking, lie as still as possible for a moment, and try to recall what you have dreamt. Often it is the most startling thing or feeling which you will remember first, followed by lesser elements. Transcribe what you remember into your journal, and write the 'story' of the dream. This may well give you an initial perception which is sufficient for your needs, both in the everyday and from a spiritual perspective.

Later, list alphabetically the elements of the dream, and decide first on the individual meanings of each aspect of the dream. Then look for the theme of the dream, and which part of your life it applies to. Often the theme is presented in more than one form, so that you 'get the message'. Next, reconstruct the dream and interpret it on a deeper level so you understand what kind of dream it is – that is, whether it is giving information as to the state of things as they are at the moment, whether it is suggesting a particular course of action or whether it is offering an explanation of what is happening within your Superconscious.

GAINING INSIGHT AND CLARIFICATION

There are several ways to gain insights through dreams, and this process is not necessarily the same as interpreting the dream. We can start off by defining the conventional meaning of something which comes up in a dream which will help us to understand our situation. Let us suppose that we are standing on a clifftop looking out to sea. The conventional explanation is that we are on the edge of something, perhaps a new experience (the clifftop). This experience may be to do with the emotions, since often water symbolizes emotions in dreams.

Insight comes when we apply conscious rationality to the dream scenario. Thinking about it allows the order and clarity to be seen, rather than the fact that everything is a complete jumble. On this occasion we are aware of the vastness and depth of the sea, and therefore understand that the emotions are far deeper and more meaningful than previously realized. This is an insight into our personality. The dream has been of use when we are able to apply that insight in everyday life.

We are aware in our dream state that we cannot decide whether to jump off the cliff (take a risk) or move away from the clifftop (refuse to face the situation or move away from danger). We then discover ourselves at the foot of the cliff. The interpretation is that we have achieved what we felt was right, and have taken the appropriate risk. The insight is that it did not matter how we did it; we simply trusted our intuition. By keeping the interpretation simple, the insight may be more telling.

Given the basic meaning of the dream action or symbol, it is possible to find out the necessary information to understand the dream. Having such information offers an interpretation of the dream; working with the interpretation gives insight. The dream vocabulary is both diverse and specific to each individual dreamer, and each person is so multi-faceted that several simultaneous explanations are possible, all of which may be equally valid. It will depend on the person who has the dream which one has the greatest validity.

Working at dream interpretation with other people, whether known to us or not, can be a highly illuminating experience. Taking the time to explore all facets of the dream – and bring into conscious memory all aspects of it – can deepen the insights that we obtain as we work with our dreams. Someone who knows us well may be able to see the relevance of some image in a dream to a situation we face in everyday life, whereas we are too close to the situation to be able to understand. Someone who does not know us well may have the degree of objectivity needed to round off an interpretation so that we can move forward.

The support offered through the insights that friends gain in interpreting our dreams can make a tremendous difference to our lives and theirs. Sometimes acting out a dream with friends and perhaps including the dream in a consideration of what may happen next can be helpful and can clarify a course of action for us. This does not simply mean using the imagination. We have the opportunity to work interpretations through more fully using our own techniques. We may choose to use meditation, guided imagery or other methods since these share much of the symbolism of dream imagery.

SYMBOLOGY

Dream image as metaphor is possibly the most potent form of symbology there is – it is what people will believe in. Frequently, there seems to be no context in which to place the figures which appear. The shapes manifest apparently at random yet, as we become more and more involved in the interpretation of our dreams, we discover they contain a message in themselves. They are an aspect of sacred geometry (the measurement of perfect proportion in the physical world) and, put simply, are the way in which the physical world reflects the spiritual. There are many images which demonstrate such a concept; below are the ones that are most likely to appear in dreams:

Circle – the circle symbolizes the Universe; a circle with a dot in the centre can signify the soul in its entirety and is sometimes taken to represent Woman or the essential feminine. A circular object – such as a ring – has the same meaning as the circle.

Crescent – information on the origins of this symbol are difficult to ascertain, but most sources agree that ancient celestial symbols were in use by the peoples of Central Asia and Siberia in their worship of sun, moon, and sky gods many thousands of years ago.

Crooked Line – deviance from the norm in a spiritual sense can be a falling away of the standards we have set ourselves. If we are aware of this on a spiritual level, a crooked line will often appear in a dream. The line may be any sort of line, such as a queue of people, a line of cars or whatever.

Cross – the cross shape gives rise to many images. Moving through the symbol of the sword with the crossbar at the bottom through the equal-armed cross, from there to the cross of suffering and crucifixion and finally to the Tau of perfection, the cross symbolizes the lessons the soul must learn. Through experience it overcomes the obstacles to spiritual progression. The arms of a cross signify conflict, anguish and distress, finally reaching perfection. The intersection signifies the reconciliation of opposites. The three upper arms are said to stand for God the Father, Son and Holy Ghost, but more properly they indicate any Divine Trinity. The hung cross with the figure of Christ represents the sacrifice of self for others.

Spiral – when the spiral moves towards its centre, it shows we are approaching our own spiritual centre via an indirect route. A clockwise spiral, moving outwards to the right, is a movement towards consciousness and enlightenment. If the spiral is moving anti-clockwise, it shows a degree of introspection towards the unconscious, and possibly regressive behaviour. The spiral convolutions on a shell have often been associated with perfection and therefore plenty. The conch shell was, and still is, used as a trumpet in certain societies, hence it may be seen as a warning. The spiral representing a flow of energy has a connection with the navel or solar plexus as the centre of power.

Square – a figure within a square is the Self or Perfect Man, perhaps the most recognizable image is Leonardo da Vinci's representation. A simple square signifies energy given expression within the physical world. A square within a circle suggests the actual act of 'becoming' or taking on form. Any square object signifies the enclosing and feminine principle.

Star – the five-pointed star or pentagram evokes personal magic, and all matter in harmony. Ideally, the star should point upwards. In dreams it signifies our acceptance of our own magical qualities and aspirations. If it is pointing downwards, it symbolizes evil and misuse of power. The six-pointed star, or Star of David, is made up of one triangle pointing upwards and another pointing downwards: the physical and the spiritual are thus joined together in harmony to create wisdom. Human nature moves towards the Divine and Spirit seeks expression through the physical. Twelve stars signify both the Twelve Tribes of Israel and the Apostles.

Swastika – this is a form of cross which, revolving clockwise, symbolizes positivity and the Wheel of Life. Revolving anti-clockwise it has a more negative connotation often connected with the misuse of power.

Tau Cross – spiritually, the Tau Cross signifies the key to Supreme Power and living a truly successful life. In the psychological sense, it signifies the meeting of the physical and the spiritual and all that that entails. Worn as a talisman, it protects from evil, and will often be perceived in this way in a dream.

Triangle – the triangle can represent family relationships, that is, father, mother and child. If the triangle points upwards, it is reaching towards the Divine, and symbolises Duality reaching Unity. If it is pointing down, it is any two polarities finding expression through the act of creation.

SPIRITUAL IMAGERY

Below we explain archetypes. For the purpose of this section we have defined these spiritual images and imagery as those which have arisen from the various systems of belief around the world. These frequently surface in dreams and are part of what Jung called the Collective Unconscious. These images are often recognizable, half-remembered and, once we have identified them, easily understandable. Obviously, in a book of this size we regrettably have not been able to include all such images, but hope that this short cross-section will whet your appetite for further research of your own.

So that it gives you, the reader, a proper flavour of how the entries in the book are laid out, we should point out that first part is a spiritual explanation, the second a slightly more emotionally slanted one – in these cases the popular meaning – which has developed over a number of years. Finally, the third section gives more down-to-earth information as to why we need these images in our lives and our dreams. Below that is a section on spiritual imagery, an important part of any dreamer's vocabulary. Some of the images also have individual entries in the body of the book which will further enhance your understanding.

✦ If spirituality is taken to be an inner truth, and religion as that which links us back to Source, then it must be the case that religious, or perhaps more accurately, spiritual imagery partly assists us in recognizing truths which we have long accepted as genuine. They are archetypal images which belong to everyone but resonate – or have a particular effect on each of us – in slightly different ways. Dreams have a way of introducing – or rather reintroducing – us to these images and when they begin to surface it is time to widen our appreciation of them perhaps by reading, perhaps by study, but probably most importantly by simple contemplation which helps decide what relevance they have to us. Using images that seem primarily to have a spiritual application allows us to integrate spirituality fully into our lives and does away with the idea that it is something separate from our daily lives but is, and always will be, an intrinsic part of who we are. Because the images are so specific they may be startling, but having the patience to work with them enhances first our understanding of ourselves and then our dream lives.

❤️If we are prepared to accept that each truth will have its own personal slant, and that we must get back to the basic Truth, all dreams can be interpreted from a spiritual point of view. This is especially true of spiritual imagery. Most interpretations here are stated only in general terms and are given only as guidelines. When you feel like throwing away the book and saying that the interpretations are not valid, then you will be able to take on personal responsibility and will only need the book for verification.

Angel – in spiritual terms the angel symbolizes pure being and freedom from earthly matters. Angels tend to be androgynous, and are not recognized either as male or female. There is a hierarchy of angels: Angels (the realm closest to the physical), Cherubim, Seraphim and finally the Archangels, Michael, Gabriel, Raphael and Uriel. As more and more people seek spirituality, there are those who have become more aware of the angel form, particularly in dreams. It is vital that we are able to differentiate between the personalized aspect of the Higher Self and the angelic form, since they are similar but different. To put it as simply as possible, the aspect known as the Higher Self has a stronger affiliation with the physical domain, while the Angels have a greater affiliation with the spiritual. The Dark Angels are reputed to be those angelic beings who have not yet totally rejected the Ego or earthly passions. When this image appears in a dream, we are being alerted to a spiritual transgression, which often has already happened. Angels who issue warnings usually symbolize what should not be done in the future.

Buddha – the figure of Buddha appearing in dreams highlights the necessity to be aware of the Qualities of Being which Buddha taught. These are the four Noble Truths. It links us to the power of renunciation and of suffering, but in the sense that experience of suffering is valid.

Breastplate – the breastplate of Aaron was a jewelled protection where the jewels had certain esoteric meanings and were also said to represent the Twelve Tribes of Israel. When we experience ourselves as wearing some form of protection around the heart, we are usually protecting our right to love unconditionally and protect ourselves spiritually. If we are particularly aware of the gems or jewels, they can also have a great deal of relevance

Ceremonies/Rituals – ceremony and ritual are all part of the heightening of awareness which occurs on the path to spirituality. In dream ceremony the images are even more vivid.

Consecration – any act of consecration, blessing or prayer is dedicating an aspect of ourselves to the service of our God. In dreams, consecrating an object is ensuring that it is used solely for spiritual purposes.

Christ – the ideal Christ is that part of ourselves which is prepared to take on our portion of the sufferings in the world by working within the world. We do not need to be crucified physically to suffer. Appearing on the cross, Christ signifies redemption through suffering. The anarchic Christ is the part of us whose love and lust for life permit us to break through all known barriers. The cosmic Christ is the part that is prepared to take on Cosmic Responsibility – that is, to be connected with the Universal Truth. While these aspects have been spoken of particularly in Christian terms, they are also present in all religious leaders.

Church or Religious Music – these sounds, dedicated to the perception of God that we have, are sacred sounds, creating a vibration which expands consciousness. This creates a different state of awareness and is a way of expanding the spirit.

Corridor or any passage – this signifies a state of spiritual limbo, of transition, possibly moving from one state of mind to another, or perhaps between two states of being.

Crucible – manifestation of spiritual or psychic energy can be perceived as a crucible, a transforming receptacle linking with receptivity, intuition and our creative side. As a container which is capable of withstanding great heat, it is the aspect which can contain change and make it happen.

Crucifixion images – in a dream, these links typify the human being's need to sacrifice himself through passion and through pain. The image of Man hung upon a tree is a very ancient one and is seen in stories of Odin, the Norse God who hung upon the World Tree for nine days in order to obtain Knowledge.

Devil – in dreams, the Devil represents temptation. This often arises from repressed sexual drives, animal drives and the lust for life which all demand attention. It may also signify the Shadow.

Ghosts – these arise from independent forces within, which are separate from the will. It will depend on personal beliefs whether we accept the appearance of ghosts as psychological or spiritual apparitions.

Gods/Goddesses – we are each given the opportunity to make real our fullest potential. In doing so, we must undertake an exploration of, and possibly a confrontation with, our perception of gods and goddesses, whichever pantheon we may believe in.

Hell – a state of being where nothing is ever as it seems and, alternatively, this could be thought of as continually existing in a state of negative illusion. Reputedly, it is a state of spiritual agony where our worst dreams are fulfilled. It is thought that the same actions are often repeated over and over again ad infinitum.

Heaven – a state of being where the energy is of such a high frequency that there is no suffering. In dreams, it appears when we are transmuting our awareness into the spiritual dimensions. It is reputedly a place where bliss exists and is also known as Nirvana and Samadhi.

Holy Communion – the belief that Christ's body was transmuted into heavenly food – symbolized by the Last Supper – appears in dreams as the intake of spiritual sustenance. Holy Communion represents a sacred sharing. Most systems of belief have evidences of feasts and celebrations where the whole community participates in a meal which has certain rituals attached to it. This is one example of transubstantiation.

Icon - an icon is a representation of a religious figure or concept. It can, through usage, become revered as a holy object in its own right. In dreams, it can signify the belief itself.

Incense – an offering to the gods and a physical form of prayer through perfume and smoke.

Initiation – this occurs when we are ready to enhance our knowledge and understanding so that we can 'be' – that is, use the power we have – in a different, more effective, way. Spontaneous initiation can occur in dreams. We transcend something within ourselves.

Mary, the Mother of God/Virgin Mother – the symbolism of Mary, both as the maiden and as the mother, is a potent one. She epitomizes all that is Woman, and all that is holy.

Moses – appears in dreams as the holy figure who will lead us out of difficulty. He often symbolizes a flaw in our personality for which there must be some kind of 'sacrifice'.

Ouroborus – the symbol of the cycle of existence. As the snake that eats its own tail, it is circular in shape and therefore has the same symbolism as the circle. It signifies eternal existence.

Religious books and Sacred Texts – there is a repository of knowledge available to us all. In dream imagery, this will often appear in the form of books such as the Bible, the Koran or the Torah. Other sacred texts will also appear in dreams at certain stages of development to help us towards understanding.

Priest/Prophet – a priest as a man of God belongs to the present, whereas a prophet will foretell events to come. Both are interpreters of Divine Will, so in dreams, if they appear together, they represent a conflict between the present and the future.

Religious Buildings – this includes churches, chapels, mosques, synagogues and temples. We all are aware of our need for sanctuary from the batterings of the everyday world. Within the religious building, we are free to form a relationship with our own personal God. Dreams are often one of the places where we first discover this sense of sanctuary. In dreams, we may also come to the realization that our body is our temple.

Religious Festivals – each system of belief has its own celebration, whether that be the Wheel of the Year, Christian festivals, Hindu celebrations or Shinto. Associated with these festivals are certain traditions such as Diwali sweets or the sharing of food. One such tradition is the Christmas tree which initially symbolizes the tree of rebirth and immortality (the World Tree), the return of the light and the beginning of a new phase of life.

Religious leaders – appearing in dreams, they epitomize the recognition of the ability to reconcile the physical and the spiritual, God and Man. They personify Perfect Man, a state to which we all aspire. Each religious leader has their own quality or particular perspective on spirituality which will resonate with us and which will manifest unexpectedly in dreams. Most often we will first meet the religious figure who belongs to our own early system of belief later widening out to include others as our awareness increases. So someone brought up as Christian may first perceive the Christ figure, someone of the Hindu faith might perceive Lord Krishna.

Religious Service – the act of worship which is used to bring people together. It is recognized in dreams, perhaps as an act of integration of the whole self, and as an illustration that the whole is greater than the parts.

Rose/Rosette – the rose in dreams carries with it a great deal of symbolism. It suggests Perfection and Passion, Life and Death, Time and Eternity. It also represents the heart, the centre of life and as a psychological symbol symbolizes perfection. It contains within it the mystery of life and its grace and happiness.

Sackcloth – the act of mourning in olden times often indicated some public show, and so sackcloth was taken as the substance to show the spiritual poverty of the people concerned – that they had lost something very valuable. Sackcloth in dreams indicates repentance and an outward show of such repentance. We may feel that we have humiliated ourselves, and wish to show the world that we have repented of an action or deed.

Seance – we need the qualities of patience and determination to contact our own spiritual self. Dreaming of being at a seance, or sitting, can suggest a need to explore the psychic side of our nature. Remembering that psychic means 'being in touch with self', this can suggest being aware of our intuition.

Sheaf – as the symbol of the goddess Demeter, the sheaf represents Mother Nature in her guise of the nurturing mother. It can also suggest a dying world, in that Demeter refused to nurture 'her' humans when her daughter Persephone was taken into the Underworld by Pluto. Previously, a sheaf, particularly of corn, would signify a harvest or good husbandry. Now it is more likely to suggest old-fashioned ways and methods of operating.

Shaman – when this figure appears in a dream he epitomizes the ability to travel with guidance through otherworldly realms. His totem animal will transport, guard and protect him as he seeks knowledge often on behalf of others. He will, in waking life, interpret dreams and will dream on behalf of the whole community or tribe.

Spirits – during spiritual development, our perceptions widen from the ordinary everyday to other aspects and dimensions of knowledge. The spiritual self has access to the Collective Unconscious in its entirety. When spirits appear in dreams, their function may be to help us through various states of transition. A kindly or helpful spirit signifies that we can move on. Seeing the spirits of dead people generally means we need reassurance.

Tabernacle – this is a place where a sacred object is kept for safety, represents a temple and therefore becomes a World Centre. To dream of a tabernacle is therefore to be trying to understand our own need for sanctuary and safekeeping.

Talisman – mankind has a deep connection with objects he believes to be sacred. In most Pagan religions, objects such as stones and drawings were, and indeed still are, given magical powers by special techniques which empower them. They retain the ability to protect the wearer throughout time. When such an image appears in a dream we are linking spontaneously with ancient magic.

Third Eye – this represents developed clairvoyant perceptiveness, or the clarity of vision that comes with spiritual development. It is the Third Eye of Buddha and symbolizes unity and balance. It is often represented in symbolism by the Eye of Horus. In no case does it represent a physical quality, though it is thought to link with the pineal gland.

Transfiguration – this is a phenomenon which can occur during altered states of consciousness. It is as though a light enters the personality and changes it; for this to happen suggests that there is some special purpose or Divine intent. In the waking state, it is taken to suggest being used as a spiritual channel. Spiritually, we need to be aware that we are all part of a greater whole, and this dream can occur as we are working through stages of transition in our lives.

Transformation – this takes place in spiritual terms when freedom of thought or action is indicated, or when higher impulses are substituted for lower reactions. As the growth to spiritual maturity takes place, there are many transformations which occur. These are often depicted in dreams as immediate changes, rather like a time-stop film sequence of a flower opening. Transubstantiation is a form of transformation which takes place through Divine Intervention when a substance 'becomes' something else.

Totem/Totem Animal – a totem is an object or objects revered as sacred; they will have particular significance for the owner. When they are given enough spiritual power by a joint belief, the objects are perceived as taking on a power of their own. A totem animal, similar to a guardian angel, appears when we are ready to accept that there are dimensions other than our own, which can be visited with the animal's guidance.

When we, through deliberate or spontaneous neglect, deny ourselves access to the store of spiritual imagery in waking life, dreams will often react to this lack and try to compensate by jolting us back into an awareness of our inner spirit. In today's society it is very easy to fasten on to the hypocritical aspects of religion and to accept that hypocrisy. It is also easy to make the assumption that the outward forms of religion often deny the existence of a true inner reality. If spirituality – the inner truth that we all hold – is neglected, it will not go away: it will simply reappear in its negative and terrifying form. In waking life, the closest image we have to that is the Devil, or the more vengeful Indian gods. Our own personalized demons can be more frightening than those. It is not until we accept responsibility for our own existence that true spirituality emerges.

ARCHETYPES

Archetypes are basic pictures that each of us hold deep within our unconscious and belong to what Jung called the Collective Unconscious. They are, in a sense, 'psychic' blueprints. These blueprints – while potentially perfect – can become distorted by childhood experiences, socialization and even parental experience. Throughout the book you will see various cross-references to certain archetypes and characters. They are the stuff of which dreams are made and closely approximate to the 'lost' parts of the personality that Fritz Perls decreed could be rescued. Because they are universal, archetypes can present in many guises, yet ultimately with thought are totally recognizable.

Three facets of our personality show themselves separately in dreams. Sometimes they appear as people we know, sometimes as fictitious or mythical characters or beings, and sometimes as other images.

The most difficult side we all have has been called the Shadow and is the personification of our worst faults and weaknesses. It is the part of us that is the same sex as us, but has been suppressed because it is frightening and unmanageable. Then there is the Anima, or in a woman, the Animus – this represents the opposite sex within the dreamer. In a man it is all that is instinctive, feminine and sensitive. In a woman, it is her masculine attributes of logic and objectivity. Finally, there is the ideal or True Self, which holds our highest possible creative potential and is most likely initially to communicate through dreams. Although the Self first appears as potential belonging to the future, as the other aspects become properly integrated the individual may then become the whole, real and many-sided Self.

If we are prepared to work with the archetypal images and to understand them, the dream figures can help to create a sustainable reality that exists beyond any of them. They will then have fulfilled their function, and so will be unlikely to reappear in dreams except in times of stress. Because the most important quality of our inner being is energy, which can then become power, each of these dream images represents a different aspect of those vital forces we have at our disposal, and each in its own way can stimulate this energy into action.

For an understanding of the archetypal figures and their functions, it is important to keep the aim of personal growth in focus. Personal growth takes place as we learn to understand and integrate each of these facets of our character. Each aspect of the personality must grow in its own sphere without disturbing the function of the others. As each aspect matures, we are able to understand more and more about ourselves. When conflict does arise between them, while the process may be painful it should not be destructive. The interaction between them should both enhance and hone the character; those parts, having first been seen as separate entities and then understood, should become familiar and properly integrated into the whole personality. Then it really is a case of the 'whole being greater than the sum of the parts'.

The Ego

When are dreaming and are observing what is going on, the part that observes is the Ego. Because it is our most conscious aspect, we tend to be more aware in dreams of the conflicts it has with our other aspects. When it has become split off or separate from other parts of the personality, we do not experience the world correctly. When this process goes too far, other aspects 'kick back' as it were, and try to redress the balance through dreams.

The Ego assesses our external reality but, if we are not careful, the need for an 'inner rightness' – an exaggerated need for fantasy – can overtake this reality. Developing objective self-criticism, observation of our fantasies and patience can create a balance.

The proper balance necessary between the inner and the outer, between logic and intuition or reason and imagination means that the Ego must be brought under control, although it can never be given up altogether.

The Shadow (a figure of the same sex as the dreamer)

This appears in a dream as the person whom we fail to recognize, a vague instinctual figure, sometimes standing behind the dreamer. Often this figure initially appears to be the opposite sex to the dreamer and can therefore be confused with the Animus and Anima. It is only later that it is recognized as the same sex. It is the part of our potential that we have never developed; it is our neglected side. It contains those aspects of our character that have already been thwarted and frustrated, but above all parts which have never been recognized.

Everyone has his or her individual Shadow, and it is nearly always the worst side of us that we have failed to recognize. Meeting the Shadow is painful: it is the shock of seeing ourselves as we really are at our worst. When we are able to face this dreadful entity with humility, we can accept ourselves, and from that acceptance learn to see the rest of reality honestly. We can then often resurrect those normal instincts, appropriate reactions and creative abilities that we have consciously suppressed and buried along with the malicious and destructive sides of the personality. When harnessed and understood, this vital energy becomes a force for forward movement rather than a dangerous enemy.

The Shadow will often appear in dreams as someone we heartily dislike, are afraid of or envy, but whom we cannot ignore. We begin to grow when we realize that some change in circumstance has given us an opportunity to bring it to the surface rather than ignore it in the hope that it will go away. When we work with these frightening dream images, we can often stop projecting the negative aspects outwards and use the energy formerly spent protecting or suppressing them for growth and creativity. We can begin to mature and be real.

When we are not prepared to explore both sides of our personality, we lose a great deal because the way in which we have experienced life most comfortably becomes more difficult. The extrovert discovers that he is unable to cope with the outside world, and the introvert loses his sense of inner peace.

Dreaming can enable us to integrate the Shadow into the personality in such a way that we are able to live more fully both on an inner level and on an outer level. Dreams can both alert us to the need for integration and also assist in the process.

Anima/Animus (a figure of the opposite sex to the dreamer)

No one can quite approximate to the ideal feminine within the man or the ideal masculine within the woman. This confusion of the inner ideal with the outer reality can cause a problem throughout life in any male/female relationship. These inner figures have been called the Anima and the Animus. If we can come to terms with them and accept them for what they are, they become the origin of our understanding of the opposite sex as well as helping us to open up to the inner realms. If this potential for androgyny (inner union) is neglected or abused, in later life the individual is likely to be cut off from contact with the important aspects of the opposite sex. It is possible that the suppressed inner function may come to the fore, making a man behave in an unstable fashion, whereas a woman may, for instance, become quarrelsome.

Anima

This is the emotional and intuitive side of the male's nature. Principally his mother, but additionally all the women the individual has known, will help to form his image of the feminine and give focus to all the feminine forces within him. In dreams this female figure may show herself as a completely unknown woman, aspects of women the dreamer has known, or as feminine deities.

Dreams make an attempt to offset unbalanced conscious attitudes. The Anima will often appear when a man is neglecting the feminine side of himself, for instance by forcing everything he is into the masculine which puts the qualities of tenderness, obedience and sensitivity beyond his grasp. If he fails to integrate these feminine attributes of warmth and genuine feeling properly, he will be perceived as rigid, world-weary or irresponsible. The suppressed feminine may also erupt into moodiness and temper tantrums rather than the more positive attributes.

When she is thwarted, the Anima turns into the completely negative feminine illusion who destroys all around her. The Anima becomes the guide to inner wisdom only when man confronts his destructive side and learns how to handle the energy he has available.

Animus

This part of the personality is the masculine part within a woman's character. When a woman learns how to integrate this properly, she is able to develop her logical, deliberating side, along with the ability to enhance self-awareness. This inner masculine is affected by a woman's early contact with the masculine around her. Interestingly, if the men around her have not been particularly adept in their own understanding of themselves, a woman's Animus can reflect that lack of understanding.

The Animus usually manifests itself in dreams to highlight the woman's need to develop the masculine traits in her personality. Only when she is able to develop her own judgement can she then use the masculine within to good effect without over-developing the need to compete with men, or equally to be destructive to other women.

If the negative side of the Animus dominates a woman's ability to think and plan, she may become obstinate and self-seeking, feeling that life, and particularly men, owes her success. When in dreams the Animus surfaces over and over again in one form or another, she must develop that side of herself that can judge without being judgmental, create strategy without being rigid, and can deliberately rather than instinctively maintain a hold on her inner reality.

Dreams allow us access to the peculiar characteristics which make each of us unique. When we have accessed the Animus or Anima we can allow ourselves to manage them in waking life and to take advantage of the energy released. There may be conflict between the masculine attributes and the feminine ones, but once some kind of a balance is established the integration of the whole character can take place. This leads to a much greater awareness, and ease of life.

The Self

The Self is the archetype of potential. It has in fact always been present, but gets hidden behind the necessary development of the personality, and can occasionally become confused with the Shadow. While the Shadow and Animus/Anima have almost deliberately been neglected, the Self holds the true secret of the properly integrated personality, which can only be revealed by working with it. Because the true potential beckons from the future, the first experience in dream form of the Self may be a figure encouraging us to move forward. Later, it becomes a symbol of wholeness, an ideal that we can work with in the here and now to create a sustainable future for ourselves.

As man begins to reach out further and further to understand the world he inhabits, a whole area of material becomes available to him which, if he dares, he is able to access and make use of. This is the unknown, unknowable higher spiritual quality held within us all. Each experience of it is unique, but its knowledge is truly universal. It is the inner guidance which we need to understand and trust. By learning to access this information, we learn once again that we are part of a greater whole with all its attendant glories.

We are often initially aware of it as a holy figure or some aspect of the particular god we have worshipped – Christ, Buddha, Krishna and so on. We exist through time and space as an entity, but are also involved in all things. It is often perceived as a knowledge we have already had without being fully conscious of it. We interact not just with other people but also with everything – we are ultimately all part of one greater whole. It is, as it were, a two-way traffic between the uniqueness and the glory of our being.

When images of this archetype – such as a guru, a god, a saintly animal, a cross, a mandala or other geometric shape – begin to appear in dreams, we are ready to face the process of becoming whole. This non-egocentric greater reality becomes so much part of our personal experience that we stand in danger of confusion. We belong to the human race and must live within our created world. We also belong to the spiritual world and have a personal responsibility within that realm. Only by achieving a balance between the two, and a full interaction, can we hope to be whole.

When negative or destructive images occur connected with this part, we are aware that we are neglecting the power of the Self. It is often at this point that we make a decision to advance and to change for the better. If we do not, often change will be forced upon us.

The Great Mother/Mother Earth

This archetype is the embodiment of all the aspects of femininity, both positive and negative. It suggests total wholeness in a woman, and is the ability to make use of all areas of her personality. In reaching for this perfection, woman must use and clarify all the separate functions of her being. She must learn to use sensation, feeling, thinking and intuition as her tools rather than as weapons. This archetype is not the exclusively mothering side of woman, but is a much more spiritual inner sense of Self. All life, and the instinctual awareness of its processes, is her domain, and can be cultivated in many different ways.

A Woman's Self

Every woman is the embodiment of feminine energy, ultimately seeking full expression in the Great Mother. Her focus is on the intangible side of life, on instinct and on feeling. Her abilities express themselves through the functions of sensation, feeling, intellect and intuition. She knows and understands the processes of life and death and of rebirth. Her images tend to be of fullness and nurturing, but also of the erotic and earthly.

She seeks to procreate, but at the same time knows she holds within the ability to destroy. She can be ruthless when it comes to destruction, seeing no point in maintaining that which she considers imperfect. In each individual woman there is a striving to express each function as fully and completely as possible, and she will tend to compensate for what she feels to be her own inadequacies by seeking balance through her man. Thus, the mothering type of woman seeking union with a man who needs mothering is often perceived, as is the virago with the hen-pecked husband. The interesting thing is that these relationships work until such times as either partner recognizes that they can develop other sides of their personality.

The Wise Old Man

This is the prime archetype for the man's whole Self, in all its aspects. Like the Great Mother for the feminine, he is the composite figure of all the masculine attributes, properly understood and integrated. When a person recognizes that the only appropriate guidance is that which comes from within, the Wise Old Man often appears in dreams. It is as though his appearance is triggered by desperation on the part of the dreamer. By pulling on the deep reserves of the unconscious, a guardian and friend appears to be a source of inspiration and understanding, to give advice and to support necessary decisions. Within the Wise Old Man are combined the functions of sensation, feeling, thinking and intuition.

A Man's Self

A man's Self will express itself much more through intellect, logic and conscious spirit. The civilized world and a technological society can mean that men are forced into the position of having to make decisions and judgements, which completely deny the intuitive function.

Primitive tribes had a much greater affinity with the earth and therefore less need to use intellect, but there is a tendency now to have the pendulum swing totally the other way. Each individual again grows into maturity by developing the functions of thinking or intellect, sensation, emotion and intuition. In this day and age as man understands more of the process of separation from the mother as a process of individuation and growth, so also he appreciates his need to be separate from, and yet connected with, his unconscious self. Provided he does not try to overcompensate by developing the macho side of himself at the expense of everything else, he will eventually reach a state of balance which allows him to relate to the rest of the world on his own terms. He will achieve an integration which allows him to function properly as a human being. If he loses himself too much on an intellectual level, his dreams will begin to depict the danger he is in.

The unconscious mind appears to sort information by comparing and contrasting. When we are aware of conflict within ourselves – whether this is between the inner and the outer selves, the masculine and feminine or whatever – we may dream in pairs of opposites (e.g. masculine/feminine, old/young, clever/stupid, rich/poor). It is as though there is some kind of internal pendulum which eventually sorts out the opposites into a totally unified whole.

The juggling that goes on in this way can take place over a period of time. A dream clarifying the masculine side of ourselves may be followed by a dream clarifying the feminine. Often in dream interpretation, looking at the opposite meaning to the obvious can give us greater insight into our mental processes.

Functions of the Archetypes

Jung began studying archetypes and dividing function into thinking, feeling, sensation and intuition. Initially, he did not consider the feminine aspect of this work. Following various advances made by his pupils, it became possible to build up a type of 'map' of the interaction between all of these functions and to discover where distortions occur.

Each function has a 'positive' and 'negative' quality which is perhaps better described as 'greater' and 'lesser'. Each of the masculine and feminine sides of the personality has these four functions, thus there are 64 (8 x 8) interactions possible. Where a distortion has occurred, we tend to project on to those around us the archetype with which we have most difficulty (often the Shadow). Consequently, there will be a tendency to repeat situations over and over (e.g. the woman who continually finds herself in close relationships with a father figure type, or the man who continually finds himself at odds with women executives) until we learn how to cope with – and understand – our distortion. The obverse of this is that, with awareness, one is able to accept other's projections on to oneself without being affected by them. Perfect balance would be achieved by using all aspects of the personality as shown below.

♦ The feminine archetypes are:

Kindly Mother – this is the conventional picture of the caring mother figure, forgiving transgression and always understanding. Because much has been made of this side of femininity, until recently it was very easy to overdevelop this aspect at the expense of other sides of the personality.

Destructive Mother – this woman may be the 'smother-mother' type or the frankly destructive, prohibitive mother. Often, it is this aspect who either actively prevents or – because of her effect on the dreamer – causes difficulty in other relationships.

Princess – this is the fun-loving, innocent, childlike aspect of femininity. She is totally spontaneous, but at the same time has a subjective approach to other people.

Siren – this type is the seductress, the sexually and sensually aware woman who still has a sense of her own importance. In dreams, she often appears in historic, flowing garments as though to highlight her erotic power.

Amazon – the self-sufficient woman who feels she does not need the male; she often becomes the totally career-focused woman. She enjoys the cut and thrust of intellectual sparring.

Competitor – she is the woman who competes with all and sundry – both men and women – in an effort to prove she is able to control her own life.

Priestess – this is the highly intuitive woman who has learnt to control the flow of spiritual information and use it for the common good. She is totally at home within the inner world.

Witch – the intuitive woman using her energy to attain her own perceived ends. She is subjective in her judgement and therefore loses her discernment.

The masculine archetypes are:

Kindly Father – this side of the masculine is the conventional kindly father figure who is capable of looking after the child in us, but equally of being firm and fair.

Ogre – the angry, overbearing, aggressive and scary masculine figure, often arising from the dreamer's relationship with their father or father figure.

Youth – the fun-loving, curious aspect of the masculine is both sensitive and creative. This is the 'Peter Pan' figure who has never grown up.

Tramp – this is the real freedom lover, the wanderer, the gypsy. He owes no allegiance to anyone and is interested only in what lies around the next corner.

Hero – the hero is the man who has elected to undertake his own journey of exploration. He is able to consider options and decide his next move. Often he appears as the Messianic figure in dreams. He will rescue the damsel in distress, but only as part of his growth process.

Villain – the villain is completely selfishly involved, not caring who he tramples on in his own search. He is often the aspect of masculinity that women first meet in everyday relationships, so can remain in dream images as a threatening figure if she has not come to terms with his selfishness.

Priest – the intuitive man is the one who recognizes and understands the power of his own intuition, but who usually uses it in the service of his god or gods. He may appear in dreams as the Shaman or Pagan priest.

Sorcerer – this is the man who uses discernment in a totally dispassionate way for neither good nor evil, but simply because he enjoys the use of power. In his more negative aspect he is the Trickster or Master of Unexpected Change.

Spiritually, when we have access to all the archetypes, we are ready to become integrated and whole, and our dreams will reflect this.

The next section of the book – the main part – is a 'dictionary' listed in A to Z order. At times some of the entries may seem somewhat idiosyncratic and indeed what you are expecting to find may be missing. By and large, as stated previously, it should be possible to find entries similar to the ones you are looking for. You will then be able to develop your own individual slant and will begin to recognize your own very personal set of themes and motifs which occur again and again. We would suggest that, as part of your record keeping, you devote some pages of your journal to a listing of your own personal meanings. It is fascinating in later years to see how you have worked through your issues in different ways.

May I wish you Happy Searching.

ABACUS

❋ Over thousands of years numbers have taken on a mystical and magical quality, which has helped man to understand his world and eventually led to scientific discovery. Numbers and mathematics have a great deal of significance within spiritual development and thus anything which represents counting or classification bears careful interpretation. An abacus, which allows you to learn about numbers and such concepts as addition, subtraction, multiplication and division, is today more of a child's toy than a scientific instrument. Though basic, it often suggests keeping some kind of a tally.

♥ Counting is an extension of language and the psychological significance of a measuring tool such as an abacus is often linked with the idea of learning new skills. A broken abacus may signify the ending of childhood or of innocence.

▦ An abacus may simply be a reminder of times past which were perhaps less stressful than they are now.

⊞ An abacus is an introduction to logic, a masculine quality, rather than intuition, a more feminine one. When a man dreams of an abacus, it may be that he is being reminded of the more logical side of his personality, or the need to calculate risk, whereas a woman may need to become conscious of her more objective qualities rather than rely on her emotions.

Additional information can be gleaned by reading the entries for Calculator, Numbers and Toy.

ABANDONMENT

❋ There are actually several meanings of abandonment that can give rise to dream images. The first links with the idea of being able to let go completely – to be without restraint – and links with the Dionysian concept of abandoning the serious for fun, entering into a state of ecstasy and achieving an altered state of consciousness. The second meaning has a more negative connotation and deals with a sense of loss and deprivation. From a spiritual perspective this can arise from the initial separation anxiety that a baby may suffer when it is first born and realizes that it is no longer in the safe environment of the womb. There can also be a strong sense, as we progress spiritually, of having been abandoned or of having lost something important, perhaps our relationship with the Divine. Dreams can often help us to reconnect as we become more conscious of needing to find a safe haven.

✪ To be abandoned, i.e. without restraint, within a dream may mean that we are seeking freedom or have issues with the idea of being constrained in some way. We are looking for the freedom to be ourselves. .

▨ Similar to the sense of being rejected, the sense of having been abandoned represents how we experienced not being wanted or not fitting in with others when we were young. Such a feeling can occur as a result of trauma. For instance, a child having had to go into hospital may have recurring dreams in adulthood of being abandoned and may have problems in forming plans for future success. In such dreams there is seldom a sense of closure, often a sense of unfinished business. When we ourselves abandon something, we are becoming aware that we no longer need a particular way of thinking or being.

⊡ A child's first and most important relationship is with its mother, so being abandoned in a dream will have slightly different connotations in a man's dream to those of a woman. For both, however, there will be security issues. Grief at the loss of a partner or family member can trigger dreams of abandonment, perhaps bringing to the fore many unresolved issues.

You may find it helpful to read the entries for Lost, Hospital and Mother.

ABBEY – *see* **RELIGIOUS BUILDINGS IN BUILDINGS**

ABCESS – *see* **BODY**

ABDUCT

❂ Abduction in a spiritual sense suggests being taken over by a force that cannot be contained and there is a stage in development where your dreams reflect the awareness of a spiritual force far greater than anything you have ever known. Many people believe that they have been abducted by aliens, and are radically changed by their perception of the experience.

✪ Abduction signifies being taken away against our will, forced to do something that goes against the grain. The two aspects of victimization and vulnerability come together in an act of abduction, reflecting an element of powerlessness in everyday life.

▨ If we appear to be the victim of abduction in dreams, we usually have an issue with authority, whether that is in a work situation or in our personal lives. It may be helpful to explore such difficulties to be free of the vulnerability this brings. If we ourselves are doing the abducting we should explore our need for control.

⸫⸬ Often in an intense relationship there is a sense of being overcome. For a woman this may result in dreams of abduction whereas a man is more likely to actually play the part of the 'knight in shining armour'.

You may find it helpful to read the entries for Alien, Hostage, Jailer, Kidnap and Prison.

ABNORMAL

❁ The abnormal or strange traditionally has possessed magical powers, possibilities or opportunities. In dreams we tend to lose the logical scientific side of ourselves and to tap into the more aware open side. Such things used to be beyond understanding and, therefore, appear abnormal and, even today, can make us aware of potential beyond the obvious. In dreams abnormality often represents something that we instinctively feel is wrong, not balanced properly or out of kilter. With an understanding of spirituality we are more able to put the balance right.

♥ An awareness of abnormality alerts us to the fact that we should be paying particular attention to areas in life that are not in line with the way we feel they should be. To dream of a giant, for instance, can indicate that our attention is being drawn to particular issues to do with size or deformity. There is something in our life that may be too big or too distorted to handle.

▦ If the abnormality is extraordinary, such as an abnormal feeling or sound, it is the strangeness that needs to be explored. Inappropriate behaviour or distortion of what we consider to be normal can give us information helpful in managing a situation in everyday life.

⸫⸬ In the balance within us of masculine and feminine, both men and women can find that, as they reach for a better understanding of themselves, dreams bring to the surface traits of character which we consider to be abnormal or deviant.

Considering the meaning of Magic/Magician and Size may widen your understanding of your particular dream.

ABORTION

❁ Pregnancy is a time of waiting and an abortion is an enforced ending of that time. The modern phrase 'termination of pregnancy' is much closer to the spiritual implications of a dream about an abortion. Generally we must give up a cherished project or idea that has not yet come to full maturity in favour of something else, which ultimately is more important.

♥ The need to look clearly at what we have undertaken to do or to be in our lives becomes apparent. We are in a position to make decisions that will get rid of what is no longer needed, or free us from responsibilities that we cannot handle. We have internalized a new way of thinking or of being, which, on further consideration, may need to be rejected.

🔲 There may be a need to reject a feeling, emotion, belief or concept that could be troublesome in some way. A risk has been taken which has not worked – often in relationships – and we must now make a conscious decision to restore the status quo.

🔳 When a woman is pregnant and dreams of abortion, particularly during a first pregnancy, she is often trying to come to terms with her new status and any fears and doubts she may have. Such a dream is not usually precognitive. When a man has such a dream he may be beginning to come to terms with some kind of emotional trauma, feelings that he needs to understand and perhaps mourn.

Additional information might be gleaned by consulting the entries for Baby, Family and Pregnancy.

ABOVE – see POSITION

ABROAD

🌞 Going or being abroad is all about new spiritual experiences. We are moving away from mundane earthly experiences, breaking new ground and transcending boundaries. If we are aware of the country we are in or travelling to, then there is a particular quality or character trait that may be developed in us.

♦ There is a psychological need to get away from, or leave, a situation. We are perhaps travelling towards something new. Our minds are more than capable of accepting new input and experience and will often do so on a subliminal level. We then become aware through dreams of what we have learnt, or what we have to do.

🔲 To dream about being or going abroad gives us an understanding of our feelings towards the widening of our horizons, or making changes in our lives. Such dreams may also be connected with beliefs about the country in the dream (See Places). We are dreaming about personal freedom or the ability to move freely around our universe.

🔳 Where the dreamer often travels in his or her workaday life, going abroad for a man may simply signify how he gets from A to B – a logical progression. For a woman her issues may be about security and emotional commitment.

Since the method of travel may be of significance, you may like to consult the entries for Aeroplane, Boat, Car, Journey and Transport.

ABSENCE

🌞 To experience an absence, or sense of nothingness, suggests the Void. This is more easily accessed in the dream state, since our waking brain receives too much input via our senses to be able totally to shut out any stimulation.

🕉 We are in a situation where we may suffer loss or where we may reject something we need. The type of dream where we are in a familiar environment, but a much-loved article or person is missing, suggests we may have a feeling of impermanence.

🔲 A dream about someone being absent, or of the absence of something one would expect to find, indicates that the unexpected may happen. We may be looking for something that we have already lost. Our feelings about the absence (e.g. fear or anger) may also be important. A child experiences a strong sense of loss when mother is first absent from his perceived environment and this can cause extreme distress.

You might like to consult the entries for Abyss and Lose/Loss/Lost.

ABUSE

🌼 Spiritual abuse suggests that our sense of rightness has been violated. Perhaps our beliefs or faith have been held up to ridicule. We do not have the resources to be able to withstand such an onslaught.

🕉 Emotional abuse in ordinary life can be experienced in dreams as violence and brutality.

🔲 Physical abuse can give rise to nightmares and other terror dreams, further depleting our resources due to both broken sleep patterns and the over stimulation of the Fright, Fight, Flight response.

Also consult Anxiety Dreams in the Introduction.

ABYSS

🌼 The Underworld, which contains ghosts, ghouls, demons and inferior matters, has been pictured so often as frightening that it often appears in dreams as the abyss. On a very profound level, the Void or abyss is the Unknowable, that part of the Cosmos that is beyond our understanding. Considering the meaning of the Void or abyss and exploring doubts and fears may help with interpretation of your dream.

🕉 There is a fear of losing control, of a loss of identity, or of some type of failure. More positively, it is possible to go beyond our own boundaries or present experience. Also the abyss indicates our coming to terms with opposites such as right and wrong, good and bad. To be on the edge of the abyss suggests having to come to terms with our own fears.

🔲 To dream of an abyss indicates that you recognize within yourself the so-called bottomless pit or void. This is an aspect of the unknown which all of us must face at some time or another in our lives. It signifies risky action which must be taken without knowledge of what the outcome is going to be.

Consult the entry for Empty for further information.

ACCENT – see VOICE

ACCIDENT

⚙ From a spiritual perspective there is no such thing as an accident, so in dreams such an occurrence signifies Divine intervention, or interference from an authoritative source.

♥ Such dreams may highlight anxieties to do with safety or carelessness, or fear of taking responsibility. When the accident happens to us our vulnerability is highlighted, when it happens to others we are made aware of the thoughtlessness of others.

▦ Dreams of being injured, murdered or killed occur relatively frequently and seem to be a response to threat. Attention, therefore, needs to be paid to the specific circumstances of the dream. We are usually receiving a warning to be careful or to be aware of hidden aggression, either our own or others'.

Also consult the entries for Fall/Falling.

ACHE – see BODY

ACID

⚙ It is the symbolism of acid that is important in a spiritual interpretation. As a corrosive substance which may or may not have a positive effect, there is an ambivalence in any interpretation. An act of corruption and potential destructiveness eats away at our integrity, yet may leave us feeling cleansed.

♥ Psychologically there is an awareness that self-confidence and our usual sense of well-being is being eroded by outside influences.

▦ A corrosive influence in our lives may be bad but the eventual outcome can be cleansing or healing. There could be the feeling that we are being 'eaten away' by some action or concept. We should become aware of something – perhaps words or actions – that must be used with caution, depending how and on whom they are being used.

ACORN

⚙ Life, fertility and immortality are symbolized by the acorn, as is the androgynous. In the seed cup is the feminine and in the nut the potential for all life. The two together suggest individual life.

♥ The germ of an idea is present. There is also a need for patience in dealings, either with ourselves or others (the acorn requires a long gestation period to grow into the mighty oak).

▦ When we dream of acorns there is a huge growth process beginning to emerge from small beginnings. There is a new potential for strength and spirituality. Since acorns appear in autumn, there may be the need to harvest or gather up the ideas before they can be stored, in order to give them time to work.

⚏ Androgeny is inherent in the acorn along with the close relationship between the masculine and feminine principles with its potential for growth. This often means that this symbol should be interpreted by the male as fertility (normally a feminine realm) and by the female as tenacity and strength (usually perceived as masculine traits).

ACQUIT

⚙ Any dream about a judicial process is usually to do with your own internal sense of right or wrong, so to dream that you have been acquitted of a crime suggests that spiritually you feel you can justify your own actions.

⚘ Whether we have chosen to develop it or not, there is an inner mentoring process which goes on in the background of our lives. Self-justification is not always possible on a conscious level, but dreams give us the opportunity to sort out our fears and doubts about our own moral conduct.

▦ On a more mundane level, to dream that you are acquitted of a crime denotes the possibility of legal action. To see others acquitted in your dream signifies that you are able to find compassion and forgiveness over others' misdemeanours.

You may find clarification by reading the entries for Authority Figures in People, Guilt and Juror/Jury.

ACTOR

⚙ There is an idea that we write our own scripts in life, so to perceive an actor on stage suggests that we each need to take responsibility for our actions and the act of living. Such an image may also suggest that we are somewhat dissociated from reality.

⚘ We each are actors in our own play, so to see ourselves as actors suggests we may be projecting a particular persona or specific aspect of ourselves. We may not yet feel that we are in control of our own destiny, but are being ruled by the circumstances around us. We are being given the opportunity to make changes and become a different person.

▦ To dream of an actor, particularly a famous one, is to become aware of the ego in oneself. Very often we become conscious of the roles we are acting out every day and recognize that we are perhaps not playing the part we really want to in life.

⚏ In a man's dream an actor can represent the public figure while an actress will suggest one of the feminine archetypes and his Anima. In a woman's dream an actor may represent her Animus and an actress a hidden, perhaps unrecognized part of herself.

You might also like to consult the entries for Celebrity, Famous People and Theatre.

ADDER – *see* SNAKE AND SERPENT IN ANIMALS

ADDICT/ADDICTION

❀ Spiritually, this is connected with the pleasure seeking, hedonistic aspect of the Self, which seeks a change of consciousness for the better. The story of Dionysus, who taught men how to grow and tend the vine and to make wine because he felt that man deserved the ecstatic experience, epitomizes man's search for a better world, and the need to understand his own passionate nature.

♥ Awareness of addiction in dreams is an identification of the hold our own passions may have over us. We fear loss of control (that is, control over ourselves), but also our control of other people. To be with a group of addicts suggests we do not understand our own behaviour in social situations. We may be conscious of the fact that we tend to become the victim in everyday life.

▤ Such a dream allows us to recognize and acknowledge obsessive behaviour in ourselves or others. We may be subconsciously aware or have an anxiety that someone or something is taking us over. To be addicted to someone is to have abdicated responsibility for ourselves. To be addicted to a substance such as tobacco, alcohol or drugs in a dream suggests an inability to relate properly to the world we live in and that we cannot function without some sort of a prop or psychological crutch.

Also consult the entries for Alcohol/Alcoholic and Drugs.

ADDRESS – *see* EMAIL, LETTER AND PARCEL

ADOLESCENT – *see* PEOPLE

ADOPT

❀ To adopt a person or a way of life is to draw it towards you – to make it your own. From a spiritual perspective this suggests a process of learning to be comfortable within a given set of circumstances – to accept a way of being.

♥ It may be that an aspect of your life needs adjustment and the circumstances surrounding a dream of adoption need exploring. To dream of being adopted may reveal a basic insecurity over your sense of self.

▤ Dreaming of adopting a child suggests you may have doubts about taking on new responsibilities. Conversely such a dream may signify that you are now in a position to take on a new project or concept.

⊞ In a man's dream, being adopted may suggest fear of emotional closeness, whereas in a woman's dream, she may actually be seeking such closeness. Your own personal circumstances will often give further clarification.

ADVERTISEMENT

�',The dreaming mind will often use a well-known object or device to drive home its message and an advertisement is one of those devices. Information received psychically needs acknowledgement so we can move forwards.

💚 There is a need to put ourselves on the line and to be acknowledged for who we are. If we ourselves are the subject of the advertisement, we should expect to be more upfront and open about our activities. If someone we know is advertising themselves in our dream, we may have become aware that they have the ability to help us in our activities. Conversely, our subconscious may be alerting us to their need for help.

🔲 Depending on the other content of the dream, this indicates those areas in our lives that need to be acknowledged or recognized. For instance, an advertisement on a hoarding might mean a way of working in the world, whereas a television advert would represent a way of thinking. To dream of reading an advertisement in a newspaper might have a more personal impact than any other type of message.

ADVICE

� We all have an inner awareness. The Higher Self or spiritual part of ourselves will often manifest itself as a figure that is giving advice, sometimes a figure of authority or a parental figure.

💚 In dreams, accepting advice helps us to acknowledge the need for change – perhaps to be doing something you don't necessarily want to do. Giving advice is recognizing that you are aware that you have information that can be helpful to others.

🔲 Receiving advice in a dream means we should consider guidance from within, possibly from a part of ourselves that is unrecognized. A little thought will usually reveal which circumstances in our daily lives are under consideration.

🔹 In a man's dream, if he is receiving advice from a woman he may find it helpful to identify with which aspect of his Anima he is working. In a woman's dream, she may wish to consider her Animus as an ally rather than as an opponent.

Additional information can be gleaned by reading Archetypes in the Introduction and the entry for Family.

AEROPLANE

� By association with the winged chariot, the aeroplane represents a spiritual journey. However as more and more people use this form of transport, the aeroplane can simply suggest the need for quick action or change of circumstance. Like the bus, it can represent a group purpose.

An aeroplane denotes a search for psychological freedom, a move towards independent being. It also suggests transcendence of the mundane, a need to 'lift off' into new ways of thinking.

Dreams of aeroplanes can represent sudden or dramatic life changes. An aeroplane taking off represents a leap into the unknown and taking risks. An aeroplane landing indicates the success of a new venture or the outcome of a calculated risk. An aeroplane crashing suggests the failure of a venture or life dream.

In some cases the aeroplane can suggest a phallic symbol or the assertive masculine. A man may choose this interpretation at the beginning of a new relationship, whereas a woman is more likely to use this interpretation as she progresses further into the relationship and understands her partner's ambition and drive.

You may also like to consult the entries for Abroad, Airport, Bus, Journey and Transport.

AFFAIR

Dreaming of an affair shows we are seeking to integrate opposite polarities within ourselves: male/female, drive/receptivity, good/bad. Such integration and an understanding of the dynamics leads to wholeness and an ability to access hidden aspects of our personality.

We could be actively seeking emotional satisfaction in a way that is unacceptable in our waking lives. In dreams, to be having an affair with someone we don't know suggests that we should perhaps reassess our own needs and desires. If the affair is with someone we know but would not normally consider in that light we are perhaps looking for different sorts of satisfaction.

We need to come to terms with our own sexual needs and desires for excitement and stimulation. Dreaming of an affair allows us to release such feelings. We may feel the need to do something naughty or something that means we have to take emotional risks.

When a woman dreams of an affair, it is likely that she has registered that connection before becoming consciously aware of it. A man will tend to be more physically attracted before dreaming of an affair. Men tend to be better at analyzing systems while women tend to be better at reading the emotions of other people. They have an increased ability to bond and be connected to others.

For further clarification you might like to read the entries for Family and People.

AFRAID – *see* **ANXIETY DREAMS IN THE INTRODUCTION**

AGATE – *see* **GEMS/JEWELS**

AGGRESSION – see ANGER

AIR

☀ Spiritually, air signifies the Breath of Life and is the second element in the four creative elements of Fire, Air, Water and Earth, which together are part of the manifestation.

♥ Air represents the intellect and psychologically allows us to bridge the gap between the spiritual realm and the physical. As breath, it is a necessary part of life which tends not to be thought about until there is a problem. In dreams we will become conscious of air as a breeze or a wind of some sort.

▦ From a pragmatic point of view, air is a force which supports and surrounds all that we do, so in dreams to be conscious of bellows or a pump suggests that we need to use strategy and power to achieve our ends.

Consult the entry for Wind for further clarification.

AIR FORCE – see ARMED FORCES

AIRPORT

☀ An airport, because of its transitory nature, is a place for new experiences. We are ready to consider our spiritual progression, to move into a new way of perceiving life and all it has to offer. It signifies the desire for freedom, high ideals, ambition and hopes.

♥ Being delayed at an airport suggests that conditions are not yet right for what it is you wish to begin. We are being put in a position where our values may need to be reassessed in the light of our own – or someone else's – authority.

▦ In dreaming of an airport we are entering a stage of transition, making decisions to move into new areas of life. It may also indicate we are, or should be, making a fresh assessment of our own identity. Watching planes take off from an airport lounge suggests that we are – or fear – being left behind.

ALBATROSS – see BIRDS

ALBINO – see COLOUR

ALCHEMY

☀ Alchemy is the science of transformation and refinement, when crude material is turned into pure. While it is understood by most to be the turning of lead into gold, the spiritual significance is, in fact, the refinement of the spirit through understanding into a state of awareness approaching Divinity and the knowledge of Eternal Life.

♥ Alchemy from a psychological perspective is a philosophy of the cosmos and of mankind's place in the scheme of things. It is the refinement of thought, having the key through the Archetypes to unlocking an understanding of the innermost and unconscious part of the psyche. As an agent for change it has a relevance in dreams through both its symbolism and processes.

▦ Alchemy began as a rudimentary form of chemical technology, exploring the nature of substances, and in so doing developed a series of semi-scientific procedures in order to find the essence of those substances. It has that significance in dreams of a mundane nature when we are trying to get to the bottom of problems and situations.

ALCOHOL/ALCOHOLIC

❀ Alcohol as 'spirit' or essence is the conjunction of opposites, a combination of the principles of fire and water. It is a means of changing consciousness. In dreams where alcohol is a feature there is an element of attempting to transcend the ordinary and approach the Divine (the Essence).

♥ When the normal constraints we put on ourselves in waking life are removed, we can often reach our own truth. Alcohol as a symbol of the removal of restraint enables us to accept dream ideas we might otherwise reject. There is the recognition of the potential for emotional confusion out of which can come clarity. To dream of an alcoholic suggests that we need to look at the way we handle excess and obsession in our daily lives.

▦ When alcohol appears in a dream it suggests that in a mundane sense we may need or require a largely pleasurable experience or influence. We have available means of changing perception. We can afford to let go and 'go with the flow' of what is happening to us.

⊡ As the use of alcohol becomes more prevalent in the everyday, it can have the effect of changing the quality of dreams, bringing more frightening or incomprehensible images to the fore. Often these images need to be interpreted in the way that they were in previous times, as gremlins and hidden fears and anxieties. Men tend to be less inclined to interpret such images and to dismiss them as being irrelevant, women may choose to take note of them.

You may like to consult the entries for Abandonment, Drunk and Wine.

ALIEN/ALIENATED

❀ From a spiritual perspective an alien thought suggests one that goes against the grain. An alien being may be a manifestation of evil or, as something different and not yet understood, the Occult.

♥ To recognize that you feel alienated within a dream suggests that there is the potential in everyday life for experiencing oneself – or a part of oneself – as not belonging. To feel alienated from the dream scenario is the realization of being different from others in the way we live our lives.

◉ To dream of an alien being suggests that there is something unknown and frightening which needs to be faced. We have never encountered the strangeness of the being that appears in our dream and we must handle whatever happens.

ALLERGY – *see* **ILLNESS**

ALMOND – *see* **FOOD AND NUT**

ALONE

◉ Spiritually, dreaming of being totally alone suggests that we have reached a state of completeness, of wholeness. We have dissociated ourselves from the ordinary and the mundane.

◉ We have developed the ability to recognize the need to deal with our own emotional make-up without the help of others. By and large such a dream occurs within the framework of learning to meditate and highlights our individuality.

◉ Dreaming of being alone can highlight being single, isolated or lonely. More positively, it represents the need for independence. Loneliness can be experienced as a negative state, whereas being alone can be very positive. Often in dreams a feeling is highlighted in order for us to recognize whether it is positive or negative.

◉ In both men's and women's dreams, feeling alone can highlight the state of our relationships. When someone dies or a relationship comes to an end, such a dream can signify grief.

ALTAR

◉ In most religions the altar signifies a sacred space where we commune with the Divine In the presence of the Divine, we can give thanks and be at one. Spiritually an altar signifies both the barrier and the link between the physical realms and the spiritual.

◉ The act of sacrifice, or rather of making our lives sacred, needs to be acknowledged and can be done through ceremony. An altar is an appropriate place to carry out such ceremonies, so in dreams it signifies a special place of great meaning. What is placed on the altar is significant and can be interpreted in the light of your religious belief or lack of such belief. Psychologically, it is worthwhile considering what is being sacrificed or given up, either willingly or unwillingly, in everyday life.

◉ An altar in a dream represents the means or need to give ourselves up to something that is more important than the immediate situation. It can also represent the centre of your world, the starting point for a new life, or the giving up of an old one.

⚡ Within the framework of the differences between men's and women's dreams, working at an altar can highlight the difference between the archetype of the sorcerer, who tends to use power dispassionately, and the priestess, whose caring is more intuitive and in tune with what is needed.

Also consult the entry for Table as well as the information on Spiritual Imagery in the Introduction.

AMBER – *see* **GEMS/JEWELS**

AMBULANCE – *see* **TRANSPORT**

AMBUSH

☼ Any dream that contains an image representing a force greater than ourselves suggests an inability to handle circumstances around us. The most outstanding element of an ambush is its surprise, highlighting the unexpectedness of such a situation. Spiritually this may be, for instance, emotions and feelings about past events or traumas, with which we may consider we have come to terms but which re-emerge to trap us.

♥ Dreams of being ambushed suggest that we are subconsciously aware of being in danger. Our way forward is blocked until we deal with the problem. Waiting to ambush someone else suggests an element of cruelty in our make-up and that we are waiting for someone to make a mistake.

▦ Circumstances around us are not what they seem and we can expect the unexpected. Whether we can deal with what happens depends on our strength of character and ability to handle crises.

You may also like to consult the entry for Kidnap and Prison.

AMERICA – *see* **PLACES**

AMETHYST – *see* **GEMS/JEWELS**

AMPUTATION

☼ Spiritually any amputation signifies a loss of some sort – we may be attempting to disfigure the perfect. Often dreams show by their symbolism what is not right or good and a dream of amputation suggests that we need to take action to rectify the situation.

♥ We are suffering from a loss of power or ability and may, in the process, find that we have cut short an experience. Since pain is often a consequence of an amputation, we are trying to come to terms with pain or unpleasantness which has occurred in waking life.

▦ When we dream of the amputation of one of our own limbs, we risk or fear losing or cutting off, by repressing, a part of ourselves. There is loss of a facility or something we value. To dream of amputating someone else's limb indicates our ability to deny others their right to self-expression.

⊡ Arising from the patterning laid down in the womb, dreams of amputation of a limb can often have a sexual or gender specific meaning. In a man's dream there is an aspect of emasculation occurring, whereas in a woman's dream, she may be experiencing problems with aspects of her Animus.

You might also like to read the entries for Guillotine and Operation as well as the information on Archetypes in the Introduction.

AMULET – *see* **BADGE AND GEMS/JEWELS**

ANALYST

⚜ When we dream of visiting an analyst or therapist we are in contact with the transformative power within, the monitor that alerts us to the need to analyse our actions and reactions. Spiritually that part of us that can heal us is making itself felt.

◈ The presence of an analyst in dreams alerts us to the fact that we are not acting appropriately in a situation in waking life. Also, if we are undergoing therapy in real life, the professional person can become a figure of authority in dreams.

▣ By analysing our actions and ideas – and breaking them down into manageable parts – we can improve our everyday lives.

⊡ Often in dreams an analyst will appear as a member of the opposite sex, so it is worthwhile taking careful note of what the interaction is between you and other people in the dream scenario.

ANCESTORS – *see* **FAMILY**

ANCHOR

⚜ From a spiritual perspective the symbol of the anchor is particularly significant as it represents a boat and mast and hence the union of masculine and feminine. Its appearance in a dream shows we are working towards a time of a future tranquility. The anchor can also be the symbol of security and in Early Christian art was used as a representation of the Cross.

◈ Psychologically we need encouragement to develop the ability to 'hold fast' during a period of instability. If we can ride out the storm we shall survive. When an anchor is being dragged during a dream, the external forces are too great for us.

▣ When an anchor appears in a dream it usually means the necessity to remain stable in emotional situations. We need to catch hold of a concept or idea which will give us a point of reference in difficult situations.

⊡ In a man's dream the anchor can sometimes suggest his sexuality or perhaps his more creative urges. In a woman's dream it suggests either her nurturing side, intuitive abilities or perhaps the security of relationship, either personal or Cosmic.

You might also like to consult the entry for Boat/Ship.

ANDROGEN/ANDROGENY

☀ From the very earliest times the idea of two polarities being able to unite in perfect harmony has been inherent in all spiritual belief. The union of the masculine and feminine principle into one perfect being is a principle presented in various forms in art and literature. The androgen in dreams, at a certain stage of development, can indicate a perfect spiritual balance, a state of autonomy and primordial perfection.

♦ We need an understanding of how our emotional selves can balance our personalities. The presence of an androgen in dreams suggests that we need to reconcile opposing thoughts and feelings within ourselves to achieve a balanced progression.

▦ If we dream of someone and cannot decide if they are male or female we are making an attempt to reconcile the opposite sides of ourselves. We are searching for completion and wholeness.

⊡ In both a woman's dream and a man's dream androgeny represents a coming to terms with the dynamic that can be created when we have an understanding of all aspects of our personality. We have, on some level, succeeded in what psychologists term 'integration'.

ANGEL

☀ Nowadays, with a greater acknowledgement of the appearance of angelic figures, they are once again accepted as messengers of the Gods – heavenly powers and enlightenment. Traditionally perceived as beings of light, their appearance in dreams indicates that we are seeking a spirituality and purity of being that goes beyond the mundane. In almost all religious belief angels stand as intermediaries between us and the Divine. Archangels are a higher order of angels, each with their own responsibilities, and are more likely to appear if you are undertaking esoteric studies.

♦ From a psychological perspective the angel is the personification of the relationship with mother or mother figure and needs to be looked at as a separate entity to both her and the dreamer, i.e. as though it were a living, breathing being.

▦ Dreaming of angels indicates we are searching for a parental figure who gives unconditional love and support, or that we need to develop these qualities ourselves. We may be trying to introduce religious concepts into our lives.

◘ Angels' appearance in dreams – for both men and women – suggest that we need to look at concepts that are particularly spiritual in origin. Both angels and archangels are traditionally identifiable by their attributes.

You might also like to consult the information on Spiritual Imagery in the Introduction for further clarification.

ANGER

✷ Throughout history societies have believed that if their gods are displeased they will show their anger. If a dream figure is angry, therefore, we may feel that we are offending our own code of conduct or are suffering Divine displeasure. Often anger is symbolized in dreams by, for instance, a flaming torch or a raging animal.

✣ We can give ourselves permission to feel passion or aggression, which could be sexual or otherwise. Often the way we express emotion in dreams can give us information as to appropriate behaviour in everyday life. If someone is angry at you in dreams in an uncharacteristic way you may have offended them without consciously being aware that this has happened.

▦ Anger in a dream can often represent other passionate emotions. Aggression (an unprovoked attack) can be perceived as an extreme form of anger. We are struggling with the right to express that which is distressing us. We probably are unable to express emotion appropriately in waking life, but can do so in dreams. Annoyance is a mild form of anger which is a reaction to a perceived threat. It reflects our feeling that we are being denied what is ours by necessity or by right.

Consult the entry for Argue/Arguments.

ANIMA/ANIMUS – *see* ARCHETYPES IN THE INTRODUCTION

ANIMALS

✷ By understanding animals and their symbolism we approach life in a more simplistic and natural way. In Shamanism, one of the most ancient belief systems, animals are an intrinsic part of the shaman's (wise man or priest) journey into other realms. They are protective as well as being teachers.

✣ When we need some sort of understanding of our own psychological urges, animals will appear in dreams – and sometimes in everyday life – which symbolize those qualities. These are:

Antelope – the antelope represents speed, grace and beauty.

Badger – the badger is both well loved and much maligned. It signifies a hierarchical family structure and, because of its nocturnal habits, the basic wisdom belonging to the underworld.

Bear – the mother appears in dreams in many forms, the bear being one of them. The image may be of the possessive, devouring mother or of the all-caring mother. If it is recognized in the dream that the bear is masculine, the image may then be of an overbearing person, or possibly the father. *Also consult the entry for Family.*

Beaver – as a builder/gatherer the beaver suggests industriousness, preservation and best use of resources.

Bull – usually the bull in a dream denotes the negative side of behaviour, such as destructiveness, fear or anger (for example, a bull in a china shop). However, more positively, the bull is recognized as sexual passion or creative power. Slaying the bull indicates initiation into the world of the mature adult who succeeds in mastering his instincts, and can also represent the sign of Taurus in the Zodiac.

Cat – to dream of cats is to link with the feline, sensuous side in human beings, usually in women. Goddesses such as Bast the Egyptian cat goddess are usually represented as having two sides to their natures, one devious and one helpful, so the cat often denotes the capricious side of the feminine. The elegant but also the powerful yet overly self-sufficient aspect of woman, may also be perceived as the cat.

Chameleon – we are recognizing either in ourselves or others the ability to adapt and to change according to surrounding circumstances.

Cow – the eternal feminine, especially the mother or mother figure, is often depicted by the cow. This is partly because it provides milk and nourishment. *Also consult the entry for Family.*

Deer/Reindeer – the deer and the reindeer herd have a strict hierarchical structure. The deer symbolizes pride and nobility. We recognize our place in the world.

Dinosaurs – *see individual entry and also the entry for Monster.*

Dog – we may recognize a faithful and constant companion, a protector or, more negatively, somebody we can't shake off and who might make trouble. Dreaming of a dog we once owned or knew at a previous time in our lives shows that there may be memories associated with that period of our life, which hold clues to present behaviour. A huntress with dogs indicates we are making a connection with one of the feminine archetypes, that of the Amazon. A dog guarding gates or being near a cemetery signifies the guardian of the threshold and creatures that must be put to sleep, tamed or brought under control before there can be an initiation into the secrets of the underworld.

You may also wish to consult the individual entry for Dog.

Elephant – to see an elephant in a dream is to recognize the qualities of patience, long memory, strength and fidelity. In the more esoteric sense it signifies radiant and glowing wisdom.

Fox – a fox in a dream tells of hypocrisy, cunning and slyness. We should be aware of someone around us whom we do not particularly trust.

Frog – because a frog transforms (from a tadpole and moves on to the land), one appearing in a dream indicates a period or act of transformation. There is something unpleasant which eventually transmutes into a desirable asset (e.g. a frog into a prince). *Consult the entry for Reptiles in this section for further clarification.*

Goat – to dream of a goat is to recognize creative energy and masculine vitality. It may also represent the dark side of human nature, promiscuousness and sexuality. To be riding a goat is to be trying to come to terms with our relationship with the dark side of our nature. The goat may also represent the Devil or Satan, as seen in old woodcut images. It is also the symbol for the astrological sign of Capricorn.

Gorilla – in being so similar to the human being, gorillas have represented the more frightening aspects of mankind. As time passes, we recognize familiar aspects of a somewhat undeveloped personality coupled with a strong sense of family.

Hare – the hare highlights intuition, spiritual insight and intuitive 'leaps'. Intuition may be debased into 'madness' or capriciousness by fear or ignorance. Because of its association with the moon, the hare can, in its negative aspect, signify the Priestess/Witch aspect of femininity or the Priest/Sorcerer of the masculine. In its positive imagery, however, it is the radiant hare (often holding its baby in a cave) and thus the Mother of God. *Also consult the information on Archetypes in the Introduction.*

Hedgehog – the hedgehog can represent nastiness and bad manners, or quite literally our inability to handle a prickly situation.

Horse – the horse in a dream represents the energy at our disposal. A white horse depicts our spiritual awareness, a brown one the more pragmatic and down-to-earth side, while a black horse is the passionate side of our nature. A pale horse has the same symbolism as the figure of Death with this scythe. A winged horse depicts the soul's ability to transcend the earthly plane and, therefore, pass through the astral planes. If the horse is under strain or dying there is a severe weakening of the dynamic power that carries us forward. Too much pressure may be being experienced in our lives. If the horse is being harnessed to a cart we may be concentrating too hard on thoroughly utilitarian objectives. In a man's dream a mare will denote the Anima, a woman, or the realm of the feminine. In a woman's dream, being kicked by a horse may indicate the Animus or her relationship with a man. A horse that can get through any door and batter down all obstacles is the collective Shadow – those aspects of the personality that most people attempt to suppress. The horse as a beast of burden is often the Great Mother or mother archetype. Even though the horse has been superceded in waking life by the car, it still has huge significance in dreams. *Also consult the entry for Car as well as the information on Archetypes in the Introduction.*

Hyena – the hyena is generally taken in dreams to signify impurity, instability and deviousness.

Jackal – esoterically the jackal assists in allowing us to access past lives and the astral planes. The jackal-headed Egyptian god Anubis weighed the souls of the departed in the Judgement Hall. It is this that gives the jackal its quality of scavenger.

Jaguar – the jaguar's main qualities are its speed and balance. It stands for the balance of power between the dark and light forces.

Kangaroo – this animal often symbolizes nurturing, caring and motherhood. It also represents innate strength.

Lamb – the lamb is the innocent side of man's nature. It is said that evil cannot withstand such innocence.

Leopard – the leopard represents cruelty and aggression and traditionally the deviousness of wrongly used power.

Lion – the lion stands for majesty, strength and courage. It can also represent the ego and the passions associated with it. If we are struggling with the lion there should be a successful development as long as we are not overpowered, or the lion killed. A man-eating lion shows that an aspect of our personality has slipped out of alignment, putting both us and our surroundings at risk. A lion lying with a lamb shows there is a union, or compatibility of opposites; instinct and spirit going hand in hand.

Lizard – the lizard appearing in a dream represents instinctive action or 'one-track' thinking. *Also consult the entry for Reptiles in this section.*

Lynx – the main quality associated with the lynx is its keen eyesight, thus in a dream it can often portray objectivity.

Monkey – the monkey characterizes the infantile, childish and arrested side of our character. The qualities of mischief, impudence and inquisitiveness all belong to the monkey. While these are often seen as regressive tendencies, this quality of lively curiosity maintains a necessary lightness of spirit.

Mare – *consult the entry for Horse in this section.*

Mole – the mole is often taken to represent the powers of darkness, but can often signify the blind persistence and determination that enables us to succeed.

Mouse – the mouse's quality of timidity can often be addressed in the dreamer, if it is recognized that this can arise from turbulence and lack of understanding. *Also consult the entry for Vermin in this section.*

Otter – the otter is uniquely equipped to exist within its chosen element of water and to be able to gain subsistence from its surroundings, all things we may need to develop.

Ox – the ox depicts the ability to be patient and to make sacrifices for others.

Panther – the panther is a strong symbol for feminine energy, particularly in its freedom-loving aspect. It also signifies regenerative power: death and rebirth.

Pig – the pig is taken in Western belief to indicate ignorance, stupidity, selfishness and gluttony. We may be beginning to recognize these unattractive qualities in ourselves; without such recognition there can be no transformation or mastery of them. Ultimately, however, it is the qualities of intelligence and cunning that prevail. If we dream of pigs and jewels together it shows there is a conflict between the lower, basic urges and higher spiritual values. Perhaps there is a failure to appreciate spiritual values. Big litters of piglets can represent fruitfulness, although sometimes without result, since the sow can depict the Destructive Mother. *Consult the information on Archetypes in the Introduction for further clarification.*

Rabbit – rabbits appearing in a dream can mean one of two things: the obvious connection with fertility could be important, or it could be that the Trickster aspect is coming to the fore. A white rabbit may show us the way to the inner spiritual world and, as such, act as a guide. *Also consult the entry for Hare in this section.*

Ram – the ram is a symbol of masculine virility and power and, by association, has those qualities of the sign of Aries in the Zodiac.

Rat – the rat signifies a tainted or devious part of our personality or a situation we are in. It can also represent something that is repulsive in some way. We may also be experiencing disloyalty from a friend or colleague. *Also consult the entry for Vermin in this section.*

Reptiles – to dream of reptiles indicates that we are looking at the more frightening lower aspects of the personality. The unfeeling, inhuman aspect of the instincts, usually recognized as being destructive and alien, is often portrayed by reptiles and other cold-blooded animals. We may have no control over these instincts, and could, therefore, be easily 'devoured' by them. We learn to understand deceitful behaviour. Though we are afraid of Death or the death process, we recognize that we must go through a process of change in order to be reborn.

Seal – the seal is most beautiful in its own element of water, thus to dream of one shows that we are at one with our own domain. We are capable of progressing through our emotions.

Serpent – the serpent is a universal symbol which can be male or female, or it can be self-created. It can signify death or destruction or conversely life and also rejuvenation. It is the instinctive nature and equally is also potential energy. When the power of the instinctive nature is understood and harnessed we come to terms with our own sexuality and sensuality and are able to make use of the higher and more spiritual energies that become available. In a man's dream a serpent or snake may appear if he has not understood the feminine or intuitive part of himself, or when he doubts his own masculinity. In a woman's dream the serpent may manifest if she is afraid of sex, or sometimes of her own ability to seduce others. Because of its connection with the Garden of Eden, the serpent is the symbol of duplicity and trickery and also of temptation. *Also consult the entry for Snake in this section.*

Sheep – the sheep is renowned for its flock instinct and it is this interpretation that is most usually accepted in dreams. The helplessness of the sheep when off balance is also another aspect that is recognizable, as is the apparent lack of intelligence. The god-fearing, 'good sheep' and also the passive and 'sheepish' may have relevance within the context of the dream. To dream of sheep and wolves or of sheep and goats is to register the conflict between good and evil.

Sinister Animals – to find any animal threatening in a dream indicates the fears and doubts we have over our ability to cope with the stirrings of the unconscious. Such dreams are relatively common when starting out on personal spiritual development.

Snake – in common with serpent dreams, snake dreams occur when we are attempting to come to terms with our more instinctive self. Inevitably this has to do with the recognition and harnessing of energies that have been suppressed and thwarted. Since the most primeval urge is sexuality, the image of the snake is the most primitive one available. Because snakes are such a low form of life, while also being in some cases poisonous, they have become associated with death and all that man fears.

A snake twined around the body or limb indicates some form of bondage, possibly being enslaved to the passions. A snake, or worm, leaving a corpse by its mouth sometimes represents the sexual act (the little death), but can also signify our control of our libido. A snake in the grass image denotes disloyalty, trickery and evil. The image of a snake with its tail in its mouth is one of the oldest available to man and signifies completion and the union of the spiritual and physical. Being swallowed by a snake shows the need and ability to return to the ultimate and lose our sense of space and time. Dreaming of a snake twined around a staff or similar suggests that the unconscious forces that drive us are being released to create healing, rebirth and renewal. The colours of the snake may give additional insight into the meaning of the dream. *Also consult the individual entries for Caduceus, Colour, Eating and Shapes/Patterns, as well as Serpent in this section*

Squirrel – the squirrel represents the hoarding, acquisitive aspect of our personalities.

Tiger – the tiger signifies royalty, dignity and power and is both a creator and a destroyer.

Toad – dreaming of toads connects us with whatever we may consider ugly in life, or in our behaviour. However, implicit in that ugliness is the power of transformation and growth into something beautiful. For a toad and an eagle to appear is to note the difference between earthly and spiritual values. *Consult the entry for Reptiles in this section for further clarification.*

Unicorn – as a symbol of purity the unicorn traditionally could only be owned and perceived by virgins. It is a return to, and a resurgence of, an innocence necessary in self-understanding and it often suggests the control of the ego and selfishness.

Vermin – in dreams, vermin represent the enforced contemplation of something that is unpleasant and unnecessary or that has invaded our personal space.

Whale – as a mammal that lives within water, the whale symbolizes the power of resurrection and rebirth – man's ability to surpass personal trauma.

Weasel – the weasel traditionally highlights the devious, less than honest side of ourselves.

Werewolf – *See Sinister Animals and Transformation of Animals in this section.*

Wild animals – usually wild animals stand for danger, dangerous passions or dangerous people. There is a destructive force arising from the unconscious, threatening our safety. Such a dream may be a way of helping us understand and highlight particular anxieties. Dreaming of domesticating wild animals shows that we may have come to terms with our wilder, more unrestrained side.

Wild Boar – the wild boar depicts the archetypal masculine principal, and often the negative masculine in a woman's dream. We may be evading an issue that should be challenged and dealt with more daringly. *You may wish to consult the individual entry for Boar and also for Pig in this section.*

Wolf – dreaming of wolves may indicate that we are feeling or being threatened. This may be by a single predatory individual or by a pack of like-minded people. The she-wolf can be taken to represent the hussy, the unrestrained feminine, but also the carer for orphans and rejected young.

Zebra – this animal has much the same significance as the horse, but with the additional meaning of balancing the negative and the positive in a very dynamic way.

When animals appear in a dream they tend to represent an aspect of the personality that cannot be properly understood except on an instinctive level. Below are some common images that occur in dreams.

Animal with a cub – this represents motherly qualities and, therefore, the mothering instinct.

Baby animals – the childlike side of our personality, or possibly children known to us, can give us information about innocence and naivety.

Composite animals – to dream of composite animals could indicate some confusion in sorting out what qualities we need to use in waking life. The qualities of the various animals need to be assimilated and integrated in order to progress; there are two potentials of further development. If a half-animal, half-human is seen it shows that the dreamer's basic instincts are beginning to be recognized and humanized.

Deformed animals – the dreamer realizes that some of his impulses are out of kilter.

Domesticated (tame) animals – when we dream of domesticated animals we are aware of those parts of ourselves with which we have already come to terms. There are passions which are being used in a controlled way, although there is the suggestion that those passions were never very formidable.

Eating the animal – such an image is often about the 'demons' we create which can only be overcome by assimilating them in a constructive way. Shamanic societies believe that one takes on certain aspects of the animal that are superior – in certain respects – to ordinary human attitudes.

Godlike, talking, awe-inspiring or wise animals, or those with human characteristics – animal wisdom is simple and uncomplicated and, therefore, is innocent. In dreams and myths we personalize this quality. It is always important to pay attention to this aspect of animal life in fairy tales and dreams, since we need to be in touch with that part of ourselves.

Helpful animals – the figures of animals are an easy way for us to accept the help the subconscious and spiritual realms can offer. Your totem animal is traditionally your 'guide' through the unconscious realms.

Hurt young animals – we are perceiving a difficulty in behaving maturely or confronting issues in waking life.

Killing the animal – this is symbolic of destroying the energy derived from the instincts. It is trying to eradicate the very raw power of basic behaviour. Taming or harnessing the animal shows the efforts made to control our instincts and, if possible, make them productive and useful.

Parts of animals (the limbs, eyes, mouth, etc) – these all have the same significance as parts of the human body. If the four legs are particularly emphasized – possibly in contrast with a three-legged animal – the whole rounded personality with all four functions of the mind fully developed is being highlighted. *You may also like to consult the entry for Body for further clarification.*

Transformation of animals – in dreams, the metamorphosis of the dreamer or other people into animals and vice versa shows the potential for change within any situation. Coincidentally, magical techniques allow 'shape-shifting', permitting magicians and shamans to adopt animal form, and dreams give us an understanding of that process.

Trapped by animals – to dream of trying to find some refuge from animals, whether by building defences or perhaps by running away, is indicative of our struggle with our animal instincts and whether the action being taken is adequate. Such instincts may be threatening or damaging to aspects of our life.

Vertebrates – just as the human skeleton gives us an understanding of the 'structure' of our lives, animals with backbones often give an understanding of the organizational qualities associated with that animal. The smaller and lower orders of animal (such as rodents) signify the unconscious, the higher orders the emotions.

Wounded and/or trapped animals – this suggests that we have been wounded, either emotionally or spiritually, or perhaps that our natural instincts are not being allowed free expression and are, therefore, not functioning properly.

ANKH

❀ The ankh is a key to the way to knowledge of hidden wisdom. Traditionally it is also a symbol for life and for the universe. As you progress in spiritual knowledge, dreams bring hidden information to the surface and the ankh in dreams often signifies a new level of awareness.

The symbolism of the ankh is that of all-encircling power and protection throughout the trials and tribulations of physical life. It is the link between the human and Divine and for many is a magical symbol signifying initiation into such mysteries.

On a mundane level the symbolism is similar to that of a cross. It represents the dreamer's concept of the universe, or his religious beliefs.

Formed as it is from the symbols of Egyptian deities Isis and Osiris – and, therefore, representing the generative principle – in a man's dream the ankh can suggest the power of resurrection, whereas in a woman's dream it is more likely to suggest the power of life.

You might also like to consult the entry for Cross in Shapes/Patterns and Spiritual Imagery in the Introduction.

ANNOY – *see* **ANGER**

ANOINT – *see* **SPIRITUAL IMAGERY IN THE INTRODUCTION**

ANT – *see* **INSECTS**

ANTELOPE – *see* **ANIMALS**

ANTHEM – *see* **MUSIC AND SING**

ANTIQUE – *see* **OLD**

ANTLERS

Supernatural powers, fertility and nobleness of spirit are represented by antlers. An attribute of the primeval Horned God and his lust for life, they suggest power over nature.

Psychologically these represent awareness of the potential for conflict between our nobler self and the baser instincts. The antler with ten points is the mark of the shaman or holy man.

The deer is a noble animal, so the interpretation differs if the antlers are mounted, as in a trophy, or are seen on the animal. If the latter, then the interpretation is that of something that is supernormal and they may represent intellectual powers. If the former, then they may be interpreted as attempting to achieve high status.

Antlers in dreams may always be considered to represent virility and sexual prowess, whether in a man's or woman's dream.

Consult the entry for Horns to enhance your understanding of your dream.

ANVIL

The anvil is an attribute of the forge Gods such as Thor, Vulcan and Hephaestos. The symbolism is that of forging new life, creating new beginnings and so on, so signifies creativity in its rawest sense.

As an image associated with the spark of life and of initiation, the anvil was once a very potent symbol. As time progresses, other objects, more pertinent to the times in which we live, appear in dreams, but the anvil will still appear as we return to basics.

🔲 Depending on the dream circumstances, the anvil can represent the basic force of nature, brute force or a way of creating an initial spark. By creating a situation in our lives where we are going to be tried and tested, we are pitting ourselves against natural forces.

🔲 In both male and female dreams the anvil can be seen as a form of resistance which allows us to use our individual creativity to fashion our lives.

APE

🔆 As science discovers just how closely associated we are to the ape, it is hardly surprising that over the centuries this creature has had projected upon it aspects of our own character that we find difficult to handle. The ape in dreams, therefore, can suggest the Trickster, the mischievous side of wrongdoing, and irresponsibility. However, in Hindu belief the character of Hanuman the Monkey God teaches us of the unlimited power that lies unused within each one of us.

♥ One of the qualities of the ape is its ability to mimic, to copy and to learn by experience. To dream of apes may alert us to this ability, or for the need for us to learn by example.

🔲 Traditionally, to dream of apes or monkeys links with the mischievous side of ourselves. However, as perception changes, the symbolism is more of natural intelligence.

Also consult the entry for Monkey in Animals for further information.

APOCALYPSE

🔆 The end of the world as we know it is such a potent image that it is part and parcel of almost every religion's belief system. In dreams the apocalypse (literally 'the lifting of the veil') is often the revelation of hidden meaning. It has much to do with our fears, with the survival of the fittest and a reshuffling of those aspects of life that are important to us. In such dreams it will be your beliefs and your faith that is the saving grace. Usually there is a particular symbol associated with your own basic belief which separates you from others in the dream.

♥ Apocalyptic dreams tend to be more prevalent at times of great change, either personal or otherwise. You may need to protect yourself from others and hold fast to an inner conviction in order to overcome opposition. The sense of knowing something or having information that no-one else does is a feature of dreams of the apocalypse.

🔲 Dreaming of an apocalypse is quite simply marking a transition period, moving away from a former course of action or way of being. Instinctively you may feel that the risks you must take are too great, or that you can only effect change by a massive shift in circumstances.

You may wish to read the entries for Atom Bomb, Disaster and Nuclear Explosion.

APOLOGY

🔆 Spiritually an apology is an act of self-justification – an understanding of rightness – and it is this meaning that comes across first of all in dreams of such an act. To dream that we apologize to someone means we acknowledge a lack of integrity in ourselves. To receive an apology suggests a recognition of that same integrity.

💟 It is important that we feel good about ourselves and, as dreams are a way of righting an imbalance, we have a mechanism through apology to put right an act or deed, either our own or others', which has upset us.

▦ If we dream about giving or receiving an apology we are aware of having offended our own personal code in everyday life and can work out what we need to do to restore the status quo.

APOSTLE – *see* SPIRITUAL IMAGERY IN THE INTRODUCTION

APPLE

🔆 Spiritually the apple is the fruit of temptation, yet it is also a magical fruit containing the seeds of knowledge and awareness. An apple suggests a new beginning and a freshness of approach. In many traditions it is the fruit of immortality. Apple blossom is a Chinese symbol of peace and beauty.

💟 Eating an apple symbolizes the wish to take in information or knowledge. This has an obvious connection with Eve's temptation of Adam. As with many natural symbols, the phrases we use in the everyday can give rise to dream images. Thus to be giving someone an apple can suggest showing appreciation, whereas to pick up a rotten apple can signify meeting someone who is not good for us.

▦ Apples on a purely mundane level can signify fruitfulness, fertility, love and temptation. Sometimes in dreams they can suggest a particular time of year.

▣ It is mainly by association that the apple has come to represent the feminine principle and sometimes the maternal breast. It is more likely to have this meaning in a man's dream than in a woman's. As a symbol of carnal knowledge it represents fertility.

The entries for Food and Fruit may give further clarification.

APPOINTMENT

🔆 Time is a man-made concept so, from a spiritual perspective, when we dream of having to keep an appointment we need to make use of time in the most spiritually effective way. There may be an issue to do with our self-discipline.

◈ We can perhaps give ourselves a gift or a reward for good work. There is something that has to be accomplished within a certain time limit. Often the person we have the appointment with may be important.

▥ Dreaming of going to an appointment indicates we need to have an aim or a goal. The dream is bringing to our notice something our inner self feels we need to deal with. Missing an appointment suggests we are not paying enough attention to detail.

You might like to consult the entries for People and Time.

APPRENTICE

✹ An apprentice is technically assigned to a worker in order to learn a trade or profession. In spiritual terms, we all learn by example and, should an apprentice appear in dreams, we need only discover what it is that we should be learning.

◈ Life is a learning process and an apprentice suggests that a commitment has been given to enable us to learn more – to put our knowledge to good use and ultimately to pass on our own knowledge.

▥ To be learning as an apprentice suggests that we need more information in our working life. To be teaching an apprentice can suggest that we feel a promotion is appropriate.

⊟ Previously apprenticeships were more valid for men than for women, so to an extent the interpretation for a man or a woman will differ according to their age group. An older man might dream of his own apprenticeship whereas an older woman may feel that someone around her is lacking skill. Today's apprentices will not necessarily perceive a division in labour.

APRON

✹ An apron can represent a badge of office and, as in Freemasonry, this suggests craftsmanship; in ancient China it was part of sacrificial regalia. It also has the symbolism of dividing the body into the upper, nobler part and the lower, baser instincts.

◈ If you are wearing the apron this may indicate the need for skill. If worn by someone else the part of you that is represented by the dream person may need protecting.

▥ The apron can represent family ties, constraints or outmoded ideas.

⊟ It depends on the gender of the dreamer and the content of the dream whether this image is negative or positive. In a woman's dream it might signify her nurturing side. In a man's dream it is more likely to represent his relationship with his mother.

You may like to consult the entries for Body, Family and People for clarification.

AQUARIUM – *see* **FISH**

ARCH

⚜ Since the arch can suggest the yoni, the feminine receptive principle, this image usually suggests that we are experiencing a form of spiritual initiation. We are being born again, given a fresh start.

♥ The arch marks a turning point; if we pass through we have passed a test. If we do not then our circumstances must remain the same. We may be being protected by authority.

▦ When we dream of arches or doorways we are often moving into a different environment or way of life. We have to go through some form of initiation or acceptance ritual in order to succeed.

⊡ In a man's dream, passing through an arch suggests that he is learning to use his intuitive side more successfully, whereas in a woman's dream it is more likely to signify that she is becoming aware of her own heritage and mystery.

ARCHANGEL – *see* **ANGEL AND SPIRITUAL IMAGERY IN THE INTRODUCTION**

ARENA

⚜ Today sport is often used as an energy release, so we are more likely to dream of a sports arena or football pitch rather than an ancient arena. Spiritually an arena suggests a ritualized form of combat and sometimes sacrifice, but can also suggest the need for space in which to expand or enjoy group activities.

♥ We are developing a new focus of attention or an area of conflict. This conflict may need to be brought out into the open for due consideration.

▦ Dreaming of being in an arena, either as a player or as a spectator, highlights the fact that we may need to make the decision to move into a specifically created environment, one which gives more room for self-expression and creativity or theatricality.

You might like to look at the entries for Competition, Games and Rite/Ritual.

ARGUE/ARGUMENTS

⚜ Two aspects of an argument are worth noting from a spiritual perspective. You are trying to resolve some internal conflict or unsettled issue which may not yet have come to conscious knowledge. If you are arguing with only one person the conflict is likely to be between two polarities of thought in you; with more than one person the issue is probably one connected with a wider, more global belief or concept.

♦ When challenged it is often difficult to state our case properly. Dreaming of an argument can help us to vocalize coherently in ordinary life.

▦ Dream scenarios often mimic everyday problems, so the atmosphere during a dream argument can give us clues about our passion or real feelings over an issue. To be having an argument with someone with whom you normally have a good relationship suggests you are unsure of your motivation in actions you are taking.

▥ Arguments with members of the opposite sex suggest that some adjustment needs to be made in the way you approach relationships. Men may need to understand their own aggression whereas women may need to be less emotional. Certainly something is out of balance.

Consult the entry for Conflict.

ARMED FORCES

✦ Any armed force is a disciplined group made up of many elements. It is this bringing together of the correct balance of factors which gives us a spiritual interpretation – a strong force, usually for good, a coherent whole with a joint purpose.

♦ To be in the armed forces in dreams signifies belonging to a trained team; to be facing an army highlights our doubts about or refusal to accept a carefully thought out plan of action. While this may be for the greater good, in itself it may be dangerous. By its association with the sea, the navy in dreams signifies a more disciplined response to emotional matters, whereas the air force suggests the need for a targeted response to intellectual and philosophical matters.

▦ The idea of fighting for a common cause suggests developing qualities which we would not necessarily foster in isolation. As organizations that accept all types of people and develops their potential, the armed forces are not just fighting units but are, in theory, agents for change.

▥ In today's climate where everything is less regimented, a man dreaming of an army (or being a member of the armed forces) is likely to be about self-discipline, whereas a woman's dream is more about the aspect of belonging to a group of like minded people.

Consult the entries for Conflict, Sailor, Tank, Uniform and War for further clarity.

ARMOUR

✦ Armour, particularly the old style suit of armour, signifies chivalry, protection and the need to protect or be protected.

♦ We may be protecting ourselves from something we feel is threatening us. Our way of protecting ourselves may, however, be outdated and inappropriate in the present circumstances. In today's climate of terror, to be wearing body armour suggests trying to protect ourselves against the wrongdoing and aggressive actions of others or against our own fears.

▣ We need to be aware of emotional and intellectual rigidity in either ourselves or others around us. If we are wearing armour we may be overprotecting ourselves, whereas if others are in armour we may be overly aware of their defence mechanisms.

ARMS

✸ Arms are significant as a symbol of surrender, wisdom or action. One arm upraised denotes commitment but sometimes also suggests vengeance. Two arms raised sideways signify supplication; raised forwards suggest welcome.

♡ Arms – in the sense of weapons – are used to protect and defend. In olden times there were quite a series of rituals and stages of initiation with the Page becoming the Knight and making the transition from the arms bearer to the user of weapons. Dreams can mirror these initiatory rituals.

▣ It is worth noting the significance of the placing of the arms. If they are placed across the chest we are defending ourselves. If we are held in or by someone else's arms it suggests a need for security. A coat of arms or other such insignia suggests a form of recognition.

Also consult the entries for Body, Sword and Weapons.

ARMY – *see* ARMED FORCES

ARRESTED

✸ There are times when spiritually we are aware we are not acting according to our own beliefs. There is a need for a higher authority and we need to be stopped from coming to harm or creating problems. That higher authority is often the moral or spiritual aspect of ourselves.

♡ When in everyday life we are unsure of our motives in an action we are contemplating, dreaming of being arrested suggests we should stop and carefully consider our behaviour before we act.

▣ When we dream of being arrested, there may be a lack of integrity or good judgement. To dream of arresting someone else would indicate our instinctive disapproval of certain actions.

ARROW

✸ Arrows as weapons suggest power, energy and expertise. As a means of pointing the way we should go, they will often hint at the next steps we need to take in personal development.

◈ Communications that we make could be damaging to other people. We could either hurt or be hurt by directness. Arrows indicating direction can suggest the quickest and easiest route.

▣ If we dream of shooting arrows we are aware of the consequences of actions, either our own or other people's, that cannot be recalled or revoked. Interestingly enough, arrows can also symbolize words in dreams.

▣ The arrow often suggests masculine power in a woman's dream while it is more suggestive of drive and ambition in a man's dream.

You might like to consult the entries for Barb, Bolt, Direction, Shot/shooting and Weapons for further clarity.

ARTIST

◈ We tend to personalize our ideas of the Creator, or the Guiding Principle, and this often manifests as the artist in dreams. In the sense that an artist or creative person interprets a divine picture or idea as best he/she can, in dreams an artist represents the interpretive side of ourselves.

◈ We need to make use of our desire or ability to be creative in our own right – often not necessarily by painting pictures. We may also be linking with that part of ourselves that records events for posterity, literally leaving our mark on life.

▣ The artist in a dream makes us recognize the artist or creative ability in us. We are aware of the aspect of ourselves that is in contact with, and can interpret, the irrational, creative side of the unconscious.

Consult the entries for Broom/Brush, Paint/Painting and Picture or other creative tools as appropriate.

ASCENDING/ASCENSION

◈ We are searching for spiritual awareness. Ascension is an altered state of consciousness which can occur as a result of meditation and spiritual practices. Ascension frequently follows the experience of a descent into the Underworld. In dreams it is seen as acceptable and real and is often accompanied by symbols of Paradise.

◈ We are becoming conscious of being able to exercise control over passion or sexual pleasure. The transition from expressing our energy through sex to expressing it in self-awareness is often shown as ascending. The act of Ascension is a breakthrough to a new spiritual plane which transcends the state of being human. It is an awareness of different levels of concentration, which give a fresh perspective to being human.

▣ If we are climbing stairs, or going up in an elevator or lift, we are making a movement towards waking or becoming more aware; we are making an escape from anxiety or being down to earth and are freeing ourselves from physical constraints.

ASCETIC

❁ There is an attempt to find the spiritual in our lives and also a development of the will to be 'pure'. In a dream, to meet an ascetic or holy man is to meet our higher self and to recognize the part of ourselves that is continually seeking unity with the Divine.

❤ Psychologically we are searching for purity in ourselves or in others. Equally we may be afraid of that purity within ourselves and need to come to terms with it. As an archetype Jung frequently mentions his Wise Old Man who was present when he needed guidance.

▦ There is some conflict with natural drives. There may be an avoidance of sex or contact through fear or the need for restraint. We may be looking for simplicity.

Consult the entries for Hermit, Monk and Mystic for further information.

ASHES

❁ Ashes represent purification and death and symbolically the perishable human body and mortality.

❤ A memory or a learnt wisdom needs to be retained in order for us to use information. After an event or person has gone or disappeared from our lives we may dream of a fire that has burned out, leaving ashes.

▦ Ashes in a dream often indicate penitence and sorrow. We are aware that we have been overanxious and stupid within a situation and that there is little left to be done. That situation has outlived its usefulness. The ashes are what remains of our experience, which will enable us to make the best of a situation.

ASK – *see* QUESTION

ASP – *see* SNAKE IN ANIMALS

ASSAULT – *see* ATTACK

ASTRONAUT

❁ Any figure that is not 'of this world' alerts us to the possibilities of other dimensions of being, spiritually lifting us away from the mundane into other areas of consciousness.

❤ In that an astronaut moves among the stars but cannot do so without some sort of protective covering, we are alerted to the discipline and skill needed when working within spiritual and psychic realms.

▦ From a mundane perspective we perhaps need to recognize that before moving into the unknown we need skill and protection.

ASYLUM/ASYLUM SEEKER

☀ To be seeking asylum suggests the recognition that we need a sacred space. In the old-fashioned sense an asylum was an institution, so it may be that we are seeking safety in structure and proscribed boundaries.

♥ An enclosed space where we have to abide by rules imposed by others can give a sense of safety and security. Seeking asylum where one is not living in danger from our peers and compatriots suggests we are conscious that our thoughts and beliefs are not in tune with others. This may reflect a working situation.

▦ When an asylum seeker appears in dreams it is probable that we are neglecting part of our persona and putting it at risk.

ATLAS – *see* MAP

ATOM BOMB

☀ We have become aware of the uncontrollable forces of life and the unconscious.

♥ There is a fear of irrationality and of power that could be used wrongly. An atom bomb is a deliberately engineered explosion designed to be destructive. We may feel that someone else may destroy and nullify our carefully constructed life.

▦ Where anxiety regarding the external world is experienced, we need to be aware that the end of a particular way of life is imminent in an especially dramatic fashion. Often there is a sense of an explosion of destructive energy before everything must be rebuilt.

Consult the entries for Apocalypse, Bomb and Nuclear Explosion for further clarification.

ATTACK

☀ There is a spiritual or psychic threat. We often become aware on very subtle levels of threats or challenges to our beliefs and ideals and these can manifest as warnings of, or actual, attacks.

♥ If we are the attacker we need to defend ourselves by positive self-expression – we are making attempts to destroy some urge or feeling in ourselves or others.

▦ Being attacked in a dream indicates a fear of being under threat from external events or internal emotions. Unknown impulses or ideas force us into taking a defensive attitude. If we are being attacked by animals we are turning our own aggression and/or sexuality inwards; we have fear of our own natural urges.

▧ In a woman's dream, being attacked will often be to do with her feelings of vulnerability. In a man's dream, being attacked perhaps highlights his poor self-image. In both men's and women's dreams, playing the part of the attacker suggests frustration and lack of control.

You might also like to consult the entry for Wound.

ATTRACTION – *see* **SEX/SEXUAL IMAGES**

AUDIENCE

☀ Spiritually, an audience tends to be either the multiple parts of our personality, all of which are answerable to the Higher Self, or represents the external world to whom we are accountable in a spiritual sense.

◈ We need to be considering an aspect of our lives carefully, particularly one that takes place in public and needs expression. We are the creators of our own play and an audience may also represent the various parts of our own personality that we have created.

▦ If we are standing in front of, or broadcasting to, an audience, we are probably having to deal with important issues in our lives. We need to reach a wider audience. If we are in the audience, we are witnessing an emotion or process of change in ourselves. To dream of listening to a broadcast means we should be listening to the message that other people are trying to get across.

Also consult the entry for Theatre.

AUDITION – *see* **EXAM/BEING EXAMINED AND TEST**

AUNT – *see* **FAMILY**

AURA

☀ The aura is an energy field, perceived clairvoyantly as bands of colour, which surrounds the physical body. It is an expression of the Self. When we become conscious of an aura in dreams, we are becoming more aware of others spirituality.

◈ The aura is a representation of the power we hold within, the force field of our essential energy with which we attract and ward people off. Because in dreams we are more sensitive, we become more conscious of such subtle emanations.

▦ To perceive an aura in a dream indicates how powerful we consider ourselves, or others, to be.

Also consult Spiritual Imagery in the Introduction for further information.

AUSTRALIA – *see* **PLACES**

AUTHORITY FIGURES (SUCH AS TEACHERS, DOCTORS ETC.) – *see* **INDIVIDUAL ENTRIES AND ALSO AUTHORITY FIGURES IN PEOPLE.**

AUTOGRAPH – *see* **SIGNATURE**

AUTOPSY – *see* **OPERATION**

AUTUMN

✹ Symbolically autumn signifies a time of introspection when we can gain benefit from previous actions. We have the advantage of experience and maturity.

♦ Psychologically by recognizing the cycles of growth and decay that occur in our own lives, we learn that some of these can be brought to fruition without harm.

▣ We are being made conscious of the sense of something coming to an end. We recognize that the good in a situation can be 'brought in' and made use of, but the rest must be given up.

Consult the entries for Harvest, Spring, Summer, Seasons and Winter for additional clarification.

AVALANCHE

✹ The power of our own nature and emotions that have frozen could overwhelm us and stop our spiritual progress.

♦ Psychologically we need to regain control of forces outside ourselves. We are in a position that puts us in some kind of danger, most likely from old ideas and attitudes which have become 'frozen' by continuous use.

▣ If we witness an avalanche in our dreams we are experiencing a destructive force. If we are in the middle of an avalanche we are being overwhelmed by circumstances.

AXE

✹ The axe represents power, thunder, conquest of error and sacrifice. As a symbol it is seen in most religions usually representing divine, supernatural power.

♦ From a psychological perspective, an axe, particularly a double-headed one, represents feminine supremacy and intuitive power, often in the role of the huntress.

▣ When we dream of an axe we need to differentiate between whether it is being used against us or if we are using it. If it is used against us we feel we are being threatened by someone's greater power. To dream of using an axe indicates that we need to become aware of the destructive forces within us.

AZTEC – *see* **INDIGENOUS PEOPLES**

BABBLE

🌞 When we are conscious of a babble of noise within a dream it suggests that there is too much information for us to be able to sort out what is relevant. The significance comes from the story of the Tower of Babel when communication is said to have become impossible. Spiritually, babble has the added significance of perhaps 'speaking in tongues' – receiving information from a hidden source.

💚 Confusion in dreams usually alerts us to the need to categorize or sort out those things we do not understand. When we ourselves are babbling, we are not communicating properly; when others babble, we are not taking in information properly in everyday life.

▦ As babies are learning to speak, they tend to babble as first experiments, as though trying out language. Babbling in dreams has this same connotation. We perhaps need to speak out more clearly. Talking in your sleep seems to be the mind's way of expressing suppressed material, or concerns that you have not been able to deal with properly.

BABY – *see* **PEOPLE**

BABYSITTING

🌞 Babysitting is an activity which crosses the divide between the spiritual and the physical. Spiritually it suggests the nurturing, caring side of the personality or that part which is ready to take responsibility for others.

💚 Viewed from a psychological perspective, babysitting in dreams suggests that there may be a part of our personality which has not yet matured fully and needs looking after.

▦ For many teenagers, babysitting is an ordinary, mundane activity and thus provides a dream scenario in which they can work out their attitude to other responsibilities in their lives. For others it may highlight their attitude to family responsibilities or to parenthood.

⊡ In a man's dream, to be babysitting suggests an increase in responsibility which may not necessarily be family related, whereas in a woman's dream it is more likely to be.

BACHELOR

🌞 A bachelor or someone we know to be 'footloose and fancy free' appearing in a dream highlights the side of our personalities which prefers to have no particular ties. We are not tied down by mundane responsibility.

❦ We need to open up to the masculine side of ourselves in order to accomplish our destiny. Similar to the knight in tales of old, we sometimes have to challenge the status quo in order to achieve a breakthrough of some sort.

▣ To dream of meeting a bachelor indicates that we are searching for freedom either within our emotions or in our love life.

▣ In a man's dream it shows he may be wishing for the freedom to achieve something he might find difficult in partnership. In a woman's dream it indicates she may be feeling constrained by a relationship.

You may find further clarification in the section on Archetypes in the Introduction.

BACK

❦ Spiritually, sometimes we have to turn our back on the past and reject the known. It will be up to you to decide which elements of the past need rejecting. In certain dreams the backbone – because it is the most stable part of our structure – signifies the Self. Backache in dreams, if not due to a physical cause, suggests that we are under some pressure, vis-à-vis a moral or spiritual issue.

❦ If we dream of turning our backs we are rejecting the particular feeling being experienced in the dream. There is a possibility that we are repressing our own urges or do not want to look at our inner feelings. We are in touch with the past and with memories. Intellectually we need to consider our firmness of character and recognize what has brought us to our present condition.

▣ Dreaming of seeing someone's back suggests we should identify the more private elements in our character or those around us. We may also find that we are vulnerable to the unexpected. If the backbone is particularly noticeable in the dream we need to consider our main support structure.

You might like to consider the entries for Body and Stab.

BACKWARDS

❦ To look back into the past can sometimes be detrimental, and at other times helpful. In dreams, to be looking or moving backwards may suggest that answers to our present dilemma lie in the past. Past behaviour patterns may not be appropriate.

❦ When she looked backwards, despite being warned, Lot's wife was turned into a pillar of salt. To be looking back in dreams suggests that mentally we are not using our best faculties or are not looking to the future.

▣ To dream of going or walking backwards indicates that we may be withdrawing from a situation, or slow to learn from it. We may need to recognize that to continue in a particular situation will, at worst, stop our progress and, at best, impede it.

BAD

✹ Spiritually, anything that is bad or decaying has finished a positive cycle and is entering a negative one. Whilst a perfectly natural process, we do well to acknowledge this and dreaming of a 'bad thing' enables us to move on.

♡ If we dream of food being bad, we are not taking sufficient care of our inner needs. A bad smell in dreams could mean that our environment is not supporting us. Bad as in bad behaviour suggests we are rebelling in some way.

▦ When we dream of something being bad we are being made aware that the dream object is now worthless or defective. Feeling bad can have two meanings: one in the sense of being naughty and the other not feeling right. We are off balance in some way.

BADGE/BROOCH

✹ A badge signifies an emblem or insignia of office, an acknowledgement or reward for effort. Dreaming of such an object shows our need to be accepted, not just as ourselves, but also as part of a greater whole. A brooch also signifies an acknowledgement of value.

♡ We have been singled out for particular recognition, possibly because we have certain qualities. A badge can also have the same meaning as an amulet, a protective device against evil.

▦ To have our attention drawn to a badge makes us aware of our right to belong to a group. If a badge is recognizable in a dream we perhaps should try to assess what our feelings are about the organization or group involved. Brooches are often formed of precious or semi-precious gems and can impart a particular message.

You might like to consult the entries for Gems/Jewels, Keepsake and Jewellery.

BADGER – see ANIMALS

BAG

✹ A bag spiritually signifies the secret, the hidden and the occult. Long known as a symbol of femininity because of its association with the womb, it can also suggest intuitive wisdom. Occasionally it will suggest the elements of wind and air.

♡ Depending on the actual bag (e.g. a handbag, a shopping bag) and what is in it, we are probably hiding certain aspects of ourselves from public consideration. To be emptying a bag suggests that we are attempting to get rid of old concepts or ideas or other aspects which may be holding us back. To have lost a bag signifies that we have temporarily suppressed certain character traits.

▦ You may be having problems with the more feminine elements in your identity such as compassion or nurturing. There is an ability to use the social graces to achieve, and to cope with whatever occurs. A torn or broken bag may alert you to a health problem or to there being too much to deal with.

[⊡] Whereas previously men carrying bags were seen as effeminate, this is no longer the case, so in dreams a man carrying a bag can symbolize his attitude to his responsibilities. In a woman's dream a bag is more likely to represent her inner feelings.

BAGGAGE

❀ Feelings of sorrow or of being overburdened can manifest in dreams as baggage. The type of baggage will be important, bulky suitcases being less easily dealt with than a simple bag. The spiritual implication is that you are perhaps holding on to inherited or learned ideas, beliefs and concepts which are for you no longer valid.

❤ You are under some psychological stress and may have to decide that some projects or feelings can be left behind in waking life. When you have been carrying luggage or baggage in a dream and find it has disappeared, you have successfully dealt with the problem.

▦ To be carrying extra baggage in a dream suggests that you may be carrying an extra load, either emotional or practical. You are expecting too much of yourself or of others and are carrying past hurt or trauma, possibly from as far back as childhood.

For further clarity consult the entry for Luggage.

BAGPIPES – *see* MUSIC AND MUSICAL INSTRUMENTS

BAILIFF

❀ The bailiff in dreams signifies retribution, Karma or a backlash of some kind. Our integrity is being called into question.

❤ We have put ourselves at risk and have not fulfilled our obligations, or have not acted in an ethical manner. Unless we take responsibility for what we have done, we could be 'punished' by material loss and loss of status.

▦ When a bailiff appears in our dream, we doubt our own ability to manage our resources, both emotional and material. We are aware that we have overstepped the mark in a particular way and must be accountable to a higher authority.

You may also like to consult Authority Figures in People for further clarification.

BAIT

❀ Spiritually, when we are strong enough, we must 'tempt' negativity in some way in order to trap and ultimately control it.

❤ There is an aspect of our lives which needs bringing out into the open. We have to coerce that part of ourselves that is failing to co-operate into making progress. There is some kind of enticement which has to take place.

🎴 Baiting an animal in dreams suggests a degree of cruelty which needs addressing. If we are laying bait then the implication is that we are, at least in part, aware of the problem. If the bait is already in position then it is a warning to be careful.

🎴 In a woman's dream, putting down bait can be an indication of her doubts about her own ability to attract a partner. She may feel that she has to entrap or ensnare a partner. In a man's dream the more practical side recognizes the need to capture an elusive idea or concept.

BAKE/BAKER/BAKERY

🎴 Since baking is a creative act, combining ingredients to make something new, it suggests the Creative Urge. As a baker knows his craft, in dreams he may be seen as an aspect of the Higher Self. The bakery in dreams represents a dedicated area or sacred space.

🎴 Our creative ability may need to be enhanced or lightened in order for us to achieve success. If the ingredients we use seem strange or bizarre, we may need to transform our mindset vis-à-vis what we are doing in ordinary life.

🎴 We all have within us the ability to alter our approach or attitude to situations in our lives. Dreaming of a baker alerts us to this ability, of a bakery, to changes to our environment, and of baking, the methods we must use.

🎴 If a woman dreams of baking she will recognize this as her need to nurture. By and large in the case of a man he may be dealing with his own professionalism.

You might like to consult the entries for Cooking, Food and Oven.

BALANCE

🎴 Spiritually, balance represents fairness and impartiality. To be thrown off balance suggests that we have received a sufficiently bad blow or emotional shock for us to lose that impartiality. Balanced scales are a representation of the zodiac sign of Libra. This suggests an equilibrium between two polarities – often man's higher and baser nature. Justice – and, therefore, a balanced viewpoint – is symbolized by the scales.

🎴 To have the feeling that we are looking for the balance of a quantity of goods indicates we have more mental assets than we had first realized and need to start using them.

🎴 When we dream of trying to maintain our balance or of being balanced in a difficult position, we are searching for stability. To dream of searching for the balance in a financial account means we are looking for something which, at present, remains unrecognized and unknown.

⊡ In terms of spiritual progression in both men's and women's dreams, a representation of balance suggests an equilibrium between masculine and feminine qualities.

You may also like to consult the entries for Scales and Zodiac.

BALCONY

❁ When we dream of being raised above the ground in some way, we are beginning to recognize our spiritual competence or progression. There is perhaps an element of danger or arrogance in such a position.

♥ Psychologically we are searching for power within a situation in which we feel powerless.

▣ To dream of being on a balcony suggests that we are searching for a higher status than we have at present. To dream of being underneath a balcony indicates that we are aware of other people's need for status. At the same time we may be hiding from our own responsibilities.

⊡ In a man's dream, being on a balcony suggests an awareness of his need for status. In a woman's dream this suggests a degree of protection. In both it can represent the need for far-sightedness.

BALD

❁ Priests used to shave their heads to show they had nothing to hide. Before it became simply fashionable in today's world to be bald, baldness in a dream signified the attainment of spirituality with its attendant humility, and signified honesty.

♥ To dream of being bald when we normally have hair can be somewhat ambiguous. It suggests a loss, usually of intellectual prowess, but can also symbolize intelligence.

▣ To dream of someone who is bald when they normally have hair suggests we are being made aware of a degree of dullness in life.

⊡ Many men nowadays choose to shave their heads when they are losing their hair and are taking a practical step to deal with a problem. In a man's dream, therefore, when he is bald it will have less of an emotional impact than it will when a woman finds herself in that position.

Consult the entries for Hair and Head in Body and Hat/Cap in Clothes.

BALL – *see* GAMES AND SPORT

BALLERINA/BALLET DANCER

❁ The figure of a ballerina is dreamlike in waking life, so in dreams a ballerina symbolizes music, fluidity and the inner aspect of spiritual feeling.

♥ We are aware of the creative side of ourselves and the need for controlled movement, yet in some ways it is separate from us. We are in touch with the expressiveness of our own inner being.

▣ The fairylike appearance of the classical ballerina within a dream shows we are making a connection with the creative energy within. Also we are searching for balance and poise.

▣ Modern ballet is a powerful medium with which to signify emotion, so in a man's dream a male ballet dancer will represent his more powerful emotions, whereas a ballerina is more likely to suggest his Anima. In a woman's dream, however, the male dancer might suggest the Animus, while the ballerina suggests the more elusive side of her personality.

You might like to consult the entries for Dance and Theatre.

BALLET – *see* DANCE

BALLOON

❀ A balloon has a similar connotation as the sphere and the ball from a spiritual perspective but with the added symbolism of 'light spirited' joy, or indeed the spirit rising. Thus an ascending balloon – whether it is child's or hot-air – suggests that you may be making some kind of transition in your life.

♡ Balloons were once made of pig's bladders and were used by the court jester to lighten up the atmosphere around the king and to remind him that he was human. In dreams they may introduce a note of fun amid seriousness. A descending balloon suggests that there is a situation in life in which you need to be grounded and practical.

▣ Very often it is the colour of balloons in our dreams which are important. The number of balloons may also be significant, indicating a party mood or a celebration. A deflating or deflated balloon suggests that the energy has run out of a particular project.

Consult the entries for Colour and Numbers for further clarification.

BALLOT – *see* VOTE

BAMBOO

❀ Man is symbolized by the bamboo, inherently perfect yet able to be pliant – to bow before the storm. The bamboo also signifies gracefulness and friendship. In China, the seven-knotted bamboo denotes the seven stages of initiation undergone before becoming an adept.

♡ Intellectually, bamboo represents good breeding, long life and a fulfilling old age. On top of that, it highlights the ability to yield when under pressure.

▣ The pliability of bamboo indicates yielding but enduring strength. It is used as a cure in Feng Shui (the art of placement) because it is fast-growing, sturdy and will thrive in a variety of conditions. It will now have gained much of that significance in dreams.

🜨 In both male and female dreams the bamboo plant can suggest androgeny. *Also consult the entry for Androgen/Androgeny.*

BANANA

🜨 The banana generally symbolizes fertility and fecundity, but can also suggest sensuality. At one time it would have suggested the exotic.

🜨 In conjunction with other fruit, it can be taken to mean fertility or sustenance – a bunch of bananas signifies a good harvest. Green bananas means a plan has not yet come to fruition.

🜨 Most dreams about fruit are to do with sexuality or the harvesting of past actions. Conventionally, the banana, because of its shape, signifies the penis. However, it is also considered, because of its yielding nature, to represent the correct management of masculine sexuality.

🜨 Other circumstances of the dream will enable you to make a full interpretation. A single banana is more likely to be interpreted by a man in terms of the penis whereas a woman may interpret the same symbol as a caring (nurturing) action.

Consult the entries for Food and Fruit.

BAND

🜨 Dreaming of a band as a group of musicians suggests harmony within the Self. All parts of the personality are integrated. If the image of a band is that of a stripe, there is some limitation within your circumstances which needs to be recognized, and you may need to work within well-defined guidelines.

🜨 There is harmony on a psychological level which you can access. However, this requires practice and imagination.

🜨 A band of material or stripe may be highlighting a division between two parts. If, however, the image is that of a group of musicians, this would indicate the need for teamwork.

Also consult the entries for Orchestra/Orchestrate and Music/Rhythm.

BANDAGE

🜨 Bandages in dreams can signify preservation – as with the bandages of a mummy – as well as healing. It is likely that an aspect of your life needs caring attention.

🜨 We may have been made sick or uncomfortable by a difficulty within our lives and need to pay attention to our ability to be healed. If the bandage is coming or being taken off we may have overcome the difficulty, or we may have been careless.

🜨 If a bandage is being applied in a dream this shows the beginning of a healing process. There may be hurt feelings or emotional injuries which need attention. The area that is being bandaged may give information as to what the problem is.

For further clarification, read the section on Body and also the entries on Doctor, Hospital and Operation.

BANG – *see* EXPLODE/EXPLOSION AND SHOT

BANK/BANKER

🔅 A bank suggests a secure space, where our spiritual resources are stored and increased with effort. It may also signify a place where an exchange of energy or power takes place. The banker represents the controlling, knowledgeable part of ourselves and thus our right to have personal management of our spiritual assets.

💚 Our internal resources need to be available to us in such a way that we have energy in reserve. Our emotional resources, such as self-confidence, social ability and wisdom, are secure, although there may be some insecurity over the actual management of those resources.

▦ Money and personal resources tend to be the things with which most people have difficulty. In our everyday life our financial, mental or spiritual resources may need careful management from a professional perspective. Our sense of security, without which it is difficult to venture into the world, needs to be properly managed and monitored. Our need for an authority figure to help us deal with problems that arise are usually symbolized by the banker or bank manager in dreams.

▤ In a woman's dream a banker may represent a type of father figure and the bank, depending on her own inherent personal abilities, a secure space. A man's dream is more likely to depict his own relationship with the material world.

BANKRUPT/BANKRUPTCY

🔅 To dream of going or being bankrupt suggests that we have lost or cut ourselves off from a source of spiritual energy.

💚 Formerly, going bankrupt carried a great deal of stigma. Such a dream, therefore, highlighted our fears and doubts about our own abilities. In today's climate where there is less disgrace, dreaming of bankruptcy simply indicates a problem that needs to be dealt with – not necessarily a financial one.

▦ Since bankruptcy signifies a lack of the necessary resources, we will need to look at circumstances around us that reflect this state of mind.

BANNER

🔅 A common standard of spiritual behaviour might be expected by those who gathered under a king's or knight's banner. A banner in dreams has this connotation and can also suggest a message to be put across to others.

🟡 Psychologically we may adopt – or need to adopt – some kind of crusade or special cause. We need to know we have a common cause to fight for which is organized and specific.

🔲 If the banner in the dream is a commercial one, such as a street, advertising or protest type, it represents the need to have something, which we may previously have ignored or rejected, brought to our attention. If the banner is an old fashioned one – as used in medieval battles – it indicates a need to consolidate thoughts and actions.

You might like to consult the entry for Flag for further clarification.

BANQUET – see FEAST, FOOD AND MEAL

BAPTISM

⚫ Baptism is symbolic of many things: initiation, death and rebirth, regeneration and renewal. A rite of passage, baptism can signify acceptance by a group of people with specific knowledge. The method of baptism in the dream is also significant: water suggests cleansing, fire purification and air or wind renewal of the spirit.

🟡 When a ceremony or ritual signifies new beginnings, our way of thought needs to change in line with what we now know to be true. We can ascribe to a common belief.

🔲 To dream of being baptised indicates a new influence entering our lives, cleansing away old attitudes and opening up to many inner possibilities. To dream of baptising someone means you are ready to pass on knowledge to other people.

Also consult the entry for Rite/Ritual and Spiritual Imagery in the Introduction.

BAR

⚫ Since strength is a feature of any bar, such an image becomes the symbol of our spiritual power, and power in everyday life. Interpretations can vary; a blockade, for instance, prevents us from wrong action, whereas a public house suggests a relaxed atmosphere and attitude.

🟡 An iron bar suggests that we should look at how rigid or aggressive we are being in our behaviour. To be standing at a bar may represent a barrier to our sexual enjoyment or an awareness that we should preserve the status quo in our lives.

🔲 We need to handle ourselves with strength of purpose and are seeking acceptance from our peer group in some aspect of everyday life.

⊞ In a man's dream an iron bar might suggest an assertive nature, whereas in a woman's dream it is more likely to signify aggression or to have sexual connotations.

Also consult the entry for Barrier.

BARB/BARBED WIRE

🔅 The barb is traditionally the fork that the Devil carried with him, with which to goad us into action. Sometimes seen as the trident, it can represent the trinity of body, mind and spirit. Barbed wire might be seen as an entanglement which is not appropriate.

🛡 Intellectually, there are two potential meanings. Firstly, we are trying to be too smart. Equally we may be trying to force other people to do something they do not want to do. A barbed comment is one which is specifically designed to hurt the recipient and can take on this physical representation of a barb or barbed wire in dreams.

🔲 To be surrounded by barbed wire in a dream indicates that we are being prevented from moving forward by either our own, or others', hurtful remarks.

⬚ In both men's and women's dreams a barb can suggest aggressive male sexuality, whereas barbed wire is more likely to represent the legendary '*vagina indentata*' or all-devouring female.

BARBER

🔅 The old idea that one's spiritual power was held in the head gives rise to the idea that a barber signifies control of spiritual strength.

🛡 An influence is becoming more apparent in our lives which indicates a need for change. That change needs to be dictated by the way we perceive ourselves, rather than dictated by an outsider.

🔲 When we dream of visiting a barber we are considering a change of attitude, thought or opinion about ourselves.

Also consult the entry for Hairdresser.

BARE – *see* NUDE

BARGE – *see* PUSH AND TRANSPORT

BARK – *see* DOG, FOREST, TREE AND WOOD

BAR MITZVAH – *see* CEREMONY AND RITE/RITUAL

BARREL – *see* CASK

BARRIER

🔅 In spiritual terms, any barrier suggests a division between two states, e.g. the spiritual and the mundane, or the physical and emotional. The implication is that it has been placed there for a purpose, to alert us to a duality.

🛡 As a barrier signifies an obstacle to be overcome, or a difficulty to be recognized, the nature of the barrier and our reactions will clarify any action that needs to be taken. In our most vulnerable emotional states we may need some sort of buffer between us and the rest of the world.

If the barrier is a safety barrier we perhaps need to stop and consider our actions. To run into a buffer may indicate the need for caution. It suggests a parameter beyond which there is danger.

BASE

Spiritually, base material suggests crudeness and the unformed – something which has not yet taken shape. Our 'basic instincts' may be brought into play, requiring that we go back to original material.

To dream of base material or metal indicates that we are dealing with something that is not of the best quality and needs refining in some way.

If our attention is drawn to the base of an object we may need to go back to the starting point of a project in which we are involved in waking life. We should consider how stable we are in any situation.

You might like to read the entry for Foundations.

BASEMENT – see BUILDINGS AND HOUSE

BASKET

Baskets traditionally represent the seasons. A full one, for instance, is full fruition and abundance, a time of harvesting. As a container, a basket can also represent the feminine closing or receptive principle.

To be attempting to fill a basket can mean that we are trying to increase our talents and abilities. Somehow we feel we do not have 'enough'.

If the basket is full of bread it can represent sharing – as in a sacramental meal. If the contents are spilt, it signifies the possible failure of a venture or sometimes the premature ending of a project.

Because of its connection with the feminine, in a man's dream a basket can suggest domesticity or his caring nature. In a woman's dream, if she finds the basket heavy, she may be finding her responsibilities a burden.

BAT

A flying bat can represent discernment or obscurity of a spiritual kind. The meaning is often ambiguous, but being a nocturnal animal usually veers towards the negative interpretation. The vague unpleasantness may also suggest some idiosyncrasy within ourselves. A bat used in sports has the same interpretation as a weapon or tool.

To dream of bats attacking us shows the need to confront our fears of madness. Because of their mouselike bodies and birdlike wings, bats are seen as having a dual nature. When the image is of a sports bat, such as cricket or baseball bat, the suggestion is that we are not able to use implements without some kind of training. To dream of using such a bat indicates a learnt degree of competence.

Because popular belief has it that bats are frightening, to dream of bats indicates that there are thoughts and ideas within the unconscious that may reveal themselves with frightening potential. Dreaming of a cricket bat or other such implement will give an indication of our attitude to controlled aggression, or to how we deal with external forces.

You might like to consult the entries for Mouse in Animals, Birds, Games, Tools, Vampire and Weapons.

BATH/BATHING

⚙ From a spiritual perspective, any dream where water is involved suggests an act of cleansing or initiation. Communal bathing depicts innocence and sensuality combined.

♥ When we dream of bathing someone, it shows the need to nurture or to have an intimate connection with another person. We may have knowledge which can help or heal.

▦ When we dream of being in the bath, it may indicate the need for cleansing of some old feelings, the need to relax, to let go. We have an opportunity to contemplate what has occurred in the past and to adopt new attitudes. To be wearing a bathing costume denotes a degree of permitted exposure.

⬛ For many women a bath can be a relaxing time of contemplation and can, therefore, have that significance in dreams. For men, it is more likely to be functional and, therefore, a time of planning.

You might like to read the entries for Swimming, Washing and Water.

BATON

⚙ Symbolic of spiritual authority and rhythm, the baton is a tool to enable us to proceed in an orderly manner, under the control of a higher authority. A musical conductor's baton suggests this interpretation.

♥ If the dream is of a drum baton or stick, the dream may represent the need for self-expression in a more forceful way than normal. A baton such as those used in relay races is representative of the passing on of information or responsibility. This, of course, returns it to its original meaning, more pertinent to dreams.

▦ If the dream is of a police baton, then it can represent authority or male sexuality and our attitudes to them.

⬛ In a woman's dream the baton can suggest perfect timing, whereas in a man's dream it is more likely to suggest authority.

BATTLE/BATTLEGROUND – *see* ARENA, FIGHTING AND WAR

BATTERY

⚙ A battery symbolizes both power and energy. To dream of a battery running out of power suggests that there may be a health problem as yet unrecognized.

◈ As there are now so many different types of battery, ranging from tiny transistor types to large cells, the interpretation will vary somewhat. Largely, however, a battery is seen as a source of power.

▦ More mundanely, we may be having a problem in finding the energy to complete a project and need to find a different source of inspiration.

⊡ In both men and women's dreams, since the principle is one of a balance of positive and negative, a battery can suggest the libido or the driving force.

BAY

◈ The wolf baying at the moon shows the overcoming of basic animal instincts. The bay tree or leaves signify victory, eternity and immortality.

◈ To be keeping something at bay indicates a need to be on our guard – on some level we are feeling threatened.

▦ Traditionally to be conscious of a bay or inlet showed an awareness of a woman's sexuality and receptiveness. Since water signifies emotion, a bay or inlet can also represent a sinificant emotional connection with feminine energy.

⊡ In dreams the mind frequently gives us images that clarify our attitude to ourselves and our everyday lives. For a man, entering a bay or inlet touches on the ancient myth of Jason and the Argonauts and their search for something attainable only with difficulty. For a woman, a bay or inlet suggests her secret and private self.

Also consult the entry for Laurel/Bay Leaves.

BEACH

◈ The potential for emotional clarity is present, particularly if the beach is deserted. The sea signifies emotion and the land security or the everyday.

◈ Depending on our actions and state of mind in the dream, dreaming of a beach usually means relaxation and creativity, and also the need to understand our need for time out.

▦ To be on a beach shows our awareness of the boundary between emotion and reality, our ability to be in touch with the elements and the capacity we have for combining perception and feeling in a relaxed manner.

BEACON

◈ As a source of light, beacons take on the symbolism of illuminating the way to spiritual enlightenment and to sanctuary for the spirit.

◈ Our emotions may be 'flaring up' and need directness of communication. If the flame is unprotected a beacon may signify passion.

▦ This can show, variously, as a warning, the need for communication or a strongly held principle by which you live.

⚑ In a man's dream, without the spiritual connotations, a beacon can be a symbol for sexuality. In a woman's dream it is more likely to suggest passionate feelings.

You might like to consult the entries for Fire, Light and Torch.

BEADS

✲ Beads made from semi-precious stones are used as spiritual reminders – as in rosaries or votive beads. In many religions prayers are counted by using beads and repeated prayers are notated in order to ensure that the right number are said. In dreams we tend to be more conscious of spiritual discipline.

♥ Psychologically we are looking for perfection. To be counting beads suggests that we are enumerating our talents, blessings or skills (the number may be important).

▦ When we dream of beads strung together – for instance in a rosary – we are becoming aware of continuity or logical progression. To dream of beads breaking indicates the failure of a favourite project.

You might like to consult the entries for Gems/Jewels, Necklace and Numbers.

BEAKER – see CUP

BEAN

✲ The bean can signify immortality and magical power, containing as it does the potential for life and manifestation.

♥ Psychologically the bean can represent stored potential. We have the ability to tap into it to achieve whatever we want. Traditionally the bean was supposed to be capable of feeding, clothing and providing an object of exchange for barter.

▦ To be storing beans in a dream may show a fear of failure or a lack of confidence in our ability to carry through an objective at this point. We may, however, need to create something in the future. To be planting beans would suggest faith in the future and a wish to create something useful.

⚑ In a man's dream the bean suggests the life force, whereas in a woman's dream it will signify her own fertility.

Consult the entries on Garden, Gardener and Plants.

BEAR

✲ The bear symbolizes spiritual strength and power, both latent – for example, when a bear hibernates – and also apparent. In shamanism the bear is a very powerful totem animal – a form of guardian.

♥ Psychologically, we have recognized the need to meet the force of our own creativity. As a symbol from a play on words, it can also suggest stamina, whether we are able to bear or put up with certain difficulties.

■ To have a bear appear alive in a dream indicates aggression, or if it is dead, the handling of one's deeper negative instincts. To dream of a toy bear – i.e. a teddy bear – shows a childlike need for security.

⊞ As a protective force in both men's and women's dreams, the bear can represent maternal energy.

Consult the entries on Animals, Archetypes in the Introduction and Mother in Family.

BEARD

❀ Spiritually there is a degree of ambivalence in the symbol of the beard and the meaning will depend on the dreamer's own culture. It may mean wisdom and dignity, or alternatively it may mean deceit and deviousness. The bearded Wise Old Man of the archetypes signifies inner wisdom.

◈ We perhaps need to consider more masculine attributes in ourselves or others. To dream of cutting or having a beard cut suggests a loss of power.

■ To dream of a man with a beard generally means we must guard against cover-up and deceit, though it can also be a sign of good luck.

⊞ In a man's dream a beard suggests masculine power but in a woman's dream it suggests that someone is trying to hide information. If a woman is growing a beard in a dream it shows she needs to be more assertive.

BEAST – *see* MONSTER

BEATING

❀ Particularly if you yourself are taking a beating, humility, anguish and grief are symbolized, along with the recognition of a degree of cruelty by others.

◈ To be beaten, either physically or in a game, indicates submission on our part to a greater force.

■ In dreams the act of beating something or someone represents our need for 'power over' whatever is represented. It suggests a need to control.

BEAVER – *see* ANIMALS

BED/BEDROOM

❀ Since sleep is a way of leaving the busy world behind, a bed can represent a form of spiritual sanctuary and a sense of purity.

◈ To be going to bed with someone can variously represent either our sexual attraction to that person or indicate that we need have no fear of them – depending on other circumstances within the dream. Such an act may suggest our search for companionship and love.

■ To be going to bed alone in a dream can indicate a desire for a return to the safety and security of the womb. To dream of a bed made up with fresh linen indicates the need for a fresh approach to those thoughts and ideas that really matter to us.

⚑ For most people, the bed and bedroom signify a private place, though sometimes from different perspectives. For both men and women, dreams about beds can give an insight into our attitude to relationships, not necessarily with the opposite sex.

Also consult the entries for Buildings, Furniture/Furnishings and House.

BEDWETTING

✻ Bedwetting in dreams can suggest a need for freedom of personal expression. It can signify the need to let go but can also highlight issues of self-control.

♥ We may have worries about correct behaviour in society or of being condemned for improper behaviour.

▦ In dreams, we often regress to a former state, and to dream of wetting the bed indicates anxieties over lack of control. In some cases it may also indicate that we have concerns with sex or sexuality.

⚑ In everyday life control of the bladder during sleep can occur quite late – often later in boys than girls – so dreaming of bed wetting may arise from traumatic experiences, or from issues of self-esteem, which take the dreamer back to childhood.

BEE/BEEHIVE

✻ The bee symbolizes immortality, rebirth and order. Through a connection with the Great Mother, a beehive signifies eloquence and direct speech.

♥ To dream of a queen bee registers our need to feel, or be, superior in some way. We may possibly feel the need to be served in our chosen purpose by others. We are also aware of the need for hard work and industry. To dream of tending a beehive alerts us to the need for good management of our resources.

▦ As a symbol of something to be feared, as well as tamed and used, the meaning of bees in dreams can be ambivalent. To be stung by a bee is a warning of the possibility of hurt. Being attacked by a swarm indicates that we are creating a situation which may become uncontrollable. The beehive is said to represent an ordered community and, therefore, the ability to absorb chaos.

You might also like to consult the entry for Hive.

BEETLE

✻ The scarab beetle was an ancient Egyptian solar symbol – it is said to have rolled the sun across the sky. A beetle thus represents protection from evil. You should look at what, or who, you feels needs to be protected.

◈ The industriousness of the beetle is often taken to represent hard work, efficient planning and use of resources which needs to be undertaken.

▦ Considered by many to be dirty, in a dream the beetle carries the same symbolism as all insects – that is, something which is unclean if not given the correct attention.

Consult the entry for Insects for further clarification.

BEG/BEGGAR

◈ Begging was at one time considered a valid spiritual discipline in that people were expected to share what they had. A beggar can be a hermit and, therefore, a spiritual petitioner, someone who trusts in the universe to provide.

◈ More negatively, emotions, drives and thoughts which have been 'starved' in our waking lives can often appear in dreams personalized as a beggar – that is begging for attention.

▦ To dream of being a beggar represents our own feeling of failure and lack of self-esteem. To dream of someone known to us as a beggar indicates that on some level we are conscious that there is a lack on their part, perhaps that they make too many demands on us, or conversely that we have a resource that they need.

BEHIND – *see* POSITION

BELL

◈ The bell is an ancient charm against the powers of destruction and 'bad' spirits and is used to clear an atmosphere. A bell in dreams may forewarn us of approaching spiritual danger.

◈ Bells can indicate the conscience and our need to seek approval from others. It may also indicate that we have a desire to communicate with someone who is distanced or estranged from us.

▦ Traditionally, to hear a bell tolling in a dream was to be warned of disaster or of a death. While that meaning is less prevalent now as there are more efficient ways of communication, a bell in a dream (such as a door bell) does warn us to be on the alert.

BELLY

◈ The belly is the seat of the solar plexus, a spiritual centre or chakra which carries vitality. It can, therefore, also be a focus for appetite and earthly desires. At times it suggests an initiatory process when it takes on the symbolism of the womb.

◈ If our own belly is distended in our dream, we may be at a point where, psychologically at least, release is necessary either through anger or frank speech. To be aware of someone else's belly draws our attention to their emotions.

🔲 You may need to learn to trust your own instincts and intuition. Equally you may be coming to terms with repressed emotion and pain.

🔲 Often before she knows she is pregnant, a woman may become conscious of her belly in dreams. Body dysmorphia, such as dreaming of becoming fat, is quite common at this time.

Consult the entries for Abdomen, Stomach and Womb in Body.

BELOW – see POSITION

BELT

🔆 A belt is an insignia of power and can represent either the spiritual power we have, or the power we are able to obtain.

♡ Intellectually we may be 'hide-bound' or constrained in some fashion.

🔲 When we dream of a belt that attracts our attention, we are perhaps being bound by old attitudes, duty and so on. An ornate belt can represent a symbol of power or office (as in regimental or nurses' belts).

🔲 In a woman's dream a belt can have the same significance as a girdle – a symbol of her femininity. In a man's dream it is more likely to be a symbol of security.

BEND/BENDING

🔆 The simple explanation of a bend in a path or road is a change in spiritual direction, perhaps to accommodate new information. Whether the change is to the right or left may be important. To bend as in bowing generally acknowledges a higher power or authority.

♡ If you are bending forwards, this suggests submission or adapting to new circumstances, whereas bending backwards would signify a need to please or accommodate others.

🔲 When you are bending an object you are hoping to change – perhaps a project or way of life. When something is bent there is a distortion which needs to be understood. To find yourself bending the rules shows an element of rebellion.

You might also like to consult the entry for Bow.

BERRIES – see FRUIT

BET – see GAMBLING

BIBLE – see BOOK AND SPIRITUAL IMAGERY IN THE INTRODUCTION

BICYCLE

🔆 Spiritually the bicycle signifies duality or the balance of two aspects of belief.

♦ Psychologically, we could be looking for freedom without responsibility. We probably need to achieve some way of moving forward in a project using balanced judgement.

▦ When we dream of riding a bicycle it shows the need to pay attention to personal effort or motivation. To fall off the bicycle indicates a lack of good judgment.

▯ A bicycle in a woman's dream represents personal freedom and previously might have suggested rebellion. In a man's dream it is most likely to have links with childhood memories.

Also consult the entries for Journey and Transport.

BIG – *see* **SIZE**

BIGAMY

❀ Spiritually, bigamy can represent the choices one has to make, possibly between right and wrong. By association it may represent the astrological sign of Gemini or the union of two parts of our personality.

♥ When we dream we are married to a bigamist we need to be aware that we are being deceived by someone very close to us.

▦ To dream of being a bigamist indicates not being able to decide either between two loves, two courses of action or two loyalties. We are being presented with alternatives, both of which have equal validity.

▯ As customs change we are less likely to dream of bigamy and more likely to dream of multiple liaisons with the opposite sex. For instance, a man might dream of a harem whilst a woman is more likely to dream of serial monogamy.

You might like to consult the entries for Affair and Marriage.

BILL

❀ To be given a bill (a request for payment) suggests there is a spiritual cost in some of our actions. To be paying a bill signifies that we have accepted such a responsibility.

♥ In everyday life the exchange of payment is constantly taking place. When we find this highlighted in dreams it is necessary to give some thought to our attitude to such transactions.

▦ Often it is the emotion associated with financial transactions that is important and we would be wise to consider whether we want or need whatever is represented in the dream.

Also consult the entry for Money.

BIND/BINDING – *see* **BONDS**

BINGE

❀ Any excess in spiritual terms is an attempt to change consciousness or awareness. Since bingeing is an intermittent activity it suggests that there are attempts to impose a degree of control without actually having the correct self-discipline.

♥ Lack of self-discipline in our day-to-day lives can be very wearing. We are being reminded that excess of any sort can be harmful. Remembering that taking in food or liquid is supposed to be nurturing, we need to consider our everyday activities very carefully.

▨ When we dream of 'going on a binge' we may have to be less rigid in our approach to caring for ourselves. Such a dream may be setting the scene for a relaxed approach to problems.

BIRDS

✤ As far back as pagan times, man has been fascinated by birds and by flight. Birds were believed to be vehicles for the soul and to have the ability to carry the soul to heaven. As a result, birds were very often invested with magical and mystical powers. Birds have come to represent the Soul – both its dark and its enlightened side.

♥ Psychologically, man often needs to project human qualities onto objects outside himself, and because birds' conduct is entirely instinctive, they can be used in dreams to understand man's behaviour. Different breeds of birds have various meanings in dreams as follows:

Albatross – as one of the world's largest birds it can represent a burden or dead weight, but also self-sufficiency and tenacity.

Buzzard – *consult the entry for Vulture in this section.*

Chicken – the imagination is being used to serve a practical function. There is potential for growth, though this may also come about through belonging to a group. The chicken can also represent stupidity and cowardice.

Cock – the cock is the symbol of a new day and of vigilance or watchfulness. It represents the masculine principle and thus the need to be more upfront and courageous.

Crow – dreaming of a crow can have two meanings. Traditionally the crow warns of death, although today it is more likely to mean great change. It may also represent wisdom and deviousness.

Cuckoo – the meaning of the cuckoo is rather ambivalent. It can represent deviousness or unrequited love, yet as the herald of spring it indicates a change from old, stale energy to newness and freshness.

Dove – as the bringer of calm after the storm, in dreams the dove depicts the Soul and the peaceful side of man's nature. It is also a representation of the Anima.

Duck – in a dream a duck denote some kind of superficiality or childishness.

Eagle – as a bird of prey, in dreams an eagle signifies domination and supremacy. It can also mean perceptiveness and awareness as well as farsightedness and objectivity. If you can identify with or have sympathy for the eagle, your own wish to dominate is becoming apparent, though there may be some difficulty in reconciling other parts of your nature. If you feel threatened, somebody around you may be threatening the status quo.

Falcon – the falcon shares much of the symbolism of the eagle. As a bird of prey, it typifies freedom and hope for those who are being restricted in any way. It can represent victory over lust.

Geese/Goose – the goose is said to represent watchfulness and love. Like the swan it can denote the dawn or new life. A flock of geese is often taken to represent the powers of intuition and to give warning of misfortune. The wild goose can represent the soul and often depicts the more nature-oriented side of our personality. Geese, in common with cats, are considered to be witches' familiars.

Hen – the hen denotes providence, maternal care and procreation. When a hen crows in a dream it is taken to represent feminine domination.

Ibis – the ibis, sometimes taken to be the stork, is the symbol of perseverance and of aspiration.

Jackdaw – *consult the entry for Magpie in this section.*

Kingfisher – to dream of a kingfisher is to dream of dignity and calmness.

Lark – a lark traditionally represents the transcendence of the mundane, overcoming the everyday problems to reach a wider viewpoint.

Magpie – there is an ancient belief that magpies and jackdaws are thieves, so to dream of one indicates we believe someone will take away, or we may lose, something we value. On a more positive note, the magpie can signify good news.

Ostrich – dreaming of an ostrich indicates that we are attempting to run away from responsibility.

Owl – sacred to Athena, goddess of strategy and wisdom, in a dream the owl shares these qualities. Because it is also associated with the night-time and, therefore, the underworld, it can sometimes represent death and messages from the hidden realms.

Peacock – to see a peacock in a dream indicates a growth of understanding from the plain and unadorned to the beauty of the fully plumed bird. Like the phoenix, it represents rebirth and resurrection.

Pelican – there are two meanings to the symbolism of the pelican. One is sacrifice and devotion and the other is careful and maternal love.

Penguin – the penguin is thought to represent adaptability, although it can also indicate stupidity or, perhaps more accurately, unwise behaviour.

Pheasant – to dream of pheasants generally foretells prosperity and good fortune to come.

Phoenix – the phoenix is a universal symbol of rebirth, resurrection and immortality (dying in order to live).

Quail – the quail represents amorousness, sometimes courage and often good luck. In its negative form it can also represent witchcraft and sorcery.

Raven – the raven can be a symbol of sin. However, if it is seen to be talking it often represents prophecy. Its meaning can be ambivalent since it can represent evil, but also wisdom.

Seagull – the seagull is a symbol of freedom and power.

Sparrow – the sparrow represents business, industry and hard graft.

Stork – the stork is a symbol of new life and new beginnings.

Swallow – the swallow seen in a dream represents hope and the coming of spring, a time of new beginnings and fecundity.

Swan – as the soul of man, the swan is often taken to be the divine bird. It can sometimes denote a peaceful death or ending as in 'swansong' – at one time swans were believed to sing only at the point of death.

Turkey – the turkey is today a food for celebrations and festivals. Dreaming of one can, therefore, denote that there may be good times ahead.

Vulture – as scavengers, vultures and buzzards have an association with the feminine aspect in its destructive persona.

Woodpecker – the woodpecker is a guardian of both kings and trees in mythology. It is also reputed to have magical powers.

▨ Birds in dreams usually represent freedom, imagination, thoughts and ideas which, by their nature, need freedom to be able to become evident. Dreaming of them in particular scenarios has the following meanings:

A caged bird can indicate restraint or entrapment.

A bird flying freely represents aspirations and desires and possibly the spirit soaring towards the Divine.

A display of plumage indicates our facade – the way we see ourselves and how we present ourselves to the outside world.

A flock of birds containing both winged and plucked birds indicates confusion over bodily or material considerations, as opposed to spiritual aspirations. Birds can sometimes denote the feminine, free side of the being. **The golden-winged bird** has the same significance as fire and, therefore, indicates spiritual aspirations. **A high-flying bird** indicates spiritual awareness or that part in us that seeks knowledge.

Black/White birds – the two aspects of the Anima or Self may be represented as two opposites; the black bird signifies the dark, neglected or shadowy side; the white the open, clear, free side.

A pet bird – personal circumstances, experiences and emotions can have a profound effect on our self-image/expression, and remembered happiness can be experienced in dreams about pet birds.

⊡ In a man's dream, a bird can represent the Anima. In a woman's dream, it suggests the Self, in the sense of the spiritual self.

Consult the Introduction for further information on the Anima and Self.

BIRTH

❋ The urge to care, to love and to give birth are all suggested by dreams of birth. It may be both a spiritual – and, therefore, an unselfish – need as well as an emotional one.

♥ Psychologically, we are coming to terms with our own existence and perhaps are recognizing our own validity.

▦ We tend to dream of birth at the beginning of a new way of life, a new attitude, new ability, or a new project – also when we become aware of the death of old ways of being.

⊡ A woman will often dream of small animals and fish as she approaches pregnancy and birth. A man is more likely to dream of protecting the child or the mother in some fashion.

BIRTHDAY

❋ Any celebration is a time for a release of or change in energy, and a birthday gives an opportunity to look back and take stock, from a spiritual perspective, either of the year just past or of the decade.

♥ Dreaming of a birthday signifies that we have the right to celebrate – either an anniversary or a new phase in life.

▦ There may be a sense of anticipation about something which lifts us away from the ordinary. We may have a gift or talent which is now usable.

You might like to consult the entries for Feast and Party.

BITE/BITTEN

❋ In a dream in which we are biting a person or an object, we have returned to very basic drives of anger and aggression, and behind that is the need to protect ourselves or our personal space. Being bitten by a snake often represents some kind of initiation.

♥ To be biting into something such as fruit within a dream indicates that there is literally an idea or a concept which we need to get our teeth into.

⊞ Being bitten in a dream may show that we are experiencing aggression from someone else, or conversely that our own aggressive instincts in our waking lives are not under control. We are feeling threatened.

BIZARRE – *see* **TYPES OF DREAMS IN THE INTRODUCTION**

BLACKBIRD – *see* **BIRDS**

BLACK HOLE

✺ In spiritual terms a black hole has the same connotation as the void or the abyss.

♥ There are times when a black hole can warn of depression or of venturing into the unknown.

⊞ Experiencing a black hole in dreams can be a little like Alice in Wonderland's rabbit hole – an entry into the bizarre world of dream images. *Consult the entries for Abyss and Void.*

BLACKMAIL

✺ Blackmail suggests that there is a part of us that is aware of information that we hold. However, we have difficulty in sharing that information with others. We may also be called upon to account for past actions.

♥ For many people privacy is a very emotive issue and to dream of blackmail suggests that someone has penetrated our defences, probably in an inappropriate way.

⊞ When there is conflict between two courses of action, to dream of blackmail suggests that we are being forced in some way to take an action which goes against our natural instincts.

BLACKSMITH – *see* **ANVIL AND FORGE**

BLAZE – *see* **FIRE**

BLESS – *see* **SPIRITUAL IMAGERY IN THE INTRODUCTION**

BLINDFOLD

✺ In spiritual terms, being blindfolded is often seen as a rite of passage. It is a transition between two states. It also signifies some kind of initiation.

♥ When we cut ourselves off from visual contact with the external world we are turning inwards in order to know and understand ourselves better. Such an image in dreams suggests that we need to become introverted for a time, perhaps so that we do not try to affect the situation around us.

⊞ If we have been blindfolded in a dream, it shows a deliberate attempt is being made to deceive us. If we are blindfolding someone else, we are not being honest in our dealings with other people. This may be through ignorance on our part.

BLINDNESS

⚙ Spiritually, blindness is a form of ignorance. It can suggest the irrational. It is also a form of initiation.

♡ Intellectually we may be aware of certain facts, but choose not to use that knowledge in the most appropriate way.

▦ If we ourselves are suffering from blindness in a dream, there is an unwillingness to 'see', i.e. perceive something. We have lost sight of a goal or objective or we are seeing qualities in ourselves that we don't like.

BLOCK

⚙ A block suggests either a preventative measure or a warning to ensure that we do not make a mistake.

♡ Blocks appear in dreams when we need to make a special effort to overcome an obstacle to progress.

▦ In dreams, a block may present itself in many forms. We can experience it as a physical block – that is, something that needs to be climbed over or got round, a mental block – for instance, not being able to speak or hear, or a spiritual block such as the figure of an angel or a demon appearing in our dreams.

▣ A block as in a cube represents the physical material realm in both men's and women's dreams.

You might also like to consult the entry for Obstacle/Obstruct/Obstruction.

BLOOD

⚙ Spiritually, being aware of blood circulating through the body can symbolize the rejuvenating or life force. This is similar to *ch'i* in Chinese medicine.

♡ Emotional abuse and difficulties can translate itself in dreams into bloody wounds and can appear to be either self-inflicted or being inflicted by someone else.

▦ From time immemorial blood has represented the life carrier or the life force. To dream of a violent scene where blood appears indicates that we are being self-destructive in some way. If we are having to deal with blood, we need to be aware of our own strength. If we have been injured and someone else is dealing with the blood, we need to look at what help is necessary to overcome hurt.

▣ For a woman to dream of menstrual blood may alert her to a health problem, but may also draw attention to her essential femininity.

Also consult the entry in Body.

BLUNT – *see* INSTRUMENT

BOAR

🔆 By association with mythology and children's fables a boar can suggest evil, or rather overbearing aggression. It also suggests abundance and vitality.

♥ The boar was once much associated with feasting and festivals and can thus signify lust and gluttony.

▦ One of the ways in which the dream mind can bring matters to our attention is by a play on words, and since not many people have contact with the animal per se, for this to appear in a dream usually indicates a 'bore'.

Consult the entries for Wild Boar in Animals and also for Pig.

BOAT/SHIP

🔆 Boats represent our attitude to death and 'The Final Journey'. They can also represent fertility and adventure and in antiquity were seen as the bearers of gods and kings.

♥ To dream of being alone in a small boat means we need to consider how we handle isolation and the ability to be alone. To dream of being on a large ship alerts us to how we handle group relationships. To dream of missing a boat is often the dream of a perfectionist who fears missing chances or opportunities.

▦ To dream about a boat or a ship very often indicates how we cope with both our own emotions and those of others. It may well represent how we navigate our way through life and whether we feel that we are in control of our lives.

You may also like to consult the entries for Journey and Transport.

BODY

🔆 The body is a physical manifestation of an inner spirituality, so in theory should be almost perfect. Sometimes, rather than looking to heal the body, it is easier to heal the spirit, and dreams of the body can highlight the areas in which we need to make changes.

♥ Most experience can be translated into bodily feeling – tension or relaxation perhaps – and, therefore, becomes a rich source of symbolism in dreams. When emotions cannot be faced in ordinary everyday life, they very often become distorted dream symbols.

Abdomen/Belly/Stomach – when the dream appears to concentrate on the abdomen, there is a need to focus on emotions and repressed feelings.

Anus – the young child's first experience of control is as he or she gains control over bodily functions, particularly the anal muscles. In dreams, the mind returns to that experience as a symbol of self-realization and self-reliance and, more negatively, of suppression and defence. Such a dream, therefore, is indicating an aspect of childish behaviour or egotism. *Also consult the entry for Excrement in this section.*

Arms – we use our arms in all sorts of different ways. In dreams we may be defending ourselves, fighting or being held. We may also be showing passionate commitment. *You might also like to consult the individual entry for Arms.*

Back – dreaming of seeing someone else's back suggests we should identify the more private elements in our characters. We should also be aware that other people may not yet wish to share their thoughts with us. We may also find that we are vulnerable to the unexpected. If we dream of turning our backs, we are rejecting the particular feeling being experienced in the dream. *You might also like to consult the individual entry for Back for further clarification.*

Backbone – if the backbone is particularly noticeable in a dream, we should consider the main support structure in our lives. Intellectually, we need to consider our firmness of character.

Breasts – to be conscious of breasts in dreams indicates our connection with the mother figure and our need for nurturing. Such a dream can also indicate a wish to return to being an infant without responsibilities. *Also consult the individual entry for Breasts.*

Eyes – any dream in which the eyes play an important part is to do with observation and discrimination. Eyes are indicative of enlightenment and wisdom, protection and stability. They also have a connection with the power of light and, in ancient times, of the sun-gods. Through its connection with Egyptian symbolism, the eye is also a talisman. Loss of eyesight signifies the loss of clarity and, depending on which eye, can be either the loss of logic (right eye) or the loss of intuition (left eye). Regaining the eyesight can indicate a return to the innocence and clear-sightedness of the child.

Foot/Feet – for some cultures, to dream of the feet may symbolize divine qualities since the feet are considered the holiest part of the body. They signify taking responsibility and are the anchor or foundation in life, that which roots or grounds you. The foot also represents your whole being and is a reflection of your persona.

Hair – hair represents strength and virility. In dreams, to be combing hair is to be attempting to untangle a particular attitude we may have. To be having our hair cut is to be trying to create order in our lives. To be cutting someone else's hair may be to be curtailing an activity (it is possible that there may be some fear or doubt connected with sexuality). To be bald in a dream is to perhaps recognize our own intelligence. *Also consult the entries for Bald and Hairdresser.*

Hands – the hands are one of the most expressive parts of the body and signify power and creativity. The right hand is the 'power' hand, while the left is passive and receptive. Sometimes in dreams the left hand can represent cheating. If the hands are contrasted with each other and/or have a different object in each, it indicates there may be some conflict in us between our beliefs and feelings. A hand on the breast signifies submission. Clasped hands indicate union or friendship, while clenched hands suggest a threat. Folded hands suggest deep repose or a state of rest. The hands covering the eyes generally represent shame or horror, while hands crossed at the wrists suggest that we are being bound, perhaps by our own actions. The open hand represents justice whilst the laying on of hands signifies healing and blessing, particularly if the hand is placed on the neck. Hands placed together give an indication of defencelessness; if they are placed in someone else's it suggests a pledge of service or commitment. When the hands are raised this can indicate either adoration, prayer or surrender; if the palms are turned outwards a blessing is being given; when they are raised to the head we should give a great deal of thought and care to our current situation. Washing the hands suggests innocenceor rejection of guilt, while wringing the hands signifies grief. A huge hand, particularly from the sky, suggests that we have been 'specially chosen'. For this reason, advertising that contains such an image has a profound effect.

Head – the head is considered to be the principle part of the body. Because it is the seat of the life force, it denotes power and wisdom. Dreaming of the head suggests that we should look very carefully at the way we deal with both intelligence and folly. To dream of the head being bowed suggests supplication. When the head is covered we may be covering up our own intelligence or acknowledging somebody else's superiority. A blow to the head in a dream can indicate that we should reconsider our actions in a particular situation.

Heart – the heart is the centre of the being and represents 'feeling' wisdom rather than intellectual wisdom. It is also representative of compassion and understanding.

Heel – this suggests the part of ourselves that is strong but, at the same time, vulnerable.

Jaw – often representative of our self-expression, on a more esoteric level the jaw suggests the opening to the underworld.

Kidneys – the kidneys are organs of elimination, therefore, to dream of them is to be aware of the need for cleansing.

Knees – the knees are symbolic of prayer and supplication, and of emotional commitment.

Legs – the legs in dreams suggest support and stability, the ability to stand firm and also the capability of moving forward. The calf represents speed and control.

Limbs – whether it is partly to do with some kind of cellular memory and the growth process that takes place is uncertain, but in dreams any limb can be taken to mean sexuality and fears associated with gender issues. Being dismembered can be taken in its literal sense – we are being torn apart. Sometimes this can suggest the need to restructure our lives and begin again. At other times it can indicate that there is a way in which we are being threatened to the very core of our existence. *Consult Arms in this section and also the individual entry for Arms.*

Liver – the liver is representative of irritability and suppressed anger.

Lungs – in Chinese medicine the lungs represent grief. They are also involved in decision making. Spiritually, the lungs are the seat of righteousness and the source of thoughts concerning the Self.

Mouth – the mouth represents the devouring, demanding part of ourselves. It can also stand for the receptive side. The circumstances of the dream may give a clue to the correct interpretation. Sometimes the mouth can symbolize the feminine side of our nature.

Nose – in dreams the nose indicates curiosity and intuition.

Penis – dreaming of a penis, either your own or someone else's, usually highlights the attitude to penetrative sex.

Skin – skin in a dream stands for our persona or the facade we create for others. Hard, tough skin shows we have created a tough exterior and are trying to protect ourselves, whereas particularly soft skin indicates we are aware of our vulnerability.

Stomach – *consult the entry for Abdomen in this section.*

Teeth – popularly, teeth are supposed to stand for aggressive sexuality – although more properly they signify the growth process towards sexual maturity. Teeth falling or coming out easily indicates we are aware of going through a form of transition, similar to that from childhood to maturity, or from maturity to old age and helplessness. If we are anxious about teeth dropping out it suggests there is a fear of getting old and undesirable, or an anxiety about maturing. In a woman's dream, if the teeth are swallowed this can sometimes signify pregnancy, a wish for pregnancy, or an issue with sex.

Throat – dreaming of the throat shows we are aware of our vulnerability and also of the need for self-expression.

Thumb – dreaming of a thumb suggests awareness of how powerful we are. The thumb pointing upwards represents beneficial energy, whilst pointing downwards indicates a negative response.

Tongue – the tongue in dreams often signifies our ability to know when to speak and when to remain silent. It may also be to do with our own understanding of information that we wish to pass on to other people. We may have deeply felt beliefs we wish to share. Another explanation that is much more basic is that of the symbolism of the serpent and the phallus, and hence sexuality.

Vagina – most often, dreams of the vagina are to do with self-image. In a woman's dream it highlights her receptivity. In a man's dream it suggests his need to be penetrative, both mentally and physically. *You may also like to consult the entry for Sex/Sexual Images.*

Womb – the womb represents a return to the beginning. We all have need of basic security and shelter, and perhaps to do away with responsibility. Dreams of the womb can signify our need to satisfy those requirements. On a slightly more esoteric level the womb represents our connection with the Great Mother or Mother Earth. Dreams of returning to the womb suggest our need to reconnect with the passive, more yielding side of our nature. We may need a period of self-healing and recuperation.

▨ The body represents the individual and is his outward physical projection of all that he is. In dreams, the body often represents the Ego. Since being 'physical' is the baby's first experience of itself, the body forms the prime source of information. The various functions and unusual aspects of the body in dreams have particular symbolic significance:

Abscess – an abscess is a localized infection. This appearing anywhere in the body highlights that particular area which is in need of consideration.

Blood – dreaming of blood can have one of two meanings. It can signify that we feel that a sacrifice is being made on some level. This links into the ancient belief that the blood somehow contained the life of the spirit and, therefore, spilt blood was sacred. It can also represent renewal of life through its connection with menstruation. Many people fear blood and thus a dream about blood can highlight the need to come to terms with these fears. On a more spiritual level it represents the blood of Christ. *Also consult the individual entry for Blood.*

Constipation – retention signifies an inability to let go of the past or of previous patterns of behaviour, literally to be uptight. *Also consult the entry for Anus in this section.*

Excrement – you may not have progressed on a subconscious level beyond a feeling that anything to do with bodily functions is dirty and self-centred. There could be an element of rebellion in your waking life. Playing with excrement can represent your attitude to money and value, highlighting fear of responsibility, as well as anxiety about money. If the excrement is transformed into living animals, maybe rats, you are accepting that you are responsible for managing your own impulses. Excrement in its more spiritual meaning belongs to the realm of feelings and you may simply be trying to get rid of bad feelings. Those bad feelings can be turned into something worthwhile. Evacuation of the bowel usually highlights our need to be free of worry and responsibility, or possibly the need to learn how to be uninhibited. It can also signify the sexual act.

Fat – dreaming of becoming fat means we are recognizing the need to widen the scope of our activities in some way. More negatively, it suggests the need for protection. If we are uncomfortable with our size it indicates fear, possibly of taking on too much responsibility or of not being adequate for a task.

Urine – urine in a dream often indicates our feelings about emotional control. We may either yield to emotion or bottle it up. The way we deal with urine in dreams often also tells us a great deal about our own sexuality, because they are both instinctive behaviours.

To dream of **the upper part of the body** links with the mind and the spiritual aspects of the character, while **the lower part of the body** represents the instincts and emotional aspects. **An adult's head on an immature body, or a child's head on an adult body** is an indication that we need to recognize the differences between mature thought and emotion. If there is conflict between the upper and lower part – for instance the lower half being bigger and the top half smaller – then it indicates that there is disharmony between the mental faculties and instinctive behaviour. **The right side or right hand** being especially noticeable in dreams signifies we should take note of the logical side of our personality, whereas **the left side or left hand** indicates we need to be aware of our intuitive, creative side. *You might like to consult the entries for People and Position for further clarification.*

BOIL

The symbolism of fire applied to water to bring about a change in temperature is a strong spiritual image denoting perhaps passion and ferment. Two Elements in juxtaposition esoterically suggests power and energy. A boil as in a skin condition signifies an infection or contamination of a cherished idea.

◈ Water often signifies emotion, so to boil water suggests an increase in emotional content. To dream of being covered in boils signifies that we have offended a code of ethics and feel that we are 'unclean'.

▣ When we are boiling up – as in running a fever – in dreams we are echoing distress in everyday life. There is nowhere for excess energy to go.

◨ In a woman's dream, to be boiling a kettle suggests that she is seeking some kind of transformation in herself. For a man to have such a dream indicates he is more likely to be seeking this in someone else.

Consult the entries for Fire, Kettle and Water.

BOLT

◈ Since there is more than one meaning for bolt, you will need to decide which is appropriate. A bolt on a door may signify that you are feeling imprisoned in a situation, perhaps by your own beliefs. A bolt as in nuts and bolts suggests the masculine principle or drive, while the bolt from a crossbow signifies direct action or speech.

◈ Psychologically, dream images can highlight a state of mind, and seeing nuts and bolts is often a way of alerting us to basic ideas or how things work, so that we understand better. The idea of a bolt from the blue suggests sudden comprehension.

▣ When we are bolting a door we may be trying to shut something in or out – often a feeling or emotion. When a plant has bolted or gone to seed, circumstances around us have gone past their best.

◨ In engineering terms a nut represents the feminine and the bolt the masculine. In both men's and women's dreams the bolt can thus signify sex or the sexual act, but is more often to do with intimate relationships – perhaps where two people have an innate understanding of one another.

You might like to consult the entries for Bow, Key, Keyhole and Nut for further clarity.

BOMB

◈ A bomb exploding in dreams often forecasts an unexpected event. Dreaming of a bomb would appear to suggest a fear of sudden death or a cataclysmic event.

◈ Psychologically, we need to be aware that our own emotions are likely to get the better of us. Anger, for instance, can be a particularly destructive force.

▣ Bombs appearing in a dream usually indicate some form of explosive situation with which we need to deal. Exploding a bomb indicates the need for positive action, while defusing a bomb suggests taking care not to make a situation worse.

Also consult the entry for Atom Bomb, Explode/Explosion, Nuclear Explosion and War.

BONDS

✹ There are two meanings for bonds in dreams. One is as in savings bonds (promissory notes) and the second as in bindings and cords. Spiritually, the significance is that of an undertaking, the changing of conflict into law and order, of chaos into cosmic order. Evil can traditionally be contained by binding it, whether by magical technique, symbolism or visualization. Depending on whether the dreamer is being bound or doing the binding, it shows submission to a greater force.

♡ Depending on whether we are giving or receiving promissory bonds, we need to consider our emotional commitment to ourselves and our own concerns. To be aware of being fettered, snared or held fast by chains or other such bonds indicates the possibility that our emotional selves may be out of control.

▤ To dream of promissory notes indicates that we have a sense of commitment to a person or a principle – that we are capable of making promises which we can keep. To dream of other bonds deals with the binding or holding that can occur in situations and relationships.

You might like to consult the entries for Chains, Chaos and Halter.

BONES

✹ Bones are one of the integral parts of man, or indeed of most creatures. Spiritually, they represent structure and the basic building material of the physical realm. They often hold the key to our ideas of death and resurrection.

♡ To dream of a full skeleton indicates that we need to reconsider the structure of our lives. To be conscious of particular bones in the skeleton, particularly the joints, highlights the way we move or create.

▤ Bones appearing in a dream usually indicate that we need to be aware of fundamental material. We need to 'go back to basics'. To dream of a dog eating a bone means we need to consider our natural instincts. To dream of finding bones indicates that there is something essential we have not considered in a situation.

You might like to consult the entries for Limbs in Body as well as the entry for Skeleton/Skull.

BONFIRE

✹ Spiritually, a bonfire reflects the power of the sun and encourages the power of good. It also represents solar festivals, where the life-giving power of the sun is acknowledged and renewal is celebrated.

♥ When we are conscious of feeding a bonfire, the passionate side of our emotional selves needs to be allowed freedom of expression. Old, outdated concepts and beliefs can be let go in order to create something new.

▦ To be lighting or tending a bonfire in a dream indicates a need for cleansing some aspect of our lives. In past times, old bedding and litter was burnt with some ceremony to mark the beginning of a fresh cycle of existence. Such a fire can also represent passions that are not confined by rigidity and custom.

Also consult the entries for Fire and Smoke/Smoking.

BONUS

✿ A bonus signifies a spiritual benefit earned through hard work and application.

♥ This is a 'just reward' usually given by a higher authority, often that part of us which knows what is best for us.

▦ On a purely mundane level dreaming of a bonus, either giving or receiving it, signifies approval of some sort, which is considered to be of benefit.

BOOK

✿ A book, particularly a sacred one such as the Bible or Koran, signifies hidden or sacred knowledge. Any religious book in dreams presupposes some kind of spiritual realization or some knowledge gained. It represents our need to look into the realms of sacred or arcane knowledge or for reassurance that we are going in the right direction.

♥ Intellectually, we are searching in our dreams for ways which will help us to handle what happens in our lives. We will need to look very carefully at our religious beliefs, myths and legends, and decide what relevance they have for us. Many systems of belief have long held to there being a book in which all our deeds are recorded, and for which we are accountable.

▦ Our search for knowledge and the ability to learn from other people's experience and opinions is symbolized in dreams by books and libraries. To dream of old books represents inherited wisdom and spiritual awareness. If we dream of a Bible or other religious book it usually means that we are aware of traditional moral standards. We need a code of conduct that helps us to survive. To dream of account books indicates the need or ability to look after our own resources, practical and otherwise.

You may also like to consult the entry for Reading for further clarity.

BOOT

✿ In many ways a car boot has the same meaning as any empty vessel, a container or repository for goods. However, spiritually, it signifies a mechanized way of carrying material and perhaps the need to be aware of how much baggage we carry. Boots as in footwear suggests protection and proper grounding, the spiritual functioning within the physical realm.

🛡 It will depend on whether the boot is packed in an orderly fashion or not, but a car boot can represent the mind and all it contains: ideas, concepts thoughts and beliefs. When our attention is being drawn to footwear we should consider our hold on reality.

▦ From an everyday perspective protective footwear highlights our need to be practical and pragmatic while also being protected. To be unloading a car boot suggests the completion of a task or project. To be packing a boot signifies the need to ensure we have sufficient resources for the task in hand.

BORDER

✹ This signifies meeting a different aspect of the Self and through this a new experience in life. We need to decide if the time is right to make a transition.

🛡 Psychologically we may need to make decisive changes in the way we think and feel.

▦ A border can appear in many different ways in a dream. To have our attention drawn to the edge or border of material can indicate changes we will make in the material world. To be standing on a border between two countries would show the need to be making great changes in life.

Also consult the entry for Frontier.

BORROW

✹ To borrow something implies having to give it back at some point. So, when we use energy or resources from a spiritual perspective, we also have to give something – usually effort – back.

🛡 The transaction of borrowing suggests not yet being in the position of 'owning' ideas and concepts but being prepared to make use of them.

▦ On a purely mundane level, when we dream of borrowing articles we perhaps cannot use knowledge or information without having acknowledged that they are someone else's ideas. We must admit that we owe them a debt.

BOTTLE

✹ This is a womb symbol: the principle of containing and enclosure and, therefore, an aspect of femininity, fertility and intuition.

🛡 Opening a bottle could mean making available resources you have but may have suppressed. A broken bottle could indicate either aggression or failure.

▦ To a certain extent it depends on which type of bottle is perceived in the dream. When the image is of a baby's feeding bottle, it would indicate the need to be successfully nurtured and helped to grow. A bottle of alcohol would show the need to celebrate, or to curb an excess, while a medicine bottle might symbolize the need to look at one's own health.

🔲 In a woman's dream, given the above significances, the image of a bottle is probably to do with her own intimate feelings about herself as a woman. In a man's dream such an image will be more to do with his perception of women.

BOTTOM – *see* **BODY AND POSITION**

BOUQUET – *see* **FLOWERS**

BOW

🔅 Variously a bow can indicate superiority, the union of masculine and feminine and celebration.

◈ While intellectually we may not feel inferior, bowing in a dream shows that on an unconscious level we may actually sense someone else's need to feel superior and acknowledge that in the dream state. Such a dream could also indicate our own sense of inferiority.

▦ To perceive a bow, as in Cupid's bow, can indicate the need to be loved – the union of masculine and feminine. To see a bow made of ribbon is making a connection to the feminine principle and beauty. An archery bow represents a compulsive force.

🔲 When the arrow is taken to represent masculine energy, in a man's dream the bow – the actual means of propulsion – signifies his need to succeed. In a woman's dream it will suggest her need to procreate.

You might like to consult the entries for Arrow and Bend/Bending.

BOWL

🔅 As with many other symbols of receptivity, a bowl represents ultimate feminine wisdom and instinctive feeling as well as fertility. It thus becomes a symbol of the Great Mother.

◈ Because of its connection with instinctive feeling and intuition, a bowl can represent the ability to see the bigger picture. In ordinary life, scrying (technically, divining the future) uses the focus of intuition through the medium of a bowl of water. In dreams, such a bowl would indicate the possible development of clairvoyance.

▦ A bowl of food in a dream represents our ability to nurture and sustain others. A bowl of flowers can represent a gift or a talent, while on a more mundane level a bowl of water represents our emotional capacity.

BOX

🔅 Any enclosed space tends to signify the feminine containing principle. A box also represents the material world. A box also implies a degree of rigidity in our thinking.

❤ Various types of boxes perceived in a dream may represent different aspects of the feminine personality. Thus a decorated box can represent a flamboyant personality, whereas a plain cardboard box might suggest ordinary everyday concerns.

▣ When we feel boxed in we are being prevented from expanding in an appropriate way. To dream of packing things in a box indicates that we are trying to get rid of feelings or thoughts with which we cannot cope.

BOY – *see* **PEOPLE**

BOYFRIEND – *see* **PEOPLE**

BRAIN

☼ The brain is considered to be the seat of the soul. Spiritually it represents the coming together of power and intellect.

❤ It is unlikely that anyone will dream of a brain *per se*, however, since the brain is also the seat of learning, we may need to consider our beliefs and ideals in the light of experience.

▣ When attention is drawn to the brain in a dream, we are expected to consider our own or others' intellect. To dream of the brain being preserved indicates the need to take care in intellectual pursuits. We may be pushing ourselves too hard.

BREAD

☼ Bread has always been symbolic of life itself. In its highest aspect it is considered to be spiritual nourishment – manna. It can also represent the need to share spiritual knowledge.

❤ If the bread is out of the ordinary or has an unusual taste, we may be unsure of what we really need out of life. We may not be following the most productive course of action in our lives.

▣ Dreaming of bread connects us with our need for basic emotional and physical or material needs. To be sharing bread in a dream represents our ability to share our experience with others so that they may learn.

You might like to consult the entries for Eating, Food and Nourishment.

BREAK

☼ There are two spiritual interpretations for break. One is shattered idealism, hope and faith, while the other much more positive interpretation is a holiday, or 'holy day', to enable us to recharge our spiritual batteries.

❤ If we dream of breaking something, we need to decide whether it is worth mending or repairing what is represented. A favourite gift might suggest a lack of appreciation of that particular association.

▣ To dream of something being broken symbolizes loss or damage. On a mundane level, if a favourite object or childhood toy is broken we need to make changes and break from the past. If a limb is broken we may be prevented from moving forward or carrying out a certain action.

BREASTS

✹ Almost inevitably from a spiritual perspective breasts represent motherhood, protection and love. Considered to be one of the most often dreamed about parts of the body, it is the symbolism of the nourishment and love belonging to motherhood that is most often understood.

♥ While intellectually we may deny the need for mothering or 'smother-love', this need surfaces when we are under stress. It often appears as the dream image of breasts.

▦ Representing femininity, breasts are an important part of the anatomy. Dreaming of losing a breast may alert us to health matters, or indicate that we are withholding love and affection from someone.

⊡ For a man to dream of breasts usually indicates his unconscious connection with his mother or the nurturing principle. For a woman, changes in size may suggest that she uses her feminine attributes in a different way.

You might like to consult the entry for Body for further clarification.

BREATH/BREATHE – *see* WIND

BREEZE

✹ As a soft wind, a breeze suggests unconditional love and the presence of the divine spirit. In some senses, it can also represent purity.

♥ Psychologically, for most people a breeze indicates happy times to be savoured and remembered.

▦ To dream of a breeze being meaningful indicates a contented state of mind. Wind and anything to do with air is usually considered to belong to the intellect, so by association a gentle breeze indicates love, while a stiff breeze indicates a degree of abrasiveness.

Consult the entry for Wind for further information.

BRIDE

✹ A bride represents a change of status from the innocent maiden to a woman with responsibilities. In dreams she represents the spiritual need for, and recognition of, love, receptivity and fertility.

♥ To dream of being at a wedding, especially your own, indicates the integration of inner feeling and outer reality. We are seeking union of the unintegrated part of ourselves. We may be looking for the innocent feminine within.

▦ As marriage itself becomes less important for many, a sense of commitment is not. To dream of a bride suggests that, at some level, a commitment has been made to another human being.

◧ When a woman dreams of being a bride, she is often trying to reconcile her need for relationship and her need for independence. She needs to have an understanding of the changes in responsibility. In a man's dream, a bride indicates his understanding of the feminine, innocent part of himself.

Also consult the entries for Bridegroom and Wedding/Wedding Dress/Wedding Ring.

BRIDEGROOM

✦ A bridegroom can represent the need to take care of another person, maybe to exert a degree of control and, in spiritual terms, to commit to the continuance of the human race.

♡ The need for partnership can sometimes be more intellectual than emotional. In connecting with the drive of the masculine we can become creative in many different ways.

▦ To dream of a bridegroom usually indicates the desire to be married or to find a partner. It often shows a willingness to be more responsible or to take on responsibility for someone else, thereby becoming more mature. It is a connection with, and an understanding of, the 'romantic' side of our nature and indicates the need for integration of the intellect and the real world.

◧ In a woman's dream a bridegroom may be something of a fantasy figure, allowing her to understand the qualities she needs in a partner on a mundane level. In a man's dream, he is perhaps putting himself in touch with his finer aspects.

Also consult the entries for Bride and Wedding/Wedding Dress/Wedding Ring.

BRIDGE

✦ The bridge is one of the most commonly found images in dreams. It signifies crossing from one state of being to another, spanning the River of Life. The ancient image of crossing the River Styx accompanied by the ferryman Charon has been largely superceded by the symbol of a bridge.

♡ The symbol of a bridge signifies the emotional connection between us and other people or aspects of our lives.

▦ This almost invariably indicates the crossing from one phase of life to another, perhaps a rite of passage. The bridge may be depicted as weak or strong, sturdy or otherwise, which gives an indication of the strength of connection necessary to make changes in our lives.

BRIDLE

✦ Spiritually, the bridle has the same connotation as a halter and suggests a degree of spiritual restraint or control.

♡ The bridle, in reining us in and keeping us focussed, can indicate the need for attention to various aspects of our lives.

▦ To be bridled in a dream indicates the need for restraint and the ability to curb an excess of energy. Being yoked suggests the need to consider more than one aspect of everyday life. We may need to work in partnership or as a team.

▟ If the bridle is made of flowers it indicates a feminine, gentle way of imposing control. If the bridling is more austere – such as one of metal and/ or leather – we perhaps need to use firmness and restraint (more masculine qualities). There may also, of course, be wordplay here with the word 'bridal'. *You might like to consult the entries for Halter and Harness.*

BRIGHT – *see* **LIGHT**

BROADCAST – *see* **AUDIENCE**

BROKEN – *see* **BREAK**

BROOM/BRUSH

✺ Magically, a broom is a witch's implement. In dreams, brooms and brushes can have a similar meaning in that they clear a spiritual space of negativity in preparation for changes to be made.

♡ The idea of clearing or cleansing is as important on a psychological level as it is on the spiritual. Clearing away outmoded beliefs or habits is an important part of progression.

▦ On a mundane level, the proverbs associated with brooms and brushes – 'a new broom sweeps clean' etc. – show us the actions that are necessary to make workaday life easier.

▟ Brooms and brushes have largely given way to technological advances. In dreams, however, they still retain their old significance. In a man's dream, a broom may suggest ordinary, mundane tasks, whereas in a woman's dream it may suggest control over her environment.

BROTHEL

✺ In a bastardization of the original meaning of brothel, such an image suggests the darker, more frightening side of femininity. In fact, women as priestesses seeking union with the Divine were a potent force for life. Hence a brothel may also represent awareness of man's spiritual debt to woman.

♡ To dream of a brothel indicates the wish for sexual liberation and freedom without responsibility.

▦ Visiting a brothel suggests the need for comfort and reassurance in a somewhat unorthodox manner. Working at a brothel suggests an appreciation of how women can use their sexuality as a tool.

▟ If a woman dreams of being in a brothel, she has not yet come to terms with the sexually active side of herself. If a man dreams of being in a brothel it may show a fear of the feminine.

You might like to consult the entries for Prostitute and Sex/Sexual Images.

BROTHER – *see* **FAMILY**

BROTHERHOOD – *see* **FREEMASONRY**

BRUTALITY – *see* **ANGER**

BUBBLE

⚘ A bubble being spherical suggests perfection, in this case temporary, and, therefore, represents the illusory elements of everyday life. More specifically, it suggests the daydream in that it comes and goes.

♥ Bubbles as beautiful but fragile objects remind us of the transitory nature of human existence – that nothing is permanent.

■ We may dream of bubbles as part of our need to have fun in a childlike way. We often become aware of the temporary nature of happiness and our need for illusion.

For further clarification consult the entry for Sphere in Shapes/Patterns.

BUCKET

⚘ The bucket as a hollow object has all the symbolism of the womb and the feminine principle. In its guise as a household tool it suggests pragmatism and a down-to-earth approach to spirituality.

♥ A bucket with a hole in it signifies we are losing energy more quickly than we can replace it. An overflowing bucket suggests an excess of emotion, whereas a completely empty bucket depicts a lack of something essential in our lives.

■ When a bucket appears in our dreams, we should be considering down-to-earth, practical ways of dealing with problems. We perhaps need to consider somewhat old fashioned methods. To knock over a bucket means to put an end to previous good work and the slang phrase 'to kick the bucket' denotes losing our essential life force.

BUCKLE

⚘ A buckle can have a double meaning in spiritual terms. It can represent a protective element against the forces of evil; it can also help us to take the strain and not 'buckle' under pressure.

♥ To be fastening a buckle in a dream shows that we accept responsibility for what we do. It can also suggest 'locking in' a specific type of energy.

■ Dreaming of an ornate buckle has the same symbolism as that of a belt, in that it can represent the holding of high office or status. It can also indicate honour and can be a symbol of loyalty or membership of a particular group of people.

You might like to consult the entries for Belt and Girdle.

BUD

🔆 How the world unfolds before us – and how we can influence that – is symbolized in spiritual terms. Unfolding gently and without force is one way of developing spiritual awareness.

💗 A new idea or way of thinking holds a great deal of potential, as yet untapped. At an early stage we can only hope that it will fulfil its promise.

🖼 To dream of a bud is to recognize the unfolding of a new way of life, new experiences or new emotions. To dream of a bud dying or shrivelling up indicates the failure of a project.

Also consult the entry for Flowers.

BUDDHA, BUDDHIST – *see* **SPIRITUAL IMAGERY IN THE INTRODUCTION**

BUILDINGS

🔆 Buildings in dreams represent the constructions we make in our lives. They are attitudes and beliefs we have built from our experience, perception and often from our family habits and customs. From a spiritual perspective, buildings in dreams allow us to see clearly the constructs we put in place to keep us safe.

💗 Where in real life we can learn a lot about a person from his personal environment, so in dreams a building can also reflect the dreamer's character hopes and concerns. The environment we put ourselves in reflects our state of mind or the emotions we have about a particular situation. We all have the ability within us to construct successful lives and equally an ability to self-destruct. A dream that highlights construction or demolition gives us access to those qualities and abilities within ourselves.

There are many different types of buildings and we have included here the ones that have particular meanings in dreams:

Castle/Citadel/Fortress – the castle or fortress has been seen as a defended space since medieval times and, therefore, can be taken to represent the protected feminine. Its connection with the Great Mother and her attribute of Wisdom arises from this concept. *Also consult the individual entry for Castle.*

Church – *see Religious Buildings below and in Spiritual Imagery in the Introduction.*

Courtyard – in dreams, the courtyard is a place of refuge, if only transitory at times, and often the shape will be relevant. A square courtyard would focus on physical or material concerns for instance – perhaps the manifestation of spiritual energy in a difficult situation *(see Shapes/Patterns).*

Hotel – to dream of a hotel or any establishment that is temporary accommodation indicates that we may not feel secure within our present living conditions. The type of accommodation often gives clues as to the insecurity we are experiencing. A bed and breakfast place could be interpreted as basic but comfortable whereas a five-star hotel might suggest expensive luxury.

House (or any place of residence) – if we are aware that the house is not empty – that it is furnished in some way – those articles will mirror some aspect of our character or day-to-day concerns. *Also consult the individual entry for Furniture/Furnishings.* Being aware of someone else in the house suggests that we may be feeling threatened by an aspect of our own personality. If there are different activities going on it indicates that there is a conflict between two parts of our personality, possibly the creative and the intellectual. Being especially aware of the front of the house portrays the facade we show to the outside world, whereas going into/out of the house indicates we need to decide whether to be more introverted or more extroverted in our dealings with other people. An impressive, awe-inspiring house indicates that we are conscious of the Self or the Soul. Dreaming of moving to a larger house shows there is need for a change in our lives, perhaps to achieve a more open way of life, or even for more space. Being outside a house depicts our more public side and how we relate to external interests. Dreaming of a small house, or the house where we were born or grew up, means we are seeking security, or perhaps the safeguards of childhood, when we had little responsibility. If we find the smallness of the house constricting, we feel we are being trapped by our responsibilities. If we are aware of work being carried out on the house (cementing, repairing etc.) it implies that relationships may need to be worked on or repaired, or perhaps we need to look at health matters. We should take note of any damage, decay or difficulty that has occurred in our lives.

Igloo – an igloo is warm on the inside and cold on the outside and, therefore, signifies the difference between the internal and the external. Because of its shape, based on the sphere, the igloo stands for wholeness and protection. *You may wish to consult the individual entry for further clarity.*

Mosque – *see Religious Buildings below and Spiritual Imagery in the Introduction.*

Pyramid – considered to be a focus for power, if a pyramid appears in a dream it shows we are concentrating on the inherent power within us. *You may also like to consult the individual entry for Pyramid for more detailed information.*

Religious buildings (such as a church, mosque or temple) – as an environment for us to consider our system of belief, any religious building will suggest a place of sanctuary and refuge and a place where we can be closer to whatever concept we have of the Divine or Ultimate Power. Although we may not consciously adhere to any particular religion, most of us have principles by which we live, which will surface in dreams in recognisable images. *Also consult the information about Religious Buildings in Spiritual Imagery in the Introduction.*

Temple – *consult the individual entry, Religious Buildings above and also Spiritual Imagery in the Introduction.*

Temporary buildings – any temporary building, such as a caravan, tent or site office, suggests some degree of impermanence. In a dream, such a structure indicates a transition between two states of being.

Tower (or any similar image such as a lighthouse, obelisk, steeple etc.) – the image of a tower represents the personality (the outside walls) and the Soul within (the inner space). While there are obvious connotations that connect it with masculinity, the tower is more correctly perceived as the individual being within the wider global or cosmic context. When thought of in this way our attention can focus on other aspects of the tower, such as where windows, doors and staircases are placed. This helps us to understand the Spiritual Self and how we function in the everyday world. *You may also like to consult the individual entry for further information.*

🔲 The features of the building often mirror aspects of the dreamer's personality or what is going on on a mundane level. Sometimes buildings in dreams can become composite and, therefore, confusing. In understanding the dream we should interpret the main appearance of the building first, as its main function, and the secondary appearance as qualities to be recognized. As well as buildings themselves, the various components also have a great deal of relevance in dreams.

Balcony (or ledge, sill etc.) – we all have need for support within our lives and a balcony indicates both support and protectiveness. Being raised from the ground it can also represent the Mother in her protective guise.

Ceiling – a ceiling will often represent the division between the spiritual and mundane worlds.

Doors – doors often refer to the openings of the body and, therefore, by default, one's sexuality. The front door and back door signifies the vagina and the anus respectively. Breaking down such a door can be taken to indicate the need to deal with some kind of inhibition over privacy or sex; there can be an unwillingness to face whatever issues this may bring up. Barring the door highlights our need for self-protection, not just in matters of relationship. Opening and closing the door can show an ambivalent attitude to sex, whereas refusing to open the door represents an innocent approach to our own sexuality; we may have a virginal mentality. A door between the outer and inner rooms shows there may be a conflict between the conscious and the unconscious. If an animal or person forces his way in and destroys the lock, it shows our own protective mechanisms have let us down. Escaping by another door indicates we need to find a new solution to the one we originally thought of to solve a problem. Someone knocking on the door signifies that our attention is being drawn to an external situation. *You might like to consult the individual entry for Door.*

Hall/Passages – any passage can represent the passages within the body, for instance the vagina or the anus. Equally, on a psychological level, it signifies how we allow our personal space to be penetrated. Passages or corridors also represent the transitions between the various stages of our lives and how we handle the growth to maturity.

Lifts – these usually indicate how we deal with information. For instance, a lift going down would suggest going down into the subconscious, while a lift going up would be moving towards the spiritual or cosmic concerns. In the sleep state we are thought to leave our physical bodies behind, so, descending in a lift and getting stuck suggests the potential to lose touch with spirituality, concentrating only on the mundane.

Rooms – in a dream, these can describe various parts of our personalities or levels of understanding, but often signify either the womb or the Mother Figure. Thus the kitchen would be the home-making part of us, whereas a sitting room would be the more relaxed, comfortable side. A small room with only one door or a basement with water in it is a direct representation of the womb and may indicate a wish to return to the womb-like state of innocence, where everything is taken care of for us. A series of rooms refers to the various aspects of femininity and often to the whole soul. An upstairs room usually signifies mental or spiritual attributes, so any object within such a room will represent an idea or concept. The meaning for a basement or cellar can be ambivalent, since a cellar can represent the parts of ourselves that we have chosen to suppress. It can also represent family beliefs and habits, particularly if the basement is one that belongs to our parents. If we deliberately leave one room and go into another then it represents a change of state and of leaving something behind. Empty rooms signify that something, such as comfort or support, is lacking in our lives.

Stairs – stairs are often an indication of the steps we must take in order to achieve a goal. Climbing the stairs is indicative of the effort that we must make in order to have access to the more mystical, spiritual side of our being. More simply, it is the exertion we practise in our everyday life – the effort to be ourselves. Conversely, in order to have access to the hidden, unconscious side of ourselves, we need to 'go downstairs' into the unconscious. A golden staircase is such a basic image, with so many interpretations, that particular attention needs to be paid both to other aspects of the dream, and also our spiritual state at that specific time. Largely it represents a 'death', but not necessarily a physical death. It is more the realization that we no longer need to function solely within the physical or material realms but can move towards a more fulfilling life. It is a way out of the mundane.

Walls – walls signify a block to progress, a difficulty we have or will come up against. Often the nature of the wall will give some clue as to what the block is. For instance, a wall which looks old will signify an old problem, whereas a glass wall would indicate some difficulties with perception. Walls closing in could describe the remembered feelings of birth, but is more likely to represent a feeling of being trapped by the lifestyle we have. A brick wall, rampart or dividing wall all signify the difference between two states of reality – often the inner psychological state and the exterior, everyday world.

Windows – windows describe the means by which we appreciate the world we live in, the way we perceive reality. Dreaming that we are looking outwards through a window can suggest that we have a more extrovert view of ourselves and will tend to look at external circumstances. Looking inwards through a window indicates we are looking inwards at our own personality, and perhaps at our own motivation. The interpretation for opening a window depends on whether we are opening the window from the inside or the outside. If the former, we are dealing with our inner feelings which we may need to escape; the latter shows our attitude to outside opinion. Breaking through a window (or glass door) can suggest the first sexual experience, or the shattering of illusions. Because of the connection with religious buildings, stained glass can be accepted as picturing religious belief and ideals.

BULL

✸ The bull is connected with the moon goddesses and also represents Taurus in the Zodiac.

♥ The bull appearing in a dream can point to the dreamer's own stubbornness and tenacity.

▦ In dreams, the bull represents the masculine principle and fertility. It also can indicate the way we handle male sexuality.

You might also like to consult the entry for Animals.

BULLET

✸ Spiritually, a bullet suggests fast, decisive action, hitting a target. The symbol is a potent one as we learn to use our energies more successfully.

♥ There is a need to understand what 'ammunition' we have available – that is, in the sense of resources to be used.

🔲 To dream of bullets is often to be aware of aggression and a desire to hurt. If the bullet is being fired at us, it may be considered to be a warning of danger. If, however, we are firing the bullet, it shows we have become aware of our own vulnerability and, perhaps, lack of control.

🔳 A bullet can represent the need for, and control of, sexual impregnation. The differences in a man's and a woman's dream are self-explanatory.

You might like to consider the entry for Shot/Shooting.

BURGLAR

🔯 Intrusion – either on a physical or material level – is intrinsic to the idea of a burglar. Spiritually, there is a violation of our sacred space.

💠 A part of our psyche may have been neglected and left to fend for itself. It then intrudes on our awareness seeking attention.

🔲 When we become aware of a burglar or intruder in our dreams we are experiencing some form of unwelcome attention. This may be from external sources or from our own inner fears and difficult emotions.

🔳 Since traditionally a burglar is perceived to be masculine, in a woman's dream he may represent the wayward antisocial aspect of the men around her. In a man's dream, a burglar is more likely to represent his need to control his own sense of impropriety.

Also consult the entries for Intruder and Offence/Offend as well as the People section.

BURIAL

🔯 The obvious spiritual symbols of death, loss and pain are relevant here. Equally, burial has the connotation of transmutation – an object buried may or may not be changed. In magical practice, it is the habit to bury or return to the earth anything which has negativity attached to it.

💠 To be attending a burial in our dreams shows the need to come to terms with loss. To be burying something suggests that we are hiding an emotion or feeling even from ourselves.

🔲 To have a dream about being buried indicates a fear of being overcome, possibly by responsibility or by someone else's ill-feeling.

Consult the entries for Coffin, Death and Grave for further clarification.

BURN

🔯 Sacrificial fire and its attendant pain has many spiritual connotations. A funeral pyre suggests burning up or consuming that which is no longer spiritually necessary to us. A burning bush signifies divine knowledge imparted with passion.

💠 To be burning rubbish signifies getting rid of concepts and ideas for which we no longer have any use. When we are burning books, we are perhaps being judgemental in our appreciation of knowledge and information.

▓ A burning building signifies that we are putting an end to a particular way of life. To burn a boat suggests cutting off a means of escape.

You might like to consult the entries for Fire and Light.

BUS

🔅 To be travelling by bus can be interpreted in more than one way. Literally the omnibus is for all and, therefore, signifies the Greater Good. Also a bus suggests a spiritual journey which must be paid for in some way.

♥ We may be experiencing the need to act as an individual, undertaking our own 'journey' while at the same time belonging to a group with a common purpose.

▓ Travelling on a bus suggests that we are coming to terms with the way we handle group relationships, and the new directions we need to take in company with others.

You might like to consult the entry for Transport.

BUTCHER

🔅 The butcher has spiritual connotations with the Grim Reaper and death. The meat cleaver can be taken to represent the scythe. As people become less accustomed to seeing a traditional butcher, such an image has not so much relevance.

♥ We may need to become aware of a destructive – or rather divisive – streak in ourselves, one which at the same time has particular skills.

▓ We see the butcher as one who mutilates, but provides for us at the same time, and this is reflected in dreams when he appears as someone who separates the good from the bad. He may also be a destroyer.

BUTTERFLY

🔅 When seen in dreams or even meditation, the butterfly represents the freed soul and immortality. There is no need for the soul to be trapped by the physical body.

♥ Psychologically, the butterfly indicates a lack of ability to settle down or to undertake a protracted task. In growing from a chrysalis, however, it has transmuted into a thing of beauty and simply is itself.

▓ On a practical level, the butterfly represents light-heartedness and freedom. As a symbol of conservation we are aware that our energy needs to be used in the best, most efficient way.

BUTTONS/BUTTONHOLES

🔅 Buttons and buttonholes were simple fastenings holding two different pieces of material together. Spiritually this can represent uniting the physical and spiritual realms into one coherent whole.

♥ Buttons were originally a form of insignia, allowing easy identification of friend or foe. If our attention is drawn to buttons in a dream, it is usually to bring about such recognition.

▦ The size, shape and configuration of the button and buttonholes may be important. An ornate button will have a different relevance to a simple one; more work or effort is required for the former. A particularly decorative buttonhole suggests that more energy needs to be put into 'fastening down' a project – it perhaps needs to be more upfront.

CABLE

✦ In the sense of a rope, a cable will represent strength and security, and may have the same connotation as any binding image. However, in this technological age, from cables associated with television and computers, they also suggest efficient communication from a remote source.

♥ A cable without a plug implies that we have not yet made proper connections whereas a broken cable that we have lost contact.

▦ In joining two objects together a cable highlights the added efficiency obtained by linking two thoughts, ideas or ways of working.

⊟ In a woman's dream a cable may highlight the strength of her bonds with someone else whereas in a man's dream it can suggest restrictions within his closest relationships.

CADUCEUS

✦ The Caduceus, or double-headed snake entwined round a central staff, is an ancient spiritual symbol which signifies that there is power in uniting the opposite polarities of the spiritual and the physical realms. Once we reconcile these opposing sides, this creates healing, rebirth and renewal, universally represented as two snakes. This is a symbolic representation of the basic form of DNA, the 'building blocks' of life.

♥ The body recognizes and communicates in dream images its need and expectation of good health. To dream of the Caduceus can mean that we need to create better conditions for achieving this. This symbol often appears as we learn of our own ability to heal others.

▦ The Caduceus is the sign that is used by doctors and medical establishments as the sign of healing. Initially it was the staff carried by the Greek god Hermes. Wellbeing, our own or other people's, needs consideration.

CAGE/CELL

✦ We need to examine and reconsider ideas and beliefs, particularly about religion and spirituality, which restrict and restrain us.

♥ We are being warned that we are enforcing too much restraint on our hidden abilities. We could be allowing others to hold us back.

▦ The cage normally represents a form of trap or jail. To dream of caging a wild animal alerts us to our need to restrain our wilder instincts. To dream that we are in a cage indicates a sense of frustration and perhaps of being trapped by the past.

You may also like to look at the entries for Jailer and Prison.

CAKES

🌑 Cakes or buns used in religious and magical rites and marked with the cross originally symbolized the round of the moon and its four quarters. Such cakes later became Eastertime Hot Cross buns and in dreams suggest spiritual celebrations.

♥ Baking cakes indicates our need to care for others or to nurture an inner need.

🔳 When we dream of celebration cakes – such as a wedding or birthday cake – we are being shown that there is cause for celebration in our lives.

🔳 Traditionally, baking cakes was a particularly feminine activity, and therefore such dreams had more relevance to nurturing. As men develop their more caring side, cakes take on this meaning in their dreams.

To interpret the meaning of candles on a cake consult the entries for Candle and Numbers.

CALCULATOR

🌑 As a modern day counting device the calculator can signify the complexities of the choices we make as we undertake spiritual development.

♥ The symbol of a calculator alerts us to the possibility of risk. It is wise for us to be able to weigh up the risks or to be able to assess what the outcome of a situation might be.

🔳 In more mundane terms the presence of a calculator in dreams may signify that the focus of the dream is work related. The numbers and totals may be significant.

You may like to consult the entry for Numbers for further information.

CALENDAR

🌑 A calendar is initially a way of naming periods of time, usually days, though also of particular cycles such as the seasons. Cycles in a calendar are often measured by the motion of planets and stars. This allows celebrations and festivals to be calculated. We should become more aware of these timetables.

♥ Because time is a self-imposed constraint, when anything that marks time appears in a dream we are being warned of the potential for limitation.

🔳 If a calendar appears in a dream there can be more than one meaning. Our attention may be being drawn to the past, present or future and something significant in our lives, or we may be being warned of the passage of time in an important scheme.

CALF – see BABY ANIMALS IN ANIMALS AND LEG IN BODY

CAMCORDER/CAMERA

🔅 There is a need to be watchful and perhaps to preserve an image. Tribal cultures believed that the camera captured the soul or essential being, and may have this significance in dreams. The camcorder with its greater technological abilities has a similar meaning.

💗 There is a necessity to retain a mental picture of what is important to us. A broken camera or camcorder immediately suggests a faulty memory or distorted perception.

🔲 To be using a camera or camcorder in a dream means that we should record events or occasions in such a way that they are preserved, perhaps for posterity or as evidence. Being filmed indicates that we need to look more carefully at our actions and reactions to certain situations.

CAMEL

🔅 The spiritual significance of animals harks back to ancient times. The camel suggests dignity as the bearer of royalty.

💗 Psychologically the camel can represent stamina and self-sufficiency.

🔲 Depending on the environment in the dream the camel can represent the unusual or bizarre. It also represents available resources and obedience to a basic principle.

CAMELOT

🔅 Fairy tales and myths often seem to have arisen from dreams and vice versa, so the stereotypical vision of a place such as Camelot highlights the qualities of spirituality, chivalry and adventure inherent in each of us.

💗 Camelot is a representation of a perfect society even up to and including its downfall and ending, so such a dream will put into perspective areas in life we feel we have not reached our potential.

🔲 As legends and myths take on a life of their own, sometimes bearing little relationship to the original occurrence, they become somewhat sanitized and personalized to fit with the patterns of society, at any particular time. Archetypal images, such as the authoritative king (Arthur), the young knight (Lancelot) setting out on a journey, or Merlin the magician, thus become available through these dream characters to help us understand ourselves.

⬛ It will depend upon the dreamer's own personal development how such a dream is interpreted. In a woman's dream, for instance, it can help her come to terms with her treatment by, or of, the men in her life; whereas in a man's dream he may be dealing with his own personal journey to maturity.

You might like to consult the entry for Archetypes in the Introduction, the individual entry for Hero/Heroine, Hero in the People section, Magic/Magician and Round Table.

CAMOUFLAGE

🔅 Camouflage has the effect of making an object disappear or appear to be something else. The symbolism is therefore of information deliberately hidden or occluded.

🟡 We hide – both from ourselves and others – those aspects of our personalities with which we cannot deal. This is a defensive mechanism which when highlighted in dreams, needs to be considered very carefully.

▦ Whereas camouflage in nature is a spontaneous occurrence, in Man it is a more deliberate act and for many is associated with war or dangerous situations. There may be a threat to our integrity or sense of control.

CAMP

See Temporary Buildings in Buildings and also the entry for Tent.

CANAL

🔅 Because a canal is a man-made structure it suggests an imposed structure, definition of boundaries or rigid belief.

🟡 We need to structure our knowledge of ourselves to create a workable system.

▦ A dream about a canal usually indicates that we are inclined to be rigid insofar as the control of our emotions is concerned. We may be introducing too much structure into our lives at the expense of our creativity.

Also consult the entry for Water.

CANCER

🔅 Symbolically Cancer represents the Moon, the Eternal Mother and the astrological sign of Cancer.

🟡 Intellectually we may have worked through our fears but still be left with attitudes and beliefs that cannot be cleared away. Very often this appears as cancer or illness in dreams and equally can represent something 'eating away' at us – usually a negative idea or concept.

▦ Cancer is one of the prime fears that a human being has to deal with, so to dream of a cancer indicates we are out of harmony with our body. It also indicates fear of illness.

⬡ Since the astrological sign of Cancer represents a feminine attribute, in a woman's dream she may be considering her ability to nurture. In a man's dream his focus may be on his attitude to his mother or mothering.

CANDLE

❄ The symbolism of candles has recently taken on a whole added significance as people re-explore religion and belief more thoroughly. They have always signified illumination, wisdom, strength, beauty and now signal the end of darkness or ignorance. Lit, they suggest the enduring flame of life and the use of power. Unlit, they signify potential held in reserve.

◈ Psychologically candles can represent knowledge or wisdom that has not yet fully crystallized. Used as tools, they mark our control of personal magic and dreams will often give information as to their best use. Lighting a candle to Bridget to welcome her in was transposed in the Christian church to the celebration of Candlemas on 2 February when new candles were placed in churches signifying the end of winter.

▦ In Pagan times, the candle or taper represented the ritualistic dispersing of darkness and a way of worshipping power. To dream of candles indicates that we are trying to clarify something that we do not understand. Candles on a birthday cake can therefore indicate that we are marking a transition from the old to the new. Lighting a candle represents using courage and fortitude or asking for something which we need.

⊟ It has been suggested that the candle epitomizes masculine power (candle) and feminine passion (flame), the one being useless without the other. In a woman's dream, therefore, extinguishing a candle might suggest control of a perceived power, whereas in a man's dream it will suggest control of external factors.

You might like to consult the entries for Fire, Light and Wax as well as the information on Phallus in Sex/Sexual Images.

CANE

❄ Probably used first as a weapon, the cane took on the symbolism of strength and power and eventually authority and social prestige. Spiritually, it also came to signify self-flagellation.

◈ Because a cane also represents pliability, we may be trying to achieve a balance between our willingness and our unwillingness to accept a situation.

▦ Because many people associate the cane with some form of punishment or sadism, it can represent self-punishment or masochism. It is more likely, however, that we are trying to come to terms with some form of childhood trauma.

Also consult the entry for Staff.

CANNIBALISM

❄ From a spiritual perspective the act of cannibalism is absorbing powers or qualities belonging to someone else.

◈ Eating human flesh in a dream can mean that we are taking in wrong information in everyday life.

▣ To dream of cannibalism usually represents unsophisticated or inappropriate behaviour. To be aware of eating human flesh may indicate our dislike of unsuitable foods or actions. There is often a part of ourselves we have not 'internalized' which we need to absorb.

CANOE

❂ In Polynesia the port hull of the canoe is the 'wahine' hull and the starboard is the 'Kane' hull. The spiritual symbolism is that the male and the female forces give us life and balance each other. The older symbolism is that of a lunar barque, and the crescent moon.

◈ We may be protected from our emotions, but also at risk. A degree of skill is necessary to enable us to handle what might happen and achieve the correct balance.

▣ To dream of a canoe suggests that we can only handle our emotions by becoming immersed in them. We are possibly making efforts to control or tame the flow of our emotion. We are aware that we are capable of making changes but only by our own efforts.

⊡ By its association with the feminine, in a woman's dream the canoe represents her place within the world. In a man's dream it signifies the hunter and protector.

CANOPY

❂ Royalty or powerful people often used a canopy with a special symbol either for spiritual protection or to signify their rank. We still acknowledge this privilege on a deep internal level.

◈ A canopy protects the head which is the seat of intellect. We have a need to draw attention (or have our attention drawn) to higher ideals or aspirations.

▣ When we dream of a canopy we are looking to be protected, sheltered or loved. In olden times a canopy was used to shelter those with special duties or powers, such as kings and queens or priests and priestesses. If we ourselves are being sheltered we recognize our own abilities and potential for greatness.

CAP

❂ A cap signifies nobility and freedom. The jester's cap was said to be a parody of the king's crown demonstrating how transient power really is.

◈ The cap shows the need for respect for a person's beliefs and wisdom or knowledge.

▣ The cap has the same significance as the hat in dreams and draws attention to status or spiritual powers. If we are wearing a cap in a dream, we may be covering up our creative abilities.

Consult the entries for Hat in Clothes and Joke/Joker.

CAPITAL – *see* **MONEY**

CAR

✦ The car is very often representative of our own personal space, an extension of our being. It also stands for spiritual direction and motivation.

❦ Dream scenarios involving cars are often much to do with what we are doing to ourselves on a psychological or emotional level. Being alone in a vehicle indicates independence, while dreaming of the brakes shows our ability to be in control. The car engine indicates the essential drives with which we have to deal. A crashing vehicle suggests fear of failure in life, while a car on fire denotes stress of some sort, either physically or emotionally. To be in a car which is driven carelessly, either by us or someone else, marks a lack of responsibility, while a feeling of being left behind would be shown by your car being overtaken. To dream of reversing a car registers a feeling that we are slipping backwards into old patterns of behaviour or are having to reverse a decision.

▣ To dream of being in a car usually alerts us to our own motivation, thus driving the car can indicate our need to achieve a goal, while being a passenger could indicate that we have handed over responsibility for our lives to someone else.

You may find it helpful to read the entries for Journey and Transport.

CARAVAN – *see* **TRANSPORT**

CARDS

✦ Cards of any type signify visual communication and the ability to convey a message spiritually. The Tarot – our Inner Truth – can be used as images in dream work. To dream of giving or receiving a card such as a birthday card alerts us to the need for a specific kind of communication, perhaps celebrating our own or others' good fortune and luck.

❦ On a psychological level, card playing in a dream can be seen as taking calculated risks and alerting us to potential danger. Generally, our subconscious may be registering concern, either about ourselves or others. Business cards convey the idea that we are happy to give other people information about ourselves, or to receive such information from others.

▣ Greeting cards are quite literally an acknowledgement of a special occasion. In a dream, playing cards highlight our ability to be open to opportunity or to take chances. The cards that one deals, or is dealt, in a dream may have significance as to number or suit: Hearts indicate emotion and relationship. Diamonds represent material wealth. Spades represent conflict, difficulties and obstacles. Clubs represent action, work and intelligence. The King portrays human success and mastery. The Queen indicates emotional depth, sensitivity and understanding whereas the Jack represents impetuosity, creativity or an adolescent energy.

Also consult the entry for Numbers.

CARETAKER – *see* SECURITY PERSONNEL IN PEOPLE

CARGO

✹ In the sense that cargo is goods which require transportation, in dreams it represents thoughts, ideas and concepts which need to be considered in a different context to their original purpose.

✷ When goods are packed for cargo they are carefully protected and often stowed away, so when such articles appear in dreams it is time to become aware of forgotten dreams and ideals – of creativity 'stowed away' to be used in different circumstances.

▣ Cargo has the same significance as luggage and baggage. Unpacking cargo suggests looking hard at what assets and talents you have. Packing cargo indicates that the time may not be right for a particular plan.

⬕ In a woman's dream bearing cargo may suggest pregnancy or her feelings about this. In a man's dream it suggests responsibility.

Consult the entries for Baggage and Luggage for further clarification.

CARPET – *see* FURNITURE/FURNISHINGS

CARRIAGE/CART/CHARIOT

✹ The carriage is a symbol of majesty and power, and a chariot also represents the Sun and the Divine. The cart is a more mundane symbol signifying down-to-earth hard work.

✷ Any symbol which signifies our being moved in some way draws attention to our ability to make progressive changes in our lives. We may have to explore archetypal images for an understanding of our own motivations. The chariot in the sense of a gladiatorial vehicle can represent basic urges before they have been honed by conditioning and knowledge. Again a cart is representative of workaday concerns.

▣ In modern times most people will dream about the car or other similar forms of transport. Dreaming of a carriage, such as a horse-drawn one, could be suggestive of old-fashioned attitudes to modern thinking, and a chariot means we have to accept a very basic kind of control. A train carriage would indicate that we are taking a 'journey' that is slightly more public than a car journey.

Also consult the entry for Car and the Journey and Transport sections.

CARRY

❁ When we are prepared to 'carry' something we are taking Spiritual Responsibility – being aware of our responsibility for the world we live in perhaps. This may be either in the long-term or a short-term project.

♥ To dream of carrying someone registers the fact that we may be accepting responsibility for someone else. It is for us to decide if this responsibility is a burden or not.

▦ When we are aware of carrying an object we need to decide how we perceive our particular relationship to that object or its symbolism. If we dream of being carried, we may feel that we are in need of support.

CASH – *see* MONEY

CASK

❁ Like most containers, a cask represents the feminine principle. An apparently bottomless cask represents needless effort.

♥ It is more likely to be the content of the cask which has meaning on a psychological level and such a dream indicates our ability to be creative with raw materials – to fashion something of value.

▦ Since a cask or barrel is often hand-made, to dream of one indicates the care taken in dealing with our own emotional make-up. This is because a cask was, and is, mostly used for storage.

⊞ For a woman a cask will represent her ability to preserve her culture or ideas, but for a man it is more likely that he feels he has the opportunity to enjoy the fruits of his labours.

Consult the entry for Keg for more information.

CASTLE

❁ Dreaming of a castle links us to the principle of an enclosed and defended private space. Spiritually it suggests some kind of test or challenge or overcoming obstacles in order to gain greater understanding.

♥ Before we can be fully open to other people, we normally have to let down our barriers, and being trapped in a castle may highlight our difficulty in freeing ourselves from old attitudes. Trying to enter a castle signifies that we recognize that we ourselves create difficulties which have to be overcome.

▦ A castle can represent the fantastic, the unattainable or perhaps difficulty in obtaining our objectives.

⊞ The castle represents the essential feminine wisdom so a woman is more likely to dream of being in a castle. A man will tend to dream of trying to enter one.

You might like to consult the entries for Buildings, Camelot and Tower.

CASTRATION

⚜ Dreaming of castration means we are prepared to make a life sacrifice, to give up or control the sexual act in favour of celibacy and perhaps a more ascetic lifestyle.

♥ Conventionally, there may be some difficulty in coming to terms with the conflict between the masculine and feminine within ourselves.

▣ In any dream that contains sexual trauma, we are being alerted to our inner fears, not necessarily associated with the sexual act. The violent act of castration in a dream indicates the damage we are doing to ourselves in denying such fears, or in denying natural urges.

⊡ Castration in a man's dream suggests that his sense of self is being attacked. In a woman's dream she should take care that she is not emasculating her partner or colleagues.

CAT – see ANIMALS

CATACOMB/CRYPT

⚜ As a place of hidden forces and occult power, in dreams the catacomb will represent the unconscious. Catacombs suggest interlinking ideas or principles while a crypt is complete within itself.

♥ Our subconscious fears or feelings connected with death can show in a dream as a catacomb or crypt. Inherent in both is the idea of sanctuary for the soul.

▣ Many dreams contain images which are to do with a space underground, and to dream of a crypt or a catacomb signifies a need to come to terms with subconscious religious beliefs or training.

You might like to consult the entry for Tomb.

CATERPILLAR

⚜ The symbol of a caterpillar is of metamorphosis or the spiritual potential, largely unrecognized, which must transmute into something more beautiful. We must change and grow from what we are now into a different way of being.

♥ To dream of caterpillars would indicate that we need to remain flexible in our attitude to change. Also, because of the caterpillar's association with creeping things, it may represent evil or difficulty.

▣ The caterpillar appearing in a dream usually indicates that we are undergoing some form of major change. We may be being warned that we must undergo a complete upheaval before we can achieve our goal. There may well then be a period of transition or apparent stasis.

⊡ The caterpillar is a recognizable first symbol of the growth process. In a woman's dream it may represent an awareness of a potential pregnancy whereas for a boy such an image suggests his emerging sexuality. In a man's dream a caterpillar signifies the commencement of a journey of discovery about his spirituality.

CAULDRON

⚙ Spiritually the cauldron symbolizes renewal and rebirth. Many folk tales use the symbolism of cooking to represent the making of mankind. A cauldron can also represent the womb.

♥ Psychologically, when a cauldron appears in a dream we may need to take note of our intuitive abilities, or of our ability to create new things from simple ingredients.

▦ Almost universally the cauldron represents abundance, sustenance and nourishment. By association, the magic cauldron suggests fertility and the feminine power of transformation. To dream of a cauldron, therefore, reconnects us with our basic principles.

⊞ Originally the cauldron was round-bottomed, thus reinforcing the symbolism of the womb. In a woman's dream it therefore suggests transformation often brought about by her own power. In a man's dream he is more likely to use power beyond himself.

You might also like to consult the entry for Kettle.

CAVE

⚙ In common with many underground symbols, the cave represents spiritual shelter or sanctuary, initiation and rebirth. Meditating on the image of an inner cave gives insight into how we tackle life events.

♥ Passing through a cave signifies a change of state, transition and a deeper understanding of our own negative impulses.

▦ As with the catacombs, the cave represents a doorway into the unconscious. While initially the cave may be frightening, an exploration can reveal strong contact with our own inner selves.

⊞ In both men's and women's dreams a cave will represent exploring the subconscious, but in a woman's dream she is more likely to sense something greater than herself whereas initially a man will begin to appreciate his own intuitive senses.

Consulting the entries for Catacomb and Door will enhance your understanding.

CEILING – *see* BUILDINGS

CELEBRATION – *see* PARTY

CELEBRITY

⚙ Spiritually, as we reach for perfection we need to 'work through' various aspects of our personality. Sometimes we are able to reject such aspects as not being appropriate for the life we live. For instance, we may realize that the destructiveness of a celebrity's public life would take its toll within our own lives.

🔯 Celebrities, pop, film and sports stars may also serve in dreams as a projection of the type of person we would like to be. We may, for instance, in real life be shy and withdrawn, but deep down need to be admired and loved.

🔲 Most of us are capable of creating an ideal person on whom to project our fantasies and wishes. We are not at this stage particularly in touch with reality. In dreams a celebrity, or any public figure will represent the Animus or Anima. A young person dreaming of a celebrity may not be ready for the responsibility of a real relationship.

🔲 In a woman's dream a male celebrity may allow her to experiment with the type of person she considers worth her attention. In a man's dream the reverse will be the case.

Consult the information on Anima/Animus in the Introduction as well as the entries for Fame and Media for clarification.

CELLAR – *see* BUILDINGS

CEMETERY

🔯 A cemetery is the place of the Dead but also of spiritual regeneration. As a place where we put aside the physical but can allow ourselves to mourn, it becomes an area of transition to something better.

🔯 In dreams we can often allow our fears to come to the surface in an acceptable way. The cemetery in dreams is a place set apart, where we can confront our fears of death and dying.

🔲 The cemetery and its association with death can have a double meaning. It can represent the parts of ourselves that we have 'killed off' or stopped using. It can also depict our thoughts and feelings about death and the attitudes and traditions surrounding it.

The entries for Catacomb/Crypt, Coffin, Grave, Sarcophagus and Tomb should clarify your understanding.

CENTAUR

🔯 Traditionally, the Centaur was half-man and half-beast, and this creature is associated with the Zodiac sign of Sagittarius. It signifies vision and wisdom.

🔯 The symbol of a Centaur in a dream represents our ability to unite two complete opposites in an acceptable way.

🔲 To have a Centaur appear in a dream demonstrates the unification of man's animal nature with his qualities of human virtue and judgement.

Also consult the entry for Fabulous Beasts.

CENTRE

◉ In spiritual geometry, the centre of anything represents totality and wholeness. It is the origin or beginning of everything. At this centre is 'sacred space'.

♥ Psychologically, to be at the centre, or in the middle of a situation, shows we need to be aware of both our ability to control that situation and our ability to be flexible. Moving towards the centre shows our need for integrity in our day-to-day life.

▦ To dream of being at the centre of something, such as in the centre of a group of people, highlights our awareness of our ability to be powerful within a situation; that everything revolves around us. To be moving away from the centre indicates that part of our lives may be off balance.

You might like to consult the entries for Point and Position.

CEREMONY

◉ Ceremonies and rituals are used for initiation – to be accepted by a group – to achieve deeper awareness and to establish new order.

♥ Any major life change has a profound effect on the dreamer and this is very often shown in dream form as a ceremony or some kind of rite of passage.

▦ When we dream of taking part in a ceremony or religious ritual we are conscious of a new attitude or skill that is needed or an important change which is taking place in our lives, perhaps a promotion at work or acceptance by our peer group.

You might like to consult the entries for Altar and Rite/Ritual as well as the information on Spiritual Imagery in the Introduction for further clarification.

CERTIFICATE

◉ As a paper acknowledgement of a learnt skill, a certificate suggests awareness of the long-term benefit of spiritual knowledge – perhaps an initiation into a particular type of this knowledge.

♥ Being given a certificate or diploma suggests our efforts have been acknowledged by others. Giving someone such a document signifies that we have successfully passed on our own knowledge.

▦ Since it confers status, we may dream of a certificate when we feel we have developed a degree of competence in our everyday life.

CHAIN

◉ In religious art bondage and slavery, dignity and unity are all symbolized by chains. The links in a chain suggest that we cannot exist in isolation.

♥ In dreams, we can become conscious of beliefs or mental attitudes – both in ourselves and others – which can create problems and hold us down. The links in a chain can very often symbolize the communication that we need to free ourselves.

🔳 To dream of chains in any form indicates a type of restriction or dependency. Just as we need strength to break out of chains, this is also needed for chains which support. In becoming aware of what is holding us back, we also become appreciative of how to break free.

CHAIR – *see* **FURNITURE**

CHALICE

�“ The chalice is symbolic of the source of inexhaustible sustenance, abundance and the Holy Grail. Because of this religious significance, the chalice usually represents something that may seem to be unattainable except without a great deal of effort.

💚 From medieval times the chalice has been associated with the symbolism of the heart, containing the life-force. In the full chalice this is represented by wine – wine and blood sharing the same meaning.

🔳 In dreams the chalice represents the feminine. It can also represent an important event or ceremony.

🔛 In a woman's dream the chalice tends to represent her sense of Self and her connection to the ultimate. In a man's dream it is more likely to be symbolic of his quest for autonomy.

To enhance your understanding consult the entries for Blood, Cup, Goblet and Quest.

CHALLENGE

�“ A spiritual challenge in dreams is one which takes us outside our comfort zone. This could show as a dream about a difficult journey for instance, an apparently insurmountable object or a descent into the underground. Ultimately we may find that it is not as difficult as we first thought.

💚 We are forced to reassess our attitudes to our own concepts, ideals or deeply held beliefs when we are challenged in any way in dreams.

🔳 To be challenged in dreams perhaps by someone barring our way or having an argument suggests that we need to know and understand our skills and talents.

CHAMPION – *see* **WIN/WINNER**

CHANT – *see* **CHARM, MUSIC AND SING**

CHAOS

�“ Before the universe began it was thought there existed a disordered state of unformed matter and infinite space. Spiritually therefore in dreams chaos is a representation of Source and the beginning of all things. There is, though, an underlying pattern, which may not be immediately apparent.

◈ A disorderly mass or jumble of thoughts and ideas which have not yet crystallized is experienced as chaos. They appear erratic and unpredictable.

▣ Chaos and confusion in dreams represent the changes over which we have no control. If we find ourselves trying to establish order then we are usually gaining insight into either our own state of mind or difficult situations around us.

Consult the entry for Churning for further clarification.

CHAPEL – *see* RELIGIOUS BUILDINGS IN BUILDINGS

CHARITY

✺ Charity comes from the word *caritas* which means 'caring from the heart'. Since the heart is the seat of self awareness this caring has a very special spiritual quality about it.

◈ Charity has implications in our ability to care for and about others. Apparently altruistic acts frequently have an ulterior self-interested motive. When we dream of a charitable act it often alerts us to the wider issues that are important in our lives.

▣ To dream of giving or receiving charity has a lot to do with our ability to give and receive love. A charity box or donation in a dream usually indicates an awareness of our own needs.

CHARM

✺ Technically, a charm is a spell or object possessing magic power, and was initially empowered by chanting (rhythmic singing). In dreams, it can have any of these resonances and suggests the idea of using power beyond the norm.

◈ Continuing the idea of magic, to perceive such an object in dreams alerts us to any special powers or talents we might have and our ability to use them. A charm bracelet was initially worn for protection and to attract good fortune.

▣ One of the magical techniques is to 'charm' someone – i.e. make them do something they would not normally do. In dreams we may find ourselves using such techniques as a way of alerting us to abilities and skills we have that we might not normally use. When someone else is being charming or attempting to charm us the opposite applies – we are being expected to do something which goes against the grain.

CHASE/CHASED

✺ Spiritually the image of being chased or pursued suggests either fear of our own actions, or is a play on words, as in 'chaste', i.e. trying to preserve our innocence.

❖ Being chased by shadows shows the need to escape from something previously repressed, such as past childhood trauma or difficulty. To be chased by an animal generally indicates we have not come to terms with our own passion.

▨ Dreaming of being chased or of trying to escape is perhaps one of the most common dreams; usually we are trying to escape responsibility, our own sense of failure, fear or emotions we can't handle.

⊡ It is not unusual for a woman to dream that she is being pursued in dreams. The implication is that she has something special which she does not wish to relinquish. If a man is being chased by a woman or that which he cannot identify then it is usually in response to his fear of being 'consumed.'
Consult the section on Animals and the entry for Hunt/Hunting/Huntsman for more information.

CHASM

✺ We are faced by the Unconscious, the Void. In developing spiritually there is often a sense of having to go down into the depths to reach understanding.

❖ We are being confronted by unknown or perhaps unrecognized negative elements in our own make-up; we have no previous experience by which to judge our actions or reactions.

▨ When we dream of a chasm or large hole, we are usually being made conscious of situations that contain an element of the unknown, or are in some way risky. We are going to have to make decisions as to whether to face the risk or withdraw.
You might like to consult the entries for Cave, Cliff, Hole and Void.

CHEMIST/CHEMISTRY

✺ The alchemist is one who changes base material into spiritual gold. Each of us has the potential to turn a very basic spiritual knowledge into a tool to help us live fulfilling lives.

❖ On a psychological level the chemist in the sense of an apothecary is the part of us which looks after health concerns and self-healing. He has access to knowledge that we need in order to stay in good health. In today's technological age a chemist in a dream signifies someone who has the ability to break down complex structures into their various components.

▨ To dream of a chemist is to link with that part of ourselves that is capable of altering the way we behave in our work-a-day lives, We are in touch with the wisdom – which is inherent in us all – concerning the Self.
You might also like to consult the entry for Alchemy.

CHERUB – *see* ANGELS AND SPIRITUAL IMAGERY

CHESS

☼ Based as it is on a battle, chess highlights the conflict between the spiritual powers of light and darkness. The white pieces and squares represent the light, and the black, darkness.

♡ Playing chess and losing indicates that we have undertaken an activity in our waking lives which cannot be successful. We have not got the wherewithal, or perhaps the knowledge, to pit ourselves against greater forces.

▦ In dreams, chess can express any internal conflict. It may also indicate the need for strategy in our lives.

Also consult the entry for Games.

CHEST/BOX

☼ Pandora's Box and the story of how negativity was released into the world is the best example of a box image on a spiritual level. A chest or box represents all those things we suppress or want to keep hidden, sometimes the darker side of ourselves, sometimes aspects that we have not yet explored. We need to be aware that care must be taken when first exploring the spiritual:

♡ Emotionally, we need to give some limitation to our feelings and secret desires. In dreams a box – whether plain or otherwise – will show how we handle life. When the chest area is highlighted in the body our attention is being drawn to our ability to love and care for others.

▦ A chest or box appearing in a dream delineates the way we keep hidden or store our emotions. Additionally, our most important ideals and hopes may need to be kept secret. It may also show the best in us; our best insights. A jewel box signifies that which needs to be kept safe and only made use of when appropriate.

CHILD/CHILDREN – *see* PEOPLE

CHIMNEY

☼ Any opening in a roof of a temple, tepee, tent, etc. represents the awareness of a change of state that may be an important part of spiritual growth. Dreaming of a chimney indicates that escape to the heavens through the solar gateway – that is, access to the gods – is possible. Rising smoke, such as that seen with incense, is also a symbol for prayer.

♡ Psychologically, a chimney and the passage of smoke portrays the channelling of energy in a more productive way than is presently occurring.

▦ When we dream of chimneys we are linking with a very old concept, that of escape from the mundane and ordinary into freedom.

⊟ In a man's dream the chimney may symbolize his sense of his own potency. In a woman's dream it will suggest her drive and desires.

CHISEL

✿ In sacred architecture the chisel is the active, masculine principle in relationship with the passive and feminine. In spiritual terms, therefore, the chisel signifies activity as opposed to waiting.

♡ Our intellectual need to succeed may put us in a position of trying to break through a barrier in order to complete a favourite project.

▦ The meaning of a chisel in a dream would depend on whether or not you are a craftsman in waking life. In such a case it will depict pride in achievement and specialist knowledge. If you have no such skill it will depend on other symbolism in the dream, but will probably indicate the need to use some force in a situation recognizable to you – literally to chip away at the structure.

⊟ In modern times the use of tools is not so gender specific as it used to be so in both men and women's dreams using a chisel suggests properly applied energy.

CHOCOLATE

✿ In the Mayan culture chocolate was food fit for the gods. This puts it in the framework of food for the soul and the release of our best efforts.

♡ Emotionally comforting, chocolate in a dream has a soothing effect. If we are eating or being given chocolate we need such soothing. If giving to someone else we are capable of soothing hurt and distress. The quality of the chocolate may be important.

▦ It is now well known that chocolate contains an essential amino acid called tryptophan which is essential to our wellbeing. Dreaming of chocolate may highlight a very real need for the beneficial effects of such a food.

⊟ Often highlighted as a suitable gift for lovers, in a woman's dream such a gift may signify an unrecognized potential in a relationship. In a man's dream he may recognize in himself the need to care for and appreciate others.

CHOICE/CHOOSE

✿ Choice in dreams suggests that we must weigh up two alternatives – right or wrong, spiritual or material, good or bad, individual or community.

♡ Decision-making can be difficult for many people. Being forced to choose in a dream suggests that we are not yet emotionally ready to make choices.

▦ When in our working or personal life we choose a particular course of action, yet are aware that we are unsure, this can present itself in dreams as confusion or dual images.

⚁ Most women will make choices from an emotional perspective and most men from a logical one. In dreams this is often reversed.

CHOKE

❀ Choking can indicate spiritual conflict and restraint. Choking in a dream highlights that we need to learn wisdom – when to speak and when to remain silent.

♥ Being choked suggests that we are being stifled by people or circumstances and are not in control of either. Choking on food suggests that there is something unpalatable in our lives.

▨ When we find ourselves choking in a dream we are coming up against our inability to express ourselves appropriately. There is some conflict between our inner and outer selves, perhaps some indecision over whether we should speak out or remain silent.

CHOP – see AXE AND TREE

CHRYSALIS

❀ Metamorphosis and Magical Powers are symbolized by the chrysalis. That which is intrinsically ugly and therefore apparently spiritually unacceptable goes through a process of inactivity to become something new.

♥ Change is taking place within us, but on a very subtle level which is not immediately recognizable.

▨ There are two ways in which a chrysalis can be interpreted within a dream. Firstly, as potential for action, which has not yet been realised, and secondly protection in a situation that must wait until the time is right.

⚁ As a period of gestation, the chrysalis may appear in women's dreams to alert her to the possibility of pregnancy.

You might also like to consult the entry for Butterfly.

CHURCH – see RELIGIOUS BUILDINGS IN BUILDINGS

CHURNING

❀ Ultimately, chaos must give way to order. One school of thought is that form arose out of churning the Chaos. In dreams such an idea has some merit, since many dream images appear to arrive from nowhere.

♥ We very often need to become conscious of a very deep-rooted sense of churning or movement within ourselves in order to become appreciative of our capacity for order.

▨ Most dreams in which there is a liquid being churned, boiled or made to move in some way link back to a very primitive sense of chaos (lack of order). This indicates we may need to reassess our creative abilities to make use of the energy available to us.

You might like to consult the entry for Chaos.

CIRCLE – *see* **SHAPES/PATTERNS**

CIRCUMAMBULATION

🔆 We symbolize creating the centre of our universe by circumambulation. Many religions use walking around an area in a circle more than once to signify a magical or sacred space.

💙 Psychologically we all need to have a place which is ours alone. To dream of circumambulation signifies taking responsibility for ourselves and our actions.

🔲 To be walking around a building or a particular spot in a dream is to be creating a 'universe' in which action can take place. It is to be designating that place as having a particular significance.

CIRCUMCISION – *see* **SEX/SEXUAL IMAGES**

CIRCUMFERENCE

🔆 Spiritually the circumference of a circle delineates a dividing line between two worlds. It suggests limitation and is a line between the spiritual realms and the physical material world.

💙 We are on the edge of new knowledge or information and could move in either direction.

🔲 To be held within the circumference of a circle is to be made aware through dream images of the limitations we may have set ourselves. To be shut out of the circumference of a circle is to be unworthy, or perhaps unknowing.

Also consult the entry for Circle in Shapes/Patterns.

CITY

🔆 A spiritual community to which we belong can be represented in dreams by a city, since a city was originally given status because it had a cathedral.

💙 A city usually has a core community, and we sometimes represent the place of work or opportunity in this way.

🔲 Dreaming of a city, particularly one known to us, is to be trying to understand our sense of community; of belonging to groups. We will often, through dreams, give ourselves clues as to what we require in the mental and emotional environment in which we live, and a bustling city may show our need for social interaction. A deserted city may portray our feelings of having been neglected by others.

Also consult Religious Buildings in Buildings and Spiritual Imagery in the Introduction.

CLAMP

🔆 Any kind of clamp implies restraint – to dream of one indicates we are being prevented from making progress in our spiritual aims.

❦ To find ourselves using a clamp such as a woodworking tool suggests having to make an extra effort to hold a situation stable.

▦ A car being clamped in dreams suggests a deliberate bar to movement. This may be because a particular task has taken too long, because authority has stepped in or because we have not paid enough attention to detail.

CLEAN/CLEAR

❧ Cleanness or clarity represent spiritual purity. Cleanliness, in the sense of having been cleansed, signifies one way of getting to that state. Baptism is a ceremony indicative of this.

❦ To be cleaning an article suggests that we are not satisfied with its original state. Making a clear statement suggests a deeply held belief.

▦ When dirty water runs clear or we have a sense of clarity we have an opportunity to clarify misunderstandings and difficulties in everyday life.

CLIFF

❧ The cliff edge denotes a step off into the Unknown. A cliff equally can suggest an obstacle to be scaled.

❦ There may be a step we need to take which will psychologically put us either on edge or on the edge in such a way that we must overcome our own fears in order to proceed through our own limitations.

▦ To be on the edge of a cliff in a dream indicates the dreamer is facing danger. It shows the need to make a decision as to how to deal with a situation, and possibly be open to taking a risk. We are often facing the unknown.

Consult the entries for Edge and Mountain for further clarification.

CLIMATE

❧ Nature and natural occurrences have always played an important part in man's spiritual understanding. Changes which were previously attributed to the gods, such as thunderstorms and floods, tend to have a more prosaic explanation in the present day. In dreams they represent disturbances.

❦ Climate changes in dreams can often reflect our own emotions and moods.

▦ As the world is seen to undergo climate change through human intervention, dreams can take on a more apocalyptic feel. We seem to be less in touch with the effect we have on the world we live in.

CLIMB

❧ Ascension, in the sense of climbing to achieve enlightenment, is an often perceived spiritual symbol.

❦ Climbing upwards suggests we are trying to reach new heights in our lives, and are possibly having to make greater efforts than before to succeed.

Climbing down, in the sense that it uses a different technique, suggests having to assess the risks of a change in position.

■ To dream of climbing is to dream of getting away from something, possibly to escape. We may be avoiding trouble.

CLOAK – *see* **CLOTHES**

CLOCK – *see* **TIME**

CLOSE/CLOSED

◉ Spiritually to be close to someone is to have empathy with them. A closed door suggests that an opportunity has passed.

♥ We can indicate to ourselves in dreams the fact that we are emotionally closed within a situation. This often manifests as a sense of being closed in.

■ To be close to someone in a dream can mean we are looking for intimacy, or perhaps protection. To close a door acknowledges the fact that we must make a decision to put the past behind us.

Consult the entries for Door and Trap/Trapped for further clarification.

CLOTHES

◉ Clothes can suggest spiritual protection. For instance, certain types of clothes will highlight roles and status. The priest's habit or judges robes are two such examples.

♥ Clothes often act as a form of protection, particularly against being touched. This protection may also be against having our real self violated. Clothes can also conceal or reveal: in covering up nudity they conceal our perceived imperfections and, by implication, disguise our sexuality. In revealing certain parts of our bodies our dreams may show in what ways we are vulnerable.

Various articles of clothing have certain symbolic meanings in dreams:

Coat/cloak/shawl – any type of coat can suggest warmth and love, but also protection. This protection can be either physical or emotional, and particularly in the case of a cloak, can be the spiritual protection of Faith. A sheepskin coat may emphasize this significance Fear of losing the coat can suggest the fear of losing faith and belief. If the coat is too short or not thick enough it shows we may be fearful that our love, or the protection we have, is not adequate for our needs. *Also consult the entry for Sheep in Animals.*

Gloves – the meaning of gloves can be ambivalent in dreams. They can represent covering and protection, but also 'showing one's hand' and challenging the status quo. *Also consult the individual entry for Gloves.*

Hat/cap – a hat or cap is a symbol of wisdom and the intellect and also of protection. It can also signify both spirituality and sexuality, depending on the other aspects of the dream.

Pyjamas/nightclothes – pyjamas or any type of nightclothes suggest relaxation and hence openness.

Raincoat – in common with other types of coat, a raincoat holds the symbolism of protection, but more specifically this time against other people's emotional onslaught. Very occasionally it may suggest some kind of wish to return to a womb-like state.

Shirt – a shirt can suggest appropriate action; correct for the occasion or casual, more relaxed. Wearing a hair shirt denotes grief and penitence.

Shoes – our ability, or otherwise, to be grounded and in touch with everyday life is symbolized in dreams by shoes. Shoes that we, or others, are wearing in a dream are there to alert us to an adjustment that needs to be made in our attitude to life. Lacing up shoes in a dream was once thought to be a well-known symbol of death as were shoes on a table. Today, these images are much more likely to indicate change is necessary.

Tie – a tie has two main significances in dreams. For some it can represent correctness and good behaviour, whereas for others, presumably because of its shape, it will signify the phallus and thus masculine power.

Underclothes – when we dream of underclothes – whether our own or other people's – we are considering hidden attitudes to self-image or sexuality.

Veil or veil-like garments – when we, or others, are wearing a veil we are either trying to hide something, or are only partially accepting knowledge about ourselves or our relationship to others. *Also consult the individual entry for Veil.*

▨ The clothes we wear in a dream can often depict the facade, or persona, we create for other people. We have certain roles that we adopt in response to others' reactions. Clothes which others are wearing in our dreams can also set the scene for an acting out of some of the confrontations which take place. Some common images which have particular relevance are:

Getting undressed can suggest the shedding of old beliefs and inhibitions whereas losing one's clothes or being naked highlights our vulnerability and fears.

Dressing inappropriately, perhaps wearing formal clothes on a casual occasion and vice versa, shows we are conscious of our own difficulty in 'fitting in' with other people. It will depend on the dream scenario whether we are surprised or distressed, and it is often the emotion that we experience which gives us the correct interpretation. We may be deliberately not conforming to others' perception of us, or trying to conform too much in adopting a certain role. The colour of the clothing is often significant.

Clothes being worn by someone to whom they do not belong indicate there is confusion in the our mind as to which roles are appropriate for each character. If a man is wearing woman's clothing it shows that we need to be more conscious of our feminine side. A uniform on a woman highlights the need to be aware of the more disciplined and masculine side of our personality. If we are changing clothes we are attempting, or perhaps need to consider how, to change our image. Clothes that have been cut short indicate that we may be outgrowing former pleasures and need to look to pastures new for our entertainment, whereas particularly pretty clothes show we have much to appreciate in our lives. If we are aware that clothes belonging to a particular person then we are being reminded of that person, even though we are aware that they cannot necessarily be with us.

CLOUDS

❄ Being unreachable, clouds symbolized the potency of the Ultimate. Similar to smoke, they were previously considered to be the vehicle for Divine Power. They retain this significance in dreams today.

❤ We may have a hidden depression, shown by dark clouds, which can be dealt with only after it has been given form in a dream. White clouds suggest contentment, but may also suggest a transitory awareness of an idea.

▦ Dreaming of clouds can have two meanings, depending on the other circumstances in the dream. It can either indicate uplifting or religious feelings, or can show that we are feeling overshadowed by someone or something. It can also warn of the possibility of difficulty or danger to come.

CLOVER

❄ The three-leaved clover is an example of body, soul and spirit, or any representation of the triad of divinity such as Father, Son and Holy Spirit. The four-leaved clover includes the feminine principle, and therefore the quaternity which predates the Christian religion.

❤ We need to look at our ability to bring the various parts of our personality back into harmony with one another. The four-leaved clover symbolizes the balance of the Ego functions: thinking, sensing, feeling and intuition.

▦ Traditionally the clover plant is considered to be lucky, so to find clover in a dream denotes good fortune is on its way. The three-leaved clover suggests the past, the present and the future.

▣ In a woman's dream clover generally highlights the psyche and her intuitive abilities. In a man's dream the focus will be on his ability to use his talents to the full.

CLOWN

⚜ Spiritually the figure of the clown has the same significance as the jester, that being the ability to laugh at our foibles and idiosyncrasies.

♥ The clown will often suggest the ability to see and sense the ridiculous in life. Often there is a tinge of sadness in this, however.

▦ In life a true clown must register his mask after which no-one else can use the same make-up and a clown can have this same significance in dreams. We must 'register' the performance we put on for the world.

CLUB (PEOPLE)

⚜ Organized Ritual and dance as an expression of an inner rhythm is an important part of the progression to spiritual awareness

♥ It requires a certain level of maturity to be at ease being part of a group, so to dream of being with a crowd and enjoying the interaction, particularly in a public place, can indicate our awareness of ourselves.

▦ When we dream of being in a club such as a night-spot or sports club, we are highlighting the right of every human being to belong to a group with common aims and beliefs.

CLUB (WEAPON)

⚜ The club as a weapon is a stereotype of masculinity, although rather crudely expressed in this instance. The type of club used in the game of golf for instance suggests the ability to use masculinity in a more refined way.

♥ We have great strength at our disposal, for which we need to find an outlet.

▦ To dream of using a weapon to club someone denotes an inner turmoil that has remained unexpressed. It may also depict our feelings of violence against ourselves.

⟠ Rather obviously, a club can be taken as a symbol of the penis in both male and female dreams.

You might also like to consult the entry for Weapons.

COBWEB

⚜ It will depend on the state of the cobweb as to the spiritual interpretation. A spider's web can suggest the symbol of the eight pointed star, the mandala – an aid to meditation – and hence the Buddhist eightfold path to spiritual enlightenment. A dirty cobweb, however, denotes that spirituality is contaminated in some fashion.

♥ The cobweb, because it is easily damaged, signifies indecision, perhaps an idea that has not quite crystallized yet.

▦ On a purely practical level the cobweb symbolizes unused talents and potential which has been allowed to go stale.

You might like to consult the entries for Spider and Star in Shapes/Patterns for further clarification.

COCK

The masculine principle, the spiritual Bird of Fame and the dawn are all part of the significance of this bird.

We may need to be more up front and courageous in what we are doing.

The cock has always been a symbol of a new day, and of vigilance or watchfulness, so to have one appear in a dream forecasts a new beginning or warning to be vigilant in one's daily work.

There is obvious significance in the slang word for the penis in a man's dream and there may be a similar word-play in women's dreams.

The section on Birds will give you additional information.

COCOON – *see* CHRYSALIS

CODE

A spiritual code may appear in dreams as an unrecognizable language which requires deciphering. It can also be a code of behaviour by which one must live.

To be deciphering a code in dreams suggests that we need some understanding of the 'key' to our own or others' behaviour or that there is knowledge at present hidden from us.

To be using a door code or some kind of numerical combination suggests that we have the necessary information to gain access. Not to know the code or to have forgotten it indicates that we must be more careful in future. This meaning holds good if we do not know the correct code of behaviour.

COFFIN

Redemption, resurrection and salvation are all symbolized by the coffin. Contemplation of the death experience can lead to dreams of a coffin, in this case symbolizing the physical body, though we may be attuned to the unseen spiritual world.

We are perhaps shutting our own feelings away and therefore causing a part of ourselves to die. There may be a dull, unaware state of consciousness which is lacking in spiritual insight.

When we dream of a coffin, we are reminding ourselves of our own mortality. We may also be coming to terms with the death of a relationship and feelings of loss. This may also be the first warning of a weakened state, a total lack of vitality.

Consult the entries for Catacomb/Crypt, Cemetery, Dead People, Death and Hearse for more information.

COINS – *see* MONEY

COLD

❖ The loss of our connection to the spirit realms can be felt in dreams as extreme cold. Equally, this can signify the presence of a spiritual energy.

♡ A physical feeling in dreams often reflects our inner feelings or our emotions. To feel cold is one such way of highlighting a state of mind.

▦ To be conscious of cold in a dream is to be aware of feeling neglected, or of being left out of things.

COLLAPSE

❖ Anything which collapses suggests there is not enough energy to hold a structure together – in this case spiritual energy.

♡ When an object in dreams collapses we need to be aware of situations in our lives which are damaged or under threat if we do not take care. Seeing a person collapse suggests that there may be a health issue around which needs attention.

▦ If a barrier or wall is seen to collapse without assistance it signifies that two aspects of life are coming together and there is no longer need for division.

COLOURS

❖ Colour affirms the existence of light. In spiritual terms, red is the colour of self-image and sexuality, orange is relationship – both with ourselves and others. Yellow is the emotional self, green is self-awareness and blue is self-expression and wisdom. Indigo is the colour of creativity, while violet depicts cosmic responsibility. Pure white suggests absolute spirituality.

♡ The symbolism of colour is very relevant in dreams since we know that these colours are not physically produced, but are a mental image. Some meanings given to colours are:

Black – holds within it all colour in potential. It suggests manifestation, negativity and judgement.

Blue – the colour of the clear blue sky and is the prime healing colour. It suggests relaxation, sleep and peacefulness.

Brown – the colour of the earth and of commitment. It also symbolizes death.

Green – the colour of nature and of plant life. It signifies balance and harmony.

Grey – there is probably no true grey, it being a combination of black and white. Sometimes the colour of nuns' habits, it means devotion and ministration.

Magenta – in some ways a colour which links both the physical and spiritual. It signifies relinquishment, selflessness, perfection and meditative practice.

Orange – an essentially cheerful uplifting colour. The qualities associated with it are happiness and independence.

Red – vigour, strength, energy, life, sexuality and power are all connected with this colour. A beautiful clear mid-red is the correct one for these qualities; if there is any other red in dreams, its attributes may not be totally uncontaminated.

Turquoise – clear greeny blue. In some religions it is taken to be the colour of the freed soul. It means calmness and purity.

Violet – while found by some to be too strong, means nobility, respect and hope. Its purpose is to uplift.

White – contains within it all colours. It suggests innocence, spiritual purity and wisdom.

Yellow – the colour that is closest to daylight. Connected with the emotional self, the attributes are thinking, detachment and judgement.

Colour is a vital part of symbolism, dream and otherwise. By learning to work with our own colour spectrum, particularly in the dream state, we can maintain and enhance our physical wellbeing. This is partly to do with the vibratory frequency which each individual colour has, and partly to do with tradition. Experiments have been carried out to ascertain what effect colour has, and have proved what occultists and healers have always known. In working with the colours of the rainbow, we discover that the warm, lively colours – which give back light – are yellow, orange and red. Cold passive colours are blue, indigo and violet. Green is a synthesis of both warmth and cold. White light holds within it the whole colour spectrum and its potential.

COLUMN

Spiritually a single column has the same significance as a tower, a structure to enable us to reach the heavens or the Divine. It may be an object of worship or a memorial. A column of light denotes an awareness of spirit or spiritual energy. Boaz (strength) and Joachim (beauty) are the two columns which stood at the entrance to King Solomon's temple in Jerusalem.

Single columns could represent strength or single mindedness. Two stone columns in the distance indicate a doorway to the future or a way into the unknown.

A column will suggest the penis but also masculinity. It is also structural or emotional support.

You might like to consult the entry for Pillar for further clarification.

COMB

Fertility, the rays of the sun, entanglement and music are all represented by the comb.

♦ We may be conscious of the fact that we need to work with our self-image.

▦ A comb is a many-toothed implement and often emphasizes the need to neaten or tidy something up in our lives. We need to tidy up our thoughts.

⊟ In a man's dream, a comb can indicate seduction or sensuality. In a woman's dream it perhaps has more to do with her devouring nature – the ability to destroy.

COMBAT – *see* ARGUE/ARGUMENTS, CONFLICT, FIGHT AND WAR

COMBINE – *see* CONNECT

COMET

✷ The coming of calamity, war, fire or danger can be seen in dreams as the comet. Comets were once thought to be divine messengers.

♦ As an intense, rare occurrence when we are most under pressure, a comet appearing in a dream indicates the answer to a problem may be about to appear to us at the speed of light.

▦ To dream of seeing a comet is to recognize the possibility of circumstances very quickly arising over which we have no control. The outcome may be unavoidable.

COMMITTEE

✷ A committee is a group of people brought together for a specific purpose. Dreams often produce such an image when our commitment is required for a particular spiritual task.

♦ When a consensus of opinion or a concerted effort needs to be made we will often dream of a committee in order to highlight the issue.

▦ In working life, a committee in dreams signifies a shared responsibility. Discussion and good management rather than personal concerns will carry the day.

COMMUNE

✷ A commune suggests a group of like-minded people who have chosen to live together to achieve a particular spiritual objective.

♦ Finding ourselves living in a commune in dreams signifies our understanding that a group of people with a common purpose are exponentially more powerful than the sum of the individuals.

▦ In dreams a commune may represent any 'family' to which we belong – a religion, our work colleagues, a hobby group. It is the shared passion that is important.

COMMUNICATION

✷ Any tool of communication – telephone, mobile or cellphone, email, fax machine, computer, internet, television – suggests that the veil between the spiritual and physical worlds can be penetrated. We are capable of better and wider communication than previously.

◈ The computer can symbolize spiritual records and the past, present and future. A database would, for instance, suggest the ordering of information. Text messaging might suggest brief but necessary information, whereas a fax, being slightly outdated, requires us to bring what we know up to date. The telephone signifies communication with unseen people and might therefore highlight communication with the spirit world. The television is, quite literally, a medium through which information is passed. The internet will tend to signify wider, more global, communication and available information.

▦ Communication occurs on so many levels that images of modern technology can now accurately mimic in dreams the way we communicate. A stored document suggests that we are making a link with past memories or stored information which we may need to access in order to progress. The computer and other high technology images are now such a part of people's lives that it very much depends on other circumstances in the dream as to the correct interpretation of the image. A computer crashing, for instance, suggests that there is a problem with the means of communication rather than communication itself.

As modern day technology spreads, such an image may simply be a means of conveying a message from the unconscious to the conscious mind, whereas in other cases it will be a reminder of personal potential or abilities. A keyboard, requiring a certain degree of skill, can suggest the stages of proficiency we need to acquire in order to communicate our ideas efficiently.

Also consult the entries for Email, Telephone, Text and Web.

COMMUTE

❀ Since commuting implies changing – perhaps moving from personal concerns to work-orientated matters – the significance is shifting from a relaxed to a more focused state.

◈ Just as our mindset must change as we travel to and from work from personal to work concerns, substituting one way of thinking for another, in essence changing perspective, can lead to radical changes in lifestyle.

▦ In modern-day life commuting has turned into a time of transition, a way of covering distance and a time for planning. Dreaming of such an occurrence can highlight any of these activities.

For further clarity see Journey and Transport.

COMPASS

❀ When we are trying to find direction, and overcome our own spiritual limitations and boundaries, we will dream of a compass.

❤ Often having the same significance as the circle, the compass can represent the source of life, or sometimes justice. Instinctively, compass directions suggest certain states of being such as north suggesting coldness and south suggesting warmth.

▦ Dreaming of a compass is often an attempt to find a new direction or activity. We need to be able to understand the differing opportunities offered to us, and to follow the one that is right for us.

⊡ In magical work the compass is used to help define the four most powerful directions. In both men's and women's dreams a compass may suggest the search for magical power.

You might like to consult the entries for Position and Map.

COMPETE /COMPETITION

✿ Any competition suggests a struggle between two polarities, though in the spiritual sense it is actually a joint effort to overcome a challenge.

❤ To be competing in a dream is to perhaps look for a better performance from ourselves than we have managed hitherto.

▦ As today's world is highly competitive our dreams may highlight competitiveness in ways that we do not consciously recognize. Dreaming of running a race might highlight such competition in the workplace.

⊡ Competition in both men's and women's dreams will highlight their area of competitiveness. A woman for instance might find herself competing against another woman for recognition, whereas a man may simply find himself in competition with all and sundry.

COMPUTER – *see* COMMUNICATION, EMAIL AND MICROCHIP.

CONCH – *see* SHELL

CONCUBINE – *see* SIRENS IN ARCHETYPES IN THE INTRODUCTION

CONDEMN – *see* JUDGE/JUDGEMENT AND JUSTICE

CONFER/CONFERENCE

✿ A conference holds the symbolism of a group meeting together to achieve a consensus either of opinion or action.

❤ To find ourselves at a conference suggests that we need to ensure that all aspects of our personality are in agreement.

▦ Conferring signifies a bringing together of perhaps differing opinions to reach a sense of common ownership. In everyday terms this image will arise when such a consensus is important to progress. The image of a conference can also come up when we find ourselves at odds with the majority.

CONFESS/CONFESSION

✿ Confession is a recognition of those aspects of our lives which are not within a particular code of conduct, whether spiritual or otherwise.

◉ To be confessing to someone else signifies that we have not been acting with integrity. To have someone make a confession suggests that we are judging a particular behaviour – our own or people around us.

▦ We feel that we are carrying a responsibility which we need to share with someone else more competent.

⬕ When the other person is known in dreams or of the opposite gender both men and women will need to monitor their own integrity. This is an aspect of the Animus or Anima and suggests that the physical being is not in alignment with the spiritual self.

CONFLICT

✷ When two opposing forces meet, particularly in the spiritual sense, this is pictured in dreams as conflict.

◉ Conflict suggests that two aspects of our personality are having difficulty in reconciling their needs and requirements. Conflict arises when the conscious self needs to make a choice between their differing needs.

▦ The dream image of conflict arises when we are at odds with others in our everyday life. Sometimes a resolution can be reached in dreams which points the way to managing the external conflict.

⬕ It is supposed that men are more logical in their thought processes and women more intuitive. However, when a woman dreams of a strategic response to a conflict she is accessing her more logical side. Conversely, when a man follows his own instincts he will be seeking an intuitive answer.

You might like to consult the entries for Argue/Arguments, Fight and War.

CONNECT/COMBINE

✷ Part of the process of spiritual development is integration – making connections between various aspects of our personality and combining them to make a more coherent whole. We tend to search for how things fit together, how they interact, how they contribute to the whole.

◉ When we dream of connecting or combining two articles, for instance two opposing forces, we are attempting to dispense with duality and perhaps achieve a better use of energy.

▦ Making connections in dreams can signify forming relationships. Missing a connection when travelling suggests that we have not linked timing and effort. Dreaming of combinations of things creates a composite, combining qualities from each of them.

For further clarity read the information on Composite Animals in Animals, as well as the entries for Journey and Transport.

CONSECRATE – *see* **SPIRITUAL IMAGERY IN THE INTRODUCTION**
CONSERVATION

Conservation suggests that we are aware of global issues and spiritual responsibilities.

Conservation implies the best usage of the resources available to us. By looking at symbols of resources which appear in dreams we are given the opportunity to become more efficient.

As the issue becomes more noticeable in everyday life conservation can have two meanings. On a personal level it can represent the best use of our talents and abilities. In a wider sense it will suggest our responsibilities towards others – family, colleagues and others. To dream of working for an organization dealing with conservation may mean that we should seek out others of a like mind.

CONTAGION/CONTAGIOUS – *see* **INFECTION**
CONTAMINATE/CONTAMINATION – *see* **DIRTY**
CONTRACEPTIVE – *see* **SEX/SEXUAL IMAGES**
CONTRACT

A contract suggests a spiritual commitment.

In that a contract is a binding agreement between two parties it signifies having made a promise to carry out a particular task, which should be easily identifiable after a little thought.

A work contract denotes a commitment of our working life. A contract to buy signifies a long-term commitment, whereas an unsigned contract suggests that we are unable to make any commitment at this stage.

As women are able to exercise more autonomy over their lives, signing a contract such as a prenuptial agreement suggests the making of a deeper commitment to themselves. In a man's dream a contract can have a more workaday connotation.

CONVENT – *see* **SPIRITUAL IMAGERY IN THE INTRODUCTION**
CONVICT/CONVICTION/CONVINCE

A conviction in the sense of a firm belief is a necessary part of spiritual commitment. A convict on the other hand is someone who has offended against others' deeply held beliefs.

All three aspects (convict, conviction and convince) presuppose an emotional connection with our own beliefs. To be convinced in a dream means that we have been deeply impressed and to have a conviction follows this same idea. To convict someone, however, suggests that we have a deeply held belief that that person has committed some wrongdoing.

🔲 To receive a conviction, therefore, means to be at the mercy of other people's opinions, whereas convincing someone means that we have converted them to our way of thinking.

CONVOLVULUS – *see* **BINDING AND FLOWERS**

COOKING

🔆 Cooking can symbolize creativity. There is a delightful fable which tells how God baked the various ethnic races into being.

◈ To be able to move forward in our lives we may need to blend certain parts of our existence in new and original ways in order to succeed. We may need to nurture a new ability. This is often brought to our attention by dreams of cooking.

🔲 To be cooking in a dream is to be preparing nourishment or to be satisfying a hunger, whether our own or other people's. This may not simply be a physical hunger, but something more subtle such as a need to make use of the varied opportunities available to us.

⊞ In a woman's dream cooking may suggest work-a-day activities as well as domestic ones, a metaphor for the way she constructs a project. A man's dream may be a way of refocusing on a creative problem.

You might like to consult the entries for Bake/Baker/Bakery, Food and Hunger.

COPY

🔆 Copying in spiritual terms signifies reproducing the perfect, producing duality where there was previously only one. It represents emanation, flowing out from the Divine.

◈ To be copying an action in dreams suggests we need to learn from others.

🔲 When we find ourselves making copies we are aware that we need to retain information for ourselves. Such a dream can suggest the idea of reproduction.

Consult the entry for Forge for further clarification.

CORD

🔆 The Silver Cord – that subtle energy which holds the life force within the body – is an image which manifests in dreams as we begin to recognize spiritual progression.

◈ There is a need to be appreciative of the ties of duty and affection.

🔲 Within any relationship there are certain restrictions or dependencies that become apparent, and these may be depicted in dreams as cords or ties. These emotional bonds can be both limiting and freedom-giving.

Also consult the entries for Bonds, Chains and Umbilical Cord.

CORN

�֎ The Great Mother, or Mother Nature, in her nurturing aspect is always shown with corn representing fertility and fecundity.

♡ To be harvesting corn is to be reaping the rewards of hard work. We may be linking with some very primeval needs and requirements.

▦ Most dreams containing images of corn or wheat symbolize fertility or fruitfulness. They may also represent new life – either pregnancy or new developments in other ways.

⊞ Women are much more in touch with the natural forces so tend to dream of goddesses and their attributes.

You might also like to consult the entries for Harvest and Mill/Millstone.

CORNER

✖ To turn the corner spiritually is to gain a new perspective on our own spiritual indecision.

♡ We are making available a hidden or little admitted aspect of ourselves. We no longer need to feel trapped or restricted. We can handle the unexpected or the new experience.

▦ To turn a corner in a dream indicates that we have succeeded in moving forward into new experiences, despite what may have seemed to be obstacles in front of us. Turning a right-handed corner indicates a logical course of action, to turn a left-handed one indicates a more intuitive approach.

CORNUCOPIA

✖ The Horn of Plenty is an image common in one form or another in all spiritual work. The abundance may be for us or the rest of the world.

♡ Within ourselves we have unlimited potential to create both an acceptable present and a sustainable future.

▦ Like the conch shell, to dream of a cornucopia can denote abundance, endless bounty, fertility and fruitfulness. It may be more than we are used to or can handle.

Also consult the entry for Horns for further information.

CORPORATE

✖ A corporate environment in dreams will suggest a diverse group of people who are brought together for a common purpose – a perhaps bureaucratic approach to spirituality.

♡ A corporate environment will not necessarily have visible within it a passion for overall success and therefore suggests a competitive spirit which may or may not be in line with our own aims as individuals.

🌑 This can simply represent our everyday workplace or a task which we have undertaken.

You might like to consult the entry for Work.

CORRIDOR – *see* BUILDINGS

CORRUPTION

🕸 Any kind of corruption suggests deliberate interference in a negative way. Morally, we have moved beyond acceptable behaviour.

♥ Corruption denotes a tainting or spoiling, particularly of our integrity, so any such image signifies something which is imperfect or has been made so by a negative influence.

🌑 An article which is decaying or corrupted is now no longer useful so from a mundane perspective we may need to look at aspects of our lives which have outlived their usefulness.

COSMETICS

🕸 The personality can and does show itself in many guises. From a spiritual perspective we find a need to cover up or disguise blemishes in our character.

♥ Psychologically we may feel that we have a problem with our public image, and need to put on some sort of front before we can be seen by others.

🌑 To be using cosmetics in a dream can have two meanings. We register the fact that we are covering up our features or that, conversely, we are enhancing our natural beauty. If we are using cosmetics on someone else, we literally need to 'make up' with that person.

You might like to enhance your understanding by consulting the entry for Make-Up.

COUNT – *see* ABACUS AND NUMBERS

COUNTERFEIT – *see* FAKE/FALSE

COUNTRYSIDE

🕸 The forces of nature in us can be symbolized by scenes of the countryside. We can return, without feeling guilty, to a very relaxed state. As our lives become more frenetic we need an image which induces good feelings.

♥ There is, in most people's minds, a type of freedom and openness about the countryside which is not necessarily available in towns and cities. Such an image appears shows we may need to clarify our own feelings about our lifestyle.

🌑 When we dream of the countryside we are putting ourselves in touch with our own natural spontaneous feelings. We may have memories of the countryside that invoke a particular mood state or way of being.

Also consult Places.

COUP – *see* **WAR**

COURT

🔅 A court in the sense of a legal arena suggests judgement by a higher authority. This implies that we are not necessarily acting with integrity. A games court represents a degree of team spirit.

💟 Appearing in court suggests that we have committed a misdemeanour of some sort and must expect to be judged or held to account by our peers.

▥ Taking someone to court for a debt or a minor offence is a way of dealing through dreams with a perceived hurt or indiscretion. A court such as a tennis or squash court suggests an acceptable way of acting out our competitive instincts.

Consult Authority Figures in People, Crime/Criminal, Debt, Games, Judge/Judgement and Justice for any further information you might need,

COUSIN – *see* **EXTENDED FAMILY IN FAMILY**

COVEN

🔅 A coven is a gathering of a group of people with a common belief, particularly Wiccan. Capable of calling on natural forces for either good or bad, it gathers to enhance the vibration of both the individual and the group.

💟 When we dream of belonging to a coven we are becoming aware of the 'power of the many' and thus share our knowledge with others.

▥ The popular image of a coven of witches can appear in dreams when relationships with work colleagues or family require a common focus.

⬒ Since coven also means a religious assembly in both men's and women's dreams it will depict a heightening of both emotional and spiritual vibrations.

Consulting the entries for Magic/Magician and Witch as well as Spiritual Imagery in the Introduction will enhance your understanding.

COVER

🔅 Covering something suggests obliterating it or hiding that which we do not want others to know about us. Burying something in the earth in a dream suggests hiding a misdeed of some sort.

💟 Covering over anything signifies making the best of or preserving what we have, perhaps ensuring that shortcomings are not recognized.

▥ It will depend what and how we are covering in dreams. Covering an article in brown paper portrays the need to be pragmatic while covering an altar signifies an act of devotion. Covering a chair suggests added comfort while covering up our actions suggests we are aware of opprobrium.

Consulting the entries for Altar, Canopy and Paper will assist in your interpretation.

COW – *see* **ANIMALS**

COYOTE – *see* **WOLF IN ANIMALS**

CRAB

☀ The astrological sign of Cancer and the Great Mother are both represented by the crab.

♥ Because the crab has a hard shell and is thus self-protective, in dreams this quality can be highlighted. When someone is 'crabby' they are irritable or morose. The crab apple is small and sour and therefore has this same connotation.

▣ A crab appearing in a dream can indicate mothering, particularly of the 'smother love' type, but can also be the qualities of unreliability and self-interest. The crab can also, because of the way it moves, denote deviousness.

⚐ In a woman's dream the crab will often represent the different aspects of the three-faceted Moon goddess, maid, mother and crone. In a man's dream it is more likely to suggest the 'smother mother'.

CRACK

☀ There may be a spiritual flaw in our make-up. A little thought should reveal what it might be.

♥ Psychologically a crack may represent the irrational or the unexpected. It may indicate our inability to hold things together mentally. Dreaming of the street drug crack will have this connotation.

▣ Dreaming of an article which is cracked indicates our recognition of something which is flawed in our lives. There may be a weakness or difficulty in the attitudes and defences we use to meet life's problems.

CRADLE/CRIB

☀ The physical as opposed to the spiritual body is sometimes represented as a cradle or baby's crib.

♥ An empty cradle can represent a woman's fear of childlessness or her fears of motherhood, depending on the other aspects of the dream. It may also suggest a lack of creativity or new ideas. A crib was initially a food receptacle, although today it can suggest a new life.

▣ To dream of a cradle or crib can represent new life or new beginnings.

⚐ As a precognitive dream a cradle can represent pregnancy, while in a man's dream it can represent the need to return to a womblike, protected state.

CRANE

☀ As a bird, the crane is a messenger of the gods. It allows communion with the gods and the ability to enter into higher states of consciousness.

T'ai chi, a form of spiritual discipline, is said to symbolize a fight between a crane and a snake.

⚕ We are capable of gaining control or status within a situation so we can build on it to our advantage.

▣ When we dream of a building crane we are often being told of the need to raise our level of awareness in some matter. We need to make an attempt to understand the overall or universal implications of our actions.

CRASH

⚘ Crashing actually suggests breaking up and signifies, therefore, a difficulty in remaining whole or complete in a spiritual sense.

⚕ A crash as in a collision suggests a traumatic occurrence, perhaps by not paying attention to detail. Crashing out would suggest losing a hold on reality.

▣ A computer crashing in dreams signifies a loss of information or power. To hear a crash is to be alerted to an imminent problem.

Also consult the entries for Car and Journey.

CREDIT

⚘ To be given credit, whether financial or otherwise, is to receive the correct recognition or approval. We are valued for who we are.

⚕ To dream about credit cards relates to our worth, value or status. Receiving a credit note suggests we have not received the correct value or have not received it at the right time.

▣ Financial transactions of any sort in dreams highlight our attitude to money, value and authority. We may need to look at who we feel either owes us or to whom we owe value.

You might also like to consult the entries for Debt and Money.

CRESCENT – *see* SHAPES/PATTERNS AND MOON

CRICKET – *see* GAMES AND INSECTS

CRIME/CRIMINAL

⚘ A crime or criminal in spiritual terms signifies an offence against spiritual law.

⚕ We all have a part of ourselves which dislikes external control. Committing a crime in dreams may be a form of rebellion. To observe a criminal at work is to recognize the potential for wrong-doing.

▣ Criminal activity offends against both personal integrity and the laws of society. When we consider the other aspects of the dream scenario we will appreciate any adjustments which need to be made in our everyday activities.

Consult the entries for Court and Justice to enhance your understanding.

CROCODILE

❁ Liberation from the limitations of the world is symbolized by the crocodile. Though we are consumed by our fear of death, or perhaps the death process. we must work through this fear in order to come to terms with physical death. Understanding brings liberation.

♥ To see a crocodile in dreams forewarns of hidden danger. We should beware of poor decision-making.

▦ To dream of crocodiles, or indeed any reptile, indicates we are looking at the frightening lower aspects of our nature. We may feel we have no control over these, and it would therefore be very easy to be devoured by them.

⊟ In the Egyptian story of Isis and Osiris the crocodile god is said to have swallowed Osiris' manhood. In a man's dream, therefore, the crocodile can symbolize emasculation. In a woman's dream it is more likely to represent an aspect of negative masculinity.

Also consult the entry for Reptiles in Animals.

CROSS – *see* **ANGER, SHAPES/PATTERNS AND SPIRITUAL IMAGERY IN THE INTRODUCTION**

CROSSING

❁ Crossing a river or chasm often depicts death. This is not necessarily a physical death but possibly spiritual change of some kind.

♥ We may encounter something we cannot control, and which may control us. To be crossing a field shows we could have a false sense of security, or may need to bring our feelings out into the open.

▦ To dream of crossing a road is recognizing the possibility of danger, fear or uncertainty. We are perhaps pitting ourselves against something that is bigger than us. Crossing someone suggests getting on the wrong side of them.

CROSSROADS

❁ A crossroads is a magical but dangerous space, full of spiritual potential, since we can go in any direction which seems appropriate. In times gone by shrines were erected at crossroads.

♥ We are in a situation where two opposing forces are coming together, not in conflict but in harmony. Many magical spells are dissipated at crossroads when they are thrown to the four winds. This image in dreams is therefore very powerful.

▦ Dreaming of crossroads indicates that we are going to have to make choices in our lives, often to do with career or life changes. We perhaps need to be aware of where we have come from in order to make intelligent decisions. Often, to turn left at crossroads can indicate taking the wrong route, though it can indicate the more intuitive path. To turn right can obviously mean taking the correct path, but can also mean making logical decisions.

You might also like to consult the entries for Journey and Position.

CROW – *see* BIRDS

CROWD

A crowd suggests a group with a popular belief, or common religious feelings. More negatively a mob has a common belief, but of a more fanatical nature.

Dreaming of being in a crowd could be indicative of the fact that we do not wish to stand out, or that we do not have a personal sense of direction at present. The type of people in the crowd may also be relevant.

We may wish to camouflage our feelings from others, to get lost or even to hide our opinions. In everyday life we need to retain our anonymity, to create a facade for ourselves. Conversely, there may be safety in numbers if we join a group of like-minded people.

You might also like to consult the entry for Group.

CROWN

A crown signifies a change into a different level of awareness, victory over death and a recognition of status. The diadem, the forerunner of the crown, was initially a simple white ribbon, ending in a knot and two stripes that were placed on the shoulders, that surrounded the head of the king to denote his authority. It signified being bound to his spiritual task.

We may have striven for something and our greatest victory has been against our own inertia. The crown can represent dedication, particularly to duty. It suggests the attainment of knowledge. When a crown is highly decorated we acknowledge our past attainments.

To dream of a crown is to acknowledge our own success, and to recognize that we have opportunities that will expand our knowledge and awareness. We may be about to receive recognition or a reward of some sort.

Consult the entry for Diadem for further clarity.

CRUCIBLE – *see* SPIRITUAL IMAGERY IN THE INTRODUCTION

CRUCIFIXION – *see* SPIRITUAL IMAGERY IN THE INTRODUCTION

CRUDE

Crude signifies the rough or unworked part of creation. It has been given form but is as yet unrefined and has not been differentiated.

Crudeness suggests the rawness of emotion which has not yet been allowed proper expression. It also suggests instinct as opposed to intelligence.

▦ In terms of everyday life, if an article seems crude in a dream, a plan or idea has not yet reached fruition or been properly considered.

CRY – see EMOTIONS AND WEEPING

CRYSTAL – see GEMS/JEWELS

CUBE – see SHAPES/PATTERNS

CUCKOO – see BIRDS

CUL-DE-SAC

❂ A cul-de-sac in spiritual terms suggests futility and sometimes lack of foresight.

❤ We are stuck in patterns of behaviour which give us no way out. We are being threatened by past mistakes.

▦ When we find ourselves trapped in a cul-de-sac it symbolizes wasted action, but perhaps also a state of inertia. Circumstance may be preventing a forward movement, and it may be necessary to retrace our steps in order to succeed.

CUP

❂ The feminine awareness of the draught of life, immortality and plenty is intuitively and sensitively used. The cup has much of the symbolism of the chalice, indicating a receptive state which accepts intuitive information.

❤ If we are open to the more feminine side, we are able to both give and receive help and assistance. The cup often signifies happiness or joy.

▦ An offering or opportunity is being offered in everyday matters which we would do well to identify. Often the feminine is offering an opportunity from the unconscious.

⊡ To some extent the interpretation depends on what kind of cup is depicted. An ordinary teacup or mug for instance focuses on mundane matters and – for a woman – her feelings about domestic concerns. In a man's dream the emphasis is more likely to be on his feelings about his wife, family and happiness.

Consult the entries for Chalice, Trophy and Win/Winning for further clarification.

CUPBOARD

❂ A cupboard was initially just that, a place to store utensils. Now it often represents a repository, perhaps in the spiritual sense, for skills or for hidden talents.

❤ Various types of cupboard can appear in dreams. A wardrobe suggests a period of transition and, because it houses our clothes, how we deal with our self-image, whereas a larder represents our ability to preserve or conserve our stores of energy. Finding a hidden cupboard suggests rediscovering something we may have forgotten. Opening a cupboard and finding it bigger than expected suggests available opportunities.

⊞ Clearing out a cupboard indicates that we may have to put our lives in order. Articles falling out of a cupboard suggest that we may be overstretched and/or overstretching ourselves.

CURE – *see* **HEAL/HEALING**

CUSHION – *see* **FURNITURE/FURNISHINGS**

CUT – *see* **KNIFE, OPERATION AND WOUND**

CYMBALS

☀ Spiritually cymbals signify two inter-dependent halves – one cannot normally operate without the other. Thus they can symbolize marriage or partnership of some sort. They may also suggest the interdependency of the sacred and the secular, the spiritual and the physical.

♦ We are reconciling passion and desire.

⊞ Cymbals are connected with rhythm and sound, so for them to appear in a dream is an indication of the need for and return to a basic vibration. In some cultures, along with the drum and tambourine, they are used to induce an ecstatic state, suggesting a need for relaxation.

⊡ Any instrument which is struck in a woman's dream suggests the coming together of her two aspects, Lilith and Eve, harlot and mother. For a man such a note signifies his life force.

DAGGER

🌑 In dreams the dagger represents an age-old instrument of blood sacrifice. Spiritually, of course, such sacrifice is no longer valid under any circumstances. If we find the dagger is turned on us in a dream we need to beware of the likelihood of self-sacrifice.

💟 Psychologically, to be penetrated by any sharp instrument in a dream is usually to do with our masculine energy and at the same time often refers to our feelings about sexuality.

▦ When a dagger appears in a dream, the meaning can either be aggressive or defensive. If you are using the dagger to attack someone then you may be trying to cut out a part of yourself or trying to get rid of something you do not like. Being stabbed highlights our vulnerability.

⊡ As with any weapon in a man's dream, the dagger represents his developing assertive behaviour, whereas in a woman's dream it will be more to do with her drives or her Animus.

Consult the entries for Knife and Weapons for further information.

DAISY – *see* FLOWERS

DAM

🌑 The image of a dam presupposes that there is a block to progress. However, one interpretation suggests that it is the conservation of a scarce resource (perhaps our spiritual awareness), until it is available in sufficient quantity. By word association the image can suggest to be damned or rendered powerless.

💟 While consciously we may need to exercise control over our emotions, in a dream sequence we will often demonstrate a natural expression of difficulty or frustration by an overflow of water or the blocking of a natural channel.

▦ When we dream of a dam its significance may vary. We may be bottling up our own emotions and drive, or conversely we could be trying to stop somebody else's emotional outburst from happening. To be building a dam indicates we are likely to be putting up defences, whereas if a dam is bursting we may feel we have no control over emotional situations around us.

For further clarity consult the entry for Water.

DAMAGE

🌑 Damage from a spiritual perspective can be very subtle, so to dream of an article, which is damaged, suggests some kind of difficulty or misperception.

A chipped vase, for instance, might signify a difficulty in perceiving the feminine correctly.

To be damaging an object in dreams suggests a strong sense of perhaps misplaced aggression. Other images in your dream should help to clarify the interpretation.

If we dream of damaged articles it may be worthwhile exploring our self-esteem in waking life. A broken bone may suggest we need to look at the way we create structure in our lives, whereas a damaged door might signify a lack of self-respect.

Damage to the self, as in self-harm, in both men's and women's dreams, signifies a lack of self-appreciation. For a man, losing a limb highlights his sense of emasculation, whereas cutting into the flesh, particularly for a woman, signifies a release from pain.

DANCE/DANCING

Spiritually, dancing has always been taken to represent the rhythm of life. The patterns created are reputed to mirror the patterns of creativity. If space and time are part of one continuum, movement and the flow of dance link the two together.

Psychologically, dance can be a reinforcement of freedom of movement, strength and emotion. Ballet in particular portrays an ethereal appreciation of mood; flamenco and other such energetic dancing reflect passion.

Dance has always represented freedom and been symbolic of other actions which were necessary for survival. To be dancing in a dream portrays the creation of happiness, feeling at one with the surroundings and possibly getting closer or more intimate with a partner.

You might also like to consult the entry for Ballerina/Ballet Dancer.

DANGER

Dreaming of being in a dangerous or precarious position can indicate a spiritual insecurity.

Dreams can often point to a danger in symbolic form, such as conflict, fire or flood. We may need to have pitfalls represented in such a way in order to recognize them on a conscious level.

When we find ourselves in dangerous circumstances in dreams, we are often reflecting the anxieties and dilemmas of everyday life. We may be conscious that our activities could be harmful to us if we carry on in the same way.

Men and women perceive danger differently in dreams. Men often confront the difficulty, whereas women may attempt to placate or work round it. Interestingly, as the differences between the genders become blurred in everyday life, these natural responses are also modified.

Consult the entry for Threat/Threaten for further clarification.

DARE – *see* **RISK**

DARK/DARKNESS

🔅 That side of the personality where chaos may reign, and where, unless some spiritual understanding can be attained, is seen as dark. Also darkness is full of mystery and part of the unknown, the obscurity which hides the Divine.

💚 Intellectually, we are in touch with the hidden side – the Shadow – and may need to deal with the darker suppressed aspects of ourselves. To be surrounded by darkness suggests that there is potential for failure in some scheme or a sense of being lost.

▦ To dream of being in the dark usually represents a state of confusion or being in unknown and difficult territory. It may point to a secret part of ourselves or a part that we do not yet know.

DART(S)

🔅 As with any penetrative weapon, a dart is seen as strength, control and capability. In a spiritual sense it also suggests focus.

💚 Since it requires expertise and practice to throw darts successfully, in dreams playing darts also suggests discipline and concentration. It is thought that the game arose in the Middle Ages when bored soldiers took to hurling arrows at the upturned covers of wine barrels, perhaps seeing who could come closest to the cork bung. The shortened form of arrow became the dart, and a slice of tree trunk the target.

▦ Darts can symbolize harsh words deliberately intended to hurt or a way of bringing something to our notice which needs understanding.

▯ In a woman's dream a dart may be seen as a direct approach from the masculine or perhaps her own attitude to achievement. In a man's dream it is more likely to be seen as a recreational pastime, or his ability to get straight to the point.

You might also like to consult the entry for Arrow.

DATE (FRUIT)

🔅 Fruit, and particularly the date, is often associated with fertility and fertility rites. In Roman times dates, because of their luscious taste and spiritual connections, were often used as an aphrodisiac during pre-nuptial activities. They are also considered to enhance the psychic senses.

💚 Our deepest emotional needs need to be cared for and looked after in a way that is different from normal.

■ Because dates are rather an exotic fruit, when we dream of them we are becoming conscious of the need for the rare or exotic in our lives. Equally, we may need sweetness and nurturing.

DAUGHTER – *see* FAMILY

DAWN/DAY AND NIGHT

✿ A form of spiritual illumination is quite often felt within this type of dream. There is a gradual awareness rather than a blinding flash of illumination. A new dawn can bring a great sense of hope. Day and night can represent opposites, as in black and white, boy and girl etc. Indeed, any two opposites may have relevance, and it is up to us to decide what opposition there is in our lives.

♥ Psychologically we are aware of the passage of time, of darkness or difficulty passing and perhaps the need to mark or celebrate this in some way. We often differentiate between two states in dreams, and the contrast between day and night highlights this.

■ To dream of a dawn or a new day represents a new beginning or a new awareness in circumstances around us. We are looking for different ways of dealing with old situations. Dreaming of both day and night indicates the cycle of time or of changes that will inevitably take place. Sometimes indication is given of the nature of a period of time.

DAY/DATE

✿ A certain date or day could point to information about a spiritual festival or anniversary that we have subconsciously retained and that may have relevance for us. When we dream of a day passing, or register that time has passed, we are alerting ourselves to the fact that we need to gauge time in some activity, or that action needs to be taken first before a second thing can happen.

♥ Very often the psyche gives us information in dreams which is precognitive and it is possible to be alerted to particularly important events in dream form. Time has no real meaning in dreams, so to note that time is measurable suggests that we are contemplating the validity of our lives.

■ In dreams, a day may also represent a much longer period of time than first thought. When a particular date is highlighted in a dream, we are either being reminded of something particularly significant – or possibly traumatic – in our lives or perhaps to consider the symbolism of the numbers contained in the date itself.

Consult the entries for Numbers and Time for more information.

DEAD PEOPLE

🔱 To dream of dead people may suggest a link of a spiritual nature to our long-forgotten ancestors, and may deal with family patterns of belief. Loved ones who have died appearing in dreams show that the veil between this world and the next is very thin.

💠 Memories can remain buried for years and often when people who have died appear in dreams, we are being reminded of different times, places or relationships which will help us to deal with present situations.

▦ Dead people we have known appearing in dreams usually refer back to strong emotions we have had about those people, whether they are negative or positive. For instance, there may be unresolved anger or guilt we still hold and the only way we can deal with it is within a dream sequence.

Also consult the entries for Death and Hearse.

DEAL

🔱 A deal in spiritual terms is a negotiation between two aspects of Self: the 'higher' part, which knows what is right from a cosmic perspective, and the lower part, which is more concerned with everyday matters.

💠 When there is some difficulty in integrating all parts of the personality we will often dream of a deal in order to clarify what action we need to take.

▦ As so much of everyday life is taken up with deals and negotiations we will often mirror such situations in dreams. To be dealing cards may suggest taking a gamble or a calculated risk.

⊞ In a woman's dream a deal is likely to highlight aspects of her masculine, more driven side but in a man's dream it may be the more intuitive skills which come to prominence. Both, of course, are skills required in efficient negotiation in the ordinary world.

DEATH

🔱 Death is a transition from an awareness of the gross physical to the more spiritual self. It signifies the unseen aspect of life; omniscience, spiritual rebirth; resurrection and reintegration. To dream of our own death suggests that we are exploring our own feelings about death or our retreat from the challenge of life. The sensation of leaving the body is an aspect of the changes in consciousness necessary for a fuller understanding of the spiritual dimension.

💠 On an intellectual level we are becoming conscious of potentials we may have missed or not expressed fully and because of this we are no longer able to make use of them. We need to be sensitive to our ability to resurrect these talents. A change of awareness is taking place, and we may be going through some 'rite of passage' such as puberty to adulthood, maturity to old age and so on. Our own death can often be used in dreams to explore our perception of others' feelings about us.

🎴 Traditionally to dream of death indicated the possibility of a birth or a change in circumstances in one's own life or that of people around. Because in the past death held great fear, it also represented calamity, in the sense that nothing would ever be the same again. It was something that had to be experienced and endured rather than understood. In these present times, as peoples' attitudes change, death in a dream indicates a challenge we must confront. We need to adjust our approach to life and to accept that there can be a new beginning if we have courage.

Also consult the entries for Coffin, Dead People and Grave.

DEBATE

🔆 The spiritual implications of a debate within a dream are to do with ascertaining the merits of a positive versus a negative argument, where both are given an equal hearing.

💗 When we find that we are in a debate, it symbolizes some inner turmoil or conflict that is as yet unresolved. It also means that you will find closure to those unresolved issues.

🎴 Listening to a debate suggests that there are things going on that need careful consideration. Taking part in a debate signifies a more 'hands-on' approach is required in some areas of our life.

📋 Since debate often contains both logic (a masculine trait) and emotion (a feminine one), men and women will weigh up the merits of the opposite perspective in a debate in dreams.

You might like to consult the entry for Argue/Arguments.

DEBRIS – *see* DEMOLITION

DEBT

🔆 Power or energy that we feel we owe to a force other than ourselves may be depicted as a debt in dreams.

💗 Being unable to pay a debt suggests that we have run out of emotional or mental resources. Paying off a debt suggests that we have fulfilled our obligations.

🎴 As debt becomes more prevalent in everyday life, the anxieties associated with it will reflect in dreams as being chased or hounded. Figures of authority will also figure quite prominently. Dreaming of lost credit cards or cash can also symbolize debt.

You might like to consult the entries for Credit and Money for further clarity.

DECADENCE

🔆 Decadence suggests a fall from grace or a debasement of the natural laws. It describes self-indulgence rather than a concern for global matters.

💠 Decadence suggests self interest and a profligate use of the resources we have. If we are content with the sense of decadence in a dream scenario we are learning to value ourselves better. If it distresses us then we need to assess how far and how much we are moving away from our own sense of self.

🔲 As poverty becomes more of a global issue, we become more conscious of the differences between lifestyles and just how decadent, materialistic and wasteful those who have enough can be. When this is highlighted in dreams, we would do well to pay attention to such matters in everyday life.

DECAY

🔆 Decay in dreams is evidence of the natural cycle of life: growth, decline and regeneration. Out of decay comes new growth and knowledge.

💠 When something is decaying it is running out of energy. For it to appear in dreams indicates we must be prepared to allow things to run their natural course. Putrefaction is when the process of decay has gone past the point of no return.

🔲 In mundane terms, we have a situation in our lives – perhaps a work project or a relationship – that has come to a natural conclusion and does not need to be nurtured. The experience we have gained, however, can be put to good use.

You might also like to consult the entry for Mould/Mouldy.

DECEIVE – *see* LIE

DECIDE/DECISION

🔆 Decisions are an integral part of spiritual progression, and to be conscious of deciding on a particular course of action, for instance, suggests choosing between right and wrong or any other two polarities.

💠 Fear and doubt can prevent us from making the correct decisions or choices for us. Dreams will highlight these fears when often we are not even aware that they exist.

🔲 Often when we are unable to make a decision in waking life, dreams provide us with an answer to our dilemma by presenting answers in symbolic form and allowing us to observe the effect of our actions.

DECORATE/DECORATION

🔆 Decoration is a way of honouring the divine and there is much symbolism attached to this from the altar cloths in Christian and Wiccan religions to food for the spirits in Thai Buddhist spirit houses. Dreams often access such spiritual knowledge.

◈ When we dream of decorating a room or dwelling place we are aware that changes need to be made in our environment, perhaps to utilize a particular vibration.

▦ Colour may be important in the way we decorate our dream rooms, as may be the articles we choose to have in our environment. When such an article is highlighted it suggests ways of enhancing our day-to-day lives by what it represents.

⊡ Men's and women's dreams may be very different in terms of the way they adorn their rooms. Traditionally it was thought that women were more drawn to frills and men to sleeker lines. If the decoration seems out of character we probably need to develop some aspect of creativity.

You might like to consult the entries for Colour and Furniture/Furnishings for further information.

DEEP

◈ The Unknown, and therefore the unfathomable, is often symbolized by depth in some way – deep water, deep underground etc.

◈ We may be trying to understand archetypal patterns that have not been recognizable in the past. There is information available to us which we can only understand through being able to appreciate our own emotional depths.

▦ When we dream of the deep we are usually considering past family influences of which we may not be consciously aware. Patterns of behaviour are often repeated in families and it takes some dredging through family stories and myths to have us recognize such patterns.

You might like to consult the entries for Abyss and Descent/Descending.

DEER – *see* ANIMALS

DEFEAT

◈ To suffer defeat in a spiritual sense is to be overcome by negativity.

◈ To feel defeated is to recognize that opposing forces are too strong for us.

▦ To be defeated signifies that there are situations around us in the everyday in which we cannot achieve an advantage.

You might also like to consult the entries for Argue/Arguments, Conflict, Fight and War for more information.

DEFECATE – *see* EXCREMENT IN BODY

DEFEND/DEFENCE

◈ Defending anything in a dream is protecting it spiritually, perhaps from contamination or from penetration. Defending any type of sacred space would have this meaning.

◈ Defending our position suggests that there is a conflict of some sort in us, maybe of ideas or principles.

▨ Putting up a defence, perhaps a wall or barrier, signifies that we feel threatened in some way. We may have to justify our position over a situation in our waking lives.

▸▪ If a woman is defending herself in a dream she is guarding against some kind of 'assault', often of her own private space. If a man has such a dream, it shows he will defend against his own vulnerability.

DEFY/DEFIANT

❁ Originally 'to defy' meant to renounce our faith, but its more modern day meaning is to challenge belief or given wisdom.

♥ To be defiant suggests that we cannot accept and act on information we have been given.

▨ When we defy authority in dreams it is often because intrinsically we are aware that something is not right in our waking life.

DELAY

❁ Delay from a spiritual perspective suggests that the time is not right for a particular event or course of action.

♥ If we are causing delay then we are not yet ready to take action: if someone else is the cause then we must wait for outside circumstances to be right.

▨ Delay can signify a lack of organization and can also, through dreams, allow the expression of frustration.

You might like to consult the entry for Time.

DEMOLITION

❁ Fanaticism and anarchy (a need to break down or destroy an old order) can be demonstrated by demolition in a dream. Spiritually the idea of using the old debris as a foundation for the new is seen in the image of the Tower in the Tarot.

♥ We may be conscious of a build-up of emotional energy within us, which can only be handled by a breakdown of old attitudes and approaches. The 'debris' left behind after such a breakdown needs sorting through to discover what needs to be retained and what discarded.

▨ It rather depends on the circumstances in the dream whether demolition highlights major changes in the dreamer's life, or a self-inflicted trauma. If we are deliberately destroying something or carrying out the demolition we need to be in control, but if someone else is in charge we may feel powerless in the face of change. The debris in this case symbolizes the fall-out from such changes. Large amounts signify major adjustments are necessary.

Consult the entry for Ruin/Ruins for further information.

DEMON

✦ Although the word 'demon' originally came from the Greek word for 'deity', for many hundreds of years it was taken simply to mean spirit. In the modern day it is taken to be an evil spirit, one at odds with God, and has this meaning in dreams.

♥ Psychologists now believe that demons in dreams are often personifications of deeply held or ingrained fears. The colour of the demons will often give information as to their relevance. Red indicates extreme and black might represent fear.

▦ Passionate beings with their own agenda, demons may represent a particular type of personality that will not allow itself to rest until a task is completed.

You might like to consult the entries for Colour, Devil, Fiend and Imp.

DEMONSTRATE/DEMONSTRATION

✦ When we take part in a public demonstration we are declaring our allegiance to a belief or ideal.

♥ To demonstrate is to prove conclusively that something is possible. Often we will dream of a solution to a problem that proves to be workable.

▦ When we find ourselves demonstrating a skill that we did not know we have, it suggests a strand of creativity that needs to be explored.

You might also like to consult the entry for Procession.

DENTIST

✦ Dreaming of a dentist, since the emphasis is on the mouth, may signify that we are having difficulty in articulating our own Spiritual truth – that in which we believe.

♥ Because of its association with pain, a visit to the dentist in dreams may highlight fears or hurt that we have hidden. A dentist may signify that a particular type of healing is appropriate, such as the removal of 'decaying' information.

▦ In everyday life the development of teeth is thought to be a step towards speech and, therefore, correct communication. A dentist in dreams suggests that a degree of care is needed in what we are saying to others.

DEPARTING – *see* JOURNEY AND LEAVE/LEAVING

DEPRESSION – *see* EMOTION AND WEEPING

DERELICT

✦ A derelict building or person signifies a lack of hope, a 'lost sheep'.

♥ Since hope and faith are two prime motivators, anything that appears derelict suggests that we have lost the ability to move away from difficult circumstances.

🔲 When the energy has gone from a project or, for instance, a relationship, and it has lost focus, we may dream of dereliction. This is when there is no hope of re-energizing the project or relationship.

Also consult the entry for Demolition.

DESCENT/DESCENDING

☀ Going down into the underworld, the quest for mystic wisdom, rebirth and immortality are all shown in dreams by descent. It is a symbol for exploring the unconscious.

♡ Descent often signifies applying practical solutions to problems. We may fear a loss of status, and yet be aware of the positive aspects of such loss which include not having to have such high expectations of ourselves and others.

🔲 When we dream of a descent, such as coming down a mountain or steps, we are often searching for an answer to a particular problem. We need to be conscious of past trauma or something we have left behind and decide what we can learn from the experience.

You may also wish to consult the entries for Deep and Fall/Falling

DESERT

☀ A desert can symbolize desolation and abandonment, but also a place of contemplation, quiet and divine revelation.

♡ Desertion implies that all support has been removed or rejected so the idea of deserting a post, task or friend suggests a sense of inadequacy. Experiencing ourselves as having been deserted signifies being left to our own devices.

🔲 To dream of being alone in a desert signifies a lack of emotional satisfaction, loneliness or perhaps isolation. Dreaming of being in a desert with someone else may show that particular relationship is sterile, or going nowhere.

You might also like to consult the entry for Abandoned.

DESERT ISLAND – see ISLAND

DESK – see ALTAR AND TABLE

DESTINATION

☀ A Spiritual goal or aspiration is signified in dreams by knowing what our destination is.

♡ Destinations such as exotic and faraway places could signify our need for excitement and stimulation, or hopes we may have for the future.

🔲 Dreaming of trying to get to a particular destination would normally indicate a conscious ambition and desire. If the destination is not known to us, we may be moving into unknown territory, or be attempting something new and different. If we have difficulty in reaching our destination there may be difficulties associated with our aspirations.

Also consult the entry for Journey.

DESTROY – *see* DEMOLITION
DEVIL

⚙ The Devil tends to be seen as the personification of Evil, or Lucifer, who, incidentally, was originally supposed to bring enlightenment to the world. It does need to be borne in mind, however, that the Devil also represents the Ego, or part of us that refuses to 'return to the light'.

♥ In order to deal with the out-of-control side of ourselves, we often need to have an object or image to confront. In dreams, as in fantasies, the Devil allows us to do this. If we fear our own wrongdoing, that fear can also manifest as the Devil.

▦ In previous times, the figure of the Devil was one to be feared and hated. Our wilder, more instinctive side will often appear in dreams as the conventional figure with horns and a tail. Once it is understood as something to be confronted, as something belonging to all of us, the Devil loses its potency.

⊡ The Devil as Satan used to appear with some frequency in both men's and women's dreams. Now the image is more likely to be that of one of the Nature Gods such as Pan, and represents basic instincts and urges.

You may also wish to consult the entries for Demon, Fiend and Imp.

DEVOUR

⚙ Clearing evil or decay, or taking in good, is symbolized as devouring it – that is, eating it greedily. Kali, the Hindu mother goddess, as the keeper of the graveyard, demonstrates this, as do the devouring Gods such as Dionysus. Such clearing is a way of returning to source and receiving spiritual upliftment. Shamanic belief puts forward the theory that we take on the power of that which we eat. We are not allowed to eat our own totem animal, however.

♥ If we ourselves are devouring something in a dream we may need to consider the way we nurture ourselves. We perhaps are not paying attention or giving enough respect to what we are doing.

▦ When we dream of being devoured we are facing our fear of losing our sense of identity; of being consumed by something such as an obsession, an overwhelming emotion or drive, or of having to deal with something we cannot control.

Also consult the entry for Eat/Eating.

DEW

⚙ Spiritual refreshment, benediction and blessing are all symbols connected to dew.

♥ We may need to accept that gentle, and not forceful or overpowering, emotion can cleanse us of whatever is troubling us.

■ Dew or gentle rain falling in a dream can represent a sense of newness and refreshment we have perhaps not been able to obtain, except from an external source.

DIADEM

✷ The diadem or tiara is perceived as an emblem of the Queen of Heaven and the circle of continuity. It often has 12 jewels, which are said to represent the 12 Tribes of Israel.

♡ There is always a magical feeling or sense of wonder associated with the diadem or tiara, and it can be taken to represent the magical and unknown. In dreams as in real life it is felt to confer status.

■ The diadem or tiara in a dream often acknowledges the power of the feminine, or the ability to use the mental or intellectual abilities to obtain supremacy.

⊟ In a woman's dream she is more likely to be wearing a tiara, this being a feminine image. In a man's dream he is more likely to wear a crown or coronet – a less elaborate form of crown.

You might like to consult the entry for Crown.

DIAMOND – *see* **GEMS/JEWELS**

DICE/DIE

✷ Dice or a die, through the play on words, is a way of taking chances, which, in the spiritual sense, may be irrevocable and may lead to a 'death' – perhaps of an opportunity, for instance.

♡ If someone else is rolling the dice, we are leaving our fate in the hands of other people and must, therefore, consider whether we should run our lives according to their rules.

■ To be playing with dice in a dream emphasizes the fact that we are playing with fate or taking chances in life, which we really ought to be considering more carefully.

You may also like to consult the entries for Games and Gambling.

DICTATOR – *see* **PEOPLE**

DIGGING/EXCAVATION

✷ Spiritually we need to have access to the characteristics of the unconscious. It will always take effort to uncover such aspects and this is symbolized by digging. Excavating, perhaps in the form of an archaeological or other professional type of digging, would suggest a more structured approach.

♡ On a creative level we may have realizations that are hard to access and must be dug out. Excavating objects can also imply that there is 'buried treasure' which belongs to the past.

■ Often when we begin the process of learning about ourselves we need to uncover those parts we have kept hidden, and this is shown in dreams as excavating a hole or digging up an object. If the act of digging is important then we are required to make an effort rather than simply wait for information to come to the surface.

Also consult the entry for Mine/Miner.

DINOSAURS

❀ We all have within us a chaotic past which has been a huge part of our lives. Spiritual progress, however, dictates that we understand that this part can be changed and our present selves can grow from that ability to change. Old standards are now extinct and will no longer stand up to scrutiny.

♥ We are in touch with an archaic or outmoded part of ourselves. Remembering that dinosaurs are extinct, and that for most people they are perceived as fossils, such a dream can recognize the part of ourselves that has become set in stone.

■ When we dream of monsters or prehistoric animals we are touching into very basic images which have the power to frighten and amaze us. Because they are considered to be so large, we need to be aware of whether it is their size or their power which is frightening. Urges as basic as this can threaten our existence, by either their size or power.

You might also like to consult the entry for Prehistoric.

DIRECTION – *see* **POSITION**

DIRTY

❀ Evil or negative impulses are often represented in dreams as things or people being dirty. In the search for spirituality we may often feel dirty or contaminated by such negativity.

♥ To be dirty in a dream may indicate that we are not at ease with our own bodily functions. If someone we know has made us dirty or contaminated us it is an indication not to trust that person.

■ We will dream of being dirty when we are not operating within our own principles or when someone else's action has put us in a situation which we find compromises us.

DISAGREE – *see* **ARGUE/ARGUMENTS, CONFLICT AND WAR**

DISASTER

❀ A disaster in dreams is any negative event that tests our beliefs and finer feelings. We do need to remember that the heightened sensations take us into areas within our psyche where we have perhaps not ventured before.

❤ Disasters such as crashing aeroplanes, falling buildings or other such images are presented to highlight extreme emotions such as fear, anger and anxiety.

▣ Many disasters in dreams echo difficulties in everyday life, pictured in such a way that they allow us to work through the problems. An exploding mine, for instance, depicts undue pressure or stress placed on an individual.

You might like to consult the entries for Aeroplane, Buildings and Mines for additional clarification.

DISCIPLE – *see* **PEOPLE**

DISCRIMINATION

❀ Being able to discriminate suggests that we have sufficient vision to be able to make spiritually correct choices, of choosing right rather than wrong, for instance.

❤ If we find we are being discriminated against in dreams we need to recognize and honour our own uniqueness.

▣ The need to discriminate and take the best option often comes up on a day-to-day basis. We often have to compare and contrast our alternatives. This reflects in dreams perhaps more vividly than in real life and allows us to discriminate in our choices.

You might also like to consult the entry for Choice/Choose.

DISCOVER

❀ There is much spiritual information that is revealed only when we are ready for it; the sense of discovering our own truth is part of progress.

❤ Discovering the unexpected in dreams highlights information that is needed. The symbolism of the object or the idea will be important. Discovering a jewel, for instance, suggests something that is precious from an emotional perspective.

▣ When the correct method or information needed for carrying out a task on a work-a-day basis is not forthcoming it is possible that dreams will offer information that points us in the right direction and allows us to discover the answer.

DISEASE – *see* **ILL/ILLNESS**

DISK

❀ Divinity and power are represented spiritually by the disk, through its connection with the sun. It represents perfection and the renewal of life.

❤ The disk in a dream has emotionally the same significance as the sun, and can be considered both as a powerful source of information and initially of life itself.

🖼 A computer disk suggests that there is a great deal of information and knowledge available to us. As other forms of storage become available such knowledge enters the realms of the everyday.

DISMEMBERMENT

✦ Dismemberment of the body, or indeed any dream where some type of fragmentation takes place, is largely to do with being rendered powerless. It is the death, or rather dissolution, of the Self before reintegration and rebirth take place.

♡ Psychologically we need to take our old feelings and ideas apart to make sense of what is going on. This process has to take place before we can rebuild our lives.

🖼 A situation may be tearing us apart and drastic action may be necessary before we can recover our equilibrium.

You may also like to consult the entries for Amputation and Limbs in the Body section.

DISSECT/DIVIDE

✦ Any division or deliberate dissection into two parts or more suggests a movement away from unity, from a state of perfection.

♡ To divide into parts signifies creating manageable portions, perhaps breaking down a series of actions to understand them better. Crossing a divide is similar to crossing a chasm: we must face our own fears.

🖼 When we are dissecting a body or animal we are trying to learn how something works or what relationships the various parts might have with one another. This might apply to a task or project in waking life.

You might like to consult the entries for Chasm and Half.

DIVING

✦ Diving suggests the taking of spiritual risk. Skydiving suggests pitting ourselves against natural forces.

♡ We need to be extremely focused and attentive to dive successfully and must bring these qualities into play in a situation we are in in our waking lives.

🖼 To dream of diving can represent the need for freedom within our lives, although we may associate freedom with taking risks. We may need to burrow into our unconscious to find the ability to face anxiety.

Also consult the entry for Water.

DIVORCE

✦ To dream of divorce would suggest that there is a loss of integration in our personality and a potential difficulty in understanding spiritual matters.

♡ Divorce – that is, a sense of the severance of some kind of link – may also indicate the necessity to clarify our own relationship between the various facets of our personality. We are becoming conscious of the need to express emotion if we are to maintain our own integrity. We are moving into a new way of life, perhaps without the old support systems we have used.

■ Dreaming of divorce may actually refer to our feelings about the other person in the dream, and perhaps our need to be free of responsibilities. It may simply highlight the need for a change in the relationship structure.

⊟ In any dream where the differences between male and female are highlighted, both men and women may be struggling with the conflict between logic and intuition.

DOCTOR

✹ The presence of a doctor in dreams suggests the appearance of the healer within. We each have within us an aspect of spiritual knowledge, which is capable of reminding the physical body of its right to be well.

♥ It will depend what sort of doctor appears in our dream as to the correct interpretation. A surgeon would suggest the need to cut something out of our lives. A physician would indicate that careful consideration should be given to our general state, whereas a psychiatrist or psychologist signifies the need to look at our mental state. If the doctor is known to us he may stand as an authority figure.

■ When we dream of a doctor we are aware that we need to give way to a higher authority in health matters. For older people the doctor may also represent the professional classes.

⊟ By and large a woman will tend to dream of the doctor as masculine, and a man the opposite. Only when the Shadow – the repressed parts of our personality – is understood will true healing take place.

You might like to consult the entries for Analyst and Medication/Medicine as well as the information on Authority Figures in the People section.

DOG

✹ A dog symbolizes the guardian of the underworld. In Egyptian mythology this is depicted by Anubis, the dog-headed god, who guided the souls of the dead to the underworld – our most secret part.

♥ To dream of a pack of wild dogs portrays emotions and feelings of which we are afraid. To be chased by a black dog suggests a fear of depression.

■ Dreaming of a dog depends on whether it is one known to us (such as a childhood pet), when it then may represent happy memories; if unknown it may signify the qualities of loyalty and unconditional love associated with dogs.

Also consult the entry for Dog in Animals.

DOLL

🌑 The doll can be a representation of the soul of a particular person who can be helped, or harmed, by sympathetic magic or witchcraft. The puppet, far from being malign, is a doll that is fashioned for a particular purpose. In dreams it serves as a focus of energy.

🌑 We tend to learn through play, and for a doll to appear in a dream usually indicates the need to relearn some childhood lessons that we have forgotten. A puppet rather than a poppet can suggest that we are being manipulated.

🌑 A doll can depict either how we felt as a child, or a need for comfort. It may also express an undeveloped part of our personality.

Consult the entry for Puppet for additional information.

DOLPHIN

🌑 In dreams the dolphin represents spiritual sensitivity and safety. They are known to be highly intelligent and to act instinctively in a supportive way.

🌑 The dolphin may portray the more playful side of our personality, but at the same time may make us aware of the trickster and behaviour that is unexpected. Dreaming of swimming with dolphins suggests putting ourselves in touch with, and appreciating, our own basic emotional nature. Coming from the depths – the unconscious – the dolphin represents the hidden side of ourselves that needs to be understood.

🌑 Dolphins are perceived by sailors as saviours and guides, as having special knowledge and awareness, and this is the image that surfaces in dreams.

DONKEY – *see* HORSE IN ANIMALS

DOOR

🌑 Spiritually a door represents the sheltering aspect of the Great Mother.

🌑 If the door in the dream is shut or difficult to open, it indicates we are creating obstacles for ourselves, whereas if the door is open we can have the confidence to move forward.

🌑 A door in a dream signifies a movement between two states of being. It can represent entry into a new phase of life, such as puberty or middle age. There may be opportunities available to us about which we must make deliberate decisions.

You might like to consult the entry for Door in Buildings and to re-read the section on Archetypes in the Introduction

DOVE – *see* BIRDS

DRAGON

🌑 The dragon is traditionally the Guardian of Power. The original of all dragons was a version of the serpent Tiamat Goddess of Chaos and

Darkness. In conquering the dragon, spiritually we become custodians of our own future.

✪ There is a heroic part in each of us which must face dangerous conflict in order to overcome the lower side of our natures and reach our inner resources. Dreaming of a dragon allows us that conflict.

▤ The dragon is a complex and universal symbol. Seen as both frightening and yet manageable, under certain circumstances it will represent in us our own untamed nature. We must come to terms with our own passions and chaotic beliefs. Often we can only achieve this through dreams, in an environment that has been suitably created.

You might like to consult the entries for Fabulous Beasts and Monster.

DRAGONFLY

✪ Though the dragonfly's physical existence is short, it symbolizes immortality and regeneration.

✪ We may be pursuing a dream, but without any real focus as to what we actually want out of life. Our reactions are instinctive rather than logical.

▤ To dream of a dragonfly is to appreciate the need for freedom, but equally to recognize that freedom can be short-lived.

DRAUGHT

✪ The Holy Spirit manifested as a rushing wind to enable the disciples to spread the Gospel. A draught suggests an unseen force or current, which creates almost imperceptible movement.

✪ Traditionally, a cold draught when working psychically indicates a visitation by Spirit. In dreams it suggests a communication from a hidden part of ourselves.

▤ To feel a draught in a dream is to be aware of an external force which could affect us or a situation we are in. To create a draught is literally to be attempting to clear the atmosphere.

Also consult the entry for Wind.

DRAUGHTS/CHEQUERS – *see* GAMES

DRINK

✪ Spiritually there is a belief that the drinking of wine is, or symbolizes, the imbibing of Divine life and power.

✪ Drinking, not necessarily of wine, in a dream may indicate our need for comfort and sustenance. Drinking – the taking in of liquid – symbolizes the interplay between the inner need to sustain life and external availability of nourishment. It also suggests our requirement for emotions that flow rather than getting stuck.

▤ To be drinking in a dream is to be absorbing or taking something in.

What we are drinking is also important, e.g. fruit juice would indicate we are aware of the need for cleansing and purity. The colour of what is being drunk is also important.

Consult the entries for Alcohol/Alcoholic and Colours for further information.

DRIVE – *see* JOURNEY

DROWNING

   ❉ Drowning symbolizes an immersion in the Sea of Life, and therefore a loss of ego. We seem to have nothing to support our efforts.

   ♦ When we are drowning in a dream this usually indicates we are in danger of being overwhelmed by emotions we cannot handle. We are fearful of allowing our emotions free expression.

   ▣ Drowning may also indicate a perceived inability to handle a stressful situation around us at the time of the dream. We have been put in a situation over which we have no control. We may be 'floundering around' with no way of being able to escape from the difficulty.

Also consult the entries for Swimming and Water.

DRUGS

   ❉ It has long been known that ingesting certain substances, particularly herbal derivatives, can alter perception. These can induce anything from a state of euphoria to a distortion of reality. This, however, can be dangerous – without knowledgeable supervision – since it is like using a crowbar rather than a key to open a door to the psyche.

   ♦ We may be attempting to avoid reality and drugs can enable us to do this. They can also be a healing agent in restoring balance. In dreams, to be given drugs by a qualified person signifies that we have accepted someone else's greater knowledge. To be sold drugs illegally indicates that we are prepared to take unnecessary risks.

   ▣ When drugs appear in a dream – whether self-administered or not – this suggests that we may need external help to enable us to change our inner perceptions. To be taking drugs suggests we feel we have relinquished control of a situation in our waking lives and are having to rely on external stimuli. To have an adverse drug reaction in dreams could mean that we fear madness. To be given drugs against our will indicates that we are being forced to accept an unpalatable truth.

You might like to consult the entries for Alcohol/Alcoholic, Drunk and Medication/Medicine.

DRUM

   ❉ The drum is an instrument that beats a rhythm. Thus it comes to represent the sound of Creation, Divine Truth and Revelation.

◆ We may be seeking a more natural form of expression or a change of consciousness from the normal, everyday methods we use.

▦ To hear a drum in a dream indicates the basic rhythm needed to keep us sane and healthy. We need to be more in touch with our natural rhythms and primitive urges. To be playing a drum is taking responsibility for the rhythm of our own lives.

You may also wish to consult the entries for Music/Rhythm and Musical Instruments.

DRUNK

❋ In previous societies it was an accepted part of life that, at certain times, drunkenness was allowed as a way of celebration or as a release of tension – hence the term a 'Bacchanalian revel'.

◆ Being drunk indicates the need to reconnect with a part of ourselves that can tolerate inappropriate behaviour. Ecstasy or extreme joy is reputedly achieved after inhibitions have been removed through getting drunk.

▦ To be drunk in a dream means that we are abandoning ourselves to irrational forces. We want to be free from responsibility and from having inhibitions. To make someone else drunk is to be forcing our irresponsibility on to someone else.

Also consult the entries for Alcohol/Alcoholic and Drugs.

DUCK

❋ The duck as a bird is said to be a symbol of superficiality, presumably because it floats on the water rather than in it. In former times religious belief was tested by the ducking stool.

◆ We may need to allow the current of life to move us rather than taking action ourselves. Knowing when to go with the flow suggests a kind of innate wisdom. In dreams, ducking to avoid an obstacle demonstrates the need to be careful.

▦ As always, other circumstances in the dream may indicate the true relevance of the symbol. A toy duck may denote the childlike part of ourselves. To be feeding the ducks may show some kind of therapeutic or calming activity is important. To be eating duck suggests a treat or celebration in store.

Also consult the entry for Birds.

EAGER

   ✹ Eagerness signifies a passionate commitment to a cause or principle.

   ♥ To be eager in dreams, for instance for a particular outcome, highlights our need for emotional support.

   ▦ When we feel deeply about a subject we become focused on the matter in hand, and able to apply concentration. Eagerness is a component of the passion we feel.

EAGLE

   ✹ The eagle represents a form of spiritual victory and the ability to be dispassionate.

   ♥ We can take authority for our own lives and have the ability to use our intellect to succeed. Using the image of an eagle as a starting point, we can become objective and take a wider viewpoint than we have done previously. This will help us to release ourselves from old ideas or attitudes.

   ▦ An eagle signifies inspiration and strength. As a bird of prey, the eagle is capable of making use of all the opportunities available to it, the implication being that we can learn to do the same.

Also consult the entry for Birds for further information.

EARLY – *see* **TIME**

EARN/EARNINGS – *see* **WAGES**

EARTH/EARTHQUAKE

   ✹ Earth is the Great Mother and is synonymous with fertility. An earthquake represents Spiritual upheaval.

   ♥ We all have the need to be grounded and practical but need support to be so. If we find ourselves under or trapped by earth in dreams it shows we need to be more aware of, and understand, our unconscious drives and habits. Old opinions, attitudes and relationships may be breaking up and causing concern. When we are conscious of an earthquake, our basic emotional stability will have been called into question.

   ▦ Dreaming of an earthquake alerts us to an inner insecurity with which we must deal before it overwhelms us. There is great inner change and growth taking place, which could cause upheaval. To dream of the planet Earth is to take account of the supportive network we have in place and those attitudes and relationships we take for granted. We are searching for some kind of parental love or social order. Soft earth particularly links with the need for mothering or tactile contact.

⚡ Symbols and images relating to earthiness and the nurturing of others will be more likely to appear in a woman's dream than in a man's. Equally, as the earth is put more at risk, men will be likely to recognize the destructive element within themselves.

Consult Archetypes in the Introduction for fuller information on the Great Mother.

EAST

☀ The East in spiritual terms has from ancient time suggested the spring, a time for hope and youth. The archangel for the East is Raphael, Healer of the world.

♥ We may be looking towards new life or a new beginning. The magical element associated with the East is Air and the colour is yellow; these significances often reveal themselves in dreams.

▦ Specifically dreaming of the East indicates we are looking at the mysterious and religious side of ourselves. We link with instinctual belief as opposed to logical reasoning.

You might also like to consult the entries for Dawn/Day and Night, Elements and Position.

EASTER EGG

☀ An Easter egg is associated with spring, rebirth and resurrection.

♥ Dreaming of an Easter egg indicates there is a great deal of potential available to us on a mental level that needs releasing. There is an element of celebration about life that needs to be maintained.

▦ The Easter egg is a pagan symbol of renewal and in dreams often takes us back to childhood feelings of promise and wonder. It may also alert us to the passage of time, since the mind will often produce symbols of times and seasons rather than actual dates.

⚡ Arising from the symbolic meaning of eggs, when a woman dreams specifically of an Easter egg her attention may be being drawn in a non-threatening way to her own fertility. For a man such a dream is more likely to be to do with his innate sense of timing.

Also consult the entry for Egg.

EAT/EATING

☀ There is a belief that we are reputed to become what we eat, so to feed ourselves spiritually we perhaps should eat the best food possible, putting ourselves as much in touch with nature as possible. This can have a holistic effect on us, putting us more closely in touch with our own spirituality, often through dreams.

♥ Dreaming of eating may denote that we lack some basic nutrient or feedback in our lives. To not eat or refuse food indicates an avoidance of growth and change. We may be attempting to isolate ourselves from others or be in conflict with ourselves over our body image. Being eaten in a dream signifies we are aware of being attacked by our own – or possibly other people's – emotions and fears or by our internal drives. Being eaten by a wild animal shows the likelihood of us being consumed by our more basic, animal nature.

▦ To be eating in a dream shows that one is attempting to satisfy one's needs or hunger. Hunger is a basic drive and we need to realize that only once such a drive is met can we move forward to satisfying our more aesthetic needs.

Consult the entries for Devour, Food and Nourishment for further information.

ECLIPSE

☼ On a spiritual level, an eclipse can represent a loss of faith, a darkening of the light which guides us.

♥ We are about to go through a period of difficulty when we could find ourselves unable to maintain our usual cheerfulness. Covering up a source of illumination and enlightenment, an eclipse can also represent being forced to cover our emotions through external circumstances.

▦ Dreaming of an eclipse signifies our fears and doubts about our own success. Others around us seem to be more important or able than we are, which does not allow us to shine or excel at what we are doing.

Consult the entries for Moon and Planets for further information

ECOLOGY

☼ As ecology is the branch of science that deals with relationship and interaction, in a spiritual sense it signifies the action between the spiritual and physical realms.

♥ As the Earth becomes more threatened, issues of climate change, conservation and preservation will become part of our everyday concerns and, therefore, part of our dreams. Any of these issues – particularly climate change – can represent a change in emotional focus.

▦ Dreams to do with ecological concerns usually focus on the efficient use of resources and it is this meaning which will often arise in dreams whether those resources are personal, work-related or of more global impact.

Also consult the entries for Climate, Conservation and Earth/Earthquake.

EDEN – *see* PARADISE

EDGE

☼ An edge suggests a changeover from one state of awareness to another, being on the brink, or about to begin a new spiritual phase.

🕸 An edge signifies a lip or rim that may seem like an obstacle or difficulty initially. The kerb on a pavement marks its edge, but can also be a hazard. To be on edge in a dream suggests we are under some emotional pressure that may not yet have surfaced in waking life.

🔲 To actually be on the edge of something in dreams may mean that we have to change our perspective about our lives.

Consult the entries for Cliff and Threshold for further information.

EDUCATION

🕸 Education can be taken as a symbol of Spiritual Awareness.

🕸 Since dreaming of education usually takes us back to a former, less responsible state, we need to apply knowledge from the experiences we have had to enable us to deal with a present situation.

🔲 To dream of a place of education, such as a school or college, indicates that we should be considering our own need for discipline or disciplined action. We are perhaps inadequately prepared for a task we are to perform, and need to access more knowledge.

Also consult the entries for School, Teacher and University.

EEL – *see* SERPENT AND SNAKE IN ANIMALS

EFFIGY – *see* STATUE

EGG

🕸 The life principle and the germ of all things are said to be contained in the Cosmic Egg, which spiritually represents our potential and power to be perfect.

🕸 We have a sense of wonder to do with the miracle of life, and a realization that there is much to plan – a gestation period – before we can enjoy life to the full. We may have to withdraw and contemplate before we can undertake new learning experiences.

🔲 The egg is the symbol of unrealized potential, of possibilities yet to come, so to dream of an egg indicates that we have not made ourselves fully conscious of our natural abilities. To be eating an egg shows the need to take in certain aspects of newness before we can fully explore a different way of life.

🔳 For a woman, an egg will usually have links with fertility, whether her own or someone else's. In a man's dream an egg more often suggests potential.

Also consult the entry for Easter Egg.

EIGHT – *see* NUMBERS

EJACULATION

🕸 From a spiritual viewpoint, ejaculation may signify a loss of power or 'the little death'.

◈ The act of ejaculation in dreams may be the giving up of old fears and doubts about ourselves and our sexual prowess.

▦ Our instinctive attitude to sex often becomes apparent in dreams through the sexual act, and to ejaculate in a dream may be an effort to understand negative feelings. It could also simply be indicative of the need for release, and the satisfaction of sexual needs.

⊞ Most teenage boys have what are called 'wet' dreams – or more properly nocturnal emissions – when they do actually ejaculate in sleep. These usually occur before the youngster has fully come to terms with the changes occurring in his body.

Also consult the entry for Sex/Sexual Images for further information.

EJECT

❀ To be ejected means to be thrown out and in a spiritual sense suggests being punished for a misdemeanour.

◈ To eject an object in dreams is to signify getting rid of a feeling or emotion – whatever is symbolized by the object – in a forcible fashion.

▦ From a purely pragmatic viewpoint, any ejection signifies complete out-of-hand rejection of a principle or idea.

⊞ The act of ejection implies the use of force. In a woman's dream such an image may imply that she must become more forceful. In a man's dream it may mean that he needs to be more focussed.

ELDER/ELDERLY

❀ The elders in a tribal society traditionally had the wisdom of age and experience. Spiritually, therefore, they had the right to guide others. This gives a similar significance to them as authority figures today. It is in this sense that the Wise Old Man represents an inner wisdom.

◈ From an emotional perspective, in dreams the elderly can be accorded respect and may represent knowledge, power and understanding.

▦ The elderly in dreams can symbolize old fashioned or outdated values and methods of operating, as well as those that are to be honoured.

⊞ In a woman's dream the elders or the elderly may suggest a more matriarchal aspect. In a man's dream this may be more paternalistic. It will, of course, depend on whether the gender of the dream figures is recognized.

You might also like to consult the entry for People.

ELECTION – *see* VOTE

ELECTRICITY

❀ Electricity symbolizes the greater Spiritual Power. Without an efficient, well-understood method of using this power, however, it can be dangerous or harmful.

⬧ If in a dream we receive what seems to be an electric shock it shows we are not protecting ourselves from danger and need to be more aware of external events. A sudden jolt can either be destructive or bring us back in line. The muscle jerk as we fall asleep might be interpreted by the dreaming mind as an electric shock.

▣ Electricity often represents power and it will depend on the context of the dream which aspect of power is being highlighted. To dream of electrical wires is to be aware of our capability and perhaps our use of energy, while to dream of switches is to be aware of the ability to control situations around us.

ELEMENT/S

✺ Since the word 'element' means first principle, spiritually this can mean the Creator. The elements Fire, Air, Water and Earth are the first principles of creation. The Chinese way of thought includes Metal as the fifth element. It is these core meanings that come across in dreams.

⬧ Water is the element most strongly associated with emotion and tends to have this significance in dreams. Air represents intellect. In magical terms each element has its own significance and direction. It is these correspondences that may first appear in dreams.

▣ Fire represents energy and power and Earth represents stability. In dreams, therefore, where these elements are prominent, we are often considering how best to use these qualities within a particular situation.

Consult the entries for Earth/Earthquake, East, Fire, North, South, Water and West.

ELEPHANT – *see* ANIMALS

ELEVEN – *see* NUMBERS

ELIXIR

✺ In alchemy an elixir is capable of prolonging life and of transmuting base metal into gold. In spiritual terms, therefore, it is the power of transformation.

⬧ A substance such as an elixir, which has undergone several processes to reach a state of purity, symbolizes a process of psychological change which many people go through, bringing understanding of ourselves and others.

▣ In mundane terms an elixir is a distillation of the essence of things, so can signify the need to return to basics and simplify matters in order to find the most efficient solution.

You might also like to consult the entry for Alchemy.

ELOPING/ELOPEMENT

✺ Elopement signifies a union – spiritual or otherwise – particularly in adversity.

◉ In a dream, planning an elopement is trying to create conditions where some sort of integration within aspects of our personalities can take place. Such changes may upset and disturb others in the meantime.

▣ Dreaming of eloping, particularly with someone you know, is trying to escape from a situation that could ultimately be painful. We must maintain a balance between the need for emotional and/or material security.

▣ Since men and women would in waking life view eloping from different perspectives – for men the 'rescuing' of the maiden and for women being rescued – such dreams can allow us to explore the need to escape from different perspectives.

EMAIL

◉ Spiritually, an email signifies fast, efficient communication.

◉ As the email – mail by electronic transfer – takes over from the letter in ordinary life, in dreams it becomes both a more immediate source and purveyor of necessary information.

▣ In dreams, a message by email has for most people moved beyond its initial use as communication in business and become, as in waking life, a way of expressing immediate thoughts and ideas. If we are sending an email in dreams we have information which others may need.

Also consult the entries for Communication and Letter for further information.

EMBERS

◉ The embers of a fire will symbolize a spiritual energy that is beginning to die down, to lose its potency.

◉ Embers suggest emotions that have moved beyond a clear expression. Whatever has been our passion is beginning to wane.

▣ As embers are what is left when material has been consumed by fire, we may need to decide whether or not a project or idea needs reviving with new input or allowed to die away quietly.

You might also like to consult the entries for Ashes and Fire.

EMBEZZLE – see STEALING

EMBLEM

◉ An emblem is a symbol, a pictorial representation of something that allows the mind to make a connection. Spiritually, therefore, it is a way of changing our perception.

◉ In a more technological age an emblem will have less connection with heraldry, a former source of emblems, and more to do with commercial concerns. A particular emblem or logo in dreams usually has some kind of personal resonance for us.

An emblem, much like the knight's standard of old, is a rallying point or a call for loyalty. It is also an easily recognized instruction as in road signs. In dreams, once we have sorted out the symbolism, it often performs this function.

Also consult the entry for Badge/Brooch.

EMBRYO

The core of physical being is the embryo, a union of masculine and feminine principles. This therefore symbolizes the centre of Creation.

We are linking back to conception, to a point where life begins and takes on meaning. We may need to look at the process of becoming consciously knowledgeable of all that we are or can be.

To dream of an embryo or foetus is to become aware of an extremely vulnerable part of ourselves. We may also be making ourselves aware of a new situation in our lives, one which has not got beyond a germ of an idea.

Since a woman is more intimately concerned with the formation of an embryo, her dreams may be more connected with the processes of development rather than the existence of a child. In a man's dream an embryo need not have the symbolism of a foetus, but rather the rudiments of an idea.

Also consult the entry for Baby in People.

EMERALD – *see* GEMS/JEWELS

EMERGENCY

Experiencing an emergency in a spiritual sense is having to deal with the unexpected, which may test our perceived limitations.

Any emergency puts our emotions under stress and so it is in dreams. If we are under stress in waking life we may dream of an emergency and equally if there is an emergency in real life we may dream of explosions and other such images.

What seems like an emergency to one person may not be so to another. Anxiety dreams often contain some element of the necessity for immediate action.

You might also like to consult Accident and Explode/Explosion.

EMIGRATE

Emigration symbolizes moving away from our perceived comfort zone.

When we dream of emigrating we are leaving behind the known for the unknown. Implicit in this is the idea of new experiences, new ways of thought and new friends. The method of emigration – train, plane or other means – may be important.

In the ordinary everyday world we do not often have the opportunity to make radical changes. Dreaming of emigration alerts us to the possibility of leaving a situation we are in and doing something completely different.

Consult the entries for Aeroplane, Boat/Ship, Journey, Train and Transport for further information.

EMOTIONS

�“ Our emotional requirement, particularly responsiveness to the more subtle energy of spirituality, allows us to begin the process of self-development. A 'lifting of the spirits' is indeed a change in consciousness and perhaps a reaching towards something beyond ourselves.

🌑 Occasionally, in order to understand a dream, it is easier to ignore the symbolisms and concentrate on the moods, feelings and emotions that have surfaced. This will often give us a clearer interpretation of our state of mind, rather than confusing ourselves by trying to interpret myriad symbols.

▦ Within the framework of a dream our emotions can seem very different to those we have in everyday life. They may be more extreme, for instance, almost as though we have given ourselves freedom of expression, or we may be able to notice that there are strange swings of mood. Thus joy is extreme pleasure and despair a lack of hope. Negative emotions such as the latter are often easier to acknowledge within dreams rather than in real life.

You might also wish to consult the entries for Anger, Hysterics and Weeping.

EMPLOYMENT

�“ Spiritual employment suggests using our talents and gifts effectively for the Greater Good.

🌑 When we are fully employed and properly rewarded our attention is very focused on what we are doing. To dream of being employed in a job other than our own can suggest that we have issues about satisfaction and lifestyle choices.

▦ Dreams about employment are often more to do with issues of personal satisfaction. Since employment can also represent the way that other people think and feel about us, such dreams will contain an element of self- assessment.

You might also like to consult the entries for Unemployment and Work.

EMPTY

�“ Spiritually, any sort of experience that brings about a sense of emptiness signifies the Void.

🌑 We may need space to be ourselves in order to come to terms with what is occurring in our lives. To be in an empty house or building denotes the fact that we have left behind old attitudes and habits.

🔲 To experience emptiness in a dream indicates there is a lack of pleasure and enthusiasm. We could be suffering from a sense of isolation, or perhaps of not having anything to hold on to. We may have had expectations that cannot be realized.

You might like to consult the entries for Abyss and Void.

ENCHANTRESS

🔆 An enchantress exudes the destructive side of the Feminine, represented by, for instance, Lilith, the first wife of Adam, who created demons in anger, or the Hindu goddess Mohini.

💠 The enchantress can appear in dreams when a woman begins to come to terms with her self-destructive side. She is to be understood rather than feared.

🔲 The enchantress is such a strong image within both the masculine and feminine psyches that she can appear in dreams in many guises. She is the feminine principle in its binding and destroying aspect; the evil witch or the beautiful seductress. She has the power to create illusion and the ability to delude others.

You might like to consult Archetypes in the Introduction as well as the entry for Siren for further clarification.

ENCLOSED/ENCLOSURE

🔆 Spiritually, any enclosure represents the protective aspect of the Great Mother.

💠 Aspects of ourselves that are too frightening, disturbing or private to be allowed full expression are often perceived as enclosed spaces. To be in an enclosed space suggests an exploration of these aspects. To be outside this space signifies a fear of them.

🔲 In dreams, the defence mechanisms we put in place to prevent ourselves from deeply feeling the impact of such things as relationships, love, anxiety or pain can often manifest as an enclosed space. Restraints and constraints can appear as actual walls and barriers.

Consulting the Introduction for information on the Great Mother and also the entries for Barrier and Walls will further help in interpreting your dream.

ENCOURAGE

🔆 Encouragement in dreams is often symbolized by a parental, authority type of figure or an easily recognized spiritual being.

💠 There is an inner aspect of our personality that knows what is right for us. This will often appear in dreams, albeit as differing characters, to encourage us when we cannot consciously make a decision.

🔲 To encourage is to 'give heart to' and from a practical perspective any positive dream images can do just that. Waking from a dream with a sense of being able to move on successfully or to take positive action comes from that sense of inner encouragement.

END/ENDING

An ending from a spiritual viewpoint indicates a successful conclusion. To be at the end can mean exploring the subconscious and sometimes the consideration of death.

A situation that may have given us problems is coming to a natural end. There need no longer be such concern.

To dream of there being an end or an ending to something signifies the reaching of a goal, or a point at which things must inevitably change. We need to decide what we can leave behind, and what must be taken forward. We must decide what we value most.

ENEMY

Any spiritual conflict may have us cast a dream character as an enemy. An enemy is 'not a friend', someone who does not have our welfare at heart.

By definition, an enemy is someone who is a threat to us, perhaps emotionally, perhaps from the point of view of integrity. Dreaming of such a figure highlights such a situation.

When we are in a confrontational situation the opponent will become the enemy, particularly in dreams. By working through the dream scenario we are able to deal with the actual situation in waking life.

You might also like to consult the entry for Oppose/Opponent.

ENGINE

An engine is symbolic of our own Spiritual inner motivations and drives.

To perceive a diesel or railway engine may be putting us in touch with our own inner power or principles. Depending on the type, the engine can sometimes represent the sexual act.

The motivating drive or energy that we need within a situation can be perceived in dreams as an engine. When the dream seems to concentrate on the mechanical action of the engine, we may need to be looking at the more dynamic pragmatic ways of dealing with our lives. To be removing the engine could indicate a health problem, perhaps putting our health at risk by overdoing it.

You might also wish to consult the entries for Car, Engine, Piston and Transport.

ENGINEERING

Spiritual engineering signifies gaining control of our own inner power and being able to make use of it.

Engineering suggests the ability, through techniques and mechanical means, to use forces that are not normally available to us. To dream of engineering in this way highlights our ability to take control of power that is external to us. We are able to manipulate (influence) events in order to achieve our goals.

🔲 To dream of engineering is to link with our ability to construct. This is our ability to create a structure that will either allow us to move forward or will make life easier for us. To dream of engineering works – as in roadworks – is to recognize the need for some adjustment in part of our lives. *Also consult the entry for Machine for further information.*

ENGRAVE/ENGRAVING

🌣 An engraving is a carving of special meaning, either because of its content or its craftsmanship. In dreams the spiritual relevance will be particularly highlighted.

♡ When we dream of engraving an article, we are creating an object that has personal meaning. We may be recording information or marking a special event.

🔲 If we dream of finding an engraved article we might consider it as a message from the past. There is the potential for it to hold secret information. Following the fashion of engraving an article to mark an achievement or special event, it will have the same meaning as an accolade. *You might like to consult the entry for Inscription for further clarity.*

ENORMOUS – *see* SIZE

ENTER/ENTRANCE

🌣 Because of the symbolism of moving from the external to an inner enclosed space, an entrance signifies the Eternal Feminine. It can also symbolize a new beginning.

♡ When we need to be in touch with the hidden side of ourselves, the intuitive or more 'knowing' side, and have the knowledge and ability to experience ourselves in new ways, we will often dream of a secret entrance, usually opening inwards.

🔲 An entrance in a dream has the same significance as a door, representing a new area of experience, or the new experience itself. Such a dream often signifies the need to make changes, to create new opportunities, perhaps to explore the unknown. The entrance, often a door, gate or similar, will often open outwards. *You might also consult the entries for Door and Gate.*

ENVIRONMENT – *see* THE INTRODUCTION AND LANDSCAPES

EPIDEMIC/PLAGUE

🌣 Spiritually an epidemic constitutes a generalized plague, infection or contamination of ideas and concepts.

❤ For an epidemic/plague to take hold people would need to be capable of being contaminated. From an emotional perspective in dreams an epidemic might suggest some kind of group hysteria.

▦ To dream of an epidemic suggests that we are under some pressure, perhaps to maintain our own viewpoint or integrity in the light of group pressure.

EQUAL/EQUALITY

✸ Any image that portrays things as being equal suggests that there is an intrinsic state of balance; spiritually, matters are as they should be.

❤ Equal suggests 'the same as' and also implies that a comparison has been made. This may be whether a particular dream emotion is valid or not, or even if we have come across similar circumstances before.

▦ Any dream of equality can highlight our relationships with siblings or with work colleagues. We may have issues that cannot be properly dealt with in waking life, and therefore our mind will try to resolve these concerns through dreams.

⊟ As women's equality has become more important, women may dream of perceived unfairness, whereas men may feel themselves to be threatened or under pressure. As equality is established, both may dream of the right to self-expression.

EROSION

✸ Erosion being the wearing down of a hard substance, it symbolizes submission to higher spiritual forces or principles.

❤ Extreme emotion can be very wearing, so often when we are under stress we can dream, for instance, of a river eroding its banks or of the sea wearing away a cliff.

▦ Such an image can suggest that, by perseverance, we are able to overcome difficulties. There may not be an immediate solution to a problem, but by working away at it, it can be solved.

You might also like to consult the entry for Cliff.

ERUPTION – *see* EXPLODE/EXPLOSION AND VOLCANO

ESCAPE

✸ Escape represents our own need for spiritual freedom and the ability to consciously move on.

❤ Trying to escape from someone signifies that we are feeling threatened. It is possible that anxiety or past trauma means we are unable to do anything other than try to escape from the situation itself.

▦ When we dream of escape we are trying to move beyond – or to avoid –

difficult feelings. We may be trying to run away from responsibility or from duty.

⊟ Broadly, escape in a woman's dream will have an emotional content perhaps triggered by fear. In a man's dream the reason is likely to be more considered.

ESTIMATE – *see* **QUOTE/QUOTATION**

EVAPORATION

☀ Fire and water combined is an alchemical symbol for the transformative power of the Spirit.

♥ By raising one's consciousness, the energy within a situation can be changed for the better. We have it within our power to create opportunities for transformation.

▨ To be aware of water in a dream and then realize that it has evaporated is to recognize the transformation that can take place, once emotion is dealt with properly.

EVENING

☀ Evening signifies old age, wisdom and many years of Spiritual experience.

♥ The evening can be a synonym for twilight and the boundaries of our conscious mind. At this time there may be 'apparitions' around, of which we do not become aware until we start working with the unconscious.

▨ When we are aware of it being evening in a dream, we need to recognize the fact that we need time for ourselves – perhaps relaxation and quiet peace.

Also consult the entries for Dawn/Day and Night and Time.

EVIL

☀ Evil in the sense of moral wickedness is often personified in dreams by the figure of the Devil – itself a corruption of Lucifer the light bearer.

♥ Evil is an expression of disapproval of that which cannot be explained away. Any violent action might be interpreted as evil – against the norm. Any darkness can also be seen as evil since for some time the colour black has been associated with it.

▨ To experience evil in a dream is usually to be conscious of our own urges, which we have judged to be wrong. Other aspects of evil, such as inappropriate action by others, may be experienced as dread and disgust.

You might like to consult the entries for Dark/Darkness, Demon and Devil.

EVOLUTION

☀ Evolution in the spiritual sense is the opening out to a new and better state of being.

To experience evolution in dreams is to be part of a process of growth. To evolve is to progress from one stage of existence to another. The whole process of dreaming could in itself be said to be a process of evolution, particularly when we dream in series.

Dreaming of evolution and its associated issues such as the natural development of flora and fauna can be a way of reminding ourselves of the steps needed to develop a project from start to finish.

EXAM/BEING EXAMINED

There is recognition of the need for spiritual examination and a degree of objectivity in the way we deal with problems.

We may be in the habit of setting ourselves tests of self-value, or habitually be concerned with our accomplishments. To be late for an examination or to be unable to take it suggests fears and doubts about our own competence. There are many instances recorded of people having been abducted by 'aliens,' of having been examined, and then returned to earth. Opinions vary as to whether these were dreams or not.

Dreaming of examinations (particularly educational ones) is usually connected with self-criticism and the need for high achievement. We may be allowing others to set our standards of morality and success for us. Being examined by a doctor indicates concerns over our own health.

Also consult the entries for Aliens/Alienated and Tests.

EXCHANGE

Spiritually any exchange signifies the idea of give and take.

In dreams, as in real life, to be making an exchange suggests we are not satisfied with what we had originally. Dreaming of the stock exchange signifies the excitement of taking a calculated risk.

An exchange suggests that someone or some circumstance has initiated the need for change. To be exchanging clothes with someone signifies our need for a new persona.

EXCOMMUNICATE

Technically, to be excommunicated is to be denied access to the sacraments, so in dreams signifies being prevented from communicating with the Divine

Emotionally, to find ourselves excommunicated in dreams suggests being cut off from a source of comfort.

As humans we have a strong need at times to belong to groups. When we dream of being excommunicated we must cope with feelings of rejection, and perhaps of disapproval.

EXCREMENT

✹ In ancient times the power of the person was said to be contained in his excrement. Now, dreaming of it is more likely to indicate a sense of relief, a letting go of old beliefs.

♡ Dreams of excrement suggest that there are certain aspects of our lives which we have used up and need to expel. Large quantities of excrement indicate that we may be feeling overwhelmed.

▦ When we dream of faeces or excrement we are returning to an infant level of expression and pleasure in bodily functions. Experiences we have had may have been relevant at the time but we now need to let them go. More negatively, we may feel that we have to process other peoples' negativity.

You might like to consult the entries for Excrement in Body and for Toilet.

EXECUTE

✹ An execution often suggests a violent conclusion. Its secondary meaning (completing a duty or task) has more resonance with the spiritual significance of such a dream.

♡ There is a sense of coercion – of having to – in the idea of execution of a task. If we tend to be driven by our emotions this will come across in dreams

▦ Violence of any sort in dreams usually signifies that something is badly out of balance, so to dream of an execution may signify that we are acting (wrongly) more from an intellectual viewpoint than from a feeling perspective.

You might also like to consult the entries for Guillotine, Punish/Punishment and Violence.

EXHIBIT/EXHIBITION

✹ To dream that we are being exhibited probably means that our spiritual identity is being questioned. When we are at an exhibition we are being presented with new ideas.

♡ Psychologically we do not appreciate being inspected like an exhibit, so this type of dream may show some disquiet about the way people regard us.

▦ An exhibition hall tends to be a place where similar objects are grouped together, so from a mundane perspective would denote such a situation in working life, possibly uncovering a difficulty with being managed too closely.

Consult the entry for Exam/Being Examined for further clarification.

EXIT

✹ Spiritually an exit can suggest that we must consider leaving a situation that is not giving us the sanctuary we need. This may mean that we must consider our concept of death. This does not suggest death itself, merely the concept.

❤ An exit is a way out, so for this to be highlighted suggests that we need to be aware of the ability to bring an end to an emotional problem.

▦ If an exit is barred, there is little that we can do except find another way out. If in dreams we seem to have a choice of exits then we have a number of possibilities that will move us into a different space. If we cannot see the exit, we need to consider our options in a workaday situation.

You might also like to consult the entries for Death, Door and Leave/Leaving.

EXORCISE/EXORCISM

✴ Spiritually exorcism depicts a rite or ceremony deliberately designed to get rid of negativity and evil. It was specifically designed to expel evil spirits, but now has the symbolism of getting rid of negativity.

❤ When emotion becomes unbearable, specific action needs to be taken to exorcise the bad feeling. In dreams we can find ourselves banishing evil, which gives us the clarity to function properly.

▦ Dreaming of exorcism suggests that there is a situation or occurrence in waking life that needs dealing with promptly. Whether we choose to use dramatic methods is a choice we must make.

You might also like to consult the entries for Ceremony, Evil, Rite/Ritual and Spiritual Imagery in the Introduction.

EXPLODE/EXPLOSION

✴ An explosion in a spiritual sense would suggest a revelation of some sort, a welling up from the depths rather than caused by external factors.

❤ A forceful explosion of an emotion – anger, fear or sexual release for instance – can accomplish a cleansing. A dream may be a safe space in which to accomplish this, the emotion having been suppressed for some time.

▦ An explosion in a dream usually indicates a release of energy in a forceful way, which will allow us to make changes in the way we express ourselves or in the life we live. Apparently destructive, the outcome may be positive in that the debris has to be cleared away.

You might like to consult the entries for Atom Bomb, Bomb, Demolition, Earth/Earthquake and Nuclear Explosion.

EXPOSE/EXPOSURE

✴ Exposure has two connotations spiritually. The first suggests vulnerability and the second the ability to reveal – for instance, a truth.

❤ When we feel exposed in dreams it suggests that we have been made emotionally vulnerable, that the defences we put up have been stripped away. To expose an object or information ourselves suggests that something is hidden that will be revealed.

⬛ When a particular task or project is not going well, we may find our self doubts prevent us from making progress. A dream that helps us deal with these doubts and fears often has elements of exposure in them, such as digging for treasure or emptying a cupboard.

⬛ Of necessity in relationships, we have to open up to someone else. In both men and women this may lead to dreams of exposure.

EXTINCT

☼ When energy is perceived as extinct it has been deadened for some time.

♥ An extinct volcano suggests that we have become aware of old feelings and emotions that are not relevant in the present circumstances.

⬛ Dreaming of extinct animals such as dinosaurs suggests that we are aware of attitudes and behaviours that are no longer relevant.

You might also like to consult the entries for Dinosaur and Volcano.

EXTINGUISH

☼ Extreme suffering – spiritual, emotional or physical – may be perceived as having extinguished or sapped spiritual passion.

♥ Usually extinguishing suggests putting out a fire or a light, having the symbolism of smothering emotions or covering up deeper feelings.

⬛ When we dream of extinguishing fire or light it is often worthwhile to look at how this is done. Dreaming of switching off a light suggests that we have cut off a source of energy, with the potential for it to be reinstated. For instance dousing a fire with a blanket suggests suppressing a powerful energy. *You might like to consult the entries for Fire, Embers and Light for further clarification.*

EXTRA-TERRESTRIAL

☼ Extra-terrestrial beings in spiritual terms are those that do not have the same qualities as human beings. They are not 'of the ordinary'. Such images suggest that we have access to other realms of being in the dream state.

♥ Emotionally, anything that is beyond our normal experience may be depicted as extra-terrestrial. We need to give such emotions some kind of form in order to be able to deal with them. It is possible that in feeling different to others we sense ourselves to be alien and not of this world.

⬛ From a practical perspective, there is no reason to suppose that extra-terrestrial beings do not exist, or that there is no such things as UFOs (Unidentified Flying Objects). However, opinions vary as to whether the objects and beings we encounter in dreams are figments of the dreaming mind or aspects of our own personality, or are indeed extra-terrestrial. *You might also like to consult the entry for Alien/Alienated.*

EYES – *see* **BODY**

FABRIC

❄ Material or fabric in spiritual terms is that which has become tangible or has a reality of its own. Fabrication in the sense of lying is making something up, creating a Spiritual untruth.

♥ Originally simply any manufactured substance – and only later specifically textile – fabric in dreams is symbolic of the physical world. The colour and texture may be important in interpretation.

▦ In mundane parlance, fabric in dreams is a tactile representation of something we need to know or remember. A rough fabric might denote a difficulty and a smooth fabric or material a carefully crafted project. Seeing fabric which has been mended or patched suggests that our original thoughts perhaps had an inherent flaw. A patch of the same colour may be an attempt to cover this up, whereas one of a different fabric or texture highlights a perhaps innovative solution.

You might like to consult the entry for Colour for further information.

FABULOUS BEASTS
(SUCH AS CENTAURS, GRIFFINS, MINOTAURS AND UNICORNS)

❄ Fearsome and terrifying powers of nature were often previously represented as fabulous creatures. In addition, they were given animalistic qualities. Learning to control these qualities within ourselves is a large part of the spiritual development which can take place through dreams.

♥ Given the freedom to create, the mind can produce both the fantastic and the grotesque, particularly in dreams. There are many combinations which are possible and we, therefore, have an almost unlimited potential to use our creative abilities. By and large, the appearance of fabulous beasts is the result of trying to reconcile two apparently diverse polarities.

▦ In dream imagery, in order to draw the dreamer's attention to certain qualities, fabulous beasts are shown as having dual characteristics. The centaur represents the combination of man with beast whilst the minotaur does the reverse – that of beast with man. These combinations are intended to show that we are able to combine two basic principles.

▶ The unicorn has its horn representing mysticism, the griffin has the qualities of both the lion and the eagle. These representations are of the best qualities of masculinity and femininity. Only the purest of women (the virgin) can tame the unicorn and only the bravest of men can tame the griffin. (It is sometimes said that only the female griffin has wings, yet the griffin is also said to draw the chariot of Nemesis, goddess of justice, across the sky.)

FACE

🔅 Traditionally the face represented, or rather symbolized, the basic powers of the Soul; the eyes are the mirror, the mouth represents expression, the forehead knowledge.

♥ We learn most about people from their faces, so to be particularly conscious of faces in dreams suggests that we may be seeking knowledge or information not otherwise available to us. If any part of the face seems particularly prominent or outstanding that should be interpreted separately.

▦ To concentrate on somebody else's face in a dream is an attempt to understand the outward personality. To be looking at our own face reflected in a mirror means that we may be trying to come to terms with the way we express ourselves in the ordinary, everyday world. We may also be attempting to understand our own ulterior motives. When the face is hidden or has no features, we are hiding our own power, or refusing to acknowledge our own abilities.

Consult the entries for Eyes, Hair, Head and Mouth in Body for further clarification.

FACTORY

🔅 Being a commercial building a factory suggests manifestation from the spiritual to the ordinary mundane world.

♥ A factory is often a large, busy space, so it is often representative of our own lives and the way we fill our inner space.

▦ Depending on what seems to be happening in a dream a factory can actually represent the workplace and our attitude to our employment. An assembly line might suggest a sense of boredom for instance.

FAIL/FAILURE

🔅 When we have a sense of failure in dreams this may be highlighting depression or spiritual frustration. Such a feeling may indicate, before we are consciously aware of it, that we have not come up to our own expectations and feel we have let others down.

♥ The fear of failure is almost universally present in one form or another. To dream of failure at least gives us the opportunity to face that fear in a manageable fashion.

▦ Personal failure in a dream indicates a degree of competitiveness and will also highlight different ways of operating in everyday life. Failure in a dream is not necessarily personal. If, for instance, lights fail or refuse to work, we need to be aware of a lack of energy, power or enthusiasm around us.

FAIR/FAIRGROUND

☀ A metaphor for life itself, with its merry-go-round and its spiritual 'ups and downs', is the image of a fairground.

♥ The fairground has a dreamlike quality of its own. It is a sort of enclosed world, a place where the trials and tribulations of the external world can be forgotten for a time. When we dream of such a place we are becoming more aware of the more hedonistic side of our nature. We are more wrapped up in our own pleasures.

▦ To dream of being in a fairground may represent a reconnection with our light-hearted childlike nature. We can afford to be less inhibited in public. To be attending a carnival or fiesta means we can drop whatever constraints or restraints we may impose on ourselves or others.

FAIRY

☀ Fairies are a specific group of otherworldly beings with mystical abilities found in most folklore, particularly in Celtic and Teutonic tales. Usually known for being mischievous, it is this aspect that becomes important for us in dreams. As a branch of Neopaganism the increase of belief in fairies may well lead to a greater awareness and appreciation of these nature spirits and their qualities. As archetypal figures they may appear more frequently in dreams.

♥ Fairies are known to be capricious, and on a psychological level they may represent the side of our being that does not wish to be controlled, and wishes to have the freedom to react and be spontaneous.

▦ Because fairies are representations of the elemental forces of nature, for them to appear in a dream signifies our connection with those forces within ourselves. There is a need for control, otherwise the mischievous side in us can run riot.

Consult the entry for Nymph for additional information.

FAKE/FALSE

☀ Anything that is fake or false is counterfeit (made in imitation of the original). This echoes the idea that man was made in the image of God, a spiritual concept. In dreams we can become acutely aware of humanity as opposed to divinity.

♥ When we become aware that something is a fake or is false in dreams it is time for us to assess our own integrity. There are flaws or misperceptions in the way we regard ourselves.

▦ A counterfeit object is one that in comparison with the original is seen to have flaws. We can admire the fake for its own intrinsic beauty while accepting the flaws. Actually fashioning fake objects suggests that we are conscious that our creativity is not being best used. Projects and tasks all have flaws that can be improved upon, and dreaming of fakes and false objects give us the opportunity to iron out difficulties before they develop into problems.

FALCON

Ascension and freedom from Spiritual Bondage are represented by the falcon, a bird of prey.

To dream of a falcon or any trained bird can represent energy fully focused on a particular project with complete freedom to act. Such a dream may allow us to concentrate on our aspirations, hopes and desires.

The power that we have to succeed must be used in a contained, directed way. A falcon – as a trained bird and one of the fastest fliers – can depict this. *Consult the entry for Birds for more information.*

FALL/FALLING

Spiritual fear or forgetfulness is symbolized here, particularly the Fall from Grace, from a state of innocent bliss to a state of sinful understanding, with its attendant consequences We may feel we are slipping away from a situation, essentially we are losing our place. This can be because of others' negative influence.

Falling has come to be interpreted as surrender (particularly sexual) and with moral failure, of not being as one should. Statistically, dreams of falling are one of the most common types of dream. They tend to occur during the first stage of sleep and are often accompanied by muscle contractions of the arms and legs, sometimes the whole body. These are known as myoclonic jerks.

A fall in a dream outlines the need to be grounded, to take care within a known situation. We may be harmed by being too pedestrian. To dream of falling shows a lack of confidence in our own ability. We may feel threatened by a lack of security, whether real or imagined. We fear being dropped by friends or colleagues.

FALSE – *see* FAKE

FAME

Spiritually, fame suggests the need to accept our own integrity, our ability to be ourselves under all conditions.

The Ego – our sense of individual existence – is a very powerful tool and the human being's need for recognition arises from this. If we are trying to make decisions as to how to move forward within our lives, we have to recognize our potential to stand out in a crowd – or not as the case may be. To dream of fame allows us to crystallize our attitude to our own unique sense of being.

▣ Dreaming of being famous, or of achieving fame within a chosen field, signifies that we ourselves need to recognize and give ourselves credit for our own abilities. In waking life we may be relatively shy, but in dreams we can often achieve things we would not believe we were capable of. Often such a dream gives us the courage to attempt what seems impossible.

You might also like to consult the entries for Celebrity and Famous People.

FAMILY

✦ The family symbolizes the Spiritual Triangle, the unification of Love and Wisdom from which arises Power. It is also a group in which we feel safe.

✿ Psychologically the struggle for individuality should take place within the safety of the family unit. This, however, does not always happen. In dreams we are able to 'manipulate' the images of our family members, so that we can work through our difficulties without harming anyone else (it is interesting to note that one person working on his own dreams can have a profound noticeable effect on the interactions and unconscious bondings between other members of his family). Almost all of the problems we encounter in life are reflected within the family, so in times of stress we will dream of previous problems and difficulties that the family has experienced. Dreams about the family figure so prominently because most of the conflicts and problems in life are experienced first within that environment. It is as though a pattern is laid down which, until it is broken willingly, will continue to appear. Individual members and their position within the family can also symbolize the various archetypes – father can represent the masculine principle and authority, whereas mother represents the nurturing, protective principle. For ease of reference the relevance of each figure in men's and women's dreams is included under each heading. Because we have had an intimate connection with members of the family they become easy targets for projection as dream images. We do have to decide whether they are in our dreams as themselves or whether they are there in a symbolic capacity.

The family relationships in more detail can be interpreted thus:

Brother – a brother can represent both feelings of kinship and of rivalry. In a man's dream an older brother can represent experience and authority, while a younger brother suggests vulnerability and possibly lack of maturity. In a woman's dream, a younger brother can represent a sense of rivalry, but also of vulnerability, whether her own or her brother's. An older brother can signify her extrovert self.

Daughter – when the relationship with a daughter is highlighted in dreams, it often represents the outcome of the relationship between the dreamer and their partner. In a woman's dream, the relationship with the daughter usually suggests a mutually supportive one – although rivalry and jealousy can arise and needs to be dealt with. Sometimes this can safely be done in dreams. In a man's dream his daughter may represent his fears and doubts about his own ability to handle his vulnerability.

Extended family (such as cousins, aunts, uncles) – members of the extended family usually appear in dreams either as themselves, highlighting our relationship with them, or typifying various aspects of our own personality that are recognizable.

Father – if the relationship with father has been successful in waking life, the dream image will tend to be a positive one. Father represents authority and the conventional forms of law and order. If the relationship with father has been a difficult or negative one, there may be some resistance in waking life to resolving the various conflicts that will have arisen. Often this can be accomplished spontaneously in dreams. In a man's life father becomes a role model, whether appropriate or not. It is often only when the individual realizes that he is not being true to his own nature that dreams can point the way to a more successful life and perhaps an understanding of his father. In a woman's life, father is the 'pattern' on whom she bases all later relationships with men. When she appreciates that she longer need use this pattern, she is often able to work out in dreams a more appropriate way to have a mature relationship. This can lead to dreams of her perhaps walking away from her father or leaving him behind.

Grandparents – if grandparents appear in dreams it can highlight our attitude to them, but also to the traditions and beliefs handed down by them. It is often said that grandparents do not know whether they have done a good job of raising their children until their sons and daughters have children of their own. In dreams grandparents can offer security, but this will often depend on the relationship our parents have had with them.

Husband/Live-in partner – crucial within the husband/wife relationship are the wife's feelings about her own sexuality and intimacy of body, mind and spirit. Her view of herself will have been formed by her connection with her father and any subsequent partnering may well be coloured by that attachment. If her doubts and fears about validity are not properly expressed, they will surface in dreams about the loss, or death, of her husband. Such fears may also be projected onto other women's husbands, almost as though her own husband is too close to her.

Mother – our relationship with mother is pivotal in our development and will often give rise to her appearance in dreams. Largely it is the first relationship we develop, probably should be perceived as a nurturing, caring one, and allows us to develop such relationships with other people. If this does not happen, fears and doubts may arise. In a man's life this may result in continually developing dependent relationships with older women, or denying his right to a relationship completely. His dreams may highlight this difficulty until such times as he is prepared to address the problem. As he grows to maturity he may experience dreams that highlight the loss of his mother. In a woman's life, her relationship with her mother will colour all other relationships. Negatively, she may find herself pushed into nurturing the needy male, or in forming relationships with both men and women that do not satisfy her basic needs. There are many ways through dreams of working through relationships with mother, both symbolically and otherwise, and much can be gained by daring to take this step. Provided we have come to terms with and understood this relationship, much material and spiritual success can be achieved. Positive images of mothering and motherhood may also give us access to archetypal material that is connected with Mother Earth and our place in the world.

Sister – the sister in dreams usually represents the feeling side of ourselves. We have the ability to make links with that side of ourselves through being able to understand our sister's personality. In a man's dream if she is older, the sister can represent the potential for persecution, but also of caring. If she is younger then she can epitomize the more vulnerable side of him. In a woman's dream if the sister is younger, she can represent rivalry. If older she stands for capability.

Son – in dreams the son can signify our need for self-expression and for extroversion. He can also signify parental responsibility. In a mother's dream he may represent our ambitions, hope and potential. In a father's dream he can highlight unfulfilled hopes and dreams.

Wife/Live-in partner – the relationship between husband and wife is often based on how the man perceives himself to be, and can be enhanced through his dreams. Dreaming of a partner sometimes signifies the part of our personality that we cannot quite make full use of without help. A man will often attempt to prove himself a good husband through his dreams. He may experience in dreams the potential loss and death of his partner with the same intensity as he experienced the first 'loss' of his mother.

⬛ The family is the first basic security image that we have. Often, through circumstances not within our control, that image becomes distorted, and dreams will either attempt to put this image right or will confirm the distortion. Thus we may dream of an argument with a family member, but the interpretation will depend on both the circumstances of the dream and our everyday relationship with that person. All future relationships are influenced by the ones we first develop within the family.

Since relationships in the family are so important, dreams containing family members can have extra significance. Some typical dreams are:

A man's mother being transformed into another woman – a man's first close relationship with a woman is with his mother or mother figure. This transformation indicates some change in his perception of women. Depending on the circumstances of the dream, such a transformation can be either positive or negative. For instance he may dream of his mother turning into his boss. This suggests he may have certain expectations as to how he should be treated. It can be a sign of growth for him to realize, through dreams, that he can let mother go.

A woman's father, brother or lover turning into someone else – similarly, a woman's first relationship with the male is usually with her father or father figure. She must learn to walk away from that relationship in order to progress onto fuller relationships. When she can handle her Animus she is ready for that transformation.

A man's brother or a woman's sister appearing in a dream – this often represents the Shadow. Often it is easier to project the negative side of our personalities onto members of the family. If this projection is allowed to continue, and not understood, it can cause difficulty with family relationships. Often the solution will present itself in dreams to enable us to come to terms with our own projections. The pattern of aggressions between family members is fairly typical, but oddly is often easier to work through in dreams than in everyday life.

Confusion of family members (e.g. mother's face on father's body) – this suggests that we may be having problems in deciding which parent or person is most important to us.

Family members suffering from injury or trauma or appearing to be distorted in some way – may reflect our fear for, or about, that person.

A family member continually appearing in dreams or, conversely, not appearing when expected – shows that the relationship with that person (or our concept of them) needs to be better understood.

Dreaming of an incestuous relationship – may indicate that we have become obsessed in some way with the other person. We are searching for integration of their qualities within ourselves.

Parents crushing us and thus forcing rebellion – this suggests that we need to break away from learnt childhood behaviour and develop as an individual. Dreaming of a parent's death can also have the same significance. When a parent appears in our own environment, we will have learnt to change roles within the parent/child relationship and perhaps will accept our parents as friends. Parents behaving inappropriately in dreams can indicate our need to recognize that they are only human, and not as perfect as we had first perceived. In tribal societies the rite of passage between childhood and adulthood is clearly marked, by initiation. Rivalry with one or both parents is highlighted in dreams when such a transformation is not properly handled and our feelings and emotions have not been given due validity.

Dreaming of conflict between a loved one and a member of our family – this shows we have not fully differentiated between our needs and desire for each person. Learning how to love outside the family is a sign of maturity. The figure of a family member intruding in dreams suggests that family loyalties can get in the way within our everyday life. Rivalry between siblings in dreams usually harks back to a feeling of insecurity and doubt, possibly as to whether we are loved enough within the family framework.

Dreaming of being adopted – suggests that we feel out of place and in some way different to other members of the family. This dream often occurs as teenagers are growing towards maturity.

Dreaming of having any family member – e.g. a brother – when we do not have one in waking life denotes our search for completion and 'missing' parts of our personality.

FAMINE

❀ A famine symbolizes a lack of Spiritual sustenance, which should give us enough energy to remain active within the physical.

♡ Famine from an emotional perspective signifies a lack of love or appreciation. In waking life those in authority may seem to withhold approval or approbation.

▨ In the Western world famine is not so prevalent but as a dream image it may signify a concern over global matters. On a more personal note, such an image suggests that a project or task is no longer receiving the attention it deserves and, therefore, lacks nurturing.

▧ In both men's and women's dreams famine suggests a lack of resources, though which particular ones will depend on everyday circumstances.

You might also like to consult the entries for Eat/Eating, Fasting, Food and Nourishment.

FAMOUS PEOPLE

❀ Spiritually, as we reach for perfection we need to 'work through' various aspects of our personality. Sometimes we are able to reject such aspects as not being appropriate for the life we live. For instance, we may realize that the destructiveness of a public life would take its toll within our own lives.

♥ Famous people, pop and film stars and sporting celebrities may also serve in dreams as a projection of the type of person we would like to be. We may, for instance, in real life be shy and withdrawn, but need to be admired and loved. In today's climate of media celebrities, both minor and otherwise, such figures can also be targets for opprobrium.

▦ Most of us are capable of creating an ideal person on whom to project our fantasies and wishes. We are not at this stage particularly in touch with reality. In dreams a film, pop star or public figure will represent the Animus or Anima. A young person dreaming of a film star may not be ready for the responsibility of a real relationship.

⊡ In a woman's dream a male pop star or famous person will most likely represent the 'knight in shining armour' destined to take her away from her mundane life. In a man's dream a female star is more likely to represent a desired type of femininity.

Consult the information on the Animus/Anima in the Introduction and also the entries for Celebrity and Fame for more information.

FANATIC

❁ A fanatic was initially 'one who was inspired by God', zealous in all he did in the service of his god. Only later did this become debased into the more negative meaning of someone who has no sense of respect for physical life. It is, unfortunately, this latter interpretation that surfaces in many of today's dreams.

♥ When we find ourselves in dreams being totally focused to the point of fanaticism on a particular outcome it is perhaps wise to consider and appraise our commitments.

▦ Without determination and tenacity many tasks cannot be completed. Dreaming of a known fanatic or act of fanaticism can help us to complete our projects.

You might also like to consult the entry for Martyr.

FARE

❁ A fare-paying dream often occurs when one feels that past actions have not been paid for or taken into account. Before we can move on we must pay our dues and come to terms with them.

♥ Demands may be being made on us and we have to decide on their appropriateness. To be paying a fare suggests acknowledgement of help we have received on our 'journey' through life. To be receiving a fare indicates that we have facilitated someone else's passage.

🔲 To be paying a fare in a dream is acknowledging the price that is paid in order to succeed. A taxi-fare would imply a more private process than a bus fare. From a mundane perspective, wordplay suggests that a transaction that we have undertaken is 'fair'.

FARM/FARMYARD

🔅 A farmyard is an enclosure in which we may feel safe and, to some extent, looked after. Dreaming of such a place shows that we are within safe Spiritual boundaries.

♡ Our natural drives such as a need for physical comfort, herd behaviour and territorial rights are best expressed in a safe, conserving environment, symbolized by the rural idyll of a farm. As time goes on the image of a farm or farmyard is superceded by the commercial requirements of a working farm, analogous with our own working environment.

🔲 To be in a farmyard in a dream (if it is not a memory) shows us as being in touch with the down-to-earth side of ourselves. There are many facets of behaviour that can be interpreted in animal terms and often this type of dream has more much impact than one including people.

🔳 The agricultural environment is an easy way to learn about procreation and conservation. In both men's and women's dreams a farm or farmyard may symbolize such issues.

You might like to consult the entry for Animals for further qualification.

FAST – *see* SPEED

FASTING

🔅 Fasting is a very old way of bringing about a change in consciousness, and also a move towards self-realization through resistance to temptation. It is considered to be the most powerful spiritual discipline there is, but should not be indulged in in everyday life without properly qualified support. Dreaming of fasting suggests that some kind of spiritual discipline may be required.

♡ Dreams while actively fasting can be particularly vivid or lurid. If we have what we consider to be a grievance, self-denial may manifest as the image of fasting (doing without sustenance). This may be the psyche's way of making this grievance known.

🔲 Deliberately depriving the body of sustenance in a dream may be an attempt to come to terms with some perceived trauma, such as a lack of love, or to draw attention to the need for cleansing in some way.

You might like to consult the entries for Eat/Eating, Famine, Food and Nourishment for additional clarification.

FAT

🔅 Pharaoh's dream of seven fat cows being devoured by seven lean ones is a perfect illustration of fat representing a surplus or surfeit of anything. The spiritual significance can be of energy, power or knowledge.

💟 Depending on how we think of our bodies in the waking state, we can often use the dream image of ourselves to change the way we feel. Body dysmorphia (distortion) in dreams is not uncommon, particularly in lucid dreaming. Dreaming of being fat can also suggest the carrying of a weighty burden.

🔳 To dream of being fat alerts us to the defences we use against inadequacy. Equally, we may also be conscious of the sensual and fun side of ourselves we have not used before.

🔳 A woman will sometimes dream of becoming fat before she is consciously aware of being pregnant.

FATHER – *see* FAMILY

FAX MACHINE/FAX – *see* COMMUNICATION

FEAST – *see* FESTIVAL

FEATHER

🔅 Feathers, particularly white ones, are said to symbolize the Heavens and messages from the Angelic realms and the Soul. Spiritual triumph is shown by a display of plumage.

💟 Feathers often represent flight to other parts of the Self, and because of their connection with the wind and the air, can represent our more spiritual side. A bird's plumage is its protection, but it is also its power and strength. Used in this sense, it is alerting us to the fact that we can use our own strength and ability to achieve what we want to do in the future.

🔳 Feathers in a dream could denote softness and lightness, perhaps a more gentle approach to a situation. We may need to look at the truth within the particular situation and to recognize that we need to be calmer in what we are doing. In a dream, plumage being drawn to our attention can often stand for a display of power and strength. It may also be a signal of defiance; we need to stand firm and show our colours.

FEED/FEEDING – *see* EAT/EATING

FEET/FOOT – *see* BODY

FENCE

🔅 A fence can represent spiritual boundaries. We need to be aware of what checks and limitations there are to our spiritual progress.

💟 When we come up against a fence or a barrier there is extra effort needed for us to overcome whatever that barrier represents.

When we dream of fences we are dreaming of social or class barriers or perhaps our own need for privacy. We may be aware of boundaries in relationships that can prevent us from achieving the proper type of connection we need. We may have difficulty in expressing ourselves in some way.

You might like to consult the entries for Barrier and Edge.

FERMENTATION

Fermentation in alchemy symbolizes spiritual transformation and transmutation. It has this same symbolism in dreams and we become aware of changes that are both necessary and are taking place. Fermentation is living inspiration.

A process of fermentation shows the ways in which we can transform and transmute aspects of our personality that do not necessarily serve us well into new and outstanding characteristics.

To dream of the process of fermentation indicates that events are occurring in the background, of which we are aware but we must wait for them to develop. Often a project will lose energy before it takes on a new lease of life.

FERRY

The ferry is one of the oldest symbols associated with death. It signifies transition, often from the physical realm to the spiritual. We may be undergoing a spiritual 'death' or change of some kind, moving on from present knowledge.

The old idea of being ferried across the River Styx, the boundary between life and death, gives an image of making major change, when we may have to leave behind all that we have known.

To dream of being on a ferry indicates that we are making some movement towards change. Because the ferry carries large numbers of people it may also represent a group to which we belong needing to make changes, needing to change its way of working and take responsibility for moving as a group rather than as individuals.

You might like to consult the entries for Boat/Ship and Death.

FESTIVAL

A festival is a church or religious feast, as in harvest festival. This was originally a pagan feast to honour the fertility gods and give thanks for a good harvest. It signifies a spiritual celebration.

Festivals are very specific for a number of cultures. While in many cases they have become somewhat secularized, in dreams they mark the need for family or group gathering in order to celebrate an event or happening. Such rituals and occasions help to cement both individual and community relationships.

▦ Nowadays music and art festivals take the place of religious festivals. When we dream of such a festival it is the common bond and how we fit in which is important.

Also consult the entry for Meal and Party.

FIEND

☀ Technically the opposite of friend, a fiend is a manifestation of Satan as the enemy of mankind. In dreams a fiend can symbolize the enemy within, that part of us that resists spiritual development.

♥ We may be afraid of our own passions, anger and fear. As a fiery creature and initially a symbol for evil, the fiend is a manifestation of those emotions. It is possible in dreams to confront such a creature.

▦ To dream of a fiend or devil usually means that we have got to come to terms with a part of ourselves that is frightening and unknown. We need to confront this part and make it work for us rather than against us.

⊞ In a woman's dream a fiend may manifest as all the unexpressed frustration that she is experiencing. In a man's dream such a figure will be more overtly aggressive.

Also consult the entries for Demon, Devil and Imp.

FIG/FIG TREE

☀ The fig is known to enhance psychic ability and also has a direct connection with the beginning of physical life. The Sacred fig is the Bo tree and is revered by Buddhists and Hindus alike. It was beneath this tree that Guatama Buddha received enlightenment. Jesus is said to have blasted the fig tree, when it would not provide him with nourishment. The fig tree in dreams usually suggests that we are in touch with a deeper spiritual awareness of which we have previously had no conscious knowledge.

♥ Because the 'fruit' of a fig is actually a specialized structure, an involuted (nearly closed) receptacle with many small flowers arranged on the inner surface, it has come to represent intuition and wisdom and their application in the ordinary world. This gives it an association with the Tree of Knowledge, the beginning of duality, and ultimately with masculinity and femininity.

▦ Often because of its shape, the fig is associated with sexuality, fertility, masculinity and prosperity. To dream of eating figs may well be a recognition that some kind of celebration is necessary although equally that a situation holds more potential than at first thought.

⊞ Because it holds many seeds, the fig is seen as a potent fertility symbol. In a woman's dream this image may represent her partner's fertility and, therefore, his ability to father children. In a man's dream it is more likely to suggest his virility.

FIGHT

✵ A fight in dreams is quite literally a spiritual conflict. We need to work out where and why there is a conflict and perhaps deal with it in a subtle way.

♥ If we dream that we are in a fight, it usually indicates that we are confronting our need for independence. We may also need to express our anger and frustration and the subconscious desire to hurt a part of ourselves. We also may wish to hurt someone else, although this would be unacceptable in the waking state.

▦ To fight back is a natural defence mechanism, so when we are feeling threatened in our everyday lives, we will often dream of taking that situation one stage further and fighting it out. To throw a punch in a dream is to recognize our own distress or aggression. To be punched is often to have invited such aggression.

◧ Fighting tends to be a masculine response to a problem so in a man's dream he may well be attempting to deal with his own reactions. In a woman's dream she will be developing her own assertiveness and must decide whether her actions are appropriate.

You might like to consult the entry for Conflict for further clarification.

FILM

✵ Film in dreams symbolizes the spiritual Akashic Records, which are understood to have existed since the beginning of Creation. Being able to access these gives us more understanding of Divine Will.

♥ Film as recording images is an important part of modern man's make up and to be viewing film within a dream is to be creating a different reality from the one we presently have. This usually applies to the waking self, rather than to the sleeping self. If we are making a film, when this is not our normal occupation, we may need to question the reality we are creating, but may also be being warned not to try to create too many realities.

▦ To dream of being at a film – as in the cinema – indicates we are viewing an aspect of our own past or character that needs to be acknowledged in a different way. We are attempting to view ourselves objectively or perhaps we may be escaping from reality.

FIN – *see* FISH

FIND

✵ Finding something after a deliberate search in a dream signifies that we have enough spiritual awareness to move forward. Finding something by chance suggests an element of spiritual assistance. A found object is something to be treasured.

❧ The mind has an uncanny knack of drawing our attention to what needs to be done to enable us to achieve our aims. It will use hiding, searching and finding as metaphors for effort we must make in the waking state. So to find something without having to make too much effort would show that events will take place that will reveal what we need to know.

▦ If we dream of finding a precious object, we are becoming aware of some part of ourselves that is, or will be, of use to us. We are making a discovery or a realization, which may be about us or about others.

FINGER

✺ A hand with a finger pointing the way signifies the spiritual direction to be taken. When the thumb and middle finger are held together it suggests suppression of the Ego (the conscious self).

❧ When we become conscious in dreams of the fingers on a hand we are often being given important information. A beckoning finger is encouragement, whereas if the fourth or ring finger is more noticeable, love of a selfless kind is suggested. If the little finger is crooked traditionally there may be some deviousness around.

▦ When the fingers are splayed, this can suggest openness and honesty; when curled towards the palm, information is being hidden. If bunched into a fist there is aggression against us. If the fingers on both hands are interlaced, some self-control is necessary.

You might also like to consult the entry for Hand in Body.

FIRE

✺ Being aware of the heat of a fire is to be aware of someone else's strong feelings. Baptism by fire signifies a new awareness and awakening of spiritual power and transformation created sometimes through extremes of emotion. Fire is a valid Western symbol of the spiritual energy known as Kundalini, which rises from the base of the spine to the crown of the head and brings with it a shift in perception. A fire bucket, as with any hollow vessel, can represent the feminine principle.

❧ Psychologically, fire often appears in dreams as a symbol of cleansing and purification. We can use the life-giving and generative power to change our lives. Sometimes fire indicates the need to use our sexual power to good effect. To dream of being burnt alive may express our fears of a new relationship or phase of life. We may also be conscious that we could suffer for our beliefs. As a symbol, the fire bucket indicates that we may have a situation around us that is out of control. The interpretation will depend on whether the bucket is full or empty for it is often only by a display of 'dampening' emotion that there can be any progress.

Fire in a dream can suggest passion and desire in its more positive sense, and frustration, anger, resentment and destructiveness in its more negative. It will depend on whether the fire is controlled or otherwise on the exact interpretation. To be more conscious of the flame of the fire would be to be aware of the energy and strength that is available to us. A fire basket draws our attention to the fact that these energies can be contained; whereas a fire bucket, particularly if it is filled with sand, suggests such energies should be smothered.

FIREWORKS

There is an excess of spiritual emotion, which needs to be channelled properly in order to prevent it shooting off in all directions. Various fireworks may have specific significances. The Catherine wheel signifies the martyrdom of St Catherine of Sienna, so in dreams could represent oppression of the feminine, while the rocket suggests aiming for the unknown.

Fireworks can have the same significance as an explosion. Such a release of energy or emotion can have quite a spectacular effect on us, or on people around us.

Fireworks are generally accepted as belonging to a happy occasion or celebration, though they may also be frightening. When we dream of fireworks we are hoping to be able to celebrate good fortune, although there may be a secondary emotion associated with that celebration.

FISH

Fish signify temporal and spiritual power. When pictured as two fish swimming in opposite directions, it is recognized as the sign of Pisces. The Collective Unconscious as Jung has called it – that part of life everyone shares, the common experience, awareness and knowledge that we all have – is becoming available to us.

Dreaming of fish connects with the emotional side of ourselves, but more our ability to be wise without being strategic. We can often simply respond instinctively to what is going on, without needing to analyze it. The salmon symbolizes wisdom; a cooked fish is a completed task and other fish represent prosperity. The fin of a fish signifies positive movement and 'going with the flow'.

In dreams the fish tends to represent anything – an idea or project – that is taking on form but at this point has not yet become conscious. Catching a fish is to get hold of such an idea. The fish and fishing can also represent the actual process of dreaming itself.

It has been thought that small fish represent semen in a woman's dream and larger fish suggest children. In a man's dream, small 'fry' suggest problems with self-image – he has not yet integrated certain aspects of his personality. The rod probably represents the penis.

FISHERMAN

🔅 Because of its Christian connection a fisherman can symbolize a priest or holy man in dreams. Equally, he is one who has the patience to sit out a situation without anticipating any particular outcome.

� We may be trying to 'catch' something, such as a job or a partner.

▦ Whenever one of our dream figures is carrying out a specific action we need to look at what is represented by that action. Often a fisherman will represent a provider, or perhaps bravery, as with a deep-sea fisherman, whilst a fresh water fisherman may indicate the need for rest and recuperation.

You might like to consult the entry for Occupation.

FLAG

🔅 Spiritual crusades and journeys often require certain standards of behaviour and flags in dreams will often symbolize an idea or principle.

♅ Any national flag will signify a degree of patriotism that may be necessary, or possibly the need to be more militant. Now with its connection to international sport, a flag can suggest an opportunity for exhibitionism.

▦ A flag in a dream will have the same meaning as a banner – that is a standard or a place round which people with common aims and beliefs can gather. It may represent old-fashioned principles and beliefs.

You might like to consult the entry for Banner for further clarification.

FLAME – see FIRE

FLASH

🔅 The lightning flash is a function within Jewish Kabbalist belief when something to be manifested is drawn very quickly through the Sephiroth (spheres of existence) to become real in the physical world. As we become more aware of spiritual matters this symbol becomes part of our vocabulary.

♅ A flash in dreams signifies a build up of energy, which may be emotional, warning us that such energy, while potentially destructive, can be used positively.

▦ Concentrated light is significant on the mundane level as a flash of inspiration in a particular project or a moment of clarity when circumstances are particularly obscure.

You might like to consult the entry for Lightning for further information.

FLEAS – see INSECTS

FLIES – see INSECTS

FLOAT/FLOATING

⚙ From a spiritual perspective floating in dreams is often a precursor to out of body experiences. In lucid dreaming we can learn to control flight, and to Astral travel (deliberately change consciousness).

◈ Because we are not taking charge of our own direction, we are being indecisive and perhaps need to think more carefully about our actions and involvements with other people.

▦ Floating in a dream was considered by Freud to be connected with sexuality, but is probably much more to do with the inherent need for freedom. Generally we are opening to power beyond our conscious self, when we are carried along apparently without our consent. We are in a state of extreme relaxation and are simply allowing events to carry us along.

FLOCK – see GROUP

FLOGGING

⚙ Flogging with a whip or scourge suggests punishment and the atonement of sins.

◈ Flogging someone else means we have to be careful that we are not attempting to impose our will on or torture the dream figure. Flogging in the sense of selling something suggests that we have to be aggressive in promoting our ideas.

▦ Any violent act against the person usually indicates some form of punishment. To dream of being flogged would indicate that we are aware that someone is driving us beyond our limits, often in an inappropriate manner. Flogging ourselves would highlight a type of masochism in our own personality, which may be inappropriate and suggest self harm.

FLOOD

⚙ A flood signifies the end of one cycle and the beginning of another. Old grievances and emotional difficulties are washed away, leaving a clear head and a clear way forward.

◈ If we are not good at expressing ourselves verbally, dreaming of a flood may allow us to come to terms with our anxieties and worries in an appropriate way. An overflow of repressed or unconscious feelings needs to be got out of the way before progress can be made.

▦ Flood dreams are fascinating, because while frightening, they often indicate a release of positive energy. To be in the middle of a flood indicates we may feel we are being overwhelmed by feelings or circumstances, while watching a flood suggests we are simply watching ourselves. Sometimes a flood dream can indicate depression.

You might also like to consult the entry for Water.

FLOWERS

☼ Spiritually flowers signify love and compassion, both that which we may receive and that which we give to others.

♦ The feminine principle is often represented in dreams by flowers, as is childhood. The bud represents the potential available, while the opening flower indicates development. To be given a bouquet – and the colour of the flowers may be important – means that we are being rewarded for an action, perhaps a spiritual offering of some sort.

Each individual flower has a particular symbolism in dreams and below are just a few. These meanings arise from often ancient symbolism.

Anenome – forsaken by love. **Arum Lily** – intensity of love and nowadays also mourning. **Bluebell** – humility. **Buttercup** – childishness, innocent action. **Carnation** – fascination. **Clover** – the Holy Trinity, completion. **Chrysanthemum** – cheerfulness and friendship. **Daffodil** – deceitful in love. **Daisy** – wakefulness and awareness. **Forget-me-not** – memories of true love. **Forsythia** – anticipation of good times. **Geranium** – foolishness. **Honeysuckle** – affectionate ties. **Iris** – courage, faith and hope. **Jasmine** – charming and loveable. **Lime/Linden** – married love. **Marigold** – trouble and jealousy. **Mistletoe** – clinging affection. **Myrtle** – love and marriage. **Narcissus** – selfishness and egotism. **Peony** – shame and distress. **Poppy** – sleep and sweet oblivion. **Primrose** – total devotion. **Rose** – love, and perhaps a wedding. **Snowdrop** – consolation. **Tulip** – the perfect lover. **Violet** – modesty and faithfulness.

▦ Flowers in a dream usually give us the opportunity to link to feelings of pleasure and beauty. We are aware that something new, perhaps a feeling or ability, is beginning to come into being and that there is a freshness about what we are doing.

Also consult the entry for Colour and Garden.

FLUTE

☼ The flute generally signifies celestial music. In many cultures, ceramic instruments express the desire to unite earth and music in order to supplicate the benevolent spirits and elicit their favour. Bamboo or wooden flutes call forth the sounds of the wind or spirit.

♦ As a way of expressing the sound of the spirit, and therefore harmony, the flute can be seen in dreams as a symbol of happiness and joy. A further aspect of the flute's symbolism is its portrayal of nature and rural life.

▦ Many musical instruments – particularly wind instruments – indicate extremes of emotion, enticement and flattery. Because of its shape the flute is often taken as a symbol of masculine virility, but could also be taken to stand for anguish since its music is somewhat plaintive.

Also consult the entry for Musical Instruments.

FLYING/FLIGHT

✦ Flight is a common image when seeking spiritual freedom. To be flying upwards is to be moving towards a more spiritual appreciation of our lives, while to be flying downwards is to be making an attempt to understand the subconscious and all that entails.

◈ Flying in dreams denotes freedom from physical inhibitions and is a recognized aspect of astral travel – the soul's ability to transcend its physical existence – and of lucid dreaming. In the latter, until proficiency is gained, the realization that we are flying is enough to have us lose the ability.

▨ Conventionally to dream of flying is to do with sex and sexuality, but it would probably be more accurate to look at it in terms of lack of inhibition and freedom. We are releasing ourselves from limitations that we may impose on ourselves.

Consult the entries for Aeroplane and Wings as well as the sections on Journey and Transport for further information.

FOG – *see* WEATHER

FOLLOW/FOLLOWER

✦ We are aware of either the need for, or the recognition of, 'discipleship' in life. In undertaking our own spiritual development there is a path that we must follow.

◈ When we dream of being followed we need to identify if what is following us is negative or positive. If it is negative, we need to deal with past fears, doubts or memories. If positive, we must recognize our need to take the initiative, or to identify what drives us.

▨ If we are following someone or something in a dream we may need a cause or crusade to help give us a sense of identity. We are looking for leadership or are aware that we can be influenced by other people. It also indicates that, particularly in a work situation, we are perhaps more comfortable in a secondary position rather than out in front.

⊡ In previous times and in many cultures the woman generally followed the man. When this image surfaces in a woman's dream she must look at how she feels subservient. In a man's dream he will become aware that he is adopting a protective, more assertive role.

FONT

✦ A baptismal font is a symbol both of acceptance into a spiritual life and of a washing away of the past and of initiation into a new way of being.

⊕ The two meanings of font come together on an emotional level. As a font is a receptacle for water it suggests feeling and security, as a typeface used in printing it suggests knowledge.

▦ The commercial meaning of font as a form of lettering can give rise to images in dreams particularly in relation to the workplace. To be changing a font would suggest doing things differently, whereas not being able to load the correct font suggests a difficulty in getting matters into perspective.

FOOD

✺ Food in dreams always symbolizes spiritual sustenance – what we need to continue on our journey through life.

⊕ Our need – or enjoyment – of food fulfils certain psychological needs. The meanings of various foods are as follows:

Bread – we are looking at our experiences and our basic needs. Unleavened breads, such as chappatis, matzos, pancakes and tortillas, have symbolic importance in a number of religions. Fancy breads can show a recognition of cultural diversity.

Cake – sensual enjoyment and celebration is represented in dreams by cakes.

Chocolate – as something considered to be the food of the gods and of the spirits, chocolate suggests sensuality and enjoyment and freedom from the mundane.

Fruits – the potential for prosperity is shown in dreams as ripe fruit. The results of our efforts and experiences – the fruits of our labour – can be represented in dream form by fruit. The colour can also be significant.

Ham/Cured Meat – our need for preservation of the status quo is represented by cured meats.

Meals – depending on whether we are eating in a group or alone, meals can indicate the desire for acceptance by our peers, sociability, a fear of not being part of a greater whole, or a need to be alone.

Meat – physical or worldly satisfaction or needs are shown often in dreams as meat. At one time raw meat supposedly signified impending misfortune, although today it is more likely to represent the need to make sure we are fully prepared for impending activities.

Milk – as a basic food, milk will always signify simple nurturing and giving to oneself.

Onion – that we all have different levels, or layers, to our personalities is often shown in dreams as an onion. If we are peeling an onion we perhaps need to examine each part of our personality.

Picnic – the informal nature of a picnic tends to represent freedom, connection with nature and choice.

Sweets – these tend to represent sensual pleasure, cosseting and the sweetness of life.

Vegetables – our basic needs and material satisfaction are represented in dreams by vegetables. They also suggest the goodness we can take from the Earth and situations around us. The colour may also be important.

▦ Food signifies a satisfaction of our needs whether those are physical, mental or spiritual. It is something we might take or are taking into ourselves. Frequent dreams about eating suggest a great hunger for something, not necessarily food. Food that is mouldy suggests that we are seeking sustenance in the wrong fashion or from the wrong direction.

Consult the entries for Bread, Cakes, Colour, Eat/Eating, Fruit, Nourishment and Onion for further clarification.

FOOTPRINTS

❀ We may be aware, on a subconscious level, of a Divine presence. This we may follow or perhaps feel supported by. Interestingly if the footprints are of bare feet we need simplicity, if the feet are shod then a more sophisticated approach is called for.

♥ In dreams, if we see footprints going in opposite directions, we need to consider carefully what has happened in the past and what is going to happen in the future. We are standing in the here and now and must consider the confusion of the present, how it may affect our future and what choices we must make. We also need to consider what actions we have initiated in the past that will enable us to move into the future.

▦ To see footprints in a dream indicates that we need to follow someone or their way of being. If those footprints are stretching in front of us, there is help available to us in the future, in the sense that someone has experienced similar circumstances. If the footsteps are behind us or seem to be our own then perhaps we need to look at the way we have acted in the past, who we have affected and what we still need to be responsible for.

Also consult the entry for Foot/Feet in Body.

FORCE

❀ Force implies strength greater than our own, in this context spiritual strength and awareness. Psychic disturbance and spiritual presence is often felt by many sensitives as an inexorable force.

♥ Often in dreams we become aware of energies and forces that seem to be beyond our control. These may often be potentials that we can understand and manage with greater understanding.

▦ Pressure and stress in day-to-day living may show itself in dreams as a force that needs to be controlled.

FOREST

☀ The forest symbolizes the psyche and the hidden realms, the place of original experience. The dark or enchanted forest that very often appears as an image in fairy tales and dreams is a threshold symbol. It is the soul entering the areas it has never explored before, working with intuition and with our own ability to sense and feel what is going on around us.

♡ Dreaming of forests or a group of trees usually means entering the realms of the feminine. A forest is often a place of testing and initiation. It is always to do with coming to terms with our emotional self, of understanding the secrets of our own nature or of our own spiritual world.

▦ We may find that a dream of forests can be interpreted as being lost and unable to find direction. As conservation of the earth's resources becomes more of an issue, the forest becomes synonymous with our care of the land.

⊟ Traditionally women tend to be more in touch with their own inner resources so a forest in a woman's dream suggests her exploration of these resources. In a man's dream, dreaming of a forest suggests an aspect of his hero's journey through his own hidden and perhaps more frightening sensitivities.

You might also like to consult the entries for Trees and Wood.

FORGE

☀ The forge represents the Sacred Fire or Spirit that resides in all of us. This is an idea common in many cultures, the power or ability to transmute that which is base and unformed into something sacred.

♡ The forge represents the masculine and active force. To dream of a forge indicates that we are changing internally and allowing our finer abilities to be shown. The forge Gods such as Thor and Vulcan were an important aspect of ancient belief and often represented the ability to change.

▦ When the forge and the blacksmith were a part of normal, everyday life this particular dream would indicate some aspect of hard work or desire to reach a goal. Now it is more likely to mean a ritual action. Forging in the sense of counterfeiting an object in dreams suggests we do not trust our own creativity.

FORK

☀ We may have come to a fork – a divergence – on our spiritual path and development and need guidance as to which direction to take. A fork, particularly a three-pronged one, is often considered to be the symbol of the Devil and, therefore, can symbolize evil and trickery.

♡ Psychologically the fork can signify the same as a barb or a goad – something that is driving us, often to our own detriment.

🖼 In dreams, a fork denotes duality and indecision. A garden fork suggests hard work coupled with responsibility, whereas a kitchen fork signifies perhaps nurturing and management of assets.

FORTRESS – see BUILDINGS, CASTLE AND TOWER

FORWARD – see POSITION

FOSSIL

🌼 A fossil, from a spiritual perspective, represents the need to preserve perfect form.

♨ When emotion becomes too rigid and reflective of the past, we may dream of fossils.

🖼 If an idea or project has got stuck in outmoded ideas, we may dream of fossils. We need to be able to take the best of the old and incorporate it in different ways.

You might also like to consult the entries for Dinosaur and Prehistoric.

FOUND – see FIND

FOUNDATIONS

🌼 When we become conscious of the foundations of buildings, we become aware that spiritual practice needs a good basis from which to start.

♨ Foundations are often formed from the rubble of previous building and when this image appears we need to remember that we have available all our previous experience on which to draw.

🖼 In everyday life strategy and planning are good foundations from which to start. When we become aware that there is something wrong with the foundations of our dream building, we may need to go back to the planning stage.

You might also like to consult the entry for Buildings.

FOUNTAIN

🌼 Spiritually a fountain symbolizes Eternal Life and is a direct reference to the Fountain of Immortality, an image seen in many systems of belief.

♨ In dreams, the fountain, by its association with water, often represents the mother figure or perhaps the source of our emotions.

🖼 To dream of a fountain means that we are aware of the generative principle, the process of life and 'flow' of our own consciousness. Because of its connection with water, it also represents the surge of our emotions, and often our ability to express this. The fountain can also represent an element of play in our lives and the need to be free-flowing and untroubled.

▸ To some extent it will depend which part of the fountain is more noticeable in dreams as to its relevance. The bowl or pool usually represents the feminine and the fountain itself the masculine.

Consult the entry for Water for further clarification.

FOX – *see* ANIMALS

FRACTION/FRAGMENT

✿ Any fragmentation perceived from a spiritual perspective suggests that integration has not yet taken place or has broken down. We have only partial information available to us.

♥ When we recognize that we can see only a fraction or fragment of a dream object we need to take further action to gain control of emotions and feelings associated with whatever is represented. The shape of the fragment might be relevant.

▦ It may be unusual to be aware of fractions in dreams except in the sense of 'things half-done' However, when allowing dreams to help us work through our problems fractions and fragments become much more relevant. A dream in three parts may give us the information we need.

Also consult the entry for Shapes/Patterns.

FRAME

✿ When an object such as a picture is framed, our attention may be being focused with intensity or we may have to become aware of some spiritual limitation.

♥ If the frame is somewhat ornate, we are perhaps being somewhat neurotic in our approach; if it strikes us as very simple then we need to simplify our way of thinking.

▦ Frames give a defined border to objects, making us aware of limitations and restrictions. Within the workaday world these are often not of our own making but put in place by others. An inappropriate frame will highlight a restriction on our creativity. Being 'framed' for an activity we have not done suggests that we are conscious of an injustice in waking life.

Consult the entries for Border and Edge for more ideas.

FRAUD

✿ We should look at our true spiritual aims and be true to them. Pious fraud – which is deception as a means to a good end – may reveal itself in dreams.

♥ If we accept that the various figures appearing in a dream are parts of our personality, a person who is fraudulent means that we should guard against being dishonest with ourselves and, therefore, deceiving others.

▦ When fraud appears in a dream, particularly if the dreamer is being defrauded, there is the potential to be too trusting of people. If the dreamer is the one committing fraud, he or she runs the real risk of losing a good friend.

FREEMASON

✿ Spiritually we gain support by belonging to a group of people who think and feel the same way as us. Freemasonry is not a religion as such but it is rich in symbolism, much of which is perceived in dreams as archetypal images. Truly holy men seek harmony and balance in the universe and as Freemasons are self-initiated, they will symbolize this quality in dreams. They may also symbolize esoteric knowledge.

♥ Any grouping of the masculine usually alerts us to the many sides and aspects of the masculine personality. The four prime beliefs of Freemasonry are: the Fatherhood of God; the brotherhood of man; relief to others; and the search for truth. When these qualities are required in our lives we may dream of Freemasonry or of someone of this belief.

▦ Dreaming of belonging to a brotherhood, a mystery school or a closed (secret) society indicates our need to belong to a group of like-minded people. We all need approval from our peers, and such a dream indicates the way we handle ritualized group behaviour.

For further clarification you might like to consult Spiritual Imagery in the Introduction.

FREEZE/FROZEN

✿ When something appears frozen in dreams it has been rendered immobile and usually requires some spiritual effort to free it from its rigidity.

♥ To be freezing something – for instance food – suggests that we are attempting to preserve an emotion or feeling, perhaps to keep a memory pure. It may not be appropriate to do this, however.

▦ In the mundane world a project may be 'frozen' either because of time constraints or to prevent it degenerating. This may translate itself in dreams as something being frozen.

Consult the entry for Ice/Icebergs/Icicles for further help in interpretation.

FRIEND/FRIENDSHIP

✿ A friend is someone we have special feelings for; friendship is much valued in spiritual work. We can continue on our spiritual search in the knowledge that we are being supported.

♥ In dreams friends often highlight a particular part of our own personality that we need to look at, and perhaps understand or come to terms with, in a different way. The concept of friendship appearing in dreams clarifies how we relate to other people.

▦ Friends appearing in our dreams can signify one of two things: firstly we need to look at our relationship with that particular person, and secondly we need to decide what that friend represents for us (for instance security, support and love). Childhood friends may signify innocence, whereas a best friend might be an identification of the best in us.

⊡ Often in male/female relationships we will dream that lovers have changed to loving friends and vice versa before this has actually occurred in waking life.

Also consult the entry for People.

FRINGE – *see* EDGE

FROG

⚙ The frog is a well-known symbol of transformation and transmutation. The Chinese money frog in *feng shui* (literally the science of wind and water) is a mythical creature, which is said to appear every full moon near homes that will receive good news of increased wealth or monetary gain. For this reason many homes will have a figurine depicting Chan Chu, as it is known, and this will appear as a dream image.

♡ The frog is a symbol of fertility and eroticism. In dreams it is also representative of a perhaps slightly unpleasant aspect of character that can be changed. This image is seen in myths and legends where the frog becomes a prince.

▦ Many people associate the frog with a visible growth pattern, which mirrors the growth to maturity of the human being. In dreams, to see a frog at a particular stage of its growth depicts the feeling we have about ourselves. For instance, to see it at the stage where it has grown its back legs would suggest that we capable of moving forward in leaps and bounds

You might like to consult the entries for Frog and Reptiles in Animals.

FRONT – *see* POSITION

FRONTIER

⚙ Spiritually, as a frontier is a borderland, we have a new experiences and explorations of the unknown ahead of us. This may lead to new ways of living and being.

♡ Psychologically when we cross from one way of life to another – such as changing from puberty to adulthood or from middle age to old age – we need to depict this by creating an actual marker. In dreams, for a frontier to appear it means crossing a barrier within ourselves. Initially a frontier was a military term signifying the front line of foot soldiers, so the idea of strategy and planning is appropriate.

▦ To dream of crossing a border or frontier from one place to another represents making great changes in life, actively instigating a change from one state to another, into unknown territory. Perhaps we are taking ourselves from the past to the future, or causing other people round us to make those changes.

You might also like to consult the entry for Border.

FRUIT

🌐 Almost inevitably fruit suggests creativity and a natural growth process towards the spiritual.

💚 Psychologically, when we have worked hard we ought to be able to recognize the fruits of our labour. Dreaming of fruit in this way indicates that we have succeeded in what we set out to do. Below are some symbolisms of various fruits.

The apple is a symbol of nourishment and growth to maturity of the intuitive Self.

The apricot symbolizes self-fertilization and, therefore, the androgynous.

Berries in general signify a good harvest and also peace.

Blackberries denote sorrow and arrogance, said to date from when Lucifer fell into a bush when he was sent to Earth from Heaven.

Cherries are thought to represent youth and innocence and sometimes even virginity.

Cranberries stand for the earth's abundance, yet tinged with bitterness and responsibility.

The orange is a wish for good fortune.

The pineapple is known in some societies as 'anana' or 'excellent fruit', and displays wealth.

The pomegranate symbolizes fertility; it was the fruit offered to Persephone to tempt her to remain as Queen of the Underworld.

Quince is a symbol of love and happiness.

Raspberries denote kindness.

The strawberry, as the only fruit to carry its seeds on the surface, signifies honesty and love.

▦ To dream of fruit, particularly in a bowl, very often indicates the culmination of actions that we have taken in the past. We have been able to 'harvest' the past and to make a new beginning for ourselves. Unripe fruit suggests that a plan or project has not yet reached a point where it can be used. Rotting fruit suggests that we have missed an opportunity.

You might also like to consult the entry for Food.

FUNERAL

🌐 As a ritual that marks the end of life, a funeral is a Rite of Passage. Spiritually in dreams it signifies that we can put behind us matters that belong to the material world and can move into a more spiritual life. In allowing others the opportunity to honour their memories, they may make their own adjustments to a change of status. When we appreciate that the funeral is a wake, the symbolism is literally of coming awake to the validity of other realms.

Dreaming of our parents' funeral indicates a move towards independence, or of letting go of the past, which may be painful. We may need to let our childhood – or childhood experiences – go, and mark that by some ritual or ceremony, being prepared to take responsibility for our own lives. A teenager will often dream of a parent's funeral, as they themselves pass into adulthood.

To dream of being at a funeral indicates that we need to come to terms with our feelings about death and our attitude to loss. This may not simply be our own death but our issues over the death of others. It may also indicate a time of mourning for something that has happened in the past. This ritual perceived in dreams can allow us to move forward into the future. To dream of our own funeral can indicate a desire for sympathy. It may also indicate that a part of us is dead and we have to let it go.

In a woman's dream when a relationship ends she may need the finality of such a dream image to allow her to come to terms with the break-up. In a man's dream a funeral may highlight his own emotional make-up and perhaps his feelings of inadequacy in such a situation.

For further clarification consult the entries for Coffin, Death, Hearse, Mourning and Wake.

FUNNEL

The symbol of a funnel suggests energy and power running from the upper realms (the spiritual) to the lower (the physical).

As a funnel channels material placed within it in a controllable way, this image can suggest control of spiritual or creative energy, for instance in healing, but also control of the emotions in certain situations.

From a mundane perspective, a funnel suggests focusing your energies in a specific way in order to get the best out of any circumstances. A blocked funnel signifies either a lack of receptivity or too much information being given at one time.

In dreams, material placed in the funnel may be seen as the power available for a particular project, whereas the flow from the bottom is more the power to take action.

The former is a more feminine attribute, the latter masculine.

FURNITURE/FURNISHINGS

🔆 Furniture usually symbolizes our inheritance or revered objects. It also reflects our 'inner landscape', that part of ourselves to which we retire when seeking sanctuary.

♥ Sometimes the furniture that appears in a dream can highlight our need for security or stability, particularly if it is recognizable from the past.

Different articles of furniture have various meanings:

Bed/mattress – this can show exactly what is happening in the subtle areas of our close relationships. We can get an insight into how we really feel about intimacy and sexual pleasure. For some people the bed is a place of sanctuary and rest, where they can be totally alone.

Carpet – often when carpets appear in a dream we are looking at our emotional links with finance. The colour of the carpet should also be noted.

Chair – a chair can indicate that we need a period of rest and recuperation. We may need to deliberately take time out, to be open to other opportunities and openings.

Cupboard/Wardrobe – cupboards and wardrobes may depict those things we wish to keep hidden, but may also depict how we deal with the different roles we must play in life.

Cushion – this suggests support and comfort.

Table – for a table to appear in a dream is often to do with communal activity and with our social affiliations.

Rugs and other soft furnishings may show what we need in the way of cosseting, and may reflect our tactile nature.

🖼 The furniture that appears in our dreams, particularly if it is drawn to our attention, often shows how we feel about our family and home life, and what attitudes or habits we have developed. It also can give an indication as to how we feel about ourselves. For instance, dark, heavy material would suggest the possibility of depression, whereas brightly painted objects could testify to an upbeat mentality. Broken furniture or that which breaks as we use it can indicate a lack of security and support, or fears about the future.

You might also like to consult the entries for Altar, Colour and Table.

FUTURE

🔆 When we are aware of dreaming of the future we begin to understand the process of Spiritual Manifestation – that the past creates the present and the present is the foundation for the future.

♥ Psychologically, if we are to be in control of our lives, we often need to feel that we have to be aware of the future, and dreams can give an insight into best courses of possible action. Dreams allow us to play out certain scenarios, to explore possibilities without coming to any harm.

There are several aspects to dreaming about the future. We may be aware within the dream itself that the events will take place in the future and are usually to do with actions we need to take in waking life. We also may have precognitive dreams, which is when we dream of events – sometimes symbolically – before they take place, and then recognize that we already have the information: we 'knew' about it. The past, present and future co-exist side by side, as it were, and it is possible to 'read' these records in the dream state. Our experience of them is subjective, although we are in the position of observers.

FUZZY

When an image is indistinct or fuzzy, from a spiritual perspective this can mean that an aspect of knowledge or awareness has not yet become clear. The 'third eye', which is the ability to perceive the truth, will sometimes operate in dreams before we are aware of this faculty in waking life.

Emotional difficulties can make our thought processes confused, symbolized in dreams by a fuzziness in the images we perceive.

As a reflection of real life, when projects or concepts and ideas have not been properly clarified, dream images will appear fuzzy and indistinct in an effort to make us aware of a problem.

GAG

✹ From a spiritual perspective a gag is anything that stops us from communicating effectively. This will encompass both negative and positive aspects; that is, when prudence dictates that we say nothing or when an external condition forcibly restrains us.

♥ Many people have difficulty in expressing their emotions, so a gag in dreams may symbolize the underlying emotional difficulty that prevents us from doing so. This might, for instance, be childhood trauma or the feeling that we will not be listened to. To gag, as in experiencing nausea, suggests we are trying to get rid of negative feelings.

▦ If we are being gagged in a dream then there is a strong possibility that in waking life we are being prevented from expressing an opinion over something we feel to be important. If we are doing the gagging then we will be suppressing our ability to speak clearly or honestly.

You might also like to consult the entries for Talking and Vomit.

GALAXY

✹ The term 'a galaxy of stars' originally applied to what we now call the Milky Way. In that sense, it symbolizes a potent part of our own universe, and a concept the magnitude of which is not easily grasped.

♥ A galaxy is a huge collection and thus symbolizes vastness and depth in dreams, and not only one emotional response but many. Since we in dreams are usually observing the phenomena, there is an element of objectivity in being able to view our emotions in this way.

▦ A galaxy of celebrities, in the sense of a group of people, most of whom have some importance in their own field, are perceived as powerful. In dreams, if this image is present we perhaps need to decide what the common factor is between them and how this might relate to our lives.

You might like to consult the entries for Celebrity, Crowd, Group, Planets and Shapes/Patterns.

GALE – *see* WIND

GAMBLING

✹ Man has, since time began, attempted to discover the will of the Divine. Spiritually, therefore, to dream of gambling offers us an opportunity to do just that. It represents taking a risk that has been assessed as far as we are able.

⊘ To dream of gambling indicates that we may need to look at something in our lives that is figuratively a gamble; we may need to take risks, but in such a way that we have calculated them as best we can.

▦ From a practical perspective, gambling dreams can represent not taking life seriously. They can show how we work within the competitive field and give us some kind of insight into our own sense of winning or losing.

Consult the entries for Dice/Die, Games, Lottery and Win/Winning for further information.

GAMES

✺ Spiritually, games are a form of ritualized conflict between two opposing forces. Wars and tribal localized fights were used previously by elders and priests to channel aggression. In the same way, because they are mock fights, games in dreams can be used as expressions of aggression against other people.

⊘ Specific games such as football, baseball, rugby and cricket (which are team games) represent for many the strong ability to identify with a 'tribe' or a group of people. They indicate the way in which we gain identity and how we connect with people. A referee in such a game signifies the monitoring of our behaviour. In dreams, games that require the power of thought and strategy – such as chess or draughts – often give some idea of how we should be taking a situation forward. Decisions may need to be made where we have to gauge the result of our action and take into account our opponent's reaction.

▦ Playing a game such as golf in our dream indicates that we are taking note of how we play the game of life. If we are playing well we may take it that we are coping well with circumstances in our lives. If we are playing badly we may need to reassess our abilities and identify which skills we need to improve in order to do things better.

Consult the entries for Chess, Gambling and Win/Winning for further information.

GANG – *see* GROUP

GARAGE

✺ We all have certain spiritual tools, such as compassion, empathy and perception, which we can call upon at certain times; they are part of our motivation. A garage is a symbolic reminder that we have them in storage and they can be utilized at any time.

⊘ A car repair garage – remembering that a car represents the way we handle our external life – can indicate the need for personal attention and perhaps bodily maintenance.

▦ A garage appearing in a dream may indicate how we store our own personal abilities. It is the workshop from which we need to move out into the world in order to show what we have done. We are looking at our reserves of drive and motivation and possibly at our abilities.

You might also like to consult the entries for Car, Engine, Transport and Workshop.

GARBAGE – *see* **RUBBISH**

GARDEN

🔆 A garden can represent a form of paradise, as in the Garden of Eden. We are able to allow ourselves some spiritual relaxation and life need not be too much of a trial. Dreaming of herbs in a garden is often to do with the magical and mystical.

♥ The garden is often a symbol of the wilder feminine attributes, which need to be cultivated and tamed in order to create clarity. Enclosed gardens particularly have this significance and traditionally have represented virginity.

▥ Dreaming of a garden can be fascinating because it may indicate the area of growth in our own lives, or it can be that which we are trying to cultivate in ourselves. It often represents our inner life and that which we totally appreciate about our own being.

▣ In a woman's dream a garden signifies her own personal space or territory, whereas for a man it will suggest a shared space.

You might also like to consult the entries for Flowers, Gardener, Magic/Magician, Paradise, Plants and Weeds.

GARDENER

🔆 A gardener helps us identify with our wiser aspects such as correct speech and careful thought. We need to tend to these gifts of wisdom and not let them become stagnant.

♥ If we find ourselves looking after a garden within a dream, we are nurturing those aspects of ourselves that we have carefully cultivated and that we need to keep 'tidy', in order to get the best out of ourselves.

▥ Whenever a person appears in our dream in a certain role it is important to look at what he is actually doing. The gardener can represent the insights that we have gathered through our experience in life and can equally represent wisdom, but of a particular sort. Often the gardener indicates someone on whom we can rely, who will take care of those things with which we do not feel capable of dealing.

You might also like to consult the entries for Flowers, Garden, Plants and Weeds.

GARLAND

🔆 A garland is symbolic of the need for dedication, either spiritually or physically. It may also represent an element of our subconscious Holiness, or rather undeveloped spirituality, which we need to acknowledge.

◈ Psychologically, a garland can represent honour and recognition and can form a link or bond with the people who honoured us. In dreams, it will be important to interpret what the garlands are made of, since this may help us to identify our best abilities; for instance, garlands of bay laurel were used to honour Apollo and his many attributes.

▨ Depending on the type of garland in the dream, we are recognizing some distinction or honour for ourselves. If we are wearing the garland, such as a Hawaiian flower garland, we are looking at various ways of making ourselves happy. We are looking at dedication, and at some way of setting ourselves apart from others. Winners in sports contests are often honoured by garlands, so in dreams these would signify competition.

Consult the entries for Bridle, Flowers, Laurel/Bay Leaves and Wreath for further information.

GARLIC

✿ Garlic is considered a herb of Magic. As a protective amulet, particularly against the evil eye, it is of significance against negativity. In Chinese lore it also symbolizes luck, health and many children, so in dreams may signify all of these.

◈ Garlic is now known to help all sorts of physical conditions – including strengthening the heart – and therefore protects one against fear. Dreaming of garlic may be a way of our body alerting us to a need for such protection from infection.

▨ Garlic in olden times had much significance. Because of its shape and its many parts it was often seen as a symbol of fertility; because of its smell it was seen as protection. Dreaming of garlic may, therefore, link back to either of these meanings. In practical magic, garlic is a specific against witches.

⊟ As a fertility symbol a full head of garlic in a woman's dream may symbolize the testicles. In a man's case such a dream is more about essential masculinity.

You might also like to consult the entries for Magic/Magician, Protect/Protection and Witch.

GARTER – *see* WEDDING/WEDDING DRESS/WEDDING RING

GATE

✿ The gate in dreams is a potent image of the transition between the physical and spiritual realms, not just in the sense of death, but also as we learn more about spirituality. It is used as a 'gateway' for communication, and as a visualization before sleep can help us to access much information. It will sometimes signify the half-aware hypnogogic and hynopompic states between sleeping and waking.

◉ Dreaming of a gate usually signifies some kind of change, often in awareness. We are passing a threshold in our lives, perhaps trying something different or moving from one phase of life to another. Often the awareness of change is highlighted by the type of gate. For instance, a farm gate would tend to indicate a work change, whereas a garden gate might represent pleasure.

◉ In everyday life the image of passing through some kind of barrier appears often in dreams. An ornate gate might suggest a somewhat structured change, whereas an old gate, particularly if it is broken, suggests a well-worn way of working, which may need updating.

Also consult the entries for Barrier and Door.

GATHERING – *see* **MEET/MEETING**

GAUGE – *see* **MEASURE AND WEIGHING/WEIGHT**

GAZELLE – *see* **DEER IN ANIMALS**

GEAR

◉ In spiritual terms a gear signifies a change of consciousness. Moving up a gear suggests moving towards the spiritual and moving down, towards the physical or material.

◉ Psychologically we sometimes need to change perspective. This can be seen as changing gear in a vehicle, to alert us to changes that need to be made.

◉ In the vernacular, gear can represent both the paraphernalia associated with drug-taking and also clothes. We shall need to make some kind of link with the circumstances in our everyday lives. For instance, if in the drug-taking 'gear' a component is missing, we may be creating difficulties for ourselves. Insofar as clothes are concerned, we probably need to act more appropriately.

You might like to consult the entries for Clothes, Drugs and Transport.

GEMS/JEWELS

◉ From a spiritual point of view, gems and jewels have always had esoteric significance. The understanding and use of gems and jewels can greatly enhance personal development. In most dreams it is the better-known stones which appear, but when the lesser-known ones are seen, there is much benefit to be gained by learning more on a conscious level. Many stones have healing properties.

◉ If, in dreams, the jewels are set – made up into wearable articles – we are aware of some of the uses of whatever the jewel signifies. For instance, to find an emerald ring might suggest that we have completed one of the stages of growth towards immortality. There are different interpretations for each gemstone, and opinions do vary. The significances of some well-known jewels and gems that have particular relevance in dreams are:

Agate (black) symbolizes wealth, courage, assurance and vigour; (red) peace, spiritual love of good, health, prosperity and longevity.

Amber represents crystallized light. There is an element of magnetism in it.

Amethyst is the healing gem. Connecting us with the spiritual, it represents the influence of dreams and also humility, peace of mind, faith, self-restraint and acceptance.

Aquamarine embodies the qualities of hope, youth and health.

Beryl is believed to hold within it happiness, hope and eternal youthfulness.

Bloodstone holds the qualities of peace and understanding. It is also reputed to grant all wishes.

Carnelian highlights friendship, courage, self-confidence and health.

Chrysolite represents wisdom, discretion, tact and prudence.

Chrysoprase symbolizes gaiety and unconditional happiness. It is also the symbol of joy.

Crystal symbolizes purity, simplicity and magical power.

Diamond has a number of influences: light, life, the sun, durability, incorruptibility, loyalty, sincerity and innocence.

Emerald embraces immortality, hope, youth, faithfulness and also the beauty of spring.

Garnet can help energy levels and indicates devotion, loyalty and grace.

Jade represents 'all that is supremely excellent', the yang power of the joyful heavens.

Jasper holds the qualities of joy and happiness.

Jet is usually associated with darker emotions such as grief and mourning, although it also controls safety within a journey.

Lapis Lazuli is a favourable stone said to evoke divine favour, success and the ability to show perseverance.

Lodestone holds within it the qualities of integrity and honesty; and is also said to influence virility.

Moonstone/Selenite symbolizes the moon and its magical qualities, tenderness and the romantic lovers.

Onyx is for perspicacity, sincerity, spiritual strength and conjugal happiness.

Opal not only represents fidelity, but also religious fervour, prayers and assurance of spiritual beliefs.

Pearl symbolizes the feminine principles of chastity and purity, and also the moon and the flow of water.

Ruby represents all that is traditionally associated with royalty; dignity, zeal, power, love, passion, beauty, longevity and invulnerability.

Sapphire holds within it worldly truth, contemplation of the universe, heavenly virtues and chastity.

Topaz holds the beauty of the Divine: goodness, faithfulness, friendship, love, sagacity. Topaz also symbolizes the sun.

Tourmaline represents inspiration and imagination as well as friendship.

Turquoise symbolizes courage – physical and spiritual – fulfilment and also success.

Zircon holds within it much worldly wisdom as well as the virtues of honour and the prestige (or otherwise) of riches.

▦ Jewels appearing in dreams almost invariably symbolize those things that we value. These may be personal qualities, our sense of integrity, our ability to be ourselves, or even our very essential being. When we feel we know what we are looking for, we are aware on some level of its value to us or others. When we simply register that we are looking for jewels, sometimes up a mountain, otherwise in a cave, we are attempting to find those parts of ourselves that we know will be of value in the future. Counting or in some way assessing them would suggest a time of reflection is needed. One system of belief suggests the following practical meanings:

Amethyst promotes healing and influences dreams.

Diamond signifies human greed, hardness of nature and what we value from a cosmic perspective.

Emerald highlights personal growth.

Opal suggests the inner world of fantasies, dreams and psychic awareness.

Pearl signifies inner beauty and value.

Ruby informs on emotions, passion and sympathies.

Sapphire highlights religious feelings.

You might also like to consult the entry for Jewellery.

GERMS – *see* **DIRTY AND INFECTION**

GHOST

� If a ghost – i.e. a shadowy shape – appears in a dream we may be alerted to our past states of being and ways of behaviour. We need to identify these and acknowledge that we have moved on.

♥ We may be resurrecting old memories or feelings in order to understand our own actions. By putting ourselves in touch with what is dead and gone we can take appropriate action in the here and now. If we dream of being haunted by a ghost we have probably not handled an emotional trauma well.

■ Actually dreaming of a ghost links us to old habit patterns, or buried hopes and longings. There is something insubstantial in these, possibly because we have not put enough energy into them.

You might like to consult the entry for Spirit for further information.

GIANT

❀ A giant represents primordial power, somewhat overwhelming in its force.

♥ Giants and ogres often represent the emotion of anger, particularly masculine anger. This can be confronted in dreams where perhaps we cannot do this in waking life.

■ Dreaming about giants may mean we are coming to terms with some of the repressed feelings we had about adults when we were children. They may have seemed larger than life or frightening in some way.

You might also like to consult the entries for Anger, Monster and Size.

GIFT/GIVE/GIVING

❀ In a spiritual sense, dreaming of a gift may be pointing us towards our creative talents, of which we may not yet be aware. We need to acknowledge the gifts and talents we have and use them appropriately. In a spiritual sense giving in is submitting to a higher authority.

♥ Each of us has a store of unconscious knowledge, which from time to time becomes available to us and may appear in dreams as gifts. Some of these gifts we are able to share with others. This satisfies one of the fundamental needs of the human being: to be able to give to others. Psychologically this represents our ability to belong to a community, to have others belong within our lives and to assume responsibility for other people.

■ Giving is all about the relationships we have with ourselves, the environment and with others. So to dream of giving somebody something in a dream indicates our need to give and take within a relationship – our need to give of ourselves, perhaps to share with others what we have, and to create an environment that allows for give and take. To receive a gift within a dream is to recognize our talents and abilities.

You might also like to consult the entries for Present/Presents for further information.

GIG – see DANCE/DANCING, MOVEMENT AND MUSIC/RHYTHM

GIGGLE – see LAUGH

GIRDLE

❀ A girdle represents spiritual wisdom, strength and power. Its appearance in dreams indicates we are progressing in the right direction, with some degree of protection. The girdle is a length of material which symbolizes time, yet, because it encircles the body, it also symbolizes completeness. It thus represents the inevitability of life and death.

♥ Like a belt, in dreams a girdle can represent an insignia of honour or of power, but perhaps of a more intuitive feminine kind. Mythologically, the magical girdle of Aphrodite had the power to influence desire.

▦ For those who have an interest in magic and magical practices, the cingulum or witch's girdle – in itself a magical tool – will often appear in dreams.

⬦ In a woman's dream the girdle may depict her sense of her own femininity, for instance when she feels bound or constricted by it. In a man's dream it is more likely to show his understanding of his power over his own life.

You might also like to consult the entries for Belt, Magic/Magician, Witch and Wizard.

GIRL – *see* **PEOPLE**

GIRLFRIEND – *see* **PEOPLE**

GLACIER – *see* **ICE/ICEBERG/ICICLES**

GLASS

✿ Glass, being transparent, symbolizes the barrier between ordinary life and the life hereafter and between the physical and spiritual realms. It can also suggest the transparency of truth as we understand it.

♥ To dream of breaking glass is to be breaking through barriers. We are shattering the emotions that keep us trapped and moving into a clearer space where we do not allow barriers to build. Frosted or smoked glass can indicate a desire for privacy, or our obscured view of a particular situation within our lives.

▦ Dreaming of glass indicates the invisible but very tangible barriers we may erect around ourselves in order to protect ourselves from meaningful relationship with other people. They may also represent the barriers that other people put up and also be those aspects of ourselves that we have built up in our own defence.

Also consult the entries for Barrier, Break, Mirror and Reflection as well as Windows in the Buildings entry.

GLASSES/SPECTACLES

✿ Spiritually, a dream of glasses or spectacles may be urging us to take a different viewpoint – on a physical as well as spiritual level.

♥ Psychologically, when we are able to wear glasses we are more able to look at that which is external to ourselves rather than turning inwards and becoming introspective. So, in dreams, glasses can represent the need for extroversion within a situation.

🔲 For glasses or spectacles to stand out in a dream indicates a connection with our ability to see or to understand. Equally, if someone is unexpectedly wearing glasses, it is to do either with our lack of understanding or perhaps their inability to see where we are coming from.

Also consult the entry for Goggles and Lens.

GLOBAL WARMING – *see* **CLIMATE**

GLOBE

🔆 Dreaming of a globe or sphere is to dream of power and of dignity and symbolizes our need for wholeness. It also suggests concern for global matters such as conservation or global warming. Spiritually a globe suggests completion.

💗 It is a representation of the wholeness of life We have certain powers within us that will enable us to create a sustainable future, and for this we need to be able to understand and take an objective world view.

🔲 To dream of looking at a globe, particularly in the sense of a world globe, indicates our appreciation of a wider viewpoint. We can cultivate the ability not only not to be narrow-minded but to be more globally aware. If we are looking at, for instance, a glass globe we may be looking at a lifestyle that is complete in itself.

You might also like to consult the entry for World.

GLOOM

🔆 Gloom usually indicates the presence of negative feelings, which will be dissipated as we become more spiritually aware. Light and lightness are symbolic of spirituality, so the opposite can suggest a movement – whether involuntary or otherwise – towards emotional distress.

💗 If in dreams we find ourselves enclosed in gloom while others appear to be in the light, we may be being warned of an aspect of depression that is affecting us, but not affecting them. Conversely if we are in light while other people are in shadow we may have information that will help them to enhance their lives.

🔲 Gloom is less pervasive than darkness, so if it is around in a dream, it can indicate difficulty in being able to see or comprehend things from an external viewpoint. There may be negativity around in waking life of which we have to be aware in order to be able to dispel it – to create light and clarity – so that we can make progress.

Also consult the entries for Dark/Darkness and Light.

GLOVES

🔆 Spiritually, since hands are symbolic of our innate creativity, gloves can symbolize the need to protect our creative ability. In dreams, they may also signify an impediment to full creative expression, our ability to give form to our ideas.

◈ To some extent it will depend what sort of gloves are represented. Working gloves will suggest protection from harm, whereas dress gloves denote enhancement of our abilities. Surgical gloves signify a degree of sterility in our dealings with other people. Throwing down a gauntlet or glove means we are challenging belief.

▦ Often in previous times the glove had greater significance than it does nowadays. Because it was so much part of social etiquette it represented honour, purity and evidence of good faith. Now being aware of gloves in a dream often represents some way in which we are hiding our abilities from people around us. To take off the glove signifies respect and an act of sincerity. To dream of boxing gloves could indicate that we are trying too hard to succeed in a situation where there is aggression.

Consulting the entries for Clothes and also Hands in Body will give further information.

GNAW – *see* BITE/BITTEN

GNOME/GOBLIN

🔆 The name 'gnome' was given by the medieval scholar Paracelsus to describe the most important of the earth spirits. Goblins are a different, more grotesque, malicious variety of gnome. Visible to some who have developed clairvoyance, they are manifestations of nature's power.

◈ Gnomes are said to guard the treasures of the earth, living underground, whereas goblins have no real home. In dreams, therefore, the former will signify contentment but the latter stands for discontent.

▦ When gnomes or goblins appear in dreams we are linking with the inherent powers of nature and perhaps the personalization of parts of our own psyche. The hidden instinctive aspect is seen in the gnome and the well-buried malicious persona in the goblin. We perhaps should look at how our actions are affecting others.

You might also like to consult the entries for Fairies and Nymphs.

GOAD

🔆 Power and Spiritual authority often act as a goad so we can improve our knowledge. The trident depicted in images of the God Neptune is a goad and represents illusion, intuition and inspiration – a threefold spur towards understanding.

♦ Psychologically, we are all goaded by our own more aggressive and negative parts. Often a dream can reveal how we are making things difficult for ourselves and indicate which part is becoming too aggressive.

▦ The goad can be shown in many ways, not just as the conventional spiked stick. Often if we are goading somebody to do something they do not want to do, we must take care that we are not creating circumstances that could rebound on us. We may be trying to force people to take action to move forward but we must also be aware that we need to be in control of that particular movement.

GOAL

✿ Our spiritual aspirations are being highlighted. If we are aware of our goal then we can make tremendous inroads towards attainment. The dream image is not then just a pictorial representation, but can be used as a visualization of our success.

♦ To set life goals – or to be conscious of doing this in a dream – indicates that we are in touch with our own internal sense of our ability to achieve. The external is often a reflection of the internal, and goals can indicate that we instinctively know how much – and what – we are capable of doing.

▦ To dream of scoring a goal may indicate that we have set ourselves external targets. In achieving those targets we may also recognize that the goals we have set ourselves in life are either short-term or long-term and we may need to adjust them in some way. To miss a goal or target indicates that we have not taken all the circumstances within a situation into account and need, perhaps, to reassess our abilities to achieve.

You might like to consult the entry for Target for additional clarification.

GOAT – *see* ANIMALS

GOBLET

✿ In dreams the goblet has similar significance to the chalice. It represents the feminine, receptive principal and our ability to achieve enjoyment in different ways. As with all hollow vessels, spiritually it suggests also the Cup of Life.

♦ To dream of a set of goblets (as in wine glasses) rather than just a single one signifies the diversity of our own emotions and the value to us of social occasion. If a goblet is broken we may have made an error of judgement.

▦ We may be able to make a celebration out of something that is quite ordinary. To be drinking from a goblet indicates allowing ourselves the freedom to enjoy life to the full. If the goblet is decorated we may find that it signifies a particular skill or ability.

Consult the entries for Chalice and Cup for further clarification.

GOBLIN – *see* **GNOME/GOBLIN**

GOD/GODS

🔅 Spiritually, we are aware of a greater power (the Divine). Christian belief holds to one God, although manifesting in three forms – Father, Son and Holy Ghost. Other religions attribute the powers to various Gods. As we grow in understanding, we can appreciate the relevance of both monotheistic and polytheistic beliefs and can begin to understand God as an all-pervading energy.

♥ The powerful emotions we sometimes experience may be connected with our tremendous childhood need for love and parental approval. Often these emotions can be personalized and recognized in the figures of gods from the numerous belief systems around the world.

▦ When we dream of God we are acknowledging to ourselves that there is a higher power in charge. We connect with all humanity and, therefore, have a right to a certain set of moral beliefs. We all have needs for love and approval, which can only be met through our understanding of our childhood.

▸ In a woman's dream, dreaming of the gods will help her to understand various aspects of her own personality. In a man's dream he is linking with his own masculinity and his sense of belonging to himself, and therefore to the rest of humanity.

For further clarification consult the information on Archetypes and Spiritual Imagery in the Introduction.

GODDESS/GODDESSES

🔅 Spiritually, a woman is able to make intuitive links with the essential aspects of her own personality. She then achieves a greater understanding of her own make-up, and is able to use all facets of her being within her normal everyday life. Sophia (meaning 'Wisdom') is a personalization of an aspect of the Divine.

♥ There are many goddess figures in all cultures. There are those perceived as being destructive, such as Kali, Bast and Lilith, and also beneficent ones such as Athena and Hermia.

▦ Dreaming of goddesses from various cultures connects us with our archetypal images of femininity. In the waking state, it is the sense of mystery – of a shared secret – which is such an intangible force within the woman's psyche. This enables women to create a sisterhood or network among themselves in order to bring about a common aim. To dream about goddesses, therefore, is to accept our right to initiation into this group.

▣ In a woman's dream a goddess will clarify both the connection through the unconscious that exists between all women and female creatures and which particular archetypal aspect of femininity she favours. In a man's dream the goddess figure signifies all that a man fears in the concept of female power. It usually also gives an insight into his earliest view of femininity through his experience of his mother.

For further clarification consult the information on Archetypes and Spiritual Imagery in the Introduction.

GOGGLES

✺ We may be covering up, or denying, the existence of negativity. The eyes are believed to be the seat of the soul and to reflect our inner feelings.

♡ In today's climate of androgynous dressing, goggles and sunglasses in dreams can appear both menacing and in some cases reflective. We must therefore decide whether we are intimidated or intrigued. If we are wearing goggles our vision of the future may be impaired in some way.

▦ Goggles in a dream can have the same significance as spectacles and a mask. The meaning can be ambivalent since goggles can be used either to cover up the eyes or to enable us to see events occurring around us better. Under most circumstances it can be taken as the latter, but the dream image of goggles may indicate the protective shield that we may need in real life.

▣ For a woman to dream that she meets a man with goggles formerly meant that she could not trust that man to be honest with her. It can still have the same significance today. In a man's dream, to be wearing goggles suggests that some important matter is being hidden.

You might also like to consult the entries for Glasses/Spectacles and Mask.

GOLD

✺ Gold in dreams can represent our sacred, dedicated side thus symbolizing Spirituality on a supreme level. The old saying of 'everything that glitters isn't gold' certainly doesn't apply in the spiritual sense.

♡ In an emotional context, gold seldom stands for material wealth. It is more the spiritual assets that we have, such as incorruptibility and wisdom, love, patience and care. These enable us to apply the principles of alchemy and turn base emotional dross into 'gold' and finer feelings.

▦ Gold in dreams suggests our best, most valuable practical aspects, such as integrity and honesty. Finding gold indicates that we can discover those aspects in ourselves or others. Burying gold shows that we are trying to hide something – perhaps information or knowledge – that we have.

Also consult the entries for Alchemy, Metal and Treasure.

GOLF – *see* **GAMES**
GOOSE – *see* **BIRDS**
GOSSIP

🜨 Gossip, in the sense of needless chatter might be called spiritual 'static'. When we are developing spiritually we can become rather like badly tuned radios and can pick up needless information.

💟 Within the framework of personal development there is often what could be called the 'gossip' in the background – the chatterbox – that which is part of our personality but which prevents us from moving away from previously held ideas and behaviour. Thus, to be gossiping in a dream may mean that we have to complete certain actions before moving on.

▥ To be gossiping in a dream can mean that we are spreading information, but in a way that is not necessarily appropriate. To be in a group of people and listening to gossip generally means that we are looking for some kind of information, but perhaps do not have the ability to achieve it for ourselves. We have to use other people to enable us to achieve the correct level of information.

Consult the entry for Talking for further information.

GOUGE – *see* **INJURE/INJURY AND WOUND**
GRADUATE/GRADUATION

🜨 Dreaming of graduating has the same spiritual significance as winning an accolade and of initiation.

💟 To graduate is to have reached a certain stage of knowledge or proficiency and in dreams, particularly on an emotional or psychological level suggests an element of self-control.

▥ Taking part in a graduation ceremony means we are receiving acknowledgement for our proficiency in having completed a project or task. We are now ready to move on to the next stage.

You might like to consult the entries for Initiation and Win/Winning.

GRAFFITI

🜨 Graffiti in dreams may be one way of the unconscious trying to get a message across. It may also suggest that some information we have received is inappropriate.

💟 As a means of self-expression, the liveliness of graffiti may suggest a need to 'lighten up' and show a creative streak.

▥ Graffiti in dreams is something 'writ large', albeit in an inappropriate place. This means we have to consider more than one aspect of a task or project, before committing it to paper.

GRAIL

�*/* The Holy Grail was thought to be the cup used at The Last Supper and to have contained the blood of Christ. The search for it has, from a spiritual perspective, become part of the Hero's Quest on his journey of self-discovery. Often in dreams it represents the achievement of spiritual success, but can also represent the cup of happiness or fulfilment.

🌣 The Holy Grail, as a chalice or goblet, is such a strong mythical image that in dreams it can appear as something miraculous, something that fulfils our wish and allows us to move forward into our full potential. We are searching for something that we may feel at this particular moment is unattainable, but that, by putting ourselves through various tests, we may eventually reach.

🔲 The Grail appearing in a dream would indicate that we can expect some form of satisfaction and change to occur within our lives. For our own peace of mind we need to sort out truth from fiction for ourselves and use such an image to help us toward success.

Consulting the entries for Camelot, Chalice, Goblet, Knight and Quest will enhance your understanding.

GRAIN

🌣 Grain can represent the very seeds of life and our need to discover the Hidden Truth. As an offering to Nature it honours the abundance of Mother Earth.

🌣 To dream of grain growing in a field can indicate that we are more or less on the point of success, that we have tended our lives sufficiently to be able to achieve growth.

🔲 Dreaming of grains such as wheat, oats, barley, etc. can indicate some kind of a harvest. We have created opportunities for ourselves which can now come to fruition. Provided we look after the outcome of these opportunities, we can take that success forward and create even more abundance.

🔳 Grain and the sheaf of corn are old symbols for fertility and for nurturing. In a woman's dream she will recognize her essential nature through these symbols. In a man's dream, he will appreciate Nature and nurturing.

You might also like to consult the entries for Bread, Food and Harvest.

GRANDPARENTS – *see* FAMILY

GRAPES

🌣 Grapes, representing the food of the Gods, can symbolize Spiritual wisdom and the search for immortality.

🌣 Grapes appearing in a dream can represent sacrifice, in the sense of making something sacred. We need to give something up in order to achieve what we are really looking for. Wine is often taken to represent such sacrifice because it has a close religious affiliation with blood and, because of its colour, with blood sacrifice.

▦ To see grapes in a dream generally indicates that there is a need for celebration. The grape is the fruit most closely associated with the Roman god Bacchus or, in his Greek form, Dionysus who was the god of conviviality. To dream of grapes indicates we are searching for fun, laughter and creativity in our lives.

You might also like to consult the entries for Fruit and Wine.

GRASS

✤ Changes of Spiritual awareness can be indicated by grass appearing in a dream. Sacred, hallowed or consecrated ground might be represented by turf.

♥ Grass can often denote our native land, and dreaming of our association with a particular piece of ground can activate memories and feelings connected with happy times. It can also suggest that we need to surrender deeply held beliefs, and thus will clarify a particular problem or situation.

▦ Grass is often a symbol of new growth and of victory over barrenness. In old dream interpretations it could represent pregnancy, but is now more likely to signify new ideas and projects. To dream of being on 'sacred' turf – ground that is revered because of its association, such as particular sports grounds – is to wish for supreme success.

You might also like to consult the entry for Harvest.

GRASSHOPPER

✤ In Chinese history the grasshopper is often associated with enlightenment. Thus, it represents some form of Spiritual freedom.

♥ A grasshopper mind (one which flits all over the place) shows an inability to settle to anything and can actually be seen in dreams as a grasshopper. We should perhaps concentrate more on important matters so we can achieve our aims.

▦ The grasshopper is a symbol of freedom and capriciousness, and in dreams it can often indicate a bid, or our need, for freedom.

You might also like to consult the entry for Insects.

GRAVE

✤ Spiritually, we may fear not just physical death but also its consequences, particularly if we have no particular belief in the after-life. Dreaming of a grave is an indication that we must have regard for our feelings about, or our concept of, death.

♥ A grave may signify the loss of emotion or of feeling. Part of our personality may, quite literally, have been killed off, or is dead and buried to the outside world.

▣ Such a dream may also be attempting to deal with our feelings about someone who has died. Falling into a grave is an old symbol for initiation. Digging a grave suggests that we need closure over an aspect of everyday life; it may mean that we can go no further with a particular task. Pushing someone into a grave signifies some very negative feelings, which need to be consciously dealt with and not buried.

You might also like to consult the entries for Burial, Coffin, Dead People, Death, Funeral and Initiation.

GRAVITY

✧ In dreams, gravity is a force that draws us towards the physical or material realms, rather than the spiritual, almost despite ourselves. As we wake up to the ordinary, everyday world, we can experience gravity as a tangible physical pressure.

♦ Emotionally, gravity symbolizes a lowering of emotion in dreams towards the more negative feelings of fear and depression. In such dreams there can seem to be an actual physical force present.

▣ A sense of gravity can inject an aspect of seriousness into our dreams if there are problems or difficulties in waking life. These can be experienced as heavy or weighted objects.

Also consult the entry for Weighing/Weight.

GREENHOUSE EFFECT – *see* CLIMATE

GREYHOUND – *see* DOG IN ANIMALS

GRIEF – *see* MOURNING

GRIFFIN

✧ In antiquity the griffin was a mythical beast with the body of a lion and the head and wings of an eagle. In dreams it is an archetypal symbol and guardian of divine power.

♦ Combining the qualities of wisdom and bravery, emotionally in dreams the griffin advocates right speech and correct action.

▣ Symbolic of fire and air combined, the griffin is used in everyday life as an emblem, so can appear in dreams in the form of a logo. It will represent the need for intelligent communication.

You might like to consult the entry for Fabulous Beasts for further clarification.

GRIP – *see* HOLD

GROOM – *see* BRIDEGROOM

GROUP

✧ A group – usually of people – is a number of different individuals often from different backgrounds with a common aim. Spiritually it is usually this aim that will bind them together. Gangs will develop signs and language peculiar to themselves and will tend to anarchic or criminal behaviour. In dreams, therefore, a group will largely be peaceable and a gang noisier.

🜨 Emotionally in dreams a group will tend to be supportive while a gang will be confrontational. Either can appear if we have problems in fitting in socially, and how we deal with them will provide information useful to us in everyday life.

▦ At some point in our lives, social skills become important to us. Groups and gangs in dreams show us how good we are at handling ourselves and others. If we are members of either then we have passed some kind of personal test; in the case of gangs we may feel we have passed through some kind of initiation ceremony. If we are rejected in dreams we ourselves may not yet be ready to belong.

GROW/GROWTH

🜨 Growth in a dream can be the recognition of a new Spiritual maturity, from which we can take heart.

🜨 Often when we dream of childhood we are able to put ourselves in touch with the growth process, and can have a sense of growing, usually larger, but sometimes smaller. This can give a strong sense of being very small within the Universe or very large and giant-like within the everyday world.

▦ The changes in us that bring about new ways of relating to other people, who we ourselves are or situations around us, are all stages of growth. They can be pictured in dreams as the growth of a plant or something similar.

You might also like to consult the entries for Giant and Size.

GUARD/GUARDIAN

🜨 A guardian is one who watches over us and spiritually this usually means a guardian angel. This belief in guardian angels can be traced throughout all antiquity and as we become more aware of the existence of the spiritual realms we become able to sense their presence in dreams. As we progress it is natural to meet our own guardian spirits and those who are the guardian spirits of Nature.

🜨 In dreams, when we become conscious of someone standing guard or guarding an object we perhaps need to be careful of our actions. If it seems that we are being guarded, then we are being protected from harm. If we are the guardian then we should consider our responsibilities.

▦ To be a guard in dreams suggests a sense of duty or obligation, either towards someone or to whatever the object is that we are charged with looking after. This also suggests a particular code of conduct or behaviour.

You might also like to consult the entry for Angel.

GUERRILLA – *see* **TERROR/TERRORIST**

GUILLOTINE

⚜ A guillotine represents a severance of some kind in dreams. Since it severs the head from the body, it suggests that we may have become severed from our spiritual sources.

♥ From an emotional perspective, a guillotine indicates that there is the potential for us to lose contact with the part of ourselves that is capable of love, or, in reality, with someone we love. A short, sharp shock in our lives may cause severe disruption.

▦ A guillotine in a dream indicates an irrational aspect in our personality, which is trying to queer our pitch. We may be afraid of losing self-control in an everyday situation, or of having part of our personality amputated. We could be aware of an injury to our person or to our dignity.

You might like to consult the entries for Amputation, Execute, Injure/Injury Weapon and Wound for further clarification.

GUILT

⚜ Spiritual guilt is self-reproach for inadequacy or wrongdoing and arises out of an internal struggle between what we perceive to be right and wrong. In dreams the feeling can be more powerful than in everyday life.

♥ The emotion of guilt is such that, rather than blame others, we will often take the feeling to a very profound level. This can disturb our dreams until we have had the courage to truly forgive ourselves.

▦ When guilt arises in dreams it is usually because our instincts tell us that we have not been true to our own principles of truth and integrity. When we have done something that may result in us being judged, or committed some minor misdemeanour, in waking life we will experience guilt in dreams.

You might also like to consult the entry for Judge/Judgement.

GUITAR – *see* **MUSIC/RHYTHM AND MUSICAL INSTRUMENTS**

GULLS – *see* **SEAGULL IN BIRDS**

GUN

⚜ The symbolism here reverts to a basic attribute – that of overt masculinity and a strong degree of aggression. Such an attribute can be a positively spiritual one in that Truth is incontrovertible and has to be dealt with.

♥ It will depend on the other circumstances in the dream how we interpret the use of a gun. We may be using it to protect those things we feel are important to us. Particularly in today's climate of criminal culture, a gun can be seen as a badge of honour and in dreams may signify arrogance and power.

▣ When under pressure in waking life, the gun in dreams can signify a particularly aggressive action and the result of that aggression. Obviously it can also signify both the actual sexual act and the result.

▣ If a woman is firing a gun she is aware of the masculine, aggressive side of her personality. If she is being shot at she perhaps feels threatened by overt signs of aggression or sexuality. For a man to be being shot suggests conflict which may, in fact, be territorial.

You might also like to consult the entries for Injure/Injury, Shot, Wound and Weapons.

GURU

❁ For many of us, God is too remote for us to be able to have a personal relationship with him. A guru therefore becomes the personification of all wisdom made available to us through his perception and is a representation of the wisdom of the unconscious. He will help us to access our own innate wisdom.

♥ Psychologically, we all need a symbol for a father or authority figure (a Wise Old Man) and this is one such representation. In searching for knowledge of a specific sort, we need an external figure with whom to relate. In Eastern religions, this is the guru – who performs the same function as the priest in Western religion.

▣ A guru appearing in a dream nowadays need not only be a holy figure, but more a person whose words can be heeded. Thus, someone who is considered to be knowledgeable in the field of business might be seen as a guru.

Consult the information on Archetypes and also Religious Leaders in Spiritual Imagery in the Introduction for further clarification.

GYM

❁ In dreams, from a spiritual perspective the gym is a place where we face ourselves and our own foibles; its original meaning was a place where one trained naked. Today this can be translated as hard work with honest effort.

♥ The gym is an environment where emotions can become raw and we are able to work out our problems, both from a physical perspective and from many others. In dreams, it will therefore represent a safe space, but also one of focused power.

▣ In dreams the gym represents a place that is not work-oriented and yet requires effort, so may identify what needs to be tackled from a social perspective. These need not be problems, but perhaps a structured series of actions that can enhance our lives.

HAG

🌞 The hag or crone is a representation of the Wise Woman, someone who has with age achieved wisdom through understanding her own feminine traits.

💚 In dreams, the hag is variously the cantankerous old woman or that aspect of femininity that aspires to use intuition and understanding for the benefit of her community. If the former, we need to come to terms with what appears to make her cantankerous in the dream – pain or disillusionment perhaps. If the latter, then the Greek goddess Hecate, as keeper of the crossroads, is worth studying.

▣ In the everyday world when we are struggling to come to terms with what appears to be interference in our affairs, the hag will appear in dreams.

⊡ In a woman's dream the hag will manifest either as mentor and friend or as a judgemental personality. In a man's dream she will tend to be more of a figure of fear. In the Hero's journey he must overcome his fear and gain her blessing.

Consult the entries for Goddess/Goddesses and Witch for further clarification.

HAIR – *see* BALD AND BODY

HAIRDRESSER

🌞 In terms of spirituality there is an obvious connection between self-image and beauty; we cannot grow spiritually unless we like ourselves. A hairdresser in dreams may also signify that our ego needs some attention.

💚 Psychologically and intellectually, the hairdresser can represent the healer within us. Developing an intimate yet objective relationship, with ourselves or others, can be valuable and a hairdresser appearing in dreams would signify this.

▣ In dreams the hairdresser may appear as the part of ourselves that deals with self-image and the way we feel about ourselves. We perhaps need to consider ways in which we can change our image or how we look at things.

⊡ For many women, her hairdresser is someone with whom she can communicate freely. In her dreams, therefore, this will represent freedom of speech. In a man's dream, as grooming becomes more important, his hairdresser will suggest a feel-good factor.

HALF

🌞 When we look at what our expectations are, there is a degree of spiritual indecision around. There is an incompleteness in us, a sort of in-between state, which means that we have to make decisions – perhaps either looking forward into the future or back into the past: completion or non-completion.

⚕ To have only half of what we feel we should have – for instance, perhaps only to have half of the food or drink we had expected – indicates that we are selling ourselves short. We are not allowing ourselves to have what we need. To dream of being half way up a hill or a mountain or halfway down a river would indicate that there is some lack of motivation. We have made an initial effort but more is needed in order for us to be where we want to be. To continually dream of slipping back, until we are only halfway through our task, to be repeating it over and over again, would indicate that we do not have the ability to complete it. There is perhaps an extra skill that we need to enable us to achieve success.

▦ Dreams can often have a very peculiar quality in that our image may only be half there or we perhaps only experience half an action. For instance, in waking life we may be aware of having only half-completed a task, but do not know how to finish it. Often the dream images that appear can show us how to do this. Conversely, if in a dream we have only partially completed a task and are left feeling dissatisfied with what has happened, we perhaps need to consider in waking life what needs to be done to enable us to complete the action in the dream.

Also consult the entry for Pair/Pairs.

HALLOWEEN – *see* **SPIRITUAL IMAGERY IN THE INTRODUCTION**

HALLUCINATIONS – *see* **INTRODUCTION**

HALO

✸ The force field – or electro-magnetic energy – that emanates from each of us has a particular quality in those who have undertaken to develop themselves spiritually. To the clairvoyant eye it can appear as a type of mother-of-pearl radiance, which seems to be brightest around the head and forms a halo.

⚕ The charisma that many world and spiritual leaders have is felt by many, and can be experienced as a sort of cloudy radiance. This 'nimbus' is usually slightly more subtle – and therefore more far-reaching – than the ordinary person's aura; the halo, particularly when it is seen in dreams, is an intensification of this energy.

▦ In religious pictures it is the convention to picture this divine radiance around Christ-like or saintly people as the halo. As an archetypal image, therefore, when seen in dreams we can accept the presence of a spiritual power. *You might also like to consult the entries for Angel and Mystic to enhance your understanding.*

HALTER

◉ We may be experiencing some spiritual restraint and should take time consciously to consider what it is that we require spiritually.

◉ When we are moving into new areas of growth we sometimes need to be shown the way, and the halter is a symbol of this leading forward into new creativity. We are, as it were, being led and shown what we need to see.

◼ The halter shares the symbolism of bonds, since under normal circumstances it often controls the head. We are dreaming about reining back on the intellect, instead of allowing our creative energy to flow freely. We are not allowing ourselves the freedom to create to the best of our ability. The halter usually represents restriction of one form or another, although interestingly enough it may indicate restriction that is tolerated by the wearer. *You might also like to consult the entries for Bonds, Bridle, Chains and Harness for further information.*

HAM – *see* **FOOD**

HAMMER

◉ The hammer is a symbol of the old Forge gods such as Thor and Vulcan and with a head of iron is a symbol of craftsmanship and good work. When the hammer is a double-sided one known as the labrys it signifies justice and vengeance. It was used by the Amazons, a race of warrior women, and has been adopted as a symbol by some gay women.

◉ In dreams the hammer will signify the judicial application of force rather than out-and-out aggression. Haephestos, a Greek Forge god, crafted beautiful artefacts for his fellow gods with the use of the hammer.

◼ Dreaming of hammers or blunt instruments highlights the more aggressive and masculine side of our nature. There may be the feeling that there is an aspect of our personality that needs crafting or shaping if we are to function effectively.

◗ In a woman's dream the hammer may signify masculine authority, though in a man's dream it will be more to do with his creativity. The labrys may appear when we are attempting to balance the various drives and motivations we have. *Consult the entries for Labyrinth and Mallet for additional information.*

HAND – *see* **BODY**

HANDCUFFS

◉ Handcuffs are a binding symbol and spiritually would suggest that we are being hampered, probably by our own doubts and fears.

◉ If we are putting handcuffs on someone, we may be attempting to bind that person to us and assert our supremacy over them or what they represent in the dream. We may be being overly possessive.

Dreaming of being in handcuffs denotes that we have been restrained in some way, possibly by an authority figure. We may ourselves feel that we need to be more circumspect. 'Joke' handcuffs are often taken as symbols of marriage or committed partnership. In dreams their deeper meaning may signal some doubts about the relationship.

Also consult the entries for Authority Figures and Police in People as well as Hands in the entry for Body.

HANDSHAKE

Traditionally a handshake symbolizes a welcome into heaven and a farewell to earthly existence. Our spiritual journey contains many welcomes and goodbyes, and today the handshake symbolizes the transitions we make. Equally the handshake can suggest the touch of healers and is also a sign of good faith.

A handshake is a mark of appreciation and of acknowledgement. In dreams it suggests that an emotional bond has been forged, which cannot easily be broken.

Agreements are often sealed by a handshake, the idea being that we are not going to attack our opposite number if we have shaken hands. In dreams, shaking hands will represent at least a partial bond with the other person since, from the times of chivalry, we remove our gloves in order to do so.

If the sleeves of the two hands are masculine and feminine in the dream, or the hands are bound by cords, the handshake may symbolize matrimony, the latter by pagan rites.

You might like to consult the entries for Bonds, Cord, Gloves and Wedding/ Wedding Dress/Wedding Ring for further information.

HANG/HANGING

Suppression of an inclination towards the spiritual may be evident. This will prevent us from moving forward, so it will be as well to find the root cause of our difficulty. It may originate in a bad religious experience or from family pressure.

If we are conscious in our dream of something hanging up, there may be word association, in that literally there is a 'hang up' in our lives. If something is hanging over us, then we are feeling threatened by circumstances around us. To be watching a hanging suggests a sense of insecurity. If there are a large number of people present, our reputation may be at stake.

Hanging is a violent act against a person, therefore if we are present at a hanging we are being party to some kind of unpleasantness and perhaps should reconsider our actions. If we ourselves are being hanged, we are being warned of some difficulty ahead.

Consult the entries for Knot, Noose and Rope.

HAPPY – *see* EMOTIONS

HARASS/HARASSMENT

⚜ A sense of harassment from a spiritual perspective suggests some kind of compulsion. The drive will come from external sources rather than internal.

♥ When pressure is put on us emotionally, the feeling may be exaggerated in dreams to a sense of harassment, behaviour which is offensive to us. We may dream of stalkers or being hunted.

▦ Stress is one of the biggest disturbers of dreams and sleep. It can translate into dreams of harassment, for instance being worried or jumped on by a dog. Once the cause is identified it can be dealt with by confronting the dog image either in the dream or in a waking visualization.

▒ To be harassed in a dream by the opposite sex suggests that a man must pay attention to his softer side and a woman to her more assertive aspects. By a figure of the same sex suggests that a better balance needs to be established between the Archetypes. The dream character will usually indicate what needs attention.

Consult the entry for Hunt/Hunting/Huntsman as well as the information on Archetypes in the Introduction for further clarification.

HARBOUR – *see* BAY

HARE – *see* ANIMALS

HAREM

⚜ Any group of women appearing in dreams will signify femininity in one form or another and often the many facets of femininity. A harem will therefore symbolize the Great Mother in her more playful aspects.

♥ It will depend on whether we can relate to a particular person in the scenario for a deeper interpretation. The harem may be representative of the feminine aspects of our personality and one dream character may come to the fore more than the others.

▦ In a work situation a group of female colleagues can bond in a way that gives the appearance of a harem. While bowing to authority, there is also a connection between the women that gives a degree of solidarity. Dreaming of a harem can give information that helps to deal with the dynamics of the relationships.

▒ For a man to dream that he is in a harem shows that he is struggling to come to terms with the complexities of the feminine nature. For a woman to have the same dream shows that she is understanding her own flamboyant and sensual nature. On a different level, she is recognizing her need to belong to a group of women – a sisterhood.

Also consult the Female Archetypes and Great Mother in the Introduction.

HARNESS

✦ Spiritually, we need to harness our energy. This means using what we have available in the most efficient way possible. When we have done this, we are then able to control the more wayward side of our personality.

✦ To harness something is to make it usable in a controlled fashion, so in dreams to be aware of this type of control implies that emotional restraint is necessary to enable the correct things to happen. As a horse is controlled by a harness, so our emotions can be used constructively.

✦ Like the halter, the harness indicates some form of control or restraint. It may be that we are actually being restrained by our own limitations, or that we are being controlled by external circumstances. To be wearing a harness often takes us back to periods in childhood when we were not allowed the freedom we would have liked.

You might also like to consult the entries for Bridle, Bonds, Chains, Halter and Horse in Animals for further information.

HARP

✦ The harp as 'the ladder to the next world' is an image that can be used both in dreams and meditation. It is one that often appears as we explore our spirituality and signifies harmony and healing.

✦ To harp on about something in a dream – that is, to keep repeating what is going on – recognizes that we have a need for acknowledgement or praise in our waking life, and also need to be noticed, perhaps in some activity we are undertaking.

✦ The harp as a musical instrument indicates the correct vibration that we need in order to create harmony within our lives. We ourselves are very much in control of this and since the harp is also a national symbol of music, rhythm and harmony we often link back to our own basic selves.

Consult the entries for Music/Rhythm and Musical Instruments for further information.

HARVEST

✦ Any kind of a harvest represents fruitfulness and fertility, particularly spiritual, and most systems of belief choose to acknowledge the gathering of a harvest. Summer and the feeling of warmth and happiness it generates are connected with spiritual progress.

✦ As harvesting become more mechanized we lose our connection with the community spirit it once engendered. To be taking part in a harvest, or perhaps a harvest festival, indicates that we are celebrating our own life energy – that energy we all have available to us. Happy memories and good feelings may be represented in dreams by stereotyped romantic scenarios such as the hayfield when those feelings need to be reproduced.

To be dreaming about a harvest indicates that we will reap the rewards of previous care we have taken. We are able to work hard, and in working hard we take care of the future. So, to dream of a harvest can actually have two meanings. It can mean looking back into the past and reaping the rewards, or it can mean looking towards the future in order to use what has happened previously. In previous times, for many the hayfield represented fun, relaxation and irresponsibility. Nowadays it is more likely to represent irritation – as in hay fever – and an unknown quality.

In a woman's dream harvest time suggests the realization of a dream. For a man it may suggest prosperity, though not without hard work and some element of sacrifice.

You might also like to consult the entries for Countryside, Food, Grass and Places.

HAT – *see* CLOTHES

HAUNT – *see* GHOST

HAWK – *see* FALCON IN BIRDS

HEAD – *see* BODY

HEAL/HEALING

Healing from spirit can take many forms. A dream may give information that allows us to take action. We may dream, among other things, of a laying-on of hands or of a strange light or spiritual figure which brings us comfort.

Emotional hurt can often be healed through dreams when it seems that another part of our being takes over to bring us understanding. If we ourselves are giving healing and easement to someone else in dreams we perhaps need to explore such abilities in waking life.

Dreams of any healing environment, such as a hospital or doctor's surgery, can start a process of healing, as can a character such as a nurse or therapist linked with such places.

You might also like to consult the entries for Analyst, Doctor, Hand in Body, Hospital and Nurse/Nursing for further information.

HEAR/HEARING

Spiritually, hearing clearly suggests being able to understand what is being said or conveyed to us. To be able to hear is somewhat different to listening, which suggests assimilating information at the same time.

♥ Sound suggests a particular vibration is created and hearing that we have responded to that vibration. In dreams this can occur on a psychic level when we are conscious on waking that our perception has altered.

▦ In practical terms a hearing in a legal sense suggests that we will be listened to and understood. Not to be able to hear in dreams suggests an unwillingness to listen, whereas someone not hearing us suggests that we need to alter the way we are communicating.

HEARSE

❄ A hearse will always symbolize an ending of some sort, not necessarily death itself but the carrying away of material or physical aspects of life for we no longer need them. We may be aware that a part of ourselves is no longer 'alive' and it is better to let it go rather than resurrect it.

♥ In an emotional sense a hearse signifies a legitimate period of mourning for something that is dead and gone. A relationship may have come to an end, or we need closure in a matter that could affect our future.

▦ To dream of a hearse indicates that we recognize that a time limit has been imposed, either on ourselves or on a project we are connected with. It is coming to a natural conclusion and we need to have regard to our feelings about such finality in order to understand ourselves.

⊞ In that following the hearse was once a man's prerogative, such a dream will signify his acceptance of death or change. For a woman, a hearse may signify her innate and intimate connection with the processes of death itself.

Consult the entries for Coffin, Dead People, Death, Funeral, Mourning and Wake for further clarification.

HEART – *see* BODY AND MACHINE

HEARTH

❄ The hearth is considered to be the centre, or heart, of the home. Hestia, goddess of the hearth and the sacred fire, was a virgin goddess so spiritually her domain signifies the Anima, that part of ourselves which guards the feminine spirit.

♥ We may be, or need to be, linking with our passionate wilder nature – the seat of our passions. This is not in a confrontational way, however, but gently, as a hearth needs to be tended properly in order for the fire to burn brightly but safely.

▦ To dream of a hearth or fireplace is to recognize the need for security and nurturing. This may be of two different types. One is knowing that the home, our place of existence, is secure. The other is recognizing the security of the inner self, the interior feminine which gives warmth and stability.

⊞ The hearth in a woman's dream will suggest her own domesticity and gentleness, whereas in a man's dream it will be more to do with the feminine in his life and his motivation to provide security.

Consult the entries for Fire, Goddess/Goddesses and Home for further clarification.

HEAVEN – *see* **SPIRITUAL IMAGERY IN THE INTRODUCTION**

HEAVY – *see* **WEIGH/WEIGHING**

HEDGEHOG – *see* **ANIMALS**

HEEL – *see* **BODY**

HELICOPTER – *see* **TRANSPORT**

HELL – *see* **SPIRITUAL IMAGERY IN THE INTRODUCTION**

HELMET

✸ As a heraldic device, the helmet denotes wisdom and security in defence, and will have this significance in dreams. It symbolizes both protection by, and of, the Spiritual Self.

♥ In olden times, the helmet was the attribute of the warrior or hero. Whilst it covered the face, it often had the eye pieces highlighted in order to scare the enemy. Even today – as with the motorcycle helmet – it is still in dreams largely a representation of the masculine.

▦ In dreams, it will depend on whether the helmet is being worn by someone else or by the dreamer. If the former, it may have the same symbolism as the mask in that it prevents the wearer being seen. If the latter, then it is a symbol of protection and preservation.

⊞ In a man's dream the helmet will represent his own virility. In a woman's dream it will symbolize her attitude to the masculine. The type of helmet will be relevant, since there are now cycle and sports helmets – among others – which do not cover the face, but do protect the head, the seat of the intellect.

You might also like to consult the entries for Head in Body, Hat in Clothes, Goggles, Hide/Hidden and Mask.

HEN – *see* **BIRDS**

HERB – *see* **GARDEN AND PLANT**

HERMAPHRODITE

✸ Spiritually this represents the Divine union or sacred marriage and suggests the masculine and feminine aspects of God united in perfect balance. It is the balance sought by all alchemists, and is an image that occurs in dreams as we become more spiritually proficient.

♥ As we grow and mature, we begin to understand that certain behaviour is appropriate or acceptable. This may mean that other natural emotions, reactions and sensitivities are suppressed and can surface as difficulties later on in life as we search for autonomy. These may cause us a great deal of confusion and can be perceived in dreams as hermaphrodism, with either the masculine or feminine attributes becoming noticeable.

⊞ When we dream of a hermaphrodite, we may be having uncertainties about our ability to adjust to the roles usually played by our own sex or about our own individual gender profile. Interestingly, as we learn and understand more about ourselves, we attempt to achieve a balance between the logical and the sensitive sides of our nature. This can appear as hermaphrodism in a dream as we sort ourselves out.

You might also like to consult the entries for Alchemy, Balance and Sex.

HERMIT

✺ A holy man, or the Wise Old Man, will often appear in dreams as the hermit, suggesting that we are discovering the dimension in ourselves which has a spiritual awareness.

♡ There are two types of hermit: one withdraws from life in order to live an entirely spiritual existence and knows that others will care for his bodily needs, whereas the other travels throughout the world using his knowledge and expertise to help others.

⊞ There is a kind of loneliness and singularity within many people, which prevents us from making relationships on a one-to-one basis. This may manifest in dreams as the figure of the hermit.

⊡ In a woman's dream the hermit may represent one of her links with the Divine in the same way as a priest does. In a man's dream the hermit will often highlight his own links with his god, whatever form that takes.

Also consult the entries for Ascetic, Monk and Wanderer/Wandering.

HERO/HEROINE

✺ The hero is the spiritual archetype who shows courage in adversity and determination in the carrying out of his duties. He was initially a defender or protector.

♡ The hero sets out on his quest or journey knowing that he will undergo trials and tribulations that will have him mature from a youth to a man. In dreams, aspects of that process – such as the knight's conflict with the dragon or the witch – will often appear. The heroine or princess is the counterpart of the hero and has a similar journey to under go albeit in a somewhat more emotional way.

⊞ In today's world a hero is considered to be anyone who is held up to public acclaim. This would suggest that it is the quality of determination that has become important and would, therefore, have him become an icon to others.

⊡ In a woman's dream a hero will largely appear as a protector and as an aspect of her Animus. As she herself moves towards autonomy she will develop the qualities of bravery required by the heroine. The Princess will appear in a man's dream as an aspect of his Anima, whereas the hero will allow him to acknowledge his maturity.

Consult the entries for Animus and Anima in the Introduction, Celebrity, Icon, Knight and Quest for further clarification.

HEX

🔱 To hex someone is to cast a malicious spell and is not within the correct use of spiritual energy. It is a deliberately conscious direction of negative energy and is said to rebound upon the perpetrator threefold.

♥ When we dream of being hexed we are probably being coerced in waking life to do something which goes against our own personal code of conduct.

▦ To hex someone is to unduly influence a person or result. Usually this has negative connotations so to dream of having a hex put on us will signify an instinctive dislike of someone, which may or may not be reciprocated. If we are performing such an action in dreams we probably need to take a long hard look at our motivation.

HEXAGON – *see* SHAPES/PATTERNS

HEXAGRAM

🔱 When spiritually we attempt to reconcile two energies – the spiritual and the physical, or the active and the passive – we may experience that union in dreams in the form of patterns. One significant group of patterns are the hexagrams, said to have been discovered on a tortoise shell by an ancient Chinese sage. A hexagram consists of six lines and symbolizes the union of the spiritual and physical worlds.

♥ Technically, according to the Chinese system of I-Ching, the hexagram is a figure of six lines on top of one another. Broadly, the three at the top represent the spiritual world and the three at the bottom the physical. These two forces unite together and seem to exert a profound influence in the ordinary world. In dreams the hexagram provides a diagram of how the two forces come together and with study can help us to live our lives successfully.

▦ In the ordinary world we frequently become aware that two energies combined are far more powerful than each individually. When we need a boost in energy our dreams will often give directives as to how to do this. The hexagrams are a potent image both in dreams and for meditation.

▣ Yang is the masculine or active principle that controls Heaven, the day's activities, the Sun's heat, action and hardness. Yin is the feminine more passive aspect that controls the Earth, the night's mystery, the cool Moon, softness and stillness. In both men's and women's dreams, when a hexagram appears some kind of balance is being established.

HIDE/HIDDEN

🔅 When information is hidden in a dream it is most likely that at this stage we have not progressed enough spiritually to be able to handle it.

💟 In waking life we become very good at hiding our emotions. A dream in which we must make an effort to uncover something suggests we perhaps need to understand why we do this. When an object is hidden in dreams we may have to first give ourselves permission to reveal whatever it represents. To find a hidden jewel perhaps suggests a hidden talent.

▦ To be hiding something suggests we have issues over our own personal privacy or sense of value. If we dream that someone is hiding something from us it may suggest a lack of trust in either direction.

HIEROGLYPHICS

🔅 True hieroglyphics in dreams are symbols and pictorial representations with hidden meanings, which connect us with a particular stream of knowledge that belongs to the Egyptians. Egyptian magic is a system of belief that gave access to the will of the divine and, once the symbology is understood, can greatly enhance our knowledge. The name originally meant sacred carvings.

💟 In dreams we will often register a symbol as being a hieroglyphic because it is an idea presented in pictorial form. It is only after conscious thought that the meaning becomes clear and is retained in memory. Hieroglyphics were developed before the written word and, therefore, often represent basic ideas.

▦ Practically, when a dream contains symbols it helps to work out what it looks like. We can then apply the relevance in everyday life. When we have a definite sense of Egypt about these symbols we probably need to access old knowledge to help us in waking life. Whether we choose to use ancient magic then is our choice.

Also consult the entries for Mummy (Egyptian) and Magic/Magician.

HIGH – *see* POSITION

HIJACK

🔅 To hijack or steal while in transit has the spiritual meaning of taking over without permission. If we do not have a good life/work balance we may feel we have been hijacked.

💟 When we are heavily involved with someone, both professionally and personally, we may dream of our emotions being hijacked. We may feel that our motivation or emotions have been sapped and this manifests in dreams as a hijacking.

▦ When a task or project is taken away from us in waking life there is often a sense of resentment that may lead to dreams of being hijacked. If we ourselves are the hijacker in dreams then we need to take care that we are not being unnecessarily overbearing.

Also consult the entries for Abduct, Hostage and Kidnap.

HILL

A hill in dreams suggests that extra effort is needed in order to achieve the perception necessary for us to continue to progress spiritually.

To be climbing a hill in the company of others often indicates that we have a common goal, that a journey we possibly thought was ours alone is actually connected with other people. We can use their knowledge and comradeship to enable us to reach where we are the best we can be. To dream that we are going downhill would indicate we feel that circumstances are pushing us in a certain direction. We may be moving from a level of attainment and now feel that – with relaxation of effort – we are not so much in control of our own abilities.

To be on top of a hill in dreams – and therefore high up – indicates that we have become aware of our own expanded perception. We have made an effort to achieve something and are able to survey the results of what we have done, to assess the effect on our environment and the people around us. We have achieved those things that we previously thought impossible and are able to undertake further tasks in the light of the knowledge we have attained.

You might also like to consult the entry for Mountain.

HINGE

A hinge initially meant the Axis of the Earth – that which kept everything stable. Any object in dreams that has two parts to it tends to represent the links between the spiritual and physical realms; a hinge particularly symbolizes that link. Neither part works efficiently without the other.

From an emotional perspective a hinge signifies our primary emotions upon which everything hang. A broken hinge in dreams suggests that we are quite literally 'unhinged' – not able to function properly emotionally.

In some ways a hinge has the same significance on a practical level as a hook. In dreams if a hinge is prominent we probably need to look at what the transition stages are between tasks. Too small a hinge on a door, for instance, suggests that planning is defective. A large or ornate hinge would suggest that the actual transition itself is an integral part of the process.

In both men's and women's dreams a hinge can represent a relationship with the opposite sex. The left hand side may represent the feminine and the right the masculine.

Consult the entries for Door and Hook for further clarification.

HIT

☀ Hit initially meant 'to meet with' and it is this meaning that we can apply spiritually. When a revelation occurs or some truth becomes obvious, it can hit with the force of a blow, as in 'it hit me all of a sudden'.

♡ A hit is the application of some force, so to be hit by someone in a dream or to be hitting someone suggests an aggression or emotion that we find difficult to deal with. To be hitting an object suggests frustration and finding an interpretation for the object may be of assistance.

▦ A hit may have the slang meaning of food, drink or drugs giving a false sense of bonhomie, which is short-lived, so in dreams a blow, hit or thump can suggest such a feeling. Phrases that contain hit, such as 'hit the ground running', suggest short, sharp action.

HIVE

☀ The feminine power in Nature is represented by the hive. The symbol of a hollow vessel holding nourishment or sustenance links with Mother Earth.

♡ The old belief that one told one's sorrows to the bees still manifests in dreams today. Any hive may represent the activity that is needed to get ourselves out of a situation.

▦ The hive usually represents an area of work where there is considerable industry and activity going on, and where the best use is made of all possible resources. To dream of being near a hive can represent the effort that is needed to be made to create fertility – or fertile situations – for ourselves. The hive can also represent protective motherhood within the everyday world.

Consult the entry for Bee/Beehive to enhance your understanding of your dream.

HOAX

☀ A hoax is a deliberately created illusion and spiritually suggests that we may be fooling ourselves. An action that we consider to be spiritual may actually be self-centred or negative.

♡ In dreams to become conscious of a hoax suggests that we do not trust our ability to sort out the real from the unreal. If we often find ourselves the butt of practical jokes in waking life our dreams may enable us to deal with this with humour.

▦ In practical terms a hoax is a deliberately engineered set of circumstances, which has no basis in truth. We may dream of such a thing when we are dissatisfied with circumstances in our lives. We may need to make radical changes in order to be true to ourselves.

You might also like to consult the entry for Joke/Joker.

HOG – *see* PIG IN ANIMALS

HOLD – *see* ARMS

HOLE

    ⚙ A round hole traditionally represents the Heavens, a square hole represents the Earth. This symbolism arises from the very simple representations developed to present complex ideas. A hole in the roof of any sacred building, or any hole which allows steam or smoke to escape, is the opening upwards to the celestial world and is the door or gateway to other dimensions.

    ♡ A hole in dreams can very often represent the feminine and the emptiness one feels as one moves towards an understanding of the Self. Without access to the vastness of the heavens – and as central heating, living in flats and in conurbations becomes more commonplace – we tend to feel more and more enclosed and less in touch with the natural order of things.

    ▦ A hole usually represents a difficult or tricky situation. It can also be a place where we may hide, or feel protected in. To dream of falling into a hole indicates that we are perhaps getting in touch with our unconscious feelings, urges and fears. To walk round a hole suggests we may need to get round a tricky situation. We may also need to become aware of the other parts of ourselves that are buried beneath our surface awareness.

    Consult Circle in the Shapes/Patterns, Door, Gate and Hollow for more information.

HOLIDAY

    ⚙ A holiday is literally a holy day – one dedicated to the Divine – so spiritual replenishment, rest and relaxation are all part of such a time.

    ♡ Our need to be independent and to be responsible only for ourselves often comes across in dreams as a holiday. It is time set apart for our own concerns. We may need to heed the warning that we require time off to create space for ourselves and restore our own emotional balance.

    ▦ To be taking a holiday in a dream indicates a sense of relaxation and of taking a break from responsibilities. In theory we do not have to be concerned about ordinary everyday matters.

HOLLOW

    ⚙ Any hollow article tends to represent the feminine. Hollowness can indicate a lack of motivation, particularly on our spiritual journey.

    ♡ Hollowness can come across in a dream in several ways. We can be conscious that we are in a hollow state – reaching an understanding of the Abyss or Void, or of being hollow inside – devoid of emotion. We are in a position where nothing is happening, where we do not feel in control and need to reassert our control of the scope we have been given.

⊞ Dreaming of feeling hollow connects with our feelings of emptiness, lack of purpose and inability to find a direction in our lives. To dream of being in a hollow in a field would indicate that we need some kind of protection from what is going on around us in our ordinary everyday life.

⊡ In a woman's dream hollowness may simply be highlighting her ability to be pregnant. In a man's dream hollowness may signify a sense of inadequacy.

You might also like to consult the entries for Abyss, Empty, Hole, Jar and Vase.

HOLY COMMUNION – *see* RITE/RITUAL AND SPIRITUAL IMAGERY IN THE INTRODUCTION

HOME

⚙ Spiritually, home always represents sanctuary – a place where we can feel safe and be ourselves without fear of reprisal. Literally, in dreams we are inside ourselves and home signifies this spiritual state. Spiritualists and those who believe in an afterlife often speak of death as 'going home', but this should not be seen as a precognitive dream.

♥ Dreaming of a safe environment such as our own home, or sometimes a parental one, suggests that we have the opportunity to integrate learned behaviour with primary personality traits – those qualities with which we are born.

⊞ The human being's primary needs of shelter, warmth and nourishment are initially met (or not) within the home, so a dream about a home on a mundane level suggests a known environment or set of standards – comfortable or otherwise.

To enhance the interpretation of the dream consult the entries for House in Buildings and this section, Parent in Family and Shelter.

HOMOSEXUALITY

⚙ Integration of parts of our personality on an internal level moves us towards spiritual maturity. As this integration takes place we may dream of homosexuality.

♥ Very often, to dream of a homosexual affair is an attempt to learn to love a part of our personality that is not much used in waking life. Often when we come to terms with such a part it will enhance our ability to have successful relationships of any sort. For some people it shows an inherent reluctance to relate fully to the opposite sex either through some trauma or fear.

⊞ Dreaming of having intercourse with somebody of the same sex as oneself often indicates a conflict or anxiety about our own gender roles. We may find ourselves attracted to someone of the same sex in dreams because we are looking for either parental love or a depth of mature love. We may also be looking for love of a different sort – a nurturing rather than sexual love.

◈ In a woman's dream a lesbian affair does not mean the dreamer is gay, simply that she seeks understanding. In a man's dream there may consciously be a degree of homophobia and a fear of his more sensitive side, but it is more likely that he is seeking approval of some sort from his peers.

HONEY/HONEYCOMB

◈ As a healing substance, honey has the power to regenerate. It symbolizes both immortality and rebirth. The honeycomb symbolizes the perfect construction.

◉ Honey is thought by some to impart fertility and virility. To be dreaming of honey would indicate that we are perhaps entering a much more productive time on all levels.

▣ Honey almost inevitably represents pleasure and sweetness. To dream of honey – and particularly eating it – can be to recognize that we are needing to give ourselves pleasure. Equally, it can indicate the essence of our feelings, that we have been through some kind of joyful experience, which can now be assimilated and become part of our everyday existence.

Also consult the entry for Bee/Beehive.

HOOD

◈ The hood represented all things hidden and therefore came to represent death and, by association, invisibility. It would now indicate that certain aspects of spiritual knowledge are held invisible until the time is right.

◉ Traditionally, for a woman to be wearing a hood in dreams suggested that she was keeping her motives hidden and may have been being deceitful. It still largely has this symbolism today. If a man is wearing a hood, it suggests that he is withdrawing his energy from a situation. Equally, in its more advanced sense, the hooded figure of a monk can indicate the more reflective side of us as it begins to become more evident in our everyday lives.

▣ A figure wearing a hood in a dream will always appear to be slightly menacing. While not necessarily being evil, there may be a part of us that has been threatened. The hood can also represent that part of ourselves that, if withdrawn, is creating a problem. An aspect of our personality may be invisible to us and may need to be uncovered in order for us to function in an acceptable fashion.

Consult the entries for Hat in Clothes, Monk and Veil for further information.

HOOK

◈ A hook is anything that grabs us and in the spiritual sense suggests that we can become obsessive about our beliefs. At the same time to become hooked is an opportunity to make a commitment to an idea or principle even though it initially feels insecure.

❤ In childhood dreams the hook can represent the hold that a parent or authority figure has over us. This symbolism can continue into adulthood, depicting the way that we allow people to take control within our lives.

▦ When we dream of a hook we are generally understanding that the power to draw things towards us can be either good or bad according to our disposition. As a visualization following such a dream we can use the image to draw positivity and success towards us. It can equally indicate that we are being 'hooked in' or coerced by someone and thus not being allowed the freedom to which we feel we have a right.

HORIZON

✺ The horizon was once considered to be the edge of the world and in dreams can still have that connotation, though now it is the boundary of the visible physical world. Beyond that is the Abyss or Void.

❤ When a new idea strikes and we become conscious of the narrowness of our viewpoint, we may literally dream of a widening of our horizons. Our perspective changes.

▦ In everyday life when change is the order of the day we will become conscious of changes on the horizon in our dream – perhaps a new building or other object – which may need interpreting, to give us clarity in our prospective actions.

You might also like to consult the entries for Abyss, Globe and World.

HORNS

✺ In a spiritual sense, because horns are associated with the head, they represent intellectual as well as supernatural power. Because they rise above the head, they also symbolize Divinity and the power of the soul. The Horn of Plenty or cornucopia symbolizes gifts from the Gods. The Gate of Horn was a classical concept – dreams that passed through this portal were said to be terrifying but true.

❤ Horns in a dream suggest superiority, either earned or conferred. It is interesting that horns are supposed to bestow the powers of the animal on the wearer. In Pagan times, as well as some tribes today, the donning of horns signifies a particularly senior position within the tribe. Often the wearer is a shaman who, through dreams, can connect with other realms. In Chinese medicine, rhinoceros horn is reputed to be an aphrodisiac. This is possibly because of its association with masculine power. All of these significances, as we become more aware, can appear in dreams.

▦ Horns appearing in dreams hark back to the idea of the animal in the human. The god Pan, who represents sexuality as well as life force, wore horns and will appear in dreams as we become more aware of the power of nature. A musical or hunting horn suggests a call to action or a warning in dreams.

⚎ In both men's and women's dreams a horn can also represent the penis and masculinity. Because it is penetrative, it can also signify the desire to hurt. Protectiveness is also a quality of horns since the male animal will use his horns to protect his territory.

You might also like to consult the entries for Animals, Antlers, Cornucopia, Gate and Shaman.

HORSE – *see* ANIMALS

HORSESHOE

⚎ Spiritually, we can link the horseshoe with a talisman or amulet that protects us and our personal space. The crescent form of the horseshoe links the symbol to pagan Moon goddesses of ancient Europe such as Artemis and Diana, and the protection invoked is that of the goddess herself. The horseshoe is always taken as a lucky symbol and, traditionally, if it is turned upwards it represents the moon and protection from all aspects of evil. When turned downwards, the power is reputed to 'drain out' and therefore be unlucky.

⚎ In ordinary everyday life, symbols that have a long history become fixed in, and used by, our unconscious – often to represent other happier times or times when there has been more happening. Nailing an iron horseshoe to a door is said to repel evil spirits, ghosts and witches, iron being a folkloric specific against such things. It will generally have this significance in dreams; each belief system has developed its own particular myths and stories.

⚎ The horseshoe is also connected as a lucky symbol to weddings. Traditionally, dreaming of a horseshoe indicated there would shortly be a wedding in your family or peer group. Nowadays it is more likely to signify the commitment of a meaningful relationship.

You might also like to consult the entries for Iron, Goddess/Goddesses, Moon and Wedding/Wedding Dress/Wedding Ring.

HOSPITAL

⚎ A healing environment where things can be brought into a state of balance is signified by a hospital. Spiritually it symbolizes a safe environment, where the energy that we need is available to us.

⚎ Dreaming of being in a hospital as a patient may be mentally creating a transition period between something that has not gone well, and an improved attitude where things can get better. To dream of visiting someone in hospital indicates that there is an imbalance or depletion in us, is 'dis-eased' and needs attending to in order to give us clarity.

🔲 Depending on our attitude to hospitals, when one appears in a dream it can either represent a place of safety, or a place where our very being is threatened and we become vulnerable. Taken as a place of healing, it represents that aspect within ourselves that knows when respite is necessary from cares and troubles – when we can allow ourselves to be cared for and nurtured and put back into one piece. If we find hospitals threatening, it may be that we are conscious of the fact that we have to 'let go', to put ourselves at the mercy of others and allow things to happen for us, in order that a situation can be improved.

You might also like to consult the entries for Doctor, Ill/Illness, Nurse/Nursing and Operation.

HOSTAGE

🔆 A hostage is a person held as security. Spiritually, therefore, this has the same connotation as kidnap since it would constitute a crime against the right of the individual. Hostages held for religious reasons in dreams suggest that we are unsure of our own beliefs.

♡ An emotional hostage is that part of us that in dreams recognizes that it has had the ability to think and feel for ourselves taken away, either through trauma or neglect.

🔲 In dreams, to find ourselves taken as hostage suggests that we have put ourselves in the position of being a victim and do not feel that we are able to resist. There may be a higher purpose at stake rather than just our own freedom.

Consult the entries for Abduct, Hijack, Kidnap and Victim for further information.

HOSTILITY

🔆 Spiritual opposition – or rather opposition to our spiritual beliefs – can generate a tremendous amount of hostility. We need to be aware that others may not necessarily agree with our beliefs.

♡ When we experience hostility within ourselves in a dream, it is often an accurate expression of an emotion we consciously have. It is simply safe to express it in a dream, whereas we may not dare do this in waking life. Hostility is one of those emotions that can be worked through within a dream itself.

🔲 If we can identify what is making us feel hostile in a dream, then we can usually draw a parallel in our waking lives and deal with whatever the problem is. If the feeling is appropriate in a particular situation, and we can justify it, then we can handle it in a conscious state without confrontation. If, however, someone is being hostile towards us, it very often means that we need to be aware that we are not acting appropriately, that others may feel we are putting them in danger.

Consulting the entries for Anger, Argue/Arguments, Conflict and War should help with clarification.

HOT

🌞 Spiritual passion is a deeply held feeling. It can be experienced in a dream as a feeling of warmth and can symbolize unconditional love. We can afford to move positively in search of this heat.

💗 Psychologically, feelings of cheerfulness and hopefulness can create an awareness of warmth and can be interchangeable. Occasionally, extreme emotion can be interpreted as a physical feeling – so anger, jealousy or other such feelings can be experienced as heat. Encountering something as hot which should be cold – for example, ice – indicates that we are perhaps having difficulty and experiencing confusion in sorting out our feelings.

▦ Pleasurable feelings can be translated in dreams to a physical feeling of heat or warmth. To dream of being hot indicates warm – or perhaps passionate – feelings. To be conscious of the fact that our surroundings are hot indicates that we are loved and cared for.

Consult the entries for Emotions and Ice/Icebergs/Icicles for further clarification.

HOTEL – *see* BUILDINGS

HOURGLASS

🌞 The hourglass measures time and is a spiritual symbol for the length of our physical lives. In former times, the hourglass was frequently taken as a symbol of death. More properly it is now seen as a measurement of the passage of life.

💗 When we are particularly under stress, we can be overly aware of the running out of time; that it can become an enemy. This is often symbolized in dreams as an hourglass. It is probably from the hourglass that we get the word deadline; when the sand runs out the energy has gone.

▦ In dreams, time is irrelevant. To experience something that measures time is often to alert us to the need for measuring our thoughts and activities. When such a symbol is old-fashioned – as in an hourglass – our perception of time and its management may be old-fashioned. We need to use different, and more precise, ways of measuring those activities.

You might also like to consult the entries for Sand and Time.

HOUSE

🌞 The house is popularly known as the seat of the soul, and in spiritual terms links us to the way we are in the world. A house represents security and safety, and therefore signifies protection and the Great Mother.

💗 In psychological terms, the house also signifies the life we live, the protections we create and the 'structure' we present to other people.

▣ In dreams, the different rooms and parts of houses represent the various aspects of our personality and life experiences. There are several interpretations and given below is one such set:

Attic – dreaming of being in an attic is to do with past experiences and old memories. Interestingly, it can also highlight family patterns of behaviour and attitudes that have been handed down.

Basement/cellar – the cellar most often represents the subconscious and those things we may have suppressed through an inability to handle them. A basement can also highlight the power that is available to us provided we are willing to make use of it. Often associated with self-image and self-confidence, we may not have come to terms with our own charisma and personal power and prefer to keep it hidden.

Bathroom – in dreams our attitude to personal cleanliness and our most private thoughts and actions can be shown as the bathroom or toilet. It is the place where we can let go of our negativity in safety.

Bedroom – the bedroom portrays a place of safety where we can relax and be as sensual as we wish.

Chimney – as a passage from one state to another and a conductor of heat, in dreams the chimney can indicate how we deal with our inner emotions and warmth.

Hall – the hallway in a dream is illustrative of how we meet and relate to other people.

Library – our minds, and how we store the information we receive, can appear as a library.

Also consult the entries for Chimney, Home, House in Buildings and Toilet.

HUNGER

✹ Hunger in the spiritual sense is a yearning to be filled with spiritual awareness. In dreams this can be experienced as an actual physical feeling of hunger.

♡ Emotionally when we are tired or upset we have the need to be comforted and cherished. There is something lacking and the dreaming mind can translate this into hunger.

▣ From a completely practical perspective, if we go to bed hungry our dreams are likely to reflect this fact and register that we need food or sustenance.

Consult the entries for Emotions, Food and Yearn for clarification.

HUNT/HUNTING/HUNTSMAN

✹ An extremely old symbolism of the hunter or huntsman is linked with death, particularly a death containing an aspect of ritual killing or sacrifice.

This 'making sacred' and an understanding of the process of ritualized killing is part of the spiritual journey.

⊘ To dream of being a huntsman alerts us to the part of ourselves that can be destructive and vicious. To dream that we are hunting, denotes that we are seeking or pursuing some inner desire, either emotional or physical. We may be looking for a solution to a problem.

▦ Dreaming of being hunted is mostly taken to be to do with our sexuality. To dream of a hunt is to register the necessity for a change of state in everyday life. To be hunting a boar, for instance, could have two interpretations: firstly, to eradicate the boring parts of our lives, and secondly, to root out the uncouth part of our personality. Other animals will have their own symbolism.

⊟ In a man's dream the hunter pursuing his quarry is an image drawn from chivalrous times and epitomizes his struggle for his lady's favour. In a woman's dream she will become the hunted one.

You might also like to consult the entries for Animals, Chase/Chased, Kill and Sacrifices.

HURRICANE – *see* WIND

HUSBAND – *see* FAMILY

HYENA – *see* ANIMALS

HYMN – *see* MUSIC/RHYTHM AND SING

HYPODERMIC – *see* SYRINGE

HYSTERICS

❈ From a spiritual perspective hysterics signifies the loss of control that can occur when the link to innate wisdom is lost and there is an overemotional reaction.

⊘ In dreams emotions can become exaggerated and a hysterical response suggests that we need to consider very carefully what has thrown us so comprehensively off-balance. Often we can express in dreams what we dare not in waking life. While disturbing, such a dream scenario can lead to healing.

▦ When a dream figure appears to be hysterical, we need to identify a situation in everyday life where loss of control, either our own or others', will be detrimental. Since hysterical energy can be highly destructive we may need also to decide what needs to be deconstructed and rebuilt without the highly emotional charge.

You might also like to consult the entry for Emotions.

IBIS – *see* **BIRDS**

ICE/ICEBERG/ICICLES

🌞 Spiritually, ice symbolizes a part of ourselves that has become frozen and needs to thaw out before we can progress. Ice cream is an image which can be used to signify impermanence. We need to decide if we wish to go for the transitory or permanent. Spiritual isolation – that is, existing in isolation because of the way our lives have gone – can be symbolized by icicles.

💙 Ice is also a representation of rigidity, of the brittleness that comes from not understanding what is going on around us, of creating circumstances where people cannot get – or be – in touch with us. Depending on how the ice appears in a dream, it can indicate a state of impermanence. To see icicles melting indicates that the troubles that have been around us will literally disappear within a short space of time. Whether the fault is our own or other people's, it would appear that outside circumstances give the ability to overcome whatever has been troubling us.

▦ When we dream of ice we are usually looking at the emotions. We are aware that perhaps we are colder than we should be, shutting off any display of warmth and compassion. We are thereby enclosing ourselves in a situation from which it may be difficult to free ourselves. Often in dreams icicles can appear to hang in a certain fashion – it is the pattern that is important as much as the icicle itself. We may be aware that we are having problems with our environment and that it is not supporting it in a way we would expect – thereby creating difficulties.

You might also like to consult the entries for Thaw, Water and Winter.

ICON

🌞 The icon is a small spiritual picture, which symbolizes a greater whole. In dreams it can often represent the threefold aspects of being: body, mind and spirit. For this reason an image received in dreams can often be used as a focus in the use of magic.

💙 Usually icons are representations of a belief system and, therefore, portray the way we feel about a number of other issues. In a dream, when an icon appears to have a religious picture but in actual fact it contains pictures of our own family, it indicates the ability to idolize the family. Modern day celebrities are often thought of as icons, people who are to be respected for their positions, perhaps with a power they do not have.

▣ Dreaming of any religious symbol usually indicates our very deep connection with old ideas and principles. The icon usually symbolizes the microcosm within the macrocosm – that is, the small world reflecting the larger world. The human being often needs something tangible to represent what is simply a principle or a concept, and the icon performs this purpose. The now popular icon in computer use signifies the gateway to an idea and in dreams suggests that a concept can be expanded.

Also consult the entries for Celebrity and Magic/Magician as well as the information on Spiritual Imagery in the Introduction.

IDOL – *see* **RELIGIOUS IMAGERY IN THE INTRODUCTION**

IGLOO

☀ The feminine principle, in the sense of sheltering and nurturing, is depicted by the igloo.

♥ The igloo is interesting as a symbol in dreams. It can equally represent a cold exterior containing a very warm interior, or the coldness of the construction itself. It can appear as though someone is uncaring and, therefore, creating an unloving home environment, although in fact there is warmth within that person.

▣ In mundane terms the igloo can represent our own construction, the way in which we fashion our environment in order to work, or rather operate, most effectively.

⊞ The igloo can often represent the feminine and the womb in dreams. Sometimes, in a woman's dream, it represents frigidity, but at other times the ability of a woman to relax and be herself once her barriers have been overcome. In a man's dream it may represent his own domain or space.

You might also like to consult the entries for Buildings and Ice/Iceberg/Icicles.

IGNITE/IGNITION

☀ The symbol of igniting a light or fire represents the beginning of an exploration of the Spiritual realms. Kundalini – the energy of consciousness or spiritual energy – is perceived as heat at the base of the spine, which may be intensely hot or pleasantly warm. Dreams often picture a spontaneous awakening when the energy, having been ignited, travels up the spine to the top of the head, bringing certain awarenesses along the way.

♥ When the ignition on a car will not fire properly we have not been able to provide the emotional 'spark' that allows us to begin a journey or task. When a huge conflagration, such as a forest fire, is ignited in dreams it symbolizes passion. When we are reigniting a fire we must return to and perhaps adjust our original ideas.

▦ More mundanely, dreaming of igniting or lighting a fire suggests that an initial surge of energy or power is needed to start a project or task. In this case what we use to begin the burning will be important. A match might suggest less effort than a firebrand, for instance.

Consult the entries for Car, Fire, Light and Spark for further clarification.

ILL/ILLNESS

✸ Lack of spiritual clarity can often be experienced in dreams as illness. We are not putting ourselves in touch with a force that can help us to overcome difficulties.

♥ Often when we are ill in a dream we are grappling with part of our personality. Part of us is out of balance and perhaps needs to be dealt with. Often the dream will give the method of dealing with it – perhaps by taking medication, having surgery or a combination of both. Illness also often represents our fears of not being looked after properly, our need to be allowed to heal properly.

▦ Whatever life has to offer, we may be left with painful memories, feelings of anger and difficulties. In a dream these memories and feelings can surface as illness. Most of the time, such a dream image gives us information as to how we should deal with the difficulty. Illness that has manifested on a physical level can trigger vivid or frightening dreams.

You might also like to consult the entries for Doctor and Hospital.

ILLUMINATE/ILLUMINATION – *see* LIGHT

IMITATE/IMITATION

✸ Spiritually this is a representation of the microcosm of the macrocosm, the small imitating the large.

♥ If we are imitating someone else we are usually conscious that we have the ability to be as they are. To be imitating one's superiors is to recognize their greater knowledge. To be mimicking someone may show that we doubt our own integrity.

▦ To dream of being imitated is ambivalent. It can mean that we are aware that what we have done is the correct thing and that other people can learn from our example. It can equally mean that other people are perceiving us as being leaders.

IMMERSION

✸ Transformation and rebirth can only be accomplished by a total immersion in spirituality, which is where the symbolism of total immersion in baptism came from, as well as that of being washed clean.

♥ To dream of being totally immersed in water generally indicates the way we handle our own emotions, that we are attempting to find the more innocent part of ourselves that does not need to be affected by external circumstances.

🔳 To be totally immersed – totally focused – on something in a dream indicates we need to be able to concentrate entirely on one particular thought or idea to help us understand ourselves We are attempting to clarify situations and to cleanse ourselves, perhaps of ideas and attitudes that have been suggested to us by other people.

You might also like to consult the entries for Baptism and Water.

IMMIGRANT – *see* REFUGEE

IMMOBILITY

🔆 Immobility in the spiritual sense is dynamic stillness. It is The Unconditioned State, or the Self, liberated from the physical. In Sanskrit this is known as *pratyahara* – withdrawal from the external world into the interior self.

💠 To be immobilized in a dream usually indicates that we have created circumstances around us which are now beginning to trap us. Often such a dream comes when we are facing the darker side of ourselves – that which could be called evil. A superhuman effort needs to be made to overcome what is holding us down.

🔳 Immobility in a dream can be extremely frightening. A feeling of oppression and of not being able to move usually indicates that we need to sit still and be immobile within our ordinary everyday lives. We need to achieve a kind of stillness which is foreign to most people, and therefore initially frightening, while later on it can be a state of peace and tranquility.

Also consult the entry for Paralysis.

IMP

🔆 The Devil as the Tempter can appear in dreams as an imp, or as a manifestation of a particularly irritating type.

💠 The imp can represent the uncontrolled negative part of ourselves, that part that instinctively creates chaos and takes great joy in doing so. It is perhaps an aspect of loss of control.

🔳 An imp appearing in a dream usually foretells disorder and difficulty. The imp often has the same significance as the Devil in its aspect of tormenting us, of creating difficulty and harm within our life.

Also consult the entries for Demon, Devil and Fiend.

IMPRISONED

🔆 Imprisonment can suggest that we are spiritually too introverted or self-involved. We need to 'open ourselves up' to new influences. We may need assistance in doing this – and have to look to an outside influence to release us.

♥ When we experience imprisonment in a dream, we are usually becoming conscious of old attitudes and beliefs, which are imprisoning us.

▣ Being or feeling imprisoned in a dream often means that we are trapped by circumstances, often those we have created through our own fear or ignorance. We feel that other people are creating circumstances around us which will not allow us to move forward. We will often need to negotiate our freedom.

Consult the entries for Jailer and Prison for further information.

INAUGURATION – *see* **INITIATION**

INCA – *see* **INDIGENOUS PEOPLES**

INCENSE

☼ Spiritually, incense is used as a vehicle for prayer and as a symbol for the subtle body or soul. In dreams we can become aware of our need to use spiritual symbolism in our work. When we begin to appreciate the use of incense as part of our daily routine we will often intuitively know through dreams what is appropriate for our purpose.

♥ Incense is used in order to raise consciousness, or to cleanse atmospheres and sacred spaces. In dreams, when we become aware of it being used in this way, we need to consider how best to improve ourselves or our environment.

▣ Physically, incense is designed to perfume a room. In dreams, it is possible to be aware of the smell of incense, particularly if it has associations for the dreamer. For instance, it may hold childhood memories of church or religious buildings.

Also consult the entries for Odour and Smell as well as the information on Spiritual Imagery in the Introduction.

INCEST

☼ In legend and myth, incest among the gods and goddesses was an attempt to maintain the purity of the energy. Spiritually, therefore, when we dream of incest we are attempting to purify or keep clear our own power.

♥ Since self-image and sexuality are so closely connected, incest in dreams is much more likely to be an effort to sort out our feelings about ourselves than anything else. Dreaming of incest with brothers or sisters may symbolize an attempt to unify the masculine and feminine aspects within us. We are attempting to make a link with the part of our own personality most closely reflected by that person. We can only do this within the safety of a dream.

▣ Incest is such a taboo subject that to dream of it seldom actually refers to the physical act. It usually represents the need and desire we have to be in control, either of ourselves or of our relationships within the family. It is possible that incest in dreams occurs because the child has not yet been allowed, or had the opportunity to sort out, his or her feelings so far as the family are concerned.

⊞ Dreams of incest with a parent for both men and women may be an attempt to sort out, understand and ultimately be free of the early dependent relationship with that parent.

Also consult the entry for Sex/Sexual Images.

INCOME

�か Our income represents reward for our efforts in relating to the world in which we live. Spiritually, this reward will not just be monetary. It will include feedback and a sense of satisfaction.

🜂 Dreaming of receiving a private income – such as a trust fund – suggests we perhaps need to look at our relationships with other people. We are aware of what people have to offer us, and also what we have to do in order to be rewarded for our efforts.

▦ Any dream connected with the income we earn – an important part of our support structure – will highlight our attitude towards our wants and needs. To dream of an increased income shows we feel we have overcome an obstacle in ourselves and can accept that we have value. A drop in income signifies our neediness, and perhaps our attitude to poverty.

You might also like to consult the entries for Money and Wages for more information.

INCUBATE/INCUBATOR

�か Incubation implies bringing something into existence, or rather to a point where it can survive without assistance. Spiritually, therefore, this represents the act of creation.

🜂 An incubator supports life that might not be viable otherwise, so from an emotional perspective will represent a new emotion which needs careful nurturing, such as love for someone else.

▦ In everyday terms, when we are incubating a new idea or project we may find that our dreams include just such an image.

⊞ As a woman becomes used to becoming pregnant she may have dreams that hold an image such as an incubator. This does not suggest that her baby will be ill, simply that she is aware of herself in that role as the baby grows.

Consult the entry for Baby in People for further clarification.

INCUBUS – *see* DEMON AND DEVIL

INDIGENOUS PEOPLES

�か Indigenous people might be defined as those who belong to a particular area of the Earth and have over many centuries developed their own spiritual practices in order to ensure survival. These practices often resonate in dreams.

◈ Since everybody has their own view of indigenous people, inevitably dreams will be coloured by our conscious awareness. However, as our knowledge of cultures and customs becomes greater the appearance of indigenous people in dreams take on different shades of meaning. Below are a few possible interpretations:

Aborigine – dreams are the soul's journey to another world, where we can enlist the help of spirits and animals. The aboriginal can represent intuitive wisdom, because they experience their dreamtime as the past, present and future co-existing – known as 'all-at-one' time.

African – Africa is now thought to be where the human race began, so dreams of Africa and the Africans may refer to our own personal origins.

Aztec – because of the Aztecs' emphasis on warfare, the warrior class was highly valued, and often warriors would volunteer for the most important sacrificial rituals. These were needed because they believed the gods had sacrificed themselves for mankind, that their blood had given Man life, and that the Sun was nourished with the blood of human hearts. In dreams, such a figure may signify supreme personal sacrifice.

Chinese – traditionally Chinese people often followed a combination of religious beliefs, including Confucianism, Taoism and Buddhism. Practices such as ancestor worship and meditation, together with the worship of gods and magical rituals, still take place and in dreams, as our knowledge increases, can give rich imagery.

Inca – politics and religion are forever intertwined and the gods are worshipped as forces of nature. The Sun God is recognized as the supreme civil ruler, so in dreams the figure of an Incan suggests a system where social responsibility is paramount.

Inuit – the Inuit traditionally believed in a god-like power that is contained in all of Nature. The Shaman is an important figure in their belief structure, being able to converse with the spirits. In dreams, the Inuit reflect the harshness of life lived as hunters close to Nature.

Japanese – many Japanese follow the Shinto religion where tradition and the family, love of nature, physical cleanliness, and *Matsuri* – the worship and honour given to the *Kami* (gods) and ancestral spirits – are important. The oriental woman often appears in dreams as the epitome of feminine, gentle qualities.

Maori – three important parts of Maori religion are what they call the life force, spirit (*Wairua*) that can be found in all people and spiritual power or prestige. This means that ancestor worship is important. The Maori stress the importance of growth and change, of working closely with nature, and will signify this in dreams.

Maya – many Mayans today believe, as the original Mayans did, in the influence of the Cosmos and the need to pay homage to the gods through rituals of many types. It is this element of ritual that will often surface in dreams today.

Native American – the Sun Dance amongst the Plains Native Americans is perceived as a replay of the original Creation. Their religion is Shamanic and as more people become aware of their culture and practices, dreams will reflect the richness of their beliefs and their closeness to nature. Ceremonies such as the sweat lodge give rise to much imagery.

▦ Becoming aware of other cultures and religious practices has the effect of opening our perception to what Jung called the Collective Unconscious, a library available to all of us. From a mundane perspective, the imagery available to us then becomes useful in remaining close to natural activity and living life mindfully.

Also consult the entry for Shaman for further clarification.

INFECTION

❂ In spiritual development, and particularly when dealing with outside influences, we can become contaminated – or infected – by ideology and spurious beliefs. We need to be aware of the possibility that we can be 'taken over' by wrong thought and negativity.

◉ When we are made uncomfortable by external circumstances in waking life, this may appear as an infection in a dream.

▦ Dreaming of having an infection suggests that there is the possibility of us having internalized negative attitudes from other people. Depending on where in the body the infection appears, there is information as to the type of 'infection'. For example, an infection in the leg may indicate that we feel we are being prevented from moving forward quickly enough in waking life.

Consult the entries for Injure/Injury and Wound for further information.

INFINITY

❂ The closest representation to infinity that can be experienced spiritually is the Abyss or Void. In dreams as we progress spiritually we can have a sense of limitlessness.

◉ For most people, infinity is beyond understanding, so when in dreams we have no sense of boundaries or a realization that we are not separate from anything else, this is a sense of infinity.

In dreams, the concept of infinity can make us feel very small and insignificant and occasionally without meaning. Conversely, it can make us appreciate how powerful we really are.

Also consult the entries for Abyss and Void.

INHERITANCE

To dream of an inheritance suggests that spiritually we have at our disposal all the knowledge and cultural input that our ancestors have accrued. This includes cultural family and religious knowledge.

Emotionally, our inheritance consists of the influences from the past from members of our family as to how we think and feel. Unless we understand those influences we cannot break free of them.

Dreaming of an inheritance suggests that we have been bequeathed something of value, not necessarily monetary. It will be much more to do with strong character traits and perhaps ways of tackling problems.

INITIATION

Initiation is a rite of passage ceremony marking entrance or acceptance into a group or society. An initiation or inauguration ceremony in a spiritual sense can mark a new beginning, the taking of new spirituality, perhaps Cosmic Responsibility.

Often a ceremony is necessary to mark the fact that we have succeeded in one thing and can now move on, putting that knowledge to the test in the outside world. To be dreaming of such a ceremony indicates that we can be pleased with ourselves and what we have achieved, that we have literally inaugurated a different way of being, and can now move forward into the future.

We have many opportunities to make new beginnings, and initiation – in that it indicates a change of status – is one such symbol. This may be important to us in terms of either personal growth or within the work situation. To dream that we are being given such an honour means we can receive acclaim for something that we have done, for our ability to make the transition from the lesser to the greater.

Rites of passage often require a formal acknowledgement and this may well be reflected in dreams. By tradition, initiation for men is more overt and physical, whilst for women it is more intuitive.

INJECT/INJECTION

Spiritually, to find ourselves accepting an injection indicates that we are prepared to create circumstances within ourselves which will help us to progress. More negatively, an injection can indicate short-term pleasure rather than long-term gain.

♥ An injection may be an attempt to heal, or to make us better. We may feel that we need external help in order to function more successfully. It will depend on our attitude to conventional medicine whether this is seen as co-operation or resistance.

▦ To dream of being given an injection is to be feeling that our personal space has been penetrated. Other people's opinions, needs or desires may be forced on us leaving little option but to co-operate. To dream of giving an injection suggests that we are attempting to force ourselves on other people.

❋ Obviously, because an injection is penetrative by nature, such a dream for both men and women may have sexual connotations.

You might also like to consult the entries for Needle and Syringe.

INJURE/INJURY

❀ Spiritually, an injury or scar may suggest that something negative and harmful has occurred, which is an external force rather than internal. We may not have dealt with it as well as we might.

♥ It will often be significant which area of the body is harmed in the dream. The nervous system can develop ways of giving information without us being conscious of it. This may give some indication of the area of life that is affected by the trauma. To have an arm broken, for instance, might suggest that our ability to hold on is compromised. If we see someone else who has been hurt or scarred we have probably been the ones who have hurt others in the past. If this is so, there are various techniques we can use in the waking state to help us release others from the hurt we have inflicted. The healing that subsequently takes place may then be recorded in further dreams by the loss of the scar.

▦ An injury will suggest a recent hurt, whereas a scar in a dream suggests that there are old hurts, which have not been fully dealt with. These may be mental and emotional as much as physical, and can remain unnoticed until we are reminded of them. Just as in physical injury there can be many kinds of scars, so there can also be in the other areas. We may, for instance, be left with a pattern of behaviour which is irritating to other people, but without the clear connection given by the dream image, we are unable to understand it.

INK

❀ Ink has significance, particularly in magical practices, when it is used to reflect powers that are outside the norm. In written magical spells it is often important to use particular inks in order to achieve the required results. Spiritually this creates the correct vibration and this concept often surfaces in dreams.

♥ On a more intellectual level, ink signifies the ability to transcribe and understand knowledge in a more sophisticated way. When a particular flow of energy or information is needed, ink can symbolize that flow.

▥ Since very few people now use fountain pens, the significance of ink on a physical level is no longer quite so valid. As a child, learning the art of handwriting could be difficult and pen and ink thus became 'instruments of torture' and can often appear as such in difficult dreams in later life. Formerly in dreams, ink also suggested the ability to communicate in a lucid fashion. *The entries for Paper/Parchment, Pen and Writing will help with further clarification.*

INQUEST

🌣 An inquest in dreams from a spiritual perspective is an attempt to understand something that is, for the time being, incomprehensible.

♥ Emotionally in dreams an inquest may signify the need to study events and feelings so that we understand our own reactions.

▥ Sometimes in everyday life we fall short of what we expect of ourselves or others. Dreaming of an inquest – a proper inquiry – will help us to work out what we must do. It is as though we need someone in authority to sort us out. *You might like to consult the entries for Death, Law and Authority Figures in People.*

INSANE – *see* MAD

INSCRIPTION

🌣 The image of an inscription often appears in dreams as we reach a certain stage of spiritual development, almost like a message from beyond. Spiritually, this usually indicates the type of knowledge that needs to be recorded and can be passed onto other people.

♥ In dreams, an inscription appearing on, for instance, a rock would suggest old knowledge or wisdom. An inscription appearing in sand would suggest that the knowledge is either impermanent, or must be learnt quickly.

▥ Any inscription in a dream is information that needs to be understood and internalized. Reading an inscription can suggest that something is understood in some way already, whereas not being able to read it suggests that more information or knowledge is required in order to complete a task. *Also consult the entries for Ink, Paper/Parchment, Stone and Writing.*

INSECTS

🌣 Psychically, insects can appear in dreams as some kind of threat. This is one reason why they are often used in psychological thrillers and science fiction. Some form of spiritual 'infection' may have taken place. Fleas are symbolic of the type of disruption that is likely to hurt, rather than destroy, such as gossip. A mantis represents deviousness, particularly of a spiritual kind. It is that Trickster part of us that can create problems when things are effectively working out for us; it is that aspect of our personality which perhaps preys on the other parts and will not take its place within our overall integration. More positively, insects such as ants can appear in dreams as reminders of instinctive behaviour.

◈ Insects tend to signify negative feelings and link us to primal instinctive behaviour, that of survival against all odds. In dreams, we often translate a quality or a situation we are struggling with into an object such as an insect; psychologically, insects can represent feelings we would rather do without. This could be something niggling at our consciences, or guilt. We may additionally be aware that we are not being treated properly and that people who should be our friends are not being fair. To be aware of a predatory insect such as a mantis may indicate that we are conscious of trickery around us. Whatever threatens us does so on a very basic level, and we may have no defences, except those of our own nature.

▦ Insects in dreams can reflect the feeling that something is irritating or bugging us. They may also indicate our feelings of insignificance and powerlessness and it will depend on the particular insect in the dream as to the interpretation. Thus, a wasp might indicate danger, whereas a beetle could mean either dirt or protection. Fleas are an irritation; there may be people or situations in our lives that are causing us difficulty, or that we feel are being parasites, and we need to go through a process of decontamination in order to be free. Flies are always associated with something nasty, which does not allow for the fact that they also devour rotten material, and thus are cleansing. So to dream of flies is to be aware that we have certain negative aspects of our lives that need dealing with. To dream of a swarm of flies indicates the deliberate intention of a large group of individuals. Where one insect may appear to be moving aimlessly, large numbers do not. Often we can only succeed in changing matters by group behaviour. As with most insects, the mantis often represents something devious within our lives.

INSIDE (IN)

◈ Spiritually, inside may have connotations of protectiveness and of a degree of introversion. Being inside suggests the need for some spiritual awareness, of being permitted to enter an inner sanctum.

◈ Being shut in suggests that we are emotionally restricted and may feel we cannot express ourselves properly. Going into a building in dreams, for example, suggests we should explore the structure of our lives.

⬛ In dreams, exploring the inside of something as opposed to the outside suggests that we need to explore motivation in some way. Being stuck inside suggests we are aware of circumstances around us that are preventing us from moving forward. This may, of course, be due to our own attitudes.

INSERT

☀ To be inserting an object into a space or area is trying to ensure that it, or whatever it represents, is drawn to our attention and given relevance in a spiritual sense.

♡ Dreaming of an insert in a paper or making an insertion in a document signifies that there is an idea or concept that we must include in our considerations.

⬛ With relevance to working life, making an insertion suggests that we are wishing to influence an outcome. For someone else to be doing so suggests that there is an influence we have not considered.

⬚ In both men's and women's dreams, insertion frequently has the same connotation as penetration, albeit from their different perspectives.

Consult the entry for Penetration for further clarification.

INSTALMENT

☀ Spiritually, when we recognize that something – payments perhaps, or information – is occurring in instalments we must understand that what is represented must happen, or occur to us, gradually. Perhaps we need to learn in bite-sized chunks.

♡ In dreaming of instalments, from an emotional perspective we must accept that there is a degree of conditional acceptance, either in ourselves or others. We may not be ready to make a full commitment.

⬛ To install something is to put it into position. A new programme on a computer in dreams would, for instance, mean accepting a new way of working. A new instalment of a story suggests a different phase in a project.

INSTRUMENTS – *see* MUSIC/RHYTHM, MUSICAL INSTRUMENTS AND SURGERY/SURGICAL INSTRUMENTS

INSULATE – *see* WADDING

INSURE/INSURANCE

☀ Spiritual insurance is a sure and certain knowledge that we are protected from harm. We may also be trying to protect ourselves against trauma.

♡ When we feel emotionally secure and safe against any loss we may dream of insurances or of trying to take out insurance. While to insure our possessions against loss and theft is natural in everyday life, to dream of doing so probably means that on some level we feel insecure.

▨ On a mundane level, insurance is trying to mitigate against possible loss in the future. It will often have this meaning in dreams, though the loss we are protecting ourselves against need not be financial.

You might also like to consult the entry for Lose/Loss/Lost.

INTERMEDIARY

❀ An intermediary is someone who can plead our case or relay information. In spiritual terms this might be represented by a religious teacher or a medium (spiritual channeller). As we try to achieve a balance between the demands of the spiritual and physical realms, an intermediary such as an angelic figure may appear in dreams.

❤ When emotions run high we need someone who can 'filter' our energy to the point where it becomes manageable. Dreaming of an argument or conflict where an intermediary is present allows us to regain control and listen to reason.

▨ In working life an intermediary performs the function of a negotiator. In dreams dealing with mundane matters, when two points of view need to be balanced, such a figure may appear.

You might like to consult the entries for Angel, Argue/Argument and Conflict for further clarification.

INTERNET – *see* COMMUNICATION AND WEB

INTERSECTION

❀ When we meet an intersection in dreams, for instance two roads or paths crossing or meeting, we are having to make choices which may have a greater impact on others than they do on us.

❤ If we are conscious of an intersection – perhaps in a pattern that appears in a dream – we are being offered choices, and perhaps have to differentiate between right and wrong.

▨ An intersection that appears in a dream – such as a T-junction – indicates there is a choice of two ways forward. Two opposites may be coming together in our waking lives, and we are able to make changes and move forward in a more focused way.

You might also like to consult the entries for Crossroads, Path and Road in Journey for further clarification.

INTERVIEW

❀ An interview in the spiritual sense suggests some test of worthiness for a task, particularly one that is for the Greater Good or has spiritual overtones.

❤ There is always a fear that we may be found wanting, so in dreams an interview may be seen as testing our belief in ourselves.

🔲 Dreaming of an interview suggests we may be questioning whether the work we do is satisfying us and giving us the feedback we need.

📑 In a woman's dream, if she is being interviewed by a panel of men, she may be confronting aspects of her own drive and tenacity. In a man's dream, if his interviewers are feminine he is coming to terms with his sensitivities and softer skills. Women being interviewed by women, and men by men, suggests that they are being judged by their peers.

INTESTINES – *see* ABDOMEN AND EXCREMENT IN BODY

INTOXICATION – *see* ALCOHOL/ALCOHOLIC, DRUGS AND DRUNK

INTRUDER

☼ Spiritually it is possible to put ourselves in danger of being open to desecration. The Self is a sacred space, but until we understand that it is inviolable, we can be open to challenge. The appearance of an intruder in dreams can indicate this.

♥ To dream of an intruder has an obvious connection with sex and threats to one's sexuality. The intruder is also that part of ourselves that does not handle our fears and doubts properly, but makes us feel insecure. In dreams, this figure needs to be challenged.

🔲 As human beings, we are very conscious of our own personal space. Dreaming of an intruder or prowler indicates that we are feeling threatened in some way.

📑 Particularly in women's dreams, the intruder is often masculine, indicating a need to defend ourselves. In a man's dream an intruder is more representative of his unruly side.

Also consult the entries for Burglar and People.

INVADE/INVASION

☼ An invasion in spiritual terms is a desecration of our own spiritual space, that part of us that we hold sacred and normally free from harm. When rendered insecure by too many demands, we can feel invaded and under attack.

♥ When we are ourselves invading somewhere in a dream, this presupposes that a degree of force is necessary, particularly on an emotional level. Normally an invasion suggests that there are many aspects involved, which could be feelings, needs or ideas.

🔲 To invade is to plan an organized movement or takeover and this can have relevance in dreams of a business environment. An invasion suggests a concerted movement against us or, if we are one of the invaders, against a weaker opponent.

📑 Dreams of an invading force in a woman's dream suggest a violation of her personal space. In a man's dream he is perhaps more likely to dream of himself as the invader, particularly if he is aware of his partner's sensitivities, whatever their gender.

Consult the entries for Armed Forces and Force for further clarification.

INVENT/INVENTOR

⚜ The inventor in us is the part that takes spiritual responsibility for our progress. He often signifies our ability to 'create' new ways of being, but needs assistance from us on a conscious level.

♥ When we dream of an inventor, psychologically we are linking with that side of ourselves that is wiser but at the same time perhaps more introverted than our waking selves. We can give ourselves permission to be creative.

▦ Dreaming of an inventor or a professor type links us with the more creative sides of ourselves. Usually this is more the thinker rather than the doer; someone who is capable of taking an idea and making it tangible.

You might also like to consult the entry for Laboratory.

INVEST – *see* MONEY AND WEALTH

INVESTIGATE/INVESTIGATION

⚜ An investigation in the spiritual sense suggests that concepts, precepts and beliefs need to be very carefully looked at.

♥ Many people do not like to look too closely at their own emotions, but to be investigating a building, for instance, can suggest that we are trying to understand ourselves and our own reactions.

▦ When we are unsure of our own position within a work hierarchy or family structure we may dream of an investigation in order to feel comfortable. If we are being investigated in dreams we may feel we have not fulfilled a task to our own satisfaction. Such a dream may also suggest that we are being too closely monitored for our own liking.

You might also like to consult the entry for Question.

INVISIBLE

⚜ Spiritually, the Invisible is God Unmanifest, that is, prior to Creation. Also known as the Absolute, it is invisible because it is not experienced or comprehended by any of the five conscious senses.

♥ When we are conscious that something is invisible in a dream, it indicates that we simply need to be aware of the image's presence, without necessarily having to interpret it immediately.

▦ Actually becoming invisible in a dream – disappearing – would indicate either that we are not ready to face the knowledge that understanding would bring us, or that there is something we would rather forget.

⊡ Sometimes a figure (either a man or woman), though seeming to be invisible, can represent the Shadow. In both men's and women's dreams it will have the same gender as the dreamer.

Also consult the information on the Shadow in Archetypes in the Introduction.

IRIS – *see* EYE AND FLOWERS

IRON

🔆 Iron usually symbolizes power. In a dream it can signify the part of ourselves that is capable of discipline – an iron will. However, before being tempered by fire (life's challenges) and made into hard steel, iron requires protecting against corrosion. It is this quality of the development of protection against spiritual 'corrosion' (eating away) that needs to be dealt with so we can progress.

♡ When we dream of using a clothes iron we are attempting to make ourselves more presentable to the outside world. We may also be trying to 'smooth things over'.

▦ When the metal iron appears in dreams, it usually represents our strengths and determination. It can also signify the rigidity of our emotions or beliefs. We should consider being more flexible.

You might also like to consult the entry for Metal.

IRRITATION – *see* ANGER, INFECTION AND INSECTS

ISLAND

🔆 In dreams an island can signify a spiritual retreat – somewhere which is cut off from the world – which will allow us to contemplate our own spiritual Self.

♡ Occasionally we all need to recharge our batteries, and to dream of an island can help, or warn us, to do this. Dreaming of a desert or treasure island indicates there is something to be gained by being alone and exploring our ability to cope with such a situation. We may actually function better in some way.

▦ Dreaming of an island signifies the loneliness one can feel through isolation, self-imposed or otherwise. We may feel out of touch with others or with situations around us. An island can also represent safety in that, by isolating ourselves, we are not subject to external pressures.

Also consult the entry for Isolate/Isolation.

ISOLATE/ISOLATION

🔆 Spiritual isolation signifies the hermit, or recluse – any person living in seclusion, whether through religious belief or not. This suggests the need to spend time alone in tranquility.

♡ When we isolate ourselves (for example, on an island) it suggests that we do not wish or need to become emotionally involved with someone.

🔲 When we find ourselves in isolation in a dream we should decide if it is by our own volition or because of others. If by our own wish, then there is a quality in us which has difficulty in relating to others; if because of others, we perhaps need to explore rejection and our feelings about it.

IVY

🔅 Spiritually, ivy symbolizes immortality and eternal life. It also represents fertility. It is a plant sacred to Bacchus and, therefore, in dreams can suggest Joy.

🔖 Because ivy has the symbolism of constant affection, we can recognize that, psychologically, we are in need of love and affection. In dreams it may signify a binding promise.

🔲 Dreaming of ivy harks back to the old idea of celebration and fun. It can also symbolize the clinging dependence that can develop within relationships.

⬛ In a woman's dream ivy may represent relationships, but in a man's dream may signify responsibility.

Also consult the entries for Bonds, Plants and Weeds.

JAB

✤ A jab, whether in the sense of a punch or an injection, may be seen as an act of aggression. From a spiritual perspective we may need to ascertain what is causing that aggression.

❦ By its nature a jab is a short sharp action, often containing an element of surprise. It will depend on other circumstances in the dream how this element of surprise is interpreted. We may need a short sharp shock to move us from our present emotional stasis.

▦ Jabs are straight, arm-length punches thrown from the leading hand. In dreams we must decide whether the action is defensive or offensive before we interpret them in terms of what is occurring in everyday circumstances. If the fight is structured as in a boxing match this action may refer to working difficulties.

You might like to consult the entries for Fight, Inject/Injection and Vaccination.

JACKAL – *see* ANIMALS

JACKET – *see* COAT IN CLOTHES

JADE – *see* GEMS/JEWELS

JAGUAR – *see* ANIMALS

JAIL – *see* PRISON

JAILER

✤ We may be feeling a degree of spiritual difficulty, a sense of being held back.

❦ To dream of a jailer suggests we feel we are being restricted in some way, maybe by our own emotions or by somebody else's personality or actions. There will be a sense of self-criticism and of alienation which makes it difficult to carry out our ordinary, everyday tasks.

▦ When we are in a situation from which we cannot escape, the personality that appears in our dream often gives information as to how we have got ourselves into that situation. For instance, being unfairly treated by our jailer would indicate that not only may we have been party to the entrapment, but also that we have become victims of our own circumstances.

Also consult the entries for Authority Figures in People and Prison.

JAM/JAMMED

✤ If a door or machine is jammed we recognize that there may be spiritual obstacles ahead of us.

⚔ To be in a traffic jam suggests that other people's concerns may be, or seem to be, more important than our own.

▨ If we have caused the jam – that is, stopped the movement or flow – we must work out what is causing the difficulty and take avoiding action. Jam as a fruit conserve (a mixture of fruit and sugar) suggests that only by blending the components of a project can we come up with something fresh and new.

JAR

✹ The Ancient Egyptians preserved the bodily organs of the dead in canopic jars to ensure that when the soul returned to the physical realms it had everything it needed. A jar thus symbolizes a receptacle for the Soul.

⚔ To be conscious of being jarred – of being shaken in some way – indicates that we are not controlling the way we are moving forward. We are putting ourselves in a position where we can be knocked about, hurt or put off balance. While this may be shocking or upsetting it can also present opportunities for us to gain understanding.

▨ A jar very often represents the feminine containing principle, perhaps some aspect of mothering or of conservation which we recognize within our lives. It often has the same symbolism as the vase – that is, an article which is beautiful in its own right and also the receptacle for something beautiful or necessary. If the jar is broken, it suggests that something essential has been lost.

⊟ In a woman's dream a jar will represent her own femininity whereas in a man's dream it is more likely to signify a nurturing nature or need.

Also consult the entry for Vase.

JAVELIN – *see* SPEAR

JAW – *see* BODY

JAZZ – *see* MUSIC/RHYTHM

JEER

✹ To be jeered at for our beliefs is often part of a spiritual testing, so experiencing it in dreams helps to clarify those beliefs.

⚔ To experience being taunted or mocked in dreams may be interpreted as an attack on our self-esteem.

▨ When we do not seem to be experiencing success in waking life that part of our personality which inhibits that success may appear in dreams to jeer at us.

⊟ In a man's dream the one who jeers may often appear as a parental figure, sometimes of the opposite sex. In a woman's dream it may be her Shadow which mocks.

JESTER – *see* JOKE/JOKER

JET – *see* AEROPLANE

JEWELLERY

🌞 Jewellery represents honour and self-respect without the attendant posturing. Spiritually, it usually indicates that we have, or can have, something valuable in our lives. Jewellery can also indicate love given or received.

💚 Very often, jewellery can represent our own feelings about ourselves, and how we present ourselves to the world. For it to appear in a dream – either as something which is very valuable or as something we know to be false (such as costume jewellery which masquerades as something valuable) gives an indication of our own self-esteem. It may also give an indication as to how others feel about us.

▦ Being given jewellery suggests that someone else values us; giving jewellery signifies that we feel we have something to offer to other people. Those qualities we have learnt to value in ourselves through hard experience are those that we display most easily to other people.

⬚ For a woman to be giving a man jewellery in dreams usually indicates that she is attracted to him and perhaps is able to offer him her own sexuality and self-respect. In a man's dream if he is giving a woman jewellery, he may be offering commitment.

You might like to consult the entries for Gift or Gems/Jewels.

JEWELS – *see* GEMS/JEWELS

JIGSAW

🌞 A jigsaw puzzle in dreams suggests a spiritual conundrum, a difficult problem to be solved.

💚 A jigsaw tool is capable of cutting around shapes. It is this interpretation which may be relevant in dreams, we are able to circumvent a difficulty.

▦ To see a jigsaw puzzle in dreams represents a mental challenge or a problem in waking life that needs to be solved. If there are pieces missing in the puzzle, then it suggests that we do not have all the facts in order to make a considered decision. If the pieces do not fit we may be at odds with a given way of working.

JINX – *see* HEX

JOKE/JOKER

🌞 A joker in dreams is a free spirit or a self-actualized personality, one who has come to terms with life on the physical plane of existence.

💚 Emotionally, a joke can bring about a release of tension and a bizarre occurrence in dreams which causes amusement can do the same. The aspect of our personality which shows itself as a joker has the same meaning as a jester – someone who can make us laugh at ourselves and arouse a sense of the ridiculous.

🔳 A joke in dreams can be an image presented in an odd way. It is as though the mind develops the oddity in order to have us remember what it is attempting to present.

You might also like to consult the entries for Balloon and Clown.

JOURNAL/JOURNALIST

🔅 As a record of our daily lives a journal allows us to keep track of our spiritual progress. In dreams it signifies a tool that we might need in order to understand and monitor our own way of taking in knowledge. A journalist symbolizes the recorder and observing part of our Higher Self which witnesses how we maintain our spiritual integrity.

💠 An actual journal in which we record our dreams keeps track of our 'inner' life – what is going on in the unconscious while we live in the real world. When this image occurs in a dream it is time we paid more attention to this hidden side of ourselves. The journalist in this context makes judgements as to how much of this can be shared with others.

🔳 In ordinary mundane terms a journal or any type of manual keeps track of the progress of a particular task or project. To be writing in such a book suggests that we may need to monitor what we are doing more carefully. A journalist or newspaper reporter in such a dream suggests that care needs to be taken in putting across the right information and ensuring that detail is not lost.

🔸 In both men's and women's dreams a journal suggests a private part of the psyche and perhaps the need for privacy. The gender of the journalist will suggest a more emotional approach if the figure is female and a more logical approach if male.

JOURNEY

🔅 The idea of life being a journey or of journeying towards maturity is a large part of spiritual discipline. There is the Hero's journey as he (or she) discovers the meaning of life, overcomes challenges and reaches autonomy. In addition there is the journey as depicted by the Major Arcana in the Tarot which illustrates the main processes that the incarnate soul (living being) goes through in the search for spirituality. The image of a journey becomes more apparent as time goes on and death approaches. We become more aware of reaching our final destination.

💠 The image of a journey is a very potent one in dream work. Any time the idea of a journey becomes apparent, it is to do with the way that we carry on our everyday lives and how we move forward. Every step that we take towards understanding ourselves and the world we live in can be pictured in terms of a journey, and the dreams that a person has reflect that movement. Making a long journey, for example, suggests leaving friends and family, as would running away to sea. Making a short journey would be investigating an idea or principle in the short term. A difficult journey now behind us means we have come through the difficulties and set-backs of the past. In our ordinary everyday speech we use idioms to suggest our understanding. We speak of the ups and downs of life, of being at a standstill and so on. Each moment is totally unique, and that uniqueness is reflected in our dreams. Mostly dreams are about the here and now and give a snapshot picture as to what is happening at this particular moment, on our individual journey and are therefore a rich source of information as to our psychological or inner state.

▨ The images that appear in dreams will reflect how we are feeling, what obstacles there are, possible courses of action and what our ultimate goal should or may be in our everyday lives. The dream will bring in images from the past or recognizable scenes to help us interpret what is going on and move forward to meet our destiny. The mode of transport we use for our journey is also important. *Consult the entry for Transport.*

Some important images to do with journeys are as follows:

Avoiding an accident means we are able to control our impulses, whereas collisions or other such accidents represent arguments and conflicts which are often caused by our own aggression. *Also consult the entry for Accident.*

Completing a journey – arriving home, touching down and so on – indicates the successful completion of our aims.

Corner – this shows we have accepted the need for a change of direction. We may have made a major decision. *Also consult the entry for Corner.*

Departures from airports, stations, etc. – formerly all departures were interpreted as death. Nowadays the symbolism is much more of a new beginning. We are leaving our old life in order to undertake something new. When someone in our lives leaves us, we may dream of departures and the grief that parting causes. In certain circumstances, to dream of wanting to leave but not being able to suggests that there is still further work to be done. To be conscious of the time of departure might suggest that we are aware of a time limit within an area of our lives. *You may also like to consult the individual entries for Airport and Departing.*

Destinations, when they become apparent, will give some ideas about the aims and objectives we have. Our declared hopes and ideals may not correspond with those we subconsciously have – our inner motivation may be totally different to our outer behaviour – and dreams will highlight this discrepancy. The exact nature of our objective is often not known to us until after we have confronted the obstacles and challenges along the way. It is often enough just to have an aim for that particular section of the journey.

Hills – going uphill suggests extra effort is necessary, while going downhill will suggest lack of control. *Also consult the individual entry for Hill.*

Obstacles ahead – these indicate that we are aware of difficulties which may occur. We do need to be aware that we ourselves create the problems. Our own attitude to life is perhaps responsible.

Passenger – it will depend if we are a passenger in a vehicle or are carrying passengers as to the interpretation. If the former, we may feel that we are being carried along by circumstances, and have not really thought out our own way forward. If the latter, we may have knowingly or inadvertently made ourselves responsible for other people in some way. Travelling with one other passenger suggests we may be considering our relationship with that person or whatever they represent. *Also consult the individual entry for Passenger.*

Road or path – the road or path in a dream suggests our own individual way forward. Just as in dreams, an individual vehicle represents the dreamer's body and external way of being, so the road reflects the way of doing. Any obstacle in the road will reflect difficulties on the chosen path whereas turns in the road will suggest changes of direction. Crossroads will offer choices, while a cul-de-sac would signify a dead end or non-success. If a particular stretch of road is highlighted it may be a period of time, or may mean an effort. *Also consult the individual entries for Crossroads, Cul-de-sac and Path.*

Road rage – road rage appearing in dreams is an aspect of suppressed anger. It signifies a complete loss of control, both of our emotions and of common sense. It will depend on whether we are the victim of such rage or the perpetrator as to the interpretation.

Standstill – being at a standstill or blocked in some way indicates we are being prevented, or are preventing ourselves, from moving forward. This needs handling with care, since to stop may be appropriate. Frequently finding ourselves stopping and starting suggests there is conflict between laziness and drive or ambition.

Walk – if in our dreams we are aware of having to walk, it usually suggests that we are capable of making a part of our life journey by ourselves without any help. Hill walking or similar outdoor activities suggest that we enjoy challenging ourselves. Going for a walk shows we can enjoy the process of recharging our batteries and clearing our minds.

JUBILEE

✺ The time of a jubilee represents a fresh start. This has particular significance in some systems of belief in that it is the 49th part of the life cycle. After 7 x 7 years, the fiftieth year becomes sacred and gives a new beginning and additional insights.

♥ Dreaming of a jubilee or jubilant occasion can represent the natural spontaneity with which we greet changes.

▦ To be dreaming of a jubilee or jubilee celebrations would indicate a rite of passage – a passing from the old into the new, perhaps evidence of having reached the age of discretion. This image might be present after a promotion at work or a change of job.

JUDGE/JUDGEMENT

✺ Though from a spiritual perspective it is not right to judge others or to make judgements, in dreams we often find that we tend to do this. We need to be sufficiently spiritually advanced in order to accept matters as they present themselves, without passing an opinion.

♥ Our own experience and, for that matter that of our families, can lead to problems with authority figures such as judges in dreams. These experiences can equally make us judgemental of others' difficulties and peccadilloes.

▦ Within work situations our judgement is often an integral part of decision making. We must, for instance, evaluate whatever criteria are being applied and act accordingly, just as a judge in court must be as fair as possible.

You might also like to consult the entry for Authority Figures in People.

JUG – *see* JAR AND VASE

JUGGLE

✺ Juggling presupposes a learned response and an expertise which we may need spiritually to balance our lives.

♥ The image of a juggler or of someone juggling suggests that we need to keep control of our own emotions or of those around us.

▦ In waking life we often find we have to carry out a number of tasks at the same time. This may translate in dreams as juggling, The colour of the balls may help us to interpret the relevance.

You might like to consult the entry for Colour

JUMBLE

✺ The jumble of images in dreams are spiritually a little like tasters at a meal, and sometimes not easily interpreted. As we become more proficient in understanding we begin to understand the themes of our dreams.

♥ A jumble of objects in dreams suggest that there is some kind of mess or confusion in our waking lives which needs to be sorted out.

▦ Jumble can have the same meaning as junk in that there is no particular order – it is a confused mess. If in everyday life there are aspects which have this quality we may be wise to try to create some kind of order, and decide what is worth keeping or continuing with and what is better discarded.

JUMPING

❀ In certain religions, spiritual ecstasy is induced by jumping. This is a way of employing physical action in order to reach spiritual realms, and has this significance in dreams.

♡ Repetitive movement of any sort in a dream usually indicates the need to reconsider our actions, to look at what we are doing and perhaps to express ourselves in a different way. On a psychological level, jumping up and down in a dream may indicate being caught up in a situation without having the power to move either forwards or backwards.

▦ The act of jumping can be somewhat ambiguous in a dream. It can indicate either jumping up – attempting to attain something better for ourselves – or jumping down, which can mean going down into the unconscious and those parts of ourselves where we may feel we are in danger. Jumping on the spot can indicate joy and has the same significance as dance.
You might also like to consult the entry for Dance/Dancing.

JUNCTION

❀ Because a road is such a potent image in a spiritual journey, a junction has equal resonance. It suggests that there are choices to be made which may well change the whole course of our lives.

♡ When in dreams we come to a junction, a joining together of more than one way, we perhaps need to look at what has brought us to this particular point. With this in mind, assessing what happened in the dream, such as hesitating before moving or having the feeling that we are waiting for someone can then be interpreted. Emotionally we may have to wait for others to catch up.

▦ Dreaming of a junction presupposes that there is an element of duality in a project. We will have to weigh up the various options and make a decision as to which course of action we should take. If the way is clearly indicated the choice is obvious. If less clearly marked or the way is obscured, there will be other factors to be taken into consideration.
You might like to consult the entries for Crossroads and Journey for further clarification.

JUNGLE

❀ The jungle can symbolize spiritual chaos due to its unpredictability. It suggests a rite of passage – a journey which must be taken to reach maturity.

◈ Psychologically, without the ordering of information that we receive, our minds can simply become a jungle of information. We need to use logic to apply order so that we can make sense of ourselves and our environment. To be trapped in a jungle indicates that we are trapped by negative and frightening feelings from the unconscious, perhaps from those areas which could be considered to be uncivilized. To be conscious of having come through a jungle would indicate that we have passed through, and overcome, those aspects of our lives which we have never dared approach before.

▣ The jungle in dreams is an image belonging to mysticism and fairy tales, often representing chaos, which can be either positive or negative depending on the circumstances of the dream. In myths the jungle symbolizes an obstacle or barrier that has to be passed through in order to reach a new state of being. With this meaning it has the same significance in dreams as the enchanted forest.

▧ In a man's dream of a jungle he is often helped by a feminine figure – his Anima – in his search for a clear passage. In a woman's dream she must frequently overcome the negative aspects of femininity before she can reveal her true identity or power.

You might also like to consult the entries for Animals and Forest.

JUNK

❀ Spiritually junk represents outmoded or unwanted concepts and ideas. A Chinese junk has the same significance as the lunar barque or boat.

◈ From an emotional perspective we all tend to accumulate a great deal of rubbish which periodically needs sorting and disposing of. A cupboard or room full of junk would suggest we need to take action to clear ourselves of hang-ups and difficulties.

▣ When 'mental' junk accumulates we are not able to think clearly and dreams have the facility of enabling us to create order so that we can sort out our lives. Being able to categorize what seems to be rubbish in dreams means we can plan or decide on a course of action.

You might like to consult the entries for Baggage, Boat/Ship and Rubbish.

JUROR/JURY

❀ Often in the process of personal development we may have to make judgements which are not popular. We sometimes have to act as our own juror. Provided we adhere to our own inner spiritual truth, we cannot be judged.

◈ Sometimes in life we may not feel we can go along with a group decision. If in dreams we are a member of the jury, a juror, it will depend on other aspects of the dream whether we can agree with the rest of the jurors or not.

We might have to decide to 'go it alone' and make a unilateral decision. Such a dream would probably reflect a situation in our everyday lives. Conversely, in dreaming of trying to reach a consensus of opinion, we must carefully consider our own beliefs as to how we should live our lives, perhaps taking into account all aspects of our personality.

▣ When a jury appears in a dream on a mundane level we are usually struggling with an issue of peer pressure. We may fear that others will not understand our actions, that they could judge us and find us wanting.

Also consult the entries for Justice and Verdict.

JUSTICE

✸ In spiritual progression there needs to be a balance between our more spiritual selves – what might be called ideal behaviour – and the physical or material realm. This balance can be difficult to both attain and maintain. Such a difficulty can be symbolized by the figure of Justice.

◈ Often when we are attempting to balance two different states or ways of being, Justice – complete with scales – can appear within a dream. This shows that we need to use both sides of ourselves successfully. To be brought to justice can signify that we must pay attention to our actions or to our attitude to authority. It may be that we are offending against some aspect of society.

▣ Very often in a dream we do not seem to be capable of expressing our right to be heard, to articulate those things we believe are correct. Therefore, to dream of either justice or injustice can indicate that the unconscious mind is trying to sort out right from wrong. This is usually on a personal level, although it can have a wider implication as to what is morally right and the norm within society.

You might like to consult the entries for Authority Figures in People, Balance, Juror/Jury and Verdict.

KALEIDOSCOPE

✦ In dreams we are able to appreciate the beauty of basic patterns. In a kaleidoscope, any arbitrary pattern of objects shows up as a beautiful symmetrical pattern because of the reflections in the mirrors from which the kaleidoscope is constructed. The patterns, both regular and irregular as seen in nature, can symbolize the patterns and matrices that we make to comfort ourselves in times of self-doubt.

♥ The magnification and myriad reflections of the patterns created by small objects as they are tumbled together permits us to recapture the sense of wonder that is felt in being human. We become aware of our own 'smallness' within the larger scheme of things.

▦ A kaleidoscope connects us with our childlike selves, and the patterns that such a toy creates reminds us of the Fibonacci perfect ratios that occur in nature, symbolizing the perfection of natural form. Just as a child is fascinated by the pattern that a kaleidoscope creates, so the dream image can introduce us to our own creativity, which can often become trapped.

Consult the entries for Colour, Mirror, Mosaic, Reflection and Shapes/Patterns for further information.

KANGAROO – *see* ANIMALS

KARMA

✦ Karma is a man-made spiritual law, which dictates that any action, good or bad, brings upon oneself inevitable results, either in this life or in a reincarnation. Dreaming of karma suggests that we are aware of the consequences of our actions.

♥ Emotions in waking life are difficult to control. Through a belief in Karma we can use our dreams to help us gain control of those emotions.

▦ In pragmatic terms karma is the law of cause and effect – what goes around comes around. When we have not always acted with integrity we may find that dreams warn us of what the effect might be.

KEEPSAKE

✦ A keepsake in the spiritual sense is an object which, because of the high regard the owner has for it, is sacred. It will probably have been blessed in some way and when it appears in dreams highlights its sacred nature.

♥ Romantic memories loom large in dream imagery. To dream of something that is very precious to us, has been given by someone else in recognition of their regard for us, or signifies a relationship which stands the test of time, allows us to appreciate and understand the beauty we hold within.

🔲 A keepsake in olden times was something which was often exchanged by lovers. To be conscious of having such an object in a dream signifies our ability to love and be loved. Any object that links with the past reminds us of what we have been capable of doing or being, and can take us back to perhaps happier times.

You might like to consult the entries for Camelot and Jewellery.

KEG

�';️ As a hollow vessel, which helps in the preservation of food and nourishment, a keg is another symbol of spiritual nourishment. A beer keg in particular may also be a symbol of pure hedonism.

♡ A keg will often symbolize our emotions and family loyalties. A broken keg may suggest lost dreams and ambitions.

🔲 A keg, particularly an old wooden one, suggests craftsmanship. If it is full, craftsmanship and expertise have fulfilled their purpose. If it is half full or empty, there is much work to be done. A beer barrel will have the same significance.

Consult the entry for Cask for further information.

KERB − *see* **EDGE**

KERNEL − *see* **NUT**

KETTLE

🌀 A kettle, being a hollow vessel, can symbolize magic and magical forces working for the Greater Good, and can have the same significance as a cauldron. It is often taken to symbolize transformation and change.

♡ A kettle just coming to the boil suggests that a plan or project is about to come to fruition. To dream of a kettle in this context suggests that we need to accelerate a process of learning and growth.

🔲 Because a kettle is such a mundane, everyday object, to dream of one indicates our more practical, pragmatic side. Perhaps we are taking certain things for granted. If the kettle is unusual − such as an old fashioned copper kettle − it denotes outworn, but still appreciated, beliefs.

🔳 As a cooking utensil, a kettle combines the power of fire and water to create usable nourishment. In a woman's dream a broken kettle, or one with a hole in it, can signify a perhaps temporary loss of energy or power. In a man's dream a kettle may denote aspects of interdependency within his relationships − a kettle is no use without fire or power.

You might also like to consult the entry for Cauldron and Magic/Magician.

KEY

⚙ A key can represent our need for liberation from a stressful situation and then the initiation of a positive spiritual move. Silver and gold keys represent – respectively – temporal and spiritual power. These keys crossed are part of the Papal regalia and signify belonging to both realms.

💮 We hold within us many of the answers to our own difficulties, but often in dreams need a down-to-earth, mundane symbol to trigger off our ability to work out solutions. When we experience ourselves as trapped, the key to freedom symbolizing what action we must take can often appear as if by magic. The image of a simple key can indicate that the solution is easy. An ornate key can suggest a more complex solution. When we cannot find a key in dreams we may have to wait until the time is right or circumstances are working in our favour.

▦ Keys often appear in dreams. They represent fresh attitudes, thoughts and feelings which are capable of unlocking memories, experiences and knowledge which we have previously hidden. If we can decide which way we turn the key, we can decide whether we are locking things up or freeing them. A bunch of keys signify responsibilities and success and the need to open up the whole of our personalities to new experiences.

▣ In a woman's dream a key can suggest that her own assertiveness needs to be sensitively used. A man may need to understand the 'mechanism' of his assertiveness and how to use it without force.

Consult the entries for Keyhole, Lock and Prison for further information.

KEYBOARD – *see* COMMUNICATION

KEYHOLE

⚙ A keyhole can symbolize our tentative entry into the Sublime or transcendent state. Our vision is somewhat restricted and even in dreams we do not yet have confidence to remain in that state, but must accept the need to remain grounded.

💮 Since a key usually requires a keyhole, to dream of one without the other indicates some kind of confusion between the inner and outer self. A keyhole by itself can represent gossip or treachery by a close associate.

▦ When we dream that we are peering through a keyhole, we are conscious of the fact that our ability to see and understand is somehow impaired. Conventionally, the keyhole has been taken to represent the feminine, so that impairment could result from our attitude to the feminine and to feminine qualities such as intuition.

When a woman dreams of a keyhole without the key she will be conscious of her own vulnerability. In a man's dream he will need to look at the sensitivities of people around him. Not being able to find the keyhole suggests he has not yet quite understood those sensitivities either in personal or work relationships.

You might also like to consult the entries for Key and Lock.

KICK

A kick can be taken symbolically as a need for spiritual motivation; it may be the kick that we need in order to continue (or maybe even begin) our spiritual journey.

Kicking a ball around in a dream signifies our need for self-control, but also our control of external circumstances. To dream of being kicked highlights a propensity to be a victim.

Aggressiveness can be represented in many ways, and to dream of kicking someone often allows the expression of aggression in an acceptable way. There will be some anxiety in everyday life that cannot be properly expressed. Being kicked in a dream may reveal a feeling of being bullied or made to react to situations that are not to our liking.

For many men, ball games such as football or rugby are simply a release of tension and will appear as such in dreams. For women, any action of kicking will be more to do with her own aggression.

Consult the entries for Games and Sport for further clarification.

KIDNAP

Spiritually, dreaming of a kidnapping suggests that someone or something is draining our essential energy and possibly using it in an inappropriate way. This might, for instance, be a family argument or an anxiety that we are not able to deal with properly.

In dreams, we may find ourselves trying to kidnap someone, suggesting that we are trying to influence someone else, perhaps trying to absorb some quality that is not freely available, or making demands that they are not prepared to meet.

If we find ourselves being kidnapped within a dream, we are conscious of the fact that our own fears and doubts can make us victims. We feel out of control and perhaps need to 'negotiate' with the frightened part. We are being overcome by our own 'demons', which have ganged up on us and caused us to become insecure.

You might like to consult the entry for Abduct.

KIDNEYS – *see* BODY

KILL

💮 Killing almost inevitably symbolizes a violent ending of some sort. Often there is a struggle involved and spiritually it is important in dreams that we are the one who overcomes our opponent.

💮 Killing is an extreme answer to a problem. It is such a final act that in dreams it can often represent our perception of the need for an act of violence. In particular this may be against ourselves or a part of our personality that is no longer acceptable. The impulse may not be correct, though some adjustment needs to be made.

▦ To dream of being killed suggests we are under an influence – usually external – which is making us, or an aspect of our personality, ineffective in everyday life. Killing someone in a dream is attempting to be rid of the influence they have over us.

Also consult the entry for Murder/Murderer.

KING – *see* PEOPLE

KINGFISHER – *see* BIRDS

KISS

💮 A single kiss (particularly on the forehead) has often had spiritual and religious undertones, and here the image symbolizes a blessing of a spiritual kind. A kiss represents tranquility, peace and harmony.

💮 We are sealing a pact – perhaps coming to some sort of agreement or recognizing different ways of co-operating with others. We may also be moving towards unity and acceptance within ourselves. Being kissed indicates that we are appreciated and loved for our own qualities.

▦ When we dream about kissing someone, whether of the same gender as ourselves or not, it can suggest an acceptance of a new relationship with that person. Such an act can also signify that, on a subconscious level, we are seeking to develop a quality belonging to that other person in ourselves.

🖽 For both men and women a kiss in dreams is an acknowledgement, often of aspects of our personality that we have not been able to integrate successfully. Women may choose to understand their own drive and assertiveness and men their more sensitive side.

KITCHEN

💮 The rituals associated with the hearth and with fire were, and still are, a significant part of spiritual development. Even in today's climate of convenience foods there is the sense of work in the kitchen being a spiritual offering. There are folk tales in most cultures to do with the kitchen, and spiritually it represents transformation and transmutation. This is much more to do with desired transformation, rather than one that is enforced.

The kitchen is a place of creation, and usually of warmth and comfort. It has, therefore, come to represent the nurturing aspect of woman. In dreams, the kitchen can often represent the mother, or rather the mothering function.

For most people, the kitchen represents the 'heart' of the house. It is the space from which we go out into the world and to which we return. It is the place that is usually busiest and, therefore, where many relationships are cemented, and where many exchanges take place.

In a man's dream, a kitchen is more to do with the way that he is, or has been, nurtured and the effect this has on him, whereas in a woman's dreams a kitchen symbolizes how she nurtures others.

Also consult the entries for Fire, Hearth, House and Oven for further clarification.

KITE

A kite represents our need for, or recognition of, forthcoming spiritual freedom. In Chinese lore, the kite symbolized the wind. We need to be free of constraints and to be 'pulling our own strings', while remaining grounded. The bird of prey also soars with the wind, and again represents freedom.

While flying a kite, we are at the mercy of the wind unless we have a fair degree of expertise. In dreams it is recognizable that we have some expertise in our everyday lives and that that expertise needs recognition.

To dream of flying a kite can remind us of the carefree days of childhood when we were without responsibility. Often the colour is important, as may be the material from which it is made. In more mundane terms, to be flying a kite may suggest ambition and career goals.

Consult the entries for Colour and Wind for further clarification.

KITTEN – *see* BABY ANIMALS IN ANIMALS

KNEAD

As bread is the 'staff of life', to dream of kneading bread suggests working hard on our own lives on order that we ourselves can effect change.

Kneading has the same symbolism as cooking: that is, combining ingredients to make something else. It also signifies working with tension to relieve pain as in massage.

In waking life, the act of kneading can be therapeutic. In dreams, this significance can be highlighted, allowing us to work at a problem or resolve a difficulty.

You might like to consult the entries for Bread and Cooking.

KNEE/KNEELING – *see* BODY

KNIFE

    ✿ A knife is a symbol of division. There may be something in life that needs to be cut out and got rid of. Alternatively, the knife may be representative of the need to view something from a dual perspective – the spiritual and the physical.

    ♡ It can be important in a dream about a knife to notice what type is being used. For instance, a table knife would be interpreted very differently to a Swiss Army knife. Both are functional, but the former would only be appropriate under certain circumstances, whereas the latter might have a more universal application. To dream that we are carrying a knife signifies anger, aggression and/or separation. We may be attempting to cut ties or feel that we need protection.

    ▦ If we are using a knife we may either be freeing ourselves from restrictions or trying to sever a relationship. If we are being attacked with a knife, it indicates either violent words or actions may be used against us. If we are aware that the knife is blunt, the words may be particularly hurtful. If sharp, matters can be dealt with quickly.

    ⊟ In a woman's dream the symbol of a knife is probably more to do with her own fear of penetration and violation, whereas in a man's dream it is highlighting his own aggression.

You might like to consult the entries for Dagger and Weapon for further information.

KNIGHT

    ✿ A knight is a follower, or someone who has taken an oath of allegiance. Hence in dreams such a figure signifies initiation, in order to develop our finer spiritual qualities.

    ♡ Psychologically, the knight in a dream signifies the guiding principle. He is that part of ourselves that is sometimes known as the Higher Self, the spirit guiding the physical. The black knight is often seen as the embodiment of evil. It is interesting that often the white knight appears with his visor up, whereas the black knight appears with his visor down.

    ▦ In pragmatic terms, a project or task may require dedication and focus. Since a knight is expected to show loyalty he may appear signifying this in dreams. Being made a knight in the modern day is still considered to be something of an honour and may have this meaning in dreams.

    ⊟ A knight appearing in a dream, particularly a woman's, can have the obvious connotation of a romantic liaison: the knight in shining armour. This actually is a manifestation of her own Animus – her own inner masculine –

and is to do with her search for perfection. In a man's dream it indicates he may be searching for the Hero in himself.

You might also like to consult the entries for Camelot, Castle, Hero/Heroine and Quest as well as the information on Hero in Archetypes in the Introduction.

KNITTING

✸ Knitting, as with weaving and knotting, can symbolize a form of creativity, the ability to form something new out of raw material.

♥ We are working on emotions, or at creating a relationship.

▣ The primary symbolism connected with knitting is that of creating something new out of available material, often having a pattern from which to work. If the pattern is intricate much care needs to be taken. A project or idea that is being worked on is beginning to come together. To be unravelling knitting suggests that a project that is being worked on needs reconsideration.

⬧ In a woman's dream knitting can represent the basic feminine skills. As many women become more business-oriented, knitting as a recreation – embodying a different form of creativity – may surface in dreams representing domesticity.

Also consult the entries for Colour, Knot, Weaving and Wool.

KNOB

✸ Since a knob of any sort is usually used to gain access to something, spiritually it can suggest changes occurring in the way we approach our unconscious self.

♥ To be dreaming of a knob such as a doorknob can indicate some kind of turning point in our life. A noticeable contrast between the door and the knob can present the dreamer with certain insights. For instance, a very plain knob on an ornate door may indicate that the process of moving forward from a situation is very easy. The knob coming off in our hands suggests a missed opportunity. We may need to turn or change issues or conditions.

▣ When we are turning a knob we need to decide whether we are turning it clockwise or anti-clockwise. Clockwise will signify a positive move, anti-clockwise perhaps an initially more difficult one, but one which will ultimately present further opportunities.

⬧ Since many people still have difficulty in calling 'private parts' by their correct name, a knob appearing in a dream can represent the penis or, if the dreamer is a man, his masculinity.

You might also like to consult the individual entry for Door and also Door in Buildings.

KNOCK/KNOCKING

✲ To hear knocking suggests we are being given permission from our spiritual self to progress on our current journey. Some believe that it is a way of alerting the psyche to the realms of spirit.

♡ If we ourselves are knocking on a door, we may be wanting to become part of someone's life, looking for a particular type of information asking for help or seeking different opportunities. We are waiting for permission before moving forward.

▣ To hear knocking in a dream generally alerts us to the fact that our attention needs to be re-focused. For instance, we may be too introverted when in fact we need to be paying more attention to external matters.

KNOT

✲ The knot symbolizes spiritual continuity or connection. It suggests a pause, perhaps for contemplation or assessment. As something to hold, a knot suggests capturing a fleeting idea or concept.

♡ A simple knot seen in a dream could represent the need to take a different direction in a project. A more complex knot could indicate that we are bound to a situation by a sense of duty or guilt. Ultimately the only way to escape from such restraint is by loosening the ties in our relationship with someone else, or with a work situation.

▣ A knot is one of the most interesting symbols to appear in dreams, since it can have so many meanings. Negatively, particularly if it is seen as a tangle, it can represent an unsolvable problem or difficulty. The answer can only be 'teased out' gradually. Positively, a knot can represent the ties or bonds that we have to family, partner, friends or work.

⏸ In a man's dream tying the knot is likely to have some aspect of being restrained or bound to a partner. In a woman's dream it is more likely to represent commitment.

You might also like to consult the entry for Tangle.

KNOW/KNOWLEDGE

✲ Spiritual knowledge and awareness can develop gradually. If we are prepared to allow it, this knowledge can come intuitively through dreams.

♡ In dreams we often know something without being sure of how we do. Many believe that in the dream state we have easier access to the collective Unconscious – the repository of all knowledge – than when we are awake.

▣ In mundane terms knowledge and experience go hand in hand. In dreams the mind may trigger an association, which allows us to reach viable conclusions.

LABEL

🔥 In the spiritual sense a label can give us a sense of spiritual identity.

♥ Having the wrong label suggests that we are aware that we are not perceiving something in the correct way. To be re-labelling something suggests that we have rectified a misperception.

▦ Often, dreaming of labels links with our need to name things. Our sense of identity comes from the name we are given, and our 'label' is much to do with the way that others see us and understand us.

LABORATORY

🔥 Dreaming of a laboratory indicates that we may need to make a more objective or perhaps scientific (knowledgeable) assessment of what is going on in our lives.

♥ A laboratory can suggest a very ordered existence, and it will depend on whether we are working in or are specimens in a laboratory how we interpret the dream. To be a specimen suggests that we feel we are being monitored in some way.

▦ Dreaming of working in a laboratory indicates that we need to be more ordered in our approach to life. We may have certain talents that need to be developed in an objective fashion, or we may need to develop our thinking faculty further.

You might like to consult the entry for Invent/Inventor.

LABOUR

🔥 The 12 labours of Hercules are reputed to represent the passage of the sun through the 12 signs of the Zodiac. They are also the hardships and effort man uses to attain self-realization.

♥ To be labouring at something, in the sense of working hard, suggests that we have a goal we wish to achieve. We are prepared to put effort in to achieve success.

▦ To dream of 'hard labour' will alert us to a tendency towards self-flagellation or self-punishment in our personality.

▦ If a woman dreams of being in labour she should look at her wish and desire to be pregnant. If a man dreams of his wife or partner being in labour, it may show his readiness to take on the responsibility of a family, or even new responsibilities at work.

Also consult the entry for Work.

LABYRINTH

⚜ Spiritually the labyrinth experience marks a watershed. It is a symbol for the transition stage between the physical, practical world and a deeper understanding of all mankind. The route in one type of labyrinth is 'unicursal' – that is, it goes by a straightforward route, which covers maximum ground straight to the centre and out again. The second type is designed with the intention to confuse, and has many blind alleys and unexpected twists. This can represent spiritual progress in dreams, through having to work out the key or code. Many trials and tribulations are met and overcome or negotiated on the path to attainment and the labyrinth may be a recurring image. Each individual will undertake his or her own route to the centre of his existence.

♥ Psychologically, in undertaking our own life journey, we must at some point go through a form of labyrinth experience. It is undertaken at a point when we must travel into the differing areas of our subconscious and come to terms with our fears and doubts, before confronting our own Shadow.

▥ On a purely practical level, the labyrinth appearing in dreams signifies the need to explore the hidden side of our own personality. With its many twists, turns and potential blind alleys when it is not unicursal, it is a very potent representation of the human being.

▤ In dreams the labyrinth can be suggested by any dream that has us exploring a series of underground passages. It is held by some to be an exploration of the hidden feminine, whether in the sense of Sophia (eternal wisdom) or the Anima in men.

Also consult the entries for Maze and Minotaur.

LACE

⚜ As a handworked adornment in vestments and altars within religious rites, lace has an extremely ancient history. In dreams, therefore, it comes to symbolize worship and perhaps the capturing of Spirit in craft of knotting. When joining two pieces of material such as linen, it signifies the transition between the physical and the spiritual realms

♥ Much symbolism can be worked into lace, so it is useful to note what, if anything, is depicted pictorially in this manner in dreams. Altar cloths, for instance, might contain Christian images such as the cross or fertility symbols might be included in Wiccan robes. As a creative art, which is less practised nowadays, lace may alert us to our own creativity.

▥ As a pastime, which kept women usefully employed and indeed was often the only source of income, from a practical perspective lace signifies gainful employment. More mundanely, to be tying our shoelaces suggests careful preparation. To be untying them suggests relaxation and informality. To lose shoelaces suggests insecurity.

Also consult the entries for Linen and Shoes.

LADDER

☼ In a dream, the rungs of the ladder are often either seven or 12 in number, these being traditionally the stages of growth towards spirituality. Jacob's dream of a ladder is one such potent image.

۞ The ladder denotes our ability to break through to a new level of awareness, moving from the physical to the spiritual, but also being able to move downwards again. It also suggests communication between the physical and spiritual realms as a stage of transition. Occasionally it may also represent death, though this is more the death of the old self, or way of being, rather than a physical death.

▨ The ladder in dreams denotes how secure we feel in moving from one situation to another. We may need to make a considerable effort to reach a goal or take an opportunity. Often this dream occurs during career changes and so has obvious connotations. If the rungs are broken we can expect difficulty. If someone else is carrying the ladder it could suggest that another person, perhaps a manager or colleague, has a part to play in our progression.

You might like to consult the entry for Levels/Layers for additional clarification.

LAGOON/LAKE

☼ A lagoon or lake represents our inner world of feeling and fantasy. It is the unconscious side, which is a rich source of power when it can be accessed and understood. The primordial substance is often pictured as a lagoon or lake. The Chinese concept of a kind of soup from which came all existence, links with the lagoon, a stretch of water that has become enclosed.

۞ Often thought to be the home of the magical feminine and of monsters, the lagoon stands for the darker side of femininity, and this is seen clearly in the legends of King Arthur and those of the Siren. This type of image will appear in dreams as we lose our fear of the depths of our own emotion.

▨ If the lake is contaminated, we have taken in ideas and concepts that are not necessarily good for us. A clear stretch of water would indicate that we have clarified our fears and feelings about ourselves.

⚐ Perhaps one of the reasons that a lake or lagoon is so enticing is because of its association with relaxation and ease. In both men's and women's dreams this quality will often come across albeit from slightly different perspectives; a stormy lake, for instance, may well signify a woman's anger, whereas for a man it is likely to represent his partner's distress.

Also consult the entry for Water.

LAMB – see ANIMALS AND SPIRITUAL IMAGERY IN THE INTRODUCTION

LAME

⚙ Lameness in the spiritual sense suggests the imperfection of creation, when an imperfect world is formed. Haephestos, one of the forge gods, was lamed when he was thrown out of heaven by his father Zeus.

♡ To be aware that someone else is lame has two meanings. If the person is known to us, we need to be aware of their vulnerability and uncertainty. If they are not known, it is more likely to be a hidden side of ourselves, which is insecure or perhaps damaged. If the left side is damaged the sensitive side is affected, if the right, then the more assertive side is in trouble.

▦ Dreaming of being lame suggests a loss of confidence and strength. If we ourselves are lame there can be a fear of moving forward or a fear of the future.

You might like to consult the entry for Limp.

LAMP

⚙ Spiritually the lamp can suggest the idea of a personal guiding 'light in darkness'. The hermit in the Tarot demonstrates this in his protectiveness of the light and his need to be able to move forward despite the darkness around him. The lamp can also signify the light of the Divine and immortality.

♡ The lamp in dreams often signifies guidance and wisdom. If it is an old-fashioned lantern, it can also represent previously held beliefs, which may need to be updated.

▦ In dreams a lamp or a light can represent life. To be moving towards a lamp suggests a clarity of perception, which may be slightly old-fashioned. The lamp in its most practical aspect in dreams signifies the intellect and perception.

You might like to consult the entries for Candle and Light.

LANCE

⚙ The lance is a phallic image initially of solar, and later of spiritual, power.

♡ A lance as a surgical instrument is penetrative and thus has a healing connotation. It is designed to release the negative, as in lancing a boil. We may need to take short, sharp action in order to improve a situation.

▦ A lance – as in a Knight's lance – in a dream suggests an aspect of masculine power, penetration and, therefore, sometimes the sexual act.

▯ In a woman's dream a knight with a lance will signify chivalry and dedication. In a man's dream a lance will suggest his own ability to fight his own corner.

Also consult the entries for Arrow, Knight and Weapons.

LANDSCAPES

❀ Spiritually, the landscape in a dream can suggest improvements that we can make in handling our own moods and attitudes.

❤ Dream landscapes can have a bizarre quality about them in order to highlight a particular message. For instance, there may be trees made of ice, or rocks made of sugar. The plot of the dream may be important in arriving at the correct interpretation of these symbols. The landscape in a dream can also indicate how we relate to other people. To be in a desert might represent loneliness, whereas to be in a jungle might represent a very fertile imagination. If the landscape changes between the beginning and end of the dream, we perhaps need to make corresponding changes in everyday life.

▦ The landscape in a dream can be an integral part of the interpretation. It usually mirrors feelings and concepts that we have and, therefore, reflects our personality. A rocky landscape would suggest problems, whereas a gloomy landscape might suggest pessimism and self-doubt. A recurring scene may be one where in childhood we felt safe, or may reflect a feeling or difficulty with which we have not been able to come to terms. Landscapes do tend to reflect habitual feelings rather than momentary moods.

Also consult the entry for Places for further clarification.

LAPSE

❀ Any kind of spiritual lapse or falling away from our beliefs will reflect itself in dreams, sometimes by a sense of foreboding or other negative image.

❤ A slip of the memory or an inability to hold on to information can manifest in dreams as a lost object or a sense of searching for something we know we have once had.

▦ When we have not been totally true to our own principles we may experience this in dreams as a lapse of attention or lack of attention to detail.

LAPTOP – *see* **COMMUNICATION**

LARGE – *see* **SIZE**

LARK – *see* **BIRDS**

LASER

❀ Because of its intensity, a laser beam has the image of light cutting through the non-essential to reveal complete truth.

❤ As it can be focused with pinpoint accuracy, from an emotional perspective this represents a kind of healing – that of cutting out emotional 'demons' and the pain associated with them.

🔲 Any laser beam suggests a clarity of perception is required. This can have an intrinsic danger, however, in that if the insights gained are not sensitively handled it can be hurtful.

Also consult the entry for Light.

LASH – *see* WHIP

LAST

🔅 There are two spiritual interpretations for last. The last supper, as in the sense of the final time, suggests the time just before we have completed one of our earthly tasks. A shoe last signifies a pro-forma from which we can achieve a better fit, albeit after some effort.

💠 When we realize that we are last, for instance in a queue, we should perhaps decide whether we are following all others or bringing up the rear. In the latter sense this requires some courage because our back is exposed. Following others may mean that others take the risk.

🔲 If we are last in a dream there may be a situation in reality where our feelings are not being taken into account. Being the last to be chosen highlights an insecurity about our viability which may be a legacy from childhood.

You might also like to consult the entries for Running and Win/Winning.

LATCH – *see* KEY AND LOCK

LATE – *see* TIME

LAUGH

🔅 Laughter in the spiritual sense signifies pure joy. It is now known that laughter has a healing quality, so to be conscious of it in dreams suggests that a healing has taken place.

💠 If we ourselves are laughing we may be experiencing a release of tension. Often the object of our amusement will give a clue to the relevance of the dream in everyday life. It can also be seen as a sign of rejection. To hear a crowd laughing suggests a shared enjoyment, if we do not have a sense of being laughed at.

🔲 Being laughed at in dreams suggests we may have a fear of being ridiculed, or may have done something which we feel is not appropriate. We may find ourselves embarrassing.

LAUNCH

🔅 In the sense of setting a boat afloat, a launch picks up the spiritual significance of a boat and also suggests some kind of initiation or the beginning of a process.

💠 Launching is associated with throwing – particularly a lance – and, therefore, emotionally represents perhaps an initial enthusiasm or enjoyment.

⊞ Launching a project in a dream suggests the beginning of an exciting time. A launch was initially a smaller boat for use on a larger one, so therefore can suggest an offshoot of a task or idea.

Consult the entries for Boat/Ship, Lance and Spear for further clarification.

LAUREL/BAY LEAVES

✿ The laurel or bay tree symbolizes chastity and eternity. It also suggests immortality.

♡ The laurel wreath is often used to indicate triumph and victory and, therefore, is an acknowledgement of success. Traditionally, the laurel or bay is difficult to grow, so it will symbolize triumph over difficulty.

⊞ The laurel or bay tree is less likely to appear in dreams nowadays with a mundane explanation, unless the dreamer is either a gardener or has a particular knowledge of symbolism. In former times, it would have represented a specific type of success.

LAVA – *see* VOLCANO

LAVATORY – *see* TOILET

LAW

✿ A law is an instruction or way of working deliberately laid down or fixed so a spiritual law is a universal code which works for all mankind, sometimes more accessible in dreams than in reality.

♡ When our emotions are called into question, we can find that an appropriate way of operating is offered in dreams. We work according to unwritten laws that are correct for us. The Law in the guise of a policeman is an aspect of a higher authority there to give guidance.

⊞ Any aspect of the law appearing in dreams is as much to do with our own code of behaviour in waking life as with 'the law' in the sense of authority. In dreams, our own internal sense of justice tends to take precedence over the laws of society.

You might also like to consult the entries for Judge/Judgement, Juror/Jury and Justice.

LAYERS – *see* LEVELS

LEAD (METAL)

✿ Lead in spiritual symbolism stands for a consciousness of the physical realms as opposed to the spiritual. It is the metal of Saturn and has this planet's symbolism of blocking progress unless it is moving forward in the correct way for ultimate success. As we become more spiritually proficient, the old magical and alchemical definitions become more relevant.

♡ Lead as a substance is less used nowadays than it used to be, but still has the connotations of a base metal. In dreams it can indicate that the time is ripe for transformation and transmutation. We need to instigate changes to give a better quality to our lives.

🎴 The conventional explanation of lead appearing in a dream is that we have a situation around us, which is a burden to us. We are not coping with life as we should, leaving us heavy-hearted. Lead, as in a lead of a pencil, has obvious connections with the life force and masculinity.

Also consult the entries for Alchemy and Metal.

LEAD/LEADING/LEADER

🌣 We are able to take authority by virtue of our spiritual knowledge, though with humility and without ego. In dreams we will often find ourselves taking the lead before we are consciously able to do so.

♡ Leadership qualities are not necessarily ones that everybody has or will use. Often we can surprise ourselves in dreams by doing things that we would not normally do, and becoming a leader is one of them.

🎴 Dreaming of a dog lead symbolizes the connection between ourselves and our lesser nature. To have lost the dog lead would indicate a loss of control. Leading someone in a dream pre-supposes that we know what we are doing and where we are going. Being led suggests that we have allowed someone else to take control of a situation around us.

You might also like to consult the entries for Harness and Halter.

LEAF/LEAVES

🌣 Leaves signify fertility and growth. Since each leaf is completely unique, we may be becoming aware of the beauty of creation and the perfection of spiral patterns in Nature.

♡ When looking at our lives as a whole, leaves can signify a particular period of our lives – perhaps a period that has been meaningful and creative, a period of growth. Following a dream about leaves we may need to assess how to go forward in order to avail ourselves of the opportunities offered.

🎴 A leaf very often represents a period of growth and can also give a measurement of time. Green leaves can suggest hope and new opportunities, or the Springtime. Dead leaves signify a period of sadness, barrenness or Autumn.

Also consult the entries for Autumn and Trees.

LEAK

🌣 A leak of any sort suggests spiritual wastefulness and inattention to resources.

♡ A leak can indicate carelessness. We may not be paying attention to necessary repairs either on a physical, emotional or mental level.

▦ Dreaming of a leak suggests we are wasting or losing energy in some way. If it is a slow leak we are perhaps not aware of the drain on our energies. If it is gushing we need to look at 'repairing' the leak, perhaps by being more responsible in our actions.

⊡ There are times in a man's dream when a leak may suggest the sexual act. In a woman's dream it is more likely to have an emotional connotation.

Also consult the entry for Water.

LEAP

❀ Making a leap of faith suggests a degree of trust in whatever we might consider to be a divine plan.

♥ Leaping in dreams suggests a longer or more difficult action than a simple jump. Emotionally it signifies the need for courage or conversely a degree of foolhardiness.

▦ A leap suggests a particular kind of action, both taking a calculated risk in facing danger, and movement that is somewhat exaggerated – a running jump rather than a standing start. These conditions in an everyday project can be symbolized in dreams. In that a leap year changes the measurement of time, causing fixed festival days to 'leap' ahead one day in the week, this image suggests that we may need to adjust a schedule.

Also consult the entry for Jumping for further information.

LEARN

❀ To learn is to accrue knowledge, and to be learned spiritually is to have acquired knowledge through study. Dreams are a way for us to link with other levels of consciousness and acquire knowledge.

♥ As we gather experience we learn more, and dreams can be a way of internalizing what we have learned. As a child learns more of the world in which he or she exists, dreams become a way of dealing with everyday experience.

▦ When life is stressful we are able to learn methods of coping through dreams, not just through interpreting images but also by practising different behaviour through techniques like lucid dreaming. When we find ourselves in a learning situation in dreams, we should perhaps look at how these lessons can be applied in everyday life.

You might also like to consult the entries for Education, Teacher and School.

LEASE

❀ A lease implies an agreement between two parties, in spiritual terms between the spiritual and physical selves.

♥ When the various aspects of our personality are able to act in harmony we may dream of signing a lease or other type of contract.

🔲 Legal papers of any sort suggest contractual arrangements. As a lease is usually to occupy premises or to apportion cost in a manageable way, we may have to decide on the long-term validity of a project or course of action.

LEAVE/LEAVING

🔅 To leave a situation may suggest conscious rejection of the past in order to create spiritual progression.

🔅 To be departing from a known situation, such as leaving home, indicates a breaking away from old or habitual patterns of behaviour. We may need to give ourselves the freedom to be independent.

🔲 We may have a strong desire to get away from responsibility or difficulties, but must be careful how we handle it.

Also consult the entries for Journey and Transport.

LECTURE

🔅 A lecture suggests the imparting of spiritual knowledge by an authority – one who has expertise.

🔅 A lecture is a way of passing on information, often specialized or newly accrued, so such an image suggests there is something we need to know.

🔲 In waking life, knowledge may be passed on in an environment geared for study or research. The need for such a situation translates into the dream image of a lecture or lecture theatre.

You might also like to consult the entries for Education, Learn, Teacher and School.

LEDGER – *see* **BOOK AND RECORD**

LEFT – *see* **LAST AND POSITION**

LEG – *see* **LIMBS IN BODY**

LEGITIMATE

🔅 In spiritual terms a legitimate act is one that has been sanctioned by a higher authority.

🔅 When we offend against our own moral code we may have dreams about being legitimate and working within the framework of the law.

🔲 Working within societies that are not particularly permissive in outlook, we may dream of needing to have our actions sanctioned if our autonomy is threatened in waking life. We may also in dreams find ourselves rebelling through illegal acts.

⊟ Dreaming of being illegitimate for both men and women suggests a lack of self worth and sometimes a questioning of our right to a place in society.

LEND/LENDING/LOAN

🔅 In spiritual terms, the concept of lending is connected with healing and support.

◈ If we are lending money, we are creating a bond of obligation within our lives. If we are being lent money we need to look at the way we are managing our resources, but more importantly what help we need to do this.

▦ If in a dream we are lending an object to someone, we are aware that the quality that object represents cannot be given away; it is ours to have but we can share it. If someone is lending us an article then we are perhaps not responsible enough to possess what it represents on a full-time basis. Conversely, we may only need it for a short time.

LENS

✿ A lens symbolizes concentration and visionary clarity.

◈ When a lens appears in a dream we need to be clear as to whether it is enlarging the object being looked at, or is intensifying it. Enlarging it suggests taking a wider viewpoint, intensifying it requires that we pay attention to detail. A full interpretation can only be made in the light of other circumstances in the dream. It is the context of the dream that is important.

▦ Just as in everyday life a lens helps to focus the attention, so in dreams it can signify our need to perceive something very clearly.

You might also like to consult the entries for Glasses/Spectacles, Goggles and Magnifying Glass.

LEOPARD – *see* ANIMALS

LEPER

✿ Spiritually, a leper in a dream can suggest that we are having to deal with a moral dilemma that takes us away from compassion and caring. This image is less prevalent today as such diseases become more treatable.

◈ If we are caring for a leper we need to attend to those parts of ourselves we consider unclean, rather than trying to dispose of them. If the leper is offering us something, it may be that we have a lesson to learn about humility.

▦ To dream of a leper suggests that we are aware of some aspect of ourselves that we feel to be unclean. We feel that we have been rejected by society without quite knowing why. We may also feel that we have been contaminated in some way.

You might like to consult the entries for Heal/Healing and Ill/Illness.

LETTER

✿ In dreams, hidden and perhaps private psychic information often comes in the form of a sealed letter, which we must make the effort to understand.

◈ Often we dream about a letter without knowing what the contents are. This suggests some information that is at present being withheld. If a particular letter of the alphabet is highlighted, we may understand more if we can name someone with that initial.

■ If we receive a letter in a dream we may be aware of some problem with the person it is from. It is possible that the sender is known to be dead, in which case there are unresolved issues with that person or the situation connected with them. If we are sending a letter we have information we feel may be relevant to that person.

Also consult the entries for Communication, Email and Reading for further information.

LEVELS/LAYERS

✵ A level in sacred architecture represents knowledge out of the norm. All religions are based on worshipping a cosmic order, which means that a key aspect of religion is trying to recreate this order, something we often try to do in dreams. A *stupa*, for instance, a memorial instigated by Buddha himself, is essentially made up of the following five levels:

a) A square base
b) A hemispherical dome
c) A conical spire
d) A crescent moon
e) A circular disc

Each of these components is rich in spiritual significance and is identified with one of the five cosmic elements of creation. These are, from the base up, Earth, Water, Fire, Air and Space.

♥ There are many levels of awareness that are available to us in the dream state. It will depend on our stage of advancement at which level we choose to interpret our dreams. As a child grows in maturity he will go through different ways of understanding his world, commensurate with his particular stage of growth, which will be reflected in dreams. These levels of understanding resonate even in adulthood.

■ Usually a level surface suggests ease and comfort. Dreaming of a road being level would indicate our way ahead is fairly straightforward. A level crossing suggests that we are approaching a barrier or blockage that requires our attention. We may not yet have enough information to take avoiding action.

LEVER

✵ A lever may appear as a symbol in dreams when we are attempting to reach a different level of spiritual awareness.

♥ A lever implies that we need to use some mechanical means to raise or lower an object. From an emotional perspective, this signifies that we need help in handling our emotions at this time.

▦ To be levering an object in dreams – for instance, using a crowbar – suggests that a project or idea needs to be freed up from some kind of restriction.

▣ A lever is a mechanical means of altering position, so in both men's and women's dreams such an image can suggest manipulation from an outside source.

LIBRARY

✷ A library represents the Collective Unconscious – all that is, was and ever shall be. It is often taken as the Akashic records – the spiritual records of existence. At a certain stage in psychic and spiritual development, the library is an important symbol. It suggests both the wisdom and skills that we have accumulated, but also the collected wisdom available to all humanity.

◈ As we are able to look more objectively at our lives we have more access to universal knowledge. A chaotic, untidy library would suggest that we have difficulty in dealing with information and emotion.

▦ A library in a dream can often represent the storehouse of our life's experience. It can also represent our intellect and the way we handle knowledge. A well-managed library would suggest the ability to create order successfully.

LICE – *see* INSECTS

LID

✷ A lid closes a container and can, therefore, symbolize the division between the physical and spiritual realms.

◈ To be trying to open a lid suggests that we may need some kind of emotional release. To be closing a lid indicates that we are repressing some aspect of our personality.

▦ To be keeping a lid on a container indicates that we suspect that some task or situation may run out of control.

LIE/LYING

✷ To lie, as in speak falsely, is to speak against a truth, though interestingly not necessarily against what we believe to be true. If we have sworn to tell the truth and do not, this would be spiritual perjury.

◈ We can become conscious of deliberate falsehood in dreams when our emotions are called into question and we are not true to our principles. To be lying prone suggests that we should adopt a different perspective.

▦ In waking life there is lying by commission and lying by omission; this is a deliberate manipulation of the truth. Dreams can often help us to clarify our awareness. We often can rely only on intuition to reveal the real truth.

LIFEBOAT

✹ There is always risk in undertaking a difficult task. When we make mistakes or the risk is too great, spiritually we can only be 'rescued' by a greater knowledge and wisdom.

♥ Since a lifeboat requires a degree of dedication from the members of the crew, we may be alerted to the need for such selfless dedication in our lives. We may also be becoming aware of the degree of skill we require to navigate life's difficulties. Because the sea can represent deep emotion, in dreams a lifeboat may be of help in learning to handle our own emotions.

▦ Dreaming of a lifeboat could indicate that we have the feeling that we need to be rescued, possibly from our own stupidity or from circumstances beyond our control. If we are at the helm of a lifeboat we are still in control of our own lives, but are perhaps aware that we need to offer assistance to someone else.

You might also like to consult the entries for Boat/Ship and Sea in Water.

LIFT

✹ A lift is an enclosed space and can, therefore, symbolize the physical body from a spiritual perspective. Being lifted up suggests Ascension.

♥ Going up in a lift suggests aspiration and a desire for something better. Going down may indicate difficult or depressing circumstances.

▦ A lift, particularly in a work situation, may indicate the possibility of promotion or demotion, but may also indicate the way to achieve this. An old-fashioned lift might signify the need for effort or, conversely, perhaps an out-of-date attitude.

LIGHT

✹ Spiritually in dreams a bright light symbolizes the manifestation of divinity, truth or direct knowledge. Often this knowledge is beyond form and, therefore, appears as energy, which the dreaming mind translates as light.

♥ When light appears in dreams we are usually in process of trying to improve who we are. A very bright light often symbolizes the development of intuition or insight. There are various techniques using candle flames and other sources of light, which can be used in the waking state to enhance this faculty.

▦ Light in a dream usually means illumination. For instance, 'light at the end of the tunnel' suggests coming to the end of a difficult project. 'He saw the light' means recognition of the results of actions. It is much to do with confidence. To feel lighter signifies feeling better about ourselves.

Also consult the entry for Lamp.

LIGHTHOUSE

✦ A lighthouse highlights the correct course of action to help us achieve our spiritual goals. It can also take on the symbolism of the tower.

♥ A lighthouse can act as a beacon and can lead us into calmer waters. It is also a warning system, and in dreams it tends to warn us of emotional difficulties. It can often have this significance in dreams whether emotionally or spiritually.

▣ It will depend on whether we are aware in the dream of being on land or at sea. If we are on land we are being warned of difficulties to come, probably from our own emotions. If we are at sea we need to be careful not to create misunderstandings for ourselves by ignoring problems and be sure to steer the right course.

You might also like to consult the entries for Beacon, Light and Tower.

LIGHTNING

✦ Spiritually, lightning denotes some form of spiritual enlightenment, literally something which had not 'struck us' before. In dreams, a lightning flash can also represent the Holy Spirit or the travelling of energy through the various planes of existence into manifestation.

♥ When we dream of lightning we are marking a discharge of tension in some way. There may be a situation in our everyday lives that actually needs to be 'blasted' – apparently negatively – in order for something to happen which will change the circumstances. If we take all the known facts into account, our intuition will make us aware of the correct action.

▣ Lightning in a dream denotes unexpected changes, which are taking place or are about to take place. This may be the sudden realization of a personal truth, or of a more universal awareness. Often such a revelation has the effect of knocking down the structures we have built in as safeguards in our lives. Alternatively, we may have to make changes in the way we think while leaving our everyday structure and relationships in place. Lightning can also indicate strong passion – such as love – which may strike suddenly but be devastating in its effect.

You might also like to consult the entries for Thunder/Thunderbolts and Weather.

LILY

✦ Spiritually, lilies are a symbol of resurrection and of everlasting life. They are often used in religious ceremony to denote this and are a symbol of the Virgin Mary.

♥ One symbol of lilies is that of purity and, particularly in a teenager's dream, lilies can suggest virginity. Lilies in dreams, other than the white funerary arum lily, can also suggest aspects of femininity.

🏛 Because of their connection with funerals, for some people lilies can symbolize death. They can also, however, symbolize nobility and grace, and the interpretation needs to be carefully thought out. If we are planting lilies we are hoping for a peaceful transition in some area within our lives.

🔹 If we are gathering lilies, particularly in a woman's dream, we are developing a peaceful existence. In a man's dream the fleur-de-lys has a connection with heraldry representing faith, wisdom and chivalry.

LIMB – *see* BODY

LIMP

🌞 Limp, as in being lifeless, suggests that there has been a loss of essential spiritual energy.

♡ To have a limp in dreams suggests that we are out of balance in some aspect of our lives. It may be worthwhile trying to remember which leg is favoured, since the right side represents the assertive masculine and the left the more equable feminine.

🏛 Recognizing that a character in a dream is limping suggests that there may be a problem in waking life with a project or relationship. It may need rethinking or reassessing as to its viability.

You might like to consult the entry for Lame.

LINE

🌞 Spiritually in dreams a line can have great significance. The straight line can represent time and the ability to go both forward and back. When horizontal the line is the earthly world and the passive point of view; when vertical it is the spiritual world, the active aspect and the cosmic axis.

♡ Psychologically, we tend to need boundaries or demarcation lines, and those lines can be demonstrated in dream symbolism in ways that might not be feasible in everyday life. For instance, jumping over a line would suggest being brave enough to take risks. A line of objects might signify the choices we are offered. Line dancing implies synchronized movement.

🏛 A line in a dream often marks a boundary or denotes a measurement. In dreams, it can also signify a link between two objects to show a connection that is not immediately obvious. A straight line suggests a direct approach, the shortest way between two objects or places. A line of people or queue would suggest an imposed order for a particular purpose. If we are waiting in line, the purpose of the line will be important in interpretation.

LINEN

🌞 Spiritually, fine linen signifies purity and righteousness. By its fineness and the care it needs it suggests reverence and love.

❤ In today's world, where everything is done as quickly and as easily as possible, linen appearing in a dream would suggest a slowness of pace and caring, which enables us to appreciate our lives better.

▨ Linen in dreams on a purely practical level can suggest an appreciation of fine things. Linen tablecloths, for instance, may suggest some kind of a celebration in the sense of only using the best. Linen bed sheets might signify sensuality.

Also consult the entry for Fabric.

LION

✿ Spiritually, the lion symbolizes all those attributes that belong to the fiery principle. However, it is also an ambivalent symbol, since it represents both good and evil. It plays a part in the recognition of the four Elements – Fire, Earth, Air and Water – and represents Fire.

❤ In psychological terms, the lion represents all those qualities it shows: majesty, strength, pride, courage and so on. It is easier to recognize the necessity for such qualities in ourselves when symbolized in something else.

▨ The lion in dreams signifies both cruelty and strength. It also symbolizes the astrological sign of Leo and epitomizes the qualities of leadership depicted in that sign.

You might also like to consult the entry for Animals.

LIP – *see* EDGE

LIQUID

✿ A strong symbol in spiritual development is golden liquid which can represent both power and energy. Its appearance in dreams suggests we have reached a certain level of understanding.

❤ Liquid in dreams can have more than one meaning. Because it is always connected with 'flow', it can represent the idea of allowing feelings to flow properly. The colour of the liquid in the dream can be important since it can give an indication of exactly which feelings and emotions are being dealt with. For example, red might represent anger, whereas violet might signify spiritual aspiration.

▨ When something is unexpectedly liquid in a dream, we need to be aware that in everyday life we are in a situation that may not remain stable. At that point we need to be ready to 'go with the flow' in order to maximize the potential within that situation. One of the symbols of liquid is to do with liquidity – that is, having assets or possessions that can be realized. This can be on either a physical or emotional level.

You might also like to consult the entries for Colour and Water.

LIST

�*/* Dreaming of a list of any sort suggests an attempt to create some kind of spiritual order.

🖤 In dreams, lists can represent logical or linear thought, in that there is a progression from one item to another.

▦ To be making a list suggests trying to impose some sort of order in our lives. To be given a list suggests that order has been reached but we must take steps to implement whatever is suggested.

LITTER

�*/* Litter in dreams can alert us to a disorderly mess, a spiritual problem not properly thought through.

🖤 Just as a newborn litter of puppies has not yet developed individual qualities, so such an image in dreams suggests perhaps unformed or undifferentiated thought. Interestingly, a litter was initially a portable bed; it may be that we need to look at how permanent we feel an aspect of our lives to be.

▦ Recognizing litter as thrown away objects suggests that some aspects of day-to-day life are no longer of use to us and a degree of clearing unnecessary problems is important.

LITTLE – *see* SIZE

LIVE/LIVING

🌱 When something is live it is full of – perhaps unspent – spiritual energy. Considering such energy may alter our perception of the life we live.

🖤 If we consider that to live is to use energy effectively, any image in dreams that highlights this, constitutes a reminder. Live ammunition, for instance, suggests that care and control of danger is necessary.

▦ The implication that an animal or person in dreams is living suggests that it still exists. To dream of a dead relative as being alive suggests either their existence in memory or within the spiritual dimension, depending on our beliefs.

LIVER – *see* BODY

LIZARD – *see* REPTILES IN ANIMALS

LOAD/LOADED/LOADING – *see* BAGGAGE AND LUGGAGE

LOAN – *see* LEND/LENDING/LOAN

LOCK/LOCKED

🌱 A lock can suggest that either a new spiritual freedom is being offered to us or that the way forward is barred. Our actions are not appropriate.

🖤 It is very easy to lock away the emotions, supposedly to keep them safe. A lock appearing in a dream may alert us to the fact that we need to free up whatever we have shut away. To force a lock would indicate that we need to work against our own inclinations to lock things away in order to be free of inhibitions. To be mending a lock suggests that our personal space has been trespassed upon and we need to repair the damage.

▨ To recognize in a dream that a part of our body has become locked suggests that we are carrying extreme tension. We need to release that tension in a physical way in order to be healthy. To realize a door is locked suggests that somewhere we thought of as sanctuary is no longer available to us. It may also be that a course of action is not right.

Also consult the entries for Key and Prison.

LOCUST

❁ Spiritually, locusts signify divine retribution, a force that cannot be opposed, and also a misuse of resources.

◈ As a flying insect, the locust can signify scattered thought and concepts that have not been properly thought out and marshalled. Put together, they may be a very powerful tool, albeit somewhat dangerous.

▨ The image of a plague of locusts is so strong in Western thought that even in dreams it has come to represent retribution for some misdemeanour.

You might also like to consult the entry for Insect.

LOG – *see* TREE

LOOK – *see* SEARCH

LOOM

❁ The loom in spiritual terms symbolizes Fate, time and the weaving of destiny.

◈ A loom picks up on the symbol of weaving and the idea of creating our own lives. We are given certain basic materials that can lay down an elementary pattern, but we must add our own touches through knowledge and experience, which give individuality to the overall 'woven' existence.

▨ A loom in dreams will obviously have a different significance if it is a work tool, or if one is a creative artist. By and large a loom suggests creativity, whether more mechanical or craft-oriented. We all have the ability within ourselves to create beautiful objects and the loom is one of these symbols.

Consult the entry for Weaving for further clarification.

LORD – *see* AUTHORITY FIGURES IN PEOPLE

LORRY – *see* TRANSPORT

LOSE/LOSS/LOST

❁ The search for the lost object or the lost chord epitomizes the search for enlightenment. In spiritual terms we do not know what we are looking for until we have found it.

♥ To experience ourselves as being lost denotes confusion and perhaps a sense of rejection. This may be emotionally or mentally as much as physically. We have lost the ability or the motivation to make clear decisions.

▣ To lose something in a dream may mean that we have forgotten matters that could be important. This may be an opportunity, a friend or a way of thought that has previously sustained us. To suffer loss suggests that part of ourselves or our lives is now dead and we must learn to cope without it.

LOTTERY

☀ Spiritually, a lottery represents our ability to take chances, to rely on fate rather than good judgement. The 'lottery of life' has the same basic meaning as the luck of the draw, in that certain conditions seem to be predestined through our genetics, our way of life or our intrinsic decisions. We appear not to be in control.

♥ A lottery can highlight all sorts of belief systems, some valid and some not. The idea of random selection – particularly mechanically – links with belief in a mechanistic universe. The lottery also denotes our attitude to greed and poverty and to the principle of winning through luck rather than effort.

▣ A lottery suggests the idea of gaining through taking a risk with money. Gambling is part of human nature almost since time began, but a lottery is less immediate and in today's society much less to do with trying to guess the will of the Divine. To dream of winning a lottery would suggest that one has either been lucky or clever in waking life. To dream of losing might suggest that someone else was in control of our destiny.

You might like to consult the entries for Gambling, Ticket and Win/Winner.

LOUD – *see* NOISE

LOVE – *see* EMOTION

LOW – *see* POSITION

LUCK/LUCKY – *see* DICE/DIE AND GAMBLING

LUGGAGE

☀ Spiritually, if we are to travel 'light' we must often find a way of unburdening ourselves. Luggage in a dream, particularly as luggage on wheels becomes more available, can help us to envisage this.

♥ When luggage appears as a symbol in our dreams we should perhaps look at whether it is ours or someone else's. If ours, it signifies those views, attitudes and behaviours that we have brought through from the past. If it is someone else's, then we may be looking at family or global concepts that no longer are useful to us.

▓ Luggage in a dream can be slightly different to baggage in that luggage will symbolize what we feel is necessary to have us go forward. It can be those habits and emotions that have helped us in the past, but which can now be reappraised before being 'repacked' for more efficient use.

▐ As more people travel on business, luggage in both men's and women's dreams can signify work problems or information needed in that environment.

Consult the entry for Baggage for further clarification.

LUMINOUS

✹ If an article is luminous it contains its own light, which is a spiritual attribute.

♥ Usually in dreams, when something appears as luminous, what is represented is transparent, easily understood and with a quality beyond the norm.

▓ As a reflection of a piece of work or project that has been well executed, an image may appear in dreams as filled with its own light, i.e. luminous.

▐ In both men's and women's dreams, love and passion can give a luminous quality to images. It is as though the energy has taken on a different quality.

LUNGS – see BODY

LUXURY

✹ Spiritually, in a dream luxury signifies sinful self-indulgence, which might be counted as a spiritual misdemeanour.

♥ To be in luxurious surroundings suggests that we have given ourselves permission in some way to have a degree of comfort in our lives. To be uncomfortable in such surroundings suggests a poor self-image.

▓ Luxury tends to equate with wellbeing, so from a mundane perspective suggests that we are trying to create such feelings.

LYNCH

✹ A violent act such as lynching – sentencing to death by mob rule – suggests an abrupt end to a great negativity.

♥ Lynching appearing in a dream indicates that there is a complete lack of control of our emotions and we are unable to put a stop to our own destructiveness.

▓ When we are having to defend our own corner, our way of working, or our own beliefs, a violent reaction can lead to dreams of lynching. Such dreams are less likely in this day and age, but could be classed as nightmares when we are under extreme pressure.

LYNX – see ANIMALS

MACHETE – *see* **AXE AND WEAPON**

MACHINE

☼ A machine may well represent the machinations of life, which would be interpreted as The 'Life Process'. In Chinese medicine *ch'i* or spiritual energy flows in certain ways around the body and the life process aids in that flow.

♥ In dreams, machines represent the brain and the logical thinking processes, so psychologically it is the actual process of thinking that is important in this context, rather than what we are thinking about. If a machine seems large and overpowering, we perhaps need to reassess the effect our actions are having, both on us and those around us.

▨ When a machine of any sort – particularly one that operates automatically like a robot – appears in a dream, it is often highlighting the body's automatic functions. These are the ordinary everyday actions that take place, such as breathing, heartbeat, elimination – those mechanical drives towards life that help us to survive. The 'mechanics' of the body are an important part of our well-being and often when we perceive a machine breaking down in dreams, it warns us that we need to take care, that perhaps we are over-stressing a particular part of our body, such as the lungs or the intestines.

You might also like to consult the entries for Body and Engine.

MAD

☼ Madness can be translated into feelings of Spiritual Ecstasy, an altered state of consciousness.

♥ Being mad in a dream represents the uncontrollable – and out of control – aspects of extreme emotion. If we are conscious of being at odds with other people, and therefore considered to be mad, we are not integrating fully within society or the group to which we belong.

▨ When we are confronted by madness in a dream, we are confronting those parts of ourselves that, within our present situation, have not been integrated internally or properly focused. We are facing an aspect that is out of control and that, under certain circumstances, can be frightening if allowed to 'escape' or take us over.

You might like to consult the entry for Emotions for further clarification.

MAGGOTS

✹ Maggots in dreams may reflect our own fears about death and illness. No-one likes the idea of the physical body being consumed by maggots, although, in fact, the spiritual does remain whole.

◈ Though the old use of maggots to cleanse wounds is receiving attention today, maggots can represent impurities in the body. They also link with the sense of being eaten up from the inside by something – such as an idea, feeling or emotion – that is alien to us and can, therefore, overtake and overcome us.

▦ Maggots appearing in dreams in their correct context can represent the feelings we have about death. If a fisherman was using maggots we would be referring to power and energy, but if someone else was using maggots, their use of nastiness might be in question.

Consult the entry for Death, Dead People and Ill/Illness for further clarification.

MAGIC/MAGICIAN

✹ Magic and the use of powers beyond ourselves has always had an appeal. Classified as any extraordinary or mystical (beyond oneself) influence, charm, or power, in dreams this power can seem more easily accessible than at other times.

◈ Psychologically, when there is magic in a dream it indicates our ability to link with our own deepest powers. Initially, they can be the powers of sexuality, the powers of control, or of power over our surroundings. By learning, often through dreams, to control our emotions and channel them properly we are able to access energy beyond our own little world and use it to improve our own, or others', lives.

▦ When we are using magic both in dreams and in everyday life, we are using our energy to accomplish something without effort or difficulty. We are capable of controlling the situation that we are in, to have things happen for us and to create from our own needs and wants. The figure of a magician appearing in a dream signifies the arrival of a wise guardian and counsellor, whether that is from an internal perspective or in everyday life.

You might also like to consult the entries for Mystic, Witch and Wizard.

MAGISTRATE

✹ Spiritual authority coupled with spiritual knowledge is often represented by a dream of a magistrate. It signifies that we can be susceptible to both.

◈ It may well be that a part of us knows best what we should be doing, and our conscious, everyday working self is deliberately flouting that inner authority. A magistrate in dreams has sufficient authority to correct our misdemeanours.

▦ There are times when we need to be told what to do, or perhaps to have somebody who is more powerful than we are take control within our lives. A magistrate in everyday life imposes the laws of society for the good of the community in which we live. A judgement must be made as to what is for the good of all. In dreams, this figure will perform the same function, generally guiding us towards more acceptable behaviour.

Also consult the entries for Authority Figures in People and Judge/Judgement.

MAGNIFYING GLASS

🔅 Making Spirituality manifest would initially mean being more aware of our own actions. We need to examine ourselves minutely.

🔅 Where it strikes us that the magnifying glass itself and not what we are looking at is important, we are recognizing our own abilities, our own power within a situation.

🔅 When anything is magnified in a dream it is being brought to our attention. To be using a magnifying glass indicates that we should be making what we are looking at conscious. It needs to be made part of our everyday working life and we do have the power to create something out of the material that we have.

You might also like to consult the entry for Lens.

MAGPIE – *see* BIRDS

MAIL

🔅 Mail in dreams is communication from the spiritual realms.

🔅 Emotion is one of the most difficult things to communicate, so 'wrapping it up' in letters or emails is a strong dream image. Trying to send mail may be trying to communicate how we feel.

🔅 Mail in the sense of armour suggests defences that we put up, but may also signify the masculine gender. Retrieving lost mail suggests that we need to increase our motivation.

🔅 In a woman's dream mail may represent her more assertive side, whereas in a man's dream he may wish to reveal his true self.

You might like to consult the entries for Armour, Communication, Email and Letter for further information.

MAIM – *see* ACCIDENT, INJURE/INJURY, TRAUMA AND WOUND

MAKE-UP

🔅 Spiritually, we must be aware of the way we are 'made-up' (constructed) and must be conscious of the facade we present to other people. In dreams we can become conscious of that facade and whether it differs greatly from the person we feel ourselves to be.

🔅 To be dealing with make-up means that we have a choice as to the sort of person we want to be. We can choose our outward appearance and can create an impression that perhaps is different from the one we naturally make use of. To make-up, in the sense of bringing about a reconciliation, in our dreams suggests that we need to allow positive emotion to flow more fully.

Make-up indicates our ability to change the impression we make on others. If we are making ourselves up it can very often indicate a happy occasion. We need to put on a facade for people – we may even need to put on a facade for ourselves – so that we feel better about our own self-image. If we are making someone else up, then often we are helping them to create a false – or perhaps better – impression.

You might also like to consult the entry for Cosmetics.

MALLET

A mallet, usually made of wood, suggests a form of spiritual power and energy. However, because of the symbolic qualities, particularly evident in Freemasonry, of the mallet – those of authority and ownership – we need to be assured that power and energy are being channelled correctly.

The mallet is a symbol of the will correctly directed and to have such an item in a dream indicates that we may be attempting to make things happen in a particular way. Rather than brute force, finesse can be used, for correctly applied the mallet and chisel are shaping tools.

For something like a hammer or a mallet to appear in a dream indicates that we may be using undue force or power to achieve a certain outcome. A mallet is a hammer for a particular purpose, and in dreams will suggest that we choose tools that are right for our task.

Also consult the entry for Hammer.

MANDALA

The mandala is a sacred shape, which is so powerful that it is found in one form or another in most systems of belief, but most frequently in Eastern religions. Typically, it is a circle enclosing a square with a symbol in the centre representing the whole of life. It is mostly used as an aid to meditation. It moves us into a space that enables us to create a whole new concept of the principles of existence.

In dreams this pattern often appears without us knowing what it really represents. It is only when it is drawn afterwards that is it recognizable as a mandala. This would suggest that it is a true expression of our individuality and connection with Unity, whatever we consider this to be.

The mandala is often consciously depicted as an eight-pointed star and represents both Man's aspirations and his burdens. It often appears in recurring dreams in this form and then becomes a personal symbol of the journey from Chaos to Order. It has also been found that in a healing process this symbol will occur in dreams over and over again. The particular shape, number of sides and colours in a mandala will be significant.

Consult the entries for Chaos, Colour, Meditation, Mosaic, Numbers and Shapes/Patterns for additional information.

MANE – *see* HAIR AND HORSE IN ANIMALS

MANIA/MANIAC/MANIC

✷ Mania suggests behaviour that is without reason, and previously was thought to be a visitation by the Gods or spirits. In dreams such behaviour is a warning of spiritual overload.

♡ Manic behaviour, such as hyperactivity, in dreams suggests that the emotions are having a bad effect on us and causing us to be out of control.

▦ In dreams, a maniac is a personalization of that destructive part of our personality that is not properly under control.

Consult the entry for Emotions for further information.

MANSION – *see* HOUSE IN BUILDINGS

MANTRA

✷ Spiritually, sound repeated over and over induces a change of consciousness and awareness. The Mantra is the creation of a sound, corresponding to a name or an aspect of God, and is a creative vibration, frequently used in meditation. Often it is three syllables long, and is an aid to becoming closer to the centre of both oneself and the universe. As such, in dreams it opens up possibilities for enhanced wisdom and knowledge.

♡ If dreams are considered to be alert restfulness, the use prior to sleep of Mantra – using intense concentration and constant repetition – can have a profound effect on the dream state in allowing us to be more focused in our dreaming. We fill the mind with one concept of God, whatever that might be – coupled with a sense of spiritual union.

▦ In dreams we frequently hear the sound of our own name and can develop this into a mantra. It is (or rather becomes) the personal 'key' to universal knowledge. When the images evoked by Mantra in waking life also appear in dreams, we are thus able to accept their validity.

You might also like to consult the entry for Meditation as well as the information on Spiritual Imagery in the Introduction.

MANUSCRIPT – *see* INK, PAPER/PARCHMENT AND WRITING

MAORI – *see* INDIGENOUS PEOPLES

MAP

✷ A map can obviously help us in our quest to find the spiritual way forward. It is worth remembering that though others can read the map for us, ultimately we must make the journey ourselves and, therefore, we are our own guides.

◈ When we first set out on the journey of discovery that makes us grow into capable human beings, we often need clarification of the way that we must undertake the journey. In dreams this often appears as a map, whether this is an old-fashioned map denoting perhaps out-of-date information, or a computer-generated one symbolizing that others have made the same journey. The direction we are being shown to take is important: i.e. forwards, backwards, left or right and we are often helped by the idea of having a course to follow.

▣ For a map to appear in a dream often indicates the clarification of the direction we should be taking in life. We may feel that we are lost and need something to indicate the way forward, particularly so far as ambition or motivation is concerned. A map that has already been used by other people would, therefore, indicate that we are capable of taking a direction and learning from those people.

Consult the entry for Position for further clarification.

MARATHON – *see* RACE AND RUNNING

MARE – *see* HORSE IN ANIMALS

MARKET/MARKETPLACE

❀ A marketplace can be viewed as a place of spiritual exchange in dreams. We can establish a balance between our everyday reality and our spiritual or inner world.

◈ A market is a bustling, happy place and to dream of one may indicate that we need to look after ourselves more and to spend time with more people. An open air or farmers market suggests that we should pay more attention to the good things in life. It could also suggest that we need to become more commercial in the work that we are doing, or perhaps to be more creatively influenced, rather than doing something purely and simply because it is commercial – thus it has quite an ambivalent meaning.

▣ Dreaming that we are in a market indicates our ability to cope with everyday life, of being able to relate to people, but particularly to relate to crowds. It is also the place of buying and selling and, therefore, often gives us some sort of indication as to how we value our various attributes, whether we have something to sell or whether we are buying.

You might also like to consult the entry for Food.

MARRIAGE

❀ Spiritually there is a process of integration that needs to come about. This is usually known as a Mystic Union or mystic marriage. Here the physical and spiritual sides need to harmonize and when they do we are suffused by a sense of bliss. The sense of rightness is sometimes felt first in dreams.

🖤 Firstly the masculine and feminine sides (drive and receptivity) of our personality need to unite, then emotions are allowed to settle. In dreams this can manifest as a sense of peace.

▦ On a more mundane level, as these processes of integration are taking place we will often dream of marriage. In previous times, the sexual act was seen as symbolizing the union of the sacred and the secular. The concept of the sacred marriage or sacred love ceremony originated with the ancients, who enacted annual ceremonies to bring fertility and prosperity, signifying commitment. Today dreams of marriage have that symbolism of dedication to someone else.

⊡ As an actual wedding ceremony tends to become less important but commitment is, both men and women may dream of an act of commitment, a proposal or making a vow when they feel secure within a relationship. Dreaming of monogamy highlights this commitment.

You might like to consult the entries for Propose/Proposal, Vow and Wedding/ Wedding Dress/Wedding Ring.

MARSH

🌣 A marsh being a mixture of earth and water suggests spiritual and emotional conflict. Water symbolizes emotion and earth symbolizes security, so an excess of emotion is not allowing us to feel at ease.

🖤 Dreaming of marshy ground very often represents difficulty on an emotional level. Our emotions are clouded by practical concerns. Perhaps we are creating emotional difficulties for ourselves – or even having them created for us – which make it difficult for us to feel secure.

▦ When we dream of a marsh or a swamp, it can indicate that we are feeling 'bogged down'. We feel that we are being held back in something we want to do, and perhaps we lack either the self-confidence or emotional support that we need to move forward. A marsh or a swamp can also indicate that we are being swamped by circumstances, being trapped in some way by the events round us.

Also consult the entries for Mud, Earth/Earthquake, Swamp and Water.

MARTYR

🌣 In previous times being a martyr inevitably meant that suffering was involved. We may perceive the need, spiritually, to become a victim, sacrificing ourselves on others' behalf and thus give our life some meaning. Such actions can be perceived as honourable provided they arise from the correct motivation.

♥ Dreaming of a religious martyr often signifies that we need to question our own religious beliefs and upbringing, and our strength of purpose and commitment. We are perhaps allowing excessive enthusiasm to guide us.

▦ Actually experiencing ourselves in dreams as playing the martyr highlights our tendency to do things without being sufficiently assertive to say no, and to act from a sense of duty. When we are aware of someone else being a martyr we may have too high expectations of that person.

You might also like to consult the entries for Fanatic and Victim.

MASK

☸ In primitive Shamanistic societies, to wear an animal mask gave the wearer the powers of that animal. If we dream of wearing such a mask, we may need to consider that animal's qualities and how they can be, or are, applied in our waking lives. The Death Mask, either our own or another's, can appear in dreams as a signal that it is time to put an end to a spiritual game we are playing.

♥ When we are trying to protect ourselves and prevent other people knowing what we are thinking or feeling, we 'mask' ourselves. A mask appearing in a dream can, therefore, represent concealment, perhaps of emotion, perhaps of finer feelings.

▦ Most people have a facade they put on for others, particularly at a first meeting. To dream of a mask often alerts us to either our own or other people's facade. When we are not being true to ourselves we can often experience this in dreams as a 'negative' or frightening mask.

You might also like to consult the entries for Animals and Shaman.

MASOCHISM

☸ Spiritual masochism suggests an act of self-inflicted pain, such as self-flagellation. The pain perversely brings pleasure. It can be an aspect of martyrdom.

♥ Pleasure from pain, in the emotional sense in dreams, can alert us to our propensity to be a victim, albeit through a self-inflicted injury.

▦ In a mundane sense masochism in dreams can highlight our tendency towards lugubrious acceptance that we can do nothing about the circumstances we are in.

▯ Sado-masochism in dreams, while seemingly sexual in nature, may well show a propensity to tolerate an extreme attitude within a relationship, for both men and women.

You might like to consult the entry for Martyr for further clarification.

MASS – *see* **RITE/RITUAL AND SPIRITUAL IMAGERY IN THE INTRODUCTION**

MASSACRE

⚙ A massacre is an indiscriminate killing and is of little spiritual value except to alert us to the violence of others' belief.

♥ Indiscriminate killing in dreams suggests that emotions have been allowed to get out of control and taken over from reasonable behaviour.

▦ In mundane terms, when business methods become both heartless and ruthless this can be translated into dreams as a massacre. This may also suggest that there is little we can do personally to prevent this.

You might like to consult the entries for Death and Kill.

MATTRESS – *see* BED/BEDROOM AND ALSO THE INFORMATION ON BED/MATTRESS IN FURNITURE/FURNISHINGS

MAUSOLEUM – *see* CATACOMB/CRYPT, MEMORIAL AND TOMB

MAYPOLE

⚙ The maypole in a spiritual sense is a representation of the phallic, of masculine spirituality and of life-giving energy.

♥ Psychologically, festivals, celebrations and occasions for ceremony are necessary for the human being to be at ease with himself. Often the maypole may be one such symbol – of celebration, of new life. It may also represent time in a dream and the way in which a dream indicates the type of timing that is necessary within certain situations.

▦ A maypole in a dream can very often represent the masculine and may indicate the 'dance' that we go through when coming to terms with our own universe. It is the central pole of the world that we create for ourselves; thus to dream of a maypole may have sexual connotations, but also may indicate the way in which we handle our own lives.

⊡ As a symbol of fertility, the maypole can appear in a woman's dream as a promise of things to come. In a man's dream it may well mark the taking on of responsibility. In former times, relationships begun on Mayday, when the maypole dances took place, lasted for a year and a day, thus honouring the goddess of fertility.

MAZE

⚙ A maze is a path of initiation into divine knowledge. It also represents the feminine, and in its twists and turns signifies – at one and the same time – confusion and innate wisdom.

♥ Psychologically, the maze may represent the variety of opinions and authoritative beliefs that we come up against in our ordinary, everyday world. We may be trying to find our own way through this mass of detail and we picture this in a dream as actually trying to find our way through a maze.

▦ A maze often represents a confusion of ideas and feelings. There are conflicting urges and opinions and we often discover that, in attempting to find our way through the maze, we have learnt something about our own courage, our own ability to meet problems. Often there is the apparently irrational fear and doubt that arises from not being able to find our way in and out of the maze. This can allow us to release feelings of self-doubt and fear. *Also consult the entries for Initiation and Labyrinth.*

MEAL

✵ The sacred meal has always been an integral part of most systems of belief. Food is such a vehicle for the life force and for sharing in community that this type of meal becomes an important spiritual concept. It carries this significance in dreams.

♡ Banquets, festivals and feasts in dreams all represent man's capacity for enjoyment. A meal, whether in company or alone, signifies our appreciation of the gifts of nature.

▦ From a purely practical viewpoint a meal eaten alone represents an aspect of self-nurturing; when eating in company, a convivial social process. In dreams, such images help to widen our perspective to encompass the needs of others. Offering a meal to a beggar would signify our need to share what we have.

You might also like to consult the entries for Festival, Food and Party.

MEANDER

✵ It was Jung who recognized that dreams appear to meander (wander) all over the place, and it is only by perceiving the overall spiritual picture that we can make sense of them. The Spiritual Spiral is a concept whereby physical manifestation takes place, moving very quickly from the spiritual to the physical realms. In dreams this can often be perceived as a slow-motion meandering. We should look at whether it is a downward spiral, an aimless wandering or a purposeful – if indirect – exploration.

♡ Water moves in its own way, and often to be conscious of a river or a road meandering around us indicates that we should be more aware of our own emotions, that we are capable of dealing with these emotions in a much gentler way than by being very direct. This may also refer to our relationship with other people. It could be that we need to recognize that other people cannot be as straightforward as we are.

▦ In a dream, to have a path or the road in front of you meandering – that is, not going in any particular direction – suggests that we very often have to 'go with the flow', to simply follow what happens without actually thinking of the direction in which we are going. Sometimes the meandering has a kind of purpose, in that by wandering about in an apparently aimless fashion we are learning to live in the moment and understand our own reactions and responses to the outside world.

You might also like to consult the entries for Journey, Path, Wander/Wandering and Water.

MEASURE

☼ A measure in dreams – whether of capacity, length or weight – suggests a comparison, often against some kind of spiritual standard.

♥ Emotionally, when we attempt to find some kind of tranquility we will measure it against previous experience. In dreams this may come across as an overflowing cup, gauge or measuring stick.

▦ In waking life, we will try to measure our performance against correct practice or a set standard. This will surface in dreams with actual physical instruments of measurement such as rulers, scales and other measuring devices. To be measuring standards is to be applying a preset code of behaviour.

You might also like to consult the entries for Cup, Scales and Weighing/Weight for further clarification.

MEDAL

☼ Just as a medal acknowledges our prowess, from a spiritual perspective it reminds us to adhere to a spiritual code of conduct.

♥ Human beings both like and need to feel good about themselves. A medal in a dream acknowledges our talents and/or successes – not just in the immediate moment – but gives a permanent reminder of what we have done.

▦ A medal is often a reward for good work or for bravery, so when one appears in a dream it is recognition of our own abilities. If we are giving someone else a medal then we are honouring that part of ourselves represented by the dream character.

You might also like to consult the entries for Badge/Brooch and Win/Winning.

MEDIA

☼ In its truest meaning 'the media' signifies all means of mass communication. Spiritually, therefore, in dreams it comes to mean the dissemination of knowledge, particularly from a cosmic perspective.

♥ Radio, television and other media all feed our need to know and emotionally give a false sense of ownership, particularly of celebrities and their lives. In dreams, where once media would have meant the possession of facts, now it can symbolize a form of intrusion on our part. To be aware of any of the tools of the media suggests that we need to be conscious of our sense of responsibility towards other people.

▣ Dreaming of hearing information through any forms of media indicate that we need to pay due regard to events beyond our own everyday concerns giving careful consideration to community and worldly matters.

You might also like to consult the entries for Actor, Celebrity, Communication, Newspaper, Radio and Television.

MEDICATION/MEDICINE

◈ The spiritual need for a healing influence in our lives is indicated by medicine appearing. It may be symbolic of spiritual healing or of the need to potentize (make more powerful) any medicine we have to take so that it can work to our best advantage.

◈ When in waking life we need medication and either cannot take it, or have difficulty in obtaining it, our dreams will often present a way – or the courage – to overcome the difficulty in waking life. Sometimes an experience that we have in waking life can be unpleasant in the immediate moment, but ultimately is good for us. In dreams, medicine can stand as such a symbol.

▣ To be taking medicine in a dream suggests that on some level we are aware of part of ourselves, possibly our self-image, that needs healing. Often we are aware of what the medicine is for and are thus alerted either to a potential health problem, or to a situation that can be changed from the negative to the positive.

You might also like to consult the entries for Doctor, Drugs, Hospital, Nurse/Nursing and Tablet.

MEDITATION

◈ As a discipline, meditation helps us to become more aware of changes in consciousness. It also has the effect of opening our minds to dreaming as a spiritual learning tool. After learning meditation, our dreams take on a different depth and clarity. For instance, the mandala seen in dreams can become a gauge for spiritual progression.

◈ Often on an unconscious level we are aware of the need to change consciousness or attitude. To dream of meditating, particularly when we first learn this art, can highlight this for us. We can access our more creative, spiritual side and thus mandala and mantra become second nature, both asleep and awake.

▣ Interpreting the act of meditation will depend on whether we meditate in real life. In someone who does, it will suggest a discipline that is helpful, putting them in touch with intuition and spiritual matters. In someone who does not, it may indicate the need to be more introverted in order to understand the necessity to be responsible for oneself.

Consult the entries for Mandala and Mantra for further clarification.

MEDIUM

❁ Mediumistic aspects in a dream can represent our wish to be in contact with the dead. This does not necessarily have to be dead in literal terms, it can merely be what is 'dead' in our life, that which we may wish to resurrect. During spiritual development, our perceptions widen from the ordinary everyday to other aspects and dimensions of knowledge that have become available to us. Whether these are aspects of our own personality or of the spirit realm is immaterial, since ultimately their function is to help us progress. The spiritual self has access to the Collective Unconscious in its entirety.

♦ To dream of being mediumistic would indicate that we are aware of greater powers than we believe we have in ordinary everyday life. When spirits appear in dreams, their function may be to help us through various states of transition. While we cope with everyday fears, there are many unconscious memories and feelings, which can surface unexpectedly. When we are conscious of a kindly or helpful spirit we are aware that we can move on. When we see the spirits of dead people we usually need reassurance.

▦ Dreaming of visiting a medium very often means that we are looking for some kind of contact with our own unconscious, or with the dead. We may also be attempting to alert our own intuition and use it differently to a way we have done previously. At a very basic level, we all have fears and feelings about death, and the actual appearance in dreams of spiritual entities can help us to come to terms with these.

You might like to consult the entry for Dead People.

MEET/MEETING

❁ As part of our spiritual learning process, in dreams we at some point will meet (come face to face with) a figure who is representative of a spiritual teacher.

♦ A meeting is a gathering of people with a common aim or purpose. In dreams, this can often signify the integration of several aspects of our personality.

▦ A work meeting or consultation in dreams may signify an attempt to gain a consensus of opinion or an agreed course of action. This may be a way of dealing with our own inner confusion, or that which is actually in an everyday situation.

Also consult the information on the Wise Old Man in the Introduction.

MELT

❁ On a spiritual level, melting suggests losing form and has sometimes had connections with the overcoming of negativity and evil. This is pictured most successfully in horror movies and dream images often follow the same format.

◈ To see something melting in a dream is an indication that our emotions may be softening. We are perhaps losing the rigidity we have needed to face the world with previously. We are undergoing a change and are becoming softer.

▦ When we feel ourselves to be melting we may be becoming more romantically inclined and less likely to drive ourselves forward. We perhaps need to sit and simply let a situation develop around us to the point where it is safe for us to give up control.

You might also like to consult the entry for Ice/Iceberg/Icicles.

MEMORIAL

◈ A memorial is a tangible representation of homage and esteem. Seeing the Cenotaph, or indeed any other war memorial, in dreams is a timely reminder of the sanctity of life.

◈ A memorial may simply be recognition of a happier time that needs to be remembered. A mausoleum in a dream, since it holds many tombs, may be a memorial to family and inherited values.

▦ To see a memorial such as a war memorial in a dream takes us back to a previous time, to a memory that may be 'cast in stone'. We need to be able to come to terms with this memory in order to move on.

You might also like to consult the entries for Catacomb/Crypt, Inheritance and Tomb.

MEND/MENDING – *see* REPAIR

MERLIN – *see* CAMELOT AND WIZARD

MERMAID/MERMAN

◈ The mermaid and merman symbolize the ability to integrate the spiritual aspects of the personality with the emotional. In being part fish and part human, they also symbolize the evolutionary journey from pure instinct to wisdom.

◈ Mermaids and mermen are feminine and masculine representations of the link between the darker forces – which we do not necessarily understand – and the conscious self. In dreams the mermaid epitomizes how difficult it is to integrate the two sides of our nature. This lack of integration can result in capriciousness. The merman, however, is said to be less 'intrigued' by humans so, therefore, represents unification, but in a way that is more isolated.

▦ Traditionally, the mermaid or merman belongs to the sea as well as being able to exist on land. This symbolically represents an ability to be deeply emotional and also entirely practical. Until these two separate parts are properly integrated, the human being cannot fully exist in either the emotional or practical realms.

⊡ Many stories exist of the human's attempt to mate or link with these creatures of the sea, though the merman is less fascinated than his counterpart by humans. Most attempts end in hurt and distress for one party or the other and men's dreams of such a creature of fantasy in particular can reflect this. Women's dreams may contain an element of coming to terms with her own capriciousness.

You might also like to consult the entry for Sea in Water.

MESSAGE

☼ Receiving a message – by whatever means – in dreams signifies communication, probably from the Higher Self. Sending a message from a spiritual perspective suggests trying to make contact with Spirit.

♥ Dreams themselves were, and still are, considered to be messages from the gods or spiritual realms. As such, they require careful interpretation; images of letters, parcels, emails and other technology can all signify messages from the unconscious or instinctive realms.

▦ In dreams, receiving or sending a message highlights the importance of information *per se*. Particularly if we work in the creative fields and information technology, messages in dreams will represent our ability to handle such input. To remember the input suggests the information is useful, to forget, that we have the information but must rediscover it. A message in a bottle signifies that contact is being made from the less accessible parts of our personality.

Consult the entries for Bottle, Communication, Email, Letter and Parcel/Package for further clarification.

METAL

☼ The ancients recognized the importance of metal, particularly as offerings to the gods, and much of that symbolism is still relevant in dreams today as we find our magical roots and progress on our spiritual journey.

♥ Most metals have symbolic meanings. They can also be connected with various planets: Sun is represented by gold, the Moon by silver, Mercury by quicksilver, Venus by copper, Mars by iron, Jupiter by tin, Saturn by lead. In dreams these ancient symbolisms begin to surface as we learn more. For instance, Mars the warrior wielding an iron sword suggests that we need to fight our own corner and become more assertive.

▦ Any metal appearing in dreams represents the restrictions of the real world. It can represent basic abilities and attributes, but also can be hardness of feeling or emotional rigidity. An article made of lead suggests a heavy responsibility.

Consult the entries for Alchemy, Gold, Iron, Lead and Planets for further information and clarification.

METAMORPHOSIS – *see* **TRANSFORMATION AND TRANSMUTATION IN THE INTRODUCTION**

MICROCHIP

🔅 In dreams a microchip will signify something that is small but powerful, such as the information we need to make spiritual progress.

💙 A microchip, being the essential driving force behind some much of today's technology, can represent the whole plethora of emotions available to us if we have the courage to access them.

🔲 Having to become aware of a microchip in dreams suggest that we need to become aware of our motivations and drives. Computers are now such an integral part of our lives that any part of them will be easily decipherable in their symbolism – for instance, a computer screen may have the same relevance for some as a picture does for an artist.

MICROSCOPE

🔅 A degree of detailed introspection is called for, either spiritual or physical.

💙 We have the ability to look at things in dreams in much finer detail than we would necessarily do in the waking state. While the mind can be creative, it sometimes also needs to apply scientific – and perhaps logical – thought to a problem, and the symbol of a microscope can draw attention to this.

🔲 A microscope in a dream very often indicates that we need to pay attention to detail. Also we may need to be somewhat introspective in order to achieve a personal goal.

Also consult the entry for Laboratory.

MIGRANT – *see* **IMMIGRANT**

MILITARY – *see* **ARMED FORCES**

MILK

🔅 One of the theories of Creation is that a celestial milk was stirred in order to create form. Milk in this context becomes a symbol for Creation and Chaos.

💙 As a nourishing food milk represents nurturing and, therefore by association, the qualities of mothering. It may also suggest the faculty of intuition.

🔲 Milk in a practical sense in dreams can represent the flow of creativity. It can also suggest a requirement for simplicity and a return to basic ideas and knowledge. Milk that has gone sour indicates there is a problem in the completion of a project.

⚁ As a symbol associated with the Great Mother, in a woman's dream milk can symbolize her own femininity, ability to nurture and her intuition. In a man's dream, it is more likely to represent his need to be cosseted and cared for, though it can also signify the flow of ideas and concepts.

Consult the entries for Chaos, Food and Great Mother in Archetypes in the Introduction for further clarification.

MILL/MILLSTONE

☼ A mill symbolizes transformative energy, turning the crude into the usable. The two large stones that make up a millstone are said to signify will and intellect, the tools we use in transformation.

♥ There is a transformation that occurs when any material is ground down and changed into a more useable material. A dream containing a mill will signify that transformation and echoes the process of Creation.

▦ A mill extracts what is useful from the crude material it is fed. It is this quality that is symbolized in dreams. We are able to extract from our experiences in life what is useful to us and what we can convert into nourishment.

MINE/MINER

☼ Mines spiritually suggest the ability to 'mine', or learn from the emerging unconscious.

♥ The word 'mine' initially signified crude ore and has since come to mean the place from which crude ore is taken. In this sense dreaming of a mine suggests prospecting for crude material, which can be refined, whether that is raw emotion or unexpressed feelings. This is also one of those symbols that can actually be a wordplay. The objects in the dream are 'mine'. Dreaming of a miner is that part of us that is prepared to explore and use the crude material.

▦ Dreaming of mines signifies bringing the resources of the unconscious into the light of day. We are able to use the potential we have available. Interestingly in dreams mines can also represent the workplace.

You might also like to consult the entries for Digging/Excavation and Metal.

MINOTAUR

☼ The Minotaur is a mythical beast – half man and half bull – that was trapped within the first labyrinth created. Spiritually, it is symbolic of man's instinctive urges overcome by sheer bravery.

♥ In dreams, depending on our personality, the Minotaur can be seen as a figure either to be pitied or feared. His conquest is part of the Hero's Journey to self-actualization or realization of our own power.

▣ As a recognizable fabulous beast, viewed from a practical perspective, the overcoming of the Minotaur denotes the solving of problems in a well thought and logical manner (mind against instinct).

Consult the entries for Fabulous Beasts, Labyrinth and Monster for further information.

MINUTE – *see* **SMALL**

MIRROR

✸ The mirror in dreams suggests self-realization, which reflects spiritual wisdom. As a means of understanding ourselves on a deeper level, we can set up a dialogue in real life between our mirror image and ourselves. Many of the insights gained can be quite startling. As a symbol in dreams it allows us to search our self-image and make whatever changes are necessary.

♥ To be looking in a mirror can signify trying to look behind us without letting others know what we are doing. We may have a concern over past behaviour. We may also need to 'reflect' on something we have done or said. When the image in the mirror is distorted we are having a problem in understanding ourselves. When the mirror image speaks to us we should be listening more closely to our inner selves.

▣ Dreaming of a mirror suggests concern over our self-image. We are worried as to what others think of us, and need self-examination in order to function correctly. There may be some anxiety over ageing or health.

You might also like to consult the entry for Reflection.

MISCARRIAGE

✸ Dreaming of a miscarriage, whether our own or someone else's, suggests that we are conscious of the fact something is not right. Spiritually, we must reject whatever is wrong.

♥ Dreaming of a miscarriage can also suggest the loss of work, a project or even a part of ourselves, and we need time to acclimatize. A miscarriage of justice suggests that all aspects of a story have not been taken into consideration.

▣ A miscarriage can represent aspects of early death and the fear it can engender. Also it can signify the early finishing of a project or task before it has really had a chance to reach its peak.

⦚ In a woman's dream it will depend on whether she has suffered a miscarriage, since nowadays she may not have given herself time to grieve properly. When a man dreams of his partner's miscarriage, it highlights fears over changes in responsibility.

MISER – see MONEY

MISSIONARY – see SPIRITUAL IMAGERY IN THE INTRODUCTION

MIST

⚙ Mist can symbolize spiritual initiation, a passage through an area where we cannot perceive things properly. Mist in a dream can indicate a transition state, a way from one state of awareness to another, and will often manifest to signify this.

♡ Mist is a symbol of loss and confusion – particularly when it comes to emotions – so when this image appears we may need to sit down and reconsider our actions, and how they may affect us, or indeed others – in waking life.

▦ In waking life, many states of confusion can arise. Swirling mist in a dream may signify that the confusion arises from others. To be moving through stationary mist suggests that we are capable of reaching our goal provided we take into account our own confusion.

MISTLETOE

⚙ Mistletoe represents the Essence of Life. In myth it was used to kill Baldur the Norse god of peace. Thought by the Druids to be an 'in between', or a gateway to other worlds, it is a divine healing substance.

♡ As a parasite, mistletoe has the ability to draw strength from its host, but also to be useful in its own right. It can, therefore, symbolize relationships where there is a dependency on one partner. It is said that mistletoe takes on some of its hosts' characteristics, apple-grown mistletoe being different to oak-grown.

▦ In mundane terms mistletoe obviously is most often dreamt of around Christmas. Conventionally, mistletoe represents a time of celebration, love and partnership. To dream of kissing under the mistletoe symbolizes a relationship that may be transitory.

You might also like to consult the entry for Flowers.

MOB – see CROWD

MOLE – see ANIMALS

MONEY

⚙ Money in dreams can represent our spiritual currency and also spiritual 'change', small or otherwise. Symbols of money such as gold coins or money bags can signify our spiritual resources, which we can call on in times of difficulty. In the spiritual sense, savings suggests those talents and abilities that we have or have developed, but have not yet used, particularly those for the Greater Good.

◈ Money can represent our own personal resources – whether material or spiritual – and our potential for success. In some circumstances a dream of money can be linked with our view of our own power. When we dream of savings we are aware of the need for conservation. This may be on a personal level or in a more global sense. A refund of money suggests that we have put effort into en emotional commitment, but have had to accept that that 'payment' is not valid. A mortgage in dreams suggests ownership of an asset – whether emotional or material – for which we must pay in the future.

▦ Money in dreams does not necessarily represent hard currency, but more the way in which we value ourselves. This symbol appearing in dreams would suggest that we need to assess that value more carefully, and equally to be aware of what we 'pay' for our actions and desires. If there is a feeling of self-denial in our making savings, particularly to the point of miserliness, we may not have managed our resources properly in the past and are having to suffer for it now. We may also fear the future. If someone else gives us their savings, we are able to use their knowledge and expertise.

You might also like to consult the entries for Debt, Lend/Lending/Loan and Wealth.

MONK

◈ In dreams, as someone who has dedicated himself to his God or Ultimate Power, a monk represents spirituality, obedience and discipline.

◈ In his devotion to the mystical life, the monk in dreams symbolizes an emotional response to a vocation, perhaps to a life of ascetism. He symbolizes holiness – and no matter what religion – that part of us that searches for the divine. He can have the same significance as the hermit or wanderer.

▦ As a shadowy representation of the part of us that prefers to exist in isolation, the monk can appear in dreams when our self-belief is under threat. When he is cowled or hooded he signifies hidden information, but with his face uncovered he represents Truth.

⟐ In a man's dream a monk can signify the need or wish for celibacy. In a woman's dream he may be a representation of the Animus.

Consult the entries for Ascetic, Hermit, Mystic and Wanderer/Wandering for further information.

MONKEY – *see* ANIMALS

MONSTER

◈ A monster is usually large and, therefore, can highlight a childlike fear – perhaps the fear of death and all that goes with it – or the fear of failure. Such an image tends to be encountered at some point in the Hero's Journey.

❤ When, in everyday life, events get out of proportion we often have to suppress our reactions. In dreams we cannot do this and so our minds create some way of dealing with the problem. Often the colour of the monster will give us some indication of what the problem is; a red monster would indicate anger (possibly uncontrolled), whereas a yellow one might suggest resentment.

▦ Any monster appearing in a dream represents something that we have made larger than life. We have personalized it so that whatever is worrying us appears as a creature. It usually indicates our negative relationship with ourselves and fear of our own emotions and drives. If we vanquish the monster, it is said that we must take care not to kill it, since we may be killing off part of our personality. Equally it should not be allowed to overcome us; self-survival kicks in and we will normally wake up before it does.

You might like to consult the entries for Colour, Dinosaurs, Fabulous Beasts, Minotaur and also the Introduction for the Hero's Journey.

MONOGAMY – *see* **MARRIAGE**

MOON

☼ The Great Mother, the darker, unknown side of Self, is symbolized by the moon. It is also symbolic of the unapproachable feminine.

❤ It has always been known that the moon has a psychological effect on the human being. In Pagan times, it was suggested that she ruled men's emotions and guarded women's intuition. Even today, that symbolism still stands. Moonlight in dreams signifies romanticism and in some cases entry into a different dimension of being.

▦ The moon has always represented the emotional and feminine self. It is the intuition, the psychic, love and romance. To dream of the moon, therefore, is to be in touch with the side of ourselves that is dark and mysterious. Often in dreams the moon can also represent our mother or the relationship with her.

⟨⟩ When the moon appears in a man's dream he either has to come to terms with his own intuitive side or with his fear of women. In a woman's dream the moon usually indicates her inter-relationships with other women through their collective intuition.

You might also like to consult the entry for Planets.

MORNING – *see* **TIME**

MORTGAGE – *see* **DEBT, MONEY AND WEALTH**

MORTUARY

☼ A mortuary may symbolize a spiritual transition phase. We are dead to the old way of life and have new spiritual awareness. When a mortuary appears in a dream, we are usually having to consider our fears and feelings about death.

◈ If we are viewing a dead body we may be having to consider a part of ourselves that has died or changed irrevocably, or perhaps a now defunct relationship. If we are the body in the mortuary, we may have induced a state of inertia that does not allow us to enjoy life properly.

▦ In everyday life, a mortuary is a frightening place, connected as it tends to be with the trauma of death or endings. A mortuary's clinical atmosphere may mean that we should simply observe without judgment what is occurring around us.

You might also like to consult the entries for Dead People and Death.

MOSAIC

✸ The Kaleidoscope of Life, with its many facets, is a potent spiritual symbol represented in dreams by the mosaic.

◈ Within a mosaic, made up of many small parts, there is a deliberate act of creation. When we are working with a mosaic in dreams we are being alerted to our abilities as a creator. The colours and shapes used will be important.

▦ Any intricate pattern appearing in dreams usually signifies the pattern of our lives. We probably need to consider life as a whole, but also to understand and respect the many separate parts of it.

Consult the entries for Colours, Kaleidoscope, Mandala and Shapes/Patterns for additional information.

MOSES – *see* SPIRITUAL IMAGERY IN THE INTRODUCTION

MOTH

✸ The moth symbolizes the Self, but perhaps in its darker, more worldly sense. As the butterfly symbolizes the soul, so the moth symbolizes Spirit trapped in the physical realms.

◈ The moth symbolizes the darker side of us that uses fantasy. The moth emerging from darkness signifies our need to recognize this shadowy self so that we can survive difficulties unscathed.

▦ The moth is largely associated with nighttime and therefore connects with the hidden side of our nature. Also, because the moth can be self-destructive when there is light around, it may highlight personal weakness. It also tends to symbolize our dream self and the more transient side of our personality – that part that finds difficulty in settling to proper tasks.

Consult the entry for Butterfly for further information.

MOTHER – *see* ARCHETYPES IN THE INTRODUCTION, FAMILY AND MUMMY (EGYPTIAN)

MOTORBIKE – *see* TRANSPORT

MOULD/MOULDY

☀ Mould or mouldiness in dreams suggests that the essential energy has dissipated. There is no longer a link to the spiritual dimension.

♡ When in dreams something has gone mouldy or has putrefied, it has been contaminated. Emotionally there is a negativity present, which indicates that we can no longer appreciate a sense of clarity; our vision is clouded and has upset our balance.

▦ There is a sense that the life has gone out of a project or task, perhaps that in waking life they have gone on too long or lost focus. If, in dreams, food has gone mouldy we no longer have some essential support. If mould is growing, for instance on a wall, there is a negative energy around, which suggests there may be difficult times ahead if it is not dealt with properly.

Consult the entries for Decay and Food for further information.

MOUND – *see* HILL

MOUNTAIN

☀ Representing the centre of our existence in earthly terms, the mountain is an image that can be worked on over and over again. It represents the higher, more spiritual aspects of the personality.

♡ We all have difficulties to face in life. Often it is how we face those difficulties that is important. The symbol of the mountain offers many alternatives and choices, such as whether to choose the apparently easier route or the more difficult. This means we can work out, through dreams, our best course of action in everyday life.

▦ In dream sequences the mountain usually appears in order to symbolize an obstacle that needs to be overcome. By daring to climb the mountain we challenge our own inadequacies and free ourselves from fear. To reach the top is to achieve our goal. To fall down the mountain indicates carelessness and that we should perhaps consider our actions more carefully.

Also consult the entry for Hill for more information.

MOURNING

☀ Mourning expresses grief, a coming to terms with loss. In the spiritual sense we may believe in life after death but we still no longer have the physical presence of the individual.

♡ In many cultures less emotionally repressed than our own, the period of mourning is seen as a way of assisting the departing soul on its way. In dreams we may find that we are helping ourselves to create a new beginning through our mourning for the old. Psychologically, we need a period of adjustment when we have lost something (for instance when a relationship ends) and need to grieve for ourselves as much as for what we have lost.

🔲 The process of mourning is an important one in all sorts of ways. We not only mourn death but also the end of a relationship or a particular part of our lives. Since sometimes mourning or grieving is seen as inappropriate in waking life, it will often appear in dreams as a form of relief or release.

You might also like to consult the entries for Death, Funeral, Weeping and Wake.

MOUSE – *see* ANIMALS

MOUTH – *see* BODY

MOVEMENT

🔅 A movement towards Spiritual Acceptance can be undertaken when the time is considered to be right. Movement in dreams is usually highlighted to make us aware of our progress. Spiritually, movement such as dance is an act of worship or adoration.

◈ The way we move in dreams can indicate a great deal about our motivations. For instance, to be moving briskly would suggest an easy acceptance of the necessity for change, whereas being moved – such as on some kind of moving walkway – would signify being moved by outside circumstances or at the wish of other people.

🔲 Moving forward suggests an acceptance of our abilities, while moving backwards signifies withdrawal from a situation. Moving sideways would suggest a deliberate act of avoidance.

Consult the entries for Dance, Immobile/Immobility and Walking for further information.

MUD

🔅 Spiritually mud represents the very basic materials of earth and water from which we are all formed, and thus its appearance in dreams indicates the need to go 'back to basics'.

◈ Mud represents the fundamental substance of life, which, handled properly, has a tremendous potential for growth but, handled badly, can be dangerous. Many cultures believe mankind was fashioned from clay mud to give him structure. In dreams, if the mud is too dry we have suppressed emotion, if too wet, like marshland, we cannot develop a proper way of working.

🔲 Mud in a dream suggests that we are feeling bogged down, perhaps by not having sorted out practicality and emotion (earth and water). Mud can also represent past experiences or our perception of them, which has the ability to hold us back.

You might also like to consult the entries for Earth/Earthquake, Marsh and Water.

MUMMY (EGYPTIAN)

The Egyptian mummy symbolizes death, but also preservation after death and, therefore, the afterlife. It also symbolizes the Self, the unbending Mother and self-preservation.

Egypt for many represents magic, and the mummy in this case its more sinister side and hidden secrets. We may be trying to understand such a concept in real life, or we may realize that life will continue despite setbacks.

The Egyptian mummy in dreams can symbolize our feelings about someone who has died. There is also an obvious connection between 'mummy' and 'mother' as a play on words. As a mummy preserves the body for life in the hereafter, its appearance in dreams indicates that we should honour the best of what our mother is or was.

MURDER/MURDERER

Murder suggests willful destruction of another life. Spiritually we need to understand what has taken us in dreams to the extreme position of trying to kill.

To be angry enough to kill suggests that we are still holding some kind of childhood anger, since it is quite natural for a child to wish somebody dead. If we are trying to murder somebody else in a dream, we first need to understand what that person represents to us before recognizing the violence of our own feelings. To dream of a murderer suggests that we are conscious of violence around us.

We may be denying, or trying to control, a part of our own nature that we do not trust. We may also have feelings about other people, which can only be safely expressed in dreams. If we ourselves are being murdered, a part of our lives is completely out of balance and we are being destroyed by external circumstances.

Consult the entries for Anger, Emotions and Kill for further clarification.

MUSEUM

The past is a learning tool that can be observed at some length, and a museum, like a library, is a place where knowledge and expertise can be accessed and given due reverence. Gaining spiritual knowledge in particular allows us to progress.

A museum can represent a place where we store our memories and, therefore, can represent the subconscious – it is that part of ourselves that we will usually only approach in an effort to understand who we are and where we came from.

▣ A museum in a dream denotes old-fashioned thoughts, concepts and ideas. We may need to consider such things but perhaps more objectively than subjectively.

You might also like to consult the entry for Old.

MUSIC/RHYTHM

✿ Sacred sound has always been used in acts of worship, as has dancing. Spiritually, music expresses ideas and emotions through the elements of rhythm, melody and harmony. Rhythm expresses the essential pulse of life, melody an individual sound and harmony a combination of several sounds to make a pleasing combination. In dreams this symbolism expresses man, his concerns and his society.

♥ Sacred music – such as chanting, drumming and pipe playing – has often been used to soothe emotions and induce an altered state of consciousness. In dreams hearing such music offers the opportunity to make such a shift in awareness. Listening to music before sleep can also heighten dream imagery. Modern day ambient music is particularly effective.

▣ Music and rhythm are both expressions of our inner selves and of our connection with life. In dreams, though in waking life we may not be musical, music gives us the opportunity to understand that connection. To be listening to music suggests that we are able to appreciate the rhythm of life and all its associations.

You might also like to consult the entries for Dance/Dancing, Musical Instruments and Orchestra.

MUSICAL INSTRUMENTS

✿ Musical instruments and the skill required to play them are both aspects of Man attempting to be close to the Divine. Ways of self-expression (for example, playing a musical instrument) are offerings of our own creativity and are spiritual acts. In dreams, we have access to vibrations and rhythms not always accessible in waking life.

♥ Sound produced by musical instruments is evocative of emotion. The symbolism of the instrument itself appearing may allow us to come to terms with that emotion in a slightly more objective way. Not being able to play a particular instrument suggests we do not have access to that emotion.

▣ Musical instruments in a dream often stand for our skills and abilities in communication. Wind instruments tend to suggest the intellect, whereas percussion instruments suggest the basic rhythm of life. Stringed instruments calm the nervous system, so when these appear in dreams we are able to act accordingly in waking life.

Consult the entries for Drum, Flute and Organ for further information.

MUTILATE – *see* **INJURE/INJURY AND WOUND**

MUTINY – *see* **CONFLICT**

MYSTIC

☼ Mysticism signifies union with the divine and the search for hidden knowledge. The mystic is someone who has dedicated their life to that search, so in dreams represents our own search for spirituality. Such a vibration in dreams opens up countless possibilities for exploration.

♡ Emotionally, mysticism requires complete submission to the idea of ultimately returning to Source, whatever our belief, and to understanding our present place in the world. In dreams, an objectivity develops that allows us to view our own and others' foibles with tolerance and dispassion. This spills over into waking life.

▦ From a mundane viewpoint, the figure of a known mystic such as Mahatma Gandhi or the Persian poet Rumi alerts us to the possibilities that are available to us if we are prepared to widen our perspectives. Mystics appear in their guise of spiritual leaders to enable us to progress.

Consult the entries for Ascetic, Hermit, Monk and Nun for further understanding.

MYSTIC KNOT

☼ The mystic knot suggests Infinity. Traditionally it consists of 8x8 knots and is never ending. As a symbol it appears in places as far apart as China and countries of Celtic origin. The mystic knot usually appears in dreams as we are attempting to understand ourselves and our relationship with the spiritual.

♡ Mystic Knots are one of the eight Buddhist symbols that symbolize long life unaffected by setback. Their traditional meaning in Celtic lore is the interconnection of life and humankind's place within the universe. Both these meanings are highlighted in dreams and will suggest that we can live life accepting what it has to offer.

▦ Traditionally, the mystic, or in mundane terms the Gordian knot had no beginning and no end. Its basic meaning suggests an unsolvable problem. We probably need to leave such a problem until it is solved either by time or correct action.

NAG

✷ To nag almost always has a negative connotation, but when a spiritual idea or feeling keeps coming back and nagging at us we would be very wise to pay attention.

♥ In dreams, if we are being nagged or scolded we will have recognized that we are not heeding our own inner truth.

▦ From a mundane viewpoint, if we are nagging someone else in dreams we may actually be trying to justify our own actions. There may be a play on words here in that a nag is also an old horse, often one that does not deviate from a particular routine.

⊟ In old-fashioned parlance a nag was a scold or cantankerous old woman. If in waking life we are used to negative reinforcement, nagging may have this relevance in both men's and women's dreams.

NAIL

✷ Spiritually the nail represents necessity and fate. Nails also signify Ultimate Sacrifice and pain and may suggest instruments of torture, either spiritual or physical.

♥ The penetrative power of the nail may be significant when we are having difficulty with issues of either masculinity or of sexuality.

▦ Dreaming of nails, as in woodworking, suggests our ability to bond things together. The holding power of the nail may also be significant. Fingernails and toenails usually suggest claws or the capability of holding on.

⊟ In a man's dream nails may signify his own sense of self or his assertiveness, whereas in a woman's dream the same things are likely to be much more representative of the masculine around her.

NAKEDNESS – *see* **NUDE/NUDITY**

NANNY – *see* **NURSE**

NARCOTIC – *see* **DRUGS**

NARROW

✷ One-pointedness and bigotry are not qualities that are particularly spiritual, but self-discipline may require us to keep to the 'straight and narrow'.

♥ A narrow bridge might suggest a difficulty in communication, perhaps in putting our ideas across. We should take care not to be narrow-minded and judgemental in our dealings with other people. We may be intolerant and parochial in our opinions.

▣ When we dream of anything that is narrow, we are aware of restrictions and limitations. Sometimes we have created them ourselves, sometimes other people will have created them for us. A narrow road would perhaps suggest some kind of restriction, and a warning that we must not deviate from our path. A narrowboat highlights the meaning of a boat with the tendency to put additional restrictions in place.

You might like to consult the entry for Boat/Ship.

NAUGHTY – *see* WILD

NAVEL

✹ The navel or solar plexus is the point of connection between the spiritual and the physical. It is our emotional centre and also, as adults, initially the seat of our inherent power. Any distress in this area in dreams signifies an imbalance of energy.

♥ The navel in a dream can signify our dependency on others, particularly our mother. Often in nightmares we become conscious of something, perhaps a Devil or Demon sitting on our navel, and this can be a personification of our own fears.

▣ To be conscious of the navel, or more subtly the solar plexus – whether our own or another's – is to be aware of the way in which we connect our inner-self with the rest of the outside world. It is through the umbilical cord that a baby in the womb first becomes aware of its physicality.

Also consult the entries for Demon, Devil and Umbilical Cord for further information.

NAVY – *see* ARMED FORCES

NAZI

✹ The figure of a Nazi still holds associations of extreme cruelty and bigotry. While the belief system was the wish for a pure race, such intense fanaticism is misplaced; it will have this significance in dreams.

♥ Emotionally such a figure will represent repression of our own emotions and often rigid self-control.

▣ If there are circumstances in waking life under which we feel oppressed, the figure in Nazi uniform – whether male or female – will often appear.

NECKLACE

✹ The necklace is an acknowledgement of honour and power. Prayer beads strung together are found in most religions to help with the recitations of devotions and prayers.

♥ Necklaces first arose from the wearing of a chain of office and, therefore, in dreams suggests a dignity or honour that has been conferred on the wearer.

The composition of the necklace may be an important part of the interpretation of the dream.

▣ A necklace suggests a special object, and thus translates into special qualities or attributes. There is a richness to be acknowledged. This may be of feeling or of emotion. An old interpretation of a man giving a woman a necklace was that he would soon ask for her hand in marriage.

You might also like to consult the entries for Beads and Gems/Jewels.

NEEDLE

✦ The needle can often suggest masculine sexuality, but also the type of penetrating insight that changes our view of life. A sewing needle will suggest spiritual repair, a knitting needle may suggest creativity and a hypodermic healing, or sometimes self-harm.

♥ The ability to have some penetrating insights about our own state of being can help us to cope with everyday life. It will depend if the needles are being used by us or on us in dreams. By us suggests that we have a need for others to share our viewpoint; on us suggests that we must internalize some kind of knowledge, unpleasant or otherwise, before matters improve.

▣ In dreams hypodermic needles suggest irritations, but can also signify the power to heal through penetration. A concept or knowledge has to be introduced from the outside, which may hurt, but will ultimately improve our wellbeing.

⬚ In a woman's dream using needles will probably require assessment of her more creative aspects, whereas for a man the assessment will be of his softer skills such as communication, listening and negotiation.

Consult the entries for Inject/Injection and Syringe for further information.

NEGATIVE/NEGATIVITY – *see* THE INTRODUCTION AND REFUSE

NEIGHBOUR – *see* PEOPLE

NEPHEW – *see* EXTENDED FAMILY IN FAMILY

NEST

✦ The spiritual significance of a nest is that of security within our known environment.

♥ It is perhaps interesting to note that just before giving birth many women have what is known as a nesting instinct, the need to clean, tidy and make ready. This will sometimes emerge in dreams before it is recognized in waking life.

▣ The nest symbolizes safety and perhaps home life. We may be emotionally dependent on the people around us and afraid of 'leaving the nest'. A nest egg was initially a device to improve a hen's ability to lay eggs and carries with it the idea in dreams of improving a situation.

NET/NETWORK

🔅 A network, like a spider's web, symbolizes relationships unlimited in their scope.

♥ Women are often more able to create a network of 'sisters' through the use of intuition, and often will symbolize this in their dreams as a tangible bonding. In modern day technological parlance a network – particularly the internet – suggests a number of people working or playing together with a common aim

▦ A net in dreams usually indicates that we are feeling trapped and entangled in a scheme or situation. A network, on the other hand, may be more supportive.

▣ In a woman's dream she will be aware of her own seductive power, whereas in a man's dream he will be conscious of his fear of women. As old crafts die out, the physical act of netting as the old fisherwomen did has less relevance. In olden times it was said that a witch could catch the wind in a net.

Also consult the entry for Web.

NEW

🔅 What seems to be new to us may be information that comes to us at the right time to enable us to progress spiritually. It has impact because we have not previously been aware of it.

♥ To be doing something new in a dream highlights the potential in a fresh learning situation. We are stimulated and excited initially. When we first move into a new situation in waking life our dreams can highlight our fears and difficulties. We may often dream of possible scenarios where we are not functioning as well as we should, or of actions we might take to enhance our performance.

▦ Dreaming of something that is new suggests a new beginning, a new way of looking at or dealing with situations, or perhaps even a new relationship. Thus, new shoes might suggest either a different way forward or a way of connecting with the earth. A new hat might suggest a novel intellectual approach, whereas new spectacles indicate a fresh way of seeing things.

NEW YEAR

🔅 Spiritually, in any culture, the New Year with its attendant celebrations can signify enlightenment or new knowledge becoming available. We are no longer in the depths of darkness.

♥ Psychologically, when there is a need for renewal or a new growth in understanding, we need to acknowledge the effort we must make. This is often symbolized as a New Year, a new beginning.

▣ To dream of the New Year is to recognize the need for a fresh start. It may also signify the measurement of time in a way that is acceptable, or a time when something can happen.

NEWSPAPER

✺ Spiritually, we should be aware that what we do needs to be for the Greater Good. We probably need to be more publicly visible, though we are not particularly comfortable with this.

◈ Newspapers in dreams signify new information available to us of which we are now aware rather than it being held subconsciously. A blank page in a newspaper can have two meanings: firstly, the information may not be available to us for various reasons; secondly, it may be for us to provide the information for other people to make use of.

▣ Largely in dreams a newspaper will suggest knowledge that is in the public domain. It might be information that we require in order to make sense of the world around us, or something that is specific to us. A tabloid newspaper in theory may suggest sensational material, whereas a quality one would suggest better researched data. A Sunday newspaper indicates that we have the ability to assimilate the knowledge we need in periods of rest and relaxation. A local newspaper signifies that the facts we require are close to hand.

You might like to consult the entries for Communication and Media.

NICHE

✺ The niche in most religions is consecrated so that it itself is a fit place to contain the Divine. It then symbolizes the holiness and special powers relevant to the particular deity. If an icon is placed within the niche, then the god or goddess is there also.

◈ In new situations we have a need to understand the world we are entering. Often our dream scenarios can open up possibilities by showing us what niche we need to find for ourselves. Not only must we find the space where we belong but we must also know which external factors are going to help us and which will hinder. Dream images connected with the niche will give us such information.

▣ Everyone has a basic need to belong and often we are conscious in dreams of finding our particular place. It manifests itself in dreams as a place where we are protected on all sides except from the front. It has been suggested that this is a return to the childhood state prior to the age of four, when the child begins to realize that he is vulnerable from the rear. A niche is, therefore, our 'spot' – the place where we are safe.

Consult the entries for Icon and God/Gods for further information.

NIECE – *see* **EXTENDED FAMILY IN FAMILY**

NIGHT

☀ Night symbolizes the intense darkness that occurs before rebirth or initiation. There is a disintegration, which has to occur before there can be any possibility of enlightenment. Night can also signify death or drastic change.

☿ Physiologically, night is a time when the body is supposed to be renewing itself. Dreams at different times of the night may highlight emotions formerly associated with various organs.

▦ Night signifies a period of rest and relaxation, both in dreams and in ordinary life. It can, however, also suggest a time of chaos and difficulty. More positively, it is a period that allows us to create a new beginning with the dawning of the new day. Used constructively, night is, therefore, the fallow period before fresh growth.

Also consult also the entries for Dawn/Day and Night and Time.

NIMBUS – *see* **AURA AND HALO**

NO – *see* **REFUSE**

NOAH/NOAH'S ARK – *see* **SPIRITUAL IMAGERY IN THE INTRODUCTION**

NOISE

☀ Any noise in dreams is a way of catching our attention, of focusing our minds. 'White noise' is a noise containing all of the audible frequencies of vibration; it is a good 'masking' agent when meditating or preparing for sleep used as a spiritual discipline.

☿ Any external noise can often be incorporated into dreams as part of the dream content. A bell ringing, for instance, might become a school bell.

▦ When we hear a strange noise in our dreams, we can expect the unexpected and the unknown in waking life.

NOMINATE/NOMINATION

☀ To nominate or be nominated suggests calling or being called for a special task often of a spiritual nature.

☿ When in dreams we are nominated by someone we perhaps should look at the level of commitment we have to our various tasks. When we are nominating someone else, it may be that we do not feel up to a particular emotional responsibility.

▦ From a purely mundane perspective a nomination is quite literally a naming, so a dream where this occurs may have a great deal to do with who we think we are.

You might also like to consult the entry for Vote for further clarification.

NOOSE

At its simplest, the noose represents a traumatic death. In a more complex sense it can represent the binding – or capturing – of spiritual intent, and the harnessing of spiritual energy.

A noose, like the halter, harness and other symbols of restraint, suggests the taming of a perhaps wild untamed part of our personality. A noose can also imply the prevention of self-expression.

A noose in a dream suggests that we have a fear of being trapped, perhaps by others' actions. We are also aware that we can create a trap for ourselves, thereby 'putting a noose round our own necks'. Traditionally, a drawing of a hangman's noose was a threat of death and it can still have that association in dreams. As always, this 'death' may be of part of our personality being unduly restrained. For a young woman wishing to leave home, a noose might represent a fear of becoming trapped in the parental home.

Also consult the entries for Halter, Hang/Hanging, Harness and Rope.

NORTH

The North in spiritual terms suggests the winter, a time for old age and reflection. The Archangel is normally Uriel, administrator of Peace, but sometimes Ariel, Keeper of Wisdom.

We are looking towards night-time and rest and the right to use the wisdom we have accrued. The magical element is Earth and the color white. There is often the completion of a cycle associated with dreams of the North.

When we dream specifically of the North, we are searching for patience and understanding. We need firm foundations.

NOURISHMENT/NURTURING

The symbolism of nourishing the soul and conferring immortality all belong to the nurturing function of the Mother Goddess.

All symbols of containment (the vessel, cup, cauldron, bowl etc.) are symbols of nurturing and femininity. Food-producing animals are also associated with the nourishing aspects of the mother and, therefore, of Mother Earth.

In dreams, all symbols of nourishment are associated with basic needs. Firstly, we require warmth and comfort; secondly, shelter and sustenance. Initially we experience this as coming from mother. Any dream in which we become aware of our needs then has an impact on our relationship with mother. If our need for nourishment and nurturing is not met we experience rejection and hurt. In dreams these things become interchangeable.

Nourishing and nurturing are such intrinsically feminine functions that any dream containing such images are to do with survival. For a woman, nurturing is perhaps more physical in feeling, whereas for a man, his focus will be on growth to maturity.

You might also like to consult the entries for Food and Fruit.

NUCLEAR EXPLOSION

✹ Spiritually, a nuclear explosion would suggest a discharge of power, which, if not handled properly, could be destructive. Treated carelessly, that power can destroy ourselves as well as others.

♥ When we have suppressed certain parts of our personality rather than handling them, there may be some type of synergy (combined energy) that can become destructive. We would be alerted to this by dreaming of causing a nuclear explosion. The threat of such a huge explosion is enough to generate fear, sometimes unfounded.

▦ A nuclear explosion is not always an act of war, but can sometimes be accidental. Such an accident can unintentionally have very far-reaching effects. To dream of a nuclear explosion can highlight our anxiety about great change in our lives. We do not yet know what effect that change may have. We do, however, know we must undertake radical change, but would prefer it to be a more gradual process.

Also consult the entries for Apocalypse, Atom Bomb and Bomb.

NUDE/NUDITY

✹ Nudity often suggests a new beginning, a rebirth, stripping away the non-essential. It is the paradise state and the state of natural innocence we all, at one time, had. It can also represent renunciation of the material world.

♥ Nudity signifies innocence. It may be that there is a situation in our lives that requires honesty and truth. If we are sufficiently secure within our own self-image, we will not be afraid of being 'stripped' in public. Dreaming of appearing nude, for instance in a strip show, could suggest we have anxiety about being misunderstood.

▦ Freud assumed that dreaming of being nude was linked with sexuality. It is, however, more to do with self-image. We have a desire to be seen for what we are, to reveal our essential personality without having to create a facade. To interpret a dream of walking down a street naked will depend on whether we are seen by other people or not. If we are seen by others, there may be something about ourselves that we wish to reveal. If we are alone we may simply have a wish for freedom of expression

⊡ For both men and women, returning to a sense of innocent pleasure and appreciation of the human body can be perceived in dreams as nudity. If in dreaming of someone of the opposite sex they are naked but we are not, they may be more vulnerable than we are.

NUGGET – *see* **METAL**

NUMBERS

When numbers are drawn to our attention in dreams they can have either a personal or a symbolic significance. Often a number will appear that has personal meaning, such as a particular date, or the number of a house we have lived in. Our minds will often retain the significance of the number even though we do not necessarily consciously remember it ourselves.

☀ Spiritually, as we progress we put ourselves in a position to make the best use of the vibratory effect of numbers. It has long been accepted that by combining numbers in certain ways, influence can be brought to bear on our environment. The more esoteric interpretations are:

One – oneself, the Beginning, the first, Unity.

Two – duality, indecision, balance, male vs. female, two sides to an argument, opposites.

Three – the Trinity, freedom.

Four – the square, strength, stability practicality, the earth, reality, the four sides of human nature: sensation, feeling, thought, intuition. The Elements of Earth, Air, Fire and Water.

Five – the human body, human consciousness in the body, the five senses.

Six – harmony or balance.

Seven – cycles of life, magical, spiritual meaning; human wholeness.

Eight – death and resurrection, Infinity.

Nine – pregnancy, the end of any cycle and the start of something new, spiritual awareness.

Ten – new beginnings, the male and female together.

Eleven – eleventh hour, the Master Number.

Twelve – Time, a full cycle or wholeness.

Zero – the Feminine, the Great Mother, the Unconscious, the Absolute or hidden completeness.

♦ Symbolically, numbers have some kind of significance in all systems of belief and religions. Below are the most often found meanings; the positive qualities are given first, followed by the more negative:

One – independence, self-respect, resolve, singleness of purpose. Intolerance, conceit, narrow-mindedness, degradation, stubbornness.

Two – placidity, integrity, unselfishness, gregariousness, harmony. Indecision, indifference, lack of responsibility, bloody-mindedness.

Three – freedom, bravery, fun, enthusiasm, brilliance. Listlessness, over-confidence, impatience, lackadaisical behaviour.

Four – loyalty, stolidity, practicality, honesty. Clumsiness, dullness, conservatism, inability to adapt.

Five – adventurousness, vivaciousness, courage, health, susceptibility, sympathy. Rashness, irresponsibility, inconstancy, unreliability, thoughtlessness.

Six – idealism, selflessness, honesty, charitableness, faithfulness, responsibility. Superiority, softness, impracticality, submission.

Seven – wisdom, discernment, philosophy, fortitude, depth, contemplation. Morbidity, hypercriticism, lack of action, unsociability.

Eight – practicality, power, business ability, decision, control, constancy. Unimaginativeness, bluntness, self-sufficiency, domination.

Nine – intelligence, discretion, artistry, understanding, brilliance, lofty moral sense, genius. Dreaminess, lethargy, lack of concentration, aimlessness.

▨ Many people do not realize that numbers can be extremely significant in everyday life. A knowledge of numbers will enhance your ability to interpret your dreams successfully.

NUN

☼ In today's somewhat promiscuous society it is unlikely that we will dream of virgins. Nuns, however, as holy women epitomize devotion to the Divine and as a feminine archetype signify the Priestess, one who has a spiritually satisfying relationship with God.

♥ The nun, as a woman who has dedicated her life to service of her God, signifies our emotional need to commit to something beyond ourselves.

▨ For many, whose experiences of nuns in real life have not been pleasant, they will be figures of fear and disciplinary action. For others, nuns will symbolize the devoted caring of which they are capable.

Also consult the entries for Mystic and Caring Professions in People as well as the information on Priestess in Archetypes in the Introduction.

NURSE/NURSING

☼ To nurse originally meant to suckle, to keep alive, and for this reason spiritually signifies the nourishing aspect of the Great Mother.

♥ The figure of a nurse in dreams will suggest either that part of our character which cares for others who are sick, or that part of us which is off-balance and needs particular nurturing at this time.

▨ From an everyday perspective a nurse suggests that all is not well with a project or task and some kind of corrective care is needed. As the profession of nursing is given less status, the uniform unfortunately becomes less relevant than it once was.

Also consult the entries for Doctor, Hospital, Ill/Illness, Medicine/Medication and

Caring Professions in People as well as the information on Great Mother in Archetypes in the Introduction.

NUT

☀ Nuts were reputed to be the food of the Gods, and so spiritually enhance the psychic powers. Edible nuts, because of their shape, have significance as inner nourishment.

◊ It was thought that nuts fed the brain, thus giving wisdom. They can still have this significance in dreams. Again, because of their shape, there is a connection with masculine sexuality and fertility. To dream of nuts may suggest that we are trying to de-personalize issues to do with sexuality.

▣ To dream of a metal nut, as in nuts and bolts, is highlighting our ability to construct our lives in such a way that it will hold together. In engineering terms a nut is considered to be feminine, and the screw masculine.

▤ Because of their association with fertility and divinity these significances can surface in both men's and women's dreams as they move towards a more spiritual understanding of life.

NYMPHS

☀ Nymphs are Earth spirits that deal with pure energy. Their charm is their youthfulness, beauty and vitality. Their significance spiritually is that they epitomize most of the feminine qualities in their purest states.

◊ Psychologically the nymph most clearly has associations with the princess. She is the carefree, fun-loving aspect of energy that glories in movement and light. As pure energy, when we work with dreams, the nymph allows us the opportunity to connect to the qualities of purity and grace.

▣ Nymphs are personifications of feminine universal productivity. They have an innocent and carefree energy, which is naive and clear. They tend to be guardians of sacred spaces such as woods, mountains and lakes, and often manifest in dreams as such.

▤ In dreams nymphs are connected with a woman's sense of beauty and her own femininity. Each group of nymphs has their own particular role and guardianship of specific areas, such as forests and lakes, woods and valleys, mountains and grottoes, which has a certain resonance with different aspects of our personality. In a man's dream nymphs will often represent a perception of innocence.

Also consult the entry for Fairy as well as the information on Princess in Archetypes in the Introduction and in the People entry.

OAK – *see* **TREES**

OAR

☀ An oar, being a tool that both propels us forward and allows us to move in a particular direction, signifies a spiritual guiding principle.

♦ To 'put our oar in' indicates our ability to interfere with other people's lives. To lose an oar indicates the loss of an ability we have formerly valued.

▦ The oar is a tool that enables a boat to move forward successfully, but its use requires some skill. Thus it stands for our own set of personal skills. We have certain skills that help us to 'navigate' our lives.

⊡ In dreams, a woman is more likely to be passive when an oar is used. If she is using the oars she is in control of any final decision. In a man's dream, since rowing faces away from the direction of travel, he must perhaps trust his own judgement.

You might like to consult the entries for Boat/Ship, Journey and Transport for further clarification.

OASIS

☀ An oasis, in spiritual terms, represents refreshment and the idea of being able to put difficulties to one side for a time.

♦ Most people see an oasis as a place of refuge in a desert. Because of its association with water, in dreams it becomes a place where we can give and receive whatever emotional refreshment is required.

▦ When people are in difficulty, they need a place where they can express themselves – or perhaps renew their own strengths and ability to cope. In dreams, an oasis, particularly when we are lost, represents such a place. It highlights a particular type of sanctuary.

You might also like to consult the entries for Desert, Lose/Loss/Lost and Water.

OATH – *see* **PROMISE AND VOW**

OBEDIENCE/OBEY

☀ To be obedient, in the spiritual sense, suggests an acceptance of the principle of the Greater Good, and the recognition that our individual struggles are a necessary part of our development.

♦ If we find ourselves in the position of being obedient to someone we know in an unexpected situation, we can often expect to have an easier relationship with them in the future; perhaps because we are able to acknowledge them in a different way.

🔲 When in dreams we expect obedience from someone, we are acknowledging our own power and authority over others. To dream of having to be obedient to others indicates we are aware of their greater authority and knowledge, and also that a degree of disempowerment has occurred.

OBELISK

🔆 An obelisk is often representative of a Sacred Stone, a marker outlining a particular area such as a sacred space, helping us to be clear regarding our spiritual beliefs or marking a particularly sacred area within which it is safe to practise our spiritual beliefs.

💗 An obelisk is a man-made needle-shaped stone, larger at the bottom than the top. It is usually taken today to indicate old instinctive knowledge – man reaching for the unknown. In dreams it suggests just that.

🔲 Any carved stone appearing in a dream suggests we are considering how we have shaped our own basic nature. The simpler it is, the more room we have for improvement; the more ornate it is, the more successful we are at using our creative energy.

🔳 Because of its shape, the obelisk obviously has phallic connotations. In both men's and women's dreams it may also represent a hard unforgiving 'core' within the personality.

Also consult the entries for Needle and Stone.

OBESE – *see* FAT

OBJECT/OBJECTION

🔆 An object in dreams can often give tangibility to spiritual concepts. A cross, for instance, will suggests sacrifice to some, conviction to others and refusal to even more. To object to something suggests that we cannot accept information given at this time.

💗 To object to or disagree with a statement or idea in dreams suggests that we may have already formed an opinion in waking life or that the statement opposes our own code of conduct. From an emotional perspective we cannot make a commitment.

🔳 Often in waking life we are unable to speak out against an injustice or a wrong move. Our dreams will often give us the opportunity to object or protest against such things.

Also consult the entry for Opponent/Oppose.

OBSCURE/OBSCURITY

🔆 Obscurity originally signified the absence of light, so spiritually has that connotation. The truth has not yet been revealed.

💗 When we have not clarified how we feel about something, a representative image can often be obscured in dreams.

◼ In the sense of being dark or dim, anything obscured in dreams requires us to uncover what is hidden and to discover the relevance in everyday life. We may not have the full facts of a situation. If we are able to admit in waking life that something is unknown, an image in recurring dreams, which has previously been obscured, becomes clear.

OBSERVE – *see* **WATCHING AND WITNESS**

OBSESSION

✺ Obsessive behaviour, regarded from a spiritual perspective, would indicate an imperfect link between the spiritual and the physical realms. Spiritual possession was once seen to manifest as obsession. A real-life stalker will be acting out the belief that they have the 'right' to possess their victim.

♥ Obsessive or repetitive behaviour in dreams is often used to ensure that we have fully understood the message being conveyed by the unconscious.

◼ Obsession is an unnatural focusing on a feeling, belief or object, and may simply indicate that we need to take time to work a difficulty through. There is often anxiety about a past occasion or deed, with which we have not been able, or allowed, to deal. When such an unnatural feeling appears in dreams we can appreciate how harmful this can be.

OBSTACLE/OBSTRUCT/OBSTRUCTION

✺ Difficulty, indecision and doubt are the three main blocks we will come up against in any spiritual journey or quest. We will have to overcome each of these blocks at some time if we are finally to achieve our spiritual goal. Indecision and self-doubt can often translate themselves in dreams into actual physical objects, and the difficulty manifests in how we deal with these obstructions.

♥ At times, our own inhibitions and anxieties cannot be faced unless they are first given tangible forms in dreams. In allowing ourselves a visual representation, these anxieties can become more manageable. What has seemed to be a huge obstacle in dreams can be consciously made smaller until we feel capable of dealing with it. For example, a patch of weeds in dreams might be cut back until we can continue on our way.

◼ Obstacles and obstructions in dreams can take many forms – a wall, a hill, a dark forest perhaps. The object will be symbolic of the problem in waking life. Largely we are aware that these obstacles need to be overcome. How we do this in a dream can often suggest how to tackle a problem in everyday life.

You might like to consult the entries for Block and Quest for further clarification.

OCEAN – *see* BAY AND WATER

OCTAGON – *see* SHAPES/PATTERNS

ODOUR

⚙ If a sweet odour is particularly noticeable in dreams it will signify saintliness and spirituality. Traditionally, incense and other sweet smelling herbs are ways of connecting with the Divine and will have this meaning in dreams.

♥ Our sense of smell is extremely delicate, but just as the other senses such as touch and sound are suspended or transmuted into something slightly different in dreams, an odour in a dream may be a way of reminding ourselves of another time or place. Odour is highly evocative and for the dreaming self to register a known smell or perfume suggests that we are trying to make some sort of connection with conditions we have known in the past.

▦ If there is an odour in a dream at all and we become aware of it, it is usually highly significant. If it is a pleasant one it suggests good times; if a bad one then it is more likely to be a warning of bad things.

Also consult the entries for Incense and Smell.

OFFENCE/OFFEND

⚙ A suggestion of spiritual wrongdoing may be relevant. A sin is a moral evil, but a wrongdoing is less culpable and in dreams may simply manifest as a warning, which allows us to assess the seriousness of the offence in waking life and then to act accordingly.

♥ To be committing an offence suggests that we are not, either consciously or unconsciously, following our own code of moral behaviour. We have put ourselves outside the norms of society.

▦ To take offence in a dream is to allow a display of emotion and feeling about our own sensitivity, which may not be appropriate in waking life. To give offence to someone in a dream is to recognize that we are not as aware of other people's feelings as we should be.

Consult the entries for Burglar, Intruder and Vice for more information.

OFFICER/OFFICIAL – *see* ARMED FORCES AND ALSO AUTHORITY FIGURES IN PEOPLE

OGRE – *see* GIANT AND MONSTER

OIL

⚙ Oil, particularly that containing fine perfumes, represents consecration and dedication. Chrism or Holy Oil is of the highest spiritual vibration. Initiates were anointed (literally, smeared with oil) to signify that they were especially blessed and oil will often have this significance in dreams.

♥ Psychologically, we may recognize that a situation can only be dealt with by removing the stress – 'pour oil on troubled water'. Ointment was initially either oil- or grease-based, so today to dream of massage oil or ointment suggests caring and pampering.

▦ It will depend on which type of oil is being used in the dream. Cooking oil, for instance, will often signify the removal of friction, or a way of combining different components, whereas engine oil will highlight our ability to keep things moving. As the world becomes more polluted by petroleum oil products, dreams of oil may suggest contamination rather than purity.

You might also like to consult the entries for Engine and Odour.

OINTMENT – *see* HEAL/HEALING AND MEDICINE

OLD

✸ The Wise Old Man is a part of ourselves, which is not always consciously available to us. An old man appearing in our dreams puts us in touch with this part of ourselves. He can also represent our feelings about time and death.

♥ Old people in dreams tend to suggest traditional thought or wisdom arising from experience. We may also need to consider our attitude to death. Old buildings can signify a past way of life, which we thought we had left behind. Antiques will often represent elements of our past experience, which might be worth keeping. If something seems particularly ancient, the meaning may be ambiguous; either it has outlived its usefulness or has been imbued with special significance because of its antiquity.

▦ When we dream of old things, we are touching into the past and perhaps need to bring some kind of knowledge forward, so that we can make use of it in the present day. Dreaming of historical figures usually means we are aware of the qualities that those people possessed. Perhaps we need to develop those qualities within ourselves.

Also consult the entries for Death, Museum and People as well as Wise Old Man in Archetypes in the Introduction.

OLYMPICS – *see* GAMES, RITUAL AND SPORT

ONION

✸ In its many-layered aspect the onion symbolizes the Cosmos, and revelation. In dreams, we find that what we are doing with the onion reveals our intrinsic way of exploring creation. In removing each layer we come to an understanding of how we create from small to large.

♥ Chopping onions can signify an attempt to increase the energy available to us in some way. We quite literally want to ensure that we have allowed the essence of our being to permeate throughout our lives. As a reflection of the various levels of understanding we explore as we mature, the onion provides an apt symbol. If the onion is dried or dried up we have to make more emotional effort to understand.

▨ Oddly enough, the onion can appear in dreams and meditation as a symbol of wholeness, but a wholeness that is many-layered. Peeling an onion can suggest trying to find the best part of ourselves, or of somebody else. It may also indicate attempting to understand the various facets of our own personality.

Consult the entry for Food for further information.

OPAL – see GEMS/JEWELS

OPERATION

🔆 An operation is a carefully planned procedure, whether that is a military or surgical one. Spiritually, therefore, it represents incisive healing, or the restoration of equilibrium. An operation in dreams can, therefore, highlight the need for healing of the spirit, the eradication of 'dis-ease'.

◈ If we are performing an operation we are recognizing our own level of skill within a situation in waking life. If the operation is being performed on us we are attempting to access some inner knowledge but are possibly fearful of the outcome. Modern surgical methods are less invasive than early surgery and when these appear in dreams will suggest more subtle ways of managing distress.

▨ An operation in hospital is usually frightening and invasive. In dreams it can signify our awareness of our own fears of illness and pain, but also a recognition of our need to be healed on some level. A military operation signifies the need for careful planning and management and the establishing of order.

Also consult the entries for Heal/Healing, Hospital, Surgery, Waiting and War.

OPPONENT/OPPOSE

🔆 An opponent in dreams, from a spiritual perspective, is that part of us that is not co-operating in the grand scheme of things and is, therefore, introducing an element of negativity. It is also, as we become more aware, negative elements, which we may be required to confront and overcome, or at worst understand, before there can be progress.

◈ When we find ourselves opposed to someone in dreams, we often have some kind of emotional difficulty, which prevents us from understanding a conflict within ourselves. Once identified, we are able to resolve our problem in waking life.

▨ In mundane terms, any conflict in waking life could manifest as a personalized opponent or as opposition in dreams. How that opponent presents itself will often give us the information we need to deal with the problem. For instance, an imp as an opponent might mean that we will have to deal with minor irritations first.

OPPOSITE – *see* **POSITION**

ORACLE

☀ An oracle is a divine pronouncement and, therefore, suggests Hidden Knowledge. Prediction and foretelling both work on the assumption that the person concerned has received knowledge prior to the event.

◈ The need to know is very strong and the assumption is that an oracle – in this case an actual person – has more information than we do. Often that information has to be unscrambled, since particularly in dreams, it is presented in odd ways. Sometimes it cannot be made sense of until such time as we have considered it in waking life, taking into consideration our own personal circumstances.

▦ Most of us like to know what is going to happen to us and also like to be told what to do, so dreaming of an oracle links us with that part of ourselves that knows what our next moves are. Often an oracle can appear as a person, for instance as a goddess or wise old man, or we can dream that we are using one of the many systems of prediction that are available in everyday life.

ORANGE – *see* **COLOUR AND FRUIT**

ORCHARD – *see* **TREE/TREES**

ORCHESTRA/ORCHESTRATE

☀ Originally a place where dancers and musicians gathered, an orchestra now symbolizes the group of musicians itself. Such an image suggests that we are capable of operating in spiritual harmony.

◈ When we wish to orchestrate something, we want to make it happen. This means that we must take action that enables us to be heard and to have people understand us. When we find we are conducting an orchestra in a dream, we feel we can accept we are in control. When we are a member of an orchestra we are simply part of a greater task.

▦ We all have certain aspects of our personality that must work in harmony with one another for us to function properly. Dreaming of an orchestra represents ways in which we are capable of bringing all those aspects together and making a coherent whole. A discordant orchestra suggests that we have not succeeded in integrating all aspects successfully. A disciplined orchestra suggests that we have succeeded in that integration.

You might also like to consult the entries for Music/Rhythm and Musical Instruments.

ORDER

☀ Spiritually, to be trying to establish order suggests that we are attempting to make sense of something. We are trying to establish a logical progression when apparently there is no such thing. To be in holy orders suggests that we are imposing a degree of discipline on ourselves.

◈ Ordering others around in dreams suggests that we recognize the need for leadership. Emotions that are under pressure or difficulty can cause havoc in our lives. Dreams will often help us to establish a natural order by reflecting the order and method we need to deal with such chaos.

▣ Lists and such techniques help us to maintain order in our everyday lives, Dreaming of such things often allows us to prioritize basic tasks. In dreams, finding that we are being ordered to do something suggests that we have instinctively recognized a greater authority.

You might also like to consult the entries for Chaos, List, Nun and Monk for further information.

ORE – *see* **METAL**

ORGAN

◈ In theory, perfect health of mind and body would be possible provided we understood the workings of the physical body – how the organs inter-relate. Spiritually, if through dreams we can become aware of what perfect is, then self-healing ensures proper working of the organs. A musical organ has a richness of sound that is capable of changing a person's consciousness, so in dreams will tend to highlight or heighten our views and feelings about union with the Divine.

◈ In Chinese medicine, the different organs of the body represent different qualities. For instance, the gall bladder deals with the ability to make decisions, while the liver is the seat of irritability. In dreams, therefore, being conscious of a bodily organ would require us to be aware of what is bothering us and learning how to deal with it in an appropriate manner in waking life.

▣ The various organs of the body can represent the different aspects of the self. In dreams they can signify diverse weaknesses and strengths. A musical organ, having many systems to produce sound, often symbolizes the bodily organs. Anything that is organic is characterized by a natural arrangement of parts, so in dreams comes to mean anything that is natural rather than manufactured. To dream we are growing food that is organic suggests we need to pay attention to the quality of our lives.

ORGY

◈ An orgy was initially an esoteric religious ritual, characterized by wild dancing, singing and drinking. It has, therefore, from a spiritual perspective, come to mean any spiritual excess.

◈ Behaviour that would not necessarily be appropriate in ordinary, everyday life can be used in dreams to balance a difficulty. Since many people struggle with their self image, which can be closely connected with their sexuality, dreaming of an orgy or licentious behaviour can indicate the way in which we can release the blocked energy.

🔲 An orgy relates to a tremendous release of energy, which can take place when we give ourselves permission to access our own basic passion. This permission will often be given subconsciously first, and can be expressed in dreams more fully than we would allow ourselves to do in everyday life. To dream of an orgy can also highlight the way we relate to other people. The need for other people to love and understand us is quite strong and, when seen as an orgy, can perhaps indicate that we are afraid of loss of control.

🔳 While most people will think of an orgy as being sexual in nature, in dreams it is more about letting go of our inhibitions. In a woman's dream an orgy may show her a way of releasing her emotional hang-ups, whereas for a man it may be more about being able to express himself properly.

ORIENT – *see* **INDIGENOUS PEOPLES**

ORPHAN

🔅 From a spiritual perspective the one thing that we all fear is rejection. To dream of being an orphan highlights this spiritual desertion, a moving away from Source into the uncharted waters of being human.

♥ We have to come to terms with our ability to grow up and to move away from our parents. When our lives force us into losing them at any age, either through death or other circumstances such as moving away, we may experience the feeling of being orphaned.

🔲 To dream of an orphan indicates that we may be feeling vulnerable and possibly abandoned and unloved. If we are looking after an orphan we are attempting to heal that part of us that feels unloved. If we experience ourselves as having been orphaned it may indicate that we need to be more independent and self-sufficient.

Consult the entry for Family for further information.

OSTEOPATH – *see* **THERAPY/THERAPIST**

OSTRICH – *see* **BIRDS**

OTTER – *see* **ANIMALS**

OUIJA BOARD

🔅 Spiritually, the ouija board was – and indeed still is – a rather crude way of communicating with the spirit world. In dreams, it shows we may be aware of our need to communicate with spirit, rather than have the spirit world communicate with us. We are the instigators of communication.

♥ Psychologically, we all need some way of making contact with the unconscious side of ourselves. To dream of the ouija board alerts us to different ways of accessing the unconscious. It may be a symbol for all we have suppressed and refused to recognize.

▦ The use of the ouija board holds within it certain inherent dangers. Dreaming of one may simply be a way that the psyche has of alerting us to further exploration of those things we do not understand. To be playing with the ouija board in dreams – as well as in waking life – denotes being prepared to take certain risks, particularly with our own peace of mind. When the ouija board seems frightening we are touching in on our deep fear of the unknown.

OUROBOROS – *see* **SPIRITUAL IMAGERY IN THE INTRODUCTION**

OUT/OUTSIDE

✺ Any sense of being outside in dreams – in the open air – will suggest a degree of spiritual freedom. We are free from the restrictions of the mundane world.

◈ Being shut out suggests rejection by others but if we ourselves are shutting something out then we are not prepared to include what is represented in our lives.

▦ In the mundane world a sense of not belonging to a peer group can lead to a feeling of isolation, of being an outcast. In waking life we are aware of restrictions and boundaries that are not necessarily self-imposed. Any sense of being beyond some kind of boundary can mean one of two things: either we have deliberately put ourselves 'beyond the pale' or we have inadvertently offended against the rules of the society or group.

OUTLAW – *see* **THIEF**

OUTLINE

✺ Spiritually, to be conscious of a line marking the perimeter of an object suggests that we are recognizing a duality – the existence of two things. To be outlining an idea suggests that we have some basic concepts that are worth exploring.

◈ An outline is usually a brief statement of intent, and with practice in dreams we are often able to formulate such a statement. An outline document in dreams can symbolize this. The problem is that when we wake up, unless we are used to recording our dreams, such a statement of intended action can be lost.

▦ An outline in dreams is intended to give emphasis or to mark the edge of something. Under these circumstances we should consider our actions in waking life a little more carefully.

OVAL – *see* **SHAPES/PATTERNS**

OVEN

✺ The oven's function of cooking represents spiritual change – the transformation of raw basic ingredients or qualities into something usable.

It thus suggests spiritual transmutation through the application of heat (fire).

◈ As a hollow object, in dreams an oven can also represent the womb. With its ability to change ingredients into something else, the oven can also represent the process of gestation and birth. In dreams, this can suggest the ability to transform character traits and behaviour from something coarse to the more refined.

▦ An oven is representative of the human ability to deliberately start a process of the adaptation of raw material into something that is functional. This can apply within a work situation, for instance at the beginning of a project or in personal life. The oven thus symbolizes a creative process.

⊟ In a woman's dream a warm oven might signify her willingness to become pregnant or to begin a new relationship. In a man's dream it might signify positive change.

You might also like to consult the entries for Bake/Baker/Bakery, Fire and Kitchen.

OVERDOSE – *see* **ALCOHOL/ALCOHOLIC, DRUGS AND DRUNK**

OVERFLOW – *see* **WATER**

OWE – *see* **DEBT**

OWL – *see* **BIRDS**

OX – *see* **ANIMALS**

OYSTER

✸ The oyster represents spiritual transformation. In nature it is almost unique because of its ability to transform a grain of sand into a pearl. It is this quality that tends to be brought to notice in dreams to demonstrate how we can change an irritant into something beautiful. We can spiritualize it.

◈ The oyster symbolizes our ability to make use of difficulty and negativity and create a new positive focus. In dealing with an irritant we are able to protect ourselves from further harm.

▦ Practically, the oyster is reputed to be an aphrodisiac food; in fact, this is because of its high zinc content, which affects the production of semen. For this reason a dream about oysters may be highlighting fertility issues. In dreams, as nowadays they can be expensive, they may well also represent the act of seduction.

⊟ In a woman's dream oysters may signify seduction, but can also suggest sacrifice. Hypatia, an Alexandrian mathematician and philosopher, was flayed to death by Christians using oyster shells in 415 CE for her beliefs. In a man's dream, oysters themselves may symbolize his own sexuality.

You might also like to consult the entries for Food, Sacrifices and Sand.

PACKAGE – *see* **PARCEL**

PACKING

⚙ With packing, as with any act of preparation, we need to make a choice about what spiritual information needs to be retained and what is relevant for the task in hand.

♥ We need to establish some kind of order in our lives. To dream of packing suggests an internal selection process must be undertaken in order to decide what is important to us. To dream of unpacking suggests qualities which may have been hidden from view.

▦ When we dream of packing suitcases, as though going on a journey, we are highlighting the need to prepare carefully for the next stage of our lives. There is a need, or want, to get away from past ideas and difficulties. To be packing a precious object very carefully indicates we are aware of the intrinsic value to ourselves, or others, of what is represented by that object.

You might like to consult the entries for Baggage, Luggage and Wadding.

PACT

⚙ When we make a pact in dreams we are usually making a treaty or agreeing to a particular course of action.

♥ When two parts of our personality are at odds with one another, dreams of a pact can show us how to have them working in harmony, bringing about a state known as integration.

▦ Reconciling two opposing ideas or principles is an integral part of day-to-day living. Reaching agreement is often a process of negotiation, which works itself out in dreams.

PADDLE – *see* **WADING AND WATER**

PADLOCK

⚙ We are preserving or, quite literally, locking up our spiritual integrity sometimes for future use.

♥ Often when our security is threatened, a symbol which reinforces our need for defence mechanisms appears, and the padlock comes into this category. It offers sanctuary and an element of control. If the padlock is of an ornate design, such control may be more complicated than we first thought.

▦ Dreaming of locking a padlock suggests that we are attempting to shut a feeling or emotion away. We are not able to explore these at this time. This may either be through fear or possessiveness. Conversely, if we are opening a padlock we may be trying to open up to new experiences.

You might also like to consult the entries for Key and Lock.

PAGAN

🔆 From a spiritual perspective a pagan is one who does not belong to a major religion, but believes in all gods. However, in dreams such a figure is likely to suggest someone who worships, and is in touch with, the forces of nature.

💟 In returning to basic beliefs about the world in which we live we can reveal our pagan side, in its true meaning. This part reacts and responds to natural forces. This tends to happen when we begin a journey of self-exploration.

▦ When a work or personal situation contains elements that we have difficulty understanding, this may be symbolized by the appearance of a pagan type of figure. Intrinsic in this is the idea of going back to very simple beliefs.

⊞ For many people the concept of paganism is of a somewhat chaotic freedom oriented religion, which deals with the balance of masculine and feminine. For this reason, both men's and women's dreams will reflect whatever rebalancing is required. Dreaming of the various Gods and Goddesses, for instance, highlights those qualities that need to be developed.

Consult the entry for God/Gods and Goddess/Goddesses for further clarification.

PAGE

🔆 The symbolism of a Book of Life in which our lives are recorded for assessment is a strong image in spiritual work. It might be said that we have our own special page.

💟 A blank page suggests a fresh start in our emotional make-up. We have no given course of action and the freedom to begin again. A page that we cannot read suggests that guidelines are available but have not yet become apparent.

▦ Manuals and procedures are an integral part of today's world, so being unable to find the right page in such a booklet suggests there may be a problem with how to complete a task in a working environment. The page being missing suggests we have not been given the correct information in the first place. Such dreams can be categorized as anxiety dreams.

⊞ There is a supplementary meaning of page, which can surface in dreams. In medieval times the page was the youth preparing to be a knight, hence the immature male. This image occurs in both men's and women's dreams as an archetype.

You might like to consult the section on Archetypes in the Introduction and also the entries for Book and Paper/Parchment.

PAGODA – *see* **RELIGIOUS BUILDINGS IN BUILDINGS**

PAINT/PAINTING

☀ Often we do not recognize our own creative ability and thus the potential we have to be in touch with the spiritual dimension. We each have the capability of 'reflecting' the Divine. This allows us to live mindfully – with awareness.

♡ Because painting has such a lot to do with self-expression, the way that we are painting in a dream may be important. If, for instance, we are painting miniatures we may need to concentrate on detail. If we are painting large pictures we may need to adopt a more global perspective. Colour in a painting is also important, as is the subject.

▣ We may not actually have the ability to paint successfully in everyday life, but such a dream may alert us to other talents we have not realized we possess. To be looking at paintings in dreams indicates that we are questioning or paying attention to different ideas and concepts. Painting as in decorating suggests we are making recognizable changes in how we think and feel. A picture that we ourselves have painted might have more emotional impact than an Old Master – an Old Master can also suggest our attitude to the past.

You might also like to consult the entries for Colour and Decorate/Decoration.

PAIR/PAIRS .

☀ The use of pairs in dreams is drawing attention to the idea of duality. We are trying to achieve a balance between the spiritual and material realms.

♡ A dream clarifying the masculine side of ourselves may be followed by a dream clarifying the feminine. The juggling that goes on in this way can take place over a period of time. Often in dream interpretation looking at the opposite meaning to the obvious can give us greater insight into our mental processes.

▣ The unconscious mind appears to sort information by comparing and contrasting. Particularly when we are aware of conflict within ourselves, we may dream in pairs (e.g. old/young, masculine/feminine, clever/stupid). It is almost as though there is some kind of internal pendulum, which eventually sorts out the opposites into a unified whole.

▣ It is quite natural for us to seek partnership, and in dreams both men and women will dream of duality as a way of sorting out emotional and spiritual complementary aspects.

You might like to consult the entries for Numbers and Partner/Partnerships for further clarification.

PALACE – *see* **CASTLE**

PAN/POT

🌑 As always, any receptacle suggests the containing Feminine Principle, usually the nurturing side. A pot can have the same spiritual significance as a jar.

🜨 Just as a cauldron can be taken to indicate the transformative process, so a pan or pot can symbolize the ability to combine several 'ingredients' to make something completely different. This can apply under any circumstances.

🔲 In dreams a pan or a pot signifies nurturing and caring. It can also suggest a receptive frame of mind.

🔳 In a woman's dream it will depend upon what stage of life she has reached as to the symbolism of pans. The three stages of femininity of Maid, Mother and Crone or Wise Woman are recognizable. In a man's dream a pan is more likely to represent his attitude to the feminine.

You might like to consult the entries for Cauldron and Jar for further clarification.

PANCAKE – *see* **BREAD**

PANE – *see* **WINDOWS IN BUILDINGS**

PANEL

🌑 There are several symbolisms of panel that might occur in dreams. The first is that of a spiritual picture – an icon such as a triptych, which may reflect aspects of our spiritual state. Such a picture has been thought to protect against visitation by the Devil.

🜨 The second image is that of a control panel. This suggests that we have the ability to make adjustments in our lives, some of which may be only small but are important.

🔲 A panel of people such as an interview panel or a panel of judges signifies that we have a situation in our lives where we are being judged or are allowing our fate to be decided by others in authority.

PANTHER – *see* **ANIMALS**

PANTOMIME – *see* **CLOWN AND THEATRE**

PAPER/PARCHMENT

🌑 There is potential for Spiritual growth through both learning and creativity. A parchment scroll suggests acknowledgement of in-depth study or ancient knowledge.

🜨 Blank writing paper points to a lack of communication, or need to communicate with someone, but can also suggest a new beginning. Brown paper can highlight the utilitarian side of our nature. Old-fashioned parchment scrolls (which were originally made from animal skins) would suggest longlasting information.

▦ Paper is one of those images that, in dreams, are dependent on the circumstances in the dreamer's life. For instance, in a student's life, paper would suggest the need to pay attention to the studies, whereas festive wrapping paper could indicate the need for, or the possibility of, celebration. The art of making paper or creating parchment indicates a highly skilled individual.

You may also like to consult the entry for Page.

PARADE – *see* PROCESSION

PARADISE

✺ To dream of Paradise is to be aware of the perfect Soul. In this state there is no right and no wrong, only completion and totality. Paradise is used instead of Heaven to describe the ultimate pleasurable place after death. It is the part from which we can develop perfect union with the universe.

♥ Psychologically, Paradise is that part of ourselves that is enclosed within and does not need to be available to anyone else – it is an unblemished, sacred space.

▦ To dream of Paradise is to link with our innate ability to take pleasure in being perfect. We can experience total harmony within ourselves and be totally innocent. When this is reflected into everyday life our universe co-operates with us.

⊟ In both men's and women's dreams, Paradise reflects a perfect relationship both with ourselves and others.

You might also find it helpful to consult the entry for Garden.

PARALYSIS

✺ Paralysis can signify a sense of spiritual inadequacy, the inability to create movement, and inertia. There is a condition, which sometimes occurs during psychic development, when sleep paralysis – a state which has a neurological explanation – forces us into facing our own fears.

♥ Imagination can often play tricks on us, and we experience as real some kind of reaction we would not normally allow ourselves. Strong emotional feelings may be experienced as paralysis in dreams in order to highlight the effect those feelings can have within the physical realm.

▦ When paralysis is felt in a dream we are probably experiencing great fear or suppression. Literally we are unable to make a move in any direction. Dealing with conscious fears will allow us access to those fears that have only been available in the dream state.

You might also like to consult the entry for Immobility.

PARAPET – *see* BALCONY
PARASITES – *see* INSECTS
PARCEL/PACKAGE

🌞 Parcels and packages can suggest latent potential gifts, skills and talents They can equally suggest opportunities offered from a spiritual perspective.

💙 Parcels and packages in dreams can also represent the gifts and assistance that we receive from others. Whether we are directly receiving the parcel from the person concerned or whether we are simply aware who the donor is is worth noting. It is something that we can receive with joy. The wrapping may also be important, brown paper being more utilitarian than a more festive kind.

▣ When we receive a parcel in a dream, we are being made aware of something we have experienced but not explored. At this stage, we do not quite know what the potential of the 'gift' is, but by exploration can find this out. If the address is wrong or we discover that the parcel is not for us we have probably some doubts about our own abilities. When we are sending a parcel or package we are sending our energy out into the world.

Consult the entries for Paper and People for further clarification.

PARCHMENT – *see* PAPER
PARENTS – *see* ARCHETYPES IN THE INTRODUCTION AND FAMILY IN PEOPLE
PAROLE

🌞 Parole strictly means our word of honour and in that sense signifies a promise to conform to whatever laws are appropriate – with awareness, spiritual laws.

💙 To be on parole indicates that there is some way in which we feel we have offended against natural laws. When we give someone else parole we are aware that we can trust them to act with honour.

▣ To have been judged by a higher authority and then to have been put on parole suggests that someone who in real life has some kind of authority over us is trusting us to do our best, but that trust is conditional on a job well done.

PARROT – *see* BIRDS
PART/PARTING

🌞 Recognizing that there is a part of something rather than a whole signifies that spiritually we have not seen the whole picture. Parting suggests division, as in the parting of the waters.

💙 When in dreams it strikes us that we can only see part of something it is the unseen part that needs careful consideration. A parting in the hair signifies a duality in our nature. Parting from a dear friend suggests there may be some difficulty to overcome in that relationship.

▣ When an object or drawing is divided into parts we can decide to break an everyday task into its various components to help us succeed. The number of parts may be significant.

Consult the entry for Hair in Body, Friend and Numbers for further clarification.

PARTNER/PARTNERSHIP

☀ Partnership of any sort in dreams signifies a joint spiritual responsibility. Being aware of having a partner highlights the fact that burdens and difficulties can also be shared.

♡ Most of us look for qualities in others that enhance or complement our own, so whether we dream of our actual partner or of being in partnership we are searching for such attributes. We require some kind of integration within ourselves.

▣ From a mundane perspective, partnership often denotes a shared task, ideal or project. Such a dream suggests that looking at the work in hand from a different perspective might bring about a solution to problems.

▣ In both men's and women's dreams, dreaming of a partner, particularly in a mixed gender relationship, will probably highlight the Animus or Anima. In many cases, a partner will represent the Shadow, a ready recipient for aspects of our own negativity.

You might like to consult the entry for People as well as the information on Animus and Anima in Archetypes in the Introduction.

PARTY

☀ When a group celebrates a belief, which can be spiritual, it is an occasion for a party or festival. The joining up of several people enhances the atmosphere and creates additional power.

♡ The human being often has need of celebration in his or her life. To be attending a party such as a dinner party or other specific purpose in a dream can indicate our need for celebration, for joining with other people to create a potentially happy atmosphere.

▣ When we find we are attending a party in a dream, we are often alerted to our social skills – or lack of them. In waking life we may be shy and dislike such gatherings, but in dreams if we are coping with the groups involved, we have a greater awareness of our own ability to belong and to take enjoyment from that. To belong to a political party would indicate that we are prepared to stand up for our beliefs, that we have made a commitment to a particular way of life.

PASS

☀ A pass signifies that permission has been given to move in selected areas and, therefore, that we have reached a certain level of spiritual recognition.

♥ To lose a library pass suggests that we have not been careful to keep our knowledge up to date. To lose a bus or travel pass signifies that we have not planned our next moves carefully. To pass an examination or interview means that we have worked hard and well enough to have gained approval.

▣ As nowadays many workplaces use electronic passes to gain entry, to forget a pass might denote a lack of interest in what we are doing or that if we are honest we do not feel our work is good enough or of value. To find a pass that is not our own signifies that we feel we have a right of entry but others do not necessarily feel the same way.

PASSAGE – see HALL/PASSAGES IN BUILDINGS

PASSENGER

☀ When we take responsibility for someone else's spiritual development we may dream of carrying a passenger.

♥ If we feel that someone known to us is drawing on our resources we may dream of having a passenger. If we are ourselves a passenger we should take warning that we are not taking full responsibility for ourselves or our actions.

▣ Often in teamwork or family life one or more individual has to be 'carried' for a time to ensure success. This might give rise to images of carrying passengers on a journey in either party.

You might like to consult the entries for Car, Journey and Transport to enhance your understanding.

PASSPORT

☀ A passport to a better life can be achieved by Spiritual Awareness. Such a document suggests that permission has been given by a higher authority – that some kind of initiation has taken place.

♥ Often the passport can appear as a symbol of the permission we need to give ourselves or others to move on to new things or situations. To lose a passport suggests we are not committed to such an action.

▣ The passport is normally regarded as proving our identity, to prove that we have reached the age of maturity or acceptance as a valid member of society. In waking life, we may experience difficulty in maintaining a good self-image and in dreams may reassure ourselves by producing a passport. Not being able to obtain a passport suggests that there is a lack of trust.

The entries in Journey may give you a greater understanding of your dream.

PAST – see TIME

PATCH – see FABRIC

PATH

☀ A path in a dream can indicate the direction that we should take spiritually. The idea that there is a path in life resonates with Chinese thought, which calls the Tao 'The Way'. In some schools of thought the left hand path represents evil or black magic.

◈ Often a path can represent the way we feel a relationship or situation is developing. It can also suggest a way of following up a concept or line of enquiry. A pavement introduces the idea that the path is already prepared for us.

▦ A path in a dream signifies the direction we have decided to take in life. The type of path, e.g. whether it is smooth or rocky, meandering or straight, may be just as important as the path itself. In waking life, it is often the way a clairvoyant 'sees' the way in which the enquirer's life is changing.

Also consult the entries for Journey, Line, Meander and Rock.

PATTERN – *see* **SHAPES/PATTERNS**

PAY/PAYMENT

✺ In spiritual terms, to pay for something is to be accountable for it. To make payment signifies taking responsibility.

◈ If in dreams we are paying a bill we may be accepting that we have received something of value. It may be that we must make good use of our resources.

▦ Payment, as in a monetary transaction, can often show our attitude to finance. To be paying cash suggests a more immediate use of our money and resources, whereas paying by credit card signifies a need to satisfy our immediate needs without thought of the consequences. A cheque nowadays could well show a slightly outdated attitude.

PEACE – *see* **TRANQUILITY**

PEACOCK – *see* **BIRDS**

PEAK

✺ A peak experience is one that takes us beyond our normal capabilities. From a spiritual perspective we have not allowed the limitations of the mundane world to hold us back.

◈ Reaching the peak of a mountain or hill in dreams signifies that we have put in a good deal of effort to reach for the best that we can be.

▦ In the sense that a peak is a high point, after which the energy begins to fall away, such a dream image may show that we have reached a point of completion and the next stage of the journey will be easier.

⊞ Men's and women's perceptions of a peak experience will differ in dreams, although both will transcend the self-imposed boundaries and limitations that occur.

PEARL – *see* **GEMS/JEWELS**

PEEP/PEERING – *see* **INSPECT**

PELICAN – *see* **BIRDS**

PEN/PENCIL

⚜ The ability to transcribe and translate spiritual knowledge into recognizable images and to keep a record of that information is a necessary part of personal development. Such records and especially the ability to keep a journal are an invaluable part of dream recording. Dreaming of a pen or pencil may also suggest that we could attempt automatic or inspired writing.

♥ We all have an ability to learn but need to have some way of transmitting our learning to other people. A pen would suggest the learning would be more permanent than a pencil. Learning through dreams is an increasing part of modern day understanding of the psyche.

▦ If a pen or pencil appears in a dream we are expressing or recognizing the need to communicate with other people. If the pen will not work we do not understand information we have been given. If we cannot find a tool to write with we do not have enough information to proceed with an aspect of our lives.

You may also wish to consult the entries for Ink, Inspire, Paper/Parchment and Writing.

PENALTY

⚜ Incurring a penalty in the spiritual sense indicates that we have transgressed against a particular code of behaviour. We may not necessarily be aware of this code.

♥ A penalty is in normal parlance a fine levied for a misdemeanour. It is a punishment imposed by others, often our peers, and will have this meaning in dreams. We will have upset someone without necessarily being prepared to take the consequences.

▦ Dreaming of a penalty goal can mean, if we are shooting this goal, an opportunity to be in the limelight because of someone else's mistake. If the opportunity for such a goal is our fault, it is a warning to be more careful.

PENANCE – *see* SPIRITUAL IMAGERY IN THE INTRODUCTION

PENDANT – *see* NECKLACE

PENDULUM

⚜ A pendulum is both a measurer of time and of energy. Spiritually it represents the rhythm of life. It is for this reason that a weighted object can be used in divination.

♥ A pendulum in dreams may be a symbol of indecision, swinging from one course of action to another. It may also suggest the oscillation between two states of emotion.

🔲 In the dream image of an old-fashioned clock, a pendulum can signify outdated ideas. It can also suggest that a period of time must pass before a plan is allowed to come to fruition. On its own a pendulum signifies a swing between two polarities; if it comes to rest in our dream we have resolved a dilemma.

Also consult the entry for Time.

PENETRATION

💠 Any article that penetrates or pierces another, such as a knife or laser beam, signifies that the normal boundaries and limitations by which we live are illusions when viewed from a spiritual perspective.

💟 In today's world people tend to view penetration from a purely sexual viewpoint. In dreams it usually signifies getting to the heart of a matter. Any pointed object represents male sexuality but can also be interpreted in the above manner.

🔲 Inherent in the idea of penetration is a piercing of defences and this meaning is one which arises frequently in dreams. When we are feeling particularly vulnerable or at risk, dreams such as of castle walls being penetrated can occur.

📳 Myths and fairy tales often give information that resonates in dreams. Women and men exploring their sexuality or their need for partnership can have dreams that highlight both penetration of a sexual nature and that of personal space.

Consulting the entries for Castle, Dagger, Knife and Sex/Sexual Images might help with further clarification.

PENGUIN – *see* BIRDS

PENTACLE/PENTANGLE/PENTAGRAM – *see* MAGIC/MAGICIAN

PEOPLE

💠 When we begin to work spiritually with ourselves, there is a gargantuan store of knowledge that can be worked on, and with, to enhance our lives. By and large it can be accepted that dream characters are aspects of ourselves and that the dream is first and foremost about us. It often helps, therefore, to view the dream through not just our own eyes but as though we are experiencing it as our dream character. The interaction that takes place between us and our dream character is an attempt either to understand that aspect of ourselves or to achieve some kind of integration with it in order to have a wider perspective on life. As such integration progresses we achieve a wholeness and awareness, which enable us to work in a more spiritual focused fashion.

💟 In order to disentangle the various types of 'information' that each · character brings to the dreamer, it is often necessary to decide what or who each one makes us think of. That way we will reveal the deeper meanings and connections. Some of the following entries can also be found in the individual letters and we suggest that you consult these entries for extra information. Where archetypes such as the Anima, Animus, Great Mother, Shadow, Self and Wise Old Man are referred to, please consult the relevant section in the Introduction.

Adolescent – if we dream we are an adolescent we are focusing on our undeveloped side. Dreaming of an adolescent of the opposite sex usually means dealing with a suppressed part of our development. The emotions associated with adolescence are very raw and clear and such emotions are accessible often only through dreams. There may be conflict over issues of freedom.

Ancestors – our customs, ways of behaving, morality and our religious feelings are all handed down from generation to generation. When we become conscious of our ancestors in a dream we are focusing on our roots. We may understand ourselves through our relationship with the past.

Authority figures such as judges, teachers etc. – our concept of authority first develops through our relationship with our father or father figure. Depending on how we were treated as children, our view of authority will be anything from a benign helper to an exploitative disciplinarian. Most authority figures will ultimately lead us back to what is right for us, although not necessarily what we might consider good for us. Authority figures in dreams initially appear to have power over us, though – if we are able to work with them properly – will generate within us the power to succeed.

Baby – to dream about a baby that is our own indicates that we need to recognize those vulnerable feelings over which we have no control. We may be attempting something new. If the baby is someone else's in the dream, we need to be aware of that person's ability to be hurt, or that they may be innocent of something. Psychologically we are in touch with the innocent, curious side of ourselves, with the part that neither wants nor needs responsibility. Dreaming of a baby can indicate that, on a spiritual level, the dreamer has a need for a feeling of purity.

Boy – to have a dream about a boy shows the potential for growth and new experience. If the boy is known to us he reflects recognized qualities in the dreamer. Psychologically, we may need to be in touch with ourselves at that age and with the innocent youthfulness and enthusiasm that a boy has. We are contacting our natural drives and ability to face difficulties.

Boyfriend – to dream of a boyfriend, whether present or former, connects with the feelings, attachments and sexuality connected with him. To dream of having as a boyfriend someone whom you would not anticipate, indicates the need to have a greater understanding of the way you relate to men. Consideration may need to be given to the loving, nurturing side of masculinity. We are still searching for the ideal lover.

Caring professions such as nurses, nuns etc. – often these characters represent the side of us that has been 'called' or has a vocation; this suggests the more compassionate, nurturing side. When such characters appear in a man's dream the relationship that is represented is often non sexual in nature.

Child (who could be one of the dreamer's own children) – dreaming of a child gives us access to our own inner child. We all have parts of ourselves that are still child-like and curious. When we are able to get in touch with that side of ourselves we give ourselves permission to return to a state of innocence, which we may not previously have wished to do.

Dictators (Hitler, Stalin etc.) – if we have, or had, an overbearing father, a known dictator may appear in dreams as representing that relationship. It is as though our dreaming self cannot face confrontation with father as such. Such a figure may also appear where issues affecting the community in which we live are of concern to us.

Emperor or Empress – *see King and Queen in this section.*

Esoteric figures (Astrologers, Magicians etc.) – any character within our dreams who appears to have knowledge of magical practices or similar types of knowledge is usually our first introduction to the Higher Self. It is as though we can only become privy to this deeper knowledge by meeting our teacher first. *Also consult the individual entries for Magic/Magician, Witch and Wizard.*

Girl – if a girl of any age appears in our dreams it shows we are attempting to make contact with the more sensitive, innocent side of ourselves. Those qualities of intuition and perception may be somewhat undeveloped but can be made available. If the girl is known to us we probably are aware of those qualities, but need to explore them as though we were approaching them from the girl's point of view. If she is unknown, we can acknowledge that a fresh approach would be useful.

Girlfriend – when a girlfriend or ex-girlfriend appears in a man's dream there are usually issues to do with masculinity and femininity involved. There may be fears to do with sexuality. If a girlfriend appears in a woman's dream, there can either be a concern about her in our mind, or we need to search for – and find – qualities belonging to the friend in her.

Hero or any heroic figure – in today's world the hero has taken on many guises, particularly in psychological parlance. For many people their own heroic figure, from footballer to successful businessperson, will act as a role model in the journey of life. *Also consult the individual entries for Hero/Heroine and Quest.*

Inadequate Person – we would be unwise to ignore this aspect of ourselves and shouldn't dismiss such an image when it appears. We must acknowledge this dream figure as a reflection of ourselves in order to deal with a learnt sense of inferiority. If we do not, we will be continually faced in life by our own sense of inferiority. It is a lot easier to confront our own inadequacies in the dream state where we are safe. Often this is the first opportunity we have to meet the Shadow.

Indigenous Peoples such as Aboriginal, Maori, Native American – *see individual entry.*

Intruder – the intruder in a woman's dream is often a personification of her own Animus. In a man's dream it characterizes his Shadow. In either case it suggests the need for a change in attitude in order for the dreamer to be able to have a full and meaningful relationship with himself. *You may like to consult the entry for Burglar as well as the individual entry.*

King – almost invariably a king appearing in a dream represents the father or father figure. A personality such as an emperor may indicate that some of the father's attitudes are alien to the dreamer, but should perhaps be accepted. When the king is old or on the point of dying the dreamer will be able to reject outworn or old-fashioned family values.

Magistrate – *see individual entry.*

Man – any man appearing in a dream shows an aspect or facet of our character in a recognizable form. Each of us has a repertoire or portfolio of behaviours, some of which are acceptable and some of which are not. In dreams those behaviours and characteristics can be magnified so that they are easily identified, often as personalities. By working with the characteristic, more energy and power becomes available. Even when we are threatened by a negative character trait, we can still access room for improvement. A man in a dream can identify the Shadow for a man, and the Animus for a woman. An older man (if the man is white-haired or holy) can represent the innate wisdom we all have. Such a person can also signify the father in dreams. When a large man appears in our dreams we are usually appreciating the strengths, certainties and protection that our basic beliefs give us. A man in a woman's dream signifies the more logical side of her nature. She has, or can develop, all the aspects of the masculine that enable her to function with success in the external world. If the man is one she knows or loves she may be trying to understand her relationship with him. An unknown man is generally that part of the dreamer's personality that is not recognized. In a woman's dream it is the masculine side of herself, and in a man's dream it is the Self.

Old People – in dreams, old people can represent either our ancestors or grandparents, hence wisdom accrued from experience. If the old person is male – depending on the gender of the dreamer – he will stand for either the Self or the Animus. If female then she will signify the Great Mother or the Anima. All father figures, or representations of the father, will often appear old as if to highlight their remoteness. A group of old people often appears in dreams. Usually this signifies the traditions and wisdom of the past – things sacred to the 'tribe' or family. Older people usually stand for our parents even though the dream figures may bear no relationship to them. *Also consult the entries for Man and Woman in this section.*

Pirate – the pirate can represent the anarchic part of our personality, which in flouting convention causes us difficulty and tends to separate us from our own integrity.

Police – dreaming particularly of police can indicate a kind of social control and a protective element for us as members of society. Often a policeman will appear in dreams as one's conscience. We may feel that our wilder, more renegade side needs controlling.

Priests, priestesses and ministers of all religions – these figures all hold a special place in the dream hierarchy. Sometimes intermediaries between an ultimate power and Man, and sometimes authority figures, their power comes from beyond themselves. There is, therefore, a sense of 'otherness' about them, and in dreams it is usually the former function that they perform. *Also consult the entries for Archetypes in the Introduction and Authority Figures above.*

Prince/Princess – these figures represent those parts of ourselves, or others, who exist by right; that is, those aspects that have been brought into conscious awareness and authority. As the hero has taken responsibility for his own journey, so the prince and princess take responsibility for the lives they live. *Also consult the entry for Camelot.*

Queen – this usually represents our relationship with our mother or mother figure, and thus with women in authority generally. This applies to a dream image of any regal figure – not only the present queen, but also a historical one such as Victoria. An empress will also have the same connotation.

Security personnel (including caretakers) – in performing a dual function, that of authority figures and guardians of property, security personnel appearing in dreams tend to represent a curb on enjoyment.

Stranger – the stranger in a dream represents that part of ourselves that we do not yet know. There may be a feeling of awe or of conflict with which we need to deal before we can progress. *Also consult Shadow in the Introduction.*

Twins – twins in a dream can suggest two sides of our personality. If they are identical we may be recognizing our ambiguous feelings about ourselves. If not identical they suggest the inner self and the outer reality. Twins may also signify our projections into the world of our own personalities. These interpretations are also valid if there is a mirror image of a dream figure. *Also consult the individual entry for Twin.*

Woman – in a woman's dream a woman, such as a family member or friend is often representative of an aspect of her own personality, but often one she has not yet fully understood. In a man's dream such a figure denotes his relationship with his own feelings and with his intuitive side. It may also show how he relates to his female partner. A goddess or holy woman signifies the highest potential for working with the Greater Good that the dreamer has. Oriental women appearing in dreams usually suggest the mysterious side of the feminine. In a man's dream such a figure will often reveal his attitude to sexuality, while in a woman's dream it will reveal more about her own intuitive transcendent powers. An older woman mostly represents the dreamer's mother and her sense of inherited wisdom. An unknown woman in dreams will represent either the Anima in a man's dream, or the Shadow in a woman's. It is the qualities of surprise and intrigue that allow us to explore further the relevance of that figure. We can gain a great deal of information because the figure is unknown.

The people who appear in dreams are the characters with which we write our 'play'. Often they appear simply as themselves, particularly if they are people we know or have a relationship with in the here and now. We may introduce them in order to highlight a specific quality or characteristic. We may also permit them into our dream scenario as projections of our inner life or state of being, or as ways of handling problems in our everyday life. Sometimes, rather than trying to decipher the meaning of the dream, it is enough to look at what bearing the dream character's actions have on our everyday life. Below are interpretations of some of the most common interactions with people in dreams.

Crowds in dreams can indicate how we relate to other people, particularly in a social sense. They may indicate how we can hide ourselves, or indeed how we hide aspects of ourselves and do not single out any one attribute. We may also be attempting to avoid responsibility. A huge crowd suggests information that we may not be able to handle.

An individual from the past could link us with that period of our lives and with specific memories that may, or may not, be painful.

A neighbour or close associate usually appears in a dream to highlight a particular quality in that person.

Somebody else's mother, father, brother etc. may suggest our own family members or possibly jealousy. To interpret why we have adopted a particular role we would need to examine their lifestyle.

When there is some conflict within us between **love and aversion for a particular person** we are more likely to dream about them. Often in dreams there may be a noted difference between two of the participants to illustrate two sides of our thoughts and feelings. Similarly there may be a marked contrast in the way we handle a situation with two of our dream characters. It is as though two options are being practised.

As with composite animals, **the composite character** will emphasize one characteristic or quality in order to draw our attention to it. The fact that it is not just one person emphasizes the many-faceted human being. Every character who appears in our dreams is a reflection of a facet or part of our own personality and can often be better understood if we put ourselves in the position of that person.

PERFECT/PERFECTION

🌣 Our search for perfection is an effort to return to our spiritual source. In dreams this is often signified by a sense of wonder.

♦ If we subscribe to the belief that everything is inherently perfect, dreams are one way in which we try to understand that perfection. They are also a way of coming to terms with anything in life that is less than perfect, of becoming aware of those things that need adjustment.

▦ Frequently in dreams we are aware of the ephemeral nature of perfection, a sense or feeling that is difficult without practice through meditation or other disciplines to retain in working life.

PERFUME – see ODOUR

PERFORM/PERFORMANCE – see ACTOR AND THEATRE

PERJURY – see LIE

PERMIT/PERMISSION

🌣 A permit suggests that recognition has been given by authority. In spiritual terms this indicates that permission has been given, or initiation has taken place to enable us to act in a certain way.

♦ When we permit certain actions this suggests that we approve of what is being done.

▦ When we find ourselves seeking permission in dreams it may be that we are uncertain of a particular course of action and feel that we need to have our decisions validated.

▣ In both men's and women's dreams, a permit can suggest the right to a relationship. Permission may be required from either party or from others for such a relationship. A backstage permit indicates the ability to get to know somebody better.

PERSECUTE/PERSECUTION – *see* **TORMENT**

PET

✤ Pets will offer us unconditional love and acceptance without question. In many ways this is a lesson in spirituality. In being sensitive to our immediate emotional distress or pain, they can be of comfort. It has been recognized also that they frequently channel healing energies.

♡ On a subliminal level, when dreaming of pets we may be aware that someone else has control over our lives. Conversely, if we own a pet in a dream we perhaps need to question or recognize our ability to look after something or someone more vulnerable than ourselves.

▦ Whereas in the waking state we may not be aware of our need for love and affection, when a pet appears in a dream we are reacting to a natural drive in ourselves to give or receive love.

You might like to consult the individual entries for various animals as well as the entry for Animals to discover their qualities.

PETITION

✤ A petition is a supplication, request or prayer and has this meaning in a spiritual sense. Nowadays it has the additional meaning of a request from like-minded people.

♡ It is worthwhile deciding which is more important in the dream, the petition itself, the cause or the people with whom we are working. We can then consciously decide where our loyalties lie in what is represented.

▦ To be signing a petition indicates committing to a deeply held belief. To refuse to sign means we question our commitment. To have a petition refused signifies disappointment in a working environment.

PETROL – *see* **OIL**

PEW – *see* **SPIRITUAL IMAGERY IN THE INTRODUCTION**

PHEASANT – *see* **BIRDS**

PHOENIX

✤ A mythical bird of great beauty, the phoenix is often an emblem of immortality or of resurrected idealism and hope.

♡ Since the phoenix rises from its own ashes ready to live its life all over again, it signifies our ability to pick ourselves up and begin again, after what appears to be disaster.

▣ The phoenix was believed to live for 500 or 600 years, then to burn itself on a funeral pyre, knowing it would rise again. In dreams, therefore, it can symbolize knowing when to move on, when to let the past go, being aware that there is more energy available if we do so.

Also consult the entry for Birds.

PHOTOCOPY – *see* COPY

PHOTOGRAPHS

✦ Photographs in dreams can represent a spiritual need to understand the past. In a sense they are a microcosm within a macrocosm – a small part within a greater whole.

♥ Obviously photographs represent memories, past occasions, perhaps past difficulties. To be looking at photographs of someone from the past is to be looking at that person's qualities – perhaps bringing them forward into our own lives – and making use of those same qualities within. In magical work a photograph is used as a representation of someone else and can have this meaning in dreams, rather than dreaming about the person concerned.

▣ When we dream of looking at photographs we are often looking at an aspect of ourselves, perhaps our younger self or a part of ourselves that we no longer feel is particularly valid. To be given a photograph of oneself would indicate that we need to be taking an objective view of situations round us or perhaps of ourselves within that situation. We need to stand back and look very clearly at what is going on.

You might also like to consult the entry for Picture.

PHYSICIAN – *see* DOCTOR

PIANO – *see* MUSIC/RHYTHM AND MUSICAL INSTRUMENTS

PICK – *see* CHOICE/CHOOSE

PICKET – *see* DEMONSTRATE/DEMONSTRATION

PICNIC – *see* FOOD

PICTURE

✦ A picture can be a visual depiction of a person or object, an icon – in itself a sacred object – or a representation of spiritual significance.

♥ The condition of the picture may be important, as may also the colours. A torn picture suggests that what is depicted has been damaged. The subject matter may give us suggestions as to what we should be 'looking at' in our lives more objectively.

▣ A picture in a dream is usually an illustration of something that is important to us at that time. If the picture is framed we may assume there is a degree of protection. The interpretation will depend on whether the picture is painted, a print of another picture, or perhaps a photograph.

For further clarification consult the entries for Colours, Frame, Icon and Photograph.

PIERCE – *see* **STAB AND PENETRATION**

PIG – *see* **ANIMALS AND BOAR**

PIGEON – *see* **BIRDS**

PILL – *see* **MEDICATION/MEDICINE AND TABLET**

PILGRIM/PILGRIMAGE

�});A seeker of Spirituality must always undertake a journey of some kind. This is often represented in dreams by a pilgrimage to a holy place of any denomination.

🌀 A pilgrim can often represent the hermit or Wise Old Man within. That part of our personality that is secure and may not need much input from others has the ability to direct our lives, provided we create the correct circumstances.

▦ When we are undertaking a pilgrimage in a dream we are recognizing the purposeful, directed side of our personality. We have a goal in life, which may require faith to achieve.

Consult the entry for Journey and the information on Archetypes in the Introduction.

PILLAR

🌱 The contrast between spiritual and material power is seen as two pillars in dreams. Esoterically, for there to be two pillars in a dream highlights the difference between the masculine and the feminine. The left pillar represents the feminine, and is often seen as being black. The right is masculine, and is seen in dreams as white.

🌀 Pillars mostly indicate a sort of support, so to become aware of supporting pillars indicates that the structure that we have given our lives may need some attention.

▦ One symbolism of a pillar is phallic, but another one is probably more accurate. We are able to create stability and to stand firm in the presence of difficulty. In dreams, to find that we are a pillar of the community suggests that we should be taking more responsibility for our actions.

You may also wish to consult the entry for Column.

PIMP – *see* **PROSTITUTE**

PIMPLE – *see* **SPOT**

PIN

🌱 We may not be able to solve a spiritual difficulty immediately. A temporary solution may be necessary and this can be symbolized by the use of a pin.

🕉 Occasionally in a dream we are reminded of a feeling we have in everyday life. To experience a feeling of pins and needles in our dream suggests that we are not ensuring an adequate flow of energy in a situation around us. A PIN (Personal Identification Number) suggests the need for a sense of security and recognition.

🔲 It depends whether the pin is holding something together or is being used to pierce us, or an object, in our dreams. If it is holding something together it indicates the emotional connections or bonds we use. If it is piercing an object a trauma is suggested, although it may be quite small.

PIPE

🕉 A pipe of any sort suggests some kind of spiritual conduit.

🕉 When we are in difficulty in everyday life, a simple symbol such as a pipe will indicate how making connections between the various aspects of a situation will help resolve it.

🔲 On a purely practical level a pipe can symbolize many things. A water pipe can give information as to how we might handle our emotions (the size and type in this case will be significant); a clay pipe might suggest former times or an old-fashioned attitude. A tobacco pipe or chillum might suggest a means of escape, whereas a musical pipe indicates our connection with the rhythm of life.

PIRATE – *see* **PEOPLE**

PISTOL – *see* **GUN, SHOT/SHOOTING AND WEAPONS**

PISTON

🕉 The spiritual drive – that is, the need to be complete – requires effort which can be enhanced by using our resources properly. A piston symbolizes this drive.

🕉 A piston may also represent a person's drive for success. We need to assess the amount of effort that is necessary for us to be able to achieve our goals. We may need to recognize that concentrated effort – which is fairly mechanical – may, at this stage, achieve more than creative flair. The piston, being only part of an engine, does require the rest of the components to operate successfully. Often a great deal of help can be gained by considering the way in which the piston works. In other words, though at a particular stage of development our actions may have to be mechanical, we do have to consider the 'engine', not just its component parts.

🔲 A piston in a dream can be taken to mean sexual drive or activity. In this context it is more of a mechanical action than a loving act, and may show a particular attitude to sex.

🔧 In a woman's dream a piston may reveal her fear of being hurt sexually. She may also be aware that she is simply being used, and that there is no tenderness. In a man's dream such an image may indicate his sense of identity and masculinity. If the piston is not rigid a man may fear impotence, whereas a woman will feel perhaps that she cannot trust her partner.

Consult the entry for Engine for further clarification.

PIT

🔆 The pit, like the abyss, represents the Void and possibly death – not necessarily a physical death, but more a death of the old self. We have no choice but to go forward, knowing that we may fail, but also that if we do succeed our lives will change for the better. To face the pit requires extreme courage.

💚 Rescuing others from a pit, particularly if they are members of our own family, suggests that we have information which may be of use to them to enable them to overcome their problems. We may also be showing our concern over certain actions, which seem irrevocable. Pushing someone into a pit indicates that we are trying to suppress a part of our personality. To be conscious that the pit is bottomless signifies that we do not have the resources to recover a previous situation.

🔲 Many people talk about the pit of despair and of feeling trapped within a situation. A pit in a dream makes us more conscious of this particular feeling. We may be in circumstances that we cannot get out of, or may find that if we are not careful we will put ourselves in such a situation. If we are digging the pit in the dream, we may be creating the situation ourselves. If others are digging the pit, we may feel we have no control over our circumstances and that doom and disaster are inevitable.

You may also wish to consult the entry for Abyss.

PLACES

🔆 In the sense that a place suggests a 'spot', places appearing in dreams allow us to orientate ourselves in order to make the best use of information we are given. Interpreting the symbolism of certain places gives us an insight into our own 'inner landscape'. A place that becomes fertile or lighter in the course of the dream indicates that an aspect that we have not previously appreciated – or have found unpleasant – is now developing possibilities and potentials, possibly for spiritual development. Dreary, unfriendly places, or tranquil favourable landscapes may well refer to our subjective view of the world. To find such landscapes changing in the course of a dream suggests that our attitudes are changing.

✪ The country where the dream takes place may have certain resonances for the dreamer. For example, America for most people will signify a rather brash, commercially oriented culture, England tends to be seen as inhibited and dutiful, while France will represent the temperamental masculine, and so on. Other places that offer information for consideration are as follows:

Our birthplace represents a secure space where we feel at ease.

A bright and sunny place suggests fun and liveliness, whereas a dark, shadowy, murky scene signifies despondency and gloom.

Darkened places can also represent the unconscious.

Countryside can suggest a particular mood or feeling, especially of freedom.

Composite scenes consisting of many images recognizable to us are usually drawing attention to particular qualities, ideals and moods. These all enhance the information content of the dream, may have particular associations for us or have been included because of frequently encountered associations.

A familiar place will often take us back to childhood or a time of learning and a particularly beautiful place may allow us to fantasize so that we can make more use of creative visualization.

Jungles connect with the labyrinth and ways of understanding our sexuality, whereas a place that feels oppressive has formerly been a sanctuary, but is no longer. A sheltered place offers peace and security. *Also see the individual entry.*

Unknown places indicate aspects of ourselves of which we are not yet aware. Such places can lead to an environment that seems familiar and yet we do not know it. This signifies a situation we are continually re-running in our lives.

Wide-open spaces offer us freedom of movement.

▦ When the environment or setting of a dream is particularly noticeable there is usually some kind of message or information being given. Sometimes the place reflects our inner state of mind or mood. It can be a reminder of a particular place, which had meaning at a specific time in our life, and sometimes a reminder of particular people.

PLAGUE – *see* **EPIDEMIC/PLAGUE**

PLAIT

✪ Very subtle influences come into play when we begin to develop spiritually. Hair plaited into the shape of a crown – or wound round the head – indicates spiritual attainment. Hair is often used as a representation of the individual in magical spells.

✪ Plaited hair was formerly a means of creating order and cleanliness. Often in dreams to see a plait reminds us of the talisman – or favour belonging to his lady – that a knight of old would carry into battle. Nowadays it is more of a lucky charm. To be plaiting string, rope, hair etc. highlights our ability to weave the different influences of our, or someone else's, life into a coherent whole.

▣ In olden times, a plait using three strands indicated the interweaving of body, mind and spirit. It also represented the influences that were assimilated by a growing girl and taken into her understanding of herself as a woman.

⊞ In dreams, a plait represents womanhood. In the present day, the more creative men will often wear their hair longer, and for this to happen in a dream suggests that they are in process of recognizing their emerging sensitivity.

To clarify this interpretation further, consult the entries for Crown, as well as Hair and Head in the Body section.

PLAN/PLANS

✹ Plans are diagrams designed to help in certain tasks, whether that is construction or in the sense of a map. They are of assistance in spiritual development in that they let us see the way forward.

♥ Normally, if we have a plan we have considered what our future actions must be. In dreams this may appear as an actual document. To be at a planning meeting signifies the need for order in our lives.

▣ As planning is such an integral part of business life today, the image or idea will surface in dreams quite frequently. When a plan or plans are dropped in a dream the significance is obvious.

⊞ When a woman dreams of visiting a family planning centre, she may be becoming aware of her wish to be pregnant. In a man's dream this may suggest his wish or need to take responsibility.

PLANETS

✹ Spiritually, once we become aware of how the subtle energies can help us live our lives successfully, we can learn to make use of planetary energy. This is a belief that goes back to ancient times and is the basis of astrology.

♥ The interpretations of the planetary significances are:

Jupiter suggests growth and expansion, and also freedom from limitation.

Mars indicates activity and war but also drive.

Mercury signifies communication, intuition and mental powers.

The Moon represents our emotions and our links with our mother.

Neptune works with illusion – but also with inspiration.

Pluto has charge of the unconscious and transformation.

Saturn is a restraining influence and rules the past.

The Sun usually symbolizes the Self and the energy that we have.

Uranus governs sudden changes.

Venus highlights love and beauty.

▦ Dreaming of planets is to be linking with very subtle energies, which surround us and have an effect on our lives, even though we may not be consciously aware of them. Often as we begin to study the esoteric arts we become more aware of these influences.

PLANTS

✺ Plants in a spiritual sense signify both the life force and the cycle of life. Because they die only to grow again, they also suggest death and rebirth.

♥ If the plants are growing wild, there is a part of us that needs freedom. If they are grown in regimented rows we are aware of too much concern for the views of other people. Many plants have both healing and magical qualities. Equally, without proper knowledge, plants can be harmful.

▦ Because of the process of growth and decay that plants go through naturally, they become a symbol for progressive change. If the plants are cultivated, then we should be aware of our ability to cultivate potential. If the plants are dying we may have reached a stage where there is no more advantage within a situation.

You might also like to consult the entries for Garden and Weeds.

PLATEAU

✺ Many dreams will hold images of climbing and of reaching a plateau. Spiritually this offers us choices. We can rest on our laurels and take time out to assess our progress, or we can use the plateau for calm and peace.

♥ If the plateau is barren, we may need some further stimulus to help us move on. If it seems to be a place of safety, we may not wish to move on and perhaps need to take time out to recuperate.

▦ After a great deal of effort we reach a place that is even and not difficult to cross. Sometimes it can represent a period of peace and quiet, sometimes stasis where there is no energy left for change. When this happens in a work situation we eventually need to decide on and initiate whatever further action is needed.

PLAY

✺ From a spiritual perspective, the life that we have creates a play, which gives us the best opportunity to learn lessons through experience. If people we know are in the play we should be aware of the 'drama' we are playing out with them.

♥ In dreams, the play that takes place is a distillation of our experiences, knowledge and abilities. The creator in us directs the performance to enable us to get the best benefit of the information it contains. Images in dreams are put together to have the greatest impact and to make the interpretation as easy as possible. Sometimes, however, to catch our attention the unexpected occurs, which means that we have to seek explanation from a source outside ourselves.

🎴 When in a dream we are watching a play, we need to decide whether it is a drama, a comedy or a tragedy. This is because we often are trying to view our own lives objectively. The content of the play may give us clues as to what our course of action should be in everyday life.

You might also like to consult the entries for Actor, Audience and Theatre.

PLEA/PLEADING

🌣 Spiritually a plea has the same meaning as prayer. It also suggests applying to arbitrators of spiritual law such as priests and holy men.

🫧 When we find ourselves pleading for something – begging or appealing – we have some extreme need for whatever is represented. This might, for instance, be some kind of assistance or sanctuary.

🎴 A strongly held feeling or principle will deepen to a plea in dreams, particularly if we feel we are not understood.

Also consult the entry for Prayer.

PLOUGHING

🌣 We are in process of creating new opportunities to develop spiritually.

🫧 We may have a situation within our lives which needs 'turning over'. By looking at it from a different perspective we are able to make the situation more productive.

🎴 As more people move away from working with the land, this symbol has become less relevant in dreams. It does mean, however, working at clearing ourselves for new growth and being able to prepare for change, particularly in regard to conservation issues.

PLUMAGE – *see* FEATHERS

PLUMBING

🌣 We are beginning to become aware of the flow of spiritual energy within our lives, though this may be in the background.

🫧 Emotional security is important to almost everybody, and mostly such feelings are hidden from view. When we are looking at plumbing we are actually looking into our subconscious to where we have stored information and emotion. We need to be able to access the subconscious in order to create clarity within our lives.

🎴 Dreaming about plumbing looks at the way we direct our emotions. It indicates how we make use of our emotions to bypass obstacles in order to create security for ourselves and to control the flow of emotions within. Another interpretation is that of the internal plumbing. Often, to dream of plumbing in this sense alerts us to something that is perhaps out of kilter with ourselves, with our bodies. A leaking steam pipe might suggest, for instance, a problem with hypertension. A pump might symbolize the heart. Obviously, such images should not be used as diagnostic tools in any way.

You might also like to consult the entry for Pipe.

PLUNGE

🔅 Spiritual risk pushes us into a situation where we must take the plunge. The Fool in the Tarot gives a visual image of this conundrum. He steps out into space secure that he will be safe.

❤ When facing uncertainty in waking life we very often need reassurance that we have both the courage and the daring to go ahead with a particular activity. Very often, to dream of plunging is to recognize that we do have the ability to go forward. To dream of a plunger – as in something that clears a blockage – usually indicates that we need to use some force to enable us to deal with difficulty. Frequently, this can be because we have internalized a problem – we have either worked too hard and don't have the energy to move the difficulty away from us or we have created a problem for ourselves in that we have not acted appropriately.

🔲 To dream of plunging into something is to recognize that we are facing uncertainty. We are going into something unknown – something that we have perhaps not done before – and are taking a risk. That risk will very often take us into our emotional depths and we will learn new things about ourselves, of which we will then be able to make use. The sports of bungee and parachute jumping epitomize this.

You may like to consult the entries for Diving and Plumbing.

POACH – *see* STEALING

POCKET

🔅 A pocket suggests hidden matters or the Occult. In a spiritual sense it is anything that occurs in the realms of the intuitive feminine.

❤ A pocket in a dream can also indicate a sense of ownership and possession. To have something in our pocket means that we have appropriated it, that we have taken ownership. This can represent a situation in the everyday world, or it can represent emotions that we may have previously hidden and now need to own, in the sense of being able to make use of them.

🔲 To dream of a pocket is to be dealing with our personal secrets or thoughts – those things that we have deliberately chosen to hide rather than done so on impulse. They are perhaps secret thoughts that we do not want to share with anyone else. There may also be thoughts about our own abilities and the value that we have within our own personal community.

POINT

⚙ A point is the Beginning of all things, the Soul or Completion, the place from which everything else emanated.

◈ Psychologically and intellectually, to have integrated ourselves means that we have reached our own centre. This is often symbolized in dreams by a point or dot.

▦ To be aware of the point of decision is to come to a resolve that something has to be done. We must bring about change in one way or another and at that particular 'point' there is nothing else to be done. From this arises all other creative solutions.

▐ Anything pointed normally refers to male sexuality and has this symbolism in both men's and women's dreams.

POINTING

⚙ A particular way forward is being indicated; there is a goal we must reach.

◈ Pointing in a dream, particularly by one of our dream characters, indicates either that we are being given a sense of direction, or that we are being pointed away from a present action and should leave it behind. If we are being pointed at we may also be being singled out for a particular task.

▦ When we dream of someone pointing, normally we are having our attention drawn to a particular object, feeling or even place. We need to take note of both who is pointing it out to us, to gain some idea of the relevance and equally what they are pointing at. We may feel that we are at the receiving end of an aggressive act or accusation – that we are being accused of wrongdoing and need to look at the validity of our conduct.

Also consult the entry for Direction in Position.

POKE/POKER

⚙ The poker in this instance suggests rigid and unbending discipline, which is sometimes necessary. There is often the necessity for aggressive action, but also rigid attitudes and behaviour in spiritual development. To poke someone is to goad them.

◈ Playing a game of poker in a dream, whether on-line or otherwise, suggests that we are taking a risk in everyday life. It may be important to note who we are playing with. A poker face is one that shows no emotion whatever the circumstances. As the game of poker becomes more popular in the field of gambling, many of the terms used have relevance in today's world.

▦ A poker obviously has links with masculinity, but also with rigidity. Inherent in the idea of such an object is that it causes a shift in perception.

When we are being poked in a dream we need to ascertain what the irritant is in our waking lives.

🔞 The use of a poker can be seen as the sexual act in both men and women's dreams but may also be seen as an inflexible attitude to the physical body.

You might also like to consult the entries for Cards and Gambling.

POLICE – *see* **PEOPLE**

POLLUTION

🔅 Pollution suggests that ideas, concepts and principles can be contaminated in some way and thus made less than perfect.

💟 In its original meaning of desecration, such a strong image makes us aware of how easy it is for us to lose sight of our aims and objectives in life. On an emotional level we can become conscious of a kind of pollution when we are not in line with our own truth.

🔲 As we become more aware of the consequences of pollution in waking life, dream images will take on a relevance that has not been evident before. On a personal level we ourselves, our bodies, can become polluted by the food we eat, the medications we need, the air we breathe and so on, giving rise to distorted dream images.

PONY – *see* **HORSE IN ANIMALS**

POOL/POND

🔅 A pool can have the same connotations as a doorway – an entry into the unconscious and our deepest emotions. A pond will tend to represent a man-made construction. Esoterically, a puddle – a small body of water – can be used for scrying, that is, looking towards the future as though into a magic mirror. To be looking into a puddle may be trying to decide what future action needs to be taken.

💟 In order to understand ourselves we may need to explore the pool by totally immersing ourselves in it, that is, to become involved in our own emotions. How we deal with what arises (in more senses than one) will teach us a lot about ourselves. The pool may suggest a form of cleansing, particularly of old traumas and emotions or of past misdeeds. The most potent image of that is baptism by immersion.

🔲 Dreaming of a pool deals with our need for the understanding of our own emotions and inner feelings. A pool in a wood, for instance, would suggest the ability to understand our own need for peace and tranquility. An urban swimming pool might signify our need for structure in our relationships with other people, whereas a pool in the road would suggest an emotional problem to be got through before carrying out our plans. A pond might suggest the emotions associated with the workplace in that this is an environment where relationships are artificially constructed.

Consult the entries for Lagoon/Lake and Water for further clarification.

POOR – *see* POVERTY

POPE

☀ Our spiritual mentor or Higher Self will sometimes be seen as the Pope. He may also be someone to whom we have given authority.

☯ The Pope often appears in dreams as a substitute for the father, or as a personification of God.

▦ Often to meet the Pope in a dream is to meet the side of ourselves that has developed a code of behaviour based on our religious beliefs. He may be benign or judgmental, depending on how we perceive the head of the Catholic church. It will also depend on how the figure of the Pope was presented in childhood.

POSITION

☀ When a particular position is highlighted in a dream it usually signifies our moral or spiritual standpoint, or our position in life. It can also give an indication of how we are handling situations in our lives. For instance, something in the wrong position means we are going about things in the wrong way.

☯ Status is an important aspect of self-esteem. In dreams we often picture our sense of self by becoming conscious of our position relative to other dream objects. Often in dream interpretation position is not considered. However, much additional information can be gleaned by carefully considering these such placings:

Higher or above – our spirit, intellect, ideals and consciences are being brought to our attention. This applies also when dreaming of the upper part of anything (of a building or body, for example). Our altruism may be being brought into question.

Underneath, below or downstairs – this signifies the anarchic or immoral side of our personalities. The sexual impulses can also be characterized in this way.

Upside down – the potential for chaos and difficulty is being emphasized.

Ups and downs – the personality has a need to balance the heights and depths of its experience, and if this does not happen a warning will usually appear in dream form. Situations in life can be experienced in dreams as the actual movement of our position.

Back and front – the back of anything signifies rejection, and the front acceptance. Conflict between rejection and acceptance can be shown in a dream as seeing both the back and front of something.

Backward/forward – when a backward and/or forward movement is prominent this usually indicates a regressive, backward-looking tendency. We may want to retire into the past, rather than tackling fears and moving ahead.

Centre – to be particularly conscious of the centre of any aspect of a dream indicates we are aware of a goal or objective, or perhaps even of our real Self. We may need to be the centre of attention whatever the circumstances. *Also consult the section on Archetypes in the Introduction.*

Far/Near – in dreams, space and time can become confused. Dreaming of something that is far away may indicate that it is far away in time. This may be future or past, depending on the dream. A long way in front would be future, a long way behind would be past. Near or close would mean recently, or in the immediate future.

Horizontal and Vertical – the horizontal usually symbolizes the material world whereas the vertical in dreams tends to represent the spiritual realm.

Left – the left side suggests the less dominant, more passive side. Often it is taken to represent all that is dark and sinister and those parts of our personality that we try to suppress. It is, however, more to do with instinctive behaviour, what feels good inside, and with personal behaviour without attention to moral codes.

The left side is supportive in expression, and receptive by nature, so anything appearing in dreams on the left side can be accepted as a symbol of support. Any pain experienced on the left side is interpreted in terms of sensitivity. The left expresses the more feminine attributes and often the past. Any conflict between right and left indicates the differences between logic and intuition. Indecision over left or right suggests an inability to decide whether to rely on drive or instinct. Feelings of being left behind suggest a sense of inadequacy, of disintegration and of having to leave the past behind.

Low – in dreams, feeling 'low' can suggest a sense of inferiority or humility. Often we will give way to submissive behaviour, and put ourselves in a lower position than others. Occasionally, to be below something or someone can indicate a need to explore the underside or negativity of a relationship or situation.

Opposite – anything in a dream that is opposite us may suggest difficulty in reconciling two paradoxes (good/bad, male/female etc.). This can sometimes suggest conflict. One thing deliberately put opposite another suggests a deliberate attempt to introduce discord. When something is deliberately moved from being opposite in a dream, any differences that we have may be reconciled.

Right – the right side represents the more dominant, logical side. It is the consciously expressed, confident side that perceives the exterior world in perhaps a more objective sense. It is to do with 'rightness' – that is, correctness and moral and social behaviour. Anything observed on the right side in dreams usually becomes more significant as we progress. Any pain experienced on the right side can also be interpreted in terms of drive. It also expresses the more masculine attributes. Movement to the right indicates that something is coming into conscious awareness.

Top – to be at the top of anything shows we have succeeded in our endeavours. Trying to reach the top suggests more effort is needed, whereas to be on top is to have assumed control.

Under/underneath – being underneath something suggests either taking shelter or submitting to someone else's handling of us. It may also represent the part of us that we hide, or the part that is less capable.

Up/upper – this shows that we have the capability of achieving a degree of supremacy. We are capable of getting the 'upper hand' in particular situations. We can move away from the mundane, ordinary, everyday world into a more spiritual way of life.

▓ When any direction is indicated or particularly noticeable in a dream, we need to consider the esoteric implications and how these are applicable in our everyday lives. Based on the Chinese method of interpretation and used by those systems of belief that adhere to the natural forces, the points of the compass can be read symbolically. **The North** signifies the Unknown, and hence sometimes darkness. It is spirituality within the world. **The East** traditionally suggests birth and mystic religions. It also represents becoming 'conscious'. **The South** is representative of earthly passion and sensuality. **The West** can symbolize death, but more properly the state after death when there is increased spiritual awareness. Traditionally, it can also represent the more logical side of our natures.

POST

✿ A post in spiritual terms may signify a support or a marker. As a marker it has the same meaning as flag or banner. As a support it will be useful to look at what help we need to advance our spiritual understanding.

◈ To be posting a notice suggests making a declaration. When in dreams we are posting a letter it is to communicate information or intention.

▓ To be 'in a post' suggests that someone else has made the decision to employ us – we become a support. A large quantity of post being delivered in a dream may indicate that we are under pressure.

POVERTY

    ✺ Spiritual poverty occurs when we become conscious that there is something lacking in our lives. It can also be recognized as self-denial.

    ❦ Poverty can be conveyed by poor surroundings in a dream. It may be that we need to deal with our surroundings; there is something lacking in our environment rather than ourselves. When we feel poor we do not have the wherewithal to look after ourselves properly.

    ▦ To experience poverty in a dream highlights a sense of being deprived of the ability to satisfy our basic needs. We may feel inadequate, either emotionally or materially. Often we need to go right back to basics to discover what our real needs are.

You might also like to consult the entries for Money and Wealth.

POWDER – see MIX

PRAYER

    ✺ There are two aspects of prayer. One is supplication – asking for something – and the other is worship – acknowledging the supremacy of the Ultimate.

    ❦ Psychologically, the human being has always needed to feel that there is a greater power than himself available to him. To be praying in a dream reinforces this, since we need to use our own inner sense of self to access the Greater Power.

    ▦ Prayer suggests the idea that we need to seek outside help for ourselves. We may need someone else's authority to succeed in what we are doing. It also can indicate our ability to draw on our own inner resources.

You might also like to consult the entry for Spiritual Imagery in the Introduction.

PREACH – see PRIEST/PRIESTESS AND MINISTERS OF ALL RELIGIONS IN PEOPLE

PRECIPICE

    ✺ A precipice will indicate a perceived spiritual danger. In fact, there is no way forward except to acknowledge that danger and continue on our way.

    ❦ The image of the Fool in the Tarot shows him at the beginning and the end of his journey. He is unmindful of the precipice and initially is not aware of the danger he is in. Conversely, he does not care because he is aware he is capable of stepping off the edge and taking flight. This type of dream often appears when we are in a position of great risk.

    ▦ The fear of failure is a very strong emotion. Often it can be represented in dreams by a precipice. To step off a precipice is taking risks, since we do not know the outcome of our action. To try to climb a precipice is to be making a tremendous effort to overcome obstacles that have arisen.

Consult the entry for Cliff to help with clarification.

PREGNANCY

⚜ There is always a gestation period in spiritual work. We may have to be patient and wait for a natural process to take place so that we can fulfil a task.

♡ To dream of someone else being pregnant suggests that we are in a position to observe part of ourselves developing new skills or characteristics. We may be unaware of what the outcome of this process will be. To dream of a man being pregnant, particularly if it is a woman's dream, is probably a projection of her own wish for the man to take responsibility within her life.

▦ Dreaming of pregnancy usually denotes a fairly protracted waiting period being necessary for something, possibly the completion of a project. A new area of our potential or personality is developing.

⚄ Interestingly enough, for a woman to dream of pregnancy seldom actually means her own pregnancy, although it can indicate pregnancy in someone around her. For a man, dreaming of the pregnancy of his wife or partner can indicate his willingness to take on extra responsibility.

PREHISTORIC

⚜ Spiritual progression requires us to understand our physical, emotional, mental and spiritual urges. The prehistoric images indicate either the lack of ability to integrate the various parts of ourselves successfully, or to integrate with society. There are still aspects perhaps of family history that need to be understood.

♡ Often in dreams the landscape or scenario appears to be prehistoric. This is 'before thought' and before we had the ability to properly record our impressions. If we believe that babies are conscious of the world they will enter before birth, then these impressions can appear in later life as prehistoric images. For instance, a barren landscape might indicate a lack of love.

▦ Being aware in a dream that something is prehistoric is to recognize that feelings and emotions we have arise literally from before the time we were able to understand ourselves. When we have not fully integrated and comprehended the basic urge for survival, it is possible for us to be self-destructive without necessarily appreciating why.

You might also like to consult the entry for Dinosaur.

PRESCRIPTION – *see* HEALING

PRESENT/PRESENTS

⚜ One of the requirements of spiritual advancement is that we learn to live in the present (literally the pre-sent). We need to be able to take advantage of anything that life offers us – to use it for ourselves, but also to recognize that it has relevance for other people and can affect the way that they live.

To present something in a dream (as in making a presentation) is offering work that we have done for approval and recognition. We appreciate that the work we have done is more important than we ourselves are.

When a present appears in a dream, it can first of all be a play on words. We are being given a 'here and now'. We are being reminded to live in the moment and not the past or future. A present can also indicate a talent or gift. If we are receiving a present we are being loved and recognized and are also gaining from the relationship. If we are giving a present, we appreciate that we have characteristics we are able to offer other people. A pile of presents in a dream can signify as yet unrecognized talents and skills. If the presents give some indication of time – e.g. birthday presents – we may expect some success around that time.

Consult the entry for Gift/Give/Giving for further information.

PRESERVE – *see* PROTECT/PROTECTION

PRIEST/PRIESTESS – *see* ARCHETYPES IN THE INTRODUCTION, MONK, NUN AND PEOPLE

PRINCE/PRINCESS – *see* ARCHETYPES IN THE INTRODUCTION, HERO/ HEROINE AND PEOPLE

PRISON

Duty and guilt are opposite sides of the same coin in a spiritual sense. Duty can be a liability and therefore a trap, and guilt can prevent us from seeing a way forward. When we feel trapped either by duty or guilt we will dream of a prison.

Often we create a 'prison' for ourselves through a sense of duty or guilt and this can often be shown in dreams. The types of locks and bolts we perceive in our prison may show us how we are imprisoning ourselves. For example, a lock with a key would suggest that we know how to escape, whereas a bolt shows that we have to make a greater effort. A barred window would suggest that we are being prevented from using that which is external to us.

We may feel that outside circumstances are making life difficult, but in actual fact we are creating those circumstances ourselves. This can be on an emotional, material or spiritual level and is translated into the dream image of a prison.

Also consult the entries for Bolt, Key and Lock.

PRIZE

In spiritual terms, gaining a prize or accolade in a dream means having used our instincts and intuition in harmony and so can use inspiration.

♥ To prize an object (as in a prize possession) is to give it its proper value. This does not necessarily mean being materialistic, but being able to gain from an appreciation of its intrinsic value. This may indicate the need to concentrate on the material world for a time.

▥ In dreams, to win a prize is to have succeeded in overcoming our own obstacles. We are also being acknowledged by other people for having made the effort to succeed and achieving what we set out to do. To be giving away prizes suggests that we are giving public acknowledgement to efforts others have made.

▤ In a woman's dream a prize often suggests emotional satisfaction. In a man's dream it will signify success.

PROCESSION

☼ Spiritually, a procession is indicative of a group of like-minded people but also of people who have great knowledge. In dreams we are recognizing the importance of whatever system of belief or religion we belong to. We recognize respect must be paid.

♥ A procession is often a way of marking a special occasion with pageantry and dignity. In dreams such an image can often represent our need to have our own successes and abilities recognized. To be taking part in a procession is acknowledging our need to belong to a like-minded group. To be watching a procession is to appreciate other people's single-mindedness.

▥ A procession means an orderly approach and often makes a statement of intent. In a dream, to see a line of people who all appear to have a similar goal or set of beliefs in mind, indicates that it is the intention behind the group which is important. Often a procession is hierarchical, with the most important people either first or last. This could be important in a dream in enabling us to adopt priorities for ourselves.

PROFIT

☼ In spiritual terms, profit is energy or power gained commensurate with the amount of effort we are prepared to put in, in anything we do.

♥ Simply, if we profit from something we gain benefit. In dreams we are made aware of possible emotional or material benefits through the symbolism of profit.

▥ The idea of profit and loss comes from the material world and the need to control resources. In dreams the meaning is widened to all sorts of resources not just financial, though if there are financial worries we may well dream of some kind of accounting procedure.

You might also like to consult the entries for Money and Wealth.

PROPOSE/PROPOSAL

☯ A proposal is a statement of intent and spiritually represents the sacred marriage, the union of spiritual and physical. To propose in the spiritual sense is to make an offer or offering of our abilities.

♢ To propose an action in a dream is to promote it as a good idea, as something that should be considered. In the sense of a marriage proposal we are marking the potential integration of two sides of our personality.

▤ A business proposal in dream parlance is a properly thought out course of action to bring about some kind of merger or autonomy. It is often the first step in a new understanding of the world we live in.

∛ Both men and women will dream of proposals with personal and business connotations. The type of proposal made or given will highlight the seriousness or emotional impact of the integration that is taking place. Contrary to popular belief, it does not necessarily mean that a proposal will take place in real life.

Consult the entries for Contract, Marriage and Wedding/Wedding Dress/Wedding Ring for further information.

PROSECUTE – *see* TRIAL

PROSTITUTE

☯ Spiritually we need to accept other people's values. A prostitute originally meant 'one who stood before', and in ancient times was a woman who initiated men into the mysteries of the sacred marriage, a rite of sacrifice.

♢ In dreaming of prostitution, we may actually be connecting with a poor self-image. We are minimizing our abilities and talents – this may be in a work situation as much as in our personal life. Very often, when we are expected to 'perform', inadequacy or ego makes us feel that we are 'prostituting' our talents.

▤ Dreaming of a prostitute often suggests a hidden sexual need. Often, dreaming of a prostitute forces us to look at our own sense of guilt or uncertainty about ourselves. A pimp is one who procures business for a prostitute and this has obvious resonance in the business world. To be paying a prostitute may suggest that we do not trust our own abilities, sexual or otherwise. To be paid for the sexual act may suggest that we feel relationships will cost us. In both cases there may be a fear of loving relationships.

∛ The appearance of a prostitute in a woman's dream can highlight her own unexpressed need for sexual freedom. In a man's dream it may signify his need for relationship at any cost.

PROTECT/PROTECTION

☯ Spiritual protection appears in many guises in dreams from images such as a cloak to a mist. It will depend on the type of protection needed – a cloak would suggest a closer, more intimate level than a mist, which is more ephemeral or disparate.

🕉 It is a natural reaction to need to protect ourselves from harm and for many people an emotional attack will cause us to dream of trying to find some sort of protection. When we feel that a principle or idea needs preserving we will often dream of protection of something.

🔲 When we have been made vulnerable in daily life our dreams will offer an image in order to help us deal with the problem. The mind has a habit of imaging the necessary type of protection needed.

Also consult the entry for Garlic.

PROTEST – *see* **ARGUE/ARGUMENT AND DEMONSTRATE/DEMONSTRATION**

PROVOKE – *see* **GOAD**

PROWL/PROWLER – *see* **THE INDIVIDUAL ENTRY FOR INTRUDER AND ALSO THE ENTRY IN PEOPLE**

PSYCHOLOGIST/PSYCHIATRIST – *see* **ANALYST**

PUDDLE – *see* **LAGOON/LAKE, POOL/POND AND WATER**

PULL/PULLING

🕉 At a certain stage of spiritual development, we can find ourselves being pulled in a certain direction. We may be compelled to do certain things without necessarily knowing where the impulse comes from. The call could be, for instance, because of someone's distress or to give us information we need. Dreams are a very effective way of implanting such ideas into our psyche.

🕉 We may in everyday life find ourselves being pulled by our emotions and feel that we are powerless to resist. This can translate into the dream image of being pulled. We may feel that we have to go along with something and do not have the ability to refuse.

🔲 Pulling suggests a positive action. We are being alerted to the fact that we can do something about a situation. In dreams, if we are pulling we are making the decisions within a project. If we are being pulled we may feel that we have to give in to outside pressures. Extra effort to have something happen may be necessary. The object we are pulling, and the means by which we are pulling it, may be important. *For examples, see Bridle, Rope etc.*

🔳 In slang terms, pulling means picking up a potential partner. In dreams this can actually translate itself into a physical feeling.

PUMP – *see* **PLUMBING**

PUNCH – *see* **FIGHT**

PUNISH/PUNISHMENT

🕉 The concept of Divine Retribution – that is, being punished by a force greater than ourselves – suggests a judgemental God. Spiritual punishment is much more, however, the idea of self-flagellation for not having achieved what is required of us. When in dreams we are punishing another, the inference is that we are standing in judgement over them.

🕉 When there is conflict in our lives, if we cannot resolve it we will often dream of being punished. This may be the only way out of our particular dilemma. We would rather suffer pain than resolve the difficulty. Inflicting punishment suggests that we feel some aspect of our personality is out of alignment.

🔲 When a child recognizes that he or she is not conforming to what is expected, the threat of punishment is often present. In later life, when there is fear of retribution from an external source, we will often dream of being punished when there is no evidence of such. Self-punishment occurs when we have not achieved the standards we expect of ourselves and in many ways might be considered self-abuse.

PUPPET

🕉 At certain stages of development, we can become aware that we are powerless without a spiritually motivating force behind us. We are like puppets in the greater scheme of things.

🕉 When a puppet appears in a dream there is perhaps a sense of being able to manipulate circumstances or people around us. A puppet can also represent the more mechanical processes of our being, those activities that go on automatically in the background.

🔲 If someone else is working the puppet, we may feel that we are being manipulated. It would be wise to look at how we are co-operating in everyday life in becoming a victim. If the puppet is manipulating us we have become aware that bureaucracy is causing us difficulty. What should be working for us has, in fact, turned into some kind of manipulation.

The entry for Toys may give further clarification.

PUPPY – see ANIMALS

PURPLE – see COLOURS

PURSE

🕉 One symbolism of a purse is the same as that of a bag: the feminine and the containing principle. We are attempting to conserve our Spiritual energy or power.

🕉 The material that a purse is made from can have an important significance. A fine material could suggest affluence and a purse that is not appropriate for the occasion symbolizes literally being out of our comfort zone. The old saying 'You cannot make a silk purse out of a sow's ear' has relevance in dreams.

■ A purse is normally used to hold money, or something of value to us. In dreams it therefore becomes something of value it its own right. To find a purse would suggest that we have found something of value, whereas to lose a purse suggests that we may be being careless.

◆ For a woman to lose her purse in dreams would suggest that her essential nature as a woman is being compromised, whereas in a man's dream he may be losing the security he finds in his primary relationship.

PUSHED/PUSHING

❈ When one is developing psychically, it is possible to become aware of the subtle forces and energy around. This can be experienced as being pushed.

◆ When in a dream we are being pushed, there is an energy around us that enables us to achieve what we want. If we are pushing, then we are usually exerting our will positively. Pushing something uphill, such as a car or snowball, suggests that we are trying to resist natural forces.

■ When in everyday life we are aware of pressure, this can surface in dreams as being pushed and can sometimes indicate a fear of illness. In certain forms of mental illness, the patient experiences a feeling of being pushed around and made to do something he does not want to do. Occasionally, when experienced in dreams, this can actually be a form of healing.

PYJAMAS – see CLOTHES

PYRAMID

❈ Spiritually, the pyramid is a symbol of integration of the Self and the Soul. In dreams it can represent death, but also indicates rebirth. It is a guardian of power.

◆ The pyramid always signifies a wider awareness of power and energy. There is a point inside the pyramid where all the planes intersect. This will regenerate any matter that is placed there, for instance razor blades will become sharp again. In a larger pyramid, that particular spot can be used for enhancing mystical experiences. In dreams, to enter a pyramid is to be searching for the meaning of life.

■ A pyramid is a very powerful image. On a physical level, it is a building of wonder. On a mental level, it is a structure of regeneration. It will depend on our level of awareness as to which interpretation is valid.

PYTHON – see SNAKE

QUADRUPLE

🌼 When a thing is quadrupled it is made four times as large or four times as important as previously. In spiritual terms this suggests that there is four times the amount of power available – it is power 'squared'.

💚 The symbolic meaning of number four deals with stability and invokes the ability of all things to be grounded, so anything that is quadrupled is linked to the proper manifestation in the physical realm. Things must manifest through the four elements of Fire, Air, Water and Earth to become real.

🖼 As we become more aware, the ancient symbolisms become more relevant. Anything which is represented as being quadrupled in size or power picks up on the symbolism of numbers. Fours represent solidity, calmness and home in the sense of sanctuary. On a mundane level, this means we may need to consider our need for security.

Consult the entries for Elements and Numbers.

QUAINT

🌼 When something is considered to be quaint it is old-fashioned but with a charm of its own. The spiritual significance of this is that ideas may be outmoded but still worth pursuing for their intrinsic value. Many folk tales are seen as quaint yet have within them a grain of truth or self-awareness.

💚 Any object seen as quaint in dreams bears further scrutiny in order to understand its relevance. We may be dealing with behaviour patterns from the past which are charming but out of date.

🖼 On a mundane level an image that is quaint is perhaps a curiosity – of interest but not much use. In today's technological age, dreaming of an old typewriter, for instance, might highlight an antipathy to new technology.

QUAIL – *see* BIRDS

QUAKER

🌼 The name 'quaker' was initially given to religious sects given to fits of shaking during religious fervor. Only later did it become a popular name for those of the Society of Friends who 'trembled at the Word of the Lord'. Religious beliefs and the acceptance of an ability to cope because of those beliefs is a great part of spiritual development.

💚 The human being has a need for a belief system that can support them in times of difficulty. To dream of being a Quaker allows us to link with our own inner self-sufficiency.

◾ To dream of somebody else being a Quaker indicates the recognition of the ability to maintain a strongly held belief, come what may. It indicates a tranquility and peacefulness that is not necessarily available to us in the waking state.

QUALIFY/QUALIFICATION

✦ In spiritual terms, a qualification suggests that we have been invested with a particular quality or ability. This suggests effort on our part to understand and make use of the hidden meaning in those things we have learnt.

♡ To dream that we have qualified – that is, passed an examination – suggests that we have been tested by an external authority and given permission to use our abilities.

◾ In purely mundane terms, to qualify an action or project is to justify its existence. In dream parlance, we may find that tasks or projects that have given us difficulty sort themselves out in dreams and enable us to move forward.

QUALITY

✦ Quality suggests the best that we can be. Poor quality means we are falling below our own spiritual aspirations. Good quality being highlighted in a dream can suggest some hidden approval.

♡ When quality is an issue in dreams we are perhaps not certain that we have put our best efforts into what we are doing. Emotion may be getting in the way.

◾ When we find ourselves in dreams dividing things into separate groupings – for instance into good and bad, or best and worst – we are questioning our own ability to differentiate.

QUANTITY – see AMOUNT

QUARANTINE

✦ Quarantine, in a spiritual sense, means isolation; that is, retreating from the world for a time, perhaps to gain a different perspective, perhaps to preserve our own truth or belief.

♡ When in waking life we feel isolated, this may translate itself in dream language into being in quarantine. We are aware that we have been cut off from normal contact with others. It would seem that some internal 'authority' has taken over to give us a breathing space or time to consider our actions. While frightening, this can be a time of rest and replenishment.

◾ Dreaming of having to put an animal into quarantine signifies our inability to look after a vulnerable part of ourselves or others. It may also indicate our awareness of having to cut off the lower, more animal side of ourselves. To put someone else in quarantine suggests that we cannot handle what that dream character represents.

QUARREL

⚛ Spiritual conflict or a conflict between the spiritual self and the physical can appear in dreams as a quarrel. It is a passionate dispute, so suggests that there is extreme feeling.

♥ Depending on the other aspects of the dream, quarrelling can suggest that there is conflict between what we have been taught and what we believe, or rather what we have come to believe. Often such a conflict can only be resolved through an outburst of emotion.

■ To dream that we are quarrelling with someone indicates an inner conflict. To be quarrelling with authority, e.g. police, indicates a conflict between right and wrong.

□ For a man to be quarrelling with a woman, or vice versa, signifies a conflict between drive and intuition.

Consult the entries for Argue/Argument, Conflict and Police in People for additional clarification.

QUARRY

⚛ Both in the sense of something which is hunted and that which is dug out, a quarry signifies a spiritual search which may require us to unearth information in order to progress.

♥ Seeking a quarry (that is, pursuing someone or something) in a dream can indicate that we know what we are looking for and have a goal in mind. It is the act of finding it that is important, however.

■ Dreaming of a quarry means quarrying the depths of our personality, 'digging out' the positive knowledge and perceptions we may have. Often dream symbols are created which link with childhood or past experiences which we may have buried and which now need to be brought into conscious understanding.

You might like to consult the entries for Chase/Chased, Digging/Excavation, Hunt/Hunting/Huntsman and Mine/Miner.

QUARTER – see FRACTION/FRAGMENT

QUARTET

⚛ Spiritually the quartet – a set of four similar things considered as one object – links with the Quaternity, which signifies manifestation on the physical plane. The Quaternity, from a theological perspective, is the Holy Trinity – Father, Son and Holy Ghost – plus the feminine principle of Wisdom.

♥ Anything repeated more than once emphasizes the significance of that object to the dreamer. The dream object will be reproduced four times at the same moment, rather than being seen sequentially, in order to make the emphasis apparent.

▦ Dreaming of a quartet of any kind signifies a link with the material or practical aspects of other objects in the dream. It could be necessary to concentrate on pragmatic solutions to a problem. A musical quartet symbolizes harmony.

Also consult the entry for Four in Numbers.

QUARTZ

☼ The quartz is recognized as both receiving and transmitting spiritual energy.

♥ The crystallization process was seen by the Ancients as the trapping of light and, therefore, power, and, on a subliminal level, this is still recognized by many dreamers. To dream of quartz, therefore, signifies a recognition of developing power.

▦ Quartz seen in dreams tends to represent the crystallization of ideas and feelings. It touches into our deep internal processes, often enabling us to express that which we have found impossible before.

You might like to consult the entry for Gems/Jewels.

QUAY

☼ Spiritual progress can be suggested by a quay, since it is a point of departure. This image has obviously had more relevance in the past when travel by sea was more prevalent than air travel.

♥ Because anything associated with water is connected with emotion and how we feel about things, being on a quay can indicate how we need to handle other people's emotions as we move into a new phase of life. It also signifies being prepared to participate in the flow of life.

▦ Standing on a quayside in a dream can indicate either moving forward into a new phase of life or leaving an old one behind. If looking forward with a sense of anticipation, it is the new phase that needs understanding. If looking back, there may be something in the past which needs attention before we can move on.

▯ Oddly, a quay, presumably because of its shape, can represent the masculine principle. In a man's dream it is the quay itself which will be relevant; in a woman's dream it will be the water and her emotions.

You might like to consult the entries for Boat/Ship, Journey and Water.

QUEEN – *see* PEOPLE

QUEST

☼ Undertaking a spiritual quest in order to understand our place in the world and the pursuit of spiritual knowledge is a way of developing our own personal attributes.

♼ Often, the trials and tribulations we have to go through in achieving something we feel to be important are translated in dreams into a quest or search. The way these events are faced is as important as the actual achievement itself.

▦ Many fairy stories and mythological tales have as their main theme the search for something rare or magical (e.g. Jason and the Argonauts). Such themes can be translated into dreams in a personally applicable way. We eventually find the rare and magical within ourselves.

⊞ The Hero's Quest for both men and women is a fundamental pattern of human experience which can appear in many guises in dreams. It is a rite of passage and usually signifies some kind of initiation. To be searching for something usually indicates that we are aware that we must undertake a frightening task in order to progress.

Also consult the entries for Hero/Heroine, Initiation, Knight, Rescue, Search and Task.

QUESTION

❀ Spiritual questioning and enquiry lead to greater knowledge. The question of the meaning of life is, of course, a perennial one. Questions of any type will often appear in dreams when we are reaching a new stage of spiritual awareness.

♼ If we have a question in waking life which needs answering, by keeping it in mind before going to sleep we may often find the answer through dreams.

▦ When we ask questions in a dream we are indicating a degree of self-doubt. To have someone asking us questions in dreams shows that we are aware that we have some kind of knowledge available to us. If the question cannot be answered, we may need to seek the answer ourselves through other means.

QUESTIONNAIRE/QUIZ

❀ Questioning the inevitable is a way forward spiritually. A questionnaire suggests a formalized form of questioning, whereas a quiz tests knowledge.

♼ A questionnaire depicts the use of our mental faculties in a focused, decision-making way. By being rational, we are able to evaluate a problem. Taking part in a pub quiz suggests a group activity which tests awareness and knowledge.

▦ To be answering a questionnaire or quiz in a dream suggests we may be making an attempt to change our circumstances without being certain of what we should actually do to bring about the change. We may also be trying to come to terms with other aspects of our personality.

QUEUE – *see* **LINE**

QUICK

❂ Formerly, quick was used to designate full of life and it is this meaning that can be used from a spiritual perspective.

❤ The word 'quick' is often used as a command to speed up an action or process. It will tend to have this connotation in dreams and it is worth considering what actions are taking too long in waking life.

▦ In pregnancy, a baby 'quickens' when it makes its presence felt in its mother's womb. A project or idea in workaday life takes on a life of its own and this is symbolized in dreams by a sense of speed.

QUICKSAND

❂ Spiritual quicksand suggests a situation where we may be on insecure ground insofar as our beliefs are concerned.

❤ To find ourselves trapped in quicksand suggests that we have been put in a difficult situation which is not necessarily of our own making.

▦ In old-fashioned dream interpretation, quicksand represented business difficulties – often due to circumstances beyond our control. Today it tends to signify a lack of security. This is represented by the ground beneath our feet not being stable and indeed being somewhat dangerous.

QUIET

❂ Peace and tranquility give us the opportunity for contemplation.

❤ Becoming aware of how quiet it is in a dream shows that we need to cease being active for a while, perhaps in order to restore our emotional or spiritual balance.

▦ Experiencing a need for quiet in a dream suggests that we need to listen more carefully to either ourselves or others in waking life. Our lives may be lived at such a pace that we have no time to 'stand and stare'.

QUILT

❂ Spiritual comfort and caring can be suggested by a quilt.

❤ Old fashioned patchwork quilts often told a story, both in their materials and the way they were constructed. They therefore became heirlooms and treasured objects. Modern day quilts tend to be more functional and, therefore, the colour and patterns will have less significance. The colour, material and pattern of a quilt in a dream, however, may have more significance than the quilt itself.

▦ The quilt or duvet can often represent our need for security, warmth and love. To be aware of one in a dream, therefore, is our identification of that need. A particular quilt may have a special significance. For instance, a childhood quilt in an adult dream would suggest the need for some kind of reassurance.

The entries for Colour, Fabric and Shape will enhance your understanding.

QUIT

🔅 Somehow quitting has a different impact to leaving. To quit suggests a premeditated action, one in which we have considered the spiritual consequences of our action.

💧 Quitting a responsibility or feeling is to gain a sense of freedom from concern and it is this sense of freedom that allows us to experience new ideas and concepts.

🔲 If in dreams we find ourselves quitting a job, it suggests that a task we have set ourselves in waking life is not fulfilling its purpose. Such a dream may also be among what is classed as anxiety dreams.

QUIVER

🔅 A state of spiritual ecstasy can be induced which is accompanied by quivering, a kind of shivering. This was initially how the Quakers got their name, as did the Shakers. A quiver in the sense of an arrow holder may be a symbol of words being used as weapons.

💧 A physiological reaction can be translated into dreams as an action. To be quivering in a dream may simply be the effect of feeling cold.

🔲 Quivering indicates a state of extreme emotion. Such a reaction in a dream would signify that we need to consider the emotion and deal with it in everyday life. For instance, an extreme fear reaction may be the residue of something that has happened to us previously and can only be dealt with in waking life.

QUIZ – *see* **QUESTIONNAIRE/QUIZ**

QUOTE/QUOTATION

🔅 A quote in a spiritual sense signifies Truth.

💧 To utter or hear a quote – e.g. Shakespeare – indicates that we should consider the sentiment and power expressed within the quote.

🔲 To be giving a quote – as in a building estimate – can signify the value that we put on our services or talents. We may have difficulty with the accuracy – or the acceptance – of the quote and, therefore, in waking life, will need to reconsider not only our own self-image, but also how we think others see us.

RABBIT – *see* **ANIMALS**

RABBLE – *see* **CROWD**

RACE – *see* **RUNNING**

RADAR

⚜ Radar in a dream represents our own personal intuitive faculty. It is our way of picking up subtle messages and signals that other people are giving out, often on a subliminal level.

♥ For many, radar will register in dreams as a sort of 'Big Brother is watching you' feeling. We are monitoring ourselves, perhaps as to whether our behaviour or thoughts are appropriate.

▦ In today's surveillance society we are conscious of being watched and observed. In dreams this can translate into the image of radar. Its appearance shows that our personal 'antennae' are on the alert for trouble.

Consult the entries for Watching and Witness for additional information.

RADIANCE

⚜ True radiance, being a quality of light, is a sign of pure spirituality. It is pictured in representations of Holy figures and has the ability to dazzle us – to stop us in our tracks – and at the same time draw us in and enlighten us. Radiance represents something out of the ordinary or supernatural. It also suggests purity of thought, wisdom and the transcendence of the mundane.

♥ When something appears as radiant in a dream it is being marked as having some kind of special quality, which we may need to explore further. Heightened emotion in dreams can be seen as radiance and charisma also has its own quality of light.

▦ Filmic images of extraterrestrials give a stereotypical image that is often characterized by a type of radiance and this can be carried over into dreams. Whether it is menacing or not will depend on other dream content, but the eeriness will certainly need to be considered.

Consult the entries for Halo, Light and Extra-terrestrials for further clarification.

RADIO

⚜ A radio is symbolic of spiritual communication. We should be alert and aware of all the subtler vibrations at this time and be open to any eventuality.

♥ Often in dreams a radio can stand for the voice of authority, or of commonly held ideas and ideals. As a method of communication, a radio suggests information that is available to everyone and therefore is widely understood.

■ To dream of hearing a radio playing suggests a form of connection with the outside world. What we are hearing is also important: speech would suggest the transmission of information whereas music would indicate a more subtle vibration.

You might also like to consult the entries for Communication and Media.

RAF – *see* **ARMED FORCES**

RAFFLE – *see* **GAMBLING**

RAFT

❀ The raft is an image connected with the spiritual transitions we must make in life. It is less secure than the idea of a boat, but more secure than doing it alone. If we are feeling 'lost' and can see no respite, then we may dream of a raft, a solid – yet impermanent – structure beneath us.

◈ It can sometimes be meaningful to find out what the raft is made of. It can often appear in dreams as a symbol of transition, so the material can give us some idea of how to act. If it were made of wood, for instance, it would suggest a readily available rigidity; if of car tyres or other waste material we need to recycle, or reuse the information we already know.

■ A raft is a place of safety, often amid turbulence. While it may not be overly secure, it has the ability to support us. This is the kind of dream that occurs when we are dealing with emotional upset or difficulties.

You might like to consult the entries for Boat/Ship, Journey, Transport, Water and Wood.

RAGE – *see* **ANGER**

RAILWAY

❀ Spiritually, the railway suggests a chosen direction that is usually fairly straightforward. It may also indicate a predictable routine.

◈ Psychologically, a railway points to the idea of keeping to one goal (which may be a group one) and being single-minded about it. One early symbolism of the railway was the facility of being able to ignore obstacles, to go round, through or over anything that stood in the way. Seeing the points on a railway line change would signify a change of direction.

■ A railway in a dream signifies the way we wish to go in life. We can take a way forward and can make informed choices. A single track suggests that there is only one way to go, whereas a multiple track suggests many more opportunities. A railway station would suggest a planned break.

Also consult the entries for Journey and Trains in Transport for further information.

RAIN

☀ Rain, by virtue of its 'heavenly' origins, symbolizes divine blessing and revelation. It brings about creativity and growth.

♥ Rain can also have a more universal meaning, in that it is the realization of potential on a group level. We should all be able to make use of the fertility that it can bring. The various types of rain have different meanings: heavy rain suggests depression and perhaps isolation whereas gentle rain indicates a time of relative prosperity. Realizing that rain has passed can indicate fresh opportunities are available.

▦ In its simplest meaning, rain stands for tears and emotional release. We may have been depressed with no way to release our feelings in everyday life. Rain in dreams often becomes the first realization that we can let go

⚬ Rain in a woman's dream can suggest the sexual act and the release that that brings. For a man it may bring understanding of his own and his partner's emotions.

You might also like to consult the entries for Emotions, Water and Weather for further information.

RAINBOW

☀ A rainbow symbolizes the spiritual glory that is available to us through understanding and learning. More esoterically, a rainbow is said to represent the seven steps of awareness necessary for true spirituality. It is the connecting 'bridge' between the physical and the spiritual realms.

♥ The raising of consciousness and appreciation of something as ethereal as a rainbow suggests the need for a heightened sense of awareness. When it was realized that white light could be split into its component parts the various colours came to have meaning. For instance, red indicates passion, green fertility, and purple dignity.

▦ A rainbow appearing in a dream is the promise of something better to come. The old story of the pot of gold at the end of the rainbow is so firmly entrenched in folklore that this meaning often comes across in dreams.

Consult the entries for Cauldron, Colour, Gold and Light for further information.

RAM – *see* ANIMALS

RAPE – *see* SEX

RARE

☀ If an object is rare it is rendered so by its scarcity, so spiritually suggests ancient knowledge and practices, which we have not yet uncovered.

♥ If something is rare it is precious and thus not seen often. This can be translated in dreams into emotions that we do not often allow to surface.

▦ In dreams, as in waking life, if meat is rare it is only partially cooked and thus represents ideas that are not yet fully formed or concepts that have been put forward without having been finalized. This does not mean that they are any less valid and this would be the same if we dreamt of any other rare article or object.

RAT – *see* ANIMALS

RAVEN – *see* BIRDS

RAW

☀ Raw as in tender or sore is recognized spiritually in, for instance, martyrdom where all pretence is stripped away and there is an element of suffering for our beliefs.

◈ Raw emotion is present in dreams when we are able to access hose things we choose to cover up in everyday life. Where we have difficulty in expressing this, such feelings can be given vent to in dreams.

▦ Images in dreams that highlight a state of rawness may be bringing to our attention that elements of our lives have not been worked on or worked with to their best advantage. Raw meat might represent a wound and raw vegetables a dietary deficiency, particularly if they are those we do not like.

You might also like to consult the entries for Food and Martyr.

REACHING OUT – *see* YEARN

READING

☀ Reading, or being in a library, appears in dreams as a symbol of the realization of spiritual truths. Reading a Holy Book in dreams suggests that we are attempting to understand a particular belief system, or that there is information in it pertinent to us at this time.

◈ Until comparatively recently, the only way to record events was to write them down. Reading is an activity that assists us in recalling things from memory – our own or joint memories. To be aware that we are reading a novel is to begin to understand our own need for fantasy. A psychic reading often works with the symbolism of many basic dream images. To dream of having such a reading suggests a need to understand ourselves on a deeper level.

▦ Reading a book in a dream suggests that we are seeking information. Reading a letter signifies receiving news. Reading a list – e.g. a shopping list – indicates a need to give some order to our lives.

Consult the entries for Book, Letter, Library, List and Medium as well as the information on Spiritual Imagery in the Introduction.

REALITY TELEVISION – *see* MEDIA AND TELEVISION

REAPING

☀ The scythe was an ancient symbol for Harvesting – gathering in. The Grim Reaper – Death – is always pictured as carrying a scythe.

♦ The saying 'as ye sow, so shall ye reap' can be interpreted as – if we do good deeds, then that good will be returned. When we dream of reaping a reward for something we have done, we approve of our own activities. More negatively, a harmful act will return to haunt us.

▣ In former times, the whole community took part in the reaping (gathering) of the harvest. This ensured that everybody gained in some way from this activity. Nowadays, to dream of reaping suggests a way of gaining from our activities.

Also consult the entries for Harvest and Scythe and also the information on Spiritual Imagery in the Introduction.

REBEL/REVOLUTION

✿ A rebel is someone who sets his face against the norms of society and held belief, so spiritually is one who cannot accept given teachings. A revolution takes place when a number of rebels can bring about a change in belief.

♦ We will only rebel if we feel sufficiently strongly about something. For there to be a rebel or anarchist in our dreams suggests that we have allowed that part of ourselves a 'voice'. We can then understand it and decide on the validity of the feelings.

▣ In working situations we are not often able to express our rebelliousness, perhaps at being asked to perform a particular task we don't consider necessary. As a dream character we can find out from the rebel what it is that is really disturbing us. A rebellion or revolution would occur in dreams if a position became completely untenable.

Consult the entry for Conflict for further clarification.

RECLUSE – *see* HERMIT

RECORD/RECORDS/RECORDING

✿ The idea of keeping spiritual records is quite a powerful one. These may range from the Akashic records, an accounting of our personal thoughts words and actions in a Cosmic sense, through to keeping notes of our own progress as we travel the spiritual path. The first is an idea that exists in most religions in one form or another and the latter allows us to take full responsibility for who we are and also to chart our progress.

♦ The content of dreams is, in a sense, a record of those things that have affected us on an emotional level, which become accessible to us through dream images. The ability to access those records becomes almost like that of a computer. Keeping records in dreams highlights our need to have some kind of order in our lives.

▦ When we dream of consulting records we are trying to access information. To be consulting company records would suggest we need to know how the company, or the community in which we live, functions. To be consulting public records may mean we need to know how to fit in. To be recording music or other material indicates that there is something we need to remember.

You might also like to consult the entries for Communication, Order and Music/Rhythm.

RECYCLING – *see* **RUBBISH**

RED – *see* **COLOURS**

REDUCE – *see* **SIZE**

REDUNDANT

☼ Spiritually to be redundant is not to be needed, to be surplus to requirements – which is the challenging of the basic human need to be wanted and a fear of rejection.

◈ In dreams, to be redundant can be equated with being rejected and will often reflect such a situation in our personal lives.

▦ To dream of being made redundant can be interpreted as an anxiety dream, not so much about our job situation but more to do with our own self-worth. In today's climate, when employment is less secure, redundancy is a risk, so such a dream may also reflect our ability to take risks.

You might also like to consult the entry for Work.

REFEREE – *see* **GAMES AND SPORT**

REFERENCE

☼ Reference books in a spiritual sense can symbolize knowledge or the Akashic records. A personal reference suggests a record of how we live our lives.

◈ To be asking for or receiving a reference is to be seeking some kind of validating process. We need to know we are 'fit for purpose'.

▦ When we are giving someone else a reference in dreams, we are giving approval to some of our own ideas and beliefs. If giving references is a normal part of our everyday behaviour, to do so in dreams may suggest we need to question some of our own beliefs. To be reluctant to give a reference suggests a lack of trust.

You might also like to consult the entry for Work.

REFLECTION

☼ Symbolically Spiritual truth that is available to us at any particular stage of understanding is often shown to us as though in a reflection. It is as if we need an image that gives us tangibility.

◈ Often, to see a reflection in a dream is to try to be understanding the inner self and the way that we cope with the outside world. If in a dream the two images do not correspond, we will need to make some kind of adjustment in order to live comfortably within the everyday world. Our inner self must give the impetus to the outer reality.

▦ A reflection seen in a dream has a great deal to do with the way we see ourselves at that particular moment. Our self-image is important to us, as is the way other people see us. If the reflection is in a mirror, then our image will be perhaps more 'solid', whereas one seen in water will be more transient. The story of Narcissus and the way he fell in love with himself (or rather his own image) is a warning to all of us against self-worship.

You might also like to consult the entry for Mirror.

REFRIGERATOR

❂ As a preserver of basic sustenance, a refrigerator will symbolize the asceticism or dispassion which is developed by some seekers of spirituality.

◈ To dream of refrigerating leftover food indicates we are storing up resentment. This, in turn, will 'cool down' our own responses to love and affection.

▦ The refrigerator is a symbol of preservation. In dreams this becomes self-preservation and suggests we may be turning cold emotionally or sexually. To dream of rotten food in a refrigerator suggests we feel we may not be being sustained properly by those around us.

You might also like to consult the entries for Ascetic, Decay, Food and Mould/Mouldy.

REFUGE/REFUGEE

❂ Dreaming of needing refuge suggests the need for some kind of sanctuary for the spirit. Spiritually, dreaming of being a refugee indicates that we are trying to escape from some anxiety or terror or from some authority greater than ourselves.

◈ If in dreams we are conscious of a place being a refuge, we can assume that we are temporarily emotionally secure. Dreaming of giving refuge indicates that we are capable of offering others that security.

▦ In more mundane terms only those who have been refugees themselves can know what it truly feels like, so any dream of being a refugee is going to be a dramatization of our circumstances. We need to identify the feeling and deal with it. Being in a refugee camp in dreams will highlight our feelings of displacement.

REFUND – *see* MONEY

REFUSE/REFUSAL

⚜ To refuse in the spiritual sense is not to recognize the long-term benefit to ourselves or others of what is being offered or suggested. We may need to identify what fears are holding us back. Intuitively we may feel something is wrong.

♡ Emotionally many people find difficulty in saying 'no' so any refusal in dreams will come from a strongly held inner feeling. Refuse in the sense of abandoned material may be a pictorial representation of such a feeling and may highlight our own fears of abandonment.

▦ To be aware in dreams of a refusal suggests that on some level we have not given ourselves the necessary permission. If an authority figure refuses us something, we may assume that we are not acting in the way we should in waking life.

REHEARSAL/REHEARSE – *see* THEATRE

REINDEER – *see* DEER IN ANIMALS

RELATIONS – *see* FAMILY

RELEASE

⚜ When we release a previously strongly held belief we are moving into a different stage of spiritual awareness. The release of birds, for instance at funerals, has the symbolism of letting the soul go free.

♡ Emotional release in dreams can give rise to a number of images, such as rushing water, a raging fire or a mighty wind.

▦ To be released in dreams from an institution such as school, prison or hospital is to gain a type of freedom. Whatever was bothering us is now behind us and we can move on.

Also consult the entry for Emotions for further information.

RELIGION/RELIGIOUS BUILDINGS/RELIGIOUS IMAGERY – *see* SPIRITUAL IMAGERY IN THE INTRODUCTION

REMOVE

⚜ When a dream object is deliberately removed it can be thought of as being spiritually unnecessary. However, we need to decide if we are being possessive over it, or what it represents.

♡ In dreams, to be removing an object suggests that we do not appreciate the principle of sharing. If someone else is removing it we should reassess our need for whatever it represents. A removal as in changing location suggests that we need change in our lives.

▦ It will depend on whether a dream object seems to have disappeared or has been deliberately removed. The interpretation if it is deliberate will suggest that we are rejecting some aspect of our waking life.

RENT

✤ Often, in spiritual terms, we must relearn how to handle money and value. We are 'on loan' to the physical realm. The image of paying rent gives this concept a focus.

✤ There comes a time when, if we wish to maximize our potential, we must find a space of our own. Paying rent allows us to be independent within someone else's space.

▦ Paying rent in dreams is to undertake a personal responsibility. We are prepared to look after ourselves and to take responsibility for who we are. Receiving rent suggests that we have entered into a transaction that will benefit us.

You might like also like to consult the entries for Home, Money and Tenant.

REPAIR

✤ An older meaning of repair was 'to go back' and it is this meaning that is most spiritually relevant. The idea of going back to where we came from – to Source – is an accepted spiritual belief.

✤ Dreaming of repairing something suggests that we still have needed of whatever the dream object represents.

▦ Making repairs from a mundane perspective suggests that we are not satisfied with what we have done in a project or task. The implication is that we need to make it work better, that until we do there is an essential flaw.

REPEAT INCLUDE REPEATED BEHAVIOUR – *see* RITE/RITUAL AND TELEVISION

REPLY – *see* RESPONSE

REPTILES

✤ With understanding of the basic urges and the way to manage them we can create a firm foundation. From there we can progress spiritually.

✤ When there is a need to understand why we do things, we first need to control our basic drives. Many reptilian dreams are about control or management. Control of a crocodile would suggest some fear of an aggressive nature. Feeding a lizard or stroking a snake symbolizes taking care of our natural basic urges.

▦ Reptiles in dreams link with our basic and instinctive reactions and responses. When there is a basic urge – such as a need for food, sex, etc. – we sometimes cannot face it full on, but will symbolize it as a reptile.

You might find it helpful to consult the information for Reptiles in the Animals entry as well as the entry for Crocodile.

RESEARCH

To be carrying out Spiritual research, for instance with Holy Books in dreams, suggests a need to understand accepted thought.

To be doing research in dreams, particularly if it is beyond our field of knowledge in waking life, indicates that we need to widen our focus, take in extra knowledge and not be narrow minded.

Research and development in waking life is a large part of many companies way of working, so in dreams we will often find that this concept points us to new ways of operating, not just in our working but also in our personal lives.
You might also like to consult the entries for Invent/Inventor and Laboratory.

RESCUE

Rescuing someone in the spiritual sense is saving someone who is less fortunate than we are, whether that is through compassion or otherwise. Spiritual rescue is a technique where the souls of the departed are turned towards the Light – direct knowledge – and helped to move on.

When we have put others in danger, we are required to rescue them in dreams. We are then able to show a degree of nobility and courage that engenders a feel-good factor and allows us to have the capability to reach for the best within ourselves.

Being rescued in dreams is a powerful image, since it leaves us indebted to our rescuer. Rescuing someone else, particularly someone known to us, often suggests that we wish to have a, or form a different type of, relationship with that person. If we do not know them, then the character may represent part of our own personality that we need to pay attention to. The knight rescuing the maiden signifies the idea of the untouched feminine being rescued from her own passion.
Also consult the entries for Danger, Knight, Light, Quest and Threat/Threaten for further information.

RESIGN

Spiritual resignation is the giving in to inevitability if possible with patience. We no longer have any need or wish to fight back any more.

Resignation is a state of mind brought about through having to face difficulties in life. It is as though we come to a point where we are not capable of making any further effort or decision. Indeed, it may be better not to, but simply to resign ourselves to whatever may happen. In dreams this resignation is recognizable as not wanting to go on.

In dreams to resign is to give up. To dream of resigning from work means we are aware of major changes in our lives. We perhaps need to look at our lives and accustom ourselves to the idea that there are areas that would bear improvement. To be resigned to something suggests that we have accepted the status quo in our lives.

You might also like to consult the entry for Work.

RESPONSE

☀ A spiritual response is one that affects every part of our being and is a reaching out to whatever we deem the Ultimate to be. An instinctive response is often one drawn from us by a situation that has personal resonance.

♡ If a response is needed or if a reply is given there must have been a question. This will often have been a subconscious one. In dreams it is unfortunate that we sometimes have one without knowing the other.

▦ To reply is to respond, usually in words to a question or an action. In dreams any response we make should be carefully considered as to whether it reflects our feelings accurately in a waking situation.

Also consult the entry for Question.

RESTORATION

☀ When something is restored it is made whole again and in spiritual terms such an image can suggest healing or a return to a former state.

♡ Carrying out a restoration in dreams suggests that we are still connected with the past and are trying to recreate it in some way.

▦ There is an interesting anomaly from a mundane perspective since in carrying out a restoration we are referring to the past but working for a future, towards the tangibility of something permanent.

You might also like to consult the entries for Old and Repair.

RETREAT

☀ A spiritual retreat is a place that allows us an environment and ambience in which to meditate and contemplate. To dream of such a place suggests we have need of peace and quiet.

♡ When we dream of retreating from something we may need to decide whether it is a forced withdrawal or a strategic move. If the former then we may be under pressure, if the latter then we must formulate new plans.

▦ When in dreams we are conscious of retreating from a previously held position this may be because we need to reassess our resources.

REVEAL

☀ A revealed (law-giving) religion is one that is considered to have been disclosed by God to Man. This presupposes an intimate relationship between the two. Revelation is that which has been revealed, and is often received in dreams.

♡ To reveal something is to make it plain. Dreams will often uncover our hidden truths, which we cannot necessarily deal with in waking life.

▣ The meaning of a symbol can often be revealed in dreams and needs to be consciously retained. Such a symbol will often have relevance to what is happening in our daily lives though we may need to follow up with research.

REVERSE – *see* **BACK AND FRONT AND BACKWARD/FORWARD IN POSITION**

RHYTHM – *see* **MUSIC/RHYTHM**

RIBBON – *see* **BRIDLE, HALTER AND HARNESS**

RICE – *see* **SPIRITUAL IMAGERY IN THE INTRODUCTION**

RIDE – *see* **TRANSPORT**

RIGHT – *see* **POSITION**

RING

☀ Like the circle, the ring signifies eternity and divinity. It represents totality and infinity.

♥ We all need some kind of continuity in our lives, something that gives a sense of long-term comfort. A ring holds this symbolism because it is never-ending and is self-perpetuating. To be ringing someone in a dream suggests we are trying to make contact with something important.

▣ A ring appearing in a dream usually signifies a relationship of some sort. A wedding ring suggests a union and a promise. A ring belonging to the family would represent old traditions and values. An engagement ring suggests a more tentative promise of devotion. An eternity ring would be a long-term promise. A signet ring would indicate setting the seal on something. A bullring suggests an element of cruelty.

You might like to consult the entries for Hole, Telephone, Wedding/Wedding Dress/Wedding Ring as well as the information on Circle in Shapes/Patterns.

RISK

☀ Spiritually we run into danger if we do not pay attention to perceived knowledge or accepted behaviour. Daring to question the status quo is a calculated risk.

♥ In dreams, an emotional risk can make itself felt if we have not acknowledged such a possibility. Then we may dream of some kind of potential disaster or breakdown.

▣ In today's business climate there are many risks to be taken. This will often reflect in dreams as personal risk, such as standing on a cliff edge or drowning. *Consult the entries for Cliff, Danger, Disaster and Drowning for further clarification.*

RITE/RITUAL

☀ Spiritually we are able to focus our energies in such a way that we can work for the Greater Good. Repetition helps to concentrate the power we are calling on, whatever our system of belief, and is used in prayer and in Mantra.

A rite is a customary form for a religious ceremony and in dreams is only distinguishable from a ritual in that it is given credence by its long usage. Such a rite would be that of baptism.

⬥ Such rituals as getting up in the morning, because they are habits, simply have the purpose of getting us focused. Religious rituals have taken on a life of their own and help concentrate the power of the many. Magical rituals have become 'power centres' in their own right.

▣ Rituals can range from the 'sublime to the ridiculous'. They are actions that are repeated over and over again in order to achieve a certain result. In dreams, such an action can be a comfort mechanism or a way of learning a required behaviour.

⬦ Magical ritual often concentrates on the union of two polarities – male and female, drive and receptivity. Ancient religions symbolized this in the sacred marriage and many dreams – particularly as we begin exploring spirituality – echo this. Men will most often play the role of priest and women as priestess in such dreams – that is, fulfilling their gender roles.

You might like to consult the entries for Baptism, Ceremony, Magic/Magician, Mantra and Ziggurat, as well as the information on Spiritual Imagery in the Introduction.

RIVER – *see* **WATER**

ROAD – *see* **JOURNEY**

ROB/ROBBER – *see* **BURGLAR, STEAL AND THIEF**

ROBE

🌑 In spiritual terms the white robe is innocence and the seamless robe represents holiness, and in dreams would tend to represent different spiritual awarenesses. Magical robes with different symbols and of different colours would signify esoteric knowledge and the ability to use power correctly.

⬥ A robe can suggest our attitude to sex and relationships. If it is clean we have a good self-image, if dirty, the opposite. A dirty robe could also suggest depression. A new robe might signify a new approach to the way we present ourselves, whereas an old one might suggest the comfort of a previous way of working.

▣ Dreaming of a robe such as a bathrobe can have two meanings: one is that of covering up vulnerability and the other is of being relaxed and at ease. The dream will indicate the correct significance. To be dressing someone else in a robe is to protect them.

You might also like to consult the entries for Clothes, Colour and Magic/Magician.

ROBOT – *see* **MACHINE**

ROCK

🌑 Spiritually we will need, at some point, to go through a transition that requires careful management This often presents itself as a rock barrier. Dual rocks through which we must pass suggest the same image as the passage between two pillars, such as the Pillars of Hercules; that is, passing from one state of awareness to the next. It is similar to an initiation.

♡ On an intellectual level, all the images that we think of in relationship to rocks prevail. There is reliability, coldness, rigidity and a foundation on which we can build. We need to recognize these qualities within ourselves so that we give ourselves the best options possible. We can find ourselves 'between a rock and a hard place', in a difficult situation in dreams.

▦ To dream of rock suggests stability in the real world. If we are on firm ground we can survive. We may also be aware that we must be firm and stand 'rock-like', and not be dissuaded from our purpose. Seaside rock can remind us of happier, more carefree times.

You might also like to consult the entries for Barrier, Initiation and Stone.

ROCKET

🌑 Because of the spiritual symbolism of reaching heights to which none have been before, and 'shooting for the stars', the rocket represents spiritual searching and adventure.

♡ Nowadays any symbol of power connects with our ability to do, or be, better than before. The rocket in this sense will have much of the same symbolism as the aeroplane except the destinations will be less easily accessible. The explosive power and energy available is something to be carefully looked at, since we need this type of power in order to make radical changes in our lives.

▦ The energy that is available to us in dreams can be indicative of what we have available in waking life. In popular parlance, to be given a rocket suggests recognizing that we are not functioning the way we should. To take off like a rocket means moving very fast in terms of some project we have. Giving someone else a rocket in dreams may mean we are trying to motivate a part of ourselves or that we know more can be done by others.

⊟ The rocket in basic terms has a connection with male sexuality and can have this significance in both men's and women's dreams.

Consult the entries for Aeroplane, Journey and Transport for further information.

ROD – *see* STAFF

ROOF

🌑 The roof is protection from the elements and suggests the sheltering aspect of the feminine as the 'guardian of the hearth'.

♦ A roof is a basic requirement in man's need for comfort. Psychologically, it is important to be protected against the elements. The various types of roofs have different significances in dreams. A pitched roof signifies our ability to reach for the sky and attain our goals. A pagoda, with its many roofs, signifies a holy place.

▨ To concentrate on, or be aware of, the roof of a building in a dream is to acknowledge the shelter and protection it affords. If the roof leaks then we are open to emotional attacks. If we are on the roof we are not being protected and, therefore, could be vulnerable.

Consult the entries for Hearth and Goddess/Goddesses for further information.

ROOMS – see BUILDINGS

ROOT – see TREE

ROPE

✿ A rope, as in a mountaineer's rope, can offer security and also a sense of spiritual freedom. As a noose, such as a hangman's noose, it may suggest despair and possibly our attitude to death.

♦ If we are tied to the rope, something is holding us back from expressing ourselves. Being tied by a rope to something or someone else means we are bound to them and need to look at the ties that bind us – what holds us together. We should look at the limitations of that particular relationship and how much mutual freedom there is.

▨ A rope can suggest strength and power, though the power can turn against us. A rope and pulley suggests using the forces of weight to help us; a frayed rope signifies a lack of care. If the rope is made of an unusual substance such as hair or material, or is fashioned in a strange way, this will be a representation of the uniqueness of the bonds we have.

You might also like to consult the entries for Hang/Hanging, Noose and Weighing/Weight.

ROSARY – see NECKLACE, BEADS AND SPIRITUAL IMAGERY IN THE INTRODUCTION

ROSE/ROSETTE – see SPIRITUAL IMAGERY IN THE INTRODUCTION

ROT – see DECAY AND MOULD/MOULDY

ROUGH – see TEXTURE

ROUND TABLE

✿ Spiritually the table suggests a centre, but one from which all things can begin. Partly because of the tales of King Arthur, there are various myths associated with a round table, but essentially it indicates that everyone is equal in status and has an equal right to express an opinion.

◈ The round table is a representation of the heavens, since the 12 knights are the signs of the Zodiac. It also suggests resolution since it gives no one person status over another. In dreams we are continually trying to create perfection and this is one such dream that calls on archetypal images.

▦ A round table in a dream is a symbol of wholeness. In mundane terms it can suggest negotiation, since it is used to allow everyone the opportunity to express an opinion.

You might also like to consult the entries for Camelot, Knight, Table and Zodiac as well as the information on Archetypes in the Introduction.

ROW – *see* **ARGUE/ARGUMENTS AND LINE**

RUBBISH

✺ We may need to dispose of spiritual rubbish – outdated perceptions and truths that are no longer relevant. A dream about rubbish or garbage can indicate that now is the time to perform that task.

◈ Very often, rubbish or garbage is the remains of food preparation. Often we are being alerted to what we need to do in order to remain healthy – how we need to treat our bodies and make space for new experiences which will allow us to act for the Greater Good. Recycling of both rubbish and garbage suggests making best use of our resources.

▦ Rubbish in our dream creates a scenario where we are able to deal with those parts of our experience or our feelings that need to be sorted through in order for us to decide what is being kept and what can be rejected so we can progress. To be collecting rubbish or garbage can indicate that we are making wrong assumptions. To be recycling old rubbish suggests that we have learned the lessons we needed to.

RUINS

✺ We sometimes have to understand a destructive streak in ourselves if we are to move forward, perhaps building on mistakes from the past.

◈ If we have deliberately ruined something we need to clarify a self-destructive element in us. Sometimes by looking at the symbolism of what has ruined an object or an occasion will give us insight into our own processes. If someone else has ruined one of our possessions in dreams we should look at an emotional difficulty in waking life.

▦ When something is in ruins we have to discover if it is through neglect or vandalism. If the former, we need to pull things together. If the latter, we need to look at how we are making ourselves vulnerable.

Also consult the entries for Buildings, Demolition and Wreck.

RUNNING

☀ Running in dreams suggests the potential for anxiety or distress. Spiritually we may be trying to do something too quickly. The original marathon signalled victory and was a trial to the death. Running races or marathons in dreams are, therefore, tests of endurance.

♥ Obviously in dreams of running, time and place are significant. Running a marathon is today a group activity and will in dreams suggest competition. Where we are going will perhaps indicate why speed is needed. If we are being pursued this will also give some kind of reason. To be running something – managing – is to be taking responsibility.

▦ To be running in a dream suggests speed and flow. To be running forwards suggests confidence and ability. To be running away from someone or something signifies fear and an inability to do something. Running back to something indicates that a readjustment or reassessment is necessary. If we do not know our destination we may not have thought through a plan properly.

You might like to consult the entries for Chase/Chased, Time and Win/Winning.

RUSH

☀ Interestingly, rushes or reeds are an ancient symbol of Time. In both spiritual work and dreams, time and space are interchangeable. Thus, if we use our space successfully then we also use time properly. If we are rushing we do not see the best of our world.

♥ We need to learn how to manage time successfully in order to succeed, and to be rushing suggests that we have not done so.

▦ To be in a rush suggests that we are having to contend with outside pressures. To be rushing suggests that we ourselves are putting the pressure on. The pressure would be on our time.

You might also like to consult the entries for Hourglass, Time and Quick.

RUST

☀ Rust signifies old outdated attitudes. Spiritually, we may have to reconsider ideas that are harmful (corrosive) before we can progress.

♥ To dream of cleaning up rust suggests that we recognize our own negligence. Dreaming of rust appearing as we look at an object signifies that a project has reached the end of its useful life.

▦ Rust represents neglect and negligence. We have not looked after the quality of our lives properly and should look to address this oversight.

Consult the entries for Iron and Metal for further information.

SACK

☀ Formerly the appearance of a sack in a dream was taken as an indication of death. Today, it is more likely to indicate the liberation (freeing up) of part of our personality or difficulties that need to be overcome so we can progress spiritually.

◊ A sack shares much of the significance and symbolism of the bag, or any such receptacle, in dreams; the womb is often symbolised in dreams as a bag or sack. As an everyday object it acts as a container and its appearance in a dream can indicate that we should look making the best use of our resources.

▦ At its simplest, to dream of a sack can link with word play such as 'getting the sack'. It brings a period of our lives to an end, possibly in a rather negative way. Perhaps in an effort to move on, we have created circumstances within our lives that make us feel bad about ourselves for a time.

⊞ In a woman's dream a bag can represent her feelings about pregnancy, while, interestingly enough, in a man's dream it is more likely to mean some kind of womb experience.

Consult the entry for Bag as well as the information on Womb in the Body entry for further information.

SACKCLOTH – *see* SPIRITUAL IMAGERY IN THE INTRODUCTION

SACRIFICES

☀ Sacrifice is an important aspect of spiritual growth and signifies the renunciation of the lesser for the rewards of the greater. As a rule, sacrifice has two meanings. Firstly, it is to give something up and secondly to make something sacred or holy. When those two things are possible within a dream scenario we are prepared to give up our ego or individuality for the sake of something greater or more important than ourselves.

◊ There is usually some expectation of a forthcoming just reward (often spiritual) for having made sacrifices. There may be an element of deferred gratification in that we do not expect an immediate reward, except that of feeling good or knowing we have done the right thing. There is always an element also of giving up egotistic behaviour, which is no longer appropriate, and going with the flow of life.

▦ Sacrificing an animal in dreams suggests that we are aware that our lower, more basic instincts can be given up in favour of spiritual power. We have to be prepared to recognize our own human fallibility, but to give up extravagance. A sacrificial altar may appear, or it may just be a question of killing and cooking an animal ritualistically. If the animal is willing to be sacrificed, then we are ready to transmute instinct into spiritual energy. If the animal is a hare or a rabbit, the symbolism is that of rebirth.

You might also like to consult the entries for Animals, Hunt/Hunting/Huntsman and Rite/Ritual.

SADISM

Sadism appearing in a dream would suggest that it is probably a counterbalance to our conscious way of being in, and dealing with, the world.

It will obviously depend on whether we are being sadistic or if someone is being sadistic towards us as to the interpretation. We know that in dreams other people can represent parts of ourselves, so we need to consider whether we are causing ourselves harm deliberately or inadvertently. We may feel that we wish to punish ourselves for some supposed misdemeanour and, as a displacement activity, we dream of sadistic behaviour. The very fact that it is sadistic may also mean that it is masochistic – that is, self-involved.

Sadism often arises because of anger still held – but suppressed – from childhood hurts. It is the wish to hurt or provoke a reaction – often in someone we love. In waking life most of us are not capable of being sadistic, but in dreams we can do what we like, so sadism becomes acceptable.

Sadistic behaviour that is not sexual in nature signifies a degree of childish cruelty in both men's and women's dreams. That cruelty may well be gender specific.

SAILING/SAILS

Sails represent the Spirit – as in a force that moves us. Sailing suggests a sense of spiritual freedom and the ability to use our intellect.

To be tacking – sailing against the wind – suggests that we have created difficulties, possibly by setting ourselves against public opinion. To be sailing with the wind means we are using opportunities to the best of our abilities. Because a boat or ship is usually thought of as feminine, the sails in dreams can represent pregnancy and fertility. By association, they can also signify how a woman will use her intellect.

Sails suggest the idea of making use of available power. Often the type of sail will be relevant. Old-fashioned sails would suggest out-of-date methods, whereas racing sails might suggest the use of modern technology. The colour of the sails may also be important. When we dream of sailing, we are highlighting how we feel we are handling our lives. We can either work with the currents or against them. If we are sailing in a yacht there is more of a sense of immediacy than if we were sailing in a liner. The former is more to do with one-to-one relationships, while the latter suggests a group effort.

Also consult the entries for Boat/Ship, Colour, Journey, Transport, Wind and Water.

SAILOR

🜚 Spiritually, the sailor can signify communication. The aspect of freedom links with a quality of the god Mercury who, having been given a task, then forgets what it is.

♡ Most people have a rather antiquated idea of the sailor. It is this image that usually appears in dreams. He represents freedom, both of movement and of spirit, and is a representation of the Tramp archetype.

▦ The sailor suggests someone who is totally in control of his own destiny, who 'sails with the tide'. A modern-day sailor in waking life would have the added benefit of being in control of his own environment and it is this image that is likely to surface in the dreams of the modern entrepreneur.

⊟ If a sailor does appear in a dream, particularly in a woman's, he is usually a somewhat romanticized figure and can represent the Hero. In a man's dream he represents the part of himself which seeks freedom, but that needs to be given permission or authority to take that freedom.

Also consult the information on Hero and Tramp in the information on Archetypes in the Introduction.

SALMON

🜚 A potent image in mythology is the Salmon of Knowledge, which signifies knowledge of other worlds (the lands beneath the sea) and of other-worldly things. This conforms to Shamanistic belief that creatures have the ability to visit other dimensions.

♡ In common with most fish when they appear in dreams, the salmon signifies our basic urges – most often the need for survival. By being able to put in effort we reap the rewards of our actions.

▦ In modern medicine the omega 3 oil that is in salmon is a powerful brain food. When the salmon appears in dreams we may need such a substance or be being warned that we need to pay attention to our intellectual pursuits.

⊟ The salmon signifies abundance and masculinity and is also phallic. In its fight to mate by swimming upstream it can also symbolize the sperm and may do so in men's dreams. Often a salmon can appear in a woman's dream as a symbol of her wish for pregnancy, whether this is a conscious wish or not.

You might also like to consult the entry for Fish as well as the information on Shaman in Spiritual Imagery in the Introduction.

SALT

☀ As a distillation of everything we know, salt represents wisdom. As a symbol of permanence and incorruptibility, spilt salt is thrown over the shoulder, supposedly in the face of the Devil.

◊ As in the old days salt was paid as salary, so nowadays to be given salt in a dream shows we are aware of our value. There are many customs associated with salt. In Scotland, along with coal and bread, it is the first thing to pass over the threshold to greet the New Year, symbolizing health, wealth and happiness and will also appear in dreams as a symbol of the savour of life.

▣ In dreams, salt highlights the subtle qualities we bring to our lives, those things we do to enhance our lifestyle. We run most of our lives through our emotions but the more subtle aspects are just as important. It has been suggested that if the water was removed from the human body there would be enough minerals and salt left to cover a fifty pence piece.

SAND

☀ Spiritually, sand represents the impermanence of the physical life and can suggest having to approach death or change in some way. The sands of time is an image much used in poetry and lyricism.

◊ Sand in a dream suggests a degree of instability and lack of security. When sand and sea are seen together we are not feeling particularly emotionally secure. When the sands are shifting we are probably unable to decide what we require from life. If we are conscious of the sand in an hourglass we are aware of time running out; we perhaps need to be certain we are making best use of our resources.

▣ Sand can represent impermanence. Because they will inevitably be washed away by the tide, building sand castles in dreams suggests that there is some doubt about the validity of a project in which we are involved. They also indicate that the structure we are trying to give to our lives does not necessarily have permanence and may be an illusion.

You might also like to consult the entries for Beach, Digging/Excavation, Hourglass and Time.

SARCOPHAGUS – *see* **TOMB**

SATAN – *see* **DEVIL**

SATELLITE

☀ A satellite can represent spiritual communication from a discarnate source.

◊ A satellite can appear in a dream to indicate the dependency that one person can have upon another. Often in relationships one partner is considered to be more important than the other and either could, therefore, recognize the symbol of the satellite.

Before satellites were invented, the stars were used as fixed points in communication. Nowadays a satellite would suggest efficient, effective contact. We are more globally aware of the effect we can have both on our environment and on other people around us.

You may also find it helpful to consult the entries for Astronaut, Communication and Space.

SATYR

The satyr is a spirit of nature and of natural power. When man was less civilized than he is now, his animal nature was closer to the surface. It was possible for him to see and identify patterns of energy or spirits, both in himself and in nature, which then took on human or semi-human form. As we progress and learn more spiritually this ability can resurface in dreams.

From a psychological standpoint the satyr is that part of nature that is not controlled, and is beyond restraint. It owes allegiance to no one and is completely anarchic. If perceived as destructive then it will be so. If accepted as helpful then it will be equally obliging.

While most of the time in the waking state we suppress such figures, in dreams – where there is no conscious control – they will sometimes appear. The satyr is usually pictured with the horns, legs and tail of a goat and is recognizable as Pan, the Horned God. He represents the wilder lustful side of our personality.

Consult the entries for Centaur, Fabulous Beasts and Horns for further information.

SAVINGS – *see* MONEY

SAW – *see* TOOLS

SCAFFOLD/SCAFFOLDING

A scaffold suggests an enforced code of spiritual behaviour and the need for self-control. Scaffolding indicates spiritual support.

Sometimes in dreams a scaffold indicates an enforced ending. This can be death, but is more likely to suggest the 'death' of part of our personality. This suggests that because at this time we cannot integrate that part, we must stop the behaviour or activity that is causing a problem. Otherwise we will have to take the consequences of behaving in such a way.

A scaffold or scaffolding in a dream usually indicates that there is some kind of temporary structure in our lives. If builders' scaffolding appears we should decide whether it is there to help us build something new or whether we are repairing something old. In either case, it indicates we need a temporary structure of some sort to help us reach the heights we wish, or achieve our goals. If we are building something new, the scaffolding will support us while we build, whereas if we are repairing the old it will support the previous structure while we make the necessary changes. A hangman's scaffold will suggest that a part of our lives must come to an end. We may, for instance, be aware that we have offended against some of society's laws and beliefs, and must be held to account. We also may need to look at our propensity to be a victim.

You might also like to consult the entries for Hang/Hanging, Martyr, Noose and Rope.

SCALES

🔅 The Scales of Justice represent spiritual balance and harmony, and also good judgement. By association, they also represent the astrological sign of Libra.

🜂 Scales in a dream suggest the necessity for balance and self-control. Without that balance we cannot make a sensible decision as to potential courses of action. We must 'weigh up' all the possibilities. Scales will also suggest standards – for instance, standards of behaviour – to which we are expected to adhere. We may be weighed and found wanting. If the scales are unbalanced in a dream we need to search our conscience and discover where we are not functioning properly in our lives.

🔲 The various types of scale we see in our dream will have slightly differing meanings. For example, bathroom scales would suggest a more personal assessment than a public machine, whereas a weighbridge might suggest that we need to take our whole lives into consideration. If they were doctor's scales we may be alerting ourselves to a potential health problem.

You might also like to consult the entries for Justice, Weighing/Weight and Zodiac.

SCALP – *see* **HEAD IN BODY**

SCAPEGOAT – *see* **VICTIM**

SCAR – *see* **INJURE/INJURY**

SCEPTRE

🔅 The sceptre is representative of royal power and sovereignty. Spiritually it signifies the transmission of divine power from above rather than below.

🜂 The sceptre can represent the magic wand and in dreams can indicate our right and ability to use such magic. If we are holding the sceptre we have the ability to transmit the life force. If someone else is using the sceptre and is bestowing honour or power on us, then we can accept that we have succeeded in a particular project.

▦ When it appears in dreams a sceptre indicates that we have given someone authority over us. We have abdicated responsibility to the point where the inner self has to take over.

◔ The sceptre has the same symbolism as most rods and staves: that of a phallic object. In a woman's dream it suggests the power for action. In a man's dream it signifies the power to take authority.

Also consult the entries for Magic/Magician, Staff and Wand.

SCHOOL

✺ Spiritually it is often considered that life itself is a school. It is an arena for learning and experiencing so that we can maximize our best potential; life is a testing-ground for the reality that comes afterwards.

◈ The school or classroom will often appear in dreams when we are re-learning how to deal with our own personalities idiosyncrasies. Such images will often appear at times when we are attempting to get rid of old outmoded ideas and concepts. Also, when we are learning different ways of dealing with authority and with feelings of inadequacy, our feelings about school will surface.

▦ School is an important part of everyone's life. In situations where we are learning new abilities or skills, the image of a school will often surface in dreams. It is also the place where we experience associations that do not belong to the family, and can in dreams, therefore, suggest new ways of learning about relationships. School may also be indicative of how we learn about competitiveness and belonging to groups.

Consult the entries for Education, Teacher and University for further information.

SCISSORS

✺ Spiritually, scissors can have two meanings. They can cut the Thread of Life, but can also represent unity and the coming together of the spiritual and physical.

◈ Scissors in dreams suggest the idea of cutting the non-essential out of our lives. This may be feelings we do not think are appropriate, emotions that we cannot handle, or mental trauma that needs to be excised. To dream of a hairdresser using scissors signifies our fear of losing strength and status.

▦ Scissors can also suggest a sharp, hurtful tongue or cutting remarks. Dreaming of sharpening scissors suggests that we need to be more precise in our communication, whereas using blunt scissors suggests that we are likely to create a problem through speaking too bluntly. The type of scissors may also be important. Kitchen scissors would, for instance, be more utilitarian than surgical scissors, which would suggest the necessity to be more precise.

Consult the entries for Kitchen, Surgery and Thread for further clarification.

SCROLL

🌞 A scroll can signify the letter of the law and the respect that it deserves. If we are given a scroll in dreams, we are deemed responsible enough to use the information we have gained.

🛡 A scroll can represent hidden knowledge, and also the passing of time. Thus, in most dreams, dreaming of a scroll signifies having to wait until the knowledge we have gained can be used at an appropriate time. The type of script used in the scroll may also need interpreting.

▦ Nowadays, a scroll will represent an acknowledgement of a learning process – i.e. the scroll presented to graduating students. We are endorsing either our own knowledge or information that has been given to us, so that we can enhance our lives.

Consulting the entries for Ink, Paper/Parchment, Seal, Time and Writing will give further information.

SCYTHE

🌞 The scythe, like the hourglass, is often held by the figure of Death and represents the ending of physical existence. We are becoming aware of the fact that the cutting off of life – or energy – may be imminent around us, although it need not be our own death.

🛡 The scythe is a very old-fashioned symbol for the passage of time. Its appearance in dreams shows we are linking with very deeply held concepts and ideas. It is time to harvest our own experience and ensure that we can acquire all that we need.

▦ The scythe is a cutting instrument, and therefore has the same significance as a knife. In dreams it usually suggests that we need to cut out non-essential actions or beliefs. We need to be fairly ruthless in order to achieve a desired end.

You might also like to consult the entries for Death, Harvest, Hourglass, Knife, Reaping and Time.

SEA – *see* WATER

SEAL

🌞 Spiritually a seal suggests hidden knowledge. Not all esoteric and occult information is available to everyone; such information is only entrusted to someone who has the courage to break the seal.

🛡 When we dream of legal documents, and are particularly aware of the seal, it can indicate that a conclusion has been reached in waking life which is both binding and secret. To be breaking a seal indicates that we are possibly breaking a confidence or someone's trust in us. In dreams, the possession of a seal gives us the authority to take responsibility for our own actions.

▦ Historically, a wax seal confirmed authority and power. It was also a symbol of identity. Nowadays in dreams it is much more likely to signify legality or correct moral action.

⊡ It has been suggested that in a woman's dream a man breaking a seal suggests that she will lose her virginity or purity at some level. In his own dreams, it will suggest that he is aware of the seriousness of his actions.

You might also like to consult the entry for Wax as well as the information for Seal in Animals.

SEANCE – *see* MEDIUM AS WELL AS SPIRITUAL IMAGERY IN THE INTRODUCTION

SEARCHING

◉ The movement towards spirituality often begins from a feeling of searching for something.

◈ Searching in a dream for something we have lost can suggest either that we need information from the past, or that we feel we have lost our identity. Searching also suggests more of a commitment to actually finding than just simply looking.

▦ To be searching in a dream is an attempt to find an answer to a problem. If we are searching for someone we may be conscious of our loneliness. If we are searching for something we may be aware of an unfulfilled need.

Consult the entries for Find and Lose/Loss/Lost for further clarification.

SEARCHLIGHT – *see* LIGHT AND TORCH

SEASONS

◉ The division of the year into Spring, Summer, Autumn and Winter gives occasion for celebrations and festivals which are vehicles for knowledge and inspiration.

◈ The need for us to be able to divide time into periods or phases arises initially from the necessity to co-operate with the seasons from a survival point of view. Given deadlines and limitations, the human being is able to survive through striving. In dreams we instinctively link with this inherent ability and need to live by the natural calendar.

▦ When we become conscious of the seasons of the year in dreams, we are also linking with the various periods of our lives; spring signifies childhood; summer, young adulthood; autumn, middle age; winter, old age.

⊡ When we understand the natural cycle of the year, dreams by both men and women will link with the union of the God and Goddess.

You might like to consult the entries for Autumn, Festival, Rite/Ritual, Spring, Summer and Winter for further information.

SEED – *see* GRAIN
SERPENT – *see* SERPENT AND SNAKE IN ANIMALS
SEX/SEXUAL IMAGES

   Dreams will often allow us to explore physicality in a safe way. Real spiritual growth takes place when we are not afraid of the curiosity that allows innocent exploration of our own body. When a child is first born, its first awareness is of itself as an individual. It has to learn that it is now separate from its mother and cope with the separation. It begins to become 'conscious' of itself, and of its need for warmth, comfort and love.

   Dreams highlight the whole range of the individual's sexuality. One vital stage of growth is the baby's fascination with its own body and the ability to be physical. Only if later we ignore our own sexual nature and fail to appreciate his own life force do the negative aspects make themselves obvious in dreams. This is a natural attempt to balance the waking state, which may have been over-intellectualized, or over-dramatized. Contact with others then becomes necessary, and often this need will manifest in dreams. There are many aspects of sex and sexuality that can surface in dreams unexpectedly or in an apparently bizarre fashion and they can generally be interpreted as follows:

Bisexuality – within us we all hold both masculine and feminine potentials. One is more overt than the other and when there is conflict between the inner and the outer selves this can sometimes show itself in dreams as bisexuality.

Castration – in a dream this suggests fear of loss of masculinity and sexual power.

Clothes – being fully clothed would suggest feelings of guilt or prudery.

Contraception – dreaming of contraception can indicate a fear of pregnancy and birth.

Ejaculation/Emission – the conflicts that arise in us because of our sexual desire for someone can be dealt with in the dream state through dreaming of emission or orgasm.

Fetishes – a fixation on an external object, in sexual terms it appears that there can be no sexual act without it – akin to a child being without its comforter. In dreams, therefore, a fetish can highlight fear, immaturity and lack of capability.

Hermaphrodite – dreaming of a hermaphrodite (someone who is both masculine and feminine) signifies our attitude to bisexuality, or androgyny – the perfect balance within one person of the masculine and feminine qualities.

Homosexuality – in dreams this is a desire for someone who is the same as oneself, i.e. has the same energies, thought processes etc. If we can identify similarities with the dream character that are not purely sexual, the dream can be fully interpreted.

Incest – usually characterizes the need for love expressed in a more tactile way. In dreams incest can highlight the guilty feelings we have about our parents or members of the family.

Intercourse (or petting) – the wish or need to be able to communicate with someone on a very intimate level can translate itself into intercourse in a dream. If intercourse is interrupted we may have inhibitions of which we are not consciously aware. Often intercourse in a dream can mark the integration of a particular part of our personality. If a child is then born in the dream that integration has been successful.

Kiss – this can indicate a mark of respect or a desire to stimulate the dream partner. It suggests we should be aware of what arousal we ourselves need.

Masochism – the desire to hurt or be hurt in dreams through sex arises from two causes. The first is to be a martyr (to suffer for one's 'sins') and the second to feel extreme emotion of one sort or another. We may not allow ourselves to feel deeply in everyday life.

Masturbation – the child learns to comfort himself through masturbation, so such a dream shows a need for comfort.

Perversion – when sexual perversion appears in dreams we are avoiding, or attempting to avoid, issues to do with closeness and bonding.

Phallus – any image either of or to do with the phallus signifies everything that is creative, penetrative and masculine. It is vitality and creativity in both its simplest and most complex form. It is resurrection and the renewal of life.

Rape – any image of rape appearing in dreams can be as much to do with violation of personal space as with the sexual act. Rape may only appear as an image when we as adults are ready to deal with trauma of any kind.

Sadism – in everyday life we may be very timid, in which case sadism in a dream is an escape mechanism. If we have to be dominant and controlling in everyday life, the unconscious shows its need to be controlled by such dreams.

Semen – the sign of masculinity and of physical maturity, semen is often seen in dreams as some other milky fluid. Dreams have an odd way of manifesting images of primitive rites and practices of which we may have no conscious knowledge, such as depositing semen in the earth.

Transvestism – signifies a confusion so far as gender is concerned in dreams.
Venereal Disease – in a dream this can suggest awareness of some kind of contamination. This need not necessarily be of a sexual nature, but could also be emotional.

■ In dreams, sexuality, in the sense of feeling desire for someone else, is a basic, primeval urge for closeness and union. It is as though we are searching for a part of ourselves that we have lost and the other character in the dream represents the closest we can get to that part. If we were a fully integrated human being, we would have no need for sex with someone else, but most of us have an inherent desire to be united with everything that is not part of our own ego. Sexual activity is either the highest expression of love and spirituality between two people or, if purely physically based, is entirely selfish. It would be up to us and our understanding of ourselves to determine which it is.

Consulting the entries for Androgen/Androgyny, Castration, Clothes, Hermaphrodite, Homosexuality, Incest, Kiss, Masochism and Sadism will help you clarify your dream.

SHADOW – *see* ARCHETYPES IN THE INTRODUCTION

SHAMPOO – *see* SOAP/SHAMPOO

SHAPES/PATTERNS

✿ At a certain stage of spiritual development, geometric shapes that will give us a greater understanding of the abstract world begin to appear in dreams. It is as though our old perceptions of form are beginning to take on new meaning and interpretation.

✪ The number of sides a shape has will be significant, as will the colours. Considerable symbology has grown up around shape. Various shapes and patterns can be interpreted as follows:

The centre symbolizes the point from which everything starts. In relation to shape, it is the point from which the pattern grows.

Circles represent the inner being or the Self. They are also unity and perfection.

Crescents (including the sickle and crescent moon) signify the feminine, mysterious power that is intuitive and non-rational. The crescent is also recognized as the symbol of the Islamic faith.

Crosses signify the realization (in the sense of making real) of spirit into matter.

Cubes – *see Square.*

Diamond shapes in a dream indicate that we have both greater and lesser options available to us.

The hexagon is the geometric figure that makes the most efficient use of space. The cells of a honeycomb are hexagonal for this reason and this shape epitomizes nature's best use of resources.

The hexagram is a geometric figure that symbolizes the harmonious development of the physical, social and spiritual elements of human life and its integration into a perfect whole.

Ovals are symbolic of the womb, and also of feminine life. Called the *Vesica Piscis*, it is the halo that completely encircles a sacred figure.

Patterns of any sort that appear in dreams as part of the scenario can categorize how we handle the repeated patterns and behaviours in our lives.

Spheres have a similar meaning to globes and indicate perfection and completion of all possibilities.

The spiral is the perfect path to evolution. The principle is that everything is continually in motion, but also continually rising or raising its vibration.

Square or Cube – the square and cube both signify the manifestation of spirit into matter. They represent the earthly realm as opposed to the heavens. The cube is a more tangible representation of this.

Stars, particularly bright ones, indicate our hopes, aspirations and ideals. The star represents those things we must reach for.

The swastika, with its arms moving clockwise, portrays Ideal Man and the power he has for good. In Eastern symbolism it signifies the movement of the sun. The swastika moving anti-clockwise signifies all that is sinister and wrong.

The triangle represents Standing Man with his three parts: body, mind and spirit (or being). Consciousness and love manifest through his physicality. There is potential still to be realized.

▣ We can accept the nature of things as they are and can look at the fundamental structure of our nature. We can appreciate the basic shape our lives are taking without placing inhibitions in the way. There is a game based on shapes in which you draw a square, a circle and a triangle, and then get someone else to elaborate each of the basic shapes into a drawing. Whatever they make of the square is supposed to relate to their outlook on the world, the circle to their inner being and the triangle to their sex life. Such images give potent material for dream work.

You might also like to consult the entries for Archetypes, Colours, Globe, Labyrinth and Numbers, as well as the information on Spiritual Imagery and Symbols in the Introduction.

SHAWL – *see* COAT IN CLOTHES

SHEAF – *see* INTRODUCTION

SHEARS – *see* SCISSORS

SHEEP – *see* ANIMALS

SHELLS

✸ Spiritually a shell is a miniature representation of the process of life and death.

♡ A shell carries within it a great deal of symbolism. It can be seen as a magical symbol which holds within it the power of transformation. The spiral of the shell suggests both going inwards and coming outwards. The ability to shelter is also symbolized, and as a receptacle it also links with the feminine, emotional side of nature.

▣ In dreams a shell represents the defences we use in order to prevent ourselves from being hurt. We can create a hard shell in response to previous hurt, or a soft shell, which would indicate that we are still open to being hurt. Shells were also once a unit of currency and in dreams can still be seen as this.

You might also like to consult the entry for Snail as well as the information for Spiral in Shapes and on Transformation in the Introduction.

SHELTER

✸ Shelter in the spiritual sense suggests sanctuary – a space wherein we will not be harmed but can be ourselves.

♡ The other image of shelter is protectiveness – that is, actively participating in giving shelter or sanctuary. If we are giving shelter to someone in dreams, we may be protecting a part of ourselves from hurt or difficulty. If we are being given shelter we are aware that there is protective power in our lives.

▣ Any shelter signifies protection. We are all aware of the need for a safe space, and this symbolism comes across in dreams quite strongly. The images used could be anything from a snail shell to an umbrella. Usually dreams about shelter highlight our needs or insecurities.

You might also like to consult the entries for Shells and Umbrella.

SHIELD

✸ In spiritual development the shield appears as a symbol of a particular stage of growth. It is at this point that we need to appreciate that we have control over our own destiny. This symbol often first appears in dreams representing this stage of development.

♡ In myths and legends the Amazonian woman is shown carrying a shield. This symbolizes woman's ability to be both protective and assertive.

A shield is a symbol of preservation. It can appear in dreams as a warrior's shield, or as a barrier between the dreamer and the rest of the world. If we are shielding someone else, then we need to be sure our actions are appropriate and supportive. If we are being shielded, we need to be clear as to whether we are erecting the shield or whether it is being erected for us.

Consult the entries for Barrier and Warrior as well as the information on Amazon in Archetypes in the Introduction for further clarification.

SHIRT – *see* CLOTHES

SHOE – *see* CLOTHES

SHOP – *see* MARKET/MARKET PLACE

SHOT/SHOOTING

Directed explosive energy, such as that from a gun, is a very effective spiritual tool, although it must be used with care. If we are noticeably aggressive we would have to be aware of our own motives and perhaps be a little more objective in taking action.

To be conscious of hearing a shot in dreams or of shooting someone highlights the need for a targeted release of energy, perhaps to clear the air or to achieve a particular end result. Being shot in a dream suggests that we may need to be aware of someone else's ill feeling towards us.

Unconsciously you may be feeling threatened in some way and need to be consciously pro-active in coming to terms with the fear that this brings. The type of weapon being used may have significance. When in a dream we are shooting someone we need to come to terms with aggressive or destructive tendencies which cannot be dealt with satisfactorily in waking life. Being in an environment where shooting is permitted, such as a shooting range or a war zone, indicates that certain safeguards should be put in place before planning on making any sort of assertive move.

In a woman's dream being shot or shot at can symbolize the sexual act and all that goes along with the idea of penetration. She might wish to explore her own feelings, particularly whether she feels targeted or victimized. In a man's dream the same idea of victimization or aggression can be apparent, but will be much less to do with the sexual act and more to do with everyday matters and his place in the world.

Consult the entries for Explode/Explosion, Gun, Victim, War and Weapon for further clarification.

SHOVEL/SPADE

A shovel is an implement or tool which can be used to help us uncover what is spiritually correct.

❦ Since a shovel or spade can suggest a degree of introspection, of covering up, what is being moved is important. We need to be mindful of the content of our lives. Digging compost, for instance, would mean considering the sum total and most fertile aspects of our lives, whereas shovelling sand, with its attendant dangers, might suggest trying to manipulate time.

▦ A shovel in a dream will signify a need to dig into past experiences for information. We may need to uncover a past joy or trauma, or possibly even a learning experience. The type of spade or shovel will be of relevance. A garden spade would suggest being totally pragmatic, whereas a fire shovel would indicate a need to take care.

You might also like to consult the entries for Digging/Excavation, Sand, Time and Tools.

SHRINK

❂ Following the psychological recognition of our smallness, we equally can become aware of the sense of belonging to a much greater cosmic whole. This is represented in dreams by a feeling of shrinking.

❦ Psychologically we can learn to handle who we are by recognizing both how necessary and also how small we are in the general scheme of things. The latter can be accompanied in dreaming by a feeling of shrinking. We therefore become less threatening to ourselves and others.

▦ In dreams, to shrink is to have a desire to return to childhood, or to a smaller space in order to be looked after. In everyday life we may be aware of losing face or of feeling small and this can be translated in dreams as shrinking. To see something – or somebody – shrink can indicate that it is losing its power over us.

Consult the entries for Analyst and Size for further information.

SHROUD

❂ In spiritual terms a shroud is a mark of respect for the dead. As a garment, it is meant to convey decency.

❦ In a dream a shroud can be a frightening image, since it is associated with death. It can also signify the covering up of something we do not fully understand. We know that it is there, but we do not wish to confront it.

▦ If we recognize that by shrouding something it becomes hidden, then the image is more manageable. In times gone by, the shroud was a set of ropes used by sailors. This image surfaces in dreams when we deliberately tie something up in order to make it safe – shrouded from view.

You might also like to consult the entry for Sailing/Sails.

SICK – *see* ILL/ILLNESS AND VOMIT

SICKLE – *see* SCYTHE

SIGNATURE – *see* WRITING

SILENCE

⚜ Spiritually, silence is a 'space' where there is no need for sound. Many religious orders are silent on the basis that there is then closer communication with God. In dreams it may suggest that contemplation and withdrawal from the everyday world is necessary.

♥ When we are silent in dreams we are unable to voice our feelings or opinions. We are either inhibited by our own selves or by outside influences. Conversely in silence we have no need to express ourselves.

■ Silence in a dream can suggest uneasiness and expectancy. There is a waiting for something to happen or not. If a dream character is silent when we expect them to speak, we are unsure as to how we ourselves will react in waking life to external circumstances.

You might also like to consult the entries for Hear/Hearing and Sound.

SILVER

⚜ Spiritually, silver is said to represent the feminine aspect, gold being the masculine. This came initially from the gold of the sun and the silver of the moon. Metals were thought to be 'reflections'.

♥ Silver on a more psychological level has been taken to represent the emotional qualities of the moon. This may be in the sense that we are available, yet remote. The moon and silver both represent a quality of attraction and self-sufficiency at the same time.

■ On a practical level, silver coins appearing in a dream suggest finance or money. Silver bars are metal in its raw state. In any case, silver is something of value that can be held in reserve against possible difficulty.

⦿ In a woman's dream, silver will often represent her essential core. In a man's dream it is more likely to represent his rather more diffuse qualities.

The entries for Colours, Gold, Metal, Money and Moon will further enhance your understanding.

SING

⚜ Spiritually when we sing we are capable of raising the vibration, either for ourselves or other people. We are in touch with the Higher Self.

♥ Singing as an act of worship is a vital part of many systems of belief. Singing as chanting has a valid place in religion – as in the Gregorian chant – where certain tones achieve a shift in consciousness. To hear this in dreams is to be in touch with a high vibration. Chanting of a mantra also achieves the same end. If we are singing alone, we have learnt to be skilled in our own right.

To hear singing in a dream is to link with the self-expression we all have. We are in touch with the flowing, feeling side of ourselves and of others. To be singing is to be expressing our joy and love of life and our need to perform and star in our own show. To be in a choir suggests our ability to worship or express ourselves in a peer group. To be singing a football anthem creates a fellow feeling. To find ourselves singing in a talent contest suggests that we wish for other people to become aware of our perceived abilities.

You might also like to consult the entries for Mantra, Music/Rhythm, Musical Instruments and Worship.

SINKING

Both spiritually and physically, to be sinking is to be getting into a situation where we are unable to see clearly or to perceive the best course of action. For sensitives, this may be when the negativity of others threatens to overwhelm us.

A sinking feeling in dreams usually suggests worry or fear. Emotionally we are unable to maintain our usual happiness. We may feel that we are not in control, and that we cannot maintain forward movement. To see an object sinking may suggest that we are about to lose something we value. A sink as a water receptacle symbolizes the way we hold onto our emotions.

To be sinking in a dream suggests a loss of confidence. We may be unhappy at something we have done, and feel hampered by the circumstances around us. We may feel we are losing ground within a relationship or situation. To see someone else sinking would suggest we are aware of a difficulty that perhaps needs our help. What we are sinking into could be important. To be sinking in water would suggest a particular emotion is threatening to engulf us. To be sinking in quicksand or a bog indicates that we feel there is no safe ground for us. Becoming conscious of a sink or basin suggests that some kind of cleansing is necessary.

The entries for Drowning, Emotions, Quicksand and Water will provide additional information.

SIREN

As an archetype, it is only when it is understood spiritually that the Siren can ultimately restore man to himself that she becomes acceptable and can be worked with. After having rejected her enchantment, we are free to become whole.

The Siren suggests deception and distraction of man from his purpose. In dreams this is usually sexually oriented and difficult to handle. In psychological terms she is Temptation and often appears in Greek or Roman attire, as if to enhance the erotic image. She can often be pictured in dreams sat by water, since she works mainly with the emotions.

🔲 To hear a siren – as in an ambulance or fire engine – is to be warned of danger. For some, the sound of a siren will evoke images and memories of war and destruction, triggering feelings of anxiety.

📳 In a woman's dream, if she has not come to an understanding of the Siren within her, such a character can appear ultimately to be destructive. In a man's dream, the Siren is generally an aspect of his Anima, initially alluring, then recognizably destructive, before he finally discovers how to handle her. For both men and women it is vital that they learn to integrate, or come to terms with, this part of the personality.

You might also like to consult the entries for Emotions, War and Water as well as the information on Siren in Archetypes in the Introduction.

SISTER – *see* **FAMILY**

SIZE

🔆 Spiritually size is irrelevant. It is more the appreciation of feeling that becomes important. A 'big' feeling is something that consumes us, whereas a 'little' perception may be only part of what really exists.

💠 A child learns very early on to make comparisons, and this is one of the things that we never lose, particularly in dreams. Something is often bigger (taller) or smaller rather than simply big or small. In dreams size is relative. We might recognize somewhere we know, but find it is larger or smaller than we thought it to be. It is the size within the dream that is relevant.

🔲 To be conscious of size in a dream highlights how we feel in relation to a person, project or object. Big or tall might suggest important or threatening, whereas small might indicate vulnerability or something 'less than' ourselves. Thus a big house would be an awareness of the expansion of oneself, whereas a small house would indicate an intensity of feeling. The contrast between fat and thin, or thick and thin, is a subjective evaluation that will often depend on cultural differences. The issue of size in dreams is dependent on our own personal evaluation. To be actively reducing an article may mean that we are trying to make a project or task manageable.

SKELETON/SKULL

🔆 A skeleton in dreams alerts us to our attitude to the macabre. We are aware that the physical must 'die' or change, but that there is still a framework left. The skull in dreams can sometimes represent major changes such as death and all the adjustments necessary.

⚕️ Psychologically, we sometimes need to be aware of our feelings about death. The obvious image of the skeleton appearing in our dreams forces us to be aware of this. It can also suggest feelings or talents that we have forgotten and that, therefore, seem to have died. To be conscious of our own skull in dreams is to appreciate the intellectual structure that we have given our lives. To perceive a skull where there should be a head suggests that we are not using our intellectual abilities as well we might. When a skull is talking to us, a part of us that we have rejected or denied is beginning to 'come back to life'. To be talking to a skull is recognizing the need to communicate with those who are lost to us in any way; if we believe in life after death, we may feel that spirit is talking through the skull.

🔲 A skeleton in a dream suggests the 'bare bones' of something, perhaps an idea or concept. A skeleton in a cupboard represents a past action or shame, both in dreams and waking life, we wish to hide. A dancing skeleton is an awareness of the life we have lived or are living. To dig up a skeleton is to resurrect something – perhaps a talent – we have buried or hidden away. The skull and crossbones in dreams could represent either a somewhat romantic appreciation of a pirate or freedom-lover, or perhaps is a symbol of danger. Since the skull is a representation of the head it can also symbolize intellectual ability, or rather lack of it.

Also consult the entry for Death and the information on the Head in the Body entry as well as the information on Tramp in Archetypes and Spirits in Spiritual Imagery in the Introduction.

SKIN – *see* **BODY**

SKULL – *see* **SKELETON**

SKY

☀️ The sky spiritually suggests infinity and that which is above and beyond us – a representation of the Ultimate. It also signifies order, particularly that applied to the intuitive function.

⚕️ The sky signifies the unattainable. Whatever effort we make we can never make the sky tangible. This is one reason why the sky gods were so important in more primitive cultures.

🔲 In dreams the sky can represent the mind and signify our potential. Floating or flying in the sky can be ambivalent, since it can either mean trying to avoid the mundane, or exploring a different potential. If the sky is dark or cloudy it may reflect our mood of gloominess; if it is bright, our mood of joy.

You might also like to consult the entries. for Clouds, Float/Floating, Flying/ Flight and Order

SLOW – *see* **SPEED**
SMALL – *see* **SIZE**
SMELL

🔆 As our spiritual senses develop, the ability to sense and recognize smells from the past on a clairvoyant level can be rather alarming. In dreams, provided this ability is recognized merely as a means of identifying a time, place or person, we need not be afraid.

💚 Childhood is a time when smell is very significant. Many smells that are associated with that time, e.g. baking bread, burning oil, flowers, school dinners, can still be very evocative for us as adults. A pleasant smell could represent happy times or memories, whereas a bad smell can hold memories of particularly traumatic times.

🔲 To be conscious of a smell in a dream usually means that we are trying to identify an object or its source. Most other senses are sharpened in dreams, but the sense of smell is made available only if a specific interpretation is needed.

Also consult the entry for Odour.

SMOKE/SMOKING

🔆 Spiritually, smoke signifies prayer rising to heaven and is used with that significance in those belief systems that use incense. It also represents the raising of the soul to escape from space and time and the restrictions of the physical dimension.

💚 Smoke in dreams can represent passion, although it may not have 'flared' properly into being. Smoke can also represent either cleansing – as with incense – or contamination of some sort. If we are smoking tobacco or any other substance, we are trying to control our anxiety. If we smoke in real life, but recognize in dreams that we no longer do so, we have overcome a difficulty. Smokers who are attempting to give up in everyday life will often have many dreams focused around the issue of smoking.

🔲 Smoke in dreams suggests that there is a feeling of danger around, especially if we cannot locate the fire. As smoking in public become less acceptable, in dreams it may be seen as an act of rebellion or deliberately choosing to go against the norms of society.

Consult the entries for Fire, Incense, Rebel/Revolution and Tobacco for additional information.

SNAIL

🔆 The snail shell symbolizes the perfection of nature's creativity, which is also echoed in mathematical fractals (repeated patterns). The spiral shape of the snail shell is symbolic of the labyrinth.

❤ From a psychological point of view, the snail suggests steadiness and self-containment. To be moving at snail's pace suggests direct planned, careful movement.

▦ The snail appearing in dreams may engender, because of its sliminess, a feeling of repulsion in some people. It does, however, also represent vulnerability and slowness, along with the type of apparent rootlessness seen in the Wanderer.

You might also like to consult the entries for Labyrinth, Shell, Spiral and Wanderer.

SNAKE – *see* **SERPENT AND SNAKE IN ANIMALS AND ALSO SPIRITUAL IMAGERY IN THE INTRODUCTION**

SNOW

❀ Snow represents spiritual purity, beauty and the melting away of difficulties.

❤ Psychologically snow in dreams can suggest emotional coldness or frigidity. When snow is lying on the ground it can symbolize a protective covering. When blowing around its interpretation is similar to that of rain.

▦ Snow is a crystallisation of water, and as such represents the crystallization of an idea or project. When melting, it can represent the softening of the heart.

You might also like to consult the entries for Cold, Ice/Iceberg/Icicles, Rain, Weather and Winter.

SOAP/SHAMPOO

❀ From a spiritual perspective, soap and shampoo represent cleansing. It is an attempt to get back to basics and to clear our wants, needs and requirements. We are trying to make a new connection with the Spiritual Self.

❤ Psychologically soap can indicate a need to clean up our act. We may feel a sense of having been contaminated by an experience and situation and our dream mind is alerting us to the fact that we need to deal with it. Because shampooing is connected with the head – which of itself represents intellect – there is a connection psychologically with needing to have clarity of thought. We may feel that our thought processes have been slowed down, or dirtied, by outside influences.

▦ Soap in dreams suggests the idea of being cleansed. We perhaps need to create an environment of cleanliness – both of physical cleanliness and appropriate behaviour. Shampoo in dreams has an obvious connection with cleansing and washing. On a practical level, we are trying to 'clear our heads' in order to think or see clearly.

▣ Often in emerging male sexual dreams soap and shampoo represent ejaculated semen. A woman will often dream of shampooing her hair when a relationship breaks down; presumably she is instinctively aware that she must intellectually free herself.

You might also like to consult the entries for Clean/Clear, Dirty and Washing as well as the information on Hair and Head in the Body entry.

SON – *see* FAMILY

SOUND

❂ Sound in the spiritual sense is vibration from which everything is created. In dreams, purity of sound is a prerequisite of awareness.

♡ To the waking mind, sound is necessary – and is sometimes somewhat irritating. Sound can be a marker for the natural changes that occur in focus in the dream state and, therefore, becomes part of the dream scenario. A particularly sharp sound – such as a desk bell pinging – would suggest sudden change, whereas an apparently long, drawn-out sound – such as a foghorn – would signify a slower process.

▦ Literally, if what we do in waking life resonates with us – that is, satisfies our inner and outer being – we may become particularly aware in dreams of sound. A discordant note would signify difficulty, and a purer one success.

Consult the entry for Noise for further information.

SOUP – *see* EATING, FOOD AND NOURISHMENT

SOUTH

❂ The South in spiritual terms suggests the summer, a time for fun and laughter. The Archangel is Michael, the Soldier of God.

♡ We are looking towards midday and the right to use the energy we have available. The magical element is Fire and the colour red. Dreams of the South often signify the high point of any endeavour.

▦ When we dream specifically of the South, we are looking to be able to direct our energies successfully. It is the will to do and to be, so a time for action.

You might also like to consult the entries for Colour, Elements, Fire and Summer.

SOWING

❂ Sowing in a spiritual sense suggests creating the correct environment in which growth can take place. It is, above all, the creative act.

♡ The image of laying down a framework for success is implicit in sowing. The actions that have to be gone through – such as preparing the ground, tilling the soil and so on – are all evocative images even in today's technological society. When this image appears in dreams, we need to look at circumstances around us and decide what we can gain most.

🔲 Sowing is a symbol that has certain basic ideas attached to it. It can represent the planting of an idea, the beginning of a new project or the careful planning of a multi-faceted task.

🔲 Originally, sowing seed was taken to be a feminine occupation. With mechanization that emphasis has shifted. However, in women's dreams, the primary image of nurturing may be that of sowing seed. In a man's dream it is more likely to signify the sexual act, and well as suggesting good husbandry.

The entry for Harvest will help to clarify your dream.

SPACE

💠 Space is a representation of a cosmic centre – a place that 'is, was and ever shall be'. When it appears in a dream it shows we need to widen our present view of the world.

💚 Psychologically we often need space to make the best use of opportunities. We should be capable of going beyond our own concepts of limitation and restriction. As the exploration of space takes us beyond our own little world, we become more conscious of the need for best use of resources.

🔲 In dreams, when we are aware of the space we occupy we are in touch with our own potential. We may be aware that our personal space is being, or has been, penetrated. To be 'spaced out' is to have widened our personal boundaries artificially through the use of stimuli.

You might also like to consult the entries for Astronaut and Rocket.

SPADE – *see* SHOVEL

SPARK

💠 The spark suggests fire and therefore love. The 'essential spark' is the vital principle in life; we need to appreciate our own lust for life.

💚 The spark of an idea suggests the germ of a creative potential that, given the opportunity, will become much bigger. Since the spark also represents the basic life force, emotionally we can accept the myriad possibilities offered to us.

🔲 A spark in a dream represents a beginning. Being aware of a spark is to be conscious of the germ of an idea that may be brought to fruition in waking life. From a physical perspective it is a small thing that gives rise to a greater one.

You might also like to consult the entries for Electricity, Fire and Lightning.

SPEAR

💠 Spiritually, the spear signifies directness and honour. It has the power of life and death.

💚 The spear is psychologically that part of ourselves that is fertile and assertive. To see a warrior with a spear is to recognize the aggressive male. To put a spear in the ground is to mark one's territory. If we are throwing a spear we perhaps need to be aware of our more assertive tendencies.

🔲 The spear has many meanings from a mundane perspective. It can represent the cut and thrust of business life or the wit of social interchange. In its more negative sense it can suggest sarcasm and bloody-mindedness.

⚏ A spear represents the masculine in dreams and is a phallic symbol. Whether it appears in a man's or a woman's dream, it allows us to be conscious of the need to cut out nonsense and get straight to the point.

The entries for Arrow and Weapons will provide further information.

SPECTACLES – *see* **GLASSES/SPECTACLES**

SPEED

🔆 There is a point when, as we are developing spiritually, we lose our sense of time. Speeding things up may appear as slowing things down, and vice versa. This is all part of the spiritual growth process. The polarities of fast and slow – that is, speed and inertia – are a duality that, when handled properly, create a balance.

🛡 Travelling at speed suggests trying to achieve a fast result. Speeding – as in a traffic offence – suggests being too focused on an end result, and not the method of getting there. However, as the opposite to fast, being slow in dreams gives a sense of greater tranquillity than such frenetic behaviour. To be taking, or to be given, speed (amphetamines) in a dream may have two meanings. If the substance is used in everyday life, we could be being alerted to a gift or talent that should be developed. If we do not normally use the drug, then we are putting ourselves in danger in some way. We may be trying to force an issue or pre-empt results.

🔲 Speed in dreams identifies an intensity of feelings that is not usually available in waking life. Because everything is happening too quickly, it engenders anxiety in us, which creates problems. In dreams, when everything slows down or seems to be going in slow motion, we need to consider very carefully each aspect of our lives at that particular moment. To be moving slowly suggests taking greater care.

Also consult the entries for Drugs, Quick and Time as well as the information on Anxiety Dreams in the Introduction.

SPHINX

🔆 Spiritually the sphinx stands for vigilance, power and wisdom as well as dignity.

🛡 Psychologically, and because even today little is known about it, the sphinx in dreams represents our enigmatic side. It will highlight the mysterious power that becomes available to us, particularly in times of trouble.

▣ The sphinx, for most people in dreams, will represent Egypt and all the mystery it contains. It may also represent a hardened attitude.

You might also like to consult the entry for Mummy (Egyptian).

SPIDER

❀ Spiritually the spider represents the Great Mother in her role as the Weaver of Life. She weaves Destiny from the body of her self and is, therefore, the Creator. In coming to terms with this aspect, we become weavers of our own destiny.

◈ In psychological terms the spider connects with the principles of the Mandala. The spider has the ability to create a perfect pattern, which both nurtures and protects at the same time.

▣ On a very mundane level spiders are generally disliked, perhaps because of their scuttling movement but also because of its association with dirt. In dreams it can also suggest deviousness, harking back to the innate fear of the Destructive Mother archetype.

⊟ In a woman's dream a spider will often reconnect her with her essential femininity, whereas in a man's dream such an image is more likely to generate fear.

Consult the entries for Insects, Mandala and Web as well as the information on Great Mother and Destructive Mother in Archetypes in the Introduction.

SPINE – *see* BACKBONE IN BODY

SPIRAL – *see* SHAPES

SPIRE

❀ As a representation of our spiritual progression, the spire suggests the movement from the secular to the sacred. It has represented this from time immemorial.

◈ The spire represents ambition and striving. A fallen spire would suggest the collapse of hopes. To be building a tower or spire has connotations with the Tower of Babel and shows a need for more – or better – communication.

▣ To see a spire in a dream is to recognize a landmark, whether personal or more universal. In previous times, people oriented themselves by churches. Now a pub tends to be a marker, but in dreams the spire still persists.

⊟ The spire can often be taken in dreams as a phallic symbol, particularly – and somewhat obviously – the erect one. In a woman's dream, the spire will usually represent her sense of the Ultimate, whereas in a man's dream it is more likely to represent his ambition.

Consulting the entry for Tower as well as Religious Buildings in Buildings and also the information for Spiritual Imagery in the Introduction should help provide further clarification.

SPIRITS – *see* **SPIRITUAL IMAGERY IN THE INTRODUCTION**

SPIRITUAL IMAGERY – *see* **INTRODUCTION**

SPORT

⚜ From a spiritual perspective, sport in dreams suggests the ability to keep the 'temple' of the physical body in peak condition. To be the best requires discipline and means calling on reserves of power and energy we may not know we have. Sporting activities were, and indeed still are, used to channel excess energy.

♥ Psychologically, any sport requires us to overcome our own inadequacies and to have courage beyond the norm. Taking part in competitive sport in dreams will signify our ability to be competitive in other areas in life. Tackling an opponent is confronting a problem, whereas fishing tackle is a means to an end.

▣ Sport, as a dream symbol of business and working life, is a potent image. Team games will represent the ability to work in harmony with others, whereas athletic activities in dreams may suggest personal excellence. Acting as a referee highlights our ability to control circumstances around us. To challenge the referee is to be challenging authority.

Consult the entries for Compete/Competition, Games, Running and Win/ Winning for further information.

SPRING

⚜ Spiritually within the cycle of nature, spring is a time of rebirth and rejuvenation. We can now afford to make a new beginning, particularly insofar as emotion is concerned.

♥ The saying 'spring forward, fall back' is also applicable in psychological terms, since effort and new energy is required to progress. To walk with a spring in one's step is to be looking forward to something.

▣ Springtime in a dream can suggest new growth or opportunities. Perhaps there is a fresh start in a relationship. A spring of water suggests fresh energy, whereas a bedspring or other type of coil would indicate latent power for movement.

You might also like to consult the entries for Autumn, Seasons, Summer, Water and Winter.

SPRINKLE/SPRINKLING

⚜ Spiritually we are aware of basic concepts and abilities. In some cultures, semen is sprinkled on the ground to propitiate the Mother Goddess and ensure a good harvest. In protective magical rituals herbs and salt are sprinkled.

♥ Sprinkling suggests the symbolism of impregnation, of conception and gestation. Psychologically we need to make a link with our creative side in order to function properly as human beings.

🔲 Sprinkling as a symbol in dreams suggests an attempt to make a little go a long way. Perhaps we need to get the best out of situations around us, by putting a little effort into many things.

Consult the entries for Goddess/Goddesses, Harvest, Magic/Magician and Rite/Ritual for further information.

SQUARE – *see* **SHAPES/PATTERNS**

SQUIRREL – *see* **ANIMALS**

STAB

✹ When we realize that we can use particular skills, they can assume an almost ritualistic feeling. Fighting and stabbing movements (as in martial arts) are a means of spiritual discipline. We need to understand appropriate behaviour.

🜊 When we make ourselves vulnerable we are open to being hurt. Often a stab is a quick way of achieving a result. For instance, to be stabbing at something rather than somebody would suggest the need to break through some kind of shell or barrier in order to proceed.

🔲 To be stabbed in a dream indicates our ability to be hurt. To stab someone is, conversely, to be prepared to hurt but also with the faculty of being able to get straight to the point.

⦂ Since a stab wound is penetrative it has obvious connections with aggressive masculine sexuality and will have this meaning in feminine dreams. In a man's dream it is more likely to be to do with his ability to get straight to the point.

Consult the entries for Dagger, Knife, Rite/Ritual and Wound/Wounding for further information.

STAFF

✹ Spiritually the staff is a symbol of the support we have, or will need, on our spiritual journey. As we progress, we move from using it as a support to using it as a tool and finally as a sign of authority.

🜊 The staff in dreams symbolizes the journeying and pilgrimage that we must undertake. It also represents magical power in the form of a wand.

🔲 A staff, in the sense of a stick, is a support mechanism; staff, as in office staff, a support system. Dreaming of either should clarify our attitude to the support we require in life. It is worthwhile noting that one is passive in its use (the stick) and one is active.

You might also like to consult the entries for Sceptre, Tool and Wand.

STAG – *see* **DEER IN ANIMALS**

STAGE – *see* **THEATRE**

STAIRS – *see* STEPS AND ALSO STAIRS IN BUILDINGS

STAR – *see* CELEBRITY, FAME, FAMOUS PEOPLE AND SHAPES/PATTERNS

STATION – *see* DEPARTURES IN JOURNEY AND TRAIN IN TRANSPORT

STATUE

⚜ There is a basic side of nature that needs to look up to something and this can be symbolized in dreams by a statue, which is representative of an idea or concept rather than a person.

♥ When emotion is not allowed proper expression it is 'dead' and, therefore, has solidified. Often in dreams this will take the form of a statue. If the statue comes to life, the emotion can be rescued.

▦ Dreaming of a statue is to be linking with the unresponsive, cold side of human nature. We may be worshipping or loving someone and not getting any response. We come up against the knowledge that we have given value to something that no longer has significance.

You might also like to consult the entry for Stone.

STEALING

⚜ Spiritually, stealing is using energy inappropriately. At each level of awareness we have certain power available to us that must be used wisely and well. For instance, 'black' magic could be interpreted as stealing. Psychic 'vampirism' is another form of stealing.

♥ Stealing is a very emotive word for most people, and it will depend on the dreamer's background as to how they feel about inappropriate behaviour. This image also comes up when dealing with the emotions. For instance, a 'needy' person may feel they are stealing affection.

▦ To dream of stealing suggests that we are intent on taking something without permission. This may be love, money or opportunities. If someone steals from us we may feel cheated. If in dreams this act is by someone we know, then we need to work out how much we trust that person. If it is by someone we don't know, it is more likely to be a part of ourselves that we don't trust. However, if we belong to a gang of thieves, then we should carefully look at, and consider, the morals of the peer group that we belong to.

You might also like to consult the entries for Burglar, Group and Thief.

STEAM

⚜ We are looking at, and are aware of, the all-encompassing power of the Spirit.

♥ Because it is two substances uniting into one (fire and water), steam suggests transformation. It also suggests a transitory experience, since steam also melts away.

🔲 Steam in dreams can suggest emotional pressure. We are passionate about something without necessarily knowing what it is.

Also consult the entries for Fire, Machine/Machinery, Piston and Water, as well as the information on Transformation in the Introduction.

STEEPLE – *see* SPIRE

STEPS

🌣 There is still perceived to be a hierarchical structure in spiritual progression. We can achieve certain things at each level before moving on to the next.

♥ Steps in dreams almost invariably suggest an effort made to succeed. Going up steps suggests trying to make things better and improve them, whereas going down means going either into the past or the subconscious.

🔲 Steps represent changes in awareness within a project, quite literally the steps necessary. Steps also represent communication of a progressive kind.

Also consult the information for Stairs in Buildings.

STERILIZE/STERILITY

🌣 Sterilization in a spiritual sense is somewhat ambivalent. It can either suggest purity of spirit or a belief in austerity, which does not allow the Self to grow.

♥ To dream of sterilizing something suggests a need for cleansing at a deep level. We wish to get rid of hurts or traumas and are prepared to put in the effort to do so. 'Sterilizing' a situation may be taking the emotion out of it.

🔲 Sterility suggests an absence of ideas and motivation. The need not to be sidetracked in everyday life can present in dreams as a sterile environment. Dreams of alienation, or of being captured by aliens, often have such an image.

🕂 For a woman to dream of being sterilized, either by an operation or otherwise, may be connecting with her feeling of powerlessness. In a man's dream sterilization may suggest sexual dissatisfactions or doubts about his self-image.

You might also like to consult the entries for Abduct, Alien/Alienated and Operation.

STONE

🌣 Stone, as basic material, signifies the imperishability of Supreme Reality. Ultimately it is indestructible and returns to Source.

♥ Stone has many connotations on an emotional level. For stone to be broken up signifies being badly hurt. Being turned to stone would suggest that we have had to harden up our attitudes. Being stoned in dreams is being punished for misdemeanours.

■ Dreaming of stone can suggest stability and durability, but also a loss of feeling. To be carving stone is to be attempting to create a lasting monument. *You might also like to consult the entries for Break, Emotions, Gems/Jewels and Statue.*

STORM

✿ Spiritually a storm symbolizes the Creative Power. Thunder and lightning are the tools of the storm gods.

◐ When we are in difficulty, for instance, in a relationship, a storm can bring release. When an argument is not appropriate in everyday life, in dreams a storm can clear our 'emotional air'.

■ In dreams a storm indicates a personal emotional outburst. We may feel we are being battered by events or emotions. It can also signify anger. *Consulting the entries for Anger, Emotions, God/Gods, Lightning, Rain, Thunder/Thunderbolts and Weather will provide further information.*

STRANGER – see PEOPLE

STRANGLE

✿ Spiritually, wisdom arises out of learning how to hold back inappropriate speech. In dreams the feeling of being strangled suggests a deliberate act of suppression.

◐ Strangulation suggests a violent act of suppression. Emotionally, our more violent, aggressive side may not allow us to act appropriately in certain situations. In dreams this can appear as strangling.

■ To dream of strangling someone is an attempt to stifle our own emotions. To dream of being strangled is to be aware of our difficulty in speaking out about our emotions. *You might also like to consult the entries for Kill, Murder/Murderer and Violence.*

STREAM

✿ The image of a stream is often quoted as being blessed by Divine Power. Spiritual energy is often experienced as a stream of light.

◐ Emotionally if we are to function properly we must feel loved and appreciated. To be in the flow of things suggests being part of a social group that will enable us to interact with people. This image often surfaces as a stream.

■ Dreaming of a stream suggests the awareness of the flow of our emotions. To be in a stream suggests being in touch with our sensuality. *Also consult the entry for Water.*

STRING

✿ String theory is a scientific attempt to explain a spiritual anomaly. Anything that binds suggests a direct relationship with our inner self. This is traditionally seen as the Silver Cord that holds the spiritual and physical together.

♥ In a psychological sense, string – like rope – can be seen as a link between two objects or aspects of our lives. We may not have made the connection before in waking life.

▦ String appearing in dreams signifies some sort of binding, perhaps to make something secure. It may also represent trying to hold a situation together.

You might also like to consult the entries for Hold and Rope.

SUBMARINE

☼ Dreaming of a submarine indicates we have a spiritual need to understand the depths of our emotions.

♥ If we are to be comfortable with ourselves, we need to understand our unconscious urges. Since there can be some fear with this – and perhaps a need for protection – the submarine becomes quite a potent image.

▦ A submarine in dreams indicates the depth of feeling that is accessible to us. Usually we are looking at the subconscious depths rather than the spiritual heights.

The entries for Boat/Ship, Deep, Torpedo and Water will provide further information.

SUCCUBUS – *see* DEMON AND DEVIL

SUCKING/SUCKLE

☼ The snake that sucks its own tail – the Ouroboros – is a potent image of spiritual completeness and will appear as we become more spiritually advanced.

♥ Emotionally we all have needs which are left over from childhood. These may be unfulfilled desires or the need to be whole and complete. This need can surface in dreams as sucking something.

▦ To be conscious of sucking in a dream suggests a return to infantile behaviour and emotional dependency. Sucking a lollipop alerts us to a need to bring ourselves some sort of comfort. Sucking a finger symbolizes the primitive urge to suckle.

SUFFOCATING

☼ Suffocation may appear in dreams when negativity is too strong for us to deal with and threatens to overwhelm us.

♥ If in waking life we are struggling within a relationship we may find that dreams of suffocation occur. Fears connected with the sexual act can also surface in dreams as suffocation.

▦ When we feel we are suffocating in a dream, it may be that our own fears are threatening to overwhelm us. It can also indicate that we are not in control of our own environment. To be suffocating a dream character may mean we wish to shut someone up in waking life.

SUICIDE

☀ Often on the path of spirituality we must let go of the old Self. This can occur in dreams as suicide. It is also a sign of anger against the Self.

♥ Emotionally, when dreams of suicide occur, we may have come to the end of our ability to cope with a particular situation in our lives. It does not actually mean that we are suicidal. It simply marks the end of a phase.

▦ Dreaming of suicide alerts us to the sudden ending of something, perhaps a project or relationship. It may also signify the end of a business or business relationship, but one that we ourselves terminate.

Also consult the entries for Anger and Death as well as the information on Self in Archetypes in the Introduction.

SUITCASE – *see* BAGGAGE AND LUGGAGE

SUMMER

☀ Esoterically, summer represents the mid-life. This is a time of spiritual success and of the ability also to plan for the rest of our lives. We have learnt by experience and can now put that experience into practice.

♥ The significance of summer on a psychological level is twofold. Because of its association with holidays and with fun and laughter, we are able to be more relaxed. We also have opportunities to meet with other people and to form new associations.

▦ To be aware in a dream that it is summer suggests that it is a good time in our lives. We can look forward to success in projects we have around us. We have the ability to make the most of what we have done to date.

You might also like to consult the entries for Autumn, Seasons, Spring, Sun and Winter.

SUN

☀ The sun can symbolize spiritual enlightenment and radiance. The dreamer can 'soak up' and use the sun's power for further spiritual development. Because the sun is such a powerful image on its own as a life source, it can also appear in dreams as a symbol for other life energy.

♥ The sun in dreams suggests warmth and conscious awareness. If dreaming of a Native American Sun Dance, or any such worship, we may be wishing to acknowledge the sun for its all-encompassing power and energy. We are using the energy of the sun for guidance and vitality.

▦ A sunny day suggests happiness. To be drawn to the sun indicates we are looking for enlightenment. In turning towards the sun, the sunflower could be said to be a symbol of obsession, but also of worship. With its many seeds it also represents fertility.

⊞ There was an ancient belief that the sun was masculine and the moon feminine. The image of the sun and the moon appearing together in a dream follows that belief and suggests integration of masculine and feminine energies.

You might also like to consult the entry for Planets.

SUNGLASSES – *see* GOGGLES

SURGERY

⚜ Spiritually we may feel that we have too much to deal with or that something needs altering.

♥ Surgery is a necessary, though unpleasant intrusion into our lives. Dreaming of having surgery performed on us shows we need to accustom ourselves to changes that may initially be difficult, but ultimately are healing and to our benefit.

⊞ To find ourselves in a doctors' surgery in dreams would indicate that we should be considering our health and health matters. Performing surgery indicates that we need to 'cut out' contamination or a 'sick' part of our personality.

Also consult the entry for Operation.

SWAMP

⚜ A swamp can symbolize the vast amount of spiritual knowledge that there is to be taken in. A swamp is so-called primordial material, out of which everything emerges; at this stage we have no idea what our potential is.

♥ Emotionally, when a swamp appears we are putting ourselves in touch with very basic feelings and emotions. The sheer vastness may leave us feeling utterly hopeless and out of our depth, but with perseverance we can pull ourselves through and have a much clearer outlook.

⊞ To be swamped is to be overwhelmed by a feeling or emotion. A swamp in a dream symbolizes feelings that can undermine our confidence and wellbeing. To be swamping someone else in a dream may suggest that we are being too needy.

You might also like to consult the entries for Marsh and Mud.

SWAN – *see* BIRDS

SWASTIKA – *see* SHAPES/PATTERNS

SWEEPING

⚜ We have attained much spiritual knowledge on which we are now reflecting and need to consider all options and how to make best use of them.

❀ Sweeping is a traditional image that symbolizes good management and clearing of our environment. In psychological terms it suggests an attention to detail and correctness, as much as to cleanliness. In modern-day technological symbolism it could suggest searching for viruses.

▦ To dream of sweeping suggests being able to clear away outmoded attitudes and emotions. To be sweeping up suggests putting things in order. There may be certain elements of confusion, which we can take time to clear away.

You might also like to consult the entries for Broom/Brush and Clean/Clear.

SWEETS – *see* **FOOD**

SWIMMING

❀ Swimming is an archetypal dream image. It suggests that spiritual energy is being used as we are moving towards a particular goal. It is said in dreams to symbolize the womb experience.

❀ To dream of being a good swimmer shows the ability to be able to handle emotional situations well, whereas being a poor swimmer in a dream could indicate the need to learn how to handle our emotions in a more positive way. Swimming in water will always be symbolic of the emotions, whereas swimming through the air connects with intellectual ability.

▦ Dreaming of swimming has much the same symbolism as immersion. To be swimming upstream in a dream would indicate we are going against our own nature. Swimming fish can have the same symbolism as sperm and, therefore, can indicate the desire for a child. Swimming in clear water indicates being cleansed, whereas dark water could symbolize the possibility of depression.

Consult the entries for Drowning and Water for clarification.

SWINE – *see* **PIG IN ANIMALS**

SWORD

❀ Spiritually the sword signifies the power of authority and protection. In dreams, to be given a sword signifies that we have the protection of the sacred. We are able to make our own decisions.

❀ The sword symbolizes justice and courage as well as strength. For the image of a sword to appear in a dream indicates there is an element of the warrior in us, and that we are prepared to fight for our beliefs.

▦ The sword in dreams invariably suggests a weapon of power. We may have the ability to create power and use energy properly through our beliefs. A ceremonial sword will confer status.

Also consult the entries for Knight, Warrior and Weapon.

SYMBOLS – *see* INTRODUCTION

SYNAGOGUE – *see* RELIGIOUS BUILDINGS IN BUILDINGS AS WELL AS
SPIRITUAL IMAGERY IN THE INTRODUCTION

SYRINGE

✹ Penetrative awareness, as symbolized by the syringe, can suggest a
particular way of approaching our own spiritual selves.

♥ Dreaming of a syringe can indicate that we need to be conscious of the
way we influence other people. We can be very specific and hit the right spot,
or we can have a more 'scatter gun' approach. Those who use syringes
regularly may well dream of contamination or associated problems.

▦ In dreams the syringe suggests an awareness of the influence that other
people can have over us. It will depend on whether the syringe is being used
to take something out or put something in as to the particular significance.
A garden syringe (as in a fly spray) in dreams can suggest either masculine
energy or decontamination.

*Consult the entries for Contamination, Injection and Needle for
further information.*

TABERNACLE – *see* **SPIRITUAL IMAGERY IN THE INTRODUCTION**

TABLE

🔅 A table can represent spiritual judgement and legislation. As a dividing line between those with authority and those without, it signifies a barrier to be crossed.

💛 To dream of dealing with a table or list of objects, or perhaps actions, instils a sense of order in our lives. It represents our ability to create order out of chaos. In sitting around a table if rectangular the top end will suggest higher status than the bottom end.

🔲 A table being a focus for meeting, whether socially or professionally, is usually recognized in dreams as a symbol of decision making. There can be an element of ritual associated with the image of a table. As a place for a family rendezvous, we may consider meals eaten around a table to be an important aspect of family life. In business and professional terms, the boardroom table can also introduce an element of ritual around it such as hierarchy of position.

You might also like to consult the entries for Altar, Furniture/Furnishings, Rite/ Ritual and Round Table.

TABLET

🔅 We all have access to esoteric and hidden knowledge. This can be represented in dreams by the Tablets of Moses. Taking tablets in dreams may suggest that spiritual or alternative methods of healing may be appropriate in a given situation.

💛 In magical terms, a tablet presupposes knowledge greater than our own and, therefore, represents an element of trust. We trust our destiny to someone else. Taking a pill in a dream may alert us to our ability to heal ourselves. We may also be conscious that we need to be careful over what we choose to include in our lives.

🔲 Taking medicine in the form of tablets signifies we recognize our need to be healthy and suggests doing something to make ourselves feel better. We need to 'heal' something that is wrong. In dreams, taking such a course of action will signify putting ourselves through an experience we need in order to improve our performance or potential. If we are giving tablets to someone else we may be aware that their needs are not being satisfied.

You might also like to consult the entry for Medication/Medicine.

TACKLE – *see* **SPORT**

TADPOLE

✿ Spiritually, the tadpole represents the Germ of Life. Dreaming of tadpoles links to an awareness of the simplicity of life.

♡ A tadpole is the beginning of an idea, an opportunity, something that has not yet had time to grow. We are aware that there is growth, but either we, or someone else, has not yet reached full maturity of thought.

▦ To dream of many tadpoles can suggest a number of business opportunities, some of which will come to fruition and some which will not. If the tadpoles are already growing legs we should look at which options in waking life have the best chance of survival.

⊞ In a woman's dream tadpoles may represent either her wish, or her ability, to become pregnant. In a man's dream tadpoles are more likely to symbolize his virility.

TAIL

✿ The tail symbolizes the completion of a spiritual action, the finishing touches. It brings our involvement to an end.

♡ The tail is necessary to the animal for balance, and thus in dreams can be recognized as a means of adjustment in difficult circumstances.

▦ To dream of a tail can signify some residue from the past, something we still carry with us. Just as our tailbone (coccyx) can be vulnerable to injury, so we also can be affected by the past.

⊞ In a man's dream the tail can indicate sexual excitement, or possibly, by association, the penis. For a woman it will initially suggest her own basic energy, and perhaps later on her way of linking with her own latent powers. *For an additional interpretation consult the entry for Follow/Follower.*

TALISMAN – *see* **SPIRITUAL IMAGERY IN THE INTRODUCTION**

TALKING

✿ Talking in dreams signifies spiritual communication, whether that is the passing on of spiritual knowledge or communication from spiritual entities.

♡ We are perhaps afraid of not being listened to properly in waking life and this anxiety can express itself through hearing someone else talking in dreams. It is not necessarily the words that are important, more the sense of what is being said. If we cannot hear them properly we are perhaps not ready consciously to accept the information.

▦ To be conscious of people talking in a dream gives a sense of being in contact with our own ability to communicate. We are able to express clearly what we feel and think, whereas in waking life we may not feel confident. Stopping people from talking means we wish some information to be kept hidden. Translating what is being said suggests we view ourselves as an intermediary, or in some cases the medium for understanding.

You might also like to consult the entry for Hear/Hearing.

TALL – *see* **SIZE**

TAMBOURINE – *see* **MUSIC/RHYTHM AND MUSICAL INSTRUMENTS**

TAME

⚜ Spiritual energy is quite powerful and as part of our discipline we must learn self-control, to tame it.

◈ To find that something is extremely tame – in the sense of being dull and boring – in dreams suggests that we should reconsider the way we live our lives. We should perhaps do more to ensure that we are interested and stimulated.

▦ To dream of taming an animal indicates our ability to control or develop a relationship with the animal aspect of ourselves. The animal may be of note, the lion representing courage for instance. To dream of being tamed, as though we ourselves were the animal, signifies the need for restraint in our lives.

Consult the entries for Animals and Wild for extra information.

TANGLED

⚜ Cutting through a tangle of trees or undergrowth in a dream is part of the Hero's Journey towards spiritual autonomy. He must work hard to overcome chaos in order to succeed.

◈ When something like hair is tangled, we need to be aware that our self-image or projection is coming across to other people as distorted, and not how we wish them to see us.

▦ Sometimes when we are confused in everyday life, we may dream of an object being entangled with something else. Often the way that we untangle the object indicates action we should take in waking moments. We can cut straight through quickly or patiently work at it.

You might like to consult the entries for Chaos, Hero/Heroine, Knot, String and Rope.

TANK

⚜ There are times when we need to be something of a 'Spiritual Warrior' and yet have our defences in place. A tank, as both a defensive and defended vehicle, would be likely to appear at this time in our dreams.

◈ Often in dreams we become aware of our need to overcome objections and difficulties. Sometimes the only form of expression we have is to ride roughshod over those objections. The image of a war tank helps to highlight our ability to do this without ourselves being hurt.

🔲 Dreaming of a water tank is putting ourselves in touch with our inner feelings and emotions. Dreaming of a military tank connects us with our own need to defend ourselves, but to be aggressive at the same time. Such a dream would indicate that we are feeling threatened in some way.

You might also like to consult the entries for Armed Forces, Conflict, War and Water.

TAO – *see* **SPIRITUAL IMAGERY IN THE INTRODUCTION**

TAP

🔆 A tap is a means of controlling the flow of Spiritual energy. As visualization before sleep it can be a way of controlling imagery in dreams.

🔯 Water is considered to be a symbol of emotion, so a tap is representative of our ability to use or misuse emotion in some way. To be able to turn emotion on and off at will is indicative of great self-control. A dripping tap would indicate a difficulty in controlling emotions.

🔲 The tap is an image of being able to make available universal resources. To dream of not being able to turn a tap either on or off highlights our ability – or inability – to control those things we consider to be rightfully ours. To be tapping something suggests that we are trying to free up our energies. Tap dancing highlights a rhythmic approach to life.

Consult the entries for Dance/Dancing, Emotions and Water for additional information.

TAPE

🔆 The image of a tape – particularly the slightly old-fashioned recording tape – is spiritually a way of recording and measuring life's processes. This ties in with the idea of the Akashic records – when everything that is, was or ever shall be is noted.

🔯 Masking or parcel tape could be considered to be restraining – to create boundaries – within which movement becomes difficult. In dreams we become aware of the limitation we impose on ourselves in everyday life.

🔲 Dreaming of a measuring tape indicates our need to 'measure' our lives in some way. Perhaps we may need to consider how we communicate with, or 'measure up' to, other people's expectations. Equally, if we are doing the measuring we may be trying to create order in our lives.

You might also like to consult the entries for Communication, Measure and Record/ Records/Recording.

TAPESTRY – *see* **THREAD AND WEAVING**

TAR

🔆 The symbolism of tar in a spiritual sense, because it is black and viscous, would suggest some kind of evil or negativity. Dreaming of tar on the road would suggest the potential to be trapped by such difficulties as we progress.

🍃 Dreaming of tar on a beach might suggest that we had allowed our emotions to become contaminated in some way. As tar was a basis for road-making and comes from oil it is now of concern to conservationists and may surface in dreams as a pollutant.

▦ To be mending a road might signify that we can be repairing wear and tear in our everyday lives. To be tarring a fence could mean we must protect ourselves and also to reinforce our personal boundaries.

Consulting the entries for Beach and Fence as well as the information on Road in Journey will enhance your understanding.

TARGET

✦ Spiritually a target with its concentric circles can symbolize the total Self. The soul is in the middle, surrounded by spirit, mind, body and finally environment. To be shooting at a bull's-eye could be interpreted as a search for perfection.

🍃 Most of us need some kind of motivation in life, and a target as a symbol of our intellectual aspirations may not make much sense until we study the context of the dream. Aiming at a target in dreams would suggest we have a particular goal in mind. To be aiming at a person could suggest 'targeting' them on an emotional level for our own gratification.

▦ In a work sense in dreams a sales or performance target might suggest our goals are imposed on us by others. On a more personal note, we will set our own targets – for instance health or education goals. If we were setting someone else a target in dreams, we would need to understand that the other person in the dream is a reflection of part of ourselves.

You might also like to consult the entries for Arrow, Goal and Shot/Shooting.

TASTE

✦ As we become more sensitive and aware, our tastes become more refined. As we progress spiritually we may find the crass and the gross harder to deal with.

🍃 In waking life we usually know what we like and what our personal standards are. In dreams those standards may be distorted in order to highlight a change. For instance, to discover that we like a colour in a dream that would not normally be appreciated in real life could suggest that we need to study the new colour more fully in order to discover what it has to offer.

▦ When something is not to our taste in a dream, it does not conform to our ideals and standards. To be aware of a bad taste in dreams suggests that whatever is signified by what we are eating or experiencing does not nourish us. If we find something a bit tasty we are aware of fine living. To recognize that our surroundings are in good taste suggests an appreciation of beautiful things.

Consult the entries for Colour and Food for further information.

TATTOO

🔆 Polynesian peoples believe that a person's *mana*, their spiritual power or life force, is displayed through their tattoo. In spiritual terms a tattoo can suggest a group identity, belonging to a tribe or cult. It will be on a more intimate level than wearing a badge.

💛 A tattoo in dreams can also signify something that has left an indelible impression. This could be great hurt, but could also be a good memory. Sometimes, the image that is tattooed is worth interpreting if it can be seen clearly. The colour and design can be important and, while fashions vary, the symbolism is evident.

📟 On a physical level, a tattoo will stand for an aspect of our individuality. We wish to be seen as different. To be having a tattoo done in dreams suggests that we are prepared to suffer for this. To be having a tattoo removed indicates that we have rejected some former belief or credo.

🔧 As both men and women will now have tattoos done, the symbolism of any particular dream tattoo will be easily interpreted. The position of the tattoo and its spiritual symbolism – its connection with a system of belief – may give us insights.

You might also like to consult the entries for Badge/Brooch, Colours and Picture as well as the information on Symbols in the Introduction.

TAU CROSS – *see* SPIRITUAL IMAGERY IN THE INTRODUCTION

TAX

🔆 Spiritually, any tax levied in a dream would indicate our attitude towards working for the greater, or communal, good. We need to take some responsibility for the universe we live in.

💛 In real terms, a tax represents the extra amount of effort necessary to enable us to belong to society. Thus, dreaming of car tax would indicate that greater effort is needed to move forward. To be paying income tax suggests that we may feel we owe a debt to society. To be paying council tax may suggest that we feel we have to pay for the 'space' in which we exist. Refusing to pay any taxes suggests an unwillingness to conform.

📟 In everyday life, a tax represents a sum of money exacted from us in return for the right to live a certain lifestyle. In dreams, therefore, having to pay a tax suggests some kind of a penalty for living the way we choose.

Consult the entry for Money or further clarification.

TAXI

✲ A taxi can represent spiritual knowledge, coupled with practical know-how. This is an important attribute in spiritual and personal development.

◈ A taxi is a public vehicle in the sense that it is usually driven by someone unknown to us. We therefore have to trust the driver's awareness and knowledge. In dreams, therefore, a taxi can suggest having the need to reach a destination without knowing how we will do so.

▣ In a dream, calling a taxi signifies recognizing the need to progress – to get somewhere. We cannot be successful without help, for which though there may be a price, it is worth paying.

Also consult the entry for Car as well as the information on Destination in Journey and Car in Transport for further clarification.

TEA

✲ Tea as a symbol suggests spiritual refreshment – based on a reverence for nature and the creation of a perfect moment in time.

◈ The Japanese tea ceremony suggests a unique way of caring for and nurturing someone – as does afternoon tea, each having their own rituals associated with them. Dreaming of teacups in particular links with our need to know the future (reading tea leaves). A tea break in a work environment suggests a need for rest and relaxation from concentration.

▣ It will depend on whether the dream is about tea as a commercial commodity, or a social occasion. On a practical level, tea as a commodity represents a unit of exchange, whereas the social occasion – and the ceremonies associated with this – suggests inter-communication and the gift of our time.

You might also like to consult the entries for Ceremony and Rite/Ritual.

TEACHER

✲ A spiritual teacher usually appears either in dreams or in person when the individual is ready to progress. There is a saying in the Hindu religion, 'When the *chela* (pupil) is ready, the teacher will come.' Often that teacher will not appear as a Wise Old Man or Woman, but as a person appropriate to the level of our understanding.

◈ When we are looking for guidance, the Animus/Anima can present itself in dreams as a teacher. Often the figure will be that of a headmaster or headmistress (someone who 'knows better'). If we dream of ourselves as a teacher we will need to look at what information we have that should be passed on.

▣ For many people, a teacher is the first figure of authority they meet outside the family. That person has a profound effect on the child and the teacher is often dreamt about in later years. Teachers can also generate conflict if their expressed views are very different to those learnt by the child at home. This may be something that has to be resolved through dreams in later years.

Consult the entries for Education, School and Authority Figures in People, as well as the information on Animus, Anima and Wise Old Man in Archetypes in the Introduction.

TEAM – *see* GAMES AND GROUP

TEAR/TEARS/TORN

✴ Tears can represent hurt or compassion, and it is often this latter meaning that applies spiritually. Experiencing compassion in a dream can make us more aware of the necessity for it in waking life.

♥ To dream of being in tears and then to wake up and discover that we are actually crying, suggests that some hurt or trauma has come sufficiently close to the surface to enable us to deal with it on a conscious level. To interpret tearing something up in dreams will depend on whether the action is destructive or one of division in order to share. If the article is already torn, then there is an aspect of our lives that is less than perfect and has been damaged in some way.

▣ Tears in dreams can indicate an emotional release and a cleansing. If we are crying we may not feel we are able to give way to emotion in everyday life, but can do so in the safe scenario of a dream. If we dream of someone we know in tears we perhaps need to look at our own conduct to see if it is appropriate. If we do not know them then we have offended against our own code of behaviour.

Consult the entries for Emotions and Weeping for further information.

TEASE – *see* TORTURE/TORMENT/TEASE

TEETH – *see* BODY

TELEGRAM – *see* COMMUNICATION, EMAIL AND LETTER

TELEPHONE

✴ Because communication via the telephone usually means that we are not able to see the recipient, using the telephone in a dream can signify communication with Spirit or with Guardian Angels.

♥ When we are aware of the telephone number we are ringing, it may be the numbers that are important. We also may be aware of the need to contact a specific person who we can help, or who can help us. If we are searching for a telephone number we are having difficulty in co-ordinating our thoughts about our future actions. Using the telephone suggests a direct one-to-one relationship. The type of phone will also have relevance; an old-fashioned one suggests ancient ideas or concepts. A modern up-to-date digital or mobile phone indicates we are easily able to make ourselves understood in various situations.

🔳 Using a telephone in a dream suggests the ability to make contact with other people and to impart information we feel they may need. This could actually be communicating with someone in our ordinary everyday lives, or establishing contact with a part of ourselves. Being contacted by telephone in dreams suggests there is information available to us at some level of awareness that we do not yet consciously know.

You might also like to consult the entries for Angel, Communication and Numbers for further information.

TELESCOPE

🔅 Interestingly enough, a telescope in spiritual terms can signify the art of clairvoyance – the ability to perceive the future from an immediate perspective.

💟 Using a telescope in a dream may mean that we should look at things with both a long- and short-term view. Without taking account of a long-term view, we may not be able to succeed in the short term. Conversely, by looking at the long-term view, we may be given information which will help us to 'navigate' our lives in the here and now.

🔳 Using a telescope in a dream suggests taking a closer look at something. A telescope enhances our view and makes it bigger and wider. We do need to make sure, however, that we are not taking a one-sided view of things.

You might like to consult the entry for Lens.

TELEVISION

🔅 There are some aspects of spiritual learning that require an element of practicality about them. Often this will appear in dreams as a medium such as television. It is as though the dreaming mind requires a recognizable intermediary in order to accept the information.

💟 Television, with its many repeats and 'reality' programmes, gives a rich source of dream images, from celebrities to fantasy scenarios. Many such images can, with a little thought, be identified as archetypal; football stars, for instance, representing both the Hero and the Tramp as freedom lover.

🔳 Dream images connected with television drama series and 'soaps' where we are able to follow a story are much to do with our ability to recognize archetypes that we can relate to, or situations that have resonance with us in our work or personal life.

Consult the entries for Celebrity, Fame, Famous People and Media as well as the information on Archetypes in the Introduction for further information.

TEMPLE

🔆 Both as a sanctuary for human beings and as a place where the Divine resides, a temple reflects the beauty of Heaven. It is a microcosm (small picture) of what is, after all, infinite.

💗 Psychologically, wherever there is a temple there is a sense of awe associated with creativity. Perhaps the biggest significance in dreams is the fact that it takes many to build one temple. This links with our awareness of the many facets of our personality that go to make a coherent whole.

🔲 Often in dreams a temple can signify our own body. It is something to be treated with reverence and care. It has the same significance as a church since it is an object built to honour and pay respect to a god or gods.

Also consult the information for Religious Buildings in Buildings and in Spiritual Imagery in the Introduction.

TEMPT/TEMPTATION

🔆 Temptation is one of the biggest spiritual barriers we must overcome. Often it is a conflict between the Self and the Ego.

💗 Intellectually, when presented with options of action we may tend to go for a result that gives short-term rather than long-term satisfaction. The idea of giving in to temptation suggests that it is stronger or more powerful than we are. Often dreams can show us the course of action we should be taking. If we are being the tempter we need to be very sure of our own motives in waking life.

🔲 Temptation is a conflict between two different drives. For instance, in dreams we may experience a conflict between the need to go out into the world and the need to stay safe at home. Temptation is yielding to that which is the easiest, and not necessarily best, course of action.

Consult the entry for Siren and also the information on Ego, Self and Siren in Archetypes in the Introduction for further information.

TENANT

🔆 Dreaming of having a tenant would link with the idea that within us we all have many aspects of personality that must be synthesized into a spiritually complete being. Evicting a tenant might signify the need to get rid of a belief or aspect that we cannot work with.

💗 If we follow up the idea of a tenant being someone with whom we have a commercial relationship, then we will have some insights into how we handle such transactions. As more people invest in buy-to-let property to give themselves security, a tenant in dreams will simply represent a means to an end.

▣ To dream of being a tenant suggests that at some level we do not want to take responsibility for the way we choose to live. We do not want to be burdened by having full responsibility for our living space. To have a tenant signifies that we find it expedient to have someone be involved in what we consider to be our 'space'. This may also be the type of dream that occurs as we are preparing to become involved in a full-time relationship.

⊟ If the dreamer is a man and the tenant a woman then the tenant is likely to represent his Anima. If the situation is reversed then the tenant will epitomize her Animus.

You might also like to consult the entries for Home and Rent as well as the information on Anima and Animus in Archetypes in the Introduction.

TENT

✵ The biblical and nomadic image of being able to pack up one's tent and steal away is the spiritual meaning here. We are not tied to any one place, but can move to where we need to be at short notice, thus satisfying the requirements of the Wanderer and the ascetic.

◐ We perhaps need to get away from everyday responsibilities for a time, and rediscover our relationship with the forces of Nature. There is benefit to be gained by being self-sufficient and not dependent on anyone.

▣ A tent in a dream would suggest that we feel we are on the move, and not able to settle down at this time and put down roots. Anywhere we settle is only going to be temporary. This might be so in a work situation as much as a personal.

You might also like to consult the entries for Ascetic and Wanderer/Wandering as well as the information for Temporary Buildings in Buildings and Tramp in Archetypes in the Introduction.

TENSE/TENSION – *see* ANXIETY DREAMS IN THE INTRODUCTION

TERROR/TERRORIST

✵ Spiritual terror could be identified as extreme fear of perceived evil. The fanaticism of a terrorist could be seen to be an effort to handle this extreme fear. This exaggerated reaction leads to drastic action and the endurance of the inevitable results.

◐ Terror in a dream is often the result of unresolved fears and doubts. It is only by experiencing such a profoundly disturbing emotion that are we likely to make an attempt to confront those fears. If someone else is terrified in our dream we are in a position to do something about it, and need to work out what course of action should be taken. The appearance of a terrorist is a negative manifestation of our predisposition to be intensely emotional.

▣ Fear or terror dreams can be one of the triggers towards a deeper understanding of oneself. If we know we are fearful we can do something about it. Terror in dreams is more difficult to handle since in that state we will not know what the cause is and may well be paralysed by the feeling itself. When we are able to identify what prompts it in waking life, we can again take action to disperse it.

Also consult the entries for Fanatic, Immobility, Paralysis and War as well as the information on Terror Dreams in the Introduction.

TESTS

✷ A spiritual test is one that is created from the circumstances around us, perhaps to test our resolve. Having to justify a course of action in dreams might be one such test.

♡ Testing something in a dream suggests that there has been some form of standard set, to which we feel we must adhere. This need not mean that we are setting ourselves against others, simply that we have resolved to maintain a certain standard.

▣ Dreaming of tests of any sort can indicate some form of self-assessment. Medical tests may be alerting us to the need to watch our health. A driving test would suggest a test of confidence or ability, whereas a written test would signify a test of knowledge.

You might also like to consult the entry for Exam/Being Examined.

TEXT

✷ A spiritual text is an encouraging message to enable us to progress. For a text such as this to appear in a dream would signify the need for encouragement and perhaps wisdom. An elaborately illustrated text or manuscript gives us access to ancient knowledge and belief.

♡ Text from a book or play indicates the need for us to carry out instructions in a particular way in order to achieve success. A manual of instruction in dreams suggests we need to take particular care over our actions.

▣ A text is taken to mean a collection of words that have a certain specific meaning. As mobile phone texting catches on, such an image suggests short pithy communication.

Consult the entries for Book, Communication, Telephone and Writing for extra information.

THAW

✷ A spiritual thaw would suggest the ability to come to terms with old barriers and constraints and to become warm, loving and less rigid in our judgements.

❤ Psychologically we have the ability to 'warm up' a situation, and to melt coldness away. If we are aware of coldness within ourselves, on an emotional level we need to discover what the problem is or was, and why we have reacted as we did.

▣ In dreams, to be conscious of a thaw is to note a change in our own emotional responses. We no longer have a need to be as emotionally distanced as previously.

You might also like to consult the entries for Emotions, Ice/Iceberg/Icicles and Water.

THEATRE

✺ Spiritually the idea of a theatre in a dream highlights the idea of the microcosm within the macrocosm – the small within a larger framework. A stage is a representation of our own life play. We are able to observe and be objective about what is going on. By externalizing the 'play' into a particular framework such as a rehearsal we can manipulate our lives.

❤ The theatre is a scenario that has meaning for many. Because it is a social venue, it has relevance in people's relationships with one another. To be in the spotlight, for instance, might signify our need to be noticed. To be up in 'the gods' might suggest that we need to take a long-term view of a situation. To be on stage in a dream is to be making ourselves visible.

▣ In dreams about the theatre it will depend which part of the theatre is highlighted: if the stage, then a current aspect of our lives being drawn to our attention. If it is the auditorium, then our ability to listen and understand the relevance is what is significant. An open-air stage suggests communication with the masses rather than a selected audience. A moving stage signifies the need to keep moving, even while performing a role. The play we create in our dreams as an aspect of our lives is particularly relevant. If we are not involved in the action, it indicates we are able to stand back and take an objective viewpoint. If we are very involved it will be from an emotional perspective.

You might also like to consult the entries for Actor and Audience.

THEFT – see THIEF AND STEALING

THERAPIST – see ANALYST

THIEF

✺ A spiritual thief is that part of us that has no respect for our or others' beliefs.

❤ When a thief appears in dreams, we are aware of part of our personality that can waste our own time and energy on meaningless activity. It literally steals from us.

🔲 Dreaming of a thief links with our fear of losing things, or of having them taken away from us. We may be afraid of losing love or possessions.

Also consult the entry for Stealing.

THIGH – *see* LIMBS IN BODY

THIN – *see* SIZE

THIRD EYE – *see* SPIRITUAL IMAGERY IN THE INTRODUCTION

THIRST

🔆 Thirst in a dream is symbolic of our quest for spiritual knowledge and enlightenment. It may well be an unquenchable one.

♡ To satisfy a thirst indicates we are capable of satisfying our own desires. By being prepared to take in what we need, we are able to experience life in the best way possible. If we are thirsty in a dream we need to look very carefully at either what we are being denied, or what we are denying ourselves, in waking life.

🔲 Dreaming of being thirsty suggests we have an unsatisfied inner need; we may be emotionally at a low ebb and need something to give us a boost. Anything that gives us emotional satisfaction – whether short- or long-term – would suffice.

Consulting the entries for Drink, Emotions, Quest and Water will provide further information.

THISTLE

🔆 The thistle can represent our spiritual defiance in the face of physical adversity and difficult conditions. This is one of the reasons why it became the emblem of Scotland. Magically it is a fire herb and, therefore, represents courage.

♡ The thistle has a meaning of rebelliousness and spite, but also of affording protection. When dreaming of a thistle we may be being made aware of those qualities, either in people around us or in ourselves. The colour of the thistles may also be important.

🔲 To be conscious of thistles in a dream is to be aware of some discomfort in waking life. A field of thistles would suggest a difficult road ahead. A single thistle would indicate minor difficulties.

You might also like to consult the entries for Colour, Plants and Weeds.

THORN

🔆 The thorn may signify that we are dedicating ourselves to a difficult element of our spiritual quest – we are suffering for our beliefs.

♡ The thorn stands for physical suffering in dreams. In matters of health, it may indicate a vulnerability to infection.

To dream of being pierced by a thorn or splinter signifies that a minor difficulty has got through our defences. If the thorn draws blood, we need to look at what is happening in our lives that could make us vulnerable.

In a woman's dream a thorn, being penetrative, could represent the sexual act, or rather fear of intercourse. For a man thorns may represent sacrifice of some sort.

Consult the entries for Crown, Sacrifices and Weeds for further information.

THREAD

Thread is a vivid image in dreams and in spiritual work. We have the thread of life spun for us by the Fates who determine the life and death of all mortal beings; Klotho spins the thread; her sister Lachesis determines the length of it and Atropos cuts the thread when the proper time has come for death. The various threads of our spirituality are being interwoven into the Tapestry of Life.

To be aware of thread is to be aware of the way our lives are going. A tangled thread suggests a difficulty that needs unravelling. A spool of thread suggests an ordered existence; the colour of the thread is also important. The image of tapestry or weaving suggests a degree of competence and creativity. The relevance of the 'picture' we produce may well represent emotional concerns.

Thread in dreams represents a line of thought or enquiry and, in today's way of communicating, a blog. In terms of our ordinary everyday lives we perhaps need to remain focused on our goals. Threading a needle has an obvious sexual reference. It can also, because of the perceived difficulty in threading a needle, suggest incompetence in ways other than sexual, such as hitting work targets.

In a woman's dream a basket full of spools suggests the various aspects of her personality. This is because of its association with the Archetypal feminine. For a man, such an image may represent his attitude to the complexity of the feminine.

You might also like to consult the entries for Colour, Needle, Sew, Tangled and Weaving.

THREAT/THREATEN

A spiritual threat is one that forces us to reassess our beliefs. Most often it will contain options of action that lead to a degree of inevitability either way. Once on that particular path we have no choice but to continue. In dreams the image of a divided path or road will often occur at this time, or of going up or down.

◈ To feel threatened in dreams approaches anxiety and nightmare. Taking us out of our comfort zone whether emotionally or otherwise results in fear and distress, which we can suppress in waking life but often not in dreams. If we ourselves are threatening someone in dreams we perhaps need to seek out the source of our own negative emotions and what it is we feel so strongly about.

▦ A threat to our security or way of life can translate itself in dreams to an image of a threatening situation or environment. The Shadow – that part of us which contains a great deal of negativity – can manifest in dreams literally as a dark shadow and at that point needs to be confronted either through working with the dream or by careful analysis.

⊞ In both men's and women's dreams the opposite gender can pose a threat. Thus a man might feel threatened by the image of a vengeful goddess (an aspect of the Anima) and a woman by an overbearing Ogre (an aspect of the Animus).

You might also like to consult the entry for Path as well as the information on Archetypes, Anxiety Dreams and Nightmares in the Introduction.

THRESHOLD

✦ We may be standing on the threshold of a new spiritual awareness. We need to be particularly alert as to what changes are occurring. At this time we are often aware of a personal guiding force known as the Guardian of the Threshold. The Guardian of the Threshold to the Underworld (a different entity) is often seen in dreams as a dog.

◈ When we are about to take on new responsibilities, we can dream of standing on a threshold. We may be moving into a new life, or perhaps a new way of living. The threshold experience is a particularly strong one in Masonic imagery and Initiation rites and surfaces in dreams when we are emotionally ready for such a ceremony. Even in Parliament, permission must be asked to cross the threshold.

▦ Crossing the threshold in dreams indicates new experiences. To be lifted across a threshold may suggest marriage, or in this day and age, a new relationship.

Consult the entries for Ceremony, Edge, Freemason, Initiation and Rite/Ritual for further information.

THROAT – *see* BODY

THRONE

✦ Spiritually we could be at a point where knowledge and understanding are finally within our grasp at last. A throne, as a symbol of power, epitomizes this.

❤ A throne is a seat of authority or power. In dreams it can represent our ability to belong to groups, or even to society; we may need to take the lead in a project or scheme. The throne usually suggests that we have attained an element of control on all levels of existence, both spiritually and physically.

▦ When we dream of sitting on a throne, we are acknowledging our right to take authority. When the throne is empty, we are not prepared to accept the responsibility for who we are. It may be that we are conscious of a lack of parenting. When someone else is on the throne, we may have passed over authority to others.

You might like to consult the entry for Crown as well as the information on King and Queen in People.

THUMB – *see* BODY

THUNDER/THUNDERBOLTS

☀ Spiritually, the rumblings of thunder can demonstrate deep anger, or in extreme cases Divine anger. This originates from the ancient belief in the Thunder Gods.

❤ Thunder has always been a symbol of great power and energy. In conjunction with lightning, it was seen as a tool of the gods. It could bring doom and disaster, but also was cleansing and has this significance in dreams.

▦ Hearing thunder in a dream can give a warning for the potential of an emotional outburst. We may be building up energy that eventually must reverberate. Hearing thunder in the distance signifies that there is still time to gain control of a potentially difficult situation.

Also consult the entries for God/Gods, Lightning, Storm and Weather for further information.

TIARA – *see* CROWN AND DIADEM

TICKET

☀ Spiritually, a dream of a ticket will symbolize our recognition that all knowledge must be somehow 'paid for' and that we have a right to that knowledge.

❤ One interpretation of a ticket – in the form of a certificate or voucher – is that of us requiring recognition of the effort we have put in. To dream of receiving such a ticket indicates it is we who are being recompensed. A winning lottery ticket would have the same significance.

▦ Generally, a ticket suggests that there is a price to pay for something. A bus ticket would indicate that there is a price for moving forward, as might a train ticket. A ticket to a theatre or cinema may suggest we need to take a back seat and be objective over a part of our lives. Tickets to a football or rugby match might mean that we will have to pay for some area of conflict in our lives.

You might also like to consult the entries for Gambling, Lottery and Win/Winning.

TIDE

🌞 Spiritually, it may well be a simple image, such as the tide turning, which indicates that we are finding our way and can progress on our spiritual journey with confidence.

♥ In waking life there are two times in the year when there are very high tides – the spring and the autumn. Thus, in dreams, an exceptionally high tide might signify those times or that our emotions are running at a particularly high level. A moon over a moving tide would, at a certain stage of development, suggest the powers of the feminine.

▦ Dreaming of a tide is attempting to go with the ebb and flow of life or, rather more specifically, with the emotions. As a tide also removes debris, the symbolism of cleansing is relevant. A high tide may symbolize high energy, whereas a low tide would suggest a drain on our abilities or energy.

Consult the entries for Autumn, Emotions, Moon, Spring and Seasons as well as the information for Seas in the Water entry.

TIDY – *see* ORDER

TIE – *see* BONDS, CHAINS AND HALTER

TIGER – *see* ANIMALS

TILL

🌞 A till is symbolic of the resources we have accumulated spiritually, not necessarily financially. They are being stored up until such times as we need them.

♥ When we put money in a till, it is being put there for safe-keeping and will allow us to quantify how much we have accumulated. Nowadays this accumulation will be deposited with a bank for safe-keeping. This is where the more practical and psychological meanings coincide. We need to save or conserve what we have – both energy and resources – to get best benefit. To be withdrawing money from a cashpoint in a dream signifies our need to make use of those resources.

▦ There are two meanings of 'till'. One is to till or tend the ground, and while that is a less potent image nowadays, the image still appears in dreams in the sense of cultivating opportunities. The other meaning is as a safe, temporary repository for money. It is this symbolism of a commercial transaction which is the one most understood. In dreams, a broken cash register would symbolize the breakdown of our ability to accumulate resources and also possibly signify debt.

You might like to consult the entries for Debt, Garden and Money for further information.

TIMBER – *see* **WOOD**

TIME

🌑 In a spiritual sense time has no relevance, being a man made construct. The Realization of Age and Time, being a valid concept, is signified by a clock. The image of Father Time as an old man signifies changes brought about by the passage of time.

💚 For time to be significant in a dream there is usually the necessity to measure it in some way, or to use a period of time as a measurement. Usually we are only aware of the passage of time – often symbolized by a clock or watch – or that a particular time is meaningful in the dream, it is part of the dream scenario. The time in the dream may symbolize a particular period in our life as follows:

The daylight hours will thus suggest our conscious waking life. Where **several days (or other long periods)** appear to have passed we are conscious that some other activity, which is not particularly relevant to us, has been going on in the dream.

If we think of our lives as being a day long, the hours of the day will refer to a specific time in our lives. Thus, **afternoon** is a time of life when we can put our experience to good use; **evening** shows a more relaxed time; **mid-day** indicates we are fully conscious and aware of our activities. **In the morning** the first part of our life or our early experience is being highlighted, whereas **night** may be a period of depression or secrecy. We may be introspective or simply at rest. **Twilight** can indicate a period of uncertainty and possible ambivalence insofar as our direction in life is concerned.

🔲 Watching the clock indicates the necessity to make time work for us. The clock hands or digital numbers in a dream may be indicating those numbers that are important to us. To be early for an appointment in a dream suggests having to wait for something to happen before we can carry on our lives. Being late shows our lack of attention to detail or the feeling that time is running out. *Consult the entries for Calendar, Dawn/Day And Night, Evening, Night and Numbers for further information.*

TITANS – *see* **GIANT AND GOD/GODS**

TOAD – *see* **REPTILES IN ANIMALS**

TOBACCO

🌑 We may be interested in the idea of spirituality, but as yet have not found the right stimulation. The symbolism of tobacco as a giver of visions may be relevant to our situation.

🜨 Native Americans are reputed to use tobacco to drive away bad spirits, and it is true that initially tobacco will give the person a mood lift. In dreams it is this symbolism of impending change that is meaningful. Trying to give up smoking in dreams suggests that we are attempting to live without false stimulation. Tobacco appearing in dreams will have different meanings depending on whether we smoke in waking life or not. If we do, then tobacco, in the dream, is probably a comfort tool, though nowadays something of a guilty pleasure. If not, then the symbolism is probably more to do with the idea of using tobacco to achieve a particular state of mind. If the dreamer is smoking a pipe, there may be issues of masculinity to deal with.

Also consult the entries for Indigenous Peoples and Smoke/Smoking.

TOILET

🜨 Spiritually, a toilet suggests that we have the means at our disposal to cleanse away negativity we have taken in.

🜨 Something wrong with the toilet could suggest that we are emotionally blocked. If it is overflowing, the blockage is causing a difficulty in controlling our emotions at the present time. Going to an unfamiliar toilet suggests we are in a position where we do not know what the outcome to a situation will be. Cleaning a dirty toilet suggests we are losing our 'prudish' attitude, and may have gone through some kind of internal epiphany.

▦ For many people the toilet has in dreams been until recently a symbol for dirt and lack of appreciation. There has also been the inevitable association with sexuality. Nowadays the symbolism is much more to do with notions of privacy, and the ability to reach a state where we can release our feelings in private.

⊟ In both men's and women's dreams, toilet dreams can often be about self-worth and clearing childish confusion.

You might also like to consult the entries for Clean/Clear and Dirty as well as the information for Bathroom in House.

TOMB

🜨 Spiritually we may feel that we have entered into a world that is all at once mysterious and dark – dark in the sense of the light being obscured. Although we perhaps fear this darkness, we are also excited. It is worth remembering that we are not trapped, but in a brief state of panic which can be overcome by belief.

🜨 If we are trapped in a tomb in a dream we may be trapped by fear, pain or old outdated attitudes in our waking life. If there are bodies in the tomb, these are usually parts of ourselves we have either not developed or have killed off. If one of those bodies comes alive, the attention we have given to that aspect of our personality has been sufficient to resurrect it, and a little thought will allow us to identify it.

▨ Going into a tomb suggests going down into the darker parts of our own personality. We may be fearful to begin with, but later more at ease. Finding ourselves in a tomb suggests we are ready to face our intrinsic fears of death and dying. A sarcophagus is similar to a tomb, but is much more of a memorial, marking how important the occupant is or was. To dream of such an edifice is to recognize the importance of death and the rites of passage associated with it.

Consulting the entries for Catacomb/Crypt, Death and Skeleton/Skull will provide further information.

TONGUE – *see* **BODY**

TOOLS

✷ Spiritual tools which can be symbolized in a practical way are love, hope, compassion and charity. As tools of understanding, Tarot cards, Runes and other divinatory devices will appear in dreams as our knowledge increases.

♦ Each tool will have its own significance in dreams A drill suggests working through emotions and fears as well as attitudes that have become hardened. Both a hammer and a mallet provide the energy to break down old patterns of behaviour and resistances. A saw suggests being able to cut through all the rubbish we have accumulated in order to make something new. The garden spade is another such tool.

▨ Tools in dreams suggest the practical tools we have at our disposal for enhancing our lifestyle. Our profession or work will give ready images of tools we use and to be using tools that are not ones we normally use will highlight skills or abilities we may need to develop.

Consulting the entries for Chisel, Hammer and Mallet will provide further information.

TOP – *see* **POSITION**

TORCH

✷ We may feel that we need some spiritual guidance, and this can sometimes be symbolized as a torch. A searchlight, in pinpointing and lighting the way ahead, enables us to reject the unnecessary.

♦ A torch can be used not only for ourselves, but also for other people. Dreaming of a torch shows we can have the confidence to know that, because of our own knowledge, we have the ability to see the way forward. A searchlight, being more focused, can symbolize the insights we need.

▣ In dreams, a torch can represent self-confidence. It can also suggest the need to be able to move forward, but at the same time carry our own light. Firebrands, having an open flame, will have the same symbolism as fire, whereas a battery torch signifies a more contained energy. If a searchlight or torch is trained on us we need to consider our actions and behaviour and whether they are appropriate.

You might also like to consult the entries for Fire and Light.

TORMENT – *see* **TORTURE/TORMENT/TEASE**

TORN – *see* **TEAR/TEARS/TORN**

TORNADO

✷ Our early ventures into spirituality may make us feel powerless, and at the mercy of all the elements. This can be symbolized by the tornado. However, within the centre there is peace and tranquillity.

♡ While a tornado can be very destructive, interestingly it can also be very cleansing and it is in this context that it is often met on a psychological level. It sweeps all in front of it, but after its passage there is the potential for new life and new beginnings.

▣ A tornado appearing in a dream is a symbol of violent energy of one sort or another. Often it is emotions and feelings against which we feel powerless. It is a recognizable symbol of energy, which has turned in on itself, and has therefore become destructive.

Consult the entries for Weather and Wind for additional clarification.

TORPEDO

✷ A torpedo is symbolic of spiritual directness. In terms of being able to home in on its target, the torpedo suggests directed energy.

♡ Since a torpedo passes through water to reach its target, the symbolism is of using emotion as a means to an end. This may be the type of honest getting to the point which we can do with friends, or it may be a warning that such directness could be harmful or upsetting.

▣ In dreams the torpedo may signify destructive power, often unrecognized until too late. In waking life we may 'expect the unexpected' though, as a torpedo is a missile, there will have been an element of pre-planning in that unexpectedness.

⊞ The torpedo, because of its shape, has obvious connections with masculine aggressiveness and will have this significance in both men's and women's dreams. It will depend on whether we are on the receiving end or are firing it. Rather obviously, men are more likely to be firing a torpedo, whilst women will be receiving it.

You might also like to consult the entries for Submarine, Target and War.

TORTOISE

🔆 In Chinese lore the tortoise is a revered figure of wisdom and knowledge. He is said to carry the pattern of all existence on his back. He also represents Creation.

🜚 The tortoise may, of course, simply be an image of a pet as an object that is loved. It may also, however, be a symbol for long life. For those undertaking esoteric studies, the tortoise in dreams may signify the need to consider Chinese systems of belief.

▦ The tortoise for most people suggests slowness but also perhaps thoroughness. It also in dreams signifies a shell that perhaps we – or others round us – have put up in order to protect or defend ourselves.

Consult the entries for Chinese in Indigenous Peoples and Pet as well as the information on Reptiles in Animals.

TORTURE/TORMENT/TEASING

🔆 Spiritual torture can be a conflict between right and wrong and spiritual torment is the mental agony, which ensues when we must make choices between two or more courses of action. Often the idea of such torture for the benefit of the majority – that is, the Greater Good is part of the process of growth. Spiritual teasing is the sort of irritation engendered by the imp.

🜚 Being teased in dreams may reveal a fear of becoming a laughing stock. If we are being physically tortured in dreams, we need to look at the other images and personalities in the dream to discover what significance such action has in our everyday life. It may be that we tend to put ourselves in the position of victim without realizing it. Torment has a hugely emotional charge behind it and reveals an element of sadism in our dream tormentor. This can amount to persecution and is the sort of dream that will surface in Post-Traumatic Stress Disorder.

▦ When an image connected with torture appears in a dream, often we are trying to come to terms with a great hurt. This does not need to be on a physical level – indeed, it hardly ever is. It is more likely to be emotional or mental pain. If we are unable to deal with the hurt, the dream may escalate into one of torment.

You might also like to consult the entries for Imp, Sadism and Victim as well as the information on Nightmares in the Introduction.

TOTEM/TOTEM POLE

🔆 Both in its symbolic meaning of a protector and as a representative of spiritual matters, the totem pole suggests strength and power. In a dream a totem pole can link us back to a very basic human need for protection. It is not the protection afforded by a father, but by those natural forces whose energy is powerful enough to be used by us.

⚕ When an object revered as a sacred article is given enough power by a joint belief, the thing itself is perceived as taking on a power of its own. One such object is the totem. When it appears in dreams we need to be looking at our belief systems to discover whether we are really living according to those beliefs.

▦ In ordinary everyday terms, a totem pole in dreams will signify a standard or representation of ethics. It suggests a hierarchy of importance that may or may not have seemed significant to us thus far.

You might also like to consult the entry for Native American in Indigenous Peoples as well as the information on Spiritual Imagery in the Introduction.

TOURIST

⚕ The tourist in a dream in spiritual terms represents the Hermit or Wanderer.

⚕ To play the tourist in a dream is to be aware of the fact that we have the necessary information to do what we want, when and how we want but that ultimately we are choosing not to do so.

▦ A tourist in a dream is someone who does not know his way around. If we are the tourist then we need to look at that aspect within ourselves. If someone else is the tourist then we need to be aware of what help we can give other people.

Consult the entries for Hermit and Wanderer/Wandering for further information.

TOW – *see* TRANSPORT

TOWER

⚕ The tower has duality in the spiritual sense, since it can be feminine in the shelter it affords and masculine because of its shape. It suggests ascent to the spiritual realms, but also descent to the practical. The inner aspects of the tower represent our inner life, whereas the outer signify the structure we present to the world.

⚕ A tower in a dream usually represents the construction of our lives – our inner attitude, outer life or both. The tower or tall building is such a rich source of imagery that it is feasible to give only the most easily identifiable. Familiarity with our own tower in the waking state will act as a trigger for many other potent images. Thus:

To dream of a tower with no door suggests we are out of touch with our inner selves.

A tower with no windows signifies that we are unable to see and appreciate either our external good points or our inner ones.

An ivory tower suggests an innocent approach.

A square tower signifies a practical approach to life, whereas a round tower is more spiritually geared.

A round tower at the end of a square building is the combination of the practical and spiritual.

▨ From a mundane perspective if we are to live life as fully as we can, we need to understand our own tower. In dreams it may appear initially as far away and later coming closer. How we get into the tower is also important. Shallow steps indicate that we have easy access to our inner self. More difficult steps suggest that we are fairly private individuals. If the door is barred or particularly difficult to open we are not yet ready to explore our unconscious self. If the door is closed we must make an effort to get in. If inside the tower is dark, we are still afraid of our subconscious. The hidden room in the tower would have the same significance as in a house.

Also consult the entries for Escape, Rescue, Shapes and Trap/Trapped as well as the information on Tower in Buildings for further clarification.

TOWN – *see* **PLACES**

TOYS

✺ Toys, as small copies of larger objects, symbolize the microcosm within the macrocosm. Appearing in dreams, they may be alerting us to our ability to create our own lives. Just as a child will imagine himself creating his own little world through his toys, so also can we create as dreamers.

◈ When there are toys in a dream we may be aware of children around us, or of our more childlike selves. Toys will highlight the creative side of ourselves, and the more playful innocent part.

▨ Perhaps we need to look at the types of toys that appear. They often give some indication of what we are playing with. We may be mulling over new ideas or new ways of relating to others. Equally we need to 'play' more, to relax and have fun.

⯳ It will depend on whether the toys are gender specific in dreams. Boys' toys in men's dreams indicate the need to learn different masculine skills and girls' toys suggest learning about sensitivity. Girly toys in women's dreams might suggest that she needs to rediscover her hidden femininity, whereas boys' toys would show that she needs to appreciate her more assertive side.

You might also like to consult the entries for Doll and Puppet.

TRACK – *see* **PATH AND ALSO TRAIN IN TRANSPORT**

TRAFFIC – *see* **TRANSPORT**

TRAIN – *see* **TRANSPORT**

TRAITOR

   ☀ Spiritually, to be a traitor is to deny our basic beliefs. We do not have the courage of our convictions.

   ♡ When in a dream we are betrayed by others with whom we thought we shared beliefs – and discover that they have let us down – it would mean they are traitors to the relationship.

   ▦ To dream of a traitor suggests that we are subconsciously aware of deviousness. This may be in someone else, or it could be a part of our personality that is letting us down. We may feel that our standards are not appreciated by others.

TRAMP

   ☀ Spiritually, although this image initially appears to be negative, if we are prepared to work with it, it can have great positivity – since ultimately he is always in the right place at the right time for the right reasons.

   ♡ The tramp personifies in us the wanderer, the freedom lover. In dreams he will often appear at a time when we need freedom, but can also show that that need can bring difficulty and sadness. He can also appear in dreams as the jester or fool. There is a part in all of us that is anarchical, and the tramp represents this aspect.

   ▦ To dream of a tramp in the sense of a decrepit old wanderer links us back to the part of ourselves that is seldom expressed fully in real life. It is the 'drop-out' or gypsy within us. We may be conscious of our need for irresponsibility.

Also consult the entry for Wanderer/Wandering as well as the information on Tramp in Archetypes in the Introduction.

TRANQUILLITY

   ☀ Tranquillity is sought by all those – such as the ascetic or monk – who search for the spiritual within themselves. Known by many names, it is one concept which spans all religions, and is the 'peace which passeth all understanding'.

   ♡ As a sanctuary from the hurly burly of waking life, tranquillity in dreams can be encouraged by choosing to empty the mind of daily concerns before sleep. This gives the dreaming mind the ability to work more efficiently to process the material of the unconscious and reach for true peace.

   ▦ Tranquil environments and landscapes in dreams have the facility to allow us to rebalance ourselves and our mental processes. Stress in daily life requires us to take in more and more information and at a certain point chaotic dreams can often be contrasted or followed with peaceful ones as though the mind is demonstrating the possibilities.

You might also like to consult the entries for Ascetic, Chaos, Landscape and Monk.

TRANSCRIBE – *see* WRITING

TRANSFIGURATION – *see* INTRODUCTION

TRANSFORMATION – *see* INTRODUCTION

TRANSLATE – *see* TALKING

TRANSPARENT

🔆 Transparency in the spiritual sense represents honesty, integrity and responsibility.

💚 When we are aware in dreams that things around us are transparent, we become our ability to 'see through' situations and people's behaviour. We are able to be discerning in our judgement.

▥ When something is transparent in a dream we may be feeling vulnerable, but may also be aware of insights we would not normally have. To be inside a transparent bubble, for instance, would suggest visibility and vulnerability in our lives, perhaps taking on new responsibilities. For a dream character to be behind a transparent shield suggests they or what they represent are somewhat remote and unavailable to us.

TRANSPORT

🔆 In a spiritual sense transport is being carried from one state of consciousness to another. This change in consciousness is not necessarily by our own volition. Riding either a horse or a vehicle suggests that we are happy to have the changes take place. The lift in mood can just as easily be due to external circumstances such as a beautiful day or extreme emotion and this can be reflected in dreams.

💚 The type of transport used in dreams may suggest how we are moving through this particular stage of our lives. Previously the horse was used as an image to depict how we dealt with life, although nowadays the car, the aeroplane and other more modern forms of transport have been substituted. A vehicle that appears in our dreams often conforms with the view we hold of ourselves. For instance, we may be driving a very basic type of car or a Rolls-Royce. In today's modern world there are so many diverse means of transport that each has developed its own symbolism. Some of these are given below.

Aeroplane – an aeroplane suggests a swift easy journey with some attention to detail. We may be embarking on a new journey of discovery about ourselves or someone else. An airman or pilot is a romanticized picture of either the Animus or of the Self. *You might also like to consult the individual* *entry for Aeroplane and the section on Archetypes in the Introduction for further information.*

Bicycle – this suggests youth, freedom and movement without a supporting structure. With two wheels and, therefore, a symbol of duality, it can suggest the first forays into relationship and adult behaviour.

Boats – it will depend on what kind of boat is in the dream as to its interpretation. A ferry or piloted boat holds all the symbolism of the journey across the River Styx after death. Today it signifies the giving up of selfish desires. Having been able to do this, we may be 'reborn' into a better life, or way of living. A small rowing boat would suggest an expedition of emotional discovery but one often undertaken alone. A yacht might suggest a similar journey done with style, whereas a large ship would suggest creating new horizons but in the company of others. Early seafarers referred to their ships as 'she' largely, it is thought, because of the close dependence they had on them for life and because they were difficult to manage. Today ships have lost that personal association. What a boat does in the dream will have relevance as a reflection of our waking life, e.g. running aground, pulling into harbour etc. To dream of disembarking indicates the end of a project, successful or otherwise. If we dream of missing a boat it shows we have not paid enough attention to detail to a project in our waking lives. *Also consult the individual entry for Boat/Ship.*

Bus – a bus signifies that part of our life journey that we are able to undertake in the company of others. More public than private, we perhaps have a common aim with the people with whom we travel. Trouble with timetables, missing the bus, arriving too early, missing a connection all indicate we are not in control of our lives and perhaps should sit down and replan how we wish to continue. Dreaming of getting on the wrong bus, or it going the wrong way, shows that there are conflicting aims or desires that need to be considered and we should listen to our own intuition. This is usually a warning of a wrong action, and we do not need to get carried away. To dream of not being able to pay the fare signifies we do not have enough resources to set out on a particular course of action. It may be that we have not paid enough attention to detail. *You may also like to consult the individual entry for Bus.*

Car/carriage/cart/chariot – any wheeled vehicle is by tradition a reflection of us and how we handle life. Carts, chariots and carriages tend to have a more old-fashioned resonance, whereas a car is more up to date and in keeping with modern thinking. All such vehicles reflect the physical body, so anything wrong with the vehicle may alert us to a problem. A car in particular is a reflection of a person's self-image and possibly sexuality and indeed any part of a car has significance. The back tyres might suggest our support system, the steering wheel the way we control our lives and so on. If the brakes are not working we are not exercising proper control over our lives. Too many people in the car would suggest that we feel overloaded by responsibility. *Also consult the entries for Car, Carriage/Cart/Chariot, Passenger and Wheel for additional information.*

Caravan or motor home – a caravan that is static will represent temporary security on a small scale, being similar in meaning to hotel. A moveable caravan or motor home will have the same symbolism as that of a snail, in that we are able to carry our security with us, giving us a sense of freedom.

Driving any sort of vehicle – this symbolizes our self-control and awareness of how external circumstances can affect us.

Engine – this represents our basic motivation our instinctive drives and possibly the sexual impulse. If the engine is not working properly we are not able to summon up enough energy to go on. If the starter motor is not working this would suggest that we need help to start a project. It is for us to be able to translate the symbolism into our own lives. *Also consult the individual entry for Engine.*

Lorry/Van – a lorry or van in a dream will have the same significance as a car, except that the drives and ambitions will be connected more with our work and how we relate on a business basis to the world in general. Being towed by a lorry or vehicle more efficient than our own suggests we need some kind of assistance with our motivation.

Motorbike – the motorbike is a symbol of masculine youth and daring. In dreams it is an image of independent behaviour and a symbol of freedom. A group of Hell's Angels would suggest some kind of anarchical behaviour, which may or may not be appropriate.

Trains – a train will often highlight our attitude to social behaviour and relationships with other people. It will also clarify our attitude to ourselves. A steam train would suggest that we feel ourselves to be somewhat outdated and old-fashioned but still viable, whereas an up-to-date electric turbo might suggest speed and efficiency. Catching the train shows we have been successful in having outside circumstances co-operate with us in achieving a particular goal, whereas missing the train indicates we do not have the resources to enable us to succeed in an appropriate way, either because we have forgotten something or because we have not been sufficiently careful. We fear that we will miss an opportunity. Equally, we may feel that external circumstances are imposing an element of control over us. Often dreams of missing a train and then catching either it or a later one, suggest that we are managing our inner resources better. Dreams of missing a train, alternating with those of catching one, show we are trying to sort out our motivations. Getting off the train before its destination or it has reached a station implies we are afraid of succeeding at a particular project. We do not appear to be in control. Getting off the train before it starts suggests that we have changed our mind about a situation in waking life. Railway lines and tracks will have significance as ways of getting us to our destination. Being conscious of the way the track runs ahead may give us an inkling as to what direction we are going. Recognizing the signals up ahead would have the same significance. Coming off the rails might suggest doing something inappropriate or of not being in control. Not wanting to be on the train might indicate we feel we are being unduly influenced by outside circumstances. Arriving at a station indicates we have completed a stage of our life journey. We may be ready for a new relationship with the world in general. The carriages on a train suggest the various compartments or sections of our lives and the way we feel about them. For example, if a carriage is untidy or dirty, we are aware that we need to 'clean up' an aspect of our lives.

🖼 Images of vehicles and methods of transport often represent either our physical body or our personality. If we are driving, we perhaps feel more in control of our own destiny. If a passenger, we feel others are trying to control our life. If we are with friends we may be aware of a group goal whereas if we do not know the other people we may need to explore our ability to make social relationships. Heavy traffic symbolizes external pressure and stress. Traffic accidents and offences can arise in dreams when we have perhaps not been paying sufficient attention to detail. We have offended a code of conduct that is important for our own safety. *Consult the entries for Accident and Passenger for additional clarification.*

TRANSVESTISM – *see* SEX/SEXUAL IMAGES

TRAP/TRAPPED

🜨 Spiritually we are holding ourselves back. We may also be aware of being trapped by the restrictions of the physical body. As we gain in spiritual knowledge, the wider perspective makes us more aware, particularly in dreams, of our lack of freedom.

♡ When we feel trapped in dreams, we are not usually able to break free of old patterns of thought and behaviour. We need outside help. The type of trap will give an indication of our psychological state. A gin trap would, therefore, suggest something is biting us and, rather obviously, a box trap that we are restricted in thought. We can gain insight into what is restricting us by taking careful note of our surroundings if we are trapped or locked in a room.

▦ To be in a trap in a dream signifies that we feel we are trapped by outside circumstances. To be aware of trapping something or someone is attempting to hold on to them. To be trapping a butterfly is to be trying to capture the inner self.

⊞ The mythology surrounding the princess in the ivory tower has resonance in both men's and women's dreams. A woman is often trapped by her own imperturbability and needs help to escape and a man needs to find and release his trapped feminine.

Consult the entries for Box, Escape, Lock/Locked, Key, Keyhole and Tower as well as the information on Rooms in Buildings for further information.

TRAVELLING – *see* **JOURNEY AND TRANSPORT**

TREASURE

✺ To search for treasure symbolizes man's search for enlightenment, his search for the Holy Grail. Expecting treasure and finding a negative as in the story of Pandora's box is part of our learning how to deal with disappointment.

♥ To find a box that has treasure such as gems and jewels in it is to understand that we must break through our own limitations before we find what we are looking for. The search for treasure epitomizes the search for tangible value in the everyday world.

▦ Treasure in dreams always represents something that is of value to us. It is the result of personal achievement and effort. To find buried treasure is to find something we have lost, perhaps a part of our personality. To be burying treasure is to be trying to guard against the future and potential problems.

You might also like to consult the entries for Box, Chest/Box, Digging/Excavation, Gems/Jewels and Money.

TREES

✺ Spiritually the tree symbolizes the Tree of Life and represents the union of heaven, earth and water. When we learn and understand our own Tree we are able to live life successfully on all levels.

♥ The tree is symbolic in dreams of the basic structure of our inner lives. When one appears in our dreams it is best to work with the image fairly extensively. A tree with wide branches would suggest a warm loving personality, whereas a small close-leafed tree would suggest an uptight personality. A well-shaped tree would suggest a well-ordered personality, while a large, messy tree would suggest a chaotic personality. Branches signify the stages of growth we go through, and leaves suggest the way we communicate to the rest of the world. To be climbing the tree suggests we are looking at our hopes and abilities, in order to succeed. To be chopping a tree down indicates the need for a complete overhaul of our beliefs and ideals and symbolizes radical change.

🔲 The roots of a tree are said to show our connection with ourselves and the earth. It could be more accurate to suggest that they signify our ability to belong to the practical side of life, to enjoy being here. Spreading roots would indicate an ability to relate well to the physical, and, conversely, deep-rootedness would suggest a more self-contained attitude. The trunk of the tree gives an indication of how we use the energies available to us, and also what exterior we present to the world. A rough trunk suggests obviously a rough and ready personality, whereas a smoother trunk would indicate more sophistication.

Consult the entries for Trees and Wood for further information.

TRESPASSING

🔅 We are approaching areas of knowledge where we cannot go without the permission of a higher spiritual authority. Trespassing indicates that we have not yet been initiated into the correct level of awareness.

💠 If it is our personal space or area that is being trespassed upon, then we need to look at our own boundaries and whether we are comfortable with them in waking life. Sometimes it is interesting when interpreting the dream to find out whether we feel that the trespasser is there voluntarily or has just wandered in. We can then work out whether we are a victim or not.

🔲 When we find ourselves trespassing in a dream, we are perhaps intruding on someone else's personal space or area of expertise in waking life. This may also suggest that there is a part of ourselves that is private and feels vulnerable. We should respect those boundaries.

You might also like to consult the entries for Initiation, Intruder, Invade/Invasion and Victim.

TRIAL

🔅 A trial in the spiritual sense is anything that tests our spiritual beliefs and understanding to the limits. Often such a dream will highlight our weakest points – sometimes ways in which we can be most judgemental – in which case we have the opportunity to reach more understanding in waking life.

💠 To dream of a scenario where we are being prosecuted suggests that we feel that authority has us on trial and we must justify ourselves, usually from an emotional perspective, but sometime in our actions or demeanour. Trial by ordeal, such as the supposed witched went through in previous times, appearing as a dream image signifies that we may be feeling persecuted.

🔲 When in waking life we are on trial, such as on probation at the beginning of a job, images of legality such as justice, judges and so on can appear in dreams. Understanding the relevance of these images can help us to overcome our own doubts.

You might also like to consult the entries for Judge/Judgement, Juror/Jury and Justice for further clarification.

TRIANGLE – *see* SHAPES/PATTERNS AND TRIO

TRICKSTER

✹ This is the spiritually irresponsible part of our nature. We have not yet put ourselves on the correct spiritual path and need to do so.

◈ Psychologically, if we have been too rigid in our attitude to life – for instance, struggling to be good the whole time or always taking a moral stance – the trickster can appear in dreams as a counter-balance. When we are under stress this personage can present himself in dreams as the character who points us in the wrong direction, answers questions with the wrong answers etc.

▣ In dreams, the trickster is literally that part of ourselves that can create havoc and chaos in our lives. A kind of practical joker, possibly presenting as the jester or fool, he symbolizes the anarchic aspect of the personality. It is our choice as whether we choose to confront or integrate him.

Consult the entries for Chaos and Joke/Joker as well as the information on Villain in Archetypes.

TRIGGER – *see* WEAPONS

TRIO

✹ Spiritually any group of three – e.g. triplets or a musical trio – appearing in dreams symbolizes The Divine Trinity. Events or situations should be looked at carefully in terms of physical wants, emotional needs and spiritual requirements, then there can be the development of spiritual stability. Negative energy challenged three times is banished.

◈ The triangle in dreams can represent the family – mother, father and child – with all its attendant relationships. It then represents emotional stability. It can also suggest the process of realization – making something tangible. Anything in triplicate or repeated three times in dreams signifies an enhanced sense of awareness. In magic, any ill wish is returned to the originator threefold.

▣ In mundane terms, when there are three similar articles in dreams, they represent body, mind and spirit. If one of the three is different to the others, what is different will give information that we require to help us.

You might also like to consult the entries for Family, Magic/Magician and Numbers.

TRIP – *see* FALL/FALLING AND JOURNEY

TRIPLETS – *see* TRIO

TROPHY

✹ A trophy would signify a Peak Experience (having moved into an expanded state of awareness) in order to achieve a spiritual goal.

◉ Formerly, trophies such as animal heads were much sought after. This is no longer so, but the symbolism of overcoming our basic fears, inadequacies and idiosyncrasies in order to achieve and be rewarded still remains.

▣ Dreaming of a trophy is to recognize that we have done something for which we can be rewarded. It depends on what the trophy is for as to its significance. The trophy will take on the significance of the object being presented. A cup would suggest receptivity and a shield, protection.

▶ A common dream that men have is the presentation of a football cup. They are the 'first among men'. Women will give trophies a totally different connotation and will give symbolism to a much more individual memento.

You might also like to consult the entries for Cup, Shield and Win/Winning.

TRUE/TRUTH/TRUST

✹ A spiritual truth is seldom provable but is one that has been given credence through belief over time or through subjective observation. It is something that, for most people, they 'just know'. In dreams such intuition is valid. Trust is belief in such truth.

◉ Perceived truth in dreams is a reality which works within the context of the dream. We believe it to be true at the time.

▣ In the mundane world we have to learn to trust our own truth. In dreams we will often receive information that helps us to verify – or not – our own appraisal of a situation.

TRUMPET

✹ The trumpet sounds a spiritual vibration, which requires awareness. The trumpet is closely associated with power. Representations of angels are often shown blowing trumpets, a stylized depiction of the trumpet's dominion over lesser spirits.

◉ As a wind instrument, the trumpet in dreams represents the call to maximize our potential, particularly our intellectual expertise. We reach for the best within ourselves to have the maximum effect and benefit in our lives.

▣ A trumpet in a dream will most often suggest either a warning or a 'call to arms'. From a practical point of view it will often be alerting us to some potential danger. When there is conflict around us we may need some kind of warning to be ready for action and a trumpet can be one such symbol. The sound of the trumpet is an invitation to sheer joy.

You might also like to consult the entries for Angels, Music/Rhythm, Musical Instruments and Sound.

TRUNK

�â Dreaming of a trunk has the same connotation as a treasure chest and indicates that spiritually we need to explore our hidden depths and the knowledge we have stored in order to get the best out of ourselves.

♡ We have the ability to store all sorts of rubbish, useful or not – both physically and mentally. When a trunk appears in a dream it is time to 'open the box' and have the courage to sort out what is there, what we can keep and what we can now reject. Often, when we should do this but do not do so, the image of the trunk will appear over and over again in different dreams. To find a jewel in a trunk indicates the good that can be found in doing a personal spring-clean.

▦ In previous times to dream of a trunk was supposed to foretell a long journey. Nowadays, as people tend to travel light, it is much more likely to represent the baggage that we have accumulated in our day-to-day life. An elephant's trunk, by association with the idea that elephants never forget, could signify memories.

Consult the entries for Animals, Baggage, Box, Chest/Box, Gems/Jewels, Luggage and Treasure for additional information.

TUG OF WAR

�â A spiritual tug of war suggests the need to resolve the conflict between two polarities and make intelligent informed spiritual choices.

♡ A tug of war may indicate the need to maintain balance through tension between opposites. To be on the winning side suggests that what we wish to achieve can be managed with help. To be on the losing side requires us to identify the parallel situation in everyday life and decide whether to continue.

▦ To dream of a tug of war suggests a conflict between good and bad, male and female, positive and negative – any two opposites. In everyday life our personal ethics may be at odds with the ethics of the group we belong to.

⊣ In both men's and women's dreams a tug of war may represent a degree of tension between the more assertive side of the personality and the more passive. Much information can be gained by noting whether the two teams are male, female or mixed.

You might also like to consult the entries for Balance, Conflict, Lose/Loss/Lost and Win/Winning.

TUMBLE – *see* **FALL**

TUNNEL

�â A tunnel in dreams at times represents the birth canal and, therefore, the process of birth, the transition between the spiritual and physical realms. The image of a tunnel both helps us to escape from the unconscious into the light and also to go down into the depths.

💠 A tunnel in a dream usually represents the need to explore our own unconscious and those things we have left untouched. If there is a light at the end of the tunnel in dreams, it indicates we are reaching the final stages of the exploration we have undertaken. If something is blocking the tunnel, some past fear or experience is stopping us from progressing.

▦ Finding ourselves in any kind of a tunnel in dreams suggests some kind of constriction in our everyday lives. We may need to focus on an end result to the exclusion of everything else. Going backwards into a tunnel suggest we may have to review the past for answers while working 'blind'.

You might also like to consult the entries for Block and Light.

TURF – *see* GRASS

TURKEY – *see* BIRDS

TURN

🏵 To turn in dreams is to change direction spiritually. A right turn may be towards good and a left turn towards wrongdoing. A right turn may also be towards the logical while the left is to the intuitive.

💠 Turning round or back in dreams is to look to the past for information. Turning on the spot suggests reaching for a different state of awareness. To turn our bodies over signifies attempting to gain a different viewpoint, whilst turning an object over is to try to uncover hidden information or ideas.

▦ In mundane terms to turn a project round is to make it viable. The image of turning a lever or wheel may symbolize this in dreams. We make it work. To be turning our cupboards or draws is an attempt to clarify our ideas.

Consult the entries for Lever, Positions and Wheel for further clarification.

TWILIGHT – *see* GLOOM AND TIME

TWINS

🏵 Twins illustrate the idea that two spiritual concepts or ideas, while separate at the moment, can achieve unity. A spiritual conceptualization is that while Unity is the Original State and splits into Duality, Duality must eventually reunite into Unity.

💠 Often in everyday life we come up against conflicts between two opposites. Twins in dreams can actually represent two sides of our personality acting in harmony.

▦ In dreams twins may, if known to us, simply be dream characters. If they are not known to us then they may represent two sides of one idea.

Also consult the information for Twins in the People entry.

TYPHOON – *see* STORM AND WIND

UFO – *see* **ALIEN/ALIENATED AND EXTRA-TERRESTRIAL**

ULTIMATUM

☼ We become aware of a spiritual ultimatum – a final demand – when we realize that we have no option but to conform to our inner beliefs; we must follow the path of spiritual integrity.

♥ To be given an ultimatum in dreams signifies that we must bring a situation to a conclusion. Often there will be considerable emotion, either negative or positive, attached to such action.

▦ We may dream of an ultimatum – a final proposal or statement of conditions – when all other methods of working have not borne fruit. This will often contain the germ of an idea that eventually solves our problem.

You might like to consult the entry for Choice/Choose.

UMBILICAL CORD

☼ The Silver Cord is an image seen psychically as the connection between body and soul, and is also perceived in dreams. As we begin to grow spiritually this is often seen as being connected at, or near, the solar plexus or belly button.

♥ The umbilical cord particularly represents the life-giving force and the connection between mother and child. Severing the umbilical cord often appears in teenage dreams as the child grows into adulthood.

▦ Often in life we can develop an emotional dependency on others, and the umbilical cord in dreams can signify that dependency. We have perhaps not yet learnt to take care of our own needs in a mature way.

▐ In a woman's dream, an umbilical cord is more likely to be about her subtle connection to someone else, particularly if she has been pregnant, whereas for a man it is more likely to be about their connection to him. Some men will dream of the umbilical cord when trying to escape from an over-possessive mother.

Also consult the entry for Navel.

UMBRELLA

☼ As a sunshade conferred status and power, along with the need to protect, so does the umbrella.

♥ As we mature we need to develop certain emotional coping skills. In dreams these can be seen as a protective covering, hence the image of the umbrella.

An umbrella is a shelter and a sanctuary, and it is this symbolism that comes across in dreams. Often in a work situation we need to work under someone's teaching, and this feeling of safety can be recognized in dreams. Occasionally, as in the term 'umbrella organization', the umbrella is seen as all-encompassing.

UMPIRE

As an umpire in sport has the right to a final decision, he takes on the function of the Higher Self in dreams.

In sport, an umpire or referee must take a number of factors into consideration before making a decision. It is this need for objectivity that surfaces in dreams of an umpire.

The umpire or referee must arbitrate between several differing opinions, and it is this function that gives rise to dreams of such a figure. This may mirror work or family disputes. As spectators in waking life we are at liberty to disagree, yet we must abide by his decision.

You might like to consult the entries for Games and Sport.

UNCLE – *see* EXTENDED FAMILY IN FAMILY

UNDER/UNDERNEATH – *see* POSITION

UNDERGROUND

The subconscious or the unconscious is often perceived in dreams as a cave or place underground. We usually need to explore the unconscious before embarking on our own spiritual journey.

To be on the underground or subway usually signifies the journeys we are prepared (or forced) to take towards understanding who we are.

Just as Alice dreamt of falling down the rabbit hole in *Alice in Wonderland*, so we all have opportunities to explore our own hidden depths through dreams. We cannot usually access the unconscious in waking life, unless we practise some form of meditation or other technique, and to dream of being underground will often allow us to come to terms with the unconscious in a very easy way.

UNDERWORLD

Almost every culture has a concept of the underworld, a place we go to after death. Dreams of the underworld, Hades or Hell are thought to help us come to terms with the illusions we have developed on the physical plane of existence and to prepare us ultimately to cope with death. The Underworld or Afterlife was once thought to be a place that was full of terrifying monsters and dangerous animals, which had to be traversed before one was free of karma.

Any dream of a descent into an underworld signifies a journey into the unconscious and a way of coming to terms with inappropriate emotions or actions. Possibly the best known such journey is that of Persephone when she was captured by Hades or Pluto and thus became Queen of the Underworld.

🔲 There are two meanings that might be given from a practical perspective to dreams of the underworld. One deals with the criminal underworld, an area of organized flouting of the law; the other is the more frightening transitional stage. Dreaming of the first suggests that we instinctively feel we are doing something wrong, whereas the other suggests that we are hampered by fears and doubts.

You might also like to consult the entries for Death and Hell.

UNDO

🔵 Spiritually, to be undoing something suggests we are trying to reverse a process. This action is not always negative in that we recognize that a situation was better previously.

💗 We often recognize through the medium of dreams that an action will have unforeseen circumstances. To be undoing a knot or tangle suggests the necessity to sort a problem out.

🔲 Pragmatically, when matters in everyday life have taken a turn for the worse, we may dream of undoing or loosening a stuck object to allow matters to move more smoothly.

You might also like to consult the entries for Knot and Tangle.

UNDRESS

🔵 To be undressing suggests a need for Spiritual openness and honesty.

💗 To be watching someone else undressing often indicates that we should be aware of that person's sensitivity. To be undressing someone else suggests that we are attempting to understand either ourselves or others on a very deep level.

🔲 When we find ourselves undressing in a dream, we may be putting ourselves in touch with our own sexual feelings. We may also be needing to reveal our true feelings about a situation around us, and to have the freedom to be totally open about those feelings.

You might also like to consult the entries for Clothes and Nude/Nudity.

UNEARTH

🔵 Spiritually, when we are prepared to move on we are able to confront the hidden Self. Dreams of unearthing objects are not unusual around this time.

💗 Occasionally, we may be aware of knowledge and potential within ourselves or others that requires hard work to realize. It has to be properly unearthed lest it remains hidden.

🔲 When we are trying to unearth an unknown object in a dream, we are attempting to reveal a side of ourselves that we do not yet understand. When we dream that we know what we are searching for, we are trying to uncover aspects of our personality that we may have consciously buried.

Also consult the entries for Digging/Excavation and Hide/Hidden.

UNEMPLOYMENT

🜚 A sense of spiritual inadequacy and inability can translate itself into the image of unemployment. This is more to do with not being motivated enough to accept a spiritual task.

♡ Unemployment is a fear that almost everyone has. When an event connected with unemployment occurs, e.g. redundancy, dole payments etc. in a dream, our feelings of inadequacy are being highlighted. We need to experience that fear in order to deal with, and overcome it.

▦ Dreaming of being unemployed suggests that we are not making the best use of our talents, or that we feel our talents are not being recognized. Equally such a dream may highlight a level of stress that requires we take a break from responsibility.

You might like to consult the entries for Employment and Work.

UNHAPPY – *see* EMOTIONS AND WEEPING

UNICORN

🜚 The unicorn signifies unconditional love and symbolizes high ideals, hope and insight in a current situation. It also suggests power, gentleness and purity.

♡ There is a story that unicorns missed being taken into Noah's Ark because they were too busy playing. They represent intuitive knowledge; in this context we need to be mindful of what is going on in the real world if we are to survive.

▦ Traditionally, the only people who were allowed to tend unicorns were virgins. When a unicorn appears in a dream, we are linking with the innocent, pure part of ourselves. This is the instinctive, receptive feminine principle.

Also consult the entries for Animals and Fabulous Beasts.

UNIFORM

🜚 Identification of a common spiritual goal and an agreement as to 'uniform' behaviour is an important aspect in spiritual development.

♡ Often, in collective groups, the right to wear a uniform has to be earned. Dreaming of being in a group of uniformed people indicates that we have achieved the right to be recognized.

▦ Dreaming of uniforms is all to do with our identification with a particular role or type of authority. However rebellious we may be, a part of us needs to conform to the ideas and beliefs of the social group to which we belong. Seeing ourselves in uniform confirms that belonging.

Consult the entry for Clothes for further information.

UNION/UNITY

🌞 Unity in a spiritual sense is usually perceived as a return to Source, to the One. Union presupposes that there are two (duality) that need to be brought together.

💧 We all attempt to achieve unity from duality – to create a relationship between two parts or opposites. Dreaming of achieving union depicts this relationship. Psychologically, the human being is consistently looking for a partner.

▦ Union indicates a joining together, and this can be of pairs or of multiples. Union in pairs suggests the reconciliation of opposites and the added energy this brings. A union, in the sense of a trade union, suggests collective action that is for the good of all.

UNIVERSITY

🌞 Spiritual Knowledge and the ability to use it can only be achieved in 'The University of Life'. Often we need to graduate or be initiated with some ceremony, such as a rite of passage, into such learning.

💧 Since a university is a place of 'higher' learning, we are being made aware of the breadth of experience and increase in knowledge available to us. Dreaming of being at university signifies that we need to move away from the mundane and ordinary into specific areas of knowledge and awareness.

▦ Dreaming of being in a university highlights our own individual potential and learning ability. We may not be particularly academic in waking life, but may be subconsciously aware of our ability to connect with people of like minds. As universities nowadays become somewhat less selective, they can also in dreams represent a potentially carefree transition between childhood and adulthood.

Also consult the entries for Education and School.

UNKNOWN

🌞 The hidden or the Occult in spiritual terms remains both unknown and unknowable unless we have the courage to face it. This we can often do through dreams.

💧 When we are conscious of the unknown in dreams, we should try to decide whether it is threatening or whether it is something we need to know and understand. It is the way we handle the information – rather than the information itself – which is important.

▣ The unknown in dreams is that which has been hidden from us, or that which we have deliberately made secret. This may be the 'occult' – that is, knowledge that is only available to initiates. It may also be information that we do not normally need, except in times of stress.

UP/UPPER – *see* **POSITION**

URINE – *see* **BODY**

URN

✻ The urn represents the feminine receptive principle.

◈ Just as all receptacles signify the feminine principle, so does the urn, although in a more ornate form. In earlier times, a draped urn signified death. That symbolism is still carried on today in the urn used in crematoriums. Thus, to dream of an urn may alert us to our feelings about death.

▣ For many people the tea urn is a symbol of community life. To dream of one suggests our ability to belong to a community and act for the Greater Good.

Consult the entries for Death, Jar and Vase for further information.

VACCINATION

✺ Vaccination in dreams suggests spiritual indoctrination, knowledge we must have if we are to be protected.

♥ Vaccination indicates that we can easily be affected and influenced by other people's ideas and feelings.

▣ In normal everyday life, vaccination is an action that initially hurts but is ultimately for our benefit. To dream that we are being vaccinated therefore suggests we are likely to be hurt by someone (perhaps emotionally), though ultimately it will be for our own good.

Consult the entries for Injection and Needle for further clarification.

VALLEY

✺ Fears of death and dying are often translated in dreams as entering into a valley – the so-called Valley of Death. The less fear we have over dying the easier our transition, which is symbolized by the valley, will be. In Spiritual terms it is simply recognizing that death is inevitable for all of us.

♥ Being in a valley can represent the sheltering, feminine side of our nature and also being down to earth. Leaving a valley suggests coming out of a period of introversion in order to function properly in the everyday world.

▣ Dreaming of going down into a valley can have the same significance as going downstairs – that is, going down into the subconscious or unknown parts of ourselves. The result of this can be two-fold, sometimes depression and gloominess and sometimes finding new areas of productiveness.

VAMPIRE

✺ Negativity, which has the effect of draining our essential energy, is represented by the vampire in dreams, particularly if there is an assault on our spirituality and beliefs.

♥ Often the fear of emotional and sexual relationships can be represented in dreams as a vampire. Because the human being still has a fear of the unknown, ancient symbols that have represented this fear can still appear in dreams.

▣ When heavy demands are made on us that we do not feel capable of meeting, a vampire can appear in a dream. We are figuratively being 'sucked dry'. The vampire or blood sucker is such a fearful figure that it is accepted as an embodiment of total negativity.

⊟ The succubus, a female demon believed to have sexual intercourse with sleeping men, and the incubus (the opposite) preying on a dreamer's vital energy has traditionally been pictured as a vampire in both men's and women's dreams. Such dreams may originally arise from childhood trauma. *You might also like to consult the entry for Blood.*

VAN – *see* LORRY IN TRANSPORT

VANDAL/VANDALIZE

🜚 Spiritual vandalism takes place when our basic beliefs are destroyed or trashed. Under these circumstances the dream content will have a sense of violence and violation.

♥ Vandalism suggests a degree of mindless damage and a vandal is the perpetrator of such mindlessness. From an emotional perspective such a dream may manifest when there has not been a natural respect for our feelings.

▦ When in waking life there are so many examples of wanton destruction, it is not surprising that such images become part of our dream content. When perhaps our professional integrity is called into question we may translate that as vandalism. That part of our being that has no respect for the norms and customs of society may be pictured in dreams as a vandal. *You might like to consult the entries for Damage and Violence.*

VANISH

🜚 One of the most annoying things about dreams is that images will vanish unexpectedly. The mind has a great capacity for 'magic'; to dream of things vanishing, and then possibly reappearing, means that we have to work a little harder from a spiritual perspective to understand.

♥ Just as a child believes in the world of magic, so the dream state is one that at the time is totally believable. When images vanish in a dream, they will very often become more tangible in the waking state and available for interpretation.

▦ There is also the tendency for us to forget various parts of the dream on waking. The reason is that the subject of the dream has not yet fully fixed itself in consciousness. Working with dreams on first waking can help to 'fix' the information our subconscious is attempting to give us.

VAPOUR – *see* WEATHER

VASE

🜚 The Great Mother in all her glory is represented. Symbolically any hollow vessel has been taken to represent feminine spiritual qualities.

♥ The accepting, receptive, intuitive aspect of the feminine is often suggested by a hollow object such as a vase. Because of its association with the womb a vase can symbolize the potential for growth. When we dream of a vase containing plants or flowers they may also help to clarify the information we are being given in the dream.

■ As a holder of beautiful things, any receptacle such as a vase, water pot, pitcher or urn tends to represent the feminine within a dream. Such an object can also signify creativity, and may suggest practical or emotional help in a project. If the vase is cracked or chipped our basic premise may be faulty.

You might like to consult the information for Great Mother in Archetypes in the Introduction and the entries for Flowers, Jar and Urn.

VAULT

☼ A vault represents the meeting place of the spiritual and physical. Consequently a vault can also symbolize death, though this may not necessarily be a physical death but rather a leaving behind of non-essential material.

◉ Collective wisdom (or the Collective Unconscious – information available to all of us) often remains hidden until a real effort is made to uncover the knowledge available. While a vault can represent a tomb, it also represents the 'archives' or records to which we all have access. As a transition image it suggests darkness and perhaps fear of the unknown.

■ In dreams any dark, hidden place suggests sexual potency or the unconscious. It can also represent our store of personal resources, those things we learn as we grow and mature. To be going down into a vault represents our need to explore those areas of ourselves that have become hidden. We may also need to explore our attitude to death.

You might also like to consult the entries for Catacomb/Crypt, Death and Tomb.

VD – see INFECTION

VEGETABLES – see FOOD AND HARVEST

VEGETATION

☼ Vegetation in a dream symbolizes abundance and the capacity for growth on a spiritual level.

◉ While the obstacles we create for ourselves in life may cause difficulty, vegetation suggests that there is also an underlying abundance and fertility that is available to us. In dreams, a pictorial image can help us to understand this. To be clearing vegetation, for instance in a vegetable garden, can suggest clearing away that which is no longer of use to us. If vegetation is sparse enough in dreams for this to be noticeable there is a lack of emotion or passion in us.

■ Vegetation in a dream can often represent the obstacles that we put in front of ourselves in order to grow. For instance, a patch of brambles can suggest irritating snags to our movement forwards, whereas nettles might represent people actually trying to prevent progress. The image of vegetation also links with the forest and with the archetypal image of the jungle.

Consult the entries for Forest and Jungle for further clarification.

VEIL

❁ A veil can represent all that is hidden and mysterious – and this often translates into aspects of the Occult. To take the veil suggests becoming a nun and, therefore, adopting a spiritual path. The veil is also a way of shrouding the feminine in order to avoid temptation and is for many women a badge of faith.

❂ The mind has different ways of indicating hidden thoughts in dreams. The veil is one of these symbols. When an object is veiled in a dream, there is some kind of secret, which cannot be revealed except to the initiated or those 'in the know'.

▥ We may, as dreamers, be concealing something from ourselves, but we could also be being kept in ignorance by others. Depending on our own attitude the veil may symbolize submission to an external authority.

Also consult the entry for Clothes.

VERDICT

❁ A verdict in a dream suggests that a judgement from a more spiritual source has become relevant. The spiritual law of cause and effect results in a 'ruling' being made.

❂ To dream we are on trial and a verdict has been given means that we have become aware that we have been judged, perhaps by our own moral code, perhaps by others.

▥ When we feel subject to scrutiny or judgement by others in waking life, perhaps having done something that could get us into difficulties, in dreams judges, courts and juries may hand down a verdict on our behaviour.

You might also like to consult the entries for Judge/Judgement, Juror/Jury and Justice.

VERMIN – *see* ANIMALS

VERTICAL – *see* POSITION

VETO

❁ In dream terms a spiritual veto – the right to forbid an action – can be experienced in many ways: a straightforward refusal, a withdrawal of approval or a definite denial of rights.

❂ In emotional terms a veto happens in dreams when we have a strongly felt reason for not agreeing to a particular course of action. Sometimes it is not until the dream action occurs that we realize the strength of our feeling.

◼ When or if an action offends in real life against a code of behaviour, we may find our dreams directing us to operate the right of veto.

VICAR

◉ A vicar is a man of God and spiritually has authority over us. He is often the authority figure to whom we have given control.

◈ When a vicar appears in a dream, we are usually aware of the more spiritual, knowledgeable side of ourselves – that part that sits in judgement on our own actions.

◼ Just as the priest was given spiritual authority over many, and was often a figure to be feared, so the vicar is also given this authority. He is perhaps less daunting than the priest in dreams.

Also consult the entries for Priest in the Archetypes section in the Introduction and in the People section.

VICE

◉ A moral fault or wickedness is a sin regularly practised and a basic moral code offended against. Unacceptable behaviour may manifest in the form of vice in dreams. The Cardinal (principal) Vices are considered to be: Lust, Sloth, Pride, Greed, Envy, Wrath and Gluttony.

◈ Often dreams allow us to behave in ways that are not those we would normally try in waking life. Being conscious of a particular vice, e.g. sloth, envy, apathy etc., in one of our dream characters may enable us to handle that tendency within ourselves.

◼ There are obviously two meanings to the word vice. One is a tool which clamps and the other a wrong action. Dreaming of a vice in its first sense may suggest that we are being constrained in some way. The second indicates that we are aware of the side of ourselves which is rebellious and out of step with society. We may in both cases need to make adjustments in our behaviour.

You might also like to consult the entry for Offence/Offend.

VICTIM

◉ If we are repressing our ability to develop spiritual potential, we will experience ourselves in a dream as a victim, often of our own doing.

◈ When we are continually creating 'no-win' situations this tendency is highlighted in dreams, but may be done so somewhat dramatically. We may find we are victims of burglary, rape or murder, for instance. These will not necessarily be precognitive dreams apart from alerting us to the potential to become a victim. The nature of our particular difficulty may reveal itself through the dream content.

◼ In dreams we are often aware of something happening to us over which we have no control. We are the victim – in the sense that we are passive or powerless within the situation. Sometimes we are aware that we are treating others incorrectly. We are making them victims of our own internal aggression, and not handling ourselves properly in waking life.

You might also like to consult the entries for Burglar, Intruder and Martyr.

VICTORY – *see* **WIN/WINNING**

VIDEO – *see* **CAMCORDER/CAMERA, FILM, RECORD/RECORDS/RECORDING**

VILLAGE

🔆 Often village life was centred around the church and the pub, providing many contrasts. Spiritually, we often have to look at balancing two parts of our lives. A village appearing in a dream suggests a fairly tightly knit community. It may illustrate our ability to form supportive relationships and a community spirit.

🕸 A village can present certain problems. For instance, everybody knows everybody else's business – which can become trying. In this case we may be highlighting the oppression felt in close relationships.

▦ A village can symbolize restriction and an unsophisticated attitude. Because the pace of life is slower, we may find that the village in a dream in today's busy world is a symbol of relaxation.

VINE/VINEYARD

🔆 A vine or vineyard can symbolize growth of a spiritual nature. We are linking with the more spiritual side of ourselves that has grown through shared, rather than individual, experience. It can also represent fertility.

🕸 When we dream of the vine we are often referring to the various members of our family, including our ancestors. Quite literally we are making a link with our family tree and all that has gone before.

▦ The vine in dreams can suggest growth and fruitfulness. This can be of one's whole self, or the various parts. A vineyard can symbolize our place of work as well as the effort we put in. A fruitful vine or vineyard suggests success and prosperity, whereas a neglected vineyard signifies that we have not previously taken enough care. Matters may have gone beyond our control.

VIOLENCE

🔆 A sense of spiritual injustice may be represented by scenes or acts of violence in a dream. A violent reaction to something in dreams suggests some kind of spiritual distress.

🕸 When we are unable because of social pressures or circumstances to express ourselves properly, we can find ourselves behaving violently in dreams. If others are behaving violently towards us we may need to take care in waking life not to upset others, or it may be that subconsciously we are aware of others' distress.

▨ Any violence in dreams is a reflection of our own inner feeling, sometimes about ourselves, sometimes about the situations around us. Often the type of violence – fighting or extreme behaviour, for example – is worthy of notice if we are fully to understand ourselves.

Also consult the entries for Anger and Fight.

VIPER – *see* **SERPENT AND SNAKE IN ANIMALS**

VIRGIN

☼ Spiritually there is a kind of innocence and purity which can often be dedicated to the service of mankind. This quality can often manifest more clearly in dreams than in waking life. In ancient Rome Vestal Virgins served the goddess Vesta as priestesses for thirty years, after which they were free to leave and marry. Most Vestal Virgins preferred to remain single after retirement. Before that, they had to maintain chastity or face a frightening death.

♡ In dream parlance, the virginal mind – that is, a mind that is free from deception and guile – is perhaps more important than physically being a virgin. It is this freedom that often becomes evident in dreams. Dreams of the loss of virginity can suggest the ending of all innocence.

▨ To dream of being a virgin suggests a state of dedication and purity, and may symbolize the life of a single, unromantically attached woman, one perhaps known to us. To dream that someone else is a virgin highlights the ideals of integrity and honesty.

⊡ In a woman's dream such a figure suggests she is in touch with her own psyche, her own essential being. In a man's dream a virgin may symbolize an innocent understanding of romance or a chivalrous approach.

VIRGIN MOTHER – *see* **SPIRITUAL IMAGERY IN THE INTRODUCTION**

VIRUS

☼ A virus is an infectious agent so from a spiritual viewpoint is a pollution or corruption of information or knowledge.

♡ Dreaming of an infectious virus has the connotation of us having caught a contaminant or had it passed on to us. Our emotions and feelings may be out of sorts.

▨ Dreaming of a computer virus suggests that a system of communication has broken down or been contaminated and we should perhaps try a different approach. A health virus suggests something a little more personal and is more concerned with our own reaction to actual physical infection.

You might also like to consult the entries for Ill/Illness and Infection.

VISA

🌞 As a visa gives permission to be in a certain place, the spiritual interpretation is that we are in the right place at the right time for the correct spiritual reason.

♀ A visa signifies a permission given by an authority, which is not the normal one under which we operate. Interestingly this image can manifest when we are embarking on a new course of action.

▦ From a purely mundane perspective, a visa signifies that we have given ourselves permission to undertake a new project or task, have sought permission from a higher authority and are ready to begin.

VISIONS – see HYPNOPOMPIC AND HYPNOGOGIC IN THE INTRODUCTION

VISIT

🌞 Our spiritual guide often first makes itself available by a visit in the dream state. Any visitation by an apparently discarnate being or a dead relative suggests information from the Higher Self.

♀ To be paying someone else a visit in a dream signifies that we may need to widen our horizons. It requires us to move beyond our own boundaries towards other people. This may be physically, emotionally or spiritually.

▦ To be visited by someone in a dream can suggest that there is information, warmth or love available to us. If it is someone we know then this may apply in a real-life situation. If it is not, then there may be a facet of our personality that is trying to make itself apparent.

VOICE

🌞 The Voice of God is a term that is used to describe the energy and seriousness of a summons – a call to spiritual duty.

♀ A voice that speaks through, or to, us as in trance work (an altered state of consciousness) has two areas of significance. Through us suggests information for others, whereas to us is more personal. If we believe in the spirit realm, this is communication from a discarnate spirit. More psychologically, when we suppress certain parts of our personalities they may surface in dreams as disembodied voices. This does not constitute a form of madness.

▦ The voice is a tool that we use to express ourselves. We all have inner awareness of our own state that is sometimes difficult to disclose. In dreams we are frequently able to use our voices in more appropriate ways, for instance in singing and chanting, which we would not normally do in waking life. Many times we are spoken to in dreams so that we remember the information given.

VOID – *see* **ABYSS**

VOLCANO

⚙ A volcano is representative of spiritual deeply held passion. This can sometimes erupt with frightening results, if we do not learn to express ourselves properly. Frustration often gives rise to the image of an active volcano.

♥ An erupting volcano usually signifies that we are not in control of a situation or of our emotions – of which there may be a hurtful release. If the lava is more noticeable, feelings will run very deep. If the lava has cooled there has been a deep passion that has now cooled off. If the explosiveness is more noticeable, and seems more recent, anger may be more prominent.

▦ The image of a volcano in dreams is a very telling one, partly because of its unpredictability. To dream of a volcano being extinct can indicate either that we have 'killed off' our passions, or that a difficult situation has come to an end. This may be one that has been around for some time.

You might like to consult the entries for Eruption and Explode/Explosion.

VOLUNTEER

⚙ In spiritual terms by volunteering for something we are promising to make a commitment – apparently an anomaly, since we are promising to make a promise. To volunteer, however, requires dedication (setting aside) of what resources we have.

♥ Volunteering in dreams shows that we have made an emotional commitment to whatever is represented.

▦ In everyday life there are certain projects and tasks that require more effort than others. Dreaming of volunteering suggests that we are aware of the extra effort required. We have decided to take part before we have consciously registered that fact.

VOMIT

⚙ Vomiting is a symbol of a discharge of negativity. We may have held on to bad feeling for so long that it has caused our spiritual system some difficulty.

♥ Intuitively, we can often be aware of problems around us and be affected by them. When we become overloaded, we may need to 'throw up' (or away) the distress it is causing us. To wake up feeling sick intimates that we have been affected on an emotional level by any release that occurred in the dreams that we have had.

▦ To dream of vomiting suggests a discharge of disagreeable feelings and emotions. It is the cleansing of inner distress that makes us extremely uncomfortable. To dream of watching someone else vomit indicates that we may have upset them or what they represent in our lives and need to have compassion and understanding.

VORTEX – *see* **WHIRLWIND**

VOTE

🕸 Spiritually when we have given unconditional acceptance to something, we have placed our trust in it. A votive offering is a spiritual request.

🕉 While the process of voting is supposed to be fair and just, when we dream of this we may question the process or the decision. To dream of being elected to a position is to seek power.

🔲 Dreaming of voting in an election, whether general or within the workplace, highlights our wish and ability to belong to groups. Being voted for signifies acceptance by our peers. If we are conscious that we are voting with the group we are happy to accept group practice. Voting against the group indicates a need to rebel.

Also consult the entry for Election.

VOUCHER

🕸 Spiritually, a voucher signifies acceptance of our wants, needs and requirements and denotes our right to have these satisfied.

🕉 A voucher opens up our opportunities and suggests that these are a gift. Because it is usually an exchange between two people, it can indicate the help that others can give us. In today's more commercial society, a voucher in dreams can also signify a way of pacifying distress.

🔲 A voucher – in the sense of a promissory note – can be taken in dreams to suggest our ability to give ourselves permission to accrue resources. If, for instance, it is a money-off voucher we may not be valuing ourselves properly, or alternatively we could be looking for an easy option.

VOW

🕸 A vow is a spiritual promise made between us and our universe, a pact between two people or between ourselves and God.

🕉 Because a vow is normally made in front of witnesses, we need to be aware of the effect that it will have on other people. In dreams we are expecting others to help us honour our promise. To be listening to or making marriage vows indicates our commitment to totality.

🔲 A vow is dedicating ourselves to a course of action and to dream of making a vow is to be recognizing responsibility for our own lives. It is more solemn than a simple promise and the results are consequently more far-reaching.

VOYAGE – *see* **BOAT/SHIP AND JOURNEY**

VULTURE – *see* **BIRDS**

WADDING

☀ Wadding, in spiritual and psychic terms, suggests security. It is an image that often arises when we are looking for protection.

♥ Sometimes bodily changes can be reflected in the images that we produce in dreams. Wadding can represent a fear of getting fat or becoming ungainly.

▦ In dreams our need for security can become more noticeable than we allow it to be in ordinary, everyday life. Because wadding is normally a protective material, we may decide that we should take action to protect ourselves rather than defend ourselves.

Also consult the entry for Fat and Packing.

WADING

☀ Spiritually, wading suggests a cleansing process, which ties in with baptism. Many meditations also use the symbolism of walking through water.

♥ Often the feeling associated with wading can be more relevant than the action of wading itself. To recognize that we are not actually in water – for example, we are wading through treacle or another substance which impedes our progress – can give us a clue to how we feel about ourselves or our circumstances.

▦ Dreaming of wading puts us in the position of recognizing what effect our emotions can have on us. If we are impeded by the water then we need to appreciate how our emotions can prevent us from moving forward. If we are enjoying our wading experience, then we may expect our connection with life to bring contentment. Sometimes the depths to which our bodies are immersed can give us information as to how we cope with external circumstances. For instance, if the water is chest high we should consider how much our knowledge of ourselves is being threatened.

Consult the entries for Baptism, Emotions and Water for further clarification.

WAGES

☀ Spiritually, wages can represent recompense for our actions and the reward we so richly deserve coming our way after all our hard work. Initially, wages were paid for work already done, whereas salary was initially an allowance to buy salt in advance – a basic commodity.

♥ Most actions we take have a result. Often when we are doing something that we do not want to do – or that we do not enjoy – the only pay-off is in the wages we receive. To dream of wages may signify that this is all we can expect from a situation in everyday life. In dreams, we tend to think of wages as a short-term payment and salary as long-term reward.

▣ Wages are normally paid in exchange for work done. In dreams, to be receiving wages signifies that we have done a good job. To be paying somebody wages implies that we feel we have to pay for services rendered. To receive a wage packet suggests that our value is tied up with other things such as loyalty and duty. To receive a salary in dreams suggests an element of trust between ourselves and our employers in waking life.

Also consult the entry for Money.

WAIL

❂ The making of sounds in mourning is used spiritually to banish bad spirits and summon the good. In dreams, therefore, wailing can suggest that we are trying to get in touch with a power that is greater than ourselves. We should look at what we feel needs 'banishing' from our lives.

♡ Wailing is reputed to be a method of summoning the spirits used in ancient times by the Oracles. It is also a long, protracted way of releasing emotions. When we hear someone wailing in a dream, we become conscious of another person's sadness.

▣ When we ourselves are wailing in dreams, we may be allowing ourselves an emotional release which would not be seen to be appropriate in everyday life. We may be attempting to make contact with a part of ourselves that has stopped functioning. It may also be a way of expressing frustration that we have not yet consciously recognized.

You might also like to consult the entries for Emotions, Mourning and Weeping.

WAITER/WAITRESS

❂ Spiritually we must learn two lessons – service and patience. These must be learnt before we can really progress.

♡ When such a person appears in a dream, there may be a play on words and we must become a 'waiter'. Part of us needs to be conscious that for complete fulfilment in any task we need to wait and be less anxious.

▣ The interpretation of this dream depends on whether we ourselves are waiting at table, or whether we are being waited upon. If we are in the role of waiter, we are aware of our ability to care for other people. If we are being waited on, we perhaps need to be nurtured and made to feel special.

WAITING

❂ In developing spiritually we must often learn to wait until the time is right for a particular event. We have to wait for the passage of time and develop patience in the interim.

◈ When we become aware that something is expected from us, and other people are waiting for appropriate action, we may need to consider our own leadership qualities in waking life. When we dream of waiting lists such as that for operations we become aware that we must wait our turn, though not necessarily over a health issue. We perhaps feel that we are not sufficiently important.

▣ To be waiting for somebody, or something, in a dream implies a need to understand the relevance of anticipation. We may be looking to other people, or outside circumstances, to help us move forward or make decisions. If we are impatient, it may be that our expectations are too high. If we are waiting patiently, there is the understanding that events will happen in their own good time.

Consult the entry for Time for further clarification.

WAKE/WAKING UP

❀ Spiritually, to wake up signifies becoming aware. The dream state alerts us to various ideas and concepts we should be looking at, although it may take us a little time to 'wake up' to them. A wake signifies appropriate grief and watching over the body of a loved one so they come to no spiritual harm.

◈ In most religions, there is a period around a death when it is appropriate to express our feelings. Sometimes it is easier to do this in company and with the support of other people. A wake such as this in a dream indicates we may need support to overcome a disappointment. To seem to wake up in a dream can indicate that we have become more aware of our selves and have come out of a period of emotional withdrawal.

▣ A wake, in the sense of a funeral rite gives us an opportunity to grieve properly. When in dreams we find ourselves attending such an occasion, we need to be aware that there may be some reason in our lives for us to go through a period of grieving. We need to let go that which we hold dear.

You might also like to consult the entries for Death, Funeral, Hearse and Mourning.

WALKING

❀ A walk becomes spiritual when it is a journey of exploration into unknown realms. Walking the labyrinth is a spiritual exercise in contemplation.

◈ Walking may be used as a relaxation from stress, and it is this significance that often comes up in dreams. If we are alone in our dream then our walk can be silent and contemplative. If it is in company, then we are able to communicate and converse with anyone without fear of interruption.

▣ In a dream, walking indicates the way in which we should be moving forward. To be walking purposefully suggests we know where we are going.

To be wandering aimlessly suggests we need to create goals for ourselves. To take pleasure in the act of walking is to return to the innocence of the child. To be using a walking stick is to recognize our need for support and assistance from others.

You might like to consult the entries for Labyrinth and Journey for further clarification.

WALL

⚜ A wall symbolizes the boundaries of a sacred space. We need to be aware of what our limitations are, not just spiritually but also emotionally.

♥ A wall has the symbolism of a dividing line – a marker between the inner and the outer, privacy and open trust. A hole in a wall suggests a breach of trust or privacy. If the wall is imprisoning us we are being held prisoner by our own fears, doubts and difficulties. If the wall appears and disappears, we have only partly dealt with our problem.

▦ In dreams, walls usually indicate the limits we have set ourselves. These may be created as defence mechanisms or support structures, and it is sometimes helpful in the interpretation to decide whether the walls have been created in order to keep ourselves in, or other people out.

Also consult the entry for Walls in Buildings.

WALLET

⚜ A wallet has the same significance as a bag, so spiritually represents our life and all it contains. As something that carries money, symbolically it signifies the value we place upon ourselves.

♥ The wallet, through its development from a money bag, can also suggest the feminine aspects of care, prudence and containment. It can highlight our attitude to intuition and awareness.

▦ In dreams, the wallet is a representation of where we keep our resources safe. These need not simply be financial resources, but can be of any kind. Many dreams can suggest our attitude to money, and to dream of a wallet is one of those dreams.

You might also like to consult the entries for Bag and Money.

WALNUT – *see* NUT

WALTZ – *see* DANCE

WAND

⚜ Obviously a wand works in tandem with magic, so to dream of a wand can symbolize 'magical' powers that may influence us or that we are capable of using. It is only when we fully understand these powers that we can use them effectively.

❤ Conventionally the wand is an instrument of supernatural forces, and it is often this image that is the most important. We are aware of some force external to ourselves, which needs harnessing. From an emotional perspective, learning to use and direct the innate power we have gives us the ability to change our circumstances.

▣ When we dream of using a wand we are aware of our influence over others. Conversely, if someone else uses a wand we are aware of the power of suggestion, either for negative or for positive within the situation.

▸ As an instrument of power, the wand can rather obviously suggest the penis. However, as more people become intrigued by magic it will revert to its older meaning of a magically charged tool. In a woman's dream it is possibly used from a more emotional perspective, whereas in a man's dream its use will be dispassionate.

Consult the entries for Magic/Magician, Witch and Wizard for further information.

WANDERER/WANDERING

❀ Wandering as a spiritual concept means going wherever life's path takes us. It is particularly recognized in the Taoist religion and signifies going with the flow.

❤ As we learn to live in the moment we are prepared to listen to our intuition and not to plan. Wandering in dreams may be alerting us to this faculty within.

▣ Meeting the wanderer in dreams is actually learning to understand that part of us that is the freedom lover, who on a practical level can take life as it comes and not be thrown by external circumstances.

You might also like to consult the entries for Hermit and Tramp as well as the information on Tramp in Archetypes in the Introduction.

WAR

❀ As a symbol, the disintegration of order inherent in war signifies some kind of conflict in us. The natural order is breaking down and identifying the source of the conflict – often a difficulty in achieving some kind of balance between the inner and outer selves – will help to bring a sense of peace or closure.

❤ War is ultimately a way of dealing with distress and discomfort. In theory, the outcome should be the re-establishing of order, but this can often only happen over an extended period of time. In dreams, when war breaks out we are dealing with destructive feelings that cannot easily be expressed in any other way.

▣ War is often deliberately engineered rather than spontaneous and tends to have a more global effect than mere skirmishes. It therefore suggests that we need to be fully aware of the consequences that our actions may have on others.

🕃 Dreams of war will depend on the experiences in waking life of the dreamer. In a woman's dream traditionally she would have been on the periphery though this may no longer be true. In a man's dream he is much more likely to be combative.

Additional information might be gleaned by consulting the entries for Argue/Argument, Armed Forces, Conflict and Fight.

WARDEN – *see* JAILER

WARDROBE – *see* CUPBOARD/WARDROBE IN FURNITURE/FURNISHINGS

WARMTH – *see* HOT

WASHING

✹ A spiritual cleansing may be necessary in order to preserve our integrity, such as before a magical ritual. Such an image will often arise spontaneously as our knowledge increases.

◈ Since water is a symbol for emotion and the unconscious, washing stands for achieving a relationship with our emotional selves and dealing successfully with the results.

▦ Dreaming of washing either ourselves or, for instance, clothes suggests getting rid of negative feelings. We may need to change our attitude, either internally or externally. Washing other people touches on our need to care for others.

Consult the entry for Water for further information.

WASP – *see* INSECTS

WASTE

✹ To be conscious of waste may mean that we are becoming aware of problems beyond our own small concerns and becoming aware of global issues. Equally, our spiritual energy may have calls upon it of which we are not consciously aware.

◈ If we are being wasteful in dreams we need to reassess how we are running our lives. We may be giving too much in relationships, or putting too much effort into trying to make things happen.

▦ Waste in dreams signifies matter or information we no longer need. It can now be discarded. Often the colour will have significance. Waste can also suggest a misuse of resources – we may initially be using too much energy on a particular project.

You might also consult the entries for Colour, Climate and Rubbish for further information.

WATCH – *see* TIME

WATCHING

✸ There is a need for us to monitor our own actions, to be objective in our self-assessment, particularly if new forms of spiritual discipline have recently been taken on.

♥ In dreams, we are often conscious of the Self or the observer in us, which is both watching and participating in the dream. If we are to achieve the best interpretation, we probably need to be aware of both perspectives.

▦ To be aware of being watched in a dream suggests that we feel threatened by someone's close interest in us. This may be in a work situation, but could also be in personal relationships.

You might also like to consult the entry for Witness.

WATER

✸ Water is such a life giving force that it symbolizes the flow of life energy itself. It is a rather mysterious substance, given that it has the ability to flow through, over and round objects. It has the quality of being able to wear away anything that gets in its way. It can symbolize spiritual rebirth. In baptism, water is a cleanser of previously held 'sins', often also those inherited from the family.

♥ Water symbolizes our emotions under all sorts of different circumstances so images associated with it are very evocative. Below are some such representations:

Bathing suggests purification.

Canals symbolize the birth process.

Dams, islands and other obstacles are conscious attempts to control the force of the water, and, therefore, our emotions.

Diving represents going down into the unconscious, or perhaps trying to find the parts of ourselves that we have suppressed.

Drowning highlights our ability to push things into the unconscious, only to have them emerge as a force that can overcome us.

Floods represent the chaotic side of us, which is usually uncontrollable. This side requires attention when it wells up and threatens to overwhelm us.

Fountains suggest womanhood, and particularly the Great Mother.

A lake, like **a pool**, can signify a stage of transition between the conscious and the spiritual Self. When come upon unexpectedly it can give us the opportunity to appreciate and understand ourselves. To be reflected in a pool indicates we need to come to terms with the Shadow. We must learn to accept that there will be a part of ourselves that we do not like very much but, when harnessed, it can give much energy for change.

Overflows and overflowing can signify an excess of energy, often emotion that is too much to be contained.

Rivers or streams always represent our lives and the way that we live them. It will depend on our attitude as to whether we see our life as a large river or a small stream. If the river is rushing by we may feel that life is moving too quickly for us. If we can see the sea as well as the river, we may be aware that a great change needs to occur or that attention must be paid to the unconscious within. Crossing a river indicates great changes. If the river is very deep we should perhaps be paying attention to the way we relate to the rest of the world. If the river is frightening we are perhaps creating an unnecessary difficulty for ourselves. If the water in the river appears to be contaminated we are not doing the best we can for ourselves.

Seas or oceans very often represent Cosmic Consciousness – that is, the original chaotic state from which all life emerges. Inherent in that state is all knowledge – i.e. completeness – although that may be obscured by our fear of deep emotion; we do not fear that which we understand. A shallow sea suggests superficial emotion. The waves in the sea represent strong emotion and passion. A calm sea suggests a peaceful existence, while a stormy one signifies passion, either negative or positive. To be conscious of the rise and fall of the tides is to be conscious both of the passage of time and of the rise and fall of our own emotions.

Waterfalls symbolize any emotion that reaches the stage where it must 'spill over' in order to become manageable.

▣ Water is usually taken in dreams to symbolize all that is emotional and feminine. Water can also stand for our potential and our ability to create a new life for ourselves in response to our own inner urgings. Water also represents cleansing, being able to wash away the contamination that we may experience in everyday life.

Water appears so often in dreams as an image, with so many different meanings, that it is possible only to suggest some probable ones. **Entering water** suggests new beginnings and **being immersed in water** is a return to the womb and can suggest pregnancy and birth. **Flowing water** signifies peace and comfort, while **rushing water** can indicate passion. **Deep water** suggests the unconscious and can also indicate that we feel out of our depth, while **shallow water** represents a lack of essential energy. To be **on the water** (as in a boat) can represent indecision or a lack of emotional commitment, while to be **in the water** but not moving can suggest inertia. **Going down into water** indicates a need to renew one's strength, to go back to the beginning, while **coming up out of the water** suggests a fresh start.

You might also like to consult the entries for Boat/Ship, Drowning, Emotions, Lagoon/Lake and Swimming as well as the information on Great Mother and Shadow in Archetypes in the Introduction.

WEALTH

�','*⚛* There is a wealth of spiritual knowledge to be gained, and to dream of pecuniary wealth indicates that this knowledge is within our grasp. Symbols of finance such as accounts or bills suggest that we should record very carefully what we do know and also what we pass on to others.

◈ Wealth and status usually go naturally together, so often when we are having problems in dealing with our own status in life we will have dreams about wealth. It can also often indicate the resources that we have or that we can use from other people. We have the ability to draw on our experiences or feelings and to achieve a great deal within the framework of our lives. Our savings may represent resources, either material or emotional, that we have hidden away until such times as they are needed. They can also represent our sense of security and independence. To dream of savings we did not know we had would suggest that we are able to summon up extra energy or time, perhaps by using material or information from the past.

▦ Dreaming of being wealthy is to dream of having in abundance those things that we need. We have possibly come though a period where we have put in a lot of effort and to dream of having a great deal of wealth indicates that we have achieved what we have set out to do. A mortgage in dreams can suggest a false sense of security in that we apparently have access to a resource that is only comparative in value and not readily realized. If we are aware of our goal in making savings in a dream we should perhaps be making long-term plans in waking life. If we are giving our savings away, we no longer have need of a particular practical resource.

The entries for Debt, Lend/Lending/Loan and Money should help with clarification.

WEAPONS

🌠 Various weapons can suggest differing degrees of spiritual power. This power should always be used with relevant caution.

◈ To have a weapon used against us means that we have to look at how we are party to people being aggressive around us. It may be that we have done something to upset the other person, which results in aggression, or it may be that we have put ourselves in a position of becoming the victim of circumstance. Different weapons have various meanings:

An arrow indicates being pierced by some kind of powerful emotion, of being hurt by someone else through words or actions. In order to make ourselves feel better we must turn our attention inwards.

The gun or pistol traditionally represents male sexuality and for a woman to dream of being shot often indicates her thoughts about sexual aggression. If we are shooting the gun ourselves we may be using our masculine abilities in quite an aggressive way, in order to defend ourselves.

A knife represents the ability to cut through debris, to 'cut into' whatever is bothering us and to cut out the hypocrisy that perhaps is prevailing in a situation.

The sword has more than one meaning. Because of its hilt – which is a cross shape – it often represents a system of belief that is used in a powerful way. Equally it can be used to suggest spiritual strength, creating an ability to cut away the unnecessary more powerfully than the knife. The sword when sheathed is the soul or the Self in the body.

To dream of weapons usually suggests our desire to hurt someone or something. We have internalized our aggression and it is marginally more acceptable to dream of weapons and of using them against people, than actually having to deal with such circumstances in everyday life. Depending on the weapon that we use we may get a fairly good idea of what the real problem is in the waking self. To dream of squeezing the trigger of a gun, for instance, suggests that we may be at fault.

Consult the entries for Armour, Arrow, Dagger, Gun, Knife and Sword for further information.

WEASEL – *see* **ANIMALS**

WEATHER

Different types of weather may be symbolic of a spiritual response. Sunshine suggests good feeling and happiness, whereas rain might suggest tears. Wind symbolizes the intellect, a windy day might suggest a time for intellectual pursuits.

Weather can indicate our internal responses to situations. If, for instance, there was a storm in our dream our emotions would be stormy, perhaps angry and aggressive. If we are watching a very blue, unclouded sky, we may be recognizing that we have the ability to keep the situations that we are in under control. We do possess the ability to control internal moods and emotions that may not have been possible in the past. Being aware of the weather would indicate that we need to recognize that we are part of a greater whole rather than just individuals in our own right.

🎑 Weather, as being part of the 'environment' of the dream, usually indicates our moods and emotions. We are very much aware of changing external situations and have to be careful to adjust our conduct in response to these. *You might also like to consult the entries for Emotions, Lightning, Rain, Storm, Thunder/Thunderbolts and Wind.*

WEAVING

🌞 Weaving is one of the strongest spiritual images there is. In most cultures there is an image of our fate being woven in a particular pattern. We are not supposed to be in control of that pattern, but must accept that the gods or God know what is best.

💎 Weaving is taken to signify life itself and often symbolizes our attitude to the way we run our lives. The fabric of our emotions is what we have to work with; the patterns that we weave consist of our experiences as we go through life.

🎑 Weaving is a very basic symbol and suggests the need to take responsibility for our own lives. Handicrafts of any sort symbolize our hold on life and on the situations around us. To make a mistake in weaving suggests that we need to take a situation back to its roots and rework it. *You might also like to consult the entries for God/Gods, Knitting and Web.*

WEB

🌞 The spider's web is the Cosmic Plan. It is within the 'web of life' that the divine powers have interwoven fate and time in order to create a reality in which we can exist. There is a belief that we are the spiritual entrapped within the physical and not able to 'escape' back to our own spiritual realm.

💎 When we dream of a web we are linking into one of the most basic of spiritual symbols. Interestingly in today's technological age it will also symbolize a network of communication as in the world wide web on the internet. In dreams this 'web' can stand for our own personal group of friends and acquaintances.

🎑 In everyday life we may well be caught up in a situation that could trap us. We could be in a 'sticky' situation and not quite know which direction to move. This can result in the symbol of a web appearing in the dream. We are 'caught in the middle' or we are trapped. Because the situation is extremely complex we have no idea which way is going to be most advantageous for us. *Consult the entry for Communication for further clarification.*

WEDDING/WEDDING DRESS/WEDDING RING

🌞 A wedding can symbolize the sacred union between the spiritual and physical. In former times it was seen as a ritual that brought fertility to the earth. Within the human being there is the need to make vows, to give promises and above all to symbolize the making of those promises Traditionally, the wedding ring was a symbol of total encircling love because it is in the shape of a circle. It is complete, with no beginning and no end.

♦ To dream of a wedding can give some indication of the type of person we are looking for as a partner. We may, for instance, dream that we are marrying a childhood friend – in which case we are looking for somebody who has the same qualities as that person. We may dream we are marrying a famous figure and again the qualities of that particular person will be important. The wedding ring, worn on the finger that represents the heart – that is, the fourth finger of the left hand – suggests that we have made a commitment or promise. To dream of a wedding ring being on any other finger than that particular finger may indicate that the promise is not valid or we feel the wedding ring to be a constriction or an entrapment in some way.

▦ A marriage or a wedding in a dream often indicates the uniting of two particular parts of us which need to come together in order to create a better whole. For instance, the intellect and feelings – or perhaps the practical and intuitive sides – may need to be united. To be dreaming of wearing a wedding dress is to be trying to sort out our feelings and hopes about relationships and weddings. To be dressing someone else in a wedding dress can indicate one's feelings of inferiority – 'always the bridesmaid, never the bride'.

To dream of losing our wedding ring would very often symbolize a problem within a marriage, or perhaps highlight a problem in our commitment. To dream of finding a wedding ring might well indicate that a relationship is being formed that could result in marriage. To be attending a wedding in dreams when we are not expecting to attend one in waking life suggests that we are aware of a relationship between two people, but it has not yet registered on the conscious level.

You might also like to consult the entries for Marriage, Partner/Partnership and Propose/Proposal.

WEEDS

🌑 Weeds, by courtesy of their irritating qualities and refusal to be quickly eradicated, symbolize spiritual difficulties.

♦ Mental attitudes and old patterns of behaviour that clog us up and do not allow us to move forward can very often be shown in dreams as weeds. We may need to decide which of these weeds are helpful to us – that is, which could be composted, transferred into something else and made use of to help positive growth – or which need to be thrown away. Often plants growing wild have healing properties and by using these properties we can enhance our lives. Such information can be given intuitively in dreams.

▦ Weeds are generally plants that grow on waste ground and their symbolism in dreams reflects this. They may indicate misplaced trust, misplaced energy or even misplaced attempts at success. They do not contribute a tremendous amount to our lives and if allowed to run riot or to overgrow can stop our own positive growth. To be digging up weeds would show that we are aware that by freeing our life of the non-essential, we are creating space for new growth and new abilities.

You might like to consult the entries for Garden and Plants.

WEEPING

☀ Weeping suggests mourning for some spiritual quality we have lost. Something exuding moisture so that it seems to be weeping is often deemed to be miraculous, and this dream can appear quite often in stages of transition as we are moving from one state of awareness to another. The excess energy can be shown as a weeping plant, tree or some such image.

♥ Weeping suggests uncontrollable emotion or grief, so to experience either ourselves or someone else weeping in dreams is to show that there needs to be a discharge of such emotion. We may be sad over past events or fearful of moving into the future.

▦ It is worthwhile exploring the quality of weeping. Are we sobbing and, therefore, not able to express ourselves fully? Are the tears that we shed for ourselves or others? We may simply be creating difficulty within ourselves, which enables us to express the feelings we have bottled up.

Consulting the entries for Emotions, Mourning, Tear/Tears and Wail should help your understanding.

WEIGHING/WEIGHT

☀ Weight in a dream indicates gravitas and seriousness. We may wish to make clear in our conscious minds our own spiritual worth. Anubis, the Egyptian god, assumed the role of the guide who holds steady the scales on which the hearts of the dead are weighed against the feather of Ma'at, goddess of Truth.

♥ Weighing something up is to be trying to make an accurate decision to assess what the risks are. If we are trying to balance the scales we are looking for justice and natural balance within our knowledge. Weight in a dream may well indicate the need to be practical and down-to-earth in waking life. We need to keep our feet on the ground.

▦ To be weighing something in dreams is to be assessing its worth. This image connects with the calculation of our needs and what is of value to us, whether materially or spiritually. Experiencing a weight or heaviness in a dream is to be conscious of our responsibilities. It may also suggest that we should assess the importance and seriousness of what we are doing.

Consult the entries for Measure and Scales for additional information.

WELL

☀ A well can symbolize a form of contact with the depths – possibly the depths of emotion. It is also a symbol for the Abyss, though perhaps less frightening. We can access its vastness through our emotions.

♥ The image of a well in a dream suggests our ability to be 'well'. We have the ability to be healed and to fulfil our dearest wish, if we so desire. By putting ourselves in touch with our intuitive, aware selves we open up the potential and possibilities for healing and success.

▦ A well in dreams is a way of accessing the deepest resources of feeling and emotion that we have. Without such access we are not going eventually to be whole and completely understanding ourselves. If there is something wrong with the well – we cannot reach the water for example – it indicates that we are not able to get in touch with our best talents.

Consult the entries for Abyss, Emotions and Water for further clarification.

WEREWOLF – *see* SINISTER ANIMALS IN ANIMALS

WEST

☀ The West in spiritual terms, from ancient times has suggested Autumn, a time for harvesting. The archangel is Gabriel, keeper of Wisdom.

♥ We may be looking towards a time of rest and reward. The magical element associated with the West is Water and the colour is blue. These significances will often reveal themselves initially in dreams.

▦ Specifically dreaming of the West indicates that we are looking at the sensitive creative side of ourselves. We link with the flow of life and the wisdom of experience.

Consulting the entries for Colour, Elements, Harvest and Water will provide additional information.

WET – *see* WATER

WHALE – *see* ANIMALS

WHEAT – *see* GRAIN

WHEEL

☀ In Buddhist teaching the Wheel of Life symbolizes the ideal way to live life, and how we see ourselves fitting in. As Eastern religion becomes more widespread this image becomes both more present and more pertinent.

♥ To lose a wheel from a vehicle is to lose motivation or direction – to be thrown off balance. A large wheel, such as the Ferris Wheel in a fairground, suggests an awareness of life's ups and downs.

🌑 A wheel in a dream indicates the ability and need to make changes – to move forward into the future without being thrown off course. It is also used in business and therapy as a symbol for work/life balance.

You might also like to consult the information for Circle in Shapes/Patterns as well as the entries for Mandala and Transport.

WHIP

🌑 A whip suggests corrective punishment and self-flagellation. We need to consider whether such behaviour is appropriate as we progress spiritually.

💜 Because the whip or lash is an instrument of punishment we need to be aware that in trying to force things to happen in waking life, we may also be creating problems for ourselves.

🔲 The whip is an instrument of torture. For it to appear indicates we have either the need to control others, or to be controlled by them. We may be trying to control by using pain – either physical or emotional.

WHIRLPOOL/WHIRLWIND

🌑 These images are symbols of the vortex, a representation of life and natural energy. Harnessed, this energy gives rise to a whirl of creativity. Unharnessed, it can be destructive.

💜 Intellectually we may know that we have control over our lives, but are caught up in an endless round of activity that appears to be unproductive, but in fact contains a tremendous amount of energy.

🔲 There are usually conflicting currents in both the whirlpool and the whirlwind. When they appear in dreams we are aware of the quality of power we have within. The whirlpool, being made up of water, will more properly represent emotional energy, whereas the whirlwind (air) will suggest intellectual power. We perhaps need to consider which one is most appropriate to use.

Consult the entries for Water and Wind for further information.

WHISTLE

🌑 A whistle can signify a spiritual summons and shares the significance of a wind instrument.

💜 A whistle may be heard and recognized in dreams about games. As a means of imposing control and training, it may be relevant as to how it is blown. For instance, if it is blown harshly, we may be being made aware that we have transgressed a known code of conduct.

🔲 A whistle being blown in a dream can mark the end of a particular phase of time. It can also sound as a warning to alert us to a particular event.

To clarify your interpretation consult the entries for Games and Musical Instruments.

WHITE – *see* **COLOURS**

WIDOW/WIDOWER

⚛ A widow can signify the Crone or Wise Woman and the widower the archetypal Wise Old Man. They have the wisdom of experience.

♥ Psychologically we all seek within ourselves complete harmony in partnership. This is a security that allows us to express parts of our personality which are not normally accessible otherwise. Dreaming of being a widow or widower when we are not suggests that we have lost part of ourselves. A husband represents the masculine principle, the drives and ambition, and a wife the intuitive sensitive principle, so to have lost either is to have lost an essential part of the Mystical Union that everyone requires in order to become spiritually complete.

▦ Dreaming of being a widow or widower can suggest loss and sadness, but can also suggest the independence of old age. Sometimes such a dream can mark the change in a woman's awareness as she moves towards the 'Crone' or Wise Woman. A woman to dream of a widow highlights her ability to be free and use her own innate wisdom.

⌨ In a man's dream a widow may signify a deeper understanding of a woman's needs. He may recognize that all women do not necessarily need to become dependent on him. In a woman's dream a widower may signify her awareness that she has a right to companionship without losing her ties to her husband.

Consult the entries for Marriage and Wedding/Wedding Dress/Wedding Ring as well as the information on Family in the People entry.

WIFE – *see* **FAMILY**

WIG

⚛ A wig, as in a judge's wig, is a symbol of Spiritual authority and judgment. In Jewish belief a woman was expected to hide her hair lest anyone other than her husband saw it. Nowadays it would be under a wig.

♥ Sometimes a wig highlights the fact that we have something to hide. We are perhaps not as competent, as youthful, or as able as we would like others to believe.

▦ In previous times, covering the head was considered to be a way of hiding the intellect, of giving a false impression, yet also of indicating wisdom and authority. A judge's wig can suggest all of these on a temporal level. A hairpiece or toupée highlights false ideas or an unnatural attitude.

You might also like to consult the entries for Bald and Hairdresser as well as the information for Hair in the Body entry.

WILD

☀ In a dream to be, or feel, wild often suggests a lack of spiritual control. Within each of us there is a part that dislikes being controlled in any way. It is the part of ourselves that needs to be free, and is creative and independent.

♡ Anything that grows wild is not subject to the same constraints which normal society puts upon us, so in this context wildness may signify anarchy and lack of stability. In its more positive sense, there is profusion and promise in whatever we are trying to do.

▣ In dreams anything wild always represents the untamed. A wild animal will stand for that aspect of our personality that has not yet committed itself to using rational thought.

▣ Depending on whether the dreamer is masculine or feminine, a wild woman will represent the Anima or the Shadow.

Also consult the entries for Animals, Flowers, Tame and Weeds, as well as the information on Anima and Shadow in Archetypes in the Introduction.

WILL

☀ Determination in spiritual matters is represented here. This can also suggest the resolution of a problem with which we have been dealing.

♡ We may dream of a will at a time when we need everything to be done properly and with certain levels of correctness. There is the obvious play on words where a will would indicate the will to do or to be – the determination to take action, for instance. Because for many making a will is a very final action, in dreams it can indicate a recognition that we are entering a new phase of life.

▣ To dream of a will or any legal document is connected with the way in which our unconscious side can push us into taking notice of our inner needs. To be making a will is to be making a promise to ourselves over future action. It may also have overtones of attempting to look after those we love and care about. To inherit from a will means that we need to look at the habits, characteristics and morals we have inherited from our ancestors.

You might also like to consult the entry for Inheritance.

WILLOW – *see* **WOOD**

WIN/WINNER

☀ In spiritual terms a winner is someone who has overcome their own fears and doubts to 'win through' to their own personal excellence.

♡ To win in dreams is to be able to acknowledge our own supremacy. To be a champion is to be best overall, to have competed and won.

▣ In the everyday world there is much competition and to dream of winning a contract, for instance, may suggest that, though this may not be our normal function, we have done a good job. To win a race signifies we have the application and dedication needed to come out on top.

⊞ In both men's and women's dreams winning can be a potent image. For a woman to win in a dream when the other competitors are women indicates that she has the right to a high opinion of herself. To win over men can signify that she has overcome her own fears of inadequacy. For a man, winning over other men may suggest he is aware of his abilities. To come in before women highlights his own ability to use the softer skills. Such dreams would need to be carefully interpreted.

WIND

❀ Wind signifies the Power of the Spirit and the movement of Life. Just as the Holy Spirit in Christianity was said to be 'a mighty rushing wind', so such a dream can represent a Divine revelation of some sort. A gale can be symbolic of the spirit we have within us. The intensity and power of our spiritual belief is depicted by a hurricane – an unpredictable force. To be winding something up, such as a clock, suggests that we are priming ourselves for action.

◈ On a slightly more psychological level, wind in a dream can suggest the beginning of a new, much deeper awareness of ourselves. Since wind in a dream often denotes spiritual matters, if we are conscious of a gale or strong wind we may be taking ourselves too seriously. We are allowing those forces within us, that will lead us forward of their own accord to something else, to have too much meaning. A hurricane can represent the power of our own passion, or passionate belief, which picks us up and carries us along.

▦ In dreams, wind symbolizes the intellect. It will depend on the force of the wind how we interpret the dream. For instance, a breeze would suggest gentleness and pleasure. An idea or concept we have is beginning to move us. A gale might indicate a principle we feel passionately about, whereas a north wind might suggest a threat to our security. Actually being in a gale indicates that we are being buffeted by circumstances that we feel are beyond our control. We are allowing those outside circumstances to create problems for us when actually we may need to look at what we are doing and either take shelter – to withdraw from the situation – or battle through to some form of sanctuary. When we experience a hurricane in a dream, we are sensing the force of an element in our lives that is beyond our control. We may feel we are being swept along by circumstances – or possibly someone's passion – and are powerless to resist.

You might also like to consult the entry for Breeze.

WINDOWS – *see* **BUILDINGS AND GLASS**

WINE

🌑 Wine can represent potential spiritual abundance (as in the parable of turning water into wine). It can also signify the taking in of spiritual power.

♥ As a symbol of 'the liquid of life', wine highlights our ability to draw the best out of our experiences and to make use of what is gleaned to provide fun and happiness. The wine glass can have two meanings. Firstly, it stands for the container of our happiness and secondly it can stand for pregnancy. Because of wine's association with blood, a broken wine glass and spilt wine can depict sorrow, or in a woman's dream, miscarriage.

▦ In dreams, wine can suggest a happy occasion. As a substance it has an influence on our awareness and appreciation of our environment. A wine cellar, therefore, can represent the sum of our past experiences, both good and bad. A wine bottle, as a source of enjoyment, is taken by some to indicate masculinity.

You might also like to consult the entries for Alcohol/Alcoholic, Blood and Drunk.

WINGS

🌑 Wings generally symbolize the protecting, all-pervading power of God. An angel's wings would depict the power to transcend our difficulties, as also would the wings of a bird of prey.

♥ Wings can be protective, and this symbolism often appears in dreams. Folded wings can suggest sorrow, whereas open wings would seem to signify unconditional love.

▦ Because wings make us think of flight, to dream of, for instance, birds' wings would suggest attention is being drawn to our need for freedom. A broken wing indicates that a previous trauma is preventing us from 'taking off' and progressing in our lives.

You might also like to consult the entries for Angel, Birds and Flying/Flight.

WINTER

🌑 Within the cycle of nature, winter can represent a time of lying fallow before rebirth; hence winter can mean death as part of the inevitable spiritual cycle of death and rebirth.

♥ At a period in our lives when we are emotionally cold, images associated with winter – such as ice and snow – can highlight the appropriateness, or otherwise, of the way we feel. In clairvoyance, the seasons can also indicate a time of year when something may happen.

▦ In dreams, winter can represent a time in our lives that is unfruitful. It can also represent old age, a time when our energy is running down.

You might also like to consult the entries for Autumn, Ice/Icebergs/Icicles, Seasons, Spring, Snow and Summer.

WIRELESS – *see* RADIO

WISH

☼ A wish is a statement of intent and when looked at from a spiritual perspective is often in dreams a directive from the Higher Self.

♥ Emotionally, we are able to 'power up' our wishes in dreams. By bearing our intent in mind prior to sleep, we can add the additional energy of the unconscious to making things happen. This is called manifestation.

▦ By regarding a wish as an appeal to the powers that be, from a mundane viewpoint we need to be very clear that what we wish for is what we want. Dreams can have the function of sorting out what we really want and getting rid of the non-essential.

WITCH

☼ Spiritually a witch is someone who has come to understand the intrinsic power they have and learnt to use it properly. Because this power, which is based in strongly held beliefs and codes of behaviour, is perceived as dangerous there are many ideas as to the protection necessary, such as hanging garlic.

♥ The conventional picture of the warty-nosed old crone is actually a personification of malevolence. Any blemish that comes to our attention in dreams can be accepted as evidence of there being a distortion in our view of the world. In dreams we have the opportunity to confront our fears, overcome them and use the power thus generated successfully.

▦ In mundane terms we may dream of witches when we do not fully understand the use of personal power. Dreaming of warts, which are often associated with witches, links with that part of ourselves which remains superstitious and afraid of an energy we have not fully comprehended.

▤ In dreams a woman will recognize the appearance of the witch as the opportunity to come to terms with the sacred duty she has to pass on her knowledge. A man may use the appearance of the witch to overcome his fears of the powerful woman.

Consult the entries for Magic/Magician, Wand and Wizard as well as the information on Witch in Archetypes in the Introduction.

WITNESS

☼ We are acknowledging a degree of Spiritual Testament or statement of truth in our life, which we need in order to continue along our spiritual path. Witnessing is a term used when spiritually we observe without judgement.

🛡 Testifying as a witness suggests that we feel we are being called to account for our actions or beliefs. We may feel somewhat insecure until we have been accepted by our peers.

🔲 When we find ourselves in the position of being a witness to, for instance, an accident, it may be that our powers of observation are being highlighted. We need to take very careful note of what is going on around about us. Our interaction with authority may also be being called into question.

Also consult the entries for Court and Crime/Criminal.

WIZARD

☀ The figure of a wizard in dreams is he who has learned to use his powers of manifestation in a dispassionate manner. He is Merlin, the sorcerer and the magician. As a stage on the journey to Wise Old Man, he is a recognizable Archetype.

🛡 Conventionally pictured in long flowing robes with a long beard, he tends to be seen as somewhat otherworldly. In dreams he appears when we are struggling with the idea of being able to use natural power in a magical way. He usually epitomizes the alchemical idea of transmutation – turning the crass into the beautiful.

🔲 In a workaday environment a wizard is a set of computer instructions which enables you to complete a task. Both practically and magically this image is one that can enable us to use the expertise we inherently possess.

🔲 In a man's dream the wizard may well represent his own sense of power and control of the energies. In a woman's dream he will suggest the non-emotional use of authority.

Consult the entries for Alchemy, Magic/Magician, Wand and Witch as well as the information on Sorcerer in Archetypes in the Introduction.

WOLF – *see* ANIMALS

WOMAN – *see* PEOPLE

WOMB – *see* BODY

WOOD

☀ The wood is often a manifestation of the Spirit. If it is a wild wood, it suggests the untamed spirit – as in nature – and we perhaps need to exercise some self-control.

🛡 When our behaviour becomes rigid or wooden, dreams will often attempt to make us aware of this and of the necessity to balance our feelings. We might then dream of willow, a tree that bends in the wind.

🔲 Dreaming of wood, in the sense of prepared timber, suggests our ability to appreciate the past and to build on what has gone before. We are capable of building a structure, which may or may not be permanent. Dreaming of a wooden toy highlights our connection with the more natural side of ourselves.

You might also like to consult the entries for Forest and Trees.

WOODPECKER – *see* BIRDS

WOOL

⚙ Wool is symbolic of Spiritual Protection. Lamb was sacrificed by the Jews at Passover, Christ was the Lamb of God so the spiritual significance of wool is obvious.

♡ Wool has, from earliest times, represented warmth and protectiveness. Nowadays it particularly represents gentleness and mothering.

▦ How we interpret wool depends on whether the image we have is of lamb's wool or of knitting wool. Lamb's wool may stand for blurred thoughts and feelings. We have not really sorted our thoughts out. 'Pulling the wool' over someone's eyes, though generally accepted as being devious, can also be a protective act.

Also consult the entry for Knitting.

WORD

⚙ Spiritually the Word is the Logos, the Sacred Sound, the beginning of creation. In dreams we can appreciate words of power, such as Mantra and the Names of God.

♡ Certain words have esoteric meanings, such as the Hebrew word *JHVH* (Jehovah). Such words are more likely to appear initially in the dream state than in ordinary everyday life at a particular stage of development. We are more open to such information while we are asleep.

▦ The repetition of words creates a particular vibration. When in dreams we are conscious of a word being repeated, we must decide whether it is the sound or the meaning that is significant.

Also consult the entries for Sound and Talking as well as the information on Spiritual Imagery in the Introduction.

WORK

⚙ There may be some degree of activity of the spirit ahead. We could be being moved towards new spiritual tasks.

♡ Often what we do as a job or daily occupation bears no relation to what we consider to be our real work. Dreams can very often help us to change our situation by giving information as to our real talents and gifts. When we dream of working at something which does not have a place in our ordinary everyday lives, it may be worth exploring how we could use those skills to enhance our lives.

▦ Dreaming of being at work highlights issues, concerns or difficulties we may have within the work situation. We could be actively trying to make changes in our lives and these changes, in dreams, become reflected into the work situation.

⊞ There used to be a strong division between men's and women's work. In dreams if we find ourselves doing work that traditionally belonged to the opposite gender we perhaps need to develop some of the qualities of that occupation. For instance, to dream of being an engineer might suggest we need to use precision and vision.

WORKSHOP

✺ A workshop often holds within it creative outlets – this creativity can be used for our spiritual progression.

◈ A workshop may often be where we meet others of like mind, people who are creative in the same way as we are. It therefore represents group interaction and talent.

▦ A workshop is a place that is productive. In dreams it symbolizes the part of ourselves that creates projects which then become profitable for us, though not necessarily financially.

You might also like to consult the entry for Garage.

WORLD

✺ As we progress spiritually we become conscious that, just as on an individual level we belong to the family, so the world belongs to the Cosmos. Being aware of the world in this sense means we must take responsibility for the way the world functions.

◈ To dream of other worlds and dimensions suggests different ways of experiencing our own lives. We perhaps need to become less rigid in our opinions.

▦ The world represents the area of experience in which one lives, and our everyday activities. Often to dream of a world beyond our sphere of influence suggests the necessity to take a wider viewpoint in a situation around us.

Consult the entry for Globe for additional information.

WORM

✺ 'Being given to the worms' is a metaphor for death, so we need to be aware that on a spiritual level changes – not necessarily death – may shortly be taking place.

◈ The worm in dreams can also highlight our feelings of ineffectiveness and insignificance (whether this is about ourselves or others). If the worm is bigger than we are then this would suggest that our own sense of inferiority is a problem. If we are particularly conscious of a wormcast – that is, the earth the worm has passed through its body – then this is a transformation image and indicates we are capable of changing our lives into something more fertile.

🔲 Most dreams about worms are fairly ambivalent. The worm is not necessarily seen to be particularly clean, so phrases like 'the worm turning' suggests that we have decided to state our case. A can of worms could be transformative or a difficult mess.

🔲 At its very basic interpretation, the worm can suggest the penis. Depending on the dreamer's attitude to sexuality and gender, there may be a sense of threat.

WORSHIP – see ALTAR, ICON, RITE/RITUAL AS WELL AS SPIRITUAL IMAGERY IN THE INTRODUCTION

WOUND

🔆 A wound symbolizes an experience, which may have been unpleasant, that we should take note of and learn from.

♥ Any wound or trauma in dreams will signify hurt feelings or emotions. If we are inflicting the wounds, our own aggression and mistrust are being highlighted, if the wounds are being inflicted on us we may be making ourselves into, or being, the victim.

🔲 The type of wound will be important in interpreting the dream. A large, ugly wound will suggest more violence, whereas a small one may indicate a more focused attack. This wound may be to our reputation, self-esteem or pride.

You might also like to consult the entries for Attack and Weapon.

WREATH

🔆 A wreath has triple spiritual significance – dedication, sacrifice or death (change). The shape, often circular, will be important as thus signifying continuity and completeness, as well as everlasting life.

♥ A wreath in dreams can have the same significance as any of the binding symbols, such as a bridle. It forms a bond that cannot be broken, or an acknowledgement that must be accepted.

🔲 A wreath in a dream can suggest honour and celebration. Dreaming of being given a wreath suggests being singled out, perhaps for some honour. It formerly warned of the potential for one's own death, which is why wreaths are still part of funeral rites. Dreaming of giving someone else a wreath – not a funerary one – validates our relationship with that person.

Consult the entries for Bridle, Flowers and Laurel/Bay Leaves for further information.

WRECK

⚙ A wreck of any kind symbolizes a spiritual defeat. Although frustrated on this occasion, we should continue to 'battle' through to reach our intended goal.

◇ Since a wreck can happen due to circumstances beyond our control, such a dream can indicate a greater need for control, or management of resources.

▣ Dreaming of a wreck – such as a car or shipwreck – indicates that our plans may be thwarted in some way. It is necessary to decide in waking life whether we are at fault for the failure of our plans or someone else is.

You might also like to consult the entries for Accident and Disaster.

WRITING

⚙ We may not be consciously aware of our spiritual progression. A manuscript would suggest some aspect of ancient knowledge. Dreaming of writing suggests a subconscious record is being kept. Spiritually our signature is a reflection of ourselves; it is a representation of who we perceive ourselves to be.

◇ Writing as a creative art is meaningful, and as a form of self-expression it perhaps allows us to communicate when spoken words are inadequate. In dreams we may learn how to communicate with ourselves in differing ways. Computers are a way of writing just as much as pens. Transcribing information in a dream signifies committing it to memory. At those times when we are arranging legal matters or agreements, but are actually not sure if we are doing the right thing, our signature can appear in dreams as obliterated or illegible.

▣ To dream of writing is an attempt to communicate information that we have. Sometimes the instrument we are writing with is important. For instance, a pencil would suggest that the information is less permanent than with a pen. Our signature in a dream suggests that we have an appreciation of ourselves. We are prepared to recognize who we are and to make our mark in the world.

Also consult the entries for Ink, Paper/Parchment and Pen/Pencil for further information.

X

🌞 Perfect Man within the Cosmos is depicted with arms and legs outstretched in the shape of an X. As a point of power and the Roman numeral ten it suggests new beginnings or potential. It may also signify balance.

💗 If a cross appears in the shape of an X, this usually represents the idea of sacrifice or perhaps of torture.

▣ If an X appears in a dream, we are usually 'marking the spot'. It can also represent an error, a misjudgement or possibly something we particularly need to note. Written as a kiss it signifies unification of two entities.

Also consult the entry for Cross in Shapes/Patterns.

X-RAYS

🌞 Spiritually, an X-ray can symbolize a new clarity that you are about to experience. This 'clear-sightedness' should enable you to move ahead more confidently and face the future with equanimity.

💗 Within waking life, it may be that there is something we need to 'see through'. This can be a play on words, in that we need to finish off a task, or we may need to have a very clear view of the situation around us.

▣ Dreaming of X-rays can be significant in a number of ways. There may be something influencing your life on an unconscious level which needs to be revealed. If you are carrying out the X-ray it may be necessary to look more deeply into a situation. There may also be a fear of illness, either in yourself or others. This image is obviously more likely to occur when you have health concerns or work in a hospital situation.

Y

⚙ The Y is said to represent the human form with outstretched arms, reaching to the Cosmos, sometimes in supplication, otherwise in glorification. It is also thought to represent the choices that Man must make between good and evil.

♥ Moving from the bottom upwards, the point at which the Y forks suggests the point at which you may demand autonomy for yourself, the right to make your own choices. From the other perspective, in two halves coming together it suggests androgeny or a perfect blend of two polarities.

▦ On a purely mundane level this letter may denote the dividing of the ways or a change in direction.

You may also like to consult the entry for Androgen/Androgeny.

YACHT – *see* BOAT IN TRANSPORT.

YARN

⚙ In former times storytellers were known as weavers of stories, which is where the symbolism arose. The myths and stories of the old heroes who undertook their own spiritual journey are archetypal and can help us identify a strategy for life.

♥ A yarn – as in a tale or story – is most often to do with our sense of history or of continuity. To be being told a yarn or story links with our need for heroes and heroines, and perhaps our need for a mentor.

▦ Yarn in the sense of knitting yarn or twine often signifies our ability to create order out of chaos. In olden times it suggested spinning, an archetypal symbol for life, and often in dreams it is this image that is portrayed. Tangled yarn may suggest a complex situation. We fashion our lives out of what we are given.

▕▏ It was once said that yarn in a woman's dream signified that she would marry well, but in a man's dream suggested that he would find himself a dutiful wife. It has less such significance nowadays, but yarn always has the overtones of industriousness and hard work.

You might like to consult the section on Archetypes in the Introduction.

YAWN

⚙ In the physical world a yawn is a way of taking in more oxygen. In the spiritual sense it is our inner selves attempting to assimilate more knowledge or power.

◈ In the animal kingdom a yawn often is a warning against aggression, and to actually be yawning in dreams may be a way of controlling our own or other's abusive or overly assertive behaviour.

▦ If we become conscious of yawning in a dream it can indicate boredom and tiredness in the everyday. We may also be attempting to communicate with someone, but have not yet thought through what we wish to say.

YEAR – *see* **TIME**

YEARN

❁ To yearn is to long for. One stage of spiritual development is a yearning to free yourself from mundane matters. You may have become impatient in a seemingly never-ending search for your spiritual self. This feeling is often heightened in a dream.

◈ If we have suppressed our needs through long habit or self-denial, an urgency may emerge in dreams for the very thing that we have consciously denied.

▦ Feelings in dreams are often heightened in intensity. A need which may be perfectly manageable in ordinary everyday life becomes a yearning and seeking in dreams. Such a dream would highlight an emotion which we may need to look at in order to understand.

▣ In some senses yearning is a more feminine feeling than masculine. However, it is also a somewhat chaotic feeling, and therefore somewhat adolescent. In both men's and women's dreams it can be given this interpretation.

YELL – *see* **SHOUT**

YES

❁ We are being given – or have given ourselves – permission to spiritually grow and flourish. With this permission, you can look towards a more directed lifestyle.

◈ Often, before we are able to make changes in our ordinary, everyday lives, we need to give ourselves permission on an unconscious level. Recognizing this in the dream state can be an important part of our growth process.

▦ Occasionally in dreams and in the hypnogogic state, we become aware that we have 'said' yes. This is an instinctive acceptance or acknowledgement of the validity of whatever has been happening.

Consult the Introduction for clarification.

YEW

❁ A yew tree outlives most other trees, and regenerates when its branches take root, so even if the main trunk dies it still continues. Thus it symbolizes transformation, great age and spiritual immortality. Ancient peoples were in the habit of planting yew trees as acts of sanctification near to where they expected to be buried.

◈ Considered to be the most powerful tree for protection against evil, the yew is a means of connecting to your ancestors and a bringer of dreams and journeys into other dimensions. There can also be an aspect of word-play here as sometimes happens in dreams, in that the 'yew' is focusing your attention away from yourself as the dreamer to some other aspect of the dream.

▦ In former times the yew tree symbolized mourning and sadness and was a symbol of the old magic. While few people would necessarily recognize a yew tree, there is, on an unconscious level, awareness of such knowledge in everyone. Such a symbol can surface as instinctive awareness in dreams.

You may also like to consult the entry for Tree.

YIELD

◈ You may have been contemplating the idea of a more spiritual existence for some time, and have now finally yielded, or submitted, to the notion. In *T'ai Chi* (an art of personal discipline) knowing when to yield in order to succeed in the end is an important lesson.

◈ Yielding is one of the more feminine attributes and signifies our need to let go and simply 'go with the flow'.

▦ To yield in a dream is to become aware of the futility of confrontation. To understand this we may need to look at situations within our everyday lives.

⦂ In a man's dream yielding suggests submission to the inevitable, whereas in a woman's dream it suggests submission to a stronger force.

YIN AND YANG

◈ Perfect Spiritual Balance is created by the energy created between two complementary opposites, the passive feminine principle and the active masculine. Each contains within itself the 'seed' of the other, creating a state of inner stability. This image occurs in dreams when we begin to approach such a state.

◈ We are continuously searching for balance, though not necessarily a state of inertia. The yin-yang symbol signifies a state of dynamic potential, the sense that anything is possible.

▦ A representation of the Cosmic egg, the beginning of all things, this symbol has become much better known in the last thirty years in the West as the balance of two complementary opposites. In dreams it indicates the balance between the instinctive, intuitive nature of the feminine and the active, rational nature of the masculine.

⦂ As a symbol, this will only appear in both men's and women's dreams when a certain state of internal equilibrium is becoming apparent.

YOB

✦ In spiritual terms the yob, as in the uncontrolled and uncontrollable youth, signifies a quality of waywardness seen in gods such as Loki and Mercury. It is an untamed part of the psyche.

♥ In not having respect for the rules laid down by society, the yob draws our attention to those aspects of ourselves and others which refuse to conform.

▦ More mundanely, such a figure in dreams can highlight a threat or difficulty in our work or personal field of endeavour.

YOGA/YOGI

✦ The word 'yoga' comes from Sanskrit language and means union or merger. The practice is in itself a spiritual discipline and in dreams symbolizes that which is needed to achieve union with the Divine.

♥ The practice of many of the different forms of yoga actually opens many pathways to perception and can enhance our dreams, allowing us access to universal truths. To be dreaming of doing yoga suggests a need for a deeper understanding of our own impulses.

▦ Yoga can play an important role in maintaining a balance between work and healthy mind. Because yoga is a physical discipline, a philosophy of mind/body connection and a spiritual way of life, any or all of these significances can become apparent in dreams. A yogi (spiritual practitioner) in dreams is a representation of a wise person or teacher and alerts us to the need in us to find such a person.

You might also like to consult the entry for Yin and Yang.

YOUTH – *see* ARCHETYPES AND PEOPLE

YULE/YULE LOG

✦ In Pagan times a log was decorated and burnt at the time of the Winter solstice (Yule) in order to clear away the Old Year, and to celebrate the return of the sun. In dreams it is seen as a symbol of light and new life.

♥ In modern times, the Yule log is often symbolized by a celebration cake. Decorated in a traditional fashion with greenery and candles, it honours the Holly King, who dies at this time, giving way to the Oak King who brings light. Therefore it tends to suggest the New Year and new beginnings in dream language.

▦ A Yule log represents an offering or sacrifice, particularly at the time of a spiritual or religious celebration when we pay homage to the gods. Originally the bringing in of the Yule log was a whole ritual in itself, requiring special prayers and offerings to ensure the next year's prosperity. In dreams such an image may suggest a time of celebration or of prosperity.

Also consult the entry for Fire as well as Spiritual Imagery in the Introduction.

ZEAL/ZEALOT

It is more likely that we would dream of a terrorist rather than a zealot, yet they both have the same fanatical belief in and love for one principle. There comes a time in spiritual development where we can, if we are not careful, develop extremist behaviour. The presence of a zealot in dreams can help us focus.

Zeal is love in action and in the psychological sense suggests service to others and denial of the self. In dreams it suggests that some of our behaviour may be 'over the top'.

Historically, the Zealots were a group who objected to Roman rulership and sought to violently eradicate it. This kind of 'love in action' has relevance in today's world when we come up against fanaticism in all its forms. Dreaming of a zealot suggests that we may need to act more circumspectly to achieve our aims.

ZEBRA – *see* **ANIMALS**

ZEN – *see* **SPIRITUAL IMAGERY IN THE INTRODUCTION**

ZERO – *see* **NUMBERS**

ZIGGURAT

The ancient ziggurats of Mesopotamia were temples built by kings to celebrate their sacred marriage with the Divine, which at that time was matriarchal. Spiritually, when this image appears, therefore, it celebrates our awareness of our own potential for such union.

The seven steps or stages up to the entrance into the secret chamber at the top of the ziggurat, leading where union took place, correspond to the different stages of awareness in Eastern religions known as chakras. So to find ourselves in dreams at, say, the fourth step or stage would signify the need to come to terms with our ability to love and be loved.

On a purely mundane level the ziggurat symbolizes a sacred secure space and the ability to access that space within ourselves.

Because the ziggurat signified union, in a woman's dream it suggests her receptivity, while in a man's dream it suggests his willingness to be of service to mankind.

You might like to consult the entries for Pyramid and Temple.

ZIGZAG

❋ A zigzag is symbolic of a lightning flash which represents new potential and growth. It is the transmission of energy between the spiritual and physical realms – in essence, a revelation.

♡ In a psychological sense, we are able to achieve a new level of awareness which will radically change our perceptions.

▥ When we see a zigzag in dreams there is the potential to be struck by some mishap, such as in a bolt of lightning. Usually an event will occur which brings about a discharge of energy; circumstances will then be brought back into balance.

ZIP

❋ A zip fastener symbolizes spiritual connections and the interlocking of the physical and spiritual realms. In technology, a zip drive is an efficient means of storing information and can therefore represent the Akashic Records – all of life's vicissitudes.

♡ Psychologically, we are capable of being either open or closed to our friends and family. Often a zip can highlight this in a dream.

▥ A zip appearing in a dream may indicate our ability – or difficulty – in maintaining relationships with other people. A stuck zip suggests a difficulty in keeping our dignity in an awkward situation. As computers themselves become more efficient, a zip drive in dreams can symbolize our working environment.

ZODIAC

❋ The zodiac wheel is symbolic of our relationship with the universe. Sometimes the signs of the zodiac are used in dreams to demonstrate time or time passing, and also suggest courses of action we might take. Each sign also rules (has responsibility for) a particular part of the physical body, and any imbalance is reflected into dreams through the symbolism of the zodiac.

♡ Hidden information often comes to us through dreams. As we become more knowledgeable these symbols tap into arcane wisdom which allows us to live our lives in tune with the universe. The spheres of influence of the planets were first described by Plato and modern astrology stills tend to follow his teachings.

By then using the correspondences we can harness the energy of the zodiac in everyday life – its colours and gemstones. Below are some of the most important correspondences:

Aries – the symbol is the Ram and it governs the head. The colour associated with the sign is red; its specific gemstones are amethyst and diamond.

Taurus – the symbol is the Bull and it governs the throat. The colours associated with the sign are blue and pink; its specific gemstones are moss agate and emerald.

Gemini – the symbol is the Twins (often shown as masculine and feminine) and it governs the shoulders, arms and hands. The colour associated with the sign is yellow; its specific gemstones are agate and beryl.

Cancer – the symbol is the Crab and it governs the stomach and higher organs of digestion. The colours associated with the sign are either violet or emerald green; its specific gemstones are moonstones and pearls.

Leo – the symbol is the Lion and it governs the heart, lungs and liver. The colours associated with the sign are gold and orange; its specific gemstones are topaz and tourmaline.

Virgo – the symbol is the Virgin and it governs the abdomen and intestines. The colours associated with the sign are grey and navy blue; its specific gemstones are pink jasper and jade.

Libra – the symbol is the Scales and it governs the lumbar region, kidneys and skin. The colours associated with the sign are blue and violet; its specific gemstones are opal and lapis lazuli.

Scorpio – the symbol is the Scorpion and it governs the genitals. The colours associated with the sign are deep red and purple; its specific gemstones turquoise and ruby.

Sagittarius – The symbol is the Archer and it governs the hips nervous system. The colours associated with the sign are orange; its specific gemstones are carbuncle and amethyst.

Capricorn – the symbol is the Goat and it governs the associated with the sign are violet and green; its specific black onyx.

Aquarius – the symbol is the Water-Bearer and it go ankles. The colour associated with the sign is gemstones are garnet and zircon.

Pisces – the symbol is The Fishes and it gover associated with the sign are sea-green and r coral and chrysolite.

Everyone has a fascination for understanding the significance of the begin the journey of self-discovery t will appear in dreams. Frequently, own star sign will appear, almos

we deal with that image will give us insight into how we really feel about ourselves.

ZOO

✷ Dreaming of being in a zoo suggests the need to understand some of our natural urges and instincts. We perhaps need to be more objective in our appraisal than subjective.

♡ There may be an urge to return to simpler, more basic modes of behaviour. Some people are natural observers, and we may be being alerted to the fact that we also need to be capable of participating in conduct appropriate to the group to which we belong. We also, of course, may be conscious that we ourselves are being observed, perhaps in the work situation.

▦ Dreaming of a zoo can alert us to the necessary and appropriate customs and behaviour or the hierarchical structure in an impending situation.

You might also consult the entry for Animals for further clarification.

10,000 Dreams EXPLAINED

HOW TO USE YOUR DREAMS TO ENHANCE YOUR LIFE AND RELATIONSHIPS

The most authoritative, comprehensive and up-to-date book available on dreams and dreaming, *10,000 Dreams Explained* enables you to tap into a whole new level of knowledge and understanding. The author, Pamela Ball, is one of the world's foremost dream interpreters and in this, her latest book, she gives you the opportunity to heal previous trauma, to enhance the way you live and to reach for the best within yourself.

ISBN 978-1-84837-087-6

9 781848 370876 >

The Mammoth Book of

BEST BRITISH
MYSTERIES

EDITED BY MAXIM JAKUBOWSKI

ROBINSON

ROBINSON

First published in Great Britain by Robinson,
an imprint of Constable & Robinson Ltd, 2008

Reprinted by Robinson in 2017

7 9 10 8 6

A CIP catalogue record for this book
is available from the British Library.

UK ISBN: 978-1-84529-711-4

Printed and bound in Great Britain by
CPI Group (UK) Ltd., Croydon CR0 4YY

Papers used by Robinson are from well-managed forests
and other responsible sources

Robinson
An imprint of
Little, Brown Book Group
Carmelite House
50 Victoria Embankment
London EC4Y 0DZ

An Hachette UK Company
www.hachette.co.uk

www.littlebrown.co.uk

CONTENTS

COPYRIGHT AND ACKNOWLEDGMENTS

INTRODUCTION

Welcome to a new beginning, or should that be a new life of crime?

Six years ago, slightly peeved that various best of the year anthologies published in America deliberately restricted themselves to publishing only stories by US authors, I made a proposal to a London publishing house for a similar series but this time exclusively devoted to British crime and mystery authors. Not only did I believe there was enough good material out there in magazine, anthology, radio and Internet territories to fill a respectable annual volume, but was also aware that many of these stories were, for market reasons, only available in the USA and thus unknown to a specifically British readership. Talk about not being a prophet in your own country!

The initial volume, titled BEST BRITISH MYSTERIES, was a runaway success and was even advertised on TV come that Christmas and earned deserved plaudits for both the book's concept and many of its illustrious contributors. The series has gone from strength to strength since then, adding first the number of the year from which the stories came from and, later, just a series number to distinguish the respective volumes. Rewardingly, many of the stories, albeit by British authors, had only appeared previously in the USA and thus became eligible for the Crime Writers' Association best short story Dagger award, and have since dominated a large proportion of the annual shortlist.

The principle is the same every year: read virtually all the crime and mystery stories published in a variety of sources, some predictable, others much less so, and I select the best. You will find, in these gripping pages, hardboiled tales, grisly murders, ingenious puzzles, cosy traditional tales of sleuthing and derring-do, memorable characters, heroes and dastardly villains, psychological landscapes of evil, thrills and spills and even laughs, etc . . . The idea is to present the whole breadth of what is being written in the mystery field today and a large field it is indeed, which continues to surprise and delight me on a daily basis.

Some authors are indeed big names and familiar to many readers, while others are talented newcomers I expect you to hear more about as their next books confirm their undoubted talent, but first and foremost it is the intrinsic quality of their storytelling that caught my attention, and will I hope please you. Shock you maybe, surprise you even, but principally entertain you. The settings of the stories range far and wide both geographically and historically and demonstrate how far ranging the crime and mystery field can be in the hands of its superior craftsmen and craftswomen.

Colin Dexter returns to the familiar and popular world of Inspectors Morse and Lewis, while Len Deighton – in his first short story in almost 20 years – welcomes back the familiar figure of Sherlock Holmes. Bill James ventures out again with those devious cops Harpur and Iles and many other favourite authors trip the murderous light fantastic with glee and dark resolve. There is so much talent in British crime writing these days and I would encourage you to pursue some of these authors well beyond this book and explore full-length books by them, should their respective story catch your eye (or your gut . . .).

Help British writers make crime pay and have a ball in the process. What a noble mission!

Maxim Jakubowski

THE .50 SOLUTION

Lee Child

Most times I assess the client and then the target and only afterward do I set the price. It's about common sense and variables. If the client is rich, I ask for more. If the target is tough, I ask for more. If there are major expenses involved, I ask for more. So if I'm working overseas on behalf of a billionaire against a guy in a remote hideout with a competent protection team on his side, I'm going to ask for maybe a hundred times what I would want from some local chick looking to solve her marital problems in a quick and messy manner. Variables, and common sense.

But this time the negotiation started differently.

The guy who came to see me was rich. That was clear. His wealth was pore-deep. Not just his clothes. Not just his car. This was a guy who had been rich forever. Maybe for generations. He was tall and grey and silvery and self-assured. He was a patrician. It was all right there in the way he held himself, the way he spoke, the way he took charge.

First thing he talked about was the choice of weapon.

He said, "I hear you've used a Barrett Model Ninety on more than one occasion."

I said, "You hear right."

"You like that piece?"

"It's a fine rifle."

"So you'll use it for me."

"I choose the weapon," I said.

"Based on what?"

"Need."

"You'll need it."

I asked, "Why? Long range?"

"Maybe two hundred yards."

"I don't need a Barrett Ninety for two hundred yards."

"It's what I want."

"Will the target be wearing body armor?"

"No."

"Inside a vehicle?"

"Open air."

"Then I'll use a three-oh-eight. Or something European."

"I want that fifty-caliber shell."

"A three-oh-eight or a NATO round will get him just as dead from two hundred yards."

"Maybe not."

Looking at him I was pretty sure this was a guy who had never fired a .50 Barrett in his life. Or a .308 Remington. Or an M16, or an FN, or an H&K. Or any kind of a rifle. He had probably never fired anything at all, except maybe a BB gun as a kid and workers as a adult.

I said, "The Barrett is an awkward weapon. It's four feet long and it doesn't break down. It weighs twenty-two pounds. It's got bipod legs, for Christ's sake. It's like an artillery piece. Hard to conceal. And it's very loud. Maybe the loudest rifle in the history of the world."

He said, "I like that fifty-caliber shell."

"I'll give you one," I said. "You can plate it with gold and put it on a chain and wear it around your neck."

"I want you to use it."

Then I started thinking maybe this guy was some kind of a sadist. A caliber of .50 is a decimal fraction, just another way of saying half an inch. A lead bullet a half inch across is a big thing. It weighs about two ounces, and any kind of a decent load fires it close to two thousand miles an hour. It could catch a supersonic jet fighter and bring it down. Against a person two hundred yards away, it's going to cut him in two. Like making the guy swallow a bomb, and then setting it off.

I said, "You want a spectacle, I could do it close with a knife. You know, if you want to send a message."

He said, "That's not the issue. This is not about a message. This is about the result."

"Can't be," I said. "From two hundred yards I can get a result with anything. Something short with a folding stock, I can walk away afterward with it under my coat. Or I could throw a rock."

"I want you to use the Barrett."

"Expensive," I said. "I'd have to leave it behind. Which means paying through the nose to make it untraceable. It'll cost more than a foreign car for the ordnance alone. Before we even talk about my fee."

"Okay," he said, no hesitation.

I said, "It's ridiculous."

He said nothing. I thought: *Two hundred yards, no body armor, in the open air. Makes no sense.* So I asked.

I said, "Who's the target?"

He said, "A horse."

I was quiet for a long moment. "What kind of a horse?"

"A thoroughbred racehorse."

I asked, "You own racehorses?"

He said, "Dozens of them."

"Good ones?"

"Some of the very best."

"So the target is what, a rival?"

"A thorn in my side."

After that, it made a lot more sense. The guy said, "I'm not an idiot. I've thought about it very carefully. It's got to look accidental. We can't just shoot the horse in the head. That's too obvious. It's got to look like the real target was the owner, but your aim was off and the horse is collateral damage. So the shot can't look placed. It's got to look random. Neck, shoulder, whatever. But I need death or permanent disability."

I said, "Which explains your preference for the Barrett."

He nodded. I nodded back. A thoroughbred racehorse weighs about half a ton. A .308 or a NATO round fired randomly into its center mass might not do the job. Not in terms of death or permanent disability. But a big .50 shell almost certainly would. Even if you weigh half a ton, it's pretty hard to struggle along with a hole the size of a garbage can blown through any part of you.

I asked, "Who's the owner? Is he a plausible target in himself?"

The guy told me who the owner was, and we agreed he was a plausible target. Rumors, shady connections.

Then I said, "What about you? Are you two enemies, personally?"

"You mean, will I be suspected of ordering the hit that misses?"

"Exactly."

"Not a chance," my guy said. "We don't know each other."

"Except as rival owners."

"There are hundreds of rival owners."

"Is a horse of yours going to win if this guy's doesn't?"

"I certainly hope so."

"So they'll look at you."

"Not if it looks like the man was the target, instead of the horse."

I asked, "When?"

He told me anytime within the next four days.

I asked, "Where?"

He told me the horse was in a facility some ways south. Horse country, obviously, grand fields, lush grass, white fences, rolling hills. He told me about long routes through the countryside, called gallops, where the horses worked out just after dawn. He told me about the silence and the early mists. He told me how in the week before a big race the owner would be there every morning to assess his horse's form, to revel in its power and speed and grace and appetite. He told me about the stands of trees that were everywhere and would provide excellent cover.

Then he stopped talking. I felt a little foolish, but I asked him anyway: "Do you have a photograph? Of the target?"

He took an envelope from his inside jacket pocket. Gave it to me. In it was a glossy color picture of a horse. It looked posed, like a promotional item. Like an actor or an actress has headshots made, for publicity. This particular horse was a magnificent animal. Tall, shiny, muscular, almost jet-black, with a white blaze on its face. Quite beautiful.

"Okay," I said.

Then my guy asked me his own question.

He asked me, "How much?"

It was an interesting issue. Technically we were only conspiring to shoot a horse. In most states that's a property crime. A long way from homicide. And I already had an untraceable Barrett Ninety. As a matter of fact, I had three. Their serial numbers stopped dead with the Israeli army. One of them was well used. It was about ready for a new barrel anyway. It would make a fine throw-down gun. Firing cold through a worn barrel wasn't something I would risk against a human, but against something the size of a horse from two hundred yards it wouldn't be a problem. If I aimed at the fattest part of the animal I could afford to miss by up to a foot.

I didn't tell the guy any of that, of course. Instead I banged on for a while about the price of the rifle and the premium I would have to pay for dead-ended paperwork. Then I talked about risk, and waited to see if he stopped me. But he didn't. I could tell he was obsessed. He had a goal. He wanted his own horse to win, and that fact was blinding him to reality just the same way some people get all wound up about betrayal and adultery and business partnerships.

I looked at the photograph again.

"One hundred thousand dollars," I said.

He said nothing.

"In cash," I said.

He said nothing.

"Up front," I said.

He nodded.

"One condition," he said. "I want to be there. I want to see it happen."

I looked at him and I looked at the photograph and I thought about a hundred grand in cash.

"Okay," I said. "You can be there."

He opened the briefcase he had down by his leg and took out a brick of money. It looked okay, smelled okay, and felt okay. There was probably more in the case, but I didn't care. A hundred grand was enough, in the circumstances.

"Day after tomorrow," I said.

We agreed on a place to meet, down south, down in horse country, and he left.

*　　*　　*

I hid the money where I always do, which is in a metal trunk in my storage unit. Inside the trunk the first thing you see is a human skull inside a Hefty One Zip bag. On the white panel where you're supposed to write what you're freezing is lettered: *This Man Tried to Rip Me Off*. It isn't true, of course. The skull came from an antique shop. Probably an old medical school specimen from the Indian subcontinent.

Next to the money trunk was the gun trunk. I took out the worn Barrett and checked it over. Disassembled it, cleaned it, oiled it, wiped it clean, and then put it back together wearing latex gloves. I loaded a fresh magazine, still with the gloves on. Then I loaded the magazine into the rifle and slid the rifle end-on into an old shoulder-borne golf bag. Then I put the golf bag into the trunk of my car and left it there.

In my house I propped the racehorse photograph on my mantel. I spent a lot of time staring at it.

I met the guy at the time and place we had agreed. It was a lonely crossroad, close to a cross-country track that led to a distant stand of trees, an hour before dawn. The weather was cold. My guy had a coat and gloves on, and binoculars around his neck. I had gloves on too. Latex. But no binoculars. I had a Leupold & Stevens scope on the Barrett, in the golf bag.

I was relaxed, feeling what I always feel when I'm about to kill something, which is to say nothing very much at all. But my client was unrelaxed. He was shivering with an anticipation that was almost pornographic in its intensity. Like a paedophile on a plane to Thailand. I didn't like it much.

We walked side by side through the dew. The ground was hard and pocked by footprints. Lots of them, coming and going.

"Who's been here?" I asked.

"Racetrack touts," my guy said. "Sports journalists, gamblers looking for inside dope."

"Looks like Times Square," I said. "I don't like it."

"It'll be okay today. Nobody scouts here anymore. They all know this horse. They all know it can win in its sleep."

We walked on in silence. Reached the stand of trees. It was oval-shaped, thin at the northern end. We stepped back and forth until we had a clear line of sight through the trunks. Dawn light was in the sky. Two hundred yards away and slightly downhill was a broad grass clearing with plenty of tire tracks showing. A thin grey mist hung in the air.

"This is it?" I said.

My guy nodded. "The horses come in from the south. The cars come in from the west. They meet right there."

"Why?"

"No real reason. Ritual, mostly. Backslapping and bullshitting. The pride of ownership."

I took the Barrett out of the golf bag. I had already decided how I was going to set up the shot. No bipod. I wanted the gun low and free. I knelt on one knee and rested the muzzle in the crook of a branch. Sighted through the scope. Racked the bolt and felt the first mighty .50 shell smack home into the chamber.

"Now we wait," my guy said. He stood at my shoulder, maybe a yard to my right and a yard behind me.

The cars arrived first. They were SUVs, really. Working machines, old and muddy and dented. A Jeep, and two Land Rovers. Five guys climbed out. Four looked poor and one looked rich.

"Trainer and stable lads and the owner," my guy said. "The owner is the one in the long coat."

The five of them stamped and shuffled and their breath pooled around their heads.

"Listen," my guy said.

I heard something way off to my left. To the south. A low drumming, and a sound like giant bellows coughing and pumping. Hooves, and huge equine lungs cycling gallons of sweet fresh morning air.

I rocked backward until I was sitting right down on the ground.

"Get ready," my guy said, from above and behind me.

There were altogether ten horses. They came up in a ragged arrowhead formation, slowing, drifting off-line, tossing their heads, their hard breathing blowing violent yard-long trumpet-shaped plumes of steam ahead of them.

"What is this?" I asked. "The whole roster?"

"String," my guy said. "That's what we call it. This is his whole first string."

In the grey dawn light and under the steam all the horses looked exactly the same to me.

But that didn't matter.

"Ready?" my guy said. "They won't be here long."

"Open your mouth," I said.

"What?"

"Open your mouth, real wide. Like you're yawning."

"Why?"

"To equalize the pressure. Like on a plane. I told you, this is a loud gun. It's going to blow your eardrums otherwise. You'll be deaf for a month."

I glanced around and checked. He had opened his mouth, but halfheartedly, like a guy waiting for the dentist to get back from looking at a chart.

"No, like this," I said. I showed him. I opened my mouth as wide as it would go and pulled my chin back into my neck until the tendons hurt in the hinge of my jaw.

He did the same thing.

I whipped the Barrett's barrel way up and around, fast and smooth, like a duck hunter tracking a flushed bird. Then I pulled the trigger. Shot my guy through the roof of his mouth. The giant rifle boomed and kicked and the top of my guy's head came off like a hard-boiled egg. His body came down in a heap and sprawled. I dropped the rifle on top of him and pulled his right shoe off. Tossed it on the ground. Then I ran. Two minutes later I was back in my car. Four minutes later I was a mile away.

I was up an easy hundred grand, but the world was down an industrialist, a philanthropist, and a racehorse owner. That's what the Sunday papers said. He had committed suicide. The way the cops had pieced it together, he had tormented himself over the fact that his best horse always came in second. He had spied on his rival's workout, maybe hoping for some sign of fallibility. None had been forthcoming. So he had somehow obtained a sniper rifle, last legally owned by the Israel Defense Force. Maybe he had planned to shoot the rival horse, but at the last minute he hadn't been able to go through with it. So, depressed and tormented, he had reversed the rifle, put the muzzle in his mouth, kicked off his shoe, and used his toe on the trigger. A police officer of roughly the same height had taken part in a simulation to prove that such a thing was physically possible, even with a gun as long as the Barrett.

Near the back of the paper were the racing results. The big black horse had won by seven lengths. My guy's runner had been scratched.

I kept the photograph on my mantel for a long time afterward. A girl I met much later noticed that it was the only picture I had in the house. She asked me if I liked animals better than people. I told her that I did, mostly. She liked me for it. But not enough to stick around.

THE DEBT

Simon Kernick

Now I've got a cousin called Kevin. Just like in that song by the Undertones. Unlike in the song, though, the Kevin I know isn't going anywhere near heaven. In fact, the no-good cheating dog's far more likely to be disappearing through a trapdoor into the fiery underworld, and deservedly so too. In fact, if I could get hold of him now, I'd gladly give a helping hand sending him there. Only problem is, there's a queue of people wanting to do just that, and I'm sitting opposite one of them now. None other than Jim "The Crim" Sneddon: gangland legend and all-round wicked hombre, renowned for his extreme cruelty to his fellow human beings, although they do say he loves animals.

The Crim leans forward in his immense leather armchair and points a stubby, sausage-like finger in my direction. I'm sitting on his "guest" sofa, a flashy leather number that's currently covered in tarpaulin, presumably in case things turn nasty, and as you can imagine, not being either cute or furry, I'm feeling less than comfortable. The Crim's thin, hooded eyes are a cold onyx, and when he speaks, the words come out in a low nicotine growl that sound like a cheap, badly damaged car turning over.

"A debt is a debt is a debt," he rumbles, speaking in the manner of a Buddhist monk imparting some great metaphysical wisdom.

"I'm aware of that," I say, holding his gaze, not showing any fear, because if you let them see your weaknesses, then you may as well throw in the towel, "but the debt in question is between you and Kevin."

"No no no no," chuckles The Crim, shaking his huge leonine head. "It don't work like that. Do it, boys?"

There are two men in charcoal black suits flanking the sofa on either side, and they both voice their agreement.

To my left, blocking out much of the room's ambient light, is one Glenroy Frankham, better known as "Ten Man Gang", a six feet six, twenty-five stone hulk of a human being, with a head so small it looks like it's been professionally shrunk, and hands that can, and probably do, crush babies. Such is his strength, he's reputed to be the only man in British penal history to tear his way out of a straitjacket, although I'm surprised they found one that fit him in the first place. His belly looks like a storage room for cannonballs.

To my right stands Johann "Fingers The Knife" Bennett, so-called because of his propensity for slicing off the digits of uncooperative debtors while The Gang holds them in place. The going rate's a finger a day until the money's been paid in full. As you can imagine, The Knife's somewhat "hands on" approach has an enviable success rate, and only once has a debt not been cleared within twenty-four hours of him being called in. On that occasion, the debtor was so broke they had to start on his toes before he finally came up with the money. The guy was a degenerate gambler and I still see him limping around sometimes, although he plays a lot less poker these days.

It's poker that's been Kevin's downfall. That, and the fact that he chose to play his games against Jim the Crim, a man whose standards of fair play leave, it has to be said, a great deal to be desired. You don't rise to multi-millionaire status in the arms and loansharking industries by adhering to the rules of the level playing field, or by being compassionate.

"It ain't my fault, is it?" continues The Crim now, "that your cousin decides to take off into the wild blue yonder without paying me the thirty-four grand he owes."

"You told me it was thirty-three."

"That was Monday, Billy. Today's Wednesday. I've got the interest to think about. It's a lot of money we're looking at here."

"And I still don't know why it's suddenly mine and my family's responsibility," I say, thinking it's time to get assertive.

The Crim bares his teeth in what I think must be a smile, it's not too easy to tell. "It's the etiquette of the matter," he says, clearing his throat, then spitting something thick and nasty into a plate-sized ashtray balanced on one of the chair's arms. "I can't be seen to be letting off a debt this size. It would do my reputation no good at all. And since there's about as much chance of your cousin reappearing as The Gang here taking up hang-gliding, someone's got to pay. And that someone's his mother."

And this, my friends, is why I'm here voluntarily. Because it is my aunt Lena – my dead mother's only sister, and the woman who brought me up from the tender age of thirteen – who is the person currently being treated as The Crim's debtor, and this is a situation that, as an honourable man, I can't allow to continue. She's prepared to pay up too by selling her house, in order to protect her only son from the consequences of his rank stupidity, but I've told her to leave it and let me see what can be done to alleviate the situation, although I'm beginning to think that it's not a lot.

"I understand your position, Jim," I say, trying to sound reasonable, "but my aunt hasn't got the money to pay you, it's as simple as that. However," I add, wanting to avoid a confrontation I know I can't win, "I haven't come here empty-handed. I've got five grand in my pocket. Consider it a deposit on what's owed. Then, when I track down Kevin, which I promise I'm going to do, I'll make sure I get you the other twenty-eight. You've got my word on that."

"Twenty-nine, you mean, and I want the lot now."

The trick in circumstances like these is always to have some room for manoeuvre. "I can get you ten by the end of tonight," I tell him, hoping this'll act as a sweetener.

It doesn't.

"I don't think you're hearing me right, Billy," he growls. "I told you what I want. Now, if you ain't got it, we'll have to see if we have better luck extracting it from your auntie."

"He came in a nice car, Mr Sneddon," says The Knife, his voice a reedy whisper, like wind through a graveyard. "It looks like one of those new BMW 7 Series."

Uh-oh, I think. Not my pride and joy. But, oh dear, The Crim's craggy, reddened face is already brightening. It is a most unpleasant sight. "Now that's what I like to hear," he says.

"And it'll cover the cost of your cousin's misdemeanours, no problem."

I shake my head, knowing I'm going to have to nip this one in the bud pretty sharpish. "That car belongs to me, Jim, and it's not for sale. I bought it with the proceeds of my last fight."

"I remember that last fight. Against Trevor 'The Gibbon' Hutton. I had a bet on it. Cost me five grand when you knocked him down in the eighth." His expression suddenly darkens at the memory, as if this is somehow my fault.

"Well, you know how hard I had to work for it then, don't you?" I tell him, making a final stand. "I'm not giving it up, no way."

The Crim nods once to The Knife and I feel the touch of cold metal in the curve of skin behind my ear.

My heart sinks, especially as I still owe fifteen grand to the finance company. I love that car.

Although I feel like bursting into tears, I keep my cool. "You've changed your weapon, Johann," I say calmly, inclining my head a little in his direction.

"A gun's less messy," The Crim replies, answering for him. He puts out a hand. "Now, unless you want The Knife here to be clearing the contents of your head off the tarpaulin, you'd better give me the keys."

So, pride and joy or not, I have no choice but to hand them over.

The Crim thinks he's doing me a favour by driving me home. Instead, it is akin to twisting the knife in a dying man.

"This really is a sweet piece of machinery," he tells me as we sail smoothly through the wet night streets of the city, the tyres easily holding the slick surface of the tarmac. As if I don't already know this. "Ah, this is what it's all about," he adds, sliding his filthy paws all over the steering wheel, and reclining in the Nasca leather seat. And he's right, too. There's nothing like the freedom of the open road, coupled with all the comforts the 21st Century has to offer; it's like driving in your own front room. The problem is it's now The Crim's front room. And it's his music too: a Back to the Seventies CD he picked up from his office, which is blaring out track after track of retro rubbish.

As we drive, a Range Rover containing The Knife and The Gang inside brings up the rear. The Crim tells me he never likes travelling in the same car as his two bodyguards. He strokes the car's panel and tells me that they're Neanderthals who don't appreciate the finer things in life, although quite how *Tiger Feet* by Mud fits into this category is beyond me. He tells me all this, even though I am hugely uninterested, and when he drops me off, he even gives me a pat on the shoulder and requests that I punch Kevin for him, next time I see the treacherous bastard.

I tell him that I will, meaning it, and clamber lonely and humiliated from the car as the Range Rover pulls up behind us. The Knife is driving and he gives me a triumphant little smirk. The Gang just stares with bored contempt, like he's viewing a side order of green vegetables. Then both cars pull away, and I'm left alone.

I used to be a handy middleweight boxer. I never troubled the top division but in a career spanning nine years and twenty-seven professional fights (seventeen wins, two draws and eight losses, before you ask), I managed to save up enough money to invest in property. I own a flat in Hackney outright, and I put down fifty percent on a house in Putney last year, which I've been doing up ever since.

But my main job these days is as a doorman. I don't need the cash particularly, but it's easy work. The place is called Stallions, not that there's much of the stallion about any of the clientèle. They're mainly middle-aged men with plenty of money. It's billed as a gentleman's establishment but, to be honest, it's more of a high-class brothel with a bit of card-playing and drinking thrown in.

Two hours after being dropped off by Jim The Crim, I arrive at the door of the club in Piccadilly, freshly showered and dressed in a dickie bow and suit, having had to get a taxi all the way down here. Needless to say, I'm not in a good mood, but I'm on floor-duty tonight, which is some compensation.

The club itself is a lavish split-level room with cavernous ceilings, and was obviously kitted out by someone who liked the colour burgundy. It's busy tonight, with all the tables taken, and the girls outnumbering the clients by less than two to one, which is rare. How it works is this: you pay an annual fee of several grand to be a member, but you don't have to sleep with any of the women. You can just come and drink and play cards if you want to, but most people indulge in the more carnal pursuits. There are private rooms upstairs to which you take your chosen girl. You pay her cash, usually along the lines of £200 an hour, and then pay a separate room fee to the management which equates to the same amount. It's pricey, but these are men without money worries and ladies with very generous looks.

As I pass the small, central dance-floor, I'm greeted by several of the girls. They wink and blow me kisses, and one – Chanya from Thailand – brushes against me like a cat as I pass, her expression inviting. But I know it's only a bit of fun. She doesn't want me. Like all the girls here, she's after a ticket out, and someone of my standing simply hasn't got the resources to provide that.

Still, the attention puts me in a better mood, and this lasts as long as it takes to round the dance-floor and take the three steps to the upper level. Because it's then I spot the man who is my current nemesis, none other than The Crim himself.

This is a surprise. I've not seen The Crim in here before. He's sitting at a corner booth talking animatedly to one of our regulars, the right honourable Stephen Humphrey MP, a former junior defence minister, who always seems to have plenty of money. There's some skulduggery afoot, I've no doubt about that, and I wonder what it might be.

I watch them from a distance for a full minute as they hatch whatever evil plot they're hatching, and I think they make a right pair. The Crim is a big lumpy ox of a man with looks to match, while the MP is tall and dapper, with every pore of his Savile Row besuited form oozing expensive education. He sports a quite magnificent head of richly curled, silver-white hair that makes him look like Julius Caesar on steroids. To be honest, I've heard it's a very expensive rug, but then you hear a lot of intimate details in a place like this, not all of them pleasant, or true.

I'm not so bothered about all that at the moment, though. What I am bothered about is getting my BMW back, since it was taken from me under duress, as I think you'll agree. Clearly, if The Crim's here then so is the car. And what's more I've got my spare keys on me. I'm taking a risk by repossessing it, of course, because The Crim is definitely not a man to cross, but I can't bring myself to do nothing when I know that it's probably in the underground car park, only yards away.

I take a look round for The Gang and The Knife, but they're nowhere to be seen.

However, when I look back at the Crim's booth, I see that one of the girls, Vanya, a tall, statuesque blonde from Slovakia with an icy smile and a model's poise, has approached the table, and is leaning over talking to Humphrey. The Crim meanwhile is surreptitiously peeking down the top of her cleavage, and trying without success to be all nonchalant about it.

As I watch, The Crim reaches into his pocket and pulls out what look suspiciously like my car keys. With a reluctant expression, he hands them over, not to Humphrey, but to Vanya, and she gives the big ox an enthusiastic peck on the cheek. What the hell's going on here, I wonder, as the politician gets up and the two men shake hands?

A second later, Humphrey and Vanya turn and walk hand in hand across the length of the club and disappear out the exit.

Not for the first time in my life, I'm confused. What's he done with my car now?

It's one of the club's rules that senior members (i.e. those the management want to keep on good terms with) can take selected girls off the premises and back to their own places, by prior agreement. Stephen Humphrey is one such member, but since he's married with a sizeable brood of kids, I doubt he's taking her back to his place for a bit of slap and tickle.

Which means they could be going anywhere.

So, what do I do now?

For the next half hour or so, I don't do a lot, just keep walking the floor of the club, making sure that everyone, clients and girls alike, feels happy and secure. But all the time I'm thinking about my car and the heinous way it's been taken from me. And, of course, what I need to do to be reunited with it.

Finally, I can take no more. I've got to have it back. It's just turned midnight when I head outside and make a call to the firm who monitor the tracking device that's installed in it. I tell the man on the other end of the phone that a friend of mine's driven off in my car for a prank. I don't want to involve the police but I do want the car back, so can he please activate the tracker and let me know where it is? He doesn't like the idea, and to be fair, it's a bit of an unusual request, but eventually, having ascertained that I am who I say I am, he does the honours and informs me that my car is currently outside Number 21 Bowbury Gardens in Hampstead.

Ah, the wonders of technology. Now all I need to do is get there.

As I turn round, putting the phone back in my pocket, I see The Crim hurrying down the steps with The Knife and The Gang in tow. They don't see me, but keep on going round to the entrance of the underground car park. Something's up, I think, but I'm no longer so worried about them. The important thing is to get my rear across to 21 Bowbury Gardens before anyone else does. So, after a quick few words with my fellow doorman, Harry "The Wolverine" Carruthers (so-called because of the thick black mat of hair that covers his body from neck to toe), he agrees to lend me his car. He's not too happy about it, obviously, since number one he's going to have to cover for me and number two, when finishing time comes round at the unearthly hour of 4 a.m., he's going to have some trouble getting home.

I tell him not to worry about this since I'll have it back well before then, and anyway, he owes me one. The Wolverine's not happy, there's no doubting that, but eventually he parts with the keys, and I drive off towards Hampstead in the hunt for truth and justice.

It's just turned quarter to one and raining when I pull into Bowbury Gardens, a quiet residential road of rundown three-storey townhouses, and I'm immediately confronted by an alarming sight. The front door of one of the houses about halfway down is open and I can see Vanya, the girl who left the club in my car, being manhandled by a number of men who all have their back to me.

Hearing my car approach, one of them turns round and I see that it's Jim The Crim. He immediately turns back and grabs Vanya by the arm, pushing her back into the house. I carry on driving, looking straight ahead, hoping they won't recognize me, and as I pass I see that they've all now disappeared inside. I also see my motor – sleek and metallic-black, like a crouching panther – parked at the side of the road.

I find a space nearby and pull in. The spare keys are in my pocket. Now is the time to pretend I never saw Vanya being

accosted by The Crim and his boys, grab my car and drive off, end
of story. Obviously, I'm going to have to get out of London for a
while, in order to escape The Crim's wrath, but I was planning a
holiday anyway, and Stallions isn't exactly a job I'll miss.

But the problem is that I'm an honourable man, as I've told
you before. I can't just walk away from a damsel in distress; it's
not right.

However, there's another problem. I am outnumbered, and if
I remember rightly (which I do), the Knife is carrying a gun.
Since I know that The Wolverine is a man who sometimes
strays on the wrong side of the law, I check in his glove
compartment for any useful accessories and, lo and behold, I
find a can of pepper spray. It's not a lot but it'll have to do.

Putting it in my pocket, I get out of the car and jog through
the rain past my car, resisting the urge to kiss the paintwork,
and carry on to the door where I saw the altercation. I try the
handle and it's locked. There's a buzzer lit up on the wall beside
it and I see that the house is split into three flats. Taking a step
back I note that the third floor's the only one with lights on, so
figure that this one's Vanya's place. I come forward again and
launch a flying karate kick at the lock on the door. It looks pretty
old and it gives easily, flying open with an angry crack.

Surprise has never been my strong point and I wonder again
why I'm helping Vanya. She's never been particularly friendly
to me. In fact, I've always thought her aloof and cold. I think
maybe I'm simply a sucker for punishment.

I shut the door behind me and move forward in the darkness,
listening. I can't hear any sounds from above so I head over to
the stairwell opposite and take the steps upwards, my shoes tap-
tap-tapping on the cheap linoleum floor. It smells of damp in
here and I suddenly feel sorry for Vanya, coming thousands of
miles to work in a brothel servicing middle-aged men, and
living in a dump like this.

There's a scream. It's short and faint, but it's definitely
coming from the top floor. Before my fights, I used to get so
nervous and pumped-up that I'd be bouncing off the walls,
counting down the seconds to the action. I get that feeling again
now. I can sense impending violence and it's weird, but I'm
actually looking forward to it. It's like I'm living again for the
first time in months, years even.

And now, of course, I know why I've come here, and why I'm defying Jim The Crim Sneddon himself. I crave the excitement. It's like a drug.

The pepper spray's in my left hand as I mount the last step, see a door in front of me, all plywood and chipped paint, and do a Jackie Chan on this one as well. It flies open as well and this time I'm confronted by a sight that's alternately hilarious and shocking.

First, the shocking part: Vanya, dressed in civvies, is sitting rigid on her threadbare living room sofa, her pale blue eyes as wide as saucers. Above her, with one foot on said sofa, stands The Knife, the tip of his trademark stiletto touching the little fold of skin just below her left eye. In his free hand, he holds a thick lock of blonde hair that he's clearly just lopped off, and it looks like he's about to embark on some more physical damage. The expression on his face is one of cold pleasure.

Now for the hilarious part, and believe it or not, there is one. Wailing like an angry baby in the middle of the room, is the right honourable Stephen Humphrey MP. Except his resplendent silver mane is no longer attached to his head, but is actually bunched up in Vanya's hand, like a sleeping Jack Russell, where she's obviously removed it with some force. So, the rumours are true. Humphrey really is as bald as a coot, and I think it must have been his screams I heard, because his shiny dome is red and raw, and laced with the remnants of torn adhesive.

The Crim is the only other person in the room, and he's having a bit of a laugh at Humphrey's plight. At least he is until he sees me bursting in like some avenging angel. The MP is the nearest to me, but I don't bother with him. As Defence Minister, he had a reputation as a tough guy in parliament. But it's one thing making the brave decisions that send other men to their deaths, and another getting in the firing line yourself. He makes his intentions admirably plain by jumping out the way very fast, and burying his newly naked head in his hands.

I identify the priority target as The Knife, since he's the one with the weapons, and as he turns my way, I let him have it with a liberal burst of the spray. He tries to cover his face but he's not fast enough, and as he chokes and splutters against the fumes, at the same time bringing his knife round in my direction, I knock him down with a swift left hook. He hits the sofa, out for the count.

But The Crim's a bit quicker, having had that much more time to react, and he yanks his head away as I fire off another burst of the spray. He's exposed in this position, and I come forward and punch him in the kidneys, twice in quick succession. He stumbles and loses his footing, and I grab him by his coat and pull him close, shoving the canister against his nose and spraying off the last of its contents straight up his nostrils.

He starts gasping for air and twisting round uncontrollably, smashing into the stereo unit, part of which falls on his head with a loud clunk. I let go of him and turn round to look for Vanya, who's giving the prone, mewing Humphrey a bit of a working over. I pull her off him and, at that moment hear the sound of a toilet flushing round the corner, just out of sight.

Oh no! The Gang! In all the excitement, I've forgotten about him, and now I'm out of spray. A second later, he comes into the room – twenty-five stone of muscle and jelly. The guy's amazingly fast for one so immense, I have to give him that.

"Run!" shouts Vanya rather unnecessarily, but he's almost upon me, leering like a demented clown and, worse still, The Knife is starting to get to his feet, obviously not quite as knocked out as I'd thought.

I strike The Gang with a three-punch combination, every blow slamming into his tiny, childlike face, but they might as well be kisses for all the damage they're doing, and he keeps coming forward, wrapping great arms round my torso, and dragging me into a vice-like bearhug that quite literally takes my breath away. I try to say something but no sound comes out. I feel my ribs giving way. I have never been in such pain in my life, and I think that if I die like this, it will be a truly terrible way to go. And it's all because of that arsehole, Kevin.

In the background, I can see The Knife rubbing his eyes. He hisses to his colleague not to kill me. He wants to end my life himself. It almost seems preferable to what I'm going through now.

But then The Gang's grip loosens, and he suddenly goes boss-eyed. I get my right arm free and deliver an uppercut that catches him under the chin. The grip loosens still more and I struggle free, bumping into Vanya, whose hand is thrust between The Gang's legs, twisting savagely. As the Americans would say, this girl has spunk.

We turn together, just in time to see The Knife slashing his weapon in a throat-high arc, and it takes all my old reactions to fend off the blow, using my right arm to block his, and my left to deliver two vicious little jabs – bang bang – right into his pockmarked mug.

He actually says "Ouch!", then goes straight over backwards, landing on the carpet, only to be trampled on by The Crim, who is still blundering around the room like a drunk gatecrashing a ballet performance.

And then we're out the door and down the stairs, taking them two and three at a time, and I can hear The Gang lumbering behind us. Vanya stumbles and I grab her arm and pull her upright. We hit the street at a mad dash, veering right in the direction of the BMW. She starts fiddling in the pocket of her jeans for the keys, thinking that's she's going to be the one driving, but there's no way that's going to happen.

"This is my car, darling!" I shout, pulling out the spares and flicking off the central locking.

Reluctantly, she jumps in the passenger side, while I leap in the driver's seat and switch on the ignition. The engine purrs into life, and I pull out into the road. I can see The Gang in the rear view mirror, coming down the road after us. He's gaining but there's not a lot he can do now and I accelerate away, feeling pleasantly satisfied, at least until Vanya tells me that the Bowbury Gardens is actually a dead end road, and I'm going in the wrong direction.

I do a quick three-point turn in the middle of the road, and swing the car back round, accelerating. Twenty yards away, The Gang is in the middle of the road, looming up like an immovable stone monolith, but this is a strong car, and a good deal more substantial than the man currently standing in front of me.

I think The Gang must belatedly realize this because at the last second, he leaps to one side, belly-flopping onto the bonnet of some poor sod's Renault Megane with a huge crash. It takes me a moment to realize that it is in fact The Wolverine's car and that now he's definitely going to be walking home tonight.

I keep driving, gliding round the bend and onto the main road. Mission almost accomplished.

"Thanks for that," says Vanya, leaning over and putting a hand on my arm. She smells nice, and I think there might be passion in her pale eyes, although to be fair, I've been wrong about this sort of thing before.

"What the hell was that all about?" I ask her, and she tells me.

Apparently, Stephen Humphrey is providing lucrative defence contracts to one of The Crim's front companies in return for cash. A very big contract is coming up and, on hearing that The Crim is driving one of the new BMWs, Humphrey wants to take possession of the car in lieu of his usual payment. The Crim reluctantly agrees and Humphrey and Vanya go for a spin. Vanya, however, has been tiring of Humphrey of late, and they end up having a violent argument. In the ensuing mêlée, Vanya physically removes the MP from the car, damaging his toupee in the process, and then drives off home, concluding that actually London life isn't for her. She decides to take the 7-Series and drive it, and her meagre possessions, back to Slovakia.

But just as she's leaving, The Crim and his boys turn up, along with a crooked-haired Humphrey thirsting for revenge. Which is where I came in.

I ask her if she's going to take the plane home now.

She looks disappointed. "Is this really your car?" she asks.

"I'm afraid it is," I tell her.

"So," she says, looking at me with an interest she's never shown before, "what are you going to do? The men you attacked are going to be pretty upset and I understand that Mr Sneddon is a very powerful man."

It's a good question, and one I haven't really given a lot of thought to. "We'll have to see," I say enigmatically.

By this time, we've pulled up outside Aunt Lena's house. I know that whatever happens, I've got to keep her out of the way of The Crim, who's going to be looking to settle scores in any way he can.

But there's something odd here. In Aunt Lena's one-car carport sits another 7-Series, brand new like mine. I park up behind it and, taking the spare keys from Vanya, just in case she decides to do another runner, tell her to wait for me.

As I reach the front door, it opens and who should I see standing there but the fugitive himself, cousin Kevin? He immediately opens fire with a barrage of excuses for his absence, as well as heartfelt apologies and gestures of thanks. The whole tirade's a pile of bullshit, of course, but you have to give him ten out of ten for effort.

"Where's your mum?" I ask him, and then remember that I actually told her to stay round her friend Marjorie's house on the next street until all this boiled over.

"Have you got The Crim's money?" I demand. "He reckons it's thirty-four grand."

"Thirty-four thousand?" he pipes up. "That's ruinous. Tell you the truth," he adds, which is usually the prelude to a lie, "I've been down in Monaco. Made some money on the tables. Had everything ready for The Crim, but then I saw this motor in the showroom near the casino . . ." He motions towards the car, "and I just had to have it. It's beautiful, Billy," he says. "Supreme engineering."

"I know," I answer, "I've got one. So, I'm taking it you haven't got the money."

He gives me a rueful expression. "Supreme engineering doesn't come cheap."

"No, it doesn't," I say, pondering the evening I've had, then clap him on the shoulder. "Look, stay here tonight, Kevin, and we'll straighten out The Crim in the morning. I'm just popping off back home."

We say our goodbyes and I get back in the car, and put a call into The Crim on my mobile as we drive away. Not surprisingly, he's none too pleased to hear from me and is full of curses and bluster until I tell him that Kevin's waiting for him at Aunt Lena's house with a present that I guarantee will make him happy, and which will simultaneously clear the debt.

I also add that it would be a lot better for everyone if my family stayed in one piece and no one got to hear about The Crim's crooked relationship with Mr Hairpiece himself, Stephen Humphrey MP.

Before he can say anything else, I end the call, settle back and turn to Vanya.

"So," I ask, as we reach the bottom of the road. "Which way to Slovakia?"

THE CASE OF THE CURIOUS QUORUM

Colin Dexter

Triply marked had been the white envelope, Personal Private Confidential; and after reading its contents, Inspector Lewis's forehead registered considerable puzzlement. Furthermore, after re-reading the two-page letter, such puzzlement appeared compounded with each succeeding paragraph.

> *53 Cumberland Place*
> *London W2 5AS*
> *0207 3736642*
> *10 April 2006*

Dear Inspector,

My only connection with you is via the late Chief Inspector Morse, who once came to talk at the Detection Club's annual jamboree at The Ritz. We had known of him because one of our number had written accounts of some of his high-profile investigations, particularly into murder, a crime ever nourishing the life-blood of our distinguished membership. Morse spoke rather stiffly, we thought, although after his speech he was somewhat more relaxed with his plentiful supply of single-malt Scotch.

It was at that point he came to speak of you, and in a most complimentary fashion. Clearly you formed an illustrious partnership and I know you will have learnt a great deal from

*him about the solving of crime. Indeed, one of our cruciverb-
alist members wrote an anagrammatic clue about his rank and
name: "Person with crimes to resolve (9, 5)". And it is in
order to resolve a crime that I write to you now. Please,
Inspector, consider the following facts.*

*I was myself, until a few years ago, the President of the
Detection Club, during which time I naturally held an open
cheque book on the Club's account. I attended a committee
meeting two weeks ago in the hotel lounge at Paddington
Railway Station, taking with me the cheque book and intending (belatedly) to surrender it to the current President.
There were five of us there, all male: our President, myself,
and three other senior members. The business was conducted
expeditiously; and before repairing to the bar with my
colleagues, I collected up my own material, consisting of a
few personal letters, the minutes of the last meeting, the
morning's agenda, my notes, etc, and stuffed them into my
briefcase.*

*On returning home and taking out these papers, I found
that the cheque book was missing, although I clearly remember that I had forgotten (yet again) to hand it over. Was my
memory playing cruel tricks on me? I am certain this was not
the case. My brain cells have not let me down for many a
decade, to be frank – eight of them almost! I did not allow this
matter to disturb me unduly, but it should have done. Why?
Because two days ago I learnt that a considerable amount had
been withdrawn from the Club's account on a cheque from
that very book, a cheque ostensibly signed by me.*

*My mind has been going round whirlygigwise this last
forty-eight hours, since I am certain that it was one of us
at the committee meeting who was responsible for the theft, as
well as for the criminal usage made of it thereafter. One of
those men is a complete monster – bit of one, anyway! One of
them is a d— arrant robber! One of them ought to be roasted
under a grill – he deserves it! Do I sound a little incoherent?
So be it.*

*Where does this leave my reputation? I used to be called the
Crime King – Father of Detection! And now I am left in
much anger and despair as I see myself the victim of a person
who is that most despicable thing – faker of cheques! He*

*would need a cheque, of course, as well as a copy of my
signature, which he could (did) practise. It may therefore be
of some help to you to have a list of those members to whom,
reasonably recently, I wrote and signed semi-official letters:
Len Deighton, Anthony Lejeune, Simon Brett, Lionel Da-
vidson, Peter Lovesey, James Melville, Reginald Hill, Robert Barnard, Jonathan Gash, John Malcolm, Ian Rankin,
John Harvey, and Robert Goddard. All men. But it was a
man. And the only reason I am not listing the names of those
members attending the committee meeting must be fairly
obvious. I find myself unwilling to point a finger at any
specific person.*

*Now that Morse is no longer with us, I am looking to you,
Inspector, feeling confident that after working for so many
years with that remarkable man, some of his skills will have
rubbed off on you. Yes, I am certain you can help me, if you
will. Alas, the resolution of this sorry affair is urgent and
imperative. We need no private eye on the assignment: let's
have it under your eye – let's prove, between us, who this
villain is!*

Yours truly,
HRF Keating

*PS On looking through what I have written, I notice that the
phrase "I am certain" is used three times. Please know that
what I tell you three times is true.*

Later that morning, rather more quickly than Lewis, it had
been Detective Sergeant Hathaway who read the letter.

"Puzzling, don't you think?" queried Lewis.

"Well, yes. I don't suppose everybody knows what a cruci-
ver—"

"*I* know," interrupted Lewis sharply. "I worked with a
chronic cruciverbalist for twenty years."

"Sorry, sir."

Lewis pointed to the letter. "Don't you find it all a bit of a
mystery?"

Hathaway hesitated. "To be truthful, sir, I don't, no. It
seems pretty clear that either it's all a joke or else this fellow's
more than halfway round the twist."

"Really? Doesn't read much like a joke to me. And I don't reckon the fellow's lost his marbles, either. I remember Morse talking about this Keating chap. Said he'd got one of the shrewdest brains in the business."

"But no one could expect us to take this sort of stuff seriously. He's told us next to nothing—"

"Except his home address and his telephone number."

"So?"

"So ring him up."

"And say what?"

"You think of something. You're a university graduate, remember."

Lewis pushed the telephone across the desk; and a few moments later both men could hear the words: "This number is not receiving incoming calls. I repeat, this . . ."

"Never mind," said Lewis. "The President – ring him."

"How do we know—?"

"The Club'll be on Google, man."

Hathaway looked up from the screen a minute later. "Fellow called Simon Brett. There's a telephone number, too."

But again both men were shortly to hear an automated voice. "The person you require is not available. Please try again later".

Lewis grinned wryly. "They all seem to be telling us next to nothing, just like you said."

But his eyes remained steadfastly on the letter as he wondered what Morse would have thought in the same situation . . .

He was still wondering a few minutes later when Hathaway interrupted whatever might have been going through the inspector's mind.

"You remember we're due out at ten o'clock, sir?"

"Yep. But just you get a copy of that letter and take it home with you tonight. You see, I'm beginning to think we may be wrong about it not telling us anything. If I'd said that to Morse, do you know what he would have said?"

Hathaway shook his head indifferently.

"He'd have said that fellow's probably told us *everything*."

"Not told us how the guilty party sorted out the transfer of the money; not told us which bank it was or how much dosh was taken out . . . Ridiculous, really, that letter!"

Lewis made no reply, and Hathaway continued:

"Tell you something else, sir. My old tutor once told me that if I kept on using as many exclamation marks in my essays as this fellow's done, he'd refuse to read 'em. And any writer who kept on using those long dashes all the time hadn't much idea on how to write the Queen's English."

Again Lewis made no reply, but something – some small, vague idea – was struggling into birth in the depths of his brain as Hathaway spoke again.

"I wonder whether Morse would think he was much of a writer, our man here. Things like 'arrant monster'—"

"Arrant *robber*," corrected Lewis.

"Ugh! Would your old boss have written that?"

"Dunno. He never wrote much. And if he had to *read* a lot of bumph, it was always the commas he was most particular about."

"Wish I'd known him, sir," said Hathaway with gentle irony as he closed the door behind him.

"A lot of people would!" said Lewis quietly to himself in the empty room.

Hathaway had finished his supper, and was looking through the evening's fare in the *TV Times* when his mind drifted back to the Keating letter. He'd won himself no Brownie points when he'd misquoted "arrant robber" from the letter. "Robber" . . . not all that different from "Robert", was it? And Lewis's Christian name must surely be Robert, with his senior colleagues always calling him "Robbie" . . . He took out the letter from his jacket-pocket: yes, there it was, "arrant robber". What *was* this stupid bloody letter all about?

But suddenly something clicked in his mind and his eyes were gleaming as he wrote out the letters of "arrant robber" and crossed them off one by one against a name on the members' list. One letter short, agreed. But there it was, immediately before those two words: the letter "d—", which he'd assumed to have been the way some people who'd never sworn in their lives expressed "damned".

"Wow!"

It was 8.45 pm and he rang Lewis immediately. Almost. But if one of the four names was hidden there in the text, in "anagrammatic" form (the very word Keating had used), yes! If one of the names was nestling there, what about the other three?

Lewis was watching the 10 o'clock news on BBC1 when Hathaway rang.

"I went through that letter line by line, sir, letter by letter, and I've found them, found all of them. All four: 'd—arrant robber' is an anagram of Robert Barnard. Next one: 'monster – bit' is an anagram of Simon Brett, our honourable President. Then we've got 'grill – he', not quite so clear, but it must be Reg Hill. The last, near the end, is 'eye – let's prove', which works out as Peter Lovesey. I checked all the other names on the list, but there's no one *else* lurking there. No one!"

After finally replacing the receiver, Hathaway felt an inner glow of forgivable pride. Yet he realised that four names didn't help all that much when the problem was deciding on just *one* name. But the other four would go down to three if the President (surely) could be shunted along with Caesar's wife into the above-suspicion bracker. Which left him with Barnard, Hill, Lovesey . . .

When Hathaway had rung, Lewis had only just got back from hearing Papadopoulos conducting the Oxford Philomusica at the Sheldonian. He felt pleasingly tired, and would have welcomed an earlyish night. But he knew he would have little chance of sleep with Hathaway's clever findings topmost in his mind, and with the idea that had begun to dawn on him that morning still undeveloped and unexamined. Unusually for him, he was aware of a strongly competitive urge to come up with something that could complement his sergeant's discovery. But who *was* that one crook on the committee? One of the four – or perhaps one of the three – for he (like Hathaway) felt prepared to pass over the President.

Think, Lewis! Think!

How would Morse have looked at the letter? Probably looked at it the wrong way round, say? How do you do that, though? Read it back to front? Ridiculous. Read the PS before the salutation? But where had he read the PS's "what I tell you three times is true" before? From Lewis Carroll, wasn't it? He located the words immediately in *The Oxford Book of Quotations*, from "The Hunting of the Snark". So what? What had *that* got to do with anything? Just a minute. Three suspects . . . but Keating hadn't mentioned any single one of the suspects three times. He hadn't mentioned *anything* three times.

Or had he?

Well, even if he had, it was past midnight, and he was walking up the stairs when he remembered what Hathaway had said about punctuation. Morse had once told him that Oscar Wilde had spent two hours one morning looking through one of his poems before removing a comma; and then spent a further two hours the same afternoon before deciding to re-instate the said comma. And after standing motionless on the third step from the top of the staircase, Lewis finally retraced his steps downstairs and looked at the letter for the umpteenth time, now paying no attention whatsoever to what things were being said, but *how* they were being said.

And suddenly, in a flash, eureka.

Thank you, Hathaway! Thank you, Morse!

Lewis took a can of beer from the fridge and drank it before finally completing his ascent of the staircase. Hathaway may have fallen asleep that night with a look of deep satisfaction on his face, but with Lewis it was one bordering on the beatific.

It was three days after the aforementioned events that Mr HRF Keating received a letter at his London address with the envelope marked "Thames Valley Police HQ, Kidlington, Oxon".

13 April 2006

Dear Mr Keating,
I write to thank you for your letter of 10 April 2006. You asked for my help.

Between us, my sergeant and I finally fathomed the anagrammatized names of the committee quorum; and leaving aside yourself, and giving the benefit of the doubt to your successor as President, we were left with three names from the list you gave us: Messrs Barnard, Hill, Lovesey. The clues were there and we spotted them. But this didn't get us very far. Which of the three men was it?

It was more difficult for us to spot the vital clue, but in reality you had made it quite complex. The three names we had, as well as the President's, were each signposted by two items of punctuation: the long em dash and the exclamation mark. It was cleverly done. But we were a bit slow to notice the full implication of this. These two punctuation marks were each used, always closely together, not four times, but seven times, and used nowhere else in your letter. Why had our suspect-list suddenly grown so much longer? The reason eventually became clear. The name of the perpetrator of the "crime" was not included in the list of club-members. But there he was, three times: "frank—eight"; "King—Father"; "thing—faker", and each of the three is a perfect anagram of the man responsible for the alleged theft of the chequebook: a man, as I say, who was not listed among the suspects. A man named HRF Keating. You, sir!

Only one problem remains, a more difficult one than that posed by your letter. Why on earth did you go in for all that rigmarole? What was the point of it? If, as we suspect, it was for sheer amusement, please remember that irresponsible wasting of police time is liable to be interpreted as a crime, and as such be liable for prosecution.

Please satisfy our curiosity about your motive, although we trust that your reply can be rather shorter than your original communication.

Yours sincerely,
R Lewis (Detective Inspector)

16 April 2006

Dear Inspector Lewis,
Thank you so much for your letter, and heartiest congratulations on your cleverness.

An American philanthropist was one of our guests when Morse spoke to us, and the two of them got on finely. This same person revisited us a month ago, and was naturally saddened to hear of Morse's death. He remembered Morse mentioning to him the work of the Police Service of Northern Ireland Benevolent Fund, and expressed the wish to make some donation to this fund. But on one specific condition. Together we amused ourselves by jointly composing the letter

I originally sent to you. The agreed condition was that the police should prove themselves still able to exhibit the high degree of mental acumen and flexibility that Morse himself had shown with crossword puzzles, and with criminal cases.

It was also agreed that I should write to you to explain the whole thing should you have shown no interest, or have been utterly flummoxed by our letter. Had such been the case, we had decided to consider the merits of the next two charities on my friend's giftlist: the Salvation Army, and the Donkey Sanctuary. I rang him immediately on receipt of your wonderfully welcome letter, and a cheque is now on its transatlantic flight to the police charity: a cheque for $25,000. This I hope should compensate in some degree for the time you and your colleague spent on the puzzle, and perhaps you can now cross my own name off the list of those potentially liable for prosecution. It remains for me only to subscribe this letter, which I now do.

A right nerk?—Ay!

PS Please note the punctuation.

THE BOOKBINDER'S APPRENTICE

Martin Edwards

As Joly closed his book, he was conscious of someone watching him. A feeling he relished, warm as the sun burning high above Campo Santi Apostoli. Leaning back, he stretched his arms, a languorous movement that allowed his eyes to roam behind dark wrap-around Gucci glasses.

A tall, stooped man in a straw hat and white suit was limping towards the row of red benches, tapping a long wooden walking stick against the paving slabs, somehow avoiding a collision with the small, whooping children on scooters and tricycles. Joly sighed. He wasn't unaccustomed to the attentions of older men, but soon they became tedious. Yet the impeccable manners instilled at one of England's minor public schools never deserted him; and besides, he was thirsty; a drink would be nice, provided someone else was paying. The benches were crowded with mothers talking while their offspring scrambled and shouted over the covered well and a group of sweaty tourists listening to their guide's machine-gun description of the frescoes within the church. As the man drew near, Joly squeezed up on the bench to make a small place beside him.

"Why, thank you." American accent, a courtly drawl. "It is good to rest one's feet in the middle of the day."

Joly guessed the man had been studying him from the small bridge over the canal, in front of the row of shops. He smiled, didn't not speak. In a casual encounter, his rule was not to give anything away too soon.

The man considered the book on Joly's lap. "*Death in Venice*. Fascinating."

"He writes well," Joly allowed.

"I meant the volume itself, not the words within it." The man waved towards the green kiosk in front of them. Jostling in the window with the magazines and panoramic views of the Canal Grande were the gaudy covers of translated Georgette Heyer and Conan the Barbarian. "Though your taste in reading matter is plainly more sophisticated than the common herd's. But it is the book as *objet d'art* that fascinates me most these days, I must confess. May I take a closer look?"

Without awaiting a reply, he picked up the novel, weighing it in his hand with the fond assurance of a Manhattan jeweller caressing a heavy diamond. The book was bound in green cloth, with faded gilt lettering on the grubby spine. Someone had spilled ink on the front cover and an insect had nibbled at the early pages.

"Ah, the first English edition by Secker. I cannot help but be impressed by your discernment. Most young fellows wishing to read Thomas Mann would content themselves with a cheap paperback."

"It is a little out of the ordinary, that accounts for its appeal. I like unusual things, certainly." Joly let the words hang in the air for several seconds. "As for cost, I fear I don't have deep pockets. I picked the copy up from a second hand dealer's stall on the Embankment for rather less than I would have paid in a paperback shop. It's worth rather more than the few pence I spent, but it's hardly valuable, I'm afraid. The condition is poor, as you can see. All the same, I'd rather own a first edition than a modern reprint without a trace of character."

The man proffered a thin, weathered hand. "You are a fellow after my own heart, then! A love of rare books, it represents a bond between us. My name is Sanborn, by the way, Darius Sanborn."

"Joly Maddox."

"Joly? Not short for Jolyon, by any chance?"

"You guessed it. My mother loved *The Forsyte Saga*."

"Ah, so the fondness for good books is inherited. Joly, it is splendid to make your acquaintance."

Joly ventured an apologetic cough and made a show of consulting his fake Rolex as the church bell chimed the hour. "Well, I suppose I'd better be running along."

Sanborn murmured, "Oh, but do you have to go so soon? It is a hot day, would you care to have a drink with me?"

A pantomime of hesitation. "Well, I'm tempted. I'm not due to meet up with my girlfriend till she finishes work in another hour . . ."

A tactical move, to mention Lucia. Get the message over to Sanborn, just so there was no misunderstanding. The American did not seem in the least put out, as his leathery face creased into a broad smile. Joly thought he was like one of the pigeons in the square, swooping the moment it glimpsed the tiniest crumb.

"Then you have time aplenty. Come with me, I know a little spot a few metres away where the wine is as fine as the skin of a priceless first edition."

There was no harm in it. Adjusting his pace to the old man's halting gait, he followed him over the bridge, past the shop with all the cacti outside. Their weird shapes always amused him. Sanborn noticed his sideways glance. He was sharp, Joly thought, he wasn't a fool.

"As you say, the unusual intrigues you."

Joly nodded. He wouldn't have been startled if the old man had suggested going to a hotel instead of for a drink, but thankfully the dilemma of how to respond to a proposition never arose. After half a dozen twists and turns through a maze of alleyways, they reached an ill-lit bar and stepped inside. After the noise and bustle of the *campo*, the place was as quiet as a church in the Ghetto. No one stood behind the counter and, straining his eyes to adjust from the glare outside, Joly spied only a single customer. In a corner at the back, where no beam from the sun could reach, a small wizened man in a corduroy jacket sat at a table, a half-empty wine glass in front of him. Sanborn limped up to the man and indicated his guest with a wave of the stick.

"Zuichini, meet Joly Maddox. A fellow connoisseur of the unusual. Including rare books."

The man at the table had a hooked nose and small dark cruel eyes. His face resembled a carnival mask, with a plague doctor's beak, long enough to keep disease at bay. He extended his hand. It was more like a claw, Joly thought. And it was trembling, although not from nerves – for his toothless smile conveyed a strange, almost malevolent glee. Zuichini must suffer from some form of palsy, perhaps Parkinson's disease. Joly, young and fit, knew little of sickness.

"You wonder why I make specific mention of books, Joly?" Sanborn asked with a rhetorical flourish. "It is because my good friend here is the finest bookbinder in Italy. Zuichini is not a household name, not even here in Venice, but his mastery of his craft, I assure you, is second to none. As a collector of unique treasures, few appreciate his talents more than I."

A simian waiter shuffled out from a doorway, bearing wine and three large glasses. He did not utter a word, but plainly Sanborn and Zuichini were familiar customers. Sanborn did not spare the man's retreating back a glance as he poured.

"You will taste nothing finer in Italy, I assure you. Liquid silk."

Joly took a sip and savoured the bouquet. Sanborn was right about the wine, but what did he want? Everyone wanted something.

"You are here as a tourist?" the American asked. "Who knows, you might follow my example. I first came to this city for a week. That was nineteen years ago and now I could not tear myself away if my life depended on it."

Joly explained that he'd arrived in Venice a month earlier. He had no money, but he knew how to blag. For a few days he'd dressed himself up as Charlie Chaplin and become a living statue, miming for tourists in the vicinity of San Zaccaria and earning enough from the coins they threw into his tin to keep himself fed and watered. But he'd hated standing still and after a few hours even the narcissistic pleasure of posing for photographs began to pall. One afternoon, taking a break in a cheap pizzeria, he'd fallen into conversation with Lucia when she served him with a capuccino. She was a stranger in the city as well; she'd left her native Taormina after the death of her parents and drifted around the country ever since. What they had in common was that neither of them could settle to anything. That night she'd taken him to her room in Dorsoduro and he'd stayed with her ever since.

"Excellent!" Sanborn applauded as he refilled his new young friend's glass. "What is your profession?"

Joly said he was still searching for something to which he would care to devote himself, body and soul. After uni, he'd drifted around. His degree was in English, but a career in teaching or the civil service struck him as akin to living death. He liked to think of himself as a free spirit, but he enjoyed working with his hands and for six months he'd amused himself as a puppeteer, performing for children's parties and at municipal fun days. When that became wearisome, he'd drifted across the Channel. He'd spent three months in France, twice as long in Spain, soon he planned to try his luck in Rome.

"I wondered about learning a trade as a boat-builder, I spent a day in the *squero* talking to a man who builds gondolas." He risked a cheeky glance at Zuichini's profile. "I even thought about making masks . . ."

"An over-subscribed profession in this city," Sanborn interrupted. "I understand why you didn't pursue it."

"Well, who knows? One of these days, I may come back here to try my luck."

"You have family?"

"My parents are dead, my sister emigrated to Australia where she married some layabout who looked like a surf god. So I have no ties, I can please myself."

"And your girlfriend?" Sanborn asked. "Any chance of wedding bells?"

Joly couldn't help laughing. Not the effect of the wine, heady though it was, but the very idea that he and Lucia might have a future together. She was a pretty *prima donna*, only good for one thing, and although he didn't say it, the contemplative look in Sanborn's pale grey eyes made it clear that he'd got the message.

"You and she must join us for dinner, be my guests, it would be a pleasure."

"Oh, no, really, we couldn't impose . . ."

Sanborn dismissed the protestations with a flick of his hand. He was old and deliberate and yet Joly recognized this was a man accustomed to getting his own way. "Please. I insist. I know a little seafood restaurant, they serve food so wonderful you will never forget it. Am I right, Zuichini?"

The wizened man cackled and nodded. A wicked gleam lit his small eyes.

"Well, I'm not sure . . ."

But within a couple of minutes it was agreed and Joly stumbled out into the glare of the sun with the American's good wishes ringing in his ears. Zuichini's small, plague-mask head merely nodded farewell; he'd uttered no more than two dozen words in the space of half an hour. Joly blinked, unaccustomed to wine that hit so hard; but the pleasure was worth the pain.

When he met up with Lucia, she made a fuss about the dinner. It was in her nature to complain; she regarded it as a duty not to agree to anything he suggested without making him struggle.

"With two old men? Why would we wish to do this? After tomorrow we will be apart, perhaps for ever. Are you tired with me already?"

Exaggeration was her stock-in-trade, but he supposed she was right and that they would not see each other again after he left the city. The plan was for him to travel to Rome and for her to join him there in a fortnight's time when she'd received her month's pay from the restaurant. He'd arranged it like that so there was an opportunity for their relationship to die a natural death. He hated break-up scenes. It would be so easy for them not to get together again in the Eternal City. If he wanted to return to Venice, he would rather do so free from encumbrances; there were plenty more fish in the sea. As for their argument, in truth she found the prospect of a slap-up meal at a rich man's expense as appealing as he did and after twenty minutes she stopped grumbling and started to deliberate about what she might wear.

They went back to her place and made love and by the time she'd dressed up for the evening, he could tell she was relishing the prospect of meeting someone new. Even if the men were old, she would love parading before them; admiration turned her on more than anything exotic he tried with her in bed. At first he'd found her delightful, he'd even managed to persuade himself that she might have hidden depths. But in truth Lucia was as shallow as the meanest canal in the city.

Against his expectations, the dinner was a success, early awkwardness and stilted conversation soon smoothed by a rich, full-blooded and frighteningly expensive red wine. Sanborn, in a fresh white suit, did most of the talking. Zuichini remained content to let his patron speak for him, occupying himself with a lascivious scrutiny of the ample stretches of flesh displayed by Lucia's little black dress. Her ankle tattoo, a small blue heart, had caught the American's eye.

"In honour of young Joly?" he asked, with an ostentatious twinkle.

Lucia tossed her head. "I had it done in Sicily, the day of my sixteenth birthday. The first time I fell in love."

"It is as elegant and charming as the lady whom it adorns." Sanborn had a habit of giving a little bow whenever he paid a compliment. "Take a look, Zuichini, do you not agree?"

The wizened man leaned over to study the tattoo. His beak twitched in approval; the gleam in his dark eyes was positively sly. Even Lucia blushed under his scrutiny.

Sanborn said smoothly, "I have long admired the tattooist's art and your heart is a fine example."

Lucia smiled prettily. "Thank you, Mr Sanborn."

"Darius, please. I like to think we are friends."

"Darius, of course."

She basked in the glow of his genial scrutiny. Joly broke off a piece of bread and chewed hard. He was revising his opinion about their host's sexual orientation. Perhaps the old goat fancied trying his luck once Joly had left town. Fair enough, he was welcome to her.

"Do you know, Zuichini, I rather think that young Lucia's heart is as elegant as Sophia's dove. What do you say?"

The bookbinder paused in the act of picking something from his teeth and treated Lucia to a satyr's grin. "Uh-huh, I guess."

He didn't speak much English and his accent was a weird pastiche American. Perhaps he'd picked it up from watching old movies. His idea of a matinee idol was probably Peter Lorre. Why did Sanborn spend so much time with him, if they were not lovers, past or present? Joly asked if Sophia was Sanborn's daughter.

"Good heavens, no. Alas, like you, I have no family. Sophia was a young lady whom Zuichini and I came to know – what? – two or three years ago. She worked behind a bar down the Via Garibaldi. We were both very fond of her. And she had this rather lovely neck tattoo, in the shape of a flying dove with broad, outstretched wings. As with Lucia's lovely heart, I have no doubt that it was carved by a gifted artist."

"You admire well-made creations?" Lucia asked, preening.

Sanborn patted her lightly on the hand. "Indeed I do, my dear. My tastes are not confined to fine books, although my collection is the most precious thing I possess."

"Tell us more," Joly said, as the food arrived.

Over the meal, Sanborn told them a little about his life. He'd inherited money – his grandfather had been president of an oil company – and he'd devoted years to travelling the world and indulging his taste for curios. Although he had never visited Venice until he was fifty years old, as he sailed into the lagoon and drank in the sights from the Bacino di San Marco, he resolved to make the city his home. By the sound of it, he lived in some grand *palazzo* overlooking the Canal Grande, and kept his income topped up with the rent from apartments that he'd been wise enough to buy up as the years passed. For all the talk of flooding, you could make good money on property in the city. Demand would always exceed supply.

"I always had a love of books, though it was not until I met Zuichini here that I started to collect in earnest. Are you a reader, Lucia, my dear?"

She shook her head. "No, I am too young. I tell this to Joly. He is of an age where there should be no time to read. He should live a bit."

"Well, books are not simply a delight for desiccated old rascals like me or Zuichini here You must not be hard on your young man. Seems to me he does pretty well for himself, living the *dolce vita* on a budget while indulging in old books whenever he finds a moment to spare."

Joly caught Zuichini peering down the front of Lucia's dress. Their eyes met briefly and the little man gave his toothless smile. Perhaps even he would find time to break off from binding books if only he could spend a night with Lucia. It wouldn't happen, though, unless Sanborn was in a mood to share. Joly savoured his swordfish. He didn't care. The American was welcome to her. If he showered her with money and presents, there was little doubt that Lucia would be content to do his bidding until she got bored. She'd confided in Joly that she'd worked in a lap dancing club in Milan and finished up living with the man who owned the joint. He was something high up in the Mafia, but after a few weeks he'd tired of her complaining and she'd managed to escape him without a scratch. Joly reckoned there wasn't much she wasn't willing to do, provided the price was right.

He felt his eyelids drooping before Sanborn snapped knobbly, arthritic fingers and asked the waiter to bring coffee. Before he knew what was happening, Lucia had accepted Sanborn's offer that they dine together again as his guests the following night. He didn't object – it was a free meal, and who cared if Sanborn was a dirty old man with an ulterior motive? Already he had spent enough time in the American's company to know that he was both persuasive and determined. If he wanted to spend his money, if Lucia wanted to sell her favours, who was Joly to stand in their way?

Sanborn insisted on paying a gondolier to take them back to a landing stage not far from Lucia's apartment. On the way home, she prattled about how wonderful the American was. Joly knew it was unwise to argue, but in the end he couldn't resist pointing out that she was the one who had been unwilling to waste her evening in the company of two old men. Now she had committed them to a repeat, on his very last night in the city, when he would have preferred them to be alone.

"And you would have been able to match Darius's hospitality? I do not think so, Joly."

The next day was even hotter. Lucia went out to work early on and was intent on shopping during the afternoon. After lunching on a ham sandwich – no point in spoiling his appetite for the evening's feast – Joly embarked on a last stroll around the gardens of Castello. Finding a seat beneath a leafy tree, he finished *Death in Venice*, then ambled back through the alleyways, absorbing the smells of the fish-sellers' stalls and the chocolate shops, wondering how long it would be before he returned to La Serenissima. He understood what had kept Sanborn here. Once you became intoxicated with the beauties of Venice, the rest of the world must seem drab by comparison. But he was keen to sample Rome and after the previous night, he was more than ever convinced that this was the right time to make a break with Lucia. Sanborn was welcome to her.

When he arrived back at the flat, Lucia was short-tempered in the way that he now associated with her rare attacks of nervousness. She was bent upon impressing Sanborn, and she'd bought a slinky new red dress with a neckline so daring it bordered on indecent. It must have cost her a month's wages. A carefully targeted investment – assuming she had footed the bill, that was. Joly wondered if she'd met up with Sanborn during the day and managed to charm the cash out of him. He wouldn't put it past either of them. So what? It was none of his business; soon he would be out of here.

. The American and his sidekick were waiting for them at the appointed time, sitting at a table inside a restaurant close to Rialto. Sanborn's suit tonight was a shade of pale cream. Zuichini was scruffy by comparison, his face more reminiscent of a scary carnival mask than ever.

"Lucia, you look dazzling!"

Sanborn kissed her on both cheeks and Zuichini did likewise. Joly had never seen the bookbinder show such animation. The little dark eyes seemed to be measuring Lucia's tanned flesh, no doubt wondering what she might look like when wearing no clothes. His attention pleased her. Perhaps she was hoping the two old men would fight over her. Even the waiter who took their order allowed his gaze to linger on her half-exposed breasts for longer than was seemly. The restaurant specialized in finest beef steak and Sanborn ordered four bottles of Bollinger.

"Tonight we celebrate!" he announced. "Over the past twenty four hours, we have become firm friends. And although Joly is to move on tomorrow, with the lovely Lucia to follow, it is my firm conviction that all four of us will be reunited before too long."

As their glasses clinked, Lucia's eyes were glowing. While they ate, the conversation turned to Joly's plans. He made it clear that they remained fluid. It was his style, he said, to trust to luck. Sanborn challenged this, arguing that even a young man needed roots.

"Learn from my mistake, Joly. Until I discovered the wonders of this marvellous city, my life lacked direction. You need something to anchor your existence. A place, firm friends, perhaps a trade."

Zuichini nodded with unaccustomed animation. "Right. That is right."

"Listen to this good man. He knows the joys of a craft, the unique pleasure that comes with creation. This is where you can steal a march on me, Joly. I am proud of my collection of books, undeniably, but I have never experienced the delight of creating a masterpiece of my own. I cannot paint, or compose, or write to any level of acceptable competence. I lack skills of a practical nature. But you, my young friend, are different. If you were to put your talents to good purpose . . ."

"I have an idea!" Lucia clapped her hands. Champagne went to her head. After a single glass, already she was raising her voice and her skin was flushed. "Once you have seen Rome, you could come back here and train as Zuichini's apprentice!"

The plague doctor's face split in a horrid smile, while Sanborn exclaimed with delight. "Perfect! There, Joly, you have your answer. How clever you are, Lucia. That way two birds could be killed with one stone. Joly would learn from a master at the height of his powers, and Zuichini would have a good man to whom he could pass on the tricks of his trade before it is too late." Sanborn lowered his voice. "And there is something else that I have omitted to mention. Zuichini, may I? You see, Joly. This good fellow here, as you may have notice, is afflicted by a dreadful malady. Parkinson's attacks the nervous system and he has been suffering stoically for some time. But it becomes increasingly difficult for him to work. An utter tragedy, sometimes I despair. Not only because Zuichini's disability saddens me, but also from a selfish motive. For who will succeed him in business, who will practise his very special skills, so as to keep me supplied in fine books? In you, perhaps I have found the answer to my prayers."

"I don't think so," Joly said slowly.

"Oh, but you must!" Lucia exclaimed. "Such an opportunity, to learn from a genius!"

Sanborn must have primed her with this idea and asked her to offer support. They'd met during the day, not only so that Sanborn could pay for the new dress. The American was, Joly thought, like the most demanding parent. He wanted to have the young folk beholden to him, at his beck and call and used his control of the purse strings to make sure they did not escape.

"I suppose I can mull it over, when I am in Rome."

He'd expected Sanborn to suggest that he abandoned his trip, but the old man surprised him, giving a broad smile and murmuring that he could not say fairer than that. Zuichini went so far as to give him a playful punch on the shoulder.

"Good apprentice, yes?"

While Joly tucked into the succulent beef, Sanborn talked about the art of binding books. He spoke of the pouch binding of Japanese books and the unique technique of *nakatoji*, of Jean Groller's leather-bound tomes covered with intricate geometric paterns, inlaid with coloured enamels and books bound in the flayed skin of murderers and highwaymen. He told them about cheverell, a goatskin parchment transformed into a binding both supple and strong with a bold, grainy pattern, popular in Italy during the fourteenth century, he described methods of fatliquoring leather, he explained . . .

"Joly, wake up!"

He became aware of Lucia's sharp elbow, digging into his side. Sanborn was beaming at him like a benevolent uncle, surveying a favourite nephew who has overdone the Christmas pudding. Zuichini was savouring his wine, still casting the occasional frank glance at Lucia's ample cleavage.

"Sorry, must have dropped off."

"Please do not apologize, I beg you," Sanborn said. "Put your sleepiness down to a combination of the wine and the weather. Perhaps accompanied by a tinge of *tristesse* – am I right, young man? This is your last night in La Serenissima for a little while and who could fail to experience a *frisson* of regret at departing from here?" He refilled their glasses, taking no notice when Joly shook his head. "So let us drink to our good friend Joly, and express the sincere hope that soon he will be back here for good!"

He reached out and patted Joly's arm. Blearily, Joly tried to focus on how to interpret the old man's behaviour. His hand did not linger. Had it been unfair to impute to him some sexual motive for such generosity? Perhaps in truth Sanborn's generosity did not amount to anything out of the ordinary. For a rich man, the cost of a couple of meals and a few bottles of fine wine was small change. Was it possible that Sanborn was no more than he seemed, a lonely old millionaire, keen to share the company of the young and beautiful, as well as that of his ailing friend, and that he had no ulterior motive at all?

Sanborn made some remark and Lucia laughed long and loud, a noise that reminded Joly of a workman drilling in the road. She had a good head for drink, Joly knew that from experience, but even she was beginning to lose control. He remembered her telling him about her last night with the Mafia boss. She'd plucked up the courage to put a small knife in her bag. If he'd attacked her, she'd steeled herself to fight for her life. Joly did not doubt the strength of her survival instinct. If she thought herself threatened, she would lash out without a moment's hesitation. What would happen if Zuichini made her afraid with the clumsiness of his overtures?

He yawned. His head was spinning and he couldn't keep worrying about what might happen between consenting adults. *Que sera, sera.*

Next thing he knew, someone was tapping him on the arm. Through the fog of a hangover, he heard Sanborn's gentle voice.

"Joly, my boy. Are you all right?"

Even the act of opening his eyes made him want to cry out, it hurt so much. Christ, how much had he drunk? He had no head for champagne, but he'd never felt this bad before. He blinked hard and tried to take in his surroundings. He was lying on a hard bed in a small, musty room. The sun was shining in through a small high window but he had no idea where he might be. Sanborn was standing beside the bed, arms folded, studying him. Suddenly, he felt afraid.

"Where am I?"

"Listen, my friend, you have nothing to fear. You just had rather too much to drink, that's all."

"The drinks were spiked." Nothing else could explain how he had come to black out; this had never happened to him before.

"No, no, no." Sanborn had a first-class bedside manner, though Joly was sure he was lying. "You overdid it, simple as that. And you threw up all over Lucia, which frankly wasn't such a good idea."

"Lucia?" He gazed at the peeling wallpaper, the unfamiliar cupboard and door. "Where have you brought me?"

"Listen, it's all right. Lucia was upset, that's all. Zuichini took care of her, no need to worry. As she wouldn't entertain you in her bed last night, I volunteered to bring you here. Now, you need to get up and dressed. I think you said you plan to take the one o'clock coach from Piazzale Roma?"

A wave of panic engulfed him. Effectively, he was the old man's prisoner.

"You haven't told me where you've brought me."

"There's no secret, Joly, keep your hair on, my dear fellow. This is an apartment I bought six months ago. Hardly the lap of luxury, but it's only a stone's throw from the restaurant. It seemed like the best solution. We could hardly leave you to your own devices, the state you were in, and Lucia was in no mood to take you back with her."

Joly coughed. "Then – I'm free to go?"

Sanborn's parchment features conveyed benign bewilderment. "I don't understand. Why should you not be? I was only striving to do you a good turn."

I've been a fool, Joly thought, this isn't a man to fear. The question is – what happened between Lucia and Zuichini? Did he try it on, did she let him get away with it?

"Sorry, Darius. I'm not myself."

"Not to worry, these things happen. There's a bathroom next door. No gold taps, I'm afraid, but you'll find the basic necessities. I'll leave you to it, if I may. Your bag's over by the door, incidentally. I went over to Lucia's this morning to pick it up."

"Thanks," Joly whispered.

"Here's the key to the front door. Would you be kind enough to lock up for me? I have a little business to attend to, but I'll be there at the coach station to see you off. It's the least I can do."

Joly stared at the old man's genial expression. Hoarsely, he said, "Thanks."

"Think nothing of it. That's what friends are for, don't you agree?"

Two hours later, Joly arrived at the Piazzale Roma, bag in hand. Within moments he caught sight of Sanborn by an advertisement hoarding and the American lifted his stick in greeting before limping to greet him. He had a black velvet bag slung over his shoulder.

"You're looking much better. Remarkable what wonders can be worked by a simple wash and brush up."

"I'm very grateful to you," Joly said humbly, handing over the key to the apartment.

"Think nothing of it." Sanborn cleared his throat. "Actually, I talked to Lucia before I made my way over here. There isn't an easy way to put this, Joly, but I don't believe she has any intention of joining you in Rome. I'm sorry."

Joly took a breath. "Maybe things had run their course."

Sanborn bowed his head. "That was rather the impression that I had gained. Well, I don't care for prolonged farewells. I hope you will reflect on our conversation last night and that soon we shall see you again in La Serenissima."

Forcing a smile, Joly said, "Who knows, I might take Zuichini up on his kind offer. There are worse ways of making a living than binding fine books, I guess."

A light flared in Sanborn's old eyes. Voice trembling, he said, "Joly, the moment I first saw you, I knew you were made of the right stuff. In fact, I'll let you into a secret. I'd seen you a couple of times at the Campo Santi Apostoli before I made so bold as to introduce myself."

"Is that so?" Joly didn't know whether to be puzzled or flattered. "So did you see Lucia as well?"

"As a matter of fact, I did. Such a pretty creature, with that gorgeous dark hair and honey skin. Oh, well, there are many more lovely girls in Venice. Despite my age, I can guess how sad you must feel. I felt the same about my friend Sophia, after I'd talked to her for the last time. But she and I were not lovers; the physical loss makes it doubly hard for you."

"These things happen."

"Yes, life goes on. And you will never forget Lucia, of that I am sure. But your life will be so much richer if you take up Zuichini's offer. Truly, his craftsmanship is unique. Think of it! You could follow in his footsteps. Make a name for yourself and earn a not inconsiderable fortune."

"Is Zuichini rich?"

"My dear fellow, do not be deceived by appearances. If – no, *when* you return, you will have a chance to visit his splendid home near the Rialto. Even though he and I are close associates, he never fails to drive a hard bargain. But I, and others like me, are willing to pay for the best. For something unique."

They shook hands and Sanborn pulled out of his shoulder bag a parcel wrapped in gift paper. He thrust it at Joly.

"I want you to have this. A token of our friendship. And a reminder of the esoteric pleasures that lie in store, should you accept Zuichini's offer to help you learn his trade."

"Thanks." Joly's cheeks were burning. He'd harboured so many false suspicions and now he couldn't help feeling a mite embarrassed. "I'm not sure that bookbinding is . . ."

"Think about it. That's all I ask." Sanborn smiled. "I have seen enough of you in a short space of time to be confident that you would relish the chance to become a craftsman in your own right. As you told me, you have a taste for the unusual. And with your love of books . . ah well, you must be going. Goodbye, my friend. Or as I should say, *arrivederci*."

Joly found himself waving at the old man's back as he limped away. At the notice board, just before he moved out of sight, Sanborn raised his stick in salute, but he did not turn his head. The bus was waiting and Joly found himself a seat by the window. As the driver got into gear, Joly tore the wrapping paper from his present. He stared at it for a long time.

The present was a book, carefully protected by bubble wrap and old newspapers and that came as no surprise. The title was *A Short Treatise on the Finer Points of Bookbinding*. But it was not the text that seized Joly's attention, though deep down he knew already that, one day, this would become his Bible.

The front cover was tanned and polished to a smooth golden brown. He'd never come across anything quite like it. To the touch, it had slight bumps, like a soft sandpaper. The spine and back cover felt more like suede. But what entranced him was not the texture of the binding.

At first sight, he thought the cover bore a logo. But with a second glance, he realized his mistake. In the bottom corner was a design in blue-black. A picture of a flying dove, with broad outstretched wings.

He held his breath as he recalled kissing Lucia's toes. Recalled the delicate heart shape traced in ink upon her ankle. Recalled, with a shiver of fear and excitement, Zuichini's admiration of the tattooist's work, the way those dark and deadly little eyes kept being drawn to Lucia's tender, honey-coloured skin.

He settled back on the hard seat. The countryside was passing by outside, but he paid it no heed. Sanborn understood him better than he understood himself. After searching for so long, he'd finally found what he was looking for. Soon he would return to La Serenissima. And there Zuichini would share with him the darkest secrets of the bookbinder's craft. He would teach him how to make the book that Sanborn craved, a book for all three of them to remember Lucia by.

TROUBLE IS A LONESOME TOWN

Cathi Unsworth

Dougie arrived at the concourse opposite the station just half an hour after it had all gone off. He'd had the cab driver drop him down the end of Gray's Inn Road, outside a pub on the corner there, where he'd made a quick dive into the gents to remove the red hood he'd been wearing over the black one, pulled on a Burberry cap he'd had in his bag so that the visor was down over his eyes. That done, he'd worked his way through the mass of drinkers, ducked out of another door and walked the rest of the way to King's Cross.

The Adidas bag he gripped in his right hand held at least twenty grand in cash. Dougie kind of wished it was handcuffed to him; so paranoid was he about letting go of it even for a second that he'd had trouble just putting it on the floor of the taxi between his feet. He'd wanted it to be on his knee, in his arms, more precious than a baby. But Dougie knew that above all else, now, he had to look calm, unperturbed. Not like a man who'd just ripped off a clip joint and left a man for dead on a Soho pavement.

That's why he'd had the idea of making the rendezvous at the Scottish Restaurant across the road from the station. He'd just blend in with the other travellers waiting for their train back up North, toting their heavy bags, staring at the TV with blank, gormless expressions as they pushed stringy fries smothered in luminous ketchup into their constantly moving mouths. The way he was dressed now, like some hood rat, council estate born and bred, he'd have no trouble passing amongst them.

He ordered his quarterpounder and large fries, with a super-size chocolate lard shake to wash it all down, eyes wandering around the harshly lit room as he waited for it all to land on his red plastic tray. All the stereotypes were present and correct. The fat family (minus dad, natch) sitting by the window, mother and two daughters virtually indistinguishable under the layers of flab and identical black-and-white hairstyles by Chavettes of Tyneside to match the colours of their footie team. The solitary male, a lad of maybe ten years and fifteen stone, staring sullenly out of the window through pinhole eyes, sucking on the straw of a soft drink that was only giving him back rattling ice cubes. On the back of his shirt read his dreams: 9 SHEARER. But he was already closer to football than footballer.

Then there was the pimp and his crack whore; a thin black man sat opposite an even thinner white woman with bruises on her legs and worn-down heels on her boots. Her head bowed like she was on the nod, while he, all angles and elbows and knees protruding from his slack jeans and oversize Chicago Bulls shirt, kept up a steady monologue of abuse directed at her curly head. The man's eyes were as rheumy as a 70-year-old's, and he sprayed fragments of his masticated fries out as he kept on his litany of insults. Sadly for Iceberg Slim, it looked like the motherfuckingbitchhocuntcocksucker he was railing at had already given up the ghost.

Oblivious to the psychodrama, the Toon Army had half of the room to themselves, singing and punching the air, reliving moment-by-moment the two goals they'd scored over Spurs – well, thank fuck they had, wouldn't like to see this lot disappointed. They were vile enough in victory, hugging and clasping at each other with tears in their eyes, stupid joker's hats askew over their gleaming red faces; they might as well have been bumming each other, which was obviously what they all wanted.

Yeah, Dougie liked to get down among the filth every now and again, have a good wallow. In picking over the faults of others he could forget about the million and one he had of his own.

Handing over a fiver to the ashen bloke behind the counter, who had come over here thinking nothing could be worse than Romania, Dougie collected his change and parked himself inconspicuously in the corner. Someone had left a copy of *The Scum* on his table. It was a bit grubby and he really would have preferred to use surgical gloves to touch it, but it went so perfectly with his disguise and the general ambience of the joint that he forced himself. Not before he had the bag firmly wedged between his feet, however, one of the handles round his ankle so if anyone even dared to try . . .

Dougie shook his head and busied himself instead by arranging the food on his plastic tray in a manner he found pleasing: the fries tipped out of their cardboard wallet into the half of the Styrofoam container that didn't have his burger in. He opened the ketchup so that he could dip them in two at a time, between mouthfuls of burger and sips of chocolate shake. He liked to do everything methodically.

Under the headline STITCHED UP, the front page of *The Scum* was tirelessly defending the good character of the latest batch of rapist footballers who'd all fucked one girl between the entire team and any of their mates who fancied it. Just so as they could all check out each other's dicks while they did it, Dougie reckoned. That sort of shit turned his stomach almost as much as the paper it was printed on, so he quickly flipped the linen over, turned to the racing pages at the back. That would keep his mind from wandering, reading all those odds, totting them all up in his head, remembering what names went with what weights and whose colours. All he had to do now was sit tight and wait. Wait for Lola.

Lola.

Just thinking about her name got his fingertips moist, got little beads of sweat breaking out on the back of his neck. Got a stirring in his baggy sweat pants so that he had to look up sharply and fill his eyes with a fat daughter chewing fries with her mouth open and to get it back down again.

Women didn't often have this effect on Dougie. Only two, so far, in his life. And he'd gone further down the road with this one than anyone else before.

He could still remember the shock he felt when he first saw her, when she sat herself down next to him at the bar with a tired sigh and asked for a whisky and soda. He caught the slight inflection in her accent, as if English wasn't her first language, but her face was turned away from him. A mass of golden brown curls bobbed on top of her shoulders, she had on a cropped leopardskin jacket and hipster jeans, a pair of pointy heels protruding from the bottom, wound around the stem of the barstool. The skin on her feet was golden brown too; mixed race she must have been and, for a minute, Dougie thought he knew what she would look like before she turned her head, somewhere between Scary Spice and that bird off *Holby City*. An open face, pretty and a bit petulant. Maybe some freckles over the bridge of her nose.

But when she did turn to him, cigarette dangling between her lips and long fingers wound around the short, thick glass of amber liquid, she looked nothing so trite as "pretty".

Emerald green eyes fixed him from under deep lids, fringed with the longest dark lashes he had ever seen. Her skin was flawless, the colour of the whisky in her glass, radiating that same intoxicating glow.

For a second he was taken back to a room in Edinburgh a long time ago. An art student's room, full of draped scarves and fake Tiffany lamps and a picture on the wall of Marlene Dietrich in *Blue Angel*. This woman looked strangely like Marlene. Marlene with an afro. *Black Angel*.

She took the cigarette from between her red lips and asked: "Could you give me a light?" Her glittering eyes held his brown ones in a steady gaze, a smile flickered over her perfect lips.

Dougie fumbled in the sleeve of his jacket for his Zippo and fired it up with shaking fingers. Black Angel inhaled deeply, closing her bronze-coloured eyelids as she sucked that good smoke down, blowing it out again in a steady stream.

Her long lashes raised and she lifted her glass to him simultaneously. "Cheers!" she said and he caught that heavy inflection again. Was he going mad, or did she even sound like Marlene too? "Ach," she tossed back her mane of curls, "it's so good to be off vork!"

"I'll drink to that," Dougie said, feeling like his tongue was too big for his head, his fingers were too big for his hands, that he was entirely too big and clumsy. He slugged down half his pint of Becks to try and get some kind of equilibrium, stop this weird, teenage feeling that threatened to paralyze him under the spell of those green eyes.

She looked amused.

"What kind of work do you do?" she asked.

Dougie gave his standard reply. "Och, you know. This an' that."

It pleased her, this answer, so she continued to talk. Told him in that smoky, laconic drawl all about the place she worked. One of the clip joints off Old Compton Street, the ones specifically geared up to rip off the day trippers.

"It izz called Venus in Furs," she told him. "Is fucking tacky shit, yeah?"

He started to wonder if she was Croatian, or Serbian. Most of the girls pouring into Soho now were supposed to be ones kidnapped from the former Yugoslavia. "Slavic" was a word that suited the contours of her cheeks, the curve of her green eyes. But how could that be? Dougie didn't think there was much of a black population in Eastern Europe. And he couldn't imagine anyone having the balls to kidnap this one. Maybe she was here for a different reason.

Images raced through his mind. Spy films, Checkpoint Charlie, the Cold War. High on her accent, he didn't really take the actual words in.

Until at some point close to dawn, she lifted a finger and delicately traced the outline of his jaw. "I like you Dougie," she smiled. "I vill see you here again, yes?"

Dougie wasn't really a one for hanging out in drinking clubs. He had only been in this one because earlier that evening he'd had to have a meet in Soho and he couldn't stand any of the pubs round there. Too full, too noisy, too obvious. This was one of the better places. Discreet, old fashioned, not really the sort of place your younger generation would go for, it was mainly populated by decaying actors skulking in a dimly lit world of memory. It was an old luvvie who'd first shown him the place. An old luvvie friend of a friend who'd been ripped off for all his Queen Anne silver and a collection of Penny Blacks by the mercenary young man he'd been silly enough to invite back for a nightcap. Dougie had at least got the silver back, while the guy was sleeping off what he'd spent the proceeds of the stamps on. He really didn't come here often, but as he watched the woman slip off her stool and shrug on her furry jacket he felt a sudden pang and asked: "Wait a minute – what's your name?"

She smiled and said: "It's Lola. See you again, honey." And then she was gone.

Dougie found himself drifting back to the club the next evening. It was weird, because he'd kept himself to himself for so long he'd felt like his heart was a hard, cold stone that no one could melt. It was best, he had long ago told himself, not to form attachments in his line of work. Attachments could trip you up. Attachments could bring you down. It was better that no one knew him outside his small circle of professional contacts and the clients they brought. Safer that way. He'd done six months time as a teenager, when he was stupid and reckless and had vowed he'd never be caught that way again.

He was mulling over all these facts as he found himself sat at the bar. He didn't quite know what he thought he was doing there, just that he felt his heart go each time the buzzer went and a new group of people clattered down the steps. Lola had come into the place alone. He supposed he could ask the Guv'nor what he knew about her, but that didn't seem very gentlemanly. After all, he wasn't a regular himself. Who knew how long she'd been making her way down here after the grind of an evening "huzzling the schmucks" under Venus' neon underskirts?

At half past one she had wound her way down the stairs towards him. A smile already twitching at the corners of her mouth, she was pleased to see him. One look up her long, bare, perfect legs to her leather miniskirt and that same leopard jacket and he felt the same.

"He-*looo*, Dougie," she said.

Dougie felt drunk, as he had ever since.

Gradually, over whisky and sodas with the ice crinkling in the glass, she'd told him her story. It was all very intriguing. Her father was Russian, she said, ex-KGB, who since the fall of Communism had managed to create an empire for himself in electronic goods. He was a thug, but a charming one – he had named her after a character in a Raymond Chandler book that he'd read, contraband, as a teenager. They had a lot of money, but he was very strict. Made her study hard and never go out. There was not a lot of emotion between him and her mother.

Her mother was an oddity, a Somalian. Lola didn't know how they met, but she suspected. Back in the old days, it was quite possible her father had bought her out of semi-slavery in a Moscow brothel. Her mother always claimed she was a princess, but she was also a drunk, so what was Lola to believe? She was beautiful, that was for sure. Beautiful and superstitious, always playing with a deck of strange cards and consulting patterns in tea leaves. She might have mastered dark arts, but never managed to speak Russian – probably she never wanted to. So Lola grew up speaking two languages, in one big, empty apartment in Moscow.

Right now, she was supposed to be in Switzerland. She looked embarrassed when she told Dougie this. "At finishing school. Can you believe? Vot a cliché." Lola had done a bunk six months ago. She'd crossed Europe, taking cash-in-hand work as she did, determined to get to London. She wanted to escape while she was in the "free West" rather than go back to what she knew would be expected of her in Russia. Marriage to some thick, bastard son of one of her father's ex-comrades. A life of looking nice and shutting up, just like her mother.

But she feared her father's arm was long. There were too many Russians in London already. Someone was bound to rat her out before long, the reward money would be considerable. So she had to get together a "travelling fund" and find somewhere else to go. Somewhere safe.

"Vere are you from, Dougie?" she purred. "Not from round here, eh?"

"What do you reckon?" he said archly. "Where d'you think I got a name like Dougie from, heh?"

Lola laughed, put her finger on the end of his nose.

"You are from Scotland, yes?"

"Aye," nodded Dougie.

"Where in Scotland?"

"Edinburgh."

"Vot's it like in Edinburgh?"

A warning voice in Dougie's head told him not to even give her that much. This story she had spun for him, it sounded too much like a fairytale. She was probably some down-on-her-luck

Balkans hooker looking for a sugar daddy. No one could have had the lifestyle she described. It was too far-fetched, too mental.

The touch of her finger stayed on the end of his nose. Her green eyes glittered under the optics. Before Dougie knew what he was doing, words were coming out of his mouth.

She had given him the germ of an idea. The rest he filled in for himself.

The Venus In Furs was not run by an established firm, even by Soho standards. Its ostensible owners were a bunch of chancy Jamaican wide boys whose speciality was taking over moody drinking dens by scaring the incumbents into thinking that they were Yardies. Dougie doubted that that was the case. They could have been minor players, vaguely connected somehow, but Yardie lands were South of the river. Triads and Micks ran Soho. He doubted these fellas would last long in the scheme of things anyway, so he decided to help Lola out and give fate a hand.

Trying to help her, or trying to impress her?

It helped that her shifts were regular. Six nights a week, six till twelve. Plenty of time to observe who came and went on a routine basis. Maybe her old man really was KGB 'cos she'd already worked out the day that the Suit came in would be the significant one.

There was this office, behind the bar, where they did all their business. Three guys worked the club in a rota, always two of them there at the same time. Lynton, Neville and Little Stevie. They had a fondness for Lola, her being blood, so it was usually her they asked to bring drinks through when they had someone to impress in there. She said the room had been painted out with palm trees and a sunset, like one big Hawaiian scene.

Like everyone, Dougie thought, *playing at gangsters – they were playing* Scarface.

Once a week, a bald white guy in a dowdy brown suit came in with an attaché case. Whichever of the Brothers Grim were in at the time would make themselves scarce while he busied himself in the office for half an hour. One of them would hang at the bar, the other find himself a dark corner with one of the girls. Then the bald man would come out, speak to no one and make his own way out of the club.

Every Thursday, 8 p.m., punctual as clockwork he came.

That proved it to Dougie. The lairy Jamaicans were a front to terrify the public. The bald man collected the money for their unseen, offshore master. With his crappy suit and unassuming exterior, he was deliberately done up like a mark to blend in with the rest of the clientele.

Dougie had a couple of guys that owed him favours. They weren't known faces, and it would be difficult to trace them back to him, their paths crossed infrequently and they moved in different worlds. On two successive Thursdays, he gave them some folding and sent them in as marks. Both confirmed Lola's story, and gave him more interesting back-up on the Brothers Grim. Both weeks, it was the same pair, Little Stevie and Neville, little and large. Large Neville, a tall skinny guy with swinging dreads and shades who was always chewing on a toothpick, sat behind the bar when the bald man showed up. He practised dealing cards, played patience, drank beer and feigned indifference to the world around him, nodding all the while as if a different, slow skanking soundtrack was playing in his head to the cheesy Europop that was on the club's PA.

Little Stevie, by comparison, always grabbed himself a girl and a bottle and made his way over to the corner booth. While Neville looked like a classic stoner, Little Stevie was mean. He wore a black suit and a white shirt with thick gold chains around his bulldog neck. A pork pie hat and thick black shades totally obscured his eyes. Ocassionally, like when the girl slipped underneath the table, he would grin a dazzling display of gold and diamond dental work. Stevie always drank proper Champagne – not the pear fizz served to the punters as such – and both Dougie's contacts copped the telltale bulge in his pocket.

Stevie's booth was the one from which the whole room could be surveyed and, even while receiving special favours, he never took his eye off the game. The minute the office door clicked open and the bald man slipped away he would knee his girl off him, adjust his balls and whatever else was down there, and swagger his way back over to the office all puffed up and bristling, Neville following at his heels.

Yeah, Stevie, they all agreed, was the one to watch.

While they were in there playing punters, Dougie was watching the door.

The Venus was based in a handy spot, in a dingy alley between Rupert Street and Wardour Street. There was a market in Rupert Street and all he had to do was pretend to be examining the tourist tat on the corner stall. The bald man went the other way. Straight to a waiting cab on Wardour Street. Each time the same.

On the night it all happened, Dougie felt a rush in his blood that he hadn't felt since Edinburgh, like every platelet was singing to him the old songs, high and wild as the wind.

God, he used to love that feeling, used to let it guide him in the days when he was Dougie the Cat, the greatest burglar in that magical city of turrets and towers.

But now he was Dougie Mackingtosh Investigates, the Private Eye for the sort of people who couldn't go to the police. He had changed sides on purpose after that first prison jolt, never wanting to be in close proximity to such fucking filth ever again. If you couldn't be a gentleman thief these days, he reckoned, then why not be a Bad Guy's PI? His methods may have differed from those used by the Old Bill, but Dougie had kept his nose clean for eighteen years, built up his reputation by word of mouth and made a good living from sorting out shit without causing any fuss. Filled a proper gap in the market, he had.

His blood had never sung to him in all that time. He supposed it must have awakened in him that first night he met Lola, grown strong that night she'd finally allowed him back to her dingy flat above a bookie's in Balham, where she had so studiously drawn out the map of the Venus' interior before unzipping his trousers and taking him to a place that seemed very close to Heaven.

Bless her, he didn't need her map. He didn't even need to know what Neville and Stevie got up to, only that they were good little gangsters and stayed where they were, in that little palace of their imagination where they could be Tony Montana every day.

He wasn't going to take them on.

All he needed was the thirty seconds between the Venus' door and Wardour Street. And the curve in the alley that meant the taxi driver wouldn't be able to see. All he needed was the strength of his arm and the fleetness of his feet and the confusion of bodies packed into a Soho night.

At the end of the alley he slipped a balaclava over his head, put the blue hood over the top of that and began to run.

He was at full sprint as the bald man came out of the door, fast enough to send him flying when he bowled into his shoulder. The man's arms spread out and he dropped his precious cargo to the floor. Dougie was just quick enough to catch the look of astonishment in the pale, watery eyes, before he coshed him hard on the top of his head and they rolled up into whites. He had another second to stoop and retrieve the case before he was off again, out of the alley, across Wardour Street, where the taxi was waiting, its engine running, the driver staring straight ahead.

Dougie was already in the downstairs bogs of the Spice of Life before the cabbie was checking his watch to make sure he hadn't turned up early. Had pulled out his sports bag from the cistern where he'd stashed it and bust the lock on the attaché case by the time the cabbie turned the engine off and stepped out of the car to take a look around. Dougie's deftness of touch was undiminished by his years on the other side. He counted the bundles of cash roughly as he transferred them into his sports bag, eyebrows raising as he did. It was quite a haul for a weekly skim off a clip joint. He briefly wondered what else they had going on down there, then chased the thought away as excess trouble he didn't need to know.

By the time the cabbie was standing over the crumpled heap in the alleyway, he had put the attaché case in the cistern and taken off the blue hood, rolling it into a ball as he nipped out of the side door of the pub. He junked it in a bin as he came out onto Charing Cross Road and hailed himself a ride up to King's Cross.

Dougie looked up from his racing pages. As if struck by electrodes, he knew Lola was in the room. She walked towards him, green eyes dancing, clocking amusedly his stupid cap and the bag that lay between his feet. Sat down in front of him and breathed: "Is it enough?"

"Aye," nodded Dougie. "It's enough."

He hadn't wanted there to be any way in which Lola could be implicated in all this. He'd had her phone in sick for two days running, told her just to spend her time packing only the essentials she needed and gave her the money for two singles up to Edinburgh.

The night train back to the magic city, not even the Toon Army could ruin that pleasure for him.

"You ready?" he asked her.

Her grin stretched languidly across her perfect face.

"Yes," she purred. "I'm ready."

Dougie gripped the Adidas bag, left his floppy fries where they lay. As they stepped out onto the road, St Pancras was lit up like a fairytale castle in front of them. "See that," he nudged her shoulder, "that's bollocks compared to where we're going."

His heart and his soul sung along with his blood. He was leaving the Big Smoke, leaving his life of shadows, stepping into a better world with the woman he loved by his side. He took her hand and strode towards the crossing, towards the mouth of Kings Cross Station.

Then Lola said: "Oooh, hang on a minute. I have to get my bag."

"You what?" Dougie was confused. "Don't you have it with you?"

She laughed, a low, tinkling sound. "No honey, I left it just around the corner. My friend, you know, she runs a bar there and I didn't want to lug it around with me all day. She's kept it safe for me, behind the bar. Don't vorry, it von't take a minute."

Dougie was puzzled. He hadn't heard about this friend or this bar before. But, in his limited experience of women, this was typical. Just when you thought you had a plan, they'd make some little amendment. He guessed that was just the way their minds worked. She leaned to kiss his cheek and whispered in his ear: "Ve still have half an hour before the train goes."

The pub was, literally, round the corner. One of those horrible, bland chain brewery joints heaving with overweight office workers trying to get lucky with their sniggering secretaries in the last, desperate minutes before Closing Time.

He lingered by the door as Lola hailed a bored-looking blonde behind the bar. Watched her take a small blue suitcase from behind the bar, kiss the barmaid on each cheek and come smilingly back towards him.

A few seconds before she reached him, her smile turned to a mask of fear.

"Oh, shit," she said, grabbing hold of his arm and dragging him away from the doorway. "It's fucking Steve."

"What?"

"This vay," she had his arm firmly in her grasp now, was propelling him through to the other side of the bar, towards the door marked TOILETS, cursing and talking a million miles an hour under her breath.

"Steve was standing right outside the door. I svear to God it was him. I told you, he is bad luck that one, he's voodoo, got a sixth sense – my Mama told me about *sheiit* like him. We can't let him see us! I'm supposed to be off sick the night he gets ripped off – he's gonna know! He's gonna kill me if he sees me."

"Hen, you're seeing things," Dougie tried to protest as she pushed him through the door, down some steps into a dingy basement which smelt of piss and stale vomit.

"I'm not, it vos him, it vos him!" she looked like she was about to turn hysterical, her eyes were flashing wildly and her nails were digging into his flesh. He tried to use his free hand to extricate himself from her iron grip, but that only served to make her cling on harder.

"Hen, calm down, you're hurting me . . ." Dougie began.

"There's someone coming!" she screamed and suddenly began to kiss him passionately, smothering him in her arms, grinding her teeth against his lips so that he tasted blood.

And then he heard a noise right behind him.

And the room went black.

"Fucking Hell," Lola looked down on Dougie's prone body. "That took long enough."

"I told you he was good," her companion pouted, brushing his hands on his trousers. "But I thought you'd enjoy using all your skills on him."

"Hmm," Lola bent down and prised Dougie's fingers away from the Adidas bag. "I knew this would be the hardest part. Getting money out of a tight fucking Jock."

That slinky Russian accent had disappeared like a puff of smoke. She sounded more like the petulant queen she was now.

"Come on." She stepped over her would-be Romeo and the pile of shattered ashtray glass he lay in. "Let's get out of here."

The car was parked nearby. As Lola got into the passenger seat, she pulled the honey-gold Afro wig off her head and ran her fingers through the short black fuzz underneath.

"I am *soooo* tired of that bitch," she said, tossing it into the backseat.

Her companion started the car with a chuckle.

"He fucking believed everything, didn't he?" he shook his head as he pulled out.

"Yeah . . . and you said he was a private detective. Well, let me tell you honey, you wouldn't believe what I suckered that dick with. My dad was a Russian gangster. My mother was a Somalian princess. I was on the run from Swiss finishing school. Can you believe it?"

Lola hooted with derision. "Almost like the fairytales I used to make up for myself," she added. "You know, I thought he might fucking twig when I told him I was named after a character in Raymond Chandler. But I couldn't resist it."

"Well," her companion smiled at her fondly. "You certainly made up for the loss of that Queen Anne silver. We've got enough to keep us going for months now. So where do you fancy?"

"Not back to Soho," Lola sniffed, as the car pulled into the slipstream of Marylebone Road. "I've fucking had it with those posing thugs. I know. I fancy some sea air. How does Brighton sound to you?"

"The perfect place," her companion agreed, "for a couple of actors."

Dougie came around with his face stuck to a cold stone floor with his own blood. Shards of glass covered him. He could smell the acrid stench of piss in his nostrils, and from the pub above, he could hear a tune, sounding like it was coming from out of a long tunnel of memory. He could just make out the lyrics: "*I met her in a club down in old Soho/Where you drink Champagne and it tastes like cherry cola . . .*"

In loving memory of Lee Hazlewood 1929–2007, who had all the best stories and all the best songs.

GREEN TARTS

Deryn Lake

God grant me grace, but I am getting on in years. I looked in the mirror this very morning and an old man stared back at me. I gazed at him in horror, hardly believing that I had come to this. But sooner or later we all have intimations of mortality. Thus I will do as my conscience dictates and set down a record of those times, so long ago, when a man met his death in the Tower and the part that I played in it all. As far as I can recall, if memory serves correctly, it all started with a bed.

It arrived in pieces, as was customary, and was carried up to the master bedroom by a team of servants, then handed over to the craftsmen to assemble. Watching them work, its new owner thought it a beautiful thing that grew beneath their hands; richly carved and sumptuously adorned. In fact he could hardly wait for them to finish that he might stretch out on it and measure his length on the silk cover, letting his eyes take in the marquetry panels on the headboard, created by German craftsmen, a number of whom now lived in Southwark. His gaze wandered over the elaborate carvings, one of which was a grinning satyr to represent fertility. It seemed to smile at him in a devilish manner. All in all, he thought to himself, this new bed summed up his status, his standing, his enviable position as the best-loved favourite of that most malleable of monarchs, James I.

Robert Carr, Viscount Rochford, took a step forward and touched the gorgeous draperies, presently being hung beneath the intricately carved oak tester. The workman responsible looked up.

"All right, my lord?"

"Splendid. I think this bed is going to be quite wonderful."

"It will indeed, my lord."

And tonight, thought Robert, I shall show it, totally complete, to my closest friend, Thomas Overbury. He gave a quiet sigh, thinking of the pleasures ahead, and turning, left the room.

As he went downstairs, Robert glanced admiringly at himself in a mirror. He was a handsome man, some twenty-four years of age, with long straight limbs and broad shoulders. He had a head of thick fair hair which he wore tightly frizzed as fashion dictated, meanwhile dressing himself to the inch in fine clothes and jewels, including a sparkling earring worn in his left ear. Unfortunately all this frippery made him appear effeminate, a feature which, no doubt, pleased his royal master enormously. For there could be no doubt that the King worshipped Robert – leaning on his arm, pinching his cheek, kissing him quite openly in full public gaze – a fact which the self-seeking young man positively encouraged, responding with melting looks and suggestive gestures. Yet, despite the love of King James, Robert had formed another liaison with Thomas Overbury, a bright young Englishman with literary pretensions. In fact the couple were devoted and it was Thomas who was to visit this very night.

In order to pass the time, Robert decided to have a bath, thus causing an army of servants to plod up and down stairs with pails of boiling water. After being towelled dry, he oiled himself then dressed in stockings and doublet, executed in silks and gold and silver thread. On his feet he put on a pair of low-heeled shoes, decorated with an enormous frill of black and yellow. Then, having shaved closely, a feature much admired by the King, he awaited Thomas's arrival. Quarter of an hour later, a thunderous knock announced his presence. Robert immediately assumed a negligent pose, his fingers idly toying with a book, the other hand supporting his chin. He looked up as his friend was announced.

"My dear Overbury," he said.

But once the bowing servant was out of the way, Robert hurried over and embraced the newcomer warmly, kissing him on both cheeks, then on the mouth.

Thomas disentangled himself. "You're pleased to see me, I take it."

"I always am. You know that."

His friend allowed a small smile to light his features, a fact which made him appear more attractive. Older than Carr, he was not so blatantly good looking yet it was a more intelligent face, though spoiled by an expression of arrogance. Now, though, he was anxious to please.

"Have you persuaded the King to like me any better?" he asked eagerly.

Robert pulled down his mouth. "No, I'm afraid not."

"You know why it is, don't you?"

"I think I can hazard a guess."

"Because he's jealous of me. He knows damn well that you love me better than him – and that is something the lecherous old beast cannot stomach."

Robert simpered and for a moment looked utterly feminine. "I think what you say is true. He cannot take his eyes off me, even at court."

Thomas Overbury scowled. "Besotted old fool."

"Shush. Someone might hear you."

"Let them." He turned to Robert. "Now, what is this surprise you have to show me?"

"Come upstairs. Come and see my new toy."

Somewhat mystified, Thomas followed him up the staircase to the master bedroom, Robert firmly closing the door behind him. A few minutes later came the sound of muted laughter as the two men sampled the new bed's delights.

"I am in despair," said Frances, Countess of Essex, bursting into a spectacular torrent of tears. "Oh, my dear, what am I to do?"

The dear in question was a small, comely widow with a pleasing face and hair like golden thread. But at present her expression was one of deep sympathy which did not totally become her.

"Think of it," Frances continued, not waiting for a reply. "Think of being wedded to a lanky brute who at first would not consummate the marriage and now expects me to lie with him, which I do not wish to do. And, sweet Anne, just at this stage I have received a love letter from another man."

Anne's expression changed rapidly to one of acute attention. "Really, my pet? Who?"

"You'll not believe it – the King's favourite! Robert Carr himself."

"Robert Carr? But surely he has other interests."

"So I always thought, but the letter was most ardent."

"What did it say?"

"How much he admires me and how much he would like to converse with me."

Anne shook her head. "I am surprised indeed."

Frances, who was one of the most beautiful women at court, looked very slightly annoyed. "Oh?"

"I'm just surprised that he had the courage to write," Anne answered swiftly.

"I see," answered the Countess, slightly mollified.

"I hold your heart close to mine as I hope you do to me," said Sir Thomas Overbury, dictating.

"Is that grammatically correct?" asked Robert Carr, pausing in his writing.

"Oh, to hell with grammar. It will certainly attract the attention of the silly bitch."

Robert laughed carelessly. "I don't know why I'm bothering with this."

"Oh, yes, you do. It's because you can't resist a challenge and the fact that the lady is in a loveless marriage appeals to you."

"What shall I do if she says yes?"

Overbury gave a careless shrug. "That, my dear, will be entirely up to you."

At that moment both men looked up as there was a noise in the corridor outside. They were in the royal palace at Greenwich, in Carr's apartments, but this did not guarantee them privacy.

"Hide the letter," hissed Overbury and Robert thrust it beneath a book as the door opened without ceremony and they saw, standing in the entrance, his royal majesty James.

He glanced at Thomas unsmilingly. Ever since the affair last year when both he and Carr had been caught laughing at the

Queen, any affection the King might have felt for Robert's friend had been totally banished. However, his feelings for Carr remained undiminished.

Now he said, "There you are, my lad. I would ask you to walk with me a little."

Straightening himself from his reverential bow, Carr smiled flirtatiously. "Of course, your Majesty."

Advancing on him, James lolled an arm round his favourite's neck and kissed him on the lips. Carr turned towards him as sweetly as any woman. "If I can do anything to please your Majesty."

The King's rheumy eyes had an inner fire. "We'll walk a little way first, eh, Carr?"

"As your Majesty pleases."

Ignoring Overbury the pair left the room, weak-legged James hanging round Robert's neck as though his very life depended on it. Thomas could not help but notice that the fingers of the King's other hand were fiddling round his codpiece as he shuffled out.

They met privately and for the first time in Carr's apartments in Hampton Court, he full of charm and prattling nonsense, she virtually tongue-tied. Looking at her, intending to use her as a plaything and then discard her, Robert was struck by how very good-looking she was at close quarters. Her hair, reddish-gold in colour, was frizzed out in the latest fashion with an aquamarine and pearl headdress, while her eyes – matching the stone – flashed shy but definite messages in his direction. As for her figure, he could see from her exceedingly low-cut gown that her breasts were truly beautiful. It was rumoured throughout the court that she was a virgin, a fact which stimulated Robert's wicked side with thoughts of deflowering her.

"Well, Lady Frances, how good of you to come."

"I come in response to your letters, Sir."

He had not written one of them; Thomas Overbury was responsible for them all. Thinking of the ribaldry as they had been composed, Robert felt himself flush and turned away.

"Would my Lady like some wine?"

"Yes, please, I would."

Carr poured two glasses and having handed her one, sat down in a chair opposite hers.

"You truly are bewitching," he said, speaking his thoughts aloud.

Frances pulled a face. "Much good it has done me."

"You are not happy?" asked Robert, hoping that this would start off the story of her marriage.

"No, Sir, I am not."

And that indeed released the floodgates. She spoke of her wedding to the Earl of Essex when she had been fifteen and he a few months younger, how her father had at first kept them apart but, following that, when her husband had returned from his trip abroad, he had failed dismally in the bed chamber. So much so that after a year of trying he had given up completely.

"And now?" Carr enquired.

"Now I would hate sexual connection. I dislike the Earl, may God forgive me."

"Why Madam?"

"Because he is not pleasing to look at, he cannot talk to me, and he is only happy in the company of other men." Tears filled the lovely bright eyes. "All in all, he is not a pretty fellow."

There was silence in the room and then Robert put down his glass and held out his hand. After a moment's hesitation, the Countess of Essex slowly put out hers and twined her fingers round his. They said nothing but sat quietly, simply looking at one another.

That evening Overbury, calling on his friend as usual, found him strangely withdrawn.

"Well, Robert, how did it go? Did you woo the hussy?"

"Don't call her that, I beg you."

Thomas was so shaken that he sat down abruptly. "God's life! Do I hear aright? Don't tell me that you have fallen under her spell."

Robert, looking at Thomas Overbury, noticed for the first time that the man had a spot with a head forming on his right cheek.

"Of course not," he said abruptly.

Thomas raised an eyebrow. "If I didn't know you a great deal better I would say that you are extremely interested in the girl. Well, don't be so I beg of you. The Howards are a poisonous bunch and you know perfectly well that her father loathes you."

"That is hardly her fault."

"Agreed. But I assure you that you will place yourself in great danger if you pursue this."

"Perhaps," Robert answered. He changed the subject. "Now, dear friend, would you care for some wine?"

"I'll have some Alicante."

"A favourite of his Majesty."

"Yes," said Thomas with much meaning. "Let us hope that he does not lose interest in it."

After he had gone, rather abruptly Robert thought – though he had been thankful, for once, to see the back of him – Carr lay on his bed. Over and over in his mind came the vision of the beautiful Countess, so young and so unhappy. A strange feeling came over him, one that he was quite unaccustomed to, and he wondered what could possibly be causing such an unusual sensation. Yet, despite it, he knew that she was indeed dangerous to him. And he also knew for certain that his original plan to use her as a plaything might well have to be abandoned.

Thomas Overbury was in a state of high alarm. There had been a definite change in his friend's attitude, all stemming from the time he had seen that wretched Howard girl on his own. It was a known fact that Thomas detested all the Howards – nobody, himself included, quite knowing why. Possibly, he often thought, he had been born hating them. But the fact remained, he had an obsessive private malice towards the entire family.

He had helped Robert write those silly letters to the Countess of Essex, born Lady Frances Howard, for one reason and one reason alone; to ruin her reputation and thus bring dishonour to her clan. But now it looked as if the entire scheme had blown up in his face. Could it even be possible that Robert Carr, Viscount Rochford, was falling in love with the woman? Alone in his room, Thomas seethed with silent rage.

Yet his position was assured. Robert, frankly, had neither the brains nor the will to wade through interminable papers, and having been raised to the role of Privy Councillor now sent various secret documents to Overbury for him to look over first. Yet this very power was making Thomas unpopular in certain quarters. And one quarter was extremely dangerous. The King himself had conceived a violent dislike of his favourite's best friend, a dislike which he barely bothered to conceal.

"I am deep in love," said the Countess of Essex, sighing.

"I am sure you are, my dear," replied Mrs Turner, wishing she were being paid a guinea for every time she had heard that remark.

"Yet I fear the situation," Frances continued. "If my husband should discover my association he would wreak havoc."

"But he is not a husband in the true sense of the word. Is he?" she added, a trifle uncertainly.

"Most certainly not," Frances replied roundly. "You know I hate the sight of him. And now I love Robert I could not bear to sleep with another man."

"But surely you and Carr have not . . ."

Anne Turner paused delicately and the Countess blushed. "No, not yet. But I fear – what am I saying? – I mean I hope that it won't be too long. That is why, my dear, I want you to take me to your Cunning Man. He has a fearsome reputation in dealing with matrimonial matters."

Mrs Turner nodded her blonde head. "He certainly has. He also has a reputation for taking his clients to bed." She laughed, a little nervously.

"Well, he won't get anywhere with me," Frances answered with asperity. And in that moment Anne saw her determination, her ruthlessness in achieving what she wanted regardless of the cost.

In this way Frances was introduced to Simon Forman, a man who combined the art of medicine with that of magic. An astrologer, a clairvoyant, and most of all a sympathetic listener, she begged him to make Robert Carr love her passionately and at the same time render her husband totally incapable in the bed-chamber. She also asked, though this in the greatest secrecy, that the Earl of Essex should die, thus leaving her free to marry again should she so desire.

Then, in the following spring, while still married to the lugubrious Earl, she and Robert met in secret at his house in London. She arrived by coach, heavily veiled, and was immediately shown into the salon. Awaiting her, in a frenzy of love, was the young nobleman, gorgeously attired as was customary but today not caring how he looked, determined, as he was, to get her upstairs to see his wonderful bed.

As soon as the servants had left the room he started to kiss her, wildly and voluptuously, knowing that she would weaken under such a barrage.

"Sweetheart," he said, close to her ear. "Oh, my darling, I want you so badly."

"But . . ." Frances protested half-heartedly.

"But what?"

"I am still married."

"To that miserable fool. To hell with him."

Robert was more aroused than he had ever been before. All his life he had found men more attractive than women but now he was in the throes of a desire so strong that it was barely containable. Turning Frances round he headed purposefully for the door.

"Where are you going?" she asked him

"There's only one place for us to go. To the bedroom."

"Oh, Robert, I'm afraid."

"So am I," he answered truthfully, making her laugh.

But once inside his bedchamber, the door locked safely behind them, she stared in wonderment at his beautiful bed.

"Oh, God's truth," she exclaimed. "I have never seen anything so glorious."

"Do you refer to me or my bed?" he asked, half seriously.

She moved round to face him. "Both," she said.

Afterwards, when they lay entwined, naked as on the day of their birth, she shuddered a little.

"What's the matter? Did I hurt you?"

"A bit. But it was worth every second."

"You belong to me now, Frances Essex."

"Don't call me by that name. I hate it. Call me Howard."

"But the Howards hate me," said Robert ruefully.

"One day they won't."

"It will take a magic spell to make them change their minds."

"Well, who knows, that might even happen."

Overbury was beside himself with anger. He was positive that his friend was deeply besotted with the wretched Howard woman, despite all his warnings of dire peril if Robert continued to associate with her.

"Abandon the bitch now," had become his war cry.

But he misinterpreted the situation. Robert had for the first time in his life fallen deeply in love – physically, mentally, and every other way. He now had one goal and that was to marry Frances as soon as she could obtain a divorce.

Things came to a head between the two men in the following March. Returning to his rooms in Whitehall in the small hours, having spent the evening in the embrace of Frances, Robert was horrified to find Overbury pacing up and down in the Privy Gallery through which he had to pass.

"Are you still here?" he asked angrily.

"Am I here? Where have you been?"

Brushing him aside, Carr went on his way only to have Overbury shout at him, "Will you never leave the company of that base woman?"

"I haven't seen her," muttered Robert.

"It is too manifest," Thomas screamed at him.

Carr wheeled about, his face livid, but Overbury was in full spate. "The King has bestowed great honours and gifts upon you and you overthrow yourself and all your fortunes in the company of that base woman. As you clearly intend to ruinate yourself I think it best if I have nothing further to do with you."

"So be it," growled Robert.

But Thomas was not done yet. "If you would kindly pay me the £1,500 you owe me then our obligations to one another are at an end. You must stand as you can, and I shall shift for myself. Good night to you." And he stormed off in a towering rage.

"Prick," yelled Robert at his departing back.

"The man is dangerous," said Frances when told of the incident next day.

"No, darling. Difficult perhaps, but not actually menacing."

"He might try and stop my suit for nullity going through."

"On what grounds?"

"On the grounds that you and I committed adultery, a fact which he knows well."

"It would be his word against ours."

"He would dig up other witnesses from somewhere."

Furthermore, thought Robert, Thomas Overbury has been thwarted in his love for me and will never forgive Frances as long as he lives. While Frances, unaware of what her lover was thinking, considered the fact that Thomas might yet reassert his power over Robert and send her packing.

"It would be better for all of us if the man could be spirited away," said Carr quietly.

"I could try and get someone to murder him," Frances remarked brightly.

Robert Carr, Viscount Rochford, merely laughed, thinking that she spoke in jest. But actually the Countess of Essex was in earnest, even going so far as to approach Sir David Wood – a Scotsman with a grudge against Overbury. Unfortunately he refused point blank, saying, "I might be accounted a great fool, Madam, if upon a woman's word I should go to Tyburn."

In the end it was the King himself who provided the solution. He decided that Overbury was to be offered an ambassadorship abroad, thus removing him and his potential for making trouble, yet at the same time treating him very fairly, for to be created ambassador was considered a good promotion.

Strangely, Overbury decided to be defiant. He believed that if he went overseas he would fade into obscurity. His prospects in England were far better, he argued. In view of the King's dislike of him and the fact that Carr had fallen out with him, this was very odd reasoning, to say the least. Yet Thomas would not budge, probably thinking that Carr was behind it all and wanted him out of the way. The possibility of blackmailing Robert – a difficult thing to do from a distance – had also crossed his mind.

King James was thrown into an almost uncontrollable rage by Thomas Overbury's contemptuous refusal of his offer.

"How dare that arrogant upstart treat me with such derision, Carr? You know I did this for you and I thought it a brave way of saving Overbury's face. And now the poxy pillock has turned down my offer. I'll have him for this, mark my words."

The spittle was running down from the King's mouth, a sign that he was labouring under some great emotion. Robert, not so keen these days on giving his Majesty whorish looks and flirtatious glances, felt genuinely alarmed. Yet alongside this alarm there rose a ray of hope.

"What do you mean, Sire?"

"I'll call him before the Council and then send him to the Tower. I'll teach him to treat me with disrespect."

Robert was so overcome that he had to sit down suddenly, despite the King being present. So their problem was going to be solved for them. Overbury was to be condemned to imprisonment.

James looked at him from a little eye. "And what do you have to say to that, eh, my Carr?"

"I say good riddance."

"I think it well if you take to your bed for a few days, Robert. And when the news does come to you, plead ignorance."

"I will, Sire, never fear." And Carr kissed the royal hand more fervently that he had done for the last several months.

At long last Frances's marriage was declared null and void. But what a terrible time she had had to endure in order to obtain her objective. The entire Howard clan had been thrown into a panic when the Court of Commissioners had insisted that she be investigated by midwives and ladies of rank to see whether she was "virgo intacta". The fact that she was having an affair with Carr was common knowledge among the family so they had substituted another girl – very young and heavily veiled – to undergo the examination. However the head of the commissioners, Archbishop Abbot, had expressed doubt about the proceedings, but once again the King had intervened. He had issued an order that each commissioner was to vote whether he was for or against the annulment without stating his reasons. Seven to five voted in favour of the Countess's marriage being annulled.

The populace at large were vaguely amused by it all and some wit wrote a ditty which went into common circulation:

This dame was inspected, but fraud interjected,
A maid of more perfection
Whom the midwives did handle, whilst the knight held the
  candle,
O there was a clear inspection.
Now all foreign writers, cry out on those mitres
That allow this for virginity
And talk of ejection and want of erection,
O there is sound divinity!

Seventeen days after Thomas Overbury was admitted to the Tower, the Governor, Sir William Wade, was dismissed and Sir Gervase Elwes was appointed in his place. Behind this extraordinary turn of events lay the hand of the Earl of Northampton, great-uncle to Frances and himself very attracted to Robert Carr. No sooner had this happened than Richard Weston, a shady character who had once worked for Mrs Anne Turner and who had latterly helped Frances and Robert to meet in secret places, was appointed as Thomas's gaoler.

Shortly after this, Mrs Turner sent for Weston to come to Whitehall to meet the Countess of Essex, as she still then was. She asked him to give Overbury "a water", insisting that Weston did not take it himself. He suspected at once it was poison but on his way to administer it he was stopped by Sir Gervase Elwes. Weston was then approached by a strange man called Franklin in the White Lion on Tower Hill, who enquired about Overbury's health. Weston told him that the man was far from well and had to have enemas regularly. Franklin immediately suggested that a strange apothecary would come and give him a poisoned glister, or enema. Weston promptly reported the matter to Sir Gervase.

Right from the start of his imprisonment, Thomas had been writing to Robert in letters that showed he had no conception of how deeply wounded Carr had been by his references to Frances. Instead he spoke blithely of plans to get him out of the Tower, most of them saying how sick he was, indeed fit to expire. In a welter of self-deception, he begged Carr to say that he – Robert – would die of a broken heart if Thomas were not released. In other letters still he tried to manage Carr's affairs, just as he once had long ago. But his greatest mistake was to refer to Frances as a "catopard"; a derogatory term that he had used about her when Robert merely regarded the girl as a plaything.

Meanwhile a steady stream of tarts and jellies had been arriving at the Tower, purporting to come from Robert. But, shortly, other foodstuffs arrived, from the Countess of Essex. Elwes kept these particular tarts, which were a bright green in shade, in the Tower kitchen and noted that after a day or two they had turned black and foul. While the jellies, left standing, grew fur on them. Then came the day when she sent another batch of emerald green tarts, this time accompanied by a letter.

In it she insisted that Sir Gervase should not allow his wife or children to taste the tarts or jelly, and that they were to be given to Thomas Overbury. "Do this at night and all will be well," she concluded.

That evening, lying next to Robert in the great and beautiful bed, she whispered, "Darling, why do you write to Overbury? Surely you must hate him as much as I do."

There was a silence, so profound that she thought her lover must have dropped off to sleep, but eventually he spoke in the darkness.

"No, I don't hate him. I just wish he weren't such an arrogant bullying creature. I truly hoped that being in prison would make him see sense and that he would swear allegiance to your family. But he continues to write in his old vein; ordering me about and . . ."

His voice died away.

"Insulting me?" asked Frances.

Carr propped himself up on one elbow. "I didn't say that."

"No, but you meant it. Oh, sweetheart, I fear that fellow. I fear his influence even from the heart of the Tower."

"What influence, pray?"

"That he will poison you against me. That he will regain his place in your heart."

"Never," answered Robert forcefully. "I swear to you that he shall never do that."

"All the same I wish he were dead and leaving us all in peace."

"Shush. You are not to say such things."

"But I think them."

The final straw in the relationship between the imprisoned Overbury and Robert Carr came in August. Thomas's brother-in-law, Sir John Lidcote wrote to him and told him of a visit he had made to Carr. Having read the letter Overbury, much enfeebled since his commital to the Tower, made a gesture of despair.

"What's the matter with you?" asked Weston, who had just come into the room.

"It's Carr. He's played me false. Listen to this. My brother-in-law told him of my plight in this place and the fellow gave a counterfeit sigh. And then do you know what he did?"

"No."

"He grinned widely in Lidcote's face. Just couldn't help smiling. And to think of my miserable condition and the number of times I have begged him to help free me. Why, I would like to kill the bastard."

"No chance of that," remarked Weston dourly.

"Indeed, indeed," replied Overbury heavily. "But at least I can put pen to paper. That is if I had any."

"I'll get you some," Weston answered, suffering an unusual moment of pity for the shambling wreck that Overbury was fast becoming.

Later he took the letter to be posted without telling Sir Gervase Elwes, little realizing that its contents would finally give Robert Carr a motive for murder, because in it Overbury threatened to expose all the secrets he and Carr had shared over the years, ending with the ominous words, "Thus, if you deal thus wickedly with me, I have provided, whether I die or live, your nature shall never die, nor leave to be the most odious man alive." He also stated that he had made copies of this indictment and sent it out to all his "friends noble".

Knowing that the contents of the letter would send Frances into a frenzy, Robert did not show it to her. But going about the Court as usual he heard nothing to make him believe that Overbury had kept his word and written to various noblemen. On the contrary, everyone was cheerful and nobody mentioned a word about receiving such a libellous document. Carr concluded that Thomas simply had threatened in vain.

But the sands of time were running out for Thomas Overbury; that arrogant bully was now seriously ill. Throughout the month of August, 1613, his condition slowly deteriorated. According to Weston, his gaoler, Thomas had a large sore on his back which he kept covered with a plaster. Apparently the changing of this caused him so much pain that he would shout and swear when Weston did it.

At the end of the month Sir John Lidcote wrote to Robert that it was virtually impossible to contact Overbury and asked if he knew anything about it. Then, almost immediately, Carr was informed that the wretched man's condition was deteriorating fast. He immediately wrote to Dr Mayerne – who was visiting

Bath at the time – and told him of the situation. The physician replied that he was sorry but there was nothing he could do at the moment. Might it not be better perhaps if Overbury wrote to him direct describing his symptoms.

But the time for writing letters was almost over. On the morning of the 14th September, Overbury begged Weston for an enema.

"It might ease me a little."

Weston looked noncommittal, his usual expression. "Aye, it might. Shall I ask Paul de Loubell, Dr Mayerne's apothecary, to make you one up?"

"If you wouldn't mind."

Two hours later an apothecary's boy had come into the room where Overbury lay, looking quite ghastly.

"You're wanting an enema, Sir?"

"Oh, God, yes. I'm in a terrible state and I'm hoping it might afford me some relief."

"Should do, Sir. Now let's to your arse."

"What's your name?" asked Weston as the boy administered the glister.

"William, Sir."

"Do you know what you are doing?"

The boy had given him a look from the eyes of a leopard. "Oh, yes, sir. I know what I am doing very well."

That evening, as Weston lay fitfully slumbering, he heard the most terrible cry from Overbury's room. Going to him he saw that the man had thrown himself half out of bed.

"What's up?" he asked laconically.

But he had to bend over Overbury to hear the reply, which came from a mouth with the lips drawn back and upwards in a kind of terrible snarl.

"I am in agony, man. For the love of Christ, help me."

"Where does it hurt you?"

"Everywhere. I have never known pain like it."

"I can change the plaster on your back if you like."

Overbury nodded. "It might help me. Can you do it beneath the bedclothes?"

"I can try."

Fumbling about beneath the sheets Weston did his best to follow Thomas's instructions as to where the ulcer was, but when sticking the plaster down he heard Overbury give vent to a terrible oath as he touched the place where it was situated. He pulled back.

"That's the best I can do."

There was no answer. Weston looked down and saw that Thomas had closed his eyes, but not peacefully. Instead there was an agonized expression on his face.

Throughout that night the gaoler kept close watch, listening to the screams and groans of the sick man. He even moved him to another bed to see if this might ease his sufferings. As dawn broke Overbury spoke to him in a feeble voice.

"Weston, go and buy me some beer, I beg of you. I have such a thirst that I think it will kill me if I don't drink."

The gaoler, paid creature of Mrs Anne Turner, took another look at the prisoner, then did what was necessary. After that he went out of the Tower for fifteen minutes. When he returned he was greeted by death. For the corpse of Thomas Overbury lay alone in the chamber to which he had been brought exactly four months previously. It was finished.

The wedding was one of the most splendid the court could remember. It took place on 26th December, 1613, exactly three months after the death in the Tower. Celebrated in the Chapel Royal at Whitehall – where Frances had married the Earl of Essex, her first husband – the service was conducted by the same man, the Bishop of Bath and Wells. Frances played the part of virgin bride by wearing her hair loose, Robert Carr – who a month before had been raised to the status of Earl of Somerset – was dressed resplendently. It was indeed a sight to behold.

The marriage was followed by extravagant festivities. A specially written masque was performed, then came dancing in which both bride and groom took part. The couple finally got to bed at about three o'clock in the morning, utterly exhausted and too tired for consummation. Acting on a whim, the new Earl had had the great bed dismantled and reassembled in his apartments at Whitehall. So that when Frances finally entered the room she exclaimed aloud in delighted surprise. And later when the groom was brought in surrounded by his male attendants, he found her sitting up in it, smiling at him.

"Oh, sweetheart, you've brought our bed here," she whispered as the last one left the room.

"Yes, goodnight, darling."

And she laughed a little as she saw that he had immediately fallen asleep.

The celebrations went on interminably. At court the entire twelve days of Christmas were taken up with masques and feasting, while poets wrote verses praising the bride's beauty and purity. On New Year's Day a tournament was held in which the teams wore the colours of either bride or bridegroom, while on the 4th January the entire court rode through the streets of London to feast with the Lord Mayor. The bridegroom went on horseback, Frances rode in a brand new coach, richly ornamented, drawn by a team of horses presented to the Earl as an additional wedding present.

It seemed as if nothing could ever go wrong for this glittering couple. Robert had made up his quarrel with Frances's family and still stood high in the King's estimation. He had estates, money, a key position, and, above all, a wife with whom he was deeply in love. Life had never been more worth living. And yet, somewhere, a worm began to turn.

Making his summer progress through the country, the King stayed at Apethorpe in Northamptonshire. And it was there that he first set eyes on George Villiers. It was love at first sight undeniably. James had never seen such a vision. For George's face and hands were effeminate yet handsome, his hair hung in chestnut curls, he was tall and well made. From that moment on the star of Robert Carr, Earl of Somerset, began to go into the descendent.

Robert's many enemies met at Baynard's Castle, four Earls being amongst their number. They determined, almost gleefully, to use Villiers to bring Carr down. They decided to clothe George, giving him spending money. The impecunious young man, owner of one threadbare suit, was now dressed in the very latest fashion. He was young, he was attractive, he was gleaming with self-awareness. At long last the Earl of Somerset had been outshone.

Furiously, Robert did everything to block his rival's rise to power. But to no avail. He had finally met his match.

"But, sweetheart," said Frances, who had been sitting patiently listening to her husband's complaints for a good thirty minutes, "surely you should try and win the King's favour back."

"I do try."

"I beg to differ. You sulk and show him open fury. You will never gain his love again like that."

Much to her surprise, her husband rounded on her. "How dare you? I know the King of old. Leave the way he is handled to me, if you please."

"Certainly," Frances replied, and stalked out of the room.

But walking down the corridor she had a frightening experience. She thought that something moved in the shadows, a dark shapeless thing.

"Overbury!" she exclaimed. And just for a second the thing took form and raised its hand at her before it vanished.

Frances ran to the bedroom and flung herself down on the bed – that wonderful bed that had accompanied her throughout her love affair with Robert Carr. She felt cold and afraid as if something unknown were rising from the grave to come and taunt her. Turning, she looked up at the woodwork but all she could see was the face of a grinning satyr.

By that summer, with George Villiers now knighted and made a Gentleman of the Bedchamber, something else, something far worse, began to worry Robert Carr. A whispering campaign had started about the death of Thomas Overbury. Talk of poison and poisoners was spreading, and all this nearly two years after the event. It occurred to the Earl of Somerset almost at once that his enemies at court had deliberately rekindled the old scandal.

Meanwhile Mrs Anne Turner, Frances's friend and confidante, to say nothing of Frances herself, was growing distinctly worried. It was widely believed that Richard Weston had been working for them and that he had insisted on being paid for his services – namely the demise of the prisoner. Had he anything to do with Overbury's death or was he demanding payment under false pretences? He continued to badger the women who had supplied him with the green tarts until the time when, in order to keep him quiet, they gave him £100 in gold, followed by another four score pounds, also in gold, both sums paid to him by Mrs Turner.

In the spring of 1615 Frances felt certain that she had become pregnant and removed herself to Greys, near Henley. Mrs Turner, who had moved in with the Somersets a short time after their marriage, accompanied her. Walking in the garden, certain that they could not be overheard, they conversed.

"My dear Anne, what are we going to do?"

"I have no idea, my dear Frances. After all, we did send in the green tarts."

"Not to mention the jelly. It was full of poison as you know."

"We must just deny everything and hope that these wretched rumours will stop."

Frances Somerset burst into tears and stamped her foot. "Horrible Thomas Overbury! He will make trouble for us yet, I swear it."

Mrs Turner made no reply but simply pursed her lips and walked steadfastly on.

Robert Carr, Earl of Somerset, had now grown frantic. He had sought from King James a pardon which would absolve him of crimes he had previously committed. But though the King seemed willing enough to sign it, it had come unstuck before the Council when the Lord Chancellor had refused to seal it. The King had become angry and had walked out of the meeting, straight to the Queen, who had, hating Somerset as she did, put the final nail into the coffin and told James not to sign.

Shortly after, His Majesty left on his summer progress. And it was while he was staying at Beaulieu that news reached him of the fact that Sir Gervase Elwes had set down an account of the events leading up to the death of Sir Thomas Overbury. Having thus been informed, it left James no option but to order a full enquiry into the death of the prisoner.

The Lord Chief Justice himself, Sir Edward Coke, who seemed to be everybody's enemy, headed the investigation, driven by his own desire to punish Somerset. He interviewed hundreds of people, everyone from the highest to the lowest – well, almost the lowest – determined to capture the big fish via the little minnows.

In mid-September Richard Weston was arrested and confessed that he had been given a phial of greenish liquid by a Doctor Franklin, a quack that both Frances and Mrs Turner had consulted to aid them with their respective love affairs. That night Franklin was summoned to the Whitehall apartments of the Countess. As he entered the room, Robert Carr, who was present with his wife, gave him a dark look and walked out, leaving him alone with the two women.

"Weston has been taken into custody," said Frances hysterically.

She looked terrible; pale, her hair wild, her body swollen by the child she was carrying.

"How very regrettable," Franklin answered, not knowing quite what else to say.

"Regrettable! It's a tragedy," she answered. "You will be next, Franklin, mark my words, and you must deny everything. If you confess anything you will be hanged. By God, if you confess, you shall be hanged for me, for I will not be hanged."

"No, Madam," said Mrs Turner in a quiet voice, "I will be hanged for you both."

Frances did not reply but left the room. In the silence that followed they could hear her speaking through the wall, and Robert answering her. When she came back again she looked slightly calmer and warned Franklin again about remaining silent when being questioned.

He bowed and left. Two days later both he and Mrs Turner were arrested and questioned.

That night, climbing into their bed, Frances and Robert hugged each other like two children.

"What shall we do?" she asked him in a tiny, frightened voice.

"Deny," he answered. "We must deny everything."

"But Weston will tell them about the green tarts, about the jelly, about the apothecaries . . ."

"Say no more, not even between these walls. All we can do is swear they are liars."

"I'm terrified, Robert."

"We should have thought of that before," he answered bitterly.

Like a rat in a trap, the Earl of Somerset did everything to defend himself; burning letters, writing to Overbury's servant, pleading with the King, objecting to the panel of commissioners investigating the case. But all to no avail. On 17 October an order was made placing him under house arrest in his apartments at Whitehall. Frances – now seven months pregnant – was similarly confined to a room in Greys.

Now, it seemed, that Overbury reached from the grave and claimed his victims. Weston was hanged by the neck until he was dead; Sir Thomas Monson, a shadowy figure who had worked behind the scenes assisting the Countess of Somerset, was arrested pending trial; Sir Gervase Elwes was stripped of office and placed in confinement; Mrs Anne Turner was taken into custody, James Franklin, the quack doctor, likewise. Somerset himself was transferred to the Tower. Because of Frances's pregnancy she was placed under house arrest in the care of Sir William Smithie, a London alderman. She was now completely isolated.

The trial of Mrs Turner proved sensational because various magic dolls were produced, all coming from the time when she and Frances had consulted cunning men about their love affairs. But in the eyes of the public it meant that she was a sorceress, a dabbler in the black arts, and it was hardly surprising when the jury found her guilty. Thomas Overbury had his second victim.

Sir Gervase Elwes was hanged, swiftly, because one of his servants took hold of one foot while the hangman's assistant tugged the other. There was a general feeling that no one thought he deserved the verdict. James Franklin was sent to the gallows and died muttering as the cart was driven away and he was left hanging. Four people had now gone to the grave.

On 9th December Frances gave birth to a baby girl after a normal confinement. The child was christened Anne a few days later. Then, on 4 April, 1616, the Countess and her daughter were parted, for the mother was taken to the Tower pending the court hearing. She lived separately from her husband – who had yet to see his baby – and it was elected that she would be the first to go to trial, to be prosecuted by no less than Sir Francis Bacon. As she entered court every man present drew breath for that day she looked radiantly beautiful. She held up her hand for the reading of the indictment.

"Frances, Countess of Somerset, what sayest thou? Art thou guilty of this felony and murder, or not guilty."

Curtseying to the Lord Chancellor, the Countess uttered a single word in a low voice, wondrous fearful. "Guilty," she said.

That, you may feel, was the end of the story. The Earl and Countess of Somerset were both found guilty and condemned to die, she by the rope and he by the axe. But, strange as it may seem, they received royal pardons and eventually walked free from the Tower.

What does that mean? Had Overbury been murdered or had he died of an illness contracted in the Tower? Had all the so-called evidence been doctored by Coke in his determination to condemn Somerset?

And what of me? You see, I was the smallest player. No one asked me what happened, but I knew all the facts.

Poor little Frances. She supplied green tarts and jellies to the prisoner, but they were intercepted by Elwes and never eaten. They were each and all so convinced of the parts they played that they trapped themselves by their own guilt.

So did anyone kill Thomas Overbury, I hear you ask?

Indeed. I killed him, dead as pork.

I, William Reeve, apprentice to Paul de Loubell, the apothecary who made up prescriptions for Dr Mayerne.

On the way to the Tower to give Sir Thomas an enema, I was approached by a shifty fellow – I have no idea who he was – and given a substance which I was asked to substitute for the one I was carrying. He offered me £20, more money than I could earn in years. So I did. I applied the enema right under the eyes of Weston, who had no idea what was really happening.

Then I fled to Paris and stayed there for several years until the whole affair was over, before returning to London and setting myself up as an apothecary. I heard the whole story from my master, Paul de Loubell, just before he died, and I have set it down for you as he told it to me.

Yet even he did not know the truth about my part in the affair. Now you alone know how I outwitted them all, even the greatest in the land. Will you find it in your heart to forgive me?

DAPHNE McANDREWS
AND THE SMACK-HEAD JUNKIES

Stuart McBride

Half past eight on a cold autumn evening and Sergeant Dumfries had his feet up on the reception desk, a mug of tea in one hand, a copy of the *Oldcastle Advertiser* in the other. Reading about the hunt for little Lucy Milne. The lobby door clattered open, letting in a howling gale, setting the posters flapping on the notice board. He sat upright with a sigh, put the newspaper away and plastered a professional smile on his face. An old lady with a walking stick was wrestling a tartan shopping trolley in through the heavy wooden doors. She had a little Westie terrier on the end of an extendible leash, barking happily as bright orange leaves tumbled in around the old woman's ankles, twirling about the police station lobby like demented Highland dancers.

"Can I help you with that, madam?"

She flashed him a smile. "No, no we'll be fine." There was something familiar about her, but Dumfries couldn't put his finger on it. Five foot two, overweight, grey-brown overcoat, tartan headscarf, granny boots, face like a wrinkled cushion . . . With one last tug she got the trolley inside, letting the lobby door slam shut. For a moment the swirling leaves hung in the air, before slowly drifting to the linoleum floor.

She trundled her shopping trolley up to the reception desk and peeled off her headscarf, revealing a solid mass of grey curls, hairsprayed within an inch of their life. "Dear, oh dear," she said, giving a little shiver. "What a dreadful evening! I was saying to Agnes this morning – we always have tea in the Castlehill Snook: they do a lovely fruit scone – and I was saying how the weather seems so much worse this year. I remember when—"

Dumfries stifled a groan as she wittered on – just his luck to get stuck with an old biddy in for a bit of a chat. "So," he said, making sure his fixed smile hadn't slipped, "what can I do for you, madam?

She stopped talking and studied at him for a moment. "Norman, isn't it? Norman Dumfries?"

"Er . . ." He shifted uncomfortably in his chair. "Yes?"

"Who would have known you'd turn out so tall! You were such a wee lad at Kingsmeath primary – see, I told you eating your greens would do you the world of good."

And that's when it clicked. "Mrs McAndrews, thought I recognized you!" This time Sergeant Dumfries's smile was genuine. "How you been?"

"Not too good, Norman," she said, leaning forward and dropping her voice to a conspiratorial whisper. "There's a naked man in my shed, and I think he's dead."

While most school dinner ladies were waxing lyrical about the exotic delights of custard creams and garibaldi biscuits, Daphne McAndrews had remained steadfast: as far as she was concerned it was homemade shortbread or nothing. Humming happily, she arranged some on the tray, next to a fresh pot of tea and six mugs, and carried it out the back door.

The police had set up a pair of huge spotlights, training them on the shed at the bottom of the garden, making the wasp-chewed wood glow. The rest of the garden was shrouded in darkness, the trees groaning and creaking in the buffeting wind. Daphne tottered carefully down the path, trying to keep the tea things from blowing away.

The shed door was propped open and half a dozen men, dressed in those white plastic over-suit things they wore on telly, were poking about inside. It was a big shed, Bill's pride and joy, but she'd barely touched it since he'd gone, just dusted from time to time. It was comforting to know that there was something of him in here: in a grey urn at the back, next to the little wooden fire engine he was working on before he died.

"Is everyone ready for a nice cup of tea?" she asked, stepping over the threshold and closing the door behind her, shutting out the wind.

Someone spun round and stared at her. "You shouldn't be in here!"

"Oh, wheesht. My Bill used to say that all the time, but a bit of shortbread always made him change his tune."

"No, you don't understand. This is a crime scene." He flapped his hands in the direction of the naked young man, sprawled against the far wall – under the shelf with Bill's urn on it – wearing nothing but a pair of argyle socks.

"It's not a crime scene, it's Bill's shed. Now stop being silly: time for tea." She started pouring. "Beside, it's not like I haven't seen a naked man before. And as a dinner lady, you get used to being around death. One lump or two?"

"Err . . ." He looked around at his companions, but no one came to his rescue. Policemen were just like little boys: you had to be firm, stand your ground, and not let them get away with anything. Cheeky monkeys. He cleared his throat and stared at his shoes for a moment, before saying, "Two please."

The shortbread was going down a treat – she wasn't a leading light of the Women's Rural Institute for nothing – when the shed door banged open again. A small pause and then someone roared, "What the hell's going on in here?" It was a man with a moustache and a thunderous expression. "Sergeant, this is supposed to be a crime scene, not a bloody tea party!" The policeman with two sugars blushed and apologized, the words coming out in a shower of crumbs. The newcomer's head looked like it was about to explode. Shouting and swearing, he dragged the policemen out into the back garden and shouted at them some more. Going on about trace evidence and short-bread crumbs and disciplinary hearings . . . Then he noticed Daphne was still in the shed, sipping her tea.

"YOU!" he said, flinging a finger in her direction. "Get back in that bloody house!"

*   *   *

A nice WPC was sent in to take her statement. "Don't worry about DI Whyte," she said, as Daphne opened a tin of Pedigree Chum Senior. "He's going through a bit of a divorce at the minute."

Daphne gave a haughty sniff and scraped a solid tube of chicken and heart into a clean dish. "If my Bill was alive today . . ." But he wasn't, so there was no point even thinking about it. She put the dish down on the floor, and whistled. "Come on darling, din-dins!" An old, yellow-white Westie dog clattered into the kitchen, little stumpy tail going at twenty to the dozen. He had Mr Bunny, his favourite, tatty old squeaky toy, clamped in his jaws.

"Oh, he's so *sweet!*" The WPC beamed. "What's his name?"

Daphne reached down and ruffled the fur between her boy's ears. "This is Little Douglas. Bill named him after my father, on account of the family resemblance. He's going to be fifteen in February. Aren't you Wee Doug, aren't you? Yes, you are! Yes, you are!" He gave a cheerful bark and stuck his nose in the dog food.

"Can you tell me when you found the dead man in your shed, Mrs McAndrews?"

"Hmm? Oh, it was . . ." Daphne frowned in concentration. "*Coronation Street*. That blonde lassie was having an affair with the Asian chap and I was thinking I could really do with a nice cup of tea. So I waited for the next advert break and went through to make one. Only before I turned on the light I saw this naked woman running climbing over the back fence. And I thought—"

"Wait, you saw a naked woman? Not a naked man?"

"Oh, yes. When you work in a school canteen you get to know the difference. Anyway, she was clambering over the fence, and I got Wee Doug and we went out and he was very brave, weren't you? Mummy's little soldier. He's very protective, you know. Anyway, I saw the shed door was open and I went to close it and there he was. So I got on my overcoat and went to the police station and reported it."

"Why didn't you just dial 999?"

Daphne shook her head sadly. Young people these days. "My dear, reporting a dead body isn't like ordering a pizza. Some things you just have to do in person."

★   ★   ★

The Castlehill Snook was nearly empty at half past ten on a Tuesday morning – just a middle-aged couple in the corner, bickering over a map – so Daphne and her best friend Agnes McWhirter had no trouble getting their usual table by the window overlooking the Castle car park. A large coach from Germany was disgorging tourists in front of the pay and display machine, all of them clutching little Scottish flags and plastic bags from the Woollen Mill. The sky was the colour of warm slate, wind making the tourists' cagoules whip and snap as they tried to get round the Old Castle ruins before the rain came on.

Daphne unclipped Wee Doug's lead and let him snuffle about the tiled floor; by the time the waitress arrived with the cake trolley, he was curled up beneath a chair. Snoring.

Agnes ordered her usual fruit scone, but Daphne shocked everyone, even herself, by asking for a slice of Battenberg instead. "Are you feelin' OK?" asked Agnes, staring aghast at the slice of yellow and pink sponge. Taking a deep breath, Daphne told her about the dead body in her shed, the naked woman clambering over the back fence, and what that nice Sergeant Norman Dumfries had said when she'd called in past the station first thing this morning to see how they were getting on.

"Fancy that!" said Agnes, pouring the tea. "Naked drug addicts in your shed!"

"I know, I'm that mortified." Daphne shuddered, took a bite of her Battenberg and chewed suspiciously. It wasn't like her to entertain baked goods involving marzipan. She fed the rest to Wee Doug.

"They were probably having kinky, drugged-up sex. That's what these people do, you know, get high and indulge in filthy sex games: it was in the *Sunday Post*. Mr McAndrews would *not* have liked that!"

Daphne nodded; her husband had been as conservative in the bedroom as she was in the biscuit department. He would never have asked her for a fig roll when there was perfectly respectable shortbread available.

"Of course, they're all at it." Agnes tapped on the window. On the other side of the castle car park a ragged figure was trying to sell copies of the *Big Issue* magazine to the scurrying German tourists. "Drug addicts the lot of them. 'Junkies' – they're everywhere these days. It was in the *Sunday Post*. I tell you, Oldcastle's getting more like that Los Angeles every day. Next thing you know there'll be drive-by shootings and prostitutes on every street corner!" She nodded sagely and the first drops of rain speckled the teashop window, getting heavier and heavier, sending the tourists scurrying back to their bus. The scruffy figure watched them in silent resignation then tromped away into the downpour.

The shed was filthy by the time the police were finished with it, covered in fingerprint powder, nothing put back in the right place. Dressed in her "Sheep of Scotland" pinny and yellow rubber gloves, Daphne scrubbed and polished and tidied until it was all good as new. She stood back and examined her handiwork with grim satisfaction – there was a lot to be said for a clean shed. She frowned. Bill's urn didn't look right.

It was a medium urn, because her husband had been a medium man. His remains would have looked short-changed in a large urn, and buying a small one would have meant leaving bits of him at the crematorium. And you never knew *which bits* they'd be, would you? The last thing she wanted was to get up to heaven and find that Bill was missing a leg, or a hand. Or his gentleman bits. He wouldn't like that. She picked the urn off the shelf and squirted it with furniture polish, buffing it up with a yellow duster until it . . . the lid was loose. With trembling hands she unscrewed it all the way.

Daphne had never felt more like a drink in her life. Not even when Bill died. Sitting at the kitchen table she poured herself a stiff sweet sherry, threw it back and poured another one. "Oh, Bill!" His urn sat on the tabletop in front of her. A big scoop of his ashes were missing. Someone had stolen bits of her husband . . . Wee Doug padded back and forth under the table, his claws clickity-clacking on the linoleum, whimpering. He knew his mummy was upset.

Biting her bottom lip, Daphne screwed the top back on the bottle. Wallowing in self-pity wasn't going to do Bill any good. If she wanted justice, she was going to have to get off her backside and do something about it. It was what Bill would have wanted.

*   *   *

Rain clattered against the cobbled street, shining like beads of amber in the yellow streetlight as Daphne trudged along Shand Street, heading back up Castle Hill to the teashop, pulling her tartan shopping trolley behind her. Wee Doug's nose poked out through a tiny opening in the top, sniffing the cold night air for a moment, before sensibly ducking back down again, out of the rain. The teashop would be closed, just like all the other shops she passed on her way up the hill, their windows glowing, but lifeless. Like the empty streets. "That's because everyone with an ounce of sense is indoors!" she told herself, stopping for a moment to rest. It was hard going and her hip was beginning to complain. Dampness seeped in through the seams of her old raincoat, her left boot squished as she walked, and her glasses were all fogged up. Sighing, she leant on her walking stick and thought about turning round and going—

A noise.

She froze, struggling to locate the sound over the rain drumming off her plastic headscarf. Nothing. She tried all the settings on her hearing aid, but it didn't make any difference. Probably just her imagination playing tricks . . . And then she heard it again, someone singing and swearing softly to themselves.

Slowly Daphne crept up the road, pulling the trolley with her, scanning the empty shop doorways on either side. A wee cobbled close disappeared off between the knitwear place and the kilt shop, the little alleyway roofed off by a hairdresser's on the first floor. It stretched away into the darkness, a link between the towering sandstone buildings on Shand Street and the dour brick of Mercantile Road. Gloomy and forbidding. That was where the noise was coming from.

Plucking up all her courage, Daphne stepped into the alley. It was dark in here, the streetlights on Shand Street barely making a dent in the shadows, but she could just make out a figure, huddled in a doorway, a grubby pink blanket pulled round his shoulders, sitting on a pile of flattened cardboard boxes. The flare of a match and she saw his face as he lit a scrawny, hand-rolled cigarette – bearded, dirty. Not the man who'd been trying to sell the *Big Issue*; but, as Agnes said, they were *all* drug addicts. He was probably doing drugs right now, chasing the rabbit, or whatever it was called. Straightening her shoulders she marched right up and said, "Excuse me?"

The man didn't answer, just kept on swearing away, so she poked him with her walking stick.

"I said, excuse me."

He squealed and scurried backwards into the wall, jittering and twitching, watching her suspiciously. "What you want?" His eyes glittered in the dim light like a snake.

"I'm looking for a woman."

The man leered. "You wanna them big fat lesbians?" She poked him with her stick again. Hard. "Ow! Cut it out!"

"This particular woman was in my shed last night, with a young man. She took someone . . . something of mine and I want it back!"

There was a silence as the man stared at Daphne – probably undressing her with his eyes. These drug addicts were all alike. Sex mad. "So . . ." he said, leaving his doorway, the filthy pink blanket still wrapped around his shoulders, smelling of urine and Marmite. "You gonnae make it worth my while, like?"

Daphne blushed. Sex mad – she knew it. Quickly, she rummaged in the damp pockets of her raincoat and came out with a half-empty bag of mint imperials. "Would you like a sweetie?"

He reached out and snatched the bag. "Got any money?"

"Manners!" Daphne bristled. "What would your mother say if she—?" He shoved her aside and she slipped, clattering down onto the cold, wet cobbles, grunting in pain. Oh, God – what if she'd broken her hip?

"Where's your purse?" He loomed over her, digging through the pockets of her raincoat, sniffing anything he found, before hurling it away into the rain. Handkerchief, lipsalve, hairgrips, the tatty old tennis ball Wee Doug liked to chase in King's Park. Then her house keys. Grinning, he held them up to the light. "Brilliant." He stuffed them in his pocket. "Now where's your bloody purse?"

Daphne raised a shaking hand and pointed at the tartan shopping trolley. The junkie rubbed his hands and unzipped the top compartment. A grumpy growl rumbled out and the filthy smile fell from his face: "What the hell's this?" Swearing, he kicked the trolley's wheels out from under it, sending it flying, spilling Wee Doug out into the gutter. Ignoring the Westie's indignant barks, he rummaged inside the trolley. Mr Bunny was hurled out into the night, closely followed by a plastic bag full of rolled-up plastic bags and a spiral-bound notebook covered in shopping lists. Wee Doug scurried off after his squeaky toy as the man grunted, "Ya beauty . . ." and settled back on his haunches to rifle through her handbag.

Gritting her false teeth, Daphne pulled herself to her knees, laddering her support stockings on the rough alley floor as she struggled upright, trembling with rage. Her walking stick was lying in the gutter; she grabbed it. "Did your parents never teach you any MANNERS?" It was a good sturdy walking stick: a shaft of tempered oak and a thick handle carved from a Stag's antlers. It made a satisfyingly wet thunking sound as she battered it off the man's head.

He yowled and she hit him a second time. Harder. He tried to say something, but she swung the handle into his face – something went crack and teeth flew, so she did it again. His cheekbone cracked. And again: his left eye spurted blood. And again: he got his hands up in time to shield his face and she heard finger bones snap. Again, and again and again . . .

Daphne leant back against the wall, puffing and panting, one hand clutching her aching chest, wondering if she was about to have a heart attack. The man lay on his side, curled into the foetal position, not moving. Wee Doug sniffed the back of the drug addict's head, then cocked his leg and peed on it. When he was all done he picked up Mr Bunny, trotted over and sat in front of Daphne, little tail wagging away sixteen to the dozen, happy as could be.

It took her a while to calm down, but eventually the pain in her chest subsided and her breathing returned to normal. She wasn't going to join Bill just yet.

She jabbed the horrible man with her stick, forcing him over onto his back. His face was all swollen and puffy, misshapen, covered with blood, a flap of skin hanging loose on his forehead. Leaking out onto the cobbles. He gave a little cough and a small plume of red sparkled in the dim light. She prodded him in the chest and he groaned. "I asked you a question, young man: who was the naked woman?"

He said something quite rude and Daphne battered the head of her walking stick off his knee. It wasn't quite a scream, wasn't quite a moan, but it sounded painful. "Who was she?"

He was crying now, tears and snot mixing with the blood and dirt. "I don't . . . I don't know . . ."

"You're lying." She hit him again, right on the ankle joint.

"Oh, God, no! Please! I don't know!" Sobbing, rocking back and forth on the ground, covering his head with his arms. "Please . . ."

Daphne scowled and counted to ten. So much for plan A. "If *you* don't know: who does?"

"I don't . . . Aaagh!" It was the elbow this time "Please! I don't . . ." Ankle again. "Aaagh! Colin! Colin'll know! He sells stuff. He'll know!"

She smiled. "And just how do I find this 'Colin'?"

Daphne had never been in a public bar on her own before – it wasn't the sort of thing a respectable lady did – but she owed it to Bill. Screwing up her courage, she marched through the doors of the Monk and Casket, a seedy-looking place at the bottom of Jamesmuir Road. It was mock Tudor on the outside, but inside it was all flashing gambling machines, vinyl upholstery and sticky floors. It wasn't a busy pub, just a handful of men and women looking somewhat the worse for drink at half eleven on a Wednesday night.

Stiffening her courage she hobbled up to the bar, taking her shopping trolley with her, and ordered a port and lemon. And a medicinal brandy – her hip was still sore and she was soaked through after walking all the way here from Castle View.

The bartender was a big hairy man with earrings and a missing front tooth. He leant forward and whispered, "We've actually called last orders, so I can't legally serve you," then slid her drinks across the bar. "If you'd like to make a donation of two pounds fifty to the lifeboat fund, that would be OK by me." Wink, wink. Blushing, Daphne thanked him and slid the money into the orange plastic lifeboat sitting on the bar.

"I'm looking for a man," she said.

The barman smiled. "Sorry, darling, I'm married."

"No, a man called 'Colin'. Do you know him? Someone told me he'd be here."

Silence from the hairy barman, and then, "Are you *sure* you're looking for Colin? Colin McKeever? Crazy Colin?"

Daphne nodded, looking around the bar, trying to see if anyone looked like a "Crazy Colin". It wasn't a big place: just a handful of tables; some framed photos of the local football team; the pinging, chattering fruit machines; and a single door leading off the room marked TOILETS, TELEPHONE AND FUNCTION SUITE. The customers were as seedy as the pub. A pair of over-made-up women cackled away in the corner with their alcopops, a fat man with a beard hunched over a pint of stout, two suspicious-looking types in black leather by the dartboard . . . "Is he the one in the hat?" She pointed at an unusual, weaselly looking man with long black hair and a baseball cap, sitting on his own.

"No, that's Weird Justin. Crazy Colin's upstairs with Stacy. Now, why don't you finish up your drink and I'll call you a taxi, OK? A nice little old lady like you doesn't want to have anything to do with the likes of Colin McKeever."

A small flutter of excitement – he was upstairs with a woman! Maybe it was the one from the shed? "Of course, of course." She downed her brandy in a single gulp, then did the same with the port and lemon. "I'll just nip off to the loo . . ."

Grabbing the shopping trolley's handle, she pushed through the door and into a stinky corridor. A door on either side said GENTS and LADIES, but right at the far end was a set of stairs with a small plaque hanging over it: TO FUNCTION SUITE. Daphne took a deep breath, and started hauling the shopping trolley up the stairs.

One floor up and the sticky linoleum gave way to sticky carpet, with just enough room at the top of the stairs for Daphne to catch her breath. Unrecognizable "music" thumped through from the other side of a battered wooden door. Why did no one know what a tune was any more? When this was all over, she was going to go home, put on some Barry Manilow and get herself a nice cup of tea.

She fiddled with her hearing aid – trying to tune down the horrible music – and opened the door to the function suite. It was about the same size as the bar downstairs, but more neglected. Ancient chairs lined the walls, fold-away tables piled in one corner, a mirror ball hanging from the ceiling, glittering over the small wooden dance floor in the middle. A man and woman rocked slowly back and forth, shambling round to the "music". She had her arms wrapped around his shoulders, he had his hands on her buttocks. Kneading away as if he was making bread.

The current song bludgeoned its way to a halt and then another one, equally dreadful, started. There was one of those "boom-box" things sitting at the side of the dance floor, so Daphne marched straight over and turned the horrible machine off. Blessed silence. The man stopped rearranging his girl-friend's underwear and scowled. He wasn't the most attractive of men – thin and short, with a scabby little beard thing, spiky hair and glasses. But he looked like a Colin.

"What the hell did you do that for?" He let go of his partner, but she continued to dance, shuffling round and round in the absence of music, on her own.

Daphne squared her shoulders. "I want my Bill!"

"I've not sold you anything."

"Don't you play games with me, young man. Your hussy broke into my shed and she stole my Bill! I want him back."

Crazy Colin looked back over his shoulder at the dancing woman. "You saying Stacy's kidnapped someone?" He laughed as Stacy tripped over her own feet and tumbled to the floor. She made an abortive attempt to get back up then gave up, sprawled on her back in the middle of the dance floor, like a dead starfish. "You've got to be kidding – she couldn't tie her shoelaces unsupervised. You got the wrong girl, Grandma."

"I said I want him back!"

"Nothing to do with me, Grandma. You got a problem with Stacy, you take it up with her . . ." He grinned. "After I've finished, like." He started to take off his shirt. "You wanna watch? No charge."

Oh . . . my . . . God . . . He was getting undressed! She didn't want to see some strange man's private parts! She hadn't even liked looking at her husband's. "I don't want any trouble; I just want my Bill back."

"Bill, Bill, Bill, Bill, Bill." He turned his back on her, unfastening his belt.

Daphne hurried back to her shopping trolley and unzipped the top, lifting out Wee Doug. He yawned and looked around the room, then sat down and had a bit of a scratch. Daphne pulled herself up to her full five foot two inches and pointed an imperious finger at Crazy Colin as he unbuttoned his fly. "Go on, Wee Doug, KILL!"

Wee Doug looked up at her, then at the end of her finger.

Daphne tried again. "Kill!"

Still nothing.

She grabbed Mr Bunny from the shopping trolley and hurled it at the undressing man. The toy rabbit landed right in the crotch of Colin's trousers as he tried to get them down over his shoes. Wee Doug growled, his little feet scrabbling on the wooden floor, not going anywhere fast . . . until suddenly his claws got purchase and he was away, tearing across the dance floor like a dog half his age. Barking.

The man spun round at the noise, eyes wide. He grabbed the waistband of his trousers and hauled them up, which was a mistake as Mr Bunny was still trapped in there – his two ragged ears sticking out of the man's fly at groin level. With a final happy bark Wee Doug leapt and clamped his jaws onto Crazy Colin's crotch. There was a high pitched scream.

Daphne took a firm grip of her walking stick and went to shut him up.

Shaking, Daphne washed the blood off her hands and face with cold water and bitter-smelling hand soap in the ladies' lavatory. Wee Doug was happily sitting up in the shopping trolley – the reclaimed Mr Bunny looking none the worst for his adventure in a strange man's trousers – watching as she stuck the head of her walking stick under the tap, the water turning pink as Crazy Colin McKeever's blood slowly rinsed away.

"No one knows . . ." she told herself. "No one knows . . ." Not even the girl – she was comatose the whole time. Couldn't have seen anything. Couldn't have – A knock on the toilet door and she almost shrieked.

"Hello?" It was the bartender, sounding concerned. "Are you in there?"

Oh, God, he's found the body! "I . . . I . . ."

"You OK? You've been in here for ages."

"I . . . I'm fine." She looked at herself in the mirror. He doesn't know. No one knows. "Just a gyppy tummy."

"That's your taxi."

She nodded at her reflection and plastered on a smile, then opened the bathroom door, taking Wee Doug and the tartan shopping trolley with her. "Thank you," she said, trying to keep the tremble out of her voice as he helped her out through the front door and into the cab.

"You take care now." He stood in the street, waving as they drove away.

It was a rumpled Daphne McAndrews who slouched into the Castlehill Snook at quarter to eleven the next day. She'd slept badly, even with a quarter bottle of sweet sherry inside her, knowing that they'd put her in prison for the rest of her natural life. The police would find Colin McKeever's body and do all that scientific stuff you saw on the telly. And they'd know it was her. Provided the nasty man who'd tried to steal her purse in the alley hadn't already reported her for thrashing him. She couldn't bring herself to use the walking stick today, not now it was a murder weapon, and her hip ached.

Daphne collapsed into the chair opposite Agnes and looked sadly out of the window at the Castle car park. Determined not to cry.

"You feelin' OK, Daphne?"

She just shrugged and ordered a fruit scone and a big mug of coffee. When the waitress was gone, Agnes leaned forward and asked, in her best stage whisper, "Did you hear about the murder?" Daphne blanched, but Agnes didn't seem to notice, "Beaten to death," she said, "a drug-dealer – in a pub! Can you believe it?"

Daphne bit her lip and stared at the liver spots on the back of her hands. "Did . . . Do they know who did it?"

"Probably one of them gangland execution things. If I've said it once, I've said it *a thousand times*: Oldcastle's getting more like that Los Angeles every day. I tell you . . ." She launched in to a long story about someone her Gerald used to go to school with, but Daphne wasn't listening. She was wondering when the police were going to come for her.

The patrol car pulled up outside the house at half past seven. At least they hadn't put the flashing lights and sirens on. She'd have died of embarrassment if the neighbours had seen that. She'd spent the day cleaning the place until it sparkled: no one was going to say she went off to prison and left a dirty house behind. With a sigh Daphne climbed out of Bill's favourite chair and answered the front door. It was Sergeant Norman Dumfries, the little boy who wouldn't eat his greens. She ushered him through to the kitchen and put the kettle on. Just because he was here to arrest her, there was no need to forget her manners.

"Tea?" she asked as he shifted uncomfortably from foot to foot.

"Er . . . Yes, that would be lovely." Adding, "Thank you," as an afterthought.

She made two cups and put them on the kitchen table, along with a plate of shortbread, telling Sergeant Dumfries to help himself. "Er . . ." he said, looking sideways at Bill's urn, still sitting on the tabletop from last night. "I'm afraid I've got something very awkward to tell you—"

Daphne nodded. There was no need to make it hard on the boy, he was doing his best. "I know."

He blushed. "I'm so sorry, Mrs McAndrews."

"You're only doing your job, Norman."

"I know, but . . ." he sighed and reached into his police jacket pocket. This was it, he was going to handcuff her. The neighbours would have a field day.

"It's all right." Trying to sound calm. "I won't put up a fight."

He looked puzzled for a moment, before bringing out what looked like a little plastic freezer bag. It was see-through, and full of grey powder. "We, um . . . the man you found in your shed had . . ." He stopped and tried again. "We did a post mortem on him yesterday. He died because he'd injected himself with . . . Er . . ." He held up the bag. "We had to take a sample to make sure. I'm sorry, Mrs McAndrews." Gently he picked Bill's urn off the table and tipped the contents of the plastic bag inside.

"Oh, God."

"I'm sorry, Mrs McAndrews. We think they were already under the influence of drugs when they broke into your shed to fool around. They discovered Mr McAndrews' remains and . . .

Well, the man had residue in his nasal passages and his lungs, so it looks like they tried snorting the . . . ah . . . deceased. When that didn't work, the man tried injecting. And then he died." It was silent in the kitchen, except for the sound of Wee Doug snoring. "I'm sorry."

She grabbed Bill's urn and peered inside. It was nearly full. "Did they both . . . ? You know?" Sergeant Dumfries nodded and Daphne frowned. She wasn't sure she liked the thought of Bill being inside another woman, and Bill would *certainly* not have been happy about being inside a naked man.

"Anyway," Sergeant Dumfries stood up. "I have to get back to the station." He looked left and right, as if he was making sure they were alone. "Just between you and me," he said in a conspiratorial whisper, "we've got a drugs war on our hands! One bloke got worked over right outside the kilt shop last night – said it was a gang with baseball bats – and the next thing you know some drug dealer gets battered to death! Mind you, at least we've got a witness to that one."

Daphne covered her mouth with a trembling hand, the girl: she was unconscious! She couldn't have seen anything – it wasn't fair!

Norman helped himself to a piece of shortbread. "We found this doped-up woman at the scene," he said, in a little spray of crumbs, "who swears blind some huge hairy bloke with a Rottweiler kicked the door down then bashed the victim's skull in with a pickaxe handle." He shook his head in amazement as Daphne went pale as a haddock. "I know," he said as she spluttered. "*Miami Vice* comes to Oldcastle, how bizarre is that?" Sigh. "Anyway, better make sure you keep your doors and windows locked tight. OK?"

When he was gone, Daphne sat at the kitchen table, trembling. Drug War. She let out a small giggle. The giggle became a snigger, then a laugh, and ended in hysterics. She'd gotten away with it. Wiping her eyes she pulled Bill's urn over and peered inside. There was only about a teaspoon missing. What would that be – an ear, a finger, his gentleman's bits? He'd miss them, even if she wouldn't . . .

With a smile she ripped the edge off a couple of teabags and poured the powdered leaves in. At his age he'd never know the difference.

ONCE UPON A TIME

Peter Turnbull

Tuesday Forenoon

It was, he thought, all too human. He was not a man who was medically qualified, but he had seen bones before, actual human bones, often in shallow graves, and much, much older than this bone, sitting there looking quite content in a curious sort of way, looked all too human. It had aged a little, he thought, it was certainly not as old as the bones he was used to examining but it was not recent either. It had a greyness about it, and had been chewed upon by his "friends." The man pondered what to do. He didn't want to appear alarmist but he also knew the value of over-reacting rather than under-reacting; and, after all, were they not told to report anything suspicious? He took the plastic bag he was carrying and walked further into the wood and emptied the contents well away from the bone. He then left the wood and walked back down the lane to the village, and to the red phone box, of the old-fashioned design because the village of Meltham was designated a conservation area, and dialled the police. Not 999; it was not an emergency, no longer life or limb – if indeed the bone ever did represent a life or limb crisis. His call was answered, eventually, by a recording of a female voice telling him that his call was "placed in a queue" and "would be answered shortly". The recording then reminded him that if his call was an emergency he should phone 999 or 112. He was then treated to a tinny recording of Beethoven's "Eroica" Symphony. Eventually, his call was answered by a stressed out and tired sounding officer who took details and asked him to wait by the phone box. This he did, wrapping his duffel coat around him and stamping his feet against the cold. It was the twelfth month of the year and the Wolds are cold, cold, cold during the winter months. It was a windless day, not a cloud in a blue sky, but cold. Very cold.

"It may be only an animal bone," he said eagerly and apologetically at the same time as the officer opened the door of the police car and stepped out.

"Take your time, sir," the officer said, calmly, but with authority as he reached for his notebook and pen.

"It's in the copse."

"Let me ask the questions, please."

The man fell silent.

"You are . . . ?"

"Coleman." The man was short, bespectacled, a mop of wild grey hair, "Clifford Coleman."

"And your address, Mr Coleman?"

"The Old Rectory, here in Meltham." He pointed. "That's my house, just there . . . well, the roof . . . you can see from here."

"You didn't phone from home, Mr Coleman?"

"I didn't, did I." Clifford Coleman scratched his head. "Now isn't that strange, I could have kept warm and had a cup of tea . . . why didn't I do that? That will puzzle me for some time."

"You found a bone, you say?" The officer interrupted Coleman's musing.

"In the small wood."

"The small wood?"

"Is the name by which it is known round here, to differentiate from another larger wood just beyond it which is known as the 'large wood'. That's the 'small wood'." Coleman turned and pointed down the pasty grey road to a copse approximately quarter of a mile distant.

"Can I ask your age and occupation, sir?"

"Why?"

"Just procedure, sir."

"Fifty-four . . . a teacher . . . at the university . . . history . . . I am a medievalist. I often see human bones in old graves that are being excavated. There is an overlap between history and archaeology, you see, and the bone I saw in the small wood looked to me to be human. There is much medieval in the village . . . the street pattern is medieval . . . though the oldest building dates only from the seventeenth century."

"Yes, yes . . . thank you, sir. Shall we walk to the wood?"

They walked to the wood. The constable taking long, effort-less, energy-preserving strides, Coleman taking short, rapid steps, but of the two it was Coleman who had to keep pace with the constable. In the wood, Coleman led the constable to where the bone lay.

"I think you were correct to call us, Mr Coleman." The constable knelt down and looked closely at the bone. "I am no doctor, but I have attended post-mortems and seen skeletons . . . certainly looks human to me. Not recently buried . . . it seems to be aged. Can I ask what you were doing in the wood? You have no dog that you were exercising, for example?"

"Feeding my friends."

"Your friends?"

"Oh, yes . . . foxes . . . badgers . . . creatures of the night. Animals enjoy foraging for their food and I never throw any-thing meaty away. Bones, fat, bacon rind . . . I bring it all to the wood and scatter it. I come at various times of the day, depending on my timetable. I'm teaching at 4.00 p.m. today and then have an evening class of mature students . . . many older than I am, doing something with their retirement. Good for them, I say . . . better than vegetating in front of day time television, I say, and their brains . . . sharp as tacks . . . get a better class of degree than many twenty-year-olds, and also . . ."

"Yes, sir."

"Well, I'll get back home too late this evening to walk up to the wood, so I came now . . . dropped the bone I had brought well away from the bone I had found . . . then phoned you. Should have phoned from my house, though . . . funny . . ."

"Not noticed it before, sir?"

"No. It has probably worked its way to the surface and one of my friends pulled it into the open. Probably a badger. Foxes are too lazy to do that – they prefer to scavenge . . . but old brock will claw anything up. Well, do you need me any more? I have some preparation to do."

"No, thank you, sir." The constable reached for the radio attached to his lapel and pressed the "send" button.

"Human, male." Louise D'Acre looked at the bone. She was clad in a green coverall, disposable hat . . . latex gloves. "Well, male is an educated guess. If it was female the lady would be very tall indeed. It's a femur, leg bone . . . and the person would be at least six feet tall in life . . . as female femurs go, it's very long."

"A six footer." D.C.I. Hennessey ran his liver-spotted hand through his silver hair.

"At least." Louise D'Acre knelt down and picked up the bone and placed it in a productions bag. "Well, there's more than one bone in the human skeleton," she said. "The rest might be around here somewhere. I'll take this to York City." She smiled a rare smile. She wore her hair short with just a trace of lipstick as her only make-up. Aged mid-forties, she was, thought D.C.I. Hennessey, a lady who knew how to grow old gracefully. "You can bring the rest along if and when you find them."

The "small wood" was, thought D.C.I. Hennessey, about one and a half acres in area of broad leafed woodland. A team of constables began to sweep across the wood, and just ten minutes into the sweep one constable stopped, held up his hand and said "Sergeant." He had found disturbed soil, and what appeared to be a bone protruding. It was about one hundred yards from where Clifford Coleman had found the bone. Hennessey looked at the disturbed soil, at the bone, and said, "Better get Scene of Crime People here . . . photograph it as you dig it up . . . bone by bone."

"Very good, sir."

Friday Afternoon

"Hard to determine age." Dr Louise D'Acre studied the bones which had been laid out in order on the dissecting table of the pathology laboratory of the City of York Hospital. "Not young, not elderly either . . . middle-aged. I'll cut a tooth in cross section and determine the age that way, but at a glance I'd say

that this is the skeleton of a middle-aged person of the male sex
. . . white European . . . there is no obvious cause of death . . .
no trauma . . . almost all the bones are here, just a few very
small bones of the feet are missing, but it has been sawn up . . .
quite neatly."

"They were found neatly too." D.C.I. Hennessey stood at
the edge of the pathology lab, observing for the police. "Stacked
one on top of the other, occupied a very small place about the
dimensions of a cardboard box that one person would take both
arms to lift."

"That's interesting." Louise D'Acre tapped the stainless
steel table with the tip of a long finger. "That means that they
were completely skeletal when they were buried. The corpse
was not merely sawn up, it was filleted as well. All tissue, all
organs were removed. Couldn't stack bones neatly otherwise."

"Or the corpse buried and then dug up some time later when
the flesh had decomposed and the bones reburied?"

"It's possible, but the interval between burial and reburial
would be measured in years. The other thing that occurs to me
is that if a skeleton was dug up it would hardly be to rebury it. I
would be inclined to throw it into the Ouse one dark night, bone
by bone. But it does tell you one thing, though: this is your
territory, not mine."

"Oh, please." Hennessey smiled. "All help gratefully accepted."

"Well, it tells you that the person or persons who did this had
a lot of space . . . some means of filleting a corpse without the
risk of being disturbed . . . can't do that in a little terrace house
. . . some means of disposing of the tissue, such as a bonfire.
Human tissue gives off a very sickly sweet smell when burned.
Anyone who has smelled it will recognize the smell again, and
be suspicious. Or alternatively, the space to bury it."

"A farmer?"

"Farm workers, farm labourers . . . again, the risk of a
witnesses. I would be inclined to think of someone who lives
alone in a large house or a smallholding. Enough space to do this
without the risk of being chanced upon." Louise D'Acre
stretched a tape measure along the spine. "It's been chopped
up, as you see, but in life he would have been about six feet tall
. . . and," she added softly, "he walked with a limp."

"He did?"

"Or he wore shoes, one of which, the left of the pair, was built up. His left femur is shorter than the right."

"That will narrow the field down, a lot."

"This is murder," Dr D'Acre said. "It can only be murder, but it's strange . . . the cause of death must have been quite mild, but the disposal of the corpse, very messy indeed. I have rarely come across anything quite like it"

"Nor I," Hennessey said. "It's usually the other way round."

"Indeed." D'Acre paused. "Well, I'll trawl for poisons, doubt I'll find any cyanide, belonged to the Victorians, and I'll determine his age by tooth extraction."

Wednesday Afternoon and Evening

George Hennessey sat at his desk and glanced out of the window of his office at a group of tourists, well wrapped up, who were walking the ancient walls of the city. That's York, he thought, a booming tourist industry year end to year end; even on cold winter days the walls will have tourists upon them. He felt satisfied. A good morning's work had been done. He had then walked the walls into the city and lunched at a pub with a wood fire and had sat underneath a reprint of an ancient map which showed "The West Ridinge of Yorkshyre, the most famous and Faire Citie Yorke described – 1610". Back at his desk, he read the report submitted by Sergeant Yellich about the man who had walked into Micklegate Bar Police Station the day previous and said to the constable on the enquiry desk, "I'm fed up of waiting to be caught. It was me that did all those burglaries." At first the man was thought to be a candidate for detention under the Mental Health Act, but then began to reveal details only the perpetrator could know. He had reached the end of Yellich's report when his phone rang. He let it ring twice before answering it. "Detective Chief Inspector Hennessey."

"Dr D'Acre, York City Hospital. I have the lab results back."

"So soon?"

"Quiet period. The deceased was fifty-three, or-four, or-five, when he died. And poisoned."

"Poisoned!"

"Self-inflicted. He was an alcoholic. It probably didn't kill him – well it would have done had he lived long enough . . . but it wasn't the murder weapon as such. But he was a very serious alcoholic in life and had been for years. It would take very heavy drinking over a long period to leave traces of alcohol in his long bones, but it's there. It's offered as an aid to identification."

Hennessey and Yellich drove out to Meltham. Neither officer had been to the village before. The turn off to Meltham, they found, could easily be missed; a narrow lane, it drove vertically between thick woodland. Upon arriving at the village they saw it to be small, nestling in a fold in the landscape. Yellich parked the car in the centre of the village, in the square which was more of a triangle in terms of its shape. The square had an ancient and preserved pair of stocks and a memorial to the three sons of the village who had given their lives for King and Country in the 1914–18 war. There was, Hennessey noted with some relief, no mention of any loss of life from the village in the 1939–45 conflict. A woman carrying a shopping bag glared at them as she walked, quite content to let the two officers see her staring at them. A burly, well-set man glanced at them suspiciously.

"This village don't like strangers," Hennessey remarked, as he nodded to the man.

"Don't, do it, boss?" Yellich locked the car.

"Well, where now?" Hennessey asked Yellich. "Where do you think?"

"Me, boss . . . tell you the honest truth, I'd try at the post office. Post mistresses in places like this know everything . . . in fact it was once my experience when I was a lad to knock on the post mistress's door at 8.00 p.m. one evening to tell her someone had died. She wasn't a relation, not even a friend of the family, but I was fourteen and the adults who were running round like headless chickens thought the best way to get the news into the community was to send me running up the lane to tell the post mistress that Mr Battie, my great uncle, had died." Yellich laughed. "Classic . . . classic . . . but it actually happened."

Hennessey laughed. "All right," he said. "Sounds good to me."

The Post Office in Meltham was located next to a small, very small, mini market and a hardware shop. It was quiet inside the shop, which had a sense of timelessness, with old-fashioned posters which had never been taken down and which advertised products priced in Imperial, not decimal currency. A youthful, very youthful, looking post mistress emerged from the gloom of the back of the shop in response to the jangling door bell.

"You'll be the police," she said pleasantly. "We thought you'd come. It'll be about the bones."

"The bones?" Hennessey raised an eyebrow.

"The bones that were found in the small wood yesterday by Mr Coleman. Mrs Innes 'does' for Coleman – he's a bachelor, you see, and Mr Coleman told her what he'd found and she told me. So we thought you'd come."

The woman seemed to be in her mid-twenties and Hennessey thought that, in terms of attitude and temperament, she had the makings of an excellent village post mistress. He asked if she had lived in the village for long.

"All my life," she replied with pride. "My husband didn't want to live here, but if he wanted me, he had to live in Meltham. He's been here nearly five years now and is beginning to get accepted."

"Lucky he."

"Well, it means he gets a game of darts in the Beggar now. For the first few years he had to stand alone at the bar."

"The Beggar?"

"The Fortunate Beggar." The woman smiled. "It's the pub, the only one in Meltham."

"I see. Well, you're right, we are here about the bones. We believe the person who was buried to have been quite tall, probably walked with a limp and had a very bad drink problem. If he was local to this area and not brought here from afar, then someone might recognize him. Our mis per records haven't shown anything."

"Mis per?"

"Missing Persons."

"Oh . . . but yes, I have heard of him. He still gets mentioned from time to time . . . the limping landlord, he disappeared . . . but that was before I was born. I'm twenty-six now."

"No wonder he's not in our records." Hennessey turned to Yellich. "If he had lived, he'd be pushing eighty now."

"He had the Beggar," the post mistress added. "Well, wait till I tell my mum. We took over the post office from her and dad when they retired. She's at the coast now, Bridlington, in a home. Your best bet now would be to try at the Beggar."

"Only by reputation." The landlord appeared to Hennessey and Yellich to be a man close to his retirement and who also subscribed to the Meltham culture of "strangers not welcome". He avoided eye contact with the officers and seemed to begrudge having to give information. "I took over the pub from him when he disappeared. That's thirty years now – thirty years last July, to be exact. He was not a happy man."

"No?"

"His flat above the pub—" the landlord looked up at the low beams above his head "– above the bar here . . . it was like a tramp's doss. The sheets on the bed hadn't been changed for months, newspapers covered the floor, empty bottles everywhere . . . My wife insisted we fumigate it. We threw everything out, stripped it right back to the bare floorboards, then we set up a brazier in the main room."

"Took a risk."

"Not really. We mounted the brazier on a bed of bricks and burned wood and damp vegetation, left all the doors open, but shut all the windows except one. Filled the flat with smoke, and crawling things began to come out of cracks in the wall and from between the floorboards; they found the open window and didn't return. Then we moved in. The lingering smell of wood smoke was better than the lingering smell of Reddick."

"A lonely man, then?"

"Yes . . . Carl Reddick, the limping, lonely landlord. Never did like that name, Carl . . . too close to 'cruel', but in this case it was apt by all accounts. Cruel Carl Reddick, not the right sort of man to be in charge of a pub."

"Irresponsible, you mean? Let youths drink too much?"

"No . . . not from what I heard. He was a soak himself, two bottles a day, and I don't mean beer."

"I get the picture."

"Apparently, so my customers told me, he used to sit on the stool at the end of the bar and be rude to everybody and anybody, customers and staff alike . . . very personally offensive."

"They didn't vote with their feet?"

"The staff did. Nobody stayed very long, but the work round here can be hard to come by, so they were easily replaced. And the customers, where could they go? The next nearest pub is in Ossley St Mary, about two and a half miles away. That could be a pleasant walk on a summer's evening if you are young and fit, but if you're getting on in years, and if it's a cold winter . . . well, it's the Beggar or nothing. So Reddick had a captive audience and he knew it . . . so he was described as spending each evening sitting there and snarling at anything that moved, with a breath so hot it was said it could ignite paper . . . then he disappeared. Here one day, gone the next. Then me and Betty took over, cleaned the place up and it became a village pub again in the truest sense of the word. I like to hear the thud of darts and the rattle of dominoes and folk laughing as they relax at the end of their day."

"Any rumours about his disappearance?"

The landlord smiled. "He got under the skin of a lot of people; a lot of people had cause to do him harm. I bet a lot of people dreamed of doing him in." The landlord broke off the conversation to serve a pint of mild to an elderly man who shuffled up to the bar with an empty glass. The landlord put the man's money in the till and returned to the officers. "So those were his bones they found in the small wood? It was all the talk in here last night."

"We believe they might be. Tell me, did anything happen over and above his abusive nature that might make someone want to murder him?"

"Well . . ." The landlord pondered. "There was the death of the lad Burgess, so I heard tell. It wasn't just that, but the attitude he was said to have taken to the incident . . . but I believe that was some years before he disappeared. Best person to talk to about that is the Reverend Price."

"Where do we find him?"

"The next village, where the nearest pub is, Ossley St Mary. His parish covers three villages, this one, Ossley St Mary and Much Haddle on Ouse. His rectory is at Ossley St Mary, large house next to the church."

"The church moves you onwards and upwards or it leaves you alone, keeps you in one place. Me it kept in one place." The

Reverend Price sipped his tea. Hennessey saw him as being late middle aged, grey hair cut neat and short. A large poster showing York Minster hung on his study wall; outside his window rooks gathered in the leafless branches of an oak tree cawing loudly. "But yes, I remember Carl Reddick's disappearance, remember it well. It was one of the first incidents in the parish of any note since my incumbency began. I've been a minister of this parish for thirty-three years now . . . and yes, I remember the sad death of young David Burgess. Now that was *the* first incident of any note since beginning my incumbency. Bad affair that. I met the Burgess family – good people, gentle-natured people, would have liked to have seen them become parishioners – but . . . well . . ."

"What happened to David Burgess?" Hennessey put his cup of tea down. The tea had been served too cold to drink by the reverend's wife who was carelessly dressed and who muttered to herself as if suffering from the onset of dementia.

"He was knocked off his bike by Reddick, who was driving his car while well under the influence."

"I see."

"Killed outright, poor lad, just fifteen years old . . . his whole life ahead of him. Reddick was fined quite heavily, and banned from driving for life, but he escaped a gaol sentence. Probably fortunate in a way because one of my parishioners is a medical man and he told me that if people have a long term and excessive drink problem, they have to be weaned off the stuff – a sudden and permanent withdrawal can be fatal – and Reddick, when I knew him, would demolish two bottles of scotch a day and would often make a start on a third. Mind you, I imagine the prisons could have given him medication to prevent death."

"They do," said Hennessey. "Massive doses of vitamins and protein given in the form of injections."

"I see."

"But what was unacceptable was Reddick's attitude to the accident. Sitting in the pub in Meltham, 'The Fortunate Beggar' – the name apparently refers to a piece of good fortune which befell a beggar in the middle ages – but he would sit in his pub boasting about how he'd got away with killing young Burgess, gloating at his 'victory' as he saw it."

"Not clever."

"Hardly. David Burgess's parents didn't ever go to the 'Beggar' again, but Meltham is a strange place; in terms of its character, it's quite different from the other two villages in my parish. In effect, it's populated by folk who belong to one of three families, with the odd incomer to make up the numbers. And the families seem to like and understand each other. It isn't a feuding village, by any means. They may not send each other Christmas cards or even say 'hello' when they pass in the street, but they know who each other is and they look after each other. So Reddick's insensitive boasts would have been heard by David Burgess's relatives, his cousins, his aunts and uncles and also other folk who knew the Burgesses but were not related to them. Reddick's trial was in January, almost a year after the accident itself, and he disappeared in the summer after the trial. Six months of drunken gloating and boasting . . . if what happened is as I think you may suspect what happened, then I have to say that it says much for the restraint of the people of Meltham."

"We'll reserve our judgement on that one, Reverend Price. A murder is still a murder. Are David Burgess's parents still alive?"

"I think his mother is still with us. No longer at home, but in the care of the local authority in York."

It was a sudden reminder. On the return drive to York they were overtaken by a motorcyclist who was travelling at speed, angling at 45 degrees as he leaned into the bend which lay ahead of them. As always, Hennessey was then reminded of his elder brother, Graham, who had one such machine and who had driven away on it one evening. Later, his father had woken him up and had told him that Graham had ridden his bike to heaven "to save a place for us". Hennessey had been eight years old at the time and all his life he'd felt a gap where his elder brother should have been. As a reaction to the loss, he never drove unless he had to and was convinced that the motor vehicle was the most dangerous machine ever invented, whether two wheels or four.

Later that day, in the mid-evening, after he had exercised Oscar and had left sufficient food and water to see the brown mongrel comfortably through the night, he drove to Skelton with its quaint eleventh-century church and equally ancient yew tree. He parked his car by the kerb in front of an L-shaped half-timbered house. He walked up to the front door and tapped the brass knocker gently, twice, resisting the pause, then a third tap. That would be the policeman's knock: tap, tap . . . tap. Not appropriate in this case.

"Sorry I'm a little late," he said when the door was opened by a smiling woman.

"No matter." Louise D'Acre hooked a slender finger round the knot of his tie and gently pulled him over the threshold. "The children are in bed. We can go straight up."

Thursday Morning

"I thought you'd come. I heard about the bones, you see." Mrs Burgess was frail, slight. "He'd be nearly fifty years old now, my David, had he lived. Possibly a professional. His father wanted him to be a lawyer – he had that sort of mind, you see – David, I mean. He could build a case for this or for that favour, or treat. So, you'll be wanting to know what happened to Reddick?"

"Yes." Hennessey spoke softly. Yellich remained silent.

"Well, Eddie – that was my husband – said we should move on with our lives and not let the tragedy destroy us, that would give Reddick a second victory . . . but we never went into his pub again."

"So I believe. The Reverend Price told us."

"Nice man. He buried both my son and my husband." Mrs Burgess smiled, briefly. "Nice man." Then she paused. Hennessey thought the heat in the nursing home to be turned up too high to be healthy. "But, you see, that's sometimes the way of it . . . you are often more angry about an injustice done to a loved one than about an injustice done to yourself."

"I have experienced that feeling," Hennessey said, thinking of his dear wife, who had died suddenly when she was just twenty-three years old.

"Well, Reddick's boasts and what he said about my David not being any good anyway . . ."

"He said that?"

"So I was told."

"So what happened?"

"Eddie had two brothers, Ernest and Edwin: They never married. They kept pigs on a small holding, just outside Meltham. They, went to the Beggar one morning, just as Reddick was opening up for the day's trade. They were gentlemen in every sense but they had had enough of Reddick by then, as many folk had. They bundled him into a van and drove him to the small holding. They didn't mean to kill him. They wanted to sober him up – that was their intention, to keep him off the drink so he'd listen when they gave him a piece of their mind."

Hennessey groaned. He knew what was coming.

"He had food and water and it was warm where they kept him, but one morning they found he'd died. Just went in his sleep, it seemed."

"How long was that after they had abducted him?"

"I think it was about three days."

"Do you know how they disposed of the body?"

"I don't. But they butchered their own meat. They would have known how to butcher a human body."

"Are Ernest and Edwin still alive?"

"No . . . both gone before now. They kept what they did from Eddie, then Ernest went. Edwin knew he was dying and so he came to see me and told me what they had done. There's just me left now."

He wasn't angry. Hennessey walked into Easingwold, had a pint of mild at the Dove Inn and walked home. It had all happened thirty years ago, all players, save one, deceased. It was an incident which had happened in a strange, inward looking village once upon a time. And what had happened to Reddick didn't make him angry, unlawful as it may have been. It was a cloudless sky and he glanced up at the Great Bear and followed the pointers to the North Star. Then he noticed for the first time that one of the seven stars of the Great Bear had begun to flicker. It was dying, and he was witness to the ending of a celestial age.

THAT'S THE WAY HE DID IT

Amy Myers

"Why won't you play the Maplechurch pitch, *omi*?" This time Toby Wellaway decided he was going to get an answer out of his father. He had a right – he was as much part of the family Punch and Judy show as his dad, especially since he'd been saddled with the name of the Buffer, the show's traditional Toby dog. If a pitch was going to be rejected, he wanted to know why.

Sam Wellaway sighed. "*Omi*, I've been thinking. It's about time I taught you the squeaker, and handed the show over to you. You've bottled for me long enough and I'm sixty now. The jokes don't come so easy as they used to. Time to step aside, and see the world with her in the kitchen. Your mother could do with a change without old Punch tagging along."

He'd be Professor Toby Wellaway! His son grinned in pleasure. Dad step aside? Dad to teach him that most precious of trade secrets, how to master the swazzle in his mouth to produce Punch's voice? He'd never thought to see the day. "I'll let you bottle for me any time you like, Dad."

"Maybe, but not on the Maplechurch pitch, eh?"

"Because of what happened? That pop star's death?"

"Disappearance," Sam reminded him.

"I wasn't even born then. Sixty-seven, wasn't it? 'Course, she's dead. Fay Darling would never have given up singing, nor her partner neither." Toby pressed his luck. "You were there, *omi*, tell me about it."

Sam reflected. The past was the past, and he was more interested in the present. Old Punch had been his life for over fifty years, man and boy. They'd been good times; they'd used live dogs as the Buffer then, not stuffed ones. That wouldn't pass unchallenged nowadays, but he still remembered his first Toby. How he'd loved that dog. He'd changed the show to keep up to date, but the heart of it still remained: Joey the clown, the Crocodile, the old Mr Punch, his wife Judy, and sometimes still the hangman. He'd introduced new puppets though, TV characters or other famous figures, kept up with the times by using modern catch phrases, gearing the performance according to the pitch. Like Maplechurch. He'd played that for six successive years at the annual charity fête, when the grounds of the Manor were thrown open. He had become quite chummy with the pop singer Fay Darling, who lived there with her husband Peter Browning, a brute of a man, jealous and greedy. Some said he had reason enough. Fay was one half of the famous duo Darling Dan, and it was rumoured she was madly in love with her partner, Dan Smith, who had moved with his wife into a house directly opposite the Manor, across the Thames which flowed between their two gardens.

"Tell me what happened, *omi*," Toby pressed him. "There's no reason I can't play the Maplechurch pitch, is there, even if you don't want to?"

Sam deliberated, then made up his mind. "Mozzy," he called to his wife. Punch language came naturally to him, about to retire or not. "What did you do with the Darling Dan puppets?"

Ada Wellaway placidly strolled in from the kitchen, holding a potato in one hand and a peeler in the other. "Up in the attic where they belong, love, having a barney with all your other has-beens. And if you want them you can get 'em yourself," she added amiably. "Ada may mean the happy one, but don't push it, mate."

"Has-beens? Ma, you can't say that." Toby was appalled at such ignorance. "Their records are still selling in their hundreds of thousands. If you took the slightest interest in the pop scene, you'd know it." His generation had grown up with the music of the singing duo.

His mother snorted and returned to the kitchen.

"Tell you what, son," Sam said. "You go to play Maple-church, and I'll tell you the story on one condition. You find out what really happened. Which of them did it? I'd like to know."

"Did what?"

"Made off with her. Did the husband murder her, or did she run away with Dan? Or did Dan do her in, come to that? And *how* was it done?"

"*Me* find out?" Toby blinked. "Don't be daft. How can I?"

"You'll manage. You can take old Ned with you to bottle for you this time. He was there in '67; maybe he can help. All water under the bridge to me. Now, listen to me, *omi*, and I'll tell you the story. The husband did it, that's what the gossip is. Every-one was sure of it, though they couldn't pin anything on him. Pete Browning was her manager as well as her husband and was greedy and jealous with it. He'd grown accustomed to her money, so he pushed Fay to keep right on singing, and she grew to hate it. There was only one problem for Pete Browning: Fay's fame went hand in hand with Dan Smith, and Pete was convinced that Fay was in love with him. He wanted her to go solo. She refused, said she'd give up altogether if he forced her, and of course that confirmed his suspicions, especially since Dan had just moved in opposite with his wife.

"Anyway, Dan Smith never appeared at the fête that day, and there was a terrible row between Fay and the husband. Every-one could hear it. That had me shivering in my shoes, for when Ned and I got down the evening before to test the pitch's acoustics, I heard Dan and Fay were due to open the festivities, so I planned the whole show round the new puppets, now residing in our loft. Instead, Pete opened the fête, with Fay singing solo. Dan never turned up."

"What was she *really* like, pa?"

"Lovely, just as lovely as her pictures, all delicate and fair, and gentle, not a bit like you imagine a sixties' hippy pop star. With her husky voice, well, she was spell-binding. Since I'd played the pitch ever since they lived there, she'd talk to me sometimes. I reckon she was scared of her husband. She wanted to have kids, but Pete wasn't having any of that. Money, that was all that mattered. I don't know whether she was in love with Dan or not, but I wouldn't have blamed her if so, the life she

led. He was a handsome devil, with more than a streak of
Romany in him. That's why their signature tune was that
pop version of 'The Raggle-Taggle Gypsies oh'. And since
she sang it solo that day, just before she disappeared, some folks
think she knew she would shortly be 'off with her raggle-taggle
gypsy' like the song says. Most think Pete murdered her,
though."

"She actually disappeared during the fête, didn't she?"

"That's right, *omi*. The grounds run down to the Thames,
and on the far side of the lawns from where I put the booth there
is – or was – a boathouse with a longish landing stage running
out over the water, and a sort of covered porch and passageway
round the building on the far side. Fay and Pete were such
having such a humdinger in the boathouse, just before she sang
her song, that everyone was listening. It grew very silent
because folks had already gathered by the river bank to listen
to the formal opening of the fête. Fay's voice being higher, you
could hear every word she was saying. 'What have you done?'
she kept shouting. I remember that. I was just getting Mr
Punch and his chums sorted to be ready for Ned when he began
banging the drum after the fête was officially open.

"Fay and Pete both came out onto the landing stage, as
though they'd just remembered what they were supposed to
be doing. Pete introduced her – he was black in the face with
rage – and it got blacker when she sang 'Everything but you' –
that's the song jazzing up Glück's 'What is life to me without
you' and then the 'Raggle Taggle Gypsies'. She didn't need any
accompaniment, not Fay. You could have heard a pin drop.
Then Fay went back into the boathouse, while Pete declared the
fête open. After that he went in, and a minute later there was a
terrible scream that chilled me to the marrow. Inhuman it was.
We all, and I mean all, rushed to the boathouse, thinking he was
strangling her, but when we got there, we found Pete there
alone. 'She's gone,' he blurted out, putting on a good show of
amazement. 'Gone back to the house.'

"But she hadn't. She'd have been seen coming out of the
boathouse door. Besides, Pete was a tightwad, and he made sure
you couldn't get into or out of the fête without passing the cash-
points. Even Fay would have had to go through them. No, there
was only one place she could have gone, over the side of the far

passageway into the river. You couldn't see far because there was a bend in the river, so folks started spreading out along the bank, and another party went to search the fête grounds. I ran through the trees, followed by all the world and his wife, to see if Fay's body had been swept round the bend, for there was a fair old current running. Then I saw her lovely hat, all white and flowers on it, bobbing along the river. A few of the better swimmers plunged into the water, but no trace of her was found. When there was no news by evening, Pete called in the police. The river was dredged eventually, but no body turned up. Only that blessed hat again. Months later a body was dredged up, but it was too far gone to identify, and there weren't no DNA testing in those days. So it was case unproven against Pete."

Sam paused, then continued. "Except in Maplechurch. I stopped in for a drink at the pub that evening."

"And for the gossip, I bet," Toby put in.

"Right, *omi*. That was flowing even faster than the beer. She would never have killed herself. Most reckoned Pete had strangled her and pushed her over the side into the river. Others reckoned she jumped in herself, and swum off to join Dan. He was never heard of again either. Rumour has it they're still busking on a Greek island, singing their hearts out for pennies. Fay had left a will, so it turned out, that in the event of her death – which was presumed in due legal course – all her royalties from her music should go to charity. Dan's went to his wife of course, but Fay wouldn't want Pete to touch a penny of hers. He could have the house, that was all. Fay was mighty scared of Pete. There was no question of divorce, you see, and she knew he'd come after her if she just ran away.

"A few of them thought it was Dan murdered her, however, because she was planning to go solo. He knew that would end his career and preferred to end with a bang, not a whimper. Fay was the leader in the partnership, of course. He was a passionate, headstrong chap, and they too had a stormy relationship, if you believed the tabloids of the day.

"The police questioned Pete endlessly, but in the end there was nothing they could do. There was no body to prove she'd been strangled and if he'd just pushed her into the river in the hope she'd drown, there was no proof of that either."

"So he got away scot free?"

"Oh no, son. Only Mr Punch does that. The whole of Maplechurch had Pete marked down as a murderer, and worse, murderer of both Fay *and* Dan. Where was Dan, they asked, if Fay alone had been killed? Dan's wife hadn't heard a dickey bird from him. He'd just vanished. Pete shut himself up in the house and drank himself to death. The next time I passed that way, five years later, I heard he was dead. Even so I never played the pitch again when the new folk bought the house. It seemed somehow disrespectful to Fay."

"What do you think happened, dad?"

"I'm a *swatchel omi*, son, a Punch and Judy man, not a blooming Sherlock Holmes."

"All right, I'll take you on. I *will* be a Sherlock. I could even do a show based round it." Toby's eyes gleamed. "Think of the publicity for the show, if I sort out what happened."

Sam laughed. "You'll do, *omi*, you'll do. You just come back with the answer. I want to know which of 'em did it."

"This where the booth was, Ned?" Ned was well past seventy now, and ready to throw in his drum and collection hat. He grumbled incessantly, but Toby knew that if his father didn't bottle for him, he'd never have the heart to find someone else, since he had a shrewd idea that talk of retiring was all for show. He'd die in his bottling boots, would Ned.

Ned grunted in his usual fashion, and banged down one of the pegs as answer.

"What do you think happened, Ned?" Toby asked when the booth was up. His first pitch as professor. He'd mastered the swazzle, written his show, and was bursting to get going. At the end of the day he'd have another show to plan: the true story of Fay and Dan. And then he'd be on the map.

"I don't think. I bottles." Ned snorted.

Shortly the gates would be thrown open, and the crowds would throng the grounds. There was no charge now to attend, for the present owners were a benevolent couple in their sixties. There were other changes too, Toby reflected, from the last time his father played here. There was a double-glazing stand here to start with, and what would old Punch make of a bouncy castle? Still, Punch had survived because he kept up with the

times, and Toby uneasily wondered whether in the excitement
of taking up his father's challenge he had given enough thought
to that aspect in his first regular show.

"Point out to me where it happened, Ned, while we can leave
the booth."

Ned shot him a look but complied. "Not sure as I know."

"Come on, Ned," Toby said patiently. "You were there."

Grumbling under his breath, and playing up his stiff leg as he
hobbled along, Ned took him over to the far side of the lawns.

The boathouse looked derelict, and was roped off, whether to
avoid accidents with rotting boards or to prevent morbid curiosity from fans of Fay Darling. Toby looked at the landing stage
from where his father had seen it, according to Ned, and then
walked past the front of the boathouse to peer at the passageway
from which it was presumed Fay had disappeared. His father had
been right. If Fay had come through the front entrance to the
boathouse, she'd have been seen by at least some of the crowd,
and so she must have gone over the side, of her own volition or
not. Had she planned her disappearance? The story had all the
hallmarks. No identifiable body, singing those particular songs,
Dan's disappearance. Fay had had good reason to vanish. She'd
probably swum round the bend past the boundary to the gardens,
climbed ashore and met her Dan. Romantic, really.

"What was Dan's wife like?" he asked Ned.

Ned shrugged. "Never met her, did I?"

Toby sighed. "I thought Dad said you were to give me all the
help I needed. You're sure you were here that day?"

Ned looked pained. "Certainly I was, *omi*. Bottling, weren't
I? And now I'm a-helping. Just you follow me. This is the way
everyone ran, led by your dad." Making great play of his
hobbling, he led the way over the hillock of land around which
the river curved. "The 'at your dad saw were over there." He
pointed to the middle of the river.

Toby looked at the rows of grand houses opposite, and the
reed-fringed edges of the river, trying to imagine the scene
thirty-odd years ago. Then he turned his attention to the
wooded valley garden bordering the river with its stream
trickling down to join it. "I think she just landed there, met
Dan and left. No one would have seen her if she kept away from
the lawns."

Ned sighed. "Good job you're a Punch professor, not the real kind. You ain't got the brains you was born with, young Toby. They'd still have to get out of the grounds. There was a blooming fifteen-foot fence to keep her little ladyship in when her hubby got mad. And the grounds were searched thoroughly, believe me."

"Then suppose she swam as far as the next property?"

"That's what some said." Ned seemed pleased. "To meet her lover," he added with relish. "Funny thing is that with all the publicity in the papers, no one claimed to have seen them leave the village. You'd have thought *someone* might have noticed. What's more, their cars were still here, and no one came forward to say they'd given a lift to two familiar-looking hitchhikers in disguise. How'd they do it?"

"She swam across the river to Dan's house?"

"Listen, *omi*, if I'd been Fay and there was a wife like Dan's ready to stick a knife in my gullet, I'd have opted for Pete to strangle me and have done with it."

This was getting him nowhere, and the show was about to start. Toby was getting frustrated.

"Who could be here today who would have been present in sixty-seven – at the house, I mean? Not the villagers. They're no more use than—" Toby stopped himself in time from saying "you".

Ned looked pleased. "Now you're talking. There's a gardener I ran into. He was only a lad then, he's head gardener – you can have a talk to him after the show. I'll mind the booth."

The show! Toby had almost forgotten his debut was only minutes away.

"Oh, it was him what did it." Adam Dale took off his sunhat, wiped his brow and sat down in his potting shed. Here, he said mysteriously, they could talk away from the crowds. Talk he could, Toby thought to himself. If Prince Charles was right and growing things responded to being spoken to, Manor Court must have the biggest vegetables and flowers in the country.

"Oh yes," he continued, "that gypsy. Underhand, mean-looking Dan Smith was. The master had a temper, but he loved Mrs Fay. He wouldn't have hurt a hair on her head."

"What about blacking her eyes?" Toby began to recall the footage he'd seen of Fay Darling in huge dark sunglasses on a winter's day.

Adam hardly paused. "They had their differences, but murder – no – not even a *crime passion fruit* or whatever they call it. Mrs Fay – everyone loved her and so did the master. Broke his heart when she disappeared."

"She left her royalties to charity, not him," Toby pointed out. "Doesn't sound like a happy marriage."

"Master told me afterwards that was his idea. He'd plenty to live on, and it would all go in tax anyway. No, it was that Dan was the joker in the pack, believe me."

"You think Fay loved him?"

"Why else would she run off with him?"

"There was no proof she did."

"They both disappear at the same time, to different places? Not on your nelly."

"Would you tell me what you remember, Mr Dale?"

Adam was only too willing, but it matched his dad's account almost exactly. "What you so interested for?" he asked curiously. "Writing a book, are you? We get 'em here quite often. I talk to everyone." Toby could well believe it.

"I want to do a new show with the Darling Dan puppets," he explained. "I need a new angle. An ending. Now everyone is dead—"

"*She* ain't," Adam interrupted.

"Fay? You know that for sure?" Toby stuttered.

"Not Mrs Fay. Dan's missis. Madam bloody Serena Smith. You'll find her out there somewhere hobnobbing with the gentry. Ned'll point her out."

"Ned?"

"She was here that day. Didn't he tell you? I'd have my money on her. Not the late master."

"*Ned*!" Toby roared, as he rushed back to the booth which Ned was minding till the next show. "Why didn't you tell me Dan's wife was here that day?"

Ned paused to disentangle the crocodile's strings. "Didn't think of it, Toby. Anyway, she didn't have anything to do with it. Too busy drinking at the bar. Couldn't be two places at once."

"But she might have seen something. At least it suggests she was expecting to see Dan."

Ned shrugged, and returned his concentration to the crocodile.

It was evening before Toby could talk to Serena Smith. It took some time to track her down, and when he did discover her, at the bar, she refused to speak to him, eyeing him up and down and suggesting he came to the house later.

She couldn't have been more than in her mid-fifties but her face, coarsened with drink, looked much older. As the drink had obviously flowed, so had her figure, though not unattractively so. She probably had Romany blood in her, as Dan had, Toby thought, as the rounded curves bulged in the chair she had dropped into with a heavy sigh. He was a little nervous, knowing what some women could be like, alone in the house with a man, but she didn't appear to have sex on her mind. Or, if she did, it wasn't with him, he realised with relief. He could see she wasn't a woman to be crossed, though.

"'Course it was him did it," she snorted. "That Pete Browning. I'd put my money on his doing in both of them, my Dan too."

"You don't believe the gossip that Dan is still alive, then?"

"Look, Dan was a rover. Of course he was. He'd Romany blood in him. But they always come back sooner or later. Thirty years is *too* late. Besides, he was mad about me, not her. He loved me. No, he's dead, and Pete Browning did it. That's what the row was about. I could hear her yelling from the bar. 'What have you done?' I didn't realize what she meant then."

"Did you know Fay Darling well?" Toby asked cautiously.

"Of course I knew her *well*," she mimicked. "I wasn't taken in by that fragile appearance, either. Tough as nails was that lady. She ruled the roost in the Darling Dan duo. Sure they were a success, but Dan loved me, not her. Miss Fay liked all the attention on her and she went on getting it, even after her death. Her own husband wasn't enough for our little angel. She got what was coming to her, in my humble opinion, when Pete strangled her."

"Where was Dan that day, then, if you were at the fête and he was missing?"

"He'd done it before, I wasn't too worried. Another tiff with Madam Nose in the Air, I thought. He'd been away for a few days

– he did that when he could, to get away from it all. I never knew where he was going, but I always knew he'd be back sometime. I expected him to turn up for the fête though, since he and Fay were opening it. I wasn't too surprised when he didn't, though, for he could be an awkward cuss at times. I asked Pete where he was, but he said he'd no idea. With your missus in the hay, I reckon, I told him. That was before the fête opened, and I was already half-seas over with booze. He might as well know the truth, I reckoned. He went bananas. 'I haven't seen him,' he shouted. 'That clear? And I don't want to.' I suppose," Serena added, as though thinking of it for the first time, "I might have put the idea in his mind to bump them off. First Dan, then her." Then she cheered up. "No, I couldn't have done. Dan was already missing, but I'm still sure Pete did for them both." She looked at her empty glass. "When you ain't got love, money's the next best thing, and I've plenty of that. One of these journalists, are you? How much are you paying me?"

"I'm no journalist." Relaxed after the drink, Toby explained about his new show, the one that would finally reveal the truth, and now he thought he knew it. He didn't tell her what he'd worked out, but she didn't take it well, all the same.

She listened to him in silence and, when he finished, announced pleasantly: "You do that, dear, and you'll land up in the river with them."

"I'm back, *omi*." Toby burst through the front door next day, full of excitement.

Sam put down his newspaper. "How did it go, son?"

"I know how it was done and why."

"Tell me, *omi*."

"I can do better than that. I'll give you my new show. That'll tell you who did it." Toby was highly pleased with his efforts. Not a bad day for his first time with the swazzle. That was a mere rehearsal for the show he'd decided he'd better confine to the limited audience of his parents for the moment. It was going to knock 'em cold.

"Right, son. There's nothing decent on telly. Why not?"

Toby didn't mind being laughed at. He was sure of his ground, if somewhat nervous. He'd decided there was no need for Ned's services with a small cast and no bottling required.

He set up the puppets while Dad went to call Mum to watch. She couldn't miss this one, he heard Sam say to her. Not Toby's first show, and in she came, apron on, and teacloth in hand. Toby nipped round to the front of the booth to give a welcoming roll on the drum, then dived into the back again. He was keyed up, but still remembered to use the indoors swazzle Dad had given him, not yesterday's outdoors caller for Punch's voice. He was so het up he nearly choked on it at first, as he screeched, "Hallo folks" and popped Punch up to join the rest of the cast lined up to greet the audience. Then he came out front again: "Right, *omi*, Mr Punch plays the wicked husband as usual, Judy plays his wife Fay, Scaramouche, Punch's neighbour, is Handsome Dan, and the crocodile is his wife Serena. We've a few other players: Joey of course, the policeman, the ghost, the buffer, the baby – even the publican."

"That's a surprise, son." Sam was impressed. "Haven't heard of a couple of those for years."

"You'll have a few more surprises coming, I reckon," Toby said complacently, and went back inside the booth again.

"Come on then, let's be having you," Sam shouted. "Where's old Judy?"

"Change of routine, Dad," came Toby's muffled voice. "Back to the old Piccini script." In this famous eighteenth-century version, the neighbour had come on first. Sam nodded, surprised, but he couldn't fault that. After a burst of song, "Where are my sausages, Scaramouche?" Punch chased after him, then disappeared while Scaramouche and Judy sang a duet, in Toby's falsetto voice, one of the old Darling Dan hits, their version of "The Gypsy's Warning".

"Do not trust him, gentle maiden . . ." Toby boomed as Judy.

"I'll truss him like a chicken; I'm not scared of him," squealed Scaramouche.

"Oh ho. What's all this? Not content with wanting my sausages, you're after my wife, too. I'll show you." Punch hit Scaramouche with his stick, who promptly lay down and died, then popped up again to berate Judy who was by now nursing the baby. He took it from her and flung it over the edge. "Ha, ha, no babies for you. That's the way to do it."

"Oh, Punch, how can you be so cruel?" sobbed Judy.

"Easy! I'll show you how!" squawked Punch in triumph, turning to whack her. But by now not only Joey the Clown was on the scene, but Jack Ketch the hangman, and Punch hastily changed his mind. "My wife," he squawked. "Isn't she lovely?" As soon as their backs were turned, he swiped at Judy again, but this time Joey the Clown appeared and pulled her away, leaving a string of sausages in her place for Punch to thump. The crocodile swallowed them up, and quickly pretended to be dead when he saw Punch. Jack Ketch appeared to hang Punch, but the publican saved him by handing him a large bottle of whisky, and Jack Ketch joined the row of bodies lying at Punch's feet.

"What's he playing at?" Ada whispered. "I don't understand. It's daft. This isn't a proper Punch and Judy."

"Give the lad time, mozzy," Sam said quietly.

"Let me see now, how many have I killed?" Punch began the body-counting routine, confused this time not only by Joey the clown but by the ghost who kept lying down to complicate matters.

Finally the policeman loomed over him. "Mr Punch, I've a warrant to cart you off for killing your wife."

"But I didn't," squealed Punch. "Honest. She warrant *there*."

"Oh." The policeman threw the warrant away, and just as Punch was chuckling with relief, popped up again: "Never mind. I'll have you anyway."

He called the publican back on – and the curtains closed.

"What did you think of it, Dad?" Toby strolled out.

His father cleared his throat. "Very neat, son. I take it you're saying Mr Punch was innocent of killing Judy, but he killed Scaramouche, but escaped the law, although he got his comeuppance in the end. That right?"

"Yes, *omi*," Toby said. "I think Fay engineered the row beforehand, when she was yelling 'What have you done?' so that everyone would think Pete was mad enough to kill her. By the time he got back in the boathouse, she had already vanished – slipped into the river, round the corner, and landed where she gave out that terrible shriek – which brought Pete into the boathouse right on cue."

"And what *had* he done, *omi*?" Sam asked.

"Murdered Dan. Fay knew it, but didn't know where the body was – so she couldn't prove it. She wanted revenge, and how better to get it than to have people think Pete had murdered her?"

"What did she do after she climbed onto the bank then?" Even his mother was getting interested now. "She still had to escape."

"No Dan to help her, was there?" Sam pointed out. "Scaramouche was dead, and his ghost couldn't help."

"No, but Joey the clown could."

There was a split-second silence, then Toby said quietly to his father: "*That's the way you did it*, omi."

A split second silence, broken by Sam's loud laugh. "How's that, then?"

"I think you helped her, Dad. Fay was friendly with you, and she came to you for help when you arrived the evening before. She told you that she knew Pete had killed Dan, and that she would never be free of him if she tried to get away, so she had to disappear for good. You helped her. You lent her the outdoor swazzle for that scream. When you led the chase over the hillock to look for her body, no one noticed that there was one extra person coming back. Why should they? It was only your bottler. Not Ned, though, he was making himself scarce in the bar. That's what put me on to it. He insisted he'd been at the boathouse with you, but there's no way he could have left you there to go back to the bar, and that's where he met Serena Smith. I think Fay wore a hat and blazer over a pair of her own trousers and a shirt. The hat hid her short hair, and no one's going to look at the face of a bottler; mentally they only see the hat. She stayed dressed like that till you went home."

"And what happened to her then, son?"

"I don't know, but you probably do. Maybe she's still singing her heart out somewhere in the world. After all, it doesn't take much in disguise when folks aren't expecting to see you any longer. Bit of hair-dye, and different hair-do, change of name and no one would recognize her now. *Do* you know, Dad? Have you ever seen her again?"

"Oh yes, son."

"So where is she?"

"Right here, *omi*. She's your ma."

THE LONG BLACK VEIL

Val McDermid

Jess turned fourteen today. With every passing year, she looks more like her mother. And it pierces me to the heart. When I stopped by her room this evening, I asked if her birthday awakened memories of her mother. She shook her head, leaning forward so her long blonde hair curtained her face, cutting us off from each other. "Ruth, you're the one I think of when people say 'mother' to me," she mumbled.

She couldn't have known that her words opened an even deeper wound inside me and I was careful to keep my heart's response hidden from my face. Even after ten years, I've never stopped being careful. "She was a good woman, your mother," I managed to say without my voice shaking.

Jess raised her head to meet my eyes then swiftly dropped it again, taking refuge behind the hair. "She killed my father," she said mutinously. "Where exactly does 'good' come into it?"

I want to tell her the truth. There's part of me thinks she's old enough now to know. But then the sensible part of me kicks in. There are worse things to be in small town America than the daughter of a murderess. So I hold my tongue and settle for silence.

Seems like I've been settling for silence all my adult life.

It's easy to point to where things end but it's a lot harder to be sure where they start. Everybody here in Marriott knows where

and when Kenny Sheldon died, and most of them think they
know why. They reckon they know exactly where his journey to
the grave started.

They're wrong, of course. But I'm not going to be the one to
set them right. As far as Marriott is concerned, Kenny's first
step on the road to hell started when he began dating Billy Jean
Ferguson. Rich boys mixing with poor girls is pretty much a
conventional road to ruin in these parts.

Me and Billy Jean, we were still in high school, but Kenny
had a job. Not just any old job, but one that came slathered with
a certain glamour. Somehow, he'd persuaded the local radio
station to take him on staff. He was only a gofer, but Kenny
being Kenny, he managed to parlay that into being a crucial
element in the station's existence. In his eyes, he was on the fast
track to being a star. But while he was waiting for that big break,
Kenny was content to play the small town big shot.

He'd always had an eye for Billy Jean, but she'd fended him
off in the past. We'd neither of us been that keen on dating.
Other girls in our grade had been hanging out with boyfriends
for a couple of years by then, but to me and Billy Jean it had felt
like a straitjacket. It was one of the things that made it possible
for us to be best friends. We preferred to hang out at Helmer's
drugstore in a group of like-minded teens, among them Billy
Jean's distant cousin Jeff.

Their mothers were cousins, and by some strange quirk of
genetics, they'd turned out looking like two peas in a pod. Hair
the colour of butter, eyes the same shade as the hyacinths our
mothers would force for Christmas. The same small, hawk-
curved nose and cupid's bow lips. You could take their features
one by one and see the correspondence. The funny thing was
that you would never have mistaken Billy Jean for a boy or Jeff
for a girl. Maybe it was nothing more than their haircuts. Billy
Jean's hair was the long blonde swatch that I see now in Jess,
whereas Jeff favoured a crew-cut. Still does, for that matter,
though the blond is starting to silver round the temples now.

Anyhow, as time slipped by, the group we hung with thinned
out into couples and sometimes there were just the three of us
drinking Cokes and picking at cold fries. Kenny, who had taken
to drifting into Helmer's when we were there, picked his
moment and started insinuating himself into our company.

He'd park himself next to Jeff, stretching his legs to stake out the whole side of the table. If either of us girls wanted to go to the bathroom, we had to go through a whole rigmarole of getting Kenny to move his damn boots. He'd lay an arm across the back of the booth proprietorially, a Marlboro dangling from the other hand, and tell us all about his important life at the radio station.

One night, he turned up with free tickets for a Del Shannon concert fifty miles down the interstate. We were impressed. Marriott had never seen live rock and roll, unless you counted the open mike night at the Tavern in the Town. As far as we were concerned, only the truly cool had ever seen live bands. It took no persuading whatsoever for us to accompany Kenny to the show.

What we hadn't really bargained for was Kenny treating it like a double date right from the start when he installed Billy Jean up front next to him in the car and relegated me and Jeff to the back seat. He carried on as he started, draping his arm over her shoulders at every opportunity. But we all were fired up with the excitement of seeing a singer who had actually had a number-one single, so we all went along with it. Truth to tell, it turned out to be just the nudge Jeff and I needed to slip from friendship into courting. We'd been heading that way, but I reckon we'd both been reluctant to take any step that might make Billy Jean feel shut out. If Billy Jean was happy to be seen as Kenny's girlfriend – and at first, it seemed that way, since she showed no sign of objecting to the arm-draping or the subsequent hand-holding – then we were freed up to follow our hearts.

That first double date was a night to remember. The buzz from the audience as we filed into the arena was beyond anything we small-town kids had ever experienced. I felt like a little kid again, but in a good way. I slid my hand into Jeff's for security and we followed Kenny and Billy Jean to our seats right at the front. When the support act took to the stage, I was rapt. Around us, people seemed to be paying no attention to the unknown quartet on the stage, but I was determined to miss nothing.

After Del Shannon's set, my ears were ringing from the music and the applause, my eyes dazzled by the spotlights glinting on

the chrome and polish of the instruments. The air was thick
with smoke and sweat and stale perfume. I was stunned by it all.
I scarcely felt my feet touch the ground as we walked back to
Kenny's car, the chorus of "Runaway" ringing inside my head.
But I was still alert enough to see that Kenny still had his arm
round Billy Jean and she was leaning into him. I wasn't crazy
about Kenny, but I was selfish. I wanted to be with Jeff, so I
wasn't going to try to talk Billy Jean out of Kenny.

Kenny dropped Jeff and me off outside my house, and as his
tail lights disappeared, I said, "You think she'll be OK?"

Jeff grinned. "I've got a feeling Kenny just bit off more than
he can chew. Billy Jean will be fine. Now, come here, missy,
I've got something for you." Then he pulled me into his arms
and kissed me. I didn't give Billy Jean another thought that
night.

Next day when we met up, we compared notes. I was still
floating from Jeff's kisses and I didn't really grasp that Billy
Jean was less enamoured of Kenny's attempts to push her well
beyond a goodnight kiss. What I did take in was that she
appeared genuinely pleased for Jeff and me. My fears that she'd
feel shut out seemed to have been groundless, and she talked
cheerfully about more double-dating. I didn't understand that
was her way of keeping herself safe from Kenny's advances. I
just thought that we were both contentedly coupled up after
that one double date.

All that spring, we went out as a foursome. Kenny seemed to
be able to get tickets to all sorts of venues and we went to a lot of
gigs. Some were good, most were pretty terrible and none
matched the excitement of that first live concert. I didn't really
care. All that mattered to me was the shift from being Jeff's
friend to being his girlfriend. I was in love, no doubting it, and
in love as only a teenage girl can be. I walked through the world
starry-eyed and oblivious to anything that wasn't directly connected to me and my guy.

That's why I paid no attention to the whispers linking
Kenny's name to a couple of other girls. Someone said he'd
been seen with Janine, who tended bar at the Tavern in the
Town. I dismissed that out of hand. According to local legend, a
procession of men had graced Janine's trailer. Why would
Kenny lower himself when he had someone as special as Billy

Jean for a girlfriend? Oh yes, I was quite the little innocent back in the day.

Someone else claimed to have seen him with another girl at a blues night in the next county. I pointed out to her that he worked in the music business. It wasn't surprising if he had to meet with colleagues at music events. And that it shouldn't surprise her if some of those colleagues happened to be women. And that it was a sad day when women were so sexist.

I didn't say anything to Billy Jean, even though we were closer than sisters. I'd like to think it was because I didn't want to cause her pain, but the truth is that their stories probably slipped my mind, being much less important than my own emotional life.

By the time spring had slipped into summer, Jeff and I were lovers. I'm bound to say it was something of a disappointment. I suspect it is for a lot of women. Not that Jeff wasn't considerate or generous or gentle. He was all of those and more. But even after we'd been doing it a while and we'd had the chance to get better at it, I still had that Peggy Lee "Is that all there is?" feeling.

I suppose that made it easier for me to support Billy Jean in her continued refusal to let Kenny go all the way. When we were alone together, she was adamant that she didn't care for him nearly enough to let him be the one to take her virginity. For my part, I told her she should hold out for somebody who made her dizzy with desire because frankly that feeling was the only thing that made it all worth it.

The weekend after I said that to her, Billy Jean told Kenny she wasn't in love with him and she didn't want to go out with him any more. Of course, he went around telling anybody who would listen that he was the one to call time on their relationship, but I suspect that most people read that for the bluster it was. "How did he take it?" I asked her at recess on the Monday afterwards. "Was he upset?"

"Upset, like broken-hearted? No way." Billy Jean gave a little "I could give a shit" shrug. "He was really pissed at me," she said. "I got the impression he's the only one who gets to decide when it's over."

"You know, I've been wanting to say this for the longest time, but he really is kind of an asshole," I said.

We both giggled, bumping our shoulders into each other like big kids. "I only started going out with him so you and Jeff would finally get it together," Billy Jean said in between giggles. "I knew as long as I was single you two would be too loyal to do anything about it. Now I can just go back to having you both as my best friends again."

And so it played out over the next few weeks. Billy Jean and I hung out together doing girl things; Billy Jean and Jeff went fishing out on the lake once a week and spent Sunday mornings fixing up the old clunker her dad had bought for her birthday; we'd all go for a pizza together on Friday nights; and the rest of the time she'd leave us to our own devices. It seemed like one chapter had closed and another had opened.

Jess turned fourteen today. Seems like yesterday she came into our home. It wasn't how we expected it to be, me and Ruthie. We thought we'd have a brood of our own, not end up raising my cousin's kid. But some things just aren't meant to be and I'm old enough now to know there are sometimes damn good reasons for that.

I remember the morning after Jess was conceived. When Billy Jean told Ruthie and me what Kenny Sheldon had done, I didn't think it was possible to feel more angry and betrayed. I was wrong about that too, but that's another story.

It happened the night before, when Ruthie and I were parked up by the lake in my car and Billy Jean was on her lonesome, nursing a Coke in one of the booths at Helmer's. According to her, when Kenny walked in, he didn't hesitate. He came straight over to her booth and plonked himself down opposite her. He gave her the full charm offensive, apologizing for being mean to her when she'd thrown him over.

He claimed he'd missed her and he wanted her back but if he couldn't be her boyfriend he wanted to be her friend, like me. He pitched it just right for Billy Jean and she believed he meant what he said. That's the kind of girl she was back then – honest and open and unable to see that other people might not be worthy of her trust. So she didn't think twice when he offered her a ride home.

She called me first thing Sunday morning. We were supposed to be going fishing as usual but she wanted Ruthie to come along too. I could tell from her voice something terrible had happened even though she wouldn't tell me what it was, so I called Ruthie and got her to make some excuse to get out of church.

When we picked her up, she was pale and withdrawn. She wouldn't say a word till we were out at the lake, sitting on the jetty with rods on the water like it was any other Sunday morning. When she did speak, it was right to the point. Billy Jean was never one for beating about the bush, but this was bald, even for her.

"Kenny Sheldon raped me last night," she said. She told us about the meeting at Helmer's and how she'd agreed to let him drive her home. Only, before they got to her house, Kenny had driven down an overgrown track out of sight of the street. Then he'd pinned her down and forced her to have sex with him.

We didn't know what to do. Fourteen years ago, date rape wasn't on the criminal agenda. Not in towns like Marriott. And the Sheldons were a prominent family. Kenny's dad owned the funeral home and had been a councilman. And his mom ran the flower arranging circle at the church. Whereas the Fergusons were barely one step up from white trash. Nobody was going to take the word of Billy Jean Ferguson against Kenny Sheldon.

I wanted to call Kenny Sheldon out and beat him to within an inch of his life. I wanted him to beg for mercy the way I knew Billy Jean had begged him the night before.

But Ruthie and Billy Jean stopped me. "Don't stoop so low," Billy Jean said.

"That's right," Ruthie said. "There's other ways to get back at scum like him."

And by that afternoon, I had started the rumour that Janine from the Tavern in the Town had stopped sleeping with Kenny because she'd found out he had a venereal disease. I don't know how long it took to get back to the shitheel himself, but I do know he'd had quite the struggle to get anyone to sit next to him in Helmer's, never mind hang out at gigs with him. That cheered us up some, and Ruthie said Billy Jean was starting to talk about getting over it. That was so like her – she wasn't the kind to let anybody take her life away from her. She was always determined to control her own destiny.

But all her good intentions went to shit about six weeks after the rape. I'd been helping my dad finish off some work in the top pasture and both girls were sitting on the front porch when I got back to the house. We all piled into my truck and headed out to the lake. We hadn't gone but half a mile when Ruthie blurted out, "She's pregnant. That bastard Kenny got her pregnant."

I only had to glance at Billy Jean to know it was true and the knowledge made me boiling mad. I swung the truck around at the next intersection and headed for the Sheldon house, paying no mind to the girls shouting at me to stop. When we got there, I jumped out and marched straight up to the house. I hammered on the door and Kenny himself opened it.

I know that violence isn't supposed to solve things, but in my experience, it definitely has its plus points. I grabbed Kenny by the shirt front, yanked him out the door and slammed him against the wall. I swear the whole damn house shook. "You bastard," *I yelled at him.* "First you rape her, then you get her pregnant."

I drew my hand back to smack him in the middle of his dumbfounded face, but Billy Jean caught my arm. She was always strong for a girl and she had me at an awkward angle. "Leave him," *she said.* "I don't want anything to do with him."

"You say that now, but you're going to need his money," *I snarled.* "Babies don't come cheap and he has to pay for what he's done."

Before anybody could say anything more, Mrs Sheldon appeared in the doorway. She looked shocked to see her golden boy pinned up against the wall and demanded to know what was going on.

My dander was up, and I wasn't about to back off. "Ma'am," *I said,* "I'm sorry to cause a scene, but your son here raped my cousin Billy Jean and now she is expecting his baby."

Mrs Sheldon reared back like a horse spooked by a snake. "How dare you," *she hissed.* "My son is a gentleman, which is more than I can say about you or your kin." *She made a kind of snorting noise in the back of her throat.* "The very idea of any Ferguson woman being able to name the father of her children with any certainty is absurd. Now get off my property before I call the police. And take your slut of a cousin with you."

It was my turn to grab Billy Jean. I thought she was fixing to rip Mrs Sheldon's face off. "You evil witch," *she screamed as I pulled her away.*

Ruthie stared Mrs Sheldon down. When she spoke her voice was cold and sharp. I know I hoped she'd never use that tone of voice to me. "You should be ashamed of yourself," *she said,*

*turning on her heel and walking back to the truck, head high. I
never knew to this day whether she meant Kenny or his mother or
both of them.*

*What happened that evening must have had some effect, though.
A week later, Kenny was gone.*

Back in the early Sixties, being an unwed mother was still about
the biggest disgrace around and most girls who got into trouble
ended up disowned and despised. But Billy Jean was lucky in
her parents. The Fergusons never had much money but they
had love aplenty. When she told them she was pregnant and
how it had happened, they'd been shocked, but they hadn't
been angry with her. Her father went round to see old man
Sheldon. He never told anybody what passed between them,
not even Mrs Ferguson, but he came back with a cashier's check
for ten thousand dollars.

Nobody knew where Kenny was. His mother told her church
crowd that he'd landed a big important radio job out on the
coast, but nobody believed her. Truth to tell, I don't think
anybody much cared. We certainly didn't.

Jeff and I were married three months later. I guess we were
both kind of fired up by Billy Jean being pregnant. We wanted
to start a family of our own. We moved into a little house on
Jeff's daddy's farm and Jeff started working as a trainee sales
representative for an agricultural machinery firm.

Half a mile down the track from us there was an old double-
wide trailer that had seen better days. Jeff's dad used to rent it
out to seasonal workers. We persuaded him to let Billy Jean
have it for next to nothing in return for doing it up. We knew
there wasn't enough room in her parents' house for Billy Jean
and a growing kid and I wanted her to be close at hand so we
could bring up our children together.

Jeff and I spent most of our spare time knocking that trailer
into shape. Billy Jean helped as much as she could, and by the
time Jess was born, we'd turned it into a proper little home for
the two of them. They moved in when Jess was six weeks old,
and Billy Jean looked relaxed for the first time since Kenny had
raped her. "I can never thank the two of you enough," she said
so many times I told her she should just make a tape of it and
give us each a copy.

"It was Ruthie's idea," Jeff said, acting like it was nothing to do with him.

"I know," Billy Jean said. "But I also know you did more than your fair share to make it happen."

We settled into a pretty easy routine. I worked mornings on the farm, helping Jeff's mother with the specialty yogurt business she was building up. Afternoons, I'd hang out with Billy Jean and Jess. Then I'd cook dinner for Jeff, we'd either watch some TV or walk down to have a beer and a few hands of cards with Billy Jean. Most people might have thought our lives pretty dull, but it seemed fine enough to us.

There was one thing, I thought, that stopped it being perfect. A year had gone by since Jeff and I had married, but still I wasn't pregnant. It wasn't for want of trying, but I began to wonder whether my lack of enthusiasm for sex was somehow preventing it. I knew this was crazy, but it nagged away at me.

Finally, I managed to talk to Billy Jean about it. It was a hot summer afternoon and Jess was over at her grandma's house. Billy Jean and I were lying on her bed with the only a/c in the trailer cranked up high. "I love him," I said. "But when we make love, it's not like it says in the books and magazines. It doesn't feel like it looks in the movies. I just don't feel that whole swept away thing."

Billy Jean rolled over on to her back and yawned. "I'm not the best person to ask, Ruth. I only ever had sex the once and that sure wasn't what you would call a good experience. I don't guess it's the kind of thing you can talk to Jeff about either."

I made a face. "He'd be mortified. He thinks I think he's the greatest lover on the planet." Billy Jean giggled. "Well, you have to make them feel like that."

Billy Jean yawned again. "I'm sorry, Ruth. I don't mean you to feel like I'm dismissing you, but I am so damn tired. I was up three times with Jess last night. She's teething."

"Why don't you just have a nap?" I said. But she was already drifting away. I made myself more comfortable and before I knew it, I'd nodded off too.

I woke because someone was kissing me. An arm was heavy across my chest and shoulder, a leg was thrown between mine and soft lips were pressing on mine, a tongue flicking between my lips. I opened my eyes and the mouth pulled back from mine. A face that was familiar and yet completely strange hovered above mine. *Jeff with long hair*, I thought stupidly for a moment before the truth dawned.

Billy Jean put a finger to my lips. . . . "Ssh," she said "Let's see if we can figure out what Jeff's doing wrong."

By the end of the afternoon, I understood that it wasn't what Jeff did that was wrong. It was who he was.

Kenny came back a couple of weeks before Jess's fourth birthday. It turned out his mother hadn't been lying to the church group. He had landed a job working for a radio station in Los Angeles. He was doing pretty well. Had his own show and everything. He rolled back into town in a muscle car with a beautiful blonde on his arm. His fiancée, apparently.

All of that would have been just fine if he had left the past alone. But no. He wanted to impress the fiancée with his credentials as a family man. The first thing we knew about it was when Billy Jean got a letter from Kenny's lawyer saying he planned to file suit for shared custody. Kenny wanted Jess for one week a month until she started school, then he wanted her for half the school vacations. If he'd been the standard absent father as opposed to one who had never even seen his kid, it might have sounded reasonable. And we had a sneaking feeling that the court might see things Kenny's way.

Justice in Marriott comes courtesy of His Honour Judge Wellesley Benton. Who is an old buddy of Kenny Sheldon's daddy and a man who's put a fair few of Billy Jean's relatives behind bars. We were, to say the least, apprehensive.

The day after the letter came, Billy Jean happened to be walking down Main Street when Kenny strolled out of the Coffee Bean Scene with the future Mrs. Sheldon. I heard all about it from Mom, who saw it all from the vantage point of the quilting store porch.

Billy Jean just lit into him. Called him all the names under the sun from rapist to deadbeat dad. Kenny looked shocked at first, then when he saw his fiancée wasn't turning a hair, he started to laugh. That just drove Billy Jean even crazier. She was practically hysterical. Mom came over from the quilt shop and grabbed her by the shoulders, trying to get her away. Then Kenny said, "I'll see you in court," and walked his fiancée to the car. Billy Jean was fit to be tied.

Well, everybody thinks they know what happened next. That night, Kenny was due at a dinner in the Town Hall. As he approached, a figure stepped out of the shadows. Long blonde hair, jeans and a Western shirt, just like Billy Jean always liked to wear. And a couple of witnesses who were a ways off but who knew Billy Jean well enough to recognize her when she raised the shotgun and blew Kenny Sheldon into the next world.

That was the end of her as much as it was the end of him.

I knew Billy Jean was innocent. Not out of some crazy misplaced belief, but because at the very moment Kenny Sheldon was meeting his maker, I was in her bed, moaning at her touch. That first afternoon had not been a one-off. It had been an awakening that had led us both into a deeper happiness than we'd ever known before.

If I'd been married to anyone other than Jeff, I'd have left in a New York minute. But I cared about him. More importantly, so did Billy Jean. "You're both my best friend," she said as we lay in a tangle of sheets. "Until this afternoon, I couldn't have put one of you above the other. You gotta stay with him, Ruth. You gotta go on being his wife because I couldn't live with myself if you didn't."

And so I did. It might seem strange to most folks, but in a funny kind of way, it worked out just fine for us. Except of course that I still couldn't get pregnant. I began to think of that as the price I had to pay for my other contentments – Jeff, Billy Jean, Jess.

Then Kenny came back.

They came for Billy Jean soon after midnight. A deputy we'd all been at school with knocked on our door at one in the morning, carrying Jess in a swaddle of bedclothes. He looked mortified as he explained what had happened and asked us to take care of the child till morning when things could be sorted out more formally.

Jess had often stayed with us, so she settled pretty easy. That morning, I drove into town, leaving Jess with her grandma, and demanded to see Billy Jean. She was white and drawn, her eyes heavy and haunted. "They can't prove it," she said. "You have to promise me you will never tell. Don't sacrifice yourself trying to save me. They won't believe you anyway and you'll have shamed yourself in their eyes for nothing. Just have faith. We both know I'm innocent. Judge Benton isn't a fool. He won't let them get away with it."

And so I kept my mouth shut. Partly for Billy Jean and partly for Jess. We'd already made arrangements with Billy Jean and her parents for me and Jeff to take care of Jess till after the court case, and I wasn't about to do anything that would jeopardize that child's future. I sat through that terrible trial day after day. I listened to witnesses swearing they had seen Billy Jean kill Kenny Sheldon and I said not a word.

Nor did Billy Jean. She said she was somewhere else, but refused to say where or with whom. Judge Benton offered her the way out. "Woman, what is your alibi?" he thundered. "If you were somewhere else that night, then you won't have to die. If you're telling the truth, give up your alibi." But she wouldn't budge. And so I couldn't. It nearly killed me.

But I never truly thought he would have her hanged.

I never truly thought he would have her hanged. I thought they'd argue she was temporarily insane because of the threat to her child and that she'd do a few years in jail, nothing more. And I was selfish enough to think of how much my Ruthie would love bringing up Jess for as long as Billy Jean was behind bars.

Sure, I wanted to make her suffer. But I didn't want her to die. She was my best friend, after all. A friend like no other. I swear, I always believed we would lay down our lives for each other if it came to it. And I guess I was right, in a way. She laid down her life rather than destroy my marriage.

When the sentence came down, it hit me like a physical blow. I swear I doubled over in pain as I realized the full horror of what I'd done. But it was too late. The sacrifices were made, the chips down once and for all.

I saw the way she looked at me in court. A mixture of pity and blame. As soon as she heard those witnesses, recognized the conviction in their voices, I think she knew the truth. With a long blonde wig and the right clothes, I could easily be mistaken for her.

There was an excuse for the witnesses. They were a way off from Kenny and his killer. But there's no excuse for Ruthie. She was no distance at all from Billy Jean that afternoon I saw them by the lake shore. She could not have been mistaken.

Why didn't I confront her? Why didn't I walk away? I guess because I loved them both so much. I didn't want to lose the life we had. I just wanted Billy Jean to suffer for a while, that was all. I never truly thought he would have her hanged.

Jess turned fourteen today. She's not old enough for the truth. Maybe she'll never be that old. But there's one thing she is old enough for.

Tonight, there will be two of us standing over Billy Jean's grave, our long black veils drifting in the wind, our tears sparkling like diamonds in the moonlight.

THE CURIOUS CONTENTS OF A COFFIN

Susanna Gregory

London, 1663

Thomas Chaloner, spy for the Lord Chancellor, hated assign-
ments like the one he had been given that morning. He did not
mind the physical labour of excavating a tomb in the hour
before dawn – although he would have been happier had it not
been raining so hard. And he enjoyed the challenge of disguising himself as a gravedigger – donning the filthy clothes of the
trade and staining his teeth brown, so that even his own mother
would not have recognized him. He did not even mind man-
handling corpses. But what Chaloner didn't like was causing
distress to the dead woman's son and daughter, who had
objected strenuously to their mother's final resting place being
disturbed. Nor did he like the possibility that he might be
ordered to steal what was in the coffin with her.

"How much longer?" demanded John Pargiter, wealthy
goldsmith and husband of the deceased. He was a tall man,
with a long nose and a reputation for dishonesty – the Goldsmith's Company had fined him several times for coin-clipping
and shoddy workmanship. "My arm aches from holding this
lamp and I'm soaking wet."

"This foul weather is a sign of God's displeasure," declared
Pargiter's son Francis, hugging his sobbing sister closer to

him. "This is an evil deed, and you will pay for it on Judgment Day."

"Please, father," begged the weeping Eleanor. "Stop this. Let our mother rest in peace."

Chaloner waited to see if Pargiter would agree. He was nearing the casket, and knew he would have to be careful not to step through it. The man who usually dug graves for St Martin's Ludgate – currently insensible after the copious quantities of ale with which Chaloner had plied him the previous night in the hope of learning a few useful tips – had confided that there was an art to dealing with rotting coffins, but had then declined to elaborate. Chaloner would have to rely on his own ingenuity to perform the grisly task, and only hoped he would convince Pargiter that he knew what he was doing. The goldsmith had brought two burly henchmen with him, and Chaloner suspected they might turn nasty if he failed to impress.

He exchanged a hopeful glance with the parish priest, Robert Bretton, a short fellow with a mane of long, shiny black curls. Bretton was chaplain to King Charles, as well as Rector of St Martin's, and it was because of him that this particular assignment had been foisted on Chaloner. When he had learned what Pargiter intended to do, Bretton had approached the King in a fury of righteous indignation – the poor woman had been in the ground for more than three years, and it was shameful to disturb her rest. With a shudder of distaste, the King had passed the matter to his Lord Chancellor to sort out.

But the Lord Chancellor said there was nothing he could do to stop the exhumation, because Pargiter had the necessary writs. What he *had* been able to do, however, was lend Bretton one of his men, assuring the agitated chaplain that Thomas Chaloner would not only ensure the exhumation was carried out decently, but could be trusted not to gossip. When Bretton had demurred, the Lord Chancellor had pointed out that he would have an ally at the graveside should he need one, and the family would be suitably grateful to him for "hiring" a man who knew how to be discreet. And, the Lord Chancellor had added slyly, he wanted his spy present anyway, because he was curious to know what Pargiter thought he might find among his wife's rotting bones.

Bretton peered at the goldsmith in the gloom, to see whether he was having second thoughts. He sighed unhappily when he saw he was not, and nodded down at Chaloner, telling him to continue. The spy began to dig again, pretending not to listen to the furious altercation that was taking place above his head. The family had kept their voices low at first, unwilling to let a stranger hear what they were saying – even one vouched for by Rector Bretton. But as time had crept by and Chaloner's spade came ever closer to the coffin, they had grown less cautious, and the foul weather and their increasing agitation encouraged them to forget themselves. In addition, Chaloner had excellent hearing – a valuable asset for a spy – and a decade of eavesdropping in foreign courts meant he was rather good at hearing discussions not intended for his ears.

"This is very wrong," said Pargiter's cousin and business-partner, an overweight man named Thomas Warren, who was the last of the graveside party. His plump face was pale and unhappy, and the hair in his handsome wig had been reduced to a mess of rat-tails in the rain. "Had I known you'd cached our gold in Margaret's grave, I'd *never* have asked for it back. I don't want her defiled."

"You're deep in debt," said Pargiter with a sneer. "You lost a fortune in Barbados sugar, and your creditors snap at your heels. Would you rather go to prison? Besides, Margaret won't be defiled. Once the coffin is reached, I shall jump down and remove the gold myself. I was her husband, so she won't object to me touching her."

Francis snorted his disdain. "She would. She hated you – and with good cause." He added something else in a low, venomous hiss that Chaloner could not quite catch. The spy supposed someone – probably his sister – had warned him to keep his voice down.

"Why are *you* so eager to retrieve the hoard, Father?" asked Eleanor softly, so Chaloner had to strain to hear her. "*You* don't need your share of this gold: you're already rich – certainly wealthy enough to lend Warren what he needs."

"Yes," said Warren, sounding relieved. "That's the best solution. Fill in the hole and I'll have papers—"

"I've lent him too much already," interrupted Pargiter roughly. "No, don't you flap your hand at me to be quiet, Warren! I shall talk as loudly as I please. And, to answer my daughter's question, our cache has been playing on my mind of late. Gold can't earn interest if it's buried, and I want it where it can do me some good."

"Tainted money," said Rector Bretton in disgust. Chaloner had noticed his increasing distress as the exhumation had proceeded, and now he sounded close to tears. "It won't bring you happiness, and I strongly advise you to leave it where it is."

"You did a dreadful thing, burying gold with our mother," said Eleanor in a broken, grief-filled voice that made Chaloner wince at his role in the distasteful business. The gravedigger's disguise had been Bretton's idea, and Chaloner heartily wished the rector had thought of something else.

Francis murmured something Chaloner did not hear, and Pargiter responded with a sharp bark of laughter that had Francis spluttering in impotent rage. The spy glanced up and saw Eleanor rest a calming hand on her furious brother's arm.

"Francis is right, cousin," said Warren in a low voice. "I cannot imagine what you were thinking when you performed an act of such heartless desecration."

"I was desperate," replied Pargiter with an unrepentant shrug. "You and I supported Cromwell, but when the monarchy was restored, Royalists surged into London and started confiscating Roundhead goods. Margaret's death from fever provided me with a perfect opportunity to hide our gold where no one would ever think to look."

"That's certainly true," said Bretton unhappily. "But only a monster would have devised such a plan – and only a devil would consider retrieving the hoard."

"Our mother was right to despise you," said Francis. Chaloner saw Eleanor was hard-pressed to restrain him as he glowered at their father. "And so are we."

Pargiter did not care what his son, daughter, rector and cousin thought, and when Warren took a threatening step towards him the two henchmen blocked his path. But the goldsmith did not so much as glance at his kinsman: his attention was focussed on the grave. Chaloner's spade had made a hollow sound, as metal had connected with wood.

"At last," said Pargiter. "Now, climb out and let me take over."

"You don't want me to open the coffin first?" asked Chaloner.

Pargiter shook his head. "I told you: I don't want anyone to see her. I'm not the heartless fiend everyone imagines and, by retrieving the money myself, I shall spare her the indignity of being gawked at. Then we can cover her up again, and be done with this business. Take my hand."

Scaling the rain-slicked sides was not easy, and Chaloner was muddy from digging. He was not halfway out before his fingers shot out of Pargiter's grasp, and he fell backwards, landing feet-first on the ancient casket. There was a crackle of shattering wood, and the top third of the lid disintegrated. Eleanor cried out in horror, and Bretton began to pray in an unsteady voice.

"Clumsy oaf!" yelled Pargiter, while Chaloner danced around in a desperate attempt to regain his balance without doing any more damage. "You've exposed her for all to see!"

Warren looked as though he might cry. "This has gone far enough, cousin. I don't want the gold any more – I'll find another way to pay my debts."

"I'm not leaving without my money," declared Pargiter, climbing inside the hole himself. He soon discovered it was not easy, and slithered down in a way that broke more of the coffin. One of his men handed him a lamp. "Everyone stay back. I'll finish quicker without an audience."

Sobbing, Eleanor appealed to Chaloner. "Please stop him. You must see this isn't right."

"If you have any compassion, you'll do as my sister asks," added Francis in a heart-broken voice. "I'll pay you – twice what my father offered."

"And I'll pray for you for as long as I live," said Bretton. He sounded distraught. "Poor Margaret doesn't deserve this."

Supposing a real gravedigger would at least consider their offers, Chaloner moved forward. He stopped when he saw the body for the first time. Margaret Pargiter had been buried in a lacy shroud and a veil that covered her hair. Her face was much as he would have expected after three years, but it was the glitter of gold that caught his attention. Coins covered her chest and shoulders – too many to count. Pargiter was busily collecting them. The goldsmith glanced up and saw his order had been ignored: everyone, even his two henchmen, was gazing open-mouthed at the spectacle.

"The bag must have broken," he said in an oddly furtive way that made Chaloner sure he was lying. "I put it under her head."

But Chaloner had spotted something beside the hoard, and he edged around Pargiter to be sure of it. "Gold isn't the only thing to have shared her tomb – there's another body beneath her."

Pandemonium erupted after Chaloner's announcement. Warren accused him of being a liar, although his furious diatribe faltered when Chaloner pointed out the grinning skull under Margaret's shoulder. Francis and Eleanor clamoured for the strange body to be removed and their mother reburied alone. Pargiter wanted his gold out and the two bodies left as they were. But Bretton had the authority of the Church behind him, and once he declared his bishop would want both bodies excavated while an investigation took place, the argument was over.

Knowing the frail coffin would disintegrate if he tried to lift it, Chaloner raised the two bodies separately, using planks of wood, although his task would have been easier if Pargiter had not been in the grave with him, grabbing coins. When he had finished, and the corpses lay in the grass next to the tomb, Chaloner reached for his spade.

"Don't bother to fill it in," ordered Pargiter. "Margaret will be back in it soon. Here's a shilling for your trouble – you're dismissed."

But Chaloner had no idea how much gold Pargiter had retrieved, and the Lord Chancellor would be annoyed if he was not told a precise sum. He thrashed around for an excuse that would allow him to lurk long enough to see the money counted. "For another shilling, I'll find out who was the second corpse," he offered rashly.

Pargiter gazed contemptuously at him. "And how would a gravedigger know how to do that?"

"Fossor used to work for Archbishop Juxon," announced Bretton, before Chaloner could fabricate a story of his own. "And he solved all manner of crimes on His Grace's behalf. Don't let his shabby appearance deceive you. Fossor possesses a very sharp mind."

Warren peered at the spy in the darkness. "You've fallen low, then, if you were in the employ of an archbishop, but now you dig graves for a living."

"He does more than that," said Bretton, before Chaloner could prevent him from inventing anything else. "He hires himself out to many of my clerical colleagues, because we all know him as a man of intelligence and discretion. Why do you think I dispensed with my usual gravedigger and hired him instead? Whatever happened here *must* be investigated and the results reported to the proper authorities – and I would rather Fossor did it than some half-drunk parish constable."

Chaloner wished he would shut up, not liking the increasingly elaborate web of lies or the fictitious name. But Bretton gave him an encouraging nod, and Chaloner supposed he was hoping to curry favour with the Lord Chancellor by supporting his spy's proposal. However, all Chaloner wanted was an excuse to see the money counted, after which he would dispense with his disguise and disappear from the Pargiter family's lives for ever. He had no intention of mounting an investigation – Bretton would have to resort to his "half-drunk parish constable" for that.

"I will discover the truth," he said, hoping he did not sound as unenthusiastic as he felt. "I shall uncover the corpse's identity, and you can make an official report to your bishop."

"Well, *I* don't want to know who it is," said Pargiter firmly. "It is common knowledge that Margaret made a cuckold of me, and one of her lovers must have contrived to be buried with her. And this *is* a man – he's quite tall and look, the fellow was buried wearing spurs."

"Our mother had no lovers!" declared Francis hotly, shooting Chaloner an uncomfortable glance. "How dare you defame her good name in front of strangers!"

Eleanor tried to pull him away, to talk to him privately, but he resisted. "You know she did, Francis. It was her way of defying the husband she didn't love. And I cannot find it in my heart to condemn her for it. And nor should anyone – including strangers who did not know her and so have no right to judge." She gazed coolly at Chaloner, who pretended to be absorbed with the skeletons.

"Nor me," said Warren. His chubby face was wan in the faint gleam of approaching dawn. "Do you mind if we just count this gold and go home? I feel sick."

"We can't," said Bretton angrily. "Something evil happened in poor Margaret's grave, and my bishop will want to know what. We are duty-bound to discover both this man's identity *and* how he came to die."

Eleanor sighed. "Rector Bretton is right. Once he reports the matter to his bishop, it will have to be investigated. He will think we have something to hide if we object."

"How do we know you can be trusted?" demanded Warren of Chaloner. "We have never met you before today."

"*I* trust him," said Bretton, before Chaloner could point out that anyone could be trusted if enough gold changed hands. "And you have known *me* for a long time. That should be enough for you."

Eleanor nodded slowly, staring hard at the spy. "Very well. If there must be an enquiry, then I suppose I would rather this Fossor did it than that horrible Constable Unwin."

"So would I," said Francis, glaring at his father. "Unwin hates us because *someone* made a fool of him over a consignment of clipped coins, and we don't want *him* poking into our affairs. He'll invent something to harm us, and who can blame him?" He turned to Chaloner. "If Bretton says you're all right, then I suppose you'll do. I'll pay you your shilling, if you find out the corpse's name."

"No," countered Warren shakily. "You might not like what he learns. Margaret was a sociable lady, and you should let matters lie while her reputation is still intact."

"It was *not* a lover," snarled Francis, rapidly losing what small control he had. "And I want to know why my mother has spent the last three years with a stranger. Do your work, Fossor."

"Let sleeping dogs lie," argued Pargiter irritably. "Folk will have forgotten her infidelities by now, and I don't want to be labelled a cuckold again, thank you very much."

"You were unfaithful yourself," said Bretton sharply. "And if Fossor needs to ask you questions to solve this wicked business, you *will* answer them. It is your Christian duty."

"You can't order *me* around!" cried Pargiter. "I'm a City goldsmith—"

"Then we shall summon Constable Unwin instead," said Bretton coldly. He nodded his satisfaction when there were resentful glares from Pargiter and his cousin, but no further objections. "Good. Fossor, you may begin."

Chaloner knelt next to the bodies. First, he inspected Margaret, recalling how her graveclothes had been carefully arranged to hide the corpse beneath – someone had been to considerable trouble. Then he turned his attention to the second body. There was nothing left of his face, and the only thing of use was a charm on a chain around his neck.

"Does anyone recognize this?" he asked, removing it. The pendant was made of jet, and was in the shape of a bird. There were shaken heads all around, although a brief glimmer of alarm flashed in Warren's eyes.

Chaloner began the distasteful business of peeling away the decaying clothes, hoping to discover how the stranger had died. Revolted, Bretton invited the others to his house, where they agreed to wait until "Fossor" had finished. From the worn teeth, Chaloner concluded the stranger had been an older man, and his silver spurs suggested he had been wealthy. The only injury was a triangular puncture-wound, clearly visible in the bones of the chest and what little skin still clung to them.

The spy gazed at the bodies and reviewed what he had been told. Margaret had died of a fever three years before, and Pargiter had taken advantage of her burial to keep some of his and Cousin Warren's money from acquisitive Royalists. The grave had been opened because Warren was in debt, although the man had become increasingly unnerved as the exhumation had proceeded. Had Warren's unease derived from the fact that an old crime was about to be exposed? And what about his hesitation when Chaloner had asked about the charm? Finally, it had been Warren who had objected to an enquiry that promised to reveal the dead man's name.

Next, Chaloner turned his thoughts to Pargiter, who did not need more money, but could no longer bear the thought of it lying uselessly underground. From the very start, the goldsmith had made it clear that only *he* was to collect the coins from the coffin, and he had issued all manner of threats to ensure he was obeyed – until Chaloner's fall had inadvertently spoiled his plan. Had he been so determined no one should see the contents of the coffin because he knew what else was in it? He had tried to persuade the others to ignore the grisly discovery, and had joined with Warren in objecting to an investigation. Was it because he had no desire to be ridiculed as a cuckold again, as he had claimed, or did he have a more sinister motive for wanting the matter quietly forgotten?

Then there were Francis and Eleanor, who had loved their mother – or at least, had not wanted her grave disturbed. Were they devoted children, who had taken her side against a hated father? Or had they made use of her death to conceal crimes of their own? But then, surely they would not have asked Chaloner to investigate the stranger? They would have taken the opportunity supplied by their father to have the matter shoved quickly underground again. Or were they afraid that might have looked suspicious?

Finally, there was Bretton, who had also objected to the exhumation. As the family rector, he would have had access to Margaret's coffin three years before. Had he encouraged Chaloner's investigation because to do otherwise would have looked odd – especially in front of the Lord Chancellor's spy? He had always referred to the dead woman as "Margaret", rather than "Mrs Pargiter". The more Chaloner thought about it, the more convinced he became that the rector might have offered her more than spiritual comfort. Did that mean Bretton had dispatched a rival for her affections?

"Anyone could have killed him," said one of Pargiter's henchmen, who had lingered to watch. "Although I suspect *you* think it was Pargiter, because this man was probably one of her paramours."

Chaloner shrugged. "No one likes his wife sleeping with another man, and Pargiter *is* violent – he has been threatening me all night. But I imagine Margaret would have been too ill to entertain lovers immediately before her death."

"She *did* die of fever – I saw her shivering and sweating myself. But I've been thinking. About the time she passed away, there was a fellow who lurked around a lot, talking to Warren. He disappeared after, and I never saw him again."

"Do you know his name, or what he was doing?"

The henchman shook his head. "All I know is that he was tall with a big nose and a stoop."

Chaloner was thoughtful. "There are two peculiar things about Margaret's burial. First, the presence of an additional corpse. And second, the coins were not in a bag, as Pargiter said they would be, but were scattered across her body."

"Worms," said the henchman. "They do odd things under-ground."

"Not that odd," said Chaloner.

Chaloner did not want to spend too much time with the bodies, in case he missed the counting of the money. He trotted across the sodden churchyard to the Rectory, a grand house boasting ornamental drainpipes of lead – few owners bothered, leaving rainwater to cascade from the roof – and was admitted to a warm, comfortable room with a blazing fire. Piles of gold pieces sat on the table.

"I found these caught in the stranger's clothes," he said, producing two coins he had pocketed earlier, in a sleight of hand no one had noticed. "Are you missing any more?"

Pargiter snatched them from him. "Good. That makes three hundred pounds exactly. It's all there." He had spoken spontaneously and then regretted it in Chaloner's presence. Chaloner wondered how much Pargiter would have left once the find had been reported to the Lord Chancellor – the Court had expensive tastes.

"Tell me about the day Margaret was buried," he said, supposing he had better make a show of investigating the stranger's death, even though he had no intention of furnishing them with answers. His work was done, and he was more than ready to change out of his filthy, wet clothes and move on to the Lord Chancellor's next assignment.

"She died in May, three years ago," replied Bretton with genuine sorrow. "But the churchyard was flooded, and she had to stay in the charnel house for two days until the water had gone down."

"So *anyone* could have shoved that fellow in her coffin," elaborated Warren. "You'll never prove his identity *or* discover what really happened – and if you try, you'll be wasting your time."

Chaloner regarded him thoughtfully. Was it wishful thinking that made him so sure?

"It is a lover," said Pargiter harshly. "Almost certainly."

"No – some felon must have hidden the victim of a robbery," argued Warren, swallowing hard. "And now I must pay my creditors." He took a step towards the door, but stopped uneasily when Francis approached Chaloner and gazed earnestly at him.

"My mother's honour is at stake here, and I want you to prove this was *not* a beau. Perhaps the fellow *was* murdered by felons, as Warren suggests. Go to the local taverns and ask known thieves whether he was one of their victims."

"That will see him killed," said Pargiter scornfully. "Let the matter lie, Fossor. I'll give you *two* shillings, if it's a love of money that makes you persist with this nonsense."

"Margaret's coffin would have been heavy with a second person inside it," said Chaloner, declining to be bribed. "Who were the pallbearers?"

Pargiter sighed irritably when he saw Chaloner was not going to do as he was told. "I was one. My children objected, since Margaret and I were estranged when she died, but I overrode them. The box *was* weighty, now you mention it."

"I was another," said Francis softly. "But I've never carried a casket before, so can't say whether it was abnormally heavy or not."

"We ordered a leaded one," explained Eleanor. Tears began to flow, and Francis put his arm around her. "We wanted her to have the best."

But the one Chaloner had uncovered had been plain wood. Had the killer removed the metal lining, so the extra weight of a second body would go undetected? It seemed likely.

"I understand a tall, stooped man visited you at Mr Pargiter's house around the time of Margaret's death," he said to Warren. "Who was he?"

Warren scowled. "I don't recall. But you're talking about things that happened three years ago, so what do you expect?"

"The visitor was a paramour, I expect," said Pargiter carelessly. "And he was there to see Margaret, not Warren. She often used such devices in an attempt to deceive me."

"That's unfair," said Eleanor, grabbing Francis's sleeve to prevent him from responding with violence. "She was desperately ill, and in no position to entertain anyone. Visit these taverns, Fossor, and talk to robbers. We should at least give this stranger a grave with his own name on it."

Chaloner promised to do his best, and took his leave, knowing there were two reasons why no robber was responsible. First, he would have stolen the gold and the silver spurs at the same time. And second, he would not have gone to the trouble of arranging the two bodies with Margaret on top. The more he thought about it, the more Chaloner became certain that the murder was connected to Margaret's family, and that someone she knew had committed the crime.

It was still raining when Chaloner headed for his home on Fetter Lane. He scrubbed the mud from his face and hands, and shoved his filthy garments in a chest that held the clothes he used for his various disguises. Then he sloshed his way to the palace at White Hall, where he was told the Lord Chancellor was with the Swedish ambassador and would not be able to see him that day. Loath to leave a written message in a place that seethed with intrigue, he decided to return the following morning, and deliver his information in person.

With nothing else to do, he walked to Cripplegate, where his friend Will Leybourn owned an untidy bookshop with cluttered shelves. Leybourn ushered him into his steamy kitchen. He wrinkled his nose in disgust when he heard what Chaloner had been doing, but became thoughtful when he learned one of the bodies had been Margaret Pargiter. As a shopkeeper, Leybourn knew a lot of people and listened to a lot of gossip.

"Margaret's affairs were common knowledge – and so were her husband's."

"Was one of her lovers Rector Bretton?"

Leybourn nodded. "He visited her regularly, long before she became ill of the fever that killed her, although Pargiter didn't know the meetings were far from pastoral. I heard she was faithful to Bretton, though, because he was special to her. So, your stranger may have been a *previous* paramour, but he certainly wouldn't have been a *current* one."

Chaloner rubbed his chin. "Well, that explains why Bretton went to such lengths to prevent her from being excavated. No wonder he was upset – it must have been a grim business for him."

"But you say *he* was the one who urged you to investigate? That should mean you could eliminate him from your list of suspects. He wouldn't demand an enquiry if he had secrets to hide."

"Not so, Will. If he'd agreed to shove both corpses back in the ground with no questions asked, it would have looked suspicious to say the least. He's a priest, supposed to uphold the law, so could hardly turn a blind eye to something so manifestly sinister – especially in front of the Lord Chancellor's spy."

"I suppose not," said Leybourn. "What a pity. I like Bretton – although he does preach the most blustering and wordy of sermons. Never go to St Martin's Ludgate on a Sunday, unless you have a good couple of hours to spare."

Chaloner showed him the charm. "I don't suppose you know anyone who might recognize this? It was around the stranger's neck. It's a black bird, perhaps a crow."

Leybourn's jaw dropped. "No, my friend, that's a raven. And Raven is the name of the man who wore it – Henry Raven. He was in your line of work – a tall, crook-backed fellow with a beaky nose."

"A spy?" asked Chaloner. "Working for whom?"

"For the government, of course. He often came to chat to me, pick my brains – just as you do. But then he stopped, and I assumed something like this had happened. You don't need me to tell you it's dangerous work. Poor Raven!"

"Could he have been one of Margaret's past lovers?"

"Never. He wasn't interested in women – or men, for that matter. Rather, he was consumed by a passionate interest in Barbadan sugar, of all odd things."

Chaloner watched the flames in the hearth, his thoughts whirling. If Raven was a government spy, then perhaps it was not the first time the Lord Chancellor had sent an agent to investigate Pargiter and Warren – and he recalled that Warren's lost fortune had been in the sugar trade. Chaloner supposed he would have to watch *he* did not suffer a fate similar to Raven's.

The notion that it was a colleague in someone else's coffin was enough to drive Chaloner back into his gravedigger costume. The nature of their work meant spies had few friends, and it was tacitly agreed that they could rely on each other to investigate any untimely ends. First, Chaloner went to see Pargiter at his mansion on Thames Street. The coat of arms over the door was picked out with gold, and there were fine woollen rugs on the floor of the hall. Chaloner, wearing clothes that still stank of death, was not permitted inside.

"I told you: I've no idea who the stranger was," snapped Pargiter, standing in a position that kept him dry and Chaloner under the dripping eaves. It was a clever way to ensure an unwanted conversation remained short.

"His name was Henry Raven," said Chaloner, watching for any sign of recognition. He saw none. "And he may have been involved in government business."

Pargiter's eyes narrowed. "How have you learned this so quickly?"

"Archbishop Juxon introduced me to a lot of people."

Pargiter stared at him, and Chaloner wished Bretton had not saddled him with quite such a prominent master. "Well, my answer remains the same. I didn't know him."

"When you hid your gold in Margaret's coffin, *where* did you put it, precisely?"

Pargiter looked angry. "Under her head, where it wouldn't be seen by anyone paying his last respects. Look, I know hiding it with her was an odd thing to do, but I was desperate and I didn't think she would object. God knows, she spent enough of my money when she was alive."

Next, Chaloner went to visit Eleanor at an address in Cheapside. She lived with Francis and his wife in a house with a roof that leaked. When he was shown into the main room, buckets littered the floor to catch the drips, and he was told to watch where he put his feet. It was a stark contrast to Pargiter's luxurious mansion, and he commented on it.

"We would never demean ourselves by accepting our father's charity," said Francis, watching his wife rock a fretful baby. "He might be rich, but his money is dirty."

"There are better things in life than gold," agreed Eleanor, smiling at Chaloner while she played with another brat next to the fire. Chaloner heard Francis's wife snort in disgust.

"We're happier here – with our leaking roof and smoking chimney – than we would be living with *him*," said Francis, glaring at her.

"But the children have no toys," snapped his wife. "They use your carpentry tools instead – a chisel is a soldier and a hammer is a dragon. And the reason these items are available for games is because *you* can't find work. Pride is all very well, but yours is affecting the welfare of your sons."

"You can always leave us and find something better, Alice," said Eleanor coolly. She turned back to Chaloner. "Our father is a selfish man, and Francis and I are better off here. It was his wicked behaviour that led our mother to seek solace in the arms of other men. He made her miserable."

"So did her lovers," said Alice tartly. "Except perhaps Bretton."

"You make it sound as though there were dozens of them," snapped Francis, turning on her. "There were not. But if that stranger was one of them, then he received his just deserts."

Chaloner raised his eyebrows. "You sound as though you're glad he died."

Francis gave an impatient sigh. "I didn't know him, but if he defiled my mother, then, yes, I am."

Eleanor came to stand next to him, resting her hand on his arm to calm him, as she had done earlier that day. "It was a long time ago, and she's at rest now. What else do you want to know, Fossor? Bretton ordered us to cooperate, and we have nothing to hide."

"Where did your mother die? Here or in your father's house?"

"The latter," replied Eleanor. "We all lived there, until she died."

"The stranger's name was Henry Raven," said Chaloner. "Someone recognized his neck-charm."

Eleanor was startled by the speed of his discovery. "Then you've succeeded, and we owe you a shilling. Do you know any more about this Raven?"

"He wasn't your mother's lover. I have it on good authority that he wasn't interested in women."

Francis gaped at him. "Are you sure?"

Chaloner nodded. "Why? Do you believe every man was a willing candidate for her affections?"

Francis was furious, and Eleanor stepped forward to prevent him from grabbing the spy by the throat. "Of course not. But you've exceeded our expectations – learning who he was *and* finding a 'good authority' who says he wasn't one of our mother's follies. You've cleared her name."

"You haven't said why he was in Margaret's coffin, though," Alice pointed out.

"We didn't ask him to do that," said Eleanor, searching in a pot for a shilling. "We only wanted to know the stranger's identity, so he can be buried in his own grave."

Francis grunted agreement. "We should let matters rest now. I don't want an ex-agent of Archbishop Juxon poking around in my family's affairs. Juxon is a creature of the Court, and—"

Suddenly, there was a piercing howl from the child by the hearth. Eleanor bent quickly to pick him up, soothing a cut finger with kisses and croons.

A petty expression crossed Alice's face. "I've warned him before about playing with that particular chisel – it's sharp – but he's just like everyone else around here. No one ever listens."

Warren's house was shabby, although it had once been fine, indicating that its owner had recently fallen on hard times. He answered his door himself, and explained sheepishly that he had no servants.

"I invested in Barbadan sugar, but there were several bad harvests in succession. Still, if I can weather this year, I may yet survive. The crops can't fail for ever."

"Did Henry Raven tell you that?" asked Chaloner. "He had an interest in sugar from Barbados."

Warren regarded him sharply. "Who?"

"The man in Margaret's coffin – as you know perfectly well. The others didn't recognize his neck-charm, but you did. I saw it in your face."

Warren closed his eyes. "Yes, that bauble belonged to Raven, although God alone knows how he got into Margaret's casket. It was nothing to do with me."

"You argued – probably about sugar investments. Did the disagreement end in violence?"

"No! There *was* no argument! He was very knowledgeable about Barbados, so I took him to Cousin Pargiter's house – not here, because I didn't want him to see the full extent of my losses – and asked his advice. He said mine was a bad venture, and recommended I withdraw while I could. I wish to God I'd listened! But I didn't kill him and I didn't put him in the coffin."

"How did you get into Pargiter's house? Does he not keep it locked?"

Warren looked furtive. "I have a key. Margaret gave it to me, a few years ago."

A short while later, Chaloner went to see the last of his witnesses. Rector Bretton was more welcoming than the others, and offered him wine and a seat by the fire. He was clearly under the impression that the liaison forced on them by the Lord Chancellor meant he was exempt from suspicion, and was surprised when Chaloner started to ask questions.

"You can refuse to answer," said Chaloner. "But the Lord Chancellor will want to know why. Everyone else has cooperated, although not always with good grace – people don't like Archbishop Juxon very much, and you should have chosen me a more popular master."

"He is a saint," said Bretton in surprise. "Who doesn't like him?"

"Margaret," prompted Chaloner, deciding he had better change the subject before he landed himself in trouble. Francis was right: Juxon *was* a creature of the Court. "Tell me about her."

Bretton stared unhappily into the flames. "All right. Yes, I was Margaret's lover. I think I was more important to her than the others, but perhaps I flatter myself. I was with her when she died."

"When was she put in her coffin?"

"The morning after her death. Francis had ordered a lead-lined box, and we put her in it together. We left it open for another day, then Pargiter and I sealed it before taking it to the charnel house. I know the others said someone could have put the stranger in at that point, but it isn't true. I stood vigil until her funeral – although I never told *them* that – and I'd have noticed anything untoward."

"The stranger was named Henry Raven," said Chaloner.

Bretton stared at him. "The tall man with the stoop? He came to see Warren around the time of Margaret's last illness, although I have no idea why. During one visit, he told us he disliked close contact with women, because he was afraid of catching the plague. He was an odd man."

"Who was the last person to visit Margaret, before the casket was closed?"

"Pargiter. He asked for a moment alone, and when I returned, he'd placed the lid across her and we nailed it down together. But this happened in Margaret's bedchamber, and unless Raven's body was hidden under the bed . . ."

Chaloner stood. "Will you summon the others? I think I know what happened now."

It was an uneasy company that gathered in Bretton's home. Warren and Pargiter claimed they were too busy for nonsense they never wanted started in the first place, and Eleanor and Francis said the investigation should have finished when Chaloner learned Raven's name. Only Bretton said nothing. The spy began his analysis.

"At first, I assumed Warren was the culprit. He recognized Raven's charm, and it was obvious they'd known each other. They discussed sugar investments, and the debate might have ended in violence. But it was Warren who asked for Margaret's grave to be opened, and he isn't so desperate for funds that he'd risk hanging for murder to claim them."

"But he was deeply unhappy about the exhumation," Bretton pointed out. "His reaction wasn't that of an innocent man."

"That's because he was one of Margaret's past lovers, too," explained Chaloner. "He said she gave him a key to the Pargiter house a few years ago – she would not have done that without good reason. And he still harbours an affection for her. He was torn between a selfish need for money and leaving her undisturbed."

Warren hung his head. "It's true – I did love Margaret. But I didn't kill Raven. Why would I? He gave me some good advice."

"Who *is* the culprit, then?" demanded Eleanor. She turned to the rector, who was regarding Warren with open-mouthed horror at the confession. "Bretton? Perhaps he was afraid Raven would take his place in my mother's heart – that he didn't come to discuss sugar with Warren, but to court *her*."

"Bretton didn't kill Raven, either," said Chaloner, cutting across the rector's spluttering denial. "He knew – from Raven himself – that the man spurned any kind of physical contact, because he was afraid of catching the plague. Thus there was no need for jealousy, and Bretton was more concerned with tending Margaret on her deathbed than in dispatching imaginary rivals."

"Well, *I* didn't do it," said Pargiter, when the others regarded him accusingly. "I didn't even know him. You say he was in my house, but I never saw him there."

"Warren invited him when you were away, hoping Raven would think the mansion was his," said Chaloner. "But Raven was killed in your house – and he was certainly stuffed in the coffin there."

"How can you know that?" demanded Pargiter in disbelief.

"Because Bretton was in constant attendance once Margaret's casket was in the charnel house. Therefore, Raven was hidden *before* you and Bretton closed the lid. At the same time, the killer removed the lead lining, to disguise the additional weight. I suppose he concealed it under the bed, or spirited it out of the house when everyone was asleep – we may never know. But although you lied about the coins, it proves you didn't kill Raven."

"I don't see how –" began Francis, while Pargiter gaped in astonishment.

"Pargiter claimed he put his bag of gold under Margaret's head," explained Chaloner. "But if that were true, he would have noticed Raven, who was already there – and he certainly would have said something. Instead of placing the coins *beneath* her, he tossed them *over* her in an act of defiance."

"I didn't –" began the goldsmith indignantly.

"You resented the amount of money Margaret spent; you said so yourself," Chaloner continued. "You hurled the gold at her, no doubt adding a taunt about her not being able to fritter it away now."

Pargiter regarded him with dislike. "I didn't anticipate that we'd have to reclaim it in the pouring rain *or* that there'd be another corpse to consider while we did so."

"And that leaves you two," said Bretton, looking at Francis and Eleanor. "Did you kill Raven and defile your mother's grave?"

Chaloner addressed Francis. "You disliked your mother's liaisons, and you loathed the men who took advantage of her. But you loved her, and you're the only one who stalwartly defends her reputation – everyone else acknowledges her indiscretions."

"Indiscretions is putting it mildly," muttered Pargiter. "She was flagrant."

Chaloner's attention was still fixed on Francis. "You said you'd never met Raven, and that's probably true. But you were so hostile to your mother's men that you were more than willing to dispose of the corpse of one of them – especially when it was to help someone else you love."

Francis licked dry lips. "This is pure fabrication. You have no proof."

"You're a man of fierce passions, who either loves or hates – there's no middle way for you. When someone told you Raven was one of your mother's beaux, you were only too happy to get rid of his body. At first, I thought you were the killer – you objected to the opening of the coffin, and you didn't agree to my investigation until Eleanor said it was a good idea. But you're a follower, not a leader, and you hid the body because you were obeying instructions."

Eleanor gazed at him, then started to laugh. "I hope you're not implying that *I* killed Raven!"

Chaloner nodded. "I *know* you did. You see, you jumped to the wrong conclusion about Raven – you *assumed* he'd come to tarnish your mother's reputation because he visited when your father was out. But poor Raven had come to discuss sugar with Warren. You killed him because *you* misjudged Margaret. By this time, she was in love with Bretton, and had forsaken all the others."

Francis rounded on Eleanor. "You said he was—" He faltered when she glowered at him.

"Eleanor told you the man she had killed was another of your mother's conquests," surmised Chaloner. "And you believed her – which is why you were startled when I mentioned that Raven wasn't interested in women. You realized then that Eleanor had stabbed an innocent man."

"But it was Francis and I who offered to pay you if you discovered Raven's identity," said Eleanor with a bemused smile. "Why would we do that, if we were the ones who'd killed him?"

"For two reasons. First, you were confident that you'd left no clues – especially ones that could be unearthed by a mere digger of graves. And second, you knew everyone would think you were innocent *because* you'd financed the investigation."

"And how did I kill Raven, exactly?" demanded Eleanor with a sneer. "A small woman against a tall, powerful man?"

"If you never met him, how do you know he was tall?" pounced Chaloner. Eleanor did not reply. "You killed him with one of Francis's carpentry tools, which he leaves lying around for his children to play with. Raven's wound was oddly shaped, and will almost certainly match the chisel – and the chisel is sharp, because his son cut himself on it today."

Rector Bretton regarded Eleanor with cold, unfriendly eyes. "Don't you remember the Latin I taught you? *Fossor* means a digger, or a man who delves. And that's what this Fossor has done – delved until he found the truth."

"I loved my mother," said Eleanor quietly. "And she was dying. I didn't want the gossips saying that she'd entertained lovers in her last hours on Earth – and Raven came to our house when Father was out, so who can blame me for thinking what I did?"

"You admit it?" cried Bretton in horror.

"No," said Pargiter sharply. "She doesn't. Fossor has no real evidence, only supposition. But if she confesses to the crime, she'll hang. Conversely, if she keeps her mouth shut, no one can prove anything. We may have had our arguments in the past, but I'll not see my daughter on a gibbet."

He went to stand next to her, gazing defiantly at Chaloner. Francis hurried to her other side, and Warren was quick to join them.

"You won't repeat what you've heard today, Bretton," said Pargiter softly. "You won't want Margaret's name dragged through the courts – nor her beloved daughter swinging on a rope. And who'll take Fossor's word over a family of wealthy goldsmiths and the King's chaplain?"

Bretton hung his head, and Chaloner knew Raven's murder would never be avenged. Pargiter was right: without a confession, there was not a jury in the country that would convict Eleanor.

The rain had abated by the following morning, and the sun glimmered faintly through thin clouds. Eleanor and her father stood side by side at the empty chasm that had been Margaret's tomb.

"Fossor came very close to discovering the real reason why I killed Raven," she said softly. "That Raven only visited Cousin Warren because he wanted to spy on our family; that his real objective was to confiscate our gold and give it to the government. Do you think Fossor will try to do the same – for whichever churchman he is working for now?"

"If he does, I'll call on your services again," replied Pargiter. "Only this time, don't ask Francis to help. He's too stupid for games of deceit, and almost gave you away."

Eleanor smiled. "But Warren played his role well. He was very convincing as the desperate debtor, and is more than satisfied with what you paid him."

Pargiter was less complacent. "What about Bretton? Do you think he was convinced by what Fossor deduced?"

Eleanor shrugged. "He seemed to be. And why not? He loved Mother very deeply, and Fossor's erroneous conclusions made it look as though I was desperate to protect her reputation as she lay dying. As far as Bretton is concerned, I'm a dutiful daughter, prepared to kill a man and hide his body to save his Margaret from ridicule and gossip."

"Well, now the spectre of a murdered government spy is truly dead and buried, you can come to live with me again," said Pargiter, placing an arm around her shoulders. "I've missed you these last three years. Francis can live in self-imposed poverty – he'll never love me as you do – but there's no longer any reason for you to endure leaking roofs and smoking chimneys."

Both jumped when someone emerged from the shelter of the churchyard yews.

"I heard you," said Bretton in a strangled voice. "You didn't murder Raven to protect Margaret's name, but to defraud the government. That's treason!"

"Rubbish," said Pargiter scornfully. "It's business. And if anyone ever claims otherwise, we shall blame the whole affair on Margaret – say she *demanded* to be buried with the gold as a way to stop the Royalists from getting at it."

"I've been such a fool," Bretton went on brokenly. "Three years ago, you paid for my roof to be mended – not out of kindness, but to pretend to your Goldsmith's company that you were a reformed man after they fined you for coin-clipping. The repairs included fine new lead drainpipes – *lead* drainpipes. You used the lining from Margaret's coffin, didn't you?"

"It seemed a pity to waste it – lead is expensive," replied Pargiter with a careless shrug. "And we could hardly sell it as it was! People have admired those drainpipes, so don't pretend you haven't enjoyed showing them off . . ."

The rector suddenly shoved Pargiter towards the grave. With a sharp cry, the goldsmith toppled inside the hole, where his head hit the remains of the coffin. He lay still. Eleanor tried to run, but Bretton grabbed her and hurled her after her father. She spat dirt from her mouth and tried to stand. Bretton struck her with a spade, and she dropped to all fours, dazed.

"I don't want Margaret associated with any more scandal – or her liaisons discussed in a way that make her sound like a whore," said Bretton brokenly. "I still love her, and I shall protect what remains of her good name. If you're dead, you can't harm her, can you?"

He gripped the shovel and began to fill in the hole.

Note

Robert Bretton was chaplain to Charles II and rector of St Martin's Ludgate. John Pargiter was a goldsmith, whom the diarist Samuel Pepys considered a "cheating rogue". Pargiter was fined several times by the Goldsmith's Company for persistently shoddy workmanship and coin clipping, and his name was removed from the list of aldermen in 1668, presumably because of his fondness for dubious practices. A merchant called Francis Pargiter also lived in London in the 1660s, although it is not known whether he and John were kin. Thomas Warren was a merchant who traded overseas.

Shortly after the Restoration of the monarchy in 1660, there were many tales of exiled Royalists returning home to retrieve hoards they had secreted years before – some found them undisturbed, others did not. One man was alleged to have chosen his wife's coffin as his hiding place, and was reputedly delighted when he excavated her and found his money just as he had left it.

THE SIXTH MAN

Bill James

The thing about Assistant Chief Constable Desmond Iles, as many knew by now, was that at funerals he could get really a bit out of proportion. This one coming up today after the crossfire killing: dicey, dicey, dicey, Harpur thought. It had big overtones and Iles loved overtones, danced and dreamed to them. Consider: a middle-aged, born-again factory worker, out ardently slipping salvation gospel tracts through people's letter boxes on his afternoon off, gets somehow in the way of a motorized turf battle between drugs firms and picks up two .38 bullets in the back. And a spread of spent bullets around, as well as those that hit him. Iles would scent chaos: this victim, born-again but dead. Did it *look* like salvation? Harpur himself scented chaos. Iles would love to sound off to folk in funeral pews a bit about chaos, and more than a bit.

As an additional element, sure to disturb the Assistant Chief, this shooting took place very close to the spot where a young, cheery, ethnic girl, rather favoured by him, had her beat, and he would fret in a very Iles style of fretting about the danger she, also, might have been in. Iles used to meet her down there on waste ground now and then, in change-every-time, by-the-hour hire cars, for anonymity. Part of Harpur's job was to know about anonymities.

At certain funerals following criminal violence, a police presence might be necessary as a public relations duty. It indicated concern and sympathy. Harpur always hated going with the ACC, whether the service happened at a church or chapel or the crematorium direct, but felt he must be handy in case some kind of restraint were needed against Iles so as to preserve reasonable calm. After all, Harpur considered it more or less obvious that funerals should have dignity, decorum. They could be ticklish events for him. Although only a Detective Chief Superintendent, he might be required to curb and lull a superior officer while eyed aghast by the congregation and minister, possibly in parts of a church that would reasonably be considered special, such as the pulpit.

Actually, "such as the pulpit" would not really do in describing these crises. If Harpur had to reach him, and apply a degree of quietening, repressive force, it would nearly *always* be because Iles had decided to bulk out the proceedings with a personal, extra sermon, and had somehow taken over the pulpit – or its equivalent in fundamentalist meeting halls. Then, at least until Harpur's intervention with muscle and/or pleas for sense, the Assistant Chief could not be persuaded out and/or silenced. Now and then at tragic funerals he would weep thoroughly; weep blatantly and noisily before he gave an address. Today's was unquestionably a tragic funeral. There'd been bloodied tracts on the pavement. Sometimes during these episodes, Iles would slander the Home Secretary for the national state of things leading to the death, or the Prime Minister, or the Trinity, or his mother and aunts, or school attendance officers, or all of the above, or permutations. Often he slandered himself and, of course, Harpur. Generally, these onslaughts came over impressively via a pulpit microphone and amplifying system. Failing these, Iles bayed.

Naturally, he would try to fight off Harpur, or anyone else who turned physical in an attempt to suppress him: say, a vicar, if he/she thought Iles's behaviour had become too wild. The ACC was not big, but possessed craftiness and knew head-butting well from way back in his career. Always, it had seemed especially unkempt to Harpur for someone to head-butt in a place of worship, whether he, Harpur, was on the end of it, or somebody else. Against anyone who opposed or attacked him,

Iles could summon an abnormal weight of momentary but true loathing, especially against Harpur, on account not just of immediate irritation, but that past chapter with the ACC's wife. These reserves of hatred seemed to help increase Iles's hideous strength and, more often than not, gave his lips true froth during tussles. He usually went to funerals in full dress uniform, and that made him additionally ferocious, unhinged and malevolent, as though convinced he should live up to the high-grade cloth, Queen's Police Medal ribbon, superb black lace-ups and insignia of his rank.

This funeral, then, Harpur considered could be one of the worst: one of the worst, that is, from the Iles aspect. Harpur guessed that, to describe the death, Iles would have been rehearsing some of his favourite terms, such as "symbolic", "ironic" and "encapsulates", for any pastoral chat he might choose to offer. If he turned to abuse of one or several or all of his targets, the words might be "slimy", "smug", "somnolent", "supine". Yesterday, Harpur suggested to him – hopelessly – that it would be wise, in view of the extraordinary tensions, to send someone of lower rank to represent them – for instance, Chief Inspector Francis Garland. "How about thinking of it for once from *my* angle, sir," Harpur had said.

"Which angle would that be, then, Col?"

"Well, it could be stressful. If you become – I mean, I might have to do another grapple, and—"

"My soul's involved here, Harpur," Iles replied.

"That's what I'm getting at, sir."

"What?"

"The buzz will be around."

"Which buzz is that, then, Col?"

"Re your soul, sir," Harpur said. "People will tell one another: 'This funeral: another Mr Iles soul session.'"

"I do try not to make too much of it – my soul. Showiness one abhors. Performances one detests."

"But people already know you can be very souly, sir. You're famed for it. Probably it's on your Personnel dossier. 'Deeply souly.' People will realise you're likely to become uncontrollably moved . . . well . . . even berserked by the funeral, so we'll get an enormous crowd there, sightseers, not just mourners, gawking in case you put on one of your perf . . . in case your soul takes over again in that tremendous way it has. The shouting, the arc of armpit sweat, the alliteration."

"I must go," Iles replied. "*We* must go." They had talked in the ACC's suite at headquarters. Harpur occupied a leather armchair. Iles paced. He liked to concentrate on nimbleness. There was a long wall-mirror near the door for him to check his appearance in civvies or uniform before going out. Harpur noticed Iles kept his eyes away from that now, though, which must signal he had bad feelings again about how his Adam's apple looked. The ACC regarded his Adam's apple as part of a skilfully focused, foul genetic joke against him. He had on one of his navy blazers, plus narrow-cut, dark grey flannel trousers to do his legs justice, and what might be a rugby club tie. He said: "This funeral demands me, Col. My presence. Well, our."

"I—"

"Unignorable, Col. This death, this pyre – unignorable."

"I—"

"Oh, you'll reply, 'It was merely someone accidentally peppered in a gang spat.'"

"Well, no, I don't think I would ever . . . I see nothing 'merely' about any death, sir. It's just that, perhaps as far as the funeral goes, we—"

"People, Col. You mentioned *people*."

"Is that OK?"

"People in relation to my soul."

"Very much so."

"They're an interesting entity, Harpur."

"Who?"

"People."

"Absolutely sir, but—"

"Yes, it's a fact, Col. Out there, where they immemorially are, people do seem fascinated by me."

"Patent, sir."

"Many would like an, as it were, glance *into* my soul."

"I've heard more than one express this longing," Harpur said.

"How many more?"

"Or a desire to know you in what they call 'the round'. They wonder what you're like 'in the round'."

"It's something I by no means understand."

"What, sir?" Harpur replied.

"This . . . well, yes, I don't think this exaggerates . . . this fascination."

"That's because of your astonishing flair for self-effacement and—"

"Much less do I actually *seek* their fascination, Col."

"Few would accuse you of that, sir."

"Which fucking few, Harpur?" The ACC stared from this third-floor window down on to passers-by in the street, as though some of that disgusting few might be there, conspiring. In a while he turned back: "Let me ask: what was that poor sod doing when wiped out, Col?"

"This has been thoroughly covered in the reports, sir."

"I know, I know. You see it's symbolic, do you, Harpur?"

"Symbolic?"

"You spot the irony?"

"Irony, sir?"

"These are terms that always confuse your struggling little mind, don't they? But I certainly absolve you of blame for this. I think of that bloody nothing school you went to."

"Someone was shot," Harpur replied.

"Let me ask again: what was this poor sod doing when wiped out?"

"Religious tract deliveries on Valencia Esplanade and in the side streets."

"Exactly, Col. And that is surely why we must be at the funeral. This death – I have described it as symbolic. Yes, I think so. This death – I have described it as ironic, painfully ironic. Yes, I think so. Doesn't it tell of our times, Harpur? Yes, tell of our dismal, sickening times. A man, Walter Rainsford Lonton, devotedly, pro-actively taking religion to house-holders, blasted suddenly by thugs. Anarchy? Hellishness? Barbarism triumphant? Forgive me, do, Col, but here's another one you may have heard me use before and been baffled by – 'encapsulates?' It's a word. You'll find it in the dictionary. For me, this shooting *encapsulates* appalling social decline, moral decline. It's happening everywhere, Harpur, accelerating."

Symbolic. Ironic. Encapsulates. Yes, Harpur feared these perennial insights would almost certainly pop up if Iles went into his standard mode at the funeral and splurged some bounteous, thudding, possibly actionable, bum oratory. Iles liked fixing a worldwide significance to limited local incidents and crises. It could be a tic taken from the former Chief Constable, Mark Lane, who'd always feared universal disintegration might begin on his patch from some seemingly limited local incident and crisis. A doorstepping, part-time missionary holed by two .38 bullets in the back would constitute such a seemingly limited local incident and crisis. Iles saw endless ramifications. Perhaps all officers who made it to Staff College had this habit of bumper-size thinking banged into them. Iles used to mock Mark Lane for his dreads. Now, though, the ACC seemed to echo them.

"But then again, I don't suppose you suffer much anxiety about social decline, moral decline, Harpur," Iles said. His voice shifted upwards towards an agony scream or screech-owl cry. Harpur took a few steps across the room and checked the door had been properly closed. This was routine when Iles seemed on his way to a reminiscence interlude. Headquarters staff would hang about the corridor outside Iles's suite if they knew he was talking privately to Harpur, in case they could eavesdrop one of the Assistant Chief's fits. Iles said: "Social decline, moral decline – they couldn't have mattered much to you when giving one to my wife in bed-bug hotels, vehicles – including possibly even official police vehicles – and, I wouldn't be surprised, on industrial canal tow-paths."

"How's your nice leggy friend down Valencia Esplanade, sir?" Harpur replied.

"Honorée? Troubled. A kind of superstition has crept in. Fears the Esplanade area's jinxed. She likes to work other sites since the shooting."

"We think we've got several decent leads on the people involved, sir," Harpur replied. "Some locals, some not."

"My faith in you is total, Col." the Assistant Chief said.

"Thank you, sir."

"As to the job, I mean, Harpur."

In fact, Iles behaved with great and sustained sweetness at the funeral. For Harpur, the proceedings turned out significant, not on account of any outbursts by the ACC, but because suddenly, from behind, someone, a male, muttered, very close to Harpur's ear, "I guessed you and Ilesy would be here, so took a chance. Number Three. Ten tonight."

This was at the very end. The coffin had left for the crem and a general shifting about among the congregation began as people edged from their seats towards the aisles, making for the door. The place was as crowded as Harpur had expected, so this dispersal took a while. Harpur did not turn to see the man who'd whispered. Unnecessary. And it might have been unwise. Of course, he recognized the voice. Although it stayed low, and had to compete with an organ finale, Harpur knew who'd spoken to him in the throng. And, of course, he understood the message.

Iles had, indeed, given an address, but by invitation, and he made it short and heartfelt. Today, in Harpur's opinion, the Assistant Chief could be regarded by almost anyone fair-minded as virtually decent and stable, even an asset, regardless of previous form at such functions. Iles referred to the "terrible symbolic impact" and "grim, searing irony" of Lonton's death. But he ditched "encapsulates". This, after all, was a Gospel Hall service, and the congregation mainly ordinary people whose education might have been as ramshackle as Harpur's. Iles, gazing out upon them, taking their tone, probably realized that "encapsulates" would sound fruity here. Iles could be surprisingly sensitive if you had time to wait.

Gospel Halls ran without clergy or ministers, and the funeral was conducted by a gruff, middle-aged man in a black jacket and silver pinstriped trousers. After he had preached from the platform about Lonton and his certainty of heaven, he asked if anyone else wished to say something. Iles hesitated. It astonished Harpur, but he detected a definite, as if modest, reluctance: perhaps Iles recognized the salt-of-the-earth qualities in this congregation and would not impose on it any of his mad monkeying and egomaniac slobber: witness, later, that editing out of "encapsulates". The simplicity, plainness, unpretentiousness of Gospel Halls might be new to him. Not to Harpur: he'd been sent to Sunday School at one as a child. He remembered emulsion-painted walls similar to these, adorned only with large-letter Bible verses.

The ACC went forward eventually and climbed on to the platform. He'd brought with him a couple of Lonton's tracts, mud-stained from the pavement and blood-flecked. Iles held them up for a time, and then read aloud the text from their front page: "It is appointed unto men once to die and after this the judgement." Iles nodded. "Harpur will do what he can about the judgement." Afterwards, the Assistant Chief remained up near the top end of the Hall until everything finished, and then talked there for a while with some of the family.

Back home, Harpur found his two daughters had watched television news coverage of the cortège. "Some of them at school say police can't keep the streets safe any longer," Hazel told him.

"Who at school?" Harpur replied.

"You want names? You want me to fink?"

"I mean, pupils or staff?" Harpur said.

"Which would worry you more?" Hazel replied.

"Neither. They'd both be wrong," he said.

"My friends say it," Hazel replied.

"Staff as well, I expect," Harpur said.

"I hate it when people say rotten things about you, Dad," Jill told him.

"I've heard worse," Harpur replied.

"Dad, listen, I think you ought to pack something," Jill said.

"We don't talk like that," Harpur said.

"Like what?" Jill asked.

" 'Pack something', of course," Hazel said. "Do you know how dim you sound, a thirteen-year-old, with words pinched from cop dramas – corny, ancient, reshown TV cop dramas?"

"I think Dad should have a gun," Jill said. "OK? What do the all-wise and wonderful fifteen-year-old and her all-wise and wonderful friends feel about that, then?"

"*Have* you lost control of the streets, Dad? Valencia Esplanade is 'No Go?' " Hazel asked.

"Of course he hasn't lost control of the streets,' Jill bellowed at her, half about to cry. "Or he wouldn't if he packed something. It's obvious. I think he should look after himself. You should look after yourself, Dad. People blasting from cars. What could you do? What could this poor Holy Joe do? He'd got some bits of paper. What's the use of them?"

"You sound like the US gun lobby: bang-bangs for everyone," Hazel said.

"Not for everybody. For Dad."

"I have to go out later," Harpur replied. "I might be late. Lock up properly and turn in." He single-parented since Megan's terrible death, and found it a strain sometimes.

"Go out where?" Hazel said.

"Work," Harpur replied.

"Is it?" Hazel asked.

"Yes," Harpur said.

"Of course it is," Jill said.

"What work?" Hazel asked.

She liked to keep track of his morals. "Routine," Harpur said.

"Is this a one-to-one with a grass, for example?" Jill said.

"Routine," Harpur replied.

"You ought to pack something," Jill said.

"And we don't call them grasses," Harpur said. Of course, everyone *did* call them grasses, but the term seemed wrong from a child. "Informants, Jill."

"What's the difference?" she asked. "Informants grass, don't they, the same as grasses grass? Wasn't there a song – 'Why Do You Whisper Green Grass?' "

"No police force could run without informants," Harpur said. "They are valuable and often brave people."

"I didn't say they weren't, did I? I only said they grass."

" 'Grass' makes them sound contemptible," Harpur said.

"So?" Jill replied.

And, yes, it *was* for a one-to-one with an informant that Harpur left them at about 9.30 p.m., perhaps the greatest grass Harpur had ever met. Perhaps the greatest grass any detective had ever met. When Harpur did meet him, it had to be in reliable secrecy. Grasses could lose limbs for grassing, could get killed for grassing. Among villains, grassing rated as easily the greatest villainy, maybe the *only* villainy. Harpur made for an old concrete block house on the foreshore, built during the war to help throw the Germans back into the sea if they ever tried it on, and still standing. Harpur reached it just before ten o'clock. Jack Lamb was already there. Lamb seemed to like this spot best of their carefully varied rendezvous points, their Number Three, as he'd called it at the funeral.

It was dark, and darker inside the windowless block house. An occasional flash of moon poked through a loophole when the clouds cleared for a few minutes. Jack had on what might be a cavalry officer's "bum-freezer" greatcoat, designed for when cavalry meant horses, not tanks, and cut deliberately short, like a riding jacket. Jack stood six foot five and weighed over two hundred and fifty pounds, so there was a lot of bum to freeze. He also wore a green Commando beret, with some large badge on it, which Harpur could not identify in the darkness. Whenever they came to Three, Lamb liked to wear army surplus clobber, in keeping. In each hand tonight he carried a brown briefcase, perhaps also once military. These cases looked well-filled, as if he would soon be off to brief Eisenhower for D-Day. Jack put both on the filthy concrete floor, opened them and brought out six automatic pistols, which he laid alongside one another on the leather. Harpur thought they might be 9 mm Walthers.

"As to the Walter Rainsford Lonton aftermath, you'll need these, Col," he said. "You've got to pack something."

"I keep getting told that."

"Because it's right. Who by?"

"It's well intentioned," Harpur replied.

"Of course it's well intentioned. Tooling up – vital at this stage."

"That right, Jack? Which stage?"

"You've got to recruit a little private army – you and if poss five others."

"That right, Jack?"

"I don't want a big mob of police."

"Where don't you want a big mob of police?" Harpur said.

"Just you and a nice, capable, small team. And in such clandestine circumstances, you won't be able to draw official police weapons, will you?"

"Hardly."

"So, I supply. They're all loaded, of course."

"Of course."

"Fifteen-round magazine," Lamb said. "Good firepower."

"Yes, I know."

"At one time, the police used Walthers, I think."

"Some are still around," Harpur replied.

"Reliable. Stoppers."

Lamb, like some other informants, *most* other informants, went in for an amount of mystification when they presented their stuff. They let the material out slowly, perhaps to make it seem more, and so qualify for bigger cash; perhaps just as a playful, theatrical exercise by creating suspense and curiosity. With Jack, it would be the second. He did not have to worry about money. But he did enjoy acknowledgement and admiration. By puzzling Harpur and then gradually making things clear for him, Jack must feel he'd come over as abnormally bright and kindly. And it was true, he *was* abnormally bright, despite the beret. Even kindly.

Jack Lamb now did as he usually did and crouched for a while at one of the rifle apertures, gazing at what he could see of the sea, ready to take on anything Mr Hitler could chuck at him.

"What Lonton aftermath?" Harpur said.

"You know what happened there, do you?" Jack said. He abandoned his sentinel stint and came and stood over the pistols.

"He took two stray bullets," Harpur said. "Walter Rainsford Lonton had God on his side, most likely, but not luck."

"Somebody in one of the cars mistook him and panicked."

"Mistook him for what?"

"There were two cars," Lamb replied.

"That we know. Four people."

"It was to be a simple but ample deal. One car brought packets of substance – a lot of packets. The other brought cash, a lot of cash. There should have been a swap. Yes, simple, but also, as you'd expect, very nervy, very excitable. These are people who live with two-timing and rough tricks."

Ritualistically and uselessly, Harpur would always ask Jack where his information came from. Ritualistically Jack, like any other purposeful whisperer, always ignored this. Sources stayed secret, or next time there would be no sources. There might be no Jack, either, if he ever disclosed too much, or anything, about those who disclosed to him. When Jack told you something you'd better believe it, and you'd better be content with that. "Who've you been in touch with, Jack?"

"On the day, one of them in one of the cars, or perhaps more than one and in both cars, sees Lonton flitting between houses and assumes he's some sort of look-out and is alerting hit squads standing by behind a couple of front doors to dash out at the crux moment and hijack everything – substance and cash. Anyway, somebody opens fire on Lonton . . ."

"So *not* accidental, not just trapped in crossfire?" Harpur said.

"They open fire deliberately on him, and would have on anyone else who appeared from the houses, if anyone had, which, as we know, nobody did, because Lonton was a total innocent. The noise of firing convinces some of the others they're being attacked – that an attempted snatch of the substances or cash is under way – so, of course, they retaliate. But as far as I've discovered, neither car has injuries."

"I don't know," Harpur said.

"Both cars finally pull away. Only Lonton is left."

"So who, Jack? In the cars."

"No names, or you'll go and pick them up now and charges might not stick. I want them done as they are doing what they do. They'll come back. They won't let a botch muck up their trade, not trade of this scale."

"I—"

"Look, Col, I only give tip-offs when I think people have acted with real vileness and disregard. I'm not a mouth for mouthing's sake."

"Absolutely." Harpur had listened often to Jack's gospel of grassing. It was important for Lamb to feel all right about what he did. No money went to him for his help, but neither did Harpur ever ask too much about the rich art business Jack ran. That's how the arrangement worked, and overall it worked well.

"I consider it monstrous to knock over an amateur apostle on his divine rounds," Jack said. "All right, an error, but people so jumpy shouldn't be out with guns. So jumpy they can't even hit one other."

"They hit Lonton."

"I wonder how many shots it took. Did you recover other bullets?

"A quantity," Harpur said.

"A ton?"

"We're still searching."

"This kind of cruel, blast-off craziness – I see it as a symptom of something rotten nationally, Col. And it deteriorates."

"Mr Iles says that."

"There you are, then."

"He can get things right sometimes," Harpur replied.

"Yes, they'll come back," Jack said.

"The buyers and sellers?"

"That's part of their brazenness, part of the general rottenness. This is commerce, Col. This is gorgeous livelihoods, Col. A bit of a shoot-out, a mistaken shoot-out, can't be allowed to stop the free flow of merchandise – dirty merchandise, but merchandise. Yes, they'll come back, not to that particular bit of ground, obviously. But I can point you the right way."

"How the hell do you know this, Jack?"

"You, plus trusted pals – pals able to handle a Walther – will be waiting. Not a full-scale swarm operation, please. Now, *please*. Leaks can happen when too many are in the know. The business would be called off. And they'd guess how police came to find out about the new plans, the new site. How? Me. Too perilous, Col. You and your picked group can certainly manage them."

"How many?"

"Probably four again, two in each car. You'll outnumber. You'll have surprise."

"I hope."

"A big BMW. A big Volvo. These are a switch from previously. They're not going to risk the same transport, are they, especially as their previous cars might be damaged? But I've got registration numbers for you. Can you call on some good, discreet boys?" He put an encouraging, huge palm on Harpur's shoulder: "But of course you can, Col."

"Francis Garland as a start. Yes, I'll be all right."

"And as long as you scoop them all up—"

"—it won't matter if they work out who sold them," Harpur said.

"I don't like 'sold'."

"Sorry. Let's amend: It won't matter if they work out who *scuppered* them," Harpur replied.

"Because they won't be around to do anything about it."

"You want the Walthers back afterwards?" Harpur asked.

"Not if they've been used. Police can prove all sorts from a used gun. But you probably know that already."

As it would turn out, only one of the Walthers was eventually used, and, a little later than eventually, Harpur committed that

to the river. He returned the rest to Jack at a subsequent short
and joyful debriefing session at Number Three.

Harpur had found he could recruit four helpers, including
Garland, not five. The pool to draw on was small. He wanted
good marksmen ready to believe they'd be passably safe, regardless: passably safe, regardless, from the crews they had to
stalk; and passably safe, regardless, from superior ranks after
running an uncleared shooting romp. Harpur considered that to
convince four in the circumstances might be good going.
Luckily, so luckily, one of them was Garland's sergeant, Vic
Callinicos, an esteemed marvel with handguns. In the swoop,
when it came he fired ahead twice from out of the passenger
window of a Citroën moving fast over uneven ground after shots
aimed at them from the Volvo and the BMW. Their shots
missed. Vic's didn't.

Harpur's interception platoon were in the Citroën and a
Ford, both unmarked. They'd waited and watched in the dark,
unnoticeable among a string of parked cars on the road bordering a public open sports field. This had been specified by Lamb
at the block house as the new transaction site. A Vauxhall and a
Peugeot already stood at one end of the field, probably immaterial. Harpur thought they could be love buggies: a soccer
ground in the day, nooky at night. Jack had said to expect the
target cars between ten thirty p.m. and eleven. At ten fifty, the
Volvo, its registration spot-on, arrived and waited. It was at a
distance, but near enough for them to hear that the driver kept
its engine running. At two minutes to eleven the BMW came to
a stop by the Volvo.

In the Citroën, Harpur said, "We go now." He drove, with
Vic Callinicos alongside him. Harpur took the car up over the
kerb and pavement and on to the grass. The Ford with Garland
in charge followed. They had fix-on blue lamps and got them
going at once. Garland also carried a loudspeaker in the Ford
and began yelling: "Armed Police, Armed Police, get out with
your hands up." Despite this din and the cars' engine roar,
Harpur heard shots from the BMW and Volvo, and heard Vic
Callinicos's reply. He saw the driver of the BMW pitch forward
against the windscreen and the man in the Volvo passenger seat
lurch to his right. In a minute the Citroën had reached the
BMW and Harpur braked and jumped out. He had a Walther in

each jacket pocket and produced one of them now, and started howling the "Armed Police" advertisement himself. You could valve off some of the fear that way. He was on the driver's side of the BMW, its window down. With his free hand, he was about to pull the door open when the man in the passenger seat leaned across behind the body of the driver and blurted: "All right, all right. Here," and threw a Browning pistol out through the window. When Harpur did open the door, the driver's body tumbled on to the field and covered the Browning. Harpur got a grip on the front passenger's arm and dragged him out. Harpur did not recognize either of them: a supply firm from away, most likely. The packages were very neatly laid out right the way across the back seat. As Jack had said, a lot.

At the Volvo, too, resistance stalled, though the engine kept going. Vic could not only shoot, he could identify the right ones to shoot to neutralize an enemy. When Harpur went to that car, he found he did know these men, the alive and the dead: Karl Dane, arrested, and Joshua Tive-Amory, both local, both very small small-timers until now. So, perhaps Lamb's and Iles's joint theory of a fast-widening threat stood up. Garland hand-cuffed the two survivors to the BMW steering wheel while a money search of their clothes and the Volvo went on. Dane said: "Who the fuck sold us then, Mr Harpur?"

"*Sold* you?" Harpur said.

"You had us surrounded, didn't you. Four fucking cars here to swamp us. Major planning. Who sold us?"

"Just two, the Ford and the Citroën," Harpur said. "All we needed for such a soft job. The other two cars are not ours. A bit of rudimentary guesswork told us you'd be back."

"I don't believe it," Dane said.

"You'd better believe it," Harpur replied. And he decided, then, that he ought to make sure the people in those original two parked cars were all right. Salvoes had flown tonight, who knew where? The Vauxhall moved off fast as Harpur approached. Somebody, or some pair, or even some trio, hetero perhaps, homo perhaps, mixed perhaps, didn't wish to get sucked into this scene. He memorized the registration all the same, in case they'd do as witnesses.

In the back seat of the second, the Peugeot, he now recog-nized Iles and his friend Honorée, efficiently getting themselves back into presentable shape. Iles lowered a window and said: "Perhaps I mentioned previously, Col, that Honorée wanted a change of location following the Lonton business. Well, I'm not sure this *is* better, after all, are you? I think we took a shot through the driver's door and into the upholstery. One might have been sitting there, you know, Harpur."

"Probably you're a back seat person in fields, sir."

"How about you give me the Walther, Harpur?" Iles replied. "It will look to the rest of them as if I'd been duly notified of this operation – and I should, should, and *should*, have been duly notified of this operation, holding the position, as you'll recall, of Assistant Chief (Operations) – and so, having, we'll imagine, been notified of it, decided to contribute in a personal, armed capacity. That would make the illicitness of this more or less all right, I feel. And the car hirer can then charge headquarters for the bullet trouble to his car."

"The illicitness of what, sir?" Harpur replied. "You mean you and Honorée having a—"

"Let's go and chat to the baddies and their captors, shall we, Col?" Iles left the car and he and Harpur walked towards the BMW and the Volvo. Iles paused, and Harpur paused with him. The ACC said: "Sly and eternal thicko, when I call it illicit, I mean, of course, you running a damn secret, unapproved, cordite campaign in which I might have got my balls shot off. But fortunately, now this has become an official police victory, with the Assistant Chief a participant. I think we can swing that. It's why I wanted your Walther. Authenticity. But, all right, if you object, I'll—"

"I have a spare Walther, sir."

"There we are then," Iles replied.

Harpur gave him the pistol intended by Jack for the sixth man. Iles would do as the sixth man. "It has to be handed back later."

"Handed back to whom?" Iles said.

"Will Honorée disappear while we're over here, sir, with the task force, prisoners and deads? That the idea? She can sneak away to the road and a cab?"

"Disappear? Of course she won't disappear, Col. This is a fine and precious girl. This is plainly a girl I brought with me as cover. If you're masquerading as an *amour* car for the purpose of ambush, you need to have a girl with you, don't you, Harpur? She's like a theatrical prop, isn't she? It's called verisimilitude. You'll find that one in the dictionary, too."

"I hadn't thought of cover as an explanation for her, sir."

"Don't get despondent. I can think for both of us, Col. It's a habit."

"I haven't had time to congratulate you on the funeral, sir. You were very measured, if I may say."

"I think you may. I appreciated the setting. I loved that wall text."

"Which?"

"The main one," Iles replied.

" 'Without shedding of blood is no remission,' " Harpur said.

PROVENANCE

Robert Barnard

Leonid noticed the man when he was on his way to put a new label
on a Manet picture on the third floor. The picture was due to be
packed and taken away for exhibition in Lyons. The Hermitage,
since the collapse of Communism, was readier to lend its treasures for special events such as the Lyons Manet show: sometimes
they accepted loans in return, in lieu of payment, but mostly they
insisted on payment, preferably in dollars. After all, they had
more than enough pictures of their own.

The man Leonid noticed was dressed in a T-shirt and
sneakers and was walking up the Grand Staircase, looking
neither to left or right. The gilded curlicues decorating the
walls, the gods on cloud nine on the ceiling, the sturdy grey
pillars with thickly encrusted gilt at their feet went unregarded
by him. Leonid had never seen, or never noticed, him before,
but as he gained the second floor he showed no hesitation in
setting off in the direction of the Large Hermitage. The Grand
Staircase could rarely have had so summary a dismissal. The
man acted as if he knew the palace too well to notice it, but
Leonid felt sure he did not. He knew where he was going
because he was well prepared. Leonid shook his head and went
about his business.

A quarter of an hour later he descended from the French
Impressionists and found himself among the Dutch paintings in

the Large Hermitage. Perhaps curiosity about the man had something to do with his destination. Certainly he walked around without apparent goal until he spotted him in front of one of the Rembrandts which were the pride of the Hermitage collection, a jewel even among the palace's three million items. Leonid stood back and watched. The man put his face close to the bilingual label under the picture, then moved on. It could have been a picture by a teenage art student for all he cared. The next picture he stopped at, by a lesser figure, was considered, evaluated, taken in. Then the man put his head down again close to the label. A second or two later he straightened, a satisfied expression on his face.

He took out a little notebook, then wrote something in it, checking what he wrote against the label under the picture.

When the man had moved out of sight, Leonid went over to the picture, though he knew the description by heart. It was "Spring Landscape" by Cuyp, and it had been acquired by the Hermitage from the Yusupov Collection in 1922.

Leonid was more than intrigued. He was professionally interested. When a Spanish touring group swarmed into the gallery, surrounding a harsh-voiced woman holding a little banner aloft, he joined them as they went to one of the great Rembrandts. Leonid's quarry had been standing in front of it, but now he moved smartly aside to one of the small pictures hung beside it. Leonid became part of the Spanish group and managed to get the place beside the man with the notebook. In that little book there was a list, ending with the landscape by Cuyp, but headed by two intriguing entries. Leonid saw:

Renoir: Portrait of Mme. Bercy. Acquired from the Spaskov Collection, 1921.

Picasso: Young Girl With Parasol. Acquired from the Berisov-Vernet Collection, 1924.

So he had already done the twenty or thirty rooms on the top floor devoted to the French Impressionists and the moderns. Why had they provided him with so few entries for his notebook?

A possible answer floated into Leonid's mind, and his heart sank.

He turned his attention to the Rembrandt now being described by the Spanish-speaking guide. It was a painting imprinted on his heart and brain down to the last casual brush-stroke. He tried to estimate the guide's expertise by the number of words he recognised: Amsterdam, Franz Hals, Saskia, National Gallery. Leonid had no foreign language beyond a rather halting English. When the Spanish group moved on to the next preselected high spot the man he was interested in was gone. Leonid went down the central aisle of the Dutch galleries, looking in every alcove, but the man was nowhere to be seen.

Leonid was troubled. Life had been so easy in the later years of Communist rule, when he had first come to work at the Hermitage. Then he had had a clearly defined specialist area (preservation) in which he worked. He was not thanked if he let his interest stray to any other area, where he would only be trespassing on someone else's special preserve.

Now it was all so different. True, his salary was now once again (Putin be praised!) paid regularly, but so much more was now expected of him. He was *required* to have an interest in the whole spectrum of the gallery's possessions and activities–conservation, display, inter-gallery loans, the education programme, the shop and other commercial enterprises, PR . . . It was all very bewildering. They even had staff meetings, which ranged over these and myriad other topics. It was possible to make an awful fool of oneself at these meetings, and though Leonid was not aware that he had done that, he did feel he had not shone. How could he shine? He was the product of a different age. How could he talk confidently about the commercial exploitability of a Cuyp landscape or Gauguin's South Sea Island girls?

On his way back to his office on the ground floor he struck lucky. He was just passing the main cafeteria when he heard an American voice and, turning, he saw the object of his interest. He was standing at the coffee counter expostulating with the woman behind it.

"Chocolate! CHOCOLATE! I always have chocolate with a cappuccino."

The woman, one of Leonid's own generation, shrugged. Then, an idea striking her, she grabbed a small bar of chocolate from the display case, slapped it down on the counter, and held out her hand for the money.

Leonid slipped ahead of the tourists, nodded to the woman, and was given his usual minute but powerful coffee.

"You mind if I sit here?" he asked his prey, sitting alone at a table, his red T-shirt, Leonid now saw, bearing the legend KANSAS – WHAT A STATE WE'RE IN! The slogan puzzled Leonid. It seemed to have two meanings. Was it a Western-style joke? The man grunted at him and looked disgustedly at his cup.

"Freakin' natives," he muttered. "Wouldn't know a cappuccino from a milkshake."

"We like our coffee very strong, and just a little," said Leonid apologetically. The man seemed surprised to encounter a Russian in Russia. Then an idea seemed to strike him.

"Waterworks problem?" he asked.

"No. Is just how we like it," said Leonid. The man grunted again. Leonid looked around the cafeteria.

"It's getting crowded already," he said in English. "With the tourist season starting. I don't mean to offend. We in St Petersburg are very glad to see you."

The man's face twisted into something that was a sort of amusement.

"I'm no tourist. I'm here on business."

"Oh really? Something in the art world?"

"No way. All that crap just passes me by. I'm a lawyer."

Leonid's heart sank.

"Oh really? I noticed you as I passed through the Rembrandt Gallery. You're very thorough. That must be legal training."

"I like to double-check everything. That's not easy when half the labels on the pictures are in Russian."

"That's for the Russian visitors."

"Well, it doesn't help. How can I be sure that the English is a true translation?"

"The Russian is likely to be more accurate. It is a very subtle and precise language." With a faint idea of directing the visitor to other attractions he went on: "We have a church in St Petersburg dedicated to St Cyril, who gave us the Cyrillic alphabet."

"You should have thrown it back in his face," said the man, biting into an iced bun. "You're loaded down with a language no one but Balkan people can understand. I don't get it at all. Some of the letters are the same as ours. Some of them seem the same but turn out to be something different. Some of them are printed backwards. And some of them are way off the beaten track, never known as letters elsewhere. St Cyril did you no favours."

"Are you a linguist, then?"

"A linguist? What's he when he's at home? I told you, I'm a lawyer."

"I thought in your spare time."

"I don't have spare time. I'm interested in the background of this collection, where the things came from, who owned them before."

Leonid began to sweat.

"Why should you be interested in that?"

"Well, after 'Where did it come from?' I ask myself '*Should* it have come from there?' Was it legally acquired, and legally lodged in the museum that holds it? Or was it a five-dime government seizing what it had no right to?"

Leonid said in a flat voice: "So you are interested in provenance?"

"Providence? No way. Never give it a thought. I'm interested in seeing justice done. Financial justice."

"*Provenance*," said Leonid, his voice still emotionless. "The history of the piece, who has owned it in the past, how it has passed from one person to another. As one hears the history of a house or a palace."

"Right. Spot on. You're on the ball. One of the few people in this godforsaken country who is."

Fearing he was going to be the object of further attempts to spread international goodwill. Leonid downed his potent brew and – feeling rather daring – said, "Have a good day" and left the café.

But though he had left behind the brash American, the man stayed with him for the rest of the morning. He was interested in provenance, even if he didn't understand the word. Interested in whence the Hermitage had acquired the pictures it displayed. Mostly that question was quite easily answered. They had been bought by Catherine the Great or her predecessors or successors on the Imperial throne. Or indeed by her Communist successors in the 'twenties, who had acquired many of the Impressionists or twentieth-century paintings in a straightforward manner, buying them in the international market.

Which was why there were few entries from that massive collection on the third floor. They had been disapproved of and hidden away in the decades of Soviet realism, but they had been bought in the early years of the Revolution, when experiment was respectable, and now they were hung in all their glory with their provenance neatly detailed on the label.

In fact, *all* the pictures had their provenances neatly detailed. Had that been a bad mistake? Because though the upper galleries had yielded meagre results for the American lawyer, he was getting much more food for thought from the Dutch rooms. The Russian aristocrats of the nineteenth and twentieth centuries had not been in the vanguard of artistic progress: They had not bought the French Impressionists or Picasso – by and large they had probably thought them artistic frauds and impostors. Some Russians had collected them, though – specialists – and their pictures had been acquired, probably at knockdown prices, in the normal way.

The aristocrats, though, had preferred Dutch landscapes, Flemish portraits, church scenes, domestic vignettes. Also Spanish street scenes, English ladies in silks, Italian classical episodes. When the Yank (Leonid had lots of other words for Americans, and political correctness was a concept quite unknown in the new Russia) had finished with the Low Countries, fertile fields still lay ahead of him.

What had the foreign gangster said?

"A five-dime government seizing what it had no right to."

And what he had been looking for, Leonid felt quite certain, was pictures acquired during the twenties from the estates of aristocrats – probably all in exile. People whose descendants were still around, most often in the U.S.A., and anxious to reclaim what they still regarded as theirs.

Leonid was a product of the Age of Brezhnev, whose first name had been given him. He was not sorry that Communism had collapsed, but he was quite pleased it had existed. Many good things had happened in those seventy years, he felt: some because of the system, some by circumventing or questioning the system. Since its fall, Leonid had noted all over Eastern Europe the old families coming back, claiming their ancestral homes and acres, their royal status. The King of Bulgaria had been given back his palaces, and then had magnanimously given one of them back to the Bulgarian people. And then had graciously consented to become their Prime Minister. It was a better world, the larger part of Leonid's brain told him. But there was still a tiny part of it that told him that the world – *his* world – had gone mad.

What the imperialist gangster was doing, Leonid was quite sure, was identifying pictures that had been confiscated from the old aristocratic families in the early years of Bolshevik rule, so that they could claim them back in a court of law or receive their value today. Millions and millions of dollars! Billions of roubles! The idea was fantastic, repulsive! These pictures belonged to the Russian people.

He began once again prowling around *his* art gallery. He had no doubt it was the greatest in the world. He looked at his favourites, and at many pictures he had hardly noticed before but now felt he loved, because they were threatened.

What was to be done? Change the labels, for a start. There was no reason why a gallery should trumpet how its treasures had been acquired. But his heart sank. Even in brave new Russia everything took time.

Decisions were made, then passed up the hierarchy before they could be acted upon. Relabelling the collection was no more than a cosmetic change, but it would take months. No, years.

"Not now, I'm busy," he said when, his office attained, his secretary had thrust letters, requisitions, permits to sign into his hands.

But she noticed before five minutes were out that "busy" meant that he was thinking. He sat, slumped forward, his head in his hands.

He had had no impression from their talk that this man was part of a team, or a larger enterprise. On the contrary, aside from his knowledge of the layout of the Hermitage, he seemed to have come poorly prepared. A familiarity with the Cyrillic alphabet would surely have been a sensible piece of preparation, and so would a broad conspectus as to how the collection had been amassed over the centuries. This man seemed to be learning on his feet, coming from a zero position.

A maverick, then. Getting together a file of pictures that could have been confiscated in the early days of the Revolution from the estates of prominent noblemen no longer resident in their native country. Possibly his preparation had been to discover which of the main important families who escaped had descendants living in the States – men and women who could be approached with a view to representing them in a lawsuit. Leonid had heard of the expression "ambulance chaser" for rapacious lawyers eager to profit from accidents. The only stretchers involved in this kind of profiteering were the ones on which the canvases were once prepared. This was a piece of speculative moneymaking of the most blatant kind, and it threatened the collections of all the most important galleries in Eastern Europe.

Time. That was what was needed. Time. Time to prepare for the threat. To prepare in minor ways, like labels which said nothing about the provenance of the paintings. But, more important, preparing government for the threat, perhaps so it could pass special legislation, retrospective legislation, legalising the state's takeover of the property of émigré nobles decades before, and giving it democratic respectability.

He thought of how he would make these suggestions at next week's staff meeting, and what a furore his revelations about the threat to the collection would make.

Time . . . A maverick speculator working on his own.

He got up from his desk and, brushing aside his secretary, again went back into the body of the museum.

So many people. Crowds milling to and fro, almost like a revolution in the making. A people's uprising, an assertion of ownership in the great artworks of all countries and centuries that had found their home in the Hermitage. He wandered around the ground floor – the shops, the cafeteria, the children's assembly area, the cloakrooms. A city in itself.

And there he was again.

Walking purposefully towards the cafe again, but five minutes away from it, potbelly thrust forward, the legend KANSAS – WHAT A STATE WE'RE IN blazoned across the chest of his red T-shirt. His eyes were staring from left to right. Looking for somebody? An accomplice?

No, looking for a lavatory. Suddenly he swerved aside and went into the Gentleman's just outside Room 99.

Leonid waited, loosening his belt – the only weapon he had. Then he went into the small convenience and bolted the door, as the cleaner always did when she was at work inside. Then he disappeared into one of the cubicles.

The Yank was into serious business. Eventually, after sounds that made Leonid feel quite queasy, paper was torn, a flush was pulled, a door unlocked, and The Threat was out into the main part of the lavatory and running water into the basin. Leonid went out.

"Hi! You're the guy I was talking to in the cafe, aren't you?"

"That's right."

"Hey, I got an idea after you left. You're one of the gang – guys, I mean, who run this place, aren't you?"

His hands were all soapy, and he put his head down towards the water – Leonid noticed for the first time how nasty he found the little moustache, reminiscent of the last great threat to the Hermitage collection in 1941 – and washed his fat cheeks.

"Er – yes, I am."

"Seems to me we could be useful to each other. What I need is information, background, maybe classified stuff. I could pay well – in dollars, of course. Always in dollars."

He'd at least learnt *some*thing about the new Russia, Leonid thought.

"So what do you say? Mutually advantageous, that's what it would be. Is it a deal?"

He was tugging down the paper towel. Leonid slipped his belt from round his waist, quickly slipped it around the man's neck, and tightened it around his throat.

"No," he said. "No, I won't. No."

So much time it took! And so much strength. The capitalist pirate at least made a struggle of it, his face going first red and then purple, his eyes popping, his wet soapy hands flailing. At last, when Leonid's own face was red with the struggle, the man started to fail, the movements became feebler, and finally his body slumped down onto the tiled floor. For a minute or two Leonid held the belt tight around his neck, resisting the temptation to pull up his trousers, which were around his ankles. At last he straightened up, and secured them with his belt.

He looked around him. The Threat's cubicle, smelly and dirty, was the place to put him. He picked him up by his

shoulders, dragged him in, and shut the door. He couldn't lock
it, but he pushed the feet well inside. Then he went and looked
at himself in the mirror. Quite presentable, really. Quite normal. He slipped back the bolt on the door and went out into the
thronged, pulsating gallery.

He was too excited to go straight back to the office. He must
go around the great artistic domain that he had saved. He
walked with his head high, his heart throbbing with pride.
He was on cloud nine with the gods on the Grand Staircase, and
he knew it. Never had he been so prompt in decision, so
effective in action. He felt like God himself, almost like the
Museum Director.

So taken up was he with his new status as the man who saved
the Hermitage that he did not notice in the Spanish Gallery the
man with the off-white T-shirt with the barely legible slogan
which read KERRY TO WIN. Or the man in the French
seventeenth-century gallery in the green T-shirt with the slogan
which read HANG NELSON MANDELA. Both were peering
closely at the labels under the pictures, and both were clutching
small notebooks and ballpoint pens. Both were purposeful,
efficient, and smiling.

JADE SKIRT

Simon Levack

My mistress was concerned about her water supply.

This may seem an odd preoccupation for an Aztec. After all, our city, Mexico, was built on an island in a freshwater lake and was riddled with canals, one of which ran past my mistress's house. However you had only to think of all the rubbish and other things that were tipped into them by the city's thousands of households to know why the water we drank always came from springs. Some of these were within the city itself; but the city had long since outgrown them, and now the most important source was on the hill of Chapultepec, across the water on the western shore of the lake.

Years ago – before I was born – the rulers of Mexico had built a great aqueduct whose two stone channels linked Chapultepec to the city. Most households got their fresh water from men who filled their jars from the aqueduct near the point where it entered the city and carried them by canoe through the city's network of canals direct to our doors. They were paid in bags of cocoa beans and most Aztecs scarcely reckoned the cost, being happy to be spared the daily chore of fetching their own water. Merchants, however, took worldly wealth more seriously than most of us. My mistress – Tiger Lily, the lady to whom I was bound technically as a slave, although in reality our relationship was a good deal more complex than that – was a merchant. This all had something to do with why I was standing in one of the aqueduct's channels – the southern one, currently empty and closed for cleaning – with evil-smelling muck oozing between my toes and a fetid stench filling my nostrils.

"It's free water for two years, Yaotl," Lily had explained. "Just for standing around and watching a ceremony, and you can't claim you haven't done worse before. Not to mention the fact that you drink the water too."

"I know," I admitted. "It still seems like an odd request, though. What can I tell a water seller that he can't see for himself?"

Blue Feather, whose canoe brought a full jar to Lily's house every day, had asked her for my services for a day. The newly cleaned and reopened northern channel of the aqueduct was to be rededicated to the water-goddess, Lady Jade Skirt, and I was to watch the ceremony. I was to take careful note of every aspect of the proceedings, even down to precisely where the priest stood while he made his sacrifices – Blue Feather had been most particular about this.

My mistress's face, framed in a mass of dark, silver-streaked hair, wore a frown whose meaning I could catch better than anyone. She obviously thought my assignment strange too. "Does it matter?" she asked eventually. "He can't be there because he's got to make a sacrifice at Jade Skirt's temple, but he wants to be sure every detail of the ceremony at the aqueduct is right. And you have to admit you're a better person to observe something like this than most – after all, you used to be a priest."

That much was true although, as I stood in the slime watching Jade Skirt's devotee going through the ritual, I was still puzzled. This ceremony was not much like the bloody sacrifices of men and quails I had been used to when I had served in the temples.

The goddess's priest balanced precariously at the edge of the full channel. "Oh, Lady of the Jade Skirt!" he cawed in a harsh, deep voice, "Oh, Goddess of the rivers and springs, accept this, our unworthy gift!" And so saying he tossed the object in his hands into the water at his feet.

It made a soft "plop" and vanished from sight.

The Goddess had received many gifts that morning, each of them accompanied by the same self-abasing formula. Some had been humble enough: tortillas, ears of maize, drinking vessels, a ladle full of burning incense; but the priest had saved the best till last, and the offering he had just made had been splendid: a small gold statuette of the goddess with glittering emeralds for eyes. It had been paid for by the water-sellers. A small crowd of them stood around, some with the priest on the edge of the water-channel, others looking up from the empty conduit next to it. Their canoes jammed the canal running beneath us under the aqueduct. Others, including Blue Feather, were at the goddess's temple, where more offerings would be made.

It was the southern channel's turn in the regular maintenance schedule, which is why it was empty of water. I stood in it among the rest of the water-sellers and the other spectators, waiting silently for the ceremony to end and fervently wishing I were somewhere else. A fine drizzle had begun to fall. It plastered the priest's already long, lank hair to his pitch-stained temples and made his black cloak hang limply around him, and made me feel more miserable than ever.

"It always seems like a terrible waste to me," someone nearby remarked.

"A waste of time, certainly," I muttered. Then I peered around at the speaker. He had a plain, undyed cloak and the tonsured hair of a man who had never captured an enemy warrior in battle: the lowliest of commoners. I wondered whether he was one of the water sellers, but when he caught my eye he told me otherwise.

"I know what you mean." He spoke quietly, for fear of upsetting our neighbours, although they were all huddled and shivering in their cloaks and probably longing to be elsewhere too. "But we have to do it, don't we? My parish provided the work detail that cleaned out that half of the aqueduct, you see, so we have to be here."

"Cleaning these channels must be a nasty job," I remarked sympathetically. One of the quirks of slavery among Aztecs was that it freed a man from many of the onerous duties that ordinary commoners were subject to, such as taking part in public works whenever the Emperor or his officials demanded it. The only person I had to obey was my mistress. So I had no first-hand knowledge of the kind of labour that cleaning the

aqueduct or shoring up the sides of a canal or whitewashing a
palace might involve.

"Oh, it's all right, unless you have a problem with filth, stink
and a back that feels like you'll never be able to straighten it
again." The other man grinned. "Of course with this particular
job we always live in hopes – if you see what I mean. Never
comes to anything, mind you. Like I said, it's a terrible waste."

I frowned. "I don't follow."

"Stuff like that gold statue," he explained patiently. "And all
the other jewels and things that get thrown in the water as
offerings to the goddess. You'd think, wouldn't you, that some
of that would come up when we're scooping all the muck out of
the bottom? Never happens, though." He sighed regretfully.
"A man could live for years on just one find like that, but I
suppose the goddess can't spare it! All we ever get is the
rubbish. She doesn't seem so interested in the clay bowls
and tobacco tubes. Funny, that, isn't it?"

Eventually, the priest gabbled his way to the end of the ritual.
It concluded with a sacrifice of his own blood, drawn from his
earlobe with an obsidian razor and sprinkled on the water's
surface.

By the time I had returned home, Blue Feather was already
there, passing the time of day in Lily's courtyard and clearly
itching to be told exactly what I had seen. He was all polite
attention as I gave my account, but he might as well have been
asleep, since he immediately asked me to repeat it.

After he had left Lily and I agreed that we still could not
understand what he was about. Still, as Lily pointed out, that
was up to him, provided she still got her water.

She was less sanguine the next morning, when she found out
that her water-seller had vanished. And naturally it became my
job to find him.

"I was looking for him in the marketplace," she explained,
"to get our agreement witnessed. But he wasn't at his usual
place, by the canal, and no one could tell me where he was. Go
and see if he's ill, or something."

This was the start of a frustrating morning. Lily told me
where he lived, and that part was easy enough. It was a typical
Aztec house, two rooms opening onto a small square of

courtyard, fronting a canal just broad enough for a two-man canoe.

I had to skirt a small pile of trash piled against one side of the house. It looked like the usual rubbish – ash from the hearth, broken shells of turkey eggs, maize husks, and so on – and I would normally not have spared it a glance, but I was surprised to see a hollow cane, the sort used as a smoking tube. This puzzled me because tobacco was expensive, imported from the hot lowlands for priests and lords; I could not understand what it would be doing in a humble water-seller's house.

The water-seller's wife was home: a weary-looking woman, fine boned and grey haired, whose patched and frayed blouse and skirt made the idea of her husband taking his ease with a pipe even more incongruous.

She received me politely, inviting me to squat in her court-yard and offering me food, as good manners required. It was a piece of a slightly stale tortilla which I had no hesitation in declining.

She had little to tell me. "He went out last night and didn't come back."

I waited for her to add something to that, but the silence merely dragged on. Eventually I said: "He didn't say why?"

"No."

"Was he in the habit of going out at night?" Few Aztecs were. The night was widely feared: it was ruled by spirits, creatures out of dreams and fateful beasts such as owls and weasels whose appearance could foretell a man's death. Only those trained to overcome such things, such as priests and sorcerers, usually went out after dark, unless there were some very good reason.

"No, he wasn't. That's why I'm worried." The woman did not sound especially worried to me. In fact she was downright curt, considering I was trying to find her missing husband. It was almost as if she resented my questions.

"Is there anyone else at home?" I asked. "Anyone who might know where he went?"

She hesitated for long time, her eyes in her lap. I suspected she was trying to think of a reason not to answer me, but at last she said: "My son. I don't think he'll help you, though. He's probably down by the aqueduct, filling his jars."

*   *   *

Blue Feather's son was called Cloud Eagle. He was a tall, burly young man of about twenty, his muscles developed by years of hauling heavy jars about. I found him at one of the water-sellers' favourite places for filling up, close to where the previous day's ceremony had taken place. Cloud Eagle was in a canoe on a broad waterway at the point where it ran beneath the aqueduct's twin channels. He was standing upright and trying to keep his craft steady using a long wooden pole jammed into the canal's bottom, while an older man poured water down towards him using a large clay jug. Unfortunately the boat kept moving, and while some of the water went where it was supposed to, tumbling into open jars with a hollow rattle, much of it ended up in the bottom of the boat, over the younger man's head, or in the canal.

"Hold that thing still, can't you?" cried the man on the edge of the aqueduct.

"I'm doing my best!" his colleague protested. He was sweating, his muscles straining with the effort of keeping the canoe where it was supposed to be. He was clearly not accustomed to this particular task and, from where I stood, it looked as though he was making a mess of it.

"Cloud Eagle?" I called out from the bank.

"Yes," snapped the youngster. "What do you want?"

"Sorry to distract you, but . . ."

The man on the aqueduct threw his jug down in disgust: it dropped straight into the canal, missing the canoe by a hand's breadth. The young man in the boat sat down heavily.

"Sorry," I said again, "but it's about your father . . ."

With a sigh he got up and took up his pole again, using it to push the boat towards me. "All right. I'm coming. Don't think I can help you, though."

From above my head a voice snarled: "Keep it short. We've still got a living to make!"

Cloud Eagle did not get out of the boat. He was taller than I so, although the bank was raised a little above the water's surface, we were almost eye-to-eye.

"My cousin lent me this boat," he explained, indicating with a glance over his shoulder that his cousin was the elder man still glowering down at us. "He said he'd help me until Father comes back . . . or at least until we find his canoe."

I felt my eyebrows lift. "Your father took his boat with him?"
That was curious. His wife had not mentioned this. It was odd
enough for a man to wander off by night for no apparent reason,
but where could he possibly want to go that would mean he
needed his canoe? It suggested he had not merely felt the urge to
go behind the wicker screen hiding the nearest public latrine,
and maybe fallen in a canal on the way. He had had some
purpose in mind, one that meant travelling farther than he could
easily walk.

"Yes, he seems to have done. I hope the boat comes back . . . I
mean, I hope he comes back, of course, but there's no way we
could afford to replace the canoe. In the meantime, Flint Knife up
there has let us use his, and he agreed to help me fill the jars, just
for today." The lad grimaced. "I should have suggested we do it
the other way around. I'm usually the one scooping water out of
the aqueduct and pouring it out, while Father holds the boat
steady. I hadn't realized his part of the job was so difficult!"

I looked at the jars surrounding him in the boat. None was
more than half full. "I expect you're right and you can't help,
but have you any idea at all where your father might have gone?
Or if he was, well, up to anything – well, you know what I
mean . . ."

"I know," said the young man sadly. "Anything he wouldn't
want my mother to know about, you mean? No, I don't think so.
If there was anything like that he didn't share the secret with
me."

I sighed. I was going to have to go back to Lily with nothing
to report, but I could think of nothing more to ask. "All right,
thanks. If he does appear, let him know that Tiger Lily wants to
see him, won't you?"

As I turned away, and Cloud Eagle picked up his pole again, a
thought struck me. "How are you going to carry on now that
jug's gone in the water?" I asked curiously.

"Oh, that happens all the time." He laughed. "I'll just dive
down and get it again. We've lost it in deeper water than this
before! It's only waist-high here; that's one of the reasons we
use this spot."

Lily was, as I had anticipated, not particularly pleased at my
failure, and the prospect of her two years' free deliveries

vanished somewhere beyond the city limits, but she was even less pleased the next morning.

"I don't believe it!" The words, uttered in her shrillest voice echoed around the courtyard of her house. "Both of them gone, now?"

The bearer of the news was none other than Flint Knife: Cloud Eagle's cousin.

"That man owes me a good deal," Lily was saying, "and if you're telling me his son's gone missing as well . . ."

"What happened?" I asked Flint Knife. "And why are you here?"

The man was almost as angry as Lily. His face was a peculiar purple colour. "How should I know what happened? All I know is, when I went to fetch my boat this morning, it wasn't there. I though my cousin might have borrowed it so I went to his house. But his mother told me he'd vanished in the night – just like his father before him! I came here because I knew you'd been looking for Blue Feather and you spoke to his son yesterday – I thought you might have some idea where he might have gone." The man breathed heavily, and added: "I need that boat, you understand? It's all very well helping out a relative in trouble, but I have to have it back, or else how am I supposed to live?"

The pitiful note in his voice did not impress Lily. "I don't understand what made you think we could help. I've got enough troubles of my own – what?"

Her last word was snarled at me, because I had just cleared my throat. "I don't know," I said. "Maybe we can help, after all." I turned to the water seller. "Just one question, though. When you spoke to Blue Feather's wife this morning, did she seem upset at all?"

He stared at me incredulously. "What, a woman who's just had both her husband and her son vanish into thin air?" He paused, frowning. "Actually, now you come to think of it, she didn't seem all that concerned. She didn't look as if she'd been up all night crying, anyway."

"What are you thinking, Yaotl?" my mistress demanded.

I glanced up at the sky. It was cloudy, but I sensed that the sun had not yet climbed very high. "It may not be too late," I muttered to myself. "If he waited until dawn . . . And he would, he might not find the place in the dark . . ." I looked at my mistress. "We'll have to go now, though," I said. "In fact if we can run, so much the better!"

I was to regret my suggestion four hundred times over before we had come to the water-seller's house. As a former priest I had been trained to endure pain and exhaustion, by the endless round of fasts, ritual self-mortifications and vigils that our rites demanded, but that had been many years before. By the time we reached our objective my lungs felt as though they had been seared by hot smoke and my legs were twitching and threatening to double up under me. Flint Knife looked and sounded worse than I was. Lily, who had kept pace with us with her skirts gathered about her knees, seemed, surprisingly, a little better, although in truth for the last part of the journey we had all more or less slowed to a brisk walk. All the same, as soon as the little house hove into sight I realized we had got there in time.

We all paused for a moment, panting. It was Cloud Eagle's uncle who was the first to utter words, staggering two further, exhausting steps towards the canoe moored by the house. "That's . . . my . . . boat!" he gasped incredulously.

"Yes," I muttered, starting forward myself. "And there's your nephew, and look what he's holding under his arm! Stop!"

The young man wasted only a moment staring at me and my exhausted and desperate-looking companions. Then he leapt straight into his canoe, the object still cradled under his arm, and seized a paddle with his free hand. At the same time his mother appeared from the house, screeched once and ran along the bank towards us.

Cloud Eagle managed one-handed to get the boat to move. It did not get very far. Flint Knife let out an angry howl and jumped into the waist-deep water in front of it, waving his arms wildly. The canal was too narrow for the vessel to pass, and Cloud Eagle could not get enough speed up to run his cousin down. He bellowed in frustration, lashing the water with his paddle. Then he raised it to strike at Flint Knife, which was when I drew level with the canoe, jumped in and wrested the trophy from the crook of his arm.

At the same time Lily raced past me to confront Cloud Eagle's mother. Recalling the words they used to each other still makes me blush. It took Cloud Eagle's despairing voice to call an end to the brawl. "It's all right, Mother," he moaned, tossing the paddle into the canal. "It's no good. They're on to us. They've got it now."

There was barely room for all of us to squat or kneel in the courtyard of Blue Feather's house. The water-seller's wife – widow, I reminded myself – did not offer us anything to eat. She stood in the corner and glared at us.

I set the thing I had taken from her son on the hard earth in front of me. The goddess Jade Skirt's emerald eyes gleamed into mine, sparkling as if with mirth. Well, I thought, nobody ever claimed the gods had no sense of humour.

"Well, now I've got my boat back, I'll be off," Flint Knife said.

"Not so fast!" snapped Lily. "I still want to know what happened, and where's Blue Feather?" When no one else answered she turned to me. "Yaotl?"

"In the lake, near where the aqueduct enters the city, I should think." I looked at his son. "But I don't think he'll be coming back from there, will he?"

The lad said nothing.

"You'd better explain," Lily said.

"It's easy enough. You remember how the water-seller wanted me to describe the ceremony at the aqueduct in detail – even down to things like exactly where the priest was standing when he threw the idol in the water? He claimed it was because he wanted to make sure it was all done right, but of course that was nonsense. Why should it matter to him? He's just an ordinary trader, and not a very successful one at that, judging by the state of this place." The grey-haired woman hissed reproachfully. "Which reminds me – I noticed tobacco tubes in the trash heap outside, and couldn't think what they were doing in such a poor household.

"I didn't work out what was happening when the old man vanished, but when we heard his son had disappeared too, it was suddenly obvious. They were after this statue – or at least the gold and jewels in it. This is what I think happened. Both Blue Feather and Cloud Eagle went out the other night, in Blue Feather's canoe. They knew where the statue was, thanks to my description. However they were a bit wary of just going straight to the place to fish it out, because it was inside the city and someone might see what they were up to. So instead, they took their boat to the point near the shore of the island, where the aqueduct first enters the city. Cloud Eagle here climbed up to the aqueduct and made his way along it. I'm not sure how deep it is when it's full, but I suppose he used one of those tobacco tubes to breathe through.

"He would have had to grope around under the water for a while, but he obviously found what he was looking for. Then he made his way back and threw the statue down to his father in the boat."

A groan from the young man told me I had got it right. "That's where it went wrong, isn't it?" I said. "Because Blue Feather didn't catch it – and being solid gold, it went through the bottom of the boat, straight into the lake. And by the time Cloud Eagle here realized what had happened, the boat and his father had both vanished."

Lily gasped. Even Flint Knife muttered something under his breath that may have been an expression of shock. Cloud Eagle looked at the ground. Only his mother was impassive.

"And that's it, really. The young man had to go home and tell his mother what had happened. She knew about the plot all along, of course – she could hardly fail too, with both of them out overnight – and they agreed that he should go back the next night and try to retrieve the statue from where it had sunk. He's a good diver – unlike his father, alas! Blue Feather and the boat will still be there, of course." Even if Cloud Eagle could have retrieved the body, I knew he would not: the drowned were sacred to the Rain God and only priests could touch them. "They must be in the lake – someone would have noticed them in a canal."

There was a long silence, which Lily eventually broke. "So, I'm not going to get my free water." She sounded philosophical enough about it. "What do we do with these, though?" she asked, indicating our unwilling hosts. Aztecs rarely went out at night, except with good reason; but Lily and I had a good reason. Besides, I had been a priest, and knew how to fight any demons we might encounter. And we had the gods on our side, I thought, as I extended a hand to help my mistress up to the edge of the aqueduct; one of the gods, at least.

"Amazing, the risks some people will take," I mused, as I gazed for the last time into Lady Jade Skirt's glittering green eyes.

"What, us perching here, you mean?"

"No, I mean fooling around with the gods, the way that water seller was prepared to do, and for what? For something he could sell in the marketplace."

We had not reported Cloud Eagle and his mother to the authorities. Losing Blue Feather and the boat had seemed punishment enough.

I smiled, and after a brief glance at my mistress, tossed the gold statue back into the water, where it belonged.

I watched it sink with a twinge of fear. What if it were looted a second time? What about all the other precious things that were tossed into the water and, as the workman had told me, never seen again? What if, in the end, the goddess never got anything but the kind of rubbish the labourers found when they dredged the aqueduct?

If that were the case, I thought, then we had better get used to drinking lake water, after all.

THE FERRYMAN'S
BEAUTIFUL DAUGHTER

Peter Robinson

The strangers came to live on the island at the beginning of summer, 1969, and by the end of August my best friend Mary Jane was dead. The townsfolk blamed the Newcomers and their heathen ways, but I was certain it was something else. Not something new, but something old and powerful that had festered in the town for years, or perhaps had always been there.

I remember the morning they arrived. We were all in chapel. It was stifling hot because the windows were closed and there was no air-conditioning. "Stop fidgeting and listen to the Preacher," hissed Mother. I tried my best, but his words made no sense to me. Flecks of spittle flew from his mouth like when water touches hot oil in a frying pan. Something about Judgment Day, when the dead would rise incorruptible.

Next to me, Mary Jane was looking down at her shoes trying to hold back her laughter. I could see the muscles tightening around her lips and jaw. If we started giggling now we were done for. The Preacher didn't like laughter. It made him angry. He finally gave her one of his laser-like looks, and that seemed to settle her down. He'd never liked Mary Jane since she refused to attend his special instruction evening classes. She told me that when he had asked her, he had put his face so close to hers that she had been able to smell the bourbon on his breath, and she was sure she had seen the outline of his thing pushing hard against his pants. She also said she had seen him touching Betsy Goodall where he shouldn't have been touching her, but when we asked Betsy she blushed and denied everything. What else could she have done? Who would have believed her? In those days, as perhaps even now, small, isolated communities like ours kept their nasty little secrets to themselves.

Across the aisle, Riley McCorkindale kept glancing sideways at Mary Jane when he thought she couldn't see him. Riley was sweet on her, but she gave him a terrible run-around. I thought he was quite nice, but he *was* very shy and he seemed too young for us, no matter how tall and burly he was. Besides, he was always chewing gum and we thought that looked common. We were very sophisticated young ladies. And you have to understand that Mary Jane was very beautiful, not gawky and plain like me, with golden hair, delicate soft skin and the biggest, bluest eyes you have ever seen.

At last the service ended and we ran out into the summer sunshine. Our parents lingered to shake hands with neighbors and talk to the Preacher, of course. They were old enough to know that you weren't supposed to seem in too much of a hurry to leave God's house. But Mary Jane and I were only fifteen, sophisticated as we were, and everybody knew that meant trouble. Especially when they said we were too old for our own good. "Precocious" was the word they used most often to describe us. I looked it up.

And that was when we saw the Newcomers. I think Mary Jane noticed them first because I remember seeing her expression change from laughter to wonder as I followed her gaze to the old school bus pulling into the parking lot. It wasn't yellow, but was painted all colors, great swirls and blobs and sunbursts of green, red, purple, orange, black and blue, like nothing we'd ever seen before. And the people! We didn't own a television set in our house, but I'd seen pictures in magazines tourists left on the ferry sometimes, and I'd even read in Father's newspaper about how they took drugs, listened to strange, distorted loud music and held large gatherings outside the cities, where they indulged in unspeakable practices. But I had never seen any of them in the flesh before.

They certainly did look odd, the girls in loose dresses of pretty, flowered patterns, the men with their long hair over their shoulders or tied back in ponytails, wearing Mexican-style ponchos and bell-bottom jeans and cowboy boots, the children scruffy, dirty and long-haired, running wild. They looked at us without much curiosity as they boarded the ferryboat carrying their few belongings. I suppose they'd seen plenty of people who looked like us before, and who looked at them the way we must have done. Even Riley, who had clearly been plucking up the courage to come over and say hello to Mary Jane before his ferry left, had stopped dead in his tracks, mouth gaping open. I could see the piece of gum lying there on his tongue like a misplaced tonsil.

Once the Newcomers had all boarded the ferry, the regulars got on. There was no chapel on the island. Only about thirty people lived there, and not all of them were religious. The Preacher said that was because most of them were intellectuals and thought they knew better than the SCRIPTURES. Anyway, the ones who weren't businessmen, like Riley's father, taught at the university in the city, about forty miles away, and commuted. They left their cars in the big parking lot next to the harbor because there were no roads on the island.

Just because we had the ferry, it didn't make our little town an important place; it was simply the best natural harbor closest to Pine Island. We had a general store, a rundown hotel with a Chinese restaurant attached, the chapel, and an old one-room schoolhouse for the children. The high school was fifteen miles away in Logan, the nearest large town, and Mary Jane and I had to take the bus. The sign read "Jasmine Cove, Pop. 2,321" and I'd guess that was close enough to the truth, though I don't think they could have counted Mary Jessop's new baby because she only gave birth the day before the Newcomers arrived.

Over the next few days, we found out a little more about the Newcomers. They were from inland, a thousand miles away, according to Lenny, who ran the general store. There were about nine of them in all, including the children, and they'd bought the land fair and square from the government and had all the right papers and permissions. They kept to themselves and didn't like outsiders. They shunned the rest of society – that's the word Lenny used, "shunned", I looked it up – and planned to live off the land, growing vegetables. They didn't eat meat or fish.

According to Lenny, they didn't go to chapel. He said they worshipped the devil and danced naked and sacrificed children and animals, but Mary Jane and I didn't believe him. Lenny had a habit of getting carried away with himself when it came to new ideas. Like the Preacher, he thought the world was going to hell in a hand basket and almost everything he saw and heard proved him right, especially if it had anything to do with young people.

That day, as we wandered out of the general store onto Main Street, Mary Jane turned to me, smiled sweetly and said, "Grace, why don't we take a little ferry ride tomorrow and find out about the Newcomers for ourselves?"

Mary Jane's father, Mr Kiernan, was the ferryman, and in summer, when we were on holiday from school, he let us ride for free whenever we wanted. Sometimes I even went by myself. Pine Island wasn't very big – about two miles long and maybe half a mile wide – but it had some very beautiful areas. I loved the western beach best of all, a lonely stretch of golden sand at the bottom of steep, forbidding cliffs. Mary Jane and I knew a secret path down, and we spent many hours exploring the caves and rock pools, or lounging about on the beach talking about life and things. Sometimes I went there alone when I felt blue, and it always made me feel better.

Most of the inhabitants of Pine Island lived in a small community of wood-structure houses nestled around the harbor on the east coast, but the Newcomers had bought property at the southern tip, where two abandoned log cabins had been falling to ruin there as long as anyone could remember. Someone said they'd once been used by hunters, but there was nothing left to hunt on Pine Island any more.

We saw the Newcomers in town from time to time, when they came to buy provisions at Lenny's store. Sometimes one or two of them would drive the school bus to Logan for things they couldn't find here. They were buying drugs there, and seeds to grow marijuana, which made folk crazy, so Lenny said. Perhaps they were.

Certainly the Preacher found many new subjects for his long sermons after the arrival of the Newcomers – including, to the dismay of some members of his congregation, the evils of tobacco and alcohol – but whether word of his rantings ever got back to them, and whether they cared if it did, we never knew.

The Preacher was in his element. He told us the Newcomers were nothing other than demons escaped from hell. He even told Mr Kiernan that he should have nothing to do with them and that he shouldn't use God's ferryboat to transport demons. Mr Kiernan explained that he worked for the ferry company, which was based in the city, not for the Preacher, and that it was his job to transport anyone who paid the fare to or from Pine Island. The Preacher argued that the money didn't matter, that there was a "higher authority", and the ferry company was as bad as the Newcomers; they were all servants of Beelzebub and Mammon and any other horrible demon names he could think of. In the end, Mr Kiernan gave up arguing and simply carried on doing his job.

One bright and beautiful day in July around the time when men first set foot on the moon, Mary Jane and I set off on our own exploratory mission. Mr Kiernan stood at the wheel, for all the world looking as proud and stiff as if he were piloting *Apollo 11* itself. We weren't going to the moon, of course, but we might as well have been. It was only later, in university, that I read *The Tempest*, but had I known it then, Miranda's words would surely have echoed in my mind's ear: "O brave new world that hath such people in it!"

The little ferry didn't have any fancy restaurants or shops or anything, just a canvas-covered area with hard wooden benches and dirty plastic windows, where you could shelter from the rain – which we got a lot of in our part of the world – and get a cup of hot coffee from the machine, if it was working. Through fair and foul Mr Kiernan stood at the wheel, cap at a jaunty angle, pipe clamped in his mouth. Some of the locals made fun of him behind his back and called him Popeye. They thought we hadn't heard them, but we had. I thought it was cruel, but Mary Jane didn't seem to care. Our town was full of little cruelties, like the way the Youlden kids made fun of Gary Mapplin because there was something wrong with his spine and he had to go around in a wheelchair, his head lolling on his shoulders as if it were on a spring. Sometimes it seemed to me that everywhere Mary Jane and I went in Jasmine Cove, people gave us dirty looks, and we knew that if we spoke back or anything, they'd report us to our parents. Mr Kiernan was all right – he went very easy on Mary Jane – but my father was a bit of tyrant, and I had to watch what I said around him.

Riley McCorkindale was hanging around the ferry dock, as usual, fishing off the small rickety pier with some friends. I don't think they ever caught anything. He blushed when Mary Jane and I walked by giggling, and said hello. I could feel his eyes following us as we headed for the path south through the woods. He must have known where we were going; it didn't lead anywhere else.

Soon we'd left the harbor and its small community behind us and were deep in the woods. It was cooler there, and the sunlight filtered pale green through the shimmering leaves. Little animals skittered through the dry underbrush, and once a large bird exploded out of a tree and startled us both so much our hearts began to pound. We could hear the waves crashing on the shore in the distance, to the west, but all around us it was peaceful and quiet.

Finally, from a short distance ahead, we heard music. It was like nothing I'd ever heard before, and there was an ethereal beauty about it, drifting on the sweet summer air as if it belonged there.

Then we reached a clearing and could see the log cabins. Three children were playing horseshoes, and someone was taking a shower in a ramshackle wooden box rigged up with some sort of overhead sieve. The music was coming from inside one of the cabins. You can imagine the absolute shock and surprise on our faces when the shower door opened and out walked a young man naked as the day he was born.

We gawped, I'm sure. I had certainly never seen a naked man before, not even a photograph of one, but Mary Jane said she once saw her brother playing with himself when he thought she was out. We looked at one another and swallowed. "Let's wait," Mary Jane whispered. "We don't want them to think we've been spying."

And we waited. Five, ten minutes went by. Nothing much happened. The children continued their game and no-one else entered the shower. Finally, Mary Jane and I took deep breaths, left the cover of the woods and walked into the clearing.

"Hello," I called, aware of the tremor in my voice. "Hello. Is anybody home?"

The children stopped their game and stared at us. One of them, a little girl, I think, with long dark curls, ran inside the nearest cabin. A few moments later a young man stepped out. Probably only three or four years older than us, he had a slight, wispy blonde beard and beautiful silky long hair, still damp, falling over his shoulders. It was the same man we had seen getting out of the shower, and I'm sure we both blushed. He looked a little puzzled and suspicious. And why not? After all, I don't think anyone else from Jasmine Cove had been out to welcome them.

Mary Jane seemed suddenly struck dumb, whether by the man's good looks or the memory of his nakedness I don't know, and it was left to me to speak. "Hello," I said. "I'm Grace Vincent, and this is my friend Mary Jane Kiernan. We're from the town, from Jasmine Cove. We've come to say hello."

He stared for a moment, then smiled and looked at Mary Jane. His eyes were bright green, like the sea just beyond the sands. "Mary Jane," he said. "Well, how strange. This must be a song about you. The Mad Hatters."

"What?" I said.

"The name of the band. The Mad Hatters. They're English."

We listened to the music for a moment, and I thought I caught the words, "Mary Jane is dreaming of an ocean dark and gleaming." I didn't recognize the song, or the name of the group, but that didn't mean much. My parents didn't let me listen to pop music. Mary Jane seemed to find her voice and said something about that being nice.

"Look, would you like to come in?" the young man said. "Have a cold drink or something. It's a hot day."

I looked at Mary Jane. I could tell from her expression that she was as uncertain as I was. Now that we were here, the reality was starting to dawn on us. These were the people the Preacher had called the Spawn of Satan. As far as the townsfolk were concerned, they drugged young girls and had their evil way. But the young man looked harmless and it *was* a hot day. We were thirsty. Finally, we sort of nodded and followed him inside the cabin.

The shade was pleasant and a gentle cross-breeze blew through the open shutters. Sunlight picked out shining strands of silver and gold in the materials that draped the furnishings. The Newcomers didn't have much, and most of it was make-shift, but we made ourselves comfortable on cushions on the floor and the young man brought us some lemonade. "Home-made," he said. "I'm sorry it's not as cold as you're probably used to, but we don't have a refrigerator yet," He laughed. "As a matter of fact, we've only just got the old generator working, or we wouldn't even have any music." He nodded towards the drinks. "We keep some chilled in the stream out back."

By this time the others had wandered in to get a look at us, most of them older than the young man, and several of them lovely women in bright dresses with flowers twined in their long hair.

"I'm Jared," said the young man, then he introduced the others – Star, Leo, Gandalf, Dylan – names we were unfamiliar with. They sat cross-legged on the floor and smiled. Jared asked us some questions about the town, and we explained how the people there were suspicious of strangers but were decent folks underneath it all. I wasn't certain that was true, but we weren't there to say bad things about our kin. We didn't tell them what lies the Preacher had been spreading.

Jared told us they had come here to get away from the suspicion, corruption and greed they had found in the cities, and they were going to live close to nature and meditate. Some of them were artists and musicians – they had guitars and flutes – but they didn't want to be famous or anything. They didn't even want money from anyone. One of them – Rigel, I think his name was – said mysteriously that the world was going to end soon and that this was the best place to be when it happened.

Someone rolled a funny cigarette, lit it and offered it to us, but I said no. I'd never smoked any kind of cigarette, and the thought of marijuana, which I assumed it was, terrified me. To my horror, Mary Jane took it and inhaled. She told me later that it made her feel a bit light-headed, but that was all. I must admit, she didn't act any differently from normal. At least not that day. We left shortly after, promising to drop by again, and it was only over the next few weeks that I noticed Mary Jane's behavior and appearance gradually start to change.

It was just little things at first, like a string of beads she bought at a junk shop in Logan. It was nothing much, really, just cheap colored glass, but it was something she would have turned her nose up at a short while ago. Now, it replaced the lovely gold chain and heart pendant that her parents had given her for her fifteenth birthday. Next came the red cheesecloth top with the silver sequins and fancy Indian embroidery, and the first Mad Hatters LP, the one with "her song" on it.

We went often to the island to see Jared and the others, and I soon began to sense something, some deeper connection, between Mary Jane and Jared and, quite frankly, it worried me. They started wandering off together for hours, and sometimes she told me to go back home without her, that she'd catch a later ferry. It wasn't that Mary Jane was naïve or anything, or that I didn't trust Jared. I also knew that Mary Jane's father was liberal, and she said he trusted her, but I still worried. The townsfolk were already getting a bit suspicious because of the odd way she was dressing. Even Riley McCorkindale gave her strange looks in chapel. It didn't take a genius to put two and two together. At the very least, if she wasn't careful, she could end up grounded for the rest of the summer.

Things came to a head after chapel one Sunday in August. The Preacher had delivered one of his most blistering sermons about what happens to those who turn away from the path of righteousness and embrace evil, complete with a graphic description of the torments of hell. Afterwards, people were standing talking, as they do, all a little nervous, and Mary Jane actually said to the Preacher that she didn't believe there was a hell, that if God was good, he wouldn't do such horrible things to people. The Preacher turned scarlet, and it was only the fact that Mary Jane ran off and jumped on the ferry that stopped him taking her by the ear and dragging her back inside the chapel for special instruction whether she liked it or not. But he wouldn't forget. One way or another, there'd be hell to pay.

Or there would have been, except that was the evening they found Mary Jane's body on the western beach of Pine Island.

*   *   *

The fisherman who found her said he first thought it was a bundle of clothes on the sand. Then, when he went to investigate, he realized that it was a young girl and sailed back to Jasmine Cove as fast as he could. Soon, the police launch was heading out there, the parking lot was full of police cars and the sheriff had commandeered the ferry. Mr Kiernan was beside himself, blaming himself for not keeping a closer eye on her. But it wasn't his fault. He wasn't as mean-spirited as the rest, and how could he know what would happen, anyway? By the time it started to get dark, word was spreading around town that a girl's body had been found, that it was the body of Mary Jane Kiernan and that she had been strangled.

I can't really describe the shock I felt when I first heard the news. It was if my whole being went numb. I didn't believe it at first, of course, but in a way I did. So many people said it had happened that in the end I just had to believe it. Mary Jane was gone.

The next few days passed as in a dream. I remember only that the newspapers were full of stories about some huge gathering out east for folks like the Newcomers, at a place called Woodstock, where it rained cats and dogs and everyone played in the mud. The police came around and questioned everybody, and I was among the first, being Mary Jane's closest friend. The young detective, Lonnegan was his name, seemed nice enough, and Mother offered him a glass of iced tea, which he accepted. His forehead and upper lip were covered by a thin film of sweat.

"Now then, little lady," he began.

"My name's Grace," I corrected him. "I am not a little lady."

I'll give him his due, he took it in his stride. "Very well, Grace," he said. "Mary Jane was your best friend. Is that right?"

"Yes," I answered.

"Were you with her when she went to Pine Island last Wednesday?"

"No," I said.

"Didn't you usually go there together?"

"Sometimes. Not always."

"Why did she go there? There's not exactly a lot to see or do."

I shrugged. "It's peaceful. There's a nice beach . . ." I couldn't help myself, but as soon as I thought of the beach –

it had been *our* beach – the tears started to flow. Lonnegan paused while I reached for a tissue, dried my eyes and composed myself. "I'm sorry," I went on. "It's just a very beautiful place. And there are all kinds of interesting sea birds."

"Yes, but that's not why Mary Jane went there, is it, for the sea birds?"

"Isn't it? I don't know."

"Come on, Grace," said Lonnegan, "we already know she was seeing a young man called David Garwell."

David Garwell. So that was Jared's real name. "Why ask me, then?"

"Do you know if she had arranged to meet him that day? Last Wednesday?"

"I'm sure I don't know," I said. "Mary Jane didn't confide in me about everything." Maybe he did know that Mary Jane was "seeing" Jared, but I wasn't going to tell him that she had told me just two days before she died that she was in love with him, and that as soon as she turned sixteen she planned to go and live with him and the others on Pine Island. That wouldn't have gone down well at all with Detective Lonnegan. Besides, it was our secret.

Lonnegan looked uncomfortable and shuffled in his seat, then he dropped his bombshell. "Maybe she didn't tell you that she was having a baby, Grace, huh? And we think it was his. Did Mary Jane tell you she was having David Garwell's baby?"

In the end, it didn't matter what I thought or said. While the bedraggled crowds were heading home from Woodstock in the east, the police arrested Jared – David Garwell – for the murder of Mary Jane Kiernan. They weren't giving out a whole lot of details, but rumor had it that they had found Mary Jane's gold pendant in a drawer in his room.

"He did it, Grace, you know he did," said Cathy Baker outside the drug store a few days later. "People like that . . . they're . . . ugh!" She pulled a face and made a gesture with her hands as if to sweep spiders off her chest. "They're not like us."

"But why would he hurt her?" I asked. "He loved her."

"*Love*?" echoed Cathy. "They don't know the meaning of the word."

"They call it *free* love, you know," Lynne Everett chirped in. "And that means they do it with anyone."

"And everyone," added Cathy.

I gave up. What was the point? They weren't going to listen. I walked down Main Street with my head hung low and the sun beating on the back of my neck. It just didn't make sense. Mary Jane stopped wearing the pendant when she bought the cheap colored beads. Jared couldn't have stolen it from her, even if he was capable of such a thing, unless he had broken into her house on the mainland, which seemed very unlikely to me. And she hadn't been wearing it on the day she died, I was certain of that. It made far more sense to assume that she had given it to him as a token of her love.

The problem was that I hadn't seen Jared or any of the others since the arrest, so I hadn't been able to ask them what happened. The police had searched the cabins, of course, and they said they found drugs, so they hauled everybody into the county jail and put the children in care.

I was so lost in thought that I didn't even notice Detective Lonnegan walking beside me until he spoke my name and asked me if I wanted to go into Slater's with him for a coffee.

"I'm not allowed to drink coffee," told him, "but I'll have a soda, if that's all right."

He said that was fine and we went inside and took a table. He waited a while before speaking, then he said, "Look, Grace, I know that this is all a terrible shock to you, that Mary Jane was your best friend. I respect that, but if you know anything else that will help us in court against the man who killed her, I'd really be grateful if you'd tell me."

"Why do you need me?" I asked. "I thought you knew everything. You've already put him in jail."

"I know," Lonnegan agreed. "And we've probably got enough to convict him, but every little helps. Did she say anything? Did you see anything?"

I told him how Jared couldn't possibly have stolen the locket unless he went to the mainland.

Lonnegan smiled. "I don't know how you know about that," he said. "I suppose I shouldn't underestimate small town gossip. We know she wasn't wearing the locket on the day she died, but we don't know when he stole it."

"He didn't steal it! Jared's not a thief."

Lonnegan coughed. "I beg to differ, Grace," he said. "David Garwell has a record that includes larceny and possession of dangerous drugs. He should have been in jail to start with, but he skipped bail."

"I don't believe you."

"That's up to you. I could show you the evidence if you want to come to headquarters."

"No, thank you."

"It's your choice."

"But *why* would he hurt Mary Jane? He told her he loved her."

Lonnegan's ears pricked up. "He did?" He toyed with his coffee cup on the saucer. It still had an old lipstick stain around the rim. "We think they had an argument," he said. "Maybe Mary Jane discovered the theft of the pendant. Or perhaps she told Garwell that she was pregnant, and he wanted nothing further to do with her. Either way, she ran off down to that cozy little beach the two of you liked so much. He followed her, maybe worried that she'd tell her parents, or the police. They fought, and he strangled her."

"But then he'd *know* for certain that the police would suspect him!"

"People ain't always thinking straight when they're mad, Grace."

I shook my head. I know what he said made sense, but it *didn't* make sense, if you see what I mean. I didn't know what else to say.

"You're going to have to accept it sooner or later, Grace," Lonnegan said. "This Jared, as you call him, murdered your friend, and you're probably the only one who can help us make sure he pays for his crime."

"But I can't help you. Don't you see? I still don't believe Jared did it."

Lonnegan sighed. "They had an argument. She walked off. He admits that much. He won't tell us what it was about, but like I said, I think she confronted him over the gold pendant or the pregnancy. He followed her."

I squirmed in my seat, took a long sip of soda and asked, "Who else was on the island that day? Have you checked?"

"What do you mean?"

"You must have asked Mr Kiernan, Mary Jane's father, who he took over and brought back that day. Was there anyone else who shouldn't have been there? Have you questioned them all, asked them for alibis?"

"No, but . . ."

"Don't you think you ought to? Why can't it be one of those people?"

"Like who?"

"The Preacher!" I blurted it out.

Lonnegan shook his head, looking puzzled. "The Preacher? Why?"

"Was he there? Was he on the ferry?"

"You know I can't tell you that."

"Well, you just ask him," I said, standing up, "because Mary Jane told me she saw him touching Betsy Goodall somewhere he shouldn't have been touching her."

The Preacher was waiting for me after chapel the following Sunday. "Grace, a word in your ear," he said, leading me by the arm. He was smiling and looked friendly enough, in that well-scrubbed way of his, to fool anyone watching, including my parents, but his grip hurt. He took me back inside the dark chapel and sat me down in a corner, crowding me, his face close to mine. I couldn't smell bourbon on his breath – not that I would have known what it smelled like – but I could smell peppermint. "I had a visit from the police the other day," he said, "a most unwelcome visit, and I've been trying to figure out ever since who's been telling tales out of school. I think it was you, Grace. You were her friend. Thick as thieves, the two of you, always unnaturally close."

"There was nothing unnatural about it," I said, my heart beating fast. "And yes, we were friends. So what?"

His upper lip curled. "Don't you give me any of your smart-talk, young lady. You caused me a lot of trouble, you did, a lot of grief."

"You've got nothing to worry about if you're pure in heart and true in the eyes of the Lord. Isn't that what you're always telling us?"

"Don't take the Lord's word in vain. I swear, one day . . ." He shook his head. "Grace, I do believe you're headed for a life of sin, and you know what the wages of sin are, don't you?"

"Did you go to Pine Island that day, Preacher? The day Mary Jane died. Were you on the ferry? You were, weren't you?"

The Preacher looked away. "As a matter of fact, I had some important business there," he said. "Real estate business." We all knew about the Preacher and his real estate. He seemed to think the best way of carrying out God's plan on earth was to take ownership of as much of it as he could afford.

"Why haven't they arrested you?" I asked.

"Because I haven't done anything wrong. The police believe me. So should you. There's no evidence against me. I didn't strangle that girl."

"Mary Jane told me about Betsy Goodall, about what she saw."

"And just what did she see? I'll tell you what she saw. Nothing. Ask Betsy Goodall. The police did. Your friend Mary Jane was a wayward child," the Preacher said, his voice a sort of drone. "She had a vile imagination. Evil. She made up stories. The police know that now. They talked to me and they talked to Betsy. I just want to warn you, Grace. Don't you go around making any more grief for me, or you'll have more trouble than you can imagine. Do you understand me?"

"Betsy was too scared to say anything, wasn't she? She was frightened of what you might do to her. What did you do to Mary Jane?"

There. It was out before I realized it. That's the problem with me sometimes: I speak before thinking. I felt his fingers squeeze into my arm and I cried out. "Do you understand me?" he asked again, his voice a reptilian whisper.

"Yes!" I said. "You're hurting me! Yes, I understand. Leave me alone." And I wrenched my arm free and ran out of the chapel over to the ferry dock. I wanted to be by myself, and I wanted to walk where Mary Jane and I had walked. There was really only one place I could go, and I was lucky, I had only ten minutes to wait.

The day had turned hazy, warm and sticky. There'd be a storm after dark, everyone said. Mr Kiernan seemed worried about me and told me if I wasn't on the next ferry home he'd send someone looking for me. I said that was sweet but I would be all right. Then he said he'd keep an eye on the weather to make sure I didn't get stuck out there when the storm came.

I walked past the houses and through the woods to the southern tip of the island, where the Newcomers used to live. They had been taken away so fast they hadn't even had time to grab what few belongings they had. Nobody seemed to know what would happen to their things now, whether anyone would come for them. I stood behind the cover of the trees looking into the clearing, the way Mary Jane and I had done that first time, when we saw Jared come out of the shower. And there it was again, faint, drifting, as if it belonged to the air it traveled on: Mary Jane's song. "And Mary Jane is dreaming/Of oceans dark and gleaming."

But who was playing it?

Heart in my mouth, I ducked low and waited. I wanted to know, but I didn't want to go in there, the way people went into basements and rooms in movies when they knew evil lurked there. So I hid.

As it turned out, I didn't have long to wait. As soon as the song ended, a furtive head peeped out of the doorway and, gauging that all was clear, the young man stepped out into the open. My jaw dropped. It was Riley McCorkindale.

Some instinct still held me back from announcing my presence, so I stayed where I was. Riley stood, ears pricked, glancing around furtively, then he headed away from the cabins – not back towards his parents' house, but west, towards the cliffs. Now I was really puzzled.

When I calculated that Riley had got a safe distance ahead of me, I followed through the trees. I couldn't see him, but there weren't many paths on the island, and not many places to go if you were heading in that direction. Once in a while I would stop and listen, and I could hear him way ahead, snapping a twig, rustling a bush as he walked. I hoped he didn't stop and listen the same way and hear me following him.

As I walked, I wondered what on earth Riley had been doing at the Newcomers' cabin. Playing the record with the Mary Jane song on it, obviously. But why? I knew he had been sweet on her, of course, but he had always been too shy to say hello. Had he made friends with the Newcomers? After all, they were practically neighbours. But Riley went to chapel, and he seemed the type to take notice of the Preacher. His father was a property developer in Logan, so they were a wealthy and respected family in the community, too, which made it even more unlikely that Riley would have anything to do with Jared and the others.

When I reached the cliffs, there was no one in sight. I glanced over the edge, down towards the beach but saw no one there, either. I wasn't sure whether Riley knew about the hidden path Mary Jane and I used to take. He lived on the island, so perhaps he did. I stood still for a moment and felt the wind whipping my hair in my eyes and tugging at my clothes, bringing the dark clouds from far out at seas, heard the raucous cries of gulls over a shoal of fish just off the coast, smelled the salt air. Then, just as I started to move towards the path, I heard a voice behind me.

"You."

I turned. Riley stepped out from the edge of the woods.

"Riley," I said, smiling, trying to sound relaxed, and holding my hair from my eyes. "You startled me. What are you doing here?"

"You were following me."

"Me? No. Why would I do that?" I felt vulnerable at the edge of the cliff, aware of the golden sand so far below, and as I spoke I tried edging slowly forwards. But Riley stood his ground, and right now he didn't seem shy at all.

"I don't know," he said. "But I saw you. Maybe it's something to do with Mary Jane?"

"Mary Jane?"

"You know I loved her. Until that . . . that freak came and took her away from me. Still, he's got what he deserves. Let him rot in jail."

"Now, listen Riley. You don't have to say anything to me." The last thing I wanted was to be Riley's confessor with a hundred foot drop behind me. "Let's just go back, huh? I don't want to miss my ferry."

"I used to watch them, you know," Riley said. "Watch them doing it."

I didn't know what to say to that. I swallowed.

"They'd do it anywhere. They didn't care who was watching."

"That's not true, Riley," I said. "You know that can't be true. You were spying on them. You said so."

"Maybe so. But they did it down there." He pointed. "On the beach."

"It's a very secluded spot." I don't know what I meant by that, whether I was defending Mary Jane's honor, deflecting the shock I felt, or what. I just wanted to keep Riley talking until I could get around him and . . . well, getting back to the ferry was my main thought. But if Riley had other ideas there wasn't much I could do. He was bigger and stronger than me. Drops of rain dampened my cheek. The sky was becoming darker. "Look, Riley," I said. "There's going to be a storm. Move out of the way and let me go back to the ferry dock. I'll miss my ferry. Mr Kiernan will be looking for me."

"I didn't mean to do it, you know," Riley said.

I had been trying to skirt around him, but I froze. "Didn't mean to do what?" There I was again, speaking without thinking. I didn't want to know, but it was too late now.

"Kill her. It just happened. One minute she was . . ."

Now he'd told me I just had to know the full story. Unless I could make a break into the woods when he wasn't expecting it, I was done for anyway. I didn't think I could outrun him, but with the cover of the trees, and the coming dark, perhaps I had a chance of staying ahead of him as far as the ferry dock. "How did it happen?" I asked, still moving slowly.

"They had a fight. I was watching the cabin and they had a fight and Mary Jane ran out crying."

The baby, I thought. She told him about the baby. But why would that matter? The Newcomers loved children. They would have welcomed Mary Jane and her child. It must have been something else. Perhaps she wanted to get married? That would have been far too conventional for Jared but just like Mary Jane. Whatever it was, they had argued. Couples do argue. "What happened?" I asked.

"I followed her like you followed me. She went down to the beach. Down that path you both thought was your little secret. I went after her. I thought I could comfort her. You know, I thought she'd dumped him and maybe she would turn to me if I was nice to her."

"How did it go wrong?"

"She did it with him, didn't she?" Riley said, his voice raising to a shout against the coming storm. "Why wouldn't she do it with me? Why did she have to laugh?"

"She laughed at you?"

He nodded. "That's when I grabbed her. The next thing I . . . I guess I don't know my own strength. She was like a rag doll."

There was a slim chance that I could slip into the woods to the left of him and make a run for it. That was when he said, "I'm glad I told you. I've been wanting to tell somebody, just to get it off my chest. I feel better now."

I paused. "But Riley, you have to go to the authorities. You have to tell them there's an innocent man in jail."

"No! I ain't going to jail. I won't. Only you and me know the truth."

"Riley, if you hurt me they'll know," I said, my voice shaking, judging the distance between his reach and the gap in the trees. "They'll know it was you. I told Mr Kiernan I came here to talk to you." It was a lie, of course, but I hoped it was an inspired one.

"Why would you do that?" Riley seemed genuinely puzzled. "You didn't know anything about it until just now. You didn't even know I existed. You didn't want to know. None of you did."

"I mean it, Riley. If you hurt me, they'll find out. You can't get away with murder twice. You'll go to jail then for sure."

"They say killing's easier the second time. I read that in a book."

"Riley, don't."

"It's all right, Grace," he said, leaning back against the tree. "I ain't going to hurt you. Don't think I don't regret what I did. Don't think I enjoyed it. I'm just not going to jail for it. Go. Catch your ferry. See if I care."

"B-but . . ."

"Who'd believe you? The police have got the man they want. There sure as hell's no evidence against me. My daddy doesn't know where I was, but he already told them I was home all day. Last thing he wants to know is that his son killed some girl. That would surely upset the applecart. Nobody saw me. The Preacher's with us, too. He was at the house talking real estate

with daddy. I don't know if he knows I did it or not, but he
don't care. He was the one told me about Mary Jane and that
freak, what they were doing and how it was a sin. That's why I
went to spy on them. He told me he knew she was really my girl,
but she'd been seduced by the devil. He told me what that long-
haired pervert was doing to her and asked me what I was going
to do about it. The Preacher won't be saying nothing to no
police. So go on. Go."

"But why did you tell me?"

Riley paused. "Like I said, I knew I'd feel better if I told
someone. I'm truly sorry for what I did, but going to jail ain't
going to bring her back."

"But what about Jared? He's innocent?"

"He's the Spawn of Satan. Now go ahead, Grace. Catch the
ferry before the storm comes. It's going to be a bad one."

"You won't . . .?"

He shook his head. "Nope. Don't matter what you say. Go
ahead. See if I'm not right."

And I did. I caught the ferry. Mr Kiernan smiled and said I was
lucky I just made it. The storm broke that night, flooded a few
roads, broke a few windows. The next day I took the bus into
the city to see Detective Lonnegan and told him about what
Riley had said to me on the beach. He laughed, said the boy was
having me on, giving me a scare. I told him it was true, that
Riley was in love with Mary Jane and that he tried to . . . I
couldn't get the words out in front of him, but even so he was
shaking his head before I'd finished.

So Riley McCorkindale turned out to be right. The police
didn't believe me. I didn't see any point running all over town
telling Mr Kiernan, father, the Preacher or anyone else, so that
was the end of it. Riley McCorkindale strangled Mary Jane
Kiernan and got away with it. Jared – David Garwood – went to
jail for a crime he didn't commit. He didn't stay there long,
though. Word made it back to town about a year or two later
that he got stabbed in a prison brawl, and even then everyone
said he had it coming, that it was divine justice.

None of the Newcomers ever returned to Jasmine Cove. The
cabins fell into disrepair again, and their property reverted to
the township in one of those roundabout ways that these things

often happen in small communities like ours. I thought of Mary Jane often over the years, remembered her smile, her childlike enthusiasms. The Mad Hatters became famous and once in a while I heard "her" song on the radio. It always made me cry.

After I had finished college and started teaching high school in Logan, the property boom began. The downtown areas of many major cities became uninhabitable, people moved out to the suburbs and the rich wanted country, or island, retreats. One day I heard that McCorkindale Developments had knocked down the cabins on Pine Island and cleared the land for a strip of low-rise, ocean-front luxury condominiums.

I suppose it's what you might call ironic, depending on the way you look at it, but by that time the Preacher and Riley's father had managed to buy up most of the island for themselves.

TELL ME

Zoë Sharp

"So, where is she?"

Crime Scene Investigator Grace McColl ducked under the taped cordon at the edge of the crime scene and showed her ID to the uniformed constable stationed there.

The policeman jerked his head in the direction of the band shelter as she signed the log. "You'll have your work cut out with this one, though," he said.

Grace frowned and moved on. She was already dressed from head to foot in her disposable white suit and she made sure she followed the designated pathway, picking her way carefully to avoid undue contamination.

The girl was on the stone steps in front of the band shelter, no more than sixteen years old but still a child, with dirty blonde hair. As Grace approached she could see the girl had her thin arms folded, as though hugging herself against the cold. And she must have been cold, to be out in the park in this weather in just a mini skirt and a skimpy top. Unless, of course, he'd taken her coat with him when he'd left her . . .

Over to the right, the rhododendron bushes grew thick and concealing. It might have been Grace's imagination, but she thought the girl's eyes turned constantly in their direction, as though something might still lurk amongst the glossy foliage.

She squatted down on her haunches next to the girl and waited until she seemed to have her full attention.

"Hello," she said quietly. "I'm Grace. I'm going to be taking care of you now. Can you tell me who you are?"

There was a long pause, then: "Does it matter?"

Grace eyed her for a moment. The girl might have been pretty if she'd taken a little time, a little care. Or if someone had taken a little care over her. Her hair was badly cut and her fingernails were bitten short and painted purple, the varnish long since chipped and peeling.

"Of course it matters," Grace said, keeping her tone light. "Finding out about you will help us find out who did this to you. Help us to catch him. You want that, don't you?"

"'Spose." The girl shrugged, darting a little glance from under her ragged fringe to see if her attitude achieved the desired level of sullen cool. The action revealed the livid bruise, like spilt ink on tissue, that had formed around her left eye.

Grace tilted her head, considering. "He caught you a belter, didn't he?" she murmured.

"I bruise easy," the girl said, suddenly defensive now. "And I'm clumsy."

"Don't tell me," Grace said, setting her bag down and opening it. "You were always walking into doors at home, falling down the stairs." She shook her head. "Did no one stop to wonder?"

The girl's face darkened. "They knew, all right," she said. "They just didn't give a—"

"No," Grace said dryly. "I can see that." She pulled out evidence bags and swabs, and paused. "Is that why you ran away – ended up on the streets?"

The girl's head jerked up and she looked at Grace fully for the first time, scowling. "Who said I'm living rough?"

Grace regarded her calmly. "Your clothes are dirty enough," she said.

"What do you expect?" the girl snapped. She gestured angrily towards the rhododendrons. "Being dragged through the mud, having him –" She broke off, bit her lip, looked away.

"Your clothes were dirty before that," Grace said, no censure in her quiet voice. 'And you're a pretty girl. Your nails are

painted – or they were. You wouldn't have done that if you
hadn't wanted to look nice, once upon a time."

The girl's lip curled. "That's for fairy stories."

"Mm," Grace said. "Let me see your hands."

Reluctantly, the girl put both hands up, backs towards Grace,
fingers splayed rigidly. Grace almost smiled at the defiance she
read there, taking hold of one carefully in her gloved fingers,
scraping out minute debris from under the receded nails.

"Ah-ha," she said, under her breath. "You got a shot in, I
see. Marked him. Oh, well done, you."

The girl looked unaccountably pleased at this praise and it
occurred to Grace that she must have received very little by way
of approval in her short life. She thought of her own mother,
who lavished praise and nurtured self-confidence in her only
child. Ironic, then, that the pre-adolescent Grace had always
been so desperate to win the approbation of her more distant
father.

"*Your* father wasn't around much, was he?" she said absently, noting the time and date and case number on the
evidence bag as she sealed it.

The girl scowled at her again. "You're guessing," she accused. "No way can you tell that from looking at my hands."
Her mouth twisted into a sneer. "Read tea-leaves as well, do
you?"

"No," Grace said levelly, "but I've been doing this job long
enough to recognize the other signs."

The girl took her hand back and folded her arms, a challenge
in her voice. "So, go on," she goaded. "If you're so clever, *you*
tell *me*. Who am I?"

"All right." Grace sat back on her heels, oblivious to the
activity going on around her. She focused inwards, closing her
eyes for a moment.

"You can't do it, can you?" the girl jeered.

Grace's eyes opened. "Your father left when you were
young," she began. "Your mother blamed you and lost herself
in the bottle – pills or booze, or possibly both."

The girl rolled her eyes, gave a derisive laugh. "Oh, big
deal," she said. "You could be talking about half the kids round
here." She jerked her head towards the nearby high-rise. "Not
good enough."

"OK," Grace conceded. "Then you're going to tell me it's also obvious that your mother brought home a procession of one-night stands to pay the rent. How old were you when the first of them asked if *you* were for sale, too?"

The girl wouldn't meet her eyes. "None of your business," she muttered.

"Mm, I thought so." She paused again but the girl wouldn't respond. "But you didn't leave then, did you? You clung in there. For a while. Until it got too much and you attempted self-harm."

"Who says I did?"

Grace nodded towards the old scars on the girl's wrists. "You cut yourself," she said, picking her words with care. "Not a serious attempt, I don't think. A cry for help. But nobody answered, did they?"

The girl twisted the cheap ring round on her finger and didn't speak, staring across the grass to where the row of uniforms swept the parkland.

"He listened," she said at last, so quietly Grace hardly caught the words.

"Ah," she said softly. "Of course he did."

The girl's head jerked up at the tone in her voice, eyes flashing. "Don't say it like that," she snapped, harsh. "You don't know how it was. He loved me!"

"I'm sure he told you he did," Grace said, bland. "Gave you that ring, didn't he? Told you that you were his girl now. Just like all the others."

"I was. I *am*."

"So how long was it before he told you about the man he owed money to? About how it would all be all right if only you'd just have sex with this man. Did you refuse? Is that why he hit you?"

"I made him angry. He was sorry – after."

"But he still made you do it, didn't he?"

"I wanted to help him. He didn't force me or nothing."

"Not that first time, no," Grace said. "But that was just the beginning, wasn't it? When did you realize he wasn't your boyfriend any more, but your pimp? Or did you ever realize it?"

"If I'd had someone looking out for me," the girl said, her voice bitter now, "do you think something like this would've happened?"

"It might have done. If it was him – your boyfriend – who did this to you."

The girl shrugged. "Might have been," she said, dismissive. Her glance was defiant. "Might not."

"So, was he a client?"

"Client?" the girl spat. "Would that make it better for you if he was? Would that make it not so shocking, not so bad, if I was on the game? Oh well, just another hooker picked the wrong john. Had it coming."

"No," Grace said evenly. "It would just give us a better place to start looking."

"Yeah, right," the girl snorted, still surly. "You're thinking it, though. I can tell."

"I try to keep an open mind but you're not making it easy for me. You shouldn't have been here at that time of night, you see. It's where the working girls come with the men they pick up when the clubs turn out. And you could have just been trying to make the money for your next fix."

The girl opened her mouth, saw Grace's gaze on the evidence of her addiction that tattooed the crook of both arms, and shut her mouth again with a glower.

"You see too much," was all she said.

"It's my job," Grace agreed. "Just as it's my job to find out who you are, and who did this to you. To stand for you, when no-one else would."

The girl looked at her with doubt and speculation in her eyes for the first time. "And you'll do that, will you?"

"I will."

"Just for me?"

"Yes."

The girl sighed. "You'll be the first, if you do."

"Well, better late than never, then."

The girl was silent again. The sky had darkened overhead and she looked up into the gathering clouds. "It's going to rain," she said.

"I know," Grace said. She stood. "I'd better get back to work. The rain will destroy the evidence if we don't protect the scene quickly."

The girl nodded. "You'll be back, though, won't you?" she said. "You won't leave me?"

"Of course," Grace said. "They'll take you in, but you'll certainly see me again. I'll need more from you, if we're to catch him."

"That's good," the girl said and gave a small smile, rusty from lack of use.

"How are you getting on, Grace?" asked a brisk voice from behind her. Grace turned to see one of the Detective Constables who'd just arrived on scene. She bent and snapped her bag closed, then straightened.

"I'm about done," she said.

"Will you get anything useful from her, do you think?"

Grace glanced back.

The girl lay on the damp steps, arms wrapped across her body, in the position they'd first found her. Her eyes were open and glassy, her lips tinged with blue. The marks of the stranglehold that had killed her showed dark and ugly around her throat.

"I think so," Grace murmured. "The dead always talk to me in the end."

COLOUR ME BLOOD

Jerry Sykes

The side of the building had been painted in a thin coat of white emulsion, but the solid colours of more than a decade's worth of graffiti still showed through the paint like blood vessels under pale Irish skin. In front of the wall, a tall scruff of a man with thick knots of dark hair was making shapes in the emulsion with a piece of charcoal. His name was Rob Blake, a local artist, and he had been commissioned by the local residents' association to create a mural on the side of the Community Centre.

Surrounding him in a loose arc, all ADD head jerks and hot feet, was a group of around ten children aged between twelve and fourteen holding in their hands face masks and cans of spray paint in a rainbow of colours. The idea was that once the artist had laid out the basic outline of the mural on the wall, the kids would then fill in the larger shapes to create the solid cast of the image, leaving the artist to add the final details later.

Across the street from the Community Centre, Detective Sergeant Marnie Stone sat and watched from the open window of her old blue Saab. In the centre of the group surrounding the artist, little more than a short head taller than the children, she could see Kate Phillips, one of the hardier members of Camden's Social Services department and an old friend. After a couple of minutes, Marnie called out her name and stuck her hand in the air, but, like the children, Kate seemed fascinated with the workings of the artist, the fluid motion of his hand, the beats of creation, and appeared not to have heard. Marnie could not see much of what was happening through the forest of shuffling limbs, just the occasional glimpse of the hand leaking sinuous lines of soft carbon, and so she had no choice but to sit back and wait.

Marnie had read about the project in the local paper and was curious to see if it would lead to a reduction in crime on the estate, as had been promised in the tenants' association's pitch to the police and the council. There were a couple of faces that she knew for a fact were responsible for a string of robberies and muggings in the area – she had just not been able to gather sufficient evidence, and so at least a couple of old people would be able to walk home in peace tonight. But she would be fooling herself if she thought it would go further than that.

A few minutes later, the artist stood up to stretch his back and the spell he held over his audience was broken. Kate glanced around and saw Marnie watching them. She stooped and said something to one of the kids nearest her, and then walked over to the Saab. The closer she came, Marnie noticed, the deeper the lines that bracketed her mouth became. But then it had never surprised Marnie that social workers appeared to age faster than the rest of the world, including police officers.

"Hello, Marnie, what are you doing out here?" asked Kate, smiling. "You're not going to arrest Rob, are you?"

"You mean that vandal trying to make the estate a better place to live?" replied Marnie, reflecting the smile. "Sure, I just wanted to see who his accomplices were first . . ."

"Ooh, don't be cruel," replied Kate, resting her hand on the lip of the door.

"What's it going to be, anyway?" asked Marnie, pointing towards the Community Centre.

"A warning about the perils of drink and drugs," said Kate. "There's going to be the usual logo, Keep it Clean, and then a street scene with kids and families and stuff like that. I don't know, I think I also heard Rob say something about a large bin with needles and guns sticking out of it or something . . ."

"And here's me thinking Walt Disney was dead," said Marnie.

"Hey, don't knock it," Kate chastised her. "If it gives these kids some stake in the estate then it'll be worth it."

"Yeah, I know," agreed Marnie, glancing away. She still had her doubts, but she also knew that she would never be able to win an argument with Kate. She started the engine and put the car in gear. "Anyway, I better be getting back to the station. I just thought I'd drop by and see how you were getting on . . ."

"Much better than I thought," said Kate, nodding. "There are far more kids here than I thought there would be . . . Including one or two I never expected to see in a million years."

"Yeah, I know who you mean," said Marnie. "So just remember to count all the paint cans at the end of the night . . ."

Kate gave her a look of mock admonishment, and then broke into a smile. "Go and chase some real villains," she said.

The children had been filling in shapes for a little more than ten minutes when the first argument started. Calum Breen, a short kid with dark hair and a pronounced lower lip that made him look like he was sulking all the time, a mask that suited his character to the ground, had been assigned a couple of letters at the end of the slogan, but what he wanted to do was something a bit more artistic, or something a bit more real, as he put it.

"Why can't I do one of the people, or even some of the background?" he asked, a sneer pushing his lip out further.

"Because that's just the way it worked out," replied Blake, wishing that Kate was still there with him. Five minutes earlier she had told him that she had to go and see a client on the estate but would be back in an hour. He was not used to dealing with a bunch of kids on his own and, although he was loath to admit it to himself, having her there made him feel safer.

"But I don't want to do the letters," replied Calum.

"Well, how about you just do one of the letters and then we move everyone around," said Blake. "That way everyone'll get to do a figure and a letter, or a bit of background, or whatever . . ."

"He's just scared of getting it wrong because he can't read," called out a kid in the centre of the group.

"There's no need for that," said Blake.

"Yeah, piss off," said Calum.

"Come on, let's not fight about it," said Blake. He could feel the group starting to slip out of his grasp, but he wasn't quite sure what to do about it.

The two kids shuffled around in the pack for a brief moment, alternating between hiding behind their colleagues and stepping out into makeshift clearings, before squaring up to one another. Blake waited until the last moment, fearful of wounding their pride, perhaps, and then stepped between them with his palms raised. And just stood there, still and silent, waiting for them to return to the growing spread of colour on the wall. Long minutes later, egos satisfied, the pair traded final insults and then broke up and returned to the task at hand. Blake folded his arms and waited to make certain that it was indeed all over, and then stepped over to watch Calum work. It did not take him long to realize that behind the brash tongue the kid had a natural talent and that perhaps he should give him a break and let him have a bit more input to the project. Trouble was he would have to do it without looking like he was cutting out the other kids.

But fifteen minutes later, two minutes after the kids had traded shapes, Calum had another complaint.

"How come we're just doing a picture of the estate, anyway? It's pretty boring, don't you think? I mean, we live here all the time. Why can't we do something a bit more interesting?"

Blake sighed. "I thought we talked about this."

"What about a beach with horses running through the surf?" suggested Calum. "I don't know, just something different . . ."

"I thought we agreed to do a mural of what we wanted the estate to look like," said Blake.

"Calum wants it to look like a building site with sand and shit," piped up a small kid from the centre of the group.

"I never said that," replied Calum, looking for the source.

"Clubbers sleeping off their highs from the night before," said another kid, his idea of a beach.

"No, that's not the kind of beach I mean," protested Calum, still looking for the source of the first voice.

"Grannies pumping coins into slot machines," suggested another, stretching the beach connection to breaking point.

"What the hell is wrong with you people?" squealed Calum. "You've got the chance to bring a bit of colour into your lives and what do you do? Paint a cartoon version of what you've already got. Jesus, give it some imagination, won't you?"

"Imagine this," said one of the kids, giving him a finger.

"This is for all of us, not just for you," said another.

"Yeah, piss off and find your own wall," said yet another.

With faceless jibes coming at him from all directions, Calum felt a sickness rise in his throat. He took a deep breath and tried to shake it loose, dampen the tension, but it just seemed to make things worse. Seconds later, past frustration, he turned and pointed his can at the wall, pressed down on the button and held it there, as if that could relieve the pressure within himself. Dark blue paint bubbled and frothed on the wall and a thin trail soon snaked down through the white emulsion.

"Oh, for Christ's sake, Calum," said Blake.

"I knew he'd turn it all to shit," said one of the kids.

Calum continued to press down on the button.

"Give me the can," said Blake, his long fingers beckoning. But Calum just ignored him, and after one more polite request, Blake stepped forward and slammed the can out of his hand.

Calum snarled at him and watched the can as it bounced and rattled on the ground, and then stormed off across the estate.

Blake watched him go, and then ran forward a couple of steps and kicked the can into the wall as hard as he could.

Calum was still feeling a little out of sorts a few hours later. Sitting on the back of a bench in the centre of the estate with a couple of his friends who had not been part of the mural project: Match, like the name suggested – kids are nothing if not literal – tall and thin and with a shock of red hair, and Tusk, a regular-looking kid with a left canine tooth that poked out from between his lips even when his mouth was closed. The pair had been messing with his head ever since he had joined them on the bench after supper. Word had travelled fast, and he was starting to get dark and pissed off, to believe that there was nowhere left to run. At one point, Match had accused him of losing his balls, and as the night had progressed and the more he had brooded on it, the more he had started to believe that Match might in fact be right. A couple of solutions had passed through his head – for an instant he had considered damaging the mural, but then he knew that he would be the main suspect – but nothing had made itself clear. Approaching midnight, he knew that he had to act soon to distance himself from the project and therefore restore his ego.

Taking a final drag on his cigarette, Calum flicked it out into the air and climbed down from the bench. He set off across the estate, breathing hard through his nose like a minotaur.

"Yo, what's happenin', man?" Match called out, standing up and following him. "What's going on, Calum?"

"Yo, wait up," cried Tusk, setting off after them.

Match and Tusk fell into step beside Calum, and the three of them headed up through Kentish Town before cutting a right into Dartmouth Park. Here the streets were quieter, darker, and there were less people about, less traffic. Calum led them through a labyrinth of backstreets and alleys, streetlights sending shadows to track them, making no attempt to hide themselves, confident in their solid presence. Fifteen minutes after leaving the comfort of the estate, he led them behind a dark parade of shops that represented another kind of comfort.

The off-licence sat in the middle of the parade between a vet's surgery and a greengrocer's, and was well known to all the kids in the area as a cheap target. Calum himself had broken into it at least three times – three that he could remember – and almost every other kid he knew had burgled it at least once. It was like a training ground for them, a rites of passage kind of place.

Match had been following Calum in glum silence, but as soon as he figured out where Calum was going, a broad grin had spread across his face as he knew his friend was coming back to them. It had been a bad time, with Calum either buried in paint and a social conscience or in despair. Match leaned into Tusk and told him the news, watched the other kid respond in the same manner.

"You going to hit the cashpoint," said Match, his nickname for the off-licence.

"Time I felt the muscle working again," replied Calum, clenching a fist in front of his heart.

"Yo, back in the world," said Tusk.

"Oh, right, let's get it on," said Calum. He led them down the back of the buildings, their feet creating scuffles and echoes in the trash that carpeted the ground. At the back of the off-licence, he held out his right hand and gestured to Match with his left. Match lifted his jacket aside, pulled out a short-bladed knife from the deep thigh pocket in his cargo pants, and handed it to Calum. As Calum lifted the knife to jam it into the gap between the door and the frame, he noticed the line of dried blood at the base of the blade and an icicle threaded his spine. The blood was from where Match had stabbed some kid in the hand the week before when he had been too slow in handing over his mobile phone. Calum had seen the attack and, although he had been witness to unprovoked violence before, the cold action of his friend had shaken him more than he cared to admit. It had been an insight too far into the mental state of their situation.

The uncomfortable thought stilled him, and when the door creaked and opened a fraction, he thought for a moment that he must have popped it open himself without realizing it and looked at the knife for a second in disbelief. And when it creaked again and opened a little further, a slice of light falling across the ground, he was still none the wiser, even when a look of keen surprise appeared on Match's face and his friend turned on his heel and fled. Understanding what was happening, Tusk too was soon up and off on his jaundiced feet into the darkness.

Stuck in that awkward space between thought and action, it was just when the manager's scared face appeared around the door that the truth of the situation hit Calum. Shaking the indecision from his limbs, he took off after his friends, but not before the manager had caught a clear glimpse of his startled face.

At nine o'clock the following morning, Rob Blake, the artist, and Kate Phillips, the social worker, were sitting on a threadbare sofa in the living room of the flat Calum Breen shared with his mother. DS Marnie Stone had been on the phone to Kate first thing: the owner of the off-licence had recognized Calum at once but because he had not committed an actual offence she was reluctant to speak to him. Could Kate go round there and have a quiet word? "Sounds like I don't have much choice," Kate had replied, but here she was with Rob at her side for moral support.

Calum's mother was sitting in a matching chair, a cup of hot coffee in one hand and a cigarette in the other. She looked like she had a hangover, bloodshot pupils and red skin.

"So who else was there last night, Calum?" asked Kate. "The manager said he saw two other kids running off."

Calum twisted in his seat and said nothing.

"It was almost midnight," continued Kate. "Somehow I just don't think that you'd have been out there on your own at that time of night. Do you want to tell me who you were with, Calum?"

Again Calum said nothing.

"Was it Match and Tusk?"

At the mention of the names Match and Tusk, Blake glanced at Kate, a little surprised, and then turned to Calum.

"I thought you said you'd left those two behind when you signed on for the mural," said Blake, feeling a little hurt.

"Yeah, well, maybe if I'd been allowed to put something of my own in it . . ."

"Is that what all this is about?" said Kate, pressing her hands between her knees. "A cry for attention?"

"You mean you jeopardized your freedom just because you didn't get your own way," interjected Blake, incredulous.

Kate rested her hand on his forearm and tried to ease him back, but he pushed on regardless.

"If it really means that much to you then I'm sure we could work something out," said Blake, feeling the soft touch of the hand on his arm fade. "It's one thing being a tortured artist, but there's no need for you to go and get into trouble over it."

"You've torn yourself away from those bad influences before," said Kate. "It'll be easier the second time around."

"I'll think about it," muttered Calum, and Kate knew then that that was as much as they were going to get from him for now.

Kate touched Blake on the arm again, and this time he knew that it meant something different.

"It'll be good to see you again," he said, rising to leave.

Under normal circumstances, stubborn pride would have kept Calum from the mural for at least another afternoon, but knowing that it would take no more than three sessions to complete, he understood he had no choice but to swallow that pride and return to the site that afternoon if he wanted to be a real part of it.

And so four o'clock found him walking across the estate with the other kids, together but apart. Without having to ask, the other kids intuited what had happened. Most of them had been witness to his original strop, and also knew his street reputation, and so knew better than to irritate him further. When the group arrived in front of the mural, Blake also tuned into the common mood and just handed Calum a can of paint with a smile and motioned for him to do as he pleased.

For two hours Calum worked in silent concentration, the shadow of the other kids staining his back like perspiration. And the following night he was there again. Blake was impressed with his dedication and the sense of Calumness that he brought to the character of the mural, little touches that added a much-needed sense of humour – a man in an open window shaving the hair on the top of his ears, a woman in a tracksuit watching aerobics on TV with a cigarette in her mouth. At the completion, both Blake and the kids were pleased with how it had turned out. Not quite as it had been planned, but perhaps all the better for that.

As the kids were cleaning up, or rather sneaking off and leaving Blake to do the cleaning up, a tall black man in a crumpled suit named Johnson approached the scene. He stood and stared at the mural, smiling, tilting his head from side to side, and then after a couple of minutes looked across at Blake.

"That's some piece of work," he said.

"The kids did a great job," agreed Blake.

"I like the little comic touches the best."

"You mean the figures in the windows," said Blake, pointing.

"Yeah, those," said Johnson.

"Yeah, I like those too," agreed Blake, stuffing tins of paint into a canvas holdall. "A touch of original thinking."

"It wasn't part of the plan, then," said Johnson.

"That was one of the kids," admitted Blake, not too proud to give credit where due. "Nothing to do with me, I'm afraid."

"I think it was the kid with the fat lip," said Johnson, smiling and pointing at his own mouth.

"You mean Calum," replied Blake, reflecting the smile.

"And he lives here on the estate," said Johnson.

"In one of the blocks near Castle Street," said Blake.

"You think he'd be interested in a solo project – that's if it's all right with you, I mean," said Johnson.

"Depends what you have in mind, I suppose."

"You know Carlo's, the café on Kentish Town Road?

"I've been there a few times," said Blake. "Nice homemade fish-cakes if I remember right."

"The wife makes them," said Johnson, and then fell silent, regarding the mural once more. "It could be a nice place, a better place, but the trouble is I have a metal shutter that's forever covered in graffiti. If I clean it, then it's covered again the following night. I think the people who walk past at night and see the graffiti must think it's a bad place and decide never to go and eat there. You must understand what I mean. I've been thinking about what to do about it . . . You think . . . You think Calum would be interested in helping me out?"

Blake thought about Calum and what he had brought to the project. "He's got some strong ideas of his own."

"But that's what I'm looking for," said Johnson. "I wouldn't know where to start if we had to do it ourselves. As long as I have some idea of what he's going to do beforehand. Perhaps if he had one or two ideas I could choose from . . ."

"And he'd be paid for the work, of course," said Blake.

"Whatever's the going rate," replied Johnson.

"All right, I'll ask him," said Blake.

For his shutter on Kentish Town Road, Johnson chose a cartoon version of his café with cartoon customers looking out at the real people passing on the street outside. At the rear of the cartoon café were caricatures of Posh and Becks tucking into large plates of pie and mash, fat bellies pushing at their cheap clothing and raw cigarettes burning in a saucer in the centre of the table. Most of the café's trade was during the week and so Johnson shut the café for the weekend to allow Calum to complete the mural in time for opening the following week.

Just like he had learned from Blake, Calum started with painting the shutter in a coat of white emulsion and then sketching the basic shapes of the characters and the furniture with a piece of charcoal. Working hard, he had the outline of the design laid out in full ten minutes short of noon and so decided to have some lunch before starting with the paint. He walked to the newsagent's on the corner and bought a can of Coke and a cheese bagel in cling-film, but the woman behind the counter rebuffed his offer of coins, telling him that she was pleased that Johnson was at last doing something to brighten up the area and that she was thinking of following his lead. She just wanted to see how it turned out first. Calum thanked her and told her to keep him in mind. Popping the top of the Coke he stepped out onto the street and bumped straight into Match and Tusk.

"We've been wondering where you'd got to," said Match.

"Thought you might be avoiding us, like," added Tusk.

Calum ignored them and strolled back to the café. He sat on the step and unwrapped his bagel, started to eat. The other two followed him and stood on the edge of the kerb facing him, holding onto a lamp post and swinging their feet in the gutter.

"You coming out with us tonight?" asked Tusk. "Finish off what we started the other night."

Calum presumed he was referring to the humiliating episode at the rear of the off-licence in Dartmouth Park, but he had no desire for a repeat performance and, besides, he had something else to keep him occupied now. He took another bite and continued to ignore them, looking off down the street towards Camden Town.

"What's the matter, can't you hear us or something?" asked Tusk.

"He must think he's too good for us now," said Match, his head poking out of his dark hood like a poison tortoise.

Still Calum ignored them, drinking from the Coke.

"I reckon the police must've put the frighteners on him or something," said Tusk.

"Turned him back into a child," agreed Match.

"Won't be the first time. Still, it's like riding a bike. He wants to get back in the saddle, it shouldn't be too hard . . ."

"If he leaves it much longer he's going to need those whatch-amacallits, those little wheels on the back . . ."

"Stabilizers," said Tusk. "Kiddie wheels."

"If he leaves it much longer he's going to need stabilizers . . ."

Calum listened to the barrage of jibes in silence. On the one hand it hurt him, his friends attacking him like that, but on the other he just wanted them to leave so that he could get on with the mural. He finished the bagel, drained the Coke, and then put the scrunched-up cling-film into the open mouth of the can.

He stood and walked across to the kerb, and stuffed the can into one of the bulging black bin liners piled there like boulders.

"You coming with us, then?" asked Match. "Finish what we started the other night . . . You can hold the knife . . ."

"I have to finish the mural," said Calum, uncomfortable.

"That's all right, we can wait," said Tusk.

"It might be a while . . ."

"We have to wait until it gets dark, anyway," said Tusk.

"I don't know . . . Perhaps some other time," said Calum.

"Come on," said Tusk, a note of pleading in his voice.

"Oh, forget him," snapped Match, stamping his foot. "He's not going to come with us. He's just pissing us about. He's gone over to the other side. Painting, for Christ's sake . . . I bet he's not even getting paid for it . . ."

"That's not the point . . ." started Calum, frowning.

"Child," Match shouted him down, rattling his fist at the shutter. "Pissing about with a big fat colouring book . . ."

A smirk creased Tusk's face.

"What do we care?" said Match. "You know if we get caught we're going to say that you were with us anyway."

This time DS Marnie Stone came to the flat herself. She said hello to Calum and his mother, accepted the offer of coffee, and then asked Calum where he had been the night before.

"I was here," muttered Calum, looking at the floor.

"You were here all night?"

"I finished working on the mural when it started to get dark and then I came straight back here."

"And what time would that have been?"

"I don't know," replied Calum, shrugging. "I suppose it must've been about nine or so. Quarter past . . . I don't know."

"You're sure about that?"

"Half past, then," said Calum. "I don't have a watch but I'm sure it was no later than about half past nine . . ."

"You stop and talk to anyone on the way home . . ."

Calum shook his head.

". . . or call in at any of the shops?"

Calum shook his head again.

"All right, let's come at it from another direction," said Marnie, looking out across the estate for a moment. "You know the old ironmonger's on Kentish Town Road? It's about two or three doors down from the café you've been working on . . ."

"Yeah, I know it," said Calum.

"You ever been in there?"

"I suppose I must've been at some point. Getting new locks and stuff after we've been broken into . . ."

"So you'll be familiar with the layout of the place?"

"I suppose so," shrugged Calum.

"Does that include the office in the back?"

"I don't know what you mean."

"The place was broken into last night, Calum," said Marnie, leaning forward in her chair. "A large amount of cash was stolen from the office. Cash and a lot of other stuff."

Calum kept quiet, averted his eyes.

"You know anything about that?"

Calum shook his head. "No."

"You're positive about that?"

"Sure I'm positive," muttered Calum.

"All right, then, what about Match and Tusk?"

"What about them?"

"They're your friends, Calum, your comrades in arms. You must know if they had anything to do with it . . ."

"I haven't seen them in a couple of days," said Calum.

"You didn't talk to them last night?"

Calum shook his head again, glanced hard at Marnie in confirmation.

"All right," said Marnie, sighing. "Let's look at what we've got, shall we: A known thief starts working on a mural in a café down on Kentish Town Road and just a few hours later an ironmonger's shop a couple of doors down from there gets broken into – so that's just a coincidence, is it, Calum?"

"Suppose it must be," said Calum, shrugging.

"We like Match and Tusk for this one," said Marnie. "You case the place for them, Calum? You tell them how to get in?"

Calum kept silent, his attention focused on the floor.

Marnie shook her head and looked out of the window across the estate. "All right, I'll leave it there for now," she said after a short time, getting up to leave. "But just so you know . . . I don't think you were there last night, Calum, but I do think that your two friends were, and it's just a matter of time before I find

the proof. If you don't want to help me then that's your
decision. But when we do nail them, don't kid yourself that
they'll think we figured it all out by ourselves . . ."

Although he was at first pleased with himself for not telling the
police that Match and Tusk had been around earlier the afternoon before, the following morning Calum awoke to find it
troubling him like a burgeoning toothache. On the one hand he
still felt a little proud that he had not offered up Match and
Tusk to DS Stone – a solid feature of his culture, he knew – but
on the other he knew that it was just a matter of time before she
arrested them and that when she did so it was almost inevitable
that he would be lumped into the gang as the third man. And
although he did not like to think about what that might mean, at
best he knew that he would not be allowed to continue with the
murals.

The dilemma continued to trouble him long after he returned
to school, but a couple of weeks later he saw his chance to get
out of the situation on what he saw as his own terms.

On the strength of his work at the café, word spread and he
was soon offered another commission, this time to paint a large
mural on the side of a car wash at the foot of Camden Road. The
wall faced the traffic coming down the hill, a huge area, and
after agreeing the design he set to work on it one weekend.

But just as Calum might have predicted, Match and Tusk
turned up late on the third night that he was there. He had just
completed the background and was about to start on the figures
in the cars he had painted – the mural was on a side wall of the
car wash and Calum had created a full-scale cartoon version of it
as if the wall were made of glass: in the centre of the wall he had
drawn a giant foam and rain machine with a grime-streaked car
going in one end and a bright clean car coming out of the other –
and the sight of his friends made his heart sink in his chest. But
Match and Tusk seemed to have lost some of their fire, poking
Calum with sullen and blunt jibes as if taunting him had
become a bore, and it did not take him long to get rid of them.
Watching them walk across Camden Road, Calum felt a smile
touch his face.

But it was a brief success: the following morning Detective
Sergeant Stone was on his doorstep once more, the electrical

store two doors down from the car wash having been burgled the night before. She went at him harder this time, refusing to believe that he had had nothing to do with it. And the harder she went at him, the more Calum dug in his heels. But even as he did so he felt something stirring deep inside, something far deeper than a cultural mistrust of the police and a refusal to grass. This time he knew that it was nothing less than fight or flight.

Ten minutes after Stone left the flat, Calum returned to the car wash to complete the details in the mural.

A little before two o'clock the following morning, chasing up on a call that had come into the station, DS Marnie Stone pulled up in front of the mural with anger and sadness in her heart. Someone had made a good attempt at defacing it, scratching and rubbing different colours of paint across the artwork, but from what she could still make out, the mural looked to be of a police car chasing another car through the car wash. And after taking in some of the finer details the message was made clear to her: Calum was giving her the people she was looking for. In the front car were two clear characters, their features a little smudged but still recognizable: a match with human features and another face with one huge tusk curling out of its mouth. But Calum had not been clever enough, and after his old friends had seen his latest artistic efforts they had meted out their own retribution. Calum had been nailed to the wall where he had painted the chasing police car. His feet were hanging in the air about three feet from the ground and his head rested on his chest in a thick splash of blood. For a moment Marnie had the horrific thought that perhaps his tongue had been cut out, but when she climbed out of the car for a closer look she was relieved to see that he was still breathing and that he had in fact been silenced with a cork rammed in between his bloodied and swollen lips.

PROS AND CONS

Donna Moore

Barry Sheehan looked at the sparkling diamonds around the wrinkled throat of the woman in front of him and surreptitiously adjusted his Y-fronts. Wealth always gave him a hard-on and these two auld bitches were dripping with it. It wasn't so much the wealth itself, as the idea of separating it from its rightful owners. In this case La Contessa Letitzia di Ponzo and her sister Signora Teodora Grisiola.

Sheehan smiled at the two frail old dears in front of him and thought how easy this was going to be. He considered his smile to be the deal-clincher. He'd practised it in front of the bathroom mirror, and convinced himself he looked like Cary Grant, when in reality he looked more like a constipated ferret.

"Well, Mr Sheehan," the Contessa adjusted the diamond necklace with a liver-spotted hand, "I think you will do very well as our chauffeur." Her Italian accent was light and soft. It reminded Sheehan of some actress in an old black and white film he'd seen on video when he was last in Mountjoy Prison. "If you would like to come back tomorrow in the morning, we will have ready a uniform for you and you can drive us out to Fairyhouse Racecourse to meet some of our potential clients."

Sheehan's interest was piqued. "You ladies are interested in horseracing?" He patted the crumpled *Racing Post* in his pocket. Things were looking better and better. The chance to drive a Daimler, a shot at stealing some rather fine diamonds, and a day at the track.

"Gambling? No." The Contessa made a moue of distaste and her silent sister looked shocked at the thought, raising a jeweled hand to her throat as if to cross herself. "But we have an interest in fine thoroughbreds, yes. Now, Mr Sheehan. I will see you out. I apologize for the lack of etiquette, but we haven't yet got around to hiring a butler." She picked an almost invisible speck of dust off her suit – Hardy Amies, dress designer to the Queen – and Sheehan stood up. He'd been dismissed. Fighting the dual temptations of bowing to them and nutting them, he allowed the Contessa to usher him to the door of the Georgian townhouse that she and her sister were currently calling *casa*.

Back in the Drawing Room, the Contessa stood at the window and watched Sheehan strolling up Lower Leeson Street towards St Stephens Green. Her sister looked at her curiously. "Well, Letty, will he do?"

"He's a dodgy, rat-faced, little wanker who wouldn't know the word 'honesty' if it gave him a lap dance and bit him on the arse. He's perfect." Her accent was now more Isle of Dogs than Island of Venice. "Didn't he remind you of that punter you had in the 60s, Dora? The politician who liked you to dress up as a milkmaid and squeeze his udders? Assistant to the Assistant of the Minister of Agriculture, Fisheries and Foods wasn't he?"

Dora giggled. "Old Marigold? Yes, but I do hope Mr Sheehan doesn't want me to slap him on the buttocks and hit him with a fly switch. I'm getting too old for that sort of thing."

Letty removed the diamond necklace and threw it down on the table, rubbing her neck. "That cheap tat is giving me a rash. Did you see Sheehan fixing his beadies on it?" She pulled a packet of Rizlas and a pouch of tobacco out of her fake Chanel handbag and expertly rolled a cigarette one-handed, lighting it with a Zippo displaying a Hell's Angels emblem and the motto "Live Fast, Die Young." She groped under the chintz cushion of the settee for the bottle of tequila she had planked there earlier, and opened the *Racing Post* which, just a couple of minutes ago, had been in Sheehan's pocket. She still had all the old skills.

Just plain Lettice and Dora Huggins – ex-high class hookers, ex-brothel madams, ex-pickpockets, -drunk rollers and -petty criminals – had moved up in the world.

Sheehan leaned against the Daimler in the private enclosure at Fairyhouse and watched Ireland's rich and famous swarm around his new employers like bluebottles around diamond-encrusted shit. Gobshites. He had to admire the Italian pair though. Their scam was a good one. From what he'd observed today they were selling certificates of part ownership in thoroughbred horses. 50,000 euros a share. The women had the right patter, references from top names in the horseracing world, the backing of Lord This and Duke That. Most of all they were fluently talking the language of the greedy bastards drooling all over them. The language of cold, hard cash.

"A 25 percent to 30 percent return in 3 months," the Countess was saying in her clipped, lightly accented tones, as she tapped out strings of numbers on the slim laptop computer on the table in front of her. "Guaranteed. The stud fees on their own are worth a fortune in income. Why, the Duke of Chalfont was able to restore the family seat in a year from his returns. 200,000 euros, Mr Kavanagh? Certainly. Just give me your bank account details and we'll effect the transaction immediately."

These rich tossers might not be able to recognize a hoor with the clap when they saw one, but Sheehan certainly did. He'd made a fair packet from this sort of scam himself until he'd gone to jail for it. His was on a smaller scale of course, but Sheehan recognized the signs. He'd sold dodgy TV advertising (he'd even got a film student friend to film a couple of fake adverts – and they'd made a porno while they were at it; Sheehan was rather proud of his starring role – OK, it was a short fuckin' fillum and it was all wobbly cameras and badly dubbed sound, but they'd got the money shot and that was the main thing). He'd guaranteed his investors a 30 percent return every 60 days. And, of course, he'd made sure to deliver to the first few investors. They spread the word and all the other suckers signed up. Needless to say, the other suckers never got their promised returns. Or their capital back as it happened. It was risky, and you had to have balls to pull it off. For a while

Sheehan had managed to juggle those balls in the air as he robbed Peter to pay Paul, but eventually the whole thing had collapsed like a drunken sailor, and Sheehan hadn't managed to disappear before the Gardai came a-calling.

Sheehan narrowed his eyes and ground out his cigarette under the heel of his boot. He was decked out in his new green and gold uniform – knife-edge creases in the trousers, gold buttons shining, black boots polished to within an inch of their life. He was hot, uncomfortable and he'd nearly lamped the auld bitch one when she gave him the uniform. Green and gold? He was a Unionist all the way. Green and feckin' gold? If it hadn't been for that insult he might have stuck with his original plan of heisting the diamonds. Now he was going to make this job really worth his while. Sheehan had a grudging admiration for the auld wans. But it wasn't going to stop him relieving them of some of the cash. It would be like taking candy from a baby.

"Well, Dora, how much have we made?" Letty put her feet up on the rented Georgian table in the drawing room, popped the cork of a magnum of Dom Perignon and opened a packet of pork scratchings.

Dora entered the final few numbers into the laptop. "Just short of 4 million euros. Not too shabby." She opened one of the miniature bottles of Tia Maria that she'd stolen off the trolley on the EasyJet flight over from Luton the week before, clinked it against the bottle of champagne in Letty's hand and knocked it back.

"Piece of piss, Dora. Piece of piss." Two enormous trunks were open at Letty's feet, each of them half full of clothes. "I checked the flight to Rio. We need to be at the airport in an hour or so. Sheehan should be back in a few minutes to drive us."

"And here I am, *ladies*." Sheehan lounged in the doorway, a smile on his thin lips.

Letty dragged herself back into Countess mode, removed her feet from the table and gently placed the half empty champagne bottle down, burping in a ladylike manner as she did so. "Ah, Sheehan, please could you take these trunks to the car."

"Oh, I don't think so. I think you and I and Dora here need to have a nice wee chat, about an equitable sharing of the proceeds of your day at the races. It's only fair after all."

He moved to where Dora had been sitting and turned the laptop round to face him. "4 million euros, eh? And what are two auld bitches like yerselves going to do with 4 million euros? A nice old peoples' home should set you back a couple of thousand at the most. I might let you have 10,000 or so, just so you can keep yourselves in Rich Tea Biscuits."

Letty jumped up from the sofa and took a couple of tottering steps towards him. Sheehan picked up the plane tickets lying next to the laptop and laughed, as Letty and Dora stared at him wide-eyed and open-mouthed, dewlaps quivering in unison.

"And yez think yez are heading off to Argentina with your ill-gotten gains?"

"Brazil," muttered Letty, as she regained her composure, hefted the half empty magnum of champagne, and swung it at the back of his head with as much vigour as she'd once used to whip politicians and High Court judges into submission in her previous career. "Rio de Janeiro is in Brazil, you stupid fucking little twat." She dropped the champagne bottle onto Sheehan's rat-like face as he lay on the floor staring blankly upwards. As the bottle smashed his nose Letty said "That'll teach you, you little wanker," and wiped her hands on her skirt.

Colm O'Neil knocked on the door of the Georgian Townhouse, his home-made collecting tin in hand. If he'd chosen to use his IT degree wisely he could have had a future. But he didn't like to get up in the morning so, instead, he'd printed out some imposing looking business cards and brochures for a charity proclaiming itself "The Holy Sisters of Perpetual Misery" and spent his afternoons fleecing Dublin's tourists and residents alike of the odd 20 euros. Just enough to get himself a wee carry-out from the offy and a couple of ounces of the finest cannabis from his dealer in Gardiner Street.

An elderly lady opened the door and looked at him calmly, a smaller woman fluttering behind her like a stressed-out moth. Quickly sizing them up – the well-cut suits, the jewels adorning their necks and fingers, the general aura of wealth, Colm decided to go for broke. "Howya ladies. I'm collecting for The Holy Sisters, and wondered if you'd be after sparing 50 euros for a good cause?" He rattled his tin to tempt them.

"Certainly young man, do come in." The non-fluttering woman opened the door wider and he stepped into the hall. Two huge old-fashioned trunks and several smaller bags were in the hallway, coats draped over them. "You've just caught us on our way out. We're waiting for a taxi to take us to the airport." The woman looked at him appraisingly for a long moment and then rummaged in her handbag. Pulling out a large wallet she gave him a hundred euros. "A fine strapping young chap like you – I wonder if you'd do us a small favor. Would you take these two trunks here to the dump? We just . . . don't have the time. And although they're on wheels they're terribly heavy and my sister and I are not as young as we used to be. It's just some old papers and old clothes that we don't want."

Colm practically snatched off her hand to get to the 100 euro note. "Sure, and whyever not."

"I just need to put a couple more things in." The woman disappeared into a room to the left, came out a couple of minutes later and slid a fat envelope into a compartment at the side of one of the trunks.

Colm lifted the handle of the brown trunk. She was right. It was heavy. Maybe he should ask for 200 euros. Still, there might be something inside worth having – he didn't want to appear too greedy. "Have a lovely trip ladies. And thank you. The Sisters of Perpetual Misery will bless you."

Letty and Dora sat in Business Class with their feet up, watching *Ocean's Eleven* on the screen in front of them as they sipped their champagne on the flight to Rio.

Dora smiled happily. "Letty, that nice young man is going to open the trunks, isn't he, dear?"

"Of course he is Dora. He won't be able to resist."

"What do you think he'll do when he finds those nicely packaged portions of Mr Sheehan?"

"I have absolutely no idea. But hopefully the 10,000 euros I also put in the trunk will offset the horrible shock." Letty studied George Clooney on the screen as he scammed the Las Vegas casino out of a fortune. "Dora, do you know if they have casinos in Rio?"

SHERLOCK HOLMES
AND THE *TITANIC* SWINDLE

Len Deighton

It was handwritten in a bold, attractive and well-formed writing style, on a cream-coloured heavy paper. There was a small crease on the corner but there was no sign of fading and the colour was the same on both front and back. Held to the light, this single sheet revealed a watermark of a floral design that I did not recognize. The upper edge of the sheet was slightly rough as if it might have been torn from a writing pad, but it may have been because the paper was handmade. Most significantly, the writing varied in ink density. The sentences started in a strong dark greyish-blue and then faded slightly as happens when writing with an old-fashioned pen frequently dipped into a bottle of ink.

Sherlock Holmes and the *Titanic* Swindle

It was a raw and foggy night in early December when Holmes and I sat either side of a blazing fire in our sitting room in Baker Street. Inspector Lestrade of Scotland Yard was there. He was likely to call in on us of an evening, and Sherlock Holmes always welcomed him, as he liked to hear the latest news from police headquarters. On this particular evening Lestrade puffed at his cigar and was uncustomarily quiet. "It's this terrible disaster," said Lestrade, shaking his head sadly.

"Some fine old families will be mourning still," I said.

"There are fears abroad that this failure of an unsinkable vessel could deliver a crippling blow to our whole shipbuilding industry," said Holmes. "I can reveal that I have already been in contact with the captain, the helmsman and several others who were on watch at the time. I am presenting my spiritual research to the directors of the White Star Line. There remain many unanswered questions."

"Surely not?" said Lestrade. "The Titanic *struck an iceberg, was ripped open and sank. How can there be a mystery concerning it?"*

"The Titanic, *was it?" said Holmes. He waited a long time before continuing. "There is not one article; not one piece of flotsam or jetsam bearing the name* Titanic." *He watched our faces and then answered the tacit question. "'White Star Line' yes, but not one item with the word* Titanic."

He held up his hand to still our questions. "To other matters," he said.

"And where's the rest of it?" I asked.

"In his father's bank or in a private Swiss vault or in a tower of his auntie's Bavarian castle," said Percy.

"Is that what's he's like?"

"Strong London accent; almost like an Aussie, carefully trimmed black beard; brown corduroy suit; pompous, assertive; aggressive almost."

"Could be any one of our authors," I said.

"My authors are respectful," said Percy.

"Because you send the aggressive ones to me."

"And they are the ones that make the money," said Percy. "Ever since that piece in *The Bookseller*, they all want you to be their editor, you know that. Fiction writers do anyway."

I read the sheet of paper again and said nothing.

"So what do you think?" said Percy after looking around the room. "Bloody untidy; your office." He had removed a pile of books in order to sit in the soft leather chair I put authors into when I have bad news for them. One leg was resting across the other to display a red cashmere sock and handmade Oxford shoe. Percy always looked like a page from a fashion magazine even on days like today, when the rain was thrashing against the windows, and the sky was so dark that all the office lights were turned on.

"Is it a parody or what?" I said. "It has the same plodding style that I remember from all Conan Doyle's Sherlock Holmes yarns."

"Is that a recommendation? Do you mean it's genuine?"

"We have quite a big list, and it will be too late for the new catalogue, no matter how fast we move. I think we should stay out of this. Send him one of your sad rejection letters."

"Send him where? To HarperCollins? To Random House?"

"Why did he pick us?" I asked.

"He wanted to bring it to the last independent publisher in London, he said."

"You didn't tell me he was a philanthropist."

"Now, now, Carl. Don't let your nasty Teutonic streak show."

"It's been a long day," I said. Percy's Teutonic joke, a reference to my Christian name, had worn thin.

"And you've had your regular kick-boxing lesson from Princess Diana all afternoon."

"Her agent told her our contract will have to be renegotiated."

"More money. She can go to Hell and take *Footsteps to Heaven* with her."

"We did rather well with her last Sharon du Parr," I reminded him. "And she has a new agent now: Freckles. Her other agent was not commercial enough for her. New agents, Percy, always want to flex their muscles."

"Her last agent was a man," said Percy who was high enough in the command structure to be in on the deals. "Sensible enough to keep her feet on the ground."

"Was he? I never met him."

"Blonde lady bomber pilots and female secret agents toting machine guns. The artwork on her last dust-jacket haunts me. I don't know why we publish that crap."

"You don't?" I enjoyed winding him up. "She loved the dust-jacket. She wanted us to make it into a poster."

"That wretched Freckles? Has she really started her own agency? Good grief."

"I think we might be dealing with her for more of our lady writers before long. She wrote an amusing article in *The*

Author. She said men authors always got paid twice as much as women authors and she was going to fight for them. And you'd better not call her Freckles to her face, Percy."

"Let's get back to this Sherlock Holmes story," said Percy. He put a finger on to his starched shirt cuff to sneak a look at his gold Rolex. "You want me to tell him to get stuffed? He's demanding some 'token' money down before we see the rest of it."

"That's just to keep us on the hook," I told him.

"So I'll tell him we're not interested?"

"Not in as many words, Percy. You don't want to make headlines as the publisher who turned down a Sherlock Holmes story that has been locked away undiscovered for a hundred years."

He wetted his lips and then sighed. "Make up your mind, Carl."

"Everyone loves Sherlock Holmes," I said. "If it's the real thing this will make news. Not trade news; big international headline news and TV."

"The paper looks old," he picked it up and looked at it and smelled it. "But is it Conan Doyle's writing?"

"Well, I don't imagine he would bring us an autograph edition; he may have copied it out."

"You'd think he'd put it on a computer or something."

"Not very secure, computers, Percy. Put something like that on the hard drive and it's only a couple of keystrokes away from going on to the Internet. And into the Public Domain, as you lawyers say. Your – what did you say his name was? – seems to be a careful chap."

"He says he wants a definite answer, and cash on the table, by the fifteenth of the month."

"The fifteenth? Next week?"

"He's out of the country till then; a business trip he said."

"Writers all say that; they have a guilt complex about holidays."

I was very busy over the next few days. One of our best line-editors had gone sick with what they suspected was chickenpox. Her daughter phoned us to say her mother might need hospital treatment. She was having blood tests. I knew that would mean a week or more out of action. The worst of it was that she lived in deepest, darkest Cornwall and there was a tall pile of typescripts sitting on her shelf. I couldn't find time to go down there, and Percy was frightened he might catch chickenpox. Finally we decided to wait and see what the medical tests showed. And Percy found an urgent need to visit one of our writers in Ireland. As usual, this meant a diligent exploration of the local pubs and Percy running at half speed for several following days.

Once back in action, Percy took his single sheet of hand-written Sherlock Holmes all around the building, swearing them all to secrecy, as he had before showing it to me. By Thursday he must have run out of people to consult for he came back to talk to me again.

"That young fellow who does the computer stuff in accounts had a good suggestion."

"About Sherlock Holmes?"

"He said we must insist on having a sheet from the original, and then have the paper examined and tested in a laboratory to see how old it was."

"No great problem getting your hands on sheets of old paper, Percy. We could probably find some in the store room, or the slush pile, if we rooted around long enough."

"And I thought of that too, Carl. I'm not a complete fool. It might be better to get one of these computer people to compare the syntax against other stories." I suppose I did not light up in the expected fashion. "Verbs, adjectives, the length of the sentences and so on. That 'customarily', for instance. Was that a word Doyle ever used?"

"It wouldn't be conclusive. We shouldn't assume that this fellow, What's-his-name, is an untutored oaf. If he's a forger he will have looked at the stories: verbs, adjectives and the length of sentences."

"You don't have to be so bloody sarcastic, Carl. I'm trying to see some way out of this situation."

"Way out?"

"Yes, I didn't tell you but I've had the newspapers sniffing around, asking if we'd found some long-lost manuscript."

"Sherlock Holmes?"

"One of them said H. G. Wells – he'd heard it was a sequel to *Things to Come* and the other didn't have a clue about who wrote anything."

"That must have been a senior literary editor. Let me guess which paper."

"No, that's just the point. These queries are coming from the news desks. The H. G. Wells loony had heard that it was going to be a major film."

"Why doesn't your punter just put it up for auction? One of the big boys might be willing to put it into their New York auctions."

"Perhaps he's frightened of it being turned down as a fake," said Percy. "That could be a crippling setback for anyone selling it."

"Will an auction house care too much whether it's a fake? They'll get their money; then it's *cave canem* for the bidders. I sometimes think half the junk put up for auction is bogus in one way or another."

"*Caveat emptor*," Percy solemnly corrected me.

"Same goes for the film," I said. "If some sharp film man grabs it, he could ride along on the publicity generated by a controversy about whether it's genuine. And if it turns out fake that will hardly dent the takings at the box office."

"So you think we should publish it?"

"I didn't say that, Percy."

"It's all right for you. You can just move on if the firm hits a rock. I'm stuck here." Percy was determined not to be deprived of his crisis.

"I don't see why."

"Because my uncle is the chairman, Carl. Be your age. You've made enough jokes at my expense."

"Have I, Percy? I hope I have never been offensive."

"I don't mind your jokes. You can be very humorous sometimes. It's the crap I get when people have to be sacked."

"People say things they don't mean."

"They mean it all right," said Percy and I almost felt sorry for him. It was, after all, Percy who had got me the job. The ad agency let me go after they lost the breakfast food account I was working on. Percy got to his feet. "Well, I must leave you now. I have an important lunch appointment."

When I saw Percy later that afternoon he was roseate and ebullient. And it wasn't all due to the unspecified number of bottles of Chevalier-Montrachet he and his luncheon guest had consumed. "There it is," he said. He put a brown packet on my desk. His aim erred to the extent that it sideswiped my keyboard and put about three hundred z's across a letter I was concocting for the "Princess" about the bewildering way her characters were apt to change names and/or appearance and then some-times change back again. "That's it." He pointed. "That's the Sherlock Holmes story. That's your Christmas bonus and my seat on the board."

"He gave it to you?"

"It wasn't easy but lunch at the Ritz can have a magical effect upon authors. I've noticed that before."

"And this is the only copy? No photocopies in your desk?"

He hesitated. "He made me promise on my honour. I signed a piece of paper for him. It wouldn't have much effect in a court of law but he knows I wouldn't want him brandishing it if there was evidence that I'd cheated on him. So look after it. Don't leave it on the train or something. You remember how you went past your station and had to get a minicab home that night after the Christmas party?"

"Yes," I said. I wished I'd never mentioned that journey home to him. At the time I was hoping he'd offer to reimburse the cab fare but instead of that he kept using it to beat me over the head with implications that I got everything wrong. "So how much did you have to pay him?"

"Nothing. Not a penny."

"He just handed it over?"

"I said the directors would have a meeting on Monday and have an offer and a contract ready for Tuesday morning. I thought that would give you a chance to read it."

"What about you reading it?"

"I have read it," said Percy. "I read it as soon as I got back from lunch."

I noticed that the packet had been torn open and then sealed up again, so perhaps he had.

"And?" Percy was not an avid reader.

"It's damned clever; almost too clever for a Sherlock Holmes yarn. *Corpus delicti*, it all turns on that. You know what I mean?"

"You don't plough your way through a thousand whodunits without discovering what *corpus delicti* means," I told him.

Percy was not to be denied a chance to display his legal qualifications. "Body; but not necessarily a human body. It's the facts, money, physical substance, evidence of any kind that a crime has been committed."

"How does the story read?"

"You'll have to read it for yourself but at the conclusion of the story, Holmes finds there is no written evidence, no substance, no witnesses, not even this gigantic ship, to prove that any crime was ever committed. Holmes ends up baffled . . . but anyway you must read it."

"Doyle was ingenious," I admitted

"It's good," said Percy. "A page-turner. But you are the senior editor, senior fiction editor, anyway."

"Ummm," I said. I could see into Percy's mind. If it turned out well, the firm would make umpteen thousands, Percy would get his seat on the board – there was going to be a vacancy in January anyway – and I would get a small Christmas bonus. If it became the sort of fiasco that Percy feared, it would all be my fault.

"Take it home. Read it over the weekend and let me know on Monday."

"Monday is a difficult day for me, Percy."

"Your day at home, I know."

"It's the only way I can get through the backlog. Here in the office there is always something cropping up."

"Like me."

"It's not only that, Percy. I have to see Sergeant McGregor in the morning and so I asked him to come to my flat for a sandwich and a beer. I want to switch a couple of his chapters and I've drafted out a new beginning. It's not as much work as it sounds but getting an author to understand the need for revisions is always a delicate job."

"Who the devil is Sergeant McGregor?"

"Peter Cardiff. He writes the 'Copper's Diary' series. We've done six of them now. They have all been trade paperbacks but marketing think he's ready to go mass-market."

"Why do these fellows have to have nom de plumes? Isn't Cardiff a good enough name? Better, in my humble opinion."

"Not for a police series about Glasgow criminals. And when he first started he was still on the Glasgow force. He had to have an assumed name."

"Move him to Tuesday, Carl. This Sherlock Holmes decision is important."

"He's coming all the way down from the other side of Aberdeen. And he is a widower; with a school-age child. He has to arrange for someone to collect her and look after her. I really wouldn't like to throw a spanner into his arrangements. And he's one of our best authors, Percy."

"What is best about him?"

"He can spell; he puts a capital letter at the beginning of each sentence and a full-stop at the end. He knows an adjective from a verb and doesn't use flashbacks or dream sequences or try to write sexy scenes that he can't handle."

"He's old fashioned, is that what you mean?"

"Yes, exactly."

"And now I've annoyed you."

"A few more old-fashioned writers like Cardiff and I would have a weekend to myself now and again."

"A palpable hit, Carl."

"Yes, well, he's not old-fashioned, Percy. He's a fine writer who stays within his capabilities, and understands instinctively the taste and intelligence of the reading public in a way that not many people in this building do."

"I say, Carl. A streak of passion! You are always able to surprise me. Very well then; 10 a. m. Tuesday morning. And don't leave it on the train tonight." He rummaged around in the cupboard where unpublished books grow dusty before going into the bin and found a green plastic bag with a Harrods motif. He put the manuscript into it, and hung it on the bentwood stand with my raincoat.

"Red sealing wax and string." I observed.

"I wanted it to be secure. On this floor, any wrapped parcel of A4 size gets thrown into the slush pile without being opened."

"Is that your signet ring you used on the wax?"

"It looks good doesn't it? I'm going to start using it on letters too. What about on the contracts?" I gave him a wintry smile. "We worked hard at college didn't we Carl? Not many parties; not very often drunk; work, work, work." I nodded. "Well I was going through the numbers with Uncle John last week, and I noticed that only one of our top earners even got into college, and she didn't graduate."

"'There are only three things needed for writing a best-seller; but no one knows what they are.' Somerset Maugham."

"Yes it's all very well for an old buzzard like that to be sardonic but he was sitting on a barrel of cash in his villa in the south of France and lunching with the likes of Winston Churchill."

"Maugham was a doctor at St Thomas's Hospital. Doesn't that rather undermine your theory about illiterate best-selling authors?"

"And Conan Doyle was a doctor, too. So were a lot of bestselling authors but that was all long ago. Now we all know what is needed for a best-seller. Not three things, only one damned thing: TV. It doesn't matter what illiterate rubbish you write, if it becomes a TV series you'll be feted and feasted and rich, and people will say you are a famous writer."

"Not always, Percy."

"Yes, always. Good grief, Carl, who would have guessed, in Maugham's day, that any silly little cookery book could be made into a best-seller? Or a book about exercising, wriggling your *derrière*, like that one we did with that frightful athlete woman who insisted on having her photo on every page?"

"We did well with it, as I remember."

"That was because the photographer did such wonders. Or his retoucher or someone at the printer. He made her look like Jane Fonda, that's why it sold."

"For whatever reason. She asked for twice as much for her second book."

"She didn't get it from us," said Percy with some force. "She didn't get another TV series. I could see that it was going to be the end of her. Her end, perhaps I should say." He didn't need to remind me that she'd made a loud and angry scene in Percy's office before taking her book to another publisher. And they had advertised it in the Sunday papers and lost a great deal of money on it. He laughed. It was good to see him happy and there is nothing that makes a publisher happier than to have a rival company steal authors, and then lose money with them.

Peter Cardiff arrived at my flat on the dot. A result of twenty-five years on the force, I suppose. His books had the series title "A Copper's Diary" and everyone in the trade, including me, admired them as fast-moving, well-written stories. Judging by his mail, the police service liked them too. But the joke was that Cardiff had actually kept a diary right from the first day he joined up as a constable recruit. He retired with dozens of notebooks and was unhurriedly making them into a literary career.

He hadn't been to my flat before. After I took his coat, he moved around the room. There wasn't much furniture. He went to the built-in shelves and started looking at all my books in a systematic way. "Reference mostly," I said. "Specialist diction-aries and encyclopaedias, maps and so on. I do most of my editing work here, away from the telephones and interruptions."

"I thought my stuff went off to someone in the country for corrections of that sort."

"For line editing; yes it does, but if I can pick something up in the early readings I can call the author with a query. It's quicker like that." I opened two cans of beer and poured them out. Then I opened the packets of smoked salmon sandwiches and arranged them on the plates. He bent to look at one of the photos on the fireplace. "My wife," I said. "She's a wonderful woman."

"I thought you were getting divorced," he said. "I'm sorry, it's the policeman in me."

I had no doubt referred to my wife in one of my letters or emails; it was sharp of him to remember so well. "We've had our ups and downs," I explained. "She went to see her family in Brisbane. My teenage son is with her. She wants me to join her there. It's not something I want to rush into. On the other hand, if I decide to go, her fare back here and return would be money wasted."

"Looks like you were there when you were getting married," he said, pointing to our wedding photo in a silver frame on the hi-fi. "The eucalyptus trees, the coastline and the man in the bush shirt – just a guess, of course."

"Ten years back. It can get very hot in summer and I'm very fond of hot weather."

He smiled and we both listened to the wind howling in the chimney. Despite the heat turned fully on, it was cold in the flat and it had been raining on and off for almost a week. "And my son wants to go to college there."

"What will he study?"

"He'll try for a Ph D in surfing and sunning."

"I'd miss you if you moved," he said. "You are painstaking and understand what I would like to be able to do. The editor they gave me at first scribbled all over my typing, scribbled in red ballpoint. That was before I got the word processor. It all had to be typed again. It used to make me livid."

He was still looking around when I said: "I like the new one very much. You are really exploring McGregor's character now. The indecision and the anger . . . and that chapter with the kid who can't speak English. You've come a long way from your first book with the motorcycle cops." It was enough to bring him to the table where I had my notes.

"So you went back and read my first one?" he said. He sipped some beer and bit into a sandwich.

"I try to see how writers develop. And I must keep you to the continuity. We don't want you slipping up about past references; things like the new inspector going to the staff college."

"No, that was stupid. So you picked that one up? I wondered who had spotted it. I should have sent a proper thank you letter. I'm not in touch as closely as I should be."

"You need a London agent," I told him.

"That doesn't sound like a publisher speaking." He was much more relaxed now and I could hear his soft Glasgow accent; the only Scots accent that I could recognize.

"Someone who knows the way around town could get you some radio plays and maybe TV too. It would get you known to a larger public and that's what publishing is all about nowadays."

"Yes, I know but I'm a slow worker. You wouldn't believe how many hours I spend in front of that damned screen. And I've always liked to be outdoors." He tucked into the sandwiches. He probably hadn't eaten since getting off the train. I should have offered him something more substantial.

"Peter, old pal," I said. He looked up sharply. I usually kept to more distant forms of address. It made it easier to criticize if I made it a bit formal. 'I have a safe here. I was broken into over the weekend."

He looked at me as if I had gone mad. "How much did you lose?"

"There was no money there; just my lease and bank statements and passport and so on. Other than that: six silver spoons that were my mother's, and a packet."

"Packet?"

"With a small manuscript inside. Keep it to yourself. I haven't told anyone at the office about it. I didn't go to the police either."

"No, I understand. It's more or less useless reporting robberies to your local coppers. Can I look at the front door?" He got up. He was a policeman now.

We went and looked at the door and the surround. "The door shows no sign of being forced," I said. "And all the windows look OK too."

"What sort of safe?"

"Not very wonderful." I went and opened the closet in the hall to show him where the safe was hidden behind the coats. "Guaranteed fireproof; that was important to me. Four figure combination lock. No sign of it being forced either."

He ran his hands round the back of it to see if he could detect damage of any kind. "Only four digits. That's useless."

"The salesman said it meant almost ten thousand variations."

"Who else has the key to this place?"

"No one. At least, there is an extra one I keep in the main safe at the office – in case I locked myself out – and the cleaning lady has one."

"Look at it like this," he said as he sat down and swallowed the rest of his beer, "most of these combination safes have locks that are quick to operate. User friendly. That means it's quick to swing through the numbers. Try and you'll see."

"Ten thousand numbers."

"Five hundred wouldn't be too daunting, would it?"

"No, it wouldn't."

"Five hundred a day. Try it; click click click. You'd be through it in twenty visits. And your winning combination is unlikely to be at the very end. On average, a thief would find the number halfway through his search. That may not be in line with the science of probability but you see what I mean."

"Yes, I see what you mean. But I don't know what I should do."

"If it's insured you'd better report it as soon as possible. Insurance companies are always looking for an excuse not to pay out."

"I'll speak to the cleaning lady. She's Estonian. She only comes in twice a week: She's a nice young woman. She's been doing the flat for almost a year." I realised how stupid it all sounded but I suppose Cardiff knew that crime victims are likely to become a little disoriented.

"She probably met some tearaway. It's a familiar story, I'm afraid. They meet in a pub and he gets the key and makes a copy. She may not be in on it but I doubt if you will see her again. It's a nasty old world. That's why I was happy to retire to my little hovel in the highlands."

We went quickly though some literals and questions that I'd sent him in advance. Then I got to my feet. "Thanks, Peter. Your new book is very good. It will have to be finally decided by the money men and the marketing people but I would be amazed if there was any hitch about your next one going mass market. We will have the same artist. You said you were happy with the previous covers."

"I leave all that to you London laddies," he said. "That's what a publisher does, isn't it?"

"That's what a publisher does if he's lucky enough to have a sensible author," I said. "Another beer?"

He shook his head but he didn't leave. He didn't even put his coat on, he picked it up and held it awkwardly and said. "You'd better tell me about it. I might be able to help. The parcel. Why would anyone crack open a safe to get a manuscript? Is it valuable? Why?"

I didn't answer.

"Come along, man. I won't be telling any of your secrets to the sheep."

"I didn't open it," I admitted. "I thought it was a photocopy of a manuscript but perhaps it's an autograph manuscript. If it's written by a famous writer from the past, it could be valuable."

"How valuable?"

"I've no idea. Anything up to a hundred thousand pounds."

"Glasgow's full of gentry who would slit their mother's throat for a crate of scotch. London's worse. You'd better tell your local law, or someone might start thinking it's an inside job."

"That I've stolen it?"

"There's no evidence of a break-in, is there?" he reasoned.

I shivered. "I'll give it another day or so. You'll keep all this to yourself, won't you?"

He nodded but he didn't say yes. Peter Cardiff was a decent chap but once a policeman always a policeman. I had a feeling he was wondering about me. Wondering if I was trying to use him to cover some ingenious theft. All the other times I'd seen him it was in the office; so why ask him to come here today? I could see that question written in his face as he shook hands and said goodbye.

"I don't have my cleaning lady's address or phone number," I said.

He smiled and nodded and I went down to the street and said goodbye. By that time I believe he thought I was the same sort of accident-prone schlemiel that Percy thought I was.

Percy's office was almost directly below mine, so on the Tuesday morning I arrived early and then went down to tell him I was ready for the meeting. I was still wondering how I was going to tackle him and his uncle. I would have indulged myself in a stiff drink before leaving home but I didn't want to make things worse by arriving with booze on my breath. "Percy not here yet?" I asked his secretary.

"Has no one told you? He never arrived yesterday." She was flustered.

"What?"

"Poor Percy. He was waiting for a bus yesterday morning and a little car came out of nowhere." She seemed to welcome the chance to relate the story again. "The ambulance took ages apparently and you know how dreadful the rain was. They took him to the little cottage hospital near where he lives. It's not life threatening or anything. But his leg is broken. And he has what they call 'superficial injuries' – bruises and grazes. It didn't stop; the car didn't stop. What brutes people are. They're doing tests, of course, in case he has anything internal. But he sounded quite cheerful on the telephone this morning. I'll give you the number. He has a private line. You can visit him any time they say. It's only a little hospital. I sent him some nice things to eat. He's not on any special diet or anything." Finally she ran out of steam.

"So, no meeting this morning?"

"It could be days," she said. "Next week perhaps. He's got his laptop and a dozen books he wanted from the London Library."

The phone rang. When she answered it I could tell it was an author complaining about a late arriving royalty cheque. I waved goodbye and left.

At first I thought, hooray, reprieved. But then I thought of Percy in the hospital and I put aside the bundle of sentimental scribble that Princess bloody Diana expected me to transform into her next best-seller. Percy lived in a rather verdant neighbourhood on the edge of the green belt. The hospital was just half a mile away, a private one, situated in many acres of countryside. It was almost possible to forget the thunder and filth of the heavy traffic grinding along the nearby North Circular.

"I see our client is a publisher by the cruel look in his eyes. His well-nourished countenance reveals a convivial lifestyle, and the faint remains of a tan suggest either an army man lately returned from service in the orient, or a playboy who takes extended holidays in Provence. As for the casing on the lower leg, this reveals a propensity to cross the road without looking both ways."

"Hello, Carl," He was sitting up in bed with a cast on his leg and extensive dressings on one arm. I'd always thought of Percy as somewhat effete. He was continuously getting colds and was likely to be found pausing breathless on the landing when the lift was out of order. He was only slightly younger, but I'd been in the army while he was getting his law degree and somehow that made a difference to our relationship.

But today I saw a new side to Percy. Despite having had surgery, he was energetically researching the world of Sherlock Holmes. On the bedside table he had his shiny new Sony laptop open and lit up. Beside it there was a tower of books from which grew a torrent of yellow sticky markers.

I decided that the best line of defence was attack. "Look, Percy, the *Titanic* sank in April 1912 – I looked it up – and Doyle didn't become interested in spiritualism until long after that. Long after Sherlock Holmes was dead and buried."

"If the old man offers you non-fiction editing, old lad, be sure to say no."

"Then what?"

"First of all, Doyle joined the Psychical Research Society in 1893. That was the same year the *Strand* magazine ran 'The Final Problem' with Holmes tipping over into the waterfall. Doyle didn't stop writing about Holmes just because his hero had died. He wrote 'The Hound of the Baskervilles', perhaps his best and most famous, in 1902, and predated the events. He simply said that this story was something that had happened to Holmes before he wrestled with Professor Moriarty above the lethal torrent of the Reichenbach Falls."

"I see." I put a bottle of Johnny Walker on the bed and Percy grabbed it and hid it under his pillow. "You've been working hard, Percy. What are you going to be like when the anaesthetic wears off?"

He beamed. Percy was enjoying it all. Sherlock Holmes had got to him as it has done to many thousands of readers over the years. And, from my point of view this was splendid. Anything that kept Percy explaining the manuscript to me, instead of the other way around, was a relief. "Tell me what else you found out?"

"This is the interesting stuff, Carl." He tapped one of the books. "Can you believe it? A new Sherlock Holmes story was published in the August 1948 issue of *Cosmopolitan* magazine. August 1948. Doyle died in 1930, didn't he?"

"Maybe they got it from a Ouija board."

"Very good, Carl. A very good joke," he said solemnly. I think he hated jokes. He once told me that jokes diverted and diluted serious thought and conversation. He was right and that's what I liked about them. "And I went on the Internet and found some *Titanic* nutters. It seems that Holmes got that one right too. None of the remains: flotsam, jetsam, anything-elsesam, had the name *Titanic* on it. Nothing! Nothing so far retrieved can be positively identified as from the *Titanic*."

"What are they saying then? That some other ship struck the iceberg?"

"Yes. The *Olympic*. But let's not get into that just yet, Carl. *Corpus delicti*, remember what I told you? Our concern is the story we are offered. Let me tell you about another situation that might – at law – be comparable with the one we find ourselves in." Percy was really enjoying himself. "This one surfaced in 1948. This was a Sherlock Holmes story called 'The Man Who was Wanted'. It wasn't written by Sir Arthur Conan Doyle; it was the work of another Arthur; a hard-up English architect named Arthur Whitaker. He sent it to Doyle. Feeling sorry for him, Doyle sent Whitaker a check for ten pounds and a sarcastic note telling him to invent his own characters rather than using Sherlock Holmes and co. Doyle tossed the story into the waste paper basket and forgot it. But someone – Lady Conan Doyle probably, or perhaps Doyle's secretary – rescued it and filed it away with Doyle's other papers."

A woman in a white starched overall came in, bringing a tray bearing two cups of tea and four chocolate biscuits. She wanted to adjust his pillows but Percy waved her away so he could get on with his story.

"Ten years after both Doyles are dead, someone finds 'The Man Who was Wanted' tucked away in the Doyle archives. It's unpublished and the law says that trustees are obliged to maximize the income of the estate. In good faith, they sell it to Hearst Newspapers. In England the *Sunday Dispatch* published this 'new unpublished story'. January 2nd, January 9th and January 16th, 1949. It's a big circulation booster for all concerned."

"But your story hasn't come from the Doyle estate," I pointed out to him.

"I wish you would stop being such a damned wet blanket."

"I'm trying to stop you setting yourself ablaze."

"In fact, Carl, old bean, you are the one who struck the match. What you said about controversy, about a lot of people who will care less about authenticity than about wallowing in the financial benefits that widespread controversy will bring . . . well, that's it."

I held up my finger in tacit protest. "It's all very well to say that to me, Percy. But you must be very careful in expressing such ideas to other people. You're a lawyer; I don't have to tell you the implications. Conspiracy and so on."

He vigorously waved away my objections with his bandaged arm. "Just tell me one thing, Carl. Did you like the story?"

"It's all right," I said cautiously.

"It's not just all right; it's marvellous, isn't it? It would make an exciting film with all the exteriors that film people call production values. It's not just two old Victorian dinosaurs chatting by the fireplace in a Baker Street sitting room. You have the shipyards, the squalid Liverpool back streets and signing the contract in the fabulous Belgravia home of the White Star chairman. New York, too. It has enough to expand the American end of the story."

"Well, that would need a lot of extra writing and dialogue. A lot."

"Film people don't mind that, Carl. They love extra writing. It gives them a chance to make the sort of film they prefer to make. Is that tea all right?"

"Yes, the tea is fine," I took a biscuit and bit into it. "The film end is a long shot," I cautioned him.

"Ah. That's what you think. One advantage to having this private room is I can talk to New York and Hollywood while they are still awake out there."

"Hollywood?"

"Yes, Hollywood, you damned Jeremiah. A film production company has been phoning everyone they can think of to ask about the new Sherlock Holmes story."

"A big company? How did they find out?"

"Big enough to be talking about half a million dollars. And a share of the profits. What do I care about how they found out?"

"But why?"

"They need to schedule it. They need time to get the stars they want. They don't want to wait around while we stage some prolonged kind of auction. Cash: up front."

"You talked to them?"

"It's better than that, Carl. These film company idiots in California have made enough phone calls to stir up our cousins in New York. I now have two publishers – one quite small, I admit – who want to do a deal. The word will soon get out. World volume rights; film and TV rights. There are all these disks and things nowadays. It could add up to a fortune."

"I've never been a party to that sort of thing, Percy. I just edit the books."

"And if the manuscript is in Doyle's hand, it could bring an immense price at auction. It's only in the last few hours, on the Internet, that I have learned how many rich collectors of Sherlock Holmes material are still active. There's money in every aspect of this deal."

"Really?"

"Yes, really, you old misery. And don't tell me that the whole manuscript is a forgery, because I think it's kosher."

"Well, I don't know."

"Let me put it another way. Is there anything at all to suggest it's a fake?"

I pulled a face, not knowing how to proceed. "I'm not an expert."

"It's real, isn't it? It's exactly like Doyle's handwriting even to the sloping words on the title page . . . I was able to compare the writing with pages and pages of Doyle's. I went carefully through every line of that facsimile edition of a Doyle manuscript that was published in Santa Barbara in 1985."

I nodded.

"Yes, you know the one I mean: 'The Adventure of the Priory School'." Percy gave a triumphal grin. "You remember, do you? I've got it here now. My secretary found it. And do you know where my secretary found it? On the floor in your office."

"I was sorting through my books to throw some out. I need shelf space."

"On the floor in your office, Carl. On the top of a pile near the door. That's where she found it." He laughed indulgently. "You need shelf space, do you? You probably didn't even look at it."

"I was working at home yesterday."

"With that policeman, Peter Cardiff. Yes, I know. Well, now you can drop everything like that until we get this story contract in the bag. I'll want you with me when we face the board."

"You'll buy it?"

"We don't want the Americans to share the purchase. If we can get it for half a million sterling, perhaps even more, we can't lose. It's better that we have it to ourselves, and then sell it piecemeal according to the best offers. The film people are in contact with New York and desperate to conclude. We have to move fast, Carl. And, let's face it, you are not renowned as a fast mover."

"I've always been a cautious animal."

"That's why you are still an editor. I do believe that if it was up to you, you wouldn't buy this story."

"It's a lot of money, Percy."

"Uncle agrees with me. It's a business opportunity. You don't have to have a degree in English Literature to see that."

"What about provenance?"

"You are not to be swayed, are you? Personally I think this is a genuine story written, and hand-written too, by the master himself. But let's suppose it's not. You don't imagine that this fellow Whitaker was the only one ever to have sent Doyle a Sherlock Holmes story, do you?"

"I see what you mean."

"Yes, now at last, you are getting to see what I am driving at. I contend that, at the worst, this is a story that Doyle read and grudgingly approved. A story that perhaps Lady Doyle rescued and that people in his office filed away in his archive."

"Umm."

"And that's at the worst."

"We'd better keep this conversation to ourselves, Percy."

"Everyone will make money."

"And the Doyle Estate?"

"I will provoke them into denying that it's genuine, or that they have ever seen it, or handled it."

"I'm glad I'm not a lawyer, Percy."

"That's not nice. That's the sort of joke I resent."

"I'm sorry," I said. "Having a wife in Australia is not very good for the morale."

"A bonus and a long weekend will restore your morale. That new advertising girl is rather sweet on you, Carl. The one with the long blonde hair who wears those white sweaters. Did you notice that?"

"I hadn't even noticed there were girls in the advertising department."

"Exactly," he said with the triumph of a diagnosis proved correct. "It's no good sitting at home moping, Carl."

"I might go to Australia, Percy."

"That would be a blow, Carl."

"It's my marriage, Percy. She has her family there and her parents are getting old. And my son doesn't want to come back here."

"What work will you do?"

"There's an ad agency there. They would probably like the idea that I'd worked for a big London agency."

"You haven't been negotiating all this on the sly, have you?"

I shook my head and he smiled. I think he would have thought more of me if I'd said yes, I had.

When I phoned my wife, I did it on a public phone from a railway terminal. It was better done that way. It was evening in London but noon in Los Angeles where she had a temporary secretarial job in a big movie production company. At noon Irene's boss was always at lunch.

"I sold our lovely Volvo. I didn't have many offers. It went for a song but I'm using it for another few days and we did rather well on the lease of the flat. The new tenant moves in next week."

"Are you managing all right, darling?"

"It's not much fun without a cleaning lady – the dishes pile up – but it was better to let her go well in advance. She's gone home for a few weeks. I gave her half towards her plane ticket and told her it was time she visited her mother."

"Well, in that case I shall give notice this afternoon."

"You should have seen Percy," I said. "He was like a small child."

"We are going to ask for six. My brother is sure they'll pay another hundred grand. They are very keen indeed. You are so clever, darling. A regular Sherlock."

I was silent for a minute or so.

"Are you there, darling?" she asked.

"It was just a goodbye joke," I said. "You remember what we agreed."

"Why are you always such a wimp, darling? This is six hundred thousand pounds. This is a new life of high-living in a new land. We start again."

"Just a goodbye joke," I said. "Taking the money would be . . ." I trailed to a halt.

"Would be wonderful," she completed her version of the sentence. "Your son could go to Harvard the way you said you would have liked to have done." She took a deep breath and became charming. "We will live a life of ease. Be sensible."

"No, Irene. It was just an idea for a story. Then it became a joke to play on Percy."

"No *corpus delicti*, darling. It's foolproof. No manuscript as evidence. No witness to the negotiations. All concerned disappear to the other side of the globe with no forwarding addresses." There was a sudden note of concern: "Your policeman swallowed the robbery story?"

"Everything went OK," I said. "But the answer is still no. No, Irene. Do you hear me?"

"Don't 'no Irene' me, Carl. My brother and I have worked damned hard on this one. And spent good money on airline tickets. All you did is scribble a silly story and sit on your ass in London. It's going ahead no matter what you think about it. So have an aspirin and go to bed. Tell the office you have a virus and by the weekend you will have vanished."

"Very well, Irene. But I don't like it."

"You have your airline ticket. Don't forget your passport. See you on the beach, darling."

"Poor Percy," I said.

And when, six months or so later, the letters started arriving, Percy's letter was one of the first. No hard feelings, he said. No crowing. I read the letter several times; I had the feeling that he was half inclined to offer me some money towards my legal costs. But he could afford to be generous. He'd got the greater part of the money back, and the world rights on my "silly story" was eventually added to that. And there is to be a movie, too, they say. Nature follows art, I suppose.

There was no point in putting more money into my lawyer's pocket. When Irene's brother, Gordon McPhail, confessed, I had no alternative but to fill in the gaps. Most of the people who heard about it got it wrong and the newspapers did too. Even Percy, who should have known everything about it, thought that the Bali bomb in October had destroyed our "lovely restaurant". Some latecomers to the bad news thought we were victims of the tsunami, which came two years later. In fact we never did buy the restaurant we were negotiating for in Bali. We found a place we liked better, in Surabaja – Irene always said that I went for it only because of the Brecht song lyrics – and we were doing quite good business when the blow fell. "We got it for a song," she used to say before telling everyone that we had paid almost double the real value.

It was the terrorist bomb in Bali that did for us, of course. The Indonesian cops opened up the bank records to the Australian security service and they noticed the big money transfer. They became really excited. Sydney told London and Washington, and before I knew what was happening I was locked up in a prison in Jakarta with dozens of cops giving me hell on a shift for shift basis. Either they were convinced that I was the moneyman for the terrorists or they put on a wonderful act. They were rough and kept saying they'd hold me for ever and they didn't care about giving me a lawyer or bringing me to trial. They put Gordon through the wringer too. He was treated worse than me.

But ours had been a good plan. Even when they had Percy identify photos of Gordon and got their tame experts to agree about Gordon's signatures it still made a flimsy case to bring before a jury.

But my mind was changed by an avuncular old Aussie detective: "I'll tell you this much, Mohammed, old son, the only way you can avoid serving fifty years in an Indonesian clink as a terrorist is to convince me you are a thief."

I shook my head.

He gave a mirthless grin and said: "The locals tell me there are 365 islands out there. That's bullshit, of course, but there are plenty of them, fever ridden and overgrown, some of them no bigger than a football field. Ideal in fact to use as high security prisons. I went to one of them once. The local coppers were showing us how they handled local law-breakers. It was a stinking hole: dense jungle, everyone as skinny as a rake, even the guards. One of the jokers there said that either the prisoners ate the snakes and rats, or the snakes and rats ate them. It was a good joke but it didn't get much of a laugh from any of our boys. The cons never come back. The guards only do six months at a time. Any questions asked and the pen-pushers at headquarters say the paperwork got eaten by termites." He sat down and mopped his brow. "You wouldn't think it was still winter, would you?"

Perhaps it was a contrivance. No doubt the same cop did the same fatherly routine with Gordon, and they were all determined not to let us discover who cracked first. I could see it might all be a bluff at the time but I didn't feel like betting my life on it.

And all through this, Percy was decent. He told the police he'd known me all his life, and that I couldn't be a terrorist. But he wouldn't lift a finger to help Irene's brother. It was under-standable really; Gordon was the one who had duped him. He didn't have the same animosity towards me. He told the cops I was a weak character who had been drawn into crime by a shrewish domineering wife and criminal brother-in-law.

So I have no resentment concerning Gordon's confession. It was just bad luck and he managed to get Irene totally exoner-ated. They treat me quite decently now that I've got the transfer back to the UK, but I'll never eat rice, boiled fish or any of those damned fiery sambals for as long as I live. The governor here is a Sherlock Holmes devotee, so he likes to talk and display his knowledge to me, and I think I've persuaded him to try his hand at a pastiche of a Sherlock Homes story. I'll help. We are going to invent "The Adventure of the Tired Captain", a case that Doyle mentions in passing at the beginning of "The Naval Treaty" but never used. We won't be the first to have a go at it but no matter. There is no pressure of time and Percy says if it's good enough he'll publish it. And why not? He published my previous Sherlock Holmes story, didn't he?

Mind you, that's not going to be the end of the story. Next week I have a lawyer coming in to see me and that kind of visit doesn't have some big-eared warder sitting in to hear what we say. The court found me guilty of a whole string of offences, and writing that damned *Titanic* story is only one of them. So what are Percy and his uncle going to do when I claim copyright and my share of all the money they have put away? I'll get legal aid, so I won't have to find the money for the lawyers.

It's only now that I can understand why writers were always complaining to me about the way publishers treat them. Why should we writers be exploited?

LOVE

Martyn Waites

Love it. Fuckin love it. No other feelin in the world like it.

Better than sex. Better than anythin.

There we was, right an there they was. Just before the Dagenham local elections. Outside the community centre. Community centre, you're avina laugh. Asylum seeker central, more like. Somali centre.

June, a warm night, if you're interested.

Anyway, we'd had our meetin, makin our plan for the comin election, mobilisin the locals off the estate, we come outside, an there they was. The Pakis. The Anti Nazis. Shoutin, chantin – Nazi Scum, BNP Cunts. So we joined in gave it back with Wogs Out an that, Seig Heillin all over the place. Pakis in their casual leathers, Anti Nazis in their sloppy uni denims, us lookin sharp in bombers an eighteen holers. Muscles like taut metal rope under skin tight T-shirts an jeans, heads hard an shiny. Tattoos: dark ink makin white skin whiter.

Just waitin.

Our eyes; burnin with hate.

Their eyes; burnin with hate. Directed at us like laser death beams.

Anticipation like a big hard python coiled in me guts, waitin to get released an spread terror. A big hard on waitin to come.

Buildin, gettin higher:

Nazi Scum BNP Cunts
Wogs Out Seig Heil
Buildin, gettin higher –
Then it came. No more verbals, no more posin. Adrenalin
pumped right up, bell ringin, red light on. The charge.
The python's out, the hard on spurts.
Both sides together, two wallsa sound clashin intaya. A big,
sonic tidal wave ready to engulf you in violence, carry you under
with fists an boots an sticks.
Engage. An in.
Fists an boots an sticks. I take. I give back double. I twist an
thrash. Like swimmin in anger. I come up for air an dive back in
again, lungs full. I scream the screams, chant the chants.
Wogs out seig heil
Then I'm not swimmin. Liquid solidifies round me. An I'm
part of a huge machine. A muscle an bone an blood machine. A
shoutin, chantin cog in a huge hurtin machine. Arms wind-
millin. Boots kickin. Fuelled on violence. Driven by rage.
Lost to it. No me. Just the machine. An I've never felt more
alive.
Love it. Fuckin love it.
I see their eyes. See the fear an hate an blood in their eyes.
I feed on it.
Hate matches hate. Hate gives as good as hate gets.
Gives better. The machine's too good for them.
The machine wins. Cogs an clangs an fists an hammers. The
machine always wins.
Or would, if the pigs hadn't arrived.
Up they come, sticks out. Right lads, you've had your fun.
Time for us to have a bit. Waitin till both sides had tired, pickin
easy targets.
The machine falls apart; I become meself again. I think an
feel for meself. I think it's time to run.
I run.
We all do; laughin an limpin, knowin we'd won.
Knowin our hate was stronger than theirs. Knowin they were
thinkin the same thing.
Run. Back where we came from, back to our lives. Our selves.
Rememberin that moment when we became somethin more.
Cherishin it.

I smiled.
LOVED IT.

D'you wanna name? Call me Jez. I've been called worse.

You want me life story? You sound like a copper. Or a fuckin social worker. Fuckin borin, but here it is. I live on the Chatsworth Estate in Dagenham. The borders of East London/Essex. You'll have heard of it. It's a dump. Or rather a dumpin ground. For problem families at first, but now for Somalis an Kosovans that have just got off the lorry. It never used to be like that. It used to be a good place where you could be proud to live. But then so did Dagenham. So did this country.

There's my dad sittin on the settee watchin Tricia in his vest, rollin a fag. I suppose you could say he was typical of this estate (an of Dagenham an the country). He used to have a job, a good one. At the Ford plant. Knew the place, knew the system, knew how to work it. But his job went when they changed the plant. His job an thousands of others. Now it's a centre of excellence for diesel engines. An he can't get a job there. He says the Pakis took it from him. They got HNDs an degrees. He had an apprenticeship for a job that don't exist no more. No one wants that now. No one wants him now. He's tried. Hard. Honest. So he sits in his vest, rollin fags, watchin Tricia.

There's Tom, me brother, too. He's probably still in bed. He's got the monkey on his back. All sorts, really, but mostly heroin. He used to be a good lad, did well at school an that, but when our fat slag bitch of a mother walked out all that had to stop. We had to get jobs. Or try. I got a job doin tarmacin an roofin. He got a heroin habit. Sad. Fuckin sad. Makes you really angry.

Tarmacin an roofin. Off the books, cash in hand. With Barry the Roofer. Baz. Only when I'm needed, though, or seasonal, when the weather's good, but it's somethin. Just don't tell the dole. I'd lose me Jobseeker's Allowance.

It's not seasonal at the moment. But it's June. So it will be soon.

So that's me. It's not who I am. But it's not WHAT I AM.

I'm a Knight of St George. An proud of it. A True Believer. A soldier for truth.

This used to be a land fit for heroes, when Englishmen were kings an their houses castles. A land where me dad had a job, me brother was doin well at school an me fat slag bitch of a mother hadn't run off to Gillingham in Kent with a Paki postman. Well, he's Greek, actually, but you know what I mean. They're all Pakis, really.

An that's the problem. Derek (I'll come to him in a minute) said the Chatsworth Estate is like this country in miniature. It used to be a good place where families could live in harmony and everyone knew everyone else. But now it's a run down shithole full of undesirables an people who've given up tryin to get out. No pride anymore. No self respect. Our heritage sold to Pakis who've just pissed on us. Love your country like it used to be, says Derek, but hate it like it is now.

And I do. Both. With all my heart.

Because it's comin back, he says. One day, sooner rather than later, we'll reclaim it. Make this land a proud place to be again. A land fit for heroes once more. And you, my lovely boys, will be the ones to do it. The footsoldiers of the revolution. Remember it word for word. Makes me all over again when I think of it.

An I think of it a lot. Whenever some Paki's got in me face, whenever some stuck up cunt's had a go at the way I've done his drive or roof, whenever I look in me dad's eyes an see that all his hope belongs to yesterday, I think of those words. I think of my place in the great scheme, at the forefront of the revolution. An I smile. I don't get angry. Because I know what they don't.

That's me. That's WHAT I AM.

But I can't tell you about me without tellin you about Derek Midgely. Great, great man. The man who showed me the way an the truth. The man who's been more of a father to me than me real dad. He's been described as the demigog of Dagenham. I don't know what a demigog is, but if it means someone who KNOWS THE TRUTH an TELLS IT LIKE IT IS, then that's him.

But I'm gettin ahead. First I have to tell you about Ian.

Ian. He recruited me. Showed me that way.

I met him the shopping centre. I was sittin around one day wonderin what to, when he came up to me.

I know what you need, he said.

I looked up. An there was a god. Shaved head, eighteen holers, jeans an T-shirt so tight I could make out the curves an contours of his muscled body. An he looked so relaxed, so in control. He had his jacket off an I could see the tats over his forearms an biceps. Some pro ones like the flag of St George, some done himself like Skins Foreva. He looked perfect.

An I knew there an then, I wanted what he had. He was right. He did know what I needed.

He got talkin to me. Asked me questions. Gave me answers. Told me who was to blame for my dad not havin a job. Who was to blame for my brother's habit. For my fat slag bitch mother runnin off to Gillingham. Put it all in context with the global Zionist conspiracy. Put it closer to home with pictures I could understand: the Pakis. The niggers. The asylum seekers.

I looked round Dagenham. Saw crumbling concrete, depressed whites, smug Pakis. The indiginous population overrun. Then back at Ian. An with him lookin down at me an the sun behind his head lookin like some kind of halo, it made perfect sense.

I feel your anger, he said, understand your hate.

The way he said hate. Sounded just right.

He knew some others that felt the same. Why didn't I come along later an meet them?

I did.

An never looked back.

Ian's gone now. After what happened.

For a time it got nasty. I mean REALLY nasty. Body in the concrete foundations of the London Gateway nasty.

I blamed Ian. All the way. I had to.

Luckily, Derek agreed.

Derek Midgely. A great man, like I said. He's made the St George pub on the estate his base. It's where we have our meetins. He sits there in his suit with his gin an tonic in front of him hair slicked back, an we gather round, waitin for him to give us some pearls of wisdom, or tell us the latest installment of his masterplan. It's brilliant, just to be near him. Like I said, a great, great man.

I went there along with everyone else the night after the community centre ruck. I mean meetin. There was the usuals. Derek, of course, holdin court, the footsoldiers of which I can proudly number myself, people off the estate (what Derek calls the concerned populace), some girls, Adrian an Steve. They need a bit of explainin. Adrian is what you'd call an intellectual. He wears glasses an a duffelcoat all year round. Always carryin a canvas bag over his shoulder. Greasy black hair. Expression like he's somewhere else. Laughin at a joke only he can hear. Don't know what he does. Know he surfs the internet, gets things off that. Shows them to Derek. Derek nods, makes sure none of us have seen them. Steve is the local councillor. Our great white hope. Our great fat whale, as he's known out of Derek's earshot. Used to be Labour until, as he says, saw the light. Or until they found all the fiddled expenses sheets an Nazi flags up in his living room an Labour threw him out. Still, he's a tru man of the people.

Derek was talkin. What you did last night, he says, was a great and glorious thing. And I'm proud of each and every one of you.

We all smiled.

However, Derek went on, I want you to keep a low profile between now and Thursday. Voting day. Let's see some of the other members of our party do their bit. We all have a part to play.

He told us that the concerned populace would go leafletin and canvassin in their suits an best clothes, Steve walkin round an all. He could spin a good yarn, Steve. How he'd left Labour in disgust because they were the Pakis friend, the asylum seeker's safe haven. How they invited them over to use our National Health Service, run drugs an prostitution rings. He would tell that to everyone he met, try an make them vote for him. Derek said it was playin on their legitimate fears but to me it just sounded so RIGHT. Let him play on whatever he wanted.

He went on. We listened. I felt like I belonged. Like I was wanted, VALUED. Meetins always felt the same.

LIKE I'D COME HOME.

The meetin broke up. Everyone started drinkin.

Courtney, one of the girls, came up to me, asked if I was stayin on. She's short with a soft barrel body an hard eyes. She's fucked nearly all the footsoldiers. Sometimes more than once, sometimes a few at a time. Calls it her patriotic duty. Hard eyes, but a good heart. I went along with them once. I had to. All the lads did. But I didn't do much. Just sat there, watched most of the time. Looked at them. Didn't really go near her.

Anyway, she gave me that look. Rubbed up against me. Let me see the tops of her tits down the front of her low cut T-shirt. Made me blush. Then made me angry cos I blushed. I told her I had to go, that I couldn't afford a drink. My Jobseeker's Allowance was gone an Baz hadn't come up with any work for me.

She said that she was gettin together with a few of the lads after the pub. Was I interested?

I said no. And went home.

Well not straight home. There was somethin I had to do first. Somethin I couldn't tell the rest of them about.

There's a part of the estate you just DON'T GO. At least not by yourself. Not after dark. Unless you were tooled up. Unless you want somethin. An I wanted somethin.

It was dark there. Shadows on shadows. Hip hop an reggae came from open windows. The square was deserted. I walked, crunched on gravel, broken glass. I felt eyes watchin me. Unseen ones. Wished I'd brought my blade. Still, I had my muscles. I'd worked on my body since I joined the party, got good an strong. I was never like that at school. Always the weak one. Not any more.

I was kind of safe, I knew that. As long as I did what I was here to do I wouldn't get attacked. Because this was where the niggers lived.

I went to the usual corner an waited. I heard him before I saw him. Comin out of the dark, along the alleyway, takin his time, baggy jeans lung low on his hips, Calvins showin at the top. Vest hangin loose. Body ripped an buff.

Aaron. The Ebony Warrior.

Aaron. Drug dealer.

I swallowed hard.

He came up close, looked at me. The usual look, smilin, like he knows somethin I don't. Eye to eye. I could smell his warm breath on my cheek. I felt uneasy. The way I always do with him.

Jez, he said slowly, an held his arms out. See anythin you want?

I swallowed hard again. My throat was really dry.

You know what I want. My voice sounded ragged.

He laughed his private laugh. I know exactly, he said, an waited.

His breath was all sweet with spliff an alcohol. He kept starin at me. I dug my hand into my jacket pocket. Brought out money. Nearly the last I had, but he didn't know that.

He shook his head, brought out a clingfilm wrap from his back pocket.

Enjoy, he said.

It's not for me an you know it.

He smiled again. Wanna try some? Some skunk, maybe? Now? With me?

I don't do drugs. I hardly drink. An he knows it. He was tauntin me. He knew what my answer would be.

Whatever, he said. Off you go then, back to your little Hitler world.

I said nothing. I never could when he talked to me.

Then he did somethin he'd never done before. He touched my arm.

You shouldn't hate, he said. Life too short for that, y'get me?

I looked down at his fingers. The first black fingers I'd ever had on my body. I should have thrown them off. Told him not to touch me, called him a filthy nigger. Hit him.

But I didn't. His fingers felt warm. And strong.

What should I do, then? I could hardly hear my own voice.

Love, he said.

I turned round, walked away.

I heard his laugh behind me.

At home, dad was asleep on the sofa. Snorin an fartin. I went into Tom's room. Empty. I left the bundle by his bedside an went out.

I hadn't been lyin to Courtney. It was nearly the last of me money. I didn't like buyin stuff for Tom, but what could I do? It was either that or he went out on the street to sell somethin, himself even, to get money for stuff. I had no choice.

I went to bed but couldn't sleep. Things on me mind but I didn't know what. Must be the elections. That was it. I lay starin a the ceilin, then realized me cock was hard. I took it in me hand. This'll get me to sleep, I thought. I thought hard about Courtney. An all those lads.

That did the trick.

The next few days were a bit blurry. Nothin much happened. It was all waitin. For the election. For Baz to find me some more work. For Tom to run out of heroin again an need another hit.

Eventually Thursday rolled round and it was election day. I went proudly off to the pollin station at the school I used to go to. Looked at the kids' names on the walls. Hardly one of them fuckin English. Made me do that cross all the more harder.

I stayed up all night watchin the election. Tom was out, me dad fell asleep.

Steve got in.

I went fuckin mental.

I'd been savin some cans for a celebration an I went at them. I wished I could have been in the St George with the rest but I knew us footsoldiers couldn't. But, God, how I WANTED TO. That was where I should have been. Who I should have been with. That was where I BELONGED.

But I waited. My time would come.

I stayed in all the next day. Lost track of time.

Put the telly on. Local news. They reported what had happened. Interviewed some Paki. Called himself a community leader. Said he couldn't be held responsible if members of his community armed themselves and roamed the streets in gangs looking for BNP members. His people had a right to protect themselves.

They switched to the studio. An there was Derek. Arguin with some cunt from Cambridge. Least that's what he looked like. Funny, I thought people were supposed to look bigger on TV. Derek just looked smaller. Greasy hair. Fat face. Big nose. Almost like a Jew, I thought. Then felt guilty for thinkin it.

It's what the people want, he said, the people have spoken. They're sick an tired of a government that is ignorin the views of the common man and woman. An the common man an woman have spoken. We are not extremists. We are representin what the average, decent person in this country thinks but doesn't dare say because of political correctness. Because of what they fear will happen to them.

I felt better hearin him say that. Then they turned to the Cambridge cunt. He was a psychologist or psychiatrist or sociologist or somethin. I thought here it comes. He's gonna start arguin back an then Derek's gonna go for him. But he didn't. This sociologist just looked calm. Smiled, almost.

It's sad, he said. It's sad so few people realize. As a society it seems we base our responses on either love or hate, thinking they're opposites. But they're not. They're the same. The opposite of love is not hate. It's indifference.

They looked at him.

People only hate what they fear within themselves. What they fear themselves becoming. What they secretly love. A fascist – he gestured to Derek – will hate democracy. Plurality. Anything else – he shrugged – is indifference.

I would have laughed out loud if there had been anyone else there with me.

But there wasn't. So I said nothing.

A weekend of lyin low. Difficult, but had to be done. Don't give them a target, Derek had said. Don't give them an excuse.

By Monday I was rarin to get out the flat. I was even lookin forward to goin to work.

First I went down the shoppin centre. Wearin me best skinhead gear. Don't know what I expected, the whole world to have changed or somethin, but it was the same as it had been. I walked round proudly, an I could feel people lookin at me. I smiled. They knew. Who I was. What I stood for. They were the people who'd voted.

There was love in their eyes. I was sure of it.

At least, that's what it felt like.

Still in a good mood, I went to see Baz. Ready to start work.

An he dropped a bombshell.

Sorry mate, I can't use you no more.

Why not?

He just looked at me like the answer was obvious. When I looked like I didn't understand, he had to explain it to me.

Cos of what's happened. Cos of what you believe in. No don't get me wrong, he said, you know me. I agree, there's too many Pakis an asylum seekers over here. But a lot of those Pakis are my customers. An, well, look at you. I can hardly bring you along to some Paki's house an let you work for him, could I?

So sorry, mate, that's that.

I was gutted. I walked out of there knowin I had no money. Knowin that, once again, the Pakis had taken it from me.

I looked around the shoppin centre. I didn't see love any more. I saw headlines on the papers:

RACIST COUNCILLOR
VOTED IN TO DAGENHAM

Then underneath:

KICK THIS SCUM OUT

I couldn't believe it. They should be welcomin us with open arms. This was supposed to be the start of the revolution. Instead it was the usual shit. I just knew the Pakis were behind it. An the Jews. They own all the newspapers.

I had nowhere to go. I went to the St George but this was early mornin an there was no one in. None of my people.

So I just walked round all day. Thinkin. Not gettin anythin straight. Gettin everythin more twisted.

I thought of goin to the St George. They'd be there. Celebratin. Then there was goin to be a late night march round the streets. Let the residents, the concerned populace, know they were safe in their houses. Let everyone know who ruled the streets.

But I didn't feel like it.

So I went home.

An wished I hadn't.

Tom was there. He looked like shit. Curled up on his bed. He'd been sick. Shit himself.

Whassamatter? I said. D'you wanna doctor?

He managed to shake his head. No.

What then?

Gear. Cold turkey. Cramps.

An he was sick again.

I stood back, not wantin it to go on me.

Please, he gasped, you've got to get us some gear ... please ...

I've got no money, I said.

Please ...

An his eyes, pleadin with me. What could I do? He was my brother. My flesh an blood. An you look after your own.

I'll not be long, I said.

I left the house.

Down to the part of the estate where you don't go. I walked quickly, went to the usual spot. Waited.

Eventually he came. Stood before me.

Back so soon? Aaron said. Then smiled. Can't keep away, can you?

I need some gear, I said.

Aaron waited.

But I've got no money.

Aaron chuckled. Then no sale.

Please. It's for . . . it's urgent.

Aaron looked around. There was that smile again.

How much d'you want it? he said.

I looked at him.

How much? he said again. An put his hand on my arm.

He moved in closer to me. His mouth right by my ear. He whispered, tickling me. My heart was beatin fit to burst. My legs felt shaky.

You're like me, he said.

I tried to speak. It took me two attempts. No I'm not, I said.

Oh yes you are. We do what our society says we have to do. Behave like we're supposed to. Hide our true feelings. What we really are.

I tried to shake my head. But I couldn't.

You know you are. He got closer. You know I am.

An kissed me. Full on the mouth.

I didn't throw him off. Didn't call him a filthy nigger. Didn't hit him. I kissed him back.

Then it was hands all over each other. I wanted to touch him, feel his body, his beautiful, black body. Feel his cock. He did the same to me. That python was inside me, ready to come out. I loved the feeling.

I thought of school. How I was made to feel different. Hated them for it. Thought of Ian. What we had got up to. I had loved him. With all my heart. An he loved me. But we got found out. An that kind of thing is frowned upon, to say the least. So I had to save my life. Pretend it was all his doing. I gave him up. I never saw him again. I never stopped loving him.

I loved what Aaron was doing to me now. It felt wrong. But it felt so right.

I had him in my hand, wanted him in my body. Was ready to take him.

When there was a noise.

We had been so into each other we hadn't heard them approach.

So this is where you are, they said. Fuckin a filthy nigger when you should be with us.

The footsoldiers. On patrol. An tooled up.

I looked at Aaron. He looked terrified.

Look, I said, it was his fault. I had to get some gear for my brother . . .

They weren't listening. They were starin at us. Hate in their eyes. As far as they were concerned I was no longer one of them. I was the enemy now.

You wanna run nigger lover? Or you wanna stay here an take your beatin with your boyfriend? The words spat out.

I zipped up my jeans. Looked at Aaron.

They caught the look.

Now run, the machine said, hate in its eyes. But from now on, you're no better than a nigger or a Paki.

I ran.

Behind me, heard them layin into Aaron.

I kept running.

I couldn't go home. I had no gear for Tom. I couldn't stay where I was. I might not be so lucky next time.

So I ran.

I don't know where.

After a while I couldn't run any more. I slowed down, tried to get me breath back. Too tired to run anymore. To fight back.

I knew who I was. Finally. I knew WHAT I WAS.

An it was a painful truth. It hurt.

Then from the end of the street I saw them. Pakis. A gang of them. Out protecting their own community. They saw me. Started running.

I was too tired. I couldn't outrun them. I stood up, waited for them. I wanted to tell them I wasn't a threat, that I didn't hate them.

But they were screaming, shouting, hate in their eyes.

A machine. Cogs an clangs an fists an hammers.

I waited, smiled.

Love shining in my own eyes.

JUST FRIENDS

John Harvey

These things I remember about Diane Adams: the way a lock of her hair would fall down across her face and she would brush it back with a quick tilt of her head and a flick of her hand; the sliver of green, like a shard of glass, high in her left eye; the look of surprise, pleasure and surprise, when she spoke to me that first time – "And you must be, Jimmy, right?": the way she lied.

It was November, late in the month and the night air bright with cold that numbed your fingers even as it brought a flush of color to your cheeks. London, the winter of fifty-six, and we were little more than kids then, Patrick, Val and myself, though if anyone had called us that we'd have likely punched him out, Patrick or myself at least, Val in the background, careful, watching.

Friday night it would have been, a toss-up between the Flamingo and Studio 51, and on this occasion Patrick had decreed the Flamingo: this on account of a girl he'd started seeing, on account of Diane. The Flamingo a little more cool, a little more style; more likely to impress. Hip, I suppose, the word we would have used.

All three of us had first got interested in jazz at school, the trad thing first, British guys doing a earnest imitation of New Orleans; then, for a spell, it was the Alex Welsh band we followed around, a hard-driving crew with echoes of Chicago, brittle and fast, Tuesday nights the Lyttelton place in Oxford Street, Sundays a club out at Wood Green. It was Val who got us listening to the more modern stuff, Parker 78s on Savoy, Paul Desmond, the Gerry Mulligan Quartet.

From somewhere, Patrick got himself a trumpet and began practicing scales, and I kicked off playing brushes on an old suitcase while saving for the down payment on a set of drums. Val, we eventually discovered, already had a saxophone – an old Selmer with a dented bell and a third of the keys held on by rubber bands: it had once belonged to his old man. Not only did he have a horn, but he knew how to play. Nothing fancy, not yet, not enough to go steaming through the changes of *Cherokee* or *I Got Rhythm* the way he would later, in his pomp, but tunes you could recognize, modulations you could follow.

The first time we heard him, really heard him, the cellar room below a greasy spoon by the Archway, somewhere the owner let us hang out for the price of a few coffees, the occasional pie and chips, we wanted to punch him hard. For holding out on us the way he had. For being so damned good.

Next day, Patrick took the trumpet back to the place he'd bought it, Boosey and Hawkes, and sold it back to them, got the best price he could. "Sod that for a game of soldiers," he said, "too much like hard bloody work. What we need's a bass player, someone half-decent on piano, get Val fronting his own band." And he pushed a bundle of fivers into my hand. "Here," he said, "go and get those sodding drums."

"What about you?" Val asked, though he probably knew the answer even then. "What you gonna be doin'?"

"Me?" Patrick said. "I'm going to be the manager. What else?"

And, for a time, that was how it was.

Private parties, weddings, bar mitzvahs, support slots at little clubs out in Ealing or Totteridge that couldn't afford anything better. From somewhere Patrick found a pianist who could do a passable Bud Powell, and, together with Val, that kept us afloat. For a while, a year or so at least. By then even Patrick could see Val was too good for the rest of us and we were just holding him back; he spelled it out to me when I was packing my kit away after an all-nighter in Dorking, a brace of tenners eased down into the top pocket of my second hand Cecil Gee jacket.

"What's this?" I said.

"Severance pay," said Patrick, and laughed.

Not the first time he paid me off, nor the last.

But I'm getting ahead of myself.

That November evening, we'd been hanging round the Bar Italia on Frith Street pretty much as usual, the best coffee in Soho then and now; Patrick was off to one side, deep in conversation with a dark-skinned guy in a Crombie overcoat, the kind who has to shave twice a day and wore a scar down his cheek like a badge. A conversation I was never meant to hear.

"Jimmy," Patrick said suddenly, over his shoulder. "A favour. Diane, I'm supposed to meet her. Leicester Square tube." He looked at his watch. "Any time now. Go down there for me, okay? Bring her to the club; we'll see you there."

All I'd seen of Diane up to that point had been a photograph, a snapshot barely focused, dark hair worn long, high cheek bones, a slender face. Her eyes – what colour were her eyes?

"The tube," I said. "Which exit?"

Patrick grinned. "You'll get it figured."

She came up the steps leading on to Cranbourne Street and I recognized her immediately; tall, taller than I'd imagined, and in that moment – Jesus! – so much more beautiful.

"Diane?" Hands in my pockets, trying and failing to look cool, blushing already. "Patrick got stuck in some kind of meeting. Business, you know? He asked me to meet you."

She nodded, looking me over appraisingly. "And you must be Jimmy, right?" Aside from that slight flaw, her eyes were brown, a soft chocolatey brown, I could see that now.

Is it possible to smile ironically? That's what she was doing. "All right, Jimmy," she said. "Where are we going?"

When we got to the Flamingo, Patrick and Val had still not arrived. The Tony Kinsey Quintet were on the stand, two saxes and rhythm. I pushed my way through to the bar for a couple of drinks and we stood on the edge of the crowd, close but not touching. Diane was wearing a silky kind of dress that clung to her hips, two shades of blue. The band cut the tempo for *Sweet and Lovely*, Don Rendell soloing on tenor.

Diane rested her fingers on my arm. "Did Patrick tell you to dance with me, too?"

I shook my head.

"Well, let's pretend that he did."

Six months I suppose they went out together, Diane and Patrick, that first time around, and for much of that six months, I rarely saw them one without the other. Towards the end, Patrick took her off for a few days to Paris, a big deal in those days, and managed to secure a gig for Val while he was there, guesting at the *Chat Qui Pêche* with René Thomas and Pierre Michelot.

After they came back I didn't see either of them for quite a while: Patrick was in one of his mysterious phases, doing deals, ducking and weaving, and Diane – well, I didn't know about Diane. And then, one evening in Soho, hurrying, late for an appointment, I did see her, sitting alone by the window of this trattoria, the Amalfi it would have been, on Old Compton Street, a plate of pasta in front of her, barely touched. I stopped close to the glass, raised my hand and mouthed "Hi!" before scuttling on, but if she saw me I couldn't be sure. One thing I couldn't miss though, the swelling, shaded purple, around her left eye.

A week after this Patrick rang me and we arranged to meet for a drink at the Bald Faced Stag; when I asked about Diane he looked through me and then carried on as if he'd never heard her name. At this time I was living in two crummy rooms in East Finchley – more a bed-sitter with a tiny kitchen attached, the bathroom down the hall – and Patrick gave me a lift home, dropped me at the door. I asked him if he wanted to come in but wasn't surprised when he declined.

Two nights later I was sitting reading some crime novel or other, wearing two sweaters to save putting on the second bar of the electric fire, when there was a short ring on the downstairs bell. For some reason, I thought it might be Patrick, but instead it was Diane. Her hair was pulled back off her face in a way I hadn't seen before, and, a faint finger of yellow aside, all trace of the bruise around her eye had disappeared.

"Well, Jimmy," she said, "aren't you going to invite me in?"

She was wearing a cream sweater, a coffee-coloured skirt with a slight flare, high heels which she kicked off the moment she sat on the end of the bed. My drums were out at the other side of the room, not the full kit, just the bass drum, ride cymbal, hi-hat and snare; clothes I'd been intending to iron were folded over the back of a chair.

"I didn't know," I said, "you knew where I lived."

"I didn't. Patrick told me."

"You're still seeing him then?"

The question hung in the air.

"I don't suppose you've got anything to drink?" Diane said.

There was a half bottle of Bell's out in the kitchen and I poured what was left into two tumblers and we touched glasses and said, "Cheers." Diane sipped hers, made a face, then drank down most of the rest in a single swallow.

"Patrick . . ." I began.

"I don't want to talk about Patrick," she said.

Her hand touched the buckle of my belt. "Sit here," she said.

The mattress shifted with the awkwardness of my weight.

"I didn't know," she said afterwards, "it could be so good."

You see what I mean about the way she lied.

Patrick and Diane got married in the French church off Leicester Square and their reception was held in the dance hall conveniently close by; it was one of the last occasions I played drums with any degree of seriousness, one of the last times I played at all. My application to join the Metropolitan Police had already been accepted and within weeks I would be starting off in uniform, a different kind of beat altogether. Val, of course, had put the band together and an all-star affair it was – Art Ellefson, Bill LeSage, Harry Klein. Val himself was near his mercurial best, just ahead of the flirtations with heroin and free form jazz that would sideline him in the years ahead.

At the night's end we stood outside, the three of us, ties unfastened, staring up at the sky. Diane was somewhere inside, getting changed.

"Christ!" Patrick said. "Who'd've fuckin' thought it?"

He took a silver flask from inside his coat and passed it round. We shook hands solemnly and then hugged each other close. When Diane came out, she and Patrick went off in a waiting car to spend the night at a hotel on Park Lane.

"Start off," Patrick had said with a wink, "like you mean to continue."

We drifted apart: met briefly, glimpsed one another across smoky rooms, exchanged phone numbers that were rarely if ever called. Nine years later I was a detective sergeant working out of West End Central and Patrick had not long since opened his third night club in a glitter of flash bulbs and champagne; Joan Collins was there with her sister, Jackie. There were ways of skirting round the edges of the law and, so far, Patrick had found most of them: favors doled out and favours returned; backhanders in brown envelopes; girls who didn't care what you did as long as you didn't kiss them on the mouth. Diane, I heard, had walked out on Patrick; reconciled, Patrick had walked out on her. Now they were back together again, but for how long?

When I came off duty, she was parked across the street, smoking a cigarette, window wound down.

"Give you a lift?"

I'd moved up market but not by much, an upper floor flat in an already ageing mansion block between Chalk Farm and Belsize Park. A photograph of the great drummer, Max Roach, was on the wall; Sillitoe's *Saturday Night and Sunday Morning* next to the Eric Amblers and a few Graham Greenes on the shelf; an Alex Welsh album on the record player, ready to remind me of better times.

"So, how are things?" Diane asked, doing her best to look as if she cared.

"Could be worse," I said. In the kitchen, I set the kettle to boil and she stood too close while I spooned Nescafé into a pair of china mugs. There was something beneath the scent of her perfume that I remembered too well.

"What does he want?" I asked.

"Who?"

"Patrick, who else?"

She paused from stirring sugar into her coffee. "Is that what it has to be?"

"Probably."

"What if I just wanted to see you for myself?"

The green in her eye was bright under the unshaded kitchen light. "I wouldn't let myself believe it," I said.

She stepped into my arms and my arms moved around her as if they had a mind of their own. She kissed me and I kissed her back. I'd like to say I pushed her away after that and we sat and drank our coffee like two adults, talked about old times and what she was going to do with her life after the divorce. She was divorcing him, she said: she didn't know why she hadn't done it before.

"He'll let you go?"

"He'll let me go."

For a moment, she couldn't hold my gaze. "There's just one thing," she said, "one thing that he wants. This new club of his, someone's trying to have his licence cancelled."

"Someone?"

"Serving drinks after hours, an allegation, nothing more."

"He can't make it go away?"

Diane shook her head. "He's tried."

I looked at her. "And that's all?"

"One of the officers, he's accused Patrick of offering him a bribe. It was all a misunderstanding, of course."

"Of course."

"Patrick wonders if you'd talk to him, the officer concerned."

"Straighten things out."

"Yes."

"Make him see the error of his ways."

"Look, Jimmy," she said, touching the back of her hand to my cheek, "you know I hate doing this, don't you?"

No, I thought. No, I don't.

"Everything has a price," I said. "Even friendship. Friendship, especially. And tell Patrick, next time he wants something, to come and ask me himself."

"He's afraid you'd turn him down."

"He's right."

When she lifted her face to mine I turned my head aside. "Don't let your coffee get cold," I said.

Five minutes later she was gone. I sorted out Patrick's little problem for him and found a way of letting him know if he stepped out of line again, I'd personally do my best to close him down. Whether either of us believed it, I was never sure. With or without my help, he went from rich to richer; Diane slipped off my radar and when she re-emerged, she was somewhere in Europe, nursing Val after his most recent spell in hospital, encouraging him to get back into playing. Later they got married, or at least that's what I heard. Some lives took unexpected turns. Not mine.

*   *   *

I stayed on in the Met for three years after my thirty and then retired; tried working for a couple of security firms, but somehow it never felt right. With my pension and the little I'd squirreled away, I found I could manage pretty well without having to look for anything too regular. There was an investigation agency I did a little work for once in a while, nothing too serious, nothing heavy, and that was enough.

Patrick I bumped into occasionally if I went up west, greyer, more distinguished, handsomer than ever; in Soho once, close to the little Italian place where I'd spotted Diane with her bruised eye, he slid a hand into my pocket and when I felt where it had been there were two fifties, crisp and new.

"What's this for?" I asked.

"You look as though you need it," he said.

I threw the money back in his face and punched him in the mouth. Two of his minders had me spread-eagled on the pavement before he'd wiped the mean line of blood from his chin.

At Val's funeral we barely spoke; acknowledged each other but little more. Diane looked gaunt and beautiful in black, a face like alabaster, tears I liked to think were real. A band played *Just Friends*, with a break of thirty-two bars in the middle where Val's solo would have been. There was a wake at one of Patrick's clubs afterwards, a free bar, and most of mourners went on there, but I just went home and sat in my chair and thought about the three of us, Val, Patrick and myself, what forty years had brought us to, what we'd wanted then, what we'd done.

I scarcely thought about Diane at all.

Jack Kiley, that's the investigator I was working for, kept throwing bits and pieces my way, nothing strenuous like I say, the occasional tail job, little more. I went into his office one day, a couple of rooms above a bookstore in Belsize Park, and there she sat, Diane, in the easy chair alongside his desk.

"I believe you two know each other," Jack said.

Once I'd got over the raw surprise of seeing her, what took some adjusting to was how much she'd changed. I suppose I'd never imagined her growing old. But she had. Under her grey wool suit her body was noticeably thicker; her face was fuller, puffed and cross-hatched around the eyes, lined around the mouth. No Botox; no nip and tuck.

"Hello, Jimmy," she said.

"Diane's got a little problem," Jack said. "She thinks you can make it go away." He pushed back from his desk. "I'll leave you two to talk about it."

The problem was a shipment of cocaine that should have made its way seamlessly from the Netherlands to Dublin via the UK. A street value of a quarter of a million pounds. Customs and Excise, working on a tip-off, had seized the drug on arrival, a clean bust marred only by the fact the coke had been doctored down to a mockery of its original strength; a double shot espresso from Caffè Nero would deliver as much of a charge to the system.

"How in God's name," I asked, "did you get involved in this?"

Diane lit a cigarette and wafted the smoke away from her face. "After Val died I went back to Amsterdam, it's where we'd been living before he died. There was this guy – he'd been Val's supplier . . ."

"I thought Val had gone straight," I said.

"There was this guy," Diane said again, "we – well, we got sort of close. It was a bad time for me. I needed . . ." She glanced across and shook her head. "A girl's got to live, Jimmy. All Val had left behind was debts. This guy, he offered me a roof over my head. But there was a price."

"I'll bet." Even I was surprised how bitter that sounded.

"People he did business with, he wanted me to speak for him, take meetings. I used to fly to Belfast, then, after a while, it was Dublin."

"You were a courier." I said. "A mule."

"No. I never carried the stuff myself. Once the deal was set up, I'd arrange shipments, make sure things ran smoothly."

"Patrick would be proud of you," I said.

"Leave Patrick out of this," she said. "This has nothing to do with him."

I levered myself up out of the seat; it wasn't as easy as it used to be. "Nor me." I got as far as the door.

"They think I double-crossed them," Diane said. "They think it was me tipped off Customs; they think I cut the coke and kept back the rest so I could sell it myself."

"And did you?"

She didn't blink. "These people, Jimmy, they'll kill me. To make an example. I have to convince them it wasn't me; let them have back what they think's their due."

"A little difficult if you didn't take it in the first place."

"Will you help me, Jimmy, yes or no?"

"Your pal in Amsterdam, what's wrong with him?"

"He says it's my mess and I have to get myself out of it."

"Nice guy."

She leaned towards me, trying for a look that once would have held me transfixed. "Jimmy, I'm asking. For old time's sake."

"Which old time is that, Diane?"

She smiled. "The first time you met me, Jimmy, you remember that? Leicester Square?"

Like yesterday, I thought.

"You ever think about that? You ever think what I would have been like if we'd been together? Really together?"

I shook my head.

"We don't always make the right choices," she said.

"Get somebody else to help you," I said.

"I don't want somebody else."

"Diane, look at me for fuck's sake. What can I do? I'm an old man."

"You're not old. What are you? Sixty-odd? These days sixty's not old. Seventy-five. Eighty. That's old."

"Tell that to my body, Diane. I'm carrying at least a stone more than I ought to; the tendon at the back of my left ankle gives me gyp if ever I run for a bus and my right hip hurts like hell whenever I climb a flight of stairs. Find someone else, anyone."

"There's nobody else I can trust."

I talked to Jack Kiley about it later; we were sitting in the Starbucks across the street, sunshine doing its wan best to shine through the clouds.

"What do you know about these types?" Jack asked. "This new bunch of cocaine cowboys from over the old Irish Sea?"

"Sod all," I said.

"Well, let me give you a bit of background. Ireland has the third highest cocaine use in Europe and there's fifteen or twenty gangs and upwards beating the bollocks off one another to supply it. Some of them, the more established, have got links with the IRA, or did have, but it's the newer boys that take the pippin. Use the stuff themselves, jack up an Uzi or two and go shooting; a dozen murders in Dublin so far this year and most of the leaves still on the fucking trees."

"That's Dublin," I said.

Jack cracked a smile. "And you think this old flame of yours'll be safe here in Belsize Park or back home in Amsterdam?"

I shrugged. I didn't know what to bloody think.

He leaned closer. "Just a few months back, a drug smuggler from Cork got into a thing with one of the Dublin gangs – a disagreement about some shipment bought and paid for. He thought he'd lay low till it blew over. Took a false name and passport and holed up in an apartment in the Algarve. They found his body in the freezer. Minus the head. Rumour is whoever carried out the contract on him had it shipped back as proof."

Something was burning deep in my gut and I didn't think a couple of antacid tablets was going to set it right.

"You want my advice, Jimmy?" he said, and gave it anyway. "Steer clear. Either that or get in touch with some of your old pals in the Met. Let them handle it."

Do that, I thought, and there's no way of keeping Diane out of it; somehow I didn't fancy seeing her next when she was locked away on remand.

"I don't suppose you fancy giving a hand?" I said.

Jack was still laughing as he crossed the street back towards his office.

At least I didn't have to travel far, just a couple of stops on the Northern Line. Diane had told me where to find them and given me their names. There was some kind of ceilidh band playing in the main bar, the sound of the bodhran tracing my footsteps up the stairs. And, yes, my hip did ache.

The McMahon brothers were sitting at either end of a leather sofa that had seen better days, and Chris Boyle was standing with his back to a barred window facing down on to the street. Hip-hop was playing from a portable stereo at one side of the room, almost drowning out the traditional music from below.

No one could accuse these boys of not keeping up with the times.

There was an almost full bottle of Bushmills and some glasses on the desk, but I didn't think anyone was about to ask me if I wanted a drink.

One of the McMahon brothers giggled when I stepped into the room and I could see the chemical glow in his eyes.

"What the fuck you doin' here, old man?" the other one said. "You should be tucked up in the old folks' home with your fuckin' Ovaltine."

"Two minutes," Chris Boyle said. "Say what you have to fuckin' say then get out."

"Supposin' we let you," one of the brothers said and giggled some more. Neither of them looked a whole lot more than nineteen, twenty tops. Boyle was closer to thirty, nearing pensionable age where that crew was concerned. According to Jack, there was a rumour he wore a colostomy bag on account of getting shot in the kidneys coming out from the rugby at Lansdown Road.

"First," I said, "Diane knew nothing about either the doctoring of the shipment, nor the fact it was intercepted. You have to believe that."

Boyle stared back at me, hard-faced.

One of the McMahons laughed.

"Second, though she was in no way responsible, as a gesture of good faith, she's willing to hand over a quantity of cocaine, guaranteed at least eighty percent pure, the amount equal to the original shipment. After that it's all quits, an even playing field, business as before."

Boyle glanced across at the sofa then nodded agreement.

"We pick the point and time of delivery," I said. "Two days time. I'll need a number on which I can reach you."

Boyle wrote his mobile number on a scrap of paper and passed it across. "Now get the fuck out," he said.

Down below, someone was playing a penny whistle, high-pitched and shrill. I could feel my pulse racing haphazardly and when I managed to get myself across the street, I had to take a grip on a railing and hold fast until my legs had stopped shaking.

* * *

When Jack learned I was going through with it, he offered to lend me a gun, a Smith & Wesson .38, but I declined. There was more chance of shooting myself in the foot than anything else.

I met Diane in the parking area behind Jack's office, barely light enough to make out the color of her eyes. The cocaine was bubble-wrapped inside a blue canvas bag.

"You always were good to me, Jimmy," she said, and reaching up, she kissed me on the mouth. "Will I see you afterwards?"

"No," I said. "No, you won't."

The shadows swallowed her as she walked towards the taxi waiting out on the street. I dropped the bag down beside the rear seat of the car, waited several minutes, then slipped the engine into gear.

The place I'd chosen was on Hampstead Heath, a makeshift soccer pitch shielded by lines of trees, a ramshackle wooden building off to one side, open to the weather; sometimes pickup teams used it to get changed, or kids huddled there to feel one another up, smoke spliffs or sniff glue.

When Patrick, Val and I had been kids ourselves there was a murdered body found close by and the place took on a kind of awe for us, murder in those days being something more rare.

I'd left my car by a mansion block on Heath Road and walked in along a partly overgrown track. The moon was playing fast and loose with the clouds and the stars seemed almost as distant as they were. An earlier shower of rain had made the surface a little slippy and mud clung to the soles of my shoes. There was movement, low in the undergrowth to my right hand side, and, for a moment, my heart stopped as an owl broke, with a fell swoop, through the trees above my head.

A dog barked and then was still.

I stepped off the path and into the clearing, the weight of the bag real in my left hand. I was perhaps a third of the way across the pitch before I saw them, three or four shapes massed near the hut at the far side and separating as I drew closer, fanning out. Four of them, faces unclear, but Boyle, I thought, at the centre, the McMahons to one side of him, another I didn't recognize hanging back. Behind them, behind the hut, the trees were broad and tall and close together, beeches I seemed to remember Val telling me once when I'd claimed them as oaks.

"Beeches, for God's sake," he'd said, laughing in that soft way of his. "You, Jimmy, you don't know your arse from your elbow, it's a fact."

I stopped fifteen feet away and Boyle took a step forward. "You came alone," he said.

"That was the deal."

"He's stupider than I fuckin' thought," said one or other of the McMahons and laughed a girlish little laugh.

"The stuff's all there?" Boyle said, nodding towards the bag.

I walked a few more paces towards him, set the bag on the ground, and stepped back.

Boyle angled his head towards the McMahons and one of them went to the bag and pulled it open, slipping a knife from his pocket as he did so; he slit open the package, and, standing straight again, tasted the drug from the blade.

"Well?" Boyle said.

McMahon finished running his tongue around his teeth. "It's good," he said.

"Then we're set," I said to Boyle.

"Set?"

"We're done here."

"Oh, yes, we're done."

The man to Boyle's left, the one I didn't know, moved forward almost to his shoulder, letting his long coat fall open as he did so, and what light there was glinted dully off the barrels of the shotgun as he brought it to bear. It was almost level when a shot from the trees behind struck him high in the shoulder and spun him round so that the second shot tore through his neck and he fell to the ground as good as dead.

One of the McMahons cursed and started to run, while the other dropped to one knee and fumbled for the revolver inside his zip-up jacket.

With all the gunfire and the shouting I couldn't hear the words from Boyle's mouth, but I could lip read well enough. "You're dead," he said, and drew a pistol not much bigger than a child's hand from his side pocket and raised it towards my head. It was either bravery or stupidity or maybe fear that made me charge at him, unarmed, hands outstretched as if in some way to ward off the bullet; it was the muddied turf that made my feet slide away under me and sent me sprawling headlong, the two shots Boyle got off sailing over my head before one of the men I'd last seen minding Patrick in Soho stepped up neatly behind Boyle, put the muzzle of a 9mm Beretta hard behind his ear and squeezed the trigger.

Both the McMahons had gone down without me noticing; one was already dead and the other had blood gurgling out of his airway and was not long for this world.

Patrick was standing back on the path, scraping flecks of mud from the edges of his soft leather shoes with a piece of stick.

"Look at the state of you," he said. "You look a fucking state. If I were you I should burn that lot when you get home, start again."

I wiped the worst of the mess from the front of my coat and that was when I realized my hands were still shaking. "Thanks, Pat," I said.

"What are friends for?" he said.

Behind us his men were tidying up the scene a little, not too much. The later editions of the papers would be full of stories of how the Irish drug wars had come to London, the Celtic Tigers fighting it out on foreign soil.

"You need a lift?" Patrick asked, as we made our way back towards the road.

"No, thanks. I'm fine."

"Thank Christ for that. Last thing I need, mud all over the inside of the fucking car."

When I got back to the flat I put one of Val's last recordings on the stereo, a session he'd made in Stockholm a few months before he died. Once or twice his fingers didn't match his imagination, and his breathing seemed to be giving him trouble, but his mind was clear. Beeches, I'll always remember that now, that part of the Heath. Beeches, not oaks.

SAY THAT AGAIN

Peter Lovesey

We called him the Brigadier with the buggered ear. Just looking at it made you wince. Really he should have had the bits surgically removed. He claimed it was an old war wound. However, Sadie the Lady, another of our residents, told us it wasn't true. She said she'd talked to the Brig's son Arnold, who reckoned his old man got blind drunk in Aldershot one night and tripped over a police dog and paid for it with his shell-like.

Because of his handicap, the Brigadier tended to shout. His "good" ear wasn't up to much, even with the aid stuck in it. We got used to the shouting, we old farts in the Never-Say-Die Retirement Home. After all, most of us are hard of hearing as well. No doubt we were guilty of letting him bluster and bellow without interruption. We never dreamed at the time that our compliance would get us into the High Court on a murder rap.

It was set in motion by She-Who-Must-Be-Replaced, our so-called matron, pinning a new leaflet on the notice board in the hall.

"Infernal cheek!" the Brig boomed. "They're parasites, these people, living off the frail and weak-minded."

"Who are you calling weak-minded?" Sadie the Lady piped up. "There's nothing wrong with my brain."

The Brig didn't hear. Sometimes it can be a blessing.

"Listen to this," he bellowed, as if we had any choice. " 'Are you dissatisfied with your hearing? Struggling with a faulty instrument? Picking up unwanted background noise? Marcus Haliburton, a renowned expert on the amazing new digital hearing aids, will be in attendance all day at the Bay Tree Hotel on Thursday, 8 April for free consultations. Call this number now for an appointment. No obligation.' No obligation, my arse – forgive me, ladies. You know what happens? They get you in there and tell you to take out your National Health aid so they can poke one of those little torches in your ear and of course you're stuffed. You can't hear a thing they're saying from that moment on. The next thing is they shove a form in front of you and you find you've signed an order for a thousand-pound replacement. If you object they drop your NHS aid on the floor and tread on it."

"That can't be correct," Miss Martindale said.

"Completely wrecked, yes," the Brigadier said. "Are you speaking from personal experience, my dear? Because I am."

Someone put up a hand. He wanted to be helped to the toilet, but the Brigadier took it as support. "Good man. What we should do is teach these blighters a lesson. We could, you know, with my officer training and George's underworld experience."

I smiled faintly. My underworld links were nil, another of the Brig's misunderstandings. One afternoon I'd been talking to Sadie about cats and happened to mention that we once adopted a stray. I thought the Brig was dozing in his armchair, but he came to life and said, "Which of the Krays was that – Reggie or Ronnie? I had no idea of your criminal past, George. We'll have to watch you in future."

It was hopeless trying to disillusion him, so I settled for my gangster reputation and some of the old ladies began to believe it, too, and found me more interesting than ever they'd supposed.

By the next tea break, the Brigadier had turned puce with excitement. "I've mapped it out," he told us. "I'm calling it Operation Syringe, because we're going to clean these ruffians out. Basically, the object of the plan is to get a new super-digital hearing aid for everyone in this home free of charge."

"How the heck will you do that?" Sadie asked.

"What?"

She stepped closer and spoke into his ear. "They're a private company. Those aids cost a fortune."

The Brig grinned. "Simple. We intercept their supplies. I happen to know the Bay Tree Hotel quite well."

Sadie said to the rest of us, "That's a fact. The Legion has its meetings there. He's round there every Friday night for his g&t."

"G&T or two or three," another old lady said.

I said, "Wait a minute, Brigadier. We can't steal a bunch of hearing aids." I have a carrying voice when necessary and he heard every word.

"'Steal' is not a term in the military lexicon, dear boy," he said. "We requisition them." He leaned forward. "Now, the operation has three phases. Number One: Observation. I'll take care of that. Number Two: Liaison. This means getting in touch with an inside man, Cormac, the barman. I can do that also. Number Three: Action. And that depends on what we learn from Phases One and Two. That's where the rest of you come in. Are you with me?"

"I don't know what he's on about," Sadie said to me.

"Don't worry," I said. "He's playing soldiers, that's all. He'll find out it's a non-starter."

"No muttering in the ranks," the Brigadier said. "Any dissenters? Fall out, the dissenters."

No one moved. Some of us needed help to move anywhere and nobody left the room when tea and biscuits were on offer. And that was how we were recruited into the snatch squad.

On Saturday, the Brigadier reported on Phases One and Two of his battle plan. He marched into the tea room looking as chipper as Montgomery on the eve of El Alamein.

"Well, the obbo phase is over and so is the liaison and I'm able to report some fascinating results. The gentleman who wants us all to troop along to the Bay Tree Hotel and buy his miraculous hearing aids is clearly doing rather well out of it. He drives a vintage Bentley and wears a different suit each visit and by the cut of them they're not off the peg."

"There's money in ripping off old people," Sadie said.

"It ought to be stopped," her friend Briony said.

The Brig went on, "I talked to my contact last night and I'm pleased to tell you that the enemy – that is to say Marcus

Haliburton – works to a predictable routine. He puts in a fortnightly appearance at the Bay Tree. If you go along and see him you'll find Session One is devoted to the consultation and the placing of the order. Session Two is the fitting and payment. Between Sessions One and Two a box is delivered to the hotel and it contains up to fifty new hearing aids – more than enough for our needs." He paused and looked around the room. "So what do you think is the plan?"

No one was willing to say. Some might have thought speaking up would incriminate them. Others weren't capable of being heard by the Brigadier. Finally I said, "We, em, requisition the box?"

"Ha!" He lifted a finger. "I thought you'd say that. We can do better. What we do is requisition the box."

There were smiles all round at my expense.

"And then," the Brigadier said, "we replace the box with one just like it."

"That's neat," Sadie said. She was beginning to warm to the Brigadier's criminal scheme.

He'd misheard her again. "It may sound like deceit to you, madam, but to some of us it's common justice. They called Robin Hood a thief."

"Are we going to be issued with bows and arrows?" Sadie said.

"I wouldn't mind meeting some merry men," Briony said.

The Brigadier's next move took us all by surprise. "Check the corridor, George. Make sure no staff are about."

I did as I was told and gave the thumb-up sign, whereupon the old boy bent down behind the sideboard and dragged out a flattened cardboard box that he rapidly restored to its normal shape.

"Thanks to my contacts at the hotel I've managed to retrieve the box that was used to deliver this week's aids." No question: he intended to go through with this crazy adventure. In the best officer tradition he started to delegate duties. "George, your job will be to get this packed and sealed and looking as if it just arrived by courier."

"No problem," I said to indulge him. I was sure the plan would break down before I had to do anything.

"That isn't so simple as it sounds," he said. "Take a close look. The aids are made in South Africa, so there are various customs forms attached to the box. They stuff them in a kind of envelope and stick them to the outside. What you do is update this week's documents."

"I'll see what I can manage."

"Then you must consider the contents. The instruments don't weigh much, and they're wrapped in bubblewrap, so the whole thing is almost as light as air. Whatever you put inside must not arouse suspicion."

"Crumpled-up newspaper," Sadie said.

"What did she say?"

I repeated it for his benefit.

Sadie said, "Briony has a stack of *Daily Mails* this high in her room. She hoards everything."

I knew that to be true. Briony kept every postcard, every letter, every magazine. Her room was a treasure house of things other people discarded. She even collected the tiny jars our breakfast marmalade came in. The only question was whether she would donate her newspaper collection to Operation Syringe. She could be fiercely possessive at times.

"I might be able to spare you some of the leaflets that come with my post," she said.

Sadie said, "Junk mail. That'll do."

"It doesn't incriminate me, does it?" she said. "I want no part of this silly escapade."

"Excellent," the Brigadier said, oblivious. "When the parcel is up to inspection standard, I'll tell you about the next phase."

The heat was now on me. I had to smuggle the box back to my room and start work. I was once employed as a graphic designer, so the forging of the forms wasn't a big problem. Getting Briony to part with her junk mail was far more demanding. You'd think it was bank notes. She checked everything and allowed me about one sheet in five. But in the end I had enough to stuff the box. I sealed it with packing tape I found in Matron's office and showed it to the Brigadier.

"Capital," he said. "We can proceed to phase four: distracting the enemy."

"How do we do that?"

"We inundate Marcus Haliburton with requests for appointments under bogus names."

"That's fun. I'll tell the others."

Even at this stage, it was still a game, as I tried to explain later to the police. Some of us had mobiles and others used the payphone by the front door. I think a couple of bold souls used the phone in Matron's office. I don't know if we succeeded in distracting Haliburton. He must have been surprised by the number of Smiths, Browns, Jones and Robinsons who had seen his publicity. The greedy beggar didn't turn any away.

And so the day of the heist arrived. Almost everyone from the Never-Say-Die had been talked into joining in and clambered onto the bus the Brigadier had laid on. Half of them were so confused most of the time that you could have talked them into running the London Marathon. The notable exception was Briony. She wanted no part of it. She stayed put, guarding her hoard of newspapers and marmalade jars. The Brigadier called her a ruddy conchie when he found out.

In their defence, few of them knew the finer points of the battle plan. But they still amounted to a formidable squad as they alighted from the bus and listened to the Brigadier's Agincourt-style speech.

"There are senior citizens all over Britain who will think themselves accursed they were not here with us. We few, we happy few, deaf but not downtrodden, stand on the brink of victory. Onward, then."

So began the main assault, as the Brigadier called it. Four old ladies crossed the hotel foyer Zimmer to Zimmer, a vanguard forging a route for the main party, twelve more on sticks and crutches, with two motorised chairs like tanks in the rear. Inexorably they headed for the suite used by Marcus Haliburton for his consultations. Their task: to block all movement in the corridor.

Because of my supposed underworld connections I had been selected for a kind of SAS role, along with the Brigadier himself. At some time in the first hour, while all the new patients were being documented, tested and examined, a security firm would deliver the latest box of hearing aids to the hotel. One of the staff was then supposed to bring it to the suite for Haliburton to begin handing out the aids to people who had placed orders on his previous visit. Thanks to the congestion in the corridor this would not be possible.

The next part was clever, I must admit. The Brigadier had booked the room two doors up and he and I were waiting in there with our own box filled with crumpled-up junk mail. The porter was bound to come past with the box containing the expensive digital aids.

We waited three-quarters of an hour and it was a nervous time. I had my doubts whether two elderly gents were capable of intercepting a burly hotel porter, but the Brigadier was confident.

"We're not using brute strength. This is our strength." He tapped his head.

"But if it doesn't work?"

To my horror he took a gun from his pocket and gave a crocodile grin. "My old service revolver."

"That would be armed robbery," I said, aghast. "Don't even think of it."

He misheard me, of course. From another pocket he produced a flask of brandy. "You need to drink a bit? Take a swig, old boy. It stops the shakes, I find."

Before I could get through to him I heard the squeak of a trolley wheel in the corridor outside. The moment of decision. Should I abort the whole operation? Unwisely, disastrously as it turned out, I decided to go on with it. I stepped into the corridor, right in the path of the trolley, and said to the porter pushing it, "Mr Haliburton said to lock the parcel in here for the time being. He'll collect it when the people waiting have been dealt with."

He said, "I can't do that. I'm under firm instructions to hand it to Mr Haliburton in person."

I winked and said, "I work with him. It's as good as done." I pressed a five-pound note into his sweaty palm.

Persuaded, he wheeled the parcel into the room and left it just inside the door. The Brigadier meanwhile had stepped out of sight into the bathroom. The porter had the impression he was locking the parcel in an empty room. The idea was that the Brigadier would then emerge from the bathroom with our box of junk mail and make the switch, returning to the bathroom with the box containing the aids, where he would lock himself in for an hour.

My job was to shepherd the Never-Say-Die residents as quickly as possible out of the corridor and back to the bus. I was starting to do so when a man in a grey pinstripe suit came marching up and said, "What's the trouble here? I'm Buckfield, the hotel manager."

"No trouble, Mr Buckfield," I said. "The system can't cope, that's all. Some of these old people have been waiting an hour for an appointment with the ear specialist. I'm suggesting they come back next time. We've got transport outside."

He looked at me with some uncertainty. "Are you their warden?"

"Something like that."

"One of the bellboys tells me he delivered a box of valuable hearing aids to Room 104. Was that at your bidding?"

I said, "Yes. I think you'll find it's still there."

He had a pass key and opened the door and picked up the parcel that was waiting there. I gave all my attention to ushering the old ladies towards the foyer and the waiting bus. Most of them were pleased to leave and didn't understand what we had achieved. A few genuine customers for the hearing aids were just as confused, and when we got to the bus I had difficulty persuading two of them that they weren't in the Never-Say-Die party.

Finally everyone except the Brigadier was on board. It was my job to see that all was clear and help him out of Room 104 with the parcel we had requisitioned, the most dangerous part of Operation Syringe.

Trying to look like any other guest, I crossed the foyer and stepped along the corridor. It was now empty of people. I tapped on the door of 104 and immediately realized that there was a fatal flaw in our plan. How would the Brigadier hear my knocking? I tried a second time.

No response.

Along the corridor, the door of Haliburton's suite opened and an old man came out. I tried to ignore him, but he said, "Are you waiting for a consultation? It's that room I just came out of."

I thanked him, but I don't think he heard. I took off a shoe and tried hammering on 104 with it.

At last the door opened and there was the Brigadier with the parcel in his arms. For the first time since I'd known him he looked concerned. "Take this to the bus and tell the driver to put his foot down."

"Aren't you coming?" I said.

"Cunning? Far from it," he said. "I'm a silly arse. Left my service revolver on the bed and some beggar in a pinstripe picked it up."

"Leave it," I shouted into his ear. "Come with me."

"Can't do that," he said and made a little speech straight out of one of those war films when the doomed Brit showed his stiff upper lip. "That revolver is my baby. Been with me all over the world. I'm not surrendering, old boy. I'll get back to base. See if I don't."

I said, "I'm leaving with a heavy heart."

He said, "Don't be so vulgar."

No use trying to talk sense into him. He really had need of a decent hearing aid.

I carried the parcel to the bus. Everyone cheered when they saw it. Then Sadie said, "Where's the Brigadier?"

I didn't want them to know he'd brought a gun with him, so I said he was hiding up until it was safer to leave.

The bus took us back to the home and we tottered off to our rooms for a nap after all the excitement. We'd agreed not to open the box before the Brig returned.

All evening we waited, asking each other if anyone had heard anything. I was up until ten-thirty, long past bedtime. In the end I turned in and tried to sleep.

Some time after midnight there was a noise like a stone being thrown at my window. I got out of bed and looked down. There in the grounds was the Brigadier blowing on his fingers. He shouted up to me, "Be a good fellow and unbolt the front door will you? I just met a brass monkey on his way to the welder's."

In twenty minutes every inhabitant of the house except the Matron and her two night staff assembled in the tea room. The nightwear on display is another story.

"Open it, George," the Brig ordered.

They watched in eager anticipation. Even Briony had turned out. "Ooh, bubblewrap," she said. "May I have that?"

"You might as well, because you're not getting a hearing aid, you conchie," the Brigadier said.

I unwrapped the first aid. It was a BTE (behind the ear), but elegance itself. I offered it to the Brigadier. He slotted it into his ear. "God Lord!" he said. "I can hear the clock ticking."

Everyone in the room who wanted a replacement aid was given one, and we still had a few over. The morale of the troops couldn't have been higher. Even Briony was happy with her stack of bubblewrap. We all slept well.

At breakfast, the results were amazing. People who hadn't conversed for years were chatting animatedly.

Then the doorbell chimed. The chime of doom. A policeman with a megaphone stood in the doorway and announced, "Police. We're coming in. Put your hands above your heads and stay where you are."

Sadie said, "You don't have to shout, young man. We can all hear you."

We were taken in barred vans to the police station and kept in cells. Because there was a shortage of cells some of us had to double up and I found myself locked up with the Brigadier.

"This is overkill," I said. "We're harmless old people."

"They don't think so, George," he said in a sombre tone. "Marcus Haliburton was shot dead in the course of the raid."

"Shot? I didn't hear any shots."

"After you left, it got nasty. They'll have me for murder and the rest of you for conspiracy to murder. We can't expect all our troops to hold out under questioning. They'll put up their hands, and we're all done."

He was right. Several old ladies confessed straight away. What can you expect? The trial that followed was swift and savage. The Brigadier asked to be tried by a court martial and refused to plead. He went down for life, with a recommendation that he serve at least ten years. They proved that the fatal shots had been fired from his gun.

I got three years for conspiracy to murder – in spite of claiming I didn't know about the gun. Sadie was given six months. The Crown Prosecution Service didn't press charges against some of the really frail ones. Oddly, nobody seemed interested in the hearing aid heist and we were allowed to keep our stolen property.

The Never-Say-Die Retirement Home had to carry on without us. But there was to be one last squirt from Operation Syringe.

One morning three weeks after the trial Briony decided to sort out her marmalade jars and store them better, using the bubblewrap the aids had been kept in. She was surrounding one of the jars with the stuff when there was a sudden popping sound. One of the little bubbles had burst under pressure. She pressed another and it made a satisfying sound. Highly amused, she started popping every one. She continued at this harmless pastime for over an hour. After tea break she went back and popped some more. It was all enormous fun until she damaged her fingernail and had to ask She-Who-Must-Be-Replaced to trim it.

"How did you do that?" Matron asked.

Briony showed her.

"Well, no wonder. There's something hard inside the bubble. I do believe it's glass. How wicked."

But it didn't turn out to be glass. It was an uncut diamond, and there were others secreted in the bubblewrap. A second police investigation was mounted into Operation Syringe. As a result, Buckfield, the manager of the Bay Tree Hotel, was arrested.

It seemed he had been working a racket with Marcus Haliburton, importing uncut diamonds stolen by workers in a South African diamond mine. The little rocks had been smuggled to Britain in the packing used for the hearing aids. Interpol took over the investigation on two continents.

It turned out that on the day of our heist Buckfield the manager suspected something was afoot, and decided Haliburton might be double-crossing him. When he checked Room 104 he found the Brigadier's revolver on the bed and he was certain he was right. He took it straight to the suite. Haliburton denied everything and said he was only a go-between and offered to open the new box of aids in the manager's presence. We know what it contained. Incensed, Buckfield pointed the gun and shot Haliburton dead.

After our release, we had a meeting to decide if we would sue the police for wrongful imprisonment. The Brigadier was all for it, but Sadie said we might be pushing our luck. We had a vote and decided she was right.

The good thing is that every one of us heard each word of the debate. I can recommend these new digital aids to anyone.

CONTINUITY ERROR

Nicholas Royle

Christine rang Maddox on his mobile. A little accident, she said. A bump.

"Was anyone hurt?"

"No, no one was hurt."

He made his way to the side street in Shepherd's Bush where it had happened. A one-way street temporarily blocked off by roadworks at the junction with Goldhawk Road. Estate agent's on the corner. Christine had reversed away from the roadworks and at five miles an hour hit a silver Toyota coming out of the concealed exit from the sunken car park behind the estate agent's.

By the time Maddox arrived, the driver of the silver Toyota was in full magnanimous third-party mode, confident the insurance companies would find in his favour. Maddox hated him on sight. Too reasonable, too forthcoming. Like providing his address and insurance details was some kind of favour.

Maddox's son Jack had got out of the car and stood staring at the small pile of shattered glass on the road, seemingly transfixed by it. Christine was visibly upset, despite the unctuous affability of the Toyota driver and Maddox's own efforts to downplay the situation.

"It's only a couple of lights and a new wing. No one was hurt, that's the main thing."

Two days later, Maddox and Jack were walking past the top of the side street. The roadworks had been removed and a car was exiting into Goldhawk Road without any difficulty.

"Is that where the accident happened, Daddy?" asked the little boy.

"Yes."

Jack stopped, his big eyes taking in the details. The fresh asphalt by the junction, the concealed exit from the sunken car park behind the estate agent's.

"Is it still there?" the little boy asked.

"What? Is what still there?"

"The accident. Is the accident still there?"

Maddox didn't know what to say.

They were getting ready to go out. Christine was ready and Maddox was nearly ready, a too-familiar scenario. She waited by the front door, smart, made-up, tall in new boots and long coat, enveloped in a haze of expensive perfume.

"Are you nearly ready, Brian?"

That she added his name to the harmless query was a bad sign. It meant her patience was stretched too thin. But he'd lost his car key. He'd looked everywhere. Twice. And couldn't find it.

"Where did you last have it?" she shouted up the stairs.

The unhelpfulness of the question grated against his nerves.

"I don't know. That's the whole point."

He started again. Bedroom (bedside drawer, dressing gown). Jacket pockets. Kitchen.

"Have you looked in your box?"

"Yes, I've looked in my box."

They each had a box, like an in-tray, in the kitchen. Christine never used hers, but always knew where everything was. Maddox used his, but still managed to lose at least one important item every day. Wallet, phone, keys. Chequebook, bank card. Everything always turned up, sooner or later, but in this case, not soon enough.

"I can't find it. I've looked everywhere."

Heavy sigh.

If the atmosphere hadn't become tense he would jokingly accuse her of having hidden it, of trying to make him think he was losing his mind. But that wouldn't play now. They were beyond that.

"It's probably at the *flat*," she said, loading the word with her customary judgmental emphasis.

"How could it be at the flat when my car's outside?" he snapped before realizing that *she* must have been joking.

"It's a pity you don't have a spare key," she said.

"It's a pity your car's in the garage," he retorted, "about to be declared uneconomical to repair. Look, Christine, it's very late. I can't find it and I certainly won't find it with you hovering, getting all wound up, so I suggest you get a cab and I'll follow."

"But what if you don't find it?"

"I'll find it. I'll be there, just a little late, that's all. You go. You'll easily pick up a black cab on the Green. You're only going to Ladbroke Grove."

Sweating, he listened as the front door was opened and shut – slammed. Gate clanged. Fading echo of footsteps receding. He felt the tension flow out of him and collapsed on to the nearest chair. He loosened his tie and reached for a glass.

In their bedroom he pressed the power button on his laptop. While waiting, he stared blankly at the framed poster on the wall. A production he'd been in more than twenty years ago. *Colossus.* Clive Barker's play about Goya. He allowed the faces of cast members to run through his mind, particularly those who'd gone on to other things. Lennie James – you saw him on television all the time now. A part in *Cold Feet.* A one-off drama, something he'd written himself. That prison series. *Buried.* Right. Buried in the schedules.

Aslie Pitter, the most naturally talented actor in the cast. He'd done one or two things – a Channel Four sitcom, guest appearance in *The Bill* – then disappeared. Maddox had last seen him working for a high-street chain. Security, demonstrating product – he couldn't remember which.

Elinore Vickery had turned up in something at the Waterman's. Maddox had liked her, tried to keep in touch, but there was an invisible barrier, as if she'd known him better than he knew himself.

Missing out on a couple of good parts because of his size (five foot five in stocking feet, eight stone dead), Maddox had quit the theatre and concentrated on writing. Barker had helped with one or two contacts and Maddox sold a couple of horror stories. Over the years he'd moved away from fiction into journalism and book-length non-fiction. The current project, *New Maps of Hell*, hadn't found a home. The publishers he'd offered it to hadn't been able to reject it quickly enough. They didn't want it on their desks. It made them uncomfortable. That was fine by Maddox. He'd worry if it didn't. They'd want it on their lists, though, when it was too late. He'd finish it first, then pick one editor and let the others write their letters of resignation.

He read through the afternoon's work, then closed the laptop. He opened his bedside drawer and there was his car key. He looked at it. Had it been there before? Of course it had. How could it not have been? But he'd not seen it, so it might as well not have been. It had effectively disappeared. Hysterical blindness? Negative hallucination?

He pocketed the key and went downstairs. The door closed behind him and the car started first time. He sneaked past White City – the exhibition halls were gone, torn down for a future shopping centre – and slipped on to the Westway. He didn't think of Christine as he approached Ladbroke Grove, but of Christie, John Reginald Halliday. The former relief projectionist at the Electric, who had murdered at least six women, had lived at 10 Rillington Place, later renamed Ruston Close before being demolished to make way for the elevated motorway on which Maddox was now driving. The film, starring Dickie Attenborough as the killer and John Hurt as his poor dupe of an upstairs neighbour, who swung for at least one of Christie's crimes, had been filmed in Rillington Place itself. Maddox understood, from comments posted on ghoulish message boards on the internet, that the interiors had been shot in No.8 and the exteriors outside No.10. But when the police, acting on a tip-off from Timothy Evans, yanked open a manhole cover outside No.10, Attenborough could be seen peering out through the ground-floor window of the end house in the terrace, No.10, where three of Christie's victims had been walled up in the pantry, his wife Ethel being found under the floorboards in the front room. For Maddox it was the key shot in the film, the only clear evidence that they'd gained access to the charnel house itself. The only other explanation being that they'd mocked up the entire street in the studio, which he didn't buy.

The case accounted for five pages in Maddox's book. He concentrated mainly on the interweaving of fact and fiction, the merging of film and reality. Attenborough as Christie. No.8 standing in for No.10, if indeed it did. The internet also yielded a piece of Pathé film footage of the demolition of Ruston Close. Two men with pickaxes. A third man speaking to camera. A burning house. Shots of the house at the end of the street with the white (replacement) door. Clearly the same house as that in the film. But there was no sound, the reporter mouthing inaudible commentary. Maddox lured a lip-reader to the flat, a junior editor from one of the publishers that had turned down his book. She reminded him of Linzi with her green eyes and shoulder-length streaked hair. Even in heels she didn't reach Maddox's height, but she had a confident, relaxed smile, She held his gaze when he spoke to her and appeared to be looking into his eyes, but must have been watching his lips, as she relied heavily on lip-reading.

Maddox was careful to make sure she was looking in his direction before speaking to her, probably over-careful. She must have spent a lifetime compensating for situations in which people wouldn't have made such allowances. Working backwards from the first words she managed to lip-read and then having to catch up. So much information assumed rather than known for certain, but Maddox could relate to that. In some areas of life he, too, knew nothing for certain. The deaf woman's name was Karen. He assumed the proposal for his book had been rejected by someone senior who had given Karen the unpleasant job of telling the author, but he didn't know *that* for certain. Possibly she'd read it and rejected it herself and only agreed to provide lip-reading services because she felt bad about it.

When she entered the flat, Maddox felt at ease. In control. He apologised for the loud, bass-heavy music coming from the downstairs flat, but she said she couldn't hear it.

"I thought you might be able to feel it," he said.

"It's a new building," she said. "Concrete floors. Otherwise . . ."

He showed her the footage. She said it wasn't straightforward. The quality was poor and the picture kept pixellating, plus the reporter unhelpfully turned his head to the side on several occasions.

Maddox asked her if she would come back and have another go if he was able to tidy the picture up a bit.

"I don't think I'll be able to get much off it for you," she said.

"If you wouldn't mind just trying one more time, perhaps when you're less tired," he said. "It's very important to me, for my book, you know."

Maddox pulled into one of the reserved spaces outside a block of purpose-built flats in the depressed residential trapezium bordered by Green Lanes and the roads of West Green, Seven Sisters and St Ann's. He listened to the ticking of the cooling engine for a few moments as he watched the darkened windows of the second-floor flat. The top flat.

The street door had been left open by one of his neighbours. He walked up.

Inside the flat, he left the light switched off, poured himself a drink and sat in the single armchair. He pulled out his phone and sent a short text message. Orange street-lighting cast a deathly glow over the cheap bookshelves stacked with pulp novels, true crime, horror anthologies and dystopian science fiction. His phone chimed. He opened it, read the return message and replied to it. When he'd lived here, the room had been dominated by a double bed. Moving into Christine's house had allowed him to turn the tiny flat into the dedicated office he'd always wanted by burning the bed on the waste ground out the back. He'd considered giving it away, since selling it had struck him as tiresome: placing an ad, answering calls, opening the door to strangers. Easier to burn the damn thing and all the memories associated with it. So then he'd moved his desk from the east end of the room, under the Velux window, to the west-facing windows overlooking the street.

Another text arrived. He read it and closed the phone without replying.

As usual, loud music was playing in the downstairs flat.

He drained his glass and let his head fall back against the soft cushion. The Artex ceiling had attracted cobwebs and grime, but he doubted he would ever feel the need to repaint or clean it. Very few people ever came here. Linzi had spent a lot of time in the flat, of course. He laughed bitterly, then chewed his lip and stared at the ceiling, sensitive to the slightest noise in spite of the thump of the bass from the downstairs flat. Christine had hardly stepped over the threshold. She'd been once or twice soon after they'd met, but not since. There was no reason to. It was clear from the odd comment that she resented his keeping the flat, since it was a drain on resources, but as he'd argued, there was no room in the house for all these books and tapes. Not to mention the stuff stored in the loft. He chewed his lip again.

He switched on the stereo and the ordered chaos of Paul Schütze's *New Maps of Hell* clattered into battle with the beat from below. Schütze's 1992 release was the constant soundtrack to any work he did on the book in the flat. (On the rare occasions that he worked on it at the house, he played the follow-up, *New Maps of Hell II: The Rapture of Metals*.) He believed it helped. *It started out as an aid to getting the mindset right*, he sometimes imagined telling Kirsty Wark or Verity Sharp in a television interview, *and soon became a habit, a routine. I simply couldn't work on the book without having the music playing in the background. It was about the creation of a hermetically sealed world. Which, I suppose you have to admit, Hell is. Although one that's expanding at an alarming rate, erupting in little pockets. North Kensington, Muswell Hill. London is going to Hell, Kirsty.*

He opened a file and did some work, tidied up some troublesome text. He saved it and opened another file, "Dollis Hill". Notes, a few stabs at an address, gaps, big gaps. He was going to have to go back.

He replayed the mental rushes. Autumn 1986. A fine day. Gusty, but dry, bright. Walking in an unfamiliar district of London. A long road, tree-lined. High up. View down over the city between detached houses and semis. Victorian, Edwardian.

The entry-phone buzzed, bringing him back to the present with a start. He closed the file. He got to his feet, crossed to the hall and picked up the phone.

"The door's open. Come up," he said, before realising she couldn't hear him.

He remained standing in the hall, listening to footsteps climbing the interior staircase. When the footsteps stopped outside his door there was a pause before the knock came.

He imagined her composing herself, perhaps straightening her clothes, removing a hair from her collar. Or looking at her watch and thinking of bolting. He opened the door as she knocked, which startled her.

"Come in," he said. "Thanks for coming."

All Maddox had done to improve the image on the video was change the size of the Media Player window so that the reporter's mouth, while slightly smaller, was less affected by picture break-up.

While Karen studied the footage, Maddox crossed to the far side of the room. He returned with a glass of red wine, which he placed beside the laptop. Karen raised a hand to decline, but Maddox simply pushed the glass slightly closer to her and left it there. Finally, while she was watching the footage for a third time, her hand reached out, perhaps involuntarily, to pick up the glass. She took a sip, then held the glass aloft while studying the image of the jaunty reporter: Michael Caine glasses, buttoned-up jacket, button-down shirt, hand alighting on hip like a butterfly.

Maddox watched as she replayed the footage again. Each time the reporter started speaking, she moved a little closer to the screen and seemed to angle her head slightly to the left in order to favour her right ear, in which she had a trace of hearing, despite the fact there was no sound at all on the film. Habit, Maddox decided.

Karen leaned back and looked at Maddox before speaking.

"He's saying something like *newspaper reports . . . of the investigation . . . into the discovery of the burned-out bodies of two women . . . Fifteen – or fifty – years ago . . . Something of the century*. I'm sorry, it's really hard."

Her speech was that of a person who had learned to talk the hard way, without being able to hear the sound of her own voice.

'That's great. That's very helpful, Karen. It would be fifteen, not fifty. I didn't even know for certain that he was talking about Christie's house. *Burned-out*, though, are you sure? That's strange."

"No, I'm not sure, but that's what it sounds like."

Karen's choice of expression – *sounds like* – reminded him of a blind man who had asked Maddox for help crossing the road as he was going to *see* the doctor.

Maddox went to fill up her glass, but she placed her hand over it.

"I've got to go," she said. "I said I could only stop by for a minute."

Maddox stood his ground with the wine bottle, then stepped back.

"Another time," he said.

"Have you got something else you want me to look at?"

"I might have. If it's not too much of an imposition."

"Just let me know."

He showed her out, then switched the light off again and watched from the window as she regained the street. She stopped, looked one way, then went the other, as if deciding there and then which way to go. Hardly the action of a woman with an appointment. He watched as she walked south towards St Ann's Road and disappeared around the corner, then he sat down in the armchair and emptied her wine glass. His gaze roved across the bookshelves and climbed the walls before reaching the ceiling. He then sat without moving for half an hour, his eyes not leaving the ceiling, listening to the building's creaks and sighs, the music downstairs having been turned off.

He took a different route back, climbing the Harringay Ladder and going west past the top of Priory Park. He floored the pedal through the Cranley Gardens S-bend and allowed the gradient to slow the car so that he rolled to a stop outside No. 23. There he killed the engine and looked up at the second-floor flat where Dennis Nilsen had lived from October 1981 to February 1983. One of Nilsen's mistakes, which had led to his being caught, was to have left the window in the gable dormer wide open for long periods, attracting the attention of neighbours.

Maddox looked at his watch and started the engine. He got on to the North Circular, coming off at Staples Corner, heading south down Edgware Road and turning right into Dollis Hill Lane. He slowed to a crawl, leaning forward over the wheel, craning his neck at the houses on the south side. He was sure it would be on the south side. He definitely remembered a wide tree-lined avenue with views over central London. Land falling away behind the house. Long walk from the tube. Which tube? He didn't know.

He turned right, cruised the next street. He wasn't even sure of the street. Dollis Hill Lane sounded right, but as soon as he'd got the idea of Cricklewood Lane off the internet that had sounded right too. He'd gone there, to 108/110 Cricklewood Lane, after reading on the net that that was where they'd shot *Hellraiser*. When he got there and found it was a branch of Holmes Place Health Clubs, he worked out it must have been the former location of Cricklewood Production Village, where they'd done the studio work.

Some time in the autumn of 1986, Maddox had come here, to a house in Dollis Hill. A movie was being made. Clive Barker was directing his first film. *Hellraiser*. They were shooting in a rented house and Maddox had been invited to go on the set as an associate of Barker's. He was going to do a little interview, place it wherever possible. Could be his big break. It was good of Clive to have agreed to it. Maddox remembered the big white vans in the street outside the house, a surprising number of people hanging around doing nothing, a catering truck, a long table covered with polystyrene cups, a tea urn. He asked for Steve Jones, unit publicist. Jones talked to him about what was going on. They were filming a dinner party scene with Andrew Robinson and Clare Higgins and two young actors, the boy and the girl, and a bunch of extras. Maddox got to watch from behind the camera, trying to catch Barker's eye as he talked to the actors, telling them what he wanted them to do. Controlling everybody and everything. Maddox envied him, but admired him as well. A make-up girl applied powder to Robinson's forehead. A hair-dresser fixed Ashley Laurence's hair. They did the scene and the air was filled with electricity. Everyone behind the camera held their breath, faces still and taut. The tension was palpable. The moment Barker called "Cut", it melted away. Smiles, laughter, everyone suddenly moving around. Maddox noticed the hairdresser, who looked lost for a moment, diminutive and vulnerable, but Steve Jones caught Maddox's arm in a light grip and cornered Barker. The director looked at Maddox and there was a fraction of a second's pause, no more, before he said, "Brian," in such a warm, sincere way that Maddox might have thought Clive had been looking forward to seeing him all morning.

They did a short interview over lunch, which they ate on the floor of a room at the back of the house.

"We're surrounded by images which are momentarily potent and carry no resonance whatsoever," Barker was saying in transatlantic Scouse. "Advertising, the pop video, a thing which seems to mean an awful lot and is in fact absolutely negligible."

Maddox noticed the hairdresser carrying a paper plate and a cup. She sat cross-legged on the floor next to another crew member and they talked as they ate.

"What frightens you?" he asked Barker.

"Unlit streets, flying, being stuck in the tube at rush hour. Places where you have to relinquish control."

Once they'd finished, Maddox hung around awkwardly, waiting for a chance to talk to the hairdresser. When it came – her companion rising to go – he seized it. She was getting up too and Maddox contrived to step in front of her, blocking her way. He apologised and introduced himself. "I was just interviewing Clive. We've known each other a couple of years. I was in one of his plays."

"Linzi," she said, offering her hand. "I'm only here for one day. The regular girl called in sick."

"Then I'm lucky I came today," he said, smiling shyly.

She was wearing a dark green top of soft cotton that was exactly the same shade as her eyes. Her hair, light brown with natural blonde streaks, was tied back in a knot pierced by a pencil.

"Are you going to stick around?" she asked.

"I've done my interview, but if no one kicks me out . . ."

"It's a pretty relaxed set."

He did stick around and most of the time he watched Linzi, promising himself he wouldn't leave until he'd got her number. It took him the rest of the afternoon, but he got it. She scribbled it on a blank page in her Filofax, then tore out the page and said, "Call me."

The chances of finding the house in darkness were even less than in daylight. He'd been up to Dollis Hill a couple of times in the last few weeks, once in the car and once on foot. Lately, he'd been thinking more about Linzi, and specifically about the early days, before it started to go wrong. He'd spent enough time going over the bad times and wanted to revisit the good. He wanted to see the house again, but couldn't. He needed to locate it for his book. He'd rewatched the film, which contained enough shots of the house's exterior that it should have been easy to locate it, but it didn't seem to matter how many times he trailed these suburban avenues, the house wasn't there. Or if it was, he couldn't see it. He'd begun to think it might have been knocked down, possibly even straight after the shoot. It could have been why the house had been available. In the film there was a No.55 on the porch, but that would be set dressing, like the renumbering of 25 Powis Square, in *Performance*, as No.81.

He looked at his watch and calculated that if he was quick he could get to Ladbroke Grove in time for coffee and to drive Christine home, thereby reducing the amount of grief she would give him. Negligibly, he realized, but still.

In the morning, he feigned sleep while she dressed. Her movements were businesslike, crisp. The night before had been a riot, as expected. When he had turned up at the dinner, two and a half hours late, she had contented herself with merely shooting him a look, but as soon as they left she started. And as soon as she started, he switched off.

It didn't let up even when they got home, but he wasn't listening. He marvelled at how closely he was able to mimic the condition with which Karen, his lip-reader, had been born. Thinking of Karen, moreover, relaxed him inside, while Christine kept on, even once they'd got into bed. Elective deafness – it beat hysterical blindness.

When he was sure Christine had left the house – the slammed door, the gate that clanged – he got up and showered. Within half an hour, having spent ten minutes pointing the DVD remote at the television, he was behind the wheel of the car with his son in the back seat. South Tottenham in twenty minutes was a bigger ask by day than by night, but he gave it his best shot. Rush hour was over (Christine, in common with everyone who worked on weekly magazines, finished earlier than she started), but skirting the congestion charge zone was still a challenge.

He parked where he had the night before and turned to see that Jack was asleep. He left him there, locked the car and walked up. He had decided, while lying in bed with his back to

Christine, that it would be worth going up into the loft. Some-where in the loft was a box containing old diaries, including one for 1986. He had never been a consistent diarist, but some years had seen him make more notes than others. It was worth a rummage among the spider's webs and desiccated wasps' nests. His size meant he didn't bang his head on the latticework of pine beams.

The loft still smelled faintly of formalin. He suspected it always would until he got rid of the suitcase at the far end. He shone the torch in its direction. Big old-fashioned brown leather case, rescued from a skip and cleaned up. Solid, sturdy, two catches and a strap with a buckle. Could take a fair weight.

He redirected the torch at the line of dusty boxes closer to the trap door. The first box contained T-shirts that he never wore any more but couldn't bear to throw away. The second was full of old typescripts stiff with Tipp-Ex. The diaries were in the third box along. He bent down and sorted through: 1974, a shiny black Pocket Diary filled mainly with notes on the history of the Crusades; 1976, the summer of the heatwave, *Angling Times* diary, roach and perch that should have been returned to the water left under stones to die; 1980, the deaths of his three remaining grandparents, three funerals in one year, coffins in the front room, all burials; 1982, his first term at university, meeting Martin, his best friend for a while. Martin was a year older, which had impressed Maddox. The age difference hadn't mattered. Everything was changing. Leaving school, leaving home. Living in halls. Martin was a medical student. They would stay up late drinking coffee and Martin would smoke cigarettes and tell Maddox about medicine, about anatomy and about the bodies he was learning to dissect.

Maddox could listen to Martin for hours. The later they stayed up, the more profound their discussions seemed to become. Maddox watched as Martin dragged on his cigarette and held the smoke in his lungs for an eternity, stretching the moment, before blowing it out in perfect rings. When Martin talked about the bodies in the anatomy lab, Maddox became entranced. He imagined Martin alone in the lab with a dozen flayed corpses. Bending over them, examining them, carefully removing a strip of muscle, severing a tendon. Getting up close to the secrets, the mysteries, of death. Martin said it didn't matter how long he spent washing his hands, they still smelled of formalin. He held them under Maddox's nose, then moved to cup his cheeks in an affectionate, stroking gesture.

"You don't mind, do you?" he said, as his hand landed on Maddox's knee.

"Could you get me in there? Into the lab?" Maddox asked, shaking his head, picturing himself among the bodies, as Martin's hand moved up his thigh.

"No. But I could bring you something out. Something you could keep."

Martin's hand had reached Maddox's lap and Maddox was mildly surprised to discover that far from objecting, he was aroused. If this was to be the downpayment on whatever Martin might fetch him back from the dissection table, so be it.

"I've got something for you," Martin said a couple of days later, "in my room."

Maddox followed Martin to his room.

"So where is it?" Maddox asked.

"Can't just leave that sort of thing lying about. But what's the rush?"

Martin lay down on the bed and unbuckled his belt.

Maddox hesitated, considered walking out, but he felt certain he'd always regret it if he left empty-handed. Instead, he knelt beside the bed and spat into his palm.

Afterwards, Martin pulled open his desk drawer.

"There you go," he said.

Maddox withdrew a strong-smelling package. He started to work at the knot in the outermost plastic bag, but it wouldn't come easily. He asked Martin what it contained.

"A piece of subcutaneous fat from the body of a middle-aged man. If anyone ever asks, you didn't get it from me."

Maddox returned to his own room on the seventh floor, washing his hands on the way. He cut open the bag and unwrapped his spoils. The gobbet of fat, four inches by two, looked like a piece of tripe, white and bloodless, and the stench of formalin made him feel sick and excited at the same time. Maddox was careful not to touch the fat as he wrapped it up again and secured the package with tape. He opened his wardrobe and pulled out the brown suitcase he'd liberated from a skip in Judd Street.

He saw less of Martin after that. At first he contrived subtly to avoid him and then started going out with Valerie, a girl with fat arms and wide hips he picked up in the union bar on cocktails night. He wasn't convinced they were a good match, but the opportunity was convenient, given the Martin situation.

The piece of fat remained wrapped up in its suitcase, which smelled so strongly that Maddox only had to open the case and take a sniff to re-experience how he had felt when Martin had given him the body part. As he lay in bed trying to get to sleep (alone. Valerie didn't last more than a few weeks) he sometimes thought about the man who had knowingly willed his cadaver to science. He wondered what his name might have been and what kind of man he was. What he might have been in life. He would hardly have been able to foresee what would happen to the small part of him that was now nestled inside Maddox's wardrobe.

When Maddox left the hall of residence for a flat in Holloway, the case went with him, still empty but for its human remains. He kept it on top of a cupboard. It stayed there for two years. When he moved into the flat in N15, he put the suitcase in the loft, where it had remained ever since. The piece of fat was no longer in Maddox's possession, but the suitcase was not free of the smell of formalin.

Maddox's 1986 diary was at the bottom of the box. It took only a couple of minutes to find what he was looking for. "*Hellraiser*, 11:00 a.m." he'd written in the space reserved for Friday 10 October. A little further down was an address: 187 Dollis Hill Lane.

He drove to Dollis Hill via Cranley Gardens, but on this occasion didn't stop.

"Why didn't I think of checking my old diaries before, eh, Jack?" he said, looking in the rear-view mirror.

His son was silent, staring out of the window.

Turning into Dollis Hill Lane from Edgware Road, he slowed to a crawl, oblivious to the noisy rebuke of the driver immediately behind him, who pulled out and swerved to overtake, engine racing, finger given. Maddox brought the car to a halt on a slight incline outside No.187. He looked at the house and felt an unsettling combination of familiarity and non-recognition. Attraction and repulsion. He had to stare at the house for two or three minutes before he realised why he had driven past it so many times and failed to recognise it.

Like most things recalled from the past, it was smaller than the version in his memory. But the main difference was the apparent age of the building. He remembered a Victorian villa, possibly Edwardian. The house in front of him was new. The rendering on the front gable end had gone up in the last few years. The wood-framed bay windows on the first floor were of recent construction. The casement window in the top flat, second floor, was obviously new. The mansard roof was a familiar shape, but the clay Rosemarys were all fresh from the tile shop. The materials were new, but the style was not. The basic design was unchanged, from what he could remember of the exterior shots in the film, which he'd looked at again before coming out, but in spite of that the house looked new. As if a skeleton had grown new muscle and flesh.

"Just like Frank," he said out loud.

"What, Daddy?"

"Just like Frank in the film."

"What film?"

"They made a film in this house and I came to see them make it. You're too young to see it yet. One day, maybe."

"What's it about?"

"It's about a man who disappears and then comes back to life with the help of his girlfriend. It happened in that room up there." He pointed to the top flat. "Although, the windows are wrong," he said, trying to remember the second-floor window in the film. "I need to check it again."

The only part of the exterior that looked as if they'd taken care to try to match the original was the front door.

As he'd walked from the *Hellraiser* set back to the tube two decades earlier, he'd read and re-read Linzi's number on the tornout piece of Filofax paper. He called her the next day and they arranged to meet for a drink.

"Why are you so interested in this house, Daddy?" Jack asked from the back seat.

"Because of what happened here. Because of the film. And because I met somebody here. Somebody I knew before I met your mother."

*   *   *

Linzi lived in East Finchley. They went to see films at the Phoenix or met for drinks in Muswell Hill. Malaysian meals in Crouch End. He showed her the house in Hillfield Avenue where he had visited Clive Barker.

"Peter Straub used to live on the same road, just further up the hill," he told her.

"Who's Peter Straub?"

"Have you heard of Stephen King?"

"Of course."

"Straub and King wrote a book together. *The Talisman*. They wrote it here. Or part of it, anyway. King also wrote a story called 'Crouch End', which was interesting, not one of his best."

Maddox and Linzi started meeting during the day at the Wisteria Tea Rooms on Middle Lane and it was there, among the pot plants and mismatched crockery, that Maddox realised with a kind of slow, swooning surprise that he was happy. The realisation was so slow because the feeling was so unfamiliar. They took long walks through Highgate Cemetery and across Hampstead Heath.

Weeks became months. The cherry blossom came out in long straight lines down Cecile Park, and fell to the pavements, and came out again. Linzi often stayed at Maddox's flat in South Tottenham, but frowned distastefully at his true-crime books. One morning while she was still asleep, Maddox was dressing, looking for a particular T-shirt. Unable to find it, he climbed up the ladder into the loft. Searching through a box of old clothes, he didn't hear Linzi climbing the ladder or see her head and shoulders suddenly intrude into the loft space.

"What are you doing?" she said.

"Shit." He jumped, hitting his head. "Ow. That hurt. Shit. Nothing. Looking for something."

"What's that smell?"

"Nothing."

He urged her back down the ladder and made sure the trap door was fastened before pulling on the *Eraserhead* T-shirt he'd been looking for.

Whenever he went into the loft from then on, whether Linzi was around or not, he would pull the ladder up after him and close the trap door. The loft was private.

When he got back to the flat that evening, he went up into the loft again – duly covering his tracks, although he was alone – and took the small wrapped parcel from the suitcase. The lid fell shut, the old-fashioned clasps sliding home without his needing to fasten them. Quality craftsmanship.

When it was dark, he buried the slice of tissue in the waste ground behind the flats.

As the decade approached its end, the directionless lifestyle that Maddox and Linzi had drifted into seemed to become more expensive. The bills turned red. Maddox started working regular shifts on the subs' desk at the *Independent*. He hated it but it paid well. Linzi applied for a full-time job at a ladies' salon in Finsbury Park. They took a day trip to Brighton. They went to an art show in the Unitarian Church where Maddox bought Linzi a small watercolour and she picked out a booklet of poems by the artist's husband as a return gift. They had lunch in a vegetarian café. Maddox talked about the frustrations of cutting reviews to fit and coming up with snappy headlines, when what he'd rather be doing was writing the copy himself. Linzi had no complaints about the salon. "Gerry – he's the boss – he's a really lovely guy," she said. "Nicest boss I've ever had."

They spent the afternoon in the pubs and secondhand book-shops of the North Laines. Maddox found a Ramsey Campbell anthology, an M. John Harrison collection and *The New Murderers' Who's Who*. On the train waiting to leave Brighton station to return to London, with the sun throwing long dark shapes across the platforms, Linzi read to Maddox from the pamphlet of verse.

" 'This is all I ever wanted / to meet you in the fast decaying shadows / on the outskirts of this or any city / alone and in exile.' "

As the train rattled through Sussex, Maddox pored over the photographs in his true-crime book.

"Look," he said, pointing to a caption: "Brighton Trunk Crime No.2: The trunk's contents."

"Very romantic," Linzi said as she turned to the window, but Maddox couldn't look away from the crumpled stockings on the legs of the victim, Violette Kaye. Her broken neck. The pinched scowl on her decomposed face. To Maddox the picture was as beautiful as it was terrible.

Over the next few days, Maddox read up on the Brighton Trunk Murders of 1934. He discovered that Tony Mancini, who had confessed to putting Violette Kay's body in the trunk but claimed she had died accidentally (only to retract that claim and accept responsibility for her murder more than forty years later), had lodged at 52 Kemp Street. He rooted around for the poetry pamphlet Linzi had bought him. He found it under a pile of magazines. The poet's name was Michael Kemp. He wanted to share his discovery of this coincidence with Linzi when she arrived at his flat with scissors and hairdressing cape.

"Why not save a bit of money?" she said, moving the chair from Maddox's desk into the middle of the room. As she worked on his hair, she talked about Gerry from the salon. "He's so funny," she said. "The customers love him. He certainly keeps me and the other girls entertained."

"Male hairdressers in women's salons are all puffs, surely?"

Linzi stopped cutting and looked at him.

"So?" she said. "So what if they are? And anyway, Gerry's not gay. No way."

"Really? How can you be so sure?"

"A girl knows. Okay?"

"Have you fucked him then or what?"

She took a step back. "What's the matter with you?"

"How else would you know? Gerry seems to be all you can talk about."

"Fuck you."

Maddox shot to his feet, tearing off the cape.

"You know what," he said, seizing the scissors, "I'll cut my own fucking hair and do a better job of it. At least I won't have to listen to you going on about *Gerry*."

He started to hack at his own hair, grabbing handfuls and cutting away. Linzi recoiled in horror, unable to look away, as if she were watching a road accident.

"Maybe I should tell you about all the women at the *Independent*?" he suggested. "Sheila Johnston, Sabine Durrant, Christine Healey . . . I don't know where to start."

It wasn't until he jabbed the scissors threateningly in her direction that she snatched up her bag and ran out.

The next day he sent flowers. He didn't call, didn't push it. Just flowers and a note: "Sorry."

Then he called. Told her he didn't know what had come over him. It wouldn't happen again. He knew he'd be lucky if she forgave him, but he hoped he'd be lucky. He hadn't felt like this about anyone before and he didn't want to lose her. The irony was, he told her, he'd been thinking his flat was getting a bit small and maybe they should look for a place together. He'd understand if she wanted to kick it into touch, but hoped she'd give him another chance.

She said to give her some time.

He shaved his head.

He drove down to Finsbury Park and watched from across the street as she worked on clients. Bobbing left and right. Holding their hair in her hands. Eye contact in the mirror. Gerry fussing around, sharing a joke, trailing an arm. As she'd implied, though, he was distributing his attentions equally among Linzi and the two other girls.

Mornings and evenings, he kept a watch on her flat in Finchley. She left and returned on her own. He chose a route between his flat and hers that took in Cranley Gardens in Muswell Hill. He parked outside No.23 and watched the darkened windows of the top flat. He wondered if any of the neighbours had been Nilsen's contemporaries. If this man passing by now with a tartan shopping trolley had ever nodded good morning to the mass murderer. If that woman leaving her house across the street had ever smiled at him. Maddox got out of the car and touched the low wall outside the property with the tips of his fingers.

Linzi agreed to meet up. Maddox suggested the Wisteria Tea Rooms. It was almost like starting over. Cautious steps. Shy smiles. His hair had grown back.

"What got into you?"

"I don't know. I thought we'd agreed to draw a line under it."

"Yes, you're right."

At the next table a woman was feeding a baby.

"Do you ever think about having children?" Linzi asked, out of the blue.

"A boy," Maddox said straightaway. "I'd call him Jack."

Maddox didn't mention Gerry. He took on extra shifts. Slowly, they built up trust again. One day, driving back to

his place after dropping Linzi off at hers, he saw that a board
had gone up outside 23 Cranley Gardens. For sale. He rang the
agents. Yes, it was the top flat, second floor. It was on at
£64,950, but when Maddox dropped by to pick up a copy of
the details (DELIGHTFUL TOP FLOOR ONE BEDROOM
CONVERSION FLAT), they'd reduced it to £59,950. He
made an appointment, told Linzi he'd arranged a surprise.
Picked her up early, drove to Cranley Gardens. He'd never
brought her this way. She didn't know whose flat it had been.

A young lad met them outside. Loosely knotted tie, shiny
shoes. Bright, eager.

Linzi turned to Maddox. "Are you thinking of moving?"

"It's bigger and it's cheap."

Linzi smiled stiffly. They followed the agent up the stairs. He
unlocked the interior door and launched into his routine.
Maddox nodded without listening as his eyes greedily took
everything in, trying to make sense of the flat, to match what he
saw to the published photographs. It didn't fit.

"The bathroom's gone," he said, interrupting the agent.

"There's a shower room," the boy said. "And a washbasin
across the hall. An unusual arrangement."

Nilsen had dissected two bodies in the bathroom.

"This is a lovely room," the agent said, moving to the front of
the flat.

Maddox entered the room at the back and checked the view
from the window.

"At least this is unchanged," he said to Linzi, who had
appeared alongside.

"What do you mean?"

He looked at her and realized what he'd said.

"This flat's all different. I've seen pictures of it."

The story came out later, back at Maddox's place.

"You took me round Dennis Nilsen's flat?"

He turned away.

"You didn't think to mention it first? You thought we might
live there together? In the former home of a serial killer? What
the fuck is wrong with you?"

"It's cheap," he said, to the closing door.

He watched from the window as she ran off towards West
Green Road. He stayed at the window for a time and then pulled

down the ladder and went up into the loft. He pulled up the ladder and closed the trap door. He opened the big brown suitcase. It was like getting a fix. He studied the dimensions of the suitcase. It was not much smaller than Tony Mancini's trunk.

Christine was at work. Maddox read a note she'd left in the kitchen: "We need milk and bread."

He went into the living room and took down the *Hellraiser* DVD from the shelf. Sitting in the car with Jack outside the house on Dollis Hill Lane, Maddox had noticed something not quite right about the windows on the second floor. They were new windows and set in two pairs with a gap between them, but that wasn't it. There was something else and he didn't know what. He fast-forwarded until the exterior shot of Julia leaving the house to go to the bar where she picks up the first victim. The second-floor window comprised six lights in a row. For some reason, when rebuilding the house, they'd left out two of the lights and gone with just four, in two pairs. But that wasn't what was bothering him.

He skipped forward. He kept watching.

Frank and Julia in the second-floor room, top of the house. She's just killed the guy from the bar and Frank has drained his body. Julia re-enters the room after cleaning herself up and as she walks towards the window we see it comprises four lights in a row. Four windows. Four windows in a row. Not six. Four.

Maddox wielded the remote.

Looking up at the house as Julia leaves it to go to the bar. Second floor, six windows. Inside the same room on the second floor, looking towards the windows. Four, not six.

So what? The transformation scenes, which take place in that second-floor room at the front of the house, weren't shot on Dollis Hill Lane. Big deal. That kind of stuff would have to be done in the studio. The arrival of the Cenobites, the transformation of Frank, his being torn apart. It wasn't the kind of stuff you could shoot on location. But how could they make such a glaring continuity error as the number of lights in a window? Six from outside, four from within. It couldn't be a mistake. It was supposed to mean something. But what?

"Daddy?"

Maddox jumped.

"What is it, Jack?"

"What are you watching?"

Maddox looked at the screen as he thought about his response.

"This film, the one shot in that house."

"The house with the windows?"

"Yes."

"Why is it important?"

"I don't know. No, I do know." His shoulders slumped. "I don't know. Maybe it's not."

He drove to the supermarket. Jack was quiet in the back. They got a trolley. Maddox stopped in front of the newspapers. He looked at the *Independent*. Although he'd first met Christine on the *Independent* arts desk, it wasn't until they bumped into each other some years later, when they were both freelancing on TV listings magazines at IPC, that they started going out. Although they were equals at IPC, Christine had routinely rewritten his headlines at the *Independent* and while he pretended it didn't still rankle, it did. Not the best basis for a relationship, perhaps. Then a permanent position came up on *TV Times*, and they both went for it, but Christine's experience counted. They decided it wouldn't affect things, but agreed that maybe Maddox should free himself of his commitments at IPC. He said he had a book he wanted to write. Together they negotiated an increasingly obstacle-strewn path towards making a life together. If they stopped and thought about it, it didn't seem like a very good idea, but neither of them had a better one.

Maddox looked around to check that Jack was still in tow, then moved on.

He stood silently in cold meats, swaying very gently.

"Gone," he said quietly. "All gone. Disappeared."

"What, Daddy? What's gone?"

"Wait there, Jack. I'll be back. Don't move."

He walked to the end of the aisle and turned the corner. He walked to the end of the next aisle and then the next, looking at the items on the shelves, familiar brands, labels he'd seen a thousand times. All meaningless. He recognised nothing. What was he looking for? Bread and milk? Where were they? He couldn't remember. He went back to where he'd left the trolley. It was there, but Jack wasn't.

He looked up and down the aisle. The brand names that had meant nothing to him a moment ago now leapt out at him, shouting, screaming for attention. It was as if the two sides of the aisle had suddenly shifted inward. Jack was nowhere to be seen.

"Jack!"

Maddox ran to the end of the aisle and looked both ways. He looked up the next aisle, then up the next and the one after. He kept calling Jack's name. Shoppers stopped and stared, but Maddox moved faster and shouted louder. He looked at the line of tills and wondered if Jack had gone that way. He could already be out of the store, wandering around the car park, about to be run over or abducted. He told himself to calm down, that he would find him, but at the same time another voice suggested that sometimes the worst thing imaginable did happen. It had before, after all. Would this be the next case heard about on the news? A half-page in the paper. London man loses child in supermarket. Brian Maddox, 42, took his eyes off his son for one moment and he was gone. But he hadn't taken his eyes off him for just one moment. He'd gone to the next aisle, or the one after. He'd gone away. He could have been gone five minutes. Ten, fifteen.

"Jack!"

"Sir?"

A young lad, a shelf stacker, was standing in front of him. Maddox told him his son had disappeared. The shelf stacker asked for a description. Maddox gave him one and the lad said he would start from the far end of the store and advised Maddox to start from the other. They would meet in the middle and most likely one of them would have found Jack. Maddox did as he was told and neither of them found Jack. Maddox was short of breath, dry in the mouth, his chest rising and falling, unbearable pressure being exerted on his temples. He could no longer call out Jack's name without his voice breaking. More staff were on hand now. They took Maddox's arms and led him to an office where he was sat down and given a drink of water.

"Maybe the boy's with his mother?" someone suggested.

Maddox shook his head.

"Do you have a number for her?"

Maddox produced Christine's number. He was dimly aware of a phone call being made. The office was full of people. Managers, security, cashiers. They swopped remarks, observations. Some expressions hardened. "What did she say?" a voice asked. "There is no son," another one answered. "No kids at all, apparently." A security guard replayed videotape on a monitor. Grainy, vivid. Maddox entering the store on his own with a trolley. Standing in front of the newspapers, on his own. Leaving the trolley in cold meats. No unattached children.

They gave Maddox another glass of water while waiting for the police to arrive. The store didn't want to press charges. "What would be the point?" Maddox was free to go. "Has this happened before?" Shake of the head. "If it were to happen again, the store would have to consider taking action . . . Very upsetting for other shoppers . . . You *will* see someone?"

Maddox sat in the car park, behind the wheel of the car. He hadn't got what he'd come for. The milk and the bread. Maybe it didn't matter any more. He sat in the car for a long time and only turned the key in the ignition when he realized the sky over central London was beginning to get dark.

He didn't go to the house. He didn't imagine Christine would be there, but it was kind of irrelevant either way. Instead, he drove to South Tottenham. He drove through the top of the congestion charge zone. It didn't matter any more. It was rush hour. It took an hour and a half to get to N15. The street door was open. He walked up, entered the flat. Thump-thump-thump from downstairs. He took out his phone and sent a text message, then stood by the window for a while watching the street. He left the phone on the window ledge and pulled down the ladder and climbed into the loft, retrieving the ladder and closing the trap door behind him. Stooping, he walked over to the suitcase, which smelled strongly of formalin. He knelt in front of it for several minutes, resting his hands on the lid, then touching the clasps.

He released the clasps and opened the case.

It was empty.

He frowned, then sat and stared at the empty case for some time, listening to the creaks of the beams and the muffled basslines from the downstairs flat. He wondered if Karen would come, how long she might be. He wasn't sure what he would do when she arrived.

Slowly, he rose, then lowered the upper half of his body into the case, folding his legs in afterwards. Inside the case, the smell of formalin was very strong. He stared at the pine beams, the cobwebs, the shadows clinging to the insulating material. He could still faintly hear his neighbour's loud music, which Karen had been unable to hear, and then, rising above it, the clear and unmistakeable chime of his phone, down in the flat, announcing the arrival of a text message. He started to uncurl his body and the lid of the case fell forward.

He had twisted his body far enough that the hump of his shoulder caught the closing lid.

He climbed out and lay down next to the suitcase.

A minute later his phone chimed a reminder.

He thought about Linzi. Linzi had been good for him, until things went bad. He wondered where she was. He looked at the empty suitcase again and plucked a long fine strand of fair hair from the lining. He thought about Karen and her need, unacknowledged, to be looked after. He remembered how vulnerable Linzi had seemed when he saw her for the first time.

Karen would be along soon. Probably. She hadn't let him down yet.

He still had options.

THE LAST KAYFABE

Ray Banks

Don't matter what city you're in, what town. Three hundred days a year on the road, you could be in Shitsville, Ohio or New York fuckin' city. All it looks to you is another hotel room charging ten dollars for a stubby bottle of beer. Outside, you got the same old shit too: drizzle throwing a mist over the streets and their barred-up liquor stores. And you know if there's a place with Martin Luther King's name on it, that's where you're gonna score.

"That time you fucked up New Jack," says Monty. "That for real?"

They don't always recognize me. This one can't believe a white boy pinned a former bounty hunter with four justifiables. I stare at him, wish he'd move his ass and hand over the fuckin' dimes.

"No," I say. "Wasn't for real."

"*Any* of that shit for real?"

Shake my head. Apart from the blood. The blood was real. The *pain*. Shit, you wanna talk pain, we can talk pain. I got a constant steel-band ache across the back of my neck thanks to a guitar broke over my head by an Elvis-looking motherfucker called himself The Honky Tonk Man. Then Hardcore, list it out: second-degree burns on my hands and arms; been spiked so many times with barb wire I lost count; broke all my ribs, individual and all at once; broke my sternum; eight concussions and I got a total of over six hundred stitches holding me together like a beefed-up rag doll with bad dreams.

Might've been sports *entertainment*. Might've been rehearsed. Bret Hart saying he never hurt anyone – fuck Bret Hart. But just 'cause you *planned* that three-hundred-pound grizzly dropping on your ass from fifty feet in the air, didn't mean your damn bones didn't shake and break.

"What about that time – shit, musta been ten years ago – you was on RAW—"

"Your name's Monty, right?"

"Yeah."

"Just making sure, 'cause your man up the way there, he told me I should come down here and get the shit from Monty. Now I gave him the money, but you ain't given me shit but an interview. So how about we turn off the fuckin' Biography Channel and do some business?"

Run the numbers: work twenty-seven days out the month, twice daily on the weekends. Nine airplane connections a week. Adds up to a couple dimes a day. In the way-back, I didn't know a jobber who didn't pop, snort, guzzle or spike. Pills for the pain, drink or tie off to sleep, snort to wake and grapple. Better living through chemistry, and mine came boulder-shaped.

Beat those old memories like dust from a rug. No good for me in the here and now.

"You give the money to Leon?" says Monty.

I point at a stringy guy who looks like he's trying to shit his pants slowly. "That Leon? 'Cause that's the motherfucker got my money."

Monty nods. "That's Leon."

"Then we're all acquainted."

"How much you give him?"

I squint at him. He's stalling. "What's the problem, Monty?"

"Ain't no problem at all, man."

Except he's looking over my fuckin' shoulder.

I turn, get the picture in Hi-Def.

Leon's quit shifting his weight, coming down on me full-bore. Got this crazy-ass chimp face on him, grin to grimace, like he's playing heel in his own private smackdown. Hands outstretched, but I knock the lunge out of him. Grab his head, bring it to mine solid – stamp the sidewalk as I do, force of habit. Another collision, Leon totters back. Reach for his skull, grab what I can of his hair. Adjust the tape on my fingers, sneak the razor out.

In the trade, they call it a blade-job. You need to sell a pillowstrike, you cut yourself. One time I caught a gash so bad, I made a 0.7 on the Muta Scale.

Leon tries to jerk, makes me dig an artery. I let him go as he squeals and bleeds like a chiselled pig.

He ain't the only one bleeding. I spin at a spike in my leg, see something drop to the ground as I turn and grab Monty. Motherfucker's heavy, but I reckoned he'd carry it slow. No more bullshit: sometimes you got to close the fist and fuck somebody up. I tear into Monty, drop him to the concrete. The sidewalk opens his head at the scalp. I put my foot in his ribs, then pull back when the pain in my stuck leg is too much.

Hearing screams melt into hoarse breath now. Monty rolls onto his back. A blood bubble appears in his open mouth, pops when his lungs are empty. Look over at Leon, he can't see through the blood in his eyes. Curled up like a fuckin' baby on the ground. Sounds like he's crying.

I look at the ground: Monty's weapon, the one he stuck me with. It's a boxcutter.

Another word we use in the trade: *kayfabe*. Means fake. Some jobber threw for real, tried to hurt you, that was breaking kayfabe. You didn't do it unless you wanted your fuckin' papers.

These two: kayfabe fuckin' dealers, no stones to back 'em up. Broke roles 'cause they reckoned me another crackhead cracker.

Thinking now, picturing these two hanging out with their pipe-hitting pals: "That whiteboy wrestler, Babyface – you remember that motherfucker? He came round my shit wanting *rocks*, man. Me an' Leon, we fucked that boy *up*."

"This fun to you?" I say. "You having fun, boys? 'Cause you want some more, I'll stretch both you motherfuckers blue."

Leon whines.

"That's what I thought."

Look at me now, you think I'm FUBAR. Lean and old, holding my fuckin' leg like it's gonna drop off. It's why they don't recognize me. Been a long time since I was the ultimate face in the Federation. But then, I was Babyface. The crowd *popped* at me, man. I put so many heels to the mat, I was a fuckin' hero. Spin out a running DDT as a finish, hear twenty thousand people calling my name.

The ladies shouting: "Nobody puts Babyface in the corner!"

Got the men: "That Babyface ain't for crying!"

Hear it now, the applause like a fuckin' rainstorm.

And then wait for the lightning to strike. The Attitude years, hearing the cheers turn to jeers, the crowd turned vicious. They need a hero like they need a bag on their collective hip. I go up against Stone Cold, I do my gimmick – rip my T and throw it to the crowd – but they ain't having it. They throw my T back. Faces are victims, there to be stomped. Some turn heel, some leave the business to sell used cars. I take flop on flop, pin on pin. Do whatever the bosses tell me 'cause I'm a good worker and I believe that people'll want their heroes back some day.

They don't.

Clean that from my mind as I limp over to Monty and see if he's legit. Sure enough, the guy's been holding. I pull two baggies of vials out of his pockets. He whistles as he breathes, tries to speak, but he don't put up a fight. Go to Leon, get my money back and more besides. Leon's hand clamps over mine.

I bend two fingers till they snap. Leon finds the breath to scream again.

"Hush up, Leon. Listen. You know Vince?"

Leon shakes his head.

Course he don't know Vince. That's what I call him. Reminds me of my old boss. It don't matter what he's called, though, 'cause the point's the same:

"Vince says you deal on this corner, you gonna get fucked up. You feel me?"

Leon's eyes get to slits.

"You know me," I say. "I'm a *good* guy. That's why I didn't fuckin' kill you. When you get yourself stitched, you remember that. And pass it on to Monty."

I turn my back, go to the rental.

Every time playing out the same shit in my head.

I go to the car, there's gonna be a gun. These guys, if they're real dealers, they'll have a fuckin' piece between 'em.

Welcoming the gun, *hoping* for it. Some fuck wants to put this Old Yeller out his misery, they can go right ahead. I seen that movie a million times and I know. Don't matter what a good dog Yeller was. Once you get bit by the fuckin' wolf, you're a short time dying.

Ain't gonna happen with these kayfabe motherfuckers. Small time. Stick me with a boxcutter instead of shooting me. I check the leg situation as I get in the car: if I was still fighting, I'd be fucked. 'Cause the damage don't matter – you have to do what your bosses tell you to do. Vince is the same. He wants me to fuck somebody up in Detroit, Baltimore, Cleveland, fuckin' *Anchorage*, I do it. He got some wide-ranging business interests and a lot of ants trying to make off with his sugar.

Start the engine. The rental coughs. I check the count on the cash. Couple thou, should be good for gas.

And enough rocks in these bags to last me a while.

Vince wants me to hit a corner in Atlanta tomorrow night. Don't know if I can do that with my leg, but I'll see how I feel after I hit the stem.

'Cause right now I need something. All us jobbers do.

TO HAVE AND TO HOLD

Ken Bruen

"I should have married Johnny Cash."

The cop was taken aback. Of all the things he expected her to say, this was never on the table.

He looked at her, the dishwater-blonde hair, the hard mouth, the slight, jagged scar along her cheek and the air of exhaustion she exuded. The coffee he'd sent out for was before her and she moved her manacled hands to take a sip, the Styrofoam cup tilted back, and he glimpsed very white teeth. He had her statement before him and if he could just get her to sign the goddamn thing, he might beat the gridlock, get home to supper before eight. His partner had gone for a leak and the tape recorder had been shut off.

She raised her hands, asked,

"Y'all could maybe take these off for a time?"

He could see where the metal had cut into her wrists and angry welts ran along the bone. He said,

"Now, Charlene, you know I gotta keep you cuffed 'til booking is done."

She sighed, then asked,

"Got a smoke?"

He had a pack of Kools in his suit pocket, for his wife, shook his head, said,

"No smoking in a Federal building, you know that."

She gave him a smile and it lit up her whole face, took twenty years right off her. She said,

"I won't tell if you don't."

And what the hell, he took out the pack and a battered Zippo. It had the logo, "First Airborne." He slid them across the table and she grabbed them, got one in her mouth, cranked the lighter, the smell of gasoline emanating like scarce comfort. She peered at the pack, Menthol, asked,

"What's with that, you're not a pillow-biter are you? Not that I have anything against Gays but I can read folk. I'd have you down for a ladies' man."

He nearly smiled, thinking,

"Yeah, right."

In his crumpled suit, gray skin, sagging belly, he was a Don Juan. What was it his daughter would answer . . . *Not*.

She wasn't expecting an answer, said,

"Years back, I was working one of those fancy hotels, still living high on the hog, and I ran the bar. Guess who walked in, with his band?"

Her eyes shining at the memory, she continued,

"The Man in Black, he'd done a concert and they dropped in for a few quiet brews and some chicken wings."

Foley was impressed. He liked Cash, except for that prison crap he did, and in spite of himself, asked,

"No shit, the Man himself?"

She was nodding, the smoke like a halo around her head, said,

"I couldn't believe it, I never seen anyone famous, not, like, in real life. I gave 'em my best service, and in those days, I was hot, had some moves."

Foley nearly said,

"You still do."

But bit down and wondered where the hell his partner had got to. Probably gone for a bourbon, Shiner back. He'd return, smelling of mints, like that was a disguise. He asked,

"You talk to him, to Mr Cash?"

"Not at first. I was getting them vittles, drinks, making sure they were comfortable and after, I dunno, an hour, Johnny said,

'Take a pew little lady, get a load off.'"

She rubbed her eyes, then.

"He had these amazing boots, all scuffed but, like, real expensive, snakeskin or something, and he used his boot to hook a chair, pull it up beside him."

She touched her face, self conscious, said,

"I didn't have the scar then, still had some dreams. Jesus."

Foley was a cop for fifteen years, eight with Homicide and he was, in his own cliché, *hard bitten*. There wasn't a story, a scam, an excuse, a smoke screen he hadn't heard and his view of human nature veered from cynical to incredulity. But something about this broad . . . a sense of, what . . .? He didn't want to concede it, but was it . . . dignity? A few months later, a Saturday night, his wedding anniversary, he'd taken his Lottie for clams and that white wine she loved. Had a few too many glasses himself – that shit crept up on you – and told Lottie about the feeling and Lottie had gotten that ice look. He wouldn't be having any lovemaking that night; she hissed,

"You had a shine for that . . . that trailer trash?"

His night had gone south.

And c'mon, he hadn't got a thing for Charlene, but something, her face now, in the middle of the Cash story, it got to him, she was saying,

"I sat down and Mr Cash, he asked me my name, I done told him and he repeated it but with an S . . . like . . . *Shur . . . leen.* He had that voice, the gravel. Luckies and corn whiskey melt, give a girl the shivers, and then he said,

"That's a real *purty* name . . . how he said 'pretty'."

She massaged her right wrist, the welt coming in red and inflamed. She said,

"I had me a leather thong on my wrist. My Mamma done give it to me, real fancy, little symbols of El Paso interwoven on there, and I dunno, I saw him look at it and maybe it was the heat, it was way up in them there 90s, even that time of the evening, and I took it off, said,

"Can I give you this?"

"His boys went quiet for a moment, the long-necks left untouched and them fellers could drink. He took it, tied it on his wrist, gave me that smile, sent goose bumps all down my spine, said,

"*Muchas gracias, señorita.*"

"Then I noticed one of the guys give a start and I turned and June Carter came in, that bitch, full of wrath. Dame had a hard on so I got my ass in gear, got back behind the bar. They didn't stay long after, and Johnny never came to say goodbye, that cow had him bundled out of there like real urgent business. The manager, he come over to the bar, paid the tab and gave me one hundred dollars for my own self. What do you think of that, one hundred bucks, for like, real little service?"

Foley knew hookers. For fifteen minutes, they'd be lucky to get thirty and change. Charlene's face got ugly, a coldness from her eyes, mixed with . . . grief? She said,

"I was on a high, floating, my face burning, like I was some goddamn teenager, and not even that Carter cunt . . ."

The word was so unexpected and especially from a woman, that Foley physically moved back, reconsidered the handcuffs. Charlene finished with,

"I was cleaning the table, them good ol' boys sure done a mess of wings and long-necks and there . . . in the middle of the table, sliced neatly in half, was my Mama's wrist band."

A silence took over the room, she fired up another Kool, taking long inhales like she was stabbing her body, her eyes like slits in her face and she said,

"When I'd be clearing up, I'd been humming, *I Walk the Line*."

Years after, Johnny came on the juke, the radio, that tune, Foley would have to turn it off.

Go figure.

When Foley's partner got back, minted almighty, his face with that bourbon glow, he brought some sodas and if he noticed the cuffs were off, he let it slide, turned on the tape recorder, asked,

"You grew up in El Paso, am I right?"

Charlene gave him a look, a blend of amusement and malice, said,

"Cinco de Mayo."

He looked at Foley, shrugged, and Charlene took a slug of the soda, grimaced, asked,

"No Dr Pepper?"

Then,

"Damn straight, between Stanton and Kansas, you get to the bus station? . . . Turn right on Franklin, walk, like maybe a block-and-a-half? . . . Little side street there, we had us our place, me and my Mom, near the Gardner Hotel. That building is, like, eighty years old?"

Foley's partner gave a whistle, said,

"No shit?"

Like he could give a fuck.

Foley was pissed at him, felt the interview had gone downhill since he had joined them. Something like intimacy had been soiled, and he had to shake himself, get rid of those damn foolish notions. Charlene stared at him, asked,

"I know he's Foley. Who are you?"

"Darlin', I'm either your worst nightmare or your only hope, *comprende, chiquita*?"

She tasted the insult, the loaded use of the Spanish, then said, *"No me besas mas, por favor!"*

He didn't get it, said,

"I don't get it."

She laughed, said,

"The next whore sits on your face, ask her."

He leaned fast across the table, slapped her mouth, hard, and Foley went,

"Jesus, Al."

His fingers left an outline on her cheek and she smiled. The week after, when Al asked his regular hooker for a translation, she told him,

"Please don't kiss me."

Foley wound back the tape, couldn't have the slap on there, then asked,

"So what brought you back to Houston?"

She shrugged, said,

"A guy, what else."

Foley looked at his notes, double-checked, then,

"That'd be the deceased, one Charles Newton?"

She lit up the cigarette she'd been toying with, blew a cloud of smoke at Al, said,

"Charlie, yeah, he promised me he'd marry me, and he was into me for Five Gs."

Al gave a nasty chuckle, more a cackle, asked,

"The matter with you broads, you give your dollars to any lowlife that says he'll marry you?"

She looked away, near whispered,

"He had a voice like Johnny Cash."

Al spread his hands in the universal gesture of *the fuck does that mean?* Charlene was thinking of her third day in Houston: one of those sudden rainstorms hit and she ducked into a building. Turned out it was a library and she looked to see if maybe they had a book on Johnny. Passing a Literature section, she saw a title . . . *To Have and Have Not*.

For some reason, she read it as *To Have and To Hold* and was about to open it when the librarian approached, a spinster in her severe fifties, demanded,

"Are you a member, Miss?"

A hiss riding point on the *Miss*. Charlene knew the type – the dried-up bitter fruit of TV dinners and vicious cats. Charlene dropped the book, said,

"If you have anything to do with it, I'm so fucking out of here."

And was gone.

She'd have asked Foley about the book if Al wasn't there, but she shut it down. Charlie was the usual loser she'd always attracted, but he had an apartment near Rice University and she was running out of time, looks and patience. When she caught him going through her purse, she'd finally figured,

"What the hell?"

And knifed the bastard, in the neck. Then it felt so good, she stuck him a few more times . . . twenty five in all, or so they said. What, they counted? She was still holding the blade when the cops showed up and it was, as they say, a slam-dunk.

Foley said,

"You turned down the offer to have an attorney present."

She gave him what amounted to a tender smile, said,

"They'd assign some guy, and you know what? I'm sick to my gut of men."

Al was unrolling a stick of Juicy Fruit, popped it in his mouth, made some loud sucking noises, said,

"You're a lesbian, that it? Hate all men?"

She let out a breath, said,

"If I sign this, can I get some sleep, some chow?"

Foley passed over a pen, said,

"Have you some ribs, right away."

She signed and Al said,

"Now the bad news darlin'. Ol' Charles, he was the son of a real prominent shaker right here in Houston. Bet he didn't tell you that. You're going away for a long time."

She stretched, asked,

"And what makes you think I give a fuck?"

She got fifteen years. As she was being led down, Al leaned over, said,

"Come sundown, a bull dyke's gonna make you think of Johnny Cash in a whole new light."

She spat in his face.

Six months later, Foley went to see her. He didn't tell Al. When they brought her into the interview room, he was shocked by her appearance. Her frame had shrunk into itself and her eyes were hollow, but she managed a weak smile, said,

"Detective, what brings you out to see the gals?"

He was nervous, his hands awash with sweat, and he blamed the humidity, asked,

"They treating you okay?"

She laughed, said,

"Like one of their own."

He produced a pack of Kools and a book of matches. She looked at him, said,

"I quit."

He felt foolish, tried,

"You can use them for barter, maybe?"

She had a far away expression in her eyes, near whispered,

"They got nothing I want."

He had a hundred questions he wanted to ask, but couldn't think how to frame them and stared at the table. She reached over, touched his hand, said,

"Johnny was on TV last week, did a song called *Hurt*, he sang that for me."

Then she changed tack, said,

"You ever get to El Paso and want to cross the border, take the number 10 green trolley to the Santa Fe Bridge. Don't take the Border Jumper Trolley – it's, like, real expensive. Walk to the right side of the Stanton Bridge and it's twenty-five cents to cross and in El Paso, you want some action, go to the Far West

Rodeo, on Airways Boulevard. They sometimes got live rodeo, and hey, get a few brews in, you might even try the mechanical bull, that's a riot."

Relieved to have something to talk about, he asked,

"You went there a lot?"

"Never, not one time. But I heard, you know?"

He looked at his watch and she said,

"Y'all better be getting on, I got to write me a letter to Johnny, let him know where I'm at."

Foley was standing and said,

"Charlene, he's dead. He died last week."

For a moment, she was stock still, then she emitted a howl of anguish that brought the guards running. She wailed,

"You fucking liar – he's not dead. He'll never be dead to me – how do you think I get through this hell?"

As he hurried down the cellblock, he could still hear her screams, his sweat rolling in rivulets, creasing his cheap suit even further.

As he got his car in "drive," he reached in his jacket, took out the packaged CD of Johnny's Greatest Hits . . . slung it out the window, the disc rolling along the desert for a brief second, then coming to a stop near some sagebrush.

A rodent tearing at the paper exposed Cash's craggy face, and, viewed in a certain light, you'd think he was looking towards the prison.

Impossible to read his expression.

THE 45 STEPS

Peter Crowther

Luddersedge's Regal Hotel lived up to its grand name in only one way.

The building was forbidding rather than imposing, a towering grey edifice of soot-ingrained stone and stained, greasy windows that squatted alongside the traffic lights on the corner of Smithfield Road and Albert Street. The somewhat less-than-impressive facade looked more like an old mill building – examples of which could still be seen dotted around the Calder Valley landscape, all the way from Halifax to Burnley and points even further west – than like a supposedly luxurious establishment catering for visiting gentry. But then, it was highly unlikely that any gentry taking advantage of the Regal's dubious hospitality would actually be visiting Luddersedge itself. Rather, such occasional tenants would more realistically be those whose misfortune was so dire that their mode of transportation between departure and arrival points had chosen Luddersedge to give up the vehicular ghost . . . and at a time to render impossible any solution other than booking into the Regal.

On the top of the five-storey building, amongst the aerials and the blackened windows, pigeons and starlings roosted noisily beside the quieter permanent residents, a troupe of bizarre gargoyles intermittently positioned amidst the stone balustrades and fashioned by Cecil Blenkinsop at the turn of the century. These monolithic decorations – whose artistic merit was questionable at the very least – were presented by Blenkinsop to the hotel in a rare demonstration of generosity.

However, the smart money around the older citizens of the town had it that the "gift" was actually a means to eradicate the excessive gambling debts run up by the gruff mill-owner's son-cum-sculptor in the hotel's extensive gambling casino, a huge two floor area in the belly of the hotel that had since been refashioned and refurbished after the Great War into a ballroom.

To say that hotels in Luddersedge were thin on the ground was an understatement of gargantuan proportions. Although there were countless guest houses, particularly along Honeydew Lane beside the notorious Bentley's Tannery – whose ever-present noxious fumes seemed to be unnoticed by the guests – usually truck drivers, who stayed there as a mid-way point on the long haul from Glasgow to the South Coast, parking their rigs on the spare ground between Carholme Place and Carholme Drive – the Regal was the only full-blown hotel, and the only building other than the old town hall to stretch above the slate roofs of Luddersedge and scratch a sky oblivious to, and entirely disinterested in, its or even the town's existence.

The corridors of the Regal were lined with threadbare carpets, hemmed in by walls bearing a testimonial trinity of mildew, graffiti and spilled alcohol, and topped by ceilings whose anaglypta was peeling at the corners and whose streaky paint-covering had been long ago dimmed by cigarette smoke.

The rooms themselves boasted little in the way of the creature comforts offered by the Regal's big-town contemporaries in Halifax and Burnley.

Only the Albert, Calder and Bickerdyke suites on the fourth floor featured tea- and coffee-making facilities, not to mention sufficient room to swing a cat . . . should such an activity be desired (though deplorable TV reception and the absence of satellite or cable-fed hotel movies imbued even the most unusual in-room entertainment with dizzily heightened credibility and attraction).

The truth, however, was that the Regal's guests brought their own entertainment in the form of a partner whose intimate attentions they might enjoy amidst the carbolic soap-smelling bed linen rather than propped against the building walls surrounding the club district of the metropolis of Halifax or parked up in one of the pull-ins overlooking Todmorden, testing the suspension and upholstery of old cars whose MOTs had been just a little too readily granted by Pete Dickinson or Tony Manderson at Tony's garage over on Eldershot Road.

Such activities were entirely safe inasmuch that, while the Regal's facilities were often found lacking, the discretion of the staff was legendary . . . and with room rates being so modest, even with breakfast added on, an additional gratuity in the form of a folded fiver jammed into the hand of the appropriately named manager Sidney Poke or one of his team was a small price to pay for uninterrupted passion in the relative comfort and complete anonymity accorded by the Regal.

For most of the year, the Regal's register – if such a thing were ever to be filled in, which it rarely was . . . at least accurately – boasted only couples by the name of Smith or Jones, and the catering staff had little to prepare in the form of sustenance other than the fabled Full English Breakfast, truly the most obscenely mountainous start-of-the-day plate of food outside of Dublin. Indeed, questions were frequently asked in bread shop or bus stop queues and around the beer-slopped pub tables at the Working Men's Club as to exactly how the Regal kept going.

But there were far too many other things to occupy the attention and interest of Luddersedge's townsfolk and, anyway, most of them recognized the important social part played by the Regal in the lives of their not-so-distant cousins living in the towns a few miles down the road in either direction . . . just as they recognized the equally important part played for themselves by similar establishments in those same towns. There were far too many scarf-bedecked Juliets and blue-collar Romeos – some young and some not so young – who had taken advantage of such no-questions-asked solitude . . . some long ago, when their flesh seemed more artistically arranged, and some only a day or two earlier, when they had supposedly been visiting relatives in far-off Leeds or Manchester or delivering a van-load of unpronounceable grommet-type things down to Birmingham or up to Newcastle: after all, it didn't do to defecate on one's own doorstep, and the status quo could only ever be maintained by not asking awkward questions.

Not that awkward questions were not asked about other situations in which the Regal played a key role, one of which came to pass on a Saturday night in early December on the occasion of the Conservative Club's Christmas Party . . . and which involved the one hotel feature that was truly magnificent – the Gentlemen's toilet situated in the basement beneath the ballroom.

To call such a sprawling display of elegance and creative indulgence a loo or a bog – or even a john or a head, to use the slang vernacular popular with the occasional Americans who visited the Calder Valley in the 1950s, the heyday of Luddersedge's long-forgotten twinning with the mid west town of Forest Plains – was tantamount to heresy.

Listen to this:

A row of shoulder-height marble urinals – complete with side panels that effectively rendered invisible anyone of modest height who happened to be availing themselves of their facility – was completed by a series of carefully angled glass panel splashguards set in aluminium side grips and a standing area inlaid with a mosaic of tiny slate and Yorkshire stone squares and rectangles of a multitude of colours. It was an area worn smooth by generations of men temporarily intent on emptying bladders filled with an excess of John Smith's, Old Peculiar and Black Sheep bitter ales served in the bars above.

Two wide steps down from the urinals, set back and mounted on ornate embellishments of curlicued brass fashioned to resemble a confusion of vines interlinked with snakes, a row of generously sized washbasins nested beneath individual facing panels split one half mirror and the other reinforced glass. The glass halves looked through onto an identical set of basins on the other side of the partition and behind them stood the WCs.

It was these wood-panelled floor-to-ceiling enclosed retreats – with their individual light switches, oak toilet seats and covers and matching tissue dispensers, and stained glass backings behind the pipe leading from the overhead cistern – that were, perhaps, the room's crowning glory, being even more impressive than the worn leather sofas and wing-backed chairs situated on their own dais at the far end of the toilet, bookended by towering aspidistras and serviced by standing silver ashtrays and glass-topped tables bearing the latest issues of popular men's magazines.

But while these extravagant rooms – albeit small rooms, designed for but one purpose – had rightly gained some considerable fame (particularly as the town was not noted for anything even approaching artistic or historical significance) they had also achieved a certain notoriety that was not always welcome.

Such notoriety came not from merely from the time, in the late 1940s, when an exceptionally inebriated Jack Walker (father of the unfortunate Stanley, who was to meet his tragic end at the hands of his wife when she administered a lethal dose of EXTERMINATE! into his bottle of beer) pitched forward rather unexpectedly – after failing to register the aforementioned double step leading to the urinals – and smashed his head into one of the glass-panelled splashguards. The accident resulted in the loss of Jack's left eye which, Jack being reluctant to wear a patch covering the now vacant socket ("Makes me look like a bloody pirate," Jack remarked to his friend Alan, down at the steel mill one morning soon after the incident), was replaced by a strangely coloured (and shaped, for that matter) orb that more resembled the marbles his then six-year-old son Stan delighted in firing across the living room carpet than an eye.

Nor did it come only from the legendary night when Pete Dickinson was ceremoniously divested of all of his clothes on his stag night and reduced to escaping the Regal, staggering drunkenly through Luddersedge's cold spring streets, wearing only one of the toilet's continuous hand towels (those being the days before automatic hand dryers, of course), a 50-foot ribbon of linen that gave the quickly sobering Dickinson the appearance of a cross between Julius Caesar and Boris Karloff's mummy.

Rather, the toilet's somewhat dubious reputation stemmed solely from the fact that, over the years, its lavish cubicles had seen a stream of Luddersedge's finest and most virile young men venturing into their narrow enclosures with their latest female conquests for a little session of hi-jinks where, their minds (and, all too often, their prowess and sexual longevity) clouded by the effects of ale, a surfeit of testosterone, the threat of being discovered, they would perform loveless couplings to the muted strains of whatever music drifted down from the floor above.

The practice was known, in the less salubrious circles of Calder Valley drinking establishments, as "The Forty Five Steps Club". The name referred, in a version of the similar "honorary" appellation afforded those who carried out the same act on an in-flight aeroplane ("The Mile High Club"), to the toilet's distance below ground – three perilously steep banks of fifteen steps leading down from the ballroom's west entrance.

And so it was that, at precisely 10 o'clock on the fateful night of the Conservative Club's Christmas Party, it was to this bastion room of opulence and renown that Arthur Clark retired midway through a plate of turkey, new potatoes, broccoli and carrots (having already seen off several pints of John Smith's, an entire bowl of dry roasted peanuts – Planters, Arthur's favourite – and the Regal's obligatory prawn cocktail first course) to evacuate both bladder and bowel. It was a clockwork thing with Arthur and, no matter where he was nor whom he was with, he would leave whatever was going on to void himself – on this occasion, all the better to concentrate his full attention and gastric juices on the promised (though some might say "threatened") Christmas Pudding and rum sauce plus a couple of coffees, and a few glasses of Bells whisky. Arthur's slightly weaving departure from the ballroom, its back end filled with a series of long dining tables leaving the area immediately in front of the stage free for the inevitable dancing that would follow coffee and liqueurs, was to be the last time that his fellow guests saw him alive.

"Edna. *Edna!*" Betty Thorndike was leaning across the table trying to get Edna Clark's attention, while one of the Merkinson twins – Betty thought it was Hilda but she couldn't be sure, they both looked so alike – returned to her seat and dropped her handbag onto the floor beside her. Hilda – if it was Hilda – had been to the toilet more than fifteen minutes ago, while everyone else was still eating, her having bolted her food down in record time, and had spent the time since her return talking to Agnes Olroyd, as though she didn't want to come back and join them: they were a funny pair, the Merkinsons.

When Edna turned around, from listening – disinterestedly – to John and Mary Tullen's conversation about conservatories with Barbara Ashley and her husband, whose name she could never remember (it was Kenneth), she was frowning.

"What?"

"He's been a long time, hasn't he?" she said across the table, nodding to the watch on her wrist. "Your Arthur."

"He's had a lot," Edna said with a shrug. The disc jockey on the stage put on Glen Campbell's "Wichita Lineman".

"Oh, I love this me," Mary Tullen announced to the table, droopy-eyed, and promptly began trying to join in with the words, cigarette smoke drifting out of her partially open mouth. She took a long drink of wine and frowned. "Who is it again? Name's on the tip of my tongue."

Edna shook her head.

"What was it like?" the Merkinson twin who had been to the toilet said to the one who had not.

A shrug was the reply. "You've been a long time, Hilda," she said, pushing her plate forward. Hilda noted that the food had been shuffled around on the plate but not much had been eaten.

"Been talking to Agnes Olroyd."

"So I saw."

"She was asking me about the robbery," Hilda said.

"Robbery? I thought you said nothing had been taken."

Hilda shrugged. "Robbery, break-in – it's all the same thing."

Hilda worked at the animal testing facility out on Aldershot Road where, two days earlier, she had come into work to discover someone had broken in during the night – animal rights protesters, her boss Ian Arbutt had told the police – and trashed the place.

Not wanting to talk about the break-in again – it having been a source of conversation everywhere in the town the past 36 hours, particularly in the Merkinson twins' small two-up, two-down in Belmont Drive – Hilda's sister said, "How's her Eric?"

Hilda made a face. "His prostate's not so good," she said.

"Oh." Harriet's attention seemed more concentrated on Edna Clark.

As Mary elbowed her husband in the stomach, prising his attention away from a young woman returning to a nearby table with breasts that looked like they had been inflated, Betty Thorndike said to Edna, "D'you think he's all right?"

John Tullen spun around, glaring at his wife. "What?"

"Who, my Arthur?" Edna said.

"D'you know who's singing this song?" Mary asked her husband. "It's on the tip of my tongue."

"I'm surprised you can sense anything with that tongue," John said as he reached for his pint of Guinness. "You've near on pickled the bloody thing tonight. Whyn't you slow down a bit?"

Edna said, "He's fine. He always goes at this time. Regular as clockwork. Doesn't matter where he is." This last revelation was accompanied by a slight shake of her head that seemed to convey both amazement and despair.

"I know," Mary Tullen agreed, still wondering who it was that was singing. "It's common knowledge, your Arthur's regularity." She had trouble getting her mouth around the word "regularity", splitting it into three single-syllabled words with the following "ity" barely covering a watery burp. " 'Scuse me," Mary said.

"But he's been a long time." Betty nodded to Arthur's unfinished meal. "And he hasn't even finished his dinner."

"He'll finish it when he gets back," Edna said with assurance.

Behind her, somebody said, "There's no bloody paper down there."

Hilda Merkinson knocked her glass over and a thin veil of lager spilled across the table and onto her sister's lap. "Hilda! For goodness sake."

"Damn it," Hilda said.

Edna threw a spare serviette across the table and turned around. Billy Roberts was sliding into his seat on the next table.

Sitting across from Billy, Jack Hanlon burst into a loud laugh. "You didn't use your hands again, did you, Billy? You'll never sell any meat on Monday – smell'll be there for days."

Billy smiled broadly and held his hand out beneath his friend's nose. Jack pulled back so quickly he nearly upturned his chair. He took a drink of Old Peculiar, swallowed and shook a B&H out of a pack lying on the table. "If you must know," Billy said, lighting the cigarette and blowing a thick cloud up towards the ceiling, "I used my hanky." He made a play of reaching into his pocket. "But I washed it out, see—" And he pretended to throw something across the table to his friend. This time, gravity took its toll and Jack went over backwards into the aisle.

As Jack got to his feet and righted his chair, Billy said, "I flushed it, didn't I, daft bugger. But I was worried for a few minutes when I saw there wasn't any paper – course, by that time, I'd done the deed. When I got out, I checked all the WCs and there isn't a bit in any of them." He blew out more smoke.

"Aren't you going to tell somebody, Billy?" Helen Simpson asked, her eyes sparkling as they took in Billy Roberts's quiffed hair.

"Can't be arsed," Billy said. "There's some poor sod down there now – probably still down there: he'll have something to say about it when he gets out," he added as he did a quick glance at the entrance to see if he could see anybody returning who looked either a little sheepish or blazing with annoyance.

"That'll be Arthur." Edna looked over her shoulder at Betty. "I bet that's my Arthur," she said. She tapped Billy on the shoulder. "That'll be my Arthur," she said again.

"What's that, Mrs Clark?" Billy said, turning. "What's your Arthur gone and done now?"

"He went to the toilet ages ago."

Harriet Merkinson shuffled around in her handbag, produced a thick bundle of Kleenex and she held them out. "Here, why don't you take him these?"

Edna nodded. "Thanks, er—"

"Harriet," said Harriet.

"Thanks Harry – good idea." She passed the tissues back to Billy and gave a big smile. "Here, be an angel, Billy and go back down and push these under the door for me."

"You haven't been down to the gents . . . have you, Mrs Clark?" There was a snigger at the last part from Jack Hanlon. "You can't get sod all under them doors."

"Well, can't you knock on his door or something?" She nodded to the table behind her. "He hasn't even finished his meal."

Hilda looked across at Arthur's plate and noted that it didn't look much different to her sister's – the only difference was that one meal was finished with and the other wasn't.

*　　*　　*

When he got back to the toilet, Billy saw one of the waiters was already going into each cubicle to fasten a new roll of tissue into the dispenser. "Bugger me, you're already doing it," he said to the young man, whose face coloured immediately. "Somebody tell you, did they? Was it Arthur Clark?"

The boy shook his head and the colour on his cheeks darkened. "It was some bloke, don't know what he's called," the waiter said, shifting his weight from one foot to the other. "Said he'd come down and couldn't find a—" The boy paused, searching for the word.

"A trap?" Billy ventured.

The boy smiled. "Said he couldn't find a trap with any paper." He nodded to a closed door at the end of the line of cubicles. "He's all right now, though."

Outside the door to the toilet there was a sudden burst of high-pitched giggling. "There's a bloody waiter in there!" a girl's voice said. Billy chuckled. Presumably only the waiter's presence was preventing the girl from coming into the gents with her partner and not the fact that the toilet area was filled with men, young and old, either standing at the urinals or washing at the basins. Alcohol was a wonderful thing and no denying.

The chuckling continued and was complemented by the sound of feet hurriedly ascending the 45 steps back to the ballroom. A man Billy didn't know wafted through the doors unzipping his flies and grinning like a Cheshire cat.

Billy exchanged nods with the man and turned his attention back to the waiter. He was still smiling – until he saw that the door to the cubicle which had been occupied while he was down here was still firmly closed.

"Has somebody just gone in there? I mean, while you've been down here."

The boy glanced at the closed door and shook his head. "Not while I've been down here."

Billy walked across and tapped gently on the door. "Hello?"

There was no response.

"He'll be sleeping it off, lad, whoever he is," a stocky bald man confided to Billy as he held his hands under the automatic drier. "You'll need to knock louder than that."

Billy nodded slowly. He rapped the door three times and said, "Mister Clark – are you in there? I've got some tissues for you."

No answer.

The bald man finished his hands off on the back of his trousers and moved across so that he was standing alongside Billy. Although he was short, a good six inches shorter than Billy and three or four beneath the lofty height of the young waiter, the bald man had a commanding air about him. The waiter shuffled to one side to give the man more room.

The bald man hit the door several times with a closed fist and shouted, "Come on, mate, time to get up. You'll be needing a hammer and chisel if you stay in there much longer, never mind bloody toilet paper."

Still no answer.

"He must be a bloody heavy sleeper," Billy said. "Either that or he's pissed as a newt."

The bald man turned to the waiter. "Is there any way into these things? I mean, some way of getting in when they're locked."

"I don't know," the boy said.

"Well, can you find somebody who does know? And can you do it bloody sharpish?"

The boy turned around and ran to the door and disappeared, his clumping feet echoing up the steps to the ballroom.

The man lifted his hands and felt around the door. "Do you know this bloke, whoever he is?"

Billy shook his head and jammed the toilet tissue into his jacket pocket. "No. Well, I do . . . I know his name and that but I don't really know him. His wife asked me to come down."

The man nodded. "Why was that, then?" he said, turning around.

"Well, there was no paper in any of the toilets."

"How did his wife know that?"

"She heard me telling them on my table. I'd just got back from . . . you know –"

"Having a crap. I know – get on with it, lad."

Billy straightened his shoulders. He would usually square up to anyone who spoke to him like that – after all, he wasn't a lad: he was almost 25 – but there was something about the bald man that made him shrink back from confrontation. "That trap was closed when I came down here and it was still closed when I went back up."

The bald man reached into his inside pocket and removed a packet of Marlboro. As he pulled a cigarette out, he said to Billy, "Do you smoke?"

Billy nodded. "Yeah," he said, lifting his hand towards the man's cigarettes. The man closed the pack and returned it to his pocket. "Well, give it up," he said as he flicked a lighter under the cigarette and drew in smoke. "It'll stunt your growth. Did you hear anything while you were down here?"

Billy shrugged. "Like what?"

The man blew smoke out. "Groans, plops, farts, throwing up . . . the usual."

"No. No, I didn't."

The man nodded. He hammered on the door again, louder this time. "What did you say his name was?"

"Arthur Clark."

"Not the bloke who wrote *2001*, I suppose? I loved that picture."

"I don't think so," Billy said with a chuckle.

"No, me neither." He hammered again. "Mister Clark . . . if you can hear me, open the door. It's the police."

Billy was watching the door but when he heard that he turned to the man. "Are you really the police? I mean, are you a . . . a copper?"

Before the man could answer, the waiter came back into the toilet. He was trailing behind a tall man with bushy eyebrows that met over his nose. His face, which was scowling, was a mask of excess, folds of skin lined with broken blood vessels. He said, "What's going on?"

"Who are you?" the bald man asked.

"Sidney Poke. I'm the manager of the Regal."

The bald man nodded. "Any way into these things when they're locked on the inside?"

Sidney Poke said, "Who are you?"

The bald man jammed his cigarette in the corner of his mouth, pulled a credit card holder from his inside pocket and shuffled through the little plastic flaps. He found what he was looking for and held it out for inspection. "Detective Inspector Malcolm Broadhurst, Leeds CID," he said.

"What's the problem, Inspector?" Sidney Poke said, his manner suddenly less aggressive.

"Somebody's in here and we can't get them to open the door. Been here a while, this lad says," Malcolm Broadhurst said, nodding at Billy Roberts.

"Who is it? Who's in there?" Sidney Poke asked Billy.

"Never mind who he is," the policeman said. "How do we bloody well get in to him?"

Sidney Poke shrugged. "I suppose we have to knock the door down."

Malcolm Broadhurst nodded. "Why did I know you were going to say that? Right—" He threw his cigarette on the floor and ground it with his foot. "One of you go upstairs and call for an ambulance – just to be on the safe side."

A blond-haired man said, "I'll do it," and disappeared at a run out of the toilet.

The policeman took hold of Billy's left arm and squeezed the biceps. "What do you do for a living, lad?"

"I'm a butcher."

"Just the job," he said, and he stepped back out of the way. "Right, break that bloody door down – and, daft as it sounds, try not to go mad: he could be on the floor at the other side."

As he squared up to the door, Billy said, "How the hell do I do that? Knock the door down but go steady, I mean."

"Just do your best. Now, you others stand back and give him room."

The door jamb splintered on the sixth try. It came away on the eighth, still fastened but only loosely.

"Brilliant job, lad," Broadhurst said taking Billy's arm. He pulled him back and stepped close to the door, squinting through the small gap that had appeared. "It's still fastened, but only just."

He stepped back and frowned. "No time to bugger about looking for something to prise it open. If the fella couldn't hear all that din then he's in a bad way." He stepped back and nodded to Billy. "Break it down, lad."

Billy pulled himself back onto his left foot and hit the door with all his strength. The lock snapped and they heard something – a screw, maybe, or part of the actual lock – clatter inside the cubicle. The door stopped against something on the floor.

Malcolm Broadhurst pushed Billy out of the way and, holding the door, squeezed his way into the cubicle. When he was inside, the policeman closed the door again.

They heard shuffling.

"Is he all right?" Sidney Poke asked. Billy thought it was a pretty stupid question.

For a few seconds there was no answer and then the policeman said, "He's dead." Then, after a few seconds more of shuffling sounds and sounds of exertion, he said, "Bloody hell fire."

Billy said, "What is it?"

When the door opened again the policeman was rubbing his face, looking down at the floor.

Billy and Sidney Poke and the young waiter – whose name was Chris and for whom this was his first night working at the Regal – followed Malcolm Broadhurst's stare.

Arthur Clark was now sitting up against the side wall of the cubicle, the toilet paper dispenser – containing almost a full roll of paper – just above and to the side of his left ear. He was fully clothed but his shirt had been ripped apart at the stomach. Worse than that, the man's flesh looked to have been flayed . . . with thick red welts and deep gashes covering the skin, and the top of his light grey trousers seemed to have been dyed black around the waistband: but they knew the original colour had been a deep red.

Chris the waiter gagged and turned away, his hand clamped over his mouth as he made for the washbasins. He made it just in time. When he was through, he leaned his head on his hand to one side of the basin and, in a surprised voice, said, "Hey, that's where they were."

The boy crouched down and reached his hands to the deep metal basket on the floor between his basin and the one next to it. When he stood up he was holding an armful of toilet rolls, some full and still thick and some partly used.

"Bloody idiots," said Sidney Poke. "Do anything for a laugh but they wouldn't think it was so damned fun—"

"Get everyone out, Mister Poke," the policeman said. His voice sounded tired. "Get everyone back upstairs. But not you, butcher boy," he said, turning to Billy. "You can give me a hand getting him out of here."

The toilet was completely empty when they finally struggled out with Arthur Clark and laid him on the floor beside the washbasins.

"He looks like he's been got at by a wild animal," Billy said. "And scared to death, by the look on his face."

The policeman shook two Marlboros from his pack and handed one to Billy. "Give it up tomorrow," he said as he held his lighter under Billy's cigarette.

Billy drew in the smoke and watched the bald man crouch down by the body. He turned over Arthur Clark's hands one by one and said, "He was the wild animal. He did it to himself. See—" He held one of the hands up for Billy to see. The nails were caked with blood and skin – they looked like the hands of a butcher.

"Why? What did he think he was doing, do you think?"

"Looks to me like he was trying to get into his own stomach."

"Arthur?" a woman's voice shouted from outside the toilet door.

Then a man's voice said, "You can't go in there, madam."

"Arthur!" the woman's voice screamed.

There was a crash outside the door that sounded unquestionably like someone falling over.

"Shit," said Detective Inspector Malcolm Broadhurst.

The ambulance arrived with siren wailing but it left silently.

Malcolm Broadhurst sat with Edna Clark for a long time, initially with Betty Thorndike, Joan Cardew and Miriam Barrett by her side, offering consolation in the undoubtedly heartfelt but seemingly sycophantic way that people have when they feel *There but for the grace of God.* To the policeman from Leeds CID the trio was doing more harm than good and he sent them packing. "Like the bloody witches from 'Hamlet'," he said to Billy Roberts over at the bar, ordering a couple of stiff Jamesons from Sidney Poke, who had assumed bar duties for the duration.

The rest of the guests and all the staff had given their names to a couple of uniformed officers from Halifax and had gone home.

"Macbeth," Sidney Poke said quietly.

Billy looked up from his Irish frowning. He would have been happier with a pint but the policeman had ordered. "What?"

"The three witches. It was 'Macbeth', not 'Hamlet'."

"Oh."

"And what about Bill and Ben? That was a turn-up for the books."

"Who's Bill and Ben?"

"Oh, the Merkinsons. The two old women."

"Oh, the one who collapsed."

Billy nodded. "And her sister."

"Was it Bill or was it Ben?" Broadhurst mumbled.

"Huh?"

The policeman shook his head. "Which one of them was it who collapsed?"

Billy shrugged. "You can never tell. They both always look the same – dress the same, talk the same . . . it's really weird."

The two "old" women, as Billy Roberts had called them, were 53 years old. Malcolm Broadhurst wouldn't have been far out with his own estimate of 50–51. The same age, give or take a year – he always forgot his own age but he knew he'd had his fiftieth because of the stripper they'd bought for him down at the station – and he didn't consider himself as old. But then again, maybe he was. "Twins, are they?" he said.

Billy nodded.

Broadhurst had noticed them, standing by while he was talking to Edna Clark, because they were identically dressed, right down to the two-string necklace of fake pearls hanging over the first half-inch of their maroon dresses. One of them was looking after the other, the one who had collapsed, feeding her sips of brandy brought over by Sidney Poke.

"Like a couple of weirdos," Billy Roberts said, remembering the scene in vivid detail. "Funny though, her keeling over like that."

Now it was the policeman's turn to nod. "She the Hilda Merkinson who works at the animal rights centre? The one that was done in this week?"

Billy frowned. "Don't know. But she's the only Hilda Merkinson in Luddersedge."

"Cheers!" said Malcolm Broadhurst. He lifted his glass and drained it, then set it back on the bar top. "How much do I owe you?" he said to the Regal's manager.

Poke shook his head. "On the house. Think I'll have one myself."

It was one o'clock.

"What was it, d'you think?" Billy asked. He lit a B&H from the packet he'd retrieved from the table and offered it to the other two. Poke waved a hand and the policeman simply produced his Marlboros and took one out.

"We'll know when the autopsy boys know," Broadhurst said around a cloud of smoke. "His missus says he didn't have a bad heart or anything, but it's either that or something he ate."

"I thought that," Billy offered, and then wished he hadn't when he caught the glare from the Regal's manager.

"Or drunk," Broadhurst said. "I've had his meal wrapped up for tests, along with the pint he was working his way through."

"Fancy," Billy said, more to himself than to the others, "getting up for a crap halfway through your meal."

"His missus says he does it regular as clockwork," Broadhurst said.

"That's right," Billy said. "Doesn't matter where he is or who he's with. Come ten o'clock he has to disappear to do the deed. It's legendary around town – everybody knows."

"Another?" Poke said, holding the bottle of Jamesons over the policeman's glass.

Broadhurst frowned over the answer to that and other questions that were already forming in his mind.

It was almost two o'clock when Broadhurst made his way from the ballroom and along the corridor towards reception. At the steps leading down to the Gentlemen's toilet he paused. The steps were well lit but only in stages, the main house lights of the hotel having been dimmed an hour earlier. Now only single bulbs, secured behind half shells equally spaced down the flights, lit the steps leaving a well of darkness at the bottom.

The darkness seemed inviting and off-putting, both at the same time.

The policeman shook a cigarette from his packet, lit it and breathed smoke around him. It felt good . . . felt normal somehow. For there was a lot about what had happened that was not normal.

Before he even realized he was moving, Broadhurst had reached the landing at the foot of the first flight, his hand on the rail and his eyes squinting into the gloom. He took the next two flights two steps at a time but when he reached the bottom, with the ornate doors leading into the toilet right in front of him, he stopped and listened.

What was he listening for, he wondered. Was he listening for the sounds of Arthur Clark, screaming in agony? For didn't some folks say that no sound ever died but only grew faint, waiting to be heard once more by those with the most finely tuned sense of hearing? No, it was something more than that . . . something more than the late-night campfire thoughts of ghoulies and ghosties and things that went *phrrrp!* in the night.

He threw his cigarette stub to the floor and stepped on it hard, pushing open the doors and stepping inside.

The toilet was silent. There was no sound save for the distant chuckle of water moving through ancient pipes, turning over in radiators and cisterns, and *dlup dlupping* down drain holes.

He looked around.

Someone else had been in here, someone who knew more about Arthur's tragic death than he did. A lot more. Broadhurst felt it – felt it in his water, he thought, cringing at the unintentional pun. The death was neither natural nor unintentional. But he couldn't understand how it could be anything else.

He walked along the row of cubicles, their doors either fully open or ajar, and felt a sense of threat . . . as though someone was going to step out of them . . . perhaps someone recently dead come to exact his revenge . . . or someone who knew more about the death, come to prevent being caught. Broadhurst stepped away from the line of cubicles and stopped, staring at the open doors.

What was he thinking of? How could the death be anything other than natural? The cubicle walls went from floor to ceiling, the door the same . . . save for barely an inch of space top and bottom – certainly far less than would be required to get into the cubicle if the door were locked from the inside. And, of course, the same went for getting out again when the deed was done.

"What deed?" Broadhurst said softly. There was no answer, just a giggle of water over by the sofa at the far end of the room.

He leaned on one of the basins and continued to look around. He moved from the basin, reluctantly turning his back on the cubicles until he was reassured by their reflection in the mirror over the basin in front of him, and looked some more. *What are you looking for, Kojak?* a small voice whispered in the back of his head, using the name granted to him by those colleagues in Halifax CID who could remember the TV show. *It's an open and shit case, seems to me*, it added with what might have been a wry chuckle.

"Funny!" Broadhurst snapped, and he looked along the basin-tops, down to the floor and then along beneath them. There was a basket beside each one.

Hey, that's where they were.

The young waiter's voice sounded clear as a bell in his head. Broadhurst could half see him, stooping down to lift an armful of toilet rolls.

Then Sidney Poke's voice chimed in. *Bloody idiots . . . Do anything for a laugh.*

Broadhurst frowned.

The ghost of Billy's voice said, *That's right, doesn't matter where he is or who he's with. Come ten o'clock he has to disappear to do the deed. It's legendary around town – everybody knows.*

Broadhurst turned around to face the cubicles

everybody knows

and walked slowly towards them, his back straightening as they came nearer. He started at one end and walked slowly, pushing open each door and staring at the empty tissue holder

Hey, that's where they were

attached to the wall of each cubicle, right next to where an arm would be resting on a straining knee . . . where so many arms had rested on so many straining knees

It's legendary around town

until he reached

everybody knows

a cubicle with toilet paper. *The* cubicle.

He stared down at the now empty floor and closed his eyes. He saw Arthur Clark writhing in agony, crying out for help . . . so much pain that he could not simply unlock the cubicle door and crawl for help.

Broadhurst removed his handkerchief from his pocket and, stepping into the cubicle, wrapped it around the toilet roll.

Seconds later he was going up the steps away from the Regal's Gentlemen's toilet, two steps at a time . . . and wishing he could move faster.

★   ★   ★

Sundays in Luddersedge are traditionally quiet affairs but the events of the previous evening at the Conservative Club's Christmas Party had permeated the town the same way smoke from an overcooked meal fills a kitchen.

In the tiny houses that lined the old cobbled streets of the town, over cereals and toast and bacon butties, and around tables festooned with open newspapers – primarily copies of the *News of the World*, the *Sunday Mirror* and the *Sunday Sport* – voices were discussing Arthur Clark's unexpected demise in hushed almost reverent tones.

Conversations such as this one:

"I'll bet it was his heart," Miriam Barrett said from her position at the gas stove in the small kitchen in 14 Montgomery Street.

Her husband, Leonard, grunted over the *Mirror*'s sports pages. "Edna said not," he mumbled. "Said he hadn't had no heart problems."

Miriam was unconvinced. She turned the sausages over in the frying pan and shuffled the ones that looked sufficiently cooked across to the side with the bacon and a few pieces of tomato that looked like sizzling blood-clots. "All that business with his . . . *toilet*," she said, imbuing the word with a strange Calder Valley mysticism that might be more at home whispered in the *gris gris* atmosphere of a New Orleans speakeasy. "Can't have been right."

Leonard said, "He was just regular, that's all."

"Yes, well, there's regular and there's *regular*," Miriam pointed out sagely. "But having to go in the middle of your meal like that, just cos it's ten o'clock, well, that's not regular."

Leonard frowned. He wondered just what it was if it wasn't regular, but decided against pursuing the point.

But not everyone in Luddersedge was talking.

In his bedroom over his father's butcher's shop at the corner of Lemon Road and Coronation Drive, Billy Roberts opened his eyes and stared at the watery sun glowing behind his closed curtains. His mouth was a mixture of kettle fur and sandpaper and using it to speak was the very last thing on his mind. It was all he could do to groan, and even then the sound of it sounded strange to him, like it wasn't coming from him at all but maybe drifting from beneath the bed where something crouched, something big and unpleasant, waiting to see his foot appear in front of it.

Billy turned to his side and breathed deeply into his cupped hand. Then he stuck his nose into the opening in his hand and sniffed. The smell was sour and vaguely alcoholic, almost perfumed. He slumped back onto the pillows. It was those bloody whiskies that did it. He should have stuck to the beer, the way he usually did. It didn't do to go mixing drinks.

Billy had had a bad night, even after all the booze. He supposed there was nothing like messing around with a dead body – particularly one that had smelt the way Arthur Clark's had done, Arthur having so recently dumped into his trousers – to sober a person up. It had taken Billy more than an hour to drop off after getting in – despite the fact that it was three in the morning – and even then his dreams had been peppered with Arthur's face . . . and the man's ravaged stomach.

Work had been underway in the ballroom of the less than palatial Regal Hotel for several hours when Billy Roberts was beginning to contemplate getting out of bed.

The wreckage was far worse than usual somehow, even though the festivities had been cut short by the tragic events in the gentlemen's toilet. But at least most of the explosive streamers were still intact and there were fewer stains than usual on the cloths and the chairs. The most surprising thing was the number of personal possessions that had been left in the cloakroom, particularly considering the very careful population of the town. But then the unceremonious way the guests had been dispatched for home after been questioned made a lot of things understandable.

Chris Hackett had arrived after the clear-up had begun, clocking into the ancient machine mounted on the green tiled wall leading to the Regal's back door at 7.13. He didn't think anyone would object to the fact that he was almost a quarter of an hour late, not after last night.

He set to straight away, throwing his yellow and blue bubble jacket onto one of the chest freezers in the kitchen and emerging through the swing doors into the ballroom. It was a hive of activity.

Jeff Wilkinson was busy dismantling one of the trestle tables over near the stage. Several of the tables had already been folded up and were standing propped against the ornate pillar beside the steps leading up to the stage, and chairs were stacked in towering piles against the side wall.

In the centre of the floor, Mervyn Frith was adding to a huge mound of tablecloths lay jumbled up – the cloths were waiting for somebody to fold them, an unpleasant job given their size and the amount of spilled food that still clung to them.

Elsewhere, various young men and women were loading glasses and bottles and plates and cutlery onto rickety wooden trolleys, the sound of their labours dwarfed by the sound of similar items being loaded into the huge dishwashers in the kitchens.

Wondering where he should start, Chris Hackett saw a table that had been untouched, over by the far wall. He went across to it, moving around to the wall side to begin stacking the plates. Halfway along the wall he caught his foot on something and went sprawling onto the floor, knocking over two chairs on the way.

Somebody laughed and their was a faint burst of applause as Chris got to his feet and looked around for the culprit of his embarrassment.

It was a ladies' handbag.

Malcolm Broadhurst sat smoking a cigarette. He had been up since before dawn, having snatched a couple of hours' fitful nap lying fully clothed on the eiderdown.

He had watched the sun pull itself languidly over the rooftops of Luddersedge and had then spent the next 40, 45 minutes trying to get something resembling decent reception from his TV. In the end, faced with either the Tellytubbies or an Open University programme on quantum physics, he gave it up and sat waiting for the day outside to catch up with him. That and thinking about the previous evening.

The call came through at a little after ten o'clock.

A man's voice said, "You up?"

"Yeah."

"Been to bed?"

Broadhurst grunted. "Didn't sleep, though."

"Well, you were right not to," the voice said. "We've been on this all night – well, all morning would be more accurate."

"And?"

"We've not finished yet but we've got a pretty good idea."

The voice with the pretty good idea belonged to Jim Garnett, the doctor in charge of forensic science at Halifax Infirmary and who doubled as the medical guru for Halifax CID. He chuckled. "It's a goodie. You were right to be suspicious."

The policeman shook another cigarette from his packet and settled himself against the bed headboard. "Go on."

"Okay. Two hours ago, I'd've been calling you to tell you he'd had a heart attack."

"And he didn't."

"Well, that's not exactly true: he did have a cardiac arrest . . . but it wasn't brought on by natural causes." Garnett paused and Broadhurst could hear the doctor shifting papers around. "What made me a little more cautious than usual – apart from your telephone call last night . . . for which Yvonne sends her thanks, by the way – was the list of symptoms, all classical."

Broadhurst didn't speak but it was as though the doctor had read the question in his mind.

"There were too many. Profuse salivation—"

"Profuse – is that like, there was a lot of it?"

"You could say that," came the reply. "The poor chap's shirt was soaked and he'd bitten through the back left side of his tongue; he'd vomited, messed his pants – diarrhoea: most unpleasant – and there were numerous contusions to the head, arms and legs."

"Suggesting what?"

"The contusions?" Garnett smacked his lips. "Dizziness, auditory and visual disturbances, blurred vision . . . that kind of thing – and not the kind of thing you want to experience when you're stuck in a WC. It's my bet he shambled about in there like a ping pong ball, bouncing off every wall. And, of course, the pain would have been nothing to what he was having from his stomach – that's why he'd clawed at himself so much. By then, he'd be having seizures – hence the tongue – and he'd be faint."

"Why didn't he just come out, shout for help?"

"Disorientation would be my guess. And panic. He'd be in a terrible state at this point, Mal."

Broadhurst waited. "And?"

"And then he'd die. I've seen cases before – cardiac arrests – with two or three of the same symptoms, but never so many together . . . and never so intense. This chap suffered hell in his final minutes."

Garnett sighed before continuing. "So, we checked him out for all the usual bacteria – saliva, urine, stool samples . . . and there were plenty of those, right down to his ankles – and—"

"So he hadn't even been to the toilet?"

"No, he *had* been. His large bowel was empty. This stuff came as the result of a sudden stimulation to the gut and that would release contents further up the bowel passage. Anyway, like I said, we checked everything but it was no go. Then I checked the meal – bland but harmless – and the beer . . . nothing there either."

Garnett moved away from the phone to cough. "God, and now I think I'm coming down with a cold."

"Take the rest of the day off."

"Thanks!" He cleared his throat and went on. "So, in absolute desperation, we started checking him for needle marks . . . thought he might be using something and that was why he always went to the toilet so regularly. But there was nothing, skin completely unbroken. And then . . ."

"Ah, is this the good bit?"

"Yes, indeedy – and this is the good bit."

Broadhurst could sense the doctor leaning further into the phone, preparing to deliver the *coup de grâce*.

"Then we turned him over and we found the rash."

"The *rash?* All that and a rash too?"

"On his backside, across his cheeks and up into the anus . . . nasty little bastard, blotches turning to pustules even five hours after he died. At first I thought maybe it was thrush but it was too extreme for that. So we took a swab and tested it."

The pause was theatrical in its duration. "*And* . . . go on, Jim, for God's sake," Broadhurst snapped around a cloud of smoke.

"Nicotine poisoning."

The policeman's heart sank. For this he had allowed himself to get excited? "*Nicotine* poisoning?" he said in exasperation.

"Nicotine as in *cigarettes*?" He glanced down at the chaos of crumpled brown stubs in the ashtray next to him on the bed.

Garnett grunted proudly. "Nicotine as in around eight million cigarettes smoked in the space of one drag."

"What?"

"That was what killed him – not the heart attack, though that delivered the final blow – nicotine . . . one of the most lethal poisons known to man."

"And how did he get it . . . if it wasn't in the drink or in the meal, and it wasn't injected? And assuming he didn't smoke eight million cigarettes while he was sitting contemplating."

Garnett cleared his throat. "He got it in the arse, Mal . . . though God only knows how."

Broadhurst glanced across at the solitary toilet roll sitting on his chest of drawers. "I know, too," he said. "But the 'why' . . . that's the puzzler."

"And the 'who'?"

"Yeah, that too."

Edna Clark sat at her kitchen table, her hands wrapped around a mug of steaming tea. Sitting across from her was Betty Thorndike.

When the knock came on the front door, Betty said, "You stay put, love – I'll get it."

Hilda Merkinson had been in every room in the house but her sister was nowhere to be found.

Worse still, she couldn't find her handbag.

"Harry?" She had already shouted her sister's name a dozen times but, in the absence of a more useful course of action, she shouted it again. The silence seemed to mock her.

Hilda knew why Harriet had gone out. She had gone out to clear her head, maybe to have a weep by herself. No problem. She would get over it. It might take a bit of time, but she would get over it – of that, Hilda was convinced.

They had lived together, Hilda and Harriet Merkinson, in the same house for all of their 53 years . . . just the two of them since their mother, Hannah, had died in 1992.

They had a routine, a routine that Hilda did not want to see altered in any way. It was a safe routine, a routine of eating together, cleaning together, watching the TV together, and occasionally slipping along to the Three Pennies public house over on Pennypot Drive for a couple of life-affirming medicinal glasses of Guinness stout. It was a routine of going to bed and kissing each other goodnight on the upstairs landing and of waking each morning and kissing each other hello, again in the same spot; a routine broken only by Harriet's job in Jack Wilson's General Store – a sop to his love of America – and Hilda's work at the animal testing facility on Aldershot Road, where she'd been for almost seven years. The same length of time that Harriet had worked. Since their mother had slipped finally into a coma in a small side ward in Halifax General, her six-stone body reduced to wattled skin and brittle bone.

During that time, the routine had persevered.

It had been all and its disappearance was unthinkable.

Not that there hadn't been times when things looked a little shaky . . . namely the times when Ian Arbutt had cornered Hilda in the small back room against the photocopier and sworn his affection – despite Ian's wife, Judith, and his two children. But basically, Ian's affection had been for Hilda's body and Hilda had recognized this pretty quickly into the relationship – if you could call the clumsy gropes and speedy ejaculations performed by her boss on the back room carpet a relationship.

Hilda had had to think of how to put an end to it – thus maintaining her and Harriet's beloved routine – while not having it affect her position at the testing centre.

The solution had been simple, if a little Machiavellian. She had sent an anonymous letter to Judith Arbutt saying she should keep a tighter rein on her husband. "I'm not mentioning any names," the carefully worded – and written – letter had continued, "but there are some folks around town who think your Ian's affections might be being misplaced." Hilda had liked that last bit.

A very anxious and contrite Ian had suggested to Hilda, on the next occasion that they were both alone in the centre, that he felt he wasn't being fair to her. "Trifling with her affections" is what Hilda imagined he was wanting to say but Ian's pharmacological expertise did not extend to the poetic. "I hope you're not leading up to suggesting I look for other work," Hilda had said, feigning annoyance, brow furrowed, "because that would mean something along the lines of sexual harassment, wouldn't it?"

The answer had been emphatic and positive. "A job for life", is how he worded it. "You're here for as long as you want to be here, Hilda," he said. And he had been true to his word, at least Hilda could give him that.

No, Hilda would have nothing come between her and her sister. They were all either of them had and their separation was something she could not contemplate. She had thought that Harriet felt the same way.

And then came the fateful day, almost a week ago – was it really only a week? It seemed so much longer – that had threatened to change all that.

Every Thursday, without fail, Harriet always walked along to the fish and chip shop on the green – Thursday being Jack Wilson's early closing day – and had the tea all ready for Hilda when she got in. But on this particular Thursday, following four days of solid rain, when Hilda – a little earlier than usual because Ian also had flooding and wanted to get off – had gone past the General Store, she had seen Harriet helping Jack with moving boxes around due to the leakage through the front windows. He had asked her to stay back and give him a hand, and Harriet couldn't refuse . . . despite her other "commitments".

"We'll just have some sandwiches," Harriet had shouted through the locked door of Jack's shop, looking terribly flustered. "You just put your feet up and I'll make them when I get in," she added.

Hilda had nodded. Then she had gone home, put the kettle on and, at the usual time Harriet always left the house en route for the fish and chips, Hilda had embarked into the darkness on the very same journey. Imagine her surprise when, from behind the big oak tree on the green, a shadowy figure leapt out, grabbed her by the shoulders and planted a big kiss on her mouth.

It was Arthur Clark.

"Thought you weren't coming," Arthur had announced to a bewildered Hilda. "Been here bloody ages," he had added. "Edna'll be getting ideas – mind you," Arthur had confided, "it won't matter soon. Must dash." Then he had given her another kiss and had scurried across the green bound for home, calling over his shoulder, "See you on Saturday anyway, at the Christmas do."

Hilda had stood and watched the figure disappear into the darkness, and she was so flabbergasted that she almost forgot all about the fish and chips and went home empty-handed. But already she was thinking that that would not do. That would not do at all.

The "meeting" had given her advance knowledge of a potential threat to the beloved routine. And by the time she was leaving the fat-smelling warmth of the shop, Hilda had hatched a plan.

She knew all about poisons from Ian's explanations, long drawn-out monologues that, despite their monotony, had registered in Hilda's mind. Which was fortunate. She knew about nicotine, and about the way it was lethal and produced symptoms not unlike heart failure.

Getting a small supply would not be a problem. There were constant threats against the centre – notably from animal rights groups based out in the wilderness of Hebden Bridge and Todmorden – so a small break-in, during which most of the contents of the centre could be strewn around and trashed, was an easy thing to arrange . . . particularly after administering a small dose of sleeping tablets to her sister, who obligingly nodded off in front of the TV during "Inspector Morse" (Hilda didn't mind missing it because it was a repeat).

Hilda scooted along Luddersedge's late night streets, let herself in with her own key – thanking God that he had seen fit to make Ian make her a joint key-holder with him . . . undoubtedly a result of Ian's keenness to make her feel important after his calling off their "affair" – did what she considered to be an appropriate amount of damage, and removed a small amount of nicotine from the glass jar in Ian's office cabinet, to which, again, she had a key. She left the cabinet untouched by "the vandals" who had destroyed the office. Then, after resetting the alarm, she had smashed in the windows with a large stick and returned home.

It wasn't until she was almost back at the house that she heard the siren. She had smiled then – it had been long enough for whoever had broken in to do all the damage and escape without challenge. The night air had smelled good then, good and alive with . . . not so much possibilities but with continuance. Back in the warmth, she had settled herself down in front of the TV and, after about half an hour, had dropped off herself. The icing on the cake had been the fact that it was Hilda's sister who woke Hilda up. A wonderful alibi, even though none would be needed.

Two days later, on the night of the Conservative Club's Christmas Party, Hilda had bolted her meal and – though she knew she was risking things – had gone to the toilet at ten minutes to ten (Arthur Clark's toilet habits being legendary in Luddersedge). Once out of the ballroom, she had run down to the gentlemen's toilet, removed the tissue rolls from all but one WC, and had treated the first few sheets of the remaining roll with the special bottle in her handbag. It was four minutes to ten when she had finished.

She had arrived back in the ballroom at 9:58 just in time to see Arthur get up from the table and set off for his date with his maker. She had not been able to go straight back and was grateful for Agnes Olroyd catching her to talk about the break-in – there was nothing that the people of Luddersedge liked more than a bit of intrigue – and about her Eric's prostate (in the absence of intrigue, family ailments being the order of the day).

By the time she had finished talking with Agnes, Hilda's composure was fully restored and she was able to rejoin the table.

And now Harriet was nowhere to be seen. But that could wait.

The main thing as far as Hilda was concerned was to find her bag.

And she had a good idea as to where it was.

Harriet's revelations had hit Edna Clark harder even than her husband's death less than twelve hours earlier.

In Edna's kitchen, with the sun washing through the window that looked out onto the back garden and with steam gently wafting from the freshly boiled kettle, Edna sat at the table feeling she had suddenly lost far more than her life partner: now she had lost her life itself. Everything she had believed in had been quickly and surely trounced by the blubbering Harriet Merkinson when she burst through the front door, ran along the hall – pursued by a confused Betty Thorndike – and emerged in the kitchen, tears streaming down her face. And now Edna's 27 years with Arthur lay before her in tatters . . . every conversation, every endearment whispered to her in the private darkness of their bedroom, every meal she had prepared (if not always lovingly – for how can one "lovingly" make egg, chips and beans three times a week for 27 years? – at least with profound affection) and every holiday snapshot they had taken in Dorset and Derbyshire (dressed in shorts, T-shirts and walking boots, their backpacks on the ground before them) and Cornwall (sitting on the beach amidst the inevitable clutter that always resulted from such seaside expeditions).

While Harriet continued sniffling and Betty simply stood leaning against the kitchen cabinets (installed by Arthur, Edna recalled, one laughter-filled weekend in the early 1980s), her eyes seemingly permanently raised in a mask of disbelief, Edna looked around at the once-familiar ephemera and bric-a-brac of a life that now seemed completely alien. The painting on the kitchen wall; the small collection of tea pots and milk jugs on the wide window sill; the stacked plates and cereal bowls stacked behind the glass door of the cupboard – all of them. It might just as well have been the priceless jewellery and artefacts unearthed in an ancient Egyptian tomb . . . so devoid now of meaning and familiarity and understanding. These were things from another life – another *person's* life – and nothing to do with Edna Clark, newly bereaved widow of one Arthur Clark, late of this parish.

The story had been a familiar one. Even as Harriet Merkinson had been burbling it out – the clandestine meetings, the whispered affections, the promise of a new life once Arthur had built up the nerve to leave his wife – Edna felt that she had heard it all before . . . or read it in a book someplace, maybe even watched it on television. The Arthur revealed by Harriet was not the Arthur she remembered . . . save for one thing: his toilet habits. At least something was constant in her husband's two lives.

And now, while Edna's mind raced and backtracked and questioned and attempted – in the strange and endearing way of minds – to rationalize and make palatable the revelations, the "other" woman continued to burble a litany of regret and sorrow and pleas for absolution and forgiveness.

"I can't forgive you," Edna said at last, her words cutting through the thick atmosphere like a knife through cheese. "Never," she added with grim finality. "I can understand, because I know these things do happen, but I can never forgive you. You haven't taken only my husband's memory, you've completely removed my entire life." It was the most articulate statement Edna had ever made, and the most articulate she would ever make in what remained of her life. Of course, she would come to terms with what had happened, but she would never get over it.

"Edna, Edna, Edna, Ed—"

"Now get out," Edna said, cutting Harriet's ramble off mid-word. Her voice was quieter now, more composed . . . gentle even. There was no animosity, no aggression, no threats of retribution: just a tiredness and, the still silent Betty was amazed to see, a new-found strength that was almost majesterial. "I never want to speak with you again."

Minutes later, Betty and Edna heard the distant click of the front door latch closing. It sounded for all the world like the closing of a tomb door or the first scattering of soil on a recently lowered coffin. Edna leaned forward and placed her face in her hands, and she began to sob, quietly and uncontrollably.

While Malcolm Broadhurst was greeting the two uniformed policemen on the steps of the Regal's ornate front door, two things were happening . . . both of them personally involving the Merkinson twins.

For Harriet, the routine so cherished by her sister had been a chore. More than that, it had been the bane of her life.

Harriet had long wanted to get out of the repetitive drudgery of the existence she shared with Hilda, and Arthur Clark – dear, sweet Arthur, with his strange toilet habits – had been her ticket to salvation. Love was a new experience to Harriet: for that matter, she did not know – not truly, down in those regions of the heart and the soul where such things reside, safe from the prying eyes of light and Society – whether she really loved Arthur, for she had never experienced such feelings, even as a teenager and a young woman, when such experiences and experimentation are commonplace. But she did see in him the means whereby she could attain a new life, a life of relative importance . . . "Harriet and Arthur", "Arthur and Harriet" – she couldn't decide which she preferred but she preferred either to "the Merkinson twins" or "Hilda and Harriet"!

As she fished out the old clothesline from the kitchen cupboard, taking care to replace the various bottles and cartons of disinfectant and packets of soap powder, she felt a calmness come over her. Arthur's death had effectively removed her last chance for salvation, and she had been destitute. But now, thanks to the clothesline, she saw a solution. It wasn't the one she would have preferred but it was now the only one available. The only game in town. She could neither face life with Hilda nor life without the constant frisson of excitement she got prior to meeting Arthur . . . and she certainly could not face the comments and whispers around town when she walked down the high street or around the green. No, this way was best for all concerned. It was best for Edna – who might at least derive a little satisfaction when she heard – and it was best for Hilda, who would have to put up with her own share of her sister's shame.

She climbed the stairs wearily and attached one end of the clothesline to the upstairs banister rail. Then, after ensuring that the line's drop was sufficiently short to do the job, she fashioned a noose of sorts and slipped it over her head. With one final look around the landing she climbed over the rail and sat on the banister, staring down at the floor far below. As she jumped, in that fleeting but seemingly endless second or two before the line pulled taut without her feet ever touching the hall floor, she wondered where Hilda was . . . and what she would say when she came home.

"You've got something for forensics?"

Broadhurst nodded. "It's inside. I didn't want to be seen with it outside."

They started to walk.

"I came up last Wednesday," Malcolm Broadhurst explained to the two uniforms. "To check into the break-in down at the animal testing centre."

"Oh, yeah?" one of the policemen observed. His name was James Proctor and he had perfected that same aggressive and questioning response to even the most innocent facts or snippets

of information, seeming to require confirmation or substantia-
tion to anything said to him.

"Yeah," Broadhurst confirmed. They were now walking up
the Regal's steps and approaching the wide, oak-panelled revolving door. "Your Inspector Mishkin asked me up because
there were a few things he wasn't too happy about. I take it you
two aren't working on that case?"

"We didn't know it was a case," the second policeman said as
they emerged from the revolving door into the hotel's reception
area. He said the word "case" with a heavy-handed touch of
sarcasm. "Thought it was just a simple break-in."

"Yes, well," Broadhurst continued. "That's the way it
looked, and Inspector Mishkin and I decided to keep it that
way until things made a little more sense."

"And have they now?" the second policeman asked. His name
was John Dearlove and he had recently transferred from Manchester when his wife got a job at the Halifax's head office. Janet
Dearlove had a degree in computer science and she was working
on a new IT project for the bank. John didn't know anything
about IT but, while he appreciated the generous salary his wife
had always managed to secure, his resentment at feeling like a
"kept man" – as so many of his colleagues on the Manchester
force had delighted in calling him – had blossomed first into a
resentment of all women and latterly into a resentment of any
kind of authority at all.

Broadhurst hit the bell on the reception desk.

"Look at it this way," the policeman said, turning from the
desk and looking the two uniforms in the eye. "Whoever broke
in through the window managed to trash the place and then
place all the broken glass on top of the wrecked office." He
nodded, smiling. "That's a pretty good trick, don't you think?"

"So—"

"So," Broadhurst continued, watching the main staircase as a
young man appeared and started down, "the 'vandal' clearly
had access to the centre and wanted to cover up the fact that
they had been there. Now that reason could be simply a matter
of their wanting to fight the animal testing . . . kind of like a
fifth columnist, or it could be another reason. I think we now
have that reason . . . although the reason itself must have a
reason – and that's what I now bloody well intend to find out."

"Yes, sir?" the young man said as he reached the bottom of the stairs and approached the three men at the desk. "Sorry to keep you waiting."

"Is Mister Poke around?" Broadhurst asked. "I gave him something to look after for me."

The man nodded and moved around the desk. "I'll give him a call, sir," he said.

As Harriet Merkinson was swinging gently from side to side in the hallway of the house she shared with her sister, Hilda Merkinson slipped quietly into the back door of the Regal.

"Hello, Miss Merkinson," Sidney Poke said. His tone was quite reverential . . . a tone he would use when speaking with anyone who had been at the previous evening's party, and particularly those who had been closely involved with the tragic death of Arthur Clark.

Hilda nodded. "I wondered," she said, "if you had found anything this morning. When you were cleaning up, I mean."

Sidney frowned attentively. "Have you—" The ring of his mobile phone interrupted him. "Excuse me just a minute," he said, pulling his phone from his side pocket. He pressed a button and said, "Yes?"

Hilda looked around as Poke listened on the phone.

"Right," he said. "I'll get it and bring it through." He waited another few seconds and then said, "Very well, I'll meet them on the way."

"Now," Poke said as he returned the phone to his pocket. "Where we were? Ah yes . . . have you lost something?"

They started walking slowly through the ballroom which was now cleared.

Tables were folded and leaning against the far wall; chairs were stacked in towering piles in front of the stage; and an army of young men and woman were busy with vacuum cleaners, criss-crossing the floor, their attention fixed on the carpet.

"My handbag," Hilda shouted above the drone of the cleaners. "I think I must have left it last night." Poke nodded and looked around absently. "In all the excitement," Hilda added, suddenly wondering if "excitement" were the correct word to use under the circumstances.

"Ah!" Sidney Poke motioned Hilda towards a small occasional table set up by the door leading out to the toilets. "The table contained a few jackets plus an assortment of bags.

"All those were left last night?" Hilda said in astonishment.

Poke gave an approximation of a laugh which sounded more like a snort. "No, these belong to the cleaners," he said, "but your bag – if you did leave it, and if it has been found – is most likely here as anywhere."

As they reached the table, Hilda saw her bag. Her heart rose – or surfaced . . . or whatever it was that hearts did that was the opposite to sinking – and she reached out for it, careful not to appear too anxious. "That's it," she said triumphantly.

She picked up the bag and unfastened the sneck. She removed her purse, noting with grim satisfaction that the small bottle was still there, nestled in the bottom amongst Kleenex tissues, lipstick, comb and all the other rudiments of a woman's handbag, and flipped it open. "There," she announced, proudly displaying her library card, "just to show it's mine."

Hilda replaced the card and dropped the purse back into the depths of the handbag. Fastening the sneck, she said, "Well, I'll get off, then."

Sidney Poke nodded. He took her arm and gently led her towards the main door that went on to the toilets and out to the reception area.

"How are you today? I mean, how are you feeling?"

Hilda made a face. "Oh," she said, "you mean after—"

Poke nodded with the quietly attentive air of an undertaker.

"It was my sister. It was Harriet who collapsed. Not me."

"Ah." He pushed open the door and ushered her through ahead of him. "Well, I'll leave you here, if that's okay, Miss Merkinson." Poke stopped at a desk in a small recess and shuffled in his pocket. He produced a set of keys and set about opening the desk's deep drawer. "We're running a little behind, what with . . . you know."

Hilda nodded, watching Poke reach around into the drawer. Somewhere far off, but coming closer, she could hear footsteps.

"Ah, here it is," Poke grunted. "Must have pushed it further back than I thought." His back to Hilda, Poke pulled out a small bundle and closed the drawer.

The footsteps were getting closer. Hilda tried to ignore the yawning staircase on her right, the fabled 45 steps that led down to the Gentlemen's toilets. Deep in her mind, the footsteps belonged to Arthur Clark as he descended less than 12 hours earlier to empty his bowel and meet his end . . . except they seemed to be coming towards her rather than away from her. She shook her head and turned back to see the Hotel manager holding a toilet roll enclosed in a polythene bag.

"Right then," Poke was saying, though his words sounded like rushing water in Hilda's ears. Rushing water and footsteps, now getting very close . . . echoing . . . as though there were more than just Arthur coming back.

Poke moved the bag from one hand to the other as he returned the keys to his pocket.

Hilda frowned at the bag, looked at Poke, smiled awkwardly, and turned around to face the toilet steps, half expecting to see Arthur climbing up to see her . . . to ask her why she had done what she had done, and bringing other people with him, friends of his . . . friends who

wanted toilet paper.

wanted to talk to her and smooth her troubled brow with grave-cold hands. She turned sharply, took a couple of steps in the direction of the reception area and then stopped. There were figures approaching, figures making footstep-sounds. Her initial relief at discovering that the footsteps didn't belong to her sister's fancy man quickly evaporated when Malcolm Broadhurst called out to her.

"Ah, one of the Misses Merkinson." Broadhurst's tone was cheery. There were two policemen with him. "Now, which one are you?"

Hilda started to speak and then, clutching her bag tightly, she spun around. Behind her, Sidney Poke was still standing by the doors leading into the ballroom, the toilet roll in his hand.

"Miss Merkinson?"

Hilda looked all around, clutching the bag even tighter, willing it to disappear . . . willing it to be a week earlier . . . willing there to have been no rain so that Jack Wilson's General Store had not been flooded and Harriet had not had to stay and so Hilda had not gone for the fish and chips and so met Arthur who believed that she was her own sister . . . willing herself, back seven years ago, not to take the job at the animal testing centre . . . so many things. So many opportunities for her to have avoided this single instant.

But it was too late.

The footsteps were growing louder and slightly faster, moving towards her along the polished floor.

"Miss Merkinson?"

Then it all became clear.

She could escape through the toilets somehow. Escape and find Harriet and they could run off together, start a new routine . . . just the two of them.

She turned and almost leapt forward.

The piece of slanted ceiling that descended with the steps stayed straight for a second or two and then tilted.

Just as she was wondering why that was, Hilda hit her head on the side railing. She felt something warm on her cheek, spun around, and smashed her shin on one of the steps. For a second, amidst the confusion and the pain, she thought she could see a figure standing at the foot of the 45 steps, a figure patiently waiting for her to come down. She heard a crack.

Hilda slipped backwards and to the side somehow, hitting the back of her head on another step before turning over fully and ramming her face into one of the rail supports. More warmth . . .

And then blackness.

Another step broke her nose and her pelvis, another her third and fourth ribs – sending a splinter of bone into her left lung and scraping a sliver of tissue away from the second and third ventricles of her heart.

Two more steps fractured her skull, broke her left collarbone and smashed the base of her spine. The final step on the first flight sent another piece of rib through her heart.

She rolled onto the first landing and then proceeded down the second flight. And then onto the third.

It was Betty Thorndike who found Harriet.

She had called around on her way back from Edna Clark's house, just to see if Harriet was all right. Of course, she wasn't.

By Monday afternoon, it was all over bar the shouting. And as far as Malcolm Broadhurst was concerned, there would be little of that.

He had been to see Edna Clark on the Sunday afternoon, with both of the Merkinson sisters lying on metal trays in the cold and strangely smelling basement of Halifax General.

In the silent loneliness of Edna's kitchen, the widow had told him everything that Harriet had told her. Broadhurst put the rest of it together himself.

He had spoken with his boss at Halifax CID and they had agreed between the two of them that there was little to be achieved by releasing all of the gory details. They decided that Hilda had been a keen promoter of animal rights, using her position at the centre to obtain vital information of the testing Ian Arbutt was carrying out – hence the break-in.

Harriet, meanwhile, had been unable to come to terms with her sister's death and had hanged herself. Only a slight discrepancy in timing suggested that such might not be the case and nobody would hear about that discrepancy. Now the two of them were united again . . . in whatever routine they could arrange.

Edna Clark cried when the policeman explained what he had organised. It meant that her life had been partially restored. To all intents and purposes, she was still the grieving widow of a fine and upstanding member of the Luddersedge community. Betty Thorndike, who had not said anything to anyone about Harriet Merkinson's revelations – and had had no intention of doing so – consoled Edna and assured her that everything was all right.

"He was a good man," Edna whispered into her friend's shoulder. "Deep down," she added.

"I know he was, love," Betty agreed. "They all are . . . deep down."

Driving back to Halifax late afternoon on Monday, there was just one thing that niggled Malcolm Broadhurst. He could not understand why Ian Arbutt had seemed somehow relieved – albeit momentarily – when he was told of Hilda's unfortunate accident.

But the policeman did not believe Arbutt was in any way involved in either the break-in or Arthur Clark's murder. There was another story there, somewhere . . . as, of course, there always is.

STEPPING UP

Mark Billingham

I was never cut out to be the centre of attention. I never asked for it. I never enjoyed it.

Some people love all that though, don't they? They need to be the ones having their heads swelled and their arses licked; pawed at and fawned over. Some people are idiots, to be fair, and don't know what to do with themselves if they aren't smack in the middle of the fucking action.

Of course, there were times when I *did* get the attention, whether I wanted it or not. When things were going well and I won a title or two. I got it from men *and* women then, and you won't hear me say there was anything wrong with that. Blokes wanting to shake your hand and tarts queuing up to shake your other bits and pieces, well nobody's complaining about that kind of carry on, are they?

But *this*, though . . .?

The doctor had been banging on about exercise, especially as I was having such a hard time giving up the fags. It would help to get the old ticker pumping a bit, he said. Get your cholesterol down and shift some of that weight which isn't exactly helping matters, let's face it. You used to box a bit, didn't you, he said, so you shouldn't find it too difficult to get back in the swing of it. To shape up a little.

Piece of piss, I told him, then corrected myself when he smiled and straightened his tie.

"Cake, I meant. Sorry, Doc. Piece of cake."

I don't know which one of us I was kidding more.

I got Maggie's husband, Phil, to give me a hand and fetch some of my old gear out of the loft. We scraped the muck off the skipping rope and hung the heavy bag up in the garage. I thought I would be able to ease myself back into it, you know? Stop when it hurt and build things up slowly. Trouble was it hurt all the time, and the more I tried, the more angry I got that I'd let myself go to shit so badly; that I'd smoked so many fags and eaten so much crap and put so much booze away down the years.

"It was mum's fault for spoiling you," Maggie said. "If she hadn't laid on meat and two veg for you every day of her life, you *might* have learned to do a bit more than boil a bleeding egg. You wouldn't have had to eat so many take-aways after she'd gone . . ."

Once my eldest gets a bee in her bonnet, that's it for everyone. It was her that had nagged me into going to the doctor's in the first place, getting some exercise or what have you. So, even though the boxing training hadn't worked out, the silly mare had no intention of letting the subject drop.

One day, in the pub with Phil, I found out that I wasn't the only one getting it in the neck.

"Help me out, for Christ's sake," he said. "She won't shut up about it, how she thinks you're going to drop dead any bloody second. Just do *something*."

"Snooker?"

"Funny."

"Fucked if I know, Phil. There's nothing I fancy."

I'd told Mags I wouldn't go jogging and that was all there was to it. I've been there, so I know how that game works; shift a few pounds and fuck up your knee joints at the same time. Tennis wasn't for the likes of me and the same went double for golf, even though a couple of blokes in the pub had the odd game now and again. The truth is, I know you have to stick at these kind of things, and that's never been my strong suit. I had a talent in the ring, so I didn't mind putting the hours in, and besides, I had more . . . drive back then, you know? Day after day on a golf course or a sodding tennis court, just so I wouldn't look like a twat every time I turned out, didn't sound much fun.

Plus, there weren't that many people I could think of to play with, tell you the truth . . .

"There's a class," Phil said. "Down our local leisure centre. One night a week, that's all."

"Class?"

"Just general fitness, you know. Look it's only an hour and there's a bit of a drink afterwards. You'll be doing me a favour."

"Hmmm." I swallowed what was left of a pint and rolled my eyes, and that was it. That's how easily a misunderstanding happens and you get yourself shafted.

I should have twigged a couple of weeks later when Maggie came by to pick me up. On the way there I asked her where Phil was, was he coming along later and all that, and she looked at me like I'd lost the plot. See, I thought it was *his* class, didn't I? A few lads jumping about, maybe a quick game of five-a-side and then a couple of beers afterwards. When I walked out of that changing room in my baggy shorts and an old West Ham shirt, I felt like I'd been majorly stitched up. There was Maggie, beaming at me, and a dozen or so other women, and all of them limbering up in front of these little plastic steps.

A fucking *step* class. Jesus H . . .

And not just women, either, which didn't help a great deal. There were a couple of men there to witness the humiliation, which always makes it worse, right? You know what I'm talking about. There were three other fellas standing about, looking like each of them had gone through what I was going through right then. An old boy, a few years on me, who looked like he'd have trouble *carrying* his step. A skinny young bloke in a tight top, who I figured was queer straight away, and a fit-looking sort who I guessed was there to pull something a bit older and desperate.

Looking around, trying my hardest to manage a smile, I could see that most of the women were definitely in that category. Buses, back-ends, you see what I'm getting at? I swear to God, you wouldn't have looked twice at any of them.

Except for Zoe.

I met her forty-odd years back, when I was twenty-something and I'd won a few fights; one night when I was introduced to some people at a nightclub in Tottenham. Frank Sparks was doing pretty well himself at that time, and there were all sorts of faces hanging about. I wasn't stupid. I knew full well what was paying for Frank's Savile Row suit and what have you, and to tell you the truth, it never bothered me.

There weren't many saints knocking around anywhere back then.

Frank was friendly enough, and for the five or ten minutes I sat at his table, it was like we were best friends. He was one of those blokes with a knack for that, you know? Told me he was following my career, how he'd won a few quid betting on me, that kind of thing. He said there were always jobs going with him. All sorts of bits and pieces, you know, if things didn't work out or I jacked the fight game in or whatever.

I can still remember how shiny his hair was that night. And his teeth, and the stink of Aramis on him.

She was the sister of this bloke I used to spar with, and I'd seen her waiting for him at the back of the gym a few times, but it wasn't until that night in Tottenham that I started to pay attention. She was all dressed up, with different hair, and I thought she was an actress or a stripper. Then we got talking by the bar and she laughed and told me she was just Billy's sister. I said she was better looking than any of the actresses or strippers that were there guzzling Frank's champagne, and she went redder than the frock she was wearing, but I knew she liked it.

I saw her quite a bit after that in various places. She started going out with one of Frank Sparks' boys and wearing a lot of fancy dresses. I remember once, I'd just knocked this black lad over in the fourth round at Harringay. I glanced down, sweating like a pig, and she was sitting a few rows back smiling up at me, and the referee's count seemed to take forever.

You just get on the thing, then off again; up and down, up and down, one foot or both of them, in time to the fucking music. Simple as that. You can get back down the same way you went up, or sometimes you turn and come down on the other side, and now and again there's a bit of dancing around the thing, but basically . . . you climb on and off a plastic step.

I swear to God, that's it.

Maybe, that first time, I should have just turned and gone straight back in that changing room. Caught a bus home. Maggie had that look on her face though, and I thought walking out would be even more embarrassing than staying.

So, I decided to do it just the once, for Mags, and actually, it didn't turn out to be as bad as I expected. It was a laugh as it goes, and at least I could do it without feeling like it was going to kill me. It was a damn sight harder than it looked, mind you, make no fucking mistake about *that*. I was knackered after ten minutes, but what with there being so many women in the class, I didn't feel like I had to compete with anyone, you know what I mean?

Ruth, the woman in charge, seemed genuinely pleased to see me when I showed up again the second week and the week after that. She teased me a bit, and I took the piss because she had one of those microphone things on her ear like that singer with the pointy tits. They were *all* quite nice, to be honest. A pretty decent bunch. I'd pretend to flirt a bit with one or two of the women, and I'd have a laugh with Anthony, who didn't bang on about being gay like a lot of them do, you know?

Even Craig seemed all right, to begin with.

The pair of us ended up next to each other more often than not, on the end of the line behind Zoe. Him barely out of breath after half an hour; me, puffing and blowing like I was about to keel over. The pair of us looking one way and one way only, while she moved, easy and sweet, in front of us.

One time, he took his eyes off her arse and glanced across at me. I did likewise, and while Ruth was shouting encouragement to one of the older ladies, the cheeky fucker winked, and I felt the blood rising to my neck.

I remember an evening in the pub with Maggie and Phil, a few weeks in, and me telling Maggie not to be late picking me up for the class. To take the traffic into account. She plastered on a smart-arse smile, like she thought she'd cottoned on to something, but just said she was pleased I was enjoying myself.

It only took one lucky punch from a jammy Spaniard for everything to go tits up as far as the fighting was concerned. I had a few more bouts, but once the jaw's been broken, you're never quite as fearless. Never quite as stupid as you need to be.

Stupid as I had been, spending every penny I'd ever made, quick as I'd earned it.

With the place I was renting in Archway, the payments on a brand new Cortina, and sweet FA put by, it wasn't like I had a lot of choice when it came to doing door work for Frank Sparks. Besides, it was easy money, as it went. A damn sight less stressful than the ring anyway, and I certainly didn't miss the training. Your average Friday-night drunk goes down a lot easier than a journeyman light-heavyweight, but the fact is, I couldn't have thrown more than half a dozen punches in nearly a year of it. I was there to look as if I was useful, see, and that was fine. Like I said before, I was happier in the background and I think Frank was pretty pleased with the way I was handling things, because he asked me if I fancied doing a spot of driving.

And that's when I started seeing a lot more of her.

She wasn't married yet, but I'd heard it was on the cards. Her boyfriend had moved up through the ranks smartish, and was in charge of a lot of Frank's gambling clubs. Classy places in Knightsbridge and Victoria with cigarette girls and what have you. She used to go along and just sit in the corner drinking and looking tasty, but some of these sessions went on all night, and she'd always leave before her old man did.

So, I started to drive her.

I started to ask to drive her; volunteering quietly, you know? There were a couple of motors on call and we took it in turns at first. Then, after a few weeks, she asked for me, and it sort of became an arrangement.

In the image I still have of her, she's standing on a pavement, putting on a scarf as I indicate and drift across towards the curb. She's clutching a handbag. She waves as I pull up, then all but falls into the back of the Jag; tired, but happy as Larry to be on the way home.

In reality of course she was thinner, and drunker. Her eyes got flatter and the bleach made her hair brittle, and she was always popping some pill or other. That crocodile handbag rattled with them. The smile was still there though; lighting up what was left of her. The same as it was when I looked down through the ropes that time and saw her clapping.

When I felt as though I was the one who'd had the breath punched out of me.

How bloody old am I?

It's a fair question, but I don't suppose it really matters. *Too* old, that's the point, isn't it? Too old to smoke and not worry about it; to put on a pair of socks without sitting down; to think about running for a bus.

Too old to feel immortal . . .

Like you'd expect, it was mostly Diet Coke and fizzy water in the pub afterwards. I had orange juice and lemonade myself, for the first week anyway, but Zoe drank beer from the off.

Ruth didn't give a monkey's what anyone did once the class was over, but there was one woman who didn't approve; who clearly enjoyed having another reason to dislike Zoe. She was glaring across at her from an adjoining table, one night a few weeks in, and I was giving it the old cow back with bells on.

"Maybe she's jealous because she secretly fancies you," Zoe whispered.

I pulled a face. "Christ, don't put me off me pint!"

She really enjoyed that one. Her laugh was low and dirty, and it still amazes me really, to think of it coming out of a mouth like hers. A face like that.

"She's just dried-up and bitter," I said. "Hates it that she's doing this to try and change how she looks, or what have you, while others don't really have to."

Zoe smiled, leaned a shoulder against mine. "Some people just don't know how to have fun, you know? Think their bodies are temples and all that."

"My body's more of a slaughterhouse these days," I said.

She enjoyed that one too. It felt fantastic to make her laugh. We shared a big packet of crisps, which really wound up the old bag on the next table. She left early, while Zoe and me and a few of the others stayed until they rang the bell, same as always. Ruth and Anthony were giggling by the jukebox, and Maggie kept an eye on me from a table near the door, where she sat clutching her mobile phone, waiting for Phil to come and pick the pair of us up.

"Why *do* you come?" I asked her. "It's not like you need to lose weight or anything. You seem pretty fit . . ."

She leaned a shoulder into mine. "You're sweet."

"I'm just saying."

She took another swig from her bottle. "I'm lazy," she said. "I need to make myself do things, get out and do something a bit off the wall, you know? Anyway, it's a laugh, don't you reckon?"

I did reckon, and I told her.

"I work in a stupid office," she said. "The people there are all right I suppose, but I don't want to see them after work or whatever. I think it's good to meet people who aren't anything like you are. People with different lives, you know? I tried a French class, but it was too hard, and the teacher was a bit stuck-up. This is much better. Much."

She had a voice it was easy to listen to. She certainly wasn't posh, but there wasn't really an accent either. Just soft and simple, you know?

"What about you?" she asked.

I said I was basically there to keep Maggie happy, and to try and get at least some of the old fitness back. I mentioned that I used to box a bit and she said that she could see it. That it was in the way I carried myself.

I had to hide my face in my glass, and I'd all but downed the rest of the pint by the time the blush had gone away.

"Someone needed a drink," she said.

There was a burst of high-pitched laughter from Ruth and Anthony, and when I looked across, I could see that Maggie had gone from a smartarse smile to something that looked like concern.

I went up to get the two of us refills, and exchanged nods with Craig who was deep in conversation with the woman behind the bar. He was smoking which made me deeply fucking envious. If Maggie hadn't been sitting by the door, I might well have ponced one.

"Enjoying yourself?" he said.

When the barmaid went to fetch the drinks, Craig span slowly round and leaned back against the bar. He looked across at Zoe for a minute, more maybe, then turned to me. His face said "I *know*, I couldn't agree more, mate. But look at *me* and look at *you*."

Or he might just have been asking me to pass the ashtray.

Oh fuck it, who knows?

Her old man had a place in Battersea, on the edge of the park. There was a night I was driving her back from one of Frank's casinos, down through Chelsea towards Albert Bridge, when she started asking me all manner of funny questions.

"Do you actually like any of them, though? Are any of them really your mates if you think about it?"

The gin had slowed her up a little. Thickened her voice, you know?

"Any of who?" I said.

She jerked a thumb back towards where we'd come from. "That lot. The boys. They're just people you work with, aren't they? Just blokes you knock around with, right, and I don't suppose any of them give a toss about you, either. Wouldn't you say?"

I shrugged and watched the road. It wasn't like I'd never heard her talking bollocks before. Next time she spoke, her voice had more breath in it, and she kept saying my name, but that's something else people do when they've had a couple, isn't it?

"It's just London, right?" she said. "Frank doesn't own stuff anywhere else, does he?"

"I don't know. I don't think so."

"I don't think so either."

"He's been up north on business, definitely. Manchester . . ."

"It was only a few times," she said. "Just to meet people."

"Birmingham as well. I drove him to the station."

"He was just looking, though, that's what I heard. Nothing came of it. It's all here really, don't you reckon?" She said my name again, slow with a question in it. Wanting me to agree with her. "Everyone's here, aren't they?"

I heard a song I knew she liked come on the radio and I turned it up for her. That girl who did Eurovision without any shoes on. I was waiting for her to start singing along, but when I looked in the rear-view I could see that her eyes were closed.

Her head was tipped back and her mascara was starting to run.

Things really started to go pear-shaped the time Zoe turned up looking like she did and Craig didn't turn up at all.

I hadn't admitted it to myself, not really, that the two of them were seeing each other outside the class, but I had to stop being stupid and face facts when I saw her walk in like that. It was like I suddenly knew all sorts of things at once. I knew that they'd got together, that everyone else had probably sussed it a damn sight faster than me, and I knew exactly what had happened to her face.

In class, I stepped that bit faster than usual. I stamped on and off that bastard thing, and it was automatic, like I could do it all day and I wasn't even thinking. Ruth said how well I was doing and when Zoe smiled at me, encouraging, I had to look away.

Afterwards, she didn't turn towards the pub with the rest of us, and when I saw that she was heading for the car-park, I moved to go after her. Maggie took hold of my arm and said something about getting a table. I told her I'd be there in a minute, to get one in for me, but she didn't look very happy.

I tried to get a laugh out of Zoe when I caught her up; made out like I was knackered, you know, from chasing after her, but she didn't seem to really go for it. "Do you not fancy it tonight then?" I said. "Not even a swift half?"

She was fetching her car-keys from her bag. Digging around for them and keeping her head down. "I've got an early start in the morning," she said. "New boss, you know?"

I nodded, told her that one wasn't going to hurt.

She caught me looking, not that I was trying particularly hard not to. It was like a plum that someone had stepped on around her cheek, and the ragged edges of it were the color of a tea-stain. There was a half-moon of blood in her eye.

"I didn't know there was a cupboard open and I turned round into it," she said. "Clumsy bitch . . ."

"Shush . . ."

"I actually knocked myself out for a few seconds."

"Listen, it's all right," I said.

"What is?"

"Come and have one quick drink," I said. "Who am I going to share my salt and vinegar crisps with if you don't?"

It was as though she suddenly noticed that my hand was on her wrist, and she looked down and took half a step back. "I'll see you next week."

"Look after yourself." It came out as a whisper. I didn't really know what else to say.

She pressed the button on her car-keys and when the lights flashed and the alarm squawked, I saw her jump slightly.

In the pub, I couldn't blame Maggie for being off with me. I sat there with a face like a smacked arse, and I couldn't have said more than three words to anyone. After half an hour I'd had enough, and I asked her to call Phil, get him to fetch us early. That didn't go down too well either because she was having a laugh with Anthony, but I just wasn't in the mood for it.

As we were leaving, Ruth raised her glass and said something about me being her star pupil.

Zoe didn't turn up at all the following week.

We were driving, same as always. Seemed like, when it came to being close or what have you, that was the only time we ever really saw each other. Me in the front, her in the back.

"Go slowly, will you?" she'd said when she got in.

Obviously I was going to do what she wanted, right, and it was raining like a bastard anyway, so it wasn't like I could have put my foot down. Still, I wanted to get back to her place as quickly as I could. Don't get me wrong, I hated it when she got out of the car, hated it, but lately I'd taken to stopping somewhere after I'd dropped her off; soon as I'd got round the corner sometimes.

I'd pull over in the dark and sit quiet for a minute. Reach for a handkerchief. Throw one off the wrist, while I could still smell her in the car.

Sounds disgusting, I know, but it didn't feel like it back then.

I drove, slow like she wanted, along the Brompton Road and down Sydney Street. Staring at the jaguar leaping from the end of the bonnet; the road slick, sucked up beneath it.

When I turned up the radio to drown out the squeak of the wipers, she leaned forward and asked me to switch it off.

Pissing down now. Clattering on the roof like tacks.

"There's people been talking to me," she said.

"What people?"

"They've been going over my options, you know?"

"What options?"

"The choices I've got."

I looked in the mirror. Watched her take a deep breath when she saw that I didn't understand.

"Billy's fucked up," she said. "Silly bugger's really gone and dropped himself in it."

Her brother. My ex-sparring partner. Always had been a bit of a tearaway.

"What's he done?" I asked. Prickles on my neck.

"He went for some flash Maltese fucker with a knife . . ."

"Jesus."

"*Didn't really do him too much harm, but they'll happily bump it up to attempted murder. Put him away for a few years unless I decide to help.*"

I knew who she was talking about now. Coppers were the same as anyone else at the end of the day. There were plenty of stupid ones, but enough of them with brains to make life interesting.

"*There's only Billy and me,*" she said. "*The bastards know how close we are.*"

She started to cry just a little bit then. I went inside my jacket for the handkerchief I'd be using later on, but she'd already pulled one out from her handbag. I'd heard the pills rattling as she rummaged for it.

I was taking us over the bridge by now. Gliding across it. The lights swung like a necklace up ahead and the rain was churning up the water on either side of me.

"*It's not like I know a fat lot.*"

"*Fat lot about what?*" I said, but it was obvious what she was banging on about.

"*Frank. Frank's business. All that.*"

All that.

"*Obviously they think I know something.*" She raised her hands, let them drop down with a slap on to the leather seat. "*Maybe I know enough.*"

Course she did; she wasn't stupid, was she? Enough to get her little brother out of the shit and herself slap bang in it.

I wanted to slam on the anchors and stop the car right there on the bridge. To reach into the back and shake her until her fillings came loose. I wanted to tell her that her brother was a pissy little waster, and that she shouldn't be such a daft bitch, and to say absolutely fuck all to anyone about fuck all.

I was the one that kept my mouth shut, though, wasn't I? The one who just gripped the wheel that little bit tighter and manoeuvered the car like I was on my driving test. Checking the wing mirrors, hands at ten to two, watching my speed.

"*I need to go away,*" she said.

Ten to two. Both eyes on the road . . .

"*Somewhere abroad might be best. Somewhere hot, near the sea if I get a choice, but it might not have to be that far. Maybe Scotland or somewhere. I've tucked a bit away and I'm sure I can make a few bob later on. I can type for a kick-off.*"

Slowing for lights. No more than a mile away from the flat on the edge of the park. Checking the mirror and feathering the brake; moving down through the gears.

"I just don't feel like I can do it on my own, you know? That's the only bit I'm scared of, if I'm honest. It's pathetic I know, relying on someone like that, but the thought of nobody being there with me makes me feel sick, like I'm looking over the edge of something. I don't mean sex or whatever, but that's not out of the question either. It's mostly about having someone around who gives a toss, do you know what I mean?"

Waiting for the amber, willing that fucker to change.

"Someone who worries . . ."

She said my name, and it felt like I had something thick and bitter in my gullet.

Neither of us said anything else after that, but we were only five minutes away from the flat by then. The silence was horrible, make no mistake about that, but it just lay there until it sort of flattened out into something we were both willing to live with. Until she asked me to turn the radio back up.

When we pulled up, I got out to open her door, then climbed back in again quick without saying much of anything. When I looked up she was standing there by my door. She had an umbrella, but she never even bothered getting it out; just stood there getting pissed on, with the rain bringing her hair down, until thick strands of it were dead and dark against her face.

She was saying something. I couldn't hear, but I was looking at her mouth, same as always.

I thought she said: "It doesn't matter, Jimmy."

Then she put the tips of two fingers to her lips and pressed them against my window. They went white where she pressed, and I could still see the mark for a few minutes after I drove away.

I didn't stop the car where I normally did. Just kept going for a bit, trying to swallow and think straight. I drove up through Nine Elms and pulled in a mile or so past the power station.

Sat there and stared out across the shitty black river until it started to get light.

Craig looked confused as much as anything when I walked round the corner. Grinned at him. It was half way through the morning, and him and a couple of older women in blouses and grey skirts had come out the back entrance of the bank for a crafty smoke.

"All right, mate?"

"Ticking along," I said. "You?"

It must have been there in my face or the way I spoke, because I saw the women stubbing out pretty long fag-ends, making themselves scarce. Neither of them so much as looked at him before they buggered off.

Craig watched his colleagues go, seemed to find something about it quite funny. He turned back to me, taking a drag. Shook his head.

"Sorry, mate. It's just a bit strange you turning up here, that's all. How d'you know where I worked?"

"Zoe must have said, last time she came to the class, you know?"

Something in his face that I couldn't read, but I didn't much care.

"How's she doing, anyway?" I said.

"Er, she's good, yeah."

"It was a shame she stopped coming, really. We were all saying how she made the rest of us work a bit harder, trying to keep up."

"She just lost interest I think. Me an' all, to be honest." Then a look that seemed to say they were getting their exercise in other ways, and one back from me that tried and failed to wipe it off his face.

It was warm and he was in shirt-sleeves. I was sweating underneath my jacket so I slipped it off, threw it across my arm.

"Are you feeling OK?"

"I'm fine," I said.

"You've gone a bit red."

I nodded, looked at the sweat patches under his arm and the pattern on his poxy tie.

He flicked his fag-end away. "Listen, I've got to get back to work . . ."

"Right."

"I'll say hello to Zoe, shall I?"

"How's her face?"

That took the smile off the fucker quick enough. Put that confused look back again, like he didn't know his arse from his elbow.

"It's fine now," he said. "She's all gorgeous again."

"Nasty, that was. Not seen many shiners worse than that one. Door wasn't it?"

"Cupboard door."

"Yeah, that's what's she said."

"She forgot it was open and turned round fast, you know? Listen—"

I was just looking at him by now.

"What?"

I knew I still had *that*. You never lose the look.

"What's your problem?"

Breathing heavily, a wheeze in it. For real some of it, like the red face, but I'd bunged a bit extra on top, you know. Laid it on thick just to get his guard down.

"I think maybe you ought to piss off now," he said.

I bent over, suddenly; dropped the jacket like I might be in some trouble. He stepped across to pick it up, like I wanted him to, which was when I swung a good hard right at his fat, flappy mouth.

I never had her in the car again after that night. Only saw her a couple of times as it goes, and even then, when she looked over, I always found something fascinating in the pattern on the carpet or counted the bits of chewing gum squashed onto the pavement.

Spineless cunt.

She went away some time after. I suppose I should say I was told she went away. It's an important distinction, right? Told like there was actually nothing to tell, but also like there wasn't much point me asking about it again or wasting any money on postcards.

A few years ago we were having a meal, me and one of the lads I used to knock about with back then. You have a curry and a few pints and you talk about the old days, don't you? You have a laugh.

Until her name came up.

He was talking about what he thought had happened and why. Wanted to know what I thought had gone on; fancied getting my take on it. You used to know her pretty well, didn't you, he said. That's what I heard, anyway. You used to be quite close to her is what somebody told me.

I had a mouthful of ulcers at that time. It was when my old girl was suffering, you know, and the doctor reckoned it was the stress of her illness that was causing it. Ulcers and boils, I had.

When he mentioned her name the first time, I started to chew on a couple of those ulcers. Gnawing into those bastards so hard it was making my eyes water, though my mate probably thought it was the vindaloo.

You used to be quite close to her, he said.

I bit the fuckers clean out then, two or three of them. I remember the noise I made, people in the restaurant turning round. I bent down over the table, coughing, and I spat them out into a serviette.

That more or less put the tin lid on our conversation, which was all right by me. My mate didn't say too much of anything after that. Well, we'd been talking about what was happening with me and my old lady before, and when he saw the blood in the napkin, maybe he was confused, you know, thought I was the one with the lung cancer.

It wasn't the best punch I ever threw, but it made contact and I concentrated on the blood that was running down his shirt-front as he swung me round and pushed me against the wall.

"What the fuck's your game, you silly old bastard?"

I tried to nut him and he leaned back, his arms out straight, holding me hard against the bricks.

"Take it easy."

I thought I felt something crack in his shin when I kicked out at him. I tried to bring my leg up fast towards his bollocks, but the pain in his leg must have fired him right up and his fists were flying at me.

It was no more than a few seconds. Just flailing really like kids, but Christ, I'd forgotten how much it hurts.

Every blow rang and tore and made the sick rise up. I felt something catch me and rip behind the ear; a ring maybe. Stung like fuck.

I swore, and kept kicking. I shut my eyes.

My fists were up, but it was all I could do to protect my face, so I can't have been doing him a lot of damage.

But I was trying.

When the gaps between the punches got a bit longer, I tried to get a dig or two in, just to keep my fucking end up, you know? That was when the background went blurry, and his face started to swim in front of me, but as far as I'm concerned that was down to the pain in my arm. It had bugger all to do with any punishment I might have taken.

The fucker hit me one more time, when I dropped my fists to clutch at my arm. It was all over then, more or less. But it was the pain in my chest that put me down, and not that punch.

Not the punch.

There's always a *something* that gets you from one place to the next, right? That you're chasing after in some way, shape or form. Granted, some people are happy enough to let themselves get pissed along like a fag-end in a urinal, and yes, I know that some poor bastards are plain unlucky, but still . . .

OK, then, to be fair there's *usually* a something. For me, anyway, is all I'm saying. If I'm centre of attention right now, for all the wrong reasons, it isn't really down to anyone else, and I'm not going to feel sorry for myself.

That's more or less what I tried to say to Maggie and Phil when they came in, but they were in no fit state to listen, and I don't think I made myself very clear.

Fuck, they're *at* me again . . .

Loads of them, and I thought there was supposed to be a shortage. Poking and prodding. Talking over me like I'm deaf as well as everything else.

It's not pain exactly.

It's warm and wet and spreading through my arms and legs like I'm sinking into a bath or something. They've got those things you see on the TV out again, like a pair of irons on my chest. Like they're going to iron out my wrinkles.

Now they're going blurry either side of me, same as that fucker did when I was punching him. The sound's gone funny too.

And clear as you like, I can see her face. The stain around her eye and the purple bruise. The hair lying dead against her cheek in the rain.

Music as I step up and step up. Some tuneless disco rubbish while I'm sneaking looks at her in that tight leotard thing and Ruth bawls at me through her stupid microphone.

As I step up off the beach. With the sea coming up on to the sand behind me. Noisy, like the sigh of someone who's sick of waiting for something.

Stepping up on to the hot pavement, where she's stood waiting with a drink. That mouth, and her hair darker now and she looks magnificent. And we lean against each other and drink sangria at one of them places where you can sit outside.

The music's still getting louder, so I ask them to turn it up.

That song she likes on the radio.

The bird with the bare feet.

"I wonder if one day that, you'll say that you care.
If you say you love me madly, I'll gladly be there . . ."

TOM OF TEN THOUSAND

Edward Marston

12 February 1682

The crime occurred in broad daylight. When the coach reached the main street, it slowed down and rumbled around the corner, its iron-rimmed wheels slipping on the frosted cobbles. Before it could pick up speed again, it was ambushed. Coming out of nowhere, three men rode alongside the coach so that they could discharge their weapons at its occupant. Two of the attackers had pistols but it was the blunderbuss held by the third that proved fatal. It went off with a deafening bang and split the victim's stomach wide open. Blood gushed out over his velvet breeches and dripped on to the floor. Confident that the man had been killed, the villains kicked their horses into a gallop and disappeared at once from the scene.

Christopher Redmayne saw it all from a distance. He had just entered the other end of the street when the murder took place. He heard the sounds of shooting clearly and the horrified screams from passers-by. He watched the coachman pull the horses to a sudden halt and caught a glimpse of the attackers, escaping in the confusion. Christopher did not hesitate. Riding at a canter, he made straight for the coach around which a small crowd was now gathering. There was an uneasy feeling in the pit of his stomach. An aspiring young architect, he was on his way to meet a wealthy potential client at a tavern in that street.

The closer he got to the coach, the more convinced he became that it belonged to the very man with whom he had arranged to dine that day.

Having leapt down from his seat, the coachman opened the door to find his employer doubled up on the floor. He was still alive but he was fading with each second. Christopher's horse skidded to a halt and the architect dismounted at speed. He looked over the coachman's shoulder.

"Is that Mr Thynne?" he asked.

"Yes, sir," replied the other.

"Is he injured?"

Without waiting for an answer, Christopher eased the man aside so that he could see for himself. Thomas Thynne was beyond help. Face contorted in agony, he made a futile attempt to speak then his eyes rolled and he collapsed in a heap. The coachman gasped. Christopher leaned in close to examine the body. When he was certain that Thynne was dead, he offered up a silent prayer before taking control of the situation. Having sent a bystander to fetch an officer, he turned to the coachman, a stout man of middle years, deeply shocked at the murder of his employer.

"Do you know who those men were?" asked Christopher.

"No, sir."

"Have you seen any of them before?"

"Never."

"Were they lying in wait for you?"

"Yes, sir," said the coachman, wiping away a tear with the back of his hand. "As soon as we turned the corner, they were there."

"Can you think of any reason why they should do this?"

"None, sir."

"Did Mr Thynne have any enemies?"

"No, sir. He was the kindest man in the world."

Prompted by loyalty, and annoyed by people staring at the corpse with ghoulish interest, the coachman took off his coat and used to it to cover Thomas Thynne's face. Then he waved his arms to force the onlookers back.

Christopher asked for any witnesses and half-a-dozen came forward to tell the same gabbled tale. None of them, however, had been able to identify the men. It was only when a constable came running to take charge of the incident that Christopher spotted a short, thin, ragged individual, lurking in a doorway on the other side of the street. He beckoned the architect across to him.

"I might know who one of them is, sir," said the man, slyly.

"You *might* know?"

"If my memory was jogged, sir."

Christopher understood. "Who was the fellow?" he said, reaching into his purse for a coin. "Give me his name."

"I could give you his address as well," promised the other, eyeing the purse meaningfully. Christopher took out a second coin and pressed both into the man's grubby palm. "Thank you, sir." He snapped his hand shut. "The person you want is Ned Bagwell. He stays at the Feathers, not two hundred yards from here."

Christopher knew the inn by reputation. After thanking the man, he mounted his horse and urged it forward. He was soon trotting briskly in the direction of the Feathers, situated in one of the less salubrious areas of Westminster. London was a dangerous city and Christopher was always armed when he went abroad. In addition to his sword, he wore a dagger and was adept with both. He was not deterred by the fact that there had been three men in the ambush. They had not only robbed a respectable gentleman of his life. They had deprived the architect of a handsome commission to build a house for Thomas Thynne. It served to harden Christopher's resolve to find the killers.

When he got to the Feathers, he tethered his horse and went into the taproom. Filled with smoke from the fire in the grate, it was a dark, dingy, unappealing place. Customers looked up in surprise. The inn was not used to welcoming someone as wholesome and well-dressed as the young architect. Christopher went across to the man behind the counter.

"Does one Ned Bagwell lodge here?" he asked.

"Aye," came the surly reply. "What do you want with Ned?"

"I need to speak to him."

"And supposing he doesn't want to speak to you?"

"Then my sword will give him some encouragement," warned Christopher, meeting the landlord's hostile stare. "Is he here now?"

"Aye – Ned is always here."

"I fancy that he went out a little earlier."

"Then you must think again."

"He had two friends with him. Are they here as well?"

The man folded his arms. "Ned's not stirred from here all day."

"I've only your word for that," said Christopher, whipping out his dagger and holding it to the man's throat, "and I wouldn't trust you for a second. Take me to him."

"No need," said the other, unperturbed. "I'll call him for you." He cupped his hands to his mouth. "Ned! Ned Bagwell, you've a visitor!"

A string of ripe obscenities issued from the next room then Christopher heard the thump of crutches on the wooden floor. When he appeared in the doorway, Ned Bagwell was a one-legged old man who let loose another stream of abuse. Christopher had been tricked. The man to whom he had given the money was already spending it in another tavern.

"Tom Thynne shot down in the street by ruffians!" cried Henry Redmayne in dismay. "It's a devilish crime."

"I mean to solve it," vowed his brother.

"I was at Court when the news came. His Majesty was greatly upset. Tom Thynne was a leading member of the Duke of Monmouth's party. It was his money that has been helping the King's bastard to win support around the country. There's your motive, Christopher," he went on, wagging a finger. "Some scurvy Roman Catholic has set these men on to kill poor Tom."

"I make no assumptions, Henry."

"But it's as plain as the nose on your face."

"Not to me," said Christopher.

They were in the parlour of Henry's house in Bedford Street. It was he who had recommended Christopher to Thomas Thynne. The contrast between the two brothers was startling. Christopher was tall, slim and well favoured while Henry's features showed clear signs of dissipation. As one led a decent, healthy, conscientious life, the other pursued vice in every corner of the city. Though he did not approve of Henry's passion for drink, gambling and lechery, Christopher was grateful for the many introductions his brother had given him to people in search of a talented architect. Henry Redmayne knew everyone of consequence in London society.

"Tell me about Mr Thynne," said Christopher. "All that I know is that he was very rich and recently married."

"Yes," replied Henry. "We called him Tom of Ten Thousand. How I envied him! Think what *I* could do with an annual income of that size."

"You'd drink yourself to death in a fortnight."

"That was not what Tom Thynne did. He was a sober gentleman but not without an eye for the ladies. The beautiful widow, Lady Ogle, was half his age yet he wooed and won her. There was only one problem."

"Was there?"

"Yes, Christopher. She let him wed her but not bed her. Repenting of the marriage, she fled abroad to Holland and is rumoured to be staying with Lady Temple. One of the ways her husband hoped to lure his wife back was to have a new house built for her. That's why I whispered your name into Tom's ear."

"We were supposed to dine at the Golden Fleece today so that we could discuss the project. Mr Thynne was murdered on his way there."

"The blackguards must be punished."

"They will be," said Christopher, gritting his teeth, "but I may need your help to catch them."

"What can I possibly do?"

"Find out who else knew about the arrangements for dinner. Those men were waiting for him, Henry. Someone told them when and where he would be at a certain time."

"So?"

"The most likely person is employed in Mr Thynne's household. You were a guest there in the past. See what you can learn at the house. The body was taken there. You'll be able to pay your respects."

"But I'm expected at the card table within the hour."

Christopher was decisive. "Solving a murder is more important than gambling away money that you can ill afford," he argued. "Get over there at once."

"I take no orders from you."

"Then take them from His Majesty. You told me how alarmed he was by the turn of events. This news will inflame those who hate the Court and its political friends. What better way to curry the King's favour than by helping to track down the culprits? He would be eternally grateful to you. Now ride across to Mr Thynne's house."

"Very well," said Henry, peevishly. He adjusted his periwig in the mirror then preened himself. "What will you be doing in the meantime?"

"Seeing what Jonathan has managed to find out."

"Jonathan?"

"Jonathan Bale."

"That gloomy constable? A sour-faced rogue, if ever there was one. He has far too many Puritan principles to be allowed in respectable company." Henry snorted. "A hue and cry will have been granted. Westminster will be crawling with officers. Why bother to involve Bale?"

"Because he is so tenacious."

"Too damned tenacious!"

"He once helped to save your life, Henry."

"Yes," wailed the other, "then he read me a lecture on the need to abandon my evil ways. The brazen audacity of the man!"

"Jonathan Bale is a godsend," insisted Christopher. "He's not without his faults, I grant you, but he has a gift for finding out things that other men would never even sniff."

"When was this, Reuben?" asked Jonathan Bale.

"Soon after I heard the shots being fired."

"And you *saw* the men?"

"I did," confirmed Reuben Hopkiss. "The three galloped straight past me and all but knocked over our chair."

"Did you recognize them?"

"I recognized one of them, Mr Bale. We carried him from his lodging here in Westminster only yesterday."

"And where did you take him?"

"To the Black Bull."

Hopkiss was a brawny man in his fifties with the strength and stamina needed to carry heavy passengers in a sedan chair. He knew Jonathan Bale of old but was surprised to see him so far from his own parish of Baynard's Castle. Bale seemed to read his mind.

"A certain gentleman has taken an interest in this case," he explained, "and he sent me a note. I was asked to search for anyone who could put a name to the face of any of the killers."

"Lieutenant Stern – that's what he was called."

"Lieutenant?"

"A naval man."

"And a foreigner to boot, then?"

"A Swede."

"That will make him easier to find. Describe the fellow, Reuben."

"Gladly."

As the chairman gave a description of the man, Jonathan Bale memorised every detail. The constable was a big, solid, serious man in his late thirties with an ugly face that was puckered in concentration. He and Christopher Redmayne had been thrown together in an unlikely friendship, and they had solved a number of crimes together. When the request from Christopher came, Bale had responded at once. Other constables had combed the scene of the crime for witnesses. Bale was the only one to wander off into the side streets. His encounter with Reuben Hopkiss had been productive. He now had a clear description of one of the attackers. He also knew where the man lodged and in which tavern he preferred to drink.

Jonathan Bale walked swiftly off to the Black Bull, hoping to catch the Swede – if not his two confederates – at the place. He was out of luck. Stern was not there and neither were any friends of his. Bale therefore retraced his steps and made for the man's lodging. Once again, he was thwarted. The landlord told him that Stern had left early that morning and not been seen since. That worried the constable. He feared that the Swede might have quit London altogether after the crime.

The booming of a bell reminded him that he had been asked to meet Christopher Redmayne at two o'clock. Hastening to Tuthill Street, he found his friend waiting impatiently at the corner. After an exchange of greetings, Bale told him what had been gleaned so far. Christopher was impressed with his diligence.

"I've just come from my brother," he said, noting the look of disapproval in Bale's eye at the mention of his sibling. "Henry spoke to the steward at Mr Thynne's house. It appears that his master used to dine at the Golden Fleece at least four times a week. Those who lurked in ambush must have known that he would come that way sooner or later."

"Can you tell me *why* Mr Thynne was killed?" asked Bale.

"Henry believes that it may be linked to his support of the Duke of Monmouth's cause."

Bale frowned. "Yet another of the King's many bastard sons."

"The duke is claiming to be the legitimate heir to His Majesty, insisting that he has written proof that the King was legally married to his mother, Lucy Walter, at the time of his birth." Bale said nothing. Having fought against the Royalists at the Battle of Worcester, he remained an unrepentant Roundhead. "It provoked the Exclusion crisis," Christopher went on. "Monmouth is resolved to exclude the King's brother, James, Duke of York, from the succession because he is an ardent Roman Catholic."

"Then you believe this murder to be a Catholic conspiracy?"

"Henry does, certainly."

"What of you, Mr Redmayne?"

"I think that we should look to the lady."

"What lady?"

"Mr Thynne's wife," said Christopher. "No sooner did she marry him than she took to her heels and fled to Holland. Now, why should any wife do such a thing?"

Bale shook his head. "It's beyond my comprehension."

"I can't imagine your wife behaving so recklessly."

"Sarah would never let me down – nor I, her."

"Yours is a real marriage. Mr Thynne's, alas, was a sham. I think that it behoves us to find out why."

"How can we do that?"

"We begin with the Swedish gentleman, Lieutenant Stern."

"But we have no idea where he is, Mr Redmayne."

"Oh, I think I can hazard a guess," said Christopher. "Let's go to the Black Bull. He may not be there but I'll wager that someone will know where to find him. A few coins will soon loosen a tongue. If he is a hired killer, he'll have collected his payment by now."

"That was my reasoning," said Bale. "I thought that he would be spending his blood money with his accomplices."

"Perhaps he sought choicer company."

"What do you mean?"

Christopher smiled grimly. "Look to the lady," he repeated, "though this particular one may not merit that title."

Her name was Jenny Teale and she picked up most of her trade at the Black Bull. The majority of her clients were eager sailors who took their pleasure quickly in a dark alley before moving on. Lieutenant Stern was different. He bought her favours for a whole night. In this instance, he had come to her at midday and adjourned to her lodging. They had spent frantic hours in bed before falling asleep in a drunken stupor. Jenny Teale lay naked across his body. When someone pounded on her door, she did not even hear the noise at first. It was only when Christopher Redmayne's shoulder was put to the timber that she was hauled unceremoniously out of her slumber.

There was a loud crash, the lock burst apart and the door was flung wide open. Christopher stood framed in the doorway. Jumping off the bed, Jenny Teale confronted him.

"You'll have to wait your turn, young sir," she said, angrily.

"I'm here for Lieutenant Stern," declared Christopher, averting his gaze from her naked body. His eye fell on the rapier lying beside the bed and he snatched it up at once, using it to prod the sleeping foreigner. "Wake up!" he demanded. "You're coming with me."

The Swede let out a yelp of pain then swore volubly in his own language. Sitting up in bed, he saw Christopher standing over him and tried to retrieve his sword from the floor.

"I have your weapon, lieutenant," said Christopher, "and I daresay that I'll find your pistol in here somewhere as well. I'm arresting you for your part in the murder of Thomas Thynne."

"Ze devil you are!" roared Stern.

"Get dressed and come with me."

"No!"

Grabbing a pillow, Stern leapt out of bed and used it to beat back Christopher. The Swede then hurled the pillow in his face and, clad only in his shirt, opened the window and dropped to the ground below. Christopher had no need to pursue him. He had taken the precaution of stationing Jonathan Bale in the garden. When he glanced through the window, he saw that the constable had easily overpowered the suspect. Christopher gathered up the rest of the man's clothing together with the pistol that had been used in the shooting. He turned to leave but found that Jenny Teale was blocking his way.

Naked and unashamed, she gave him a bewitching smile.

"Do you have to leave so soon?" she asked.

"I fear so."

She spread her arms. "Don't you like what you see?"

"The only person I'm interested in is the man we just apprehended. He's a vicious killer," Christopher told her. "Try to choose your clients with more care in future."

Moving her politely aside, he went out of the room.

Henry Redmayne had repaired to a coffee-house near Temple Bar. He was deep in conversation with his friends when he saw his brother enter the room. Excusing himself from the table, he took Christopher aside.

"Really, sir!" he complained. "Must you always come between me and my pleasures?"

"Count yourself lucky that you are not Lieutenant Stern."

"Who?"

"One of the men who attacked Thomas Thynne," said Christopher. "I caught him in bed with his whore. He is now in safe custody. You might pass on that intelligence to His Majesty, and you can assure him that this crime did not arise from political intrigue."

"It must have done."

"No, Henry."

"The Duke of Monmouth has grown bold. The King exiled him yet he insists on returning to this country to press his absurd claims to the throne. Tom Thynne endorsed those claims to the hilt. He paid for his folly with his life."

"I think not."

Henry was petulant. "That's only because you are so ignorant about affairs of state. I move among the great and the good, and know how corrupt their greatness and goodness really is. What prompts them in the main," he said, airily, "is envy, malice and perverse ambition. There are hundreds of people who seek to pull Monmouth down. What better way to do it than by having his chief paymaster assassinated?"

"Lieutenant Stern has never heard of the Duke of Monmouth."

"Has he confessed who suborned him?"

"No," said Christopher. "He admits that he was one of the three men who shot at Mr Thynne but it's all he will tell us. That's why I must turn to you again."

"But I'm enjoying a coffee with my friends."

"Thomas Thynne was a friend of yours once."

"Yes," said Henry, blithely, "and I mourn his death."

"By carousing in here?"

"I gave you help. You can't ask any more of me than that."

"I can," returned Christopher. "Your aid is crucial. You can provide information that is way beyond the reach of Jonathan and myself. We must learn more about Mr Thynne's wife."

"Elizabeth, the former Lady Ogle? A pretty little thing."

"Why did she betray her marriage vows and flee the country? Had her husband been unkind to her? Was any violence involved?"

"Tom Thynne would not harm a fly."

"Then what made his wife desert him?"

"Covetousness," said Henry, knowledgeably. "The fault that mars all women. She left one man because another one must have offered her more than he could. Tom of Ten Thousand was outbid by someone with even more money and, most probably, with a title to dangle before her."

"We need his name."

Henry tried to move away. "I need my cup of coffee."

"No," said Christopher, restraining him. "It will have to wait, Henry. You are part of a murder hunt. Something is missing and only you can track it down."

"Am I to be allowed no leisure?"

"Not until this case is solved. We have one villain behind bars but two others remain at liberty. Additional people may yet be involved but the person who interests me most is the wife."

"Any man with red blood in his veins would be interested in *her*," said Henry with a lewd grin. "A most bed-worthy lady in every sense. Tom Thynne was by no means her only suitor."

"She must have preferred someone else."

"I told you – she covets wealth and position."

"Then give us the name of the man who offered it to her."

*   *   *

The second arrest was made early that evening. Bribed by Christopher Redmayne, the landlord of the Black Bull had not merely supplied the name and whereabouts of Lieutenant's Stern's favourite prostitute. He had told them that the Swede's closest friend was a Polish sailor called Borosky. Jonathan Bale went in search of him but not in the guise of a constable. He first returned to his house on Addle Hill to change into the clothing he had worn in his former life as a shipwright. Bale then worked his way through the various taverns frequented by sailors.

He was at ease in their company. Bale talked their language and shared their interest in a seafaring life. He met more than one man who had sailed with Stern and Borosky, but it was not until he called at the Blue Anchor, the fifth tavern on his list, that he actually came face to face with the Pole. Borosky was a sturdy man of middle height with a flat face and high cheekbones. He had clearly been drinking heavily and was off guard. Bale had no difficulty getting into conversation with him.

"Where do you sail next, my friend?" he asked.

"To the Baltic," replied Borosky.

"Under which captain?"

"Captain Vrats of the *Adventure*."

"I helped to build a ship of that name once," confided Bale. "She was a frigate of thirty-two guns with a crew of a hundred and twenty. But your *Adventure* is just a merchant ship, I daresay. What do you carry?"

Borosky talked freely about the vessel and mentioned that it would be sailing in a few days. Bale acted promptly. He enticed his new acquaintance out of the Blue Anchor with the promise of a meal at another tavern. As soon as they stepped into the fresh air, however, Bale arrested him. There was a brief scuffle but Borosky was too drunk to offer much resistance. He was marched off to join Lieutenant Stern in a dank cell.

Buoyed up by his success, Bale went immediately to Christopher Redmayne's house in Fetter Lane to tell him what had transpired. The architect was delighted to hear of the second arrest and, like Bale, guessed the name of the third suspect.

"Captain Vrats of the *Adventure*," he said.

"The Polander talked of him with affection."

"Did he say that the captain instigated the crime?"

"No," admitted Bale, shaking his head, "he swore that the man had nothing to do with it. He told me over and over again that Captain Vrats was innocent."

"What conclusion did you reach?"

"He was hiding something."

"I think we should pay Captain Vrats a visit."

"But he's aboard his ship in the Thames."

"So? You know how to row a boat, don't you?"

"Of course, Mr Redmayne."

"Then let's go out to the *Adventure*," said Christopher, reaching for his sword. "My instinct tells me that we're getting closer to solving this crime. We are entitled to congratulate ourselves – all three of us."

Bale was mystified. "All *three*?"

"Do not forget my brother."

"What has he done to help us?"

"Henry discovered that Mr Thynne was a regular visitor to the Golden Fleece in Westminster. All that the villains had to do was to lie in wait nearby, knowing that he would eventually turn up there."

"Reuben Hopkiss was far more use to us than that," contended Bale. "He guided us towards Lieutenant Stern. With respect to your brother, sir, he has not pointed us towards any of the suspects."

"But he has," said Christopher, holding up a letter.

"What's that?"

"A message from Henry. It arrived minutes before you did."

"What does the letter contain?"

"The one thing that I wanted above all else."

"And what was that, Mr Redmayne?"

"A name."

The *Adventure* was anchored in the middle of the river, its masts pointing up into the clear night sky like giant fingers. Two watchmen had been left aboard but they were too busy playing dice by the light of a lantern to see the boat that was being rowed out to them. A call from below alerted them to the fact that their ship had visitors.

"Ahoy, there!" yelled a voice.

"Who's below?" asked one of the men, leaning over the bulwark to peer at the boat. "Give me your name."

"Christopher Redmayne."

"What's your business?"

"I wish to see Captain Vrats," said Christopher. "I have news for him about a member of your crew – Lieutenant Stern."

"Has something happened to him?"

"He's been badly injured and cannot be moved. But he's calling for your captain. We promised him that we'd convey the message."

The watchman pondered. "You'd best come aboard," he said at length. "The captain is in his cabin."

Jonathan Bale secured the rowing boat then, in spite of his bulk, shinned up the rope ladder with consummate ease. Christopher found the ascent much more difficult and he was grateful that the ship was so stable. He clambered over the bulwark and stood on the deck. One of the watchmen held up a lantern so that he could study them carefully. Satisfied that they presented no danger, he led them to the captain's cabin and introduced them. The watchman returned to his post.

Two lanterns burned in the cabin, illumining a room that was small, cluttered and filled with curling tobacco smoke. Captain Vrats took one more puff on his pipe before setting it aside. He appraised the visitors shrewdly.

"What's this about Lieutenant Stern?" he asked.

"He was stabbed in a fight at the Black Bull," replied Christopher. "It seems that he was drinking with a young woman named Jenny Teale when another man tried to take her away from him. There was a brawl and the lieutenant came off worst."

"You don't look like the sort of man who'd deign to enter the Black Bull," said Vrats, suspiciously, looking at Christopher's fine apparel. "It's not for the likes of you, Mr Redmayne."

"Too true, captain," Bale put in, "but I drink there from time to time. And I saw the fight with my own eyes. I helped to carry the wounded man to Mr Redmayne's house nearby and he sent for a surgeon. There was not much that could be done, sir."

"Stern is dying?"

"He'll not live through the night."

"And he's calling for me?"

"He has something important to tell you," said Christopher. "He begged me to fetch you so I asked Mr Bale to row me out to your ship."

"I see."

Captain Vrats sat down behind a table that was littered with documents and maps. He watched them through narrowed lids. He was a handsome man with dark hair and a neatly trimmed beard. His command of English was good though he spoke with a strong German accent. He pretended to search for something on the table.

"Lieutenant Stern and I are old shipmates," he observed.

"That's what he told us," said Christopher.

"And he's no stranger to tavern brawls."

"He fought well," claimed Bale. "Then a knife was pulled on him. He was stabbed in the stomach. He's lost a lot of blood."

"You'll lose some of your own if you tell me any more lies," said Vrats, seizing a pistol from beneath a pile of papers. "I don't believe that Stern is injured at all. This story is just a device to get me ashore."

"Is there any reason why you shouldn't come with us?"

"I'm holding it in my hand."

Captain Vrats stood up and pointed the pistol at each of them in turn. Their ruse had failed. Bale bided his time, hoping for the opportunity to disable the man. Christopher took over.

"That weapon is a confession of guilt," he decided.

"I confess nothing."

"You ambushed Thomas Thynne with the aid of two others."

"I spent the whole day aboard," asserted Vrats, "and I have members of my crew who will vouch for me."

"Then they'll be committing perjury," said Christopher. "You are right about one thing. Lieutenant Stern was not injured in a brawl. He and Borosky have been arrested. They will hang for their crime and you will take your place on the gallows beside them."

Captain Vrats laughed. "Nobody will catch me."

"You can only kill one of us with that pistol," noted Bale. "Whoever survives will arrest you on the spot."

"What chance would one man have against three? As soon as they hear the sound of gunfire, the watchmen will come running."

"Then we must be ready for them," said Christopher.

He had been edging slowly towards the table and now made his move. Diving suddenly at the captain, he grabbed the barrel of the pistol and turned it upwards. The gun went off with a loud report. Bale reacted quickly. As Christopher grappled with the captain, Bale stepped forward to fell Vrats with a powerful punch to the ear. He then indicated that Christopher should stand behind the door. After blowing out both lanterns, Bale took up his position on the other side of the door. It was a matter of seconds before the two watchmen came hurrying down the steps to see what had happened. Bale knocked the first one senseless and Christopher held his dagger at the other's throat.

"Find some rope," ordered Christopher.

"No shortage of that aboard a ship," said Bale.

The constable left the cabin but came back with some rope almost immediately. He trussed up both of the watchmen then hauled Vrats off the floor. The captain was still dazed. Christopher lit one of the lanterns before holding it a few inches from the captain's face.

"Tell me where we can find him," he demanded.

"Who?" asked Vrats, clearly in pain.

"The man who set you on to kill Thomas Thynne."

"Nobody set me on."

"His name is Count Konigsmark."

Captain Vrats was astounded. "How ever did you find that out?"

"My brother, Henry, kindly provided the name," said Christopher, cheerfully. "He has a gift for smelling out scandal."

Gravesend was rimed with frost. The passengers who waited at the harbour that morning shivered in the cold. A rowing boat arrived to take them out to the ship. Before they could climb aboard, however, they heard the clatter of hooves and half-a-dozen horsemen came galloping out of the gloom towards them. Reining in his mount, Christopher Redmayne leapt from the saddle and surveyed the passengers. He was disappointed. The man he sought did not appear to be among them.

"Count Konigsmark?" he asked.

Nobody answered. Some of the passengers shrugged, others shook their heads. Christopher's gaze shifted to the man on the fringe of the group. Tall and lean, he had long, fair hair that spilled out beneath his hat to reach his waist. He was shabbily dressed but, when Christopher took a closer look at him, he saw how impeccably well-groomed he was. The man had poise and striking good looks. There was an aristocratic disdain in his eye. Christopher gave a signal and two of the riders dismounted to stand either side of the passenger.

"You must come with us, Count Konigsmark," said Christopher.

"But my name is Lindegren," argued the other, reaching into his pocket. "You may see my passport, if you wish. I am sailing back to Stockholm."

"No, you are fleeing the country to avoid arrest. The passport is a forgery. This, however," Christopher went on, producing a letter to wave in front of him, "is not. Do you recognize your own hand?"

"I told you. I am Oscar Lindegren."

"Then we will arrest you in that name, though we know full well that you are Count Konigsmark. Your countrymen will be shocked to learn that one of the leading figures in their kingdom is party to a brutal murder." He snapped his fingers. "Take him."

The two officers grabbed hold of the man. He was outraged.

"Is this the way you treat innocent people in England?" he protested. "You have made a terrible mistake."

"It was you who made the mistake," said Christopher, indicating the letter. "You should not have sent word to Captain Vrats that you were leaving Gravesend on a Swedish ship this morning. We found this in his cabin when we arrested him. I've ridden through the night to catch up with you, Count Konigsmark."

"I committed no crime."

"You paid others to do it for you and that is just as bad. And if you are as innocent as you pretend, why are you sneaking away in disguise with a false passport?"

Konigsmark was trapped. He was hopelessly outnumbered and was, in any case, unarmed. There was no point in further denial.

"Tell these men to unhand me," he said, peremptorily, "I demand the right to be treated with respect."

"You did not treat Thomas Thynne with respect."

"Mr Thynne was a fool."

"Yet it was he whom Lady Ogle married and not you." Christopher saw the flash of anger in the other man's eyes. "I know that you courted her as well for a time. Was that why you had Mr Thynne ambushed in Westminster? Were you racked with envy?"

"I would never envy such a man. He was beneath contempt."

"From what I hear, he did not have too high a regard for you either." Konigsmark scowled. "Is that what provoked your ire? Were you upset by slighting remarks that Mr Thynne made about you?"

"He should have remembered who I am," growled the other.

"Save your breath for the trial," advised Christopher, slipping the letter back into his pocket. "Captain Vrats is languishing in prison with two other villains. You will soon join them."

The officers tried to move him away. Konigsmark held his ground.

"I am a member of the Swedish aristocracy," he said with dignity, "and I insist on the privileges due to my rank."

"Of course," said Christopher with a deferential smile. "I'll make absolutely sure that you are hanged first."

In fact, Count Konigsmark did not hang at all. Captain Vrats, Lieutenant Stern and Borosky were found guilty of murder and were hanged in the street where the crime occurred. At the Old Bailey trial, Konigsmark was charged with being an accessory but he was acquitted. Captain Vrats went to his death with remarkable equanimity. His body was then embalmed by a new method devised by William Russell, an undertaker. When he was shipped back to Germany fifteen days after execution, the body of Captain Vrats was in an exceptional state of preservation.

A CASE OF ASYLUM

Michael Jecks

It had cost him a fortune, that passport. Not because it was illegal, but because his need was so obvious. Someone in his position couldn't afford to stay, not even when his wife and daughter remained. When the authorities were after you there was only limited time to escape; and the desperate have to pay.

He'd known he'd have to bolt when he realized he was being watched.

The farm had long been the centre of attention, and the dogs had patrolled his fences enthusiastically all through the hotter weather, their ridged backs terrifying his workers when they materialized from the bushes, heads lowered in truculent demonstration, brows wrinkled and glowering. Alan had loved those two, the dog and the bitch. When he found their corpses out by the boundary fence, even as he wept over them, he was reviewing his options. The two were proof that an attack would come soon.

The government didn't want his family. Others might – it was possible that they could be held and ransomed – but even here women and children tended to be safe. No, it was him they'd try to "arrest"; *him* whom they would shoot and leave in a dirt track far from anyone. Not the dignity of a grave for someone who worked against this government.

He'd escape and go to England. Where people were free.

*　　*　　*

Paul Jeffries yawned and glanced across the Arrivals hall to Jeannie.

She was wearing her "invisible" clothes today: grey trouser suit; a small briefcase of ballistic material holding her laptop hanging from her shoulder; dark hair bobbed in a vaguely professional cut; her face partly concealed behind small, rectangular glasses. But it couldn't hide her delicate bone structure. Like Michelle Pfeiffer, Paul reckoned. Really good looking, but with a sort of healthiness about her. Pfeiffer was almost unwell looking, with those big pale eyes and all. Jeannie was plain gorgeous once you noticed her – not that many did. She just blended into the background, the best of their intake.

He lifted a finger to his right eye and scratched at the eyebrow three times – "I need a pee" – saw her acknowledge tersely, and moved away from Arrivals to the toilets.

She was often short with him. Probably she'd guessed he was crap. She'd been with him almost from day one, and perhaps because she was so much older and more confident in herself, she resented his laziness and stupidity. That was his impression, anyway. Meanwhile, all he wanted to do was rip her clothes off and get sweaty with her.

It could just be the shift. Most hated this – first thing in the morning, keeping an eye on tourists, holidaymakers, businessmen, and Christ knew who else, but Paul liked it. He'd always wanted to make use of his degree, and although this wasn't the way he'd anticipated things panning out, with his good second in Anthropology and Psychology, he was happy enough. Standing about here, simply watching the folks walking back into the country was itself an education.

Sometimes the best part was watching the others who worked here. Especially cops. Jesus, he'd almost jumped a crew last month. He'd seen them shoving packets into pockets before walking to customs, and it was only when the first in the line had held up his warrant card at the gate that he'd realized they'd come over from Holland. There were enough who'd go there for a smoke, and these had brought back a small stash. Bleeding idiots, if you asked Paul. He'd never smoked, and didn't see why others should.

Jeannie smoked sometimes. It had been useful, when she'd been watching someone who was a smoker. There was a sort of fraternity among the morons. They'd stand and exchange side-long, self-effacing grins; rapport established without words. She'd been able to get closer to them by bringing out her own pack and apologetically nodding towards their lighter. Fluent in Arabic and Swahili, she'd been able to stand nearby and listen without their having the faintest idea. Not that many would look twice at her anyway. No one thought that a coloured woman would work for a disgraced government like this British one.

Yeah, she was a diamond among the watchers.

He washed his hands, fastidious to the last, left the toilets and strolled over to the concessions. Buying good filter coffee, he moved over to the farther side of the hall, from where he still had an unimpeded view of Jeannie.

"Hi, Pete! How's it hanging?"

"Dave. Nothing so far today."

David was the massively ineffectual section head of the team. More proof of the rash of urgent recruiting and promotions in recent years, and the perfect example of the *Peter Principle* – once a moderately competent operative, as manager of the team he had reached his own level of incompetence. Soon it would be noticed, and another effective watcher would be removed from the field. Daft.

After 9/11, the British government had reversed decades of under-investment in immigration and customs controls, and started making changes. The disaster of 7/7 in London added urgency to the new policy. Where politicians had floundered ineffectually, the big guns of business took their opportunity.

Weapons and surveillance companies had suffered with the peace dividend after the cold war, and turned their best sales teams onto the police and politicians. Police commanders keen to exercise more authority demanded better guns, more cameras, identity cards, new laws to ban everything from airguns to congregations larger than two people with a child; and a callow, incompetent government swallowed every worst-case scenario presented to them. The power to arrest and hold men and women, uncharged, returned for the first time in four hundred years.

With these came the need for accurate surveillance on the ground.

The Watchers had been all but disbanded under previous administrations, but suddenly they were needed. Once-redundant officers were offered new packages, tempted with golden hellos, but few wanted to return. Burned once, they were less eager to return. So Human Resources had to seek new blood, returning to the usual fertile grounds: the universities. Not only Oxbridge, either. The new government couldn't swallow that sort of injustice. The new world order demanded equality in controlling the public.

Yes, the services were taking on people from the smaller universities. The main thing was, bodies on the streets and at ports. Which was how Paul had slipped in, really. And how David had been put in charge of his own team when he was scarcely able to use a phone, let alone the radios.

"We have a new one," Dave was saying.

Paul took the file with surprise. It was not usual for his leader to present him with a file so conspicuously. Just as Paul was not allowed to have his earpiece plugged in, because the little clear plastic coil gave away his profession, all briefings were supposed to be given in the room out at the back, behind the Special Branch area. He glanced at it, and felt a little worm of anxiety moving in his belly. "What is it?"

"FARC. Watch the BA flight from Bogotà. Twenty minutes."

Andy Campbell was in the armoury already. His vest was itching, the heavy weight of the ceramic plates pulling at his shoulders as he pulled out the magazine from his H&K submachinegun, then drew back the cocking lever to empty the breech. The cartridge flew out, and he caught it with a practised snatch of his hand. He racked the breech a couple of times, from habit, pulled the trigger to ease the springs, and put the gun down on the table.

He wouldn't be here many more times. He'd been a specialist shooter here at the airport for some months, but he couldn't carry on. Not once he'd admitted what had happened.

It was last night. He'd knocked off bloody late after doing a favour and working a shift at Heathrow because they'd had a minor flu epidemic. Jack, his partner, and he'd taken overtime and given them a hand, but he'd known he had to be up at four to get to Gatwick airport for the first shift. He'd been dog tired, though. Knackered. So when he got home, he'd started undressing in his hallway, before going up to bed. He had three hours to kip before the alarm was going to go off, and the last thing he wanted was a row with the missus about his hours again. So he'd left his clothes downstairs, his handgun on the belt. The sub-machinegun he took upstairs, of course. But the Glock stayed there in the hall.

He knew he shouldn't have brought it home, but shit, when the hours were this daft, what the fuck were you supposed to do? If he'd driven to the airport armoury last night to dump his guns before going home, he'd have had no time to sleep. All the lads took risks sometimes – it was the old rule: don't get found out.

Well, he would be found out this time. Some fucker had broken into his house, gone through the stuff in the hall, and his Glock had been nicked. Bloody gone, just like that. Today he'd been able to get away without it, saying he'd left it behind, and he had the H&K, so there was little enough to be said, but when he got home tonight, he'd have to have a good hunt, just in case. Maybe it had fallen down behind the umbrellas, or got kicked along the hall . . . Andy just prayed – Jesus, please don't let it be – yes, that either the thing hadn't been taken by some crook who was going to use it to hold up a bank or something, or that it hadn't been thrown away in the road outside his house.

He'd looked, of course, he'd looked everywhere, and just now all he could feel was a cold sweat breaking out at the mere thought that he'd be discovered at any moment. He had to get back home and make sure that the thing wasn't just lying there.

God, but any moment he could be called to be asked what the fuck his gun was doing in the hands of some drugged up shite who'd been holding a hostage or . . .

"Andy? Stop that. We've got a shout on. Some wanker with bombs or something. Get tooled up again."

He had to stop thinking of his real name. Now he was Ramón, not Jean-Jacques. Ramón Escobar. The lightness in his belly was unbearable as he peered down through the window at Britain.

It was surprisingly green. He wasn't used to that. In Bogotà the city lay almost dead on the equator, although at that height it was hard to believe sometimes. The weather was not too hot. Not like Africa. The temperature in Colombia remained constant, and there was little in the way of seasonal variation. No summer and winter, just a slight change, a little cooler or a little warmer.

Like this, it was very green. You took off from Bogotà airport, and all you could see for miles around was greenhouses. The hothouses spread all over the plain, and even when the plane lifted and the ground fell away from that high plateau up in the mountains, the glass reflected the light all about the area. They said that Colombia's biggest legal export was cut flowers to America, and . . . *Ramón* could believe it. Easily.

Here, though, the plane was slowly descending through wisps of pale cloud, and beneath the greenness was . . . darker. Not so rich and blooming as the plant life of Bogotà. It looked harsher, as though the trees and shrubs were struggling more to survive, and it was easy to see why as the aircraft drew nearer to the ground. Here the greyness of concrete and tarmac was all about, but without the bright colours of jacaranda and bougainvillea to ease the sight. No, here, all was unrelenting, grey, miserable, and he felt the tears welling again to think that this place was his refuge.

His sanctuary in his exile. His new motherland.

The system was well worked out, and they swung into action as soon as the papers had been digested.

Paul walked casually away from the main hall as soon as he had checked the details in the print out and glanced up at the arrivals display. The plane was close, but not here yet. He had time.

Jeannie had seen the discussion, and now was play-acting as only she could. She looked up at the boards, and frowned at her watch, looking about her with a discontented expression, before wandering off in the direction of the women's toilets. Paul made his own way through a security barrier with a palmed card shown discreetly to the man at the gate, and into the Special Branch section. She was waiting for him.

"What's going on?"

He passed her the papers. "Terrorist, they reckon. Bloke from Colombia. He's used this ID before – it was noted when the IRA three were over there. It's fake. Why the hell he didn't get something new before taking off . . ."

"Perhaps no time?" She frowned as she absorbed the description of the man.

"He was with FARC, the terrorists who control the country out towards Venezuela," Paul said. He shivered. This was the kind of incident he had feared. "They were trained by the IRA in new bombs and mortars. This Escobar was a cousin of one of the cartel leaders from Medellin, and he escaped the crack down when his cousin was killed. He made it to Panama originally, then turned up back in Colombia with FARC. Now he's coming here."

"Why?"

"Jesus! I don't know, all right?" he snapped. "All we have to do is find him and watch, just like we always do. And when we see him, we go live on radio in case we have to call in the shooters."

Jeannie nodded, and he saw a small smile of satisfaction on her face – she liked to needle him. There was a reasonably fresh brew of coffee in the jug. She poured, added a good slug of milk, and sipped it easily, walking from the room out to the main hall again, leaving him alone with his fears.

He should have been honest about his education, but when he was interviewed, he assumed that they'd never want him for active duties. He'd said he was good with languages, because that was what his mate said they wanted, but it never occurred to him that he'd be needed. God – the nearest he'd got to languages was a smattering of Bantu and Ndebelele when he took a gap year to study anthropology in Botswana.

Anyway, when he wrote out his CV, no one had seemed remotely interested. There'd been no time for checks. Perhaps someone would spot his lying later, when they went back through the CVs they'd collected in the last years since 9/11. Probably not, though. Human Resources had been reduced as they increased the Watchers – if you spend in one area you have to cut a budget elsewhere – and now there weren't the HR people to check all the new staff, let alone trawl through existing ones.

At his interview they were more keen on his post as a prefect at school. Responsible character, they'd said. No one had guessed he'd lied about that as well.

His eyes were drawn back to the sheet of paper, to the words that were highlighted: *Paul Jeffries to keep close. Spanish essential.*

Shit!

The H&K was soon made ready again. The mag slammed into the gun and smacked with the palm of his hand to seat it. He pulled the cocking lever back and let it drive forward, stripping the first round from the magazine and leaving the gun cocked and ready. He switched on the safety, keeping his finger well away from the trigger. In the last few years more police officers had been wounded because of negligent discharges than by criminals. He had enough on his plate without that, sod it.

Jack was waiting at the door. "Shit of a day to leave the Glock behind, eh?"

"Fuck it!" Andy hissed. They both walked out together, their guns across their chests, fingers clear, and they turned their radios on as they entered the thronging main hall.

The man who called himself Ramón knew a fair amount about Bogotà, but only from reading. Not many people went to the city unless they had to. The bombs, the bullets, the murdering, the kidnapping and ransoming all dissuaded tourists, not only foreign ones. Locals were as unlikely to travel there. Anyone could be stopped and kidnapped, and a man like him, with a price on his head, would be best served keeping off the roads. Travel was very dangerous. Just like home. Except here the terrorists and guerillas were better armed than the police, whereas back home only the police and army had guns. And the President's friends.

Bogotà was beautiful. Ringed by the high, dark peaks, the place had an atmosphere all of its own. He had thought that, sitting in the *Parc de Periodistas*, waiting for the man to arrive with the new passport. There was a smell of thick smog in the air, and he could see the coal smoke rising from several chimneys in the tower blocks nearby. A sulphurous odour that caught in his throat, and yet the buildings were typical Spanish colonial in so many areas of the city, especially the older parts where the emeralds were sold for so little. Spanish, American, there were so many influences. It was a lovely country.

His contact was a scrawny man, with a sallow, pock-marked complexion and a thatch of filthy brown hair. He spoke English only haltingly, and that suited Ramón. Neither wanted to know much about the other, and Ramón had been assured he was safe. He'd paid well for the advice.

Their business was soon completed, an envelope with much of Ramón's remaining cash, all in US dollars, was passed over, and in exchange a fake passport, driving licence, and some local identification cards. With these Ramón was safe. With these he could fly from the country and not be turned away at British immigration. It was too easy for asylum-seekers to be refused now, unless they had applied before leaving their homes, but he couldn't apply back home, and no one would help in Colombia. They had other things to worry about: terrorists and drug-dealers.

The jerk of the wheels hitting tarmac brought him back to the present. In his bag in the hold there was the explosive material, and soon he would be in a position to light the touch-paper, he told himself.

Paul's first warning was the nod from immigration. There was no need for a buzzer or pager to call when a watcher was present. Only if there was an immediate danger did they "hit the tit" for the armed fuzz. Otherwise everything had to be managed silently, with a minimum of fuss to alert the bad guys that they were being followed.

At the carousel Paul stood back, watching his mark. Not tall, but well muscled, and a face that spoke of a warmer climate than Britain in November. Yes, he was the one, all right. There were plenty of Spaniard types on the place, but this one definitely fitted the photo and profile best. Jeannie was down in the carousel hall, and they had a dummy bag for her to collect. She stood near the mark, and grabbed her bag as it came round.

Paul took a deep breath, shivering with expectation. Then he walked out through the customs tunnel, walking through the red channel and waiting with his own small luggage bag in case the target came this way. Jeannie would wait until he had left, then go through green no matter what.

The customs officer was a slim blonde girl, and she waited with Paul patiently until he had the signal from another officer. Then Paul hurried through the channel and out into the main hall.

Jack and Andy were waiting idly when the call came through. "He's in the main hall now. Following him out."

Andy beckoned with his head and wandered over to the main arrivals corridor. There was a family, then a couple of teens with backpacks, long fair hair straggling. A gap, a long gap. Andy felt his palms begin to sweat. He took his pistol hand away from the H&K and wiped it down his trousers, willing himself to look a little away from the corridor, but unable to obey. The bright fluorescent glow of the arrival tunnel transfixed him. He saw the tall figure appear.

Ramòn. Ramòn. Not Jean-Jacques Bressonard. He had to remember his new name until he could get his package delivered, but the officials on all sides petrified him. There was a young brunette watching him, and he forced himself to blink slowly, smiling through his exhaustion, looking away innocently and striding on determinedly, through the wide corridor, turning right at the end, passing through the crowds. He was safe.

There were two policemen in armour ahead of him, and he hardly glanced at them. He was thinking about his ancestors. They had fled from the terror in France, first arriving here in England, then making the long and dangerous journey to Africa. There they had thrived until the independence, until the new regime.

Over the centuries, England had remained their homeland. They owed their existence to the British who welcomed his Huguenot forebears. His grandfather volunteered and died in the trenches of the first war, his father nearly died in the Battle of Britain as a Hurricane pilot. Yes, Ramón was coming home.

In his own land he had ceased to exist. When his ID card was confiscated, he became a non-person. A man with no ID was nothing. He had no rights.

He smiled and nodded to the police, but then a chill entered his blood as he took in their faces: dead; cold, inhuman. Just like at home.

Walking more swiftly, he went right, avoiding them. Ahead of him was a beautiful woman, just like his lovely Miranda, and he felt a pang in his breast at the thought. He missed his family so much . . . but hopefully he could have them rescued too. They could come here to this cold, grey country.

For a moment he thought he could hear Miranda calling to him: "Good morning!" just one instant before he saw the gun, realized it was flashing, felt the slugs hit his breast, and collapsed slowly, sinking to his knees even as the police emptied their H&Ks into him.

"Fuck, fuck, fuck!"

Andy shivered, his finger still tight on the trigger as he stood over the body.

"Cease firing! Cease firing! Cease firing!"

The terrorist was down, bullet wounds weeping all over his torso. An eye was punctured, and wept jelly, and Andy could only stare, too shocked even to feel sick yet. That would come later.

"Andy. ANDY! Get a fucking grip. Secure the place! Come on!"

"Why'd he do that? Why'd he fire?"

Paul had been hit twice that he knew of. He had been behind the target when he saw the man's body jerk and collapse, saw the bullets strike from the police guns, saw the body suddenly lifeless like a dummy, arms flailing as he was thrown to the side.

"No need for Spanish after all!" he said, almost giggling with reaction.

At his side a young girl was weeping, sprawled, a bloody mess on her back to show the exit wound. Near her a man was still and silent, an elderly woman was slumped by the wall, staring with surprise at a bloody hole in her belly, while her husband stood beside her with an expression of spaniel-like hurt and confusion. Paul gazed about him at them all, and tried to stand, but couldn't. All he could do was sit and watch as the police bellowed at the people in the area to get clear. Dazed, he looked up at the policeman with the sub-machinegun when he approached, and began to wonder what he might do. He'd just seen the man empty his magazine into a crowd.

"There's an ambulance on its way," Jack said. He stood behind Andy. "You all right?"

"I'm hit."

"I can see that."

Paul shook his head, tasted bile. "Why did she say that? Why did she call to him and shoot him?"

Jack sighed and walked off. Andy frowned. "Who did?"

"Jeannie," Paul said. He choked a little on the phlegm that had materialised in his throat. "My partner. Where is she?"

It was late when Andy returned to the gun room. He sat on the bench, exhausted. Jack walked in a few minutes later to unload his weapon.

"You all right?"

"I'm fine."

"Unload, then. Come on, Andy! Unload."

Andy stood and fumbled with the cocking lever, but there was nothing to do. His magazine was empty. Instead he pulled the mag free and stared at it dumbly.

Jack eyed him, then unloaded his own weapon. It was unfired. He set it in the safe, and as he did so, his foot kicked something under the bench. "Shit, Andy – is that your gun? You didn't lock it in the safe, you prick!"

Andy jerked awake from his nightmare and gazed at Jack dumbly. Seeing the direction of his pointing finger, he reached down and took up the Glock in its holster. He hefted it in his hand, pulled it free. It had been fired. He could smell the powder in the barrel. And when he looked closer, the serial number on the side was one he knew all too well.

His hand began to tremble.

Paul took the advice from the ambulance driver, still shivering slightly as the needle went in and he watched the clear liquid pushed into his arm. The wounds were small: one bullet had winged his shoulder, which was already as sore as hell, and a second had caught his rib, running around the outside of it, and ending up in his back after running around underneath his skin. The medic had offered to cut it loose, but he refused the offer.

"You'll need it taken out soon," the medic said. He didn't bother to add that Paul would have to have the entire bullet's track opened and cleaned to remove all the bits of material and burned powder, or risk septicaemia.

"Davie? Where is she?"

"Who? Jeannie? I told her to go home. She was in shock."

Paul shivered. Davie looked at him sympathetically. "Look, Paul, you need to rest, mate. Get on home."

"She murdered the guy."

"What?"

"She had a handgun. I saw her. She shouted something and opened fire. The cops started shooting as soon as she started. She started it, though. I saw her."

"What did she shout? Spanish?"

"*Lotjhani* – in Ndebele it means 'Hello'."

"Are you sure?"

The files in the bags were exhaustive. Details of murders, of officially sanctioned brutality. Paul shivered as he took in pictures of bodies in streets, strewn in fields, punctured with gunshots, or slashed with pangas, and he felt the sickness in his belly.

"Who is he?" Dave muttered.

"An asylum seeker. We killed an asylum seeker from Zimbabwe," Paul spat. The pain was washing through him now as he stared at the sheet of paper, and he could feel a cold sweat run over his spine. Nausea roiled in his belly. "And Jeannie murdered him."

Perhaps, he wondered, the HR team hadn't only cocked up with *his* application?

The woman he had known as Jeannie climbed out of the car with the diplomatic plates, and walked in through the guarded doors into the High Commission as the car purred round to the parking space. The lift took her up, and soon she was seated, waiting for the debriefing, running the events through her mind once more.

It had been perfect. The theft of the policeman's firearm was a calculated risk, but when she had seen the changed rotas, it seemed a good bet. All the police took their guns home occasionally, even though it was officially disapproved of, and when a man had to travel far to his next shift, it made sense for him to keep his gun nearby. And the gamble paid off.

She had waited for the man this morning, and he had passed her the Glock at the airport entrance. The theft had gone without a hitch. The fool was too exhausted to hear the two as they rifled his clothing and bags. After that all she had to do was wait until she saw Bressonard while the policeman was present. Shoot, and run. They'd said that the police expected a terrorist, so they'd shoot as soon as they heard shots, and they'd been right. They always saw what they expected, or what they feared. No one would suspect her, a "spook".

So the enemy of the country was dead. He had been led carefully down a route preplanned for him. A contact with FARC had agreed to provide obvious ID for him, and then they had known which aircraft he would take to Britain, and now he was dead. Well, now the world would see what a safe country Britain was for asylum seekers. Like the Brazilian, a white farmer had been removed, and the police were guilty of his homicide. Either the machine gun or the pistol had killed him, and both were one officer's weapons.

The woman who had been called Jeannie removed her ID and placed it carefully before her on a glass-topped table. She wouldn't need these again. No. She was looking forward to returning to her own name. Her real one.

And returning to the glorious Zimbabwe sun, of course. Perhaps she could buy a small farm. Maybe even take Bressonard's?

Life was good.

THE DEATH OF JEFFERS

Kevin Wignall

Heg the Peg was the end of it. Marty had known from the start which creek he was up; this was just the confirmation on the whereabouts of the paddle. If it had won, he'd have been in the clear, or as near as made any difference.

True to its name though, the first race had finished five minutes ago and Heg the Peg was still running. So much for Bob and his cast-iron tips, straight from the stable, the whole crowd of them laying money on it like it was the only horse in the race. If there was any cast-iron, it was in Heg the Peg's saddle.

So now Marty had two choices. First was finding some other way of raising two thousand euros by the end of the month – and frankly, that was looking about as likely as the stewards disqualifying every other horse in the last race. Second was borrowing the money off Hennessey and paying back the interest for the rest of his life.

Three choices – he could tell McKeon to sing for the money, leave Dublin, leave Ireland, and find a monastery in Bhutan that was recruiting. Four choices – his next fare could be some crazy American on his first trip to Dublin, wanting to hire him for the whole week, money no object. You never knew with the airport.

The door opened and Marty turned off the radio.

"Wynn's Hotel, please." English, in a suit, overnight bag; no big tip here. The fare leaned over and handed him a piece of paper with an address on it. "Could you stop here on the way? I'll give you a good tip."

Marty glanced at the address. It wasn't far out of the way.

"No problem. First time in Dublin?"

"Yes, it is."

Marty pulled away. He could probably take the guy around the houses and he wouldn't be any the wiser. He found himself taking the direct route though; that was why he ended up in positions like this in the first place, because he was too honest for his own good.

He looked in the rear-view. The fare looked like a civil servant, or someone who worked in life insurance, nondescript, late thirties, the kind of guy who was born to make up the numbers and get lost in the crowd. But he'd still offer him the same old patter.

"I suppose you'll be wanting to sample some of the good stuff while you're here?"

"Sorry?"

"Guinness."

"Oh." The fare smiled like it was something he wasn't used to. "Actually, I don't drink. Very rarely, anyway."

Marty nodded and said, "So what brings you here, then?"

"Business." He smiled again, but he wasn't getting any better at it. "But I've been wanting to come to Ireland for a long time. I'm of Irish stock."

Jesus, who wasn't? The day he picked up a fare at that airport who *didn't* claim to have Irish blood, that was the day he'd win the lottery. Still, he put on his best "that's amazing" smile and said, "Really? What's your name?"

"Jeffers. Patrick Jeffers."

Well, sure, anyone could call their kid Patrick, but he wasn't so sure about the Jeffers bit. Didn't sound particularly Irish to him.

"Don't know any Jeffers. Must be a name from out West."

"I think it is." End of conversation.

Jeffers kept him waiting no more than two minutes. He went into the house empty-handed and came out with a briefcase. Now that was suspicious – no other way of looking at it, particularly some guy who'd never been to Dublin having business in a regular suburban street.

By the time he got him to the Wynn's, though, there was no doubt it was his first time here – he'd been looking out of the window like a tourist for the last ten minutes.

"That'll be twenty-two euros."

"Keep the change," said Jeffers, handing him thirty.

"That's kind of you, Mr Jeffers. Enjoy your stay in Dublin."

One thousand, nine hundred and ninety-two to go.

Bryan was a charmer, all right, and there was no doubt about what he thought he'd be getting when they went out later. First day on the job, all the girls had told Kate not to fall for any of his talk, and here she was, second day behind the reception desk, going out with him tonight.

She was smiling at him now as he leaned across the desk. And he thought she was smiling at the silver words coming from his mouth, but it was how much he looked like Danny that was really tickling her. If it weren't for Bryan's blue eyes, the two of them could meet and think they were long-lost brothers.

Of course, Bryan would be the good brother. They all thought she was some naïve young slip of a thing, but twenty-four hours had been enough to tell her that Bryan was decent to the core. He was one for the girls, sure, but a good family lad at heart, working his way through college, a bright future ahead of him.

Danny, on the other hand, he was sexy and dangerous and the biggest mistake she'd made in her eighteen years. He'd come to a nasty end sooner or later and probably take a good few with him. The important thing was knowing that Danny wouldn't stick around, and that she wouldn't want him to.

Suddenly, Bryan pushed himself up and stepped away, making himself busy, and she saw one of the guests heading toward the desk, a businessman, boring-looking. She put on her best smile.

"Yes, sir, what can I do for you?"

"I checked in a short while ago?"

He sounded like he was asking a question, and she felt like telling him straight, Mister, if you don't remember, I'm sure as hell, I don't. He certainly didn't look familiar.

"That's right. Is your room satisfactory, Mr . . .?"

"Jeffers."

"Mr Jeffries, that's it."

"It's fine. But it's Mr Jeffers. Actually, it's an Irish name."

"It is so. From up north, I think, Donegal, that way."

"Yes, I think you're right." He smiled, wonky somehow, like he'd had botox and was still getting used to his face again. "How do I get to Trinity College?"

"Ah, you have to work really hard at school." His smile stayed fixed – no sense of humour. "Just a little joke there. It's just around the corner. Bryan here will point the way."

Bryan had been straightening leaflets but snapped to attention now and ushered the Englishman out onto the street. He was cute, Bryan, a tight little backside on him, and he was going to get exactly what he wanted tonight, and the dates would be close enough that he'd never think to question whether the kid was his. How could he? In all probability, it was even going to look like him.

Jeffers had listened attentively as Bryan gave him directions for the short walk across to Trinity, but he seemed in no mood to move anywhere once he'd finished. So Bryan stood in silence with him, the two of them surveying the street like they were looking out over their ranch at sunset.

Then, absentmindedly, Jeffers said, "Have *you* heard of the name? Jeffers?"

"I haven't. Sorry." Jeffers nodded but still looked straight ahead, feet planted firmly, and so Bryan tried to fill the pause by saying, "I'm a student at Trinity myself. History."

Jeffers turned and looked at him as if he'd revealed something vital. He stared at him for a few seconds, a look intense enough to be unnerving, and Bryan couldn't help but see that Jeffers looked troubled. Finally, he said, "Let me tell you something, don't ever fall into the trap of believing you don't have choices. You always have a choice, in everything."

He seemed to consider that for a moment, then nodded to himself and handed Bryan five euros before walking off along the street with Bryan's thanks lost in the noise behind him. Bryan stood there looking at the five euros, wondering what might have induced such a bizarre fit of profundity.

He was close to laughing it off as he walked back into the hotel, ready to get another smile out of Kate by telling her, and then for some reason, it made him think of Lucy and it was no longer funny. You always have a choice, in everything. Lucy – if ever a girl could have turned him into a poet.

It was strange, though – two minutes with an English businessman who didn't know how to smile, and suddenly he felt that if he didn't get in touch with Lucy right now, see her this very evening, he'd regret it for the rest of his life. What was that all about?

Kate was smiling at him as he walked toward the desk. She was a pretty girl, and Danny had said she was easy, but he wasn't sure he wanted it any more – not with her, not with any of these other girls.

"I've just got to make a call." She smiled back at him, coquettishly, he thought, but girl, it wouldn't be tonight.

"Mr Parker, you do not have to write essays on Joyce, and when we're discussing him, I will not mark you down for opting out of the conversation, but if you insist on writing essays and speaking your mind, please be so kind as to read something other than *Dubliners*."

The others laughed but Parker was smiling, too. She only teased him because she knew he could take it and because he was probably smarter than all the rest put together.

"You know, Dr Burns, I have skim-read *Ulysses*."

"Would that be the jogging tour of Dublin, Mr Parker?" That earned another laugh, but the hour was upon them and they were already putting their things together. Parker was first out the door. Clare was the last, waiting till everyone had left before shyly handing in an essay.

She started to read through it once she was on her own again, but was only a page or two in – impressive, if lacking a little in flair – when there was a knock at the door and it opened a fraction.

"Come in."

The man who stepped into the room was about thirty-five, six foot, the average kind of build that couldn't easily be read under a suit. Facially, he looked innocuous, which immediately put her on her guard.

"Dr Elizabeth Burns?" She nodded, smiling, and he closed the door behind him.

"Call me Liz, Mr . . .?"

She'd gestured at the seat across from her desk and as he sat down and placed his briefcase in front of him, he said, "Patrick Jeffers. The office sent me."

The office. It was about twenty years since she'd heard anyone call it that.

"And what office would that be?"

He didn't answer, just smiled awkwardly and relaxed into his seat.

He seemed to relax then, confident and in control as he said, "I've got a lot of admiration for people like you." She offered him a quizzical expression. No one had ever contacted her like this so, whoever he was, she wanted to draw him out a little more. "People in 14. And no, I don't expect you to admit it but, being buried deep the way you were for, what was it, four years, that really takes something."

Her expression unnerved him a little, and with no wonder, for she was wearing a look of utter astonishment. "Mr Jeffers, I have absolutely no idea what you're talking about. People in fourteen, what?"

He nodded knowingly, uncomfortable, as if he'd spoken out of turn and made himself look unprofessional, which he had. At the same time, she was unnerved herself, wondering what this Jeffers was doing here, wondering why she'd had no word that he was coming. He knew she'd been in 14, so somebody must have sent him.

"You don't sound Irish." He tilted his head questioningly. "Jeffers is an Irish name, but you don't sound Irish. Irish grandparents, perhaps?"

"Yes, I think so." He hesitated before saying, "So you've heard of the name? I think you're the first person since I arrived who recognizes it."

"There's actually a folk song, somewhere down in the Southwest, though the exact location escapes me at the moment, about the death of a Jeffers."

"Oh, I didn't know that."

"Of course, there's also the American poet, Robinson Jeffers."

"Yes." She could tell he didn't like being sidetracked. He was here on business and wanted to get on with it.

"What do you want here, Mr Jeffers? Why has your office sent you?"

"Yes, I'm really just here to deliver a message." He bent down and picked up his briefcase, but started to cover himself, saying, "Just some paperwork you need to read and sign."

Amateur! He was opening the briefcase on his lap and she had absolutely no doubt what kind of message he was about to produce from it. There were all kinds of thoughts running through her head, questions of whether she'd been double-crossed, and if so, by whom, questions of who he was working for and whether she'd have to move on, but there was something more immediate, an instinctive reflex that would never leave her.

She picked the phone up off the desk and threw it hard. It cracked him on the head with a clatter, and then a further clatter as the briefcase and the gun inside it fell onto the floor. He was dazed for only a second, but she was around the desk before he came up for air and she was pulling the telephone cord tight around his neck.

"Who sent you?"

His arms flailed, trying to strike her a body blow but unable to find her where she stood directly behind him.

"Who sent you?"

He tried another approach, trying to pull her own hands off, then trying to get his fingers under the cord, desperately tearing at his neck, drawing blood with his fingernails. He wouldn't talk; he was at least that professional. She yanked up the tension an extra notch, and the flailing of the arms gave way to a more convulsive movement through his entire body. She had to use all her strength to keep him in the seat, but she couldn't resist leaning down, whispering breathlessly into his ear.

"You know that song about Jeffers? It's a celebration. See, Jeffers was a diamond trader, and he was English!"

She couldn't get the phone working again, even after she'd disentangled it from his body. She took her cell phone and dialled. When Lambert picked up she said, "Someone came after me. I'll need removals."

"Someone from the North?"

"No, he claimed to be one of us."

"Name?"

"Patrick Jeffers. Passport backs that up." She looked at the passport she'd retrieved from his jacket. He certainly had the right look.

"Jeffers? There has to be a mistake. Let me just check something." She could hear Lambert tapping away on his computer keyboard. He was as much an old timer as she was and always hit the keys like they belonged on a manual type-writer. 'Liz, Patrick Jeffers is on his first assignment, but he's in Damascus; he's a Middle East specialist."

She looked at the throttled body, slumped in the chair like a drunk, and now that she thought of it, he hadn't seemed to recognize the name of Robinson Jeffers, and surely he would have done, as surely as she knew who Robbie Burns was.

"Well, I hope he's doing better than the Jeffers in front of me now."

Lambert laughed. She liked Lambert; he had a good sense of humour. People didn't need to look much in this game, but a sense of humour was an absolute must.

DISTILLING THE TRUTH

Marilyn Todd

The instant Marie-Claude's husband told her that he'd compiled
a dossier detailing the Chief Inspector's corruption complete
with dates, names and times, then placed the file personally in the
hands of the Commissioner, she knew it was all over. No wonder
he waited until he'd finished his *tartiflette* to tell her what he'd
done. She'd have thrown the damned dish on the floor and to hell
with dinner, and he could have whistled for his *île flottante* as
well. As it was, she didn't hear him out. What on earth was the
point of lengthy explanations?

"You're a fool, Luc. No one likes a whistle blower."

"I didn't join the police to be popular."

"It's the end of your career, you know that? They won't keep
you on in Paris after this!"

"Blackmail, extortion, what was I supposed to do, Marie-
Claude?" He laid down *Le Figaro* and turned his gaze to her.
"For years, Picard has been preying on the very people he was
meant to protect. I couldn't simply turn aside."

"And I'm sure the Commissioner shook your hand and
thanked you warmly for your efforts."

One side of Luc's face twisted uncomfortably. "Not exactly,
no."

"You see? No one likes a whistle-blower. They'd rather
close ranks and have a bastard in their midst than admit to one

bad apple, and you already know my feelings about the Commissioner."

Like when they were invited over to dinner and she overheard him talking to her husband in his study when she went to find the bathroom.

"Your wife is truculent, selfish and a pain in the *cul*, Luc—"

The rest was drowned by children's laughter upstairs, but who cared? That's the last time she'd eat at that pig's house, she told Luc, and if her husband felt bad about making excuses when future invitations arrived, then so much the better. She wanted nothing to do with a man who insulted her, and it wouldn't have hurt Luc to have stuck up for her, either.

"– couldn't agree more, sir—"

Truculent and selfish, her *cul*. She pushed her thick curls back from her face. She had married too young, that was the trouble, and to a man ten years older than herself at that. Admittedly, after six years Luc was no less handsome and his back was as strong, but that type of love can't sustain a marriage indefinitely. And when he wasn't working all the hours *le bon Dieu* sent, he had his head stuck in a file or wanted to talk politics, and not even French politics, either. Honestly! Who cared whether rich diamond deposits had been found in Siberia or how many communists this Senator Mc-Whatever-His-Name accused in the American State Department? What was going to actually change people's lives were things like the new television transmissions that were now coming out in colour, not some piece of paper signed by Egypt and Britain over a canal in Suez that Luc insisted was going to have far-reaching consequences. But however exasperated Marie-Claude got with her husband, she'd never once known him to lose his temper.

Not even when, a mere fortnight after delivering his sancti-monious dossier, the Commissioner transferred him to Cognac.

"You'll like the South," Luc said confidently, as their train pulled away. "Twice as much sunshine, warmer summers, better winters—"

"Better theatres, Luc? Will they have better street cafés and shops? Will they get subtitled versions of 'On the Waterfront', do you think?" By all accounts, it was set to scoop an Oscar. "Will they have better parks? Better gardens? Women in *peignoirs* leaning over the balconies, calling obscenities to men in the street?"

He looked at her beneath lowered lids as the train chugged through the forests of Rambouillet. "You never liked Montmartre."

"It had life," she retorted. "It had character and substance, it was always noisy, colourful, constantly changing—"

Marie-Claude broke off. Why was she referring to these things in the past tense? For heaven's sake, it wasn't as though she wasn't going back! No, no, once she'd seen Luc settled in (she owed him that) she would start a new life. A new life with a man who appreciated art, the cinema, fashion and fun. Someone who liked dancing, for sure!

"I'll bet they've never heard of Perry Como in Cognac."

"You can probably count yourself lucky if they've heard of Bing Crosby," he murmured behind his guide book. "But this is promotion, Marie-Claude. We're lucky to get it. Do you want to look through this, by the way?"

Marie-Claude shook her head. She'd seen enough of those military vines and flat-bottomed boats from upside down, thank you.

"We'll be able to afford a house of our own, instead of a poky apartment on the fifth floor where you can hear everything that happens next door. We're close to the seaside, and I'll bet the air's better, too."

There was nothing wrong with the air in the Rue de Roc, she wanted to say, but his nose was back in the pamphlet and, as Orléans rumbled past, she stroked the hat in her lap. Such a jaunty little number, as well. *Très* Audrey Hepburn with just a dash of Ava Gardner. She sighed and closed her eyes. By the time she got the chance to wear it again, it would either have too many feathers or too few, and who would be seen dead wearing green for next season? At Tours, the only other couple in the carriage got off and an old woman with a runny nose got in.

"Amazing," Luc said, turning the page of his paper to avoid creasing. "It says here construction's underway on the St Lawrence Seaway that'll allow deep-draught ships direct access to the rich industrials of the Great Lakes. Direct access. Can you imagine?"

Marie-Claude switched off. Her husband was clever, conscientious, honourable, but dull. Handsome, rugged, muscular and tall, yet he lacked passion where it really counted. And now, it seemed, he was a failure into the bargain.

At Angoulême they changed trains.

She blamed herself for marrying him.

A week later, the vineyards around Cognac sprang into leaf and an Englishman called Bannister ran a mile in under four minutes. Less than two months down the line, once the vines had been pruned and tied back, an Australian beat the Englishman's record, but by the time the summer sun was swelling the grapes on the hillsides, the Englishman had once again reclaimed his crown in Vancouver, Little Mo's tennis career was cut short by a riding accident and a pair of Italians were the first climbers to reach the peak of K2. These things seemed to excite everyone except Marie-Claude, but it didn't matter, because she kept herself busy making the house nice for Luc.

It was pleasantly located in the old quarter, halfway between the chateau and the covered market, where the streets were narrow, hilly, twisting and cobbled, and the houses built of thick stone to keep them cool in summer, retain heat in the winter, and with fireplaces large enough to secrete a small army. But an old man had lived alone here for the past twenty years and she was damned if she'd be accused of leaving her husband to a place which looked (and smelled) like a pig-sty.

A week's scrub with carbolic transformed it no end, but the shutters could use a coat or three of paint and although she'd considered returning to Paris in August, the weather was perfect for strolls along the tow-path, and whilst Marie-Claude knew of lots of people who didn't bother with curtains and just used the shutters, Luc worked so hard that the very least he deserved, if he wasn't to have a decent dinner waiting on the table, was to be able to pore over his paperwork in a house that was cosy. One or two rooms, that was all. Bedroom. *Salon*. Enough to lend a bit of warmth and character where it mattered the most.

By the time workers had been drafted in for the harvest and Pope Pius X had been canonized, the Algerians had started a guerrilla war against their French protectors, "This Ole

House" was on everyone's lips and Marie-Claude had run up another pair of drapes, this time for the kitchen, and accepted the offer of part-time work in an upmarket dress shop.

"I'll be late tonight," Luc announced one lunchtime, as he washed his hands in the sink. Close by, the bells of St Léger pealed merrily. "The proprietor of one of the smaller Cognac houses has been murdered."

Marie-Claude laid the *cassoulet* on the table and lifted the lid. "Good."

"Good?" He chuckled as he sniffed appreciatively through the steam. "Some poor woman has been battered over the head and all you can say is good?"

"Not good that she's dead." She heaped his plate. "Good that you've got some proper detective work to do at last."

All he'd been called upon to investigate over the past five months had been robbery, the inevitable smuggling and once, right at the beginning, an art theft that turned out to be a simple insurance fraud. Luc was a first-rate detective and at last this would give him something to sink his teeth into. In fact, with such a high-profile case demanding his attention, Marie-Claude doubted he'd notice she'd left, although she might as well wait until the warm weather ended. Paris was desperately wet in October.

"Marie-Claude, this duck is delicious."

It was the market, she explained, scraping out the dish for him. So close it made shopping each day easy, and you could buy the freshest produce without it having been hanging around in a vans for several days as it made its way slowly up country. Luc shot a covetous glance at the second pot on the stove.

"Tomorrow?"

"Certainly not!" Tomorrow she was planning *coq au vin*. "I made that for Suzette next door. Her husband died last year from an accident in the boiler room in one of the distilleries down on the quay, so with three small children and no work, I thought it might help."

"That's very generous."

"Nonsense. We can easily afford one extra duck. My job, your pay rise—"

"No hat bills, no theatre tickets." He wiped both *cassoulet* and smile from his mouth with a serviette. "Do you miss them, Marie-Claude? Honestly?"

"If you've finished, I need to get back to the shop," she said briskly. "Madame Garreau's visiting her mother and I'm all on my own this afternoon." She scraped the bones into the bin while he brewed the coffee. "So who died, then?"

"A woman by the name of Martine Montaud—"

"Madame Montaud?" She wiped her hands on the dishcloth and set out a plate of *palmiers* still warm from the oven. "Handsome, late forties, with dark hair?"

"You know her?"

"As one would expect of the owner of a cognac house, she was one of Madame Garreau's best customers." Marie-Claude sat on the table and began swinging her legs. "Very elegant lady," she said. "Exquisitely made up, hands neatly manicured and I wouldn't like *her* hairdresser's bill, I can tell you." She sighed. "I shall miss her coming in, though," she added. "She never took offence when I told her what didn't suit her—"

"Marie-Claude, that's the reason Madame Garreau adores you. You give her clientele an honest appraisal and you don't hold back. People respect that."

She wondered how he could possibly know her employer's opinion. As far as she knew, Luc had never met Madame Garreau, but that was beside the point. No woman wants to be told lilac suits her when it makes her look bland, any more than being sold the concept that wide stripes will flatter her hips. Especially Madame Montaud, who invariably left the shop hundreds of francs lighter, but every inch looking the successful businesswoman she was.

"She never struck me the type to get herself murdered," Marie-Claude said, sipping her coffee. "Well, not bashed on the head, anyway. It seems so . . . vulgar."

"You'd have preferred she was strangled?"

She shot him a look to say that wasn't funny. "Who killed her, do you have any idea?"

"Everything points to the cellar master," he said sadly. "Like that art theft back in May, there's very little detective work involved in this case, – oh, and talking of art, I suppose you know Matisse is dead?"

"Cellar master? Luc, the cellar master of a cognac house is just one step below God. He's not just responsible for the blend, he oversees the whole process of distillation from beginning to end, he even chooses the oak trees from which the barrels are made that will store his precious cognac, for heaven's sake!"

"And you know this because . . .?"

"Suzette. I told you. Her husband died in a boiler room fire." She brushed a curl out of her eyes with the back of her hand. "We spend a lot of time talking when she picks up the kids."

"You *babysit?*"

"Don't sound so surprised. It gives her chance to do a typing course and – *hein*. The point is, you're looking at the wrong person, Luc. The cellar master couldn't possibly have clonked Madame Montaud on the head. That wouldn't have been *his* style, either."

"Ah. You'd have preferred he strangled her?"

"That wasn't funny the first time, and besides! What motive would he have for killing his employer?"

"Something sexual probably, it usually is." Luc shrugged as he reached for the last pastry. "Money or sex lies at the root of most murders, plus his were the only fingerprints that we lifted and I found one of her ear-rings in his bed—"

"It was so obvious, you searched his house?"

"Not exactly." He leaned his weight against the back of the chair and folded his arms over his chest. "But because her body was found in the cellars, I conducted a thorough search of the entire factory, including the distillery, which happens to have a small room sectioned off that serves as the cellar master's bedroom."

"Only from November until March, when distillation takes place around the clock and he needs to be on hand night and day."

"Suzette?"

"Suzette."

"Hmm." He scratched his chin. "Well, if you know so much about the cognac process and you don't believe my suspect is the killer, why don't you go up there and tell me who is?"

Marie-Claude jumped down from the table. "I'll need a cardigan."

"What about the shop?" he called up the stairs, and look! it proved the acoustics in this house were rubbish. It sounded for all the world as though he was laughing.

"What about the shop?" she called back, reaching for her green hat with the feathers. "They're rich, these women. They can afford to wait a while longer."

Poor Madame Montaud could not.

The Domaine de Montaud lay on the north side of Cognac, protected by woodlands and snug inside a bend in the river. For almost two thousand years, its sun-kissed slopes had gazed over the valley of the Charente and the hills that unfolded beyond, but the acidic soil and low alcohol content played havoc with the wine's conservation and so, in the seventeenth century, foreign merchants hit upon the idea of importing it in spirit form and diluting it on arrival. Because of the double distillation process involved, the Dutch named this spirit *brandwijn* – burnt wine – which had the added advantage of being cheaper to ship. But no matter how economical the costs of transport, when recession hits, luxury goods are the first to suffer. Huge stocks of brandy piled up in the cellars. Things were not looking good.

Until local producers noticed that their spirit not only improved with age, it tasted even better drunk neat . . .

But as cognac was born, so evolved a world of secrets and magic. In each dark saturated cellar, the cellar master became sorcerer, blending smooth with mellow, amber with gold, elegance with subtlety, to produce a unique and individual range of cognacs, from the youngest, at under five years, to prestigious *réserves* that had been maturing in oak casks for decades.

Marie-Claude had imagined such sorcerers to be sober, unsmiling, aloof and dull. Undertakers in different suits. If they were, Alexandre Baret broke the mould.

"*Enchanté, madame.*"

Any other time and the eyes behind the spectacles would be twinkling flirtatiously. The crows' feet either side said so. But today they only viewed the inspector's assistant with mistrust, and were clouded with something else, too. Guilt? Grief? Fear? Marie-Claude couldn't say but, following him through the shadowy barrel-lined chambers, their walls black from evaporation, she felt prickles rise on her scalp. With its rigorously controlled temperature, light rationed to brief and rare visits, the okay tang to the air, it was like walking through a cathedral.

That same air of reverence. Humility. Silence. Tranquillity. The taking of life here seemed sacrilegious.

"I have informed the workforce that this area is out of bounds until further notice," Monsieur Baret said, studiously avoiding the outline of a body chalked on the flagstone floor. "But in any case, only a handful of employees have access, and I assure you it is quite impossible to enter without the necessary keys. Indeed," he added dryly, "one would stand a better chance breaking into the *Banque de France*."

"You don't think this could be a robbery turned sour, then?" Marie-Claude's voice echoed softly. "After all, there are hundreds of migrants in the vineyards right now, breaking their backs to bring in the harvest."

Alexandre Baret watched dust motes dance in the air over the spot where every trace of his employer's blood had been scrubbed clean. "No, *madame*, I do not think that."

"You're not exactly helping your case," she said, and behind her heard Luc grind his teeth.

"Why?" The cellar master swung round sharply to face him. "Am I under suspicion, inspector?"

Marie-Claude was acutely conscious that her husband didn't look at her when he replied. "Madame Montaud was found with just one emerald cluster in her left ear," he said mildly. "An identical cluster was found in your bed next to the still."

Monsieur Baret said nothing, but his eyes flickered, she noticed, as he opened the door from the cellars. Perhaps it was nothing more than passing from darkness into the light.

"I cannot explain that," he said at length. "But if you are suggesting—" he indicated the cramped sleeping quarters partitioned off with nothing more than wood and glass "—I'm sorry, inspector, you are mistaken."

Marie-Claude opened the door and peered in. There was just about enough room for the bed and a small chest of drawers. The blankets did not look very clean.

"The night watchman confirms that you have been leaving very late. Past midnight on several occasions."

"I did not conduct an affair down here with Madame Montaud," Baret insisted, "that's simply too sordid to contemplate, I am a married man. And the notion that I killed her – pff! What possible motive would I have?"

Luc drew a carbon copy from his breast pocket. Reading upside down, Marie-Claude saw that the letter bore yesterday's date, was addressed to the cellar master and had been typewritten.

"This was on top of the paperwork in Madame Montaud's desk," Luc said. "The desk, incidentally, that we were only able to open with the key that was found in her pocket."

Baret took the proffered letter and, as he read, the colour drained from his face. His jaw tightened. "I–I have never seen this before."

Marie-Claude didn't get the chance to read every last word before it disappeared back inside Luc's pocket, but the gist was enough. In the most civil of terms, Martine Montaud was dismissing her cellar master.

"Is it, do you think, too sordid to contemplate?" Luc asked, once they were alone in the distillery. "Tall, fifty, and with that thick thatch of dark hair, it seems perfectly reasonable to me that the earring of the widowed and lonely Martine would end up in his bed."

"Not this bed," Marie-Claude said, sending clouds of dust into the air as she tried to pull the curtains and found the hooks had rusted solid.

"Wouldn't the risk of discovery have been the spice, though? Two educated, articulate, respected people fired by the danger of being caught in the act?"

"If there's any danger, it comes from fleas, not ruined reputations," she said, prodding the unsheeted mattress. "And anyway, who said she was lonely?"

When Madame Montaud tried on clothes in the shop, those were not sensible foundations garments she'd been wearing underneath!

"Who else has a key to the distillery and cellars?" she asked.

"No one who doesn't have a cast iron alibi."

"While Monsieur Baret . . .?"

"Claims he went for a walk, and if you believe that, you believe anything." Luc ran his hand over the ticking on the bolster. "You know, Marie-Claude, just because they're both polite, refined individuals, it doesn't mean they don't enjoy the occasional foray into degeneracy."

She considered the new baby doll pyjamas that were all the rage at the moment. Both she and Luc agreed that these were the most depraved and decadent garments that had ever been invented, and indeed they'd considered them so depraved and decadent that they ripped them off no less than three times last Saturday night.

"So you're saying Alexandre met with Martine last night, as usual. They came down here, as usual, made love in his seedy little camp bed, as usual, where she lost an earring in the heat of their passion . . . then fired him?"

"No," he said, leaning his hip against the chest of drawers. "That's what the evidence is saying. Not me."

Marie-Claude threw her hands in the air. "Luc Brosset, you are the most impossible man on God's earth! If you suspected all along that this was a set-up, for heaven's sake why didn't you just come straight out with it and tell me you wanted my help?"

"That's funny," he said. "I thought that was exactly what I had done."

Centuries had come and gone, but the method of distilling cognac hadn't changed. The still itself, the *alambic*, was made of gleaming red copper and, with its swan neck, long pipes and balloon shape resembled more a giant oriental hookah than a boiler. For nearly four months of the year, once the grapes had been pressed and their precious juice extracted, these three pieces of apparatus would be working night and day to produce the first distillation, the *brouillis*, before undergoing its distinctive second boiling. Only after that could the "heads" and "tails" be separated from the clear "heart" of the spirit that would eventually mature into cognac.

During these four months, though, the cellar master would virtually live next to his *alambic* while, outside, the town would grow warm from so many boilers pumping round the clock, the air would become impregnated with the sweet smell of brandy, and the characteristic black on the buildings would deepen, a symbol of status and pride. Incredibly, a tenth of the cognac was lost to evaporation, a contribution known as the angels' share. Marie-Claude wondered whether Madame Montaud would be able to distinguish her own cognac from where she sat on her cloud. And how silly to get misty-eyed over someone she hardly knew!

"The way she was killed," Luc said, "hit on the back of the head with a marble bust of the founder that took pride of place next to the *alambic*, that suggests the crime wasn't premeditated."

Marie-Claude thought about the key in her pocket. The fact that Alexandre's were the only fingerprints. The way nobody else here had access.

"It suggests an earring coming off when she fell," he continued, "and the killer taking the opportunity to implicate someone else."

She wondered what the gem-smith who made Madame Montaud's jewellery would have to say about such odds.

"Or," she said, "it's a double-bluff designed to look that way."

Luc spiked his hands through his hair. "You mean Baret planned it from the outset, then left clumsy clues that pointed directly to him, leading us to think they had been planted?"

"If it was a spur-of-the-moment act, why didn't he plead *crime passionel* straight away? Cellar masters are respected all over France, Luc, and think about it. Sex, rejection, dismissal? Any one of these things are enough to make a man feel emasculated and strike out in the heat of anger, yet here we have three stacked on top of each other. Alexandre Baret could have thrown up his hands and admitted his crime, and even the worst advocate in the country would have had him walking away a free man."

She stared up at the shining copper works and saw Madame Montaud holding up two evening dresses, the navy blue and the green. *What discount will you give me, Madame Garreau, if I take both? I see. Well, thank you for your time, but I think I'll drive into Angoulême and see – Why, yes, Madame Garreau. Ten percent would be perfectly acceptable. But shall we say twelve?*

"Madame Montaud was elegant, successful, she drove a hard bargain, but by all accounts she was fair. While a man who blends cognac that not only his successor won't see sold but *his* successor either, is a man who is patient, clever and selfless."

Luc scratched his head. "Are you saying he did or he didn't?"

Marie-Claude straightened her hat in the boiler's reflection. "It's late," she said. "I have to get back to the shop."

★   ★   ★

"Some joint," she murmured as they snubbed the workforce's entrance in favour of the broad sweep of the drive.

"Twelve bedrooms, five wings and ceilings so high you can house a giraffe in each room, should you so desire," Luc said. "And to prove how handsomely this business pays, the house is surrounded by seventeen hectares of beautiful but totally unproductive parkland."

"If you think I'd live there, you're mistaken," Marie-Claude said. "Look at the number of windows for a start. And the height of them! I'd spend all my day washing them."

"You'd have people to do that for you."

"I would not," she protested.

What? Strangers trooping all over her house, snooping all over her business?

"Some people might envy the rich for their lifestyle," she said firmly. "Not me. Madame Montaud may have been successful, but the poor woman was a martyr to the business, she barely took a day off, and look at that sister of hers. Dresses like Grace Kelly, but never gets a chance to breathe, much less be her own person. No privacy, not even a house to call her own, and when her husband leaves the shop, it stinks of stale wine and cigars for simply hours."

"Oh? And what do I stink of?"

"Nutmeg and citron and cool, mountain forests," she said, and his eyes weren't just green, they crinkled at the corners and were flecked with red, grey and brown, and his mouth twisted sideways when he smiled. With his thick mop of dark hair and square practical hands, she was glad Luc would have no trouble finding a new wife once she'd gone.

"Hmm."

He stuffed his square practical hands in his pockets and whistled *Mambo Italiano* under his breath as they sauntered past the bustling vineyards down the hill towards the river. Since the Domaine was only a fifteen-minute walk from the house, they hadn't bothered with the car, and Marie-Claude was wrong about the cardigan. She hadn't needed it at all.

"I don't suppose this sudden obligation to duty has anything to do with the sister?" he asked after working his way through *Three Coins in the Fountain, Smile* and *Hernando's Hideaway*.

"Madame Montaud wasn't having an affair with her cellar master," Marie-Claude said, wondering at what point her arm had become linked with his. "She ordered far too many evening gowns for an illicit liaison."

More likely she was being courted discreetly, preferring to wait and see how things developed before going public with the relationship.

"Loose women aren't taken seriously in business," she pronounced. "But the sister, Madame Delaville, now that's a different story."

Husband reeking of stale booze and smoke, choosing all her clothes? She'd lost count of the number of times she'd seen him sitting in Madame Garreau's plush armchair, squat and potbellied like a cocky little toad, while his wife paraded in unflattering suits with slow and mechanical precision.

"Natalie Delaville is a woman of loose moral standards?"

"Exactly the opposite," Marie-Claude said, turning the key in the shop. "Her husband has the word bully all but etched on his forehead, but the more I think about it, the more I remember that her chin hasn't drooped quite so much lately, there's been colour in her pale cheeks, and miracle of miracles, Madame Delaville actually called in half a dozen times on her own over the past month. I want to look up what she – *voilà!*"

"Well?" Luc held out his hands in exasperation. "Are you going to tell me what the little mouse bought?"

"Certainly not." Such matters were private! "But I can tell you that the dresses were feminine and flattering, and I can tell you whose account they were charged to, as well." She shot her husband a sideways glance. "Alexandre Baret."

"All right . . ." Luc rubbed his jaw in thought. "But is this actually getting us anywhere?"

"It explains his unease and reluctance to provide an alibi."

"Because he was protecting Natalie Delaville."

"Absolutely." She locked the door and tested the catch. "Now all we have to do is prove how that bitch killed Martine."

"Metamorphosis is a wonderful thing," Luc observed, stretching his pace to match hers. "One minute she's a mouse, the next she's a bitch – what? What have I said?"

"Honestly!" Marie-Claude stopped outside the baker's and shook her head in disbelief. "I don't know where you get your ideas, sometimes! Not Madame Delaville, Luc. She didn't kill Madame Montaud."

It was Madame Baret, of course. Alexandre's wife.

"*And* she killed the wrong woman."

As the hills slowly turned to russet and gold and the French populace finally came to terms with defeat in Indochina, the Empire State Building had been eclipsed as the world's tallest structure, civilization was facing extinction from something called Rock and Roll, and Luc had been proved right about Suez, especially in light of that botched attempt earlier on the Egyptian president's life.

"By the way, Marie-Claude, I received a letter from the Commissioner this morning."

More and more these days Luc had taken to joining her on walks along the tow-path, although sometimes their route took them through the town hall park or onto the islands, where they would take a picnic providing they wrapped up warm.

"He writes that he has finally rounded up everyone involved in the blackmail and extortion ring. Some seven police officers are awaiting trial, he says, and commends me for a job well done."

"That the letter?" Marie-Claude tossed it into the Charente, where a squadron of ducks came steaming in, mistaking it for a bread roll. "You know my opinion of the Commissioner."

"For the life of me, I can't imagine why."

"He said I was truculent, selfish and a pain in the *cul*."

Luc laughed. "Well, if you overheard that much, you'd have also heard him qualify his statement by adding that you were spirited, funny, and I was lucky to have you."

Couldn't agree more, sir, Luc had replied, and damn those horrid children upstairs for drowning out the Commissioner's words.

"He congratulated me on the Montaud murder, as well." Luc stuffed his hands in his pockets. "Being a high-profile case, I suppose word found its way back to his desk, but what I'm getting to is that he ended by saying that, now the corruption ring's been wrapped up and my life is no longer in danger, there's a job for me in Paris, should we want it."

"You never told me your life was threatened!"

"Hell hath no fury like a Chief Inspector jailed. So, then. Do we? Want that job, I mean."

"It might have been high-profile, but it wasn't exactly brain surgery, Luc."

All those late nights in the distillery, indeed! *I did not conduct an affair down here with Madame Montaud*, the cellar master had insisted, *that's simply too sordid to contemplate.* Quite right. It may have been his employer's sister he'd been carrying on with, not his employer, but he wouldn't have dreamt of taking the delicate, browbeaten Natalie to the distillery had it not been the only place where they could meet and not be either seen or overhead. His office was too close to the main works. They dared not be seen in public. So they either sat down there, talking long into the night, or they sneaked off in his car to plan their new life together, and what a lot of planning there was. For all that cellar masters are handsomely paid and live in grand houses, they still don't live like the Montauds! There would be no majestic mansion for Natalie once she left Delaville. No parklands, no servants, no prestigious balls. Alexandre had wanted her to be one hundred percent sure before making the leap. He knew there would be no going back.

For her part, of course, Madame Baret hadn't believed for a second that her husband had been required to work late.

In the way of deceived wives everywhere, she followed him, saw the lights in the distillery, knew about the bed, heard him whispering on the telephone in the hall. She'd had no trouble tracing the number to the Domaine and knew immediately who he was carrying on with. (Who else was there, for goodness sake? Hardly that pale, downtrodden sister!) So, again in the way of deceived wives everywhere, she hoped and then prayed the affair would blow over. Until the day she overheard him talking about their new life together . . .

From that moment on, revenge was all that consumed her. Revenge on the woman who had destroyed her life. Revenge on the man who discarded her.

"The marble bust might look like the instrument of a crime of passion, a spur-of-the-moment decision, grabbing the first object to hand," Marie-Claude said, as they paused to watch the churning waters of the millrush merge with the stately river.

"But equally it smacked of a squeamish reluctance to be facing the victim."

A uniquely feminine approach to murder. As was the cold-blooded planning.

"It was easy enough to get a set of her husband's keys cut."

"One of the locksmiths confirmed it straight away, but as evidence it was still far from conclusive."

"No, but it all mounted up." She kicked the fallen leaves as she walked. Alder, willow and poplar. "Madame Baret's mistake was planting the desk key in Martine's pocket."

Good heavens, women as elegant as Madame Montaud don't use pockets! They tuck them away tidily in their *Chanel* handbags, which meant someone had used that key to get into her desk and replaced it in a hurry. And if it wasn't to take something out, then it must be to put something in.

A quick check of the keys proved that the letter had been typed on the Barets' private typewriter, not in the office at the Domaine, but it had been a clever move on Madame Baret's part. If the head of a cognac house wanted rid of their cellar master, this would not be made public knowledge. A gentleman's agreement between the two parties, however bitter underneath, would not show on the surface. Both had too much invested in the business to jeopardize their reputations.

"She was smart about fingerprints, too."

Taking care the only ones lifted were her husband's, and who would think anything odd about seeing a lady of quality going round in evening gloves? Exactly. And whatever excuse she'd used to lure Madame Montaud down to the cellars, she must have thought it was her lucky day when Martine agreed so easily. But then, of course, she didn't know she was setting a trap for the wrong woman.

"Too smart about the fingerprints," Luc said. They had stopped to watch one of the wooden, flat-bottomed *gabarres* pass through the lock, laden with casks lashed with ropes. "That was one of the things that bothered me from the outset. That if Martine Montaud was exerting so much passion in the cellar master's quarters, why weren't hers there, too?"

"She misjudged the calibre of Madame Montaud's jewellery, as well."

How cold must her heart have been, as she stood over the corpse, unscrewing the emerald cluster? Extracting the key from Martine's handbag, placing the letter of dismissal in her desk, then walking out as if nothing had happened and secure in the knowledge that her husband would not plead *crime passionel*. Why should he, after all? The man was innocent.

"Never mind Madame Baret," Luc said. "Just tell me whether we want that job in Paris."

Marie-Claude watched the *gabarre* sail round the bend and disappear from sight. Above, the sun shone through the falling leaves and blackbirds foraged in the litter. Next week "Dial M for Murder" would be running back to back with "Rear Window" and in subtitles, plus she still hadn't finished those curtains for the bathroom, the cellar really needed a new blind, the old one was a disgrace, the bedroom could use fresh wallpaper, ditto the *salon* now she came to think about it, and she'd promised Madame Garreau two more days a week with the winter collection.

"Maybe when the rains come," Marie-Claude said slowly.

Besides. She wasn't sure Luc was quite ready to live alone yet.

WISH

John Rickards

Four days since I called in sick. I think.

I've been awake for three of them straight. I think.

My fellow *gardai* would piss themselves if they could see me, no doubt. Then they'd have me committed.

But they don't know. They haven't seen. They're all out getting drunk, or off fucking their wives, or fucking their mistresses and lying about it to their wives, or passed out in front of their TVs in their nice safe homes while I'm

fucking

dead.

And I don't know if even I believe it.

It started with Michael. A mental case, low-grade nut. We have quite a few. A handful of paedophiles, stalkers, minor assaults. Care in the community jobs, not criminal enough to be locked up for good, criminal enough to be in and out of the cells on a regular basis. Since jail seems to do fuck all by way of curing them – worse, many come out of it even more damaged than they went in – my own policy is not to arrest. Talk, threaten, watch, but don't arrest if possible. Jail only makes them more of a risk to everyone in the long run.

Some of these guys are homeless, but not Michael. It's a shithole of a flat, though, overlooking the railway tracks not far from where they cross the Tolka, north of Dublin's city centre. Building that smells of boiled vegetables and cat piss. Walls the colour of boiled vegetables and cat piss.

"That woman hasn't been poisoning your kitten, Michael. She doesn't even know who you are. She wouldn't know how to poison a kitten, even if she wanted to."

"Could swear I've seen her . . ."

"No, you haven't. She hasn't done a thing. Trust me on this, OK? Jesus, they train me for this sort of thing and, believe me, if she was guilty, I'd know and I'd have dealt with her. You've got to stop yelling at the woman and threatening her, Michael."

Sullen look. A child being unfairly chided. A flash of malice. I wish for something to shut him up. I wish for something to stop this kind of shit.

So I do it. I drop the threat. Let the genie out of the bottle. Make the wish.

"And you listen good to me, Michael. You leave that woman alone from now on, or else I'll send your name, address and photo to Iron Kurt's Gay Nazi website."

Let me explain. I have a friend, Curt, who's funny, erudite, can hold his drink remarkably well, and who happens to be gay. One night in Fallon's, the conversation turns to gay rights and marriage, a subject which he understandably feels strongly about. He speaks his piece, and someone else makes some comment about him being a "fascist homo" or something. Funny in its stupidity. And so the remark resurfaces and transforms, blossoming into something so much more.

It helps that there's been trouble with a couple of Neo-Nazi crackpots in the city on TV recently, even with the NSRUS pulling out of Ireland. Nazis make the best bad guys. Ask Indiana Jones. And I see a twitch of fear or homophobia in Michael's eyes.

"I'll do it," I tell him. "And you know what'll happen then . . ."

Of course, his mind fills in the blank with its own worst fears. He promises to be good.

And over the next few weeks, he is. And I trot out the same threat to other lunatics I have to deal with. And they don't see me as a punisher. Iron Kurt is the punisher. I'm just the messenger. So they don't even resent me for it.

My fellow *gardai* find the whole thing fucking funny. Some of them start using Kurt themselves. And Dublin sleeps safer at night. Kurt's out there, watching over the city. A spectre in the fog blowing in off the harbour, creeping upriver. A paper tiger keeping evil at bay.

One afternoon, I see William, one of our deranged, sitting in the doorway of a boarded-up shop with an Iron Cross badge pinned proudly to his battered old blue Leinster rugby top. Next to him is a scratched metal strongbox.

"Hey, William."

"It's . . . you're gonna beat me."

"Leave it alone, William. What's in the box?"

"They're mine, see."

"Fine. But show me what you've got."

"It's private. Mine."

"Last time we had this conversation, you had a petrol bomb on you. I just want to make sure you don't have another one. Anything else, you can keep."

He thinks, pops open the box. Inside, an untidy pile of black fur.

"Why are you carrying a bunch of dead rats around?" I ask.

"They pay me. It's my deal. Not yours."

"I've got no ambitions of being a ratcatcher. Who pays?"

"The big red building down Castleforbes Road. Food warehouse. To set traps. Ten cents a rat."

"And you get them from somewhere else, and they pay for them."

"Yeah. It's a good job."

"Good for you. What's with the Iron Cross?" I point at his chest.

"It's protection, is what. Keith saw Iron Kurt."

I try not to smile. "Yeah?"

"And he said, you wear stuff like this and you'll be OK."

"Unless you've been posted on his website."

"Well, yeah."

"While we're on the subject, you're keeping away from that playground, right?"

He nods vigorously. "Yeah. Never meant to do anything."

"Did Keith say what Iron Kurt looked like?"

"Yeah. A big guy, tall, built like a brick shithouse. Bald. With a beard. Tattoos all over."

The real Curt is 5′5″ and built for comfort, not speed. Again, I stifle a smile. "Yeah, that sounds right. You'd better stay out of trouble, huh?"

Not long after, I see Keith himself. The shopping trolley that holds his worldly possessions has a bunch of plastic German soldiers on string looped all the way around it like fairy lights. Now I'm looking for it, I start to notice similar items on most of the other nutcases in my patch.

A belt buckle like an Iron Cross around the neck. A pencil-drawn swastika. An SS-style shoulder patch. In one house in Clontarf, a guy named Terry has a toy soldier shrine in a foil-lined cardboard box.

Votive offerings. Symbols of fear, not worship, not support. Warding off Kurt and his unholy wrath.

I shouldn't be surprised. They all gather together in Duff Alley off East Wall Road to drink Tennant's Super until someone passes out or pisses themselves. And they talk, and share stories. Chinese whispers. Some believe them, some don't. But they all listen.

They say Kurt's the son of an SS officer. They say he's raped and killed more than two hundred men. They say his website has more than a thousand followers, all over the world, who take perverse delight in making each victim last as long as possible. They say – and when I tell Curt this he practically wets himself laughing – that he has a fourteen-inch dick and that most of his victims die from blood poisoning caused by massive anal tearing.

Iron Kurt.

My creation. My Frankenstein. My cartoon monster.

And then Keith disappears. One day, gone. No one knows where. No one's seen him. They find his trolley round the corner from a soup kitchen on North Quay, but he never comes back for it. Shit happens, these people move on.

William stops picking up pay for his rats and vanishes from the hostel he's been staying at. Someone tells me he'd been beaten up and his badge taken a couple of days before.

I stop seeing Terry. When I go to his house, his toy soldier shrine is still there, but he's gone. The neighbour says the last they saw of him, he was going to get a pint of milk. A couple of the others disappear too.

Duff Alley gets very empty, and the conversation there becomes very muted. They get drunk, huddle together, and after dark they whisper that Iron Kurt has come for them. And now I'm

shit

scared.

Another trip to the piss-stained steps outside Michael's flat. He's almost the only one left, and I need to know what he knows. To find out if he can reassure me. Keith left for Cork. William found a winning lottery ticket in the street and moved to the Caribbean. Some other *gardai* told the Duff Alley crazies to get out, so they're meeting somewhere else now.

When I knock on the door, I hear a wet thudding noise from inside. When I try the handle, it's unlocked. When I should turn and run away, I push it open and walk in.

The sickly-sweet smell of blood on the air. The acrid spike of human waste. The cloying taste of someone else's sweat. Michael lies in a crimson-splashed, naked tangle in the middle of his living room floor. The carpet around him soaked black with blood. Legs splayed at an unnatural angle, and pink-yellow ribbons of intestines running from the torn and tattered gash that yawns between them.

He twitches, and I realize he's still alive.

"Michael? Can you hear me?"

Whimper. Twitch. One eye creaks open and fixes me with a stare of utter agony and shock.

"Who did this? What the fuck's going on?"

"*It . . . Kurt . . . didn't . . .*"

"Kurt? You're sure? Christ."

"*Said . . . name . . . site . . . to punish . . . I didn't . . .*"

I should be calling an ambulance. I should be calling my colleagues. "Where is he now?"

Michael's eye looks down. Pleading. Betrayed. "*You said . . .
wouldn't . . . website . . . I . . . good . . .*"

He thinks I did it. "I didn't tell him," I say. "Jesus, Michael,
I wouldn't even know how. I swear to you."

"*He . . . told . . .*" Michael smacks his lips. Dry mouth. Lost
too much fluid already. Bleeding out. Dying.

"What did he tell you?"

"*No . . . he asked . . . who . . . gave my name . . .*" Smack.
Smack. "*I . . . told him . . . you . . .*"

As Michael's head drops to the carpet, something thumps out
in the stairwell and my heart jumps into my mouth. Again I
think about running, but I don't. Again I think about calling the
station, but to tell them what? That some kind of phantom is
stalking lunatics on my beat?

I step outside, check the stairs with shaky steps and trembling
hands. And there's nothing there.

When I come back down to Michael's flat, the body is gone.
So is the blood that soaked the carpet a moment ago. Is the smell
gone as well? I can't tell. But there's no sign that Michael was
ever here. And was he – could I be imagining it? Could all this
be in my head, a product of my own fear?

Fuck. Fuck.

When I search the flat, I can't see any of the protective
trinkets the others had. He was an unbeliever.

I'm not. Not now.

When I walk away from Michael's, I see the tall figure of a
bald man watching me from the trees on the far side of the park
across the street. He's massive, and bare-chested. The dark
outlines of tattoos that litter his skin flicker and swirl like
flames. He points at me, long and hard, then slides back into
the undergrowth.

So now it's been four days since then, since I called in sick.
Since I barricaded myself into my flat to wait for the end. In the
yellow glare of the 40-watt bulb, in the air that reeks of stale
sweat and fear, I'm protected by a butcher's knife and an Iron
Cross. A spray paint swastika on every wall. A replica of one of
those Nazi imperial eagles they'd carry everywhere in those
films. Terry's foil-lined box with his tableau of half a dozen toy
German WWII soldiers.

Maybe they'll help me. I certainly won't step beyond their protective radius.

Because Kurt is coming to kill me. His creator. To close the circle. I'm the last one he's looking for here. And he won't let me go. I know it.

Soon I'll hear his footsteps on the stairs. Slow, heavy, deliberate.

Thump.

Thump.

Thump.

Be careful what you wish for, you just might get it.

THE BRICK

Natasha Cooper

It all started with the broken window. That was what was so infuriating. If those wretched children hadn't found the brick next door's cowboy builders had left in the front garden and thought it would be fun to smash a big bit of clean glass, none of it would have happened. We'd still have been OK; not in seventh heaven or anything extravagant like that, but OK.

The randomness of it still makes me swear. It needn't have happened; none of it. That's what gets to me when I let myself think about it.

There I was peacefully sitting on a beanbag on the floor (we'd sanded the boards by then but not varnished them and they looked a bit splintery; but they were clean, which was something after the state we'd found them in when we tore up the old lino) reading short stories for a prize. They were all about spouses killing each other, of course: short stories for prizes nearly always are. And I'd been congratulating myself rather because however livid I'd been with John, I'd never, even in my wildest, most secret fantasies, wanted to kill him. Stiffen him, maybe; tell him not to be such a baby and to get on out there and do his bit of the bargain, like I'd always done mine. I mean, I'd given up my job when it was clear that he needed more input than I'd been able to give him while I was working so hard.

It wasn't only the comfort and the listening and the putting-up with stress-induced sulks, you see; he'd needed a lot more practical help with all sorts of things, and meals suddenly became important to him in a way they'd never been before. We'd always just picked for supper whenever we both got back from work, but suddenly he wanted three courses with both of us sitting down at the table, whenever he got back. And my publishing salary just wasn't up to paying a housekeeper, not after tax and all the things I'd had to pay for, you know, decent clothes and that sort of thing. So I'd given up. I'd always done a bit of freelance, luckily as it turned out. So when John cracked up, I still had all my contacts in place.

Anyway, where was I? Being on my own all day means that I do get very short of chat, which is why I can't stop talking when there's any opportunity. Sorry about that. I've lost my drift. Oh, yes, the brick. Well, you see, there I was, sitting by the window, thinking that at least this titchy little South London cottage was a bit lighter than our Kensington house, when this bloody brick crashed through the window and landed by my feet. It must have been in next door's garden for a while because it was coated with mud and had woodlice clinging to it. You know, those prehistoric-looking horrid little black things.

They were all over the house when we bought it, but once we'd sorted the damp we got rid of most of them. They crunch under your bare feet. In a way that was nearly the worst thing, getting out of bed that first morning in the new house and hearing the crunch under my feet. I could have hit John then. I wouldn't have, honestly, and I never told him that's how I felt, but it was the last straw.

He was lying there with most of the pillow over his head, not getting up, hating the potty little job that was all he'd managed to get. I know he was feeling awful. And I did sympathize. I really did. You couldn't not if you loved him, and I did. But I wished he'd just pull himself together a bit. I mean, the rest of us had to.

Anyway, the brick. Well, it wasn't so much the brick as the bits of glass. One of the bigger splinters sliced through my forearm, you know, the one bit of one that stays looking reasonably firm even when the rest begins to go scraggy. It was such a shock. I was still reeling from the noise. You can't imagine how much noise one of those plate-glass windows makes when it's broken. And then there was a kind of stinging down my arm; that's all it seemed to be at the beginning, a sting. And I looked down and there was this great long red line, getting redder and wider all the time. Spreading. It was about six inches long, I think, and the lips of it opened as I looked, like a cut in a bit of steak.

Anyway, for a while I just sat and looked at it. Then when the blood started dripping down onto the beanbag – it was natural canvas, so it showed – and the planks we'd spent so long sanding, I knew I'd have to do something. It was hurting by then, too. And I felt like a child. Perhaps that was why I let her in. I felt wobbly and pathetic, nothing like Penny-who's-such-a-brick, Penny who's always kept everything going even when her husband cracked up like that and both the children went so peculiar.

She rang the bell just as I'd got to the hall, gripping the sides of the cut with my other hand. Well, it would have to be the other hand, wouldn't it? Honestly, sometimes I forget I've ever been a copy-editor. Where was I? I know, trying not to think too much about her. She'd have said I was in denial and she'd have been right. I sort of thought it must be whoever'd chucked the brick through the window who was ringing the bell and I wasn't going to answer. I was leaning against the hall wall – we hadn't painted that yet, just stripped off the awful old spriggy paper we'd found when we came – and feeling faint, really. Anyone would have. And then she called out:

"Are you all right? I saw them throw it and tried to catch them, but I was just too far away."

She did sound breathless, as though she'd been running. And she had a nice voice, rich and deepish, and very warm. It sounded so safe and sure that I came over even more wobbly than before, which was barmy. Children always do it if you're too sympathetic when they've bumped themselves, but I was old enough to know better.

"Hello? Are you all right? My name's Sophie Allen. I live just round the corner. I'm perfectly respectable. Can I come in? Give you a hand? There's a very good glazier I know who does our windows whenever we're burgled. I can give him a ring for you, if you'd like. Are you there?"

So then I stammered out something idiotic and opened the door. And there she was, just about my age but much younger looking. She wasn't having to hold down all that fury, for one thing. Or not by then. I found out later that she'd been through the same sort of thing in a way, but she'd got over it. People do. Or so they say.

"You poor thing," was all she said. But she came right in, put an arm round my shoulders and nearly pushed me towards the kitchen. I'd hated that, too, being able to see into the kitchen from the front door. It really drove the down-shifting bit home.

She knew all about the house because hers was exactly the same. They all are in those little streets between the commons. She had my arm under the cold tap in seconds. The firmness of her was lovely then, just as safe-making as her voice. The brick and the malice of it were washed off just like the blood. They came back. But for a bit they'd gone. She kept on talking and I didn't really listen to the words, just the sureness of her voice.

It sounded as though she knew everything that mattered and would always help but never ask the sort of questions you didn't want to answer. She always did see a lot, and she knew what you could take and what you needed – and offered it straight off. Always.

When she'd got me bloodless and dried out and bandaged up, she called the glazier she knew and swept up the glass, found the Hoover and sucked up the splinters from the beanbag, too, and even Hoovered my jeans. I wouldn't have thought of that, but she was right; there were chips of glass caught in some of the seams. I saw them gleaming as she sucked. It was a weird sensation, that powerful pull all down my thighs and her lovely, warm matter-of-fact voice, telling me what she was doing and why and what the shock of it all was doing to me, and why I was feeling so awful, and who she thought the children were who'd thrown the brick and how it wasn't me they were throwing it at but the old bat who'd lived there before us. She'd been a bit of a witch apparently, always complaining about ordinary noise and making a great fuss about children playing in the street. They still do that, round here. I couldn't believe it at first: roller-blading in the middle of the road, chucking balls about. As though they weren't ten minutes' walk from two huge open spaces. And they always did make a bit of a row. I saw what she meant: the old bat, I mean, who in a way caused the trouble because if she hadn't upset them in the first place, they wouldn't have chucked the brick and none of the rest of it would've happened.

"But there's a SOLD sign outside," I said at the time. I remember that. It was nearly the first thing I'd said in the torrent of all the comfort she'd poured out. I'd meant to say something about how amazing it was to find a friendly neighbour in a place where I'd never expected to, but all that came out was that peevish little protest. "Can't they read?"

"Probably not. Lots of the more delinquent ones can't. I'm a woodentop, and I see a fair amount of children like them."

"A woodentop?" I thought I hadn't heard properly, but she smiled, a great huge smile that showed off her perfect, white teeth. Mine aren't like that: crossed over at the front and a nasty grubby colour like stale clotted cream. Ugh.

"Magistrate," she said, laughing. She had a lovely laugh, too, and none of us had laughed for ages, not happily like that. "No one calls us that these days, but in the old days they did and I like it. Now, you're glass-free. You'd better have something hot. Tea? Coffee? God! I sound like an air hostess, don't I? Shall I put the kettle on?"

And so she made herself at home. I liked it, which I'd never have let myself do if it hadn't been for the brick and the blood. I sat on the beanbag, looking at the jagged great hole in the window and thought about the violence of South London and how much I hated it and how scared I was even though I couldn't afford to be. They say it's changed now, but in those days it was pretty rough. So there I was, thinking how amazing it was that she was there, and perhaps even in South London there would be people to meet and like and talk to. Damn! I'm forgetting the copy-editing again. But I can't stop once I've started. Sorry. I don't often talk as much as this. Well, I do actually, but it feels new each time I do it and I always mean not to afterwards.

There was one little bit of glass she'd missed. Even she'd managed to miss one and it lay on the scrubbed board just near a stickying puddle of my blood, glinting. It was a sunny day. All the days that summer were sunny. It seemed unfair in a way.

She came back with the tea, very strong, tea-bag tea. It tasted like her, strong and warm and helping. Then we just talked. She was still there when the woman who was doing the school run to the local comprehensive dropped my two off and she stayed to tea and made them laugh and helped with their homework. Then she went, giving me her number and telling me she'd drop in again. She only lived round the corner.

It wasn't for weeks that I got round to asking her for supper so that John could share in it all. I suppose in a way I'd wanted to keep her as my treat. But then it seemed selfish, so I fixed it so that he could meet her too.

When he took one look at her and said, "Sophie?" in that surprised but blissful voice I suppose I knew what was going to happen. I was angry with her for not telling me she knew him, but when I looked at her I saw that she was just as surprised as he'd been. She knew my married name, of course, but I never talked about John because it would have been disloyal and so she'd never made the connection; she'd been married, too, for about ten years and so he hadn't recognized her name when I'd talked about her.

That was it, really. They tried not to, I think. They really did try, but she was just so much better at making him feel all right than I was. I understood that. She did it for me, too, when he could only make me feel miles worse. In a way it wasn't what they did that made me so angry. It was what he said when he'd made his decision, as though I'd be pleased to hear it, as though he was giving me something again after all.

"If it wasn't for everything you've taught me I'd never have been able to love Sophie as she deserves. I couldn't do it when I first knew her because I didn't know enough. It was you who taught me how to know people and let them know me. It's all your doing, Penny. You've shown me how to be all the things she wanted me to be then and I couldn't. We owe it all to you and we'll never forget it."

I won't either. Not ever. You see, that was when I *did* want to kill him. But even then, if I hadn't been jointing the chickens when he said it and had a sharp knife in my hands, we'd still have been all right. I know we would.

THE KILLER BESIDE ME

Allan Guthrie

"We're long past our sell-by date." Trevor switched his grip on his cane. He'd been clutching it hard for ages now and his hand was clammy. What were the bastards up to, taking so long to get here?

"Bollocks," Harry said. "We've got a good couple of years in us yet. We've defied the odds so far. I'm looking forward to old age. Has its perks. You can spit on the floor and beat nosey children with your cane."

"But after a while," Trevor said, "you'll get tired of lying in a pile of your own shite."

"Or somebody else's."

"What're you saying? If anything, you'll lose control of your bowels before me."

"At least I can still get it up."

"Fuck you. Anyway, that's not what I mean. Just making a point," Trevor said. "We shouldn't be here. Not at our age."

"Fuck, we're not in our seventies yet. Don't write us off. I can see the day when we'll need special adult undergarments. I long for that day."

Trevor didn't move. He couldn't, not without his brother's help. The settee was too deep. A faded old two-seater, that's the best the fuckers could come up with. Stuffed out of the way in a room that was some kind of cleaning room. A hoover, mop in a bucket, stink of furniture polish. The bank manager had had to move a cardboard box full of rubber gloves and dusters before they'd been able to sit down. When he left, he'd locked the door behind him.

Where the fuck were the police?

Trevor said, "I once gave a blind man a blow job, you know."

"You did not."

"Did."

"Not."

"You were asleep."

"Shite."

"You were."

"I'd have woken up."

"You were drunk. Paralytic."

"Then you must have been too."

"You can't hold your drink. Anyway, it's true. Back at Aggie's—"

"I don't want to hear about it."

"Well, I'm telling you."

"I'm not listening." Harry started singing. But he couldn't drown out Trevor's voice. Especially after Trevor started shouting. Harry gave in, asked, "What happened?"

"He wandered into the bedroom by mistake. I heard him scuffling around, banging into things. I put on the light." Trevor adopted a high-pitched voice. "I spoke like this," he said. "Made him think he'd walked into a lady's room. Completely fooled him."

"But why?"

"For fun."

"No, why did you blow him?"

"He asked. Completely up front about it. And I felt sorry for him."

"That's fucking disgusting."

"A selfless act," Trevor said. "Some might say it was noble."

"Wonder what he'd think if he knew you were male."

"He'll never find out."

"I could tell him."

"But you don't know who it is."

"Bet I can guess."

Trevor said, "How the fuck?"

"How many blind people stayed at Aggie's?"

"Three. At least."

"One was a woman, so it wasn't her. So there's a fifty-fifty chance of me getting it right."

"Well, I'm not going to tell you."

"But I know, anyway."

"No way."

"Do too."

"Ah, away and shite, you old fuck."

The two old men were silent for a while. The sound of traffic seeped through the walls behind them.

"Who was it, then?" Trevor asked.

"Not telling."

"You don't fucking know. You were asleep. You don't remember it. So how can you know? You can only guess."

Harry shrugged. Well, as much as he was able to. "This conversation is over."

"Fine."

"Yeah, fine."

"Good."

"Well, shut up."

"I will."

"How did you turn out gay, anyway?"

"I'm not fucking gay."

"You gave a blind man a blow job."

"So?"

"That's pretty gay."

"You think so? How do you explain Edna, then?"

"Okay, so you're bisexual."

"At least I'm sexual."

"What's with you today? You've done nothing but pick on me from the minute we woke up."

Silence.

"The surgeon's in town."

"Huh?"

"The surgeon." Trevor stared at Harry's annoying blank face. "*The* surgeon. *Our* surgeon."

Harry looked away. "Shut up about that. It's not happening. You want to end up like Carslaw, back in '98?"

"Don't remember him."

"Yeah, you do. Big guy. Talked about cars all the time?"

"Vaguely."

"Went into hospital for a hip replacement," Harry said. "Never saw him again."

"Died?"

"Escaped. Outran the bastards, him and his dodgy hip."

"Yeah?"

"Course not, you thick twat. He went under the knife. Didn't have the heart for it. Went to sleep and never woke up. You don't remember?"

"Nope."

"Jesus. Maybe you're senile already."

"Fuck off."

"Can't speak to you. Don't know why I bother."

Trevor said, "Leave me alone then."

"I will."

"Give your pecker a tug."

"You sure you don't want to?"

"Fuck off, you dirty bastard."

"Well," Trevor said, after a while, "I expect an apology at the very least."

"For?"

Trevor crossed his arm over his chest. Said nothing.

"Huh?" Harry said. Shook his head. "Okay, I'm sorry I said you were gay."

"Not that. I don't care about that."

"Thought you wanted an apology."

"I do. But not for the gay remark."

"Well, what, then?"

"What do you think?"

"Fuck's sake, how am I supposed to know?"

"Take a wild guess."

"No," Harry said. Thought for a minute. "Nope. Nothing."

Trevor looked him in the eye.

"Well, maybe," Harry said. He looked down at his hand. He was better with his hand than Trevor was. Maybe because Harry was right-handed.

"Say it."

Harry sighed. "The robbery? Us ending up here?"

"Great fucking guess. You're a fucking genius."

"Sarcasm's unbecoming."

"Oh, but robbing a fucking bank without telling me is okay?"

"Didn't think you'd mind."

"Like I had any choice."

"You knew about the gun."

"Yeah, but how was I supposed to know what it was for?"

"What'd you think if was for?"

"I dunno. Self-defence?"

"Oh, yeah. You really believed that."

"Lots of kids about, what're they called, hoodies. You know they'll fuck us over, pair of old codgers like us, joined at the hip. Anyway, that's what you said."

"I lied. You always know when I lie."

"Not this time."

Silence. "So, you're claiming you had no idea? Not even an inkling?"

"That's right."

"Up until what point?"

"What do you mean?"

"At what point did you realize what was going on?"

"Once you got the gun out and said, 'Everybody freeze. This is a robbery.'"

"Pretty fucking cool, that."

"No, it wasn't. You're not cool. You'll never be cool. It's not even a proper fucking gun. You're retarded."

"Speak for yourself."

"Thanks, I will."

"So what's going to happen now?"

"Dunno. They'll fetch the police. And they'll probably come and handcuff us. Lead us off to some pokey room somewhere in a police station and bombard us with questions." Trevor paused. "I'm going to tell them the truth."

"Which is?"

"I was coerced into it."

"Coerced? Co*fucking*erced? I hate it when you know words I don't. How do you do that? I've never seen you so much as pick up a dictionary."

"You *forced* me to do it. That better?"

"Suit yourself. Doesn't bother me what you say."

"You'll back me up."

"I will?"

"Sure. You know it's the truth."

"But why should I?"

"Because you don't want to go to prison."

"What's you getting off with it got to do with me going to prison?"

"Everything. Think about it."

Pause.

"Well?"

Harry said, "I'm thinking."

"Nothing clicked?"

"If I'm guilty, they'll send me to prison."

"Yeah. But if I'm innocent, they can't send *me* to prison. So how do they arrange that, short of an operation?"

"Ah, I'm with you. Fucking nice."

A key scraped in the lock. Harry and Trevor got to their feet. Took a well-timed joint effort. A difficult operation, but they'd had lots of practice. They waddled forwards a couple of steps as the door opened. A young guy in a suit walked in tucking his bleached blonde hair behind his ear.

"Hi," Harry said. "You're the manager, right? I'm Harry. This is Trevor. Nice bank you've got. Don't like this room much, though. Smells like a summer breeze."

The bank manager ignored Harry, looked at Trevor.

Trevor said, "I'm innocent."

He nodded. "It's clear you weren't a willing participant. I could see you trying to get your brother to put down . . . this." He held up the gun. "Whatever it is."

"I was coerced." Trevor looked sideways at Harry.

"Don't you mean co-*arsed*?" Harry said. "Fucking cockjockey."

"So can I go?"

The bank manager said, "That may be problematic."

"But I'm innocent."

"I dare say." He pulled a face. "You'll have to wait for the police to decide."

"I want to go home."

"That's too bad."

"Harry can stay."

"That's impossible. Even if I could let you, it's physically impossible."

"But you've no right to keep me here."

"You have to stay till the police get here." The manager tucked his hair behind his ear again. "I have every right to insist on that."

"You're fucked," Harry said. He started laughing. "I robbed your bank. I pulled out my gun and waved it around and threatened people with it and there's fuck all you can do because I'm a Siamese twin and my brother's innocent."

"I thought," the bank manager said, "that the correct expression was 'conjoined twin'."

"To you," Harry said, "it is."

Trevor lashed out with his cane, struck the bank manager on the temple.

"Oh," Harry said. "Nice fucking shot."

"Thanks," Trevor said. The bank manager was sprawled on the floor. He groaned. "After three," Trevor said.

Together the conjoined twins lurched out of their seat. They bent over and Trevor picked up the gun. "You okay?" he asked the bank manager.

The bank manager opened his eyes, saw the gun in Trevor's hands, flinched.

"Know what it is?" Trevor said. "Humane killer. Used for killing livestock. Place the weapon to the animal's forehead like this." He placed the gun to the bank manager's forehead. "And then when you pull the trigger, it fires a steel bolt into the animal's brain."

The bank manager said, "No. For God's sake."

Trevor shrugged, straightened up. He turned, smiled at Harry. Placed the gun to his brother's forehead and pulled the trigger.

Harry jolted. A red circle beauty-spotted his brow. Blood began a slow trickle downwards. His eyes closed.

Trevor dropped the gun. "Jesus," he said.

Harry slumped to the side, dragging Trevor sideways. They fell on the floor, landing on top of the bank manager.

The bank manager cried out. Trevor struggled to get his wind back, then said, "Sorry."

No point trying to get back to his feet. That was an impossibility now.

The bank manager struggled out from beneath them, sat with his back to the wall, hugging his knees. After a while, he relaxed, gently massaged his temple. He moved forward, slowly, eyes on Trevor. Then he examined Harry. "You've killed him," he said. He picked up the gun, stared at it.

"Yeah," Trevor said. "Can you call an ambulance? Tell them they'll need to perform an emergency separation on a pair of conjoined twins. And they'll need to do it now. There's a number in my back pocket. They'll need to phone it. It's the number of a surgeon who can perform the operation."

"You planned this?"

"Harry would never agree to the op. Too risky."

"So you did agree to the robbery? You weren't as innocent as you claimed?"

"I'm admitting to nothing. Just call for an ambulance. And get the surgeon. He's in Edinburgh at the moment. But he's on standby." Trevor paused. "Hurry. I think I'm going into shock."

"What if I refuse?"

"No matter." Trevor was short of breath. "The police'll bring an ambulance with them. Where are they?"

"Ah, Trevor," the bank manager said. "You really believe a couple of geriatric Siamese – forgive me – *conjoined* twins having a public argument constitutes a serious enough threat for us to call the police?"

"But my brother asked for your money."

"And you told him to be quiet."

"But he waved his gun around." Trevor glanced at the humane killer in the bank manager's hand.

"And you took it off him and gave it to a teller."

"So, what are you saying? You didn't call the police?"

"Nope. No police." He paused. "No ambulance." He walked towards the door.

"Fuck," Trevor said. "I won't survive longer than a couple of hours on my own. Harry's dead. Don't you understand what that means?"

The bank manager turned in the doorway, said, "I understand completely."

"Come on," Trevor said. "What kind of a sadistic fuck are you?"

"I'm a bank manager." The door closed.

UNCLE HARRY

Reginald Hill

"What I need to make clear and you need to get clear is, any resemblance between me and a real terrorist is purely coincidental.

"We've nothing in common, me and those guys. My thing was personal, not ideological. The only common ground was putting the thing together, which did teach me one thing about their line of business that I'd never realized before.

"The trouble with being a terrorist is that you experience a lot of terror!

"Not perhaps if you're one of those mad sods who reckon that blowing up a busload of people on their way to work is a first-class ticket to a world full of warm sunshine, sweet music, soft couches and doe-eyed virgins.

"But for a middle-aged, rationalist, atheist humanist who claims to believe that this life is all you get – *finito* – good night Vienna – this is the end, there is no more – then sitting in your flat trying to follow the instructions on your laptop that will turn the motley assembly of chemicals, wires, batteries and clock parts strewn across your kitchen table into a lethal weapon is fraught with terror, believe me.

"You will note I say *claims* to believe.

"It never really goes away, does it, all that religious stuff you get drummed into you when you're a kid? Mature logic and experience may seem to wash it all out of your mind, but scrub as hard as you like, if you look carefully under a bright light you can still find the faint outline of an indelible *what if?*

"And a laptop screen showing a DIY bomb recipe casts a very bright light indeed.

"Now this may not be so bad if your *what if?* tunes in images of all that sweet music and doe-eyed virgins stuff. The trouble is no matter how I cut it, the *what if?* my upbringing has left me with produces pictures of fires that burn but do not consume, grinning devils, souls in paroxysms of pain, eternities of agony.

"Killing people is wrong, my dad used to say. Doesn't matter who, how, why, when or where, take a life and your soul belongs to Satan.

"Of course being a preacher, he would say that, wouldn't he?

"Not necessarily, you may think. There are plenty of preachers able to trot out any number of exceptions to the sixth commandment. Where would politicians be without them? But my dad was a fundamentalist, which was surprising, seeing that he was C of E from a good old traditional Middle England background. When he got up in the pulpit you'd have looked for skeins of soporific platitude followed by a pre-lunch sherry at the vicarage. Instead he made most Welsh chapel sermons sound like Christopher Robin saying his prayers.

"'Ten commandments there are!' he'd thunder. 'Just ten. Not a lot to remember, not a number to over-tax even the mind of a poor stockbroker wending his weary way home on the five-fifty-five after a long hard day breaking stock. No! God reviewed his Creation and He thought, *these humans look all right, most of them, even the stockbrokers, but I've got to face it, I did skimp on the brain power. So best keep it simple. Ten fingers they've got, so surely they'll be able to count up to ten?* And that's how we got the Decalogue. Ten simple commandments. No riders, no sub-clauses. You do what they say, or else! There's no Fifth Amendment saying, *honour thy father and thy mother until you become a teenager, then anything goes.* There's no Six-and-a-halfth Commandment that says, *Thou shalt not kill except in the following circumstances.* NO! These are God's rules!! Break them, and, believe me, YOU WILL BURN!!!'

"I found that gem in a bundle of his old sermons which had turned up in the Bombay Mission. They'd been moving premises and Dad's papers would have been burned with all the other rubbish if Sister Angela, the Mission's chief administrator, hadn't spotted them. She always had a soft spot for me and we've kept in touch, even though she knows I've strayed a long way from my father's path since last we met. Possibly she thought that forwarding a small selection of the sermons might nudge me back. Sorry, Angela, no deal, though they certainly brought Dad back to me, and that early one at least gave me a laugh as I imagined how sentiments like these must have gone down in the rich Surrey parish where he started his ministry! No wonder it wasn't long before his bishop suggested his talents might be better employed in a more challenging environment (i.e. one a long way away from Surrey). He probably meant anywhere north of Watford, but Dad never did things by half and that was how he came to be pastor of the Ecumenical Mission settlement in Mumbai, or Bombay as it still was back in the Seventies.

"So if we look for first causes, it was the dear old bishop who was responsible for putting my father into the predatory path of Uncle Harry. He's dead too, the bishop, so in the unlikely event of their mythology proving true, Dad will have eternity to harangue the poor chap for not letting him continue his God-given task of bashing the brokers.

"I suppose by the same token we could say that ultimately it was the bishop's pusillanimity that led to me setting out on my long bus journey from Battersea this morning, gingerly clutching an eight by four by two brown paper package on my knee.

"Dad had got it wrong, you see. In my view there definitely is a Six-and-a-halfth Commandment, and what it says is: killing's OK when the target has enjoyed the rewards of his villainy for decades and looks like he's heading for the winning post so far ahead of the Law, he no longer even bothers to glance back over his shoulder.

"Religion, if you've got it, might be a comfort here. *Vengeance is mine; I will repay, saith the Lord*, Dad liked to thunder, meaning don't worry that there's no justice in this world, there'll be plenty in the next. Well, I'd like to believe that, Dad, but despite those residual *what-if*s I mentioned earlier, I really don't. Meaning, unless I take care of the bastard, no one else will.

"So there I was carrying a bomb through the streets of London to rid the world of the villain who'd destroyed my family.

"Does that make me a terrorist? In the eyes of the Law, I suppose it does. To me, what I was planning to do was an act of justice, but I suppose that's what all the doe-eyed virgin boys say too. Though I must confess it did occur to me as I sat on the bus that if I'd got something wrong – an ingredient too volatile, a connection too loose – and we bounced over a pothole a bit deeper than the norm even on this stretch of the Earls Court Road, none of these innocent people around me would be interested in making fine distinctions.

"I had learned to clasp my package a bit tighter as a stop approached. This driver must have missed the bit on his training course about gradually applying the brakes. By this time I only had one more stop to go. I was glad to see most of the other passengers had got out. Only a perspiring bald man and his glossily veneered companion remained, and they didn't look too innocent.

"I glanced down at my package. It looked good. I never throw anything away and when I decided it would be both convincing and appropriate if the instrument of Uncle Harry's death seemed to have come from the site of his infamy, I had dug out the brown paper Sister Angela had wrapped the sermons in. Of course I couldn't simply reuse it, not with my address all over it in the Sister's fine copperplate. But with infinite care I had been able to remove the stamps and enough of the Mumbai post mark to be convincing, and transfer them to my own parcel.

"An Indian fan, he would think, an admirer on the subcontinent who has remembered my birthday. How terribly kind! And full of anticipation he would rip the package open . . .

"Surprise!

"I hoped he'd have time to take in the writing on the inside lid of the box before the bang. I'd cut it from the title page of one of my father's sermons and pasted it there.

"It read: *On Divine Retribution* by DLP Lachrymate DD.

"Yes, he was a three initial man too. Perhaps that was why it was so easy for Uncle Harry to ensnare him. *Three forenames means a man comes from a family with a pride in their past*, Dad would say. *You can always trust a man with three initials. Never buy a used car from a one initial man. Hesitate to lend money to someone with only two. But give your hand and your trust when you see that third initial!*

"Four he felt a little ostentatious except in the case of royalty.

"I have three, of course. PDL. Same as my father's only the order is changed.

"That's me all over. All the same elements as my father only the order is changed.

"I too believe in retribution and hellfire, but I want them now!

"I wouldn't like you to think that I have spent my life obsessing about my poor father's fate. I was only six when he died. To me, one day he was there, the next he wasn't. Everyone talked about him being in a better place, but how a place could be better that didn't have me and Mum in it, I could never fathom. As to how he got there, throughout my youth I was well protected from any real knowledge of what had actually happened. Certainly without him the place we were in seemed a great deal worse. My mother continued to work at the Mission. I don't think she really had a wage, just the occasional subsistence level hand out. I expect it was the same for the rest of them. It was probably believed that any complaints about wage levels could be answered by pointing to the squalor and abject poverty around us and saying, 'How can you look at that and still complain?'

"Myself, I don't think Mother gave a toss about remuneration levels. I don't even think she had any real interest in the Mission's work. All she wanted was see me through to the age of independence then, with a sigh of relief, give up the ghost and go to join her lost husband, which is exactly what she did.

"It was after the funeral, in dribs and drabs, that Sister Angela told me the story. She had to support her own memory of events from a report she had written for the Mission Trustees at the time. It was couched in a curious mixture of Indian Civil Service jargon and King James Bible English. It went something like this.

"*The comprehensive recording procedures installed at the Mission by the present writer acting on the excellent advice of CK Bannerjee (Bachelor of Law-University of Bombay) by the grace of God our legal officer, enable us to trace precisely the first appearance of the subtle serpent, Keating, on our premises. For it is clearly written in the Book of Visitors that he was a guest in our midst at tea-time on the fifteenth day of May in the year of our Lord, 1974, as testified by his own signature, HRS Keating.*

"As her narrative unfolded, it took me some time to realise that this serpent she was talking about, the architect of all our woes, was in fact Uncle Harry.

"Not really my uncle, of course. But within a very short time of his first appearance at the Mission, that's what I was calling him. I remembered him very well, and all my memories were pleasant ones. He was a merry, voluble man in his late forties, always willing to spend time with me and treat me to ices from one of the street vendors that my mother warned me against but whose wares I adored. (In fact I never had any stomach trouble all my life till I came to England and tried a Shepherd's Pie out of a pub microwave.) I knew vaguely that he was some kind of writer and Sister Angela now confirmed that the fraud by which he gained access to the Mission was that he was gathering material for a book about the disenfranchised, destitute and often criminal classes that my father worked amongst. Certainly he had real creative talent. Often when his visits coincided with my bedtime, he would fill my head with marvellous stories of high adventure and wild excitement. These were a rare treat. Mother had no narrative gift and for Father any story that did not come from the Bible was so much factitious frippery.

"Curiously, it is Dad's tales of Samson pulling down the temple, and the death of Jezebel, and the slaughter of the Benjamites, that remain with me while Uncle Harry's marvellous stories have all faded. But at the time I waited like a drug addict for the next instalment.

"But the real evidence of Uncle Harry's powers of invention lies in the way he took in my father.

"I think the trouble was – and Sister Angela confirmed this – that Dad believed his life was directed by God. When he asked a question, God answered it with the result that in decision he was incisive and in judgment, absolute. And for the twenty years of his adult life, this had worked.

"So when he asked God about Uncle Harry and he thought

he heard God telling him *Harry's OK*, that was it. In my father's eyes, friends, and enemies, were forever.

"Thus when Uncle Harry came to him in a distracted state, he didn't hesitate. The pitch was that Harry's widowed mother who lived in the States was seriously ill and her only chance of survival lay in a new transplant procedure, which only one hospital in the country could offer. Harry was on his way to see her now. He had realized his assets and managed to raise most of what was needed to pay for the procedure. But he was still short, and though he would have the rest in a fortnight's time when an investment bond matured, by then it might be too late.

"I can remember Uncle Harry's distraction, though its alleged cause was of course unknown to me till Sister Angela filled me in. My reason for remembering was purely selfish. It was 19 May, my sixth birthday, and I felt I ought to be the centre of everyone's attention.

"Not that Harry's pretended agitation prevented him from bringing me a splendid present, a wooden locomotive big enough for me to straddle which made whooping noises just like the real thing when you pulled a cord.

"It might have been this generosity, plus of course the three initials, that made my father rise to the bait.

" 'How much do you need?' he asked.

" 'Fifteen hundred pounds,' said Harry.

"Now you should understand that the Mission finances were on a very hand-to-mouth basis. Only the big charities could afford to do national appeals in those days, and even they weren't yet the streamlined corporate machines for extracting money from the public they have since become. So the Mission relied very much on local charitable donations and there was rarely much in the kitty. But just the day before, a rather dodgy local businessman had decided to spring-clean his conscience by donating a couple of lakhs of rupees. He'd been on the brink for a week or so, and the proposed act of charity had almost turned into a bazaar haggle with my father as to how much, or rather how little, would see him right with the Christian God. My father had probably entertained Uncle Harry with a description of the man's hesitations. Finally the previous day, a threat of police investigation had made the vacillating villain decide he needed help from all the deities available and he'd turned up with the cash which was now in the Mission safe.

"How much cash?

"In sterling, about fifteen hundred pounds.

"Surprise.

"To my father this was evidence of God's handiwork.

"To Angela, with hindsight, it was evidence of Uncle Harry's brilliant opportunism.

"Dad, who had a key to the safe – why wouldn't he? – gave Harry the money on the promise that it would be paid within two weeks. Harry left that night with protestations of eternal gratitude and the cash. Probably his gratitude was genuine enough, or does a con man simply despise his mark? Whatever, Uncle Harry and the fifteen hundred pounds quickly vanished from Bombay and our lives, never to be seen again.

"It evidently took my father a whole month to admit that neither was about to reappear.

"So that was it. A sting. Not a particularly big one in the grand scale of stings, though fifteen hundred was worth a lot more back then. The trustees of the Mission took it, if not in their stride, at least with the resigned philosophy of men long accustomed to dealing with humanity at its worst. They read Sister Angela's report and, judging that chances of the police catching up with Uncle Harry were remote and of recovering the money non-existent, they decided it was better to hush the whole thing up rather than risk putting off other potential benefactors.

"So, all in all, an unpleasant experience which many men after the first shock might have treated as a rough but salutary lesson.

"Not Dad.

"You see it undermined that supremely confident belief in his own God-backed judgment which had been the mainstay of his being these many years. If he'd got this wrong, what else had he got wrong? It pulled away or at least seriously damaged one of the mainstays of his faith.

"Within a fortnight of recognizing he'd been conned, a fortnight during which by Angela's account he worked like a man possessed, he went out on some errand of mercy one night and that was all that anyone saw of him till his body was pulled out of the Mazagon Docks a fortnight later. The fish had worked at it so much that cause of death could never be established. Suicide? I don't like to think so. I want to believe he just took a risk too far and paid the price.

"All these memories rolled through my mind as I sat on that bus, and the violent jolt as the vehicle crashed to a halt at my stop took me by surprise and I almost dropped the package. As I stepped onto the pavement, despite the cool autumn air I was sweating.

"I had walked the route before while making my plans so I set off at a brisk pace towards my destination. Getting the package delivered without arousing suspicion was always going to be the hard part, but I'd worked out a method. It was not without risk, but apart from knocking at Uncle Harry's door and handing it over to whoever answered, I couldn't think of anything better.

"Now the end was near, I felt only relief. Like I say, at the time of Dad's death I'd been a child, and was devastated like a child, and then had adapted like a child. Mother's death had hit me harder. And when I learned from Angela that Uncle Harry's chicanery had ultimately been the cause of both of them, I got very angry.

"But I was only eighteen and at eighteen you're very angry at a lot of things. The main long term effect of learning the true facts was to finally make me dump the religious baggage I'd been dragging after me all my short life. I looked around and saw that the world was full of goodies and the only way to get your share was to go in hot pursuit. So that's what I did, mainly in the sub-continent where I'd grown up, with occasional forays to Malaysia and the Antipodes.

"Then with youth well behind me and my fortieth birthday lumbering ever closer, I got the chance to come and work in England.

"Why not? After all I was English, that's what my passport said. So back I came to this cold, damp, unwelcoming country. After six months I was beginning to think it was a mistake. I reached the dreaded fortieth in May and in this dreadful climate, it felt more like fifty. I had to get out, but my contract bound me here at least till Christmas. By the end of September I was feeling desperate. I looked back at my life and it seemed a wasted journey, and I looked forward and saw only a road to nowhere. Then one evening as I travelled back to my lonely apartment, I picked up a bookshop magazine that someone had left on the train.

"Now I'm not a reading man myself, and it was in a mood of cynical mockery that I glanced down a list of newsworthy forthcoming events in the literary calendar. Who the hell could really be interested in dinners to award prizes to novelists or the publication of a ghosted life of some idiot sportsman too thick to write his own biography?

"Then something leapt out at me.

"*Notable Anniversaries*

"*On 31 October, the distinguished crime writer and well known figure on the London literary scene, Mr Harry Keating, best known as the creator of the famous series of books featuring Inspector Ghote of the Bombay Police, will be celebrating his eightieth birthday, to general rejoicing.*

"Keating . . . Bombay . . . it couldn't be coincidence. This had to be Uncle Harry!

"When I arrived at my station I popped into the bookshop.

"Quite a lot of his books were on the shelves. I bought a couple and took them back to my flat.

"I raced through them. The detailed knowledge of Bombay life and topography could only have come from a man who knew the city inside out. And when I looked at the author photo on the back cover of the book, I knew I was right.

"He had attempted to change his appearance by growing a rather fine bushy beard, but there was no disguising that splendid hook nose.

"Uncle Harry. The subtle serpent who had destroyed my family's personal paradise.

"I thought of my dead parents. Then I thought of this man, approaching eighty, basking in the love of friends and family, acknowledging the applause of the world of literature. And suddenly it seemed to me that here was fate offering me a chance to do at least one meaningful act before I died! I told you that Dad used to believe God spoke directly to him. It must be in the genes. For the first time in my life I heard a voice speak in my head.

"*Let him get to eighty. But make sure he gets no further!*

"God? I didn't think so. After all, I don't believe in God. I refuse to believe in God!

"But as I approached Northumberland Place I found myself thinking, this is the real test, this is where things need to go absolutely smoothly or it's all in vain. If the Almighty really reckons this is a good idea, then the next few minutes will be a stroll in the park.

"And a few minutes later, I knew I had the divine seal of approval.

"The post van which I'd watched for five mornings on the trot the previous week showed up within the usual fifteen minute range. And about five minutes before it turned into Northumberland Place, it parked in its usual spot outside a block of flats. The driver got out with an armful of letters and packages and went into the building. On previous evidence he would be in there a good five minutes, sometimes longer. Perhaps someone gave him a cup of tea, or something. I moved forward, checked there was no one watching me, opened the van door and leaned inside. There were several bags filled with mail. I pulled a couple of envelopes out of the nearest one. I was really on a divine providence roll, for they both bore Uncle Harry's name and address! As I'd anticipated from all I'd read about him, the world was so overcome with joy at the great man's eightieth birthday that his numerous gifts and greetings merited a separate bag.

"I dropped my packet into it, closed the door and went on my way.

"I thought of hanging around to listen for the bang, but there was no way of foretelling how long it would be before he opened his last present, and I didn't want to be picked up on CCTV loitering in the area. So I came home and waited for the news to come over the airwaves. *Famous writer killed by bomb on 80th birthday*. That must make the headlines, surely?

"Instead after nearly three hours just as I was getting really impatient, the doorbell rang, I opened the door, and there you were holding up your ID, and I knew things had gone seriously wrong.

"But not so wrong, Detective Inspector Gospill, that you need to treat me as a terrorist! So why not get that out of the way, then perhaps you won't need to sit here any longer waiting for this Commander Grisewood who seems to be such a very bad time-keeper.

"You could start off by telling me exactly what's happened. And where did it all go wrong?"

After my arrest, I'd been brought to Scotland Yard and left sitting in an interview room for well over an hour with a blank faced constable for company.

Finally DI Gospill reappeared, the constable left, and I waited for the interview to start. When nothing happened, I asked him what the hold-up was. He said that we were waiting for his superior, Commander Grisewood, who was returning from a conference in the Midlands. I said surely there must be enough senior officers sitting around on their thumbs in Scotland Yard for one of them to deal with the matter. What was so special about this man Grisewood anyway?

And that was when he told me, in a tone of some irritation not totally aimed at me, that Commander Grisewood was in charge of the unit which dealt with terrorist acts by British nationals and that for reasons best known to himself he wanted to conduct my interview personally, to which end he had given strict orders that nothing was to be done until he arrived, which should have been half an hour ago.

I might have been amused by the thought that Gospill was clearly missing a very important date because of this, but one word had caught all my attention and there was nothing amusing about it.

Terrorist!

That's what had launched me into my long defence and justification.

Gospill tried to interrupt me a couple of times, presumably to point out that the tape wasn't on and I'd have to say it all again. But once I got started, out it all came, and finally he sat back and listened. He never switched the recorder on but after a while he did start making notes.

When I finished he made no attempt to answer my concluding question but sat with furrowed brow in complete silence.

Then his phone rang.

He listened, said, "Jesus H. Christ!" and switched off.

I said, "What?"

"Accident on the motorway," he said, not really in answer to me but in accusation against some malevolent fate. "Twenty-mile tailback. Jesus!"

Then he picked his notes and without another word rose and left the room, to be replaced by the silent constable.

Another hour went by. I tried to provoke the constable to speech by requesting a drink. He went to the door and bellowed, "Tea!" and that was all I got for my effort at social intercourse, except for a cup of tea so foul there'd have been a riot if it had been served in India. By the time Gospill returned I was feeling very irritated and ready to be extremely uncooperative.

"Now listen, inspector," I said. "Either you start answering my questions or you'll get no answers when you start asking yours."

To my surprise he smiled.

"Certainly, Mr Lachrymate," he said. "Now let me see. I seem to recall the last question you asked me was, where did it all go wrong? Where indeed? My problem is knowing where to begin. You made more mistakes than Tony bloody Blair! But let's start with the biggest one of all, shall we? You clearly didn't stop for a moment and consider who it was you were dealing with!"

I said weakly, "Sorry, I don't understand. . . ."

"Clearly! Well, listen and learn. Now, I like watching detective series on the box as much as the next man, and I've read quite a lot of crime novels too, and I can tell you, from a professional point of view, they're mainly very ripe farmyard manure. What most of them writers know about real detection you could write on the end of a gnat's cock without arousing it.

"But this Mr Keating, he's different. He's been at it so long, there's stuff he could teach us! So there he is, on his eightieth birthday, opening his prezzies, and he sees this package from India. Or at least it looks as if it's from India. Except that he can't see a Customs Declaration.

"Funny, he thinks. So he looks closer. Now he gets a lot of mail from India, does Mr Keating. He's big out there, it seems. And he's got lots of young relatives and friends who collect stamps so he takes note of the postage. So here's what his sharp detective mind gets puzzling over. He knows the Indian Post Office Speedpost rates to the UK are 675 rupees for the first 250 grams and 75 for each additional 250 grams. So why should a package which weighs about 1200 grams only have the basic 675 rupees postage on it?"

He paused. If his intention was to alleviate his own irritation by making me feel foolish, he was succeeding. Seeing this, he smiled malevolently and pressed home his advantage.

"But there was something else, something much more basic. The very first thing that attracted his keen detective eye was the fact that you got his name wrong."

"I don't believe that," I said indignantly. "I'm absolutely sure I didn't misspell Keating."

"No, you got that right," he admitted. "It was the initials you cocked up. It's HRF, not HRS."

I checked my memory bank which is usually pretty reliable. It definitely printed out Uncle Harry's initials as HRS.

"Are you quite sure?" I asked.

"Dead sure. Look for yourself."

From his pocket he produced one of the Keating paperbacks I'd bought and dropped it on the table.

He was quite right.

HRF Keating.

"I don't know how I got that wrong," I muttered disconsolately.

"I do," he said smugly. "As soon as we were alerted to this attempt on Mr Keating's life, we contacted our colleagues in Mumbai to check if the postmark was genuine and to ask if they might be able to throw any light on the outrage. They got back to us about forty minutes ago. And it was the thing about the wrong initial that put them on to it. Very efficient record keepers, those boys. It seems that about thirty years ago, in 1973 to be precise, they had their eye on a suspected con man who was using the name Keating. Our Mr Keating's name was already getting to be well known in literary circles over there, and this fellow was obviously trying to cash in on it by implying that he was the distinguished British crime writer, without actually saying it. By using the famous three initials he put the idea into people's minds, but by changing the last one from F to S (which sounds very much the same if you say it fast) he put himself just out of reach of a charge of personation. Clever that. Of course from what you say, in your parents' case it probably didn't matter as they don't sound the types to be interested in anything so worldly as detective novels."

"No, I'm pretty sure they thought Agatha Christie was a nun," I burbled as I tried to come to terms with what he'd just said. "I'm sorry, inspector, but are you telling me that HRF Keating the writer isn't the same man as HRS Keating, my Uncle Harry, the con man?"

"Of course he's not, you moron," snapped Gospill. "Do you think a man like Mr Keating would go around conning people out of money? In any case, what happened to your father happened in 1973, right? Well, it's on the record that our Mr Keating didn't make his first visit to India till a couple of years later!"

"No, that can't be true," I objected. "From the dates on those books of his, he'd been writing about Inspector Ghote for a whole decade by then. How could a man show such an intimate knowledge of a country without visiting it? Who's to say he didn't make an earlier trip before this official one he admits to?"

"You are," he cried triumphantly. "You mentioned it was your birthday, your sixth birthday, on the day that your father let Uncle Harry con him out of them rupees. And that would be the nineteenth of May, right?"

"Right."

"Well, by one of those quirks of fate which protect good innocent people and put toe-rags like you in jail, Mr Keating, who is a meticulous record keeper, was able to tell us exactly where he was on that date. He was at a Crime Writers' Conference in Harrogate on the weekend of Friday 18 to Sunday 20 May 1973, and he was able to give us the names of several other writers of unimpeachable character and unfaultable memory who were delighted to confirm what he said. So there it is. You picked on the wrong man, stupid!"

I was beginning to be seriously annoyed by his attitude. I mean, I might be a murder suspect, but there was no need to be rude!

And in any case, now I thought about it, I wasn't actually a murder suspect, was I? From the way he was talking, the attempt must certainly have failed.

For the sake of certainty, I continued to ignore his rudeness and asked, "So Mr Keating is all right, is he? I mean, from what you say, the bomb didn't go off?"

"Yes, I'm glad to say Mr Keating is alive and well and at this very moment no doubt entertaining his friends at his birthday party with the story of the idiot who tried to blow him up. Of course, what he doesn't know yet because the bomb squad only confirmed it an hour ago was that he never was in any real danger. Don't know where you got your recipe from, Mr Lachrymate, but the experts say there was as much chance of your bomb going off as there is of Mr Keating's birthday cake blowing up when they light the candles!"

I suppose I should have felt relieved, but all I felt at that moment was an utter incompetent fool.

"So," I said wretchedly, "I got the wrong man and I made a dud bomb."

Then cheering up a little because it's not in my nature to be down for long, I went on, "But if my bomb wasn't really a bomb and no one actually got hurt, I can't have committed a crime, can I? Certainly not a terrorist crime. In fact, nothing more than a slap on the wrist, ASBO, two weeks community service kind of crime!"

He laughed.

If Bloody Judge Jeffreys laughed as he was handing down sentences, it probably sounded like that.

"Never believe it, sunshine. We've got you bang to rights. That's another little error you made. A pro knows that you burn all the stuff that could be evidence against you as you go along. But with you we've got the lot. All them notes you made planning out the attack, the hard disk from your computer showing the terrorist sites you accessed, not forgetting the bomb itself. OK, it might be a Mickey Mouse device with as much chance of working as a chocolate teapot, but it's got your prints all over it. This government may not have done much but they did pass some legislation that makes the intention as culpable as the deed. As the very old bishop said to the actress at the third time of asking, 'it's intent that counts, darling'. Way people feel about terrorist threats these days, I'd say you're looking at ten years minimum."

The shock nearly made me faint. *It's intent that counts.* That's what my dad used to say about sin. I never knew it applied in law too.

Ten years . . . I'd be fifty by the time I got out . . . I'd be an old man!

Gospill's phone rang.

He growled, "Yeah?", then suddenly sat up to attention and said, "Yes, Commander! I'm with him now, Commander. No, I haven't started the interrogation. Definitely not. Yes, I've collected all the physical evidence, and I've put it on your desk so that you can take a look at it before you start. Yes, sir, it's confirmed the device is quite safe. Commander, can I suggest . . . yes . . . what I meant was . . . thank you, sir. See you soon. Look forward to it, sir. Goodbye."

I got the impression the Commander had cut him off short and the last few phrases were for my benefit.

He caught me looking at him and snarled, "That's happy hour over, Lachrymate. Commander Grisewood's just coming into the building and he'll be along here soon as he checks out the evidence bags on his desk. And that's when your troubles are really going to begin, believe me."

I believed him. So much so that for the first time since I was a child, I found myself saying a little prayer to God. To Dad's God. Something on the lines of, "OK, God, after the crap you heaped on my mum and dad, you owe the Lachrymate family. I'd really appreciate it if you could come through now."

My lips must have moved.

Gospill said, "What?"

I said for the want of anything else to say, "So how did you get on to me so quick?"

"Easy," he said. "That sermon title you pasted on the lid of the box. *Divine Retribution* by DLP Lachrymate DD. Not many Lachrymates in London, believe me. In fact, you're the only one. With the same initials in a different order. And as soon as you opened the door, I saw you were our boy."

He looked so smug and self satisfied, I offered another little prayer, this time for a thunderbolt to come down and destroy him.

At the same moment we both heard a distant bang, like a birthday balloon being punctured. Perhaps God had taken aim and missed.

For a moment nothing happened, then came the distant shrill of an alarm bell.

Gospill sat looking at me for a moment then he rose.

"Wait there," he commanded and went to the door.

He closed it firmly behind him but I didn't hear a lock click.

After a little while I stood up, went to the door and opened it a crack.

I could see Gospill at the end of the corridor. He was talking to a uniformed sergeant who had a phone to his ear.

I opened the door a little further so I could hear them.

"What's going on, sarge?" I heard Gospill ask.

"Not sure, sir. Just checking it out. Think there's been an explosion."

"I gathered that!" snapped the DI. "Where?"

"Hang about, sir, I'm getting something now . . . yes . . . yes . . . you're sure? So no evacuation . . . that's good . . . that's very good . . . OK, thanks."

He switched off his phone and said to Gospill, "It's OK, sir, Seems a device went off, and there's been a bit of a fire and quite a lot of damage, but it's all been confined to one room and no one's hurt. So no panic and we can stay put. Reckon someone's head's going to roll though. Doesn't look good, letting a bomber get right into the heart of the Yard!"

A pause, then Gospill asked too casually, "Whose room?"

Even at a distance I could here the tremolo in his voice.

"Not absolutely sure, sir, but they think it was Commander Grisewood's. Made a right mess from the sound of it. All those lovely water colours his missus did and he was so proud of, they'll have gone. Oh, someone's in real trouble, believe me!"

I closed the door quietly and went back to my seat.

Things were looking better. I'd been very stupid but there wasn't a commandment saying *Thou shalt not be stupid.* And now with nothing of what I'd said so far on tape, and all the physical evidence against me probably burning merrily away with the Commander's desk, all I needed to do was continue to look stupid and say nothing.

Thank you, Dad's God. You came through!

The Ghote novel Gospill had produced still lay on the table. I picked it up and looked at the author photo.

No longer could I see much resemblance to the plausible crook who all those years ago had touched on my family's life then gone on his way. Probably he'd been dead for years.

IN SOME COUNTRIES

Jerry Raine

The day's work was over and the sun was sinking on the horizon. Inside the kitchen Woody Granger was eating supper on his own. He usually ate with the Cutter family but he'd been late coming back from the field where he'd been fixing fences all day and the family were next door in the living room playing cards. Woody preferred eating on his own though. He wasn't much of a conversationalist. Never had been, never would be. He was a sixteen-year-old orphan drifting through Tennessee, getting work where he could.

He finished his cup of coffee and carried his dishes to the sink. The living room door opened and Harold Cutter came in. He was a large red-faced man with thick hairy arms and a belly that hung over the belt of his jeans. Woody was a bit scared of him because he could never tell what kind of mood his employer would be in. Sometimes they would joke together, and other times, when either the work was too hard or the sun too hot, they would nearly come to blows.

"Do you want to come with me tonight Woody?" Harold asked, as he made his way to the pantry.

Finishing his dishes, Woody said over his shoulder, "Okay," when he really wanted to be going back to his room.

Harold came out of the pantry carrying a bucket with a chopper and two large knives inside. Woody's heart dipped.

He dried his hands and Harold pointed to a lantern that was sitting on the table. "Carry please," he said, then they walked out into the yard.

At the sound of the screen-door slamming, six dogs sprang out from under bushes and chairs and came running towards their master with heads bowed low and tales wagging. Woody smiled at them and patted Mickey, the eldest.

"Are we taking the horses?" Woody asked.

"No, we'll walk," Harold said. "The sheep are only in the home paddock."

Woody was disappointed. He always liked riding, especially at night. He walked alongside Harold and threw sticks for the dogs. His favourite was Snowy, who was in fact black. He also had a soft spot for Skunk, a grey and white streaked dog who was permanently chained at the back of the house. Skunk was a sheep killer and was very rarely let off his leash.

Ten minutes later and they were at the home paddock. Harold unlocked the gate and they all went through, the dogs getting excited when they saw the hundred or so sheep in the distance.

They walked to a large tree in the centre of the field. The tree had no leaves and the branches were wrinkled and crooked like the fingers of an old man. Hanging from one of the branches was a large hook and the bottom of the trunk was stained with dried blood. Harold left his bucket by the tree and called out to the dogs.

"Get back! Get back! Fetch 'em up! Fetch 'em up!"

The dogs ran towards the herd, some going right and some going left. They got right behind the sheep and barked at them and nipped their legs. The herd moved slowly forward.

Harold and Woody waited by the tree. The sun was almost down and soon it would be dark. Woody lit the lantern and hung it from a branch.

"Just watch what I do this time," Harold said, "and next time you can have a go yourself. Just give me the knives when I tell you."

Woody had only been working on the farm for six months. He'd been down on his luck, sitting in a bar in town, wondering where to go to next, when he'd overheard a conversation about work. He'd walked the five miles to the Kerren Ranch and started work straight away. He was the only person the Cutters employed.

Woody watched as the sheep came nearer and soon they were surrounding the tree with no escape, the dogs keeping them in a neat circle.

Harold walked into the middle of them still calling to the dogs, but not so loudly now. He pushed and prodded, looking for the right sheep, then grabbed one round the neck and dragged it over to the tree.

"Okay, Woody," he said.

Woody took one of the large carving knives from the bucket and gave it to him. Harold had the sheep lying backwards between his legs with his strong hands around its neck. He took the knife and started cutting into its throat. It made a crunching noise as it cut through the main arteries and Woody winced as he saw the blood coming out. It ran dark red down the sheep's stomach and then as the knife went deeper it started to bubble in the deep cut and now and then a small fountain would squirt on to the ground. The sheep's eyes stayed open for what seemed like a long time and then they shut and Harold let the body fall. It lay on the ground with the blood spreading into the ground, and then its back legs twitched and then the animal was still.

Harold wiped his bloody hands on a tuft of grass and went back to find another sheep. He killed this one the same way and then he told the dogs to back away. The sheep slowly wandered back to where they had been before, minus their two friends that lay at the foot of the tree.

Woody watched Harold go to work on the sheep. His arms were now covered with blood as he chopped off the two heads. Then he skinned the two animals by slitting open their bellies. The dogs were sniffing and looking anxiously, eager for the innards that Harold would eventually give them.

"Give me a hand here, Woody," Harold said. Together they lifted the first sheep and hung it upside down from the hanging hook. Woody turned away from the smell as Harold cut out the stomach, bright green chewed grass falling from a split. He threw it to the dogs along with the intestines. The dogs gathered around hungrily and ripped the flesh to bits. Woody was disappointed to see Snowy joining in the fun.

Harold continued cleaning out the carcass and took it off the hook and laid it out on an old rug that was lying behind the tree. Then they hooked up the second sheep and Harold went to work again.

"It's pretty easy," he said, "once you get used to the smell. The smell's the worst bit."

"Yeah, it doesn't smell too good," Woody said.

They took down the second sheep when the carcass was clean and placed it alongside the other one on the rug. They also placed the two skins on there. Although they were bloody and dirty they would be put on the shed roof and later on when they were dried out and stiff, they would be sold.

They each took a corner of the rug and started pulling it and the sheep back towards the farm. It was slow going and Harold kept shouting at the dogs to move away as they were now getting interested in the good meat.

"I usually just kill one sheep," Harold said, "but with you here I can pull an extra one back. When we've eaten this lot I'll let you kill the next two."

Great, Woody thought to himself. *I'll be looking forward to that.*

When they were back at the farm they lifted the carcasses on to one of the water tanks where they would be out of reach of the dogs. They would stay there until morning when Harold would cut them into smaller chunks and his wife Molly would then put them into storage.

From a tap in the garden the two of them washed their hands and shook them dry. They stood in the kitchen light that came across the veranda. The dogs had crept back to their bushes and chairs to sleep.

"You can knock off now, Woody," said Harold. "I'll see you in the morning."

Woody said okay, and tried to smile, but the dead sheep smell was still with him. Harold sensed how he was feeling and grinned.

"You'll get used to it," he said, and patted him on the back.

Woody went back to his room, but before he reached it, he doubled over and puked in the bushes outside.

The next day Woody was back in the field fixing fences again. He was wearing a hat to keep the sun off his face. Just last year, on one of the other farms he'd worked on, he'd been digging a ditch all day and telling the time by looking at the sun. When he'd returned to his lodgings he'd had a terrible pain in his eyes, like someone had thrown sand in them. Much to the amusement of the other workers he'd spent the whole of the next day lying in a darkened room. They'd told him he had sunstroke. Eventually the pain had disappeared, but he'd learnt his lesson.

At lunchtime, Woody saw a horse approaching, and as it came nearer, he was pleased to see the rider was Harold's daughter Jane. She was fifteen years old, pretty, with long blonde hair. She climbed down off her small horse, and carried over a bag of lunch for him.

"Hello," Woody said shyly. "How are you?"

"Fine, Woody," said Jane. "Have you recovered from last night?"

Woody decided to play it dumb. "Recovered from what?"

Jane handed him the bag of food. She was wearing a white dress with a flower pattern on it, a straw hat on her head. "The killing of the sheep. I heard you puking after."

Woody felt embarrassed. Jane's room was just behind his. He shrugged. "So I puked. So what?"

"You'll never be a farmer if you can't kill a sheep."

"Who says I want to be a farmer?"

"What are you doing here if you don't want to be a farmer?"

"I need the money. When I've saved a bit I'll do something else. Like maybe rustle cattle. Or rob trains."

Jane laughed. "Just keep dreaming, Woody. We all need our dreams. I have to get back. My dad said to come straight home."

Woody watched Jane walk back to her horse and climb on. He looked down at the lunch bag and started opening it.

"Woody?"

He looked up and Jane was still sitting on her horse. Only now she had her skirt pulled high up on her thigh and she was rubbing her leg. "Do you think I have nice legs?" she asked.

Woody was so shocked he didn't know what to say.

"If you kill a sheep for me, Woody, I'll let you see more," and then her dress fell back into place and she was riding away.

Woody was stunned. He looked at Jane until she was almost out of sight. Then he looked down at his lunch bag but he didn't feel so hungry any more.

Woody kept thinking about Jane's leg for the rest of the day. What did she mean exactly by saying she'd let him see more? Was she going to let him go the whole way? He was still a virgin and wasn't sure he knew exactly what to do. Maybe he should just forget the whole thing. Maybe she was just leading him on. And what did she mean by "kill a sheep for me"? Was this some kind of test of his manliness? Or was she trying to lead him into trouble?

Woody worked hard on the fence and then started walking home. At the dinner table that night he couldn't keep his eyes off Jane. She kept smiling at him and even winked one time. Her younger brother Billy did most of the talking, so Harold and Molly were easily distracted.

When the dishes were done Woody went back to his room. Evening times always passed slowly. His room was only big enough for a bed and a wardrobe and was right next to the back veranda. On the other side of the veranda was the washer room, and several times he had watched Jane in there, washing clothes in the sink.

He still thought of her words. "Kill a sheep for me." What was that meant to mean? Was he meant to bring the body back to her room and lay it out in front of her? What kind of a sick person was she? Or would just the head be enough? Bring me the head of a sheep and I'll let you see my body. He wished she'd been clearer in her intentions. He lay on his bed and looked at the ceiling.

After an hour of turmoil he could wait no longer. He left his room and edged round to the veranda. He crept on to it and looked into the kitchen. It was empty. He eased open the screen-door and crept into the pantry. He took a large knife and slid it under his shirt. Then he crept outside.

His heart was pounding with excitement as he made the short walk to the home paddock, the carving knife now stuck down the belt of his jeans. He had decided to kill a sheep and bring the head to Jane. Then she would show him her body. Then he would see what would happen next. He quickened up his pace.

He found the herd easily, a grey moving shape in the dark. He walked slowly up to them, but they heard him coming and moved away. He tried running at them but they ran away, faster than he'd thought they could be. He stopped to catch his breath. He tried again. They ran away.

It took him ten minutes to finally catch one, and he was so angry and frustrated he just plunged the knife straight into the sheep's chest. It seemed to have little effect, so he stabbed it in the neck and then stabbed it again. Eventually the bleating animal was still.

Woody sat on the grass next to it, catching his breath. Sweat was pouring off him and he was covered in blood. He looked at the sheep and immediately felt guilty. Why was he doing this? Taking away a life just so he could see Jane naked? He felt the same revulsion he'd felt last night. He felt his supper starting to come into his throat. He moved away from the sheep and sat down again. Then he lay on the grass and looked at the stars. He waited until he'd cooled down. There was no way he could cut off the sheep's head. He would just make his way home and forget the whole thing. He would have to throw his blood-stained clothes away.

He left the sheep where it lay. When Harold found it tomorrow maybe he would think a wolf had done it. Woody left the paddock and made the walk home, the knife stuck down into the belt of his jeans once again.

He approached his room from the privy side, where no one could see him. He walked on the path where Skunk was tied up, but as he approached Skunk began to growl.

"It's only me, Skunk," Woody said softly.

But then Skunk barked loudly and ran straight for him, his chain rattling as it took up the strain. Woody took a step backwards and then Skunk made another charge. This time, to Woody's horror, the chain broke and Skunk was on top of him. He wrestled with the dog as it went for his throat. Skunk was going berserk and Woody didn't know why. Then he thought that maybe it was the smell of the sheep's blood. Then he remembered the knife in his belt. He managed to get it free and he slammed it into Skunk's side. The dog whimpered and fell off him on to the dirt. Then Woody passed out.

When he came to, Woody didn't know where he was. He was lying on his back on something hard and he didn't recognize the ceiling. He turned his head and looked around. A sofa and some armchairs. A chest of drawers. A cabinet for plates and cutlery. He was in Harold's living room.

He was lying on a table. He had an incredible pain in his left arm. He looked down and wondered if he was imagining things.

He looked down again. His left arm was covered in a white bandage but it was much shorter than it used to be. He tried to wriggle his fingers but he didn't seem to have any. His hand just wasn't there any more.

Feeling a panic sweep over him he rolled off the table and put his feet on the floor. He held his two arms out in front of him but the left one was nearly a foot shorter.

"NO!" he screamed, and staggered out of the room.

He was in his own room now. Sedated.

He stayed there for a week while the pain in his arm lessened and his neck healed. But he wasn't too worried about his neck, he was worried about his missing hand. How was he going to get work now? No one would employ a one-armed man. Maybe Harold would be kind and keep him on. He would have to have a talk with him real soon.

Molly brought him his meals. He hadn't seen Jane at all. He tried talking to Molly as she fed him, but all she would say was that his hand had been mangled by Skunk. Skunk was dead, of course. She didn't mention the dead sheep.

Another week passed before Harold came to his room. Woody was sitting up in bed and Harold pulled up a chair and sat down.

"How's it going, Woody?" he asked.

"Not too good," Woody said. "What happened to my hand?"

Harold looked down at the floor and didn't meet his eyes. "Skunk got a hold of it. Chewed it all up. The doc said he couldn't save it."

"Are you sure?"

Harold looked up. "Sure about what?"

"Sure that he couldn't save it."

"Sure I'm sure. I saw it myself. It's just bad luck, that's all."

"Shit," Woody said. "I don't even remember Skunk attacking my hand. All I remember is him going for my throat."

"Well, it probably happened too quickly for you to remember. You probably passed out before he did it."

"Maybe," Woody said.

They were silent for a minute and then Harold cleared his throat. "I'm going to have to let you go, Woody."

Woody had suspected as much. He nodded.

"After all," Harold continued. "You won't be able to do much with one hand."

"I know," Woody said. "I'm no use to anybody now."

They were silent again.

"Sorry," Harold said, and then he stood up and reached for the door.

The day before he left Woody asked Harold for just one thing. He asked him for a pistol with just one bullet in it.

Harold said okay, but asked him why just one bullet?

Woody said, "Eventually I'll probably have to shoot myself because I won't be able to get any work. When I do it though, I want to be sure that I'm doing the right thing. If I have six bullets I'm likely to do it when I'm drunk. If I only have one bullet I won't know which chamber it's in when I'm drunk and the feeling will pass. If I kill myself I want to be sober, just so I'm sure that's really what I want to do."

Harold had looked at him with a little respect in his eyes. "That's a good idea Woody, a good idea."

Woody walked down the road away from the farm, his few belongings in a bag over his shoulder. From the front veranda Harold and Molly watched.

"Do you think he'll be okay?" Molly asked.

"I don't know," Harold said. "I really don't know."

"He was a nice boy," Molly said. "I wish you hadn't cut off his hand."

Harold didn't look at her. "He shouldn't have killed that sheep. I can't afford to have sheep killed for nothin'."

"Oh, I think you know very well it wasn't for nothin'."

Harold looked at her. "In some countries they cut off your hand if you steal something, you know. He killed a sheep. I don't see what the difference is."

Molly gave him a scornful look. "In some countries. But we're not in those countries. We don't have to do things those ways."

"The real problem," Harold said, "is that daughter of yours. That makes three we've had to get rid of because of her. This can't go on forever. We're gonna have to talk to her again."

And then he walked back inside the kitchen.

BRYANT AND MAY'S MYSTERY TOUR

Christopher Fowler

"Mr Bryant is so old that most of his lifetime subscriptions have run out." Leslie Faraday, the Home Office crime liaison officer, poked about on his biscuit tray looking for a Custard Cream. "He's far beyond the statutory working age limit, but no one has the heart to broach the matter with him."

"Sentimentality can't be allowed to stand in the way of modern policing procedures," replied Oskar Kasavian, peering from the window into the tiled Whitehall courtyard. Faraday took a quick peek to see if the new supervisor in charge of Internal Security cast a shadow, as his cadaverous pale form created office rumours of supernatural lineage. "We're not here to provide the inefficient with a living."

This last remark confused Faraday, who believed that this was precisely the purpose for which Whitehall had been created. "Quite," he replied, "but surely we must take into account his long and illustrious career working with the Peculiar Crimes Unit. He and his partner pioneered research in the field. One doesn't force admirals into retirement simply because they no longer go to sea. We benefit from their experience."

"Old generals are the cause of military disasters," said Kasavian, drumming long fingers on the window pane. "The elderly are weak precisely because they live in the past." He released a long, desperate sigh. "However, in this situation I see no other recourse than to put them on the case."

So it was that the Home Office called Arthur Bryant of the Peculiar Crimes Unit, and Bryant visited a crime scene in King's Cross, and then called his partner, John May, with instructions to meet him at 10:15 a.m. beside a bus stop in Marble Arch. It was a muggy wet morning, and May resented being summoned from his bed.

"Ah, there you are." The elderly detective hailed his partner with a wild whip of his walking stick, and nearly pruned a passing tourist. Bryant had misbuttoned his shapeless brown cardigan and dragged his moth-eaten Harris tweed coat over the top of it. He looked more like a tramp than a detective. "I got here early and had a potter through Hyde Park."

"You had your mobile with you?" asked May, surprised. Arthur was three years his senior, but two decades behind the rest of the world when it came to technology.

"I did have, yes," Bryant admitted, tugging his battered brown trilby further onto his head. "Here's our bus." He indicated the open-topped Routemaster that was just pulling up.

May was suspicious. "Then where is it now?"

"I think I dropped it in the Princess Diana Memorial Drain. Don't worry, it'll just keep going round. I'll get it when I come back. You're probably wondering what this is all about."

"And why we're boarding a sightseeing bus, yes," said May, helping his partner inside the idling vehicle. The portly driver stared at them through his windscreen.

"There was a rather sad little murder in King's Cross during the night. A 54-year-old cleaning lady named Joan March was strangled to death in her third floor flat in Hastings Street. The HO felt the case warranted our involvement."

"But this bus doesn't go anywhere near King's Cross." May checked the route, noting that it tacked through central London in a loop.

"Oh, we're not going to the murder site. I've already been there." Bryant seated himself on the arrow-patterned seat at the front of the bus, next to a gingery young man who was standing in the aisle with a microphone. His badge read; *Hi! I'm Martin!* "I wanted you here so that we could apprehend the murderer."

The Routemaster pulled away from the stop at Speaker's Corner, heading into Oxford Street. "My Uncle Jack used to get up on his soapbox over there, just after the war," said Bryant, tapping the rain-spattered window. "Less passion, less protein, ban licentious theatre, shoot the Welsh; he'd rant about anything so long as it involved getting rid of something. I suppose the preachers of Speaker's Corner still do."

"Now, does anyone know the name of the bi-i-i-g department store on our right?" Martin the tour guide was as wide-eyed as a first-time father, and as patronizing. There were no takers. "Anyone?"

Bryant raised his hand. "Selfridges, opened in 1909 by Harry Gordon Selfridge. He coined the phrase 'The customer is always right', and was the first salesman to put products out on display."

"Well, I don't know about that," said Martin.

"But I do," Bryant countered.

"We're catching a murderer on a bus?" asked May in disbelief.

"We are now heading toward Oxford Circus, which was once described by Noel Coward as the Hub of the Universe," announced the tour guide.

"This boy's a dunderhead." Bryant jerked a wrinkled thumb at Martin, who overheard him. "That was John Wyndham's reference to Piccadilly Circus." Bryant had recently given up working as a London guide in his spare time, after picking too many arguments with the tourists. He forgot most things, but never the facts he had painstakingly gathered about his city.

"I don't understand," May persisted. "Why did we get the case?" Bryant and May's division, the Peculiar Crimes Unit, only handled investigations the Home Office found detrimental to government policy. Arthur loved working with his partner John May, and revelled in the fact that they performed a service no one else in the city could offer. No one had their arcane depth of knowledge, or was able to use it in the cause of crime prevention. Across the decades they had closed the cases few could understand, let alone solve.

"There are three oddities." Bryant ticked his fingers. "One, after strangling Mrs March, the murderer ordered two pizzas, calmly eating both of them. B, he slept overnight in the apartment. And three, his victim killed someone after he left."

May considered the matter as the bus turned into Regent Street. "I'm sorry, Arthur, you've utterly lost me."

"Do try to pay attention. The murderer left the flat at 6:15 this morning, not realizing that his victim was still alive. Mrs March struggled to the window to raise the alarm, but the effort of opening it was too much for her. She lost consciousness and fell out into the street, landing on a gentleman called Sir Ian Lowry—"

"The MOD bigwig?"

"The very same, who was apparently just leaving a call-girl's flat, where he had presumably stayed the night. Mrs March broke her neck and his leg. And that's why the HO called us in. Obviously, it's a serious security breach, because Sir Ian is privy to all kinds of military secrets. The call-girl has already been brought in, and all that's left is the apprehension of her killer."

"So I'm here to help you identify him," said May, still a little confused.

"Oh, I know who the murderer is." Bryant cheerily flashed his oversized false teeth. "You were complaining about getting old the other day, so I thought this would be a chance for you to test your fading faculties."

The Routemaster stopped outside Hamley's toy store to allow a single Japanese tourist on board. There were eight passengers seated downstairs. The heavily falling rain prevented anyone from sitting on the open deck. It was now 10:44am.

"You already know the murderer's identity?"

"Better than that", said Bryant smugly. "I can tell you the precise time he'll be arrested." He checked his ancient Timex. "At 11:26 a.m."

"Are you saying we're looking for somebody on board this bus?"

"That's the general idea, yes."

The tour guide was attempting to deliver a potted history of the Haymarket, and was not happy about being distracted. "There are seats further back," he said pointedly.

"I'm quite happy here," Bryant insisted, withdrawing his pipe from his top pocket and absently striking a match to it. A middle-aged woman in a red baseball cap, a glittery tank-top and shorts reacted with horror behind him. "That's disgusting," she complained. "It's illegal to smoke in public in my country."

"But not to dress like an enormous toddler, Madam, which I find curious," Bryant turned back to his partner. "So take a look around you, and tell me who you suspect. Give me the benefit of your observational skills."

The ancient bus was now chuntering toward the rainswept plain of Trafalgar Square.

"On your left, Nelson's Column, finished in 1843, with four bronze panels at the base depicting his naval victories," said the guide.

"His left arm was struck by lightning in the 1880s, and he's only just getting it X-rayed this year," said Bryant. "That's the National Health Service for you."

"So you know exactly where the murderer will get on this bus, how long he'll stay on and where he'll get off?" asked May.

"Indeed I do." Bryant could be supremely annoying when he was holding privileged information.

At 11:02 a.m., the bus stopped near the corner of Craig's Court. "Pall Mall derives its name from a 17th-century mallet and ball game played here by, er, members of royalty," Martin the guide stated with a hint of uncertainty.

"Everyone knows that," said Bryant, fidgetting in his seat. "Tell them something new. Alleys of shops are called malls because they're shaped like the game's playing sites. Did you know that Pall Mall is only worth £140 on the Monopoly board?"

"I don't think he cares for your interruptions," whispered May. "You're unsettling him."

"Some people deserve to be unsettled," Bryant replied. "When a man is tired of London he should clear off. Oh dear, he's wearing a clip-on tie." Coming from a man as sartorially challenged as Bryant, this was a bit rich.

When the bus stopped halfway along Whitehall, May surveyed the new arrivals. One of them was a murderer, but which? There were now eleven passengers on the lower deck; four Americans, two Chinese, one Japanese and two couples of indeterminate origin. No singles. He decided that the murderer had yet to put in an appearance.

"Was this woman, Mrs March, in her own flat?" he asked.

"Correct."

May thought of the call-girl living on the ground floor. "Did she look after the other girls? Was her murderer a client?"

"No, she had nothing to do with them." Bryant sat back, pretending to listen to the tour guide's inaccurate description of the Cabinet War Rooms.

"But her killer left behind a clue to his identity."

"It was something he took with him that gave me the clue."

The bus continued along Whitehall, picking up three more passengers, and headed up toward Parliament Square. May eyed the newcomers with suspicion. A German couple – he overheard their conversation – and a fiftyish man with unmistakably Russian features and anxious, flitting eyes. May studied his shabby jacket, twisted T-shirt and unshaven chin. *A sad little murder*, Bryant had said. This man had dressed in a hurry, without stopping to shave, and looked around every time the bus came to a halt. But if he was a killer, why would he make his escape aboard a tour bus, on a trip that ended back where it began?

"Who can tell me the name of this building?" asked Martin the guide.

"Houses of Parliament," the assembly muttered faintly, as if being asked to recite a prayer in church.

"Now, many people think Big Ben is the name of the tower . . ."

"Dear God no," Bryant sighed loudly. "Can't he come up with anything more original than that?"

Martin shot him a filthy look. "But it is actually the name of the single bell housed inside . . ."

"Absolute rubbish." Bryant thumped the guide on the arm with his stick. "There are five bells in St Stephen's Tower, young man. The other four play the *Westminster Quarters*, variations of 'I know that my redeemer liveth' from Handel's *Messiah*."

"Look, who's giving this bloody tour?" The guide's cheeks were turning as red as his hair.

"It could be him," said May, pointing to the Russian. "The killer has to be alone, and he's the only one."

"I'll take over if you like," Bryant snapped back at the guide. "I'd do a better job."

"But Arthur, how could you know when he was due on the bus? That just leaves . . ."

"Listen, mate, I don't have to put up with this. My shift ends here, anyway." As the bus stopped on the corner of the square, Martin threw down his microphone and tapped on the glass, signalling to the driver.

As he made his way along the aisle, May said, "The guide, it's the guide, and he's getting away!"

Bryant did not move a muscle as a moon-faced young woman with a colourless ponytail took over from the departing Martin. "Hello, my name is Debbie, and I'll be your guide on the second half of this tour," she told them all. The bus pulled out into traffic and made its way around the square.

"Why didn't you stop him?" asked May with growing incredulity.

Bryant pulled back his sleeve and held up his watch so that his partner could read it. 11:19 a.m. There was still another seven minutes to go.

"Who can tell me the name of this building?" said Debbie, pointing to Westminster Abbey and cupping her hand around her ear.

"Is there some special nursery school where they're trained to speak in this fashion, I wonder?" said Bryant. The bus headed back onto Victoria Embankment.

"Where does the tour go from here?" asked May.

"Around Covent Garden, where Debbie will probably regale us with a re-enactment of *My Fair Lady*, then back toward Oxford Street," said Bryant.

"You said it was something he took with him that gave you a clue," May repeated.

Bryant rested his chin on his knuckle and regarded the distant stippled thread of the Thames. "She'll ask them to name the river next," he muttered.

"He was so unfazed by the thought of murdering Mrs March that he stayed all night . . ."

"I wonder if anyone knows where the lion on Westminster Bridge comes from," asked Debbie.

"Because he was used to her . . ." said May, following the thought.

"Good Lord, an intelligent question," Bryant beamed delightedly at the new guide.

"It stood on the parapet of the Lion Brewery until 1966, near Hungerford Bridge . . ." said Debbie.

"Because he was *married* to her . . ." said May.

"Yet we have come to regard it as a symbol of London . . ."

"And he stuck to his routine, getting up the next morning . . ."

"So when we photograph the lion beside Big Ben, we recreate the traditional link between members of Parliament – and alcohol." Debbie flourished a smile.

"Oh, bravo!" said Bryant. "I like her!"

"And he came to work just as he always did, driving a bus," said May as then truth dawned. "His jacket, cap and badge were missing from the flat."

Bryant rose unsteadily to his feet and pressed the stop bell. "I'm sorry, Debbie," he apologized, "but I'm afraid the tour terminates here."

May looked out of the window. The bus-stop faced New Scotland Yard. It was exactly 11:26 a.m.

"He won't run off," said Bryant. "He wants to be taken in for the murder of his wife. I imagine she never stopped nagging him about his weight."

The Japanese tourist took a very nice photograph of the detectives arresting their man.